Spain

© Malburet/ MICHELIN

Executive Editorial Director	David Brabis
Chief Editor	Cynthia Clayton Ochterbeck

THE GREEN GUIDE — SPAIN

Editor	Gwen Cannon
Principal Writer	Paul Glassman
Production Coordinator	Allison Michelle Simpson
Cartography	Alain Baldet, Michèle Cana, Peter Wrenn
Photo Editor	Brigitta L. House
Proofreader	Gaven R. Watkins
Layout	Cynthia C. Ochterbeck, Allison M. Simpson, Nicole D. Jordan
Cover Design	Laurent Muller
Interior Design	Agence Rampazzo
Production	Pierre Ballochard, Renaud Leblanc

Contact Us :

The Green Guide
Michelin Travel Publications
One Parkway South
Greenville, SC 29615
USA
☎ 1-800-423-0485
www.michelintravel.com
michelin.guides@us.michelin.com

or

Hannay House, 39 Clarendon Road
Watford, Herts WD17 1JA, UK
☎ 01923 205 240 - Fax 01923 205 241
www.ViaMichelin.com
TheGreenGuide-uk@uk.michelin.com

Special Sales :

For information regarding bulk sales, customized editions and premium sales, please contact our Customer Service Departments:

USA	1-800-423-0485
UK	(01923) 205 240
Canada	1-800-361-8236

Note to the reader

One Team...
A Commitment to Quality

There's just one reason our team is dedicated to producing quality travel publications—you, our reader. We want you to get the maximum benefit from your trip—and from your money. In today's multiple-choice world of travel, the options are many, perhaps overwhelming.

In our guidebooks, we try to minimize the guesswork involved with travel. We scout out the attractions, prioritize them with star ratings, and describe what you'll discover when you visit them.

To help you orient yourself, we provide colorful and detailed, but easy-to-follow maps. Floor plans of some of the cathedrals and museums help you plan your tour.

Throughout the guides, we offer practical information, touring tips and suggestions for finding the best views, good places for a break and the most interesting shops.

Lodging and dining are always a big part of travel, so we compile a selection of hotels and restaurants that we think convey the feel of the place, and organize them by geographic area and price. We also highlight shopping, recreational and entertainment venues, especially the popular spots.

If you're short on time, driving tours are included so you can hit the highlights and quickly absorb the best of the destination.

For those who love to experience a destination on foot, we add walking tours, often with a map. And we list other companies who offer boat, bus or guided walking tours of the area, some with culinary, historical or other themes.

In short, we test and retest, check and recheck to make sure that our guidebooks are truly just that: a personalized guide to help you make the most of your visit. After all, we want you to enjoy traveling as much as we do.

The Michelin Green Guide Team
michelin.guides@us.michelin.com

PLANNING YOUR TRIP

INTRODUCTION TO SPAIN

SYMBOLS

🖐	Tips to help improve your experience
👁	Details to consider
💰	Entry fees
🚶	Walking tours
🔑	Closed to the public
⏱	Hours of operation
🕐	Periods of closure

CONTENTS

DISCOVERING SPAIN

How To Use This Guide

Orientation

To help you grasp the "lay of the land" quickly and easily, so you'll feel confident and comfortable finding your way around, we offer the following tools in this guide:

- Detailed table of contents for an overview of what'll you find in the guide, and how it is organized.
- Map of Principal Sights showing the starred places of interest at a glance.
- Detailed maps of city centers, regions and towns.
- Floor and site plans of museums and cathedrals.
- Principal Sights ordered alphabetically for easy reference.

Practicalities

At the front of the guide, you'll see a section called "Planning Your Trip" that contains information about the best time to go, getting to Spain and getting around, basic facts, tips for making the most of your visit, and more. It includes suggested itineraries, a calendar of annual events and festivals worth planning for, and tips about national and regional cuisines, and what to expect in the way of lodging. Then comes information on shopping, sightseeing, kids' activities, sports and recreational opportunities.

LODGING

We've made a selection of hotels and classified them according to room price in high season (without tax and breakfast, except where indicated) to fit all budgets. For the most part, we've selected accommodations for their uniquely Spanish or regional character, so unless the individual hotel embodies local ambience, it's rare that we include chain properties, which typically have their own imprint. If you want a more comprehensive selection of lodgings throughout the country, see the red-cover *Michelin Guide Spain*.

RESTAURANTS

We thought you'd like to make eating part of your experience of Spain. So we selected restaurants that capture the essence of Spain and of its regions—those that are well-frequented and popular, and conveniently located. As we did with the hotels, we categorized them by price to appeal to all wallets. We've also indicated selected TAPAS bars separately, so as to include one of Spain's great food traditions. If you want a more comprehensive selection of eating places, see the red-cover *Michelin Guide Spain*, which describes hundreds of restaurants throughout Spain.

Attractions

We've organized the the major cities and towns of mainland (peninsular) Spain in alphabetical order, with references to where to find them on our Michelin maps. Separate sections cover the Balearic and Canary Islands.

We also indicate neighboring sights according to headings in this book, making it easy to find descriptions, and we give the distances in miles and kilometers. According to the locale, you'll find listings of sights Worth A Visit, or step-by-step Walking About itineraries with complete directions, including where to turn at intersections. Excursions are nearby areas accessible by car, guided tour, or on foot.

Contact information, admission charges and hours of operation are given for each attraction. Unless otherwise noted, admission prices shown are for a single adult only. Discounts for seniors, students, military personnel, etc. may be available; be sure to ask. If no admission charge is shown, entrance to the attraction is free.

If you're pressed for time, we recommend you visit the three- and two-star sights in a city or area first: the stars are your guide.

STAR RATINGS

Michelin has used stars as a rating tool for more than 100 years:

★★★	Highly recommended
★★	Recommended
★	Interesting

SYMBOLS IN THE TEXT

Besides the stars, other symbols in the text indicate tourist information ⓘ; wheelchair access ♿; on-site eating facilities ✗; camping facilities △; on-site parking Ⓟ; entry fees ⊜; hours of operation ⓒ; hours closed ⓒ; and sights of interest to children Kids.
See the box appearing on the Contents page for other symbols used in the text.
See Maps explanation below for symbols appearing on the maps.
Throughout the guide you will find peach-colored text boxes or sidebars containing anecdotal or background information. Green-colored boxes contain information to help you save time or money.

Maps

All maps in this guide are oriented north, unless otherwise indicated by a directional arrow.
See the map legend at the back of the guide for an explanation of other map symbols.
A complete list of the maps found in the guide appears at the back of this book.

Addresses, phone numbers, opening hours and prices published in this guide are accurate at press time. We welcome corrections and suggestions that may assist us in preparing the next edition. Please send your comments to:

Michelin Travel Publications
Editorial Department
P.O. Box 19001
Greenville, SC 29602-9001 USA
Email: michelin.guides@us.michelin.com
Web site: www.michelintravel.com

Principal Sights

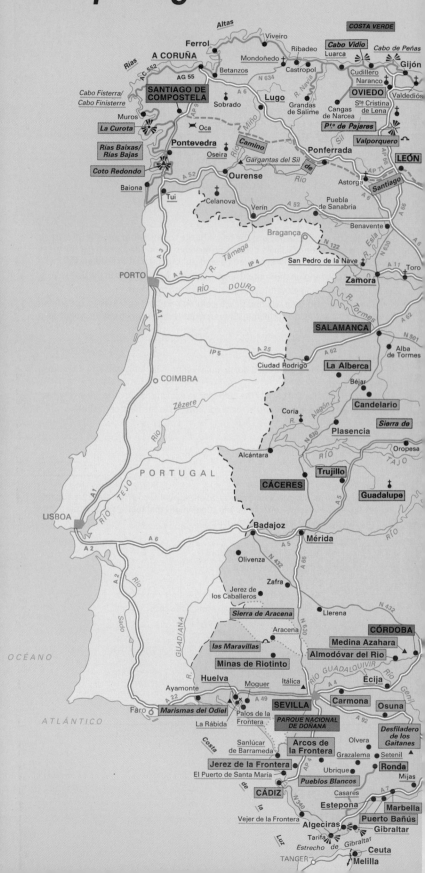

Driving tours

For descriptions of these tours, turn
to the Planning Your Trip section following.

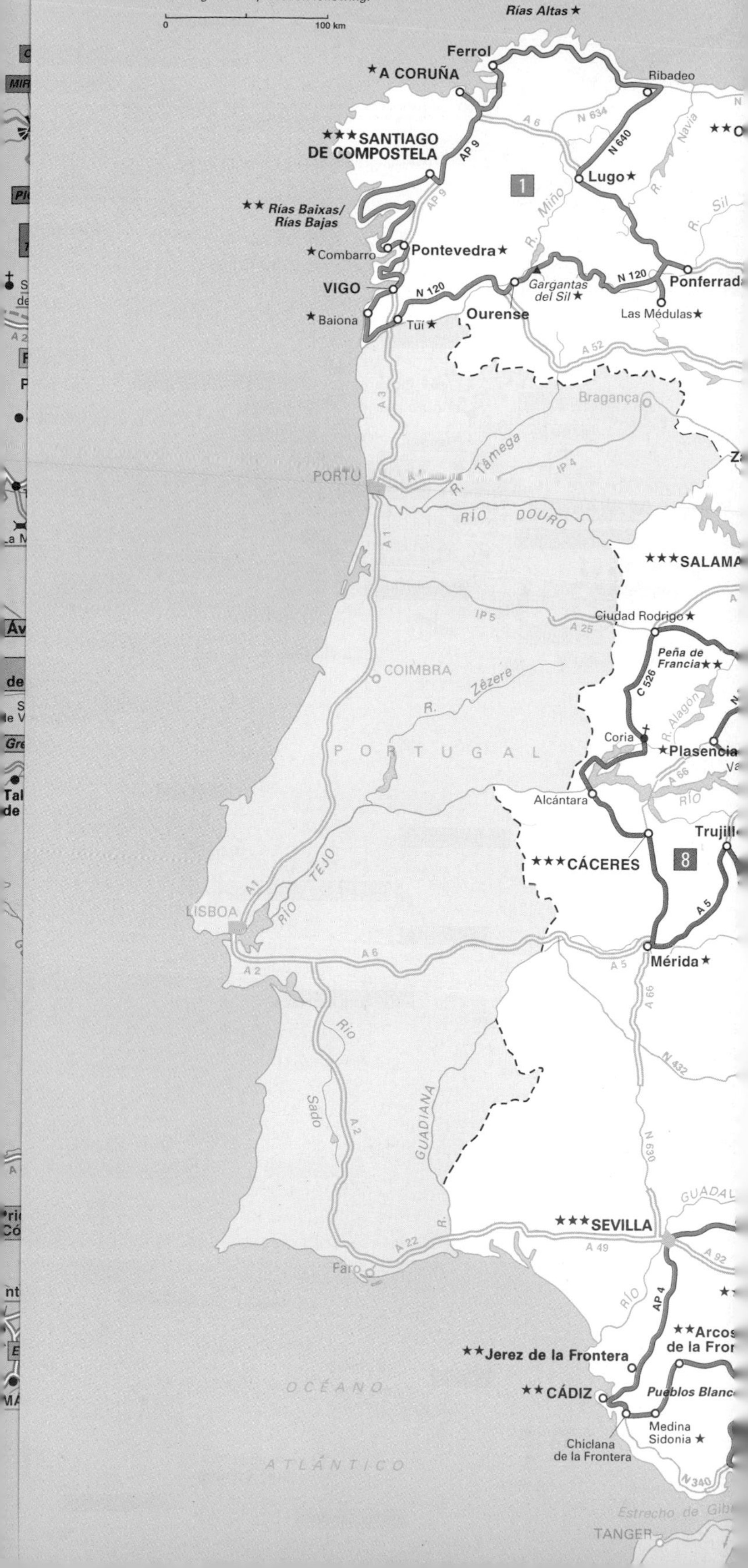

0   100 km

Rías Altas ★

Ferrol
★ A CORUÑA
Ribadeo

★★★ SANTIAGO
DE COMPOSTELA

1

Lugo ★

★★ Rías Baixas/
Rías Bajas

★ Combarro   Pontevedra ★

VIGO
Gargantas
del Sil ★

Ponferrad

★ Baiona   Tuí ★   Ourense
Las Médulas ★

Bragança

PORTU

RIO DOURO

★★★ SALAMA

IP 5
Ciudad Rodrigo ★

COIMBRA
Peña de
Francia ★★

Coria
★ Plasencia

PORTUGAL

Alcántara

RÍO

★★★ CÁCERES   **8**   Trujill

LISBOA
RIO TEJO

Mérida ★

GUADIANA

★★★ SEVILLA

Faro

GUADAL

★★ Arcos
de la Fron

★★ Jerez de la Frontera
Pueblos Blanc

★★ CÁDIZ
Medina
Sidonia ★

Chiclana
de la Frontera

OCÉANO

ATLÁNTICO

Estrecho de Gib

TANGER

BORDEAUX

TOULOUSE   MONTPELLIER

PAU   F   R   A   N   C   E

ANDORRA   PERPIGNAN

Vielha

★★ *Parc Nacional d'Aigüestortes*

Púigcerdà

N 260

★★★ *PIRINEOS CATALANES*

★ **Figueres**   El Port de Llançà

SANT PERE DE RODES ★★★

★★ **Besalú**   **Cadaqués** ★★

★★ **Girona / Gerona**   **Empúries** ★★

Lleida / Lérida ★   *COSTA BRAVA* ★★★

★★★ **POBLET** ★

★★ **Montblanc**   **BARCELONA** ★★★

★★ **Port Aventura**   **Tarragona** ★★   **Sitges** ★★

Costa Dorada ★

Peñiscola

M   A   R   M E D I T E R R A N E O

MENORCA

MALLORCA

VALÈNCIA ★★

El Saler

P. Natural de la Albufera

Cullera

IBIZA   *ISLAS*   *BALEARES*

Gandía

Alcoi / Alcoy   **Xàbia / Jávea**

Guadalest ★   Calp

Xixona   Altea

Benidorm

ALACANT / ALICANTE ★ ★

Costa Blanca

1	Galicia (1050 km)
2	Around the montes de Cantabria (800 km)
3	The Basque country, Rioja and Navarra (700 km)
4	Catalunya (1000 km)
5	Castilla y León (750 km)
6	Zaragoza, Soria, Guadalajara and Teruel (900 km)
7	Around Madrid (700 km)
8	Extramadura and the Peña de Francia (800 km)
9	The lands of La Mancha (850 km)
10	The Levant region (750 km)
11	Córdoba, Sevilla, Cádiz and Málaga (900 km)
12	Granada, Almería, and Jaén (850 km)

Ceramic tiles, Casa de Pilatos, Sevilla

H. Le Gac/ MICHELIN

IDEAS FOR YOUR VISIT

Spain's Coastlines

MEDITERRANEAN COAST

Spain has thousands of miles of beautiful coastline, with the Mediterranean continuing to attract millions of Spanish and foreign visitors every year to its delightful waters and magnificent beaches.

The rugged and indented **Costa Brava**, or Wild Coast, with its charming coves and lively resorts, extends from north of Barcelona as far as the French border.

The **Levante** coast, characterised by long sandy beaches and built-up resorts such as Benidorm, Cullera and Gandía, continues to be as popular as ever. This area is also favoured by Spanish families, and is occupied by a large number of second homes.

The **Costa del Sol**, in particular the famous stretch between Málaga and Estepona, is a succession of luxury developments and golf courses. Marbella is considered the leading resort here, reinforced by its reputation as the playground of the international jet-set.

The remainder of the Andalucían coast is generally quieter, attracting mainly-Spanish visitors.

The **Balearic Islands** are one of the country's most popular tourist destinations. Of the three main islands, Mallorca and Ibiza attract large numbers of Spanish and foreign (particularly German) visitors, who come here to enjoy their magnificent landscapes and beaches and lively nightlife. Menorca tends to be quieter, finding popularity with those in search of a more relaxing holiday.

ATLANTIC COAST

Spain's North Atlantic coast stretches from the Basque Country in the east to Galicia in the west. In general, its resorts are popular with Spanish visitors attracted by the temperate climate, delightful beaches, excellent fish and seafood, impressive landscapes and fascinating towns and cities, including renowned resorts such as Donostia-San Sebastián and Santander. With the exception of a few places, the coast of Northern Spain has escaped the frenetic development of the Mediterranean, and as such has managed to preserve its natural beauty.

Although less popular with foreign visitors, the **Costa de la Luz** (Coast of Light), stretching between the southernmost tip of Spain and the Portuguese border, has some of the country's finest beaches, dotted with charming family resorts and historic cities such as Cádiz, the oldest in Spain.

CANARY ISLANDS

The Canary Islands come into their own in winter, when thousands of visitors flock here to escape the cold of Northern Europe. High season in the Canaries runs from 1 November to 30 April.

The main tourist centres on the archipelago can be found in the south of Gran Canaria (Maspalomas, Playa del Inglés and Playa de San Agustín) and on Tenerife (Playa de las Américas to the south, and Puerto de la Cruz to the north).

National Parks

Spain is a country that acts as a bridge between Europe and Africa, and as such has a wealth of different landscapes including salt marshes, conifer forests, high mountains, desert areas and Mediterranean woodland. The country's national parks protect those areas of major ecological interest to ensure their continuing survival. The main aim of these parks is to preserve their unique flora and fauna and to control public access within them. In total, Spain has 12 national parks – seven on the mainland and five spread across the islands. For many animal and plant species, Spain's mountain parks provide the most southerly habitat in Europe.

F. Vidal/ MICHELIN

MOUNTAIN PARKS

The country's first national park was the Parque de Montaña de Covadonga, created in 1918. In 1995, this protected area was significantly extended (from 16 925ha/41 822 acres to 64 600ha/159 626 acres) and became known as the **Parque Nacional de los Picos de Europa** (*see p 401*). This magnificent park is characterised by breathtaking landscapes with glacial lakes and extensive forests of beech (between 800m/2 624ft and 1 500m/4 920ft) as well as chestnut and oak, where water, in the shape of rivers, streams, lagoons and lakes, is an ecological factor of great importance. In terms of fauna, the main species found here are chamois, mountain cats, polecats, foxes, otters, squirrels, imperial eagles and partridges, with the occasional sighting of the brown bear. The main types of fish found in the park's rivers are trout and salmon. The **Parque Nacional de Ordesa y Monte Perdido** (*see p 382*), at the heart of the Pyrenees in the province of Huesca, covers an area of 15 608ha/38 567 acres, and was also established in 1918. The park is spread across four valleys, in which the landscape is dominated by bubbling mountain rivers and streams, waterfalls, impressive precipices and forests of mountain pine, beech and fir, inhabited by polecats, wild boar, foxes, pine martens, otters etc. The present-day appearance of the **Parc Nacional de Aigüestortes i Estany de Sant Maurici** (*see p 103*), covering 9 851ha/24 342 acres in the province of Lleida, in the Catalan Pyrenees, was created by the ice that invaded this area during the Quaternary Era. The park's varied landscape includes lakes, forests of mountain pine, fir and Alpine meadows, populated by a variety of fauna, including wild boar, ermine, pine martens, dormice, imperial eagles and partridge. The **Sierra Nevada** (90 000ha/ 222 390 acres) (*see p 292*) is a mountain park with several summits over 3 000m/9 840ft, including Mulhacén, the highest peak on mainland Spain at 3 482m/11 421ft. This range is also renowned for the variety of its flora and fauna, which is the result of the unique climatic and topographical features that exist here.

PARQUE NACIONAL DE CABAÑEROS

Spread across a flatland area between two rocky formations in the Montes de Toledo, this protected national park covering some 40 000ha/98 840 acres is characterised by a Mediterranean-style wooded landscape abundant with deer, wild boar and birds of prey, in particular black and griffon vultures.

WETLAND PARKS

The Tablas de Daimiel and the Parque de Doñana are of vital ecological importance due to the protection they offer flora and fauna in danger of extinction, and their role as a breeding, migration and wintering area for numerous species of birds. The **Tablas de Daimiel** (Ciudad Real) (*see p 118*) is the smallest of Spain's national parks, with an area of just 1 928ha/4 764 acres. The flooding of the Cigüela and Guadiana rivers has resulted in the formation of areas of shallow bodies of water ideal for the creation of typical marshland vegetation that has been colonised by various species of birds, some of which migrate here for the winter or to nest (grey herons, lesser egrets, red-crested pochard etc).
The extraordinary wealth of species in the **Parque Nacional de Doñana** (50 720ha/125 329 acres) (*see p 231*) is the result of its three distinct habitats: the coastal dunes, the salt marshes, and the former hunting grounds or cotos. Its strategic location on the southern tip of Europe, almost within sight of the coast of Africa, has resulted in its development as an important wetland for migratory birds. Various birds and animals in danger of extinction can still be found here, such as the lynx, ichneumon and imperial eagle.

PARKS ON THE SPANISH ISLANDS

The **Cabrera archipelago,** in the Balearics, is Spain's only maritime and terrestrial national park, stretching across an area of some 10 000ha/24 700 acres. The remaining four parks not on the Spanish mainland are found in the Canary Islands: the Parque Nacional del **Teide**, on Tenerife; the **Caldera de Taburiente**, on the island of La Palma; **Timanfaya**, on Lanzarote; and **Garajonay**, on the island of La Gomera.

Driving Tours

For those visitors wishing to spend a few days exploring different parts of Spain by car, we have put together a number of different itineraries which appear on the map of **Driving Tours** on ♿ *p 11* and are described below. You may also wish to refer to the map of **Principal Sights** on ♿ *p 8*.

Picos de Europa

1 GALICIA

Round trip of 1 031km/644mi from A Coruña/La Coruña – This tour provides an insight into a region with magnificent towns and cities, verdant landscapes, an indented coastline and villages full of character and charm, known in ancient times as *finis terra*, or "end of the world." Galicia is also renowned for its delicious seafood. After visiting A Coruña/La Coruña, with its old quarter and attractive seafront promenade *(avenida de la Marina)*, head south to **Santiago de Compostela**, one of Spain's finest cities, to marvel at the spectacular plaza del Obradoiro, dominated by the impressive cathedral – the final destination for hundreds of thousands of pilgrims every year. The tour continues along the **Rías Bajas** to the mouth of the Miño, forming a natural border with Portugal. Along this magnificent stretch of coastline, with its genuine fishing villages and summer resorts popular with Spanish holidaymakers, the sea has created a series of beautiful inlets. Having followed the Miño as far as the historic town of **Tui/Tuy**, continue by motorway to **Orense/Ourense**. After visiting the town, the itinerary continues along the spectacular gorges cut by the Sil, before following the same road into the province of León, and the town of Ponferrada, the gateway to the magical landscapes of **Las Médulas**. Heading back into Galicia, make your way to **Lugo**, which has managed to preserve its exceptional Roman walls. Continue north to the coast, driving along the **Rías Altas** before returning to A Coruña/La Coruña.

2 AROUND THE MONTES DE CANTABRIA

Round trip of 764km/477mi from Santander – The Cantabrian mountains form a natural boundary between Castilla y León and the autonomous communities of Cantabria and Asturias. To the north, the highest summits of the Picos de Europa rise up close to the stunning coast, while in the lands of Castilla to the south you won't want to miss some of the towns and villages along the Way of St James, or two outstanding jewels of Gothic art, the cathedrals of León and Burgos. Leaving behind the seigniorial town of **Santander**, with its superb location on a magnificent bay, head west to the charming medieval town of **Santillana del Mar**, making sure you visit the replica of the **Cuevas de Altamira**, a masterpiece of prehistoric cave art. Continue along the same road to the picturesque pueblo of **Comillas**, before reaching the seaside resort of **San Vicente de la Barquera**. From here, the tour heads into the mountains, passing through the northern section of the **Parque Nacional de los Picos de Europa**, before returning to the coastal city of **Gijón**, renowned for its extensive beach, and then south to nearby **Oviedo**, with its well-maintained historical centre containing some outstanding examples of Asturian architecture. Continue inland to visit the historic city of **León**, and then east across the Meseta towards Burgos along the Way of St James, visiting Villalcázar de Sirga, Carrión de los Condes and **Frómista** en route, the latter famous for the Iglesia de San Martín, a masterpiece of Romanesque architecture. Having spent time exploring **Burgos** and its magnificent religious heritage, the tour continues towards **Aguilar de Campoo**, overlooked by its castle, and from here to Reinosa, at the foot of the Montes Cantábricos, an ideal departure point for an excursion to the **Pico de Tres Mares**; alternatively, make your way

J. Malburet/ MICHELIN

back to Santander, stopping at **Puente Viesgo** to admire the wall paintings in the Cueva del Castillo.

③ THE BASQUE COUNTRY, RIOJA AND NAVARRA

Round trip of 696km/435mi from Bilbao – This tour combines stunning coastline dotted with picturesque villages, the delightful inland landscapes of northern Spain and the Way of St James, as well as charming towns and cities renowned for their wonderful gastronomy.

The tour starts with an obligatory visit to the **Guggenheim Museum** in Bilbao before following the indented **Costa Vasca** eastwards through quaint fishing villages to **Donostia-San Sebastián**, with its majestic setting on one of Spain's most breathtaking bays. From here, continue the short distance to **Hondarribia**, a pleasant resort and fishing port with an attractive old quarter, close to the French border. The magnificent Valle del Bidasoa provides the backdrop as you head inland to **Pamplona/Iruña**, a medieval town built around its imposing cathedral and famous for the annual running of the bulls. The route then heads deeper into Navarra, past monasteries and important staging-posts on the **Way of St James** (Leyre, La Oliva, Sangüesa/Zangoza and Puente la Reina) and historic towns such as Sos del Rey Católico and Olite), before reaching **Estella/Lizarra**, one of the most important stops along the famous pilgrimage route. After visiting the nearby Monasterio de Irache, the pilgrims' path continues west to **Logroño**, the capital of La Rioja, known for its cathedral and old streets, and then through the extensive vineyards for which this region is justifiably renowned; the most famous halts on this section of the path are undoubtedly **Nájera** and **Santo Domingo de la Calzada**. Between the two, nestled in a delightful valley, is the village of San Millán de la Cogolla, the cradle of the written Castilian language. Before returning to the Basque country via the capital of the province of Álava, **Vitoria-Gasteiz**, with its atmospheric old quarter and several museums of interest, take time to visit Haro and the Museo del Vino de La Rioja. Return to Bilbao via the motorway, which winds its way through an impressive mountain landscape.

④ CATALUNYA

Round trip of 1 020km/637mi from Barcelona – This driving tour through Catalunya is characterised by high Pyrenean peaks, rugged coasts with charming coves, long sandy beaches, picturesque villages, exquisite Romanesque churches, impressive monasteries, and towns and cities overflowing with history.

Once you've spent time in the region's capital, **Barcelona**, a city with a fascinating mix of modernity and history, begin your tour along the **Costa Brava**, a beautiful stretch of coastline dotted with authentic fishing villages and summer resorts. After visiting the old Roman colony of **Empúries/Ampurias**, the Golfo de Roses, the picture-postcard small town of **Cadaqués** and the **Monasterio de Sant Pere de Rodes**, head inland to **Figueres**, home of the museum dedicated to Salvador Dalí, and **Girona/Gerona**, a city that still retains the vestiges of its Roman, Jewish, Moorish and Christian past. From here, the tour climbs up into the **Pyrenees**, a land of spectacular mountain roads, beautiful valleys and charming villages with small Romanesque churches of singular purity and simplicity. The itinerary abandons the mountains via the Valle de la Noguera Ribagorzana to reach **Lleida/Lérida**, watched over by the remains of its former Moorish fortress and by the city's cathedral (Seo). The journey back to the Mediterranean provides an opportunity to visit **Poblet**, the most famous Cistercian monastery in Spain, as well as the walled town of **Montblanc**, before arriving in **Tarragona**, capital of Tarraconensis under the Romans. Have a fun day out at the **Port Aventura** theme park before heading back to Barcelona. The final leg of the tour runs along the coast past the attractive resort town of **Sitges** on the **Costa Dorada**.

⑤ CASTILLA Y LEÓN

Round trip of 756km/472mi from Salamanca – Historic towns and lofty castles dominate this tour through the lands of old Castile. If your trip coincides with Holy Week, head for Zamora or Valladolid to witness their solemn Semana Santa processions.

After spending time exploring **Salamanca**, a lively university city teeming with sumptuous monuments, head north to **Zamora** to admire the scallop tiling on the cupola of the cathedral. The road east towards Valladolid passes through **Toro**, where the dome of the town's collegiate church is similar in style to the cupola of Zamora's cathedral, and **Tordesillas**, where the famous treaty dividing the lands of the New World between Spain and Portugal was signed. In **Valladolid**, renowned for fine examples of Isabelline art, it is well worth visiting the Museo Nacional de Escultura, Spain's national sculpture museum. Continue your journey through an extensive landscape of cereal crops, passing through Medina de Rioseco en route to **Palencia**, with its magnificent cathedral. Heading east into the province of Burgos, the itinerary takes in charming small towns and villages such as **Lerma** and **Covarrubias**. One of the highlights of this tour is the **Monasterio de Santo Domingo de Silos**, the cloisters of which are a masterpiece of Romanesque art. From here, the itinerary heads south, skirting along the banks of the Duero, to visit a series of **castles** built to defend the lands conquered by Christians from the Moors, such as the ruined fortress at Peñaranda de Duero; the impressive castle at **Peñafiel**; **Cuéllar**; and the more unusual **Castillo de Coca**, in Mudejar style. The tour continues to **Segovia**, famous for its aqueduct and fairytale castle, and on to **Ávila**, a city of convents and churches, encircled by its famous walls. Before completing your circuit, it is well worth making a last stop in the small town of Alba de Tormes.

6 ZARAGOZA, SORIA, GUADALAJARA AND TERUEL

Round trip of 869km/543mi from Zaragoza – This tour travels across several inland provinces, passing through impressive mountain landscapes, villages crowned by old castles and towns full of character and charm.
The journey begins with a foray into Navarra to visit **Tudela**, with its interesting examples of Mudéjar architecture and its fine cathedral. Returning to the province of Zaragoza, head for **Tarazona**, famous for its old quarter and cathedral, and the **Monasterio de Veruela**, which is well worth a visit. From Tarazona, continue to **Soria**, a quiet provincial capital

embellished with impressive churches, on the banks of the Duero. The itinerary then continues southwest, passing through **Calatañazor**, a picturesque village overlooked by a medieval castle, to **Burgo de Osma**, yet another charming town, renowned for its magnificent cathedral. Head across country to **Berlanga de Duero**, the site of another castle built to defend the Duero, and **San Baudelio de Berlanga**, with its unusual and remote 11C Mozarabic chapel. Once past **Atienza**, crowned by the ruins of its castle, continue to historic **Sigüenza**, whose highlights include the fortified cathedral with its impressive array of sculptures, and the castle (now a parador). Join up with the fast highway heading east towards Zaragoza, passing through attractive scenery along the banks of the Jalón, crossing the river briefly to visit the magnificent **Monasterio de Santa María de Huerta**, built in sober Cistercian style with a number of Renaissance additions. As the road passes Ateca, head directly south past the La Tranquera Reservoir to the **Monasterio de Piedra**, to enjoy a stroll through its delightful park. The tour continues via Molina de Aragón, with yet another castle, before entering the Sierra de **Albarracín** en route to the charming medieval village of the same name. The next stop on the itinerary is **Teruel**, a town enjoying a superb location, and adorned with a number of interesting examples of Mudéjar architecture. To complete the tour, head north to **Daroca**, with its 4km/2.5mi of walls, before joining the motorway for the final leg to Zaragoza.

La Granja

7 AROUND MADRID

Round trip of 689km/431mi from Madrid – The area around the Spanish capital is home to several towns of major interest, a number of royal palaces and the scenic, mountainous landscapes of the Sierras de Gredos and Sierra de Guadarrama.

One of the closest towns to Madrid is **Alcalá de Henares**, the birthplace of Miguel de Cervantes, where the major attraction is the former university, the Colegio de San Ildefonso. From here, the route passes through **Chinchón**, with one of the country's prettiest main squares, and onto **Aranjuez**, nestled in a verdant setting on the banks of the Tagus. After visiting the royal palace and pavilions and strolling through the delightful gardens here, continue your journey southwest to the historic city of **Toledo**, magnificently perched on a loop of the Tagus, with the sumptuous vestiges of its rich past. Continue your journey west to **Talavera de la Reina**, famous for its ceramics, and then north along a mountain road through the **Sierra de Gredos** en route to Ávila, visiting along the way the Cueva del Águila, a cave 4km/2.5mi from the main road via an unsurfaced track. Ávila, a city of churches and convents, and the cradle of St Teresa, has preserved intact its magnificent 11C walls. From Ávila, the tour heads east to the **Monasterio de El Escorial**, an immense monastery built by order of Philip II. On the way to Segovia, you may wish to branch off to the **Valle de los Caídos**, or Valley of the Fallen, impressively situated amid the stunning landscapes of the Sierra de Guadarrama. In **Segovia**, admire the incredible Roman aqueduct, the city's Romanesque churches and the exotic Alcázar. Close to the city, at the foot of the Sierra de Guadarrama, are the palace and magnificent gardens of **La Granja de San Ildefonso**, built by Philip IV – the grandson of Louis XIV– in nostalgia for the Versailles of his childhood. Return to the mountains, and after crossing the **Navacerrada Pass**, head northeast through a valley to the **Monasterio de El Paular**. A twisting road farther north traverses the Navafría Pass, before descending into **Pedraza de la Sierra**, a seigniorial town full of charm. Before returning by motorway to Madrid via the Somosierra Pass, the small town of **Sepúlveda** is worth a visit to admire its impressive site overlooking a deep gorge of the River Duratón.

8 EXTREMADURA AND THE PEÑA DE FRANCIA

Round trip of 780km/487mi from Plasencia – This tour through the region of Extremadura has a strong historic focus because of its links with the Romans, the great conquistadors and Emperor Charles V. The tour ends with the Peña de Francia, in the province of Salamanca.

After visiting the cathedral and old quarter of **Plasencia**, the tour starts in the verdant **Valle de La Vera**, the setting for the **Monasterio de Yuste**, to which Charles V withdrew following his abdication, and the 15C castle in **Jarandilla de la Vera** (now a parador). Leaving the valley along a country road that crosses the Valdecañas Reservoir, you come to the village of **Guadalupe**, huddled around its magnificent monastery. Following a visit to this shrine, continue westwards to the monumental town of **Trujillo**, the birthplace of several of the famous conquistadors, and the site of one of Spain's most impressive and original main squares. From Trujillo, the tour then heads southwest by fast highway to **Mérida** to admire the city's Roman remains (theatre, amphitheatre etc) and the Museo Nacional de Arte Romano, which bears witness to Mérida's importance during this period. The next stops on the itinerary are **Cáceres**, a monumental town with a stunning and superbly preserved old town where time seems to have stopped in the 16C and 17C, and **Alcántara**, whose main sights of interest are a monastery – the seat of the military order of the same name – and an exceptional Roman bridge spanning the Tagus. Head northeast to **Coria** to visit its cathedral, and then into the province of Salamanca, to **Ciudad Rodrigo**, a pleasant small town with several buildings of interest hidden behind its walls. The tour ends with a visit to the **Peña de Francia**, a crag rising to 1 723m/5 682ft, and the Sierra de Béjar, with its typical mountain villages.

9 THE LANDS OF LA MANCHA

Round trip of 849km/531mi from Cuenca – For many, La Mancha conjures up a scene of seemingly endless fields of cereal crops and vines, interspersed with the occasional village or town and the evocative silhouette of a windmill or castle. Yet it is also an area of impressive mountains and landscapes that have little in common with this image.

Cuenca, with its impressive position between the ravines of the Júcar and Huécar rivers, is the starting-point for this tour, which begins with a drive through the **sierra** of the same name, famous for sights such as the Ciudad Encantada (with its unusual stone formations), the source of the River Cuervo, and the Beteta Ravine. Returning to Cuenca, the itinerary then heads out along the flat landscapes to the southwest to **Belmonte**, with its castle and interesting collegiate church, and **Campo de Criptana**, a typical La Mancha village, whose houses are framed by the silhouette of its windmills. After passing through **Alcázar de San Juan**, the largest town in the area, continue on to **Consuegra**, where the castle and line of windmills on a hill overlooking the town offers one of the region's most enduring sights. From here, head south for a visit to the **Parque Nacional de las Tablas de Daimiel,** a wetland area at the confluence of the River Guadiana and River Cigüela. The next stop on the itinerary is in **Almagro**, a historic town that has preserved its delightful old quarter, including a magnificent main square and the Corral de Comedias, a 16C theatre. A short distance to the southeast stands **Valdepeñas**, the capital of La Mancha's wine industry. Continuing east, the tour passes through **Villanueva de los Infantes**, containing several fine examples of Renaissance and Baroque architecture, and the village of **Alcaraz**, with its outstanding main square lined by elegant buildings, protected by the mountain range in which the River Mundo has its source. The next stop is the city of **Albacete**, home to a provincial museum with an interesting archaeology section. From here, head north to **Alarcón**, impressively situated on a hill almost completely encircled by the River Júcar and crowned by an imposing medieval castle (now a parador), before returning to Cuenca.

10 THE LEVANTE REGION

Round trip of 715km/447mi from Valencia – This tour running along the coast and inland through the provinces of Valencia, Alicante and Murcia is characterised by long sandy beaches and charming villages and towns with a fascinating artistic and architectural heritage.

Having spent time exploring **Valencia**, start the tour along the Mediterranean, visiting **El Saler**, with its extensive sandy beaches, and the nearby **Parque Natural de la Albufera**, a large freshwater lake and important rice-growing area. The itinerary then passes through a series of large resorts such as **Cullera**, **Gandía**, home to the former palace of the Dukes of Borja, and Denia, watched over by its castle. **Xàbia/Jávea**, with its picturesque old quarter, is just a few miles north of the Cabo de la Nao headland, offering spectacular views of the coast, and **Calp/Calpe**, located close to the impressive **Penyal d'Ifac** rock. **Altea**, the next resort to the south, is one of the area's most attractive coastal towns with its steep and narrow streets. Continue along the coast to **Benidorm**, where the backdrop to the beach is a mass of high-rise hotels and apartment buildings, and from here to the **Terra Mítica** theme park. The tour then heads inland through the mountains to visit **Guadalest**, in a spectacular location on a rocky ridge, **Alcoi/Alcoy**, nestled in a fertile river valley, and to the south, **Xixona**, famous for its nougat, and reached via the Carrasqueta Pass. Returning to the coast, the next major city on the itinerary is **Alicante**, a pleasant and relaxed provincial capital overlooked by an imposing fortress, the Castillo de Santa Bárbara. The itinerary continues southwards, skirting the resorts of Guardamar del Segura and Torrevieja, before arriving at **Mar Menor**, a shallow lagoon separated from the sea by a long sand bar, at the southern tip of which stands the resort of **La Manga del Mar Menor**. After a visit to **Cartagena**, on the curve of a deep bay, leave the coast for the town of **Murcia**, whose main sights are its fine cathedral and the Museo Salzillo, a museum dedicated to the 18C sculptor Francisco Salzillo. Continue northeast to **Orihuela**, a tranquil town with numerous churches of interest, and then to **Elx/Elche**, famous for its palm grove. From here the itinerary heads farther inland by dual carriageway to **Villena**, protected by its imposing castle. The final stop on this driving tour is **Xàtiva/Játiva**, the town of a thousand fountains. Situated on a fertile plain, the town has preserved a number of buildings of architectural interest.

11 CÓRDOBA, SEVILLA, CÁDIZ AND MÁLAGA

Round trip of 890km/556mi from Córdoba – This tour takes in some of the finest cities of inland Andalucía, the delightful whitewashed towns and villages (*pueblos blancos*) in the provinces of Cádiz and Málaga, as well as the famous resorts along the Costa del Sol.

Córdoba, one of the three emblems of Andalucía, along with Sevilla and Granada, is one of Spain's most beautiful cities with monuments such as the Mezquita, typical whitewashed streets and a history influenced by the Christian, Muslim and Jewish faiths. From here, head west to **Écija**, the so-called "frying pan" of Andalucía, a town of churches, convents, palaces and numerous bell towers. Farther west stands the breathtaking city of **Sevilla**, a name that conjures up passion and colour, where several days are needed to explore it to the full. The itinerary then heads towards the Atlantic, pausing in the elegant town of **Jerez de la Frontera**, famous for its sherry, equestrian history, and delightful architecture, before arriving in **Cádiz**, reached via an impressive causeway. This charming provincial capital and port is one of Spain's best-kept secrets, with its 18C architecture, historic squares, impressive monuments and superb beaches. **Chiclana de la Frontera**, to the south, is the closest town to the Playa de la Barrosa, a magnificent, and seemingly endless sandy beach. From here, the tour heads inland to **Medina Sidonia**, a quaint town with a medieval quarter perched on a hill with expansive views of the surrounding area. The whitewashed town of **Arcos de la Frontera**, the next stop, has an even more outstanding location, straddling a ridge above a gorge of the River Guadalete. Arcos is one of the region's famous **Pueblos Blancos**, which include **Ronda**, renowned for its dramatic location, stunning architecture and tradition of bullfighting. From Ronda, the itinerary winds its way through stunning mountain scenery down to the coast, dominated by the impressive **Rock of Gibraltar**. The coast road east to Málaga passes through some of the Costa del Sol's most famous resorts (Estepona, **Marbella**, Fuengirola, Benalmádena etc), with their luxury developments, hotels and apartments.

Blind arches, La Mezquita, Córdoba

B. Kaufmann/ MICHELIN

From **Málaga**, follow the fast highway inland to **Antequera**, the ideal base from which to explore local nature, and from here to **Estepa**, crowned by the remains of a fortress. The hilltop town of **Osuna**, the last stage on the journey, has preserved an interesting architectural heritage with numerous palaces and noble mansions amid its old whitewashed centre. From Osuna, return directly to Córdoba.

12 GRANADA, ALMERÍA AND JAÉN

Round trip of 835km/522mi from Granada – This tour through the eastern half of Andalucía is characterised by historic towns and cities with an outstanding artistic heritage, magnificent deserted beaches, breathtaking mountain scenery and a landscape carpeted with olive trees as far as the eye can see.

For many, a visit to the Alhambra, overlooking **Granada**, is the highlight of a trip to Spain. It marks the starting-point for this driving tour, which begins with a journey across the spectacular **Alpujarras** mountain range, passing through verdant valleys and picturesque whitewashed small towns and villages to reach **Almería**, a provincial capital overlooked by a Moorish fortress perched on a hill above the city. The itinerary continues through the **Parque Natural de Cabo de Gata** and along the Almerian coast, an area of luminous skies, sand dunes, wild beaches and impressive desert landscapes that conjure up images of nearby Africa; **Mojácar**, perched on a hill, is the most attractive town in this area. From here, follow the fast highway north, cutting inland to the area known as Los Vélez, in the foothills of the Sierra de María, and the town of **Vélez Blanco**, overlooked by its unusual Renaissance castle. Once you have crossed the Sierra de María, a cross-country route leads to **Pontones**, in the province of Jaén, at the heart of the **Parque Natural de las Sierras de Cazorla, Segura y las Villas**. The tour through the park as far as **Cazorla** passes through impressive mountain landscapes cut by deep ravines, rivers and streams. Following a restorative sojourn at the heart of nature, the tour continues to **Úbeda** and **Baeza**, two monumental towns renowned for their magnificent Renaissance architecture. The last leg of the tour traverses extensive olive groves before reaching **Jaén**, spread out at the foot of the Cerro de Santa Catalina, a hill crowned by the city's imposing Arab fortress. Apart from the castle, the other major sights of interest in Jaén are its sumptuous cathedral and the Arab baths in the Palacio de Villardompardo.

Over the Border

If you're staying close to Spain's national borders, you may wish to consider a day trip into southwest France or Portugal to visit a number of sights of interest within easy distance.

The Green Guide collection covers these areas (Atlantic Coast; Languedoc Roussillon Tarn Gorges; and Portugal), in addition to the *Michelin Guide France*, the *Michelin Guide España Portugal*, and a comprehensive range of maps and plans to enhance your touring itineraries.

PLACES OF INTEREST CLOSE TO THE SPANISH BORDER

FRANCE

Across the border from the province of **Guipúzcoa**, the Basque country of France boasts some of the country's most beautiful and most famous resorts such as St Jean de Luz, Biarritz and Bayonne.
Less than 30km/18mi from **Roncesvalles** (Navarra) is the town of St-Jean-Pied-de-Port, a famous staging-post on the Way of St James. From various places in the **Pirineos Aragoneses**, such as Somport and the Portalet Pass, it is possible to

Bayonne

drive into the Parc National des Pyrénées, a protected area within the French Pyrenees. From the **Pirineos Catalanes**, it is also easy to cross the border to admire the impressive landscapes on the French side of the range.
From **Cerbère** (Girona), the coast road winds its way north to the delightful village of Collioure, where the poet Antonio Machado died, and then inland to Perpignan, the capital of French Catalunya.

PORTUGAL

Opposite the Galician town of **Tui/Tuy** (Pontevedra), and linked by a bridge designed by Gustave Eiffel over the River Miño, stands Valença do Minho, where you can ascend Monte do Faro to enjoy a magnificent view.
To the south of **Puebla de Sanabria**, in the province of Zamora, it is also well worth visiting the historic Portuguese city of Braganza, while from **Ciudad Rodrigo** (Salamanca) you may wish to explore the fortified town of Almeida.
From **Cáceres**, the N 521 runs directly west into Portugal and the attractive mountain landscapes of the Serra de São Mamede, including the fortified town of Marvão and Castelo de Vide. The walled town of Elvas is located just across the border from **Badajoz**, with Estremoz and its attractive old quarter some 50km/31mi farther west.
Ayamonte (Huelva), the closest town to Portugal in southern Spain, is the perfect starting-point from which to explore the summer playground of the Algarve, with its beautiful beaches, lively resorts and quaint fishing villages.

Leisure Activities

As a result of its climate and varied landscapes, Spain is able to offer a whole range of activities for nature-lovers and outdoor sports enthusiasts.

WINTER SPORTS

There are 31 ski resorts in Spain including 17 in the Pyrenees, six in the Cordillera Cantábrica, four in the Cordillera Central, three in the Cordillera Ibérica and one in the Sierra Nevada (near Granada). Information on these is available from the Federación Española de Deportes de Invierno, Arrofresno 3 A, 28035 Madrid, ☎ 91 376 99 30, or from ATUDEM (Asociación Turística de Estaciones de Esquí y Montaña), calle Padre Damián 43 2°, puerta 26A, 28036 Madrid, ☎ 91 350 20 20. Maps and brochures showing the major resorts, including their altitude and facilities (ski-lifts, downhill and cross-country runs), are available from tourist offices.

GOLF

There are approximately 180 golf courses across the country, a number that is steadily growing, particularly in coastal areas. For further information, contact the Federación Española de Golf, calle Capitán Haya 9, 5°, 28020 Madrid, ☎ 91 555 26 82, www.golfspainfederacion.com. A map of golf courses is also available from tourist offices.

Golf courses and their telephone numbers are also listed in the current edition of the **Michelin Guide España Portugal** under the nearest town or city.

Playing golf in Jávea

B. Kaufmann / MICHELIN

HUNTING

Spain boasts the largest hunting area of any European country, populated by large game including wild boar, deer and moufflon, and smaller prey such as partridge, pheasant, rabbits, hare and duck. The hunting season generally runs from September to February, although this varies from species to species. Hunting and fishing permits can be obtained from local autonomous community authorities. For further details, as well as information on the official hunting calendar, contact the Federación Española de Caza, calle Francos Rodríguez 70, 2°, 28039 Madrid, ☎ 91 311 14 11.

FISHING

Spain's 76 000km/47 500mi of river courses provide a wealth of options for freshwater fishing enthusiasts, although seasons can vary from one region to another. Fishing permits are issued by the Environment Agency (Agencia de Medio Ambiente) in the relevant autonomous community. For further information on sea and freshwater fishing, contact the Spanish Sea and Freshwater Fishing Federation (Federación Española de Pesca en Agua Dulce y Marítima), calle Navas de Tolosa 3, 1°, 28013 Madrid, ☎ 91 532 83 53.

SAILING

The waters of the Mediterranean and Atlantic are one of Spain's major attractions. As a result, hundreds of sailing clubs and pleasure marinas have been established along the coastlines. For further information, apply to the Royal Sailing Federation (Real Federación de Vela), calle Luis de Salazar 12, 28002 Madrid, ☎ 91 519 50 08; www.rfev.es.

SCUBA-DIVING

The Spanish coast, in particular the waters of the Mediterranean, is becoming increasingly popular with scuba-divers, with the development of diving sites such as the Cabo de Gata, the Islas Medes, on the Costa Brava, and resorts in the Balearic and Canary islands. For further information, contact the Spanish Scuba-Diving Federation (Federación Española de Actividades Subacuáticas), calle Santaló 15, 3° 1ª, 0821 Barcelona; ☎ 93 200 67 69; www.fedas.es.

B. Kaufmann/ MICHELIN

HIKING AND MOUNTAINEERING

Hiking is becoming increasingly popular across Spain. For information on hiking routes and paths, as well as mountaineering, contact the Spanish Mountaineering Federation (Federación Española de Montañismo), calle Floridablanca 75 entresuelo 2ª, 08015 Barcelona, ☎ 93 426 42 67, www.fedme.es.

HORSE RIDING

A wide choice of options is available to horse-riding enthusiasts, ranging from short excursions to treks lasting several days. Every autonomous community has a large number of companies and organisations offering equestrian activities. For further information, contact the Spanish Horse Riding Federation (Federación Hípica Española), calle Menorca 3, 4º, 28009 Madrid, ☎ 91 436 42 00; www.rfhe.com.

OTHER SPORTS

Information on clubs offering paragliding, hang-gliding, microlight flying, rafting etc is available from local tourist offices.

SPA RESORTS

The hectic pace of modern life has resulted in an increasing number of people visiting the country's spa resorts for a few days in which to relax, recharge their batteries and help ease certain illnesses and ailments through treatments that are based on the medicinal qualities of the resorts' mineral-rich waters.

Generally speaking, spa complexes are found in areas of outstanding beauty where visitors and patients are also able to enjoy the surrounding nature and leisure facilities available. In Spain, there are a number of spa resorts dotted around the country, inheriting a tradition that has been passed down from the Greeks, Romans and Moors. For information on the treatments and facilities available at individual spas, contact the National Spa Resort Association (Asociación Nacional de Estaciones Termales), calle Rodríguez San Pedro 56, 3º, 28015 Madrid, ☎ 91 549 03 00, or log onto www.balnearios.org.

IDEAS FOR CHILDREN

In recent years, the number of leisure attractions popular with families has increased dramatically with the opening of several major theme and water parks. The following list offers just a few examples of places that will guarantee a fun day out for children and their parents alike.

The country's best-known **theme parks** are Port Aventura (near Tarragona), Terra Mítica (Benidorm), Isla Mágica (Sevilla) and Warner Bros. Park on the outskirts of Madrid. The country's capital is also home to one of Spain's best amusement parks.

Wildlife parks, such as the Parque de la Naturaleza de Cabárceno (near Santander), zoos (Madrid) and aquariums (Barcelona, Madrid, Donostia-San Sebastián, and O Grove, in Galicia), continue to be popular with youngsters of all ages, as do the bird and animal parks in the Canary Islands, including the Parque Ecológico Las Águilas del Teide, Loro Parque and Cactus and Animal Park, all of which are on Tenerife; Palmitos Park, on Gran Canaria; and Tropical Park, on Lanzarote.

The Spanish coastline, particularly the Mediterranean, boasts numerous **water parks**, which are invariably full throughout the summer.

The country's **interactive science museums**, such as those in Valencia, Granada and La Coruña, offer an interesting and educational alternative to the leisure options above, as does a visit to the **Parque Minero** in Minas de Riotinto (Huelva), where visitors are transported by miners' train to discover this fascinating site.

Lastly, for those families on holiday close to Almería, a visit to **Mini-Hollywood**, where many of the early Spaghetti Westerns were filmed, is an absolute must for young and old alike.

UNESCO World Heritage Sites

In 1972, the United Nations Educational, Scientific and Cultural Organization (UNESCO) adopted a Convention for the preservation of cultural and natural sites. To date, more than 150 States Parties have signed this international agreement, which has listed over 600 sites "of outstanding universal value" on the World Heritage List. Each year, a committee of representatives from 21 countries, assisted by technical organizations (ICOMOS – International Council on Monuments and Sites; IUCN – International Union for Conservation of Nature and Natural Resources; ICCROM – International Centre for the Study of the Preservation and Restoration of Cultural Property, the Rome Centre), evaluates the proposals for new sites to be included on the list, which grows longer as new nominations are accepted and more countries sign the Convention. To be considered, a site must be nominated by the country in which it is located. The protected cultural heritage may be monuments (buildings, sculptures, archaeological structures etc) with unique historical, artistic or scientific features; groups of buildings (such as religious communities, ancient cities); or sites (human settlements, examples of exceptional landscapes, cultural landscapes) which are the combined works of man and nature of exceptional beauty. Natural sites may be a testimony to the stages of the earth's geological history or to the development of human cultures and creative genius or represent significant ongoing ecological processes, contain superlative natural phenomena or provide a habitat for threatened species.

Signatories of the Convention pledge to cooperate to preserve and protect these sites around the world as a common heritage to be shared by all humanity. Some of the most well-known places which the World Heritage Committee has inscribed include: Mont-Saint-Michel and its Bay (France, 1979), Australia's Great Barrier Reef (1981), the Statue of Liberty (USA, 1984), the Canadian Rocky Mountain Parks (1984), Durham Castle and Cathedral (UK, 1986), the Great Wall of China (1987), the Kremlin (Russia, 1990) and the Historic Centre of Brugge (Belgium, 2000).

UNESCO World Heritage sites included in this guide:

Alcalá de Henares: University and historic quarter	**Lugo**: Roman walls
Altamira: Cave	**Mérida**: Archaeological site
Atapuerca (Burgos): Prehistoric remains	**Oviedo**: Monuments in the city and the kingdom of Asturias
Ávila: Old town and extra-muros churches	**Poblet**: Monastery
Barcelona: Parque Güell, Palacio Güell, Casa Milà, Palau de la Música Catalana and Hospital de Sant Pau	**Salamanca**: Old town
Burgos: Cathedral	**San Millán de la Cogolla**: Monasterio de Yuso and Monasterio de Suso
Cáceres: Old town	**Santiago de Compostela**: Old town
Córdoba: Historic centre	**Santiago de Compostela**: Way of St James
Cuenca: Historic fortified town	**Segovia**: Old town and aqueduct
Doñana: National Park	**Sevilla**: Cathedral, Alcázar and Archivo de Indias
Elche: El Palmeral palm grove	**Tarragona**: Roman town (Tarraco)
El Escorial: Monastery	**Tenerife**: San Cristóbal de la Laguna
La Gomera: Garajonay National Park	**Teruel**: Mudéjar architecture
Granada: Alhambra, Generalife and Albaicín	**Toledo**: Historic city
Guadalupe: Monasterio Real de Santa María	**Valencia**: La Lonja de la Seda
Ibiza: Biodiversity and culture	**Vall de Boí (Lleida)**: Romanesque churches

What to Buy

Spain has always had a rich tradition of arts and crafts reflecting the character of each region as well as the influence of the various civilisations – Iberian, Roman, Visigothic, and Muslim – that have marked the country's history. Traditional wares such as pottery, ceramics, basketwork and woven goods are produced countrywide.

POTTERY AND CERAMICS

The difference between pottery and ceramics is that pottery has been baked just once. In Castilla, pottery is mainly made by women who use a primitive technique. Among their specialities are kitchen utensils, jars and water pitchers. The basic items of crockery used in farmhouses – dishes, soup tureens and bowls made of glazed earthenware (*barro cocido*) – appear in villages and on stalls in every market. Many of the techniques (metal lustre, *cuerda seca*, decorative motifs, and colour) used in ceramics have been influenced by Islamic traditions. There are two large pottery centres in the Toledo region. The first, **Talavera de la Reina** is famous for its blue, green, yellow, orange and black ceramics, while the second, **El Puente del Arzobispo**, mainly uses shades of green. Pottery from **La Bisbal d'Empordà** in Catalunya has a yellow background with green decorative motifs. The Mudéjar tradition is evident in Aragón and the Levante region where blue and white pottery is made in **Muel**, green and purple ceramics in **Teruel** and lustreware in **Manises** (Valencia). Most of the figurines used as decoration for cribs at Christmas are produced in **Murcia**. Spain's richest pottery region is Andalucía, with workshops in **Granada** (glazed ceramics with thick green and blue strokes), **Guadix** (red crockery), **Triana** in Sevilla, (polychrome animal figures, glazed and decorated), **Úbeda, Andújar** (jars with cobalt blue patterns) and in **Vera** (white pottery with undulating shapes). In Galicia, porcelain and earthenware goods with contemporary shapes and designs are factory-made at the **Sargadelos** centre in the province of La Coruña, but there is also a craft industry at **Niñodaguia** in Orense (where the yellow glaze only partially covers the pottery) and at **Bruño** (where yellow motifs set off a dark brown background). Mention should be made of the famous *xiurels*, whistles decorated in red and green from the Balearic Islands.

LACE, WOVEN AND EMBROIDERED GOODS

The textile industry was very prosperous under the Muslims and several workshops still thrive today. Brightly coloured blankets and carpets are woven in the Alpujarras region, la Rioja, the area around Cádiz (Grazalema) and at Níjar near Almería (where *tela de trapo* carpets are made from strips of cloth). Blankets from Zamora, Palencia and Salamanca are well known. The village of **El Paso**, on the island of La Gomera, in the Canary Islands, is the only place in Spain that still produces silk fabrics.

In some villages in the province of Ciudad Real (particularly in **Almagro**) female lacemakers may still be seen at work in their doorways with bobbins and needles. Lacework from **Camariñas** in Galicia is also widely known. The most popular craft, however, is embroidery, often done in the family. The most typical, geometrically patterned embroideries come from the Toledo region (**Lagartera** and **Oropesa**). Embroidery has been raised to the level of a veritable art in two thoroughly Spanish domains: firstly, in the ornaments used for *pasos* during Holy Week and secondly in bullfighters' costumes.

METALWORK

Iron forging, a very old practice in Spain, has produced some outstanding works of art such as the wrought-iron grilles and screens that adorn many of the country's churches. Blacksmiths continue to make the grilles for doors and windows so popular in architecture in the south of Spain (La Mancha, Extremadura and Andalucía).

Guadalupe, in Extremadura, is an important centre for copper production (boilers, braziers etc). Damascene weapons (steel inlaid with gold, silver and copper) are still being produced today, in **Eibar** (País Vasco) and in **Toledo** particularly, according to pure Islamic tradition. The best switchblades and knives in Spain are produced in **Albacete**, Las Palmas de Gran Canaria and Taramundi (Asturias).

Gold- and silver-smithing were developed in antiquity and throughout the Visigothic period and have retained some traditional methods. One example is filigree ornamentation (soldered, intertwined gold and silver threads) crafted in **Córdoba** and **Toledo**. Salamanca, Cáceres and Ciudad Rodrigo specialise in gold jewellery. **Santiago de Compostela** is the world's leading centre for black amber ornaments.

LEATHERWORK

Leather-making has always been an important trade, especially in Andalucía, and has become industrialised in some areas. The town of Ubrique (Cádiz) is the leading producer of leatherwork in Spain, followed by the Alicante area and the Balearic Islands. The production of the famous **Córdoba** leather, including embossed polychrome leatherwork, continues to the same high standards. Workshops specialising in the manufacture of harnesses and horse-riding and hunting accessories are predominantly found in Andalucía (Jerez de la Frontera, Alcalá de los Gazules, Villamartín, Almodóvar del Río and Zalamea la Real) .
Typically Spanish gourds and wineskin containers are made in the provinces of Bilbao, Pamplona/Iruña and Burgos and in other wine-growing areas. The wineskins produced in Valverde del Camino (Huelva) are known throughout Spain.

BASKETWORK

Basket-making remains one of the most representative of Spanish crafts. Although carried out countrywide, it is particularly rich on the Mediterranean coast and in the Balearic Islands. The type of product and the material used vary from region to region. Baskets, hats and mats are made of reeds, willow, esparto grass, strips of olive-wood and birch and chestnut bark, while furniture may be rush or wickerwork. Willow is used in Andalucía and in the Levante, hazel and chestnut in Galicia and in Asturias, and straw and esparto grass on the island of Ibiza.

Sightseeing

Opening times and entrance fees for monuments, museums, churches etc are included in the "Discovering Spain"

section of this guide. This information is given as a guideline only, as times and prices are liable to change without prior warning.
The prices shown are for individual visitors and do not take into account discounts for groups, who may also benefit from private visits. As many monuments require frequent maintenance and restoration, it is always advisable to phone ahead to avoid disappointment.
Information for churches is only given if the interior contains a sight of particular interest with specific opening times or if an entrance fee is payable. In general, religious buildings should not be visited during services, although some only open for Mass, in which case visitors should show appropriate respect.

Books

GENERAL – HISTORY

Franco – Paul Preston (Fontana 1995)

The Hispanic World in Crisis and Change, 1598-1700 – John Lynch (Blackwell Publishers 1994)

Imperial Spain 1469-1716 – JH Elliott (Penguin Books 1990)

Moorish Spain – Richard Fletcher (Phoenix Press 1994)

The Basques, the Catalans and Spain – Daniele Conversi (C Hurst & Co 1997)

The New Spaniards – John Hooper (Penguin Books 1995)

A Concise History of the Spanish Civil War – Paul Preston (Fontana 1996)

Fire in the Blood – Ian Gibson (Faber and Faber 1992)

Spanish Hours – Simon Courtauld (Libri Mundi 1996)

The Spanish Labyrinth – Gerald Brenan (CUP 1990)

Homage to Catalonia – George Orwell (Penguin Books 2000)

Admiral of the Ocean Sea: A Life of Christopher Columbus – Samuel Eliot Morison (Little Brown and Company 1991)

The Spanish Seaborne Empire – JH Parry (University of California Press 1990)

The Basque History of the World – Mark Kurlansky (Jonathan Cape 1999)

TRAVEL

A Moment of War – Laurie Lee (Penguin Books 1992)

A Parrot in the Pepper Tree – Chris Stewart (Sort Of Books 2002)

A Rose for Winter – Laurie Lee (Penguin Books 1971)

As I Walked Out One Midsummer Morning – Laurie Lee (Penguin Books 1971)

Andalucía – Michael Jacobs (Pallas Athene 1999)

A Visit To Spain and North Africa – Hans Christian Andersen (Peter Owen 1975)

Barcelona – Robert Hughes (Harvill Press 1999)

Between Hopes and Memories: A Spanish Journey – Michael Jacobs (Picador 1984)

The Charm of Majorca – Charles Moore (Colin Venton 1974)

Cities of Spain – David Gilmour (John Murray 1992)

Contrasting Spain – Charles Moore (Venton Educational 1977)

Driving Over Lemons – Chris Stewart (Sort Of Books 1999)

Homage to Barcelona – Colm Tóibín (Simon & Schuster 1994)

Iberia – James A Michener (Fawcett Books 1983)

Madrid – Elizabeth Nash, Michael Jacobs (C Hurst & Co 2001)

On the Shores of the Mediterranean – Eric Newby (Picador 1995)

Our Lady of the Sewers and Other Adventures in Deep Spain – Paul Richardson (Abacus 1999)

A Pilgrim's Road – Bettina Selby (Abacus 1995)

South from Granada – Gerald Brenan (Penguin Books 1992)

Spain – Jan Morris (Penguin Books 1986)

Spanish Journeys – Adam Hopkins (Penguin 1993)

The Face of Spain – Gerald Brenan (Penguin Books 1987)

The Pillars of Hercules – Paul Theroux (Penguin Books 1996)

The Way of St James: a Walker's Guide – Alison Raju (Cicerone Press 1998)

Wild Olives – William Graves (Pimlico 1996)

Wines of Spain – Jan Read (Mitchell Beazley 2001)

A Woman Unknown – Lucia Graves (Virago Press 2000)

Voices of the Old Sea – Norman Lewis (Picador 1996)

ART – LITERATURE

The Sun Also Rises – Ernest Hemingway (Vintage 2000)

For Whom the Bell Tolls – Ernest Hemingway (Vintage 1999)

Death in the Afternoon – Ernest Hemingway (Vintage 2000)

Spanish Short Stories Vol 1 – Jean Franco (Ed) (Penguin Books 1970)

Spanish Short Stories Vol 2 – Gudie Lawaetz (Ed) (Penguin Books 1972)

World of Art: Dalí – Dawn Ades (Thames & Hudson 1995)

The House of Bernarda Alba and Other Plays – Federico García Lorca (Penguin Books 2001)

Goya – José Gudiol (Harry N Abrams Inc 1998)

Picasso – Timothy Hilton (Thames & Hudson 1975)

Lorca: A Dream of Life – Leslie Stainton (Bloomsbury 1999)

The Assassination of Federico García Lorca – Ian Gibson (WH Allen 1979)

Federico García Lorca – Ian Gibson (Faber and Faber 1989)

Lorca's Granada – Ian Gibson (Faber and Faber 1992)

When to Go

SEASONS

As a guideline, the best two seasons to visit Spain are spring and autumn, when temperatures across the country are generally pleasant.

Spring is the best time to explore Extremadura, Castilla-La Mancha and Andalucía, which in summer are the hottest regions in Spain. Late spring is also a good time to visit the Mediterranean and Balearic Islands, as the sea temperature starts to warm up.

In **summer**, the country's north coast comes into its own, offering a pleasant climate for sightseeing and relaxing on the beach without the oppressive heat of other parts of the country. This time of year is also ideal for discovering the magnificent mountain landscapes of

Temperature chart

Maximum temperatures in black.
Minimum temperatures in red.

Month	Jan	Feb	Mar	Apr	May	Jun	Jul	Aug	Sep	Oct	Nov	Dec
	13	14	16	18	21	25	28	28	25	21	16	13
Barcelona	6	7	9	11	14	18	21	21	19	15	11	7
	9	11	15	18	21	27	31	30	26	19	13	9
Madrid	1	2	5	7	10	14	17	17	14	9	5	2
	12	12	15	15	17	20	22	22	21	18	15	12
Santander	7	6	8	9	11	14	16	16	15	12	9	7
	15	17	20	23	26	32	36	36	32	26	20	16
Sevilla	6	6	9	11	13	17	20	20	18	14	10	7
	15	16	8	20	23	26	29	29	27	23	19	16
Valencia	5	6	8	10	13	16	19	20	17	13	9	6

the Pyrenees, Picos de Europa, and the Sierra de Gredos, Sierra de Guadarrama and Sierra Nevada ranges.

Autumn is a generally pleasant season across most of Spain.

In **winter**, skiing enthusiasts can head for the Pyrenees or the Sierra Nevada, while those preferring to escape the cold wet winter in northern Europe can travel south to the Canary Islands for some winter sunshine.

For up-to-date information on **weather** in Spain, log onto the Spanish Meteorological Office website at www.inm.es.

WHAT TO PACK

Since Spain has so many days of sunshine and its temperatures are generally warmer than many other European countries, pack as few clothes as possible. Unless you choose to visit in winter, light-weight clothing is usually an ideal choice. It's a good idea to pack a sturdy pair of walking shoes, or even hiking boots. An umbrella, rainwear, a light-weight jacket and suntan lotion are good to have with you. Try to pack everything in one suitcase and a carry-on bag. Take an extra tote bag for bringing new purchases back home.

Calendar of Events

Spain's major festivals are mentioned in the list below. In order to confirm exact dates and times, which may vary slightly, contact the relevant local tourist office, which will be able to provide an up-to-date calendar of events. During the summer months, practically every small town and village in the country hosts a fiesta in honour of its own patron saint.

WEEK BEFORE ASH WEDNESDAY

Carnival festivities
Cádiz, Santa Cruz de Tenerife

1ST SUNDAY IN MARCH

International Vintage Car Rally
Sitges (Barcelona)

3RD SUNDAY IN LENT

Feast of the Magdalen; bullfights, processions
Castellón de la Plana

12-19 MARCH

Las Fallas Festival
Valencia

HOLY WEEK

Processions
Cartagena, Cuenca, Málaga, Murcia, Sevilla, Valladolid, Zamora

FIRST WEEK AFTER EASTER

Spring Festival
Murcia

APRIL

April Fair
Sevilla

22-24 OR 24-26 APRIL

St George's Festival: "Moors and Christians"
Alcoi/Alcoy

LAST SUNDAY IN APRIL

Romería (pilgrimage) to the Virgen de la Cabeza
Andújar (Jaén)

APRIL OR MAY

Horse Fair
Jérez de la Frontera

1ST FORTNIGHT IN MAY

Las Cruces Festival
Córdoba

15 MAY

San Isidro Festival
Madrid

WHITSUN

Pilgrimage to the Nuestra Señora del Rocío shrine
La Caballada Festival
El Rocío (Huelva)
Atienza (Guadalajara)

2ND SUNDAY AFTER WHITSUN: CORPUS CHRISTI CELEBRATION

Streets carpeted with flowers; competitions; processions
Puenteareas
Sitges (Barcelona)
Toledo

24 JUNE

"Hogueras" St John Festival
Alicante
Midsummer's Day Festival
Ciutadella (Menorca)

4-6 JULY

"A Rapa das Bestas" Festival
A Estrada (Pontevedra)

6-14 JULY

"Los Sanfermines" Festival with bull-running
Pamplona/Iruña

Effigies (ninots), Las Fallas Festival, Valencia

H. Levy/MICHELIN

1ST OR 2ND SATURDAY IN AUGUST

Kayak races down the River Sella
Arriondas – Ribadesella (Asturias)

11-15 AUGUST

Elche Mystery Play
Elche (Alicante)

7-17 SEPTEMBER

Fair (Feria)
Albacete

19 SEPTEMBER

America Day in Asturias
Oviedo

21 SEPTEMBER

St Matthew's Festival
Oviedo

20-26 SEPTEMBER

La Rioja Wine Harvest Festival
Logroño

24 SEPTEMBER

Festival of Our Lady of Mercy (Virgen de la Merced)
Barcelona

8 OCTOBER

Procession of the Virgin
Guadalupe (Cáceres)

WEEK OF 12 OCTOBER

Pilar Festival
Zaragoza

FESTIVALS

Holy Week
Sacred Music Festival
Cuenca

June and July
International Music and Dance Festival ☎ 958 276 200
Granada

July
Internacional Classical Theatre Festival www.festivaldealmagro.com
Almagro (Ciudad Real)

3rd week of July
Jazz Festival www.jazzvitoria.com, ☎ 945 141 919
Vitoria

Last week of July
Jazz Festival www.jazzaldia.com, ☎ 943 440 034
Donostia-San Sebastián

July – August
Classical Theatre Festival www.festivaldemerida.es ☎ 924 004 930
Mérida (Cáceres)
Castell de Perelada Festival
Perelada (Girona)

Last two weeks of September
San Sebastián International Film Festival www.sansebastianfestival.com/ ☎ 943 481 212
Donostia-San Sebastián

First two weeks of October
Catalunya International Film Festival www.cinemasitges.com/
Sitges (Barcelona)

Last week of October
Seminci (International Film Week) www.seminci.com
Valladolid

End of November
Ibero-American Film Festival
Huelva

GLOSSARY

Common words

yes, no	**sí, no**
good morning	**buenos días**
good afternoon	**buenas tardes**
goodbye	**hasta luego, adiós**
please	**por favor**
how are you?	**¿qué tal?**
thank you	**gracias**
(very much)	**(muchas)**
excuse me	**perdone**
I don't understand	**no entiendo**
sir, Mr, you	**señor, Usted**
madam, Mrs.	**señora**
miss	**señorita**

Time

when?	**¿cuándo?**
what time?	**¿a qué hora?**
today	**hoy**
yesterday	**ayer**
tomorrow morning	**mañana por la mañana**
tomorrow afternoon	**mañana por la tarde**

Shopping

how much?	**¿cuánto (vale)?**
(too) expensive	**(demasiado) caro**
a lot, little	**mucho, poco**
more, less	**más, menos**
big, small	**grande, pequeño**
credit card	**tarjeta de crédito**
Correspondence	
post box	**buzón**
post office	**Correos**
telephone	**teléfono**
letter	**carta**
post card	**(tarjeta) postal**
poste restante	**lista (de Correos)**
stamp	**sello**
telephone call	**conferencia**
tobacco shop	**estanco, tabacos**

On the road, In town

coche	car
gasolina	petrol
a la derecha	on the right
a la izquierda	on the left
obras	road works
peligroso	danger, dangerous
cuidado	beware, take care
dar la vuelta a	to go round, tour
después de	after, beyond
girar	to go round, to circle

Numbers

0	cero
1	uno / una
2	dos
3	tres
4	cuatro
5	cinco
6	seis
7	siete
8	ocho
9	nueve
10	diez
11	once
12	doce
13	trece
14	catorce
15	quince
16	dieciséis
17	diecisiete
18	dieciocho
19	diecinueve
20	veinte
21	veintiuno
22	veintidós
23	veintitrés
24	veinticuatro
25	veinticinco
26	veintiséis
27	veintisiete
28	veintiocho
29	veintinueve
30	treinta
40	cuarenta
50	cincuenta
60	sesenta
70	setenta
80	ochenta
90	noventa
100	cien
1,000	mil

Food and Wine

For further hotel and restaurant vocabulary, consult the current edition of the **Michelin Guide España Portugal.**

aceite, aceitunas.........oil, olives
sin gas .... sparkling/still water
ajo .... garlic
alcachofa .... artichoke
alergia: tengo
   alergia a.......... I'm allergic to...
alubias......................beans
anchoas.................anchovies
arroz ....rice
atún.......................... tuna
ave....................... poultry
azúcar...................... sugar
bacalao ....cod
berenjena..............aubergine/
   ....eggplant
café con leche. coffee with hot milk
café solo .... black coffee
calamares................... squid
cangrejo .... crab
carne.........................meat
cebolla......................onion
cerdo......................... pork
cerveza .... beer
chorizos............ spicy sausages
cordero (lechal) .... mutton (lamb)
crema (de leche) ....cream
ensalada .... green salad
entremeses .... hors-d'œuvre
fiambres .... cold cooked meats
gambas .... prawns
garbanzos ....chick peas
guisantes ....garden peas
helado .... ice cream
hígado .... liver
huevo; huevos
   al plato.......... egg; fried eggs
jamón........................ ham
judías verdes.........French beans
langostino .... (king) prawns
leche........................ milk
legumbres ....vegetables
limón .... lemon
mantequilla................. butter
manzana.................... apple
mariscos ....seafood, shellfish
naranja......................orange
nata..........................cream
nuez (nueces) .... nut(s)
pan ....bread
patatas.................. potatoes

pescados...................... fish
pimienta (negra)... (black) pepper
pimiento (rojo/verde).............
   .... (red/green) pepper
plátano .... banana
pollo .... chicken
postre.................... dessert
potaje........................soup
queso ....cheese
sal............................ salt
salchichas................sausages
sandía .... water-melon
setas/hongos .... mushrooms
ternera.......................veal
tortilla ....omelette
trucha.......................trout
vaca/buey................... beef
vegetariano/a.......... vegetarian
vino blanco/
   rosado/tinto ....
   .... white/rosé/red wine
zanahoria...................carrot
zumo de frutas.......... fruit juice

Places and Things to See

See also architectural terms in the Introduction.
Words in italics are in Catalan.
where is?............**¿dónde está?**
may one visit?... **¿se puede visitar?**
key ....**llave**
light .... **luz**
sacristan .... **sacristán**
guide ....**guía**
porter, caretaker .**guarda, conserje**
open, closed ..... **abierto, cerrado**
alcazaba ....Muslim fortress
alcázar..............Muslim palace
alrededores.....environs, outskirts
alto .... pass, high pass
ayuntamiento, *ajuntament* ....
   ....town hall
audiencia ....audience, court
balneario .... spa
barranco ....gully, ravine
barrio, *barri*................. quarter
bodega ....wine cellar/store
cabo, *cap* ....cape, headland
calle, *carrer* ....street
calle mayor ....main street
camino................. road, track
campanario..................belfry
capilla .... chapel

capitel . . . . capital
carretera . . . . main road
cartuja . . . . . . Carthusian monastery
casa . . . . .house
casa consistorial . . . . .town hall
castillo . . . . castle
castro . . . . Celtic village
ciudad, *ciutat* . . . . town, city
claustro . . . . .cloisters
colegio, colegiata . . . .
. . . . .college, collegiate church
collado, *coll*. . . . . pass, high pass
convento . . . . . . monastery, convent
cruz . . . . cross, Calvary
cuadro . . . . .picture
cueva, gruta, cava . . . . cave, grotto
desfiladero . . . . .defile, cleft
embalse . . . . .reservoir, dam
ermita . . . . hermitage, chapel
estación .station
excavaciones . . . . excavations
finca . . . . .property, domain
fuente . . . . fountain
gargantas . . . . .gorges
gruta . . . . cavern, grotto
hoz . . . . . .defile, narrow pass, gorge
huerto, huerta . . . . vegetable/
. . . . market garden
iglesia . . . . .church
no entry, not allowed . . . . **prohibido**
entrance, exit . . . . . .**entrada, salida**
apply to . . . . **dirigirse a**
wait . . . . **esperar**
beautiful . . . . **bello, hermoso**
storey, stairs, steps . . **piso, escalera**
imagen . . . . .religious statue/
. . . . sculpture
isla . . . . .island, isle
lago, *estany* . . . . .lake
mezquita . . . . .mosque
monasterio, *monestir* . . . monastery

monte . . . . mount,
. . . . mountain
mirador . . . . belvedere,
. . . . viewpoint,
. . . . lookout point
museo, *museu* . . . . museum
nacimiento . . . . .source,
. . . . .birthplace
palacio (real), *palau*. . .(royal) palace
pantano . . . . artificial lake
paseo, *passeig* . . . . avenue,
. . . . esplanade, promenade
paso sculptured figures: the Passion
pazo . . . . manor-house (Galicia)
plaza, *plaça* . . . . square
plaza mayor . . . . .main square
plaza de toros . . . . bullring
portada . . . . .portal, west door
pórtico . . . . portal, porch
presa . . . . dam
pueblo, *poble* . .village, market town
puente, *pont* . . . . bridge
puerta . . . . door, gate, entrance
puerto . . . . pass, harbour, port
ría . . . . estuary
río .river, stream
romano; románico . . . . Roman;
. . . . .Romanesque
santuario . . . . .church
siglo . . . . century
talla . . . . .carved wood
tapices . . . . .tapestries
techo . . . . ceiling
tesoro . . . . .treasury, treasure
torre . . . . tower, belfry
torre del homenaje . . . . .keep
torrente . . . . mountain
. . . . stream, torrent
valle, *vall* . . . . valley
vega . . . . fertile plain
vidriera . . . . .window: plain
. . . . .or stained glass
vista . . . . view, panorama

KNOW BEFORE YOU GO

Useful Websites

www.spain.info:
The official site of the Spanish Tourist Board, providing comprehensive information on all aspects of the country, including transport, accommodation, sport and leisure activities.

www.tourspain.co.uk:
The Spanish Tourist Board's site for U.K. visitors.

www.okspain.org:
The Spanish Tourist Board's site for U.S. visitors.

www.tourspain.toronto.on.ca:
The Spanish Tourist Board's site for Canadian visitors.

www.fco.gov.uk.
The British Government's Foreign and Commonwealth Office website provides up-to-date information on travel around the globe.

www.state.gov:
American visitors may check the US State Department website for travel advice around the globe.

www.fac-aec.gc.ca:
Website of Foreign Affairs Canada with relevant travel updates.

www.tourspain.es:
The business-to-business site of the Spanish Tourist Board is useful for travel professionals.

Tourist Organizations

London
22-23 Manchester Square,
London W1U 3PX
☎ (020) 7486 8077;
24-hour brochure line: 0906 364 0630 (60p per minute);
londres@tourspain.es

New York
666 Fifth Avenue,
New York, NY 10103
☎ 212-265-8822;
nuevayork@tourspain.es

Chicago
Water Tower Place, Suite 915 East,
845 North Michigan Avenue,
Chicago, IL 60611
☎ 312-642-1992;
chicago@tourspain.es

Los Angeles
8383 Wilshire Blvd, Suite 960,
Beverly Hills, CA 90211
☎ 213-658-7195/7192
losangeles@tourspain.es

Miami
1221 Brickell Avenue,
Miami, FL 33131
☎ 305-358-1992;
miami@tourspain.es

Toronto
2 Bloor St West, 34th Floor,
Toronto, Ontario M4W 3E2
☎ 416-961-3131;
toronto@tourspain.es

International Visitors

EMBASSY AND CONSULATES

American Embassy
Serrano 75, 28006 Madrid
☎ 91 587 22 40 (emergencies,
☎ 91 587 22 40); www.embusa.es

American Consulates
Paseo Reina Elisenda de Montcada 23, 08034 Barcelona,
☎ 93 280 2227.

In addition there are consular agencies in **Málaga** (☎ 952 47 48 91), **Sevilla** (☎ 954 23 18 85), **Valencia** (☎ 963 51 69 73), **Las Palmas** (☎ 928 27 12 59), **La Coruña** (☎ 981 21 32 33) and **Palma de Mallorca** (☎ 971 40 37 07).

Australian Embassy
Plaza del Descubridor Diego de Ordás 3, 2º, 28003 Madrid,
☎ 913 53 66 00;
www.embaustralia.es.

Australian Consulates
Barcelona (honourary, ☎ 93 490 90 13);
Sevilla (honourary, ☎ 95 422 09 71).

British Embassy
Calle Fernando el Santo 16, 28010 Madrid, ☎ 91 700 82 00; www.ukinspain.com

British Consulate-General
Paseo de Recoletos 7/9, 28004 Madrid, ☎ 91 524 97 00.

British Consular Offices
Alicante (☎ 965 21 61 90);
Barcelona (☎ 93 366 62 00);
Bilbao (☎ 94 415 76 00);
Granada (☎ 669 89 50 53);
Ibiza (☎ 971 30 18 18);
Las Palmas, Canary Islands (☎ 928 26 25 08);
Málaga (☎ 952 35 23 00);

Menorca, Menorca (☎ 971 36 78 18);
Palma de Mallorca, Mallorca (☎ 971 71 24 45);
Santa Cruz de Tenerife, Canary Islands (☎ 922 28 68 63); and
Vigo (☎ 986 43 71 33).

Canadian Embassy
Calle Núñez de Balboa 35, 28001 Madrid, ☎ 91 423 32 50; www.canada-es.org

Canadian Consulate
Barcelona (☎ 93 204 27 00);
Málaga (☎ 952 22 33 46).

Embassy of Ireland
Ireland House, Paseo de la Castellana 46, 4ª, 28046 Madrid, ☎ 91 436 40 93; embajadairlanda@terra.es

Honorary Irish Consulates
Alicante (☎ 965 10 74 85)
Barcelona (☎ 93 491 50 21);
Bilbao (☎ 944 23 04 14);
Las Palmas, Canary Islands (☎ 928 29 77 28);
Málaga (☎ 952 47 51 08);
Palma de Mallorca, Mallorca (☎ 971 72 25 04);
Sevilla (☎ 954 21 63 61); and
Santa Cruz de Tenerife, Canary Islands (☎ 922 24 56 71).

FORMALITIES

Despite the law which came into force on 1 January 1993 authorising the free flow of goods and people within the European Union, travellers must be in possession of a valid **passport**. Holders of British, Irish and US passports do not need a visa for a visit to Spain of less than 90 days. Visitors from some Commonwealth countries or those planning to stay longer than 90 days should enquire about visa requirements at their local Spanish consulate. US citizens should obtain the booklet *Your Trip Abroad* (US $1.75, or online at travel.state.gov) which provides useful information on visa requirements, customs regulations, medical care etc for international travellers. Apply to the Superintendent of Documents, PO Box 371954, Pittsburgh, PA 15250-7954, ☎ 202-512-1800; Fax 202-512-2250; bookstore.gpo.gov.

CUSTOMS REGULATIONS

Since the birth of the single European market and the abolition of the duty-free system on certain goods, allowances for various commodities within the EU have changed. For further information on these allowances as well as specific regulations relating to the Canary Islands, contact HM Customs and Excise, ☎ (0845) 010 9000; www.hmce.gov.uk The US Customs Service offers a free publication **Know Before You Go** for US citizens, ☎ 202 927 6724; www.customs.gov.

TRAVEL INSURANCE

British citizens should apply for **Form E 111**, issued by the Post Office, which entitles the holder to urgent treatment for accident or unexpected illness in EU countries. This form should be presented to the relevant medical services prior to receiving treatment. For further information in the UK, contact your local post office or the Department of Health and Social Security at www.doh.gov.uk. Visitors are strongly advised to take out additional travel insurance to cover against any expenses not covered by form E 111, as well as lost luggage, theft, cancellation, delayed departure etc. Non-EU travellers are advised to check with their insurance companies about taking out supplementary medical insurance with specific overseas coverage.

Pets (cats and dogs) – A general health certificate and proof of rabies vaccination should be obtained from your local vet before departure.

Accessibility

Information on facilities for the disabled within Spain is available from Polibea, Ronda de la Avutarda 3, 28043 Madrid, ☎ 91 759 53 72; www.polibea.com/turismo.

GETTING THERE

By Air

A number of Spanish and international airlines operate direct scheduled services to airports across Spain. These include:

 Iberia Airlines: ☎ 0845 601 2854; www.iberia.com. Reservations within the US and Canada: ☎ 00-772-4642 (toll-free number only within the US and Canada).

British Airways: ☎ 0870 850 9850; www.ba.com. Reservations within the US and Canada: ☎ 1-800-AIRWAYS.

A number of low-cost airlines also offer inexpensive flights to several Spanish cities from the UK. Some airlines only allow bookings to be made via the Internet, while others offer small discounts for Internet bookings:

Buzz: www.buzzaway.com

Bmibaby: www.bmibaby.com

EasyJet: ☎ 0870 6000 000; www.easyJet.com

Hundreds of weekly charter flights also operate from the UK to Spanish cities, particularly along the Mediterranean coast and in the Balearic and Canary islands.

By Sea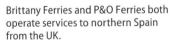

Brittany Ferries and P&O Ferries both operate services to northern Spain from the UK.

Brittany Ferries run a ferry service between Plymouth and Santander from mid-March to mid-November; journey time: approx. 24hr. For reservations, contact:

Brittany Ferries: ☎ 08705 360 360 (UK); ☎ 942 36 06 11 (Santander); www.brittany-ferries.com

P&O Portsmouth offers a twice-weekly crossing from Portsmouth to Bilbao from March to December; journey time: approx. 30hr. For reservations, contact:

P&O Portsmouth: ☎ 08705 20 20 20; ☎ 944 23 44 77 (Bilbao); www.poferries.com

By Rail

Eurostar (☎ 08705 186 186; www.eurostar.com) operates high-speed passenger trains to Paris, from where overnight train-hotel services operate to Madrid and Barcelona, with onward connections to other destinations across the country. Services from Paris, as well as train tickets within Spain, can be booked through the Spanish State Railway Network's (RENFE) UK agent, the Spanish Rail Service, ☎(020) 7224 0345; www.spanish-rail.co.uk Alternatively, log onto the official **RENFE** website at www.renfe.es.

By Coach/Bus

Regular long-distance bus services operate from London to all major towns and cities in Spain. For information, contact: Eurolines UK, ☎ (01582) 404 511; www.eurolines.co.uk

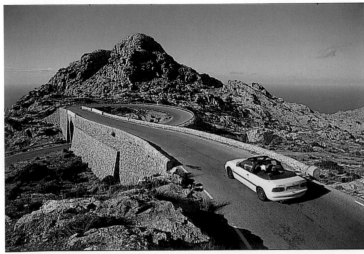

B. Pérousse/MICHELIN

GETTING AROUND

By Car

ROAD NETWORK

Spain has over 340 000km/212 500mi of roads, including 7 000km/4 375mi of divided highways and expressways. **Speed limits** in Spain are as follows:

- 120kph/75mph on expressways and divided highways;
- 100kph/62mph on the open road (with a hard shoulder of at least 1.5m/5ft);
- 90kph/56mph on the open road (without a hard shoulder);
- 50kph/31mph in built-up areas.

DOCUMENTS

In general, motorists need only have a current driving licence from their country of origin and valid papers (vehicle documentation and valid insurance) to drive in Spain, although in certain situations an International Driving Permit may be required. If in doubt, visitors should check with the AA or RAC in the United Kingdom or with the American Automobile Association in the US.

DRIVING REGULATIONS

The minimum driving age is 18. Traffic drives on the right. It is compulsory for passengers in both front and rear seats to wear **seat belts**. Motorcyclists (on all sizes of machine) must wear safety helmets. It is now a legal requirement for motorists to carry two red warning triangles, in addition to a spare tyre and a set of replacement bulbs.

Motorists should note that it is illegal to use a **mobile phone** when driving, unless the vehicle is fitted with a hands-free unit. Heavy on-the-spot fines are frequent for those caught using hand-held phones.

INSURANCE

Those motorists entering Spain in their own vehicles should ensure that their insurance policy includes overseas cover. Visitors are advised to check with their respective insurance company prior to travel. Motorists are also advised to take out adequate accident and **breakdown** cover for their period of travel overseas. Various motoring organisations (AA, RAC etc) will be able to provide further details on options available. Bail bonds are no longer necessary, although travellers may wish to take this precaution (consult your insurance company). Members of the American Automobile Association should obtain the free brochure, *Offices to Serve You Abroad*, which gives details of affiliated organisations in Spain.

If the driver of the vehicle is not accompanied by the owner, he or she must have written permission from the owner to drive in Spain.

ROAD INFORMATION

The **National Traffic Agency** (Dirección General de Tráfico) is able to provide information in English on road conditions, driving itineraries, regulations etc. For further information, call 900 12 35 05 (toll-free) or log onto the agency's website at www.dgt.es.

TOLLS

Tolls are payable on some sections of the Spanish highway network. On Michelin maps, these sections are indicated by kilometre markers in red; toll-free sections are marked in blue.

MAPS AND PLANS

Michelin's España/Portugal spiral **road atlas** and general **road maps** will assist you in the planning of your journey. These are listed in the **Maps and plans** section at the back of the guide.

MOTORING ORGANISATIONS

RACE (Royal Automobile Club of Spain) 902 30 05 05 and 902 40 45 45.

CAR HIRE

Vehicles in Spain can be hired through the offices of all major international car hire companies around the world. Alternatively, cars can be hired at major airports, train stations, large hotels and in all major towns and cities around the country:

Avis 902 24 88 24. www.avis.com

Europcar 902 40 50 20. www.europcar.com

Hertz ✆ 902 22 00 24. www.hertz.com

Visitors should bear in mind that although the legal driving age in Spain is 18, most companies will only rent out vehicles to drivers over the age of 21.

By Rail

RENFE ✆ 902 24 02 02 (24hr information line; reservations 5.15am-11.40pm); www.renfe.es.

The **AVE** (Alta Velocidad Española) high-speed trains run on two lines: Madrid (Atocha Station) to Córdoba in just 1hr 45min and Sevilla in 2hr 15min; and to Zaragoza in 1hr 58min and Lérida in 2h4 58min. ✆ 902 24 02 02.

"Green" railway stations – Dozens of stations are so designated (*estaciones verdes*) due to their location near nature reserves, or because of their suitability for hikers, mountain bikers or for nature lovers wishing to discover the beauty of rural Spain. Schedule information is available from railway stations in provincial capitals. Additional tourist information can be obtained on line at www.renfe.es/index-mapa.html.

TOURIST TRAINS

El Expreso Al Andalus – A seven-day trip across Andalucía in carriages built in the 1920s and 1930s. The tour includes excursions, meals and accommodation and operates from April to June and September to November. Departures from Madrid and Sevilla. ✆ 91 570 16 21 (from 9am-7:30pm); www.alandalusexpreso.com.

El Transcantábrico – This narrow-gauge train skirts the coastline of Cantabria from San Sebastián (Donostia) to Santiago de Compostela. The trip lasts a week and combines rail and bus travel. The service operates from June to October. ✆ 91 571 66 92 (9am-1.30pm and 4-7.30pm).

El Tren de la Fresa – The Strawberry Train operates vintage cars between Madrid and Aranjuez, Sat-Sun in spring and fall from Atocha station. ✆ 902 24 02 02 (Spanish Railways).

By Bus

The Spanish bus network is a comfortable, modern and relatively inexpensive way of travelling across the country. Numerous companies offer local and long-distance services. Information on routes, timetables and prices can be obtained from local bus stations.

Two of the companies with the largest networks are:

Alsa – Extensive routes across the country, particularly in the northwest, center, and along the Mediterranean. For information, call ✆ 902 42 22 42 or log onto www.alsa.es.

Auto Res – Numerous services in the Valencia region, Castilla y León, Extremadura, etc. For information, call ✆ 902 02 00 52 or log onto www.auto-res.net.

By Air

Spain has over 40 airports, including 12 on the islands. Information on these is available from AENA (Aeropuertos Españoles y Navegación Aérea) at www.aena.es, ✆ 902 40 47 04.

The largest airports in the country are as follows:

    Madrid-Barajas ✆ 902 35 35 70.
    Barcelona ✆ 932 98 38 38.
    Bilbao ✆ 94 486 96 64.
    Sevilla ✆ 95 444 90 00.
    Málaga ✆ 95 204 84 84.
    Valencia ✆ 96 159 85 00.
    Palma ✆ 971 78 92 08.

MAJOR AIRLINE COMPANIES:

    Iberia and **Aviaco**: Inforiberia, ✆ 902 400 500 (information and bookings); www.iberia.com

    Air Europa: ✆ 902 401 501; www.aireuropa.com

    Spanair: ✆ 902 13 14 15; www.spanair.com

By Sea

Several ferry companies operate services between the Spanish mainland and the Balearics, Canaries and North Africa.

Trasmediterránea – Daily services to the Balearics (from Valencia and Barcelona), a weekly service from Cádiz to the Canary Islands, and daily crossings to Ceuta and Melilla from Almería, Málaga and Algeciras.
    Information and reservations: ✆ 902 45 46 45 and www.trasmediterranea.es

Regional offices: Madrid: Alcalá 61, 28014 Madrid, ☎ 91 423 85 00; Barcelona: Estació Marítima, Muelle San Beltrán, 08039 Barcelona, ☎ 93 295 91 34/35; Cádiz: Estación Marítima, Muelle Alfonso XIII, 11006 Cádiz, ☎ 956 22 20 38.

Baleària – Baleària operates services to and from the Balearics and from island to island. For information, call ☎ 902 160 180 or log onto www.balearia.com

Regional offices: Madrid: calle O'Donnell 38, ☎ 91 409 14 42; Denia (Alicante), Estación Marítima, Puerto de Denia, ☎ 96 642 86 00.

WHERE TO STAY AND EAT

Address Books

Hotel and Restaurant listings fall within the description of each region in order to enhance your stay and enable you to make the most of your holiday. These recommendations have been chosen for their location, comfort, excellent value for money and in some cases for their charm. We have also made a conscious effort to cover all budgets, although some regions (for example, the Costa Brava, Costa del Sol and the Balearic Islands) are more expensive than others, and prices in Madrid and Barcelona can be as high as in other major cities in Europe.

As a general rule, restaurants serve lunch from 1:30pm-3:30pm and dinner from 9pm-11pm.

The symbols used in the Address Books are explained in the Legend at the back of the guide.

Where to Stay

This section lists a selection of hotels, hostales and pensiones based on the price of a double room in high season and generally excluding breakfast and VAT, unless otherwise indicated. The difference in rates between high and low season can be significant, particularly on the coast and islands, so it is always advisable to receive confirmation of prices in writing at the time of booking.

PARADORS

Almost all of the state-run network of luxury hotels are in restored historic monuments (castles, palaces, monasteries etc) in magnificent locations. For more information, contact Paradores de Turismo, calle Requena 3, 28013 Madrid ☎ 91 561 66 66; www.parador.es The official UK representative is Keytel International, 402 Edgware Road, London W2 1ED ☎ (020) 7616 0300; Fax (020) 7616 0317; paradors@keytel.co.uk. In the US, contact PTB Hotels, ☎ 1-800-467-0772, info@paradors.com; in Canada, ADSUM Tourism Services, ☎ 416-728-5356, paradores-ca@adsum.ws. Special weekend **offers** are often available, in addition to a five-night "go as you please" accommodation **card**.

Parador, Pontevedra

J. Malburet/MICHELIN

RURAL ACCOMMODATION

The number of visitors to Spain who wish to stay in rural accommodation is steadily increasing. Most autonomous communities publish a practical guide listing details of every type of accommodation available, including rooms in private houses, hostels for groups, entire houses for rent, and farm campsites. Contact local tourist offices listed within the Principal Sights for further details, or www.ecoturismorural.com.

CAMPSITES

The Secretaría General de Turismo publishes an annual campsite guide. Further details on camping and caravanning are supplied by the Federación Española de Campings, calle San Bernardo 97-99, Edificio Colomina, 3° planta, 28015 Madrid, ☎ 91 448 12 34. For links to current listings, 👆 *see Useful Web Sites, above.* Book in advance for popular resorts during summer.

YOUTH HOSTELS

Spain's 160 youth hostels are open to travellers with an **international card**, available from international youth hostelling offices and youth hostels themselves. For further information, contact the **Spanish Youth Hostel Network** (Red Española de Albergues Juveniles), ☎ 91 720 11 65. Information and online bookings are available at www.reaj.com.

SPECIAL OFFERS

Many chains and hotels catering to business travellers often offer reduced rates at weekends. It is also possible to purchase vouchers for one or several nights at advantageous prices. For further information on these special offers, contact the following:

NH Hoteles ☎ 902 115 116 (24 hours); www.nh-hoteles.es Special weekend rates from €55 per double room per night in over 100 hotels throughout Spain.

Bancotel ☎ 902 877 877, 00800 1001 1002 from Europe, 91 509 61 22 from elsewhere; www.bancotel.com/ing/index.htm Booklets of five vouchers on sale exclusively at travel agencies and on its website. Three-, four- and five-star hotels. Good discounts on standard rates.

Halcón Viajes ☎ 807 227 222 (information and reservations); www.halconviajes.com Individual vouchers (for a one-night stay for one or two people) with a discount on the official rate.

Hoteles Meliá ☎ 902 14 44 40; www.solmelia.com Discounts via the MAS loyalty card and special weekend offers.

DON'T FORGET THE MICHELIN GUIDE

The **Michelin Guide España Portugal** is revised annually and is an indispensable complement to this guide with additional information on hotels and restaurants including category, price, degree of comfort and setting.

Where to Eat

The restaurants listed in the Address Books in this guide have been chosen for their surroundings, ambience, typical dishes or unusual character. Coin symbols correspond to average cost of a meal and are given as a guideline only. Restaurant prices are classified into categories based on price: ☺ meals less than €14 (less than €16 in large cities); ☺☺ between €14 and €25 (€16 and €30 in large cities); ☺☺☺ between €25 and €40 (€30 and €50 in large cities) and ☺☺☺☺ more than €40 (€50 in large cities).

TAPAS

Given the country's reputation for tapas, we have also included a list of tapas bars where visitors can enjoy an aperitif or meal throughout the day and late into the evening. Prices of tapas are often not listed, although as a general rule the cost of a reasonably priced tapas lunch or supper should not exceed €12.

TAKING A BREAK, SHOPPING AND NIGHTLIFE

These headings, which appear periodically in Address Books throughout the guide, include a variety of addresses from cafés and bars to shops and theatres, as well as nightclubs and concert venues. Some may be quiet cafés during the day, transforming themselves into lively bars at night.

BASIC INFORMATION

DISCOUNTS

Consult the website of the **Instituto de la Juventud**, www.injuve.mtas. es (Calle Marqués de Riscal 16, 28010 Madrid, ☎ 91 363 77 00) for links to youth-oriented travel services; or the **Oficina Nacional de Turismo e Intercambio de Jóvenes y Estudiantes (TIVE)**, calle José Ortega y Gasset 71, 28006 Madrid, ☎ 91 347 77 78 or 91 363 78 12, injuve@mtas.es.

The **EURO<26 Card**, issued by student organisations in 27 countries, entitles young people between the ages of 14 and 25 to a whole series of discounts on travel, cultural events, accommodation etc. In Spain, some 50 000 outlets participate in the scheme. For information, see www. eyca.org

The **Student Card**, available to those aged 12 and over, also provides numerous discounts on a variety of services.

Senior citizens aged 65 and over qualify for significant discounts on transport, entrance fees to monuments, and events and shows. Many museums offer half-price entry, with free entrance to many national monuments.

ELECTRICITY

220 volts AC (some older establishments may still have 110 V). Plugs are two-pin.

Emergency services: ☎ 112
Medical emergencies: ☎ 061
Directory enquiries: ☎ 1003
International directory enquiries: ☎ 025

EMERGENCIES

TELEPHONES

Public telephones accept coins as well as phone cards (*tarjetas telefónicas*). For **international calls** from Spain, dial 00, then dial the country code (44 for the United Kingdom, 353 for Ireland, 1 for the United States and Canada), followed by the area code (minus the first 0 of the STD code when dialling the UK), and the number.

For number information, dial 11888 or 11811 for Spain, 11825 for other countries.

For calls within Spain, dial the full 9-digit number of the person you are calling.

When calling Spain from abroad, dial the international access code, followed by 34 for Spain, then the full 9-digit number.

CURRENCY

The unit of currency in Spain is the **euro**, written as €. In late 2005, the exchange rate was €1.48 to the pound (€0.83 to the US dollar). Coins come in the following denominations: 1, 2, 5, 10, 20 and 50 cents and 1 and 2 euro with notes in 5, 10, 20, 50, 100, 200 and 500 values (& *see the illustrations opposite*). There are no restrictions on the amount of currency (euro or other) that foreigners may bring with them into Spain.

Changing Money

Travellers' cheques and foreign cash can be exchanged at banks and exchange offices (*cambios*). International credit cards are accepted in most shops, hotels and restaurants. Visitors can also obtain cash from bank machines using credit and debit cards. A pin number will be required to use this service.

Banks

Banks are generally open 8.30am-2pm, Monday to Saturday. The same opening times apply in summer, except on Saturdays, when banks are closed.

Credit Cards

In the event of a **lost or stolen credit card**, contact the relevant issuer as soon as possible:

CC **Mastercard**: ☎ 800 97 1231

CC **Visa** ☎ 900 99 1124

CC **American Express** ☎ 902 37 56 37

CC **Diners Club** ☎ 902 40 11 12

PUBLIC HOLIDAYS

Because autonomous communities and individual towns and cities have their own local festivals and feast days, it is difficult to draw up a definitive list of public holidays.

The following list represents those public holidays that are taken throughout the country:

Notes and Coins

The euro banknotes were designed by Robert Kalinan, an Austrian artist. His designs were inspired by the theme "Ages and styles of European Architecture." Windows and gateways feature on the front of the banknotes, bridges feature on the reverse, symbolising the European spirit of openness and co-operation. The images are stylised representations of architecture typical of each period, rather than specific structures.

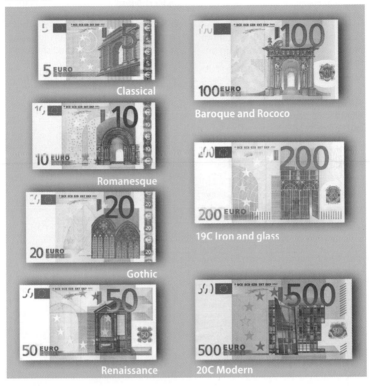

Classical

Romanesque

Gothic

Renaissance

Baroque and Rococo

19C Iron and glass

20C Modern

Euro coins have one face common to all 12 countries in the European single currency area or "Eurozone" (currently Austria, Belgium, Finland, France, Germany, Greece, Ireland, Italy, Luxembourg, The Netherlands, Portugal and Spain) and a reverse side specific to each country, created by their own national artists.

Euro banknotes look the same throughout the Eurozone. All Euro banknotes and coins can be used anywhere in this area.

1 January (New Year's Day), 6 January (Epiphany), Good Friday, 1 May (Labour Day), 15 August (Assumption of Our Lady), 12 October (Virgin of the Pillar: Day of the Hispanidad), 1 November (All Saints), 6 December (Spanish Constitution Day), 8 December (Immaculate Conception) and 25 December (Christmas Day).

POST

Post offices are open 8.30am-2.30pm, Monday-Friday, and 9.30am-1pm on Saturdays.

Stamps (*sellos*) can also be purchased at tobacconists (*estancos*). **The Red Michelin Guide España Portugal** gives the postcode for every town and city covered.

TIME DIFFERENCE

Spain is 1hr ahead of GMT. The Spanish keep very different hours from either the British or North Americans.
As a general rule, restaurants serve lunch from 1:30pm to 3:30pm and dinner from 9pm to 11pm.

SHOPPING

Shops are generally open 10am-2pm and 5-8:30pm, although an increasing number of larger stores and shopping centres do not close for lunch. The majority of shops close on Sundays, and a few still close on Saturday afternoon.

Clothing

Women							Men
	35	4	2½	40	7½	7	
	36	5	3½	41	8½	8	
	37	6	4½	42	9½	9	
Shoes	38	7	5½	43	10½	10	Shoes
	39	8	6½	44	11½	11	
	40	9	7½	45	12½	12	
	41	10	8½	46	13½	13	
	36	4	8	46	36	36	
	38	6	10	48	38	38	
Dresses &	40	8	12	50	40	40	Suits
Suits	42	12	14	52	42	42	
	44	14	16	54	44	44	
	46	16	18	56	46	48	
	36	08	30	37	14½	14,5	
	38	10	32	38	15	15	
Blouses &	40	12	14	39	15½	15½	Shirts
sweaters	42	14	36	40	15¾	15¾	
	44	16	38	41	16	16	
	46	18	40	42	16½	16½	

Sizes often vary depending on the designer. These equivalents are given for guidance only.

a. 🏨 *Luxury hotel ?*

b. 😴 *"Bib Hotel": accommodation at moderate prices ?*

c. 🛋 *Very quiet hotel ?*

Can't decide ?

Find out more with the Michelin Guide Collection!

- A collection of 13 titles
- 30 000 hotels around Europe
- 1 600 town plans
- The best addresses in every price category

Discover the pleasure of travel with the Michelin Guides

MICHELIN
A better way forward

Equestrian statue of Philip III, Plaza Mayor, Madrid

E. Baret/MICHELIN

A WAY OF LIFE

Whenever foreigners conjure up an image of Spain, their thoughts inevitably turn to a leisurely lifestyle, plentiful sunshine, noisy and lively towns and cities, and an extroverted, friendly people whose daily timetable is impossible to comprehend!

Yet, irrespective of the crazy rhythms imposed by the demands of modern life, the Spanish always attempt to extract the very maximum from life; the maxim that most applies to them is that of having to work to live rather than living for work.

Despite the differences that exist between the north and south, the coast and inland areas, and towns and cities, it can be said that a common bond exists among all Spaniards in the manner in which they approach life.

Life in the Street

There's no doubt that the excellent climate enjoyed by most parts of the country is one of the main reasons for the Spaniards' "passion" for living outdoors; there are of course others, of lesser or equal importance. Spain is a country of informal get-togethers and social gatherings, in bars, cafés, restaurants, at work, and of chance meetings of a couple of friends – any excuse is good enough to indulge in a friendly chat or animated discussion. This affection for going out as a group, meeting friends for dinner, or enjoying an aperitif or drink, is to the Spanish a sign of identity, irrespective of their age or social standing. Nor is it uncommon for Spaniards to have a relaxed drink with friends or colleagues before heading home after a long day's work.

Daily Schedule

The daily schedule of the Spanish is completely different from the rest of Europe and as such is the major characteristic that distinguishes the country from its European neighbours. Spaniards don't usually have lunch before 2pm or 2.30pm, or dinner before 9.30pm, a custom that results in long mornings and afternoons and provides ample time for them to indulge in their passion for a leisurely stroll, shopping or meeting up for a snack with friends and work acquaintances.

Tapas and Aperitif Time

This gastronomic pastime is one of the most deeply rooted traditions in Spain, with youngsters, couples and entire families heading for bars to *tapear*, either standing at the counter or, if time allows, sitting down on a café terrace. An aperitif can be a frugal affair, although

Plaza Mayor, Madrid

J. Malbure/MICHELIN

Las Ramblas, Barcelona

B. Pérousse/MICHELIN

by ordering a number of tapas you can quite easily create an alternative to lunch or dinner.

These traditional appetisers come in many guises, ranging from the small tapa itself to larger portions known as a *media ración* or *ración*. Choose a *media ración* of *manchego* cheese or Jabugo cured ham, a *ración* of chorizo sausage, or a selection of vegetarian, fish, seafood or meat dishes – washed down perhaps with a glass of draught beer (*una caña*) or a glass of fino sherry (*una copa de fino*). Every region has its own specialities and its own way of presenting tapas, yet whether you're in the Basque country, Andalucía or in the middle of the Meseta, tapas are appreciated the length and breadth of the country.

Bars

There are literally tens of thousands of bars in Spain, including in the smallest and most remote hamlets and villages. They act as a focal point for locals, who congregate here with friends or family in the evening and at weekends. During the afternoon and early evening in smaller towns and villages you're bound to come across locals playing cards or indulging in a game of dominoes over a coffee or something stronger. The mornings are busy in bars as well, with regulars stopping by for a pastry and coffee for breakfast.

Terraces

With the onset of fine weather, terraces spring up across Spain – outside restaurants, cafés, bars and ice-cream parlours, on pavements and patios and in gardens and narrow alleyways. During the warmer months, it is pleasant at any time of day to take the weight off your feet for a short while and watch the world go by in front of your table.

In summer, many of the most crowded bars and clubs, particularly those by the sea, provide outdoor terraces for their customers.

Beach Bars

These typical features of resorts along the Spanish coast come in various guises, ranging from the cheap and cheerful to the expensive and luxurious. These *chiringuitos*, as they are known, have grown in popularity, particularly given that customers can enjoy a drink or have a meal wearing only their swim suits. In the more popular tourist areas they have become a meeting-point for locals and visitors alike, with some also open for dinner.

Nightlife

The lively character of Spanish towns and cities and summer resorts is often a cause of great surprise to visitors. Nowadays, the choice of venues is often overwhelming, with something to suit every budget and taste: quiet cafés for a drink and a chat with friends; lively bars packed to the rafters, with dance floors and music played at full volume; clubs offering a variety of shows; and nightclubs ranging from small holes-in-the-wall to mega-venues where the pace doesn't stop until late the next morning.

On Thursday and Friday nights and on weekends, as well as in summer and during holidays, the action is almost constant, with nightclubbers migrating from one club or bar to the next – don't be surprised if you get stuck in a traffic jam at three or four in the morning! An example of this is on the paseo de la Castellana, in Madrid, with its numerous outdoor bars open until the small hours.

The Siesta

Although the demands of modern life prevent most people from perpetuating this healthy custom, most Spaniards long to have an afternoon nap and will make sure that they take a restorative siesta on weekends and when they're on holiday. Although less common nowadays, those Spaniards whose work schedule allows them three hours off from 2 to 5pm will try to make it home for lunch and a short sleep.

The Family

In line with other Latin countries, the family remains the bedrock of Spanish life, and is a determining factor in the behaviour and many of the habits of Spanish society at large. Without a solid family base, it would be hard to understand how a country with a high rate of unemployment and one in which children continue to live with their parents until their late-20s and even early-30s could prosper without too many problems. It should also be added that numerous Spanish celebrations and fiestas are based upon these close family ties.

The Work Ethic

Those foreigners who have chosen to live in Spain soon realise that the old image of Spain as a country where very little work is done – a view perpetuated by the country's way of life and daily schedule, and the Spaniards' well-documented liking for enjoying themselves to the full – is far removed from modern reality. Nowadays, the work ethic in Spain is similar to that in any other European country. Visitors may wonder how this is possible, given the unusual lifestyle. The answer is simple: the Spanish sleep less. Working hours are little different from those in the rest of Europe, but from an early age the Spanish are brought up used to sleeping less during the week and trying to catch up on lost sleep on the weekend.

A LAND OF CONTRASTS

Because of its geographical location, Spain acts as a bridge between two continents – Europe and Africa. The country has myriad natural attractions, ranging from long sandy beaches, sheltered coves and steep cliffs to breathtaking mountain landscapes characterised by high peaks and enclosed valleys. By contrast, the centre of Spain, known as the Meseta, is marked by seemingly endless expanses of flat terrain.

Mallorca

J. Malburet/MICHELIN

Government and Administration

The Spanish Constitution, which was approved by referendum on 6 December 1978, defines the political status of the Spanish State as a constitutional monarchy in which sovereignty rests with the Spanish people. This political system can be broken down as follows: a **Head of State**, in the shape of the King, the **Cortes Generales** (Parliament), and a **Government**. The **Cortes** are elected by universal suffrage every four years. They are divided into two chambers: the **Congreso de los Diputados** and the **Senado**. The Government (*Gobierno*) performs executive functions and comprises a head of government (*Presidente del Gobierno* or prime minister), vice-presidents and ministers. Judicial power is an independent authority administered by judges and magistrates. The Supreme Court acts as the highest tribunal in the land.

Spain can be broken down into the following administrative divisions:

Autonomous communities: Spain is divided into 17 *comunidades autónomas*, in addition to two autonomous enclaves (Ceuta and Melilla). These communities may comprise a single province or several provinces. The leading political figure in these is the *Presidente de la Comunidad*, who is elected by universal suffrage every four years. The transfer of decision-making to autonomous bodies has yet to be fully achieved; however, the system of autonomy developed in Spain is one of the most advanced in Europe.

The Iberian Peninsula, which is separated from the rest of Europe by the Pyrenees, is made up of continental Spain and Portugal. Spain covers an area of 504,750km2/194,960sq mi, including the Canary Islands and Balearic Islands, and is the fourth largest European country after Russia, the Ukraine and France. It has over 4,000km/2,500mi of coastline lapped by the waters of the Mediterranean and Atlantic. The country's population currently stands at just under 40,000,000.

Provinces: The need for greater administrative efficiency led the governments under Isabel II (19C) to establish an initial division of the country into provinces. At present, Spain has 50 provinces.

Municipalities: This is the smallest territorial division, comprising a town council (*ayuntamiento*) headed by a mayor (*alcalde*).

Given the new adminstrative system now operating within Spain, communities and municipalities are better able to administer their territory.

Regions and Landscape

Relief – The average altitude in Spain is 650m/2,100ft above sea level and one sixth of the terrain rises to more than 1,000m/3,300ft. The highest peak on the Spanish mainland is Mulhacén (3,482m/11,424ft) in the Sierra Nevada. The dominant feature of the peninsula is the immense plateau at its centre.

This is the **Meseta**, a Hercynian platform between 600m/2,000ft and 1,000m/3,300ft high, which tilts slightly westwards. The Meseta is surrounded by long mountain ranges which form barriers between the central plateau and the coastal regions. All these ranges, the **Cordillera Cantábrica** in the northwest (an extension of the Pyrenees), the **Cordillera Ibérica** in the northeast and the **Sierra Morena** in the south, were caused by Alpine folding. Other mountains rising here and there from the Meseta are folds of the original, ancient massif. They include the **Sierras de Somosierra, Guadarrama** and **Gredos**, the **Peña de Francia** and the **Montes de Toledo**. The highest massifs in Spain, the **Pyrenees** (Pirineos) in the north and the **Sierras Béticas**, including the **Sierra Nevada**, in the south, are on the country's periphery, as are Spain's greatest depressions, those of the Ebro and Guadalquivir rivers.

Climate – Despite the fact that most of Spain enjoys 300 days of sunshine a year, the great diversity of its landscapes is partly due to the country's variety of climates: the Meseta has a **continental** climate with extremes of temperature ranging from scorching hot in summer to freezing cold in winter. On the north coast, where mist often develops into drizzle, the climate is **mild and very humid**. The east and south coasts have a **Mediterranean** climate verging on a desert climate in the Almería region.

ATLANTIC SPAIN

País Vasco, Cantabria, Principado de Asturias: a maritime Switzerland – The mountain chain that borders the northern edge of the Meseta emerged in the Tertiary Era and now runs through each of the coastal provinces. The **Montes Vascos**, secondary limestone ranges, continue westwards from the Pyrenean foothills and rise to 1,500m/4, 900ft. The **Cordillera Cantábrica** farther west forms an imposing barrier which has given the province of Cantabria the name of La Montaña. The range rises above 2,500m/8,200ft in the **Picos de Europa**, less than 50km/31mi from the sea.

The **País Vasco** (Basque Country) is a markedly undulating region with small villages and isolated farms nestling in the valleys. Local architecture is very distinctive: half-timbered houses with broad whitewashed fronts. The land sandwiched between the mountains and the sea in **Cantabria** and the principality of **Asturias**, is very hilly. Roads wind along valley floors hemmed in by lush meadows, cider apple orchards and fields of maize. Dairy produce is a major source of livelihood, especially in Cantabria. Maize, originally imported from America, has since become an important crop, judging by the large number of hórreos or squat drying sheds, so typical of Asturian villages.

The coast is indented by deep inlets or rías and lined by low cliffs in many places.

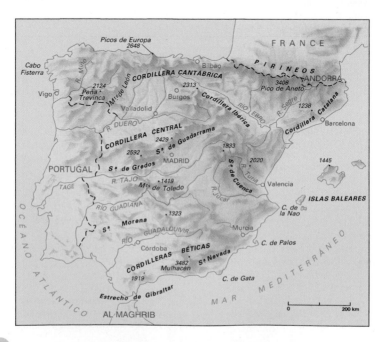

Picos de Europa

There are beautiful beaches, particularly in Cantabria.

Galicia – This remote region fronting the Atlantic on its northern and western borders is reminiscent of Ireland, Wales or Brittany. Galicia is an ancient eroded granite massif that was displaced and rejuvenated as a result of Alpine folding. Although peaks rise to 2,000m/6,600ft (that of Peña Trevinca is 2,124m/6,968ft high) the average altitude is less than 500m/1,600ft. Yet the overall impression of Galicia is that of a hilly and mountainous region.

The coast, cut by deep **rías**, is more densely populated than the interior. It is Spain's chief fishing region where most of the catch is canned. The interior is primarily an agricultural region where mixed farming is the norm: maize, potatoes, grapes and rye. The Orense province produces beef for export.

The climate is strongly influenced by the sea: temperatures are mild and vary little (the annual average is 13°C/55°F), and rainfall is abundant.

THE PYRENEES AND THE EBRO REGION

The autonomous communities of Aragón, Navarra and La Rioja are characterised by their varied landscapes and colour.

The Pyrenees (Pirineos) – **Alta (Upper) Aragón** (Huesca) embraces the Pirineos Centrales, a region of mountain valleys and piedmont vales, spring waterfalls (Parque Nacional de Ordesa) and villages of rough-stone houses with slate roofs. The main source of livelihood is farming around Huesca and stock-raising in the valleys. There are some industries in Zaragoza.

In **Navarra** the Pyrenees are watered by Atlantic rain. They rise regularly from the 900m/2,953ft of Mont La Rhune to the 2,504m/8,215ft of the Pic d'Anie (both peaks just over the French border). East of Orreaga/Roncesvalles, the terrain becomes more mountainous and the harshness of the climate becomes visible in the ruggedness of the forest cover and the steeply sloped slate roofs and stone fronts of the houses. Resemblance to the Basque provinces is apparent west of Roncesvalles where small parcels of land are used alternately as pasture or to grow maize and the houses have tiled roofs with half-timbered whitewashed fronts. To the south, beyond the limestone range of the Andía, Urbasa, Navascués and Leyre sierras, the land drops away to the Ebro basin.

Ebro depression – This clay basin was formerly a gulf that has since been filled with sediment. The terraces on either side of the river are deeply ravined, providing a sharp contrast with the lower valley, which has been transformed by irrigation into fertile market gardens or huertas.

Cereals predominate in the Cuenca region, also known as the Pamplona basin, in **Navarra**. The western **ribera**, a continuation of the famous **Rioja**, is a wine-growing area, while the well-irrigated eastern part of the province around Tudela has become a prosperous horticultural region growing and canning asparagus, artichokes and peppers. Tall brick houses are typical of the architecture in this area.

Cordillera Ibérica – The clay hills bordering the Ebro basin in **Bajo Aragón** (Lower Aragón) around Daroca and Alcañiz are planted with vineyards and olive groves. Brick villages and ochre-coloured houses merge in with the tawny shade of the deeply scored hillsides. The plateaux surrounding Teruel form part of the massive spread of the **Montes Universales**, one of Spain's great watersheds where the Cabriel, Turia, Júcar and Tajo (Tagus) rivers rise. The climate here is continental, as the mountains prevent maritime weather systems from exerting their influence this far inland.

THE MESETA

This tableland accounts for 40% of the surface area of the Iberian Peninsula, and occupies the autonomous communties of Castilla y León, Castilla-La Mancha, Madrid and Extremadura. Its horizons appear infinite, broken only here and there by a rock-brown village clustered at the foot of a castle, or by the indistinct outline of **páramos** (bare limestone heights).

The northern Meseta – The autonomous community of Castilla y León (Old Castile) in the north consists almost entirely of the Duero basin. This area is about 1,000m/3,300ft above sea level and is ringed by the Montes de León in the northwest, the Cordillera Cantábrica in the north, t he Cordillera Ibérica in the east and the Cordillera Central in the southeast. As the Tertiary sediment on the Meseta resists erosion in different ways, there are different landscape features such as wide terraced valleys dotted with rock pinnacles, narrow defiles and gently rolling hills.

Cereal growing predominates everywhere: wheat on the better land, oats and rye elsewhere. Only the southwest peneplains near Salamanca are used for stock-raising: sheep on small properties and fighting bulls on larger ones of often over 500ha/1,200 acres.

The southern Meseta – This section covers the whole of Madrid-Castilla-La Mancha (New Castile) and Extremadura. It is a vast tableland slightly tilted towards the west, watered by two large rivers – the Tajo (Tagus), which cuts a deep gorge through the limestone Alcarria region, and the sluggish Guadiana. The terrain is flatter than in Castilla y León and rises to an average altitude of less than 700m/2,300ft compared to between 800m/2,600ft and 1,000m/3,300ft in the north. The aridity of the region is particularly apparent in summer and the name **La Mancha** comes from the Arab manxa meaning dry land. Despite this there is considerable cultivation and a sweeping look across the Meseta would take in wind-ruffled cereal fields, stretches of saffron turned purple in the flowering season, and straight lines of olives and vines. The region is Spain's leading area for the production of table wines, and is also famous for its *manchego* cheese.

The bare, eroded and virtually uninhabited **Montes de Toledo** separate the Tajo basin from that of the Guadiana, while the other massifs in the region ring the borders. The **Cordillera Central** runs along the northern edge (Sierras de Gredos and Guadarrama), the **Sierra Morena** is in the south, and the **Serranía de Cuenca**, a limestone plateau pitted with swallow-holes (*torcas*) and cut by gorges (*hoces*), lies to the northeast. The **Alcarria** farther north is a region of remote villages where the Tajo and its tributaries flow through deeply eroded gullies. Its upper mountain slopes grow aromatic plants such as thyme, rosemary, lavender and marjoram from which a well-known honey is produced.

The rural character of the region persists; small towns look more like large villages with the arcaded *plaza mayor* (the main square) still acting as the nerve-centre.

Extremadura in the southwest is a schist and granite Hercynian platform that levels off at about 400m/1,300ft. The immense plateaux of the region are used for sheep grazing but lie deserted in summer when the animals are moved to higher pastures. Cork provides supplementary income as does traditional pig farming. The population is concentrated along the rivers that supply irrigation for a variety of crops including tobacco, cotton and wheat as well as market-garden produce. The Badajoz Plan that controls the flow of the Guadiana by means of a series of dams has made it possible to reafforest a large area and to develop high-yield crops such as maize, sunflowers, market-garden produce and above all animal fodder.

MEDITERRANEAN REGIONS

These comprise Catalunya, the Comunidad Valenciana, Murcia and the Balearic Islands.

Catalunya – Catalunya is a triangle of varied landscapes between the French border, Aragón and the Mediterranean. In the north, the eastern stretch of the Pyrenees, between Andorra and the Cabo de Creus headland, is a green wooded area with peaks over 3,000m/9,800ft high. The limestone foothills of the Pyrenees are similar in appearance to the sierras of Aragón.

Olive groves near Jaén

B. Kaufmann/MICHELIN

The **Costa Brava** between France and Barcelona is a rocky area with many bays and inlets. It has a Mediterranean climate as does the **Costa Dorada** (Gold Coast) farther south with its vast sandy beaches. The hinterland, separated from the coast by the Catalan *sierras*, is a drier region with harsh winters.

The southern part of the triangle is composed of green hills sloping down to an intensively cultivated plain around the lower Ebro and its delta. Although fertile (cereals, vines, olives and market-garden produce), Catalunya is primarily an industrial region with its main activities centred around Barcelona.

Levante – The whole of the Levante, including Valencia and Murcia, comprises a narrow alluvial plain between the Mediterranean coast and the massifs of the interior (the Cordillera Ibérica in the north and the Sierras Béticas in the south).

The coast, called **Costa del Azahar** (Orange Blossom Coast) near Valencia and the **Costa Blanca** (White Coast) around Alicante and Murcia, consists of dunes and offshore sand bars that form pools and lagoons.

The climate is Mediterranean but drier than average in this area. Little rain falls except during the autumn months when the rivers flood. Thanks to an ingenious system of irrigation (*acequias*) developed since Antiquity, the natural vegetation, of olives, almond and carob trees and vines, has gradually been replaced, and the countryside transformed into **huertas** (irrigated areas), lush citrus orchards and market gardens, with orange trees between Castellón and Denia and lemons near Murcia. The prosperous *huertas* are among the most densely populated areas in Spain. There are palm groves around Elche and Orihuela in the south and rice is grown in swampy areas.

The region's economy is based on the mining of mineral deposits, port activities, and the booming tourist industry.

The arid **interior** is devoted to the growing of cereal crops and the breeding of livestock. Here, the climate is cooler than on the coast, which has more abundant rainfall.

Balearic Islands (Islas Baleares) – The Balearic archipelago consists of three large islands (Mallorca, Menorca and Ibiza), two smaller ones (Formentera and Cabrera), and numerous tiny islets.

The limestone hills, none of which exceed 1,500m/4, 900ft, differ in origin. Ibiza and Mallorca are an extension of the Cordillera Bética in Andalucía while Menorca belongs to the submerged massif from which Corsica, Sardinia and the Catalan cordilleras rise.

The lush vegetation produced by the autumn rains is one of the sunny islands' greatest attractions. Pines shade the indented shores, junipers and evergreen oaks cover the upper hillsides, while almonds, figs and olives cloak the plains.

The three larger islands differ considerably in character although they share the same contrast between the tranquillity of the hills inland and the bustling tourism along the coast. Their beaches are washed by a wonderfully calm, clear sea.

ANDALUCÍA

This magnificent region is known for its varied landscapes, whitewashed villages and towns, flowers and patios, and the charming character of its people. In geographical terms, it can be divided into three distinct areas:

Sierra Morena – This mountain chain separates the Meseta from Andalucía. It is rich in minerals and thickly covered by a scrub of oaks, lentisks (mastic trees) and arbutus (strawberry trees). Jaén province's extraordinary landscape consists of row upon row of olive trees as far as the eye can see.

Guadalquivir depression – This Quaternary basin, a former gulf, opening broadly onto the Atlantic, is one of the richest agricultural areas in Spain. Cereals, cotton, olives and citrus fruit are grown on the plains, and rice and vines (around Jerez) on the coast, where fighting bulls are also bred. The centre of the region is Sevilla, Spain's fourth largest city. The whole area is a vast tract of cultivated land divided into large properties known as **fincas**.

Cordilleras Béticas – The **Sierra Nevada**, which includes mainland Spain's highest peak, Mulhacén (3,482m/11,424ft), is continued westwards by the Serranía de Ronda and Sierra de Ubrique. The range's snow-capped heights dominate a series of basins like the wide *vega* (plain) of Granada.

Despite its semi-desert climate, the province of Almería, at the eastern end of the Costa del Sol (Sun Coast), produces citrus and early fruit and vegetables which are grown on irrigated land.

CANARY ISLANDS

It would appear that these volcanic islands were created following the compression of the Atlantic plate at the time of the formation of the Saharan Atlas mountains. **Mount Teide**, on the island of Tenerife, is the highest peak in Spain, rising to a height of 3,718m/12,195ft.

As a result of the archipelago's delightful scenery and superb climate, characterised by pleasant temperatures all year round due to the influence of the trade winds and the cooler Canarian current, it has developed into one of Europe's major tourist destinations.

HISTORY

Modern Spain represents the culmination of centuries of crossbreeding, political union, exclusion and division. The country's history is a complex one, enlivened by myths and legends, and punctuated by significant historical and cultural landmarks, which have combined to create a unique people.

From Antiquity to the Visigothic Kingdom

BC

11C-5C – Phoenician and Greek trading posts founded on the eastern and southern coasts of Spain, inhabited by **Iberians** and **Tartessians** respectively. In the 9C BC, the central-European Celts settle in west Spain and on the Meseta, intermingling with the Iberians (forming **Celtiberians**).

3C-2C – The **Carthaginians** take over the southeast after conquering the Greeks and Tartessians. The capture of Sagunto by Hannibal leads to the Second Punic War (218-201 BC).

Rome expels the Carthaginians and begins the conquest of peninsular Spain (with resistance at **Numancia**).

1C BC-1C AD – Cantabria and Asturias are finally pacified in AD 19. Spain is now known as Iberia or Hispania.

AD

1C – Christianity reaches the Iberian Peninsula and begins to spread.

5C-6C – Early Suevi (Swabian) and Vandal invasions are followed by those of the **Visigoths** (411) who estabish a powerful monarchy with Toledo as capital. The peninsula unites under King Leovigild (584-85).

Muslim Spain and the Reconquest

8C – Moors invade and annihilate the Visigothic kingdom after the **Battle of Guadalete** in 711. Pelayo's victory at **Covadonga** in 722 heralds a 700-year-long Christian War of Reconquest. The first Muslim invaders are subjects of the Umayyad Caliphate in Damascus. **Abd ar-Rahman I** breaks with Damascus by founding an independent emirate at Córdoba in 756.

9C – Settlement of uninhabited land by Christians.

10C – Golden age of the emirate of Córdoba, which is raised to the status of a caliphate (929-1021) by **Abd ar-Rahman III**. A period of great prosperity ensues during which the expansion of Christian kingdoms is checked. Fortresses are built in the north along the Duero river.

11C – Christian Spain now includes the kingdoms of León, Castilla, Navarra and Aragón, and the county of Barcelona. On the death of al-Mansur in 1002, the Caliphate of Córdoba disintegrates into about 20 *taifa* (faction) kingdoms (1031). Alfonso VI of Castilla conquers Toledo (1085), and the area around the Tajo river is resettled by Christians. The taifa kings call upon the **Almoravids** (Saharan Muslims) for assistance and in a short time the tribe overruns a large part of Spain. Pilgrims begin to tread the Way of St James of Compostela. **El Cid** conquers Valencia (1094).

12C – Dissension stemming from a second age of taifa kingdoms assists the Reconquest, especially in the Ebro Valley (Zaragoza is taken in 1118, Tortosa in 1148 and Lleida in 1149), but after Yacoub al-Mansur's victory in Alarcos (1195), the **Almohads** (who routed the Almoravids) recover Extremadura and check Christian expansion towards the Guadiana and Guadalquivir rivers. Sevilla, with Córdoba under its control, enjoys great prosperity.

Great military orders are founded (Calatrava, Alcántara, and Santiago).

Unification of the kingdoms of Aragón and Catalunya (1150).

13C – The *taifa* kingdoms enter their third age. The decline of the Muslims begins with the **Battle of Las Navas de Tolosa** (1212). Muslim influence is reduced to the Nasrid kingdom of Granada (modern provinces of Málaga, Granada and Almería) which holds out until its capture in 1492.

Unification of Castilla and León under Ferdinand III (1230).

The crown of Aragón under James I, the Conqueror (1213-76), gains control over considerable territory in the Mediterranean.

THE CHRISTIAN RECONQUEST OF THE IBERIAN PENINSULA

The Catholic Monarchs (1474-1516) and the Unification of Spain

1474 – Isabel, wife of Ferdinand, succeeds her brother Henry IV to the throne of Castilla. She has to contend with opposition from the supporters of her niece Juana la Beltraneja until 1479.

1478-79 – The court of the **Inquisition** is instituted by a special Papal Bull and **Torquemada** is later appointed Inquisitor-General.
The court, a political and religious institution directed against Jews, Moors and later Protestants, survives until the 19C.
Ferdinand becomes King of Aragón in 1479 and Christian Spain is united under one crown.

1492 – Fall of Granada marks the end of the Reconquest. Expulsion of Jews.

12 October 1492 – Christopher Columbus discovers America.

1494 – The **Treaty of Tordesillas** divides the New World between Spain and Portugal.

1496 – Juana, daughter of the Catholic Monarchs, marries Philip "the Handsome" (Felipe el Hermoso), son of Emperor Maximilian of Austria (Maximiliano I).

1504 – Death of Isabel. The kingdom is inherited by her daughter, "Mad" Joan (Juana la Loca) but Ferdinand governs as regent until Juana's son Charles (b 1500), future Emperor Charles V, comes of age.

1512 – The Duke of Alba conquers Navarra, thus bringing political unity to Spain.

The Habsburgs (1516-1700) and the Conquest of America

1516 – **The apogee: Charles I** (1516-56) and **Philip II** (1556-98).
On the death of Ferdinand, his grandson becomes Charles I (Carlos I) of Spain. Through his mother, Charles inherits Spain, as well as Naples, Sicily, Sardinia and American territories. Cardinal Cisneros governs until the new king arrives for the first time in Spain in 1517.

1519 – On the death of Maximilian of Austria, Charles I is elected Holy

1492

If there were only one important date to remember in Spanish history, it would be 1492. That year, after 781 years of Muslim occupation, the Reconquest ended with the fall of Granada on 2 January. This was also the year that the Jews were expelled, the Spaniard Rodrigo Borja (Borgia) became Pope Alexander VI and on 12 October, Christopher Columbus discovered America.

Christopher Columbus (Cristóbal Colón) (1451?-1506) and the discovery of America – Born in Genoa, the son of a weaver, Columbus began his seafaring career at an early age. He travelled to Lisbon in 1476 where he developed a passion for mapmaking on discovering Ptolemy's Geography and the Frenchman Pierre d'Ailly's Imago Mundi. Convinced that the Indies could be reached by sailing west, he submitted a navigation plan to João II of Portugal and to the kings of France and England. He ultimately managed to gain the support of the Duke of Medinaceli and that of the Prior of the Monasterio de La Rábida, Juan Pérez, who was Isabel the Catholic's confessor. The Catholic Monarchs agreed to finance his expedition and, if he succeeded, to bestow upon him the hereditary title of Admiral of the Ocean and the viceroyship of any lands discovered.
On 3 August 1492, heading a fleet of three caravels (the Santa María, under his command, and the Pinta and the Niña captained by the Pinzón brothers), he put out from Palos de la Frontera. On 12 October, after a difficult crossing, San Salvador (Bahamas) came into sight and a short time later Hispaniola (Haiti) and Cuba were discovered. On his return to Spain on 15 March 1493, Christopher Columbus was given a triumphant welcome and the means with which to organise new expeditions. This marked the beginning of the great Spanish discoveries of the New World.

Roman Emperor under the name of **Charles V** (Carlos V). He inherits Germany, Austria, the Franche-Comté and the Low Countries.

1520-22 – The Spanish, incensed by Charles V's largely Flemish court advisers and the increasing number of taxes, rise up in arms. The emperor quells **Comuneros** and **Germanías** revolts.

1521-56 – Charles V wages five wars against France in order to secure complete control of Europe. In the first four he conquers Francis I (imprisoned at Pavia in 1525) and in the fifth he routs the new French king, Henri II, and captures Milan.

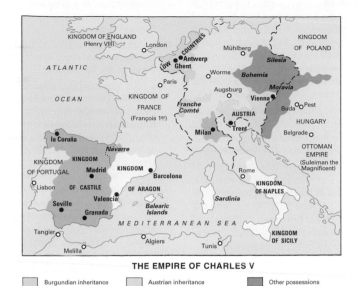

THE EMPIRE OF CHARLES V

Burgundian inheritance　　Austrian inheritance　　Other possessions

Spanish inheritance　　Charles V's conquests　　– – – The Holy Roman Empire

The conquistadores move across America. **Núñez de Balboa** discovers the Pacific; **Cortés** seizes Mexico in 1521; **Pizarro** and **Diego de Almagro** subdue Peru in 1533; **Francisco Coronado** explores the Colorado river in 1535; **Hernando de Soto** takes possession of Florida in 1539; and **Pedro de Valdivia** founds Chile in 1541.

1555 – Charles V signs the Peace of Augsburg with the Protestants in Germany after failing to suppress the Reformation.

1556 – Charles V abdicates in favour of his son and retires to a monastery in Yuste. **Philip II** becomes king, inheriting Spain and its colonies, the kingdom of Naples, Milan, the Low Countries and the Franche-Comté, but not Germany and Austria which are left by Charles to his brother Ferdinand I of Austria. Philip II turns his attention to Spain and the defence of Catholicism. He chooses Madrid as capital in 1561. Spain goes through a serious economic crisis.

1568-70 – Revolt of the Moriscos (Muslims who converted to Christianity) in Granada.

1571 – The Turks are defeated in the **Battle of Lepanto** by a fleet of ships sent by the Pope, the Venetians and the Spanish, under the command of **Don Juan of Austria**, the king's natural brother. The victory seals Spain's mastery of the Mediterranean.

1580 – The King of Portugal dies without an heir. Philip II asserts his rights, invades Portugal and is proclaimed king in 1581.

1588 – Philip II sends the **Invincible Armada** against Protestant England, which supports the Low Countries. The destruction of the fleet marks the end of Spain as a sea power.

1598 – Philip II dies, leaving a vast kingdom which, in spite of huge wealth from the Americas, is crippled by debt after 70 years of almost incessant war and monumental building projects like El Escorial.

1598-1621 – **The decline** – The last Habsburgs, **Philip III** (Felipe III, 1598-1621), **Philip IV** (Felipe IV, 1621-65) and **Charles II** (Carlos II, 1665-1700), lack the mettle of their forebears. Paradoxically, Spain enjoys a **golden age** of art and culture.

Philip III entrusts the affairs of State to the Duke of Lerma who advises him to expel the Moriscos in 1609. 275 000 Moors leave Spain with disastrous consequences for agriculture.

1640 – Under Philip IV (Felipe IV), the Count-Duke of Olivares adopts a policy of decentralisation which spurs Catalunya and Portugal to rebellion. The Portuguese proclaim the Duke of Braganza King John IV, but their independence is not recognised until 1668.

1618-48 – Spain wastes her strength in the **Thirty Years War.** In spite of victories like that of Breda (1624), the defeat in the Netherlands at Rocroi (1643) signals the end of Spain as a European power.

The **Treaty of Westphalia** gives the Netherlands independence.

1659 – The **Treaty of the Pyrenees** ends war with France. Philip IV arranges the marriage of his daughter María Teresa to Louis XIV of France.

1667-97 – Spain loses strongholds in Flanders to France during the **War of Devolution** (1667-68). The Dutch Wars (1672-78) end with the **Treaty of Nijmegen.** The **Treaty of Ryswick** (1697) concludes the war waged by the Confederation of Augsburg (Spain is a member) against France (1688-97).

The Bourbons, Napoleon and the War of Independence (1808-14)

1700 – Charles II dies without issue. He wills the crown to Philip, Duke of Anjou, grandson of his sister María Teresa and Louis XIV. Emperor Leopold, who had renounced his rights to the Spanish throne in favour of his son, the Archduke Charles, is displeased, but the appointment of the Bourbons to the Spanish throne stabilises the balance of power in Europe.

1702-14 – War of the Spanish Succession – England, the Netherlands, Denmark and Germany support the Archduke of Austria against France and Philip of Anjou. Catalunya, Valencia and Aragón also side with the Archduke and war spreads throughout Spain (1705). By the **Treaty of Utrecht**, Spain forfeits Gibraltar and Menorca (taken by the English) and many of her Italian possessions. **Philip V** (Felipe V) is proclaimed King of Spain (1714-45).

1759-88 – The reign of **Charles III** (Carlos III), an enlightened despot, is the most brilliant of those of the Bourbons. He is assisted by competent ministers (Floridablanca and Aranda) who draw up important economic reforms. Expulsion of the Jesuits in 1767.

1788 – **Charles IV** (Carlos IV) succeeds to the throne. A weak-willed king, he allows the country to be governed by his wife María Luisa and her favourite, Godoy.

1793 – On the death of Louis XVI, Spain declares war on France (then in the throes of the Revolution).

1796-1805 – Spain signs an alliance with the French Directory against England (Treaty of San Ildefonso, 1796).

Napoleon enters Spain with his troops on the pretext that he is going to attack Portugal. The renewed offensive against England in 1804 ends disastrously with the **Battle of Trafalgar** the following year.

1805-08 – Napoleon takes advantage of the disagreement between Charles IV and his son Ferdinand to engineer Charles IV's abdication and appoint his own brother, Joseph, King of Spain. The Aranjuez Revolt takes place in March 1808.

2 May 1808 – The Madrid uprising against French troops marks the beginning of the **War of Independence** (The Peninsular War) which lasts until Napoleon is exiled by Wellington in 1814. During the war there are battles at Bailén (1808), Madrid, Zaragoza and Girona.

1812 – The French are routed by Wellington in the Arapiles Valley; King Joseph flees from Madrid. Valencia is taken by the French general, Suchet.

Spanish patriots convene the Cortes (parliament) and draw up the liberal **Constitution of Cádiz.**

1813-14 – Anglo-Spanish forces expel Napoleon after successive victories.

Ferdinand VII (Fernando VII) returns to Spain, repeals the Constitution of Cádiz and so reigns as an absolute monarch until 1820. Meanwhile, the South American colonies struggle for independence.

The Disturbances of the 19C

1820-23 – The liberals oppose the king's absolute rule but their uprisings are all severely quelled. The 1812 constitution is reinstated after a liberal revolt led by **General Riego** in Cádiz in 1820, but only for three years.

In 1823 Ferdinand VII appeals to Europe for assistance and 100 000 Frenchmen are sent in the name of St Louis to re-establish absolute rule (which lasts until 1833).

1833-39 – On the death of Ferdinand VII, his brother Don Carlos disputes the right to the throne of his niece Isabel II, daughter of the late king and Queen María Cristina. The traditionalist Carlists fight Isabel's liberal supporters who, after six years, win the **First Carlist War** (Convention of Vergara). In 1835, the government minister **Mendizábal** has a series of decrees passed which do away with religious orders and confiscate their property (desamortización).

1840 – A revolutionary junta forces the regent María Cristina into exile. She is replaced by General Espartero.

1843-68 – Queen Isabel II comes of age. The **Narváez** uprising forces Espartero to flee. A new constitution is drawn up in 1845. The Second Carlist War (1847-49) ends in victory for Isabel II but her reign is troubled by a succession of uprisings on behalf of progressives and moderates.
The 1868 revolt led by General Prim puts an end to her reign. Isabel leaves for France and General Serrano is appointed leader of the provisional government.

1869 – The Cortes passes a progressive constitution which however envisages the establishment of a monarchy. Amadeo of Savoy is elected king.

1873 – The Third Carlist War (1872-76). The king abdicates on finding himself unable to keep the peace. The National Assembly proclaims the **First Spanish Republic**.

1874 – General Martínez Campos leads a revolt. The head of the government, Cánovas de Castillo, proclaims Isabel's son **Alfonso XII**, King of Spain. The Bourbon Restoration opens a long period of peace.

1885 – Death of Alfonso XII (at 28). His widow María Cristina (who is expecting a baby) becomes regent.

1898 – Cuba and the Philippines rise up with disastrous losses for Spain. The United States, which supports the rebel colonies, occupies Puerto Rico and the Philippines, marking the end of the Spanish Empire.

1902 – **Alfonso XIII** (born after the death of his father Alfonso XII) succeeds to the throne at 16.

The Fall of the Monarchy and the Second Republic (1931-36)

1914-18 – Spain remains neutral throughout the First World War. A general strike in 1917 is severely put down.

1921 – Insurrection in Morocco; General Sanjurjo occupies the North (1927).

1923 – General **Miguel Primo de Rivera** establishes a dictatorship with the king's approval. Order is restored, the country grows wealthier but opposition increases among the working classes.

1930 – In the face of hostility from the masses, Primo de Rivera is forced into exile and General Berenguer is appointed dictator.

1931 – April elections bring victory to the Republicans in Catalunya, the País Vasco, La Rioja and the Aragonese province of Huesca. The king leaves Spain and the Second Republic is proclaimed.

June 1931 – A constituent Cortes is elected with a socialist republican majority; a Constitution is promulgated in December. Don Niceto Alcalá Zamora is elected President of the Republic. Agrarian reforms, such as compulsory purchase of large properties, meet strong right-wing opposition.

1933 – The **Falange Party**, which opposes regional separation, is founded by **José Antonio Primo de Rivera**, son of the dictator. The army plots against the régime.

Oct 1934 – Catalunya proclaims its autonomy. Miners in Asturias spark off a revolt against the right-wing government and are brutally repressed.

Feb 1936 – The Popular Front wins the elections, precipitating a revolutionary situation. Anarchy hits the streets and the right promptly retaliates.

The Civil War (1936-39)

17 July 1936 – The Melilla uprising triggers the Civil War. The army takes control and puts an end to the Second Republic.

Nationalist troops based in Morocco and led by General Franco cross the Straits of Gibraltar and make their way to Toledo which is taken at the end of September. Franco is proclaimed Generalísimo of the armed forces and Head of State in Burgos. Nationalists lead an unsuccessful attack against Madrid.

While Madrid, Catalunya and Valencia remain faithful to the Republicans, the conservative agricultural regions – Andalucía, Castilla and Galicia – are rapidly controlled by the Nationalists. These latter outnumber the Republicans tenfold and the Republicans themselves are torn by dissension between anarchists and communists within their own ranks. They do, however, receive assistance from International Brigades.

1937 – Industrial towns in the north are taken by Nationalist supporters in the summer (Gernika is bombed by German planes). The Republican Government is moved to Barcelona in November. In the battle of Teruel in December, the Republicans try to breach the Nationalist front in Aragón and thereby relieve surrounded Catalunya. Teruel is taken by the Republicans and recaptured by the Nationalists soon after.

1938 – The Nationalist army reaches the Mediterranean, dividing Republican territory into two parts. The **Battle of the Ebro** lasts from July to November: the Republican army flees eastwards and Franco launches an offensive against Catalunya which is occupied by the Nationalists in February 1939.

1 April 1939 – The war ends with the capture of Madrid.

The Franco Era

1939-49 – Spain is declared a monarchy with Franco as regent and Head of State and remains neutral in the Second World War. Period of diplomatic isolation.

1952 – Spain joins UNESCO.

1955 – Spain becomes a member of the United Nations.

1969 – Prince Juan Carlos is named as Franco's successor.

20 Dec 1973 – Prime Minister Carrero Blanco is assassinated.

20 Nov 1975 – Death of Franco. **Juan Carlos I** becomes King of Spain.

Democracy

15 June 1977 – General elections – **Adolfo Suárez** is elected Prime Minister. A new constitution is passed by referendum in 1978. Statutes of autonomy are granted to Catalunya, the País Vasco (Euskadi) and Galicia.

1981-82 – Suárez resigns. There is an attempted military coup on 23 February 1981. The general elections on 28 October 1982 are won by the Socialist Party and **Felipe González** becomes Prime Minister.

1 Jan 1986 – Spain joins the **European Economic Community**.

11 March 1986 – Spain's continued membership of NATO is voted by referendum.

11 June 1986 – General elections – Felipe González, leader of the Socialist Party (PSOE), is re-elected Prime Minister.

Oct 1989 – General elections again won by the Socialists under Felipe González.

1992 – Barcelona hosts the 1992 Summer Olympics, and Sevilla hosts Expo 1992.

3 March 1996 – General election is won by the Popular Party; **José María Aznar** becomes Prime Minister.

2000 – José María Aznar is re-elected Prime Minister.

11 March 2004 – A **terrorist attack** by Islamic fundamentalists in Madrid leaves 192 dead and 1,500 injured, convulsing the country.

14 March 2004 – The Socialist Party carries the general elections. **José Luis Rodríguez Zapatero** becomes Prime Minister.

22 May 2004 – The Prince of Asturias, heir to the Spanish crown, becomes engaged to Letizia Ortiz Rocasolano, a journalist and divorcee.

ABC of architecture

Ground plan

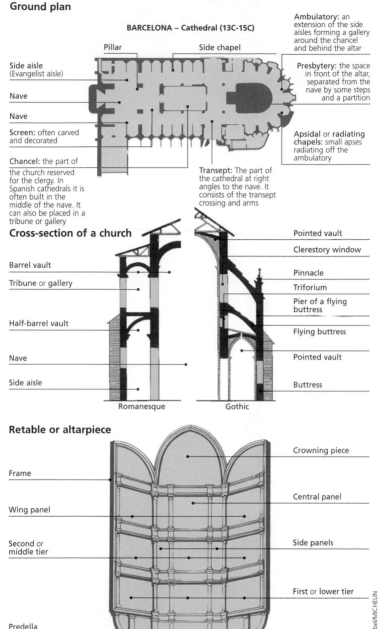

BARCELONA – Cathedral (13C-15C)

Pillar

Side chapel

Ambulatory: an extension of the side aisles forming a gallery around the chancel and behind the altar

Side aisle (Evangelist aisle)

Nave

Nave

Screen: often carved and decorated

Chancel: the part of the church reserved for the clergy. In Spanish cathedrals it is often built in the middle of the nave. It can also be placed in a tribune or gallery

Presbytery: the space in front of the altar, separated from the nave by some steps and a partition

Apsidal or **radiating chapels:** small apses radiating off the ambulatory

Transept: The part of the cathedral at right angles to the nave. It consists of the transept crossing and arms

Cross-section of a church

Barrel vault

Tribune or gallery

Half-barrel vault

Nave

Side aisle

Pointed vault

Clerestory window

Pinnacle

Triforium

Pier of a flying buttress

Flying buttress

Pointed vault

Buttress

Romanesque

Gothic

Retable or altarpiece

Frame

Wing panel

Second or middle tier

Predella

Crowning piece

Central panel

Side panels

First or lower tier

R. Corbel/MICHELIN

Arcos

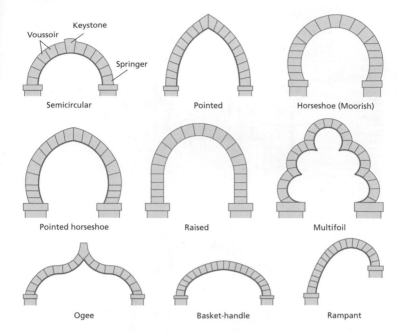

Keystone
Voussoir
Springer

Semicircular

Pointed

Horseshoe (Moorish)

Pointed horseshoe

Raised

Multifoil

Ogee

Basket-handle

Rampant

Vaults

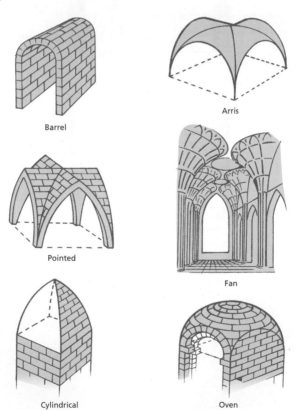

Barrel

Arris

Pointed

Fan

Cylindrical

Oven

Hispano-Moorish art

CÓRDOBA – Mezquita: Puerta de Alhakem II (10C)

Eight centuries of Moorish rule in Spain had a fundamental influence on Spanish art.

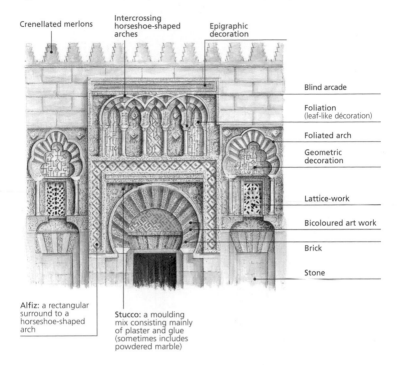

Crenellated merlons

Intercrossing horseshoe-shaped arches

Epigraphic decoration

Blind arcade

Foliation (leaf-like décoration)

Foliated arch

Geometric decoration

Lattice-work

Bicoloured art work

Brick

Stone

Alfiz: a rectangular surround to a horseshoe-shaped arch

Stucco: a moulding mix consisting mainly of plaster and glue (sometimes includes powdered marble)

GRANADA – La Alhambra (14C)

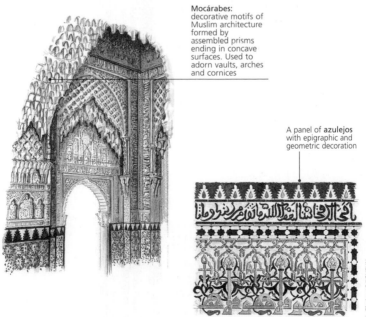

Mocárabes: decorative motifs of Muslim architecture formed by assembled prisms ending in concave surfaces. Used to adorn vaults, arches and cornices

A panel of azulejos with epigraphic and geometric decoration

H. Choimet/MICHELIN

Romanesque

SANTIAGO DE COMPOSTELA – Cathedral: Interior (11C-13C)

Santiago cathedral is a typical example of a Spanish pilgrimage church and shows clear French influence.

Barrel vault

Barrel arch: formed of a single curved member, with no diagonal ribs

Tribune: a gallery above the side aisle and of a similar width

Paired arch: arches grouped in pairs

Wall arch: an arch parallel to the length of the nave, separating it from the side aisle

Raised round arch

Organ

Corinthian capital

Abacus: the uppermost slab of a capital or column

Pillar with engaged columns

Corinthian capital

Gothic

LEÓN – Cathedral: side façade (13C-14C)

In Gothic architecture, light was considered the essence of beauty and the symbol of truth. León cathedral is the brightest and most delicate of all the major Spanish cathedrals and is viewed as the best example of this concept. The beauty and magnificence of its stained glass attracts the admiration of its many thousands of visitors every year. French influence is clearly evident in its ground plan (Reims) and sculptures (Chartres).

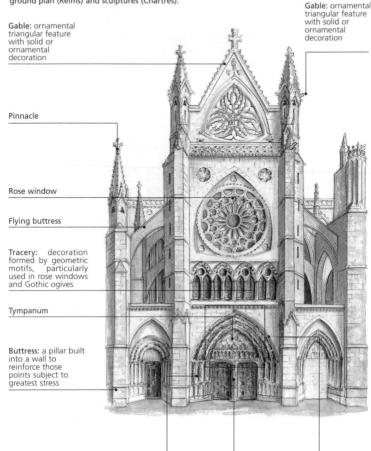

Gable: ornamental triangular feature with solid or ornamental decoration

Gable: ornamental triangular feature with solid or ornamental decoration

Pinnacle

Rose window

Flying buttress

Tracery: decoration formed by geometric motifs, particularly used in rose windows and Gothic ogives

Tympanum

Buttress: a pillar built into a wall to reinforce those points subject to greatest stress

Pier: a vertical structure, often finely decorated, supporting a door or a wall

Mullion: a vertical feature which divides in two the opening or span of a portal or window

Archivolt: ornamental moulding on the outer edge of an arch

Tympanum

Plateresque

SALAMANCA – University: façade (16C)

Although the exuberant decoration used to cover the entire façade is somewhat Gothic in style, the motifs used are Classical.

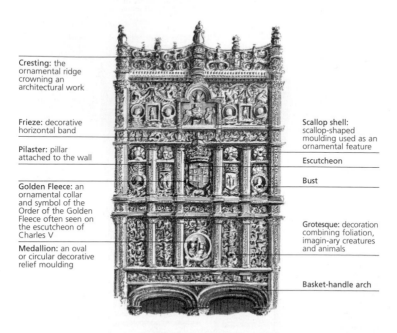

Cresting: the ornamental ridge crowning an architectural work

Frieze: decorative horizontal band

Pilaster: pillar attached to the wall

Golden Fleece: an ornamental collar and symbol of the Order of the Golden Fleece often seen on the escutcheon of Charles V

Medallion: an oval or circular decorative relief moulding

Scallop shell: scallop-shaped moulding used as an ornamental feature

Escutcheon

Bust

Grotesque: decoration combining foliation, imagin-ary creatures and animals

Basket-handle arch

Renaissance

TOLEDO - Hospital Tavera: patio (16C)

The sense of proportion, visible on both the ground and first floors surrounding the double patio of this hospital, is a typical feature of pure Renaissance style.

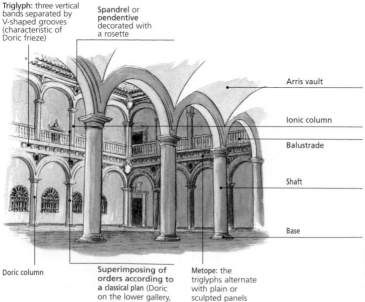

Triglyph: three vertical bands separated by V-shaped grooves (characteristic of Doric frieze)

Spandrel or **pendentive** decorated with a rosette

Arris vault

Ionic column

Balustrade

Shaft

Base

Doric column

Superimposing of orders according to a classical plan (Doric on the lower gallery, Ionic on the upper gallery)

Metope: the triglyphs alternate with plain or sculpted panels

H. Choimet/MICHELIN

Baroque

MADRID – Museo Municipal (Antiguo Hospicio): portal (18C)

The Baroque retable or altarpiece, which reached new architectural heights in Spain, was occasionally created on the façade of a building, rather than inside it.

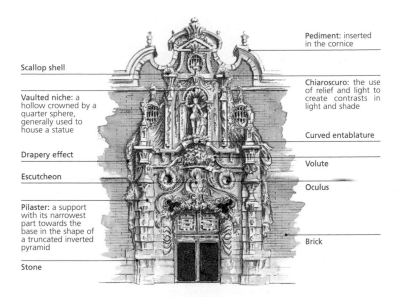

Scallop shell

Vaulted niche: a hollow crowned by a quarter sphere, generally used to house a statue

Drapery effect

Escutcheon

Pilaster: a support with its narrowest part towards the base in the shape of a truncated inverted pyramid

Stone

Pediment: inserted in the cornice

Chiaroscuro: the use of relief and light to create contrasts in light and shade

Curved entablature

Volute

Oculus

Brick

Neo-Classical

MADRID - Observatório Astronómico (18C)

This small building designed by Juan de Villanueva is a model of simplicity and purity which shows clear Palladian influence in its proportions and design.

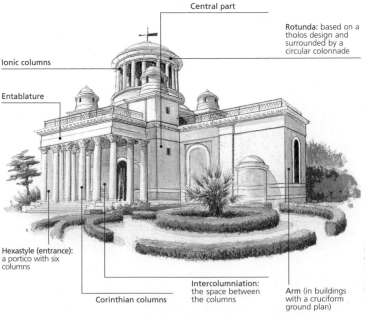

Central part

Rotunda: based on a tholos design and surrounded by a circular colonnade

Ionic columns

Entablature

Hexastyle (entrance): a portico with six columns

Corinthian columns

Intercolumniation: the space between the columns

Arm (in buildings with a cruciform ground plan)

H. Choimet/MICHELIN

71

Modernist

BARCELONA –Casa Batlló (Antoni Gaudí: 1905-07)

Modernism is a colourful, decorative and sensual style which recreates organic forms in a world dominated by curves and reverse curves.

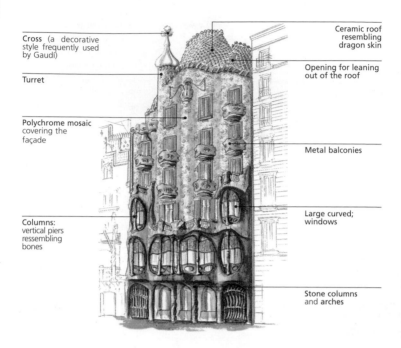

Cross (a decorative style frequently used by Gaudí)

Turret

Polychrome mosaic covering the façade

Columns: vertical piers ressembling bones

Ceramic roof resembling dragon skin

Opening for leaning out of the roof

Metal balconies

Large curved; windows

Stone columns and arches

Mediterranean Rationalist

BARCELONA – Fundació Joan Miró (JL Sert: 1972-75)

The building consists of a series of interrelated architectural features and open spaces in which natural light plays a fundamental role.

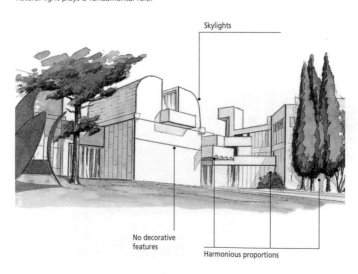

Skylights

No decorative features

Harmonious proportions

H. Choimet/MICHELIN

GLOSSARY OF ARCHITECTURE

Some of the terms below are illustrated on the previous pages. Words in italics are Spanish.

Ajimez: paired window or opening separated by a central column.

Alfarje: wooden ceiling, usually decorated, consisting of a board resting on cross beams (a feature of the Mudéjar style).

Alfiz: rectangular surround to a horseshoe-shaped arch in Muslim architecture.

Alicatado: section of wall or other surface covered with sheets of ceramic tiles (azulejos) cut to form geometric patterns. Frequently used to decorate dados (a Mudéjar feature).

Aljibe: Arab word for cistern.

Altarpiece: also retable. Decorative screen above and behind the altar.

Apse: far end of a church housing the high altar; can be semicircular, polygonal or horseshoe-shaped.

Apsidal or radiating chapel: small chapel opening from the apse.

Arch: *See illustrations p 66.*

Archivolt: ornamental moulding on the outer edge of an arch.

Artesonado: marquetry ceiling in which raised fillets outline honeycomb-like cells in the shape of stars. This decoration, which first appeared under the Almohads, was popular throughout the country, including Christian Spain, in the 15C and 16C.

Ataurique: decorative plant motif on plaster or brick which was developed as a feature of the Caliphate style and was subsequently adopted by the Mudéjar.

Azulejos: glazed, patterned, ceramic tiles.

Barrel vaulting: vault with a semicircular cross-section.

Caliphate: the architectural style developed in Córdoba under the Caliphate (8C-11C) of which the finest example is the mosque in that city.

Churrigueresque: in the style of the Churrigueras, an 18C family of architects. Richly ornate Baroque decoration.

H.Choimet/MICHELIN

Estípite: pilaster in the shape of a truncated inverted pyramid.

Gargoyle: projecting roof gutter normally carved in the shape of a grotesque animal.

Groined vaulting: vault showing lines of intersection of two vaults or arches (usually pointed).

Grotesque: typical Renaissance decoration combining vegetation, imaginary beings and animals.

Kiblah: sacred wall of a mosque from which the mihrab is hollowed, facing towards Mecca.

Lacerías: geometric decoration formed by intersecting straight lines making star-shaped and polygonal figures. Characteristic of Moorish architecture.

Lombard bands: decorative pilaster strips typical of Romanesque architecture in Lombardy.

Lonja: commodity exchange building.

Mihrab: richly decorated prayer-niche in the sacred wall (kiblah) in a mosque.

Minaret: tower of the mosque (mezquita), from which the muezzin calls the faithful to prayer.

Minbar: pulpit in a mosque.

Mocárabes: decorative motifs of Muslim architecture formed by assembled prisms ending in concave surfaces. They resemble stalactites or pendants and adorn vaults and cornices.

Mozarabic: the work of Christians living under Arab rule after the Moorish invasion of 711. On being persecuted in the 9C, they sought refuge in Christian areas bringing with them Moorish artistic traditions.

Mudéjar: the work of Muslims living in Christian territory following the Reconquest (13C-14C).

Mullion: slender column or pillar dividing an opening in a door or window.

Naveta: megalithic monument found in the Balearic Islands, which has a pyramidal shape with a rectangular base, giving the appearance of an upturned boat.

Plateresque: term derived from *platero* (ie silversmith); used to describe the early style of the Renaissance characterised by finely carved decoration.

H. Choimet/MICHELIN

Following are Spanish terms and their translations used in the guide. Words like coro are in the original Spanish; there is no equivalent in English.

Predella: the lower part of an altarpiece.

Sebka: type of brick decoration developed under the Almohads consisting of an apparently endless series of small arches forming a network of diamond shapes.

Seo or *seu*: cathedral.

Soportales: porticoes of wood or stone pillars supporting the first floor of houses. They form an open gallery around the plaza mayor of towns and villages.

Star vault: vault with a square or polygonal plan formed by several intersecting arches.

Stucco: type of moulding mix consisting mainly of plaster, used for coating surfaces. It plays a fundamental role in wall decoration in Hispano-Muslim architecture.

Talayot: megalithic monument found in the Balearic Islands, which takes the form of a truncated cone of stones.

Taula (*mesa* in the Mallorcan language): megalithic monument found in the Balearic Islands, which consists of a monolithic horizontal stone block placed on top of a similar vertical stone block.

Triforium: arcade above the side aisles which opens onto the central nave of a church.

Tympanum: inner surface of a pediment. This often ornamented space is bounded by the archivolt and the lintel of the doors of churches.

Venera: scallop-shaped moulding frequently used as an ornamental feature. It is the symbol of pilgrimages to Santiago de Compostela.

Yesería: plasterwork used in sculptured decoration.

Cabecera: the east or apsidal end of a church.

Camarín: a small chapel on the first floor behind the altarpiece or retable. It is plushly decorated and very often contains a lavishly costumed statue of the Virgin Mary.

Capilla Mayor: the area of the high altar containing the **retablo mayor** or monumental altarpiece which often rises to the roof.

Coro: a chancel in Spanish canonical churches often built in the middle of the nave. It contains the **stalls** (*sillería*) used by members of religious orders. When placed in a tribune or gallery it is known as the coro alto.

Crucero: transept. The part of a church at right angles to the nave which gives the church the shape of a cross.

Girola (also *deambulatorio*): ambulatory. An extension to the aisles forming a gallery around the chancel and behind the altar.

Presbiterio: the space in front of the altar. (The presbytery is known as the casa del cura.)

Púlpito: pulpit.

Sagrario: chapel containing the Holy Sacrament. May sometimes be a separate church.

Sillería: the stalls.

Trasaltar: back wall of the capilla mayor in front of which there are frequently sculptures or tombs.

Trascoro: the wall, often carved and decorated, which encloses the coro.

H. Choimet/MICHELIN

ART AND ARCHITECTURE

Over the centuries, Spain has amassed countless artistic and architectural treasures across the length and breadth of the country, ranging from diminutive Romanesque chapels, lofty Gothic cathedrals and exuberant Baroque churches to awe-inspiring Hispano-Moorish monuments, imposing castles, magnificent paintings and outstanding sculptures.

From Prehistory to the Moorish Conquest

PREHISTORIC ART

Prehistoric inhabitants of the Iberian Peninsula have left some outstanding examples of their art. The oldest are the Upper Palaeolithic (40000-10000 BC) cave paintings in Cantabria (Altamira and Puente Viesgo), Asturias (El Pindal, Ribadesella and San Román) and the Levante region (Cogull and Alpera). Megalithic monuments like the famous Antequera dolmens were erected during the Neolithic Era (7500-2500 BC), or New Stone Age, while in the Balearic Islands strange stone monuments known as **talayots** and *navetas* were built by a Bronze Age people (2500-1000 BC).

FIRST MILLENNIUM BC

Iberian civilisations produced gold and silverware (treasure of Carambolo in the Museo Arqueológico in Sevilla), and fine sculpture. Some of their work, such as the Córdoba lions, the Guisando bulls and, in the Museo Arqueológico in Madrid, the *Dama de Baza* and the *Dama de Elche*, is of a remarkably high standard. Meanwhile, Phoenician, Carthaginian and in turn Greek colonisers introduced their native art: Phoenician sarcophagi in Cádiz, Punic art in Ibiza and Greek art in Empúries.

ROMAN SPAIN (1C BC-5C AD)

Besides roads, bridges, aqueducts, towns and monuments, Roman legacies include the Mérida theatre, the ancient towns of Italica and Empúries, and the Segovia aqueduct and Tarragona triumphal arch.

THE VISIGOTHS (6C-8C)

Christian Visigoths built small stone churches (Quintanilla de las Viñas, San Pedro de la Nave) adorned with friezes carved in geometric patterns with plant motifs. The apsidal plan was square and the arches were often horseshoe-shaped. The Visigoths were outstanding gold and silversmiths who made sumptuous jewellery in the Byzantine and Germanic traditions. Gold votive crowns (Guarrazar treasure in Toledo), fibulae and belt buckles adorned with precious stones or cloisonné enamel were presented to churches or placed in the tombs of the great.

Hispano-Moorish Architecture (8C-15C)

The three major periods of Hispano-Moorish architecture correspond to the reigns of successive Arab dynasties over the Muslim-held territories in the peninsula.

CALIPHATE OR CÓRDOBA ARCHITECTURE (8C-11C)

This period is characterised by three types of building: **mosques**, built to a simple plan consisting of a minaret, a courtyard with a pool for ritual ablutions and finally a square prayer room with a *mihrab* (prayer-niche marking the direction of Mecca); **alcázares** (palaces), built around attractive patios and surrounded by gardens and fountains; and **alcazabas** (castle fortresses), built on high ground and surrounded by several walls crowned with pointed merlons – one of the best examples of these can be found in Málaga. The most famous monuments from this period are in Córdoba (the Mezquita and the Medina

Dama de Elche

H. Stierlin

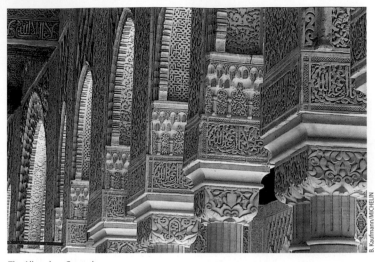

The Alhambra, Granada

Azahara palace) and in Toledo (Cristo de la Luz) where, besides the ubiquitous horseshoe arch which virtually became the hallmark of Moorish architecture, other characteristics developed including ornamental brickwork in relief, cupolas supported on ribs, turned modillions, arches with alternating white stone and red-brick voussoirs, multifoil arches and doors surmounted with blind arcades. These features subsequently became popular in Mudéjar and Romanesque churches.

The Umayyads brought a taste for profuse decoration from Syria. As the Koran forbids the representation of human or animal forms, Muslim decoration is based on calligraphy (Cufic inscriptions running along walls), geometric patterns (polygons and stars made of ornamental brickwork and marble) and lastly plant motifs (flowerets and interlacing palm leaves).

ALMOHAD OR SEVILLA ARCHITECTURE (12C-13C)

The religious puritanism of the Almohad dynasty, of which Sevilla was the capital, was expressed in architecture by a refined, though sometimes rather austere, simplicity. One of the characteristics of the style consisted of brickwork highlighted by wide bands of decoration in relief, without excessive ornamentation (the Giralda tower in Sevilla is a good example.) The style was later used in the Mudéjar architecture of Aragón. Other features that emerged at this time include *artesonado* ceilings and *azulejos*. Arches of alternate brick and stonework disappeared, the horseshoe arch became pointed and the multifoil arch was bor-

dered by a curvilinear festoon (ornament like a garland) as in the Aljafería in Zaragoza. Calligraphic decoration included cursive (flowing) as well as Cufic script to which floral motifs were added to fill the spaces between vertical lines.

The Decorative Arts

Extremely rich and varied decorative artifacts from this period include geometric wood strapwork, brocades, weapons, ceramics with metal lustre decoration and small ivory chests.

NASRID OR GRANADA ARCHITECTURE (14C-15C)

This period of high sophistication, of which the **Alhambra** in Granada is the masterpiece, produced less innovation in actual architectural design than in the decoration, whether stucco or ceramic, that covered the walls.

Surrounds to doors and windows became focal points for every room's design and the spaces between them were filled by perfectly proportioned panels. Arch outlines were simplified – the stilted round arch became widespread – while detailed lacework ornamentation was used as a border.

MUDÉJAR ARCHITECTURE

This is the name given to work carried out by Muslims while under the Christian yoke, yet executed in the Arab tradition. It was fashionable from the 11C to the 15C in different regions depending on the area recovered by the Reconquest, although some features, like *artesonado* ceilings, continued as decorative themes for centuries.

Court Mudéjar, developed by Muslim artists (in buildings ordered by Peter the Cruel in Tordesillas and Sevilla, and in synagogues in Toledo), was an extension of the Almohad or contemporary Nasrid style. Popular Mudéjar, on the other hand, was produced by local Muslim workshops and reflects marked regional taste: walls were decorated with blind arcades in Castilla (Arévalo, Sahagún and Toledo) and belfries were faced with *azulejos* and geometric strapwork in Aragón.

Pre-Romanesque and Romanesque Art and Architecture (8C-13C)

ASTURIAN ARCHITECTURE

A highly sophisticated style of court architecture, characterised by sweeps of ascending lines, developed in the small kingdom of Asturias between the 8C and the 10C. Asturian churches (Naranco, Santa Cristina de Lena) followed the precepts of the Latin basilica in their rectangular plan with a narthex, a nave and two aisles separated by semicircular arches, a vast transept and an east end divided into three. Decoration inside consisted of frescoes, and borrowings from the East including motifs carved on capitals (strapwork, rosettes and monsters) and ornamental openwork around windows. Gold and silversmiths in the 9C and 10C produced rich treasures, many of which may be seen in the Cámara Santa in Oviedo Cathedral.

MOZARABIC ARCHITECTURE

This term is given to work carried out by Christians living under Arab rule after the Moorish invasion of 711. Churches built in this style, especially in Castilla (San Miguel de Escalada, San Millán de la Cogolla), brought back Visigothic traditions (horseshoe arches) enriched by Moorish features such as ribbed cupolas and turned modillions.

Illuminated manuscripts provide the earliest known examples of Spanish medieval painting (10C). They were executed in the 10C and 11C by Mozarabic monks and have Moorish features such as horseshoe arches and Arab costumes. They portray St John's Commentary on the Apocalypse written in the 8C by the monk **Beatus de Liébana**, after whom the manuscripts were named.

CATALUNYA, HOME OF THE EARLIEST ROMANESQUE STYLE IN SPAIN

Catalunya had intimate links with Italy and France and consequently developed an architectural style strongly influenced by Lombardy from the 11C to the 13C. This evolved in the Pyrenean valleys, isolated from the more travelled pilgrim and trade routes. Sober little churches were built often accompanied by a separate bell tower decorated with Lombard bands. Interior walls in the 11C and 12C were only embellished with frescoes which, in spite of their borrowings from Byzantine mosaics (heavy black outlines, rigid postures, and themes like Christ in Glory portrayed within a mandorla), proved by their realistic and expressive details to be typically Spanish. Altar fronts of painted wood, executed in bright colours, followed the same themes and layout.

EUROPEAN ROMANESQUE ART ALONG THE PILGRIM ROUTES

Northwest Spain opened its gates to foreign influence during the reign of Sancho the Great of Navarra early in the 11C. Cistercian abbeys were founded and French merchants allowed to settle rate-free in towns (Estella, Sangüesa and Pamplona). Meanwhile, the surge of pilgrims to Compostela and the fever to build along the routes brought about the construction of a great many religious buildings in which French influence was clearly marked (characteristics from Poitou in Soria and Sangüesa, and from Toulouse in Aragón and Santiago de Compostela). The acknowledged masterpiece of this style is the cathedral of Santiago de Compostela.

In Aragón, Romanesque art was particularly evident in sculpture. The artists who carved capitals in the manner of their leader, the Maestro de San Juan de la Peña, had a seemingly clumsy style because their emphasis was more on symbolism than realistic portrayal. Disproportionate faces with bulging eyes were the means by which the sculptor illustrated the soul, while gestures such as outstretched hands conveyed religious meaning.

In the early 12C, reform of the **Cistercian Order** with emphasis on austerity brought an important change to architecture. The transitional style which heralded the Gothic (intersecting ribbed vaulting, squared apses) was introduced and the profusion of Romanesque decoration disappeared. Examples of this style may be seen in the monasteries of Poblet, Santes Creus, La Oliva and Santa María de Huerta.

The Gothic Period (from the 13C)

THE EARLY STAGES

French Gothic architecture made little headway into Spain except in Navarra where a French royal house had been in power since 1234. The first truly Gothic buildings (Roncesvalles church, Cuenca and Sigüenza cathedrals) appeared in the 13C. Bishops in some of the main towns in Castilla (León, Burgos, Toledo) sent abroad for cathedral plans, artists and masons. An original style of church, with no transept, a single nave (aisles, if there were any, would be as high as the nave), and pointed stone arches or a wooden roof resting on diaphragm arches, developed in **Valencia**, **Catalunya** and the **Balearic Islands**. The unadorned walls enclosed a large, homogeneous space in which there was little carved decoration, and purity of line supplied a dignified elegance.

Civil architecture followed the same pattern and had the same geometrical sense of space, used with rare skill particularly in the *lonjas* or commodity exchanges of Barcelona, Palma, Valencia and Zaragoza.

THE GOTHIC STYLE DEVELOPS

During the 14C and 15C in Castilla, the influence of artists from the north such as **Johan of Cologne** and **Hanequin**

of Brussels, brought about the flowering of a style approaching Flamboyant Gothic. As it adapted to Spain, the style developed simultaneously in two different ways: in one, decoration proliferated to produce the Isabelline style; in the other, structures were simplified into a national church and cathedral style which remained in favour until the mid 16C (Segovia and Salamanca).

THE LAST OF THE GOTHIC CATHEDRALS

Following the example of Sevilla, the dimensions of Gothic cathedrals became ever more vast. Aisles almost as large as the nave increased the volume of the building, while pillars, though massive, retained the impression of thrusting upward lines. A new plan emerged in which the old crescendo of radiating chapels, ambulatory, chancel and transept was superseded by a plain rectangle. Gothic decoration accumulated around doors, on pinnacles and in elaborate star vaulting; a style echoed in some Andalucían cathedrals.

PAINTING

Artists in the Gothic era worked on polyptyches and altarpieces which sometimes reached a height of more than 15m/50ft. The Primitives, who customarily painted on gold backgrounds, were influenced by the Italians (soft contours), the French and the Flemish (rich fabrics with broken folds and painstaking detail). Nonetheless, as they strove for expressive naturalism and lively anecdotal detail, their work came across as distinctively Spanish.

Iglesia de San Martín de Frómista

R. Lopez-Alonso/STOCK PHOTOS

Oronoz/ARTEPHOTO/Museo de Bellas Arte, Bilbao

Gothic art: an altarpiece painted by Pedro Serra

There was intense artistic activity in the states attached to the Crown of Aragón, especially in Catalunya. The Vic, Barcelona and Valencia museums contain works by **Ferrer Bassá** (1285-1348) who was influenced by the Sienese **Duccio**, paintings by his successor **Ramón Destorrents** (1346-91), and by the **Serra** brothers, Destorrents' pupils. Among other artists were **Luis Borrassá** (c 1360-1425) who had a very Spanish sense of the picturesque, **Bernat Martorell** (d 1452) who gave special importance to landscape, **Jaime Huguet** (1415-92) who stands out for his extreme sensitivity and is considered to be the undisputed leader of the Catalan School, and finally **Luis Dalmau** and **Bartolomé Bermejo**, both influenced by Van Eyck (who accompanied a mission sent to Spain by the Duke of Burgundy).

In Castilla, French influence predominated in the 14C and Italian in the 15C until about 1450 when Flemish artists like **Rogier van der Weyden** arrived. By the end of the 15C, **Fernando Gallego** had become the main figure in the Hispano-Flemish movement in which **Juan of Flanders** was noted for his appealingly delicate touch.

SCULPTURE

Gothic sculpture, like architecture, became more refined. Relief was more accentuated than in Romanesque carving, postures more natural and details more meticulous. Decoration grew increasingly abundant as the 15C progressed and faces became individualised to the point where recumbent funerary statues clearly resembled the deceased.

Statues were surmounted by an openwork canopy, while door surrounds, cornices and capitals were decorated with friezes of intricate plant motifs. After being enriched by French influence in the 13C and 14C and Flemish in the 15C, sculpture ultimately developed a purely Spanish style, the Isabelline.

Portals showed a French influence. Tombs were at first sarcophagi decorated with coats of arms, sometimes surmounted by a recumbent statue in a conventional posture with a peaceful expression and hands joined. Later, more attention was paid to the costume of the deceased; with an increasingly honed technique marble craftsmen were able to render the richness of brocades and the supple quality of leather. In the 15C, sculptors produced lifelike figures in natural positions, kneeling for instance, or even in nonchalant attitudes like that of the remarkable Doncel in Sigüenza Cathedral. Altarpieces comprised a predella or plinth, surmounted by several levels of panels and finally by a carved openwork canopy. Choir stalls were adorned with biblical and historical scenes or carved to resemble delicate stone tracery.

THE ISABELLINE STYLE

At the end of the 15C, the prestige surrounding the royal couple and the grandees in the reign of Isabel the Catholic (1474-1504) provided a favourable context for the emergence of a new style in which exuberant decoration covered entire façades of civil and religious buildings. Ornamentation took the form of supple free arcs, lace-like carving, heraldic motifs and every fantasy that imagination could devise (🖐 see VALLADOLID). The diversity of inspiration was largely due to foreign artists: **Simon of Cologne** (son of Johan) – San Pablo in Valladolid, Capilla del Condestable in Burgos; **Juan Guas** (son of the Frenchman, Pierre) – San Juan de los Reyes in Toledo; and **Enrique Egas** (nephew of Hanequin of Brussels) – Capilla Real in Granada.

The Renaissance (16C)

In the 16C, at the dawn of its golden age, Spain was swept by a deep sense of its own national character and so created a style in which Italian influence became acceptable only when hispanicised.

ARCHITECTURE

Plateresque was the name given to the early Renaissance style because of its finely chiselled, lavish decoration reminiscent of silverwork (platero: silversmith). Although close to the Isabelline style in its profusion of carved forms extending over entire façades, the rounded arches and ornamental themes (grotesques, foliage, pilasters, medallions and cornices) were Italian. The Plateresque style was brought to a climax in Salamanca in the façade of the Universidad and that of the Convento de San Esteban. Among architects of the time were **Rodrigo Gil de Hontañón** who worked at Salamanca (Palacios de Monterrey and Fonseca) and at Alcalá de Henares (university façade), and **Diego de Siloé**, the main architect in Burgos (Escalera de la Coronería). Together with **Alonso de Covarrubias** (d 1570) who worked mainly in Toledo (Alcázar and Capilla de los Reyes Nuevos in the cathedral), Diego de Siloé marked the transition from the Plateresque style to the Classical Renaissance. **Andrés de Vandelvira** (1509-76) was the leading architect of the Andalucían Renaissance (Jaén cathedral). His work introduces the austerity which was to characterise the last quarter of the century.

The Renaissance style drew upon Italian models and adopted features from Antiquity such as rounded arches, columns, entablatures and pediments. Decoration became of secondary importance after architectonic perfection. **Pedro Machuca** (d 1550) who studied under Michelangelo, designed the palace of Charles V in Granada, the most classical example of the Italian tradition. Another important figure, **Bartolomé Bustamante** (1500-70), built the Hospital de Tavera in Toledo.

The greatest figure of Spanish Classicism was **Juan de Herrera** (1530-97) who gave his name to an architectural style characterised by grandeur and austerity. He was the favourite architect of Philip II. The king saw in him the sobriety that suited the Counter-Reformation and in 1567 entrusted him with the task of continuing work on El Escorial, his greatest achievement.

SCULPTURE

Sculpture in Spain reached its climax during the Renaissance. In the 16C, a great many choir stalls, mausoleums and altarpieces (also known as retables or reredos) were still being made of alabaster and wood. These latter were then painted by the estofado technique in which gold leaf is first applied, then the object is coloured and finally delicately scored to produce gold highlights. Carved altarpiece panels were framed by Corinthian architraves and pilasters.

The sculptures of **Damián Forment** (c 1480-1540), who worked mainly in Aragón, belong to the transition period between Gothic and Renaissance styles. The Burgundian **Felipe Vigarny** (d 1543) and the architect **Diego de Siloé**, who was apprenticed in Naples, both worked on Burgos Cathedral. **Bartolomé Ordóñez** (d 1520) studied in Naples and carved the trascoro (choir screen) in Barcelona Cathedral and the mausoleums of Juana the Mad, Philip the Handsome (Capilla Real in Granada) and Cardinal Cisneros (Alcalá de Henares).

The home of the Renaissance School moved from Burgos to Valladolid in the mid-16C by which time the Spanish style had absorbed foreign influences and Spain's two great Renaissance sculptors had emerged. The first, **Alonso Berruguete** (1488-1561), who studied in Italy under Michelangelo, had a style which drew closely on the Florentine Renaissance and reflected a strong personality. He sought strength of expression rather than formal beauty and his tormented fiery human forms are as powerful as those of his master (statue of San Sebastián in the Museo de Valladolid). The second, **Juan de Juni** (d 1577), a Frenchman who settled in Valladolid, was also influenced by Michelangelo and founded the Catalan School of sculpture. His statues, recognisable by their beauty and the fullness of their forms, anticipated the Baroque style through the dramatic postures they adopted to express sorrow. Many of his works, such as the famous Virgen de los Siete

Cuchillos (Virgin of the Seven Knives) in the Iglesia de las Angustias in Valladolid and the Entombments in the Museo de Valladolid and Segovia Cathedral, were subsequently copied.

Most of the finely worked wrought-iron grilles closing off chapels and coros (chancels) were carved in the 15C and 16C. Members of the Arfe family, Enrique, Antonio and Juan, stand out in the field of gold- and silversmithing. They made the monstrances of Toledo, Santiago de Compostela and Sevilla cathedrals respectively.

PAINTING

Under Italian Renaissance influence, Spanish painting in the 16C showed a mastery of perspective, a taste for clarity of composition and glorification of the human body. These features found their way into Spanish painting mainly through the Valencian School where **Fernando Yáñez de la Almedina** and **Fernando de Llanos** introduced the style of Leonardo da Vinci, while **Vicente Macip** added that of Raphael and his son **Juan de Juanes** produced Mannerist works. In Sevilla, **Alejo Fernández** painted the famous *Virgin of the Navigators* in the Alcázar. In Castilla, the great master of the late 15C was **Pedro Berruguete** (c 1450-1504) whose markedly personal style drew upon all the artistic influences in the country. His successor, **Juan de Borgoña**, specialised particularly in landscape, architecture and decorative motifs. Another artist, **Pedro de Campaña** from Brussels, used chiaroscuro to dramatic effect while **Luis de Morales** (c 1520-86), a Mannerist, gave his work a human dimension through the portrayal of feelings. Ordinary people with religious sentiments responded favourably to the spiritual emotion expressed in his paintings. At the end of the 16C, Philip II sent for a great many Italian or Italian-trained artists to paint pictures for El Escorial. During his reign he introduced portrait painting under the Dutchman **Antonio Moro** (1519-76), his disciple **Alonso Sánchez Coello** (1531-88) and **Pantoja de la Cruz** (1553-1608). **El Greco**, on the other hand, was scorned by the court and settled in Toledo.

Baroque (17C-18C)

Spanish art reached its apogee in the mid-17C. Baroque met with outstanding success in its role as an essentially religious art in the service of the Coun-ter-Reformation and was particularly evident in Andalucía, then enriched by trade with America.

ARCHITECTURE

Architects in the early 17C were still under the influence of 16C Classicism and the Herreran style to which they added decorative details. Public buildings proliferated and many continued to be built throughout the Baroque period.

Public buildings of the time in Madrid include the plaza Mayor by **Juan Gómez de Mora**, built shortly before the Ayuntamiento (town hall), and the most significant building of all, the present Ministerio de Asuntos Exteriores (Ministry of Foreign Affairs) by **Juan Bautista Crescenzi**, the architect of the Panteón de los Reyes at El Escorial.

Church architecture of the period showed greater freedom from Classicism. A style of Jesuit church, with a cruciform plan and a large transept that served to light up altarpieces, began to emerge. Madrid has several examples including the Iglesia de San Isidro by the Jesuits **Pedro Sánchez** and **Francisco Bautista**, and the Real Convento de la Encarnación by **Juan Gómez de Mora**. In the middle of the century, architects adopted a less rigid style, changing plans and façades, breaking up entablatures and making pediments more elaborate. A good example of this Italian Baroque style is the Iglesia Pontificia de San Miguel (18C) in Madrid. A new feature, the **camarín**, was introduced: at first simply a passage behind the high altar leading to the retable niche containing a statue venerated by the faithful, it developed into a highly ornate chapel. Decoration of this kind may be seen in Zaragoza's Basílica de Nuestra Señora del Pilar designed by **Francisco Herrera the Younger** (1622-85). The Clerecía in Salamanca is a magnificent Baroque creation with a patio that anticipates the audacity and superabundant decoration characteristic of the Churrigueresque style.

THE CHURRIGUERESQUE STYLE

In this style, named after the Churriguera family of architects (late 17C), architecture became no more than a support for dense concentrations of ornament covering entire façades. The style is typified by the use of *salomónicas*, or barley sugar columns entwined with vines, and *estípites*, or pilasters arranged in an inverse pyramid. Early examples of this extravagance, the altarpiece of the Convento de San Esteban in Salamanca and the palace in Nuevo Baztán near Madrid, were by **José de Churriguera** (1665-1725) who was the instigator of the style but did not make any architectural changes. His brothers **Joaquín** (1674-1724) and especially **Alberto** (1676-1750) who designed the plaza Mayor in Salamanca, took greater liberties in their work. **Pedro de Ribera** (1683-1742), a Castilian architect who worked mainly in Madrid, surpassed the Churriguera brothers in decorative delirium. The other great Castilian, **Narciso Tomé**, is remembered for the façade of the Universidad de Valladolid (1715) and particularly for the *Transparente* in Toledo Cathedral (1720-32).

REGIONAL VARIATIONS

The popularity of the Baroque spread countrywide, differing from province to province. In **Galicia**, where the hardness of the granite precluded delicate carving, Baroque took the form of softer lines and decorative mouldings. The best example of the style and the masterpiece of its designer, **Fernando de Casas y Novoa**, is the Obradoiro façade of Santiago de Compostela Cathedral (1750).

In **Andalucía**, Baroque attained its utmost splendour, especially in decoration. Undulating surfaces characterised the façades of palaces (Écija), cathedrals (Guadix) and the doorways of countless churches and mansions (Jerez) in the 18C. As well as sculptor and painter, **Alonso Cano** was the instigator of Andalucían Baroque and designed the façade of Granada Cathedral. The major exponent of the style was, however, **Vicente Acero**, who worked on the façade of Guadix Cathedral (1714-20), designed Cádiz Cathedral and built the tobacco factory in Sevilla. Mention should also be made of **Leonardo de Figueroa** (1650-1730) for the Palacio de San Telmo in Sevilla and **Francisco Hurtado** (1669-1725) and **Luis de Arévalo** for La Cartuja in Granada; Hurtado worked on the monastery's tabernacle and Arévalo on the sacristy, the most exuberant Baroque works in Andalucía.

In the **Levante**, Baroque artists used polychrome tiles to decorate church cupolas and spires like that of Santa Catalina in Valencia. In the same town, the Palacio del Marqués de Dos Aguas by **Luis Domingo** and **Ignacio Vergara** is reminiscent of façades by Ribera, although its design is more like French Rococo. The cathedral in Murcia has an impressive façade by **Jaime Bort**.

THE GOLDEN AGE OF SPANISH PAINTING

This was characterised by the rejection of the previous century's Mannerism and the adoption of naturalism. The starting point was Caravaggio's tenebrism, powerful contrasts of light and shade, and his stern realism. Painters took up portraiture and still life *(bodegón)*, while allegories on the theme of *vanitas* (still-life paintings showing the ephemerality of life) reflected a philosophical purpose by juxtaposing everyday objects with symbols of decay to illustrate the transience of wealth and the things of this world and the inevitability of death. Among 17C artists were two from the Valencian School – **Francisco Ribalta** (1565-1628), who introduced tenebrism into Spain, and **José de Ribera** (1591-1652), known for his forceful realism.

Some of the greatest Baroque artists worked in Andalucía. One was **Francisco Zurbarán** (1598-1664), master of the Sevilla School; light in his paintings springs from within the subjects themselves. Other artists included **Murillo** (1618-82), who painted intimate, mystical scenes, and **Valdés Leal** whose powerful realism clearly challenged earthly vanities. **Alonso Cano** (1601-67), architect, painter and sculptor, settled in Granada and painted delicate figures of the Virgin.

The Castilian painters of the century, **Vicente Carducho** (1575-1638) and the portraitists **Carreño de Miranda** (1614-85) and **Claudio Coello** (1642-93), all excellent artists, nonetheless pale beside **Velázquez**. His aerial perspective and outstanding sense of depth are beyond compare.

SCULPTURE

Spanish Baroque sculpture was naturalistic and intensely emotive. The most commonly used medium was wood, and while altarpieces continued to be carved, pasos or statues specially made for Semana Santa processions proved a great novelty.

The two major schools of Baroque sculpture were in Castilla and Andalucía. **Gregorio Hernández**, Juni's successor, worked in Valladolid, the Castilian centre. His style was a lot more natural than that of his master, and his Christ Recumbent for the Convento de Capuchinos in El Pardo was widely copied. Sevilla and Granada were the main centres for the Andalucían School. **Juan Martínez Montañés** (1568-1649) settled in Sevilla and worked exclusively in wood, carving a great many *pasos* and various altarpieces. Alonso Cano, Granada's illustrious artist, became famous for the grace and femininity of his Immaculate Conceptions while his best-known disciple, **Pedro de Mena**, produced sculptures of great dramatic tension which contrasted with his master's understated style. The statue of Mary Magdalene (Museo Nacional de Escultura Policromada, Valladolid), St Francis (Toledo Cathedral) and the Dolorosa (Monasterio de las Descalzas Reales, Madrid) are telling examples of his work.

The 18C saw the rise to prominence of the great Murcian, Francisco Salzillo, whose dramatic sculptures were inspired by Italian Baroque.

Churrigueresque excess in sculpture took the form of immense altarpieces which reached the roof. These huge constructions took on such grand proportions that they began to be designed by architects. Their statues seemed smothered by decoration, lost in an overabundance of gilding and stucco.

Bourbon Art

Austrian imperialism was succeeded by enlightened Bourbon despotism which resulted in artistic as well as political change in the 18C. Henceforth the rules of art were to be governed by official bodies like the Academia de Bellas Artes de San Fernando.

ARCHITECTURE

During the first half of the century architecture still bore the stamp of Spanish Baroque, itself influenced at the time by French Rococo. The king and queen had palaces built in a moderate Baroque style (El Pardo, Riofrío, La Granja and Aranjuez) and began work on Madrid's Palacio Real modelled on Versailles. These buildings sought to ally French Classical harmony with Italian grace, and to this end most of the work was entrusted to Italian architects who generally respected the traditional quadrangular plan of *alcázares*, so typically Spanish. The vast gardens were given a French design.

Excavations of Pompeii and Herculaneum contributed to the emergence of a new, neo-Classical style which flourished between the second half of the 18C and 19C. It repudiated Baroque excess and aspired to Hellenistic beauty through the use of Classical orders, pediments, porticoes and cupolas. The kings of Spain, Charles III in particular, set about embellishing the capital by building fountains (Cibeles, Neptune), gates (Alcalá and Toledo), and planting botanic gardens.

The first Spanish neo-Classical architect, **Ventura Rodríguez** (1717-85), who was actually apprenticed in Italian Baroque, quickly developed an academic neo-Classical style. His works include the façade of Pamplona Cathedral, the paseo del Prado in Madrid and the Basílica de Nuestra Señora del Pilar in Zaragoza. **Sabatini** (1722-97), whose style developed along similar lines, designed the

The Third of May, Goya

Puerta de Alcalá and the building that now houses the Ministerio de Hacienda (Ministry of Finance) in Madrid. The leading architect was without doubt **Juan de Villanueva** (1739-1811), schooled in Classical principles during a stay in Rome. He designed the façade of the Ayuntamiento in Madrid, the Casita del Príncipe at El Escorial and most importantly, the Museo del Prado. Two notable town planners emerged during the 19C: **Ildefonso Cerdà** in Barcelona and **Arturo Soria** (1844-1920) in Madrid.

PAINTING

Bourbon monarchs took pains to attract the greatest painters to court and grant them official positions. In 1752 Ferdinand VI founded the Academia de Bellas Artes de San Fernando where it was intended that students should learn official painting techniques and study the Italian masters. Leading artists of the time were **Anton Raffael Mengs** (1728-79) from Bohemia and the Italian **Gian Battista Tiepolo** (1696-1770), both of whom decorated the Palacio Real. There was also **Francisco Bayeu** (1734-95) from Aragón, who painted a great many tapestry cartoons, as did his brother-in-law **Francisco Goya** (1746-1828). Goya's work, much of which may be seen in the Prado, Madrid, was to dominate the entire century.

Painters working in the post-Goya period did not follow in the master's footsteps as academic neo-Classical influences and Romanticism took over; Goya's legacy was not taken up until the end of the 19C. The following stand out among artists of the academic Romantic trend: **Federico de Madrazo**, representative of official taste in royal portraits and historical scenes, **Vicente Esquivel**, portrait-painter, and lastly **Leonardo Alenza**, and **Eugenio Lucas**, the spokesmen for **Costumbrismo** which had attained full status as a genre. (This was a style of painting illustrating scenes of everyday life which gradually developed from the simply anecdotal to a higher calling, the evocation of the Spanish soul.) Historical themes became very popular in the 19C with works by José Casado de Alisal, Eduardo Rosales and Mariano Fortuny.

Impressionist features began to appear in naturalist paintings by **Martí Alsina** and in post-Romantic landscapes by **Carlos de Haes**. The style secured a definitive hold in the works of **Narciso Oller, Ignacio Pinazo**, the best Valencian Impressionist, **Darío Regoyos** and lastly, **Joaquín Sorolla**, who specialised in light-filled folk scenes and regional subjects. The Basque artist **Ignacio Zuloaga** (1870-1945) expressed his love for Spain in brightly-coloured scenes of everyday life at a time when Impressionism was conquering Europe.

THE DECORATIVE ARTS

Factories were built under the Bourbons to produce decorative material for their royal palaces. In 1760, Charles III founded the Buen Retiro works, where ceramics for the famous Salón de Porcelana in the royal palaces of Aranjuez and Madrid were made. The factory was destroyed during the Napoleonic invasion.

In 1720, Philip V opened the Real Fábrica de Tapices de Santa Bárbara (in Madrid), the equivalent of the French Gobelins factory in Paris. Some of the tapestries were of Don Quixote while others depicted scenes of everyday life based on preparatory cartoons by Bayeu and Goya.

20C Art

FROM MODERNISM TO SURREALISM

The barren period that Spanish art in general experienced at the end of the 19C was interrupted in Catalunya by a vast cultural movement known as **Modernism**. This was particularly strong in architecture, with outstanding work by **Antoni Gaudí, Lluís Domènech i Montaner** and **Josep María Jujol**.

In the field of sculpture, **Pau Gargallo** broke new ground through the simplicity of his shapes, the attention he gave to volume and the use of new materials like iron.

Painting was varied and prolific. The following stand out among the many artists of the time: **Ramón Casas**, the best Spanish Impressionist, whose works are suffused with an atmosphere of grey melancholy, **Santiago Rusiñol, Isidro Nonell**, instigator of Spanish Expressionism, and **Pablo Ruiz Picasso** (1881-1973), the dominant figure whose innovations were to mark the entire history of 20C painting.

Picasso's attention was first devoted to academic naturalism (Science and Charity). He subsequently became a Modernist and social Expressionist. Later, once he had moved to Paris (1904), his style developed through the successive blue and rose periods to Cubism (Les Demoiselles d'Avignon), Surrealism and Expressionism (Guernica), which in turn led to a totally personal and subjective lyrical style (La Joie de Vivre).

Fundació Antoni Tàpies Barcelona/©Adagps, Paris 2003

Llibre-mur, Tàpies

In the 1920s a movement began to emerge that was influenced by Cubism and more particularly, by Surrealism. Its sculptors were **Angel Ferrant, Victorio Macho, Alberto Sánchez** and lastly **Julio González**, who strove towards abstract Expressionism through the use of iron and simple shapes. Painters of the movement included **Daniel Vázquez Díaz**, Juan Gris, Joan Miró and Salvador Dalí. **Juan Gris** (1887-1927), the most faithful analytical Cubist, worked in Paris. The works of Joan Miró (1893-1983), champion of Surrealism, are characterised by childlike spontaneity and an original attitude to everyday objects. Miró used very bright colours and magic symbols in all his paintings. **Salvador Dalí** (1904-89), a quasi-Surrealist, dreamed up his own creative method which he called the paranoic critical. Some of his best paintings were a result of his interest in the subconscious and his vision of a dream world. All his works attest to an excellent drawing technique and many show an attention to detail worthy of the best miniaturists.

POST-WAR ART

Spanish art was crucially affected by the Civil War in two ways: firstly, the fact that several artists went into exile meant that the country suffered cultural loss, and secondly, official taste in architecture developed a penchant for the monumental. This is clearly apparent in a number of colossal edifices. Many government buildings, all in Madrid, were designed in the manner of El Escorial, including the Ministerio del Aire, the Museo de América, the Arco del Triunfo and the Consejo de Investigaciones Científicas. The most striking example is the monument of the Valle de los Caídos (Valley of the Fallen) outside Madrid. However, among exponents of the nationalist style, there were several innovative architects like **Miguel Fisac**.

In 1950 the first signs of a new style, based on rational and functional criteria, began to emerge. Examples abound in Barcelona – the Vanguardia building by **Oriol Bohigas** and **José María Martorell**, the residential block by **Ricardo Bofill** in carrer de Nicaragua – and in Madrid – the Colegio Monfort by **A Fernandez Alba**, the Maravillas secondary school *(gimnasio)* by **Alejandro de la Sota** and the Torres Blancas (White Towers) by **F Javier Sáenz de Oíza**.

Post-war sculpture and painting are basically academic but there are some notable artists such as **José Gutiérrez Solana**, whose paintings are full of anguish, and the landscape painters **Benjamín Palencia**, who glorifies the country and light of Castilla, and **Rafael Zabaleta**, who is more interested in painting the region's country folk.

Avant-garde painters also began to emerge after the war. The first post-war Surrealists are members of a group called **Dau al Set** including **Modest Cuixart**, **Antoni Tàpies** and **Juan José Tharrats**. Tàpies is a veritable pioneer, one of the major abstract artists.

NEW ARTISTIC TRENDS

In the 1950s two abstract groups, with different qualities but with the common aim of artistic innovation, were formed: the **El Paso** group in Madrid with **Antonio Saura, Manuel Millares, Rafael Canogar, Luis Feito, Manuel Viola and Martín Chirino,** all representatives of what was known as action painting; and the **El Equipo 57** group in Cuenca with **Duart, Ibarrola, Serrano** and **Duarte**, who were more interested in drawing. The movement's sculptors included **Jorge Oteiza, Andréu Alfaro** and lastly **Eduardo Chillida**, who worked in iron and wood and stripped his sculptures of any figurative suggestion.

85

SPANISH GARDENS

The gardens of Spain are a further example of the country's rich culture, and bear witness to an enviable ability to adapt to a varied climate. Although Spanish landscape gardening has inherited many of its traditions from within Europe, particularly from the Greco-Roman era, the long period of Moorish occupation added a completely new dimension to the country's landscape.

The Generalife (14C), Granada

The Moors were truly gifted gardeners. The Generalife is *the* Moorish garden par excellence, despite the alterations it has undergone over the centuries. As a result of its extraordinary position it is a magnificent balcony, but above all it has been able to preserve an intimate, sensual character which was such a feature of Muslim gardens.

A Moorish garden is always an evocation of paradise; it is a feast for the senses and a harmonious whole which avoids grandiloquence. Nothing has been left to chance: the colour of the plants and flowers, their scent, and the omnipresence of water combine to create a serene ambience full of intimate charm.

The Generalife has been laid out on several levels to ensure that the trees in one garden do not interfere with the views from another. In fact, the Generalife is a series of landscaped areas and enclosures each with its own individuality yet part of an overall design. The garden's architectural features and vegetation, reflected in the water channels, blend together to create a perfect whole.

J. Helsing/STOCK PHOTOS

La Granja (18C), La Granja de San Ildefonso, Segovia

Once he came to the Spanish throne, Philip V, the grandson of Louis XIV, chose a beautiful spot in the Segovian countryside at the foot of the Sierra de Guadarrama to create these magnificent Baroque gardens. They bring to mind those of Versailles, where the monarch spent his childhood. Philip V was to make La Granja his personal retreat.

Although the Versailles influence is clearly evident, the differences are also obvious. Because of its position, hemmed in by the mountains, the grandiose perspectives of Versailles are not to be found at La Granja. The rigidity of the French garden is also lost here as there is no clear central axis; instead, La Granja consists of a succession of parts each with a certain independence, thus adopting hints of Moorish design. Although the gardeners brought with them a variety of species from France, they were able to adapt perfectly to the features of the local landscape and to preserve the somewhat wild appearance which gives it an undoubted charm. Magnificent fountains and sculptures scattered in small squares and along avenues add a theatrical touch.

A. de la Rosa

Pazo de Oca (18C-19C), La Estrada, La Coruña

A pazo is a Baroque-style manor typically found in Galicia. These large rustic residences are built on plots of land which generally comprise a recreational garden, a kitchen garden and cultivated farmland.

The Pazo de Oca garden, the oldest in Galicia, is a magnificent example of a garden in the wet part of Spain. What comes as a complete surprise is its perfect integration into its surroundings, where the damp climate has enabled vegetation to grow on rocks, creating an intimate relationship between its architectural and vegetal features. Water plays a vital role, appearing in basins or fountains or trickling through the garden. The most attractive part, with its two ponds, is hidden behind a parterre. A delightful bridge, with benches enabling visitors to enjoy this enchanting spot, separates the two sections, overcoming the difference in height between them. The lower pond contains the pazo's most representative and famous feature: the stone boat, with its two petrified sailors, planted with hydrangeas.

The combination of both climate and vegetation gives the site an unquestionably romantic air.

F. Bouillo~/MARCO POLO

Jardín Botánico de Marimurtra (20C), Blanes, Girona

Carlos Faust, the German impresario who settled on the Costa Brava, created this botanical garden in 1921 for research purposes to enable scientists to carry out studies on flora, and to catalogue and preserve plants threatened with extinction. It is situated in a delightful spot between the sea and the mountains and offers visitors magnificent views of the coast.

Marimurtra is a fine example of a contemporary Mediterranean garden, although a number of exotic species from every continent have also adapted perfectly here. It contains an interesting cactus garden, an impressive aquatic garden, as well as a collection of medicinal, toxic and aromatic plants. The scientific aims of the garden have not interfered in any way with the aesthetic direction it has taken. The only architectural feature with a purely decorative function is the small temple built at the end of the steps running down to the sea.

At present, only a third of Marimurtra is open to the public.

H. Le Gac /MICHELIN

LITERATURE

Errant knights, Don Juan characters, mystics and highwaymen occupy a hallowed place in Spanish letters. Spanish literature reached its peak during the Golden Age of the 16C and 17C, and has enjoyed a renewed period of acclaim since the beginning of the 20C, through the works of a new generation of writers from within Spain and across the Spanish-speaking world.

Roman Spain produced great Latin authors such as **Seneca the Elder** or the Rhetorician, his son **Seneca the Younger** or the Philosopher, Quintilian the Rhetorician, and the epic poet **Lucan**. In the 8C, the monk Beatus wrote the Commentary on the Apocalypse which gave rise to a series of outstanding illuminated manuscripts known as Beatus. Arab writers won renown during the same period. Works written in Castilian began to emerge only in the Middle Ages.

The Middle Ages

The first milestone of Spanish literature appeared in the 12C in the form of *El Cantar del Mío Cid*, an anonymous Castilian poem inspired by the adventures of **El Cid**. In the 13C, the monk **Gonzalo de Berceo**, drawing on religious themes, won renown through his works of *Mester de Clerecía*, the learned poetry of clerics and scholars. **Alfonso X, the Wise**, an erudite king who wrote poetry in Galician, decreed that in his kingdom, Latin should be replaced as the official language by Castilian, an act subsequently followed throughout Spain except in Catalunya where Catalan remained the written language. In the 14C, **Don Juan Manuel** introduced the use of narrative prose in his moral tales while Juan Ruiz, **Archpriest of Hita**, wrote a brilliant satirical verse work titled *El Libro de Buen Amor*, which later influenced the picaresque novel.

The Renaissance

In the 15C, lyric poetry flourished under Italian influence with poets such as **Jorge Manrique** and the **Marquis of Santillana**. **Romanceros**, collections of ballads in an epic or popular vein, perpetuated the medieval style until the 16C when *Amadís de Gaula* (1508) set the model for a great many romances or tales of chivalry. In 1499, *La Celestina*, a novel of passion in dialogue form by **Fernando de Rojas**, anticipated modern drama in a subtle, well-observed tragicomic intrigue.

The Golden Age (Siglo de Oro)

Spain enjoyed its greatest literary flowering under the Habsburgs (1516-1700), with great lyric poets such as **Garcilaso de la Vega**, disciple of Italian verse forms, **Fray Luis de León** and above all **Luis de Góngora** (1561-1627) whose obscure, precious style won fame under the name of Gongorism. Pastoral novels became popular with works by Cervantes and Lope de Vega. The **picaresque** novel, however, was the genre favoured by Spanish writers at the time. The first to appear in 1554 was *Lazarillo de Tormes*, an anonymous autobiographical work in which the hero, an astute rogue (*pícaro* in Castilian), casts a mischievous and impartial eye on society and its woes. There followed Mateo Alemán's *Guzmán de Alfarache* with its brisk style and colourful vocabulary, and *La Vida del Buscón*, an example of the varied talents of **Francisco de Quevedo** (1580-1645), essayist, poet and satirist. The genius of the Golden Age, however, was **Cervantes** (1547-1616), with his masterpiece, the universal **Don Quixote** (1605). **Lope de Rueda** paved the way for *comedia*, which emerged at the end of the 16C. Dramatists proliferated,

Beatus – El Escorial

H. Stierlin/Monasterio de El Escorial

among them the master **Lope de Vega** (1562-1635), who perfected and enriched the art form. This "phoenix of the mind" wrote more than 1 000 plays on the most diverse subjects. His successor, **Calderón de la Barca** (1600-81), wrote historical and philosophical plays *(La vida es sueño or Life's a Dream* and *El alcalde de Zalamea* or *The Mayor of Zalamea)* in which he brilliantly reflects the mood of Spain in the 17C. **Tirso de Molina** (1583-1648) left his interpretation of Don Juan for posterity while **Guillén de Castro** wrote *Las Mocedades del Cid* (*Youthful Adventures of the Cid*). Mention should also be made of works on the conquest of America by **Cortés** and **Bartolomé de las Casas** among others. Finally, the moralist **Fray Luis de Granada** and the mystics **Santa Teresa de Ávila** (1515-82) and **San Juan de la Cruz** (St John of the Cross) (1542-91) wrote theological works.

18C and 19C

The critical mode found expression in the works of essayists such as **Benito Jerónimo Feijóo** and **Jovellanos**, while elegance dominated the plays of **Moratín**. The great romantic poet of the 19C was **Bécquer** (1836-70) from Sevilla, while **Larra** was a social satirist, **Menéndez Pelayo** a literary critic and **Ángel Ganivet** a political and moral analyst. Realism was introduced to the Spanish novel by **Alarcón** (*The Three-Cornered Hat*) and **Pereda** (*Peñas arriba*) who concentrated on regional themes. By the end of the 19C, the best realist was **Pérez Galdós** whose prolific, lively work (*National Episodes*) is stamped with a great sense of human sympathy.

20C

A group of intellectuals known as the Generation of '98, saddened by Spain's loss of colonies like Cuba, pondered over the future and character of their country and, more generally, the problems of human destiny. The atmosphere was reflected in the work of essayists such as

Miguel de Unamuno (1864-1936) who wrote *El sentimiento trágico de la vida* (*The Tragic Sense of Life*), and **Azorín**, as well as the philologist **Menéndez Pidal**, the novelist **Pío Baroja** and the aesthete **Valle Inclán**, who created an elegant poetic prose style. Among their contemporaries were **Jacinto Benavente** (winner of the 1922 Nobel Prize for literature), who developed a new dramatic style, and the novelist **Vicente Blasco Ibáñez**. Henceforth Spain opened up to literary contributions from abroad. Some great poets began to emerge, including **Juan Ramón Jiménez** (Nobel Prize 1956), who expressed his feelings through simple unadorned prose poems *(Platero y yo)*, **Antonio Machado** (1875-1939) the bard of Castilla, and **Rafael Alberti. Federico García Lorca** (1898-1936) equally great as both poet and dramatist *(Bodas de sangre)*, was Andalucían through and through. His work was, perhaps, the most fascinating reflection of a Spain whose mystery **Ortega y Gasset** (1883-1925), essayist and philosopher, spent his life trying to fathom.

Post-war writing

Several years after the Civil War, writing rose from its ashes with works by essayists (Américo Castro), playwrights (Alfonso Sastre) and above all, novelists such as **Miguel Delibes, Camilo José Cela** *(La familia de Pascual Duarte)* who won the Nobel Prize for Literature in 1989, **Juan Goytisolo, Ramón Sender** and Antonio Ferres, all preoccupied with social issues.

Among contemporary authors, mention should be made of novelists Juan Benet, Juan Marsé, **Manuel Vázquez Montalbán**, Terenci Moix, Javier Marías and **Eduardo Mendoza**, and playwrights Antonio Gala, Fernando Arrabal and Francisco Nieva.

The Spanish-speaking countries of Latin America are making enormous contributions to literature in Spanish with works by Jorge Luis Borges, Gabriel García Márquez, Pablo Neruda and Miguel Ángel Asturias.

CINEMA AND MUSIC

Over the centuries, Spain has produced countless musicians and thespians of world renown. In more recent times, the genius of film directors such as Luis Buñuel, Juan Antonio Bardem and Pedro Almodóvar, composers such as Manuel de Falla, and classical guitarists such as Antonio Segovia, has thrilled audiences the world over.

Cinema

Spanish cinema dates back to a short film in 1897 which shows people leaving the Basílica de Nuestra Señora del Pilar in Zaragoza after Mass. Studios for silent movies were later set up in Barcelona.

In the 1920s, several Surrealists tried their hand at the new art form. Among them were **Dalí** and above all **Buñuel**, the master of Spanish cinema, who made *Un chien Andalou (Un perro andaluz)* in 1928 and *L'Age d'Or (La edad de oro)* in 1930. When talking films appeared in the 1930s, Spain was in the throes of a political and economic crisis and so her studios lacked the means to procure the necessary equipment.

At the end of the 1930s, when films like *Sister Angelica (Sor Angélica)* by Gargallo tended to address religious themes, Juan Piqueras launched a magazine called Nuestro Cinema which was strongly influenced by Russian ideas, and gave star billing to films such as *Las Hurdes – Land without Bread (Las Hurdes – Tierra sin pan*, 1932) by Buñuel, depicting poverty in a remote part of Spain.

During the Civil War and the ensuing Franco era, films were heavily censored and the cinema became one of the major vehicles for the ideology of the time, with historical and religious themes glorifying death and the spirit of sacrifice. One such success was *Marcelino, Bread and Wine (Marcelino, pan y vino*, 1955) by Ladislao Vajda. Change came with works by Juan Antonio Bardem like *Death of a Cyclist (Muerte de un ciclista*, 1955) and with Berlanga's *Welcome Mr Marshall (Bienvenido, Mr Marshall*, 1953) and *The Executioner (El verdugo*, 1964).

The 1960s enjoyed a period of renewal with directors like **Carlos Saura**, whose first film, *The Scoundrels (Los golfos)*, came out in 1959. More than ever before, the 1970s saw a new wave in Spanish cinema with outstanding directors and films. These were mainly concerned with the problems of childhood and youth marked by the Franco régime. Saura's *Ana and the Wolves (Ana y los lobos*, 1973) shows a young girl arriving as an outsider in a family in which three 50-year-old brothers personify the all-powerful hold of the army and religion during the Franco era. Mention should also be made of Saura's *Cría cuervos* (1975); *The Spirit of the Beehive (El espíritu de la colmena*, 1973) and *The South (El sur*, 1983) by **Víctor Erice**, *The Beehive (La colmena*, 1982) by **Mario Camus**, and films by **Manuel Gutiérrez Aragón** such as *Demons in the Garden (Demonios en el jardín*, 1982) and *The Other Half of Heaven (La Otra mitad del cielo*, 1986) which illustrate the economic changes between Spain under Franco and Spain as a democracy. **Pedro Almodóvar** breaks with this serious, nostalgic type of cinema so critical of the Franco era. His films are of a completely different, modern Spain in which the *Movida* (a fashionable, progressive anti-establishment movement in the arts during the 1980s) in Madrid is shown in a comic light, as in *Women on the Edge of a Nervous Breakdown (Mujeres al borde de un ataque de nervios*, 1988).

Three Spanish films have won an Oscar for Best Foreign Film: *To Begin Again (Volver a empezar*, 1982), directed by **JL Garci**, **F Trueba's** *Belle Epoque* (1993), and *All about my mother (Todo sobre mi*

Death of a Cyclist

Cahiers du Cinéma

madre, 1999), by **Pedro Almodóvar**. The last five years have seen a resurgence in Spanish cinema with young directors such as **Alejandro Amenabar** (Tesis, 1996), **Alex de la Iglesia** *(El día de la bestia*, 1995) and **Julio Medem** *(Los amantes del Círculo Polar*, 1998). This development has resulted in huge box office triumphs which were previously the exclusive territory of large-scale Hollywood productions, such as *The Dog in the Manger (El perro del hortelano*, 1996) by the late **Pilar Miró,** and *Secrets of the Heart (Secretos del corazón*, 1997) by **Montxo Armendáriz**. Other successful films of recent years include *The Lucky Star (La buena estrella*, 1997) by **Ricardo Franco**, *Barrio* (1998) by **Fernando León de Aranoa**, *El abuelo* (1998) by JL Garci, *The Girl of your Dreams (La niña de tus ojos*, 1998) by **F Trueba**, and *Solas* (1998) by **Benito Zambrano**.

Music

Alongside its folk music, Spain has developed an extraordinarily rich musical repertory since the Middle Ages, marked by a large number of influences including Visigothic, Arabic, Mozarabic and French. Polyphonic chants were studied in the 11C and the oldest known piece for three voices, the *Codex calixtinus*, was composed at Santiago de Compostela c 1140. During the Reconquest, the church encouraged great musical creativity in the form of liturgical chants, plays *(autos)* like the *Elche Mystery* which is still performed today, and poetry like the 13C **Cantigas de Santa María** by Alfonso the Wise.

At the end of the 15C, the dramatist **Juan de la Encina** composed secular songs, thus proving that he was also an excellent musician. Music, like the other arts, however, reached its climax in the second half of the 16C, under the protection of the early Habsburgs. **Victoria** (1548-1611) was one of the most famous composers of polyphonic devotional pieces, while among his contemporaries, **Francisco de Salinas** and **Fernando de las Infantas** were learned musicologists and **Cristóbal de Morales** and **Francisco Guerrero** were accomplished religious composers. As for instruments, the organ became the invariable accompaniment to sacred music, while a favourite for profane airs was the *vihuela*, a sort of guitar with six double strings which was soon replaced by the lute and eventually by the five-string Spanish guitar. In 1629, Lope de Vega wrote the text for the first Spanish opera. **Pedro Calderón de la Barca** is credited with creating the **zarzuela** (1648), a musical play with spoken passages, songs and dances, which, since the 19C, has based its plot and music on popular themes. The major composer of religious and secular music in the 18C was Padre **Antonio Soler**, a great harpsichord player.

In the 19C, the Catalan **Felipe Pedrell** brought Spanish music onto a higher plane. He opened the way for a new generation of musicians and was the first to combine traditional tunes with classical genres. At the beginning of the century, while works by French composers (Ravel's *Bolero*, Bizet's *Carmen*, Lalo's *Symphonie Espagnole* and Chabrier's *España*) bore a pronounced Hispanic stamp, Spanish composers turned to national folklore and traditional themes: **Isaac Albéniz** (1860-1909) wrote *Iberia*, **Enrique Granados** (1867-1916) became famous for his *Goyescas* and **Joaquín Turina** (1888-1949) for his *Sevilla Symphony*. This popular vein culminated in works by **Manuel de Falla** (1876-1946) including Nights in the Gardens of Spain, *El amor brujo* and *The Three-Cornered Hat*.

Among the best-known classical guitar players of our day, **Andrés Segovia** (1894-1987), **Joaquín Rodrigo** (1901-99), famous for his *Concierto de Aranjuez*, and **Narciso Yepes** (b 1927), have shown that this most Spanish of instruments can interpret a wide variety of music. Another Spaniard, **Pablo Casals** (1876-1973), was possibly the greatest cellist of all time. Spain holds a leading position in the world of opera with singers such as Victoria de los Ángeles, Montserrat Caballé, Plácido Domingo, Alfredo Kraus (1927-99), José Carreras and Teresa Berganza.

TRADITIONS AND FOLKLORE

Spain has kept alive its old traditions, as can be witnessed by the huge number of fiestas fervently celebrated around the country throughout the year. These unique and varied outpourings of religious sentiment and joy are a clear demonstration of Spain's rich cultural heritage and diversity.

A Land of Fiestas and Traditions

Numerous fiestas are celebrated across Spain. Unbridled joy, pomp and ceremony, and a sense of theatre are just some of the characteristics associated with these traditional aspects of Spanish life.

A detailed list of major festivals in Spain can be found in the Planning Your Trip section of this guide.

MAJOR FESTIVALS

To a greater or lesser degree, every Spanish town and city celebrates one main festival every year, normally in honour of its patron saint. These celebrations, many of which take place over the summer months, attract the entire local population, as well as inhabitants from outlying villages and rural areas. Typical events will include religious celebrations and processions, bullfights and bull-running, while many will attend just to indulge in animated discussions with friends until the early hours, or to enjoy rides on the fairground attractions that are traditional features of these events. The most important festivals in Spain include:

Los Sanfermines de Pamplona, in honour of San Fermín (7 July), which starts with the setting-off of a huge firework rocket or *"chupinazo"*. For an entire week the city is the backdrop for a non-stop celebration that enjoys its most spectacular moments during the morning running of the bulls *(encierros)* and at the early-evening bullfights.

Las Fallas de Valencia, held in March in honour of San José, is renowned for its firework displays, culminating in the *"Nit del foc"* (Night of Fire), when the impressive *"ninots"* (pasteboard figures) dotted around the city are set alight.

ANDALUCÍAN FIESTAS

Sevilla's April Fair is the most famous of these festivals, with a reputation that has stretched far beyond the borders of Spain. Andalucían fiestas are renowned for their exciting atmosphere, colourful costumes and spontaneous dance, with mountains of tapas consumed, accompanied by a glass or two of chilled dry sherry *(fino)* or *manzanilla*. The streets of the fairground area are a mass of colour as Andalucían women parade up and down on foot or on horseback dressed in the breathtaking flamenco dresses for which the region is famous.

ROMERÍAS

Romerías (pilgrimages) are an important aspect of religious life in Spain. Although each of these colourful events has its own specific characteristics, the basic principle is the same: a pilgrimage on foot, and occasionally on horseback, to a hermitage or shrine to venerate a statue. Usually, this religious peregrination will also include a procession, music, dancing and a festive meal in the countryside. The pilgrimage to El Rocío (Huelva) is the most extravagant and popular romería in the whole of Spain, attracting around one million pilgrims every year.

SEMANA SANTA

Holy Week processions are another vivid expression of the Spanish character. Numerous villages, towns and cities around the country participate in these outpourings of religious fervour, which see thousands of people taking to the streets to accompany the passion of Christ and the pain of his mother. Semana Santa tends to be a more sober affair in Castilla, and more festive in Andalucía, although across Spain the beauty of the statues (often works of art in their own right), the solemnity of the processions, some of which take place against a magnificent backdrop, and the fervour of those involved, create an atmosphere that will impress believers and non-believers alike.

Although Holy Week in Sevilla is undoubtedly the most famous, the processions in Valladolid, Málaga, Zamora and Cuenca are also worthy of particular note.

CARNIVAL

Carnival celebrations in Spain are generally extravagant affairs where the imagination is stretched to its limits and joy is

J. Malburet/MICHELIN

unbounded. They often involve many months of hard work during which performances are rehearsed and costumes made.

In the Canaries, particularly on Tenerife, Carnival is an important aspect of island tradition, involving a procession of floats and the election of the Carnival queen – events that bring the island to a standstill. The Carnival in Cádiz, which is known for its groups of musicians and folk dancers, is the liveliest on mainland Spain.

CHRISTMAS

The Christmas period in Spain is traditionally a time for family celebration. At home, where the Christmas tree and crib are essential decorative features, families congregate for dinner either on Christmas Eve or on Christmas Day, depending on the custom of their region. An equally traditional aspect of Christmas is the procession of the Kings: as a prelude to the most eagerly awaited night of the year, the Three Wise Men and their pages ride through the streets of towns and cities on the night of 5 January, handing out sweets to excited children lining their path.

BULLFIGHTING FESTIVALS

It is impossible to broach the subject of fiestas without mentioning bullfighting – a subject that raises passions and criticism in equal measure. It is impossible to deny that bullfighting festivals are just as much a part of Spanish culture as Holy Week processions; it is also true that the bullfighting world is indelibly linked with the major festivals around the country, and it is rare to find a town in which bullfighting is not present in some shape or form.

Very few cultural events are as regimented as a bullfight; consequently, a basic understanding of the various moves and stages of the contest is required to make any attempt to appreciate the spectacle. The bullfighting season runs from the spring to the autumn, and the most important festivals are those in Sevilla, held during the April Fair, and the San Isidro festival in Madrid.

Folklore

ANDALUCÍA

Flamenco, derived from gypsy and Arab sources, is a befitting expression of the Andalucían soul. It is based on the *cante jondo*, or deep song, which describes the performer's profound emotions in ancient poetic phrases. The rhythm is given by hand-claps, heel-clicks and castanets. The **sevillana**, from Sevilla, is a more popular type of dance and song. Sevilla and Málaga are the best places to see **tablaos** or performances of Andalucían music. Flamenco and the sevillana owe much of their grace to the Andalucían costume of brilliantly coloured flounced dresses for women and close-fitting short jacketed suits, wide flat hats and heeled boots for men.

The Castells forming a human pyramid in Valls

ARAGÓN

No general rejoicing here goes without a **jota**, a bounding, leaping dance in which couples hop and whirl to the tunes of a *rondalla* (group of stringed instruments), stopping only for the occasional brief singing of a *copla* by a soloist.

CATALUNYA AND THE COMUNIDAD VALENCIANA

The **sardana** dance is still very popular in Catalunya where it is performed in a circle in main squares on Sundays. The **Castells**, who form daring human pyramids, may be seen in festivals at El Vendrell and Valls.

In the Levante, the rich local costume notable for its colour and intricate embroidery is worn during lively, colourful festivals. Valencia's **Fallas** in March are a veritable institution which Alicante's **Fogueres** try to rival. Lastly, the *Moros y Cristianos* festivals – those of Alcoy are the best known – give a colourful replay of the confrontations between Moors and Christians during the Reconquest.

GALICIA, ASTURIAS AND CANTABRIA

Romerías in Asturias and Galicia are always accompanied by the shrill tones of the **gaita**, a type of bagpipe, and sometimes by drums and castanets. The gaita is played during events in honour of cowherds, shepherds, sailors and others who work in the country's oldest occupations. The most typical festivals are those held in summer for *vaqueiros*, or cowherds, in Aristébano and others for shepherds near the Lago de Enol. Common dances in Galicia include the *muñeira* or dance of the miller's wife, the sword dance performed only by men, and the *redondela*.

Bowls (*bolos*) is a very popular game.

PAÍS VASCO AND NAVARRA

The Basque Country and Navarra have preserved many of their unusual traditions. Men dressed in white with red sashes and the famous red berets dance in a ring accompanied by **zortzikos** (songs), a **txistu** (flute) and a *tamboril*. The most solemn dance, the *aurresku*, is a chain dance performed by men after Mass on Sundays. The **espata-dantza**, or sword dance, recalls warrior times while others, like the spinners' dance or another in which brooms are used, represent daily tasks. The Basques love contests, such as tug-of-war, trunk cutting, stone lifting and pole throwing. But by far the most popular sport is *pelota*, played in different ways: with a **chistera**, or wickerwork scoop, or with the very similar **cesta punta** in an enclosed three-walled court (*jai alai*), or with a wooden bat or *pala* or, finally, simply with the hand, **a mano**. There is a famous pelota university at Markina in Vizcaya.

CASTILLA

Few regions in Spain are as mystical or have such sober customs as Castilla. Traditional dances include the **seguidilla** and the **paloteo**, also known as the **danza de palos**, which is accompanied by flute, tambourine, and sometimes by a bass drum or the most typical of Castilian instruments, the local reed-pipe, or **dulzaina**. Peasant costumes around Salamanca are richly embroidered with precious stones, silk thread and sequins.

BALEARIC ISLANDS

Mallorca's traditional dances include the *copeo*, the *jota*, the *mateixes* and the *bolero*. Dances and festivals are accompanied by a *xeremía* (local bagpipes) and a tambourine. In Menorca, a festival dating back to medieval times and calling for about 100 horsemen in elegant costumes, is held at Ciutadella on Midsummer's Day. Popular dances in Ibiza have a poetical accompaniment to guide the performers' movements.

CANARY ISLANDS

The folklore of the Canaries shows influences from the Spanish mainland, Portugal and South America (the latter as a consequence of the strong links created by emigration); these in turn have become intertwined with local traditions. The **isa**, the **malagueña**, the *folía* and the *tajaraste* are the four best-known types of dance from the islands. The *timple* is a type of small guitar which is typical of the archipelago.

FOOD AND WINE

Spanish food is distinctively Mediterranean: it is cooked with an olive oil base, seasoned with aromatic herbs and spiced with hot peppers. It nevertheless varies enormously from region to region. Among dishes served throughout the country are garlic soup, cocido (a type of stew accompanied by beans or chickpeas), omelettes with potatoes, like the famous tortilla, typical pork meats like chorizo (a kind of spicy sausage), savoury rice dishes and delicious lean serrano hams. Fish and seafood are also used in a great many dishes.

No description of Spanish food should be complete without mentioning the ubiquitous tapas – the hors d'œuvres which appear on the counters of most bars and cafés just before lunch and dinner. This often vast array of colourful appetisers comes in two different forms: tapas (small saucer-size amounts) or raciones, more substantial portions. A selection of two or three tapas or one or two raciones makes for a very pleasant lunch accompanied by a glass (caña) of draught beer.

The country is also renowned for its magnificent wines, which include famous appellations such as Rioja and Penedès, and the sherries of the Jerez region.

Galicia

Galicia's cuisine owes its delicacy to the quality of its **seafood**: octopus, hake, gilthead, scallops (vieiras), mussels (mejillones), goose-barnacles (percebes), prawns (gambas), king prawns (langostinos) and mantis shrimps (cigalas). There is also el **caldo gallego**, a local soup, **lacón con grelos** (hand of pork with turnip tops) and another common traditional recipe, **pulpo gallego** (Galician-style octopus), often served as a tapa or ración. All these dishes may be accompanied by local wines such as red or white Ribeiro or white Albariño. The region's desserts include tarta de Santiago, an almond-flavoured tart, and filloas, a type of sweet fritter.

Asturias and Cantabria

In Asturias, fish and seafood are also important but the main speciality is a casserole dish called **fabada** made with white beans, pork, bacon and spicy sausages. As far as cakes and pastries are concerned, mention should be made of **sobaos**, delicious biscuits which originated in Cantabria and are cooked in oil. Cider is often drunk at meals.

País Vasco

Cooking in the Basque Country has been raised to the level of a fine art and requires laborious preparation. Meat is mostly served roasted, grilled or cooked in a sauce, while fish such as cod or hake is often accompanied by a green parsley sauce (salsa verde) or by peppers. Chipi-

D. Ball/PHOTONONSTOP

🍲 GAZPACHO 🍲

On a gastronomic level, Andalucía is renowned mainly for its fried fish dishes, and also its gazpacho, a cold soup which is particularly refreshing and tasty during the hot summer months.

Ingredients:

Tomatoes
peppers (red or green)
cucumber
garlic
olive oil

vinegar
seasoning
breadcrumbs
water.

Method: Grind the chillies, garlic and a little salt in a large pestle and mortar. The traditional method would be to add the diced peppers and tomatoes and the bread-crumbs and pound by hand until well mixed – but these days, most people liquidise everything with the help of a food processor! Slowly pour the oil onto the mixture stirring all the time. Leave to soak for a while, then add some cold water and strain the mixture through a sieve. Add a little vinegar and seasoning. Serve well chilled, with croutons, diced cucumber, red peppers and raw onion sprinkled on top.

rones en su tinta is a dish of baby squid in their own ink. *Marmitako*, a typical fishing village dish, is composed of tuna fish, potatoes and hot red peppers, and is often served with a good *txacolí*, a tart white wine.

Navarra and La Rioja

Navarra and La Rioja are the regions for game, excellent market-garden produce and the best Spanish wines, especially reds. The food is varied and refined, with partridge, quail and woodpigeon competing with trout for pride of place in local dishes. Navarra has noteworthy rosés and fruity white wines. Delicious Roncal cheese is made in the valleys from ewes' milk.

Aragón

Aragón is the land of **chilindrón**, a stew made with meat or poultry and peppers, and of **ternasco** (roast kid or lamb). These dishes may be washed down with heavy red Cariñena wines.

Catalunya

Catalunya has a typically Mediterranean cuisine. Look out in particular for *pan con tomate* (bread rubbed with a cut tomato and occasionally garlic and sprinkled with olive oil), red peppers cooked in oil, and wonderful fish dishes with a variety of sauces such as *all i oli* (crushed garlic and olive oil) and *samfaina* (tomatoes, peppers and aubergines). Among pork meats are **butifarra** sausages, various kinds of slicing sausage and the *fuet* sausage from Vic. Dried fruit is used in a great many dishes or may be served

at the end of a meal. The most wide-spread dessert is **crema catalana**, a kind of crème brûlée. Catalunya is also home to *cava*, a sparkling wine. Excellent light wines are made in the Empordà region, fruity whites in Penedès and reds in Priorato.

Castilla and Extremadura

Castilian specialities from local produce include roast lamb (**cordero asado**), suckling-pig (**cochinillo tostón** or **tostado**) and the ubiquitous **cocido**, all of which may be accompanied by a light fresh Valdepeñas red.

Rueda wines from the province of southern Valladolid are fresh fruity whites, while those from Ribera del Duero are generally acidic reds.

Castilla is also known for its cheeses, with a ewe's milk speciality from Burgos and many varieties of *manchego*, Spain's best-known cheese. Among local sweets are the famous marzipans *(mazapán)* from Toledo.

Extremadura enjoys an excellent reputation for its hams, such as those from Guijuelo (Salamanca) and Montánchez (Cáceres).

Levante

The Levante is the kingdom of rice dishes, including the famous **paella** which is cooked with a saffron rice base and chicken, pork, squid, mussels, shrimps and king prawns. As for sweets, **turrón** (made of almonds and honey or castor sugar, rather like nougat) is a Levantine speciality.

Balearic Islands

Soups are specialities in the Balearics; Mallorca's *mallorquina* has bread, leeks and garlic, while other soups are made with fish. **Tumbet** is a well-known casserole of potatoes, onions, tomatoes, courgettes and peppers. **Sobrasada**, a spicy sausage, flavours many local dishes. **Cocas**, pastries with sweet or savoury fillings, and **ensaimadas**, light spiral rolls, make delicious desserts.

Andalucía

The region's best-known dish is **gazpacho**, a cold cucumber and tomato soup made with oil and vinegar and flavoured with garlic. Andalucíans love their food fried, especially fish and seafood. Pigs are reared in the Sierra Nevada and Sierra de Aracena for the exquisite *serrano* ham. Among local desserts, *tocino de cielo* is as sweet as an Oriental pastry.

The region is especially well known for its dessert wines: the famous **Jerez** or sherries (& *see JEREZ DE LA FRONTERA*), **Montilla-Moriles** and **Málaga**.

🍲 PAELLA VALENCIANA 🍲

Paella is best prepared in a wide, shallow pan known as a *paellera*. It is essentially a dish for a festive occasion with family or friends, and can take a variety of forms. The following recipe is for a mixed meat and seafood paella:

Ingredients (serves 4):

small cup of olive oil
2 cloves of garlic (crushed)
1 green pepper (finely sliced)
half a cup of tomato purée
100g chicken (diced into medium-sized pieces)
100g pork (diced into medium-sized pieces)
250g arborio rice
1 tsp/half a dozen strands of saffron

salt and pepper
500ml fish stock
500ml chicken stock
100g clams
100g mussels
100g prawns
50g squid (cut into thin slices)
50g sweet red peppers (cut into thin slices)

Method: Heat the olive oil in a large frying pan or paella dish. Add the garlic and green peppers and fry for 2min. Add the chicken, pork and squid and cook, stirring, for a further 5min. Add the rice, saffron and tomato purée, followed immediately by the fish and chicken stock and salt and pepper. Cook for 10min, stirring occasionally. Once the rice is almost cooked, add the mussels, clams, prawns, sweet red peppers and green peas. Cook for a further 3-5min or until shellfish are cooked through. Garnish with slices of lemon.

¡Que aproveche! Enjoy!

Little Red Riding Hood

But Little Red Riding Hood had her local map with her, and so she did not fall into the trap. She did not take the path through the wood and she did not meet the big bad wolf. Instead, she chose the picturesque touring route straight to Grandmother's house, and arrived safely with her cake and her little pot of butter.

The End

With Michelin maps, go your own way.

The Mezquita, Córdoba

Aguilar de Campoo

POPULATION: 7,594.

MICHELIN MAP 575 D 17 – CASTILLA Y LEÓN (PALENCIA)

The Castillo de Aguilar stands on a rocky outcrop typical of the landscape of this part of the Meseta. The castle looks down on the old town, which has preserved something of its medieval appearance with its gateways, walls and mansions adorned with coats of arms.

Location

The town stands on the crossroads of the A 67, linking Palencia (97km/60mi S) with Santander (104km/65mi NE), and the N 627, which runs from Aguilar to Burgos (79km/49mi SE). The Aguilar reservoir *(embalse)* (2.5km/1.5mi W), fed by the waters of the Pisuerga river, is a popular water-sports centre. 🛈 *Plaza de España 30, 34800 Aguilar de Campoo*, ☎ *979 12 36 41.*

📍 *Neighbouring sights are described in the following chapters: BURGOS, PALENCIA, The WAY OF ST JAMES, SANTANDER and COSTA DE CANTABRIA.*

Worth a Visit

Colegiata de San Miguel

🕐*Open 4-7pm, Sat-Sun and public holidays 10.30pm-2pm and 4.30-7.30pm; summer 10.30am-2pm and 4-8pm.* 👝 *1.80€.* ☎ *616 99 46 51 (Mª. Carmen Gómez Simal).*

This Gothic church with Romanesque elements marks one end of the long **Plaza de España.** It shelters two fine mausoleums: the first, 16C, of the Marquessses of Aguilar praying, the second, in the north apsidiole, carved in a realistic manner, of the archpriest García González.

Monasterio de Santa María la Real

On the edge of town towards Cervera de Pisuerga. 💬*Guided tours (1 hr) noon-1.30pm and 5-8 pm; 15 Jun-15 Oct 10.30am-1.30pm and 3-6pm. 1.50€.* ☎ *979 12 22 31.*

This fine transitional Romanesque Gothic (12C-13C) monastery is known for its historiated capitals inside the church, its cloister and chapterhouse. It has recently undergone extensive restoration.

Tours

TO THE PICO DE TRES MARES VIA REINOSA *66km/41mi N*

This tour passes through a vast plain with fields of cereal crops before climbing the southern slopes of the Cordillera Cantábrica.

▶ *Follow the A 67.*

Cervatosa

The **antigua colegiata**★, a former collegiate church with an unusually pure Romanesque style, is remarkable for the richness and imaginativeness of its carved **decoration**★. The portal tympanum is meticulously patterned with a tight openwork design. There is a frieze of lions back to back while varied and audacious figures decorate the cornice modillions and those beneath the capitals of the south apsidal window. Inside there are harmonious blind arcades in the apse and, again, the carving on the capitals and the consoles supporting the arch ribs is both dense and sophisticated with entangled lions, eagles with spread wings, plant motifs and strapwork. The nave was raised with intersecting ribbed vaulting in the late 14C. 🔑*Ask for the key at the house next door (Don Julio).* ☎ *942 75 50 49.*

▶ *Continue along the same road, then turn off to the right.*

Retortillo

All that remains in the small **church** of the Romanesque period are the oven-vaulted apse and the triumphal arch with two finely carved capitals illustrating warriors. A few metres away are the ruins of a villa which stood in the Roman city of **Julióbriga**.

▶ *Return to the A 67.*

Reinosa

The proximity of the town to the Embalse del Ebro (a reservoir which is navigable for 20km/12mi) and the ski resort of Alto Campoo has resulted in its development as a tourist centre.

▶ *From Reinosa, take the CA 183 to the Pico de Tres Mares (27km/17mi).*

Pico de Tres Mares★★★

On the way, paths from the village of Fontibre lead to a greenish pool, the **source of the Ebro** (Fuente del Ebro), Spain's largest river, at an altitude of 881m/2 890ft.

 Access to the Pico de Tres Mares by chairlift. The peak (2 175m/7 136ft), one of the summits of the Sierra de Peña Labra, got its name as the source of three rivers which flow from it to three different seas (sea: *mar* in Spanish) – the Híjar, tributary of the Ebro which flows into the Mediterranean; the Pisuerga, tributary of the Duero which flows into the Atlantic; and the Nansa, which flows directly into the Cantabrian sea. From the crest there is a splendid circular **panorama**★★★: to the north, of the Nansa and the Embalse de la Cohilla (Cohilla Dam) at the foot of Monte Cueto (1 517m/4 977ft), and circling right, the Embalse del Ebro, the Sierra de Peña Labra, the Embalse de Cervera de Pisuerga and the Montes de León; due west, the central range of the Picos de Europa including the 2 618m/8 589ft Peña Vieja, and linked to it by a series of high passes, the eastern range which includes the Peña Sagra (2 042m/6 699ft). In the foreground is the eroded mass of the Peña Labra (2 006m/6 581ft).

Parc Nacional d'Aigüestortes i Estany de Sant Maurici★★

MICHELIN MAP 574 E 32-33 –

LOCAL MAP SEE PIRINEOS CATALANES – CATALUNYA (LLEIDA) ·

This national park in the Catalan Pyrenees is an area abounding in waterfalls and rushing streams. The twisting waterways, or aigües tortes, that have given the park its name wind gently through valleys between moss-covered meadows and wooded slopes. The glacially eroded landscape in the Aigüestortes National Park has a harsh type of beauty with U-shaped valleys, high mountain lakes, and impressive snow-covered peaks. The vegetation consists of a variety of coniferous trees such as firs and Scots pines but there are also birch and beech trees which provide a stunning splash of colour in autumn.

Location

The 14 119ha/34 888 acres of this national park stand at an altitude of between 1 500m/4 900ft and 3 000m/9 800ft, and consist mainly of granite and slate. The park can be reached via Espot, to the east, or from Boí, to the west. *Centro del Parque de Boí: Plaza del Treio 3, ☎ 973 69 61 89; Centro del Parque de Espot: Prat del Guarda 4, ☎ 973 62 40 36.*

 Neighbouring sights are described in the following chapters: PIRI-NEOS CATALANES and PIRINEOS ARAGONESES.

Worth a Visit

 Both entry points have adequate parking facilities.

 As private vehicles are prohibited within the park, visitors are best advised to take an organised

A landscape dominated by mountains

B. Brillion/MICHELIN

excursion by four-wheel drive with a local guide. A number of well-signposted paths are also available. In total, there are four mountain refuges within the boundaries of the park.

🕹 *Before starting your visit we recommend that you head for the Casa del Parque Nacional L'Estudi in Boí or the Casa del Parque Nacional in Espot.* 🕐 *Both open Jun-Sep 9am-1pm and 3.30-7pm; Oct-May 9am-2pm and 3.30-6pm; Sun and public hols 9-14.* 🕐 *Closed 1 and 6 Jan and 25-26 Dec. Round-trip transport through the park:* 🚍 *8€.* ☎ *973 69 61 89 or 973 62 40 36*

Estany de Sant Maurici

Reached by a tarmac road from Espot. The lake is surrounded by forest and dominated by the peaks of the Sierra dels Encantats, which can be seen reflected in its waters.

Portarró d'Espot

🚶 *3hr there and back on foot along a forest track leaving from the Estany de Sant Maurici.* The path gradually delves deeper into the Sant Nicolau Valley. When you draw level with the Redó lake, admire the splendid **panoramas**★★ of the Aigüestortes area.

Estany Gran

🚶 *3hr there and back on foot along a path leaving from Sant Maurici lake.* Beside the lake, the mountain streams and their gushing waterfalls form an impressive sight.

Estany Negre

🚶 *5hr there and back on foot from Espot or 4hr on foot along a forest track leaving from Sant Maurici lake.* The path takes you through the ravishing Peguera Valley. In its last stretch, the river throws itself into the Estany Negre (Black Lake), hemmed in by a circle of awesome summits. The lake owes its name to its dark, mysterious waters.

Aigüestortes

Western section. Reached by a branch off the Barruera-Caldes de Boí road. The track *(5km/3mi)* is practicable for private vehicles although there are also organised jeep tours. The road leads into Aigüestortes where a stream winds its way through rich pastures. There is a path to Estany Llong (🚶 *3hr there and back on foot*).

Alacant/Alicante ★

POPULATION: 275 111.

MICHELIN MAP 577 Q 28 (TOWN PLAN) – MAP 123 COSTA BLANCA –

110KM/69MI FROM CARTAGENA – COMUNIDAD VALENCIANA (ALICANTE)

Alicante has always been enjoyed for its remarkably luminous skies – the Greeks called it *Akra Leuka* **(the white citadel), the Romans** *Lucentum* **(the city of light). It is a friendly, typically Mediterranean town, where unhurried provincial calm mixes pleasantly with the bustle of a major tourist centre.**

Location

The town stretches out below the castle (Castillo de Santa Bárbara), along an immense bay between the capes of Huertas to the north and Santa Pola to the south. The city's busy port is the main shipping centre for the fruit and vegetables grown locally and in Murcia. 🛈 *Rambla de Méndez Núñez 23, 03002 Alicante,* ☎ *96 520 00 00.*

👁 *Neighbouring sights are described in the following chapters: COSTA BLANCA and MURCIA (81km/51mi SW).*

Capital of the Costa Blanca

Because of its mild climate and proximity to vast beaches (El Postiguet, La Albufereta and San Juan), Alicante has developed into the tourist capital of the Costa Blanca (👁 *see COSTA BLANCA*), with seaside resorts such as Santa Pola, Guardamar del Segura, Torrevieja, Campoamor springing up all along the southern part of this flat, sandy coastline.

ADDRESS BOOK

For coin ranges, see the Legend at the back of the guide.

WHERE TO EAT
🍽 La Taberna del Gourmet

San Fernando 10 – ☎ 96 520 42 33. Near the seafront promenade, the Taberna del Gourmet specializes in rice dishes, ham, seafood, and assorted sandwiches and tapas along the bar. Nautical decor.

🍽🍽 La Goleta

Paseo Explanada de España 8 – ☎ 965 21 43 92 – ▦.
On a busy street near the marina, this restaurant has a pleasant covered terrace and marine decor inside. It offers regional sausages, fried seafood, faultless paella, and good homemade desserts.

TAPAS
Piripi

Oscar Esplá 30 – ☎ 96 522 79 40 – ▦ – €7. Enjoy tapas and regional specialties, in the right combination of variety and quality.

WHERE TO STAY
🛏 Residencia La Milagrosa

Villavieja 8 – ☎ 96 521 69 18 – 29 rooms.
A basic pensión frequented by the young and worldly. The rooms, some sharing baths, are bright and uncluttered; the terrace is huge and flower-filled. Try for a room with a view of picturesque plaza de Santa María.

🛏 Hostal Les Monges Palace

San Agustín 4 – ☎ 96 521 50 46 – www. lesmonges.net 🅿 ▦ *– 23 rooms*. An excellent location in the heart of old Alicante, with a standard not normally found in a pensión. Features of this charming 18C building include a marble staircase and large mirrows and windows.

TAKING A BREAK
Horchateria Azul

Calderón de la Barca – Open Mon-Sat 9am-1pm and 4pm-midnight.
A tiny shop without pretension, specialising in horchata, a drink made from barley and almonds. Friendly staff.

NIGHTLIFE
Barrio del Carmen

Alicante's old quarter is pleasant by day, and after 11pm, the whole district is transformed into one huge disco.

Bodega Las Garrafas

Mayor 33 – Open Mon-Sat 9am-1pm and 4pm-2am
Authentic local bar run by a character who fought bulls and knew Dalí, Picasso and Hemingway. The decoration is on the eclectic side: with bells, pans, old photos.

Puerto de Alicante

One of the liveliest areas on summer nights. On one side are locales with Latin and Spanish rhythms, on the other the shops and cafés and terraces of the Panoramis complex.

SHOPPING
Mercado Central

Av. Alfonso X El Sabio – Open 6am-1pm.
This large covered market sells meat on the first floor and fish in the basement.

FIESTAS

Alicante celebrates its **fiestas del "foc"** (festival of fire) at midnight on 24 June, when giant pasteboard figures are set alight around the city, and the sky is lit up by a huge firework display.

Special Features
OLD TOWN

▷ *Follow the route marked on the town plan*

Explanada de España★

This is the most pleasant promenade in the region with its multicoloured marble pavement adorned with geometric designs and its magnificent palms providing shade as you sit or walk beside the pleasure boat harbour. Concerts are held on the bandstand on Sundays.

Catedral de San Nicolás

🕐*Open 7.30am-noon (1pm in winter) and 6-9pm (5.30-8.30pm in winter); Sun and public hols, 8.30am-1pm. No charge.* ☎ *96 521 26 62*. The present building, dating from the 17C, stands on the site of a former mosque – the city was not finally reconquered until 1296. The Herreran nave is crowned by a well-proportioned cupola, 45m/15ft high. Note the baroque communion chapel. On calle Labradores, with its terraces for fine weather, are the 18C Palacio Maisonnave, no. 9, which now houses the Municipal Archives; and an 18C mansion, no. 14, now a cultural centre.

Ayuntamiento (Town Hall)

This imposing 18C palace of golden stone was built in the 18C and is flanked by two towers. The façade, with its two rows of balconies, is adorned with three doorways, the middle one supported by solomonic columns. Visit the Rococo **capilla** (chapel) decorated with *azulejos* from Manises, and two Romantic reception rooms with blue silk hangings. ○*Open 9am-2pm.* ○*Closed Sat-Sun and public hols.* ☎ 96 514 91 00. Nearby on calle Gravina is the early 18C palace of the Museo de Bellas Artes Gravina (art museum), showing works of the 16-19C. ○*Open 10am-2pm and 4-8pm; May-Sep 10am-2pm and 5-9pm; Sun and legal holidays 10am-2pm.* ○*Closed Mon. No charge.* ☎ 96 514 67 80.

ALACANT ALICANTE		
Alfonso X el Sabio Av. de	AY	
Ayuntamiento Pl. del	BY	8
Calvo Sotelo Pl.	AZ	10
Castaños	AYZ	14
Constitución Av. de la	AY	21
Elche Portal de	AZ	28
Gabriel Miró Pl. de	AZ	31
Jijona Av. de	AY	33
Jovellanos Av. de	BY	35
Juan Bautista Lafora Av. de	BY	36
López Torregrosa	AY	37
Manero Mollá	AZ	39
Mayor	BYZ	
Mendez Núñez Rambla	AYZ	
Montañeta Pl. de la	AZ	41
Poeta Carmelo Calvo Av.	AY	47
Puerta del Mar Pl.	BZ	48
Rafael Altamira	BZ	50
Ramiro Pas.	BY	51
San Fernando	ABZ	53
Teatro Principal	AY	58

Ayuntamiento	BY	H	Colección de Arte del s. XX.		
Catedral de San Nicolás	BY	A	Museo de La Asegurada	BY	M¹
			MUBAG (Museo de Bellas Artes Gravina)	BY	M²

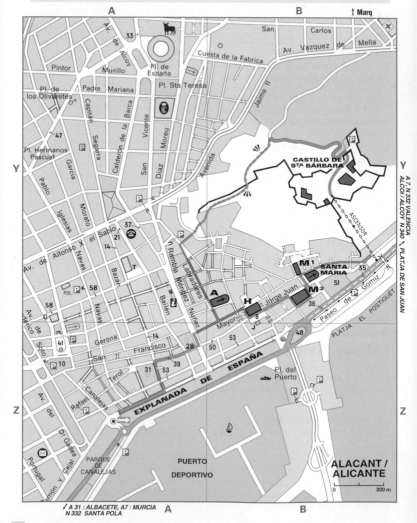

View of the city from the Castillo de Santa Bárbara

Iglesia de Santa María

⚰ *Closed for restoration.* ☎ 96 521 60 26. The church stands in a picturesque square of the same name, just below Santa Bárbara Castle. The **façade**★ is characteristic of 18C Baroque with its wreathed columns, its pillars and the breaks in its cornices. Once a mosque, the church was rebuilt in the 14C and has since been altered several times inside, particularly in the 17C when the nave was enlarged and the sanctuary disfigured by heavy Churrigue-resque decoration. Near the entrance are graceful Renaissance marble fonts and a painting on wood of John the Baptist and John the Apostle by Rodrigo de Osuna the Younger.

Museo de la Asegurada★

⚰ *Closed for restoration.* ☎ 96 514 07 68. On the same plaza, ane housed in a 17C public granary , this museum contains an interesting collection of 20C painting and sculpture donated by the sculptor Eugenio Sempere. There are works by artists both Spanish (Miró, Picasso, Gargallo, Tàpies, Saura, Genovés, Chillida and Dalí) and foreign (Vasarely, Bacon, Braque, Chagall and Kandinsky).

Castillo de Santa Bárbara

😊 *The best way to visit the castle is to go up by lift and walk back down the path, either all the way (good views) or to the halfway stop (from where you can take the lift back down).* 🕐 *Open Oct-Mar, 9am-7pm; Apr-Sep, 10am-8pm; last admission 30min before closing.* 🎟 *2.40€ if you take the lift, no charge if you drive or walk up.* ☎ 96 526 31 31.

Fortresses have been built atop strategic Benacantil hill since ancient times. The surviving complex dates from the 9C in Muslim times, though most outbuildings were raised during a 16C reconstruction. A castle visit includes entry to the **Fundación Capa sculpture collection** (mainly by 19 and 20C Spanish artists), shown in the open as well as in three halls of the castle. 🕐*Open 10am-2pm and 4-7pm; Apr-Sep 10am-2pm and 5-8pm; Sun & public hols 10am-3pm; last admission 30 min before closing.* 🕐*Closed 1 Jan and 24-25 Dec. No charge.* ☎ 965 15 29 69.

There are three different sections; the highest, the Plaza de la Torreta *(at the lift termi-nus)*, is surrounded by the oldest buildings. A platform commands a fine **view**★ of the harbour, the town, Castillo de San Fernando on another hill, and of San Juan beach. The second section is 16C *(halfway point for the lift)*, and the lowest, third perimeter dates back to the 17C. The footpath leads down into the narrow streets and tiny squares of the working-class Santa Cruz quarter of town, medieval in origin.

Worth a Visit

MARQ (Museo Arqueológico Provincial de Alicante)★★

🕐 *Open 10am-7pm; Sun and public hols 10am-8pm.* 🕐 *Closed Mon.* 🎟 *6€.* ☎ 96 514 90 00.

Can a non-specialist really enjoy an archaeological museum? MARQ makes it possible, with an entertaining and magnificently presented learning experience. The museum offers a unique opportunity to get close-up to the science of archaeology, and to get to know the beliefs, burial rites, and customs of the ancients of this area.

The museum is orgnized into three large halls (Prehistory, Iberian, Roman, Middle Ages, and Modern Era) around a great central space devoted to archaeology itself. Here you can get right into the work by visiting reconstructions of excavations in a cave, a church, and an underwater site.

Excursions

ELX/ELCHE★

24km/15mi SW. ℹ *Pl. del Parc 3, 03202 Elx,* ☏ *96 545 27 47.*

Elche (Elx in Valencian), stands on the banks of the Vinalopó river and is famed for its Dama, its palm grove and its mystery play (El Misteri).

The **Dama de Elche** (4C BC), a masterpiece of Iberian art now on display in the Museo Arqueológico de Madrid (*see Introduction to Spain: Art and Architecture*), was discovered in **La Alcudia** *(2km/1.2mi S, see below).* **El Misteri** is a medieval verse drama performed by an all-male cast which recounts the Dormition, Assumption and Coronation of the Virgin. It is played in the Basílica de Santa María on 14 and 15 August. In May 2001, the play was included on UNESCO's Oral and Intangible Heritage of Humanity list.

El Palmeral★★ (Palm Grove) – The groves, believed to have been planted by the Phoenicians and expanded by the Arabs, are the largest in Europe with more than 200 000 trees, and are a UNESCO World Heritage Site. The palms flourish in the mild climate, with the aid of a remarkable irrigation system. Female trees produce dates, and the fronds from the male trees are used in Palm Sunday processions and various handicrafts. Cereals and vegetables are grown beneath the trees outside the city limits.

Huerta del Cura★★ – ⏱ *Open 9am-6pm (8.30pm, May-Sep).* ▧ *2.40€.* ☏ *96 545 19 36.*

The huerta is a delightful garden of Mediterranean and subtropical plants set under more than a thousand magnificent palm trees. Especially notable are the imperial palm, with seven trunks, said to be 160 years old, and beautiful nooks such as the cactus garden, near the pond.

Parque Municipal★ – A leafy, well-tended garden covered with palm trees with a 50 000m²/59 800sq yd extension.

Museo Arqueológico – ⚿ *Closed for restoration.* ☏ *96 545 36 03.*

The archaeological museum, housed in the Palacio de Altamira (originally Moorish), displays finds taken mostly from excavations at La Alcudia. Among the most noteworthy items are sculpture and ceramics from the Iberian period and the *Venus of Illicis*, a delicately carved white marble Roman sculpture.

Basílica de Santa María – This monumental 17-18C Baroque basilica has a beautiful, monumental portal by Nicolás de Bussi and is the setting for the annual mystery play. Take advantage of the magnificent view of the palm groves from the tower.

Nearby are the 17-18C Almohad tower, **La Calaforra**, and the Baños árabes (Arab baths).

Baños árabes – *Access by a side door of the Convento de la Mercè.* ⏱*Open 10am-1pm and 4.30-8.30pm.* ⏱*Closed Mon.* ☏ *96 545 14 03.*

A well-prepared exhibition (with narration in Spanish, Valencian, English or French) introduces the meaning and use of these baths in the 12C.

La Alcudia: archaeological site and museum – *2km/1.2mi S.* ⏱ *Open 10am-5pm; summer 10am-2pm and 4-8pm. Sun and public hold 10am-2pm.* ⏱ *Closed Mon. No charge.* ☏ *96 661 15 06.*

The site and museum reveal the development of a city whose oldest remains date from the Neolithic period to its decline in Visigoth times. Especially notable are Iberian (the Dama de Elche was discovered here), Roman (forum, baths, and domus) remains, and a Paleo-Christian basilica.

TOUR INLAND *176km/110mi N.*

▶ *Leave Alicante and take the N 340. In San Juan, take the Alcoi road and then turn right.*

Cuevas de Canalobre

Guided tours (40min), 11am-5.50pm; 21 Jun-30 Sep and during Holy Week, 10.30am-7.50pm. Closed 1 Jan and 25 Dec. 4€. 96 569 92 50.

At 700m/2 300ft up Mount Cabezón de Oro, the caves form a maze of stalactites and stalagmites, some shaped like candelabra *(canalobre)*.

▶ *Return to the N 340.*

The road crosses dry country dotted with fig and carob trees.

Xixona/Jijona

The speciality of this small town is the manufacture of *turrón*, a sweet made of almonds and honey, exported worldwide. A small **museum** (El Lobo) and several factories are open to visitors.

Beyond Xixona the road threads its way through terraces of almond trees and up round a series of hairpin bends to a pass, the **Puerto de la Carrasqueta★** (1 024m/3 360ft), which commands a view of the entire Torremanzanas Valley with Alicante and the sea in the far distance.

Alcoi/Alcoy

Alcoi is an industrial town (textiles, paper, metallurgy and confectionery) set in magnificent mountain scenery at the confluence of the Serpis, Molinar and Barchell rivers.

At the end of April, Alcoi holds the colourful **Moors and Christians** (Moros y Cristianos) **festivals** to commemorate an attack by the Moors in 1276 which ended with a Christian victory thanks to the intervention of St George.

▶ *In Alcoi, take the CV 795 as far as Barxell, then follow the CV 794.*

Bocairent

The church in this small market town perched on a hill has an interesting **Museo Parroquial** (Parish Museum) with several works by **Juan de Juanes** (1523-79) – who died here – and his school, and a 14C Last Supper by Marcial de Sax, as well as a collection of church plate.

Guided tours (45min) by appointment. Open Sun and public hols from 12.30pm. 1.80€. 96 290 50 62.

▶ *Take the CV81.*

Villena

Castillo la Atalaya – *Guided tours at 10.30 and 11.30am and 12.30pm. Sat-Sun and public hols 11am, noon and 1pm. No charge. 96 580 38 04 (Turismo).*

This hilltop castle of Arabic origin dominates its former feudal domain. Among its owners have been two famed men of letters: **Don Juan Manuel** in the 14C, and Prince **Henry of of Aragon** (1384-1434), better known as the **Marqués de Villena**, a great poet and magic fan. Its walled keep survives, with circular towers in the corners, and the large Homenaje (homage) tower (upper section 15C). Fine views from the walls.

Iglesia de Santiago – *Visits by prior arrangement with the Tourist Office. 96 580 38 04.*

In the plaza of the same name stands this Gothic-Renaissance church (14-17C), along with the town hall. The exterior is notable for its bell tower, The interior of three naves is notable for its unusual **spiral pillars★** which support the Gothic vaults. Note the baptismal font, in Renaissance style.

Museo Arqueológico (Archaeological Museum) – *Open Tue-Fri, 10am-2pm and 5-8pm; Sat-Sun and public hols, 11am-2pm. Closed Mon, 1 and 6 Jan, 1 May, 8 Sep and 25 Dec. No charge. 96 580 11 50 (ext. 769).*

The museum is in the town hall *(Palacio Municipal)* which has a fine Renaissance façade and patio. It displays two solid gold collections dating from the Bronze Age (1500-1000 BC). One is the outstanding **Villena Treasure★★** with gold jewellery and gourds decorated with sea urchin shell patterns.

▶ *Return to Alicante on the A 31.*

Albacete

POPULATION: 135 889.

MICHELIN MAP 576 O-P 24 – CASTILLA LA MANCHA (ALBACETE)

Albacete (*Al Basite* meant "the Plain" to the Arabs), the capital of the south of La Mancha, stands on a plateau which forms an arid Castilian promontory jutting into the fertile greenery of the *huerta* country between the Beatic chains and the Iberian Cordillera. This city of contrasts has a centre that combines old buildings with modern constructions and residential districts.

Location

The city stands at the crossroads of several roads: the A 35 and A 30, leading to the Levante and Murcia respectively, and the A 32, which connects the Levante with Andalucía. 🖪 *Tinte 2, Edificio Posada del Rosario, 02071 Albacete, ☎ 96 758 05 22.*

🚶 *Neighbouring sights are described in the following chapters: CUENCA (144km/90mi N), MURCIA (147km/92mi SE) and ALACANT/ALICANTE (168km/105mi SE).*

Worth a Visit

Museo de Albacete

🕐 *Open 10am-2pm and 4.30-7pm; 1 Jul-17 Sep, 10am-2pm; Sun and public hols, 9am-2pm.* 🕐 *Closed Mon, 1 Jan, Maundy Thu, Good Fri and 25 Dec.* ⊜ *1.20 € (no charge Sat and hols).* ☎ *96 722 83 07.*

This modern building on the upper section of the Abelardo Sánchez park houses two separate museums: on the second floor, the Fine Arts Museum (Museo de Bellas Artes), dedicated to the landscape artist Benjamín Palencia (1900-80); and on the first floor, the Joaquín Sánchez Jiménez Archaeology Museum, displaying finds unearthed at archaeological sites in the province. The latter houses a rich collection of Iberian sculptures (Room 6) – including the **sphinx from Haches**, the **hind of Caudete**, and the lion from Bienservida – and above all a large **collection of Roman dolls with movable joints★** (Room 9), four dolls made of ivory and one of amber – which were among the funerary items discovered in a 4C burial-ground at Ontur in 1946.

Cathedral

Construction of the building began in the late 16C, with later, more modern additions, such as the façade and side doorway. The interior comprises three naves separated by large Ionic columns. The most interesting aspects of the cathedral are the sacristy, decorated with Mannerist paintings, and the Capilla de la Virgen de los Llanos, a chapel dedicated to the Virgin of the Plains, the city's patron saint. Inside, note a large Renaissance altarpiece by the artist known as the Maestro de Albacete.

Pasaje de Lodares

The passageway linking calle Mayor with calle del Tinte is one of the most characteristic sights in the city. This long, narrow iron- and glass-crowned gallery contains a proliferation of decorative features (columns and allegorical figures) and is lined by shops and private homes.

ADDRESS BOOK

WHERE TO STAY & EAT

⊜⊜ **Hotel-Restaurante Juanito**

Mártires 15 – La Roda – 36km/22.5mi NW of Albacete on the A 31 – ☎ 96 754 80 41 – 🖩 – 31 rooms – ⌖ 3€ – Restaurant 29€. This addition to the roadside restaurant of the same name is a new, reasonably priced hotel with comfortable, well-decorated rooms. The restaurant has an attractive menu of La Mancha specialities prepared with an innovative touch.

SHOPPING

Since Moorish times, Albacete has been famous for the manufacture of knives. Nowadays, the range of knives and penknives is vast, with a huge choice in terms of size, shape and decoration.

Excursions

Alarcón★

103km/65mi NW. ▶ *Take the A 31 to Honrubia, then turn right onto the A 3.* Alarcón, meaning Alaric's town, in honour of the Visigothic king who founded the town, stands on top of a mound of brown earth almost completely encircled by a meander of the Júcar river. The 13C-14C castle, now a parador, is one of Spain's best examples of medieval military architecture. Its magnificent **location**★★★ made the fortress practically impregnable, despite the frequent bloody battles in the area. It is of triangular construction, with a double protective enclosure of gold-coloured stone. The Infante **Don Juan Manuel** (1284-1348), into whose hands the castle ultimately fell, wrote many of his cautionary tales while living there.

The town itself has a number of attractive whitewashed façades. Note the **Iglesia de Santa María**, a Renaissance church with an elegant Plateresque doorway, Gothic vaulting and a fine sculpted 16C altarpiece. **Plaza de D. Juan Manuel** is fronted by the Ayuntamiento (town hall), with its impressive porticoed façade, the Iglesia de San Juan Bautista, a church in the Herreran style, and the Casa-Palacio, adorned with attractive grilles.

The Alarcón dam, 3km/2mi away, controls the variable flow of the Júcar river.

Alcalá del Júcar★

60km/37mi NE along the CM 3218.

From Puente Torres the road winds its way along the Júcar through a series of steep **gorges**. The river encircles the hill occupied by the village, which is spread out between its castle tower and church on a magnificent **site**★ overlooking a fertile plain that has little in common with the arid landscapes normally associated with La Mancha. A walk through Alcalá's maze of steep alleyways is worthwhile for the attractive views of the surrounding countryside. Most of the dwellings hollowed out of the rock have long corridors leading to balconies overlooking the other side of the cliff. Some of these dwellings can be visited.

Cueva de la Vieja

70km/44mi E along the A 35, via Alpera.

This is one of the rare caves in the region that is easy to reach and still has clearly visible paintings. These depict stylised human silhouettes in active poses with clear narrative themes (men hunting stags with bows and arrows, groups of individuals etc). The female figures, shown dressed in long robes, are noteworthy, as is the depiction of a figure with a plumed headdress, the best preserved painting in the entire cave.

Almansa

74km/46mi E along the A 35.

Almansa, once the Moorish *Al-Manxa*, spreads out around a steep limestone crag crowned by a medieval castle, with a maze of narrow streets and alleyways at its centre.

Iglesia de la Asunción – *At the foot of the castle.* This church standing at the foot of the castle was completely transformed in the neo-Classical period, hence its eclectic appearance. The monumental portal, attributed to Vandelvira, is Renaissance in style.

Palacio de los Condes de Cirat – *Next to the church.* This mansion, known as the **Casa Grande**, has a fine Mannerist-style doorway bearing a large escutcheon flanked by two crudely sculpted large figures. The interior is embellished with an attractive patio.

Castle – The 15C ramparts (restored), perched precariously along the rock ridge, command a view of the plain and are a pleasant place for a stroll. The keep *(torre de homenaje)* is crowned by groin vaults bearing keystones decorated with the coat of arms of the Marqués de Villena.

Alcaraz

79km/49mi SW along the A 32. Alcaraz stands isolated upon a clay rise tinted with the wine colour typical of the region, in the middle of the mountains of the Sierra de Alcaraz, a delightful landscape dotted with small forests and criss-crossed by numerous streams. The town, which grew rich manufacturing carpets, retains a Renaissance character, as can be witnessed in a number of buildings influenced by the style of the architect **Andrés de Vandelvira**, who was born here in 1509.

Plaza Mayor – The square is overlooked by the town's main monuments, all of which are similar in style: the 15C Pósito, a former municipal granary; the 16C **Ayuntamiento**

(town hall), with its emblazoned façade; the 17C **Lonja** del Corregidor, standing against the **Torre del Tardón** (clock tower); and the 15C **Iglesia de la Trinidad**, with its Flamboyant Gothic portal.

The main street or **calle Mayor** is fronted by old houses – note the façade with the two warriors and the Casa Consistorial with its Plateresque doorway, the **Puerta de la Aduana** (Customs Doorway). A series of steep, stepped alleyways head away from the right-hand side of the square.

The path leading out of the village to the cemetery passes through two archways, beyond which there are attractive views of the brown rooftops and the surrounding countryside.

Excursion to the source of the River Mundo – *46km/29mi S of Alcaraz along the CM 412*. The road winds its way through a wooded valley in the Sierra de Alcaraz, passing close to Ríopar, a village known for its bronzework. Turn right towards Siles and after 6km/4mi turn left to the Cueva de los Chorros. At the cave, a spring at the foot of the steep Sierra del Calar marks the source of the River Mundo, a tributary of the Segura, which drops down a wall of rock in a series of waterfalls. 🐾 The best time to visit is in the spring. 🛈 *For further information contact the Albacete Tourist Office.*

La Alberca★★

POPULATION: 958

MICHELIN MAP 575 K 11 – CASTILLA Y LEÓN (SALAMANCA)

La Alberca is a delightful village at the heart of the Sierra de la Peña de Francia, an isolated land of stunning scenery and villages that have managed to retain much of their traditional architecture and deep-rooted traditions. The whole area has an enviable gastronomic reputation, particularly for its meats, sausages, desserts, honey and, during the autumn, its walnuts and chestnuts.

Location

The Sierra de la Peña de Francia is situated in the extreme southwest corner of the province of Salamanca, on the boundary of the province of Cáceres and the area of Las Hurdes. In geological terms, the *sierra* is part of the Sistema Central. 🛈 *La Alberca: Plaza Mayor, 37624 ☎ 92 341 52 91.*

🐾 *Neighbouring sights are described in the following chapters: CIUDAD RODRIGO (50km/31mi NW) and SALAMANCA (76km/47mi NE).*

Walking About

La Alberca is one of the most typical villages in this area, with its winding, haphazardly laid out streets, all leading to the main square (plaza Mayor), of irregular shape and partly arcaded, with an attractive cross and fountain at its centre.

The village displays numerous examples of tradtional architecture, with unusual old houses built of stone up to first floor level, with wooden beams, ledges and attractive wooden balconies on the upper storeys. The village has also preserved its strong folklore, as can be witnessed during the Feast of the Assumption.

Excursions

Peña de Francia★★

15km/9mi W. The Peña, a shale crag of 1 732m/5 682ft and the highest point in the range, can be distinguished from a considerable distance. The approach road is spectacular, affording wide **panoramas**★★ of the Hurdes mountains, the heights of Portugal, the Castilian plain and the Sierra de Gredos. There is a Dominican monastery with a dependent hostelry *(open in summer only)* at the top.

Las Batuecas road★

To the S. This road climbs imperceptibly to the Portillo Pass (1 240m/4 068ft)

Fiestas

On 15 August, the village performs the ancient mystery play or Loa relating the triumph of the Virgin Mary over the devil, in which participants dress up in colourful and intricately embroidered costumes.

ADDRESS BOOK

WHERE TO EAT

*⊜ **Mesón La Romana***

Núñez Losada 4 – Candelario – ☎ 923 41 32 72 – open hols – reservation recommended.

This delightful restaurant, situated next to the church and behind the town-hall, in the upper part of the village, occupies a restored house, and is the ideal place to enjoy the renowned grilled meats of the region. Make sure you also try the delicious grilled fresh goat cheese.

WHERE TO STAY

*⊜ **Hotel Artesa***

Mayor 57 – Candelario – ☎ 923 41 31 11 – 9 rooms – ⊑ 4.30€ - Restaurant 11.20€.

This simple hotel occupies an old house in the centre of the village. The rooms are modest but clean and tastefully decorated. The hotel also has a pleasant terrace to the rear. Other facilities include a restaurant, a shop selling local products and various arts and crafts workshops.

before plunging through 12km/7.5mi of sharp bends into a deep, green valley in which the Batuecas Monastery lies hidden. It continues beyond Las Mestas, to the desolate and long isolated **Las Hurdes** region of Extremadura, the setting in 1932 for Buñuel's film *Land without Bread*.

TOUR THROUGH THE SIERRA DE BÉJAR AND THE SIERRA DE CANDELARIO

76km/47mi to the SE – allow one day.

This itinerary heads along minor roads, which meander through the gorges of the Alagón and Cuerpo de Hombre rivers amid impressive mountain landscapes abundant in forests of chestnut, walnut and oak.

▶ *Head E out of La Alberca. After 2km/1.2mi, take the turn off to Cepeda and onward to Sotoserrano. From Sotoserrano, head towards Valdelageve and Lagunilla until you reach the N 630 at Puerto de Béjar.*

The villages of **Baños de Montemayor**, a pleasant thermal spa, and **Hervás**, which has preserved its old **judería** or Jewish quarter, are both located in this area.

▶ *Return to Puerto de Béjar. From here, one road heads towards La Garganta, another to Candelario.*

The road passes through an attractive landscape of chestnut and oak forests and meadows full of cattle. The views of the Sierra de Candelario from the higher stretches of this road are particularly impressive.

Candelario★★

This picturesque mountain village built into the flank of the *sierra* is one of the prettiest in the entire province. It has preserved much of its traditional stone architecture, with elegant balconies and wooden ledges along its steep whitewashed streets, which act

Plaza Mayor

as conduits for the water which cascades through Candelario when the mountain snow melts in the spring. To combat this, waterproofing is provided by means of upturned tiles on whole sections of walls, and house entrances are protected by gates.

Béjar

4km/2.5mi NW. Béjar's hill site is seen to best advantage when you approach the small town from the northwest. The town (known for its sheets and woollen fabrics) stretches out along a narrow rock platform at the foot of the Sierra de Béjar.

▶ *Leave Béjar along the SA 515.*

Miranda del Castañar

34km/21mi W. The entrance to the old quarter is through the Puerta de San Ginés, reached after crossing the bullring, having passed the imposing 15C **castle** on one side. This rustic, walled settlement has preserved an interesting series of narrow streets lined by houses with wide eaves, some of which are adorned with family coats of arms.

The charming villages of **Mogarraz** (10km/6mi W) and **San Martín del Castañar** (10km/6mi N) are well worth a visit before returning to La Alberca.

▶ *Continue towards the Peña de Francia to return to La Alberca along the SA 202.*

Alcalá de Henares★

POPULATION: 162 780.

MICHELIN MAPS 575 AND 576 K 19 – MADRID

Alcalá, which re-established its university in 1977, is a pleasant town with a historic centre★ adorned with 16C-17C buildings – predominantly old colleges and convents – and attractive, spacious squares. The outstanding calle Mayor, a street whose origins date back to the 13C, is a long avenue adorned with impressive gateways.

In 1998, the university and historic centre of Alcalá were declared a World Heritage site by UNESCO.

Location

The town is on the A 2, between Madrid (32km/20mi W) and Guadalajara (25km/15mi E).
🛈 *Plaza de los Santos Niños, 28801 Alcalá de Henares, ☎ 91 881 06 34.*
🖈 *Neighbouring sights are described in the following chapters: MADRID, GUADALAJARA and ARANJUEZ (85km/53mi SW).*

Worth a Visit

Antigua Universidad or Colegio de San Ildefonso★

Guided tours (45min), Oct-Mar, at 11.30am, 12.30pm, 1.30pm, 4.30pm and 5.30pm; Apr-Sep, at 11 .30am, 12.30pm, 1.30pm, 5.30pm and 6.30pm. ◷ *Also open Sat-Sun and public hols, 11am-2pm and 4-7pm (5-8pm Apr-Sep).* ◷ *Closed 1 Jan and 25 Dec.* ⊛ *2.10€ (includes the Capilla de San Ildefonso). ☎ 91 889 26 94.*

The old university building, now used to house the university education offices, stands on the plaza de San Diego. Its beautiful **Plateresque façade★** (1543) is by Rodrigo Gil de Hontañón and comprises three sections crowned by a balustrade. On the central section, framed by the cordon of the Franciscans – Cardinal Cisneros belonged to this order – note the large imperial escutcheon of Charles V decorating the pediment. The majestic 17C **Patio Mayor**, known as the Santo Tomás de Villanueva patio, was designed by Juan Gómez de Mora, a pupil of Herrera and architect of the Plaza Mayor and Ayuntamiento (Town Hall) in Madrid; at the centre is a wellhead with a swan motif, the emblem of

WHERE TO EAT

◉◉◉ **MIGUEL DE CERVANTES**
Imagen 12 – ☎ 91 883 12 77 – 🍽.
This restaurant, well-located behind Cervantes' birthplace, is housed in a restored town house and serves traditional cuisine against a backdrop of typical Castilian decor. A few reasonably priced rooms are also available.

Cardinal Cisneros. Across the Patio de los Filósofos, around which student quarters were originally laid out, stands the delightful **Patio Trilingüe** (1557) where Latin, Greek and Hebrew were taught. This 16C Renaissance patio, a model of simplicity, belonged to the Colegio de San Jerónimo. The **Paraninfoa** (1520), a small room formerly used for examinations and degree ceremonies, is now the setting for the solemn opening of the university year and the awarding of the Cervantes literary prize. The decoration includes a gallery delicately embellished in the Plateresque style, with superb Mudéjar **artesonado**★★ work, comprising six-pointed star ornamentation.

Capilla de San Ildefonso★

Next to the university. This fine early-16C chapel was built for use as the university's church. Its single nave and the presbytery are both crowned with magnificent **Mudéjar artesonado** ceilings. The delicate **stucco** decoration shows the stylistic evolution of this technique: the work on the Epistle side of the church belongs to the late-Gothic period, while that of the Evangelist side opposite is Plateresque. The presbytery houses the **mausoleum**★★ of Cardinal Cisneros (his remains are placed to rest in the Catedral Magistral), a work by Domenico Fancelli and Bartolomé Ordóñez. Carved in Carrara marble, it is one of the finest examples of 16C Spanish sculpture.

Catedral Magistral

Plaza de los Santos Niños. Although the cathedral was built between 1497 and 1515, it has since been remodelled on several occasions. On the exterior, note the central portal, with its mix of Gothic, Plateresque and Mudéjar features. The late-Gothic interior contains some attractive wrought-iron **grilles**. The cloisters (entrance on calle Tercia) house the **Museo de la Catedral**. ◷ *Open 10.30am-1.30pm and 5-7.30pm; Sun and public hols, 10.30am-2.30pm.* ◷ *Closed Mon. €1.80.* ☎ *91 888 27 00.*

Palacio Arzobispal

Plaza de Palacio. In the 13C, the bishops of Toledo, the lords of Alcalá, erected a sizeable palace-fortress on this site. The present-day Renaissance **façade**, designed by Alonso de Covarrubias, originally fronted the courtyard of the palace. The large Baroque coat of arms was added at a later date.

The adjoining plaza de San Bernardo is lined by the **Convento de San Bernardo**, whose 17C church is crowned by an impressive elliptical dome, and the **Museo Arqueológico de la Comunidad de Madrid**, an archaeological museum housed in the 17C former Convento de la Madre de Dios. ◷ *Open 11am-7pm; Sun and public hols, 11am-3pm.* ◷ *Closed Mon. No charge.* ☎ *91 879 66 66.*

Historical Notes

Under the Romans the city was an important centre known as **Complutum** but the history of Alcalá is mainly linked to that of its university, founded by Cardinal Cisneros in 1498. It became famous for its language teaching and in 1517, Europe's first Polyglot Bible was published with parallel texts in Latin, Greek, Hebrew and Chaldean. The university was moved to Madrid in 1836. Alcalá's famous citizens include **Catherine of Aragon,** daughter of the Catholic Monarchs and first wife of Henry VIII, the Renaissance architect **Bustamante**, who designed the Hospital de Tavera in Toledo, and **Miguel de Cervantes**, whose **birthplace** is open to the public. Open 10.15am-1.30pm and 4-6.15pm. Closed Mon. No charge. ☎ 91 889 96 54.

Cervantes

Adventure and storytelling are the words that best sum up the life of **Miguel de Cervantes Saavedra** (1547-1616). As a young man he spent four years in Italy after which he enlisted and fought at the Battle of Lepanto (1571) where he was wounded. In 1575 he was captured by the Turks, taken off to Algeria as a slave and rescued after five years by the Fathers of the Holy Trinity. In 1605 he published the first part of **Don Quixote** which was an immense and immediate success. In this tragicomic masterpiece an elderly gentleman sets out as a doughty knight errant in search of adventure, hoping to redress wrongs in the terms of the storybooks he loves; he is accompanied by his simple but astute squire, Sancho Panza. The interaction of the ideal and the real, the true and the illusory, reveals the meditations of a man of 58 deeply involved in philosophy, life and the Spain of his day. His writing continued with *Exemplary Novels* or humorous stories of adventure and intrigue, comedies, *entremeses* or one-act prose farces, novels and, in 1615, the second part of *Don Quixote*. He died a year later, on 23 April 1616 – the same day as Shakespeare.

Alcañiz

POPULATION: 12,820.

MICHELIN MAP 574 I 29 – ARAGÓN (TERUEL)

Alcañiz, set amid orchards and fertile olive groves, is the capital of Lower Aragón. The region is famous for its Holy Week ceremonies accompanied by incessant drum playing known as tamborrada.

Location

Alcañiz is situated in the northeastern corner of the province of Teruel, on the boundary of the provinces of Castellón, Zaragoza and Tarragona. 🅿 *Mayor 1, 44600 Alcañiz,* ☏ *97 883 12 13.*

⚲ *Neighbouring sights are described in the following chapters: MORELLA (67km/42mi S), TORTOSA (102km/63mi E), ZARAGOZA (103km/64mi NW) and LLEIDA/LÉRIDA (116km/72mi NE).*

Worth a Visit

Plaza de España★

Two memorable façades meet at one corner of the square: the tall Catalan Gothic arcade of the **Lonja**, where a market was once held, and the Renaissance town hall *(ayuntamiento)*. Both buildings are crowned by the typical Aragón gallery with overhanging eaves.

> **Luis Buñuel (1900-83)**
>
> The film director was born in Calanda, 17km/10.5mi SW of Alcañiz.

Colegiata de Santa María la Mayor

🕐 *Open 9am-1pm and 4.30-8pm.* ☏ *97 883 12 13.*

A rhythmic interplay of vertical lines and curves marks the upper part of the façade of the collegiate church, rebuilt in the 18C, while below is an exuberantly Baroque **portal**★. The spacious interior is divided by massive columns with composite capitals reaching up to a noticeably projecting cornice.

Castillo

The castle standing on the hilltop was the seat of the Aragón commandery of the Order of Calatrava in the 12C. Most of the buildings now used as a parador date from the 18C. At the far end of the courtyard are the Gothic chapel, with its single aisle of equilateral arches, and on the first floor of the keep, 14C wall paintings.

Alicante★  see Alacant

Almagro★

POPULATION: 8,962.

MICHELIN MAP 576 P 18 – CASTILLA LA MANCHA (CIUDAD REAL)

Almagro is an attractive small town at the heart of the La Mancha countryside, its reddish earth bathed in the stunning light of central Spain. A wander through its stone-paved streets takes visitors back to the days of the Military Order of the Knights of Calatrava, and reveals elegant façades emblasoned with the coats of arms of noble families.

The 16C Convento de San Francisco, with its fine patios and delightful gardens, has been converted into a parador.

Address Book

For coin ranges, see the Legend at the back of the guide.

WHERE TO EAT

⊖⊖ El Corregidor

Plaza Fray Fernando Fernández de Córdoba 2 – ☎ 92 686 06 48 – Closed 1-7 Aug and Mon (exc Jul) – ▤. This old Castilian inn, just a few metres from the Plaza Mayor, serves tasty and innovative regional cuisine. The dining room on the first floor is crowned by an attractive glass ceiling, while the bar has been installed in the former carriage entrance. Note also the restaurant's attractive patio.

WHERE TO STAY

⊖ Hospedería Almagro

Ejido de Calatrava – ☏ 926 88 20 87 – P – 42 rooms – ☞ 2.80€ – Restaurant 8/14€.

A former 16C convent now houses this hostelry which retains a certain monastic austerity with its high-ceilinged sober rooms. The large patio is shady and pleasant.

FESTIVALS

During the month of July, Almagro hosts its **International Festival of Classical Drama**, during which the Corral de Comedias and the patios and cloisters of the town are transformed into lively outdoor theatres. For further information: www.festivaldealmagro.com.

SHOPPING

Almagro is famous for its delicious aubergines in vinegar and its traditional lacework and embroidery.

Location

Almagro is situated at the heart of the vast Campo de Calatrava plain. ▤ *Plaza Mayor 1, 13270 Almagro, ☎ 926 86 07 17; Daimiel: Plaza de España, 1, 13250 Daimiel, ☎ 926 26 06 39.*

   Neighbouring sights are described in the following chapters: ARANJUEZ (115km/72mi N) and TOLEDO (145km/90mi N).

Walking About

   The walk described below takes you through cobbled streets lined with white-washed houses where several convents and monasteries have fine stone carved doorways and grand coats of arms recalling the power of the Knights of Calatrava.

Plaza Mayor★★

This elongated square, one of the most unusual and beautiful in Castile, is the focal point of the town and was once the setting for bullfights and jousting tournaments. It has a continuous stone colonnade framing two sides, supporting two storeys of windows all with green surrounds. Two picturesque narrow streets, Toril and Villar, head away from the square.

The **Corral de Comedias**★, at n°18, dates from the 17C and is the only theatre in Europe to have preserved its original structure. The wooden porticoes, oil lamps, stone well and scenery wall combine to create a superb example of popular architecture. Every summer, performances are held here as part of the International Festival of Classical Drama. ⊙ *Open Oct-Mar, 10am-2pm and 4-7pm (6pm Sat-Sun and public hols); Apr-Jun and Sep, 10am-2pm and 5-8pm (7pm Sun and public hols); Jul and Aug, 10am-2pm and 6-9pm (8pm Sun and public hols).* ⊙ *Closed Mon, Jan 1, Dec 24-25 and 31.* ⊜*2€ (incl Teatro Municipal).* ☎ *926 86 15 39.*

Go to the end of the Plaza Mayor with the statue of Diego de Almagro and take calle de Nuestra Señora de las Nieves (which has some fine doorways) to the left. This leads to the triangular plaza Santo Domingo, surrounded by mansions. Turn

R. López -Alonso/ STOCK PHOTOS

Plaza Mayor

left into calle de Bernardas, fronted by the spectacular Baroque doorway of the **Palacio de los Condes de Valparaíso**, and then head along calle de Don Federico Relimpio. Continue to the left along calle de Don Diego de Almagro which is dominated by the imposing façade of the **Convento de la Asunción de Calatrava**, also known as the **Convento de los Dominicos**. The 16C cloister, the two storeys of which are connected by a fine Renaissance staircase, is worthy of particular note. ⏰ *Open 10am-2pm and 4-6pm (5-7pm Apr-Jun and Sep; 6-8pm, Jul-Aug); Sun and public hols, noon-2pm.* ☜ *1.50€.* ☎ *926 86 07 17.*

Return to the Plaza Mayor , and at the far end turn right onto Calle Gran Maestre, where you'll find the interesting **Museo Nacional del Teatro**, in an 18C palace. It exhibits old documents, period costumes, and models of theatre sets. ⏰ *Open 10am-2pm and 4-7pm; Sat 11am-2pm and 4-6pm; Jul 10am-2pm and 6-9pm; Sat 11am-2pm and 6-8pm; Sun and public hols 11am-2pm.* ⏰ *Closed Mon.* ☜*2.40€.* ☎ *926 26 10 14.*

Excursions

Parque Nacional de las Tablas de Daimiel

31km/19mi N along the CM 4107 and the N 420. Once you reach Daimiel, take a tarmac road to the right (7km/4.5mi). ⏰ *Open 9am-6.30 pm (9pm in summer).* ☎ *926 69 31 18.*

This wetland area covering 1 928ha/4 764 acres appears like an oasis at the heart of the La Mancha plain. The name "tablas", which translates as "wide stretches of river", refers to the areas in which local rivers frequently flood their banks. As a result, the marshland and reed beds formed by the Guadiana and Cigüela rivers provide a habitat for a huge variety of European birds. The park suffers serious variations in water level: while it is under water in winter, the opposite is true in summer, when the lack of water reaches critical levels. Observatories have been built along routes through the park, enabling visitors to admire species such as mallard duck and grebe.

Parque Natural Lagunas de Ruidera

67km/42mi NE. This park, covering an area of 3 772ha/9 320 acres, is located on the border of the provinces of Ciudad Real and Albacete. Comprising a series of 15 lagoons linked to each other via a network of streams, gullies and waterfalls, it is an area of outstanding natural beauty with crystal-clear water and extensive areas of shade, making it a perfect place to escape to during the summer months.

San Carlos del Valle★

46km/29mi E. The outstanding feature of San Carlos de Valle is its charming **Plaza Mayor**★, built in brick in the 18C. The house at no5, the former hospice, has preserved a stone doorway and a typical patio. A Baroque church, crowned with a cupola and four lantern turrets, dominates the square.

Valdepeñas

34km/21mi SE along the CM 412. Valdepeñas, the production centre of a well-known table wine, stands at the southern tip of the vast wine-growing area of La Mancha.

Life in the town centres around plaza de España, where blue and white coloured houses rise above shady porticoes. On

Soldiering Monks

In the mid-12C, the Campo de Calatrava plain was the scene of unceasing warfare between Christians and Muslims. The old Fortaleza de Calatrava, a fortress built originally by the Moors on the banks of the Guadiana, was handed over by Sancho III to Raimundo, the abbot of Fitero, around 1157. Raimundo defended the fortress from Almohad attacks and founded the **Orden Militar de Calatrava**, the first of Spain's military orders. Following the Battle of Alarcós (1195) and the capture of the castle by Al-Mansur, the knights were forced to flee to a safer haven.

one side stands the late-Gothic façade of the **Iglesia de la Asunción** (Church of the Assumption), with its harmonious tower and a Plateresque upper gallery; and a venerated hermitage, the Ermita de la Veracruz.

The cellars of the **Cooperativa La Invencible**, the largest bodega in the town, can be visited by the general public. ○ *Open 3-7pm.* ○ *Closed Sat-Sun and public hols. No charge.* ☎ *926 32 27 77.*

Las Virtudes

58km/36mi SE (24km/15mi S of Valdepeñas). The village claims that its **bullring** *(plaza de toros)* is the oldest in Spain (1641). It is square and is blocked along one side by the wall of the 14C **Santuario de Nuestra Señora de las Virtudes** (Sanctuary of Our Lady of Holy Virtue) which has a Mudéjar ceiling over the nave and a Churrigueresque altarpiece.

Castillo-Convento de Calatrava la Nueva★

32km/20mi SW. 7km/4.5mi SW of Calzada de Calatrava, turn right onto a paved road (2.5km/1.5mi). The semi-ruined citadel of the Castillo de Calatrava, with its crumbling walls crowning a magnificent **site** on top of the Alaclanejo hill, dominates the route south towards Andalucía. It conveys, as no other site, the lonely ordeals undergone by the Knights of the Reconquest.

The fortress consists of three stout perimeter walls. The first has retained its original entrance gateway, which leads into a large vaulted room that served as the castle stables; the second, built into the rock, houses the religious buildings (cloisters, refectory, chapter house and the monks' dormitories), including the impressive **church**, lit by an immense rose window, with fine brick vaulting, described as swallow's nest in design and probably the work of Moorish prisoners; the third wall, on the highest part of the site, is home to the castle, with its huge vaulted chambers in which the Order's archives were stored. The views from the towers encompass the ruins of the **Castillo de Salvatierra** on the other side of the road, as well as the reddish landscape of the La Mancha plain. ○ *Open 10am-2pm and 4-7pm; Apr-Sep, 10am-2pm and 6-9pm.* ○ *Closed Mon and public hols.* ☎ *908 62 35 48.*

Almería

POPULATION: 159,587.

MICHELIN MAP 578 V 22 – MAP 124 COSTA DEL SOL – ANDALUCÍA (ALMERÍA)

The city of Almería appears as a swathe of white between the Mediterranean and an arid hill crowned by an impressive Arab fortress.

Its magnificent climate – a line of mountains acts as a barrier to winds from inland – has resulted in its development as a major tourist destination. Life in the city centres on the paseo de Almería, an elegant tree-lined avenue bordered with shops, banks and cafés, while another oasis of greenery, the parque de Nicolás Salmerón, stretches out along the harbour beneath the palm trees. La Chanca, to the west, is the fishermen's quarter, where the houses, each with its own terrace, have been built into the rock.

Location

The city extends across an area of semi-desert which has always been considered isolated. Until the development of modern communciations, the sea acted as the city's only contact with the world at large. 🚩 *Parque Nicolás Salmerón, 04002 Almería,* ☎ *950 27 43 55.*

🔎 *Neighbouring sights are described in the following chapters: COSTA DEL SOL and GUADIX (109km/68mi NW).*

Worth a Visit

Alcazaba★

○ *Open 9.30am-6.30pm (8.30pm Apr-Oct).* ○ *Closed Mon, 1 Jan and 25 Dec.* ⊛ *2.50€; no charge for citizens of the European Union.* ☎ *950 27 16 17.*

Address Book

For coin ranges, see the Legend at the back of the guide.

WHERE TO EAT

⊖⊖ La Gruta

5km/3mi W of the city on the Aguadulce road – ☎ 950 23 93 35 – Dinner only. Closed Sun, 15-28 Feb and 15-31 Oct – ▤. The enormous caves (grutas) of a former quarry have been transformed into this unusual restaurant specialising in grilled meats and simple cooking based on high-quality products.

TAPAS

Casa Puga

Jovellanos 7 – ☎ 950 23 15 30 – Closed Sep, Sun and public hols – ▤. Almería is teeming with tapas bars, of which Casa Puga is the oldest. A huge choice of tapas, excellent wines and sausages.

WHERE TO STAY

⊖⊖ Hotel Costasol

Paseo de Almería 58 – ☎ 950 23 40 11 – ▤ – 55 rooms – ☲ 8€. The Costasol is housed in a characterless 1960s-style building on Almería's busiest shopping street, although the rooms are spacious and comfortable, some with a balcony. Private car park.

⊖⊖ Las Salinas de Cabo de Gata

Almadraba de Monteleva. Las Salinas. 4km/2.5mi SE of El Cabo de Gata – ☎ 950 37 01 03 – elmolesllarural.es – Closed in Oct – ▤ – 20 rooms – ☲ 5.40€ – Restaurant 18/29€. The hotel's location in a tranquil setting within the Parque Natural de Cabo de Gata makes this an ideal base from which to enjoy a number of excursions. All the rooms offer views of the bright-white salt pans or the beach.

On a privileged site – a little hill overlooking Almería and its bay – Abd ar-Rahman III ordered the construction of this fortress in the 10C to defend the city. It was subsequently enlarged by Almotacín, who built a splendid Moorish palace, and by the Catholic Monarchs, who erected a Christian palace after they had regained control of the town. However, its high, crenellated, ochre-coloured walls still dominate the town's white houses. A long wall, vestige of the old ramparts, links the fort to a second hill, the Cerro de San Cristóbal, which was formerly crowned by a castle.

Attractive public **gardens** have been laid out within the first walled enclosure where rivulets spring from fountains and flow between a variety of flower-beds. The bell in the Muro de la Vela, a wall separating the first and second enclosures, was used to warn the city's inhabitants of attacks by pirates. Excavations in the second enclosure have revealed the site of the royal residence, including a cistern, a Mudéjar hermitage and baths. In the third enclosure, the keep (torre del homenaje), notable for its incredibly thick walls, looks down upon the Christian alcázar.

The **view**★ from the battlements takes in the town, the Chanca district, the surrounding hills and the sea.

Catedral★

🕐 Open daily for guided tours, 10am-4.30pm. 🚫 No visits during religious services. 👓 2.50€. ☎ 609 57 58 02.

The cathedral was built in 1524 to replace the former mosque. Raids by Barbary pirates, however, decreed the construction of a fortified building – a rare necessity at the time.

In spite of its military character, the cathedral has two well-designed **portals**★ and, at the east end, a **delicately carved sunburst**★. The spacious interior is homogeneous; the high altar and the pulpits of inlaid marble and jasper are 18C, the choir stalls date from 1560 and the jasper trascoro with three alabaster statues is again 18C. The axial chapel in the ambulatory houses the venerated statue of the Cristo de la Escucha.

Historical Notes

The city was founded by Abd ar-Rahman II in the 9C, and played an important role in the 11C when it was the capital of a taifa kingdom. It was captured by Alfonso VII in 1147; however, upon his death, 10 years later, it fell into Moorish hands once more. Almería formed part of the Nasrid kingdom of Granada until 1489, the year in which it was reconquered by the Catholic Monarchs.

In the last third of the 20C, the development of advanced agricultural techniques and the opening-up of modern infrastructures have placed this provincial capital at the forefront of Spanish agriculture.

Monsul beach

Iglesia de Santiago

This 16C church in one of the city's main shopping streets (calle de las Tiendas) has a fine **Renaissance doorway**★ similar in style to the one adorning the cathedral.

Tours

In the province of Almería, nature provides an endless source of surprises: seemingly constant clear blue skies; areas of sand dunes that resemble the deserts of Africa; arid landscapes dotted with cacti, prickly pear, aloes and palm trees; as well as orchards and gardens ablaze with myriad colours.

TOUR ALONG THE EAST COAST★

Approx. 240km/150mi.

▶ *Leave Almería on the airport road and take a turn-off to the right after 14.5km/9mi.*

Parque Natural de Cabo de Gata-Níjar★★

Situated to the extreme south of the volcanic Cabo de Gata mountains, this park is a haven of isolated landscapes and wild, unspoilt beaches.

The road crosses the salt flats of Acosta before reaching this desolate cape. The lighthouse on the rocky spur faces Mermaid Reef, a popular haunt for underwater fishing enthusiasts.

On the other side of the mountain is the small, pleasant summer resort of San José with its two beautiful beaches; los **Genoveses**★ and **Monsul**★ (about 2km/1.2mi from the centre of the town).

▶ *Follow the AL 12, turning off towards Agua Amarga at Venta del Probe.*

Agua Amarga

Agua Amarga is a pleasant seaside complex with an attractive beach nestled between two rocky promontories.

▶ *Follow the coast road to Mojácar (32km/20mi).*

The road climbs up the pyramid-shaped mountains in a series of twists and bends, offering impressive views of the coast. A fortified tower dating from the 17C and a number of watchtowers built by the Moors in the 13C and 14C are visible along its path.

Mojácar★

The village of Mojácar stands in a splendid **site**★ on an outcrop offering fine **views** of the coast (2km/1.2mi away) and, further inland, a plain broken up by strange rock formations.

Its beauty mainly resides in the charm of its well-maintained popular architecture and its superb vistas. The heart of the village, spread out over the hill, shows unquestionable Arabic influence with its steep, narrow streets and secluded corners enhanced by colourful shrubs.

▶ *Follow the AL 12 back towards Almería, turning off at Níjar.*

Níjar

This old village of Arab origin is a fine example of popular architecture and carries on the craft of weaving the traditional multi-coloured *jarapas* (blankets), created using strips of already woven material *(trapos)*.

THE ROAD TO THE NORTHEAST

55km/34mi along the N 370. A tableland of sand dunes stretches for miles between Benahadux and Tabernas – it was used as the setting for *Lawrence of Arabia* and various westerns. Film sets are open to the public at **Mini-Hollywood**. ⏰ *Open 10am-9pm.* ☎ *950 36 52 36.*

Beyond Tabernas, the land is red and barren; pottery-making is the main occupation in the surrounding villages. **Sorbas** has an amazing **setting**★ with its houses clinging to a cliff, circled below by a loop in the river course.

THE ROAD TO THE NORTHWEST

71km/44mi along the A92. The road climbs to Guadix through a grandiose but desolate landscape of hills cut by great gorges. The aridity is occasionally relieved by a small green valley growing lemon and orange trees, or vines famous for their large sweet grapes. On 31 December, it is the Spanish custom to eat a grape at each stroke of midnight.

Principat d'Andorra★★

Principality of ANDORRA

POPULATION: 62,400.

MICHELIN MAP 574 E 34-35.

In recent years life in Andorra has undergone significant change on account of its large-scale town-planning schemes, the development of hydroelectric stations and the emergence of foreign tourism. However, tradition remains very much alive, both in the local economy (the terraced slopes of the Sant Julià de Lòria Valley are planted with tobacco) and in religious pilgrimages (the famous Catalan *aplec*).

Location

The seven parishes that make up the principality of Andorra occupy 464km²/179sq mi of high plateaux and valleys cut across by charming mountain roads.
Andorra La Vella is located 20km/12mi from La Seu d'Urgell. 🛈 *Andorra la Vella: Doctor Vilanova,* ☎ *00 376 82 02 14.*

👁 *Neighbouring sights are described in the 56,98/78,59 following chapter: PIRINEOS CATALANES.*

Worth a Visit

Andorra la Vella

Here, in the capital of the Andorra valleys, the houses are clustered onto a terrace overlooking the Gran Valira. Away from the main traffic routes, the streets in the old quarter of Andorra la Vella have remained almost intact, as has the **Casa de les Valls**, which continues to welcome debates on major national issues. This ancient stone building houses the seat of the Consell General de les Valls, which acts as both Parliament and courthouse to the small nation. 🚶 *Guided tours (30min, must*

Historical Notes

Until 1993 Andorra was a co-principality subject to an unusual political regime dating back to the days of feudalism. The neighboring rulers, the Bishop of Urgell and the President of the French Republic, enjoyed rights and exercised powers over this small territory, which was jointly governed by them. At present Andorra is a sovereign state – a full member of the United Nations.

be booked one month in advance), 9.30am-1pm and 3-7pm; Sun and public hols 10am-2pm. ◐ *Closed Sun and publics Nov-May, 1 and 6 Jan, 14 Mar, 1 May, 8 Sept, 1 Nov, 21, 25 and 26 Dec.* ☎ *00 376 82 91 29.*

To the east, Andorra la Vella is extended by the lively municipality of Les Escaldes, dominated by **Caldaea**, a thermal spa with futuristic lines featuring Turkish baths, jacuzzis, bubble beds, hot marble slabs etc.

Estany d'Engolasters (Engolasters Lake)

The Engolasters plateau, covered with pastures, is an extension of Andorra la Vella and is used for sporting and recreational activities. The fine Romanesque tower of the church of Sant Miquel stands out proudly against the rolling plains.

After reaching the end of the road, climb over the crest among the pine trees and then continue your descent on foot towards the dam. Prettily surrounded by trees, this impressive hydroelectric construction has raised the waters of the lake (alt 1 616m/5 301ft) by a total of 10m/33ft.

Santuari de Meritxell

After the pass of Los Bons lies a lovely **site**★ with a group of houses gathered under a ruined castle which once defended the area, as well as the Capilla de Sant Romà. Nearby stands the church of Nuestra Señora de Meritxell, a national sanctuary of the principality since 1976.

Canillo

The belltower of the church backing onto the rocks is the highest one in Andorra. At its side, you can see the ossuary, painted in white – a characteristic feature of Iberian civilisation.

Iglesia de Sant Joan de Caselles

◐ *Open Jul-Aug, 10am-1pm and 3-6pm; otherwise by prior arrangement.* ☎ *00 376 85 14 34.*

Beneath the openwork tower and its three rows of ornamental windows, this church is one of the best examples of Romanesque architecture in Andorra. Inside, behind the wrought-iron grid of the presbytery stands a painted altarpiece, executed by the master **Canillo** (1525), representing the life and visions of the Apostle St John. The Romanesque **Crucifixion**★ was restored when the church underwent renovation work in 1963: a Christ in stucco has been placed on top of a fresco illustrating a scene from Calvary.

Port d'Envalira★★

The roads are often blocked by snow but they are usually reopened within 24hr. Alt 2 407m/7 897ft. Of all the Pyrenean passes served by a reliable road, Envalira boasts the highest altitude. It lies on the dividing line between the Atlantic and the Mediterranean slopes and so commands a lovely panorama of the Andorra mountains.

Practical Information

CUSTOMS AND OTHER FORMALITIES

Visitors need a valid passport and, for those driving a car, a green card and current driving licence. There are customs checkpoints on the borders.

CURRENCY

The euro is the currency of Andorra and can be easily obtained from banks and post offices. Withdrawals can also be made from cash machines using credit and debit cards.

POSTAL SERVICE

Andorra has both Spanish and French postal services, with full-time post offices in Andorra la Vella and local offices elsewhere. There are plans to create an Andorran mail service at an as yet unspecified future date.

SHOPPING

Andorra has long held a reputation as a shopper's paradise, due to its duty-free status. A wide variety of products are on offer at very reasonable prices (food, luxury items, clothes, electronic goods etc). Shops are generally open from 9am to 1pm and 4pm to 8pm, although department stores tend to open all day.

TELEPHONING

The code for Andorra is 376 followed by the correspondent's number.

WEBSITE

www.turisme.ad

Pas de la Casa★

Alt 2 091m/6 861ft. Formerly no more than a small frontier-post, the highest village in the principality has now developed into the main ski resort of the region.

Ordino

 *Leave your car on the church square, in the upper part of town.* Ordino is a quaint village with a maze of charming alleyways surrounding the church. Inside, admire the wrought-iron grilles, similar to those that can still be seen in many sanctuaries near old Catalan forges. Not far from the church, note another fine example of wrought-iron artistry: an 18m/60ft balcony adorning the casa de Don Guillem, executed in his day by a master blacksmith.

Antequera★

POPULATION: 38,827.

MICHELIN MAP 578 U 16 – ANDALUCÍA (MÁLAGA)

This whitewashed town, a small industrial centre in the heart of a fertile valley, successfully integrates old and new buildings. Its cobblestone alleyways, windows with wrought-iron grilles, unusual roofs with coloured tiles and the many churches help to preserve its individuality. The San Sebastián belfry has fine brick Mudéjar decoration.

Location

The town lies at the foot of the Sierra del Torcal and opposite the Peña de los Enamorados, 7km/4.5mi from the A 92 highway linking Granada and Sevilla. 🛈 *Plaza de San Sebastián 7, 29200 Antequera,* ☎ *95 270 25 05.*

🚗 *Neighbouring sights are described in the following chapters: MÁLAGA (55km/34mi S), COSTA DEL SOL and OSUNA (74km/46mi NW).*

Worth a Visit

Alcazaba

🕐 *Open 10am-2pm.* 🕐 *Closed Mon.* ☎ *95 270 25 05 (Tourist Office).*

This was the first fortress captured by the Christians during the reconquest of the kingdom of Granada (1410). It could not be held, however, as the position was encircled by the Moors. Today, there is a pleasant garden within its walls, and from the towers a fine **view**★ over Antequera's roofs and church towers to the plain and the Torcal plateau beyond.

Menga dolmen

Colegiata de Santa María★

Access to this church, standing at the foot of the castle gardens, is through the 16C **Arco de los Gigantes** (Arch of the Giants). The church dates from 1514 and has a façade which is considered to be one of the earliest examples of Renaissance architecture in Andalucía.

> 😊 **A Word of Advice** 😊
>
> Given the dangerous nature of the defile and to ensure the safety of visitors, we recommend that you go no farther than the metal bridge suspended high above the El Chorro defile.

Iglesia del Carmen

🕐 *Open 10am-2pm and 4-7pm; in summer, 10am-2pm and 5-8pm; Sun and public hols, 10am-2pm.* 🎫*1.50€.* ☎ *95 270 25 05.*

The central nave of the church boasts a Mudéjar artesonado ceiling and a magnificent Churrigueresque altarpiece.

Museo Municipal

📷 *Guided tours (40min), 10am-1.30pm and 4-6pm (9-11pm 1 July-15Sep); Sun 11am-1.30pm.* 🕐 *Closed Mon and public hols.* 🎫*3€.* ☎ *95 270 40 21.*

The museum is housed in the 17C **Palacio de Nájera** and exhibits an interesting archaeological collection. The most outstanding item is the **Ephebus of Antequera★**, a bronze Roman sculpture dating from the 1C.

Dolmens★

▷ *To the left of the Antequera exit on the A 354, towards Granada.* The **Menga** and **Viera dolmens**, enormous collective tombs dating from 2500 to 2200 BC, take the form of funerary chambers beneath tumuli formed of great stone slabs. Menga, the oldest and largest of the two, is an oblong chamber divided by a line of pillars supporting enormous stone slabs. 🕐 *Open 9am-3pm (3.30pm 15 Sep-1 Jul); Fri-Sat 9am-5.30pm (6pm 15 Sep-1 Jul); Sun and public hols 9.30am-2.30pm.* 🕐 *Closed Mon, 1 and 6 Jan, 9 Apr, 1 May, 16 and 20 Aug, 1 Nov, 6, 24, 25 and 31 Dec. No charge.* ☎ *95 270 25 05.*

▷ *Continue along the A 354 and turn left onto the N 331.*

The **El Romeral** dolmen (1800 BC), the most recent chamber, consists of small flat stones so laid as to produce a trapezoidal section in the corridor. 🕐 *Open 9am-5.30pm (3.30pm Tu); Jul-15 Sep 9am-6pm (3pm Tu); Su 9.30am-2.30pm.* 🕐 *Closed Mon, 1 and 6 Jan, 9 Apr, 1 May, 16 and 20 Aug, 1 Nov, 6, 24, 25 and 31 Dec.* ☎ *95 270 25 05.*

Excursions

Parque Natural de El Torcala★

14km/9mi SE. ▷ *Take the C 3310 towards Villanueva de la Concepción, then bear right onto a signposted road leading to the* **Centro de Recepción "El Torcal".** 🕐 *Open 10am-2pm and 4-6pm.* ☎ *95 203 13 89.*

The park, spread over an area in excess of 12ha/30 acres, has some of Spain's most unusual scenery, where erosion by wind and rain have combined to create chasms, obelisks and other strange formations. Two signposted paths *(1hr and 3hr)* lead to a group of strangely shaped limestone rocks.

TOUR TO THE DESFILADERO DE LOS GAITANES★★

50km/31mi SW. ▷ *Take the A 343 as far as Álora.* After the Abdajalís valley, the corniche road crosses some superb mountain scenery to reach **Álora★**, an attractive village of narrow, twisting alleyways on a hill overlooking the banks of the Guadalhorce River. ▷ *Upon leaving Álora, take the MA 444; visitors are then advised to leave their car at the El Chorro campsite.* Continue on foot along a tarmac track (🚶 *30min there and back)* which climbs to a metal bridge offering magnificent **views★★★** of this incredible natural phenomenon.

FROM ANTEQUERA TO MÁLAGA★

62km/39mi S along the A 45, C 356 and C 345.

These pleasant well-planned roads, always within sight of majestic hills, afford splendid **views★★** beyond the Puerto del León (Lion Pass, 960m/3 150ft) of Málaga and the Mediterranean.

Aracena★

POPULATION: 6,500.

MICHELIN MAP 578 S 10 – ANDALUCÍA (HUELVA)

Aracena rises in tiers up a hillside in the sierra of the same name. This attractive town, crowned by the remains of a Templars' castle, is further embellished by whitewashed houses adorned with ornate wrought-iron grilles.

Location

Aracena is located at the heart of the Parque Natural de la Sierra de Aracena. *Plaza de San Pedro, 21200 Aracena,* ☎ *959 12 82 66.*

Neighbouring sights are described in the following chapters: SEVILLA (93km/58mi SE), ZAFRA (98km/61mi N) and HUELVA (108km/67mi SW) .

Worth a Visit

Plaza Alta, the hub of local life, is fronted by the Renaissance Iglesia de Nuestra Señora de la Asunción and the **Cabildo Viejo** (Centro de Información del Parque Natural Sierra de Aracena y Picos de Aroche). Open 10am-2pm and 4-6pm; in summer, 10am-2pm and 6-8pm. Closed Mon, 1 Jan and 25 Dec. ☎ 959 12 88 25.

The **Museo al Aire Libre de Escultura Contemporánea**, an open-air exhibition of modern art displayed in the town's streets and squares, adds a touch of modernity to this picturesque pueblo.

Gruta de las Maravillas★★★ (Cave of Marvels)

Guided tours (50 min) 10am-1.30pm and 3-6pm. 7.70€. ☎ 959 12 83 55 (advance booking recommended).

Underground rivers below the castle have hollowed out vast caves covered in concretions which mirror their size in limpid pools. The series of high chambers and increasingly narrow passages follows the line of rock faults. The concretions consist of draperies, pipes and coral formations coloured by iron and copper oxide or brilliant white calcite crystal as in the outstanding **Salón de la Cristalería de Dios★★** (God's Crystalware Chamber). The complex is also home to the **Museo Geológico Minero**, a geological and mining museum.

Castle

The castle was built in the 9C on the remains of an Almohad fortress. On the north side of the tower (the former minaret) abutting the church, note a style of decoration which is similar to that of the Giralda in Sevilla.

Corta Atalaya

B. Kaufmann/MICHELIN

Excursions

Parque Natural de la Sierra de Aracena y Picos de Aroche ★★

The park is a land of contrast with vast areas of forest, occasionally punctuated by slender peaks offering delightful views, and picturesque villages such as **Alájar**★, a whitewashed village of low houses nestled at the foot of its church, and **Almonaster la Real**★, hidden amid a dense mountainous landscape of chestnut, eucalyptus, cork and holm oak, which has preserved its old **mosque**★. ⟳*Open Sat-Sun and public hols, 11am-7pm. No charge.*

The nearby village of **Jabugo** is justifiably famous for its delicious cured hams.

Minas de Riotinto ★★

35km/22mi S. The mining tradition of this area, populated by dense plantations of holm and cork oak, dates back to Antiquity.

Parque Minero de Riotinto★★ – *Verify hours.* ⊛*15€. (includes visit to museum, Corta Atalaya and railway).* ⟳ *Closed 1 and 6 Jan and 25 Dec.* ☎ *959 59 00 25.*

This mining theme park lies within the town and in the surrounding area. It includes an interesting mining and railway museum, the **Museo Minero y Ferroviario**★, the spectacular open-cast mines of **Corta Atalaya**★★★ and **Cerro Colorado**★★, and a **tourist train** which runs along a railway line built at the end of the 19C by the British Río Tinto Company Limited.

Aranjuez★★

POPULATION: 35,872.

MICHELIN MAPS 575 AND 576 L 19 – MADRID

Aranjuez, on the banks of the Tagus *(Tajo)*, appears like an oasis at the centre of the harsh Castilian plain. The town is renowned for its greenery and leafy avenues, particularly around the royal palace.

The shaded walks described by writers, sung by composers (Joaquín Rodrigo's famous *Concierto de Aranjuez*) and painted by artists (the Catalan, Rusiñol) are now popular with Madrileños, especially at weekends.

Location

Aranjuez is situated just off the A 4 highway linking Madrid with Andalucía, 47km/29mi from both the Spanish capital and Toledo. 🔢 *Plaza de San Antonio 9, 28300 Aranjuez,* ☎ *91 891 04 27.*

👁 *Neighbouring sights are described in the following chapters: MADRID, TOLEDO and ALCALÁ DE HENARES (85km/53mi NE).*

Background

The Aranjuez Revolt *(El motín de Aranjuez)* – In March 1808, Charles IV, his queen and the prime minister, Godoy, were at Aranjuez. They were preparing to flee (on 18 March) first to Andalucía, then to America, as Godoy had allowed Napoleon's armies free passage to Portugal through Spain the year before. In Portugal, the French were fighting the Portuguese who were strongly supported by the British. The Spanish people, however, had objected to the passage of the French and Godoy had advised his king to follow the Portuguese royal house (which had fled from Lisbon to Brazil) into exile.

On the night of 17 March, Godoy's mansion was attacked by followers of the heir apparent, Prince Ferdinand; Charles IV dismissed his minister and was compelled to abdicate in favour of his son. This was not enough, however: Napoleon summoned both to Bayonne and made them abdicate in his own favour (5 May).

These intrigues and the presence of a French garrison in Madrid stirred the Spaniards to the revolt of May 1808 which marked the beginning of the War of Independence.

Special Features

ROYAL PALACE AND GARDENS★★

The Catholic Monarchs enjoyed staying in the original 14C palace, then Emperor Charles V enlarged the domain, but the present palace is mainly the result of an initiative by Philip II who called on the future architects of the Escorial to erect a new palace surrounded by gardens.

In the 18C, the town became one of the principal royal residences and was considerably embellished under the Bourbons. It was, however, ravaged by fire in 1727 and, no sooner was it rebuilt in 1728 than it burned down again. Most of the palace was then reconstructed, including the present frontage. Ferdinand VI built the town to a grid plan; Charles III added two wings to the palace and Charles IV erected the delightful Labourer's Cottage.

Practical Information

TREN DE LA FRESA

Operates Sat-Sun and public hols, Apr-Oct. ☎ *902 22 88 22.*

This small steam train (the Strawberry Train), is a charming alternative method for those travelling from Madrid to Aranjuez; It is a copy of the original train which first went into service in 1851. The journey includes a guided visit of the palace and museums.

LOCAL SPECIALITIES

Aranjuez is known for its high-quality strawberries and asparagus.

FIESTAS

The colourful Ferias del Motín, in which hundreds of participants dressed in period costume re-enact the famous revolt which took place in Aranjuez, is held during the first week of September.

Palacio Real★

Guided tours, 10.30am-5.15pm (10am-6.15pm Apr-Sep). Closed Mon, 1 and 6 Jan, 1 May, 24, 25 and 31 Dec; the palace may also close during official ceremonies. 3€; no charge Wed for citizens of the European Union. ☎ 91 892 15 32.

This Classical-style royal palace of brick and stone was built in the 16C and restored in the 18C. In spite of many modifications it retains considerable unity of style and symmetry. The court of honour, overlooking a vast outer square, is framed by the main building with wings at right angles on either side; domed pavilions mark the angles.

The apartments have been left as they were at the end of the 19C.

The grand staircase was designed by the Italian Giacomo Bonavia during the reign of Philip V. The bust of Louis XIV by Coysevox recalls Philip V's French ancestry. In María Luisa's apartments, in an antechamber, are paintings by the Neapolitan artist Luca Giordano, and in the music room, a piano presented by Eugenia de Montijo to Isabel II.

The **Salón del Trono** (Throne Room), with crimson velvet hangings and Rococo furnishings, has a ceiling painted with an allegory of monarchy – ironically it was in this room that Charles IV signed his abdication after the attack on 17 March 1808.

The **Salón de Porcelana**★★ (Porcelain Room) is the palace's most appealing and gracefully appointed room. It is covered in white garlanded porcelain tiles, illustrating in coloured high relief scenes of Chinese life, exotica and children's games, all made in the Buen Retiro factory in Madrid in 1763. They are enhanced by carved and painted wood doors, a chandelier and a marble floor.

In the king's apartments a music room precedes the Smoking or Arabian Room – a diverting reproduction of the Hall of the Two Sisters in the Alhambra in Granada. A fine Mengs *Crucifixion* hangs in the bedroom, and the walls of another room are decorated with **203 small pictures** painted on rice paper with Oriental-style motifs. At the end of the guided tour you can also visit a museum of palace life at the time of Alfonso XIII, where you will see rooms and exhibits which include a gymnasium and a tricycle.

Parterre and Jardín de la Isla★ (Parterre and Island Garden)

Open 8am-6.30pm (8.30pm Apr-Sep). Closed 1 and 6 Jan, 2 and 30 May, 16 Aug, 11 Oct, 1 Nov and 6 Dec. ☎ 91 542 00 59.

The **Parterre** extending along the palace's east front is a formal garden laid out by the Frenchman Boutelou in 1746. The fountain of Hercules brings a mythological touch to the balanced display of flower-beds and trees (cedars and magnolias).

The **Jardín de la Isla** was laid out on an artificial island in the Tajo river in the 16C. Cross the canal which once drove mill wheels to reach the park and its many fountains hidden among copses of chestnut, ash and poplar trees and banks and hedges of boxwood.

Jardín del Príncipe★★ (The Prince's Garden)

Entrance in calle de la Reina. Open 10.30am-5.45pm (6.45 Apr-Sep); Sun and public hols 9.55am (9.25am Apr-Sep)-2.25pm. Closed 1 and 6 Jan, 1 and 15 May, 9 Sep and 24-25 and 31 Dec. ☎ 91 891 13 44 or 91 891 43 32.

The garden beside the Tajo is more a vast gracefully laid-out park (150ha/371 acres). It has grilles and four monumental gateways by Juan de Villanueva. In 1763, called upon by the future Charles IV, Boutelou landscaped the park according to the romantic vision of nature fashionable at the end of the 18C. Within its bounds were a model farm, greenhouses with tropical plants and stables for exotic animals.

Casa del Labrador★★ (The Labourer's Cottage) – *Guided tours by prior arrangement, 10am-6.15pm (5.15pm in*

One of the numerous fountains adorning the gardens (detail)

J. Balanya/MICHELIN

summer). 🕐 *Closed Mon.* 💳 *5€; no charge Wed for citizens of the European Union.* ☎ *91 891 03 05.*

The so-called cottage, named after the peasant farm which originally stood on the site, stands at the eastern end of the Jardín del Príncipe and is a Versailles type Trianon built on the whim of Charles IV in a neo-Classical style similar to that of the Royal Palace but with more luxurious decoration. The wrought-iron grille and balustrade surrounding the courtyard entrance are surmounted by 20 Carrara marble busts of figures from Antiquity.

The interior, a reflection of Spanish Bourbon taste, is an excellent example of sumptuous 18C decoration: Pompeian style ceilings, embroidered silk hangings, mahogany doors, marble floors, furniture and lamps, canvases by Bambrilla, clocks and porcelain. The billiard room on the first floor has a ceiling by Maella illustrating the Four Elements and magnificent embroidered silk hangings showing views of Madrid.

The statue gallery is embellished with Greek busts and a marble floor covering inlaid with Roman mosaics from Mérida. The French clock in the middle of the gallery incorporates a reproduction of Trajan's column. The María Luisa room has remarkable embroidered hangings made up of 97 small pictures showing a variety of views. In the centre of the ballroom stand a magnificent malachite table and chair given to Charles IV by the Tsar Alexander III. The Platinum Room, or Gabinete de Platino, is decorated with gold, platinum and bronze inlays while the figure of a bird in the anteroom is carved from a single piece of ivory.

Casa de Marinos (The Sailors' House) – 🚶 *Guided tours by prior arrangement, 10am-6.15pm (5.15pm in summer).* 🕐 *Closed Mon. 3.40€; no charge Wed for citizens of the European Union.* ☎ *91 891 03 05.*

A museum beside the former landing stage contains the **falúas reales**★★ *(royal vessels)* which once made up the Tajo fleet of launches that ferried the royal family and guests to the Labourer's Cottage. The vessels belonged to six sovereigns: Isabel II, Charles IV (whose ship has paintings by Maella), Alfonso XII (whose ship is made of mahogany), María Cristina (whose ship has paintings resembling woven hangings), Alfonso III and finally Philip V, whose vessel, a gift from a Venetian count, is remarkable for its ornate decoration in gilded, finely carved wood.

Excursions

Chinchón★

21km/13mi NE along the M 305.

Chinchón is famous for its aniseed spirit and, more importantly, the Countess of Chinchón, to whom the West owes quinine. The countess, wife of a 17C viceroy of Peru, was cured of tropical fever by an Indian medicament prepared from tree bark; having proved the remedy she brought it back to Europe. In the 18C, Linnaeus, the Swedish botanist, named the bark-bearing tree chinchona, in the vicereine's honour. Aniseed, gin and other spirits are distilled in the old castle at the top of the town.

Plaza Mayor★★ – The uneven but picturesque arcaded square, dominated by its church, is surrounded by three-storey houses with wooden balconies. Bullfights are held here in summer.

The brick buildings of the former Augustinian monastery beside the square now house a parador.

Tembleque

47km/29mi S on the N IV. The picturesque 17C **Plaza Mayor**★ in this La Mancha village is a very large quadrilateral, which must have once been used as a bullring. It is framed by a graceful three-storey portico in which the lowest arches are of stone, the upper of wood. An unusual cobweb-style roof crowns one of the entrances to the square.

Ávila★★

POPULATION: 49,868.

MICHELIN MAPS 575 OR 576 K 15 – MAP 121

ALREDEDORES DE MADRID – CASTILLA Y LEÓN (ÁVILA)

Ávila stands on the banks of the Adaja river, hidden behind magnificent 11C walls. Time seems to have by-passed this town embellished with numerous convents and churches. As you wander through its silent streets in winter, when the town is smothered in a white blanket of snow, the sound of distant chants and prayers seems to echo through the air.

Location

Its position on a plateau at an altitude of 1 131m/3 710ft has a strong influence on its climate, which is harsh in winter with cold temperatures and strong winds. 🖪 *Plaza Catedral 4, 05001 Ávila, ☎ 920 21 13 87.*

👌 *Neighbouring sights are described in the following chapters: Sierra de GREDOS, Monasterio de EL ESCORIAL (64km/40mi E), SEGOVIA (67km/42mi NE), SALAMANCA (98 km/61mi NW) and MADRID (107km/66mi SE).*

Worth a Visit

Murallas★★ (City walls)

The ramparts are Europe's most striking example of medieval fortifications. The crenellated walls are punctuated by advanced bastions and towers (90 in all), eight gateways and various posterns, and enclose a quadrilateral area of 900m/2 953ft by 449m/1 476ft. Most date from the 11C; as a result, they have managed to maintain an overall impression of unity in spite of modifications in the 14C. The sentry path along the top is open to the public. The best place for a general **view** of them is a spot known as **Cuatro Postes**, or Four Posts, on the Salamanca road.

Catedral★★

🕘 *Open 9.30am-6.30pm (8pm Jun-Oct); Sat, 9.30am-6pm (8pm Jun-Oct); Sun and public hols, noon-6pm (8pm Jun-Oct).* 🕘 *Closed 1 and 6 Jan, Maundy Thu, 15 Oct and 25 Dec.* ⊛ *2.50€ (museum) ☎ 920 21 16 41.*

The fortified **east end** of the cathedral serves as an advanced bastion in the ramparts and is crowned with a double row of battlements. The use of granite and the church's defensive stance give the exterior an austere appearance despite the window tracery, portal carvings and a ball decoration along the upper outlines of the tower, buttresses and pinnacles. The 14C **north doorway** with French Gothic decoration, unfortu-

A view of the walls at dusk

R. Mattes/MICHELIN

The City of St. Theresa

Santa Teresa de Jesús (1515-82), whose visions deeply affected her contemporaries, is one of the greatest mystics of the Roman Catholic Church. Living at a time when the Reformation was gaining adherents throughout Europe, and the monastic orders, grown rich in power and possessions, were relaxing their discipline, she succeeded in widely re-establishing the strict observance of the Carmelites, gaining converts and founding convents.

Her letters are famous, particularly those to her spiritual director, St John of the Cross, as are her mystical writings and her autobiography, Life, published in 1588. She was canonised in 1622 and made a Doctor of the Church in 1970.

Several buildings in Ávila preserve the memory of the saint, including the museums in the **Convento de San José (Las Madres)** and the **Convento de La Encarnación**. The crypt of the **Convento de Santa Teresa (La Santa)**, built on the site of the house where she was born, is home to the most comprehensive museum dedicated to her life. Her remains, however, are not in Ávila but in Alba de Tormes.

nately in stone too friable to resist erosion, originally stood in the **west front** but was removed in the 15C by Juan Guas when he redesigned the main entrance there. This was remodelled in the 18C in an unusual style more suitable for a palace.

The **interior** is a total contrast to the exterior with its high Gothic nave, its chancel with sandstone patches of red and yellow and its many **works of art**★★. These include the **trascoro** (1531) which has many beautifully detailed Plateresque statues (from left to right: the Presentation of Jesus in the Temple, the Adoration of the Magi and the Massacre of the Innocents) which blend into a harmonious whole, the **choir stalls** from the same period, and two delicately worked wrought-iron **pulpits** – one Renaissance, the other Gothic.

At the end of the apse, in which the windows are still Romanesque – the cathedral's construction lasted from 1135 to the 14C – is a large painted **altarpiece** (c 1500) by Pedro Berruguete and Juan de Borgoña. It has a gilt wood surround with Isabelline features and Italian Renaissance style pilasters. Against the back and sides of the high altar which face onto the double ambulatory are five carved Renaissance panels: those on the sides show the four Evangelists and the four Holy Knights (Hubert, George, Martin and James). The central panel is the sculptor Vasco de la Zarza's masterpiece: the alabaster **tomb**★★ of Don Alonso de Madrigal, theologian and prolific writer, who was Bishop of Ávila in the 15C and nicknamed El Tostado or The Swarthy. He is shown writing before a beautiful Epiphany. The embroidery on the chasuble has been rendered with particular delicacy.

Address Book

For coin ranges, see the Legend at the back of the guide.

WHERE TO EAT

⊝ Siglo Doce

Plaza de la Catedral 6 – ☎ 920 252 885 – reservations recommended. A 12C house right beside the Cathedral, rustic, unpretentious, with charming exposed beams and peaked tile roof. Many choices, but the most popular is Ávila veal chop.

⊝⊝ Doña Guiomar

Tomás Luis de Victoria 3 – ☎ 920 25 37 09 – Closed Sun evening – 🍽. A popular choice with locals. Good views of the market on the opposite side of the street.

WHERE TO STAY

⊝ Pensión Continental

Plaza de la Catedral 6 – ☎ 920 21 15 02 – 54 rooms. Somewhat antiquated, with spartan rooms which have wood skirting and high ceilings. The presence of the

cathedral opposite adds to the monastic atmosphere of this part of town.

⊝ Hostería de Bracamonte

Bracamonte 6 – ☎ 920 25 12 80 – 24 rooms – 🍽 6€ – Restaurant 25/35€. A charming hotel right in the centre of Ávila. The decoration in this old inn includes wooden beams, attractive brickwork and pictures hanging from the walls. The pleasant guest rooms are arranged around a plant-filled inner patio. Although a little on the expensive side, the hotel is normally full at weekends.

SPECIALITIES

The city is also famous for its candied egg yolks *(yemas de Santa Teresa)*, named for Ávila's patron saint. Give them a try.

Museo – 🕐 *Open 10am-6.30pm (7.30pm Jun-Oct); Sat, 10am-7pm (7.30pm Jun-Oct); Sun and public hols, noon-6.30pm (7.30pm Jun-Oct).* 🕐 *Closed 1 and 6 Jan, Maundy Thu, 15 Oct and 25 Dec.* ✆ *2.50€.* ☎ *920 21 16 41.*

The way to the museum leads through a 13C ante-sacristy followed by a **sacristy**★★ from the same period which has a remarkable eight-ribbed vault, a massive 16C alabaster altarpiece and, in place of windows, wood sculptures of the four scenes of the Passion in imitation alabaster.

In the museum are a head of Christ by Morales painted on a tabernacle door, a portrait by El Greco, a monumental Isabelline grille, late-15C antiphonaries and a colossal monstrance 1.70m/5ft 8in high made by Juan de Arfe in 1571. The Gothic **cloisters** have recently been restored.

In plaza de la Catedral, the former **Palacio de Valderrábanos**, now a hotel, has a fine 15C doorway surmounted by the family crest.

Basílica de San Vicente★★

🕐 *Open 10am-1.30pm and 4-6.30pm.* 🕐 *No visits during religious services.* ✆ *1.40€.* ☎ *920 25 52 30.*

This vast Romanesque basilica, which took from the 12C to the 14C to build, and has ogive vaulting, stands on the alleged site of the 4C martyrdom of St Vincent of Zaragoza and his sisters, Sabina and Cristeta. The 14C south gallery with its slender columns clustered and ringed, the carved cornice extending the full length of the nave, the tall porch added to the west front and the two incomplete towers, all combine to form a harmonious whole.

The **west portal**★★ is outstanding for the statue columns beneath the richly decorative cornice and covings which seem so lifelike that they might almost be gossiping at the church entrance. The style of their clinging robes recalls that of sculptures in Vézelay, France. Inside, beneath the 14C **lantern**★, is the **martyrs' tomb**★★, a late 12C masterpiece under an unusual 15C Gothic canopy with a pagoda-shaped top. The martyrdom of St Vincent and his sisters is depicted on the tomb so masterfully, both technically and evocatively, that it has been attributed to the same unknown

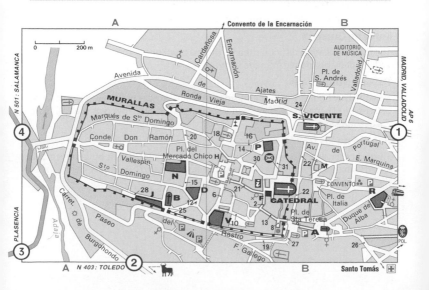

sculptor as the west portal. The scenes of the martyrs' capture below the walls of Ávila, their stripping and torture, are particularly powerful.

Monasterio de Santo Tomás★

🕐 *Open 10am-1pm and 4-8pm.* 🖼 *3€ (cloisters and choir).* ☎ *920 22 04 00.*

This Dominican monastery founded at the end of the 15C and embellished with gifts from the Catholic Monarchs, who on occasion made it their summer residence, was also the university.

The **church** façade incorporates the principal decorative motifs to be found on other buildings in the monastery: architectural details are emphasised with long lines of balls – a common feature throughout Ávila but here used profusely – and the yoke and fasces adopted by Ferdinand and Isabel as their emblem. The church, in accordance with Dominican custom of the time, has only a single aisle, its arches resting on clusters of slender columns. A rare feature are the two galleries, one on the west for the choir, the other on the east. As they are accessible only from the cloisters, the monks alone had access.

The fine **mausoleum**★ (1512) in the transept crossing is that of Prince Juan, only son of the Catholic Monarchs, who died at 19. Its alabaster table with delicate Renaissance carving is by Domenico Fancelli, the Florentine who also carved the Catholic Monarchs' mausoleum in the Capilla Real (Royal Chapel) in Granada. In one of the north chapels another fine Renaissance tomb belongs to Juan Dávila and his wife, the prince's tutors.

Claustro (Cloisters) – Beyond the unadorned 15C **Claustro de los Novicios** is the **Claustro del Silencio**★, small enough to be intimate and generously carved on its upper gallery. Beyond is the Claustro de los Reyes (Catholic Monarchs' Cloister), larger and more solemn with spectacularly bare upper arching.

From the Claustro del Silencio, stairs lead to the gallery of the *coro* containing beautiful 15C Gothic **choir stalls** carved with pierced canopies and arabesques. From the same cloister's upper gallery, more stairs go to the high altar gallery where one can see in detail Berruguete's masterpiece in high relief, the **retable of St Thomas Aquinas**★★ (c 1495).

Iglesia de San Pedro

🕐 *Open 9.30am-1pm and 6.30-8.30pm.* 🕐 *No visits during religious services.* ☎ *920 22 93 28.*

Standing on the vast **plaza Santa Teresa**, this fine Romanesque church shows early Gothic influence in its pointed arches and especially in the delicate rose window in the façade. A lantern lights the transept.

Palacio de los Verdugos

The façade of this Gothic Renaissance palace, emblazoned above the entrance and window with the family crest, is flanked by two stout square towers.

Palacio de Polentinos

This palace, now a barracks, has a finely decorated Renaissance entrance and patio.

Torre de Guzmán

The Oñates' palace is distinguished by this massive square corner tower, complete with battlements, dating from the early 16C.

Palacio Núñez Vela

Now the Law Courts, the former residence of the Viceroy of Peru is a Renaissance palace with windows framed by slender columns surmounted by coats of arms. There is a beautiful inner patio.

Palacio de los Dávila

The palace consists of several seigniorial mansions: two 14C Gothic buildings embellished with coats of arms give onto plaza Pedro Dávila and two others, belonging to the Episcopal Palace, give onto plaza de Rastro.

Badajoz

POPULATION: 130,247.
MICHELIN MAP 576 P 9 (TOWN PLAN) – EXTREMADURA (BADAJOZ)

The approach from the north provides a pleasant view of this border town on the banks of the Guadiana river. Its most impressive monuments are the walls of an Arab fortress, crowning the hill upon which the town is built, the 16C **Puente de Palmas**, a Herreran-style granite bridge, and the 16C crenellated gateway of the same name.

Location

Badajoz stands on the border with Portugal, some 17km/11mi from the Portuguese town of Elvas. The A 5 highway provides a road link with Mérida (62km/39mi W), while the EX 100 connects the town with Cáceres (91km/57mi NE). ⓘ *Plaza de la Libertad 3, 06005 Badajoz,* ☎ *974 01 36 58.*

⚷ *Neighbouring sights are described in the following chapters: MÉRIDA, CÁCERES and ZAFRA (80km/50mi SE).*

Background

An eventful history – Badajoz, in Roman times a modest town dependent on Mérida, became capital, in the 11C, of a Moorish kingdom or *taifa*. In the 16C it held a key position in peninsular strategy and was caught up in the Wars of Succession between Spain and Portugal, which meant that it was often besieged and pillaged. For centuries, the embattled town was shut away in narrow streets, protected by the Moorish fortress and medieval ramparts.

Today, Badajoz has abandoned this frontier mentality and is projecting itself as a city with an open, modern character as shown by the **Puente Real** (Royal Bridge) and its new modern art museum, the **Museo Extremeño e Iberoamericano de Arte Contemporáneo**. ⓞ *Open 10am-1.30pm and 5-8pm; Sun, 10am-1.30pm.* ⓞ *Closed Mon and public hols. No charge.* ☎ *924 01 30 60.*

The Fall From Grace of Don Manuel

Manuel Godoy Álvarez de Faria (1767-1851), the son of a modest provincial *hidalgo*, left his family at 17 for the Court where he enlisted in the Guards. Favours from Queen María Luisa assisted him in a meteoric career in politics; by the age of 25 he had been appointed Prime Minister. His rapid success earned him little sympathy from the Court, or from the common people who, outraged, accused him of being in Napoleon's pay. They insisted on his leaving the country. After the Aranjuez uprising (⚷ *see p 128)*, he followed the royal family into exile at Bayonne where he drew up Charles IV's act of abdication which was to deliver Spain to Napoleon. He died, unknown, in Paris.

Worth a Visit

Catedral

ⓞ *Open 11am-1pm and 6-8pm.* ⓞ *No visits on Sun because of religious services. Museum open Fri-Sat, 11am-1pm.* ⓐ *1.80€ (museum).* ☎ *924 22 39 99.*

The cathedral, built in the 13C in the Gothic style, was considerably remodelled during the Renaissance and is consequently full of contrasts: it has a fortress type tower as well as a delicate Plateresque decoration of friezes and window surrounds. Inside, in the middle of the nave and masking the general view, is an impressive coro for which the stalls were carved in 1557.

In the sacristy to the right of the chancel hang six fine 17C Flemish tapestries.

The War of the Oranges

At the end of the 13C, Olivenza was given in dowry to King Denis of Portugal. In 1801, it was ceded to Spain to prevent the Alentejo invasion – begun by Godoy's troops – becoming a major conflict between the two nations. The skirmish, however, left no other souvenir than the story of Godoy's futile gesture of sending oranges to Queen María Luisa from trees at the foot of the Elvas ramparts (⚷ see *The Green Guide Portugal*).

Museo Arqueológico Provincial

🕐 *Open 10am-3pm.* 🕐 *Closed Mon and public hols.* ⟨⟩ *1.20€.* ☎ *924 22 23 14.*

The 16C Palacio de la Roca inside the *alcazaba* now houses a modern museum with rich collections of local archaeological finds. These include prehistoric and protohistoric stelae and figurines; Roman mosaics and tools made of bronze; beautiful Visigothic **pilasters** carved with plant and geometric motifs; medieval artefacts, and exhibits of work from the Islamic civilisation.

Museo Provincial de Bellas Artes

🕐 *Open Sep-May, 10am-2pm and 4-6pm; Jun-Aug, 10am-2pm and 6-8pm; Sat-Sun, 10am-2pm.* 🕐 *Closed Mon and public hols. No charge.* ☎ *924 21 24 69 or 924 24 80 34.*

This fine arts museum is housed in two elegant 19C mansion houses. It contains a fine collection of paintings, sculpture and sketches, particularly from the 19C and 20C.

Excursions

Olivenza

25km/15mi SW. Five centuries of Portuguese history have left their mark on the appearance and architecture of this quiet white-walled town set in the middle of olive groves. Olivenza is one of the few places in Spain where the Manueline style can be seen. This specifically Portuguese architecture, the origins of which date back to the reign of King Manuel (1495-1521), is late Gothic in style embellished with Renaissance, Moorish and maritime features (sailors' knots, ropes and armillary spheres).

Iglesia de Santa María Magdalen★★ – The brothers Diego and Francisco de Arruda, architects of the Mosteiro dos Jerónimos and the Torre de Belém in Lisbon, are believed to have designed the church's Manueline nave. The sober elegance of the lierne and tierceron vaulting supported on cabled pillars contrasts with the sumptuous altarpieces and *azulejos* which decorate the Baroque sanctuary.

Museo Etnográfico González Santana – 🕐 *Open Oct-Apr, 11am (noon, Sat-Sun and public hols) to 2pm and 4-6pm; May-Sep, 11am (noon, Sat-Sun and public hols) to 2pm and 7-9pm.* 🕐 *Closed Mon.* ☎ *924 22 27 63.*

This ethnographic museum is housed in an 18C building known as the Panadería del Rey (King's Bakery) inside the walls of a medieval castle. A keep built by João III of Portugal in 1488 dominates the fortress and offers fine views of the town. In the museum, the workshops of several craftsmen have been re-created, including a tailor's and a blacksmith's, in addition to the inside of a 19C house.

Ayuntamiento (town hall) – The **doorway**, a delightfully graceful example of Manueline style decoration, is adorned with two armillary spheres, symbols of the discoveries by the great Portuguese navigators of the 15C and 16C.

Baeza★★

POPULATION: 17,691.
MICHELIN MAP 578 S 19 – ANDALUCÍA (JAÉN)

Historical and seigniorial Baeza stretches across a hill surrounded by fields of cereal crops and olive groves. The town is endowed with a rich architectural heritage; its churches, monuments and stately mansions built from golden stone in predominantly Renaissance style bear witness to the importance of this tranquil town in the 16C-17C.

Location

Along with its close neighbour, Úbeda, Baeza is situated in the centre of Jaén province, close to the Parque Natural de Cazorla (to the E), in an area with abundant water.
🛈 *Plaza del Pópulo, 23440 Baeza,* ☎ *953 74 04 44.*

🔎 *Neighbouring sights are described in the following chapters: ÚBEDA (9km/5.5mi W), Parque Natural de las SIERRAS DE CAZORLA, SEGURA Y LAS VILLAS and JAÉN (48km/30mi SW).*

Walking About

MONUMENTAL CENTRE★★★
Route marked on town plan – allow half a day.

Plaza del Pópulo★

Standing in the centre of the small, irregular square is the **Fuente de los Leones** (Fountain of the Lions), built with Antique remains. The former **carnicería** (abattoir), on the left, is a Renaissance building of noble appearance considering its function; the escutcheon over the first floor portico represents the imperial coat of arms of Charles V.

The **Casa del Pópulo** (now the tourist office), at the end of the square, has decorative Plateresque windows and medallions. The six doors once opened on six notaries' offices; court hearings were held on the first floor. An attractive balcony projects onto the **Puerto de Jaén**, which, along with the Villalar arch, was dedicated to Charles V. The Jaén gate was erected to mark the emperor's visit on his way to Sevilla for his marriage to Isabel of Portugal on 12 March 1526. The **Arco de Villalar** was dedicated as a gesture of submission to the king after his victory, in 1521, over the Comuneros, whom the town had supported.

Plaza de Santa María

On the left, the walls of the 17C **Seminario de San Felipe Neri** are covered with inscriptions – the ancient custom having been to inscribe in bull's blood one's name and date on graduation. Behind the **Fuente de Santa María**, a triumphal arch adorned

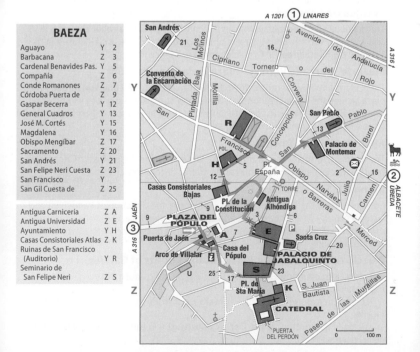

with atlantes, is the Gothic façade of the **Casas Consistoriales Altas**, emblazoned, between twin windows, with the coats of arms of Juana the Mad and Philip the Fair.

Catedral★– 🕐 *Open 10am-1.30pm and 4-6pm; Jun-Sep, 10am-1.30pm and 5-7pm. No charge.* ☎ *953 74 41 57.*

The **interior**★★ was almost entirely remodelled by Vandelvira and his followers in the 16C. Some of the chapels are outstanding: the Capilla Dorada (Gold Chapel) beside the fonts has a delicate Italianate relief; St James' has a fine Antique setting and St Joseph's is flanked by caryatids. The graceful door to the sacristy is adorned with scrollwork and angels' heads. A monumental iron grille by Bartolomé closes the first bay in the nave while a pulpit of painted beaten

B. Kaufmann/MICHELIN

Façade of the Palacio de Jabalquinto

metal (1580) stands in the transept crossing. In the Capilla del Sagrario, to one end on the right-hand side, a Baroque silver monstrance carried in procession on the feast of Corpus Christi is on display.

Four Mudéjar chapels adorned with *atauriques* and Arabic inscriptions can also be seen in the cloisters.

Palacio de Jabalquinto★
🔒 *Closed for restoration.*

The palace's **façade**★★, a perfect example of the Flamboyant-Gothic style, is best seen in the morning when the finials cast impressive shadows and the sun accentuates the Gothic decoration of the windows and pinnacles beneath slanting armorial bearings. The **patio**, built c 1600, is of more sober style, the only informal feature being the two lions guarding the monumental Baroque stairway.

Opposite the palace is the Romanesque church of Santa Cruz, the only one to remain of those built immediately after the town's reconquest. The main features of the interior are a Gothic chapel and the wall paintings in the apse. 🕐*Open 11am-1pm and 4-6pm; Sun and public hols, noon-2pm.*

Antigua Universidad

The building, which nowadays houses a secondary school, was built between 1568 and 1593 and was the headquarters of the town's university until it closed in the 19C. The plain façade conceals an elegant Renaissance patio.

Plaza del Mercado Viejo (or Plaza de la Constitución)

This square, lined by bars and cafés, is the centre of Baeza life. Buildings around the plaza include the Antigua Alhóndiga, the former corn exchange, with its porticoed façade (1554), and the Casas Consistoriales Bajas, built in 1703 as a gallery for officials attending celebrations held in the square.

Ayuntamiento★ (Town Hall)

The building, formerly used as the town's law courts and prison, has a Plateresque façade embellished with balconies and heraldic decoration.

Ruinas de San Francisco

Construction of the convent began in 1538 under the direction of Vandelvira and lasted a century. The vast transept and apse and majestic carved stone altarpieces provide some idea of the beautiful 16C church that once stood here. It is now used as an auditorium.

Palacio de Montemar (or Palace of the Counts of Garcíez)

Beautiful Gothic windows and a Plateresque style patio adorn this early-16C nobleman's palace.

A little farther along stands the **Iglesia de San Pablo**, with its Renaissance façade.

Iglesia de San Andrés (note the **Gothic paintings**★ in the sacristy); the Convento de la Encarnación.

Barbastro

POPULATION: 15,827.
MICHELIN MAP 574 F 30 – ARAGÓN (HUESCA)

Barbastro's interesting architecture bears witness to its importance during the 16C. The town is an excellent base for excursions into the Central Pyrenees and is the capital of the Somontano, a region known for its excellent wines.

Location

Barbastro stands on the edge of the foothills of the Pyrenees, at the exit point of two valleys, one of which leads to the Parque de Ordesa, the other to the Maladeta range, via a canyon known as the Congosto de Ventamillo *(see PIRINEOS ARAGONESES)*. 🛈 *Avenida de la Merced 64, 22300 Barbastro,* ☎ *974 30 0J 50.*

♿ *Neighbouring sights are described in the following chapters: PIRINEOS ARAGONESES, HUESCA (52km/32mi NW) and LLEIDA/ LÉRIDA (68km/42mi SE).*

Alquézar

B. Brillion/MICHELIN

Worth a Visit

Catedral★

The cathedral is a typical Spanish hall-church with three elegant aisles beneath richly ornamented vaulting with gilded decoration supported by slender columns crowned with capitals. The predella on the **retable** at the high altar is an important work by Damián Forment. Several of the side chapels are Churrigueresque in style; the first on the left-hand side contains a fine interesting early-16C altarpiece. The **Museo Diocesano** is open to the public. 🕐 *Open 9.30am-noon and 5-8pm.* 🕐 *Closed on public hols. No visits during religious services.* 👛 *1.80€.* ☎ *974 31 16 82 or 974 30 83 50.*

Complejo de San Julián y Santa Lucía

The former Hospital de San Julián has been converted into a complex housing the Tourist Office, a wine shop, and a **museum** dedicated to the excellent Somontano appellation. The 16C Renaissance church of San Julián opposite has been converted into the **Centro de Interpretación del Somontano**★, an exhibition centre highlighting the area and its tourist sites via an interesting film lasting 11 minutes. 🕐 *Open 10am to 2pm and 4.30-8pm.* 🕐 *Closed Sun, Mon 10am-2pm, 1 and 6 Jan, 1-8 Sep, and 25 Dec.* 👛 *1.80€.* ☎ *974 31 55 75.*

Excursions

Alquézar★

23km/14mi NW along the A 1232, following the course of the Río Vero. Alquézar enjoys a magnificent isolated **setting**★★ amid fields of red earth. The village appears to cling to a rocky promontory which is surrounded on three sides by the river.

Old quarter – The narrow alleyways of this medieval village are testimony to Alquézar's long history. The old quarter is a maze of uneven streets lined by houses adorned with rounded stone doorways and coats of arms. The village also has an enchanting arcaded main square.

Colegiata★ – *Guided tours, 11am-1.30pm and 4-6pm; in summer, 11am-1pm and 4.30-7.30pm.* Closed Tue. *2€.* 974 31 82 67. The Moors built an **alcázar** on the site which later fell to Sancho Ramírez, King of Aragón. In the late 11C and early 12C, the still visible walls were constructed together with a church which was rebuilt in 1530. The north gallery of the Romanesque cloister has fine capitals carved in anecdotal archaic style illustrating the Sacrifice of Isaac, Balaam and his ass, Adam and Eve and the Last Supper. Inside the collegiate church is a beautiful Romanesque Christ dating from the 12C.

Cañón del río Vero★ – Allow at least a day to walk up and in some places wade or swim this spectacular canyon. At the very least, hike to the Roman bridge at Villacantal (*2 hrs round trip*) for an overview and to see the impressive ochre and grey walls.

TOUR THROUGH THE RIBAGORZA

85km/53mi– allow one day

This tour follows the Esera and Isábena river valleys, passing through the historic lands of the county of Ribagorza, in the pre-Pyrenees of Aragón.

▶ *Leave Barbastro on the N 123. After 16km/10mi turn right onto the A 2211.*

Santuario de Torreciudad

In 1804, an 11C Romanesque statue of Our Lady of Torreciudad was placed in a small shrine and venerated by the local people. In 1975 a church, now a place of pilgrimage, was built for the statue under the auspices of Monsignor José María Escrivá de Balaguer (now canonised), founder of Opus Dei (1928). Preceding the brick buildings is a vast esplanade affording beautiful **views**★ of the Pyrenees and, in the foreground, the El Grado dam. The church itself has a large nave and a modern alabaster altarpiece with relief work illustrating scenes from the Life of the Virgin. The statue of Our Lady of Torreciudad stands in the lower part of the altarpiece. *Open 10am-2pm and 4-7pm (7.30pm 1 May-15 Jun; 8.30pm Jul-15 Sep).* 974 30 40 25.

▶ *From Torreciudad, return to the A 2211, heading towards La Puebla de Castro, and then take the N 123ª.*

Graus

The village huddles around the irregular-shaped **Plaza de España**, lined by old houses decorated with frescoes, carved beams and brick galleries. The most important monument in Graus is the **Santuario de la Virgen de la Peña**★, built in the middle of the 16C. The Renaissance doorway provides access to the church, its single aisle crowned by pointed vaulting. The cloisters, housing a museum of icon reproductions, opens out like a balcony over the village.

▶ *From the centre of Graus follow the A 1605 which crosses the Esera river.*

Roda de Isábenaa

26.5km/16.5mi from Graus. This picturesque village is perched on a promontory in a beautiful mountain **setting**★. Narrow cobbled streets lead to the impressive **cathedral**★, construction of which began in the 11C; the north apse, decorated on the outside with Lombard bands, dates from this period. Most of the interior, basilical in plan with three aisles, was built in the 12C. Note the central **crypt**, housing the **tomb of San Ramón**★★, with its interesting polychrome low reliefs. A 13C fresco adorns a chapel off the cloisters. *Guided tours at 11.15am, noon, 12.45pm, 1.30pm, 4pm, 4.45pm, 5.30pm and 6.15pm; in summer at 5.15pm, 6pm and 6.45pm.* *1.80€.* 974 54 45 35.

▶ *Continue for 16km/10mi N along the A 1605.*

Monasterio de Santa María de Obarra

All that is left of this monastery is the church, built by Lombard masters in the 10C-11C. The east end has three apses decorated with lesenes and blind arches. A 12C hermitage, the Ermita de San Pablo, stands to one side.

Barcelona★★★

POPULATION: 1 681 132

MICHELIN MAP 574 H 36 (TOWN PLAN) – MAP 122 COSTA BRAVA –

MICHELIN CITY PLANS BARCELONA 40, 41 AND 2040 – CATALUNYA (BARCELONA)

Barcelona is perhaps the most cosmopolitan of all Spanish cities. As the capital of an autonomous community, it has succeeded in combining the traditional and the avant-garde to forge an identity that is both open and welcoming. Barcelona is many things: a Mediterranean metropolis, a major port, a centre for modern art, and a city that lives life to the full, with cultural and nocturnal attractions which tempt millions of visitors here every year.

Location

The capital of Catalunya and one of the leading ports in the Mediterranean, Barcelona stretches along the Mediterranean shore between the hills of Montjuïc, Vallvidrera and Tibidabo. It is the hub of an important road network: the AP7 motorway runs along the Mediterranean coast from Murcia to the French border, passing through Girona; the C32 heads to the resorts north of the city and south to Tarragona; while the C 16 veers inland towards Manresa (59km/37mi NE) and the C 17 runs to Vic. El Prat airport is located 18km/11mi south of the city centre. 🅘 *Paseo de Gracia 107 (Palau Robert), 08008 Barcelona, ☎ 93 238 80 91; Plaza de Catalunya 17, 08002 Barcelona, ☎ 807 11 72 22; Sants Estació, 08014 Barcelona; ☎ 807 11 72 22. www.gencat.es/probert/indexfo. htm and www.barcelonaturisme.com.*

🖑 *Neighbouring sights are described in the following chapters: SITGES (45km/28mi SW), GIRONA/GERONA (97km/60mi NE), COSTA BRAVA (NE), VIC (66km/41mi N), TARRAGONA (109km/68mi SW) and COSTA DORADA (SW).*

A Bit of History

The growth of the city – The city was founded by the Phocaeans. It grew in the Roman era and was known as **Barcino** in the 1C BC. The Romans settled on Mount Taber (the site of the present cathedral) and a fortified wall was built in the 3C. In the 12C, Barcelona took control of most of the former Catalan earldoms and became the capital of Catalunya and the seat of the joint kingdom of Aragón-Catalunya as well as a very important market centre. It conquered considerable territories in the Mediterranean. At the same time, the Catalan Gothic style of architecture blossomed, many new buildings were erected and the city spread beyond its walls.

During the War of the Spanish Succession (1701-14), Catalunya took sides with Charles, Archduke of Austria. After the victory of the Bourbons (on 11 September 1714) Barcelona lost its municipal government and its historical independence. Montjuïc hill was then fortified, a citadel, Ciutadella, was built and the district of Barceloneta was developed. The townspeople were not allowed to build beyond the walls within a radius of 2km/1.2mi, a distance corresponding to the range of cannon fire. The town then grew upwards inside the fortifications, with an extraordinarily high population density. The ban on building was not lifted until the middle of the 19C when a decision was taken to urbanise all the no-man's land around the old city. To this end the Cerdà plan was chosen. Over a period of 30 years, Barcelona grew quickly and substantially, rapidly incorporating small neighbouring villages such as Gràcia, Sants, Horta, Sarrià and Pedralbes. Industrialisation made Barcelona one of the most active towns in Europe and two International Exhibitions were held here, one in 1888 (on the site of the Ciutadella) and the other in 1929 on Montjuïc hill. There was an explosion of Modernist architecture during this period.

Barcelona present and future – More dynamic than ever, Barcelona is not only a large industrial centre with a very busy port, it is also a university town and the seat of the Generalitat de Catalunya. It is an important cultural centre with an opera house and many museums, theatres and concert halls.

The Olympic Games, held in Barcelona in 1992, brought about the development of large-scale planning projects which have had an enormous impact on the city's appearance. Likewise, the Forum of Cultures in 2004 led to the redevelopment of the Sant Adrià del Besòs waterfront district.

Practical Information

GETTING THERE

Airport – ☎ 93 298 38 38 or 93 298 40 00. 18km/11mi from the city centre. Can be reached by local train *(tren de cercanía)* every 15min from 6am to 10pm, or by the bus service from the plaça de Catalunya and plaça de Espanya, departing every 15min from 5.30am to 11pm. By taxi, the fare from the city centre will be approximately 20€.

Taxis – The city's black and yellow taxis are an efficient, inexpensive way of getting around the city. Radio Taxi Barcelona: ☎ 93 303 30 33; Tele-Taxi: ☎ 93 466 56 56.

Metro – *Metro stations (⊙) are shown on the maps in this guide.* For further information: ☎ 93 318 70 74 or visit www. tmb.net Information on access for the disabled can be obtained on ☎ 93 412 44 44.

The network is open 5am-11pm Mon-Thu; 5am-1am Fri, Sat and days preceding public holidays; 6am-midnight Sun; and 6am-11pm on weekday public holidays. A free metro guide is available.

Metro tickets and cards can also be used on buses, the "Tramvía Blau" (a tourist tram in the Diagonal section of the city) and train services operated by Ferrocarriles de la Generalitat de Catalunya. In addition to single tickets, multi-journey cards (abonos) are also available. These include the T-1 (valid for 10 trips), T-DIA (unlimited travel for one day), T50-30 (for 50 trips in 30 days) and the T-MES (unlimited travel for one month).

Streetcars – There are three lines (T1, T2 and T3).

Regional railway network – *"Ferrocarriles Catalanes" train stations are shown on the maps in this guide.* For further information, call ☎ 93 205 15 15. Free connections to the metro system may be made at these stations: Avenida Carrilet /L'Hospitalet, Espanya, Catalunya and Diagonal/Provença.

Bus Turístic – This excellent service offers visitors a variety of bus itineraries throughout the city. Daily departures from plaça de Catalunya starting at 9am.

Boat trips – The Las Golondrinas company organises trips around the port *(approx 35min)* as well as excursions by catamaran *(1hr 30min)*. Departures from Portal de la Pau, opposite the Columbus monument. ☎ 93 442 31 06.

SIGHTSEEING

Publications – *The Guía del Ocio* is a weekly guide on sale at newspaper stands containing a list of every cultural event in the city. The city's airport and tourist offices are also able to provide visitors with a full range of booklets and leaflets produced by the Generalitat de Catalunya's Department of Industry, Commerce and Tourism.

Combined tickets and discounts – Three tickets offering discounts are available to tourists:

♦ **Barcelona Card** (1, 2 or 3 days): unlimited transport, discounts ranging from 30 to 50% in 30 museums, and other reductions for shows and in shops and restaurants. On sale at the city's tourist offices *(plaça de Catalunya and plaça de Sant Jaume)*. For further information: ☎ 807 11 72 22 or visit www. barcelonaturisme.com

♦ **Articket**: 50% savings on entry to the MNAC, Fundació Joan Miró, Fundació Antoni Tàpies, the CCCB, Centre de Cultura de la Caixa and the MACBA. ☎ 902 101 212.

♦ **Multiticket de la Ruta del Modernismo**: 🕯 see Special Features, "El Ensanche and Modernist Architecture".

DISTRICTS

Barri Gòtic – Following an intense restoration programme undertaken during the 1920s, the area containing the city's major historical buildings was renamed the Gothic quarter.

Ciutat Vella – The old city includes districts as diverse as Santa Anna, La Mercè, Sant Pere and El Raval. The latter, which used to be known as the Barri Xino (Chinatown), now contains Barcelona's leading cultural centres and is a fine example of urban renovation.

Eixample – Eixample (Ensanche) developed following the destruction of the city's medieval walls. The district personifies the bourgeois, elegant Barcelona of the end of the 19C, with its prestigious boutiques, smart avenues and some of the best examples of Modernist architecture.

Gràcia – This *barrio*, situated at the end of the Passeig de Gràcia, is one of the city's most characteristic areas. Gràcia developed from its early agricultural

La Boquería market

R. Mattes/MICHELIN

origins into an urban area as a result of the influx of shopkeepers, artisans and factory workers. During the 19C, Gràcia was renowned for its Republican sympathies. Today, it still hosts a number of popular fiestas.

Ribera – With its narrow alleyways and Gothic architecture, this former fishermen's quarter still retains an unquestionable charm. Its main attractions are the Calle Montcada and the Iglesia de Santa María del Mar.

Barceloneta – Barceloneta is famous for its outdoor stalls, restaurants and nautical atmosphere.

Vila Olímpica – The Olympic Village was built to accommodate sportsmen and sportswomen participating in the 1992 games. Nowadays, it is a modern district with wide avenues, landscaped areas and direct access to some of Barcelona's restored beaches.

Les Corts – This district is located at the upper end of Diagonal and includes the **Ciudad Universitaria** and the **Camp Nou**, the home of Barcelona Football Club and its football-orientated **Museo del Barça**.

Sarrià – Sarrià nestles at the foot of the Sierra de Collserola and has managed to retain its traditional, tranquil character. The neighbouring districts of **Pedralbes** and **Sant Gervasi de Cassoles**, at the foot of Tibidabo, have become a favourite hangout for the city's well-heeled inhabitants.

Sants – One of the city's main working class districts close to the railway station of the same name.

Horta-Guinardó – This barrio at the foot of Collserola was first populated by peasants and then by factory workers. It is home to the **Laberinto de Horta** (to the north), an 18C property with attractive gardens, and the **Velódromo**, a venue for sporting events and major music events.

For coin ranges, see the Legend at the back of the guide.

WHERE TO EAT

☺ Ca l'Estevet

Valldonzella 46 (Ciutat Vella) – ⓜ Universitat – ☎ 93 302 41 86 – Closed Sun and public hols - 🖩. A small, family-run restaurant with a friendly atmosphere, decorated with attractive azulejos and photographs of famous people.

☺☺ La Provença

Provença 242 (Eixample) – ⓜ Provença – ☎ 93 323 23 67 – 🖩. In the Eixample district, just a stone's throw from the Passeig de Gràcia, pleasant and with cheerful, tasteful, decor, serving a range of regional cuisine. Good for the price.

☺☺ Agua

Passeig Marítim Barceloneta 30 (Vila Olimpica) – ⓜ Barceloneta – ☎ 93 225 12 72 – 🖩. A spacious restaurant with designer furniture and African sculpture. Its terrace, always crowded in summer, is the perfect spot for a quiet dinner by the sea. Mediterranean cuisine and rice dishes prepared in a charcoal oven.

☺☺ Agut

Gignàs 16 (Ciutat Vella) – ⓜ Jaume I – ☎ 93 315 17 09 – Closed Sun eve, Mon and Aug – Reservations advisable. A good location in an area of alleyways, close to the Moll de la Fusta. Agut has been serving traditional Catalan cuisine for over 75 years. The environment is subtly lit, intimate and bohemian, the walls covered with paintings.

☺☺ El Tragaluz

Passatge de la Concepció 5 (Eixample) – ⓜ Diagonal – ☎ 93 487 06 21 – Closed 1 Jan, Sat, and Aug. This elegant restaurant is decorated like a greenhouse, with a moveable glass roof, unique in the city centre. It has a tapas bar, and dining room serving Mediterranean fare with avante garde touches.

☺☺ 7 Portes

Passeig d'Isabel II 14 (Ciutat Vella) – ⓜ Jaume I – ☎ 93 319 30 33 – 🖩. This late-hours restaurant in the emblematic Porxos d'en Xifre building dates from 1836, and preserves period decor. The fare is traditionally Catalan.

☺☺ Los Caracoles

Escudellers 14 (Ciutat Vella) – ⓜ Liceu – ☎ 93 302 31 85 – 🖩. Founded in 1835, this famous restaurant, one of the gastronomic emblems of Barcelona, is located on the corner of calles Escudellers and Nou de Sant Franc. The decor here consists of tiled floors, wine barrels, murals and photos. Regional and traditional cuisine.

EXPENSIVE

☺☺☺ Casa Calvet

Casp, 48 (Eixample) – ⓜ Urquinaona – ☎ 93 412 40 12 – Closed Sun, public hols and Holy Week – 🖩. This restaurant is housed inside the former offices of a textile company, in a magnificent Modernist building designed by Gaudí. The decor is dominated by iron beams and wood floors, while the traditional Mediterranean dishes show creative touches.

☺☺☺ Casa Leopoldo

Sant Rafel 24 (Ciutat Vella) – ⓜ Liceu – ☎ 93 441 30 14 – Closed Mon, evenings of public hols, Holy Week, and August. This classic Barcelona restaurant is decorated with bullfighting mementoes, signed photos of famous customers and a superb bottle collection.

TAPAS

Irati

Cardenal Casanyes 17 (Barri Gòtic) – ⓜ Liceu – ☎ 93 302 30 84 – 🖩. Near the plaza de la Boqueria, in one of the busiest districts, a typical tapas bar with a counter full of Basque skewers along with a grill room with a limited menu.

El Xampanyet

Montcada 22 (Ribera) – 🚇 *Jaume I –* ☏ *93 319 70 03 – Closed Sun evening, Mon, evenings of public hols, in Aug and during Holy Week –* €6. Famous for its anchovies and the sparkling wine of its name.

Euskal Etxea

Placeta Montcada 1-3 (Ribera) – 🚇 *Liceu –* ☏ *93 310 21 85 – Closed Sun and 15-30 Aug –* 🍴. By the church of Santa María del Mar, the perfect setting for a glass of txacolí (a Basque white wine) and some appetising Basque specialties.

WHERE TO STAY

😴 Hotel España

Sant Pau, 9 and 11 (Ciutat Vella) – 🚇 *Liceu –* ☏ *93 318 17 58 -* 🍴 ♿ *– 75 rooms* 🛏. *- Restaurant 18/27€.* The España dates from the end of the 19C and is one of the oldest hotels in the city. It is housed in an exuberant building famous for the two dining rooms designed by the Modernist architect Domènech i Montaner. Though frayed, a good central option.

😴 Hostal d'Uxelles

Gran Vía de les Corts Catalanes, 688 and 667 (at the plaza de Tetuan) - 🚇 *Tetuan -* ☏ *93 265 25 60 - www.hotelduxelles.com - 21 rooms -* 🛏 *7€.* Rooms in this inn, in two buildings, are a delightful combination of comfort, antiques, and attention to details. Most have a private terrace, all have traditional Andalusian-style baths.

😴 Hotel Medicis

Castillejos 340 (Eixample) – 🚇 *Hospital Sant Pau –* ☏ *93 450 00 53 –* 🍴 *– 30 rooms –* 🛏 *6€.* This modern hotel, opposite the Hospital de Sant Pau, near the Sagrada Familia, has functional but comfortable rooms, a good value for those who prefer to stay outside the Gothic Quarter.

😴 Hotel Granvía

Gran Vía de les Corts Catalanes 642 (Eixample) – 🚇 *Catalunya –* ☏ *93 318 19 00 -* 🍴 *– 55 rooms –* 🛏 *10€.* This impressive residence dating from the last third of the 19C was home to a wealthy banker. Converted into a hotel in 1936, it has managed to retained its seigniorial air. The room rates here are very reasonable given the charming setting.

😴 Hotel Gaudí

Nou de la Rambla 12 (Ciutat Vella) – 🚇 *Liceu –* ☏ *93 317 90 32 –* 🍴 *– 73 rooms –* 🛏. Its location opposite the Palacio Güell and the Modernist decor in the reception area evoke the artist of the hotel's name. Try for a rooms with balcony on an upper floors for superb views of the city and the Palacio Güell.

😴 Hotel Hesperia Metropol

Ample 31 (Ribera) – 🚇 *Jaume I –* ☏ *93 310 51 00 –* 🍴 *– 68 rooms –* 🛏 *9€.* This pleasant hotel close to the waterfront is situated in a narrow street in the old quarter, between the Post Office and the Basílica de La Mercè. An attractive feature

Hotel Arts and Torre Mapfre

J. Malburet/MICHELIN

here is the lobby in a covered patio. The guest rooms are comfortable, with the usual creature comforts.

😴 Hotel Arts

Moll Marina 19 (Vila Olímpica) – 🚇 *Ciutadella –* ☏ *93 221 10 00 –* 🍴 ♿ *– 397 rooms –* 🛏 *25€. – Restaurant 60/75€.* Barcelona's most luxurious hotel, with an emphasis on modern art and design. Located in the heart of the Vila Olímpica, with every room enjoying impressive views of the city and Mediterranean.

TAKING A BREAK

Café de la Opera

Rambla dels Caputxins 74 (Ciutat Vella) – 🚇 *Drassanes –* ☏ *933 02 41 80 – Open 9am-10pm.* Because of its history, Modernist façade and 19C atmosphere, this café is one of the most famous in the city. Not to be missed!

Quatre Gats

Montsió 3 bis (Ciutat Vella) – ☏ *933 17 40 33 – Open Mon-Sat, 5pm-2am.* The symbol of Modernist and bohemian Barcelona. This landmark café was a meeting-place for famous artists such as Picasso, Casas and Utrillo. Reasonable lunchtime menu.

BARS AND CAFÉS

La Fira

Provença 171 (Eixample) – ☏ *933 23 72 71 – Open Mon-Thu, 10.30pm-3am; Fri-Sat, 10.30pm-4.30am.* An attractive bar decorated with robots and fairground amusements.

Jamboree

Plaça Reial 17 (Ciutat Vella) – 🚇 *Liceu –* ☏ *933 01 75 64 – Open 10.30pm-5.30am.* The meeting point in Barcelona for jazz musicians and aficionados.

Karma

Plaça Reial 10 (Ciutat Vella) – 🚇 *Liceu –* ☏ *933 02 56 80 – Open Thu-Sun, midnight-5am.* The playlist here is dominated by rock and music from the 1980s. A popular venue for foreigners of all nationalities.

La Paloma

Tigre 27 (Sant Antoni) – 🚇 *Universitat –* ☏ *933 01 68 97 – Open Thu-Sat, 6-9.30am and 11.30am-5pm; Sun, 6-9.30am.* One of the liveliest and most packed of all the city's clubs.

Café de l'Opera

Ch. Sarramon/ MARCO POLO

London Bar

Nou de la Rambla 34 (Ciutat Vella) – Liceu – ☏ 933 18 52 81 – Open Tue-Thu and Sun, 7pm-4am; Fri-Sat, 7pm-5am. A favourite with circus performers when it first opened in 1909. Hemingway, Miró and others also came here to enjoy its lively atmosphere.

Margarita Blue

Josep Anselm Clavé 6 (Ciutat Vella) – Drassanes – ☏ 934 12 54 89 – Open Mon-Wed, 11am-2pm; Thu-Fri, 7am-2pm; Sat, 7am-3am. Margarita Blue's unusual style of decoration (mirrors of all shapes and sizes, weird and wonderful objects and antique lamps) has helped cement its reputation as one of the most popular bars in the city, hosting weekly shows and concerts. If you fancy a bite to eat, the cuisine here is Tex-Mex.

Marsella

*Sant Pau 65 (Ciutat Vella) – Liceu – ☏ 934 42 72 63 – Open Mon-Thu, 10am-2am; Fri-Sat, 10am-3am.*19C mirrors and marble tables decorate this bar, which opened its doors in 1820.

Nick Havanna

Rosselló 208 (Eixample) – Diagonal – ☏ 932 15 65 91 – www.nickhavanna.com – Open Mon-Wed, 11am-4.30am; Fri-Sat, 11.30am-5.30am. A bar famous for its modern design.

Torres de Ávila

Avenida del Marquès de Comillas 25 (Sants – Montjuïc) – Espanya – ☏ 934 24 93 09 – Open Fri-Sat, 12.30pm-7am. This popular venue, refurbished by the designers Mariscal and Arribas, attracts large crowds in summer.

Xiringuito Escribà

Platja del Bogatell (Vila Olímpica-Poble Nou) – Ciutadella-Vila Olímpica – ☏ 932 21 07 29 – Open Tue-Thu, 11am-5pm; Fri-Sun, 9am-11pm. This beachside restaurant is hugely popular during the summer months.

ENTERTAINMENT

The **Palau de la Música Catalana** (see p 148), **Gran Teatre del Liceu** (see p 151) and the recently opened **Auditorio** are the city's biggest concert halls.

Major pop and rock concerts are held in the **Palau Sant Jordi** (see p 163), **Velódromo de Horta, Plaza de Toros Monumental** and **Sot del Migdia**.

The **Festival del Grec** (end of June to early August) is held at several venues, including the **Teatre Grec de Montjuïc**.

SHOPPING

ANTIQUES

Plaza de la Catedra – *(Ciutat Vella)*

A small market with stalls selling an eclectic range of antiques is held here on public holidays.

Plaza Sant Josep Oriol – *(Ciutat Vella)*

Mirrors, furniture, paintings and household goods are all on sale at this popular Saturday and Sunday market.

Calle de la Palla and calle Banys Nous – *(Ciutat Vella)*

These two streets are well-known for their reputable antique shops.

Bulevard Antiquaris – *Passeig de Gràcia 55 (Eixample)*

An area containing over 70 shops selling a range of artwork and antiques.

ART GALLERIES

Barcelona's most prestigious galleries can mainly be found in the calle Consell de Cent **(Carles Tatché, René Metras, Sala Gaudí)**, along the Rambla de Catalunya **(Joan Prats)**, on the periphery of the Born market and around the MACBA. The **Galeria Maeght** and the **Sala Montcada** are both located in the calle Montcada.

Catalan identity – Barcelona is above all a Catalan town. This is evident in the use of Catalan which is considered the official language along with Castilian Spanish. The Catalan people are proud to speak their own language which was banned for many years under the Franco regime. A simple stroll around the city will reveal that all the street names and signs are in Catalan. The same goes for the literature, as a glance at a bookshop window will show.

A thriving centre for artists – Barcelona has been and still remains a thriving city and place of residence for great artists. Among the best-known modern artists are the painters Picasso, Miró, Dalí, Tàpies, the sculptor Subirachs and the architects Gaudí, Josep Lluís Sert, Bofill and Bohigas.

Visit

El Ensanche and Modernist Architecture★★
See general plan

The word *Eixample* (in Catalan) or *Ensan-che* (in Castilian) means enlargement. Barcelona's Eixample district was added to the city as a result of the Cerdà Plan in the 19C.

The plan adopted by Ildefonso Cerdà in 1859 consisted of a grid pattern of streets, some parallel to the sea, others perpendicular to it. The streets circumscribe blocks of houses (called *mançanes*

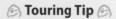

> ### 😄 Touring Tip 😄
>
> The Multiticket de la Ruta del Modernismo offers half-price entry to nine of the main Modernist sights in Barcelona (Palau Güell, Palau de la Música, La Pedrera, Sagrada Familia etc). *For further information, contact the Casa Amatller, ☎ 93 488 01 39.*

in Catalan or *manzanas* in Castilian, also meaning apples) which are octagonal in shape because the right-angled corners have been trimmed off. This plan is crossed by two wide diagonal avenues, avinguda Diagonal and La Meridiana, which meet on plaça de les Glòries Catalanes.

It was in this rational and ordered new section of the city that architects built the majority of their buildings, transforming El Ensanche into the centre of the Modernist movement in Barcelona.

La Sagrada Familia★★★(Church of the Holy Family)
🕐 *Open Jan-Feb, 9am-6pm (8pm Apr-Sep).* 🕐 *Closed 1, 6 Jan and 25 Dec.* ☞ *8€.* ☎ *93 207 30 31.*

The project, begun by Francisco de P Villar in 1882, was taken over by Gaudí in 1883. He planned a church shaped like a Latin Cross with five aisles and a transept with three aisles. On the outside, three façades were each to be dominated by four tall spires representing the Twelve Apostles and, above the transept crossing, a central spire flanked by four other spires were to represent Christ and the Evangelists. The nave was planned to look like a forest of columns. In his lifetime, only the crypt, the apsidal walls, one of the towers and the **Nativity façade**★★ were finished. The Nativity façade comprises three doorways, Faith, Hope and Charity, richly decorated with statues and groups of carved figures. After Gaudí's death, work resumed in 1940 and today there are eight spires together with the Passion façade which was completed in 1981.

Gaudí (1852-1926)

Antoni Gaudí, born in Reus, studied architecture in Barcelona. His style was influenced first by Catalan Gothic architecture with its emphasis on large areas of space (wide naves, the effect of airy spaciousness) and subsequently by the Islamic and Mudejar styles. He also studied nature, observing plants and animals which inspired his shapes, colours and textures. He gave full rein to these images – liana-like curves, the rising and breaking of waves, rugged rocks and the serrations on leaves and flowers – when designing his fabulous buildings. Part of his great originality lay in his use of parabolic arches and spirals (as can be seen in the chimneys of Casa Milà). An intensely religious man, Gaudí drew upon a great many religious symbols for his buildings, especially for the Sagrada Familia (Church of the Holy Family) on which he worked for over 40 years. He spent his last years here, hidden away in a small room in the middle of the site, until his tragic death when he was run over by a tram.

Gaudí worked a great deal for the banker **Eusebi Güell**, his patron and admirer, who asked him to design his private houses.

Gaudí's main works are the Sagrada Familia, Casa Batlló, La Pedrera, Casa Vicens, Palau Güell, Pavellons Güell and the Parc Güell.

Detail on the towers of the Sagrada Familia

From the top of the east spire there is a good overall **view**★★ of the work on the church, as well as of Barcelona beyond. One of Domènech i Montaner's main works, **Hospital Sant Pau**★, with its remarkable glazed tile roofs, may be seen at the end of avinguda de Gaudí.

Passeig de Gràcia★★

This boulevard of luxury, adorned with elegant wrought-iron **street lamps**★ by Pere Falqués (1900), contains the finest examples of Modernist architecture in Barcelona. The styles of the three most famous Modernist architects can be compared in the block of houses known as the **Manzana de la Discordia**★★ (Street of Discord): n°35 **Casa Lleó Morera**★ (1905) by Domènech i Montaner, n°41 **Casa Amatller**★ (1900) by Puig i Cadafalch, which houses the Instituto Amatller and the Centro del Modernismo (which arranges exhibitions and tours of the main Modernist buildings of Barcelona), and n°43 **Casa Batlló**★★ (1904-06) by Gaudí, as surprising on the outside, with its extraordinary mosaic façade with unusual openings and its undulating roof covered in scales, as inside, with its extraordinary beauty and esthetic coherence.

Fundaciò Arqueológica Clos: Museu Egipci de Barcelona

🕐 *Open 10am-8pm; Sun and public hols, 10am-2pm. Evening visits (Fri-Sat, except public hols) by prior arrangement, 9.30-11pm.* 🕐 *Closed 1 Jan and 25-26 Dec.* ⬡ *5.50€; evening visits, 12€.* ☎ *93 488 01 88.*

This interesting and well-presented private museum devoted to Egyptology is noted for its sarcophagi, mummies, funerary masks, collections of statuettes of divinities and of jewels, and a statue of Ramses II.

La Pedrera or Casa Milà★★★

🕐 *Open 10am-8pm; last admission 30min before closing.* 🕐 *Closed 1, 6 Jan, second week of Jan and 25-26 Dec.* ⬡ *7€.* ☎ *902 40 09 73 .*

With its undulating lines, this notable and magnificent building by Gaudí resembles an underwater cliff face. The **roof and attic**★ and a **residential floor**★ may be visited. The **Espai Gaudí** has exhibits of drawings and models by the artist, as well as audio-visual presentations on his work. A visit to the roof terrace, with its forest of chimneys and

Modernist Architecture

Modernism developed between 1890 and 1920 alongside similar movements in other parts of Europe, such as Art Nouveau in both France and Great Britain and Jugendstil in Germany. Modernist architecture sprang from artistic exploration that combined new industrial materials with modern techniques, using decorative motifs like curve and counter-curve and asymmetrical shapes in stained glass, ceramics and metal. It enjoyed great success in Catalunya at a time when large fortunes were being made as a result of industrialisation. The most representative architects of the style were Antoni Gaudí, Domènech i Montaner, Puig i Cadafalch and Jujol. A parallel movement in Catalan literature known as Renaixença also flourished during this period.

ventilation funnels, provides one of the best **views**★ of the city, and an impression of the originality of the building.

El Piso★ is a re-creation of a luxurious apartment on an upper-class family in the early 20C, along with an exhibit on Barcelona in those days, and space for temporary shows.

▶ *Turn right from plaça de Joan Carles I into avinguda Diagonal.*

Diagonal

Casa Quadras (1904), a Modernist building on the right, was designed by Josep Puig i Cadafalch. A little further along on the left, **Casa de les Punxes** or **Casa Terrades**★, by the same architect, bears the stamp of Flemish influence.

Parc Güell★★

Kids ⏱ *Open Nov-Feb, 10am-6pm (7pm Mar and Oct; 8pm Apr and Sep; 9pm May and Aug).* ⊜ *1.20€.* ☎ *93 413 24 00.*

The park is the most famous of Gaudí's undertakings commissioned by Güell. Gaudí's extraordinary imagination is particularly evident here.

Visitors have the impression that they are entering an enchanted forest peopled with mushroom-shaped pavilions, a flight of steps climbed by a mosaic dragon, and avenues leading to an extravagant fantasy world. The artful combination of architecture and nature produces a curious effect, intermingling both rustic and fantastic elements. The **Chamber of the Columns**, in which an undulating mosaic roof covers a forest of sloping columns, and the remarkable **rolling bench**★★ are telling examples of the artist's fertile imagination.

A tour of the Park Güell ends with a visit to the **Casa-Museu Gaudí**★, located in the house where the famous architect once lived. (⏱ *Open 10am-6pm (7pm Mar-Apr and Oct; 8pm May-Sep).* ⏱ *Closed 1 Jan, 6 Jan (afternoon) and 25 and 26 Dec (afternoon).* ⊜ *4€.* ☎ *93 219 38 11).*

Dragon, Parc Güell

J. Malburet/MICHELIN

Palau de la Música Catalana★★

In Carrer de Sant Pere Mès Alt. ☜ *Guided tours (1hr), 10am-3.30pm; 10am-5pm Aug and Holy Week. Visits in English, Catalan and Spanish.* ⏱ *Closed 1 Jan and 25 Dec.* ⊜ *8€. Advance sales* ☎ *93 295 72 00.*

This unusual concert hall, the seat of the Orfeó Català, is Domènech i Montaner's most famous work. It was built between 1905 and 1908. Its surroundings have recently been redeveloped, providing visitors with a better perspective of the spectacular **exterior**★, with its lavish mosaic decoration. The interior, dominated by the large **inverted cupola**★★ of polychrome glass, is profusely and artistically decorated with sculpted groups and mosaic figurines. Today the Palau de la Música Catalana is Barcelona's most important concert hall. Visitors who attend a concert in this strange venue find it to be a memorable experience indeed.

Fundació Antoni Tàpies★★

🕐 *Open 10am-8pm.* 🕐 *Closed Mon, 1 and 6 Jan and 25-26 Dec.* ∞ *4.20€.* ☎ *93 487 03 15.*

The foundation was created by the artist himself – who was born in Barcelona in 1923 – and set up in a former publishing house in the Modernist Montaner i Simó building designed by Domènech i Montaner. The brick building is crowned by a large aerial sculpture by Tàpies called Núvol i Cadira (cloud and chair), the emblem of the museum. It is a fitting example of the artist's symbolic universe.

The interior, a vast bare sober space where everything is painted in colours favoured by Tàpies (brown, beige, grey and ochre), is lit by skylights (a cupola and a pyramid) and sets off the artist's work remarkably well. The collection of over 300 paintings and sculptures tracing the development of Tàpies' work since 1948 is displayed on a rota basis. The foundation is also a research centre and the wooden bookshelves that once belonged to the publishing house have been kept for a library.

Walking About

BARRI GÒTIC★★ (THE GOTHIC QUARTER)

🔎 *See plan of old city.*

The Gothic quarter, so named on account of its many buildings constructed between the 13C and 15C, is, in fact, far older. There are traces of the Roman settlement as well as of the massive 4C walls built after barbarian invasions.

Plaça Nova

This is the heart of the Gothic quarter. The Romans built a rectangular site with walls 9m/30ft high and attendant watchtowers of which the two that guarded the West Gate remain to this day. In the Middle Ages, when the town expanded beyond the walls, the gateway was converted into a house.

Opposite the cathedral, the **Collegi d'Arquitectes** (College of Architects) stands out as an architectural surprise among the old buildings. Its modern façade has a decorative band of cement engraved by Picasso.

Catedral★

🕐 *Open 8am-1.15pm and 5-7.30pm; no visits during religious services.* 🕐 *Closed Sat afternoon, Sun and public hols.* ∞ *2€. (terrace and choir).* ☎ *93 315 15 54 or 93 315 22 13.*

The cathedral adjoins **pla de la Seu**, fronted on one side by the **Casa de l'Ardiaca**★ (12C-15C), and on the other by the **Casa de la Canonja** (16C) and **pia Almoina**, the latter housing the **Museo Diocesano de Barcelona** (🕐 *Open 10am-2pm and 5-8pm; Sun, 11am-2pm.* 🕐 *Closed Mon.* ∞ *3€.* ☎ *93 315 22 13).*

The present edifice, dedicated to St Eulàlia and the Holy Cross, was built on the former site of a Romanesque church. Construction began in the late 13C, ending only in 1450. The front façade and the spire are modern (19C) additions based on original designs by a builder from Rouen in France (hence the French influence in the gables, pinnacles and crockets).

The Catalan Gothic **interior**★ has an outstanding elevation due partly to the delicate, slender pillars. The nave is clearly lit by a fine lantern-tower above the first bay but the perspective is unfortunately broken by the **coro**★★. This features double rows of beautifully carved **stalls**. Note the fine workmanship and the humorous scenes adorning the misericords. In the early 16C, the backs of these were painted with the coats of arms of the knights belonging to the Order of the Golden Fleece during one of their many gatherings, presided over by Charles V. The artist was Juan de Borgoña, who signed here one of the most impressive achievements in the history of European heraldry.

The side chapels contain exquisite retables and marble tombs. The white marble **choir screen**★ was sculpted in the 16C after drawings by Bartolomé Ordóñez, one of Spain's greatest Renaissance artists, who may have also worked on the stalls. The statues illustrate the death of St Eulàlia, a 4C virgin and martyr born in Barcelona who became the patron of the town. Her relics lie in the **crypt**★ in a 14C alabaster sarcophagus carved in the style of Pisa.

The Capilla del Santísimo, to the right as you enter the main door, contains the 15C *Christ of Lepanto,* which is thought to have been mounted on the prow of the galley belonging to Don Juan of Austria during the Battle of Lepanto (1571). The next chapel holds a Gothic retable by Bernat Martorell, also the artist of the **retable of the Transfiguration**★ in an ambulatory chapel.

Cathedral roof visit – Ascent by elevator from an ambulatory chapel. Metal walkways under the imposing silhouettes of the cathedral towers and cupola, allow exceptional **views**★★ of the city.

Claustro★

The cloisters, dating from 1448, open onto huge bays built according to Gothic tradition. They form a restful oasis of greenery with their palms and magnolias, and are home to a flock of geese. The chapter house off the west gallery houses a museum where you can admire a Pietà by Bermejo (1490), altarpiece panels by the 15C artist Jaime Huguet and the missal of St Eulàlia, enhanced by delicate miniatures. (◷*Open 10am-1pm and 4-6.30pm; Sat, 10am-1pm.* ☞ *1€.* ☎ *93 315 15 54.*

▸ *Upon leaving the cloisters, return to pla de la Seu and head along carrer dels Comtes.*

Museu Frederic Marès★

This museum is housed in the Palau Reial Major. The entrance is located on the tiny **plaça de Sant Iu**, one of the liveliest sections of the city and always full of mime artists and street musicians *(☝ see description under Worth a Visit).*

Palau del Lloctinent

This 16C late-Gothic palace with Renaissance additions used to be the residence of the viceroys of Catalunya.

Plaça del Rei★★

On this splendid square stand some of the important medieval buildings of the city: the Palau Reial Major (at the back), the Capilla de Santa Àgata (on the right) and the Palau del Lloctinent. In the right-hand corner is the Casa Clariana-Padellàs, which houses the **Museu d'Història de la Ciutat**★★ *(☝ see description under Worth a Visit),* housed in a fine 15C Gothic mansion that was moved here stone by stone while the via Laietana was being built in 1931.

Palau Reial Major

Initially built in the 11C and 12C, the palace was gradually enlarged over the years until it acquired its present appearance in the 14C. It used to be the official residence of the counts of Barcelona and subsequently that of the kings of Aragón. The façade features huge buttresses linked together by arches. At the back of these arches lies the original Romanesque façade with its trilobate windows and Gothic rose windows.

Plaça Ramón Berenguer el Gran

From the plaza, Roman walls are visible, incorporated into the Palau Reial.

Carrer Paradis

At no. 10 stand four Roman **columns**★, remains of the Temple of Augustus. Carrer Paradis leads into carrer de la Pietat which is bordered on the left by the Gothic façade of the Casa dels Canonges. The cathedral cloister doorway opposite is adorned with a wooden 16C sculpture of a *Pietà*.

Ajuntament (Town Hall)

The town hall façade on plaça Sant Jaume is neo-Classical, while that on carrer de la Ciutat is an outstanding 14C Gothic construction.

Palau de la Generalitat (Provincial Council)

This vast 15C-17C edifice is the seat of the Autonomous Government of Catalunya. It has a Renaissance-style façade on plaça Sant Jaume (c 1600). (◷ *Open on the 2nd and 4th Sat and Sun of each month, 10.30am-1.30pm; visits on other Sat and Sun by prior arrangement.* ☎ *93 402 46 16).*

Carrer del Bisbe

The left of the street is bordered by the side wall of the Palau de la Generalitat (Provincial Council). Above a doorway is a fine early-15C medallion of St George by Pere Johan.

The right of the street is bordered by the **Casa dels Canonges** (Canons' Residence), now the residence of the President of the Generalitat. A neo-Gothic covered gallery (1929), over a star-vaulted arch, spans the street to link the two buildings.

Plaça Sant Felip Neri

The Renaissance houses surrounding this small square were moved here when via Laietana was being built, to make room for the new street. The square is home to the unusual **Museu del Calçat**, a shoe museum whose exhibits include Columbus' shoes. (🕐 *Open 11am-2pm.* 🕐 *Closed Mon.* ⊛ *2€.* ☎ *93 301 45 33.*

▶ *Return to carrer del Bisbe along carrer Sant Sever.*

LA RAMBLA★★

The most famous street in Barcelona, La Rambla, made up of five different sections, follows the course of an old riverbed bordering on the Gothic quarter. La Rambla forms a long exuberant promenade between plaça de Catalunya, separating the Eixample district from the old quarter, and plaça Portal de la Pau, where the Columbus Memorial stands. At all times of the day and night a colourful crowd of locals, tourists and down and outs moves along the street beneath the plane trees, passing the bird- and flower-sellers and the news-stands that sell papers and magazines in every language.

The upper section of La Rambla, level with plaça de Catalunya, is called Rambla de Canaletes, and the following stretch Rambla dels Estudis or Rambla dels Ocells (Avenue of the Birds).

Iglesia de Betlem

This church built in Baroque style – the interior was razed by a fire in 1936 – has retained its imposing façade, which gives onto carrer Carme.

▶ *Follow carrer Carme.*

Antic Hospital de la Santa Creu

This complex of Gothic, Baroque and neo-Classical buildings is a veritable haven of peace in the middle of a very lively district. One old hospital building now houses the Library of Catalunya. A charming planted **Gothic patio**★ (Jardines de Rubio y Lluch) can be reached through a hall decorated with azulejos.

▶ *Return to La Rambla, at the Iglesia de Betlem.*

Palau de la Virreina★

This elegant palace dating back to 1778, originally built for the Vicereine of Peru, is charmingly decorated with both Baroque and Rococo elements. It hosts major temporary exhibitions. Alongside is the traditional Mercat (market) de Sant Josep o La Boqueria.

Further down La Rambla on the right-hand side stands the city's opera house, the **Gran Teatre del Liceu**, which has been completely rebuilt following a catastrophic fire in 1994. Opposite the Liceu lies **pla de la Boqueria**, a charming little esplanade whose pavement was decorated by the artist Joan Miró.

▶ *Turn left onto carrer del Cardenal Casañas.*

Iglesia de Santa Maria del Pi★

This 14C Catalan Gothic church on the square of the same name is striking for its simplicity and the size of its single nave.

▶ *Return to La Rambla.*

Plaça Reial★★

This vast pedestrian-only square shaded by palm trees and lined with cafés is surrounded by neo-Classical buildings constructed between 1848 and 1859. With its shoe-shiners and other small tradespeople it has kept its picturesque air. The fountain in the middle is flanked by lampposts designed by Gaudí. A stamp and coin market is held here on Sunday mornings.

▶ *From La Rambla, turn left onto carrer Nou de la Rambla.*

Palau Güell★★

🕐 *Open 10am-1pm and 4-7pm.* 🕐 *Closed Sun and public hols.* ⊛ *2.40€.* ☎ *93 317 39 74.*

The former residence of the Güell family (1886-1890) is a curious building designed by Gaudí. Note the parabolic arches at the entrance and the extravagant bars so typical of the Modernist movement. The most striking feature of the interior is the **great central hall**. Also important are the innovative use of materials and the treatment of light as a design element of each space.

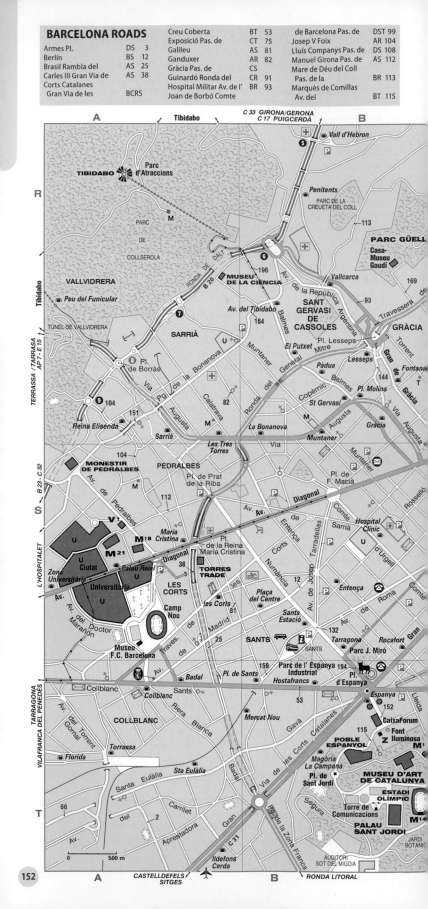

BARCELONA ROADS

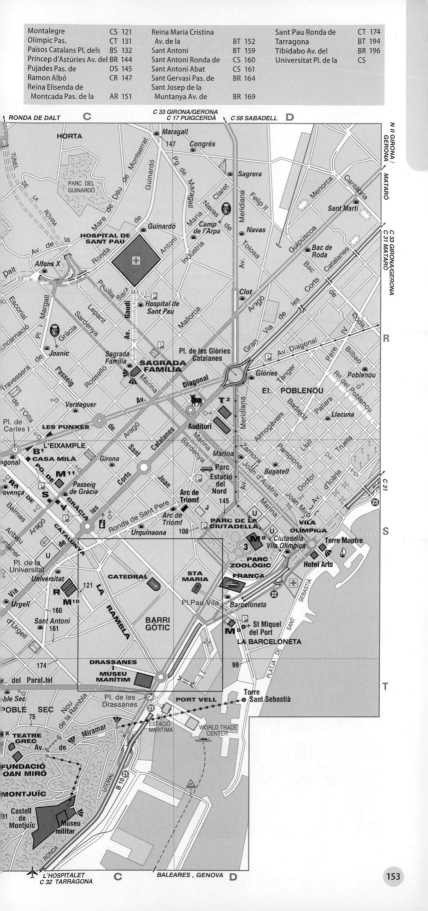

BARCELONA SIGHTS							
Casa Quadras	CS	B¹	Fundació Antoni Tàpies	CS	S	Museu d'Història	
Casas : Amatlier,			Galería olímpica	BT	M¹⁴	de Catalunya	DS	M⁹
Batlió, Bonet,			Museu Egipci			Museu dels Carrosses	AS	M¹⁸
Morera, Mulleras	CS	Y	de Barcelona	CS	M¹¹	Palau de Pedralbes	AS	M²¹
Centre de Cultura			Museu Etnológic	BT	M¹⁵	Pavelló Güell	AS	V¹
Contemporàna de			Museu d'Arqueològia			Pavelló Mies		
Barcelona			de Catalunya	CT	M⁵	van der Rohe	BT	Z
(Centre d'Estudis i			Museu d'Art			Teatre Nacional		
de Recursos Culturals)	CS	R	Contemporàni	CS	M¹⁰	de Catalunya	DR	T²
			Museu d'Art Modern	DS	M⁸			

▶ *Return to La Rambla.*

La Rambla de Santa Mònica marks the point where La Rambla meets up with the sea. Here stand the former **Convento de Santa Mònica**, now a modern art centre that hosts temporary exhibitions, and the **Museu de Cera**, a wax museum. (🕐 *Open 10am-1.30pm and 4-7.30pm; Sat-Sun, 11am-2pm and 4.30-8pm; Jul-Sep, 10am-10pm).*

Columbus Memorial

Erected in 1886, this monument commemorates the welcome that the Catholic Monarchs gave the navigator when he returned from the Americas.

Worth a Visit

BARRI GÒTIC AND LAS RAMBLAS

Museu d'Història de la Ciutat★★

Entrance on calle Veguer. 🕐 *Open 10am-7pm (Wed 8pm); Sun and public hols 10am-2.30pm.* 🕐 *Closed Mon except pub holidays, 1 and 6 Jan, 25-26 Dec.* 🎫 *3€; no charge 23 Apr, 18 May, 11 and 24 Sep.* ☎ *93 225 47 00.*

The visit is divided into two parts: the remains of the old Roman city, lying underground beneath the main square, and the outbuildings attached to the Palau Reial Major, including the Salón Tinell and the Capilla de Santa Àgata.

The Roman city★★★

An interesting stroll underneath the museum and plaça del Rei will allow you to discover the vestiges of the ancient Roman town, with the houses' foundations, canalisations, reservoirs etc. In the adjoining rooms, covered with barrel vaulting, are displayed sculptures dating from the 1C-4C (busts portraying Agrippina, Faustina and Antoninus Pius). Two 13C Gothic frescoes were discovered in the Sala Jaime I in 1998.

La Rambla

R. Camprub/GC (DICT)

Capilla de Santa Àgata★★

This 14C palatine chapel with a single nave is covered by intricate polychrome woodwork panelling. It houses the **Altarpiece of the Constable**★★, executed by Jaime Huguet in 1465, depicting scenes from the life of Jesus and the Virgin Mary. In the centre, the *Adoration of the Three Wise Men* is a masterpiece of pictorial art from Catalunya.

A side staircase leads to the **Mirador del Rei Martí**, a five-storey tower commanding a lovely **view**★★ of the old city, with the cupola of the Basílica de la Mercè looming in the distance.

Salón del Tinell

This lofty 14C room, 17m/56ft high, is covered with a two-sloped ceiling resting on six vast round arches.

According to tradition, it was here that the Catholic Monarchs received Christopher Columbus in 1493 after he returned from his first voyage to America.

Museu d'Art Contemporàni de Barcelona (MACBA)★★

🕐 *Open 11am-7.30pm; 25 Jun-30 Sep, 11am-8pm; Sat, 10am-8pm; Sun and public hols, 10am-3pm.* 🕐 *Closed Tue, 1 Jan and 25 Dec.* ⊛ *7€.* ☎ *93 412 14 13.*

The **standing collections**★ housed in large, pristine white exhibition rooms cover the major artistic movements to have emerged in the past 50 years. Exhibits include works influenced by Constructivism and Abstract art (Klee, Oteiza, Miró, Calder, Fontana), as well as creations by experimental artists (Kiefer, Boltanski, Solano) and names typically associated with the 1980s (Hernández, Pijuán, Barceló, Tàpies, Ràfols Casamada, Sicilia).

Museu d'Art Contemporàni de Barcelona (MACBA)★★

Designed by the American architect Richard Meyer, this museum is a huge **building**★★ that presents characteristics of the rationalist Mediterranean tradition while also introducing modern elements of contemporary architecture. Two significant works can be seen outside: *La Ola* by Jorge Oteiza and Eduardo Chillida's mural, Barcelona *(see description under Worth a Visit).*

Centre de Cultura Contemporània de Barcelona (CCCB)

🕐 *Open 11am-2pm and 4-8pm; Wed and Sat, 11am-8pm; Sun and public hols, 11am-7pm; 23 Jun-8 Sep, Tue-Sun, 11am-8pm; Sun and public hols 11am-3pm.* 🕐 *Closed Mon, 1 Jan and 25 Dec.* ⊛ *4€ (higher with special exhibitions).* ☎ *93 306 41 00.*

This busy arts centre (temporary exhibitions, lectures, courses etc) is set up on newly restored premises whose unusual **patio**★ combines original decorative elements (mosaics or silk-screen floral motifs) with modern characteristics, like the large central pane of glass.

The **standing collections**★ housed in large, pristine white exhibition rooms cover the major artistic movements to have emerged in the past 50 years. Exhibits include works influenced by Constructivism and Abstract art (Klee, Oteiza, Miró, Calder, Fontana), as well as creations by experimental artists (Kiefer, Boltanski, Solano) and names typically associated with the 1980s (Hernández, Pijuán, Barceló, Tàpies, Ràfols Casamada, Sicilia).

Museu Frederic Marès★

🕐 *Open 10am-5pm; Sun and public hols 10am-3pm.* 🕐 *Closed Mon, 1 Jan, Good Fri, 1 May, 24 Jun and 25 Dec.* ⊛ *3€.* ☎ *93 310 58 00.*

The collections displayed in this museum, set up in the Palau Reial Major *(enter through plaça de Sant Lu)*, were bequeathed to the city by the sculptor Frederic Marès (1893-1991). There are two parts to the museum:

Sculpture Section

This part occupies two floors of the palace and the crypt. The works are displayed in chronological order from the Iberian period up to the 19C. Note the imposing **collection of Christs and Calvaries**★ carved in polychrome wood (12C-14C), Romaneque and Gothic **Virgins with Child**★; a 16C **Holy Entombment**★ and **The Vocation of St Peter**★, a highly expressive 12C relief attributed to the master Cabestany.

Gabinete del Coleccionista

This houses an extensive collection of small everyday objects, mainly 19C. Particularly interesting are the various recreational rooms, the smoking parlour and the women's boudoir (spectacles, fans, clothes etc). The artist's studio may also be visited.

BARCELONA

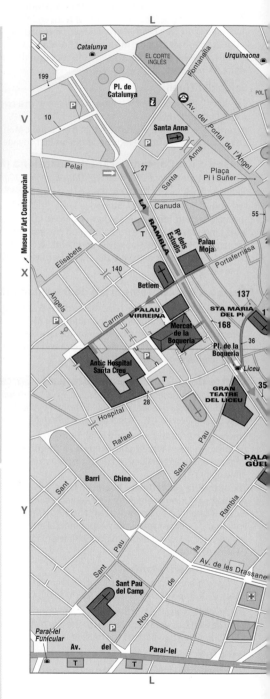

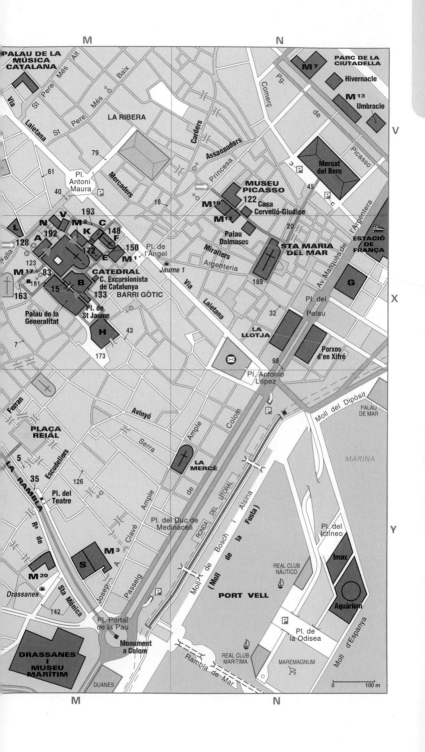

PALAU DE LA MÚSICA CATALANA

PARC DE LA CIUTADELLA

M 7

Hivernacle

M 13

Umbracle

Via Laietana

St Pere Més Alt

St Pere Més Baix

LA RIBERA

Carders

Assaonadors

Princesa

Pg. de Comerç

de Picasso

V

79

61

Pl. Antoni Maura

Mercaders

18

Mercat del Born

P 45

40

193

L N V M 2 C

A 192 K 148

172 E

128

123

M 17 83

181

163 15 B

CATEDRAL

C. Excursionista de Catalunya

BARRI GÒTIC

133

Pl. de St Jaume

Palau de la Generalitat

7

H

173

43

Pl. de l'Àngel

Jaume 1

MUSEU PICASSO

122 Casa Cervelló-Giudice

M 16

M 12

Palau Dalmases

Mirallers

Argenteria

189

STA MARIA DEL MAR

20

Av. Marquès de l'Argentera

ESTACIÓ DE FRANÇA

G

X

Pl. del Palau

32

LA LLOTJA

98

Porxos d'en Xifré

Pl. Antonio López

Moll del Dipòsit

PALAU DE MAR

Ferran

PLAÇA REIAL

Avinyó

Serra

Ample

Colom

MARINA

5

35

Escudellers

Pl. del Teatre

126

Ample

de

LA MERCÈ

RONDA DEL LITORAL

Pl. del Duc de Medinaceli

Moll de Bosch i Alsina

Pl. del Ictineo

Y

LA RAMBLA

Rª de

M 3

Clavé

Moll de la Fusta

REAL CLUB NÀUTICO

Imax

S

Josep

Passeig

PORT VELL

Aquàrium

M 20

Drassanes

Sta Mònica

142

Pl. Portal de la Pau

P

P

Pl. de la Odisea

Moll d'Espanya

DRASSANES I MUSEU MARÍTIM

Monument a Colom

REAL CLUB MARÍTIMA

MAREMAGNUM

DUANES

Rambla de Mar

0   100 m

M

N

BARCELONA — STREET INDEX

BARCELONA — SITES INDEX

La Barceloneta	DS		Museu de Geología	NV	M¹³	Pavelló Güell	AS	V¹
La Llotja	NX		Museu de la Ciència	AR		Pavelló Mies van der Rohe	BT	Z
La Mercè	NY		Museu del Calçat	MX	M¹⁷	Pia Almoina	MX	N
La Ribera	MV		Museu dels Carrosses	AS	M¹⁸	Poble Espanyol	BT	
Mercat de la Boqueria	LX		Museu militar	CT		Poble Sec	CT	
Mercat del Born	NV		Palau Dalmases	NX		Port Vell	DT	
Miràdor del Rei Martí	MX	K	Palau Güell	LY		Porxos d'en Xifré	NX	
Monestir de Pedralbes	AS		Palau Marc	MY	S	Sagrada Familia	CR	
Montjuïc	BCT		Palau Moja	LX		Saló del Tinell	MX	C
Monument a Colom	MY		Palau Sant Jordi	BT		Sant Miquel del Port	DS	
Museu Barbier-Mueller			Palau de Pedralbes	AS	M²¹	Sant Pau del Camp	LY	
d'Art Precolombi	NVXM¹²		Palau de la Generalitat	MX		Santa Anna	LV	
Museu Egipci de Barcelona	CS	M¹¹	Palau de la Música Catalana	MV		Santa María del Mar	NX	
Museu Etnològic	BT	M¹⁵	Palau de la Virreina	LY		Santa María del Pi	LX	
Museu F. C. Barcelona	AS		Palau del Lloctinent	MX	E	Teatre Grec	CT	
Museu Frederic Marès	MX	M²	Palau del Marquès de Llió			Teatre Nacional de Catalunya	DR	T²
Museu Picasso	NV		(Museu Tèxtil i de la			Tibidado	AR	
Museu d'Arqueològia			Indumentària)	NV	M¹⁶	Torre Mapfre	DS	
de Catalunya	CT	M⁵	Parc Estació del Nord	DS		Torre Sant Sebastià	DT	
Museu d'Art Contemporàni	CS	M¹⁰	Parc Güell	BR		Torre de Communicacions	BT	
Museu d'Art Modern	DS	M⁸	Parc Joan Miró	BS		Torres Trade	AS	
Museu d'Art de Catalunya	BT		Parc d'Atraccions	AR		Umbracle	NV	
Museu d'Història de Catalunya	DS	M⁹	Parc de l'Espanya Industrial	BT		Vila olímpica	DS	
Museu d'Història de la Ciutat	MX	M¹	Parc de la Ciutadella	DS				
Museu de Cera	MY	M³	Parc zoològic	DS				

CARRER DE MONTCADA★★

🕐 *1hr 30min including a visit to the Museu Picasso – see plan of old city.*

Museu Picasso★

🕐 *Open 10am-8pm; Sun, 10am-3pm.* 🕐 *Closed Mon, 1 Jan, Good Fri, 1 May, 24 Jun, 1 Nov and 6 and 25 Dec.* 🞉 *5€, free first Sun of month.* ☎ *93 319 63 10.*

The Gothic palaces of Berenguer de Aguilar and Baron de Castellet and the Baroque Palau Meca provide a wonderful setting for the museum. Many of the works of Picasso (Málaga 1881-Mougins 1973) are displayed, dedicated, in most cases, to his friend Sabartès of whom there are several portraits (including an abstract painting of him wearing a ruff).

Picasso's advanced genius is evident in work from his youth: portraits of his family, *First Communion* and *Science and Charity* (1896). Among examples of his early work in Paris are *La Nana* and *La Espera*, while *Los Desemparados* (1903) is from his Blue Period and the portrait of *Señora Casals* from his Rose Period. His **Las Meninas series**★ consists of liberal variations on the famous picture by Velázquez.

Picasso's skill as an engraver may be seen in his outstanding etchings of bullfighting and his talent as a ceramist in the many vases, dishes and plates (donated to the museum by Jacqueline Picasso) that he made in the 1950s.

Museu Barbier-Mueller d'Art Precolombí

🕐 *Open 10am-6pm (3pm Sun and public hols).* 🕐 *Closed Mon, 1 Jan, 1 May, 24 Jun and 25-26 Dec.* 🞉 *3€.* ☎ *93 310 45 16.*

The Palacio Nadal houses this collection of pre-Columbian art which includes votive figures from Amazonia.

The Ribera District

During the 13C and the 14C the Catalan fleet exercised unquestionable supremacy over the western basin of the Mediterranean. Important merchant families acquired considerable social status and the carrer de Montcada became a showcase for their high expectations and new standards of living. This street, named after the Montcada, an influential family of noble descent, is a unique ensemble of merchants' palaces and aristocratic mansions, most of which date back to the late Middle Ages. Behind the austere façades are quaint little patios with galleries and porches typical of Catalan Gothic architecture.

The following is a selection of small palaces: the 15C Palau de Berenguer de Aguilar, now the Museu Picasso, the 14C Palau del Marqués de Llió which houses the **Museu Tèxtil i d'Indumentària** (Textile and Costume Museum), the 17C Palau Dalmases at no20 with Baroque frieze decorations on the staircase, and the 16C Palau Cervelló-Giudice at no25, now the Maeght Gallery, with a fine flight of steps.

🕐 *Open 10am-6pm; Sun and pub hold 1am-3pm.* 🕐 *Closed Mon, 1 Jan, Good Friday, 1 and 31 May, 24 Jun, 1 Nov, and 6 and 25 Dec.* 🞉€3.5. ☎ *93 310 45 16.*

Iglesia de Santa María del Mar★★

🕐 *Open 10am-1.30pm and 4.30-8pm; no visits during religious services.* ☎ *93 319 05 16.*

This church is one of the most beautiful examples of the Catalan Gothic style. It was built in the 14C by local sailors who in spite of their modest means, wanted to compete with the wealthy townspeople who were building the cathedral. The result is a gracefully proportioned church, outstanding in its simplicity. The walls are unadorned in the Catalan manner and the west front deco rated only by a portal gable and the buttresses flanking the superb Flamboyant **rose window**★. The **interior**★★★ gives the impression of harmonious spaciousness due to the elevation of the nave and the side aisles divided only by slender octagonal pillars.

THE SEAFRONT★ 🕐 *allow half a day*

🚌 *Bus 14 follows the seafront to Vila Olímpica.*

The seafront runs from the foot of the Montjuïc Mountain to the mouth of the Besòs river. The whole district was completely redesigned and upgraded for the 1992 Olympic Games. Ironically, Barcelona, which has always turned its back to the sea, is now regarded as a coastal city.

Drassanes (Shipyards)★★ and Museu Marítim★★

🕐 *Open 10am-7pm.* 🕐 *Closed 1 and 6 Jan and 25-26 Dec.* 🎟 *5.40€.* ☎ *93 342 99 20.*

The **ropeworks** here are among the best examples of non-religious Gothic architecture in Catalunya. Ten sections – seven from the 14C and three beside La Rambla from the 17C – remain from the former shipyard; they are covered by a long timber roof supported by a row of sturdy arches carved in stone. Such a place was the ideal setting for a **Maritime Museum**, in which Catalan naval history is re-created through interactive displays and priceless exhibits. Among the many models of sailing boats and steamships is a lifesize replica of the **Royal Galley of Don Juan of Austria**★★, flagship of the Christians at the Battle of Lepanto (1571). The area devoted to cartography contains the **Portulan of Gabriel de Vallseca** (1439), which belonged to Amerigo Vespucci, while the Pere IV building displays a fine collection of figureheads.

The rehabilitation of the area around the port began with the refurbishment of the Moll de Bosch i Alsina, commonly referred to as **Moll de la Fusta**, a promenade lined with palm trees, flanked by a raised terrace.

Port Vell★

The old harbour has been converted into a lively leisure area featuring a great many bars, the **Maremàgnum** shopping and leisure centre, a modern **aquarium** and the **Imax**, a spectacular cinema screen showing three-dimensional films.

Aquarium★

🧒 🕐 *Open Oct-May, 9.30am-9pm (9.30pm Jun and Sep; 11pm Jul-Aug); last admission one hour before closing.* 🎟 *13.50€, 9.25€ (children aged 4-14).* ☎ *93 221 74 74.*

This is one of Europe's most impressive sub-aquatic zoos displaying a full range of Mediterranean species and exotic tropical specimens. A spectacular tunnel, 80m/262ft long, crosses this magnificent aquarium.

Basílica de la Mercè★

🕐 *Open 9am-1pm and 6-8pm (8.30 Sat); Sun and public hols, 10am-2pm and 7-8.30pm.* ☎ *93 310 51 51.*

The building such as it stands today dates from 1760. Its main façade is the only existing example of curved Baroque architecture in Barcelona. The façade giving onto carrer Ample is Renaissance and was taken from a different church. The late 19C cupola is crowned by a monumental sculpture portraying the Virgin de la Mercè, to whom a pretty Gothic statue is also dedicated in the interior, and the **Mare de Déu de la Mercè**★, attributed to Pere Moragues (1361).

▶ *After crossing vía Laietana, whose construction in the first decade of the 20C involved razing or moving a great many buildings, continue along the passeig d'Isabel II.*

La Llotja★

The building currently houses the headquarters of the Chamber of Commerce and Industry. It was completely rebuilt in the neo-Classical style in the late 18C. Of the original medieval construction there remains only the lofty **Gothic hall**★★, a huge chamber with three naves separated by triple round arches.

Estació de França★

This huge iron structure crowned by glass roofing is, as the name would suggest, a terminal for trains to France. It also stages important cultural events, such as the Annual Comics Fair.

Parc de la Ciutadella★

🕐 *Open 7.30am-9pm.* 📷 *1.20€.* ☎ *93 413 24 00.*

Originally built by Philip V to keep watch over the rebels of Barcelona, the citadel was destroyed in 1868 and replaced by gardens. Its grounds were used to host the 1888 World Fair, whose symbolic entrance was the Triumphal Arch.

Castell dels Tres Dragons★★

Domènech i Montaner built this pavilion for the World Fair in a functional, neo-Gothic style, using stark materials (brick and iron) without any form of covering. It houses the **Museu de Zoologia**★, which houses a representative collection of all zoological species. 🕐*Open 10am-2pm (6.30pm Thu).* 🕐*Closed Mon, 1 Jan and 25 Dec.* 📷 *3€ (3.90€ with visit to Museu de Geologia and Botanical Garden), no charge first Sun of every month.* ☎ *93 319 68 95.*

Waterfall

Gaudí collaborated on the design of this impressive waterfall while he was still a student of architecture.

Parc Zoològic★

🔲 Kids 🕐*Open Jan, Feb, Nov and Dec, 10am-5pm; Mar and Oct, 10am-6pm; Apr and Sep, 10am-7pm; May-Aug, 9.30am-7.30pm.* 🕐*Closed 25 Dec.* 📷*12.90€, (8.20€ child).* ☎ *93 225 67 80.*

This zoo takes up a large part of the Parc de la Ciutadella, in which animals from all over the world can be seen in their natural environment. A popular dolphin show is held in the Aquarama.

Museu d'Art Modern

🕐 *Open 10am-7pm; Sun and public hols, 10am-2.30pm. Last entry 30 min before closing.* 🕐 *Closed Mon, 1 Jan, 1 May and 25 Dec.* 📷 *3€; no charge first Thu of month, 18 May, 11 and 17 Sep.* ☎ *93 319 57 28.*

Set up in a wing of the former citadel, the museum presents the work of Catalan artists from the 19C and especially the 20C; Fortuny, Ramón Casas, Nonell, Regoyos, Gargallo, Sert etc.

▶ *Return to pla del Palau along avenida Marquès d'Argentera and take the passeig Nacional.*

La Barceloneta★

This district, known as the "Iberian Naples" and traditionally associated with fishermen, sailors and dockers, will delight visitors because of its quaint narrow streets and its typical fish restaurants and stalls, offering mouthwatering seafood dishes.

Museu d'Història de Catalunya★

🕐 *Open 10am-7pm; Sun and public hols, 10am-2.30pm.* 🕐 *Closed Mon, 1 and 6 Jan, 25-26 Dec.* 📷 *3€.* ☎ *93 225 47 00.*

This museum is housed in the former general stores of the port of Barcelona, a group of buildings which date from the beginning of the century. It provides an insight into the history of Catalunya from prehistory to the present day.

▶*At the end of the passeig Nacional, continue into the passeig Marítim.*

Vila Olímpica★

Built to provide accommodation for the 15 000 athletes competing in the 1992 Olympic Games, this is one of the most modern areas of present-day Barcelona. The overall project was entrusted to the team of architects M.B.M. (Martorell, Bohigas & Mackay), but the plans for each individual building were conceived by local architects. The Olympic Village boasts many gardens and avenues dotted with modern sculptures.

The new **marina**★★ designed by engineer JR de Clascà has become one of the city's most popular leisure areas with numerous bars, restaurants and pavement cafés. The most striking buildings are the two **towers** 153m/502ft high (Hotel Arts and the Torre Mapfre). The **view**★★★ from the top of these is truly breathtaking: on a clear day you can even glimpse the outlines of Mallorca.

MONTJUÏC★ *1 day, including museum visits – see general plan*

The "mountain of the Jews" is a 173m/568ft hill overlooking the city. When the citizens of Barcelona rose in revolt against Philip IV in 1640 they built a fort on the hill (now a military museum). The castle terraces command extensive **views**★ of the city and the harbour to the south. Montjuïc hosted the International Exhibition in 1929 and since then **plaça de Espanya**, the gateway to the exhibition, has remained a major centre for World Fairs. Among the many remaining monuments and pavilions built for the event are the illuminated **fountain** or *Font Magica* by Carles Buïgas, at the end of Avinguda de la Reina Maria Cristina, the **reception pavilion**★★ by Mies van der Rohe, outstanding for its simplicity, modernity and the variety of materials used, and the Spanish Village (Poble Espanyol in Catalan, Pueblo Español in Castilian).

CaixaForum

🕐 *Open 10am-8pm.* 🚫 *Closed Mon (except pub holidays).* ☎ *476 86 00.*

The La Caixa foundation has rescued the magnificent Modernist building of an early 20C one-time textile factory, built by Puig i Cadafalch. It now houses a great cultural center with thematic exhibits of its splendid modern art collection of more than 800 works from the Dau period to the Set, and from the El Paso group to the latest trends. Architect Arata Isozaki designed an entry through a powerful tree of steel and glass.

CaixaForum offers comprehensive cultural programming (lectures, courses, concerts, etc.).

Museu Nacional d'Art de Catalunya★★★

🕐 *Open 10am-7pm; Sun and public hols, 10am-2.30pm.* 🚫 *Closed Mon, 1 Jan, 1 May and 25 Dec.* 💶 *4.80€; 15€ for combined Articket (valid three months, offers entry to the MNAC, Fundació Joan Miró, Fundació Antoni Tàpies, the CCCB, Centre de Cultura de la Caixa and the MACBA); no charge first Thu of month.* ☎ *93 622 03 75/76.*

Housed in the Palacio Nacional that was built for the 1929 World Fair, this museum features remarkable **Romanesque and Gothic collections**★★★ taken from many churches in Catalunya and Aragón, and a selection of exhibits from the **Francesc Cambó** collection, with works from the 16C-18C. In the near future, the museum will also include Renaissance and Baroque sections, as well as a collection from the Museu d'Art Modern.

Romanesque art

In the 12C-13C the Pyrenean valleys saw the development of a highly expressive and mature art form.

The frescoes are displayed in chapels and large rooms that evoke the atmosphere of contemporary churches. Clearly influenced by Byzantine mosaics, they are characterised by heavy black outlines, superimposed frieze compositions, lack of perspective and rigidity of stance. However, the addition of realistic or expressive details lend a distinctive Catalan touch to these paintings. Note the 12C frescoes by Sant Joan de Boí *(Room II)* with *The Stoning of St Stephen, The Falconer* and *Paradise and Hell*, the late 11C lateral apses by Sant Quirze de Pedret *(Room III)*, the Santa María de Taüll ensemble (12C), presenting a host of images dominated by a fine *Epiphany* and the paintings from Sant Climent de Taüll *(Room V)* with its remarkable *Christ in Majesty*: the apse is considered to be one of the finest examples of Renaissance painting. Note the deliberate anti-naturalistic approach and the subtle geometry of the drawing.

The **altar frontals** fall into two categories: those painted on a single panel (Iglesia de Sant Martí d'Ix, Catedral de Santa María at La Seu d'Urgell, known as the Apostles' altarfront) and those carved in relief (Santa María de Taüll). In the magnificent sculpture galleries, the the polychrome *Majestad de Batlló* (13C) is notable. The museum also presents superb **collections of capitals**★ *(Room VI)*, silverware and enamels *(Room XV)*.

Last in this section are paintings from the chapter house of **Sigena** (1200), which evidence a great stylistic change.

Gothic art

This section provides visitors with an overview of Catalan Gothic art during the 13C and 14C. Exhibits include the stone retables attributed to **Jaime Cascalls** *(Rooms IV and V)*; the large collection of Catalan international Gothic art *(Room IX)*, with works by the city's most influential artists (**Guerau Gener, Juan Mates, Ramón de Mur, Juan Antigó, Bernardo Despuig** and **Jaime Cirera**); the room dedicated to **Bernardo Martorell** *(Room XI)*, an artist for whom detail and pictorial matrixes were of paramount importance; the famous *Virgin of the Councillors* by **Luis Dalmau**; the set of works by the **Master of La Seu d´Urgell** (*Room XV*) and, lastly, the section dedicated to funerary sculpture in the 14C and 15C (*Room XVIII*).

16-18C Art

Works on exhibit are currently limited to the Cambó Legacy, a small collection of the works of notable European painters (Zurbarán, Tintoretto, El Greco, La Tour, Rubens, etc.).

Poble Espanyol★ (Spanish Village)

▶ *Entry by avenida Marqués de Comillas.*

Kids ◷*Open Mon, 9am-8pm; Tue-Thu, 9am-2am; Fri-Sat, 9am-4am; Sun, 9am-midnight; last admission 1hr before closing.* ◷*Closed 1 Jan and 25 Dec.* ⊜ *7€.* ☎ *93 508 63 30.*

The village was built for the 1929 exhibition to illustrate regional styles in Spanish architecture. A walk through it will reveal a picturesque variety of local features ranging from a small Castilian square, a street in an Andalucían village with white-walled houses set off by flowering geraniums, to a Mudéjar tower from Aragón. There are also restaurants, bars, shops, and craftsmen at work making traditional Spanish wares. The village is also home to a **Collection of Contemporary Art**★, which exhibits works of the historic vanguard (Picasso, Miró, Dalí) and of leading Spanish artists from the 1950s to the present.

Anella Olímpica★

Built as a venue for the sporting events of the 1992 Olympic Games, this huge complex occupies a wide esplanade situated high up on the mountain. Basically, it consists of the **Olympic Stadium**★, with its 1929 façade and fully renovated interior, and the nearby **Palau Sant Jordi**★★, a modern sports centre designed by the Japanese architect Arata Isozaki, housed under a large metallic structure.

The **telecommunications tower** commissioned by Telefónica, the work of Santiago Calatrava, offers a pleasing combination of modernity and aesthetics.

Galería Olímpica

◷ *Open Oct-Mar, 10am-1pm and 4-6pm; Apr-Jun, 10am-2pm and 4-7pm.* ◷ *Closed Sat-Sun and public hols.* ⊜ *2.70€.* ☎ *93 426 06 60.*

This gallery commemorates the 1992 Olympic Games: it displays medals won by Spanish athletes, detailed photographs of sporting events which were particularly dramatic that year, and a host of miscellaneous objects associated with the history of the Olympic movement.

Fundació Joan Miró★★★

◷ *Open 10am-7pm (8pm Jul-Sep); Thu, 10am-9.30pm; Sun and public hols, 10am-2.30pm; last admission 30min before closing.* ◷ *Closed Mon (except pub holidays), 1 and 6 Jan and 25 Dec.* ⊜ *7.20€.* ☎ *93 443 94 70.*

Joan Miró (1893-1983) was unquestionably one of Europe's leading figures in the field of avant-garde art. His name is closely associated with Palma de Mallorca *(⌖ see PALMA de MALLORCA)* as well as Barcelona, his native town on which he has clearly left his mark. Examples of his work can be found in many different parts of the city: a ceramics mural at the airport, pavement mosaics on La Rambla, not to mention the famous logo he designed for the savings bank La Caixa, symbolising all its local branches.

Born in Barcelona, Miró spent 1921 and 1922 living in Paris, where he painted **La Masía**, a canvas that prefigured his departure from figurative art. Between 1939 and 1941 he executed **Constellations**, his famous series of 23 panels expressing his horror of the Second World War. The themes illustrated in this series (the night, the sun, women etc) were to become recurring motifs in his later work. Miró's art consists in exploring the many possibilities offered by colours, shapes and symbols. His work is a skilful combination of joy and tragedy, enhanced by a strong touch of magic and poetry *(see the video presentation of the artist)*.

Created by Miró in 1971, the Foundation was officially opened in 1976. It is housed in a modern building of harmonious proportions, designed by the architect Josep Lluís Sert, a close friend of the artist whose main concern was to conceive a building that blended in well with the surrounding landscape. The collections, totalling over 10 000 exhibits (paintings, sculptures, drawings, collages and other graphic works), bring together many of Miró's works, the majority of which were executed during the last 20 years of his life. You can also visit a small exhibition of contemporary art featuring Alexander Calder's **Fountain of Mercury**, along with works by artists such as Matisse, Tanguy, Max Ernst, Chillida, Saura, Rauschenberg etc.

People, birds, star by Joan Miró – Fundació Joan Miró

©Fundacio Joan Miro, Barcelona/© Adagp, Paris 2003

Next to the Foundation lies a small **garden of sculptures**, presenting the work of young contemporary artists.

Teatre Grec★

Based on the Epidaurus model from ancient Greece, this 1929 open-air theatre is set against a rocky backdrop belonging to an abandoned quarry. In summer it hosts dance, concerts and stage performances organised by the **Festival del Grec**.

Museu d'Arqueologia de Catalunya★

🕐*Open 9.30am-7pm; Sun and public hols, 10am-2.30pm.* 🕐*Closed Mon, 1 Jan and 24-25 Dec.* 🎫 *2.40€, no charge Sun and public hols.* ☎ *93 424 65 77.*

Catalan archaeology has a great tradition and is responsible for some important discoveries. Through the exhibits on display (implements, ceramics, votive figures, household effects etc), visitors are able to follow distinct periods in history from Palaeolithic times through to the Visigothic era, including the periods of Greek and Roman colonisation.

THE CIUTAT UNIVERSITÀRIA DISTRICT

Monastir de Santa Maria de Pedralbes★★ (Pedralbes Monastery)

🕐 *Open 10am-2pm (last admission at 1.30pm).* 🕐 *Closed Mon, 1 Jan, Good Fri, 1 May, 24 Jun and 25-26 Dec.* 🎫 *3.50€, no charge first Sun of every month.* ☎ *93 315 11 11.*

Although the village of Pedralbes has been incorporated into a residential quarter of Barcelona, it still preserves its rustic charm.

Founded in the 14C by King James II of Aragón and his fourth wife, Doña Elisenda de Montcada, the monastery has a fine Catalan Gothic **church**★ which houses the sepulchre of the foundress. The vast three-storey **cloisters**★ surrounded by cells and oratories are sober and elegant. The Sant Miquel Chapel is adorned with beautiful **frescoes**★★★ by Ferrer Bassá (1346), a Catalan artist strongly influenced by Italy whose works artfully combine the close attention to detail that characterised the Siena School with the acute sense of volume and perspective associated with the great Tuscan masters.

The **Thyssen-Bornemisza collection**★ *(access via the cloisters)* is on display in the former monks' dormitory and in the Sala de la Reina (Queen's Room). It contains 72 paintings and eight sculptures (from the Middle Ages to the 18C) which were part of the large collection (over 800 works) on show at the Museo Thyssen-Bornemisza in Madrid. Among the numerous works with a religious theme, **Fra Angelico's** magnificent *Virgin of Humility* and **Zurbarán's** *Santa Marina* stand out, as do several paintings of the *Virgin and Child* (B Daddi, 14C and L Monaco, 15C). Another room worthy of special mention is the Sala de los Retratos (Portrait Room) which contains some fine examples of various 15C and 18C schools.

Palau de Pedralbes (Pedralbes Palace)

▶ Enter from avinguda Diagonal.

🕐 Open 10am-6pm; Sun and public hols, 10am-3pm. 🕐 Closed Mon, 1 Jan, Good Fri and 25 Dec. ☞ 3.50€ (includes Museu Tèxtil i d'Indumentària). ☎ 93 280 16 21).

Between 1919 and 1929 the city of Barcelona built a residence for King Alfonso XIII which was influenced by palaces of the Italian Renaissance and surrounded by attractive gardens. This particular palace houses the **Museu de les Artes Decoratives**★, with its displays of household items from the Middle Ages through to the industrial design era. It is also home to the **Museu de Ceràmica**, with exhibits showing evolutions in this art form from the 13C to the present day. Particularly worthy of note are the collections of Catalan and Alcora ceramics (18C-19C).

Retable of Saints Abdon and Sennen, Iglesia de Santa María

R. Manet/MICHELIN

▷ Museu de la Ciència; Iglesia de Sant Pau del Camp (10C, **cloisters**★); Teatre Nacional de Catalunya (Ricardo Bofill), Auditorio (Rafael Moneo).

Excursions

Monasterio de Sant Cugat del Vallès★★

20km/12mi W along the BP 1417. 🕐 Open 10am-1.30pm and 3-7pm (8pm Jun-Sep). 🕐 Closed Mon. exc public hols, 1 Jan and 25 Dec. ☞ 3€ (to museum). ☎ 93 589 63 66.

The town is named after the Benedictine **monastery** established in the Middle Ages on the site of an earlier chapel. This had been built very early to contain the relics of St Cucufas whose throat was cut by Diocletian's legionaries on this spot eight Roman miles along the road from Barcelona around AD 304. Of the former walls there remain the church, at present used as a parish church, the cloisters (museum) and the chapter house, now serving as a chapel, the Capilla del Santísimo. The rectory, formerly the Abbot's residence, is a Gothic building that was converted in the 18C.

Iglesia★

This is a telling example of the transitional period between Romanesque and Gothic. The oldest part of the church is the 11C belfry decorated with Lombard bands incorporated into the main building when the side chapels were built (15C). A chancel had already been added in the 12C. The façade was completed in 1350. The flat, crenellated wall supported by thrusting buttresses was relieved by a radiating rose window as vast as the doorway below with its smooth covings. There are three apses, polygonal outside and with engaged pillars inside; the central one was given radiating vaulting, a feature which was to mark an alteration in style, reflected in the ogival vaulting in the lantern and above the three aisles. Among the works of art, note the 14C **All Saints Altarpiece**★ by Pere Serra.

Claustro★

The cloisters are among the largest Romanesque cloisters in Catalunya. During the 11C-12C a double row of columns (144 in all) was built around a close; in the 16C an upper gallery was added above a blind arcade decorated with sculpted modillions. The skilfully carved **Romanesque capitals**★ are Corinthian (acanthus leaves), ornamental (strapwork), figurative (birds) and historiated (biblical scenes); these last ones are grouped largely in the south gallery which abuts the church. The most interesting of all, however, is the one over the northeast corner column on which the sculptor, Arnaud Cadell, portrayed himself at work and then cut his name.

Terrassa/Tarrasa

31km/19mi NW along the C 58. This important industrial city has preserved the impressive ensemble of churches known as the Conjunto Monumental de Iglesias de Sant Pere, a splendid example of pre-Romanesque religious architecture.

Conjunto Monumental de Iglesias de Sant Pere★★

🕐 *Open 10am-1.30pm and 4-7pm; Sun, 11am-2pm.* 🕐 *Closed Mon and public hols.* ☎ *93 789 27 55.*

This fine cluster of churches, a reminder of the former bishopric of Egara (5C), constitutes a soothing haven of peace in the midst of the bustling city. These three buildings (9C-12C), of unquestionable artistic value, show Pyrenean influence but also feature a great many Roman and Visigothic ruins.

Antiguo baptisterio de Sant Miquel★

Sant Miquel, a former baptistery of square design with a heptagonal apse, was built in the 9C using late Roman remains. The dome above the font is supported on eight pillars; four have Roman capitals, four have Visigothic. Alabaster windows in the apse provide a filtered light by which to see the 9C-10C pre-Romanesque wall paintings. Below is a crypt, abutted by three small apses with horseshoe-shaped arches.

Santa Maria★

The church is a good example of the Romanesque Lombard style. Before the façade are the remains of a 5C mosaic from the original church. The present edifice is in the shape of a Latin cross, with a cimborrio (lantern) and an octagonal cupola. Inside, the 11C apsidal vaulting features vestiges of mural paintings but a 13C wall fresco in the south transept, illustrating the martyrdom of Thomas à Becket of Canterbury, has preserved its bright colours. Among the superb 15C altarpieces, note the one in the north transept by Jaime Huguet of **St Abdon and St Sennen★★**.

Sant Pere is a rustic church whose construction began in the 6C. It was built according to a trapezoid plan and has a Romanesque transept crossing. Embedded in the apse is a curious **stone altarpiece**★.

Masia Freixa★

This strange-looking Modernist bourgeois mansion (1907), which presently houses the Academy of Music, is situated inside the Sant Jordi Park. Visitors' attention will be attracted by the repeated use of parabolic arches.

Museu de la Ciencia y la Tècnica de Catalunya★

🕐 *Open 10am-7pm (2.30pm Jul-Aug); Sat-Sun, 10am-2.30pm.* 🕐 *Closed Mon and public hols.* ⊙ *3€, no charge first Sun of month.* ☎ *93 736 89 66.*

The museum occupies the premises of an old 1909 steam works (Aymerich, Amat i Jover) that is an interesting example of industrial architecture under the Modernist movement. It offers a retrospective of the various technological advances which have occurred in connection with industrialisation.

Museu Tèxtil (Textile Museum)

🕐 *Open 9am-6pm (9pm Thu); Sat-Sun, 10am-2pm.* 🕐 *Closed Mon and public hols.* ⊙ *3€, no charge first Sun of month.* ☎ *93 731 52 02 / 49 80.*

Oriental materials, including rare Coptic fabrics from the 4C and 5C, Merovingian fabrics and brocades, provide an excellent panoramic history of textile and manufacture.

Sierra de Montserrat★★

49km/31mi NW along the C 58.

The Macizo de Montserrat (Montserrat Massif) has a grandiose **site**★★★ and was, in fact, used by Wagner as the setting for his opera, Parsifal. The range is composed of hard Eocene conglomerates, which stand solidly above the more eroded surrounding rock formations. The piling up of the boulders into steep cliffs, crowned by weird pinnacles, has produced a serrated outline which has given Montserrat the nickname Sawtooth Mountain. Today, it is the principal site of Marian devotion in Catalunya. The **views**★★ of the mountain from the road are particularly impressive. Access to the Montserrat cable car is from near Monistrol de Montserrat.

The Monastery

The history of Montserrat, one of the five main hermitages on the mountain, begins in the 9C with the arrival of Benedictines from Ripoll. In 1025 Abbot Oliva founded a priory on the site which grew rapidly in importance, until by the 13C the Romanesque buildings had to be greatly enlarged. It continued to flourish and, as an abbey, declared its independence from Ripoll in 1409. It had become powerful; its monks were learned – one of the abbots, Giuliano della Rovere, the future Pope Julius II, was a scholar, artist and patron of the Italian Renaissance – and the community was rich; its pilgrims were fervent and numerous. Every century saw additions to the monastery making it an anthology of masterpieces of every architectural style.

In 1812, however, disaster struck; the monastery was sacked by the French. The present buildings, therefore, are 19C and 20C (the church façade was completed in 1968). At the end of the dark, overly ornate **basilica** (15C), stands the shrine of the Black Madonna. ○ *Open 7am-7.30pm (8.30pm Jul-Sep).* ☎ *93 877 77 01.*

La Moreneta★★

La Moreneta is the Catalan name for the Black Madonna. The polychrome wood statue is said to date from the 12C; the seated figure of the Infant Jesus was restored in the 19C. According to legend, the figure, now in a niche *(camarín)* above the high altar, and venerated annually by thousands of pilgrims as the patron saint of Catalunya, was found by shepherds in a cave on the mountainside.

Access to the *camarín* for a closer view of the statue is through the chapels in the south aisle. The church services by the monks (the Montserrat community consists of 80 members) are known for the high standard of their singing: concelebratory Mass is at 11am; Vespers at 6.45pm, there are special services at Christmas and in Holy Week. The **Escolanía**, one of Europe's oldest boys' choirs – its foundation dates back to the 13C – may be heard every day at 1pm (Virolai) and 7.10pm (Salve).

Hermitages and viewpoints

🛈 *Information from the Tourist Office. Access via the* 🚶 *mountain trails,* 🚡 *cable cars or funiculars. Sant Joan: Jan-Mar, Nov and Dec, 11am-4pm; Sat-Sun and public hols, 10am-4pm; Apr-Jun, Sep and Oct, 10am-5.40pm; Jul-Aug, 10am-7pm.* 🎫 *6.10€ round trip (service operates every 20min).* ☎ *93 205 15 15. Santa Cova: 10am-1pm and 2-5pm (4pm Nov-Feb).* 🎫 *2.50€ (service operates every 20min).*

Before the arrival of Napoleon's troops, there were 13 hermitages, each occupied by a hermit. Today, they are all deserted but some make interesting walks.

Ermita de la Trinitat

🚶 *45min on foot.* Charmingly nestled in a bucolic plain, this hermitage is sheltered by three unusually-named mountains: El Elefante (The Elephant), La Preñada (the Pregnant Woman) and La Momia (The Mummy).

Sant Jeroni★

🚶 *Access on foot (1hr 30min) or* 🚗 *by car along a forest track (1hr 30min).* From the viewpoint (1 238m/4 062ft) there is a **panorama**, on a clear day, stretching from the Pyrenees to the Balearic islands.

Ermita de Santa Cecilia

Until the 16C Santa Cecilia was a Benedictine monastery like Santa María of Ripoll, but lacked its influence. The 11C **Romanesque church**★ has a most attractive exterior with its east end circled by Lombard bands, its roof and its asymmetric, free-standing belfry.

Santa Cova

🚶 *1hr walk.* According to legend, it was in this cave that the statue of the Virgin was found. Views of the Llobregat Valley.

Sant Miquel★

🚶 *30min walk from the monastery; 1hr from the upper terminal of the Sant Miquel funicular.* General view of the monastery.

Sant Joan

🚶 *30min from upper terminal of the Sant Joan funicular.* Beautiful panorama; the Ermita de San Onofre may be seen clinging to the rock face.

Belmonte ★

POPULATION: 2 601.

MICHELIN MAP 576 N 21 – CASTILLA LA MANCHA (CUENCA)

The birthplace of the 16C prose writer Fray Luis de León is a typical La Mancha town with whitewashed houses and wide streets in which it is easy to conjure up the image of Don Quixote astride his trusty steed Rocinante. Belmonte is dominated by the imposing structure of its collegiate church and by the medieval castle crowning San Cristóbal hill.

Location

Belmonte stands alongside the N 420 linking Cuenca and Ciudad Real (142km/89mi SW), at the heart of the vast La Mancha plain. The town is approximately 1hr by road from Cuenca and 2hr from Madrid (157km//98mi NW).

⚭ *Neighbouring sights are described in the following chapters: CUENCA (101km/63mi NE) and ALBACETE (107km/67mi SE).*

A Photogenic Castle

In the past, the magnificent medieval castle of Belmonte has been the stunning backdrop for a number of films. The most famous of these was undoubtedly *El Cid* (1961), starring Charlton Heston and Sophia Loren.

Visit

The Town

Belmonte has retained part of the old wall linking the town with the castle, as well as three of its five entrance gateways. Of these, the best preserved is the Puerta de Chinchilla.

Antigua Colegiata★

This 15C collegiate church contains an interesting collection of **altarpieces** made by local artists in the 15C, 16C and 17C. The 15C **choir stalls**★, from the cathedral in Cuenca, illustrate, with stark realism, scenes from Genesis and the Passion. The font in which Fray Luis de León was christened has been preserved.

Castillo★

🕐 *Open 10am to 2pm and 3.30-6pm (Apr-15 Jun 4-7pm; 16 Jun-14 Sep 45-8pm).*
🕐 *1 Jan, 24 Aug and 25 Dec.* ✆2€. ☎ *967 17 00 08.*

This hexagonal fortress, flanked by six circular towers, was built in the 15C by Juan Pacheco, Marqués de Villena, as part of the defences of his vast domain. It was subsequently abandoned until the 19C when it was restored, although it had lost all its furnishings. In 1870 the triangular patio was disfigured by a brick facing ordered by the new owner, Eugenia de Montijo. All that remains in the empty rooms are beautiful Mudéjar **artesonado**★ ceilings – the audience chamber is outstanding – and delicately carved stone window surrounds. Follow the curtain walls to the stepped merlons for a view of the village and the austere La Mancha countryside beyond.

Excursions

Villaescusa de Haro

6km/4mi NE along the N 420. The 1507 **Capilla de la Asunción**★ (Chapel of the Assumption) belonging to the parish church is a magnificent late-Gothic construction. It has crenels, a Gothic-Renaissance altarpiece and a wrought-iron screen with a flowery Gothic design of three arches.

Bilbao★

POPULATION: 372 054.

MICHELIN MAP 573 C 21 (TOWN PLAN) – PAÍS VASCO (VIZCAYA) –

LOCAL MAP SEE COSTA VASCA

In recent years, Bilbao has undergone a major facelift with the completion of important projects such as the sleek and stylish new metro system, with its distinctive glazed station entrances by Sir Norman Foster; a new footbridge and airport terminal, both created by Santiago Calatrava (architect of Barcelona's Torre de Comunicaciones de Telefónica); and a riverside development and park by Cesar Pelli (architect of London's Canary Wharf tower). The jewel in modern Bilbao's crown, however, is the Guggenheim, its spectacular new museum of modern art designed by Frank Gehry.

Bilbao was the birthplace of the great writer and humanist Miguel de Unamuno (1864-1936).

Location

The capital of Vizcaya province is situated at the end of the Bilbao ría which forms the Nervión estuary. The city is an excellent base from which to explore the Basque country, with Vitoria-Gasteiz 69km/43mi to the south, Donostia-San Sebastián 102km/63mi to the east, and Santander 103km/64mi to the west. *Plaza Arenal 1, 48005 Bilbao, ☎ 94 479 57 60.*

Neighbouring sights are described in the following chapters: COSTA VASCA, VITORIA-GASTEIZ and DONOSTIA-SAN SEBASTIÁN.

Address Book

For coin ranges, see the Legend at the back of the guide.

WHERE TO EAT

Goizeko Kabi – *Particular de Estraunza 4* – ☎ *94 442 11 29 – Closed Sun and 31 Jul-15 Aug –* . This regional gastronomic institution near the Museo de Bellas Artes is renowned for its high-quality cuisine offering a balanced combination of the traditional and innovative, with outstanding seafood dishes.

TAPAS

El Viandar de Sota – *Gran Vía de Don Diego López de Haro 45* – ☎ *94 415 25 00* – . This complex of five different places to eat and drink is another famous landmark in the modern section of the city, also near the Museo de Bellas Artes. Take your pick from the traditional tapas bar, the sidrería, serving excellent local cider, or the vinoteca.

WHERE TO STAY

Hotel Iturrienea – *Santa María 14* – ☎ *94 416 15 00 – 21 rooms. 48€* – 4.28€. This charming hotel at the heart of the old quarter is housed in a tastefully refurbished old building with a distinctive blue façade. The emphasis here is on antiques, along with works by local artists. Although the rooms are generally on the small side, the wooden floors add to the homely feel.

Hotel Sirimiri – *Plaza de la Encarnación 3* – ☎ *94 433 07 59 – hsirimirieuskalnet.net* – – *28 rooms* – 6€. Nestled in the old quarter, on the right bank of the River Bilbao, close to the Museo de Arte Sacro. The rooms here are modern, spacious and functional with large fully equipped bathrooms.

CAFÉS

Café Iruña – *Jardines de Albia-Berástegui 5.* This café, which was founded in 1903, has become something of an institution in Bilbao. It is situated in a pleasant square and contains some attractive Mudéjar-inspired ceilings and decoration. An enjoyable place for a drink, particularly at night.

Café La Granja – *Plaza Circular 3.* This famous café dates from 1926 although its style is more in keeping with the 19C with its marble tables, wooden chairs and decadent air. On evenings during the weekend the quiet, contemplative mood is replaced by a more lively atmosphere and loud music.

FIESTAS

Bilbao's main annual festival takes place during **Semana Grande** in August with bullfights, Basque pelota championships and other events.

Background

The city – Founded in the early 14C, old Bilbao stands on the right bank of the Nervión river, up against the mountain crowned by the Santuario de Begoña (Begoña Sanctuary). It was originally named *las siete calles*, or seven streets, on account of its layout.

The modern *El Ensanche* business district (*ensanche translates* as "enlargement"), stands on the left bank of the river on the other side of the puente de Arenal; this area developed alongside the old section of the city in the 19C. The town's wealthy residential quarter is spread around the Doña Casilda Iturriza park and along Gran Vía de Don Diego López de Haro.

Industry – Local industry began to develop in the middle of the 19C when iron mined from the surrounding hills was shipped to England in exchange for coal. Iron and steelworks were subsequently established.

Greater Bilbao and the ría – Since 1945 Greater Bilbao has included all the towns along the *ría* to the sea, from Bilbao itself to Getxo. Industrial works (iron and steel, chemicals and shipbuilding) are concentrated along the left bank in **Baracaldo, Sestao, Portugalete** with its **transporter bridge** built in 1893, and in Somorrostro where there is a large oil refinery. **Santurtzi**, a fishing port, is well-known for its fresh sardines.

Algorta, a residential town on the right bank, provides an attractive contrast to the heavy industry, while **Deusto** is famous for its university.

Special Features

Museo Guggenheim★★★

🕐 *Open 10am-8pm.* 🕐 *Closed Mon (except Jul-Aug).* ⊗ *10€ (12€ for special exhibitions).* ☎ *94 435 90 80*

This important new museum, funded primarily by the Basque government, is a European showcase for the renowned collection founded in New York by wealthy art patron Solomon R. Guggenheim (1861-1949). The Bilbao institution is the youngest member of the prestigious family of museums managed by the Guggenheim Foundation that comprises two New York sites (Fifth Avenue and SoHo) and the Peggy Guggenheim in Venice.

With this stunning museum complex, inaugurated in October 1997, acclaimed California-based architect **Frank Gehry** has created what is widely considered one of the great buildings of the late 20C, making it an appropriate counterpart to the famous spiral monument designed in the 1950s by Frank Lloyd Wright to house the Guggenheim's Fifth Avenue Museum. Previous European projects by Pritzker Prize winner Gehry include the Festival Disney entertainment complex at Disneyland Paris (1988-92) and the American Center at Bercy, Paris (1994).

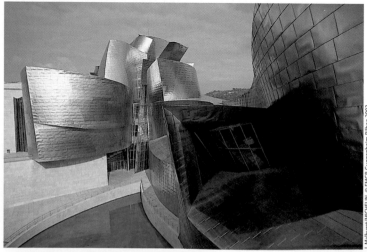

J. Malburet/MICHELIN © FMGB Guggenheim Bilbao 2003

Museo Guggenheim, Bilbao

The emblem of the city

The museum rises from the banks of the Nervión like a vast and complex ship with billowing sails. Formal geometry and symmetry are abandoned as Gehry skilfully juxtaposes free forms, creating harmony and gracefully flowing lines out of potential chaos. The resulting eye-catching architectural composition, clad in shimmering titanium, demands to be seen from all angles and takes on a different aspect with every change of light. The south entrance is made of golden limestone, used for both walls and paving. It opens into a vast, soaring **central atrium** (50m/165ft high) of glass, white walls and steel ribs, in which there are echoes of Wright's great spiral, transformed here into a whirl of smoothly moulded shapes and natural light. Access to the galleries fanning out from the central atrium on the three floors inside is by glass-fronted lifts or vertiginous suspended walkways and staircases. The galleries are spacious, ranging from 8m/25ft to 15m/50ft in height. The largest gallery measures 130m/450ft long and 25m/80ft wide, running the length of the riverside site, passing beneath the road bridge and culminating in a V-shaped metal and stone tower.

Collections

Drawing on the reserves of the vast and world-renowned Guggenheim collections in New York and Venice (more than 6 000 paintings, sculptures and works on paper), the latest Guggenheim Museum focuses on art from the 1950s to the present. Among the artists well represented in the collections are Modern masters (Picasso, Mondrian, Kandinsky) and proponents of the major movements such as Abstract Expressionism (Rothko, De Kooning, Pollock), Pop art (Oldenburg, Rosenquist, Warhol), and Conceptual and Minimalist art (Carl André, Donald Judd). More contemporary artists likely to be on view include Anselm Kiefer, Francesco Clemente and Damien Hirst. To complement the works on loan from the Guggenheim Foundation, the Basque government has budgeted for the museum to invest in its own acquisitions and has commissioned several site-specific works including a vast mural by Sol LeWitt and Richard Serra's Snake, three gigantic sheets of undulating steel standing upright and parallel. Spanish talent is also present, with works by Antoni Tàpies, Eduardo Chillida, Francesc Torres, Cristina Iglesias and Susana Solano likely to be on display.

The opening of the museum has given a new lease of life to the Basques' long-standing campaign to bring **Picasso's** *Guernica* home to the Basque capital. A special space has already been reserved for the mural in the Guggenheim Bilbao. However, concerns regarding the fragile condition of the work and the political issues that surround it prevail to date, with the result that it remains firmly in the Reina Sofía museum in Madrid.

Worth a Visit

Museo de Bellas Artes★

🕐 *Open 10am-8pm; Sun, 10am-2pm; last admission 15 min before closing.* 🕐 *Closed Mon , 1 Jan and 25 Dec.* 🎫 *4.50€, no charge Wed.* ☎ *94 439 60 60.*

The fine arts museum is housed in two buildings in the Doña Casilda Iturriza park.

In the **ancient art section**★★ *(old building, ground floor)*, pride of place is given to Spanish paintings from the 12C to the 17C. Noteworthy Romanesque works include a 12C Crucifixion from the Catalan School, while the section on 16C-17C Spanish classical painting has canvases by Morales, El Greco, Valdés Leal, Zurbarán, Ribera and Goya.

Dutch and Flemish painting (15C-17C) is also well represented with *The Usurers* by Quentin Metsys, a *Pietà* by Ambrosius Benson and a *Holy Family* by Gossaert.

The **Basque art section** on the first floor contains a comprehensive collection of works by the great Basque painters: Regoyos, Zuloaga, Iturrino etc.

The **contemporary art section** *(new building)* displays a rich collection of works by artists both Spanish – Solana, Vázquez Díaz, Sunyer, Gargallo, Blanchard, Luis Fernández Otieza, Chillida and Tàpies – and foreign – Delaunay, Léger, Kokoschka, Vieira da Silva and Bacon.

Museo Vasco (Basque Museum)

🕐 *Open 11am-5pm (4pm Sun).* 🕐 *Closed Mon and public hols.* 🎫 *3€, no charge Thu.* ☎ *94 415 54 23.*

The museum, which is housed in the former **Colegio de San Andrés** in the heart of the old town, contains an extensive collection of ethnographic exhibits providing visitors with a detailed insight into the traditional activities of the Basque people

BILBAO

Arenal Puente	EY	2	Gran Vía Don Diego		
Arriaga Pl.	EYZ	3	de López de Haro	DEY	
Arriquíbar Pl.	DYZ	4	Jado Pl. de	DY	28
Ayuntamiento Puente	EY	5	Ledesma	EY	32
Bidebarrieta	EZ	7	Lersundi	DX	36
Bilbao la Vieja	EZ	8	Marqués del Puerto	DY	38
Correo	EZ		Merced Muelle	EZ	40
Cosme Echevarrieta	DY	14	Merced Puente	EZ	41
Cruz	EZ	15	Moraza Pl. de	EX	45
			Pablo Picasso	DZ	50
			Pedro Eguillor Pl.	DY	52

Pedro Martínez Artola	DZ	53
Pío Baroja Pl.	EZ	55
Plaza Nueva	EZ	57
Puerto de la Paz Av.	DX	60
Ribera Puente	EZ	65
Santiago Pl.	EZ	71
Santos Juanes Pl.	EZ	73
Sombrereía	EZ	75
Viuda de Epalza	EY	80

Museo de Bellas Artes	DY	M

(linen weaving, arts and crafts, fishing). In the middle of the classicist cloisters the primitive, animal-like **idol of Mikeldi** may be seen. The top floor contains an immense relief model of Vizcaya province.

Museo Diocesano de Arte Sacro (Diocesan Museum of Sacred Art)
🕐 *Open 10.30am-1.30pm and 4-7pm; Sun, 10.30am-1.30pm.* 🕐 *Closed Mon and public hols.* ⊚ *3€, no charge Thu.* ☎ *94 432 01 25.*

This interesting museum, housed in the former Convento de la Encarnación (16C), contains a collection of Basque silverware and a series of 12C-15C sculptures of the Virgin and Child.

Santuario de Begoña

You can drive up along the Donostia-San Sebastián road (Avenida de Zumalacárregui) but it is easier to take the lift from Calle Esperanza Ascao. There is an interesting **view of Bilbao** from the upper terminus footbridge. *Upon leaving the Mallona park, take the main street on the right, which leads directly to the sanctuary.* Open 8am-1.45pm and 4.30-9pm; Sun and public hols, 9.30am-1.15pm and 4.30-8pm. ☎ 94 412 70 91.

The church contains the venerated figure of Nuestra Señora de Begoña, patron of the province, in a silver camarín in the chancel.

El Burgo de Osma★

POPULATION: 5 054

MICHELIN MAP 575 H 20 – CASTILLA Y LEÓN (SORIA)

This attractive Castilian town, one of the oldest episcopalian seats in Spain, acquired its present-day appearance in the 18C, a period when its porticoed streets and squares and elegant Baroque institutional buildings, such as the former San Agustín hospital on the Plaza Mayor, were built. The ruins of the town's castle crown a nearby hill. The tall Baroque tower of the cathedral is clearly visible when approaching El Burgo de Osma from the west.

Location

El Burgo de Osma is nestled between the Ucero and Avión rivers, along the N 122 highway. It lies 56km/35mi SW of Soria and 139km/87mi SE of Burgos. *Plaza Mayor 9, 42300 Burgo de Osma, ☎ 975 36 01 16.*

Neighbouring sights are described in the following chapters: SORIA, COVARRUBIAS (95km/59mi NW), BURGOS and PEDRAZA (111km/69mi SW).

Visit

Catedral★

Open 11am-1pm and 4.30-5.30pm; Jul-Nov 10am-1pm and 4-7pm. Closed Mon. 3€. ☎ 639 57 33 37.

This Gothic sanctuary was built in 1232 as a result of a vow taken by a Cluniac monk, Don Pedro de Osma, to replace the former Romanesque cathedral which had stood on the site. The east end, transept and chapter house were completed in the 13C; the late-Gothic cloisters and the chancel were embellished with Renaissance decoration in the 16C, while the large sacristy, royal chapel and 72m/236ft belfry were built in the 18C.

The Gothic decoration on the late-13C **south portal** includes on the splays, statues of (left to right) Moses, Gabriel, the Virgin, Judith, Solomon and Esther; on the lintel, a Dormition of the Virgin and on the pier, Christ displaying his wounds (late 15C).

The interior is remarkable for the elevation of the nave, the delicate wrought-iron screens (16C) by Juan de Francés, the **high altar retable** by Juan de Juni with scenes from the Life of the Virgin, and the 16C white marble **pulpit** and **trascoro altarpiece**.

The 13C polychrome limestone **tomb of San Pedro de Osma★** may be seen in the west arm of the transept. In the **museum**, among the **archives** and **illuminated manuscripts★** are a richly illustrated 1086 **Beatus** and a 12C manuscript with the signs of the Zodiac.

Excursions

Peñaranda de Duero★

47km/29mi W along the N 122 and BU 924. The small Castilian town is dominated by the ruins of its castle.

Plaza Mayor★

The square is an interesting architectural mix of half-timbered houses resting on robust stone pillars; at its centre stands a 15C pillory.

The **Palacio de Avellaneda**★, a palace with a noble façade and fully ornamented Renaissance entrance, stands on one side of the square. The interior, designed by Francisco de Colonia, makes it one of the finest Renaissance residences in Spain. There is a patio surrounded by a two tier gallery, an inner patio arch, a grand staircase and chambers with **artesonado ceilings**★. *Guided tours (30min), 10am-2pm and 4-7.30pm; Oct-Mar, 10am-2pm and 3-6pm; last admission 1hr before closing.* **○** *Closed Mon, 1 Jan and 24-25 and 31 Dec. No charge.* ☎ *947 55 20 13.*

Cañón del Río Lobos

15km/10mi N on the SO 920. This 25km/15mi stretch of canyon has been formed by the erosive action of the Lobos river (from Ucero to Hontoria del Pinar). The landscape here is riddled with caves, depressions and chasms, and has an abundance of juniper bushes, pines and young oaks. *For further information, contact the Centro de Interpretación del Parque Natural on* ☎ *975 36 35 64.*

Calatañazor

25km/15mi NE on the N 122 towards Soria. Calatañazor is one of those places in which time appears to have stood still. A stroll along its steep, stone-paved streets is quite an experience. From the ruins of the medieval castle, the view encompasses the plain on which Almanzor was said to have been defeated by Christian troops.

Castillo de Gormaz

14km/9mi S on the SO 160. The impressive ruins of this 10C Moorish castle stand on a hill overlooking the Duero river. Measuring 446m/1 463ft in length, and with 26 towers, this medieval fortress is the largest of its kind in Europe.

Berlanga del Duero

28km/17mi SE on the C 116 and SO 104. Berlanga still appears protected in medieval fashion with stout ramparts below the massive walls of its 15C castle – the town was a strongpoint in the fortified line along the Duero. In the Gothic **Colegiata**, a monumental 16C hall-church, are two chapels containing altarpieces carved and painted in the Flamboyant style and the 16C recumbent alabaster statues of its founders. *To visit the church, follow the instructions on the entrance door.* ☎ *975 34 30 49.*

Some 8km/5mi southeast in **Casillas de Berlanga** is the **Iglesia de San Baudelio de Berlanga**, an isolated 11C Mozarabic chapel with a highly original layout. At the centre of the square nave is a massive pillar on which descend the eight flat ribs supporting the roof. The gallery rests on a double line of horseshoe-shaped arches and, like the rest of the building, was covered with frescoes in the 12C. Some hunting scenes and geometric patterns can still be made out. (**○** *Open Nov-Mar, 10am-2pm and 3.30-6pm (Apr-May 10am-2pm and 4-7pm; Jun-Aug 10am-2pm and 5-9pm; Sun and public hols all year, 10am-2pm.* **○** *Closed Mon and Tue, 1 Jan and 24-25 and 31 Dec. 0.60€, no charge Sat-Sun.* ☎ *975 22 13 97.)*

Burgos★★

POPULATION: 169 111

MICHELIN MAP 575 E 18-19 (TOWN PLAN) – CASTILLA Y LEÓN (BURGOS)

Burgos sits on the banks of the River Arlanzón, on a windswept plateau at the heart of the Spanish Meseta. This impressive provincial capital is dotted with fine monuments and churches, the most famous of which is the magnificent cathedral, whose lofty Gothic spires dominate the city's skyline.

Location

Burgos is located 88km/55m from Palencia, 117km/73mi from Vitoria-Gasteiz and 120km/80mi from Valladolid. Because of its exposed position, at an altitude of 856m/2 808ft, the city is exposed to bitterly cold winds in winter. ▪ *Plaza Alonso Martínez 7, 09003 Burgos,* ☎ *947 20 31 25.*

 *Neighbouring sights are described in the following chapters: COVARRUBIAS (39km/24mi SE), La RIOJA (Santo Domingo de la Calzada: 75km/47mi E), AGUILAR DE CAMPOO (79km/49mi NW) and PALENCIA.*

Address Book

For coin ranges, see the Legend at the back of the guide.

WHERE TO EAT

Rincón de España – *Nuño Rasura 11 - ☎ 947 20 59 55 - Closed Mon-Tue evenings Nov-Mar –* 🍽️. The best feature here is two summertime terraces with views to the cathedral nearby, though there's also a covered terrace and formal dining room. Castillian fare includes house specialties prepared in a wood-fired oven.

Ponte Vecchio – *Vitoria 111 (passage) – ☎ 947 22 56 50 – Closed Mon –* 🍽️. An italiano restaurant in a magnificent locale, with murals inspired by ancient Rome. Detailed neo-Mediterranean decor, good service, and a welcoming environment where couples go to dine.

WHERE TO STAY

Hotel Jacobeo – *San Juan 24 – ☎ 947 26 01 02 – 13 rooms – 🛏️ 4.50€.* The major advantage of this small hotel, housed in a restored mansion, is undoubtedly its location in the very heart of the city's historic quarter. The rooms here are pleasant if not particularly spacious.

Landa Palace – *3.5km/2mi S along the A 1 – ☎ 947 25 77 77 –* 🅿️ 🍽️ *– 39 rooms – 🛏️ 16€ – Restaurant 38€.* The impressive facilities occupy part of a restored medieval castle. Especially notable are the majestic lobby, a great dining hall under stone vaults, individually styled and well-appointed rooms, and the spectacular covered pool. .

Background

Historical notes – Burgos was founded by Diego Rodríguez in 884 and selected as capital of the united kingdom of Castilla and León in 1037, a title it relinquished in 1492 on the fall of Granada, when the royal court moved to Valladolid. However, the loss of political involvement appears to have released energy for commercial and artistic enterprises: the town became a wool centre for the sheep farmers of the Mesta (🕯️ *see SORIA)*; architects and sculptors arrived, particularly from Northern Europe, and transformed monuments into the currently fashionable Gothic style. Burgos became Spain's Gothic capital with outstanding works including the cathedral, the Monasterio de las Huelgas Reales (Royal Convent of Las Huelgas) and the Cartuja de Miraflores (Carthusian monastery). Yet, the end of the 16C brought the decline of the Mesta and a halt to the town's prosperity.

Burgos was chosen by Franco to be the seat of his government from 1936 to 1938.

The Land of El Cid (1026-99) – The exploits of Rodrigo Díaz, native of Vivar *(9km/5.5mi N of Burgos)* light up the late-11C history of Castilla. The brilliant captain first supported the ambitious King of Castilla, Sancho II, then Alfonso VI who succeeded his brother in somewhat dubious circumstances. Alfonso, irritated at Díaz's suspicions and jealous of the prestige he had won following an attack on the Moors in 1081, banished the warrior hero although he was, by then, married to the king's cousin, Ximena.

Díaz, as a soldier of fortune, entered service first with the Moorish king of Zaragoza and subsequently fought Christian and Muslim armies with equal fervour. His most famous enterprise came when at the head of 7 000 men, chiefly Muslims, he captured Valencia after a nine-month siege in 1094. He was finally defeated by the Moors in an exploit at Cuenca and died soon afterwards (1099). His widow held Valencia against the Muslims until 1102 when she set fire to the city before fleeing to Castilla with El Cid's body. The couple were buried in the San Pedro de Cardeña Monastery *(10km/6mi SE of Burgos)*, but their ashes were moved and interred in Burgos Cathedral in 1921. Legend has transformed the stalwart but often ruthless 11C warrior, the Campeador or Champion of Castilla, El Cid *(Seid* in Arabic), into a chivalrous knight of exceptional valour. The first epic poem *El Cantar del Mío Cid* appeared in 1180 and was followed by ballads. In 1618 Guillén de Castro wrote a romanticised version of El Cid in his *Las Mocedades del Cid* (Youthful Adventures of El Cid) upon which Corneille, in 1636, based his drama *Le Cid.*

Special Features

Although Burgos is endowed with a wealth of impressive sights, the city's three most famous monuments are the cathedral, the Monasterio de Las Huelgas and the Cartuja de Miraflores.

CATEDRAL★★★ ⏱1hr 30min
🕐 Open 9.30am-1pm and 4-7pm (from 10am Nov-18 Apr). 🚻 3€. ☎ 947 20 47 12.

The cathedral, the third largest in Spain after those of Sevilla and Toledo, is a remarkable example of the transformation of French and German Flamboyant Gothic into a style that is typically Spanish through the natural exuberance of its decoration. The many works of art adorning the interior of the cathedral make it an outstanding showcase of European Gothic sculpture.

Ferdinand III laid the first stone in 1221 and there followed two principal stages of building which corresponded with distinct periods in the evolution of the Gothic style.

At the beginning of the 13C, under the aegis of Maurice the Englishman, then Bishop of Burgos, who had collected drawings during a journey through France (at that time very much influenced by the Gothic style), the nave, aisles and portals were built by local architects.

Spires of the cathedral

B. Juge/MICHELIN

The second period in the 15C saw the building of the west front spires and the Capilla del Condestable (Constable's Chapel) as well as the decoration of other chapels. These were directly influenced by foreigners from the north, through the architects and sculptors from Flanders, the Rhineland and Burgundy, whom another great Burgos prelate, Alonso de Cartagena, had brought back on his return from the Council of Basel.

These artists, from a Europe in which the influence of Flamboyant Gothic was beginning to wane, found new inspiration in Mudéjar arabesques and other Hispano-Moorish elements in Spanish art. The most outstanding among them, the Burgundian **Felipe Bigarny**, the Fleming **Gil de Siloé** and the Rhinelander **Johan of Cologne**, integrated rapidly and with their sons and grandsons – Diego de Siloé, Simon and Francis of Cologne – created what was essentially a Burgos school of sculpture.

The cloisters were built in the 14C, while the magnificent lantern over the transept crossing – the original of which collapsed after some particulary daring design work by Simon of Cologne – was rebuilt by Juan de Vallejo in the mid-16C.

Exterior

A walk round the cathedral will reveal how the architects took ingenious advantage of the sloping ground (the upper gallery of the cloisters is level with the cathedral pavement) to introduce delightful small precincts and closes cut by stairways.

West front

The ornate upper area, with its frieze of Spanish kings and its two openwork spires, pinnacled and crocketed, is the masterwork of Johan of Cologne.

Portada de la Coronería (Coronería Doorway) (1)

The statues at the jambs have the grace of their French Flamboyant Gothic originals, although the folds of their robes show more movement. The Plateresque **Portada de la Pellejería (2)**, or Skinner's Doorway, in the adjoining transept wall was designed by Francis of Cologne early in the 16C.

As you continue round by the east end it becomes obvious that the Constable's Chapel, with its Isabelline decoration and lantern with pinnacles, is one of the cathedral's later additions.

Portada del Sarmental (Sarmental Doorway) (3)

The covings are filled with figures from the Celestial Court, while the tympanum is an incredible sculpture in which each of the four Evangelists sits in a different position as he writes.

Interior

The design of the interior is French-inspired while the decoration bears an exuberant Spanish stamp.

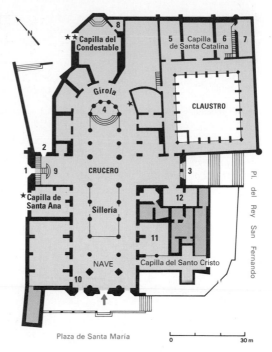

Plaza de Santa Maria

Crucero, Coro and Capilla Mayor★★ (Transept crossing, choir stalls and chancel)

The splendid star-ribbed lantern of the transept crossing rises on four massive pillars to a height of 54m/177ft above the funerary stones of El Cid and Ximena, inlaid in the crossing pavement.

The imposing unit of 103 walnut choir stalls, carved by Felipe Vigarny between 1507 and 1512, illustrates biblical stories on the upper, back rows and mythological and burlesque scenes at the front. The handsome recumbent statue of wood plated with enamelled copper, on the tomb at the centre, dates from the 13C and is of Bishop Maurice.

The high altar (4) retable is a 16C Renaissance work in high relief against an intrinsically Classical background of niches and pediments.

Claustro

The 14C Gothic cloisters present a panorama of Burgos sculpture with stone, terracotta and polychrome wood figures.

The **Capilla de Santiago** (St James' Chapel) (5) contains the cathedral treasure, a rich collection of church plate and liturgical objects.

In the **Capilla de Santa Catalina** (St Catherine's Chapel) are manuscripts and documents, including the marriage contract of El Cid. Note the 15C carved and painted consoles showing Moorish kings paying homage to the king of Castilla.

The **sacristía** (sacristy) (6) houses the *Christ at the Column* by Diego de Siloé, a supreme example of Spanish Expressionism in post-16C Iberian sculpture. The **sala capitular** (chapter house) (7) displays, besides 15C and 16C Brussels tapestries symbolising the theological and cardinal virtues, a Hispano-Flemish diptych, a *Virgin and Child* by Memling and, above, a painted wood Mudéjar *artesonado* ceiling (16C).

Capilla del Condestable★★ (Constable's Chapel)

A magnificent grille closes off the area. The Isabelline chapel founded by Hernández de Velasco, Constable of Castilla, in 1482 and designed by Simon of Cologne, is lit by a lantern surmounted by an elegant cupola with star-shaped vaulting. All the great early Renaissance sculptors of Burgos cooperated in the subsequent decoration of the walls and altarpiece. The heraldic displays in the chapel are striking. On either side of the altar, the Constable's escutcheon, held by male figures, appears to be suspended over the balustrades of the tribune.

BURGOS		Eduardo Martínez			Nuño Rasura	A	23
		del Campo	A	10	Paloma La	A	24
Almirante Bonifaz	B 2	España Pl.	B	12	Rey San Fernando Pl. del	A	27
Alonso Martínez Pl. de	B 3	Gen. Santocildes	B	15	Reyes Católicos Av. de los	B	26
Aparicio y Ruiz	A 5	Libertad Pl. de la	B	16	Santo Domingo		
Arlanzón Av. del	B 6	Mayor Pl.	AB	18	de Guzmán Pl. de	B	28
Cid Campeador Av. del	B 8	Miranda	B	20	Vitoria	B	
Conde de		Monasterio de					
Guadalhorce Av.	A 9	las Huelgas Av. del	A	21			

Arco de Santa Maria	A B	Museo Marceliano		Museo de Burgos	B M¹
		Santa María	B M²		

Statues of the Constable and his wife lie on their tomb, carved in Carrara marble, and beside them is an immense garnet-coloured marble funerary stone for the names of their descendants. On the right side of the chapel is a Plateresque door to the sacristy (1512) **(8)** where there is a painting of *Mary Magdalene* by Pietro Ricci.

Girola★ (Ambulatory)

The *trasaltar* (at the back of the high altar), carved partly by **Felipe Vigarny**, includes an expressive representation of the Ascent to Calvary.

Escalera Dorada or Escalera de la Coronería (Golden or Coronation Staircase) (9)

The majestically proportioned staircase was designed in the pure Renaissance style by Diego de Siloé in the early 16C. The twin pairs of flights are outlined by an ornately elegant gilded banister by the French master ironsmith, Hilaire.

Capillas

Each of these side chapels is a museum of Gothic and Plateresque art: **Gil de Siloé** and Diego de la Cruz cooperated on the huge Gothic altarpiece in the **Capilla de Santa Ana★** which illustrates the saint's life. In the centre is a Tree of Jesse with, at its heart, the first meeting of Anne and Joachim and at the top, the Virgin and Child.

At the beginning of the cathedral nave, high up near the roof, is the **Papamoscas** or **Flycatcher Clock (10)**, with a jack which opens its mouth on the striking of the hours.

In the **Capilla del Santo Cristo** (Chapel of Holy Christ) is a Crucifixion with the particularly venerated figure complete with hair and covered with buffalo hide to resemble human flesh.

The **Capilla de la Presentación** (Chapel of the Presentation) **(11)** contains the tomb of the Bishop of Lerma, carved by Felipe Vigarny and the **Capilla de la Visitación** (Chapel of the Visitation) **(12)**, that of Alonso de Cartagena by Gil de Siloé.

REAL MONASTERIO DE LAS HUELGAS★★
(ROYAL CONVENT OF LAS HUELGAS)

1.5km/1mi W of Burgos; take avenida del Monasterio de las Huelgas.

Guided tours (50min) 10am-1.15pm and 3.45-5.45pm; Sun and public hols 10.30am-2.15pm. ⏰ Closed Mon, 1 and 6 Jan, 9 Apr, 1 May, 18 and 29 Jun, and 24, 25 and 31 Dec. ⊚ 5€, no charge Wed for citizens of the European Union. ☎ 947 20 16 30.

Las Huelgas Reales, originally a summer palace of the kings of Castilla, was converted in 1180 into a convent by Alfonso VIII and his wife Eleanor, daughter of Henry II of England. The nuns here were Cistercians of high lineage, the abbess all-powerful; by the 13C the convent's influence, both spiritual and temporal, extended to more than 50 towns and it had become a common place of retreat for members of the house of Castilla and even became the royal pantheon.

Rearrangement over the centuries has resulted in a heterogeneous and somewhat divided building in which, although the Cistercian style of the 12C and 13C predominates, there are Romanesque and even Mudéjar features (13C-15C) as well as Plateresque furnishings.

Iglesia

The clean lines of the exterior of this church are pure Cistercian. The interior is divided into two by a screen: from the transept, open to all, you can see the revolving pulpit (1560), in gilded ironwork, which enabled the preacher to be heard on either side of the screen. Royal and princely tombs, originally coloured, rich in heraldic devices and historical legend, line the aisles, while in the middle of the nave, the nuns' *coro*, is the double sepulchre of the founders, Alfonso VIII and Eleanor of England. The rood screen retable, delicately carved and coloured in the Renaissance style, is surmounted by a fine 13C Deposition. The altar is flanked on each side by two handsome 13C and 14C tombs.

Gothic cloisters

13C-15C. Enough fragments of Mudéjar vaulting stucco remain in these Gothic cloisters to give an idea of the delicacy of the strapwork inspired by Persian ivories and fabrics.

Sala Capitular

This chapter house contains the **pendón**★, a trophy from the Battle of Las Navas de Tolosa, decorated with silk *appliqué*.

Romanesque cloisters

Late 12C. In these Romanesque cloisters, slender paired columns, topped by highly stylised capitals, combine to create an effect of elegance. Several rooms in this part of the building, Alfonso VIII's former palace, were decorated by the Moors. The **Capilla de Santiago** (Chapel of St James) retains an *artesonado* ceiling with its original colouring and stucco frieze. According to legend, the statue of the saint with articulated arms conferred knighthood upon princes of royal blood.

★★ (Museum of Medieval Fabrics)

The fabrics, court dress and finery displayed in the former loft provide a vivid review of royal wear in 13C Castilla. Of the clothes, (mainly tunics, pelisses and capes) found in the tombs, the most valuable items come from that of the Infante Fernando de la Cerda (who died in 1275), son of Alfonso X, the Wise. This tomb, one that was not desecrated by French troops in 1809, contained a long tunic, *pellote* (voluminous trousers with braces) and a very large mantle, all made of the same material embroidered with silk and silver thread. There is also a *birrete*, a silk crown adorned with pearls and precious stones.

CARTUJA DE MIRAFLORES
(MIRAFLORES CARTHUSIAN MONASTERY)

4km/2.5mi E. ⏰ Open 10.15am-3pm and 4-6pm; Sun and public hols, 11.20am-12.40pm, 1.15-3pm and 4-6pm. ⊚ No charge.

This former royal foundation, entrusted to the Carthusians in 1442, was chosen by Juan II as a pantheon for himself and his second wife, Isabel of Portugal. The church was completed in full Isabelline Gothic style in 1498.

Iglesia★

The sobriety of the façade, relieved only by the buttress finials and the founders' escutcheons, gives no indication of the richness inside. This appears in the church's single aisle with its elegant vaulting and gilded keystones and particularly in the magnificent apse.

Sculpture ensemble in the Capilla Mayor★★★ (apse)

This was designed by the Fleming, Gil de Siloé at the end of the 15C and comprises the high altarpiece, the royal mausoleum and a funerary recess.

The polychrome wood **altarpiece**, the work of Siloé and Diego de la Cruz, has a striking design: the usual rectangular compartments have been replaced by circles, each crowded with biblical figures.

The white marble **mausoleo real** (royal mausoleum) is in the form of an eight-pointed star in which can be seen the recumbent statues of the founders, Juan II and Queen Isabel, parents of Isabel the Catholic. Dominating the exuberant Flamboyant Gothic decoration of scrolls, canopies, pinnacles, cherubim and armorial bearings, executed with rare virtuosity, are the four Evangelists. In an ornate **recess** in the north wall is the tomb of the Infante Alfonso, whose premature death gave the throne of Castilla to his sister Isabel the Catholic. The statue of the young prince at prayer is technically brilliant but impersonal (compare with that of Juan de Padilla in the Museo de Burgos, 👁 *see below*).

Also in the church are a 15C Hispano-Flemish triptych (to the right of the altar) and Gothic **choir stalls** carved with an infinite variety of arabesques.

Visit

Museo de Burgos★

🕐 *Open 10am-2pm and 4-7pm (5-8pm in summer); Sat-Sun 10am-2pm.* 🕐 *Closed Mon and public hols.* 🎫 *1.20€, no charge Sat-Sun and public hols.* ☎ *947 26 58 75.*

Two sections, housed in separate buildings:

Prehistoric and Archaeological Department

Housed in the Casa de Miranda, a Renaissance mansion with an elegant patio, this section contains finds discovered in the province covering the Prehistoric to Visigothic periods.

Of particular interest are the rooms devoted to Iron Age sites, to the Roman settlement of Clunia and the collection of Roman funerary steles.

Fine Arts Department

The Casa de Ángulo houses works of art from the Burgos region covering the period from the 9C to the 20C. There are several precious items from the Santo Domingo Monastery at Silas: an 11C **Hispano-Moorish casket**★, delicately carved in ivory in Cuenca and highlighted with enamel plaques, the 12C **Frontal** or **Urn of Santo Domingo**★ in beaten and enamelled copper, and a 10C **marble diptych**.

In the section on 14C-15C funerary sculpture is the **tomb**★ of Juan de Padilla on which Gil de Siloé has beautifully rendered the countenance and robes of the dead man.

The collection of 15C painting contains a *Christ Weeping* by the Fleming, Jan Mostaert.

Arco de Santa María★

🕐 *Open 11am-2pm and 5-9pm; Sun, 11am-2pm.* 🕐 *Closed Mon and public hols.* ☎ *947 28 88 68.*

The 14C gateway once defended the city walls. In the 16C it was modified to form a triumphal arch for Emperor Charles V and embellished with statues of the famous: below, Diego Porcelos Rodríguez is flanked by two semi-legendary judges said to have governed Castilla in the 10C, and above, Count Fernán González and El Cid (right) are shown with Charles V. In the interior can be seen the **Sala de Poridad**, with its magnificent Mudéjar cupola, and the pharmacy from the former Hospital de San Juan.

Iglesia de San Nicolás

🕐 *Open in summer, 10am-2pm and 4-8pm; public hols 9am-2pm and 5-6pm; in other seasons by prior arrangement.* 🕐 *No visits during religious services.* 🎫 *1€.* ☎ *947 20 70 95.*

The **altarpiece**★ of this Gothic church, carved by Simon of Cologne in 1505, is both large and ornate with more than 465 figures. The upper part shows the Virgin crowned at the centre of a circle of angels; St Nicholas in the central part is surrounded by scenes from his life – note the voyage by caravel to Alexandria – and below, there is a back view of the *Last Supper*.

Iglesia de San Esteban: Museo del Retablo

🕐 *Open 10.30am-2pm and 4.30-7pm; Sun 10.30-2.* 🕐 *Closed Mon, Tu-Fri 1 Nov-31 May and 29 Jun.* 👓 *1.20€.* ☎ *947 27 37 52.*

The city's Retable Museum is housed in this delightful **church**★, built in the 14C in Burgos Gothic style. The interior is a magnificent setting for the 18 retables which are exhibited according to their religious significance in the church's three naves. The coro alto contains a small collection of gold and silverwork.

Iglesia de San Gil

👓 *Guided tours (45min) in summer, 10am-2pm and 5-8pm; in winter by prior arrangement.* 🕐 *Closed for visits Sun and public hols.* 👓 *1.20€.* ☎ *947 26 11 49.*

One of the city's most beautiful churches. Hidden behind its sober façade is a temple from the end of the Gothic period. Particularly worthy of note are the Nativity Chapel and Buena Mañana chapels, the latter containing a retable by Gil de Siloé.

Plaza Mayor

This delightful circular main square, typically lined by a portico, is the setting for all public festivities.

Casa del Cordón

The recently restored palace of the Constables of Castilla was built in the 15C (and presently houses the Caja de Ahorros savings bank). Still decorating its façade is the thick Franciscan cord motif which gave the palace its name. It is interesting historically as the place where Columbus was received by the Catholic Monarchs on his return from his second voyage to America and also where Philip the Fair died suddenly of a chill after a game of *pelota*, reducing to despair his already much disturbed wife, Juana the Mad.

Museo Marceliano Santa María

Open 10am-1.50pm and 5-7.50pm; Sun, 10am-3.30pm. 🕐 *Closed Mon and public hols.* 👓 *0.15€.* ☎ *947 20 56 87.*

The museum, in the ruins of the former Benedictine monastery of San Juan, displays Impressionist type canvases by the Burgos painter Marceliano Santa María (1866-1952).

Hospital del Rey

Founded by Alfonso VIII as a hospital for pilgrims. It has preserved its entrance, known as the Patio de Romeros, with its fine 16C Plateresque façade. Today, it is the headquarters of the University of Burgos

Excursion

Archaeological finds in the Sierra de Atapuerca

Take the N 120 towards Logroño. When you reach Ibeas de Juarros (13km/8mi), head for the Emiliano Aguirre hall (on the side of the main road). 👓 *Guided tours (2hr) of the caves and Museo Emiliano Aguirre by prior arrangement.* 👓 *3.01€.* ☎ *947 42 14 62.*

The construction of a trench for a railway line at the end of the last century led to the discovery of one of the world's most important palaeontological finds, which has recently been declared a World Heritage Site. Excavations at **La Dolina** have brought to light the remains of hominids who lived around 800 000 years ago. The fossil register at the **Sima de los Huesos** (literally the Chasm of Bones), is the largest in Europe dating from the Middle Pleistocene age between 400 000 and 200 000 years ago. Visitors are able to walk along the trench and visit a small archaeological museum.

Cáceres★★★

The monumental centre of this quiet provincial capital, which in 1986 was declared a World Heritag enturies. Its Almohad walls, punctuated by several towers, provided protection in the past for the unique and homogenous Gothic and Renaissance mansion houses that embellish this historic city.

Location

Cáceres is strategically situated at the heart of Extremadura and is an excellent base from which to explore the region's delightful towns, villages and countryside. *Plaza Mayor 10, 10003 Cáceres, ☎ 927 01 08 34.*

Neighbouring sights are described in the following chapters: TRUJILLO (47km/29mi E), MÉRIDA (60km/37mi S), PLASENCIA (84km/52mi NE) and BADAJOZ (96km/60mi SW).

Walking About

CÁCERES VIEJO★★★ (Old Cáceres) *1hr 30min*

Within its defensive walls and towers built by the Moors, this old quarter includes a group of Gothic and Renaissance seigniorial mansions beyond compare in Spain. The unadorned, ochre-coloured façades of the residences belonging to the noblemen of the 15C and 16C bear no ostentatious flourishes as they reflect the nature of their owners, the Ulloas, the Ovandos and the Saavedras, proud warriors all, who in their fight against the infidel – Moor or American Indian – won more in prestige than in wealth. Minimal decoration consists of a narrow fillet around the windows, a sculptured cornice or a proud coat of arms. The fortified towers which once stood guard over the mansions and proclaimed their owners' power were lowered on the command of Isabel the Catholic in 1477.

▶ *Follow the route marked on the plan.*

Pass beneath the **Arco de la Estrella** (Star Arch) which was built into the wall by Manuel Churriguera in the 18C.

Address Book

For coin ranges, see the Legend at the back of the guide.

WHERE TO EAT

El Puchero – *Plaza Mayor 9 – ☎ 92 724 54 97 – .*
A good choice for the visitor, right in the plaza before the walled enclosure. There are two dining rooms with a local flavour where you can enjoy regional specialties at an attractive price.

El Figón de Eustaquio – *Plaza de San Juan 12 – ☎ 92 724 81 94 – Closed 1-15 Jul – .* Most traditional city, superbly located on the fringes of plaza Mayor. Traditional, local cuisine served in a rustic ambience.

TAPAS

El Asador – *Moret 34 – ☎ 92 722 38 37 – .* A good location in a narrow street in the old quarter. The tapas served at this bar-restaurant have an excellent reputation with locals. There's also a modest dining room to the rear.

WHERE TO STAY

Hotel Iberia – *Pintores 2 – ☎ 92 724 76 34 – – 36 rooms– 3.50€.* This pleasant hotel just off the plaza Mayor is housed in a building dating from the 17C. Cosy rooms, a central location and excellent value for money. Highly recommended.

Parador de Cáceres – *Avenida Ancha 6 – ☎ 92 721 17 59 – caceresparador. es – – 9.70€ – Restaurant 25.30€.* The 14C Palacio de Torreorgaz has been transformed into the city's delightful parador. Tasteful furnishings, comfortable rooms and well worth splashing out on.

Plaza de Santa María★

This irregularly shaped square forms the monumental heart of the old city; rising on all sides are attractive golden ochre façades. The front of the **Palacio Mayoralgo** (Mayoralgo Palace), now restored, has elegant paired windows while the **Palacio Episcopal** (Bishop's Palace) has a 16C bossed doorway with medallions of the Old and New Worlds on either side (left and right respectively).

Iglesia de Santa María

🕐 *Open 10am-to 1.30pm (10.45am-noon Sun and public hols) and 5-6.15pm; May-Sep, 10am-1.30pm and 6-7.15pm.* 💳 *1€.* ☎ *92 721 53 13.*

This nobly styled church, completed in the 16C, serves as the city cathedral. The three Gothic aisles of almost equal height, have lierne and tierceron vaulting from which the ribs descend into slender columns engaged around the main pillars. The carved retable at the high altar (16C) is difficult to see but with its high standard of workmanship is well worth the effort.

By continuing round to the left of Santa María to the top of calle de las Tiendas, you will see the **Palacio de Carvajal** (Carvajal Palace) flanked by a 15C tower. The chambers, patio and chapel of this nobleman's residence are open to the public. 🕐 *Open 9am-9pm; Sat 10am-2pm and 5-8pm; Sun and public hols, 10am-2pm.* 🕐 *Closed 1 Jan and 25 Dec.* ☎ *92 725 55 98.*

Palacio de los Golfines de Abajo★ (Lower Golfines Palace)

This rich mansion, twice honoured by visits by the Catholic Monarchs, has a rough stone façade, Gothic in style with the Plateresque traits characteristic of civil architecture of the late 15C. The paired window derives from the Moorish *ajimez*, while the fillet, delicately framing the two windows and the door, recalls the *alfiz*. To lighten the front, a Plateresque frieze with winged griffons was added to the top of the central area in the 16C, while medallions and the Golfines coat of arms – a fleur-de-lis and a tower – complete the decoration.

Palacio de los Golfines de Abajo

Plaza San Jorge

Note the austere 18C façade of the Jesuit church of **San Francisco Javier.**

Iglesia de San Mateo

The church's high Gothic nave, begun in the 14C, was abutted in the 16C by a *coro alto* resting on an arcade with basket vaulting. The interior is bare except for the Baroque altarpiece and the side chapels containing tombs with decorative heraldic motifs. Continuing round the church by the north wall you come, in succession, on two 15C towers both of which have lost their battlements but have retained unusual parapets – they are respectively the **Torre de la Plata** (Silver Tower) and the **Casa del Sol** (Sun House) which owes its name to the elegant crest of the Solís family boldly carved over the arch.

Casa de las Cigüeñas (The Stork House)

The house, now occupied by the military, proudly sports a battlemented tower – the only one to escape the lopping decreed in the late 15C.

Casa de las Veletas (Weather Vane House)

The mansion, its fine 18C façade emblazoned with Baroque family crests, was built over a Moorish alcázar of which the cistern still remains. It houses the **Museo de Cáceres**: collections of archaeology (engraved Bronze Age steles, Celt-Iberian statues of wild boar known as verracos, Roman remains) and ethnology (local dress, arts and crafts).(🕐 *Open 9am-2.30pm and 4-7.15pm; in summer, 9am-2.30pm and 5-8.15pm; Sun, 10am-2.30pm.* 🕐 *Closed Mon and public hols.* 💳 *1.20€, no charge for citizens of the European Union.* ☎ *92 701 08 77).*

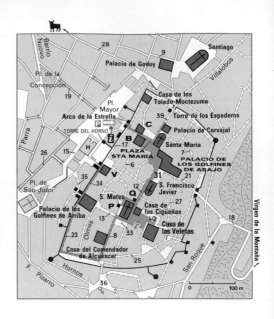

The 11C **aljibe** (Arab cistern) is still fed by a trickle of water from the roof and sloping square outside. It is covered by five rows of horseshoe-shaped arches supported by granite capitals with carving which is unfortunately barely noticeable.

Casa del Comendador de Alcuéscar

This palace, also known as the **Palacio de Torreorgaz**, is nowadays the city's parador. Its main features are the fine Gothic tower, the delicate window surrounds and an unusual corner balcony.

By taking the alley alongside the ramparts you reach the **Palacio de los Golfines de Arriba** (Upper Golfines Palace) with an austere, imposing façade and an attractive patio. The **Casa de la Generala** a little further on, houses the law faculty.

▶ *Go through the door in the ramparts opposite.*

The steps leading down to Plaza Mayor del General Mola afford an interesting view of the walls, particularly high at this point, and the Torre del Horno.

EXTRAMUROS

Iglesia de Santiago (St James' Church)
🕐 *Open 9am-noon and 6-8pm.* ☎ *92 724 49 06.*

The Romanesque church, rebuilt in the 16C, is traditionally held to be the birthplace of the Military Order of the Knights of Cáceres who in turn founded the Order of the Knights of St James. Inside, the altarpiece carved by Alonso Berruguete in 1557 bears scenes from the Life of Christ. These surround a vigorous, finely portrayed St James *Matamoros* or Slayer of the Moors.

The **Palacio de Godoy** opposite has an impressive coat of arms on the corner and a fine inner patio with decorative azulejos.

▶ Palacio de los Toledo-Moctezuma; Torre de los Espaderos.

Excursions

Santuario de la Virgen de la Montaña
3km/2mi E. 🕐 *Open 8.30am-2pm and 4-8pm (10pm in summer).* 🕐 *Closed 22 Apr-1st Sun in May.* ☎ *92 722 00 49.*

This 17C Baroque shrine, built on a hill cloaked in olive trees, shelters a famous statuette of the Virgin. A picturesque romería (pilgrimage) to the shrine is held on the first Sunday in May. The esplanade affords an extensive **view**★ across the Extremadura plateau.

Museo Vostell-Malpartida

▶ *10km/6mi along the N 521 towards Malpartida de Cáceres. The museum is located 3km/2mi beyond the town (follow the signposts). ○ Open 10am-1.30pm and 4-6.30pm; in summer, 10.30am-1.30pm and 6-9pm; in spring, 10am-1.30pm and 5-7.30pm. ○ Closed Mon and public hols. ₪ 2€, no charge Wed. ☎ 92 727 64 92.*

In 1976 the Hispano-German artist Wolf Vostell created a private contemporary art museum in this 18C-19C wool-washing factory. Vostell was the leading light in the Fluxus movement founded in 1962 by George Maciunas. The museum contains seven rooms created by Vostell, a large collection of conceptual art, including works by Canogar, the Crónica team and Saura, and a donation from the Fluxus collection by Gino di Maggio with works by Maciunas, Brecht, Higgins and Vautier.

Arroyo de la Luz

▶ *20km/12mi W along the N 521 and C 523. To find the Iglesia de la Asunción, take the tower as a bearing and proceed along the widest street.* The church has a 15C-16C Gothic nave. The altarpiece is worth looking at for the 16 **pictures**★ and four medallions it comprises which were painted on the spot by **Morales the Divine** between 1560 and 1563. As the artist's paintings are scattered, the collection here provides an opportunity to appreciate more fully than usual his delicate, elegant style.

Alcántara

65km/40mi NW along the N 521 and C 523. Alcántara stands in a countryside of ancient shale rocks through which the Tajo river has cut its course, watching over the old Roman bridge which once brought it renown and from which it took its name (*Al Kantara* is Arabic for bridge).

Puente Romano★

2km/1.2mi NW on the road to Portugal. This magnificent construction was built during the reign of the Emperor Trajan in AD 106. The bridge is made of massive granite blocks held together without mortar and was erected to withstand the most formidable flood-waters. More damage, however, has been caused by man and it has had to be restored several times. The small temple at one end and the central triumphal arch are both Roman.

> ### The Order of Alcántara
>
> The Knights of San Juan de Pereiro changed the name of their order to Alcántara when they were entrusted with the defence of the town's fortress in 1218. Like the other great orders of chivalry in Spain – Calatrava, Santiago and Montesa – the Order of Alcántara was created to free the country from the Moors in the 12C. Each order, founded as a military unit under the command of a master, lived in a community bound by the Cistercian rule. These religious militias, always prepared for combat and capable of withstanding long sieges in their fortresses, played a major role in the Reconquest.

Convento de San Benito

Guided tours (30-45min), 10am (11am Sat) to 2pm and 4-6.30pm (in summer, 5-7.30pm); Sun and public hols, 11am-2pm. ₪ No charge. ☎ 92 739 00 80.

The old headquarters of the Military Order of Alcántara stands high above the Tajo. The 16C monastery buildings include a richly decorated Plateresque church with star vaulting, a Gothic patio and, outside, a graceful arcaded Renaissance gallery used as the backdrop for plays.

Garrovillas

36km/22mi NW along the N 630 and EX 302.

In this typical Extremadura town, the Plaza Mayor is lined by arcades in which, in a delightfully artless way, fantasy has run rife with every pillar askew!

Cádiz★★

POPULATION: 143 129.

MICHELIN MAP 578 W 11 – ANDALUCÍA (CÁDIZ)

Surrounded by water on three sides, Cádiz is Spain's longest-established seafaring city, attracting settlers and mariners for over 3 000 years. It is also one of Andalucía's most delightful and engaging provincial capitals, characterised by charming parks and squares, an ordered layout of atttractive 19C streets, narrow alleyways and a quietly confident air, this tranquility is broken only by the exuberant Carnival, considered to be the best on the Iberian Peninsula. The reward for those visitors who venture here is the opportunity to discover a friendly, cosmopolitan city which, despite lacking major monuments, is one of Spain's unheralded treasures.

Location

This fortified city occupies an impressive coastal position with the waters of the Atlantic to the south and west, the Bahía de Cádiz to the north and east, and the town of El Puerto de Santa María visible across the bay. 🖪 *Avenida Ramón de Carranza, 11006 Cádiz, ☎ 95 625 86 46; Plaza de San Juan de Dios 11, 11005 Cádiz, ☎ 95 624 10 01.*

🖑 *Neighbouring sights are described in the following chapters: Costa de la LUZ, JEREZ DE LA FRONTERA (35km/22mi NE) and RONDA (123km/77mi E).*

Background

The oldest city in Europe – Cádiz, a bastion ringed by the sea, is attached to the mainland by a narrow sand isthmus. According to legend, it was founded by the Phoenicians in 1100 BC, subsequently conquered by the Romans in 206 BC, and later occupied by the Visigoths and Moors. Alfonso X reconquered the city in 1262.

Address Book

For coin ranges, see the Legend at the back of the guide.

TAPAS

Aurelio – *Zorrilla 1* – ☎ *95 622 10 31* – *Closed Mon except from Jul-Sep. –🍴.* This popular bar specialising in seafood is one of the places to eat tapas in Cádiz. Its only drawback is its size, which means that it soon fills up. A good central location close to the Plaza de Mina.

WHERE TO STAY

🛏 **Hostal Fantoni** – *Flamenco 5* – ☎ *95 628 27 04* –🍴 – *8 rooms.* Why spend more when you can stay in this simple but pleasant hostal? It's slowly being upgraded. We recommend the rooms with en-suite bathrooms that face a pedestrian lane.

🛏🍽 **Hotel Francia y París** – *Plaza de San Francisco 6* – ☎ *95 622 23 19* –▤ – *57 rooms* – ☕ *5.11€.* An early-20C hotel with pleasant rooms fronting an attractive small square in the centre of the city.

BARS AND CAFÉS

Café Parisien – *Plaza de San Francisco 1* – *Open 9am-11pm.* This old café on a quiet square is popular with people of all ages, who converge on the highly sought-after outside tables. The café also serves a selection of meals.

El Café de Levante – *Rosario* – *Open 4pm-3am.* A quiet café with tasteful modern decor on one of the old quarter's most typical streets. Its relaxed atmosphere attracts an eclectic crowd who come here to enjoy a quiet chat with friends. A variety of concerts are regularly held here on Thursday evenings.

SHOPPING

Horno Compañía – *Compañía 7.* This traditional shop sells local products such as pan de Cádiz.

FIESTAS

The **carnival** in Cádiz, the week before Ash Wednesday, is without a doubt the most famous and lively on the Iberian Peninsula.

ENTERTAINMENT

The **Gran Teatro Falla** *(plaza Falla)* organises a programme of theatre and concerts throughout the year (except in summer), while the city's five **cultural centres** (El Palillero, El Bidón, La Viña, La Lechera), host a wide range of exhibitions, workshops etc, as well as flamenco concerts at the fifth venue, the **Baluarte de la Candelaria**, on alameda de Apodaca.

During the 16C, Cádiz was repeatedly attacked by English corsairs, including in 1596, when it was partially destroyed by the Earl of Essex. In the 18C, Cádiz became one of Europe's greatest ports once it had acquired trading rights with Spanish America, hitherto the monopoly of Sevilla.

Constitution of Cádiz – During the French occupation and siege of 1812, Spanish patriots convened the Cortes which promulgated the country's first liberal constitution.

Watchtowers – Between the 16C and 18C, merchants in Cádiz built in excess of 160 towers to watch over the arrival and departure of their ships. In addition to their protective role, these towers were a symbol of the merchants' prosperity and prestige.

Walking About

Cádiz is a city with pleasant squares and gardens which are best discovered on foot. The two itineraries below include the city's most characteristic districts as well as its main monuments (see plan).

AROUND SANTA MARÍA AND THE PÓPULO DISTRICT 1

Plaza de San Juan de Dios

This 16C square is the most popular in the city. On one side stands the neo-Classical façade of the **town hall** *(ayuntamiento)* dating from 1799, a work by Torcuato Benjumeda, with the Baroque tower of the Iglesia de San Juan de Dios next to it. The square is also home to the city's tourist office, housed in an attractive neo-Classical building.

▶ *Take calle Sopranis, to the left of the Iglesia de San Juan de Dios.*

Calle Sopranis

The street contains some of the best examples of Baroque civil architecture in Cádiz, particularly the houses at nos9, 10 and 17. At the end of the street note the former **tobacco factory** a superb example of 19C iron and brick architecture, and the **Convento de Santo Domingo.**

▶ *Continue along calle Plocia as far as Concepción Arenal.*

Cárcel Real★

The royal jail, built in 1792 by the architect Torcuato Benjumeda, is one of the most important Baroque civil buildings in the whole of Andalucía. It consists of a single-section façade with a triumphal arch-style entrance bearing the escutcheon of the Spanish monarchy. Since 1990, the building has housed the city's law courts.

Iglesia de Santa María

This Mannerist-style church dates from the 17C and is crowned by a belfry with an azulejo-adorned spire.

▶ *Continue along calle Santa María, passing the 18C* **Casa Lasquetty** *to the left, then cross calle Félix Soto and head towards the 13C* **Arco de los Blancos***.*

Casa del Almirante

The outstanding feature of this 17C Baroque palace is the double-section Italian marble **doorway★★**, with its combination of Tuscan and Solomonic columns.

Iglesia de Santa Cruz★

🕐 *Open for Mass at noon and 7pm (the church is usually open beforehand).* ☎ *95 628 77 04.*

The old cathedral was rebuilt following the destruction of the city by the Earl of Essex in 1596. The finely proportioned, yet sober interior consists of three aisles separated by robust Tuscan-style columns.

The Casa de la Contaduría, home to the Museo Catedralicio, stands alongside the church (👃 *see description under Worth a Visit*).

Catedral★★

🕐 *Open 10am-1pm and 4.30-7pm (6.30pm Wed and Fri).* 👃4€ *(includes visit to the museum).* ☎ *95 628 61 54.*

Work on the new cathedral began in 1722 according to a design by Vicente Acero. However, various problems prolonged the project until 1838. The result is a building essentially Baroque in character with the occasional neo-Classical feature. The **façade★** consists of a series of concave and convex surfaces flanked by two lofty

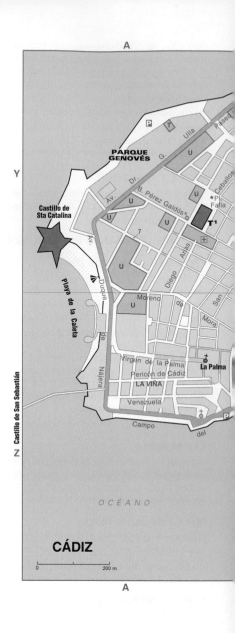

CÁDIZ

Façade, Cádix Cathedral

towers. The triple-aisle interior is surprisingly light and spacious due to the type of marble used in its construction. The crypt contains the remains of the composer **Manuel de Falla** (1876-1946).

🐾 FROM PLAZA SAN JUAN DE DIOS TO THE CATHEDRAL ②
This itinerary starts in calle Nueva, which runs into plaza de San Juan de Dios. Head along calle Nueva, turning left into calle Cristóbal Colón.

Casa de las Cadenas

This Baroque mansion is fronted by an interesting Genoese marble **doorway**★ framed by a pair of Solomonic columns.

▶ *Continue along calle Cristóbal Colón and calle Cobos as far as plaza de la Candelaria; from here, return to calle Nueva. Once past plaza de San Agustín, head along calle Rosario, to the Oratorio de la Santa Cueva (see description under Worth a Visit).*

Plaza de San Francisco

This charming plaza, lined by several lively bars and cafés, is one of the most pleasant corners of the city. The Baroque tower of the Iglesia de San Francisco rises above the square.

Plaza de Min★★★

Created in 1838 on the vegetable garden of the nearby Convento de San Francisco, this delightfully verdant square is imbued with a colonial feel. The fine examples of Isabelline-style architecture surrounding the square include the impressive **Museo de Cádiz** (👣 *see description under Worth a Visit*).

▶ *Head down calle de San José to the Oratorio de San Felipe Neri (👣 see description under Worth a Visit). The oratory stands alongside the Museo Iconográfico e Histórico de las Cortes y Sitio de Cádiz (👣 see description under Worth a Visit).*

Hospital de Mujeres★
🕐 *Open 10am-1.30pm. Closed Sun and public hols. 0.80€. ☎ 95 622 36 47.*

This distinguished Baroque building is laid out around two patios linked via an extraordinary Imperial-style **stairway**★★. The 18C Vía Crucis in the patio, created from 18C Triana azulejos, is particularly attractive.

The Battle of Trafalgar

On 21 October 1805, Admiral Villeneuve sailed out of Cádiz harbour with his Franco-Spanish fleet to confront the English under Nelson off the Cabo de Trafalgar headland. The ships were ill-equipped and poorly manned; after some heroic combat Villeneuve's fleet was destroyed and he was taken prisoner. Nelson had been mortally wounded during the course of the battle but England's supremacy at sea was established.

▷ *Continue on foot to the Torre Tavira (see description under Worth a Visit) on calle Sacramento.*

Plaza de las Flores

The numerous flower and plant stalls, cafés and shops contribute to the delightful atmosphere in one of the city's liveliest squares.

▷ *From here, follow calle Compañía to return to plaza de la Catedral.*

Worth a Visit

Museo Catedralicio★

🕐 *Open 10am-1.30pm and 4.30-7pm; Sat 10.30am-1pm.* ⊜ *4€ (includes visit to the cathedral).* ☎ *95 625 98 12.*

This complex of medieval buildings contains a fine 16C **Mudéjar patio**★, as well as a variety of liturgical objects and sacred art. The 16C **Custodia del Cogollo**★, a gold-plated silver monstrance attributed to Enrique Arfe, and the 18C **Custodia del Millón** are the museum's finest pieces.

Oratorio de la Santa Cueva★

🕐 *Open 10am-1pm and 4.30-7.30pm (5-8pm in summer); Sat-Sun 10am-1pm.* 🕐 *Closed Mon and public hols.* ⊜ *2€.* ☎ *95 622 22 62.*

The highlight of this elliptical oratory is the set of three **canvases**★★ painted by Goya in 1795.

Museo de Cádiz★

🕐 *Open 9am-8pm; Sun, 9am-2.30pm.* 🕐 *Closed Mon, Tue 9am-2.30pm (except by prior arrangement), 1 and 6 Jan, 1 May, 16 Aug, and 25 and 31 Dec.* ⊜ *1.50€, no charge for citizens of the European Union.* ☎ *95 621 22 81.*

The city's museum is housed in a small neo-Classical palace built midway through the 19C. The archaeological section contains a fine collection of vases, oil lamps and jewellery, although the outstanding exhibits are the two 5C BC **anthropoidal sarcophagi**★★; the male sarcophagus was discovered in 1887 and the female one in 1980. Both were copied by Greek artists based on Egyptian models. The fine arts section houses numerous works from the Spanish School, painted during the Golden Age by renowned artists such as Morales, Murillo, Ribera and, above all, Zurbarán, who was responsible for the series of nine **panels**★ emanating from the Carthusian monastery in Jerez, and painted between 1638 and 1639.

Torre Tavira★

🔦 *Guided tours (40 min) 10am-6pm (8pm 15 Jun-15 Sep); last guided tour 30 min before closing.* ⊜ *3.50€.* ☎ *95 621 29 10.*

What was once the city's official watchtower in the 18C has since 1995 housed the first **camera obscura** in Spain, an ingenious device capturing real-time images of the city's movements via a series of lenses.

Oratorio de San Felipe Neri

🕐 *Open 10am-1.30pm.* 🕐 *Closed Sun and public hols.* ⊜ *0.90€.* ☎ *95 621 16 12.*

This elliptical Baroque church has gone down in history as a place of liberalism, as it was here that the Cortes gathered in 1812 to proclaim the liberal Constitution of Cádiz. The interior is graced by an **Immaculate Conception** painted by Murillo in 1680 shortly before his death.

Museo Iconográfico e Histórico de las Cortes y Sitio de Cádiz

🕐 *Open 9am-1pm and 4-7pm; 15 Jun-15 Sep, 9am-1pm and 5-7pm; Sat-Sun, 9am-1pm.* 🕐 *Closed Mon and public hols. No charge.* ☎ *95 622 17 88.*

The museum's main exhibit is a marble and mahogany **model**★ of the city as it was during the reign of Charles III.

▷▷ Castillo de Santa Catalina, Parque Genovés★, Baluarte de la Candelaria, Iglesia del Carmen (Baroque façade★).

Excursions

San Fernando

9km/5.5mi SE along the CA 33. Linked to Cádiz via a narrow strip of land, San Fernando has been one of the main bases for the Spanish Navy since the 18C. The town's main monuments are all found along calle Real: the town hall (ayuntamiento), Iglesia del Carmen, and the Museo Histórico Municipal. The most important civil building is the neo-Classical **Observatorio Astronómico de la Marina**, dating from 1753.◐ *Visits by arrangement with the Patronato de Turismo de San Fernando,* ☎ *956 94 42 26.*

Medina Sidonia★

44km/27mi E on the CA 33, A 48 and A 390.

The town of Medina Sidonia sits proudly on a hill, crowned by the **Iglesia de Santa María la Mayor**★, a 15C Gothic church containing an exquisite Plateresque **altarpiece**★ sculpted by Juan Bautista Vázquez el Viejo. ◐ *10am-2pm and 4-6pm; in summer, 9.30am-2pm and 4-9.30pm.* ◐ *Closed 1 Jan and 25 Dec.* ◓ *2.50€.* ☎ *95 641 03 29.*

The Torre de Doña Blanca, a tower next to the church, provides access to the remains of the alcázar and the old quarter, with its 16C houses. The descent to the modern town passes under the Arco de la Pastora, before reaching the **Conjunto Arqueológico Romano**, an impressive Roman complex containing over 30m/98ft of underground galleries dating from the 1C AD. ◐ *Open 10am-1.30pm and 4.30-7pm; Jun-Sep, 10am-1.30pm and 5.30-8pm.* ◐ *Closed Mon.* ☎ *95 641 00 05 (tourism office).*

To complete your visit, head towards plaza de España, dominated by the 18C neo-Classical façade of the **town hall** *(ayuntamiento)*.

Parque Natural de las Sierras de **Cazorla, Segura y Las Villas**★★★

MICHELIN MAP 578 S 20-21-22 R 20-21-22 Q 21-22 – ANDALUCÍA (JAÉN)

This magnificent park is characterised by steep cliffs, deep gorges and a complex network of rivers and streams, which includes the source of the Guadalquivir river. The park's altitude and humidity favour the growth of a dense mountain vegetation similar to that found in Mediterranean regions. Fauna in the park includes deer, mountain goats, wild boar, golden eagles, griffon vultures and osprey. The Sierra de Cazorla is also an important hunting area.

Location

Spain's largest nature reserve was created in 1986 and extends over an area of 214 300ha/529 535 acres situated at an altitude of between 600m/1 968ft and 2 017m/6 616ft. Before embarking upon a tour of the park, it is advisable to head for one of the **information points**. The largest of these is at the Torre del Vinagre, although others are located at Cazorla, Segura de la Sierra and Siles. In addition to exploring minor roads, mountain-bikers, horse-riders and hikers can also follow the extensive network of forest tracks and marked footpaths. ◪ *Torre del Vinagre: Carretera del Tranco, Km 48.3, 23379 Torre del Vinagre ☎ 95 371 30 40; Cazorla: Juan Domingo 2, 23470 Cazorla, ☎ 95 372 01 15.*

  Neighbouring sights are described in the following chapters: ÚBEDA (46km/29mi NW of the town of Cazorla) and BAEZA (55km/34mi NW).

Tours

FROM TÍSCAR TO THE EMBALSE DEL TRANCO DE BEAS
92km/67mi – allow one day.

This route passes through picturesque mountains villages and superb natural landscapes within the Sierra de Cazorla.

Tíscar★

The **Santuario de Tíscar** enjoys a superb site enclosed by rocks. ◷*Open for worship 11.30am-1pm and 4.30-6pm; Jun-Sep 11am-1pm and 5-7pm.* ☎ 95 371 36 06.
Below this place of pilgrimage, which houses a statue of the Virgin Mary, appears the impressive **Cueva del Agua**★, a natural cave formation where a torrent of water emerges from between the rocks.

▶ *Follow the C 323 as far as Quesada.*

Quesada

Quesada sits on the Cerro de la Magdalena hill, its mass of whitewashed houses standing out amid the surrounding olive groves. The town was the birthplace of the painter Rafael Zabaleta (1907-60) and is home to a **museum** dedicated to his life and work. ◷ *Open 11am-2pm and 5-7pm (4-8pm in winter).* ◷ *Closed Mon-Tue.* ◉ 3€ ☎ 95 373 30 25.

B. Kaufmann/MICHELIN

The Castillo de la Iruela and Sierra de Cazorla

The Cañada de las Fuentes, a ravine situated on the outer limits of Quesada, is the **source of the Guadalquivir river** *(access via a track off the A 315, to the N of Quesada).* Wall paintings from the Palaeolithic era can be admired in Cerro Vitar and in the Cueva del Encajero, just a short distance from the town.

Take the A 315 towards Peal de Becerro, then bear right on the A 319 at a signposted junction.

Cazorla★

Cazorla occupies an outstanding **site★** nestled below the Peña de los Halcones and dominated by the silhouette of its **castle**. This attractive town is a network of well-maintained streets with whitewashed houses, flower-adorned balconies and attractive squares. At the centre of the plaza de Santa María stands a Renaissance fountain, the Fuente de las Cadenas; the ruins of the Iglesia de Santa María, a work by Vandelvira, on one side of the square, are now used as an auditorium.

Head 1.5km/1mi NE along the A 319, then turn right at a signposted junction.

La Iruela

This small town is overlooked by the remains of a Templar castle offering superb **views★★** of the Guadalquivir Valley. The Iglesia de Santo Domingo, a Renaissance-style church designed by Vandelvira, stands proudly at its centre.

The road from La Iruela to the Tranco Reservoir★

The first 17km/10.5mi stretch along the A 319 snakes its way along a corniche, providing **spectacular views★★**. The Parador de **El Adelantado** is reached via a branch road *(8km/5mi)* which winds its way uphill through forests of pine trees popular with hunters.

Continue along the A 319 running parallel to the river.

Torre del Vinagre

Open 11am-2pm and 5-8pm; in summer, 11am-2pm and 4-6pm. Closed 25 Dec.. No charge. ☎ 95 372 01 15.

A number of routes head off from the Centro de Interpretación inside the park. This information centre contains a hunting museum as well as a botanical garden where species native to the park can be seen.

A game reserve, the **Parque Cinegético de Collado del Almendral**, 15km/9.5mi further along the A 319, has several lookout points where the typical wildlife of the area (deer, mouflons, mountain goats etc) can be observed. *For information, call ☎ 95 371 01 25.*

Embalse del Tranco de Beas

⚠ Several camping areas and hotels have been created close to this reservoir, which, along with the water sports on offer, have turned it into one of the popular destinations within the park. Two islands stand in the middle of the reservoir: the Isla de Cabeza la Viña; and the **Isla de Bujaraiza**, with the ruins of an old Moorish castle. The impressive **Mirador Rodríguez de la Fuente** viewpoint offers impressive vistas of both islands.

FROM SANTIAGO-PONTONES TO SILES

80km/50mi – 🕐 *allow half a day.*

This itinerary around the Segura de la Sierra passes through several villages that have preserved vestiges of their Moorish occupation.

Santiago-Pontones

This municipality encompasses several villages scattered through the mountains. A number of archaeological sites are located within its boundaries, such as the **Cueva del Nacimiento**, a cave 9 000 years old, and the **Cuevas de Engalbo,** with their impressive wall art.

▶ *From Pontones, head NW along the A 317.*

Hornos

This settlement-cum-fortress consists of an attractive series of cobbled streets. The remains of the fortress rise above a steep cliff from where there are some spectacular **views**★ of the Tranco Reservoir and the Guadalquivir Valley.

▶ *Take the A 317, then bear right to Segura de la Sierra at a signposted junction.*

Segura de la Sierra★

This picturesque village, the birthplace of the 15C poet Jorge Manrique, straddles a hill at an altitude of 1 240m/4 067ft in the shelter of its Mudéjar **castle**, with its sweeping **panorama**★★ of the Sierra de Segura. The main buildings of note in the centre of the village include the **town hall** *(ayuntamiento)* with its Plateresque door-way; the **parish church**, containing a delicate, polychrome statue of the Virgin Mary carved in Gothic style from alabaster, and a recumbent Christ attributed to Gregorio Hernández; and the **Moorish baths** *(baños árabes)*, crowned by barrel vaults and star-shaped vault lights.

▶ *Follow the JV 7020 to Orcera.*

Orcera

The Iglesia de Nuestra Señora de la Asunción, with its sober Renaissance portal, and the Fuente de los Chorros, a 15C fountain, can be seen in the town's main square, the plaza del Ayuntamiento. The three Santa Catalina towers, the only remaining vestiges of the former Moorish fortress, are visible on the outskirts of Orcera.

▶ *Continue along the JV 7020 beyond Benatae, then take the JV 7021.*

Siles

The village has preserved several sections of its old walls. The nearby nature reserve of Las Acebeas is an area of delightful landscapes close to the source of the Los Molinos river.

Ceuta

POPULATION: 73 208.

MICHELIN MAP 742 FOLDS 5 AND 10 – NORTH AFRICA

The city, with its typically European style architecture, is situated on the narrow isthmus linking Monte Hacho with the African continent. The closest African port to Europe, it was conquered by the Portuguese in 1415, before passing into the hands of the Spanish in 1580, when Philip II annexed the kingdom of Portugal.

Location

Ceuta occupies a strategic position dominating the Straits of Gibraltar.

🛈 *Avenida Muelle Cañonero Dato, 51001 Ceuta,* ☎ *95 6956 50 14 10.*

♿ *Neighbouring sights are described in the following chapters: Straits of GIBRALTAR.*

Worth a Visit

Museo Municipal

🕐 *Open Oct-May, 10am-2pm and 5-8pm; Jun-Sep, 10am-2pm and 7-9pm; Sun and public hols, 10am (11am Jun-Sep) to 2pm.* 🎟 *No charge.* ☎ *95 651 73 98.*

This municipal museum houses a white marble Roman sarcophagus, Punic and Roman amphorae, a collection of coins and old weapons as well as various items of ceramic ware.

Parque Marítimo del Mediterráneo

🕐 *Open Oct-Apr, 11am-8pm; May-Sep 11am-8.30pm and 9-12pm; Sat-Sun and public hols 10am-8.30pm and 9pm-1am.* 🕐 *Closed Thu (Oct-Apr) and 1 Jan, 24-25 and 31 Dec.* 🎟 *Price varies by day of week.*

Palm trees, exotic plants, swimming pools, lakes, waterfalls and sculptures have all been perfectly integrated by César Manrique to create this spectacular leisure park which covers an area of 56ha/138 acres facing the sea. Several restaurants, a nightclub and a casino have been opened inside the fort which dominates the park, while a multi-cinema complex has been built in the Poblado Marinero.

Other places worthy of interest are the **Iglesia de Nuestra Señora de África** (Church of Our Lady of Africa), housing the statue of the patron saint of the town, the 18C **Catedral** and the **Foso de San Felipe**, an old Portuguese fort where San Juan de Dios, the founder of the Orden de los Hospitalarios (Order of the Hospitallers of St John), worked in 1530.

Tour

Monte Hacho★

10km/6mi – about 30min. Best visited in the morning.

Calle Independencia and calle Recintor Sur, running parallel to the seafront, lead to the foot of Monte Hacho which has a citadel at its summit. The corniche road encircling the peninsula offers beautiful **views** of the Western Rif coastline to the south and the Spanish coast and the Rock of Gibraltar to the north.

▸ *Before reaching the lighthouse (no entry), bear left.*

Ermita de San Antonio

😊 *Leave your car in the car park.* The wide flight of steps leads to a charming square fronted by the 16C Capilla de San Antonio (Chapel of St Anthony). The imposing **Fortaleza de Hacho** stands nearby, crowning the hill.

From here there is a magnificent **view**★★ of, to the left, the town spread out on its slightly curved isthmus around the port, and to the right, far off views of the peninsula coastline.

Address Book

GETTING TO CEUTA

By ferry – Trasmediterránea operates services between Algeciras and Ceuta. Journey time: 40min. For information and bookings, call ☎ 90 245 46 45.

WHERE TO EAT

MODERATE

🍽 **Parador H. La Muralla** – Plaza Virgen de África, 15 - ☎ 956 51 49 40 - ▤ - €22,10. A good place to pause during your visit, an attractive dining area with lush tropical plants and exposed beams. The cooking is Andausian with Arab influences.

Ciudad Rodrigo★

POPULATION: 14 973.

MICHELIN MAP 575 K 10 – CASTILLA Y LEÓN (SALAMANCA)

Ciudad Rodrigo appears high on a hilltop, guarded by the square tower of its 14C Alcázar (now a parador) and medieval ramparts. A Roman bridge spans the río Águeda from the Portuguese side. After the Moorish invasion it was re-established in the 12C by Count Rodrigo González from whom it takes its name; later it became a stronghold on the Spanish-Portuguese border and was involved in all the conflicts between Castilla and Portugal. Wellington's success in the bloody battle against the French in 1812 won him the title of Duke of Ciudad Rodrigo and Grandee of Spain.

Location

The surrounding region is given over to large estates of ilex trees beneath which graze black pigs and fighting bulls.

🗐 *Plaza de las Amayuelas 5, 37500 Ciudad Rodrigo, ☎ 923 46 05 61.*

🔆 *Neighbouring sights are described in the following chapters: SALAMANCA (89km/55mi NE) and La ALBERCA (50km/31mi SE).*

Walking About

The Old Town

▶Start your visit at the cathedral (plaza de las Amayuelas), where you will also find the tourist office.

Catedral★★

🕒 *Open 9.30am-1pm and 3.30-7pm.* 🕒 *No visits during religious services.* 🖼 *2€ (museum).* ☎ *92 348 14 24.*

The cathedral was built in two main stages, first from 1170 to 1230 and then in the 14C; in the 16C Rodrigo Gil de Hontañón added the central apse. The stiffness of the figures of the Disciples in a gallery in the upper part of the south transept façade contrasts with the delicate ornamentation of the surrounding blind arcades. The 13C **Portada de la Virgen**★ (Doorway of the Virgin), masked outside by a classical belfry which forms the cathedral narthex, has a line of Apostles carved between the columns beneath the splayings and the covings.

In the interior, the Isabelline choir stalls in the coro were carved by Rodrigo Alemán. The fine Renaissance **altar**★ in the north aisle is adorned with an alabaster Deposition, beautifully composed and carved in low relief, a masterpiece by Lucas Mitata.

The cloistersa are made up of diverse architectural styles. In the west gallery, the oldest part, Romanesque capitals illustrate man's original sin, while grotesques on the column bases symbolise greed and vanity. Opening off the east gallery is a Plateresque door in the pure Salamanca style decorated with medallions including one (on the right) of the architect Pedro Güemes.

A number of valuable exhibits are also on display in the **Museo Catedralicio**.
The nearby plaza de San Salvador is fronted by the 16C Palacio de los Miranda.

▶ *Return to the cathedral, in front of which stands the Capilla de Cerralbo.*

Capilla de Cerralbo

The chapel, built between 1588 and 1685, is pure and austere but harmonious in the Herreran style.

▶ *The arcaded plaza del Buen Alcalde is to the right. Take the street to the left to reach plaza del Conde.*

Palacio de los Castro★ (or Palacio del Conde de Montarco)

This late-15C palace, on plaza del Conde (Square of the Count), has a long façade punctuated by delicate windows. The Plateresque doorway is surrounded by an alfiz and flanked by two twisted columns showing Portuguese influence, which are further embellished by two protective lions. Note also the simple patio.

> *From here, head to the plaza Mayor, passing the 16C Palacio de Moctezuma to the right.*

Plaza Mayor★

Two Renaissance palaces stand on the city's lively main square: the first, now the **Ayuntamiento** (town hall), has a façade with two storeys of basket arcading forming a **gallery**★ and a loggia, while the second, the **Casa de los Cueto**, has a decorative frieze separating its first and second storeys.

> *Continue as far as calle Juan Arias, lined by the Casa del Príncipe or Casa de los Águilas, a 16C building in Plateresque style.*

Murallas (Ramparts)

The walls built on the remains of Roman foundations in the 12C, were converted to a full defensive system on the north and west flanks in 1710. There are several stairways up to the 2km/1mi-long sentry path.

> *The imposing keep of Henry of Trastámara's castle stands on the SW corner of the walls, alongside the Roman bridge spanning the Águeda river. Nowadays, the castle is home to the town's parador.*

Córdoba★★★

POPULATION: 310 388.

MICHELIN MAP 578 S 15 – ANDALUCÍA (CÓRDOBA)

Córdoba stands on the right bank of the Guadalquivir where the ranches and farmlands of the Sierra de Córdoba plateau to the north meet the wheatlands and olive groves of the southerly Campiña plains. The city owes its fame to the brilliance of the Roman, Moorish, Jewish and Christian civilisations that have endowed Córdoba with its rich and varied history. The Mezquita, the city's most precious jewel, dominates the old section of Córdoba, although it is far from being the only attraction in this delightful provincial capital, whose narrow, whitewashed streets and charming small squares are further embellished with wrought-iron grilles and flower-filled patios.

Location

The city stands in the Guadalquivir depression alongside the A 4 highway linking the city with Écija (52km/32mi SW) and Sevilla (143km/89mi SW). ▮ *Torrijos 10, 14003 Córdoba, ☎ 95 747 12 35; Caballerizas Reales 1, 14004 Córdoba, ☎ 90 220 17 74; Alcázar de los Reyes Cristianos, ☎ 95 729 95 35.*

◔ *Neighbouring sights are described in the following chapters: OSUNA (86km/54mi SW), PRIEGO DE CÓRDOBA (98km/61mi SE) and JAÉN (107km/67mi E).*

Background

The Roman city – Córdoba, capital of Baetica, was the birthplace of **Seneca the Rhetorician** (55 BC-AD 39), his son **Seneca the Philosopher** (4 BC-AD 65), who became tutor to Nero, and Lucan (AD 39-65), who was Seneca the Philosopher's nephew and companion to Nero in his student days. His writing, particularly the poem *Pharsalia* which recounts the war between Caesar and Pompey, won him great acclaim. The early Christian period was marked by the episcopacy of **Ossius** (257-359), counsellor to Emperor Constantine, protagonist of orthodoxy against Arianism and reorganiser of the Church in Spain.

The only remaining vestiges of Roman Córdoba are the mausoleum in the Jardines de la Victoria, the remains of a 1C temple, and the heavily restored bridge linking the old section of the city with the Torre de la Calahorra.

The Córdoba Caliphate – Emirs from the Damascus Caliphate established themselves in Córdoba as early as 719. In 756 **Abd ar-Rahman I**, sole survivor of the **Umayyads** of Damascus who had been annihilated by the Abbasids, arrived to found the dynasty which was to rule over Muslim Spain for three centuries and bring untold prosperity and fame to Córdoba. In 929 **Abd ar-Rahman III** proclaimed himself caliph, and Spain independent. In the 10C a university was founded which won high renown. The open-mindedness and tolerance alive at the time allowed the three communities – Christian, Jewish and Muslim – not only to live side by side but to enrich one another intellectually and culturally. On the accession, in 976, of the feeble **Hisham II**, power fell into the hands of the ruthless but remarkable **Al-Mansur** (the Victorious); his descendants, however, failed to prevent Al-Andalus from fragmenting into small warring kingdoms, the **reinos de taifas**. Córdoba itself became part of the kingdom of Sevilla in 1070. Political decline in no way diminished intellectual life, however. There lived in the city from 1126 to 1198 the Moor **Averroës**, a universal scholar – physicist, astrologer, mathematician, doctor and philosopher – who, although he was prevented from teaching by the doctrinaire Almohad leader, Yacoub al-Mansur, who opposed his theories, did much to bring the learning of Aristotle to the West. A contemporary of Averroës, the Jew **Maimónides** (1135-1204) was famed for his learning in medicine, theology and philosophy, but had to flee to Morocco and later Egypt to escape persecution.

Eventually reconquered by the Christians in 1236, the city's prosperity waned until the 16C and 17C, when Córdoba leatherwork, embossed, tooled and coloured, became the fashion for wall and seat coverings.

Other famous Cordobans – Among the city's sons are Gonzalo Fernández de Córdoba, the **Gran Capitán** (1453-1515) born in the nearby town of Montilla, who conquered the kingdom of Naples in 1504, and **Luis de Góngora** (1561-1627), the great Baroque poet and major exponent of *culteranismo*, a school of poetry characterised by its cultured verse. His main works include the *Fábula de Polifemo y Galatea*, and *Soledades*.

Address Book

For coin ranges, see the Legend at the back of the guide.

WHERE TO EAT

Taberna los Faroles – *Velázquez Bosco 1* – ☎ *95 748 56 29 – 10/30€*. This tavern owes its name to the numerous lanterns that illuminate its attractive patio at night. Specialities here include local dishes such as salmorejo (a variant of gazpacho), aubergine with honey and *rabo de toro* (braised oxtail). A cool, pleasant atmosphere is enhanced by the *azulejos* on the walls.

El Rincón de Carmen – *Romero 4* – ☎ *95 729 10 55 – Closed Mon* – . The shady garden here provides a pleasant escape from the frenzied tourist activity around the Judería. Plenty of alternatives to the traditional gazpacho and an interesting wine list.

Paseo de la Ribera – *Plaza Cruz del Rastro 3* – ☎ *95 747 15 30* – . One of the best places to eat authentic Cordoban cuisine. The dining room, nestled between stone arches, is relatively cool and brings to mind a Romanesque church. The terrace, on paseo de la Ribera, overlooks the Guadalquivir river.

Casa Palacio Bandolero – *Torrijos 6* – ☎ *95 747 64 91* – . The Bandolero has a superb location opposite the Mezquita and is popular with tourists and locals alike. Home-made tapas are served in the bar, in addition to traditional local cuisine in the medieval-style dining room indoors and on the flower-decked patio.

Almudaina – *Jardines de los Santos Mártires 1* – ☎ *95 747 43 42* - . An attractive restaurant in a central plaza, near the Alcázar. High point is the painstaking regional decor, with dining on two levels around a pleasant covered patio. The excellent food is a good introduction to Cordoban cuisine.

TAPAS

Córdoba does full justice to Andalucía's great tapas tradition with a wide range of bars offering a huge selection of tapas, providing visitors with the perfect opportunity to try the local specialities such as *salmorejo* (a type of local gazpacho), rabo de toro (braised oxtail), *embutidos* (local sausage) and sherries (finos, amontillados, olorosos).

Taberna Salinas – *Tundidores 3* – ☎ *95 748 01 35 – Closed Sun and in Aug* – . Open for more than a century, this welcoming bar consists of a counter, two rooms decorated with *azulejos* and photos of celebrities, and a small patio.

Taberna San Miguel-Casa El Pisto – *Plaza San Miguel 1* – ☎ *95 747 01 66 – Closed Sun and in Aug* – .Founded in 1886, the Taberna San Miguel is located opposite the church of the same name and is a popular choice for tapas in the city. The traditional decor is enhanced by the bullfight posters and photos on the walls.

Taberna Casa Pepe de la Judería – *Romero 1* – ☎ *95 720 07 44* – . This bar first opened in 1928 and the counter dates from this period. Several rooms serving tapas around an attractive patio. Restaurant on the upper floor. Andalucían cuisine.

WHERE TO STAY

Hostal El Triunfo – *Corregidor Luis de la Cerda 79* – ☎ *95 749 84 84* – – *55 rooms* – ☐ *3.26€ – Restaurant €6/12.75*. Most of the rooms here look onto the Mezquita, which is separated from the hotel by a narrow street. Stay on the top floor if you can to make use of the huge terrace. All rooms have a TV.

Hostal La Milagrosa – *Rey Heredia 12* – ☎ *95 747 33 17* – 🅿 – *8 rooms (doubles only)*. Good central location near the Mezquita. Attractive features are the plant-filled typically Cordoban patio and well-kept, large, cool guest rooms with full bathrooms.

Hotel González – *Manríquez 3* – ☎ *95 747 98 19 – 16 rooms – Restaurant 27€*. The rooms in this former 16C palace, located within the triangle of the Mezquita, the Judería and the gardens of the Alcázar, are spacious and well appointed. The Moorish-inspired patio doubles as the hotel restaurant.

Hostal Séneca – *Conde y Luque 7* – ☎ *95 747 32 34 – 12 rooms*. The Seneca is a quiet hostal near the Mezquita with typical Andalucían decor and a flower-filled patio. Despite the rooms being fairly basic (some without a bathroom), the hotel is often full so advance booking is recommended.

Hotel Posada de Vallina – *Corregidor Luis de la Cerda 83* – ☎ *95 749 87 50* – ☐ *4.81€ – Restaurant 17/35€*. Elegance and comfort are the main features of this small hotel housed in a tastefully restored Cordoban house, whose windows open out onto the Mezquita. The pleasant restaurant on the ground floor is particularly popular.

Hotel Casa de los Azulejos – *Fernando Colón 5* – ☎ *95 747 00 00* – 🅿 ⎕ ♿ – *8 rooms*. This charming hotel is a traditional Andalucian house with a colonial flavour. Outstanding features include a lovely interior garden with plants, and magnificent large rooms with period furnishings, iron headboards, original floors and colourful designer baths.

BARS AND CAFÉS

Málaga Café – *Málaga 3* – ☎ *95 748 63 13* – *Open Mon-Thu, 4pm-2am; Fri-Sat, 4pm-4am, Sun, 4-10pm*. A quiet café with classical decor and comfortable sofas and armchairs near the plaza de las Tendillas in the centre of the city. Highly recommended for evening drinks with friends.

Siena – *Plaza de las Tendillas* – ☎ *95 747 46 08* – *Open 8am-midnight*. A long-established café in Córdoba's main square, with one of the city's most popular outdoor terraces. A perfect venue for a morning coffee or an evening drink.

Sojo – *Benito Pérez Galdós 3* – *Open 8am-4am*. Popular with the over-25s, this avant-garde bar is open from breakfast time to late at night. The Sojo also organises concerts by soloists, as well as art, photography and video exhibitions. Highly recommended, whatever the hour.

NIGHTLIFE

Chato – *Alhakem II 14* – *Bellver de Cerdanya* – *Open 4pm-late*. A bar with a modern design in the Gran Capitán area of the city with a trendy mixed-age clientele. A pleasant location for a quiet early-evening coffee or drinks in a more lively atmosphere closer to midnight.

El Puentecillo – *Poeta Emilio Prados* – *Open in summer, 9.30pm-5am; in winter, Thu-Sat, midnight-5am*. A small venue on the way up to the El Brillante district. Warm and inviting decor inside as well as on the small patio. Tends to be frequented by a slightly older, quieter crowd. Popular for drinks early on in the evening.

B. Kaufmann/ MICHELIN

SHOPPING

The city's traditional craftwork includes embossed leather and cordovans, in addition to gold and silver filigree. Another good buy is the local wine, **Montilla-Moriles**, produced to the south of Córdoba in the area around Montilla, Puente Genil, Lucena and Baena. The excellent wines and brandies from Montilla-Moriles are similar in style to those of Jerez.

FIESTAS

At the beginning of **May**, Córdoba celebrates the Festival of the Crosses (Cruces de Mayo), when large, flower-decked crosses adorn the city's squares and street corners. The first half of May is also the time for Córdoba's traditional patio competition, while the eagerly awaited **Feria** is held at the end of the month.

Special Features

THE MEZQUITA AND THE JUDERÍA★★★ 3hr

Mezquita-Catedral★★★ (Mosque-Cathedral)

🕐 *Open 10am-7.30pm; Sun and public hols, 2-7.30pm; last admission 30min before closing.* ☞ *6.50€, includes cathedral, mosque and treasury.* ☎ *95 747 05 12 or 95 747 56 13*.

The Mezquita was built on the site of the former Visigothic basilica of San Vicente. Following the Reconquest, a Christian cathedral was built at the very heart of the mosque.

The Mezquita

The overall plan is the traditional Muslim one of a crenellated square perimeter enclosing the Patio de los Naranjos (Orange Tree Court) with a **basin (1)** for ritual ablution – in this case that of Al-Mansur – a hall for prayer and a minaret.

The mosque was built in several stages. The first Muslims to arrive in Córdoba were content to share the Visigothic church of St Vincent with the Christians. Soon, however, this proved insufficient and Abd ar-Rahman I (758-88) purchased their part of the site from the Christians. He razed the church and around the year 780 began the construction of a splendid mosque with 11 aisles each opening onto the Patio de los Naranjos. Marble pillars and stone from former Roman and Visigothic buildings were re-used in the mosque which became famous for an architectural innovation: the superimposition of two tiers of arches to give added height and spaciousness. After

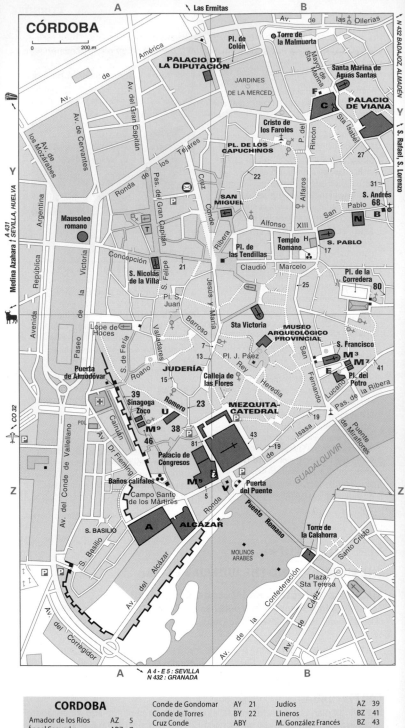

CÓRDOBA

the reconquest, chapels were built by the Christians in the west nave. These include the 17C **Capilla de la Purísima Concepción (2)**, which is completely covered with marble of different colours.

The mosque was enlarged over the years: in 848 Abd ar-Rahman II had it extended to the present-day Capilla de Villaviciosa (Villaviciosa Chapel), in 961 El Hakam II built the *mihrab*, and lastly, in 987, Al-Mansur gave it its present size by adding eight more aisles (recognisable by their red-brick pavement).

Interior

Entrance through the Puerta de las Palmas. The interior is a forest of columns (about 850) and the horseshoe-shaped arches consist of alternating white (stone) and red (brick) voussoirs. The aisle off the doorway, wider than the others and which served as the main aisle of the original mosque, has a beautiful *artesonado* ceiling. It leads to the **kiblah** wall, generally orientated towards Mecca, before which the faithful, led by the imam, would pray, and the **mihrab**★★★, normally a simple niche, but which in this case is a sumptuously decorated room preceded by a triple **maksourah (3)** or enclosure reserved for the caliph. The enclosure is roofed by three ribbed domes which rest on a most unusual series of apparently interweaving multifoil arches, as striking as the cupolas themselves, which are faced with mosaics against a background of gold. Decoration throughout adds to the richness of the architecture: on the mosaics, alabaster plaques and stucco are ornate arabesques and palm-leaf motifs sometimes framed by Cufic script.

In the 13C, conversion of the building to Christian use brought certain physical alterations: the aisles (except that off the Puerta de las Palmas) were walled off from the court; a few columns were removed and pointed arches substituted for the Moorish ones when the first **cathedral (4)** was built – fortunately nothing was done which destroyed the perspectives in the mosque. Alfonso X was responsible for the chancel in the **Capilla de Villaviciosa** or **Lucernario (5)**, and built the **Capilla Real**★ **(6)** decorated in the 13C with Mudéjar stucco which harmonised with the whole. A number of chapels were constructed in the western nave, among them the outstanding marble-faced 17C **Purísima Concepción (2)**.

Catedral

In the 16C the cathedral canons desired more sumptuous surroundings. They began by cutting away the centre of the mosque to erect loftier vaulting. In spite of the talent of the architect Hernán Ruiz and his followers, Emperor Charles V was far from pleased with the result: "You have destroyed something unique," he said, "to build something commonplace." The roof is a mix of various styles from the 16C and

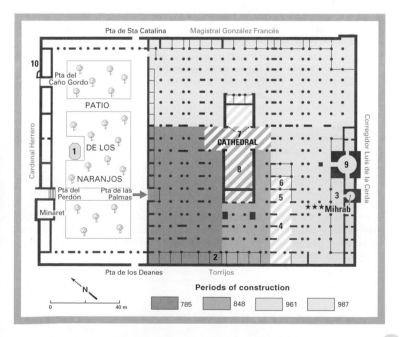

Periods of construction: 785 | 848 | 961 | 987

Cathedral vaults (detail)

17C (Hispano-Flemish, Renaissance and Baroque). Additional enrichments are the Baroque **choir stalls**★★ (8) by Pedro Duque Cornejo (c 1750) and two **pulpits**★★ (7) of marble, jasper and mahogany.

Tesoro

The treasury, built by the Baroque architect Francisco Hurtado Izquierdo, can be found in the **Capilla del Cardenal** (Cardinal's Chapel) (9) and in two adjoining rooms. A monumental 16C **monstrance**★ by E Arfe and an exceptional Baroque figure of Christ in ivory stand out in this collection of liturgical objects.

Exterior features of the complex include the **minaret**, from the top of which the muezzin called the faithful to prayer. In the 17C the minaret was enveloped in a Baroque tower. At its foot, giving onto the street, is the 14C Mudéjar **Puerta del Perdón** (Pardon Doorway) which is faced with bronze. A little further on is a small chapel to the deeply venerated **Virgen de los Faroles** (Virgin of the Lanterns) (10).

The Alcázar of the Umayyads stood at the centre of magnificent gardens facing the mosque on the site of what is now the Palacio Episcopal (Bishop's Palace), housing the **Museo Diocesano de Bellas Aartes**. (Open 9.30am-1.30pm and 4-6pm (9.30am-3pm Jun-Jul); Sat, 9.30am-1.30pm. Closed Sun and public hols. 1.50€ (no charge for bearers of Mezquita entrance ticket). ☎ 95 747 93 75).

Judería★★ (Old Jewish Quarter)

NW of the Mezquita. Narrow streets, white walls spilled over with brilliant flowers, doors half open onto cool patios, delicate window grilles, bars where a group of Cordobans may burst into song to the accompaniment of a guitar, snapping fingers or sharp handclaps – such are the features of the old Jewish quarter. A section of the walls that originally protected the old city has been preserved here.

Sinagoga

 Open 10am-2pm and 3.30-5.30pm; Sun and public hols, 10am-1.30pm. Closed Mon. 0.30€, no charge for citizens of the European Union. ☎ 95 720 29 28.

The Córdoba and Toledo synagogues are the only major synagogues which remain in Spain today. Built in the early 14C, this one consists of a small square room with a balcony on one side for the women. The upper parts of the walls are covered in Mudéjar stucco.

Not far away is the **Zoco Municipal** or souk, where craftsmen work around a large patio which in summer is the setting for flamenco dancing. Here too is the 16C Casa de las Bulas, now home to the **Museo Municipal Taurino** (Municipal Bullfighting Museum) (see description under Worth a Visit).

Worth a Visit

Palacio de Viana★★

Guided tours (1hr), Oct-May, 10am-1pm and 4-6pm; Jun-Sep, 9am-2pm. Closed Sat afternoon, Sun, public hols and 1-15 Jun. 6€; 3€ (patios only without tour). ☎ 95 748 01 34.

The Viana Palace, a fine example of 14C-19C Cordoban civil architecture, has 12 patios and an attractive garden. The city is famous for the beauty of its patios and those in this palace, with their charm and sensitivity are, without doubt, worthy of their renown.

The interior is lent a sense of harmony by its rich furnishings. On the ground floor are precious collections of porcelain, 17C-19C side-arms and tapestries. The staircase to the first floor has a beautiful Mudéjar *artesonado* ceiling made of cedar. Of the many rooms open the most interesting are the gallery of Cordoban leather with magnificent 15C-18C work; the room hung with tapestries made in the royal workshops from cartoons by Goya; the library; and the main room adorned with a rich *artesonado* ceiling and tapestries illustrating the Trojan War and various Spanish tales.
The old stables are also open.

Museo Arqueológico Provincial★★

Open 9am-8.30pm (2.30-8pm Tue); Sun, 9am-2.30pm. Closed Mon. 1.50€, no charge for citizens of the European Union. ☎ 95 747 10 76.

The archaeological museum is in the Palacio de los Páez, a 16C Renaissance palace designed by Hernán Ruiz. Displayed in rooms around the cool patios are prehistoric Iberian objects, Visigothic remains and, in particular, the **Roman collection**★ (reliefs, capitals, sarcophagi and mosaics) testifying to the importance of Córdoba at the time. The first floor galleries house examples of Córdoba's Muslim decorative arts: ceramics, a model of the mosque, capitals, and bronze sculptures including the outstanding 10C work from Medina Azahara of a **stag**★, or *cervatillo*, decorated with plant motifs. Note also the Abad Samson bell and a large collection of well copings.

Alcázar de los Reyes Católicos★

Open 10am-2pm and 4.30-7.30pm; Sun and public hols, 9.30am-2.30pm. Closed Mon. 3€, no charge Fri. ☎ 95 742 01 51.

The present edifices were built under Alfonso XI in the early 14C, and later expanded by Ferdinand and Isabel. Of the palace there remain attractively cool Moorish patios with ornamental basins and pools, baths, a few rooms with Roman **mosaics**★ and a fine 3C **sarcophagus**★. From the towers there is a **view** of the gardens, the Guadalquivir, the Roman bridge and the Torre de la Calahorra. The **gardens**★, in Arabic style, are terraced and refreshed with pools and fountains, and cypresses.

Iglesias Fernandinas★

On 29 June 1236, Ferdinand III reconquered Córdoba. The arrival of the Christians had a large impact on the city's architecture with the construction of 14 parish churches under Ferdinand (Fernando). The beauty of these churches can still be seen today, particularly in **Santa Marina de Aguas Santas** (St Marina of the Holy Waters), **San Miguel** (St Michael) and **San Lorenzo** (St Lawrence). These late-13C and early-14C temples of stone, built in primitive Gothic style, are endowed with a sober yet rounded beauty by the purely structural elements. The addition of single trumpet-shaped doorways introduces the only lighter aspect to these edifices.

Palacio de la Diputación★

The provincial Parliament building occupies the former Convento de la Merced, built in the 18C. The attractive façade is graced by a white marble Baroque doorway, while the main architectural features of interest inside include the patio, staircase and stucco-adorned church.

Torre de la Calahorra: Museo vivo de Al-Andalus

Open 10am-6pm; May-Sep, 10am-2pm and 4.30-8.30pm. 4€. ☎ 95 729 39 29.

The Moorish fortress was built in the 14C to defend the Roman bridge. It now houses a museum which, through audio-control techniques, traces the history of the Cordoban Caliphate, a period of great cultural, artistic, philosophical and scientific prosperity. Major trends in 12C Christian, Jewish and Muslim thought are illustrated through information on Alfonso X, Maimónides, Averroës and Ibn-Arabi respectively. There is also a fine **model**★ of the mosque as it was in the 13C.

Plazuela del Potro

On this square, named after the small statue of a colt *(potro)* decorating the fountain, stands the charming inn, **Posada del Potro**, described by Cervantes in *Don Quixote*. It now houses a cultural centre. ⏰ *Open 9am-9pm (1 Jul-30 Sep 8.30am-2.30pm).* ⏰ *Closed Sat-Sun and public hols.* ⚬ *No charge.* ☎ 95 748 50 01.

On the far side of the square are the **Museo Julio Romero de Torres**★, a museum containing works by this early-20C Cordoban artist (1880-1930) who painted beautiful women (⏰ *Open 10am-2pm and 5.30-7.30pm; Sun and public hols, 9.30am-2.30pm. Closed Mon.* 3€, *no charge Fri.* ☎ 957 49 19 09), and the **Museo de Bellas Artes** (Fine Arts Museum) with paintings by 14C-20C Spanish artists. ⏰ *Open 9am-8.30pm (2.30-8pm Tue); Sun and public hols, 9am-2.30pm.* ⏰ *Closed Mon.* ⚬ *1.50€, no charge for citizens of the European Union.* ☎ 957 47 33 45.

Plaza de la Corredera

The square, lined with 17C arcades, was formerly used for bullfighting.

Museo Municipal Taurino

⏰ *Open 15 Oct-1 May, 10am-2pm and 4.30-6.30pm; 2 May-14 Oct, 10am-2pm and 5.30-7.30pm; Sun and public hols all year, 9.30am-2.30pm.* ⏰ *Closed Mon, 1 Jan, Good Fri and 25 Dec.* ⚬ *3€, no charge Fri.* ☎ 957 20 10 56.

The museum, housed in a 16C mansion, the Casa de las Bulas, has collections of items related to tauromachy including engravings, posters, bullfighters' costumes and documents on Córdoba's most famous matadors: Lagartijo, Guerrita, Manolete and Machaquito.

El Cristo de Los Faroles (Christ of the Lanterns)

The Calvary surrounded by wrought-iron lanterns in the tranquil **plaza de los Capuchinos**★ is well known throughout Spain.

Excursions

Medina Azahara★★

▶ *Leave Córdoba on the A 431 (to the W of the plan). After 8km/5mi bear right onto a signposted road.* ⏰ *Open May-Sep, 10am-8.30pm; Oct-Apr, 10am-6.30pm; Sun 10am-2pm.* ⏰ *Closed Mon, 1 and 6 Jan, 9 Apr, 1 May, 1 Nov, and 24-25 and 31 Dec.* ⚬ *1.50€, no charge for citizens of the European Union.* ☎ 957 32 91 30.

The Sephardic Jews

No history of Spain is complete without a mention of the Jews whose presence may still be felt in *juderías* (old Jewish quarters) and synagogues. The main Jewish towns in the past were Córdoba, Toledo, Sevilla, Palma de Mallorca and Girona.

The Sephardim or Sephardic Jews (Sefarad is the Hebrew word for Spain) came to the Iberian Peninsula in Antiquity at the same time as the Greeks and Phoenicians. In the 8C, during the Arab occupation, they welcomed the Muslims who regarded them as sympathetic allies. The Muslims put them in charge of negotiating with the Christian community. As merchants, bankers, craftsmen, doctors and scholars, Jews played an important economic role and influenced the domains of culture and science. Some became famous, like Maimónides of Córdoba.

Maimónides

O. Torres/MARCO POLO

The Jews were particularly prosperous under the Caliphate of Córdoba (10C-11C). However, at the end of the 11C, Jews from Andalucía moved to Toledo and Catalunya, especially Girona, as a result of intolerance and persecution under the Almohads. They were often persecuted by Christians during the Reconquest (a royal decree forced them to wear a piece of red or yellow cloth). In the end they were expelled by the Catholic Monarchs in 1492. Some chose to convert, others (known as Marranos), in spite of having publicly converted, continued practising their Jewish faith in hiding, while most emigrated to other parts of the Mediterranean, to the Netherlands, to England and to America. Today the Sephardic Jews represent 60% of the Diaspora. Some of them have kept their language, Ladino, which is pure 15C Castilian.

B. Kaufmann/MICHELIN

Castillo de Almodóvar del Río

Excavations have revealed the remains of a sumptuous city built by Abd ar-Rahman III. Construction began in 936; however, hardly had the caliphs had time to complete the undertaking when it was sacked in 1013, during the war that was to end the Cordoban Caliphate, by the Berbers. The city extended upwards in three tiers – a mosque below, gardens and main reception rooms at the centre, and an *alcázar* at the top. The jewel of this archaeological site is the **Abd ar-Rahman III room**, with its magnificent decoration of carved stone and vegetal and geometric motifs embellishing the walls, arches and capitals.

Castillo de Almodóvar del Río★★

25km/15mi W along the A 431. 🕐 *Open 11am-2.30pm and 4-7pm (8pm in summer).* 👝 *3€.* ☎ *670 33 84 30.*

This imposing **castle** is perched on an impressive hill dominating the wide expanses of the Cordoban countryside. The town sits at the foot of the hill on its southern side, by the Guadalquivir river.

Although it is known that a Moorish fortress existed on the site in the 8C, the Gothic-style castle standing today was built in the 14C and consists of two walled enclosures with eight towers of differing sizes. Once inside the castle, the narrow path behind the parapet, the parade ground and the towers are all well worth a pleasant stroll.

Las Ermitas

13km/8mi N of Córdoba on the El Brillante road. 🕐 *Open 10am-1.30pm and 3-6pm; Apr-Sep, 10am-1pm and 4.30-5.45pm; Sun, 9am-1.30pm and 4.30-7.45pm.* 🕐 *Closed Mon. 1.90€.* ☎ *957 33 03 10.*

This group of 13 hermitages (ermitas) and a single church is situated in a wild, mountainous location. **Views**★★ of Córdoba, the mountains and the Guadalquivir Valley can be enjoyed from the road and from the mirador.

Andújar★

76km/47mi E along the A 4.

Andújar, Spain's major olive-producing area, has preserved many old houses and churches that date back to the 15C and 16C. On the last Sunday of April, the popular *romería* (pilgrimage) is held to the Santuario de la Virgen de la Cabeza *(32km/20mi N on the J 5010)*, situated at the heart of the **Parque Natural de la Sierra de Andújar**★, with its alternating landscape of open pasture, grazed by fighting bulls, and dark ravines of dense vegetation.

Iglesia de Santa María

The 15C-17C Church of St Mary, on the attractive square of the same name, contains El Greco's painting *Christ in the Garden of Olives*★★, on display in a chapel to the left, enclosed by a fine **grille**★ by Master Bartolomé. An *Assumption of the Virgin* by Pacheco can be seen in the north apsidal chapel.

Iglesia de San Bartolomé

This church, dating from the end of the 15C, has three **Gothic portals**★ on its main façade.

A **Coruña**/La **Coruña**★

POPULATION: 252 694.

MICHELIN MAP 571 B 4 (TOWN PLAN) – GALICIA (LA CORUÑA)

The site of this pleasant Galician city is a rocky islet, linked to the mainland by a narrow strip of sand. The lighthouse stands to the north, the curved harbour to the south, with the impressive glass tower of the marina, and along the west side of the isthmus, the sandy Riazor and Orzán beaches. Three distinct quarters testify to La Coruña's growth: the **City** (Ciudad), at the northern end of the harbour, a charming old quarter with its small peaceful squares and Romanesque churches, the business and commercial centre on the isthmus with wide avenues and shopping streets (**Avenida de Los Cantones, Calles Real and San Andrés**), and the **Ensanche** to the south, built up with warehouses and industrial premises, a reminder that La Coruña is the sixth largest commercial port in Spain as well as an important industrial and fishing centre.

Location

The region's economic capital is situated on the north coast of Galicia and has good road links with the region's cultural capital, Santiago de Compostela, via the AP 9 motorway. The A 6, which heads SE, runs past Lugo (97km/60mi SE) before continuing to Madrid. ⓘ *Dársena de la Marina, 15001 La Coruña, ☎ 98 122 18 22.*

♿ *Neighbouring sights are described in the following chapters: RÍAS ALTAS and SANTIAGO DE COMPOSTELA (73km/45mi S).*

Background

Invincible Armada – It was from La Coruña (A Coruña in Galician) that Philip II's **Armada** set sail in 1588. The fleet of 130 men-of-war, manned by 10 000 sailors and transporting 19 000 soldiers, set out for England ostensibly to punish Elizabeth for the execution of Mary, Queen of Scots. The ill-fated expedition, however, dogged by bad weather and harassed by the smaller, more easily manœuvred English ships, was a failure. Sixty-three ships and more than 15 000 men were lost. The defeat marked the end of Spanish sea power. A year later, in 1589, Elizabeth sent Drake to attack the Iberian coast. The invaders fired La Coruña but the town was saved by **María Pita** who seized the English standard from the beacon where it had been planted and gave the alarm.

The events of the 19C – Over two centuries later, during the Peninsular War, Marshal Soult led Napoleon's forces to a decisive victory over the English in the Battle of Elviña

Address Book

For coin ranges, see the Legend at the back of the guide.

WHERE TO EAT

◖◖ **Coral** – *Callejón de la Estacada 9 – ☎ 98 120 05 69 – Closed Sun –* ▤. A restaurant popular with coruñeses for its high-quality, original cuisine and professionalism. The decor here is an attractive mix of stone and wood.

◖◖ **Domus** – *Ángel Rebollo (Domus-Casa del Hombre) – ☎ 98 120 11 36 - Closed Mon and in Feb –* ▤. Situated right in the Domus Museum, with its own entry. An outstanding feature is its conservatory dining room, bordered by natural stone on one side and open to magnificent sea views on the other. The modern decor sets off fine traditional cuisine with authoritative enhancements.

WHERE TO STAY

◖ **Hostal Mar del Plata** – *Paseo de Ronda 58 – ☎ 98 125 79 62 – 27 rooms –* ⌑ 2.50€. This simple and functional family-run hotel is located just out of the city centre, near the Riazor football stadium, home of Deportivo La Coruña. The rooms here are unpretentious, but perfectly acceptable, some with sea views.

◖◖ **Plaza** – *Av. Fernández Latorre 45 - ☎ 98 129 01 11 -* ▤ ♿ *- 84 rooms -* ⌑ 7.20€ - Restaurant 10€. A hotel carefully decorated in minimalist fashion, with pure lines and light tones. Public areas are small, but the rooms are modern with designer bathrooms.

A CORUÑA LA CORUÑA		Angustias Pl. de las	15	Obispo Valero	45
		Carmen Pl. del	20	Pósito	55
		Colegio San José	25	Puerta de Valencia	58
Alfonso VIII	2	Fray luis de León	30	San Nicolás Pl.	65
Alonso de Ojeda	5	Júcar Ronda del	40	San Pablo Puente de	68
Andrés de Cabrera	8	Julián Romero Ronda de	43	Trabuco	71
Angustias Bajada a las	12	Mayor Pl.	44		

Colegiata de Santa María del Campo	BY	M¹	Museo de Bellas Artes	AY	M²

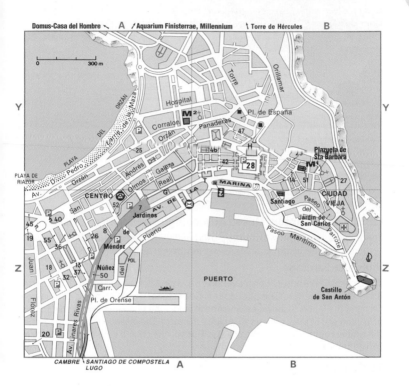

in 1809. Throughout the latter years of the 19C, during the period of frequent liberal uprisings, La Coruña consistently supported the insurgents and in consequence suffered severe reprisals.

The town is proud of being the birthplace of the novelist **Emilia Pardo Bazán** (1852-1921) and to have been a home to the poet **Rosalía de Castro** (1837-85).

Walking About

Ciudad Vieja

The old town occupies the original settlement at the northern end of the harbour. This quarter is characterised by narrow cobbled streets and peaceful squares.

Colegiata de Santa María del Campo

A Romanesque church with three barrel-vaulted naves strengthened by arches with plaster borders. Worthy of note on the exterior are the fine 13C-14C portal, the Gothic rose window and the tower. A **Museum of Sacred Art** (Museo de Arte Sacro) is housed on one side of the church. In the square, between Santa María and a fine Baroque house, stands a 15C Calvary.

Plazuela de Santa Bárbara

This peaceful square, which hosts concerts of chamber music during August (Fiestas de María Pita), lies in the protective shadow of Santa Bárbara convent's high, sombre walls. Above the doorway of the convent is a Romanesque lintel depicting the weighing of souls in the presence of Christ.

Avenida de la Marina

Jardín de San Carlos

It is in this attractive park that General John Moore, who was killed in the Battle of Elviña, is buried.

Castillo de San Antón: Museo Arqueológico e Histórico

This fortress, which dates from the period of Philip II, formed part of La Coruña's system of defence in former times (& *see description under Worth a Visit*).

Iglesia de Santiago

The church's three apses, which overlook plaza de Azcárraga, along with the north door, are Romanesque. The west door is Gothic; Santiago Matamoros or St James Slayer of the Moors is shown on horseback below the tympanum while the figures of St John and St Mark are carved against the piers. The massive arches supporting the timber roof above the nave are also Gothic. The church contains a beautifully carved stone pulpit.

EL CENTRO

The city's central district acts as a natural extension to the old quarter. Nowadays it is a lively commercial area.

Avenida de la Marina★

The avenue, facing the harbour, is lined by tall houses with glassed-in balconies typical of La Coruña. Extending it on one side is the paseo de la Dársena and on the other the attractively landscaped **Jardines de Méndez Núñez**, gardens with a variety of flowering trees.

Plaza de María Pita

The vast pedestrian square just behind avenida de la Marina is named after the town's 16C heroine. It has a great many terrace cafés and is lined on three sides by arcades upon which rest houses with glassed-in galleries.

Worth a Visit

Castillo de San Antón: Museo Arqueológico e Histórico

🕐 *Open 10am-7pm (9pm Jul-Aug); Sun and public hols, 10am-2.30pm (3pm Jul-Aug); last admission 30min before closing time.* 🕐 *Closed Mon, 1 Jan, Mon-Wed during Carnival, and 24-25 and 31 Dec.* ✎ *2€.* ☎ *98 118 98 50.*

The castle's casemates served as a prison for several famous inmates such as Malaspina. It now houses an archaeological museum, which includes a room dedicated to prehistoric gold and silverware.

Museo de Bellas Artes

🕐 *Open 10am-8pm; Sat, 10am-2pm and 4-8pm; Sun, 10am-2pm.* 🕐 *Closed Mon and public hols.* ✎ *2.40€, no charge Sat afternoon and Sun.* ☎ *98 122 37 23.*

The main feature of this modern fine arts museum is the light and spacious feel of its exhibition rooms, dedicated to art from the 16C to the 20C. Of particular note are the sketches by Goya.

Domus-Casa del Hombre

🕐 *Open 10am-7pm; Jul-Aug, 11am-9pm.* 🎟 *2€.* ☎ *98 118 98 40.*

This unusual **building**★, designed by the Japanese architect **Arata Isozaki**, is located on the Riazor bay, and has become one of the architectural symbols of the city. The façade, facing the bay, is composed of a double curve which adopts the shape of a large sail, and is covered with pieces of slate to give a scaly appearance. The building's other wall has made use of the city's old quarry to create an area of large stone blocks which act as a screen. The museum itself is dedicated to Man, and deals with various aspects of human life such as genetics, reproduction and the senses through texts, photographs, interactive displays, holographs etc.

Aquarium Finisterrae

🕐 *Open 10am-7pm (9pm Jul-Aug); Sat-Sun and public hols, 10am-8pm (9pm Jul-Aug).* 🎟 *8€ (10€ including visit to the Casa de las Ciencias, Domus).* ☎ *98 118 98 42.*

Also known as the Casa de los Peces (House of the Fish), the city's aquarium is located close to the Torre de Hércules. Its main role is to highlight to visitors the marine eco-systems in the waters off the Galician coast. Large tanks in the main exhibition room, the Maremágnum, display several of these ecosystems, including the continental shelf, banks of algae etc.

Torre de Hércules (Hercules Tower or Lighthouse)

🕐 *Open Oct-Mar 10am-6pm (7pm Apr-Jun and Sep; 9pm Sun-Thu, midnight Fri-Sat and holiday eves Jul-Aug). Last admission 15min before closing.* 🎟 *2€.*

This was built in the 2C AD and is the oldest functioning lighthouse in the world. In 1790 when Charles III modified the tower to its present square shape, the original outer ramp was enclosed to form an inner staircase. From the top (104m/341ft), there is a **view** of the town and the coast.

Excursion

Cambre

11km/7mi S. 🕐 *Open 10am-9.30pm.* ☎ *98 167 51 57.*

The 12C Romanesque **Iglesia de Santa María**★ has a lovely façade, divided into three sections corresponding with the nave and two aisles inside. Multifoil arches, emphasising the windows on either side, reflect Moorish influence as do the buttress capitals. The tympanum is carved with the Holy Lamb in a medallion supported by angels. The interior, with its great purity of style, has a feature often found in churches on the Santiago pilgrim route, an apse circled by an ambulatory with five radiating chapels.

Costa del Azahar

MICHELIN MAP 577 K 31, L 30, M 29, N 28-29, O 28-29 –

COMUNIDAD VALENCIANA (CASTELLÓN, VALENCIA)

Over the years, the sun-blessed Orange Blossom Coast has developed into one of Spain's major tourist centres as a result of its benign climate, enhanced by the protective barrier of mountains inland. Sadly, many of its resorts have become swamped by high-rise apartment blocks and hotels which appear incongruously alongside the region's long sandy beaches and orange groves. However, despite this intrusion of concrete, a number of small towns and villages have preserved their old quarters, in which history has left its indelible mark. The Costa del Azahar is also justifiably famous for its cuisine, in particular its fish, seafood and savoury rice dishes.

Location

The Orange Blossom Coast extends across the provinces of Castellón and Valencia. Resorts in Castellón tend to be more low-key and more family orientated, while the bigger, mass-market resorts are located to the south of Valencia. The AP 7 Autopista del Mediterráneo toll motorway and the A 7 and N 332 national roads run along this stretch of coast. *Castellón de la Plana: Plaza María Agustina 5, 12003 Castellón, ☎ 964 35 86 88; Gandía: Marqués de Campo, 46700 Castellón, ☎ 964 287 77 88; Peñíscola: Paseo Marítimo, 12598 Castellón, ☎ 964 48 02 08.*

Neighbouring sights are described in the following chapters: COSTA DORADA (to the NE), TORTOSA (to the N), MORELLA (NW of Vinaròs) and the COSTA BLANCA (to the S).

Tours

FROM VINARÒS TO CASTELLÓN *72km/45mi*

▷ *Follow either the N 340 or the AP 7 toll motorway.*

The northern coast of the province of Castellón, on the border with Tarragona, is separated from the interior by the mountains and canyons of the Maestrazgo chain, whose name derives from the word maestre, recalling knights from the Templar and Montesa orders who exercised control over this area during the Middle Ages. Some of the largest resorts in the Comunidad Valenciana can be found along this coast, such as Peñíscola and Benicàssim.

Address Book

For coin ranges, see the Legend at the back of the guide.

WHERE TO EAT

◷ **El Peñón** – *Santos Mártires, 22 – Peñíscola –* On the way up to the castile, next to the Ermita de la Virgen – ☎ 96 448 07 16 – Closed Christmas, Jan-Feb and early Mar. Half-hidden in one of the narrow streets of the old town, the Peñón is a friendly restaurant with attractive decor and a pleasant small terrace, where you can enjoy *dorada a la sal* (gilthead baked in salt) or an excellent grouper stew (cazuela de mero), made with fish fresh from the Peñíscola market.

◷◷ **El Coloso** – *Plaza Marqués de la Romana - Cullera – ☎* 96 174 60 76 – Closed Wed. Classic Spanish seafood emporium, with immense windows to seaward. You'll

feel as if you're on the high seas. Specialties are paella, seafood and grilled meats.

WHERE TO STAY

◷**Albatros** – *Grau 11 (near beach) - Gandía – ☎* 96 284 56 00 – [P] ▤ – 44 rooms – ⌲ 3.82€. This hotel is notable for its sharp style and amenities, rare attributes in the beach area. The coffee shop serves a limited menu in the evening.

◷◷ **Hotel Simó** – *Porteta 5 - Peñíscola –* ☎ 96 448 06 20 – Open Mar-Sep – ▤ – 10 rooms – ⌲ 5.50€. Well-located at the seaside by the old city walls. Spectacular views more than compensate for tiny bathrooms and fluorescent lighting. Ground-floor restaurant.

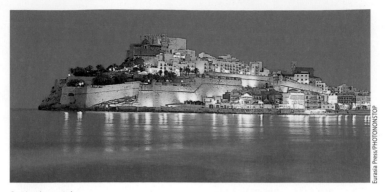

Peñíscola at night

Vinaròs

Vinaròs is the first town of any importance when approaching Castellón province from the north. It has several monuments of interest, including the 16C **Iglesia de Nuestra Señora de la Asunción**, in addition to a pleasant promenade close to the fishing port. Vinaròs is traditionally known for its prawns, which figure heavily on local menus.

Benicarló

This town with a long fishing tradition has developed into a large resort mainly as a result of its proximity to Peñíscola, to which it is linked via one of the best beaches in the area; sadly, the latter has been blemished somewhat by excessive tourist development.

Peñíscola★★

Peñíscola is without doubt the most attractive town along the Orange Blossom Coast. Its old quarter, surrounded by walls, sits on a small rocky peninsula in the shadow of an imposing fortress, while its sandy beaches extend to either side. A small **fishing port** is still active in the town.

Old town★

The *ciudad vieja* is huddled within the ramparts built during the reign of Philip II. Its narrow and winding whitewashed streets (*closed to traffic*) are lined with myriad souvenir shops.

Castillo★

⏲ *Open 16 Oct-Palm Sunday, 9.30am-1pm and 3.15-6pm; during Holy Week and 15 Jun-15 Sep, 9am-2.30pm and 4.30-9.30pm; other times 9am-8pm.* ⏲ *Closed 1 and 6 Jan, 9 Sep, 9 Oct and 25 Dec.* ✆ *2€.* ☎ *96 448 00 21.*

Built by the Templars at the beginning of the 14C, the castle was subsequently modified by Pope Luna (see right), whose coat of arms, featuring a crescent moon in allusion to his name, can be seen on one of the gates. Grouped around the parade ground are the church, a vast hall with pointed vaulting and a free-standing tower containing the conclave room and the study of the learned antipope who, among his many acts, confirmed in six bulls the foundation in 1411 of the University of St Andrew's in Scotland (👁 *see The Green Guide Scotland*) and promulgated the Statutes of Salamanca University.

Pope Luna

On the death of the antipope Clement VII in 1394, the Aragonese Cardinal Pedro de Luna (Benedict XIII) was elected successor by the French cardinals in conclave at Avignon. It was a dubious heritage, however, as his predecessor had never succeeded in establishing his claim. The withdrawal of the support of King Charles VI of France and of St Vincent Ferrer and the accusation of heresy by the Councils of Pisa (1409) and Constance (1416), in no way diminished the self-styled Benedict XIII's conviction of his right. He considered the proposal that he should abdicate and help to seal the schism inadmissible and, in the face of general hostility, sought refuge in the fortress on Peñíscola. There he remained until he died in 1422, a nonagenarian, tenacious as ever, who even named his own successor! (This prelate, however, soon abdicated in favour of the Rome-elected Martin V.)

There is a **panorama**★ of the village and coastline from the castle terrace.

Today, the castle is the setting for various musical events such as the Festival of Baroque and Ancient Music, held in August.

The road runs parallel to the coast, passing through an arid landscape with sparse vegetation. The resort of Alcossebre, a popular holiday destination for Spanish families, stands halfway between Peñíscola and Benicàssim.

Benicàssim

This resort is the other major tourist centre in the province of Castellón and is separated from the interior by the **Desierto de las Palmas** (Palm Desert), an area which has suffered badly from the effects of fire in the past few years. Benicàssim has some excellent beaches, lined by a continuous cordon of summer villas and apartments which are generally occupied by Spanish families. The quieter town of Oropesa is located to the north.

Castellón de la Plana

Just a couple of miles separate Benicàssim from the port of Castellón, whose origins date back to the 13C. The capital of the province is situated in La Plana, an extensive fertile area irrigated by the River Mijares. The town's main square (plaza Mayor) is fronted by the **Catedral de Santa María**, rebuilt after the Spanish Civil War and with only three doorways left standing; the octagonal bell-tower alongside the cathedral was erected in the late 16C. The town hall *(ayuntamiento)*, graced with an elegant façade, was built in the last decade of the 17C.

Other sights of interest include the series of paintings attributed to Zurbarán in the Convento de las Madres Capuchinas, and the Museo Provincial de Bellas Artes, with its displays of prehistoric objects and a collection of canvases and ceramics from the local area.

FROM CASTELLÓN TO VALENCIA *69km/43mi*
22km/14mi NW on the CV 10 and CV 160.

Vilafamés

This town of Moorish origin extends across a hill dominated by the ruins of a medieval castle, from where the views are particularly impressive. Villafamés is an attractive town with typical, whitewashed streets and an increasing number of artists' workshops.

Museo Popular de Arte Contemporáneo

◷ *Open 10am-1.30pm and 4-7pm (10.30am-2pm and 4-7pm Sat-Sun and public hols); Jun-Sep, 10am-1.30pm and 4-8pm.* ⊛ *1.80€.* ☎ *96 432 91 52.*

The museum, housed in a 15C palace, is the centre of a very active cultural scene. Many of the works it displays are by famous artists including Miró, Barjola, Serrano, Genovés, Chillida and Grupo Crónica.

▸ *Return to Castellón, then continue along the A 7 for 25km/15mi as far as Vall d'Uxo.*

Grutas de San José

In Vall d'Uxo, follow signs to the caves (grutas). ⏍ *Guided tours (35min), Dec-Feb, 11am-1.15pm and 3.30-5pm (5.45pm Mar and Nov; 6.30pm Apr, last*

A Legendary Siege

Sagunto has a place in Spain's heroic history. In 218 BC the Carthaginian general, **Hannibal**, besieged Sagunto, then a small seaport allied to Rome, for a period of 8 months. Seeing only one alternative to surrender, the local inhabitants lit a huge fire and women, children, the sick and the old then proceeded to throw themselves into the furnace while soldiers and menfolk made a suicidal sortie against the enemy. The event marked the beginning of the Second Punic War. Five years later, Scipio Africanus Major rebuilt the city which became an important Roman town.

The Borja Fief

Gandía became the fief of the Borja family, better known under its Italian name, Borgia, when in 1485, the Duchy of Gandía was given by Ferdinand the Catholic to Rodrigo Borgia, future Pope Alexander VI. The pope is chiefly remembered for his scandalous private life and for his children: Lucrezia, renowned for her beauty and culture, and victim of political intrigue between her father and brother; and Cesare who for political ends had his brother murdered and served as a model for Machiavelli's *The Prince*. However, the fourth duke and great-grandson of Alexander VI, who became St Francis Borja (1510-72), was to redeem the family name.

two weeks of Sep and in Oct); 1 May-15 Jul, 10am-1.30pm and 3.30-6.30pm (8pm 15 Jul-15 Sep). ◷ Closed Mon Nov-Feb, 1 Jan and 25 Dec. ⊜ 6.50€. ☎ 96 469 67 61.

An underground river, one of the largest in Europe, has hollowed out these impressive caves at the foot of the Parque Natural de La Sierra de Espadán. Guided tours by boat cover a distance of around 1.2km/0.75mi.

▶ Continue for 20km/12mi along the CV 230, then follow the N 234.

Segorbe

The **cathedral** is chiefly important for its **museum** (museo) which contains a large **collection of altarpieces painted by the Valencia School**★. There are several paintings by **Juan Vicente Macip** (d 1550) who was influenced by the Italian Renaissance style. An Ecce Homo by his son **Juan de Juanes** bears the touch of gentleness favoured by Leonardo da Vinci. There are also works by Rodrigo de Osona and Jacomart and a 15C marble low relief of a Madonna by Donatello. (◷ Open 10.30am-1pm. ◷ Closed Mon, 1 and 6 Jan, Holy Week and 25 Dec. 2.40€. ☎ 96 471 10 14).

▶ Continue along the N 234, toward the coast.

Sagunto

The historic town of Sagunto sits at the foot of a hill occupied by the ruins of a castle and Roman theatre. The port, El Port de Sagunt, home to a large industrial complex, is located 5km/3mi to the east.

Ruins

◷ Open 10am-6pm (8pm in summer); Sun and public hols, 10am-2pm. ◷ Closed Mon, 1 Jan, Good Fri and 25 Dec. ☎ 96 266 55 81.

The ruins are reached through the upper part of town, through the narrow alleyways of the old Jewish quarter.

The **theatre** was built on the hillside by the Romans to take full advantage of the local relief.

The **Acropolis** consists of the ruins and remains of ramparts, temples and houses built by Iberians, Phoenicians, Carthaginians, Romans, Visigoths and Moors. Buildings to the west date from the War of Independence, when the French general Suchet besieged the town. The **view**★ from here encompasses the town, the local countryside and the sea.

Valencia (👤 see VALENCIA)

FROM VALENCIA TO XÀTIVA 122km/76mi

▶ Leave Valencia along the coast road S.

El Saler

This long sandy beach stretches out in an area dominated by pine trees.

Parque Natural de La Albufera

This vast body of water (albufera in Arabic translates as "small sea") to the south of Valencia is the largest freshwater lagoon in Spain and is separated from the Mediterranean by an offshore bar, the Dehesa, that has been planted with rice since the 13C. It is also a fishing area; its eels appear on typical menus in restaurants in **El Palmar** (to the S) which also serve Valencia's famous dish, **paella**. ▯ For further details on the park, contact the **Centro de Interpretación del Racó de l'Olla**. (◷ Open Mon, Wed and Fri, 9am-2pm; Tue and Thu, 9am-2pm and 3.30-5.30pm; Sat-Sun and public hols, 9am-2pm and 3-5.30pm. ☎ 96 162 73 45).

El Españoleto

José (Jusepe) **de Ribera** studied in Valencia, probably with Ribalta, before going to Italy where he settled in Naples in 1616. Lo Spagnoletto, or the Little Spaniard, as Italians called him on account of his small stature, became accredited to successive Spanish viceroys of Naples, notably the Duke of Osuna, and won early and equally widespread fame in Italy and Spain. He died in Italy in 1652.

He was one of the major exponents of tenebrism, with a style that was reminiscent of Caravaggio's chiaroscuro. He is known for his paintings of monks and saints, which he depicted with a somewhat coarse energy. However, some of his later works, more serene and in mellower colours, reveal a different and surprisingly sensitive artist, probably the influence of the Venetian and Bologna Schools.

The action in the novel *Cañas y barro*, by **Vicente Blasco Ibáñez** (1867-1928), was set in the Albufera.

▶ *Continue along the CV 500.*

Cullera

This large resort stands at the mouth of the River Júcar and the foot of the Monte de Oro; its bay is demarcated to the north by a lighthouse, the Faro de Cullera. The town has preserved the remains of a 13C castle.

▶ *Head 27km/17mi S along the N 332.*

Gandía

Gandía lies on the Costa Blanca south of Valencia at the centre of a *huerta* which produces large quantities of oranges. A seaside resort has developed near the harbour along a 3km/1.8mi-long sandy **beach**.

Palacio Ducal

🖙 *Guided tours, Oct-May, 10am-2pm and 4-8pm (every hour); Jun-Sep, 10am-2pm and 5-9pm (every 30min).* 🎟 *3.50€.* ☎ *96 287 14 65.*

The mansion in which St Francis Borja was born, now a Jesuit college, underwent considerable modification between the 16C and 18C. Only the patio remains Gothic in appearance and typical of those along the east coast of Spain. The tour includes richly decorated apartments with painted or coffered ceilings, *azulejos* and marble floors. Several rooms have been converted into chapels. The last room off the golden gallery has a beautiful floor, a Manises mosaic representing the four elements.

▶ *Head inland along the CV 60. Just before reaching Palomar, bear right on the A 7.*

Xàtiva/Játiva

Known as "the town of the thousand fountains", Xàtiva stands at the heart of a delightful plain covered with a typically Mediterranean landscape of vineyards, orchards and cypress trees.

The town was the birthplace of two members of the Borja family who became popes, Calixtus III (1455-58) and Alexander VI, and, in 1591, of the painter **José Ribera**.

Plaza de Calixto III

The 16C **cathedral**, modified in the 18C, faces the **hospital** which has an ornate Gothic and Plateresque style façade.

Museo

🕐 *Open 10am-2pm and 4-6pm; 15 Jun-15 Sep, 9.30am-2.30pm; Sat-Sun and public hols all year, 10am-2.30pm.* 🕐 *Closed Mon, 1 Jan and 24-26 and 31 Dec. 2€, no charge Sun.* ☎ *96 227 65 97.*

The Almudin, which used to be a granary, now houses a collection of paintings.

In the patio is an 11C **Moorish fountain** or *pila*, one of the most interesting examples of Moorish sculpture in Spain as it depicts human figures, something which is extremely rare in Islamic art.

Ermita de Sant Feliu

▶ *On the castle road.* 🕐 *Closed for restoration.* ☎ *96 227 33 46.*

Built on the flank of the hill, this chapel contains a group of 15C Valencian primitives. At the entrance is a white marble stoup★ hollowed out of a former capital.

Castillo

🕐 *Open 10am-6pm (7pm in summer).* 🕐 *Closed Mon, 1 Jan and 25 Dec. 2€.* ☎ *96 227 42 74.*

What remains of the castle – it was demolished under Philip V – stands on the site of the original town. It commands extensive **panoramas** of the town, the surrounding countryside, the *huerta*, and the sea in the distance. Among the Castillo Mayor's distinguished prisoners was the Count of Urgel, pretender to the throne of Aragón, who was defeated by his rival, Ferdinand, in 1412.

Costa Blanca★

MICHELIN MAP 577 P 29-30, Q 29-30 –

COMUNIDAD VALENCIANA (ALACANT/ALICANTE), MURCIA

The Costa Blanca or White Coast stretches south from the shores of the Valencian province of Alicante to those of Murcia. It is mainly flat and sandy with the occasional area of high land where the *sierras* drop to the sea. The hot climate, low rainfall, dazzling white light after which the coast is named, long beaches and turquoise water attract a vast number of Spanish and foreign tourists throughout the year.

Address Book

For coin ranges, see the Legend at the back of the guide.

WHERE TO EAT

Labarta – *Conde de Altea 30 – Altea* – ☎ 96 584 51 12 – *Closed evenings in winter.* This white building on the beachfront in Altea recalls the style of local fishermen's houses. Traditional home cooking (rows of tapas, paella, tomato bread) served under an awning, with sea view.

Casa Modesto – *Playa de Finestrat – 4km/2.5mi W of Benidorm along the Playa de Poniente* – ☎ 96 585 86 37 – *Closed 15 Jan-15 Mar.* Not surprisingly, the menu at this beach restaurant revolves around fish and seafood. The sea views from this cove are splendid, although the high-rise towers of Benidorm are something of a blot on the landscape.

WHERE TO STAY

Hostal L'Ánfora – *Explanada Cervantes 8-9 – Denia* – ☎ 96 643 01 01 – ▤ – *20 rooms.* This small building with its distinctive green façade is located at the fishing port in Denia. Although small and basic, the rooms here are bright and clean. In the mornings, guests can also enjoy the sight of local fishing boats from their windows.

Miramar – *Pl. Almirante Bastarreche 12 (port) - Jávea* – ☎ 96 579 01 00 – *Closed 1-6 Jan* – ▤ – *26 rooms.* Facing the seafront drive at one end of the beach, and an excellent choice for the price. Rooms are large and updated, well-equipped with full bathrooms.

TAPAS

Calle Santo Domingo – *Benidorm*. A pedestrianised street with ten or more bars. Worthy of mention are the *Aurrerá* and the *Cava Aragonesa* (below).

La Cava Aragonesa – *Plaza de la Constitución (also entry on Calle Santo Domingo) - Benidorm* – ☎ 96 580 12 06 – *Open noon-3.30pm and 6.45pm-1.30am.* This typical bar makes a refreshing change from the dozens of neighbouring tower blocks, with its cured hams hanging from the ceiling and its good choice of tapas.

BARS AND CAFES

Casino de Torrevieja – *Plaza Waldo Calero - Torrevieja -* ◷ *Open 10am-2am.* A formidable private club of Moorish inspiration, hosting choral performances, art shows and other cultural events. Ideal for an aperitif in one of its pleasant mid-19C rooms. .

Chocolaterías Valor – *Avenida Pianista Gonzalo Soriano – La Vila Joiosa* – ☎ 96 589 09 50 –* ◷ *Open Mon-Fri, 9.30am-12.30pm and 4-6pm.* Founded in 1881 by Don Valeriano López, Valor now has more than 15 stores around Spain. Visits to the factory are available every day, while chocoholics will not want to miss the Museo del Chocolate.

NIGHTLIFE

Avenida d'Alcol – *(most of the bars can be found on the right-hand side of the Playa de Levante) – Benidorm.* During the summer, this beach area is a mass of humanity with every available inch of beach space occupied during the day and the avenue's bars, restaurants and ice-cream parlours heaving at night. For people-watching, gaze at the youthful crowd at *Ku Beach*, *KM Playa* and *Penelope Beach Club*.

Avenida Comunidad Valenciana – *Benidorm* – ◷ *Open from 12.30am.* This avenue is home to Benidorm's most popular dance venues: *Ku, KM* and *Penelope*.

Calle Apolo – *Torrevieja.* This street has no fewer than 15 bars including the *Casablanca,* the *Memfils,* the *Asteriz* and the *Pub JF,* transforming calle Apollo into one huge nightclub. The beach is often busy at night with youngsters taking a breather from the dance floor.

J. Malburet/MICHELIN

Penyal d'Ifac

Location

The main towns along this coast are well linked via the N 332 and the AP 7 toll motorway. *Altea: San Pedro 9, 03590 Alicante, ☎ 96 584 41 14; Benidorm: Avenida Martínez Alejos 16, 03500 Alicante, ☎ 96 585 13 11; Calpe: Avenida Ejércitos Españoles 44, 03710 Alicante, ☎ 96 583 69 20; Denia: Plaza del Oculista Buigues 9, 03700 Alicante, ☎ 96 642 23 67; Jávea: Plaza Almirante Bastarreche 11, 03730 Alicante, ☎ 96 579 07 36.*

Neighbouring sights are described in the following chapters: ALACANT/ALICANTE and Costa del AZAHAR.

Tours

FROM DÈNIA TO GUADALEST
115km/71mi – allow 2 days

Dènia (Denia)

The former Greek colony was taken over by the Romans who named it *Dianium*. Dènia today is a commercial port, fishing harbour, industrial centre specialising in the manufacture of toys, and a popular seaside resort. The fortress overlooking the town houses an archaeological museum.

The coast south of Dènia becomes steep and rocky with pine forests.

Cap de Sant Antoni★

From near the lighthouse on this headland, a last foothill of the Sierra del Mongó, there is a good **view**★ towards Xàbia and the Cabo de la Nao headland.

Xàbia (Jávea)

The old quarter stands on high ground, its houses closely grouped around a fortified 14C Gothic church. The resort's modern quarter has grown up near its harbour, around the sandy beach where there is a parador.

Cabo de la Nao★

The climb affords views over Xàbia at the foot of the Sierra del Mongó, before you enter thick pinewoods relieved only by villas standing in individual clearings. Cabo de la Nao is considered to be the eastern outpost of the Sierras Béticas (Baetic Cordillera) chain although in fact the formation continues under the sea to reappear as the island of Ibiza. There is a beautiful **view**★ south from the point along the indented coastline to the Penyal d'Ifac. Sea caves (approached by boat) and charming creeks such as **La Granadella** (south) and **Cala Blanca** (north) are excellent for underwater swimming.

Calp (Calpe)

The **Penyal d'Ifac**★, an impressive rocky outcrop 332m/1 089ft high, provides Calp with a distinctive setting. A path leads to the top of the Penyal (*about 1hr walk*) from which, as you climb, you will get interesting views along the coast of Calp and its salt pans, of the darkish mountain chains, and northwards of the precipitous coast as far as Cabo de la Nao.

The Sierra de Bernia road twists and turns before crossing the spectacular Barranco de Mascarat (Mascarat Ravine) in the mountain hinterland to Cabo de la Nao.

Altea

Altea, white walls, rose-coloured roofs and glazed blue tile domes, rises in tiers up a hillside overlooking the sea – a symphony of colour and reflected light below the Sierra de Bernia. A walk through the alleys to the church and then the view from the square over the village and beyond to the Penyal d'Ifac will reveal the attraction of so many painters towards Altea.

Benidorm

The excellent climate and two immense beaches (the Levante and the Poniente), curving away on either side of a small rock promontory, have provided the basic elements for Benidorm's incredible success as a tourist resort. It has grown from a modest fishing village in the 1950s to a kind of Mediterranean Manhattan with modern tower blocks overlooking the sea, all manner of entertainment and a very lively nightlife.

From the lookout on **El Castillo** point, there are **views**★ of the beaches and the Island of Plumbaria. The old quarter stands behind the point, close to the blue domed church.

Terra Mítica

Kids *3km/2mi from Benidorm. Exit the AP 7 at exit 65 A.* ○ *Open 10am-8pm (midnight Jun-Aug.* ◉ *32/day€ (45€ for 2 days; 13.50€ evenings/nights).* ○ *Closed Mon-Fri Nov-Dec and Mar, Mon-Tue in May and 29 Dec-14 Mar.* ☎ *90 2020 220.*

Opened in the summer of 2000, this vast theme park is based upon the four main civilisations in the Mediterranean: Egypt, Greece, Rome and Iberia. The park is organised into five areas: the four above are laid out around the large central lake symbolising the "Mare Nostrum", with the fifth, the Islands, appearing at the centre. Terra Mítica also has numerous attractions for visitors of all ages and tastes, as well as various shows and a good choice of shops and restaurants.

Main attractions – In Ancient Egypt, enter a pyramid in the Mystery of Cheops, or descend the Cataracts of the Nile on an exciting white-water roller coaster ride. In Greece, why not emulate Theseus in the Labyrinth of the Minotaur, or experience the sensation of falling down a waterfall in the Fury of Triton. The Magnus Colossus in Rome is a spectacular wooden roller coaster ride which dominates the park. In the Flight of the Phoenix, enjoy the excitement of a free fall from a height of 54m/177ft, or battle against currents and whirlpools in the Rapids of Argos, in the Islands section.

▶ *Take the CV 70 to Callosa d'En Sarrià and from there head along the CV 755 to Alcoi.*

On the drive inland, you pass through small valleys cloaked in all sorts of fruit trees, including citrus and medlars. The village of **Polop** stretches up a hillside in a picturesque mountain setting. Beyond, the landscape becomes more arid but the views more extensive, the mountains more magnificent.

Guadalest★

Guadalest stands out from the terraced valleys of olive and almond trees to face the harsh limestone escarpments of the Sierra de Aitana. The **site**★ is impressive, with the village, in self-defence, forced halfway up a ridge of rock, a natural stronghold accessible only through an archway cut into the stone. Walk round the **Castillo de San José** (now the site of a cemetery) of which only ruins remain of the castle fortifications wrecked by an earthquake in 1744. From here can be seen the view over the green Guadalest reservoir with its reflections of the surrounding mountain crests, the amazing site of the old village, and, beyond, the sea.

Costa Brava★★★

MICHELIN MAP 574 E 39, F 39, G 38-39 – CATALUNYA (GIRONA)

The Costa Brava or Wild Coast derives its name from its twisted, rocky shoreline where the Catalan mountain ranges form a line of cliffs which fall away into the sea. The beautiful inlets along the whole of the coast, its clear waters, quiet, picturesque harbours, fishing villages and numerous leisure and sporting activities on offer here have earned it an international reputation, attracting a great many foreign tourists in recent years.

Location

The Costa Brava comprises the entire coastline of the province of Girona, from Blanes, to the south, to Portbou on the border with France. The towns to the south (Lloret de Mar, Tossa de Mar and Platja d'Aro) are major tourist centres, while those to the north are more low-key. Visitors heading inland will also find delightful medieval towns and villages. ⓘ *Patronat de Turisme Costa Brava Girona: Emili Grahit 13, Girona, ☎ 972 20 84 01; Blanes: Plaza Catalunya 21, 17300 Blanes, ☎ 97 233 03 48; Cadaqués: Cotxe 2, 17488, ☎ 972 25 83 15; Sant Feliu de Guíxols: Plaza del Monestir, 17220, ☎ 97 282 00 51.*

ⓖ *Neighbouring sights are described in the following chapters: GIRONA/GERONA, FIGUERES and BARCELONA.*

Tours

THE ALBERES COASTLINE★★

1️⃣ *From Portbou to Roses 65km/40mi – allow half a day*

The last foothills of the Sierra de l'Albera extend right up to the sea and form huge, enclosed bays, like those of Portbou and El Port de la Selva. The route continues to wind its way upwards along the cliff tops, especially on the **road section**★★ from Portbou to Colera, offering fine views of one of the most craggy coastlines in Catalunya.

El Port de Llançà

A pleasant tourist resort located around a bay facing the sea that shelters it from offshore winds like the *tramontana* as well as sudden Mediterranean storms. The charming beach and its shallow waters are ideal for bathing.

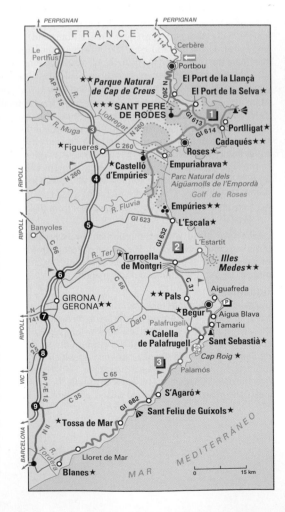

Cadaqués

▶ *Continue along the GI 612 for 8km/5mi*

El Port de la Selva★

This tourist locality lies in a natural bay that basks in golden sunlight at dusk. Besides its traditional white houses, in which the fishermen once lived, the village features newly-constructed buildings with many flats and hotels. Fishing continues to be one of the main activities of the port.

Monasterio de Sant Pere de Rodes★★★

7km/4mi from El Port de la Selva. 🅿 *Leave your car in the car park and proceed on foot for 10min.* 🕐 *Open 10am-5.30pm (8pm Jun-Sep); last admission 20min before closing time.* 🕐 *Closed Mon, 1 Jan and 25 Dec.* ⊜ *3.60€, no charge Tue.* ☎ *972 28 75 59.*

The ruins of this imposing Benedictine monastery stand on the slopes of the Monte de Sant Salvador in a beautiful **setting**★★ that dominates the Gulf of Lion and the Cabo de Creus peninsula. Its construction began in the 10C but it was subsequently pillaged and eventually abandoned in the 18C. The **church**★★★, a truly remarkable building showing pre-Romanesque influence, is a fine, if somewhat unusual, example of architectural harmony. The three naves are crowned with vaulting: the central nave with barrel vaulting, the two lateral ones with surbased vaulting. They are separated by huge pillars, reinforced with columns leaning on raised bases. The splendid **capitals**★ are delicately carved with intricate tracery and acanthus leaves, evoking the tradition of Córdoba and Byzantium. The transept has a central chapel and two radiating chapels with a narrow ambulatory and a crypt. The left arm of the transept leads to an upper ambulatory offering a sweeping view of the central nave.

The 12C **bell tower**★★ is a magnificent example of Lombardy Gothic.

The coast running between El Port de la Selva and Cadaqués features many small irregular creeks with crystal-clear waters, accessible only by sea. The road continues inland, offering lovely views of the surrounding region.

▶ *13km/8mi along the GI 613. Care should be taken along this road as it is extremely narrow in parts.*

Cadaqués★★

Tucked away behind the very last Pyrenean foothills, Cadaqués lies south of the Cabo de Creus in a delightful **setting**★ enclosed by mountains, with the sea as its only natural outlet. It used to be a humble fishing village until a bunch of contemporary artists (Dalí, Picasso, García Lorca, Buñuel, André Breton, Paul Éluard etc) took to coming here, turning it into a fashionable resort.

Built along steep, narrow streets, the white houses and their picturesque porticoes are clustered around the **Iglesia de Santa María,** whose sober exterior contrasts sharply with its interior: note the lovely **Baroque altarpiece**★★ in carved and gilded wood. Every year the town hosts an international music festival. 🕐 *Open 11am-8pm.* ☎ *972 25 85 00.*

Address Book

For coin ranges, see the Legend at the back of the guide.

WHERE TO EAT

La Gua-gua – *Platja Canyelles Petites – Roses – 2.5km/1.5mi SE of Roses –* ☎ 972 25 77 82 – *Closed Oct-Holy Week. Reservation recommended.* This delightful restaurant serves traditional fish dishes (make sure you try the *suquet de peix* – a type of fish stew) on a beachside terrace with lovely sea views. The only disadvantage is the hordes of sunbathers on the beach in summer.

Can Rafa – *Passeig 7 – Cadaqués – Exit 4 from AP 7 toward Cadaqués* ☎ 972 15 94 01 – *Reservation recommended.* Good local cuisine in a dining room covered with photos from the 1970s. Tremendous views of the port from the terrace.

Eldorado Mar – *President Irla 15 – Sant Feliu de Guíxols* – ☎ 972 32 62 86 – *Closed Wed Oct-May.* This restaurant in the upper part of town specialises in fish and seafood. Despite the dining room's plain decoration, its large windows offer stunning sea views. The fixed menu is reasonably priced.

La Brasa – *Plaça Catalunya 6 – El Port de LLançà* – ☎ 972 38 02 02 – *Closed Mon eves,Tue (except Jul-Aug) and 15 Dec-Feb* – 🔲. The Brasa has a distinct summer feel to it, particularly inside, where grilled fish and meat (the house speciality and included on the set menu) are cooked in front of guests. The restaurant also has a pleasant shady terrace for those who prefer to sit outside.

Santa Marta – *Francesc Aromir 2 – Tossa de Mar* – ☎ 972 34 04 72 – *Closed Tue (except Jun-Aug).* Located within the walls of the old town, the Santa Marta has a varied menu offering a range of fish and meat dishes. Despite its irregular shape, the dining room has a warm, relaxed feel to it. Pleasant terrace.

Ca la Maria – *Unió 5 - Mollet de Peralada – 4km/2.5mi N of Peralada –* ☎ 972 56 33 82 – *Closed nights, Tue,holiday eves 15 Feb-15 Mar* – 🔲 – *Reservation recommended.* A large restaurant in the quiet village of Mollet, 16km/10mi inland. An unpretentious setting in which to try typical Catalan cuisine. Always busy at weekends.

WHERE TO STAY

Hotel Ubaldo – *Unió 13 – Cadaqués –* ☎ 972 25 81 25 – *26 rooms.* The hotel's simple façade masks a pleasant interior of white walls, curved furniture and soft lighting. The comfortable, fully equipped rooms overlook the alleyways of the town's old quarter.

Hotel La Goleta – *Pintor Terruella 22 – El Port de LLançà –* ☎ 972 38 01 25 – 🅿 – *30 rooms* – ☞ – *Restaurant 17.50€.* Close to the port area, the La Goleta offers guests comfortable surroundings and an interesting decor of paintings and other furnishings. A friendly atmosphere and good value for money.

Hotel Diana – *Plaza de España 6 – Tossa de Mar* – ☎ 972 34 18 86 – *Open Mar-Nov – 21 rooms –* ☞. The interior of this splendid Modernist building by the sea is exquisite, with an emphasis on high ceilings, cool rooms and a patio adorned with a marble fountain. The rooms are comfortable and furnished in style.

Hotel Rosa – *Pi i Rallo 11 – Begur –* ☎ 972 62 30 15 – *Open Mar-Nov –* 🔲 – *21 rooms.* ☞ - *Restaurant.* This small hotel in a tastefully restored old stone house is mainly popular with a younger crowd who appreciate the modern decoration, functional furniture and well-thought-out lighting. By the church square.

Hotel Port Lligat – *Avenida Salvador Dalí 1 – Port Lligat –* ☎ 972 25 81 62 – 🛌 – *30 rooms –* ☞ 8€. The creature comforts in this attractive blue and white building in a cove full of fishing boats near Dalí's house are particularly popular with guests. Every room is different, and if you don't mind paying a bit extra, ask for one with a sea view.

Hotel Sant Roc – *Plaça Atlántic 2, (Sant Roc district) – Calella de Palafrugell –* ☎ 972 61 42 50 – *Open 12 Mar-8 Dec* – 🅿 🔲 – *48 rooms –* ☞ 9.55€. This charming building crowned by a small tower enjoys a peaceful, relaxing setting amid pine groves overlooking the Mediterranean. The rooms are spacious and elegant, while the restaurant terrace enjoys fine views of neighbouring coves. Half-board compulsory in summer.

Hotel Plaça – *Plaça Mercat 22 – Sant Feliu de Guíxols –* ☎ 972 32 51 55 – – 🔲 – *19 rooms –* ☞ 6€. A practical choice, both in terms of its location and its modern, functional character. Bright, pleasant rooms, some of which overlook a square that is particularly lively on market days. Outdoor jacuzzi and solarium on the top floor.

Hotel Almadraba Park – *Roses – 4km/2.5mi SE of Roses –* ☎ 972 25 65 50 – *Open 8 Apr-13 Oct* – 🅿 🔲 ♿ – *60 rooms –* ☞ – *Restaurant 37€.* A hotel offering impeccable service in a delightful natural setting amid lovely gardens. The building itself, modern in design and south facing, looks onto manicured gardens that descend to the sea in terraces. All the guest rooms enjoy wonderful views.

NIGHTLIFE

Avinguda Just Marlès Vilarrodona – *Lloret de Mar.* At nightfall, this wide throroughfare sees a mix of beautiful girls, hunky men, and flower vendors at the doors to bars. At least ten discos: *Londeners, Flamingo, Moef Gaga* and *Tropics*, one of the largest and most modern on the Costa Brava; not to forget *St Trop* (one street over), the only one that can face up to *Tropics*, with three floors, seven bars, and 200,000 watts of light.

La Frontera – *Miquel Rosset 22 – Cadaqués – Open 8pm-3am.* La Frontera, in a narrow street in Cadaqués, is a popular meeting-point for youngsters who come here to enjoy a drink on the terrace or a game of billiards.

L'hostal – *Passeig 8 – Cadaqués – ☎ 972 25 80 00 – Open 10am-5am.* This bar, which looks onto the main square, also hosts live jazz, rock and salsa concerts.

Mojito Bar – *Codolar 2 – Tossa de Mar – Open 6pm-2am.* A small cocktail bar with a relaxed air in the pedestrianised section of the resort. The Mojito mainly concentrates on salsa, flamenco and sevillanas.

Moxo – *Empuriabrava – Open 8pm-3am.* The *Moxo* is the focal point for nightlife in this modern tourist resort, which has about 20 bars, nightclubs and restaurants. The *Saloon* specialises in country music and the *Glass* in techno.

SHOPPING

Casa Bordas – *Carret. L'Escala-Orriols – L'Escala – ☎ 972 77 00 85 – Open Mon-Fri, 9am-1pm and 2.30-7pm.* This modern building on the outskirts of town is an excellent place to buy local anchovies.

▷ *Upon leaving Cadaqués, head N for 2km/1.2mi.*

Portlligat★

This small bay is home to the **Casa-Museo Salvador Dalí**★, housed in a cluster of fishermen's houses. Dalí's workshop, library, rooms and garden are all open to the public. ▱ *Guided tours (45min) by prior arrangement, 10.30am-6pm (to 9pm 15 Jun-15 Sep). Tour ticket must be retrieved 30min beforehand on day of visit.* ◷ *Closed Mon (except in summer), 1 Jan, 7 Jan-12 Mar, 2 Dec.* ▱ 8€. ☎ 972 25 10 15. *Continue 4km/2.5mi N*

Parque Natural Cap de Creus★★

4 km/2.5mi N. Steep roads and paths wind their way along sheer cliffs and around hidden bays through this attractive park. A spectacular **view**★★★ can be enjoyed from the **lighthouse** perched on the park's highest point.

▷ *Return to Cadaqués. From here, head SW on the Gl 614 and then E on the C 260.*

Roses★

It was here that the sailors of Rhodes founded a colony bearing that name. Located in a splendid natural harbour overlooked by the Golfo de Roses, the town has an important fishing fleet but is also a popular seaside resort. Its 16C Renaissance **citadel**★ was commissioned by Charles V, who feared an invasion of the Turkish army. It was designed according to a pentagonal plan and features a great many bastions. Its interior houses the vestiges of a Benedictine monastery destroyed by the French during the War of Independence.

THE EMPORDÀ PLAIN★ ☐2

From Roses to Begur 75km/46.5mi – allow one day

This stretch of the Costa Brava, at the foot of the cordillera, is taken up by the fertile Empordà plain.

▷ *Leave Roses on the C 260 towards Castelló d'Empúries.*

Empuriabrava★

A pleasant luxury marina built on top of an intricate network of canals in 1973, where boats can take people right up to their own door.

Castelló d'Empúries★

The former capital of the country of Empúries (between the 11C and the 14C) proudly stands on a small promontory at a short distance from the coast. The **Iglesia de Santa Maria**★, built in the 14C-15C, is flanked by a typical Catalan belfry. The imposing **portal**★★ is a unique example of Gothic art in Catalunya: the tympanum illustrates the Adoration of the Magi while the Apostles are represented on the jambs. The

View of Calella de Palafrugell

large central nave, separated from its lateral naves by fine cylindrical pillars, is supported by ribbed vaulting. The alabaster **retable**★ in the high altar (15C), crowned by conical pinnacles, depicts scenes taken from the Passion. (🕐 *Open 1 Jun-30 Sep, 10am-1pm and 4-8pm; Sun and public hols, 11am-12.30pm and 4-8pm; rest of the year, Sat-Sun only.* ☎ *972 25 05 19*).

The village has kept some of the administrative buildings dating from its golden age: the **Ajuntament** (former Maritime Commodities Exchange), combining Romanesque and Gothic elements, and the **Casa Gran**, of Gothic inspiration.

▶ *Leave Castelló d'Empúries in the direction of Sant Pere Pescador. From here, continue S until you reach the GI 623.*

L'Escala★

This tourist resort has a long-established fishing tradition and nice sandy beaches. Two inlets protect its harbour. Its speciality is the salting of anchovies.
The ruins of Empúries are located to the N of L'Escala.

Empúries/Ampurias★★

🕐 *Open 10am-6pm (8pm Holy Week and Jun-Sep).* 🕐 *Closed 1 Jan and 25 Dec.* ⊛ *2.40€.* ☎ *972 77 02 08.*

The Greco-Roman town of Ampurias (or *Emporion* as it was known to the Greeks, meaning market or trading station) was built on a striking **site**★★ beside the sea. Nowadays, it is still possible to make out three centres: the old town, or **Paliápolis**, the new town or **Neápolis**, and the Roman town.

In the mid-6C BC, the Phoenicians (who had already settled in Marseille), founded Paliápolis, a commercial port on the then offshore island, now joined to the mainland and occupied by the village of Sant Marti d'Empúries. Some years later, a town began to develop on the shore facing the island, and so Neápolis came into being. As a Roman ally during the Punic Wars, it saw the arrival of an expeditionary corps led by Scipio Africanus Major in 218 BC. However, it wasn't until 100 BC that the Roman town was established to the west of Neápolis. The two centres coexisted independently until Augustus bestowed Roman citizenship upon the Greeks. The colony continued to grow but suffered severely from barbarian invasions in the 3C AD. At one time, however, it was a bishopric as the basilica ruins discovered in Neápolis prove. It finally succumbed to the Moors in the 8C.

Neápolis

The piling up of different edifices over a period of 1 000 years has made an analysis of the ruins difficult. Near the gate was the **Templo de Asclepio** (Aesculapius – god of healing) and a sacred precinct which contained altars and statues of the gods. Nearby stood the **watchtower** and, at its foot, drinking water cisterns (a filter has been reconstructed). Another point of interest, the **Templo de Zeus Serapis** (a god associated with the weather and with healing), was surrounded by a colonnade. At the other end of the main street was the **Agora**, general meeting-place and heart of the town, where the bases of three statues remain. A street ran from the agora to the sea, bordered on its left by the **stoa** or covered market formed of alleyways and shops. Behind the stoa are the clearly distinguishable ruins of a 6C **palaeo-Christian basilica** with a rounded apse.

Museo Arqueológico de Ampurias

A section of Neápolis is displayed together with models of temples and finds from the excavations including a mosaic of the sacrifice of Iphigenia, a Hellenistic work from the 2C or 1C BC, a mosaic of a partridge and yet another of a mask.

The Roman town

This stands on a hill behind the museum and, unlike Neápolis, is a vast, geometrically laid out town. It has been partially excavated, with restorations to some of the walls. **House n° 1** (entrance at the back) has an atrium or inner courtyard with six columns. Around this are the residential apartments, the peristyle, or colonnaded court, and the impluvium, or basin for catching rainwater. The reception rooms are paved in geometric, black and white mosaic. At the house's northern end are the private baths.

Next door, **house n° 2B** has rooms paved with their original mosaic. One of these, near the atrium, has been reconstituted in clay (by the rammed earth method in use at the time) with its walls resting on stone foundations.

The **forum**, a large square lined by porticoes and, to north and south respectively, by temples and shops, was the centre of civic life in the town. A porticoed street led to the city gate and beyond the walls to the oval **amphitheatre** which is still visible.

▷ *Take the GI 632 to Bellcaire d'Empordà, then turn left onto the GI 640.*

Torroella del Montgrì★

This village is still arranged in the manner of a Roman encampment, with two main streets joining on an arcaded square. Despite its Baroque front, the 14C **Iglesia de Sant Genís** is a fine example of Gothic Catalan art. The **castle** which stands on the heights of the Montaña de Montgrí (1hr on foot along a signposted path among the rocks) is an extraordinary **belvedere**★★ from which you can admire the sea and the Gavarres mountain range.

▷ *Continue for 5km/3mi along the GI 641 to L'Estartit.*

Islas Medes★★

Several companies offer boat trips around the islands leaving from l'Estartit. For further information contact the Tourist Office. ☎ 972 75 19 10.

This small archipelago, consisting of seven islets and some coral reefs, is the marine extension of the calcareous massif of Montgrí. The site is particularly interesting for ecologists on account of the many different marine species and ecosystems that can be observed. The islets are extremely popular among amateurs of diving and underwater exploration.

▷ *Return to Torroella de Montgrí from L'Estartit, then follow the C 31.*

Pals★

Dominating the mouth of the Ter river, this village features an attractive old quarter, **El Pedró**, where the vestiges of fortified ramparts enclose ancient houses and winding alleyways, some of which have covered flights of steps.
Begur is located 7km/4.5mi E of Pals.

THE COAST ROAD★★ ③
From Begur to Blanes 98km/61mi – allow one day

The coastline along this part of the Costa Brava features alternately plains and mountains that extend down to the sea, giving way to a series of long beaches and **coves** of astounding beauty: **Aiguafreda, Aigua Blava, Tamariu**, forming a haven of peace sheltered by pine trees and dotted with luxury villas and exclusive hotels.

Begur★

The town overlooks a pretty series of creeks from an altitude of 200m/656ft above the sea. The castle ruins (16C-17C), the highest point of the locality, offer a nice view of Begur and its haphazard network of streets.

▷ *Leave Begur and head for Llafranc.*

Far de Sant Sebastià★

2km/1.2mi from Llafranc. Built in 1857, the lighthouse stands on a tiny isthumus surrounded by steep cliffs. The nearby hermitage commands a lovely **view**★ of the sea.

Calella de Palafrugell★

This attractive fishing port is also a popular summer resort known for its **Festival de Habaneras**, which takes places on the popular Carrer dels Voltes, facing the seafront, on the first Saturday in July. The public can enjoy Afro-Cuban songs and dances while sipping the local *cremat*, coffee laced with flambé rum.

A road leaving Calella by the south leads to a pretty farm which houses the **Jardin Botánic del Cap Roiga**. An attractively-terraced park carved out of the rock, overlooking the Mediterranean Sea, presents more than 1 200 plant species laid out along shaded avenues. These gardens offer some wonderful **views**★★ of the coast. (🕐 *Open 9am-6pm (8pm Apr-Sep).* 🚗 *3€.* ☎ *972 61 45 82).*

▷ *Follow directions to Palafrugell, then take the C 31 to Palamós. From Palamós the C 253 skirts the coast, with beaches alternating with rocky inlets. The C 31 is quicker though less scenic.*

S'Agarò★

An elegant resort with chalets and luxury villas surrounded by tidy gardens and pine forests. The camino de Ronda offers pretty viewsa of the sheer cliffs.

Sant Feliu de Guíxols★

Nestling in the curve of a bay, sheltered from the last spurs of the Sierra de les Gavarres, this is one of the most popular locations of the Costa Brava. Its famous seaside boulevard Passeig de la Mar is lined with pavement cafés and their bustling terraces. The **Iglesia-Monasterio de Sant Feliu**★ is part of a former Benedictine monastery whose vestiges tower over the small municipality. It has retained its Romanesque façade, known as the **Porta Ferrada**★★, with horseshoe arches dating back to pre-Romanesque times. The interior (14C) is Gothic in style. 🕐 *Open 8-11am and at 10.30pm; Sun and public hols, during hours of worship only.* 🕐 *Closed Mon, 1 Jan and 25 Dec.* ☎ *972 82 15 75.*

The lookout point by the chapel of Sant Elm commands beautiful **views**★★ of the coastal road.

▷ *Follow the GI 682, enjoying spectacular views of the coast.*

Tossa de Mar★

Situated in a splendid natural setting, this sandy beach curves around to Punta del Faro, the promontory on which stand the lighthouse and the 13C walls of the **Vila Vella**★, the old town and its cobbled streets. The **Museu Municipal**★ contains archaeological artefacts unearthed in an ancient Roman villa nearby, and an **exhibition of contemporary art** displaying the work of artists who visited the town in the 1930s (Chagall, Masson, Benet etc). 🕐 *Open 11am-1pm and 3-5pm; 16 Jun-15 Sep, 10am-8pm. Closed Mon (except in summer) and 25 Dec.* 🚗 *3€.* ☎ *972 34 07 09.*

Between Tossa and **Lloret de Mar** (the most important and popular tourist resort of the Costa Brava), the road follows a spectacular **clifftop route**★★ overlooking wide sandy beaches.

▷ *Continue along the GI 682.*

Blanes★

The magnificent **Passeig Marítim**★ offers a lovely panorama of Blanes and its sun-drenched beach. On a hill to the east stand the remains of the Castillo de Sant Joan: at its foot lies the 14C Gothic Iglesia de Santa Maria. To the southeast is located the **Jardin Botánic de Marimurtra**★. This botanical park presents around 5 000 plant species from countries all over the world, including many rare exotic varieties. At each new bend the twisting paths reveal wonderful **views**★ of Cala Forcadera and the coast. 🕐 *Open 9am-6pm (7pm Aug); Nov-Mar, 10am-5pm; Sat-Sun and public hols, 10am-2pm. Last admission one hour before closing.* 🕐 *Closed 1 and 6 Jan and 25 Dec.* 🚗 *2.10€.* ☎ *972 33 08 26 (prior booking available).*

Costa de Cantabria★

MICHELIN MAP 572 B 16-20 – CANTABRIA

From Castro Urdiales west to San Vicente de la Barquera the Cantabrian coast is a succession of gulfs, capes, peninsulas, *rías*, splendid bays such as those in Santander and Santoña, traditional summer resorts with long sandy beaches, and delightful towns dotted with impressive noble mansions.

This area is also rich in prehistoric caves with more than 20 bearing traces of human habitation from the Palaeolithic Age.

Location

The fast highway running slightly inland is the quickest way of travelling along this coast. Despite being considerably slower, the winding coastal routes provide spectacular views and pass through a number of charming villages. *Comillas: Aldea 6, 39520, ☎ 942 72 07 68; Laredo: Alameda de Miramar, 39770, ☎ 942 61 10 96; San Vicente de la Barquera: Avenida Generalísimo 20, 39540, ☎ 942 71 07 97.*

Neighbouring sights are described in the following chapters: COSTA VERDE (to the W), PICOS DE EUROPA (to the W) and the COSTA VASCA (to the E).

Tours

FROM EAST TO WEST

Castro Urdiales

The village, clustered round a Gothic church, a ruined castle and a lighthouse, stands on a promontory overlooking a vast bay. The annual Coso Blanco festival is held on the first Friday in July.

Laredo

The **old town** huddled around its church adjoins a long beach lined by modern buildings. It is a maze of narrow alleyways climbing up a hillside which shelters the fishing boat harbour below.

Limpias

The small fishing village on the banks of the ría Asón is known for a miracle which occurred here in 1919. The local church contains a deeply venerated Crucifix said to have shed tears of blood, a wonderfully carved Baroque figure attributed to Juan de Mena.

Address Book

For coin ranges, see the Legend at the back of the guide.

WHERE TO EAT

⊜⊜ **Mesón Marinero** – *La Correría, 23 – Castro Urdiales* – ☎ 942 86 00 05 – 🔲. As it suggests, this famous name in Cantabrian gastronomy specialises in fish and seafood of excellent quality. The choice of tapas at the bar is equally impressive.

⊜⊜ **Maruja** – *Avenida Generalísimo – San Vicente de la Barquera* – ☎ 942 71 00 77. This small, tastefully decorated restaurant resembling a private drawing room has become one of the best-known along the Cantabrian coast, with dishes based around fresh local products and traditional recipes.

WHERE TO STAY

⊜ **Pensión La Sota** – *La Correría 1 – Castro Urdiales* – ☎ 942 87 11 88 – *19 rooms.* ⌇ *2.50€.* The La Sota stands on the main square of Castro Urdiales in the heart of the old quarter. Although lacking in space, the guest rooms are adequately furnished and have modern bathrooms.

⊜⊜ **Hotel Gerra Mayor** – *Los Llaos – Gerra – 5km/3mi NE of San Vicente de la Barquera* – ☎ 942 71 14 01 – *Closed 23 Dec-1 Mar* – 🅿 – *19 rooms* – ⌇ *4€.* This simple hotel, superbly located between the sea and the mountains, is housed in a converted farmhouse and is the perfect setting for those searching for peace and quiet and a pleasant base from which to explore this beautiful stretch of coastline.

Comillas

Santuario de Nuestra Señora de la Bien Aparecida

A winding uphill road leads to the Baroque shrine. Veneration for the patron of Cantabria province dates back to 1605. Splendid **panorama**⋆ of the Asón Valley.

Santoña

The fishing port facing Laredo was selected as a military headquarters by the French in the Peninsular War. The **Iglesia de Nuestra Señora del Puerto**, which was remodelled in the 18C, has, in addition to Gothic aisles, Romanesque features including carved capitals and an old font. ○ *Open 9am-1pm and 3-8.30pm.* ○ *No visits during religious services.* ☎ *942 66 01 55.*

Bareyo

The small **Iglesia de Santa María** stands on a slope overlooking the ría de Ajo. It retains interesting features from its original Romanesque design including slender, moulded arches and historiated capitals in the apse. The **font** is probably Visigothic. *Visits by prior arrangement.* ☎ *942 62 11 22.*

Peña Cabarga

A road with a 16% gradient (1 in 6) leads to the summit (568m/1 863ft) on which stands a monument to the Conquistadores and the Seamen Adventurers of Castilla. From the top there is a splendid **panorama**⋆⋆ of Santander bay and town.

Santander⋆ (See SANTANDER)

Santillana del Mara⋆ (See SANTILLANA DEL MAR)

Museo de Altamira⋆⋆ (See SANTILLANA DEL MAR)

Comillas⋆

Comillas is a pleasant seaside resort with a delightful plaza Mayor, a local beach and easy access to the extensive sands at Oyambre – 5km/3mi west. The town was a royal residence at the time of Alfonso XII. Buildings which catch the eye include, in the vast park surrounding the neo-Gothic **Palacio de los Marqueses de Comillas**, a freakish pavilion by Gaudí, **El Capricho** (now a restaurant) and, overlooking the sea from the crown of the hill, the Universidad Pontíficia (Papal University).

San Vicente de la Barquera⋆

This resort has an unusual **site**⋆, a vast beach on the other side of the ría and interesting old houses. The **Iglesia de Nuestra Señora de los Ángeles** (Our Lady of the Angels) at the top of the partially fortified hill, has two Romanesque portals, Gothic aisles and several tombs dating from the 15C and 16C.
If you are continuing to Unquera, look back after a few minutes for a pleasing **view**⋆ of San Vicente.

Costa de la Luz★

MICHELIN MAP 578 U 7-8-9-10, V 10, W 10-11, X 11-12-13 –

ANDALUCÍA (HUELVA, CÁDIZ)

The Spanish coast in the provinces of Huelva and Cádiz is edged with beaches of fine sand interrupted by the Guadiana, Tinto, Guadalquivir and other river mouths. Although this Atlantic coast has attracted less tourism in the past than the Mediterranean coast of southern Spain, several resorts are being developed. Because of its dazzling white sand and translucent skies it is known as the Coast of Light.

Location

The Costa de la Luz extends from Ayamonte, at the mouth of the Guadiana, to Tarifa, the most southerly town on mainland Spain. ⃞ *El Puerto de Santa María: Luna 22, 11500 Cádiz, ☎ 956 54 24 13; Huelva: Avenida Alemania 12, 21001 Huelva, ☎ 959 25 74 03; Sanlúcar de Barrameda: Calzada del Ejército, 11540 Cádiz, ☎ 956 36 61 10; Tarifa: Paseo de la Alameda, 11380 Cádiz, ☎ 956 68 09 93.*

⦿ *Neighbouring sights are described in the following chapters: SEVILLA (96km/60mi E of Huelva), JEREZ DE LA FRONTERA (35km/22mi NW of Cádiz), Straits of GIBRALTAR and COSTA DEL SOL (E of Tarifa).*

Tours

THE HUELVA COAST★
From Ayamonte to the Parque Nacional de Doñana
135km/84mi – allow one day

Address Book

For coin ranges, se the Legend at the back of the guide.

WHERE TO EAT

⊖⊖ **Casa Bigote** – *Bajo de Guía 10 – Sanlúcar de Barrameda – ☎ 956 36 26 96 – Closed Sun and in Nov – ▤.* This old tavern in the river district of Bajo Guía has developed into famous gastronomic landmark. Run by the same family for the past 50 years, it is decorated with old photos, fishing mementoes and antique objects. Pride of place on the extensive menu is given to the excellent local fish and prawns.

⊖⊖ **Trafalgar** – *Plaza de España 31 – Vejer de la Frontera – ☎ 956 44 76 38 – Closed in Jan – ▤.* This welcome culinary surprise, on the attractive plaza de los Pescaítos, specialises in delicious fresh fish. Tapas are also served at the entrance. Guests can dine on the terrace in summer.

⊖⊖ **Casa Juan Luis** – *San Francisco 15 – Tarifa – ☎ 956 68 48 03 – Closed Sun except in summer – Reservation recommended – 26€.* The peculiarity of this small restaurant, housed in an old building in a pedestrianised street in the old quarter, is that everything it serves is pork based. A good menu with a surprisingly wide choice.

WHERE TO STAY

Hotel La Pinta – *Rábida 79 – Palos de la Frontera – ☎ 959 35 05 11 – ▤ – 30 rooms – ⌷ 3.01€ – Restaurant 9.62€.* Well located in the heart of Palos de la Frontera, this charming small hotel offers excellent service and pleasant rooms.

⊖ **Convento de San Francisco** – *La Plazuela – Vejer de la Frontera – ☎ 956 45 10 01 – ▤ – 25 rooms – ⌷ 3.50€ – Restaurant 20/29€.* This former convent for Poor Clares dating from the 17C is situated in Vejer's old quarter. Although soberly decorated, the rooms are pleasant, with high ceilings and exposed beams. The hotel also has a good restaurant.

⊖⊖ **Hotel Toruño** – *Plaza del Acebuchal 22 - El Rocío – ☎ 959 44 23 23 – ▤ – 30 rooms - ⌷ - Restaurant 14.50€.* At the edge of Parque Nacional de Doñana, in a traditional great house that blends perfectly into the village of El Rocío. Some rooms are placed for lovely sea views.

⊖⊖ **Posada de Palacio** – *Caballeros 11 (Barrio Alto) – Sanlúcar de Barrameda – ☎ 956 36 48 40 – Closed Nov-Feb – 27 rooms – ⌷ 6€.* This family-run hotel is housed in an 18C mansion opposite the town hall (ayuntamiento) in the upper section of Sanlúcar. The rooms, laid out around an attractive patio, are simply yet tastefully decorated with antique furniture.

Ayamonte★

This important fishing port at the mouth of the Guadiana river is a lively border town of cobbled streets and whitewashed and brightly coloured houses standing opposite its Portuguese counterpart Vila Real de Santo António on the opposite bank. The main monuments in the old quarter are the 16C colonial-style Iglesia de las Angustias, the Convento de San Francisco, with its elegant bell tower and magnificent *artesonado* work, and the 13C Iglesia del Salvador, built above the former mosque.

Tourist boats heading off on excursions across the river depart from the Muelle de Portugal.

A number of resorts line the coast between Ayamonte and Huelva including **Isla Canela, Isla Cristina, La Antilla** and **Punta Umbría**. This area also includes delightful natural environments such as the marshland of the **Marismas del río Piedras y Flecha de El Rompido★**, the El Portil lagoon, and the Enebrales de Punta Umbría, a landscape dominated by juniper trees. The marshland areas along this stretch of coastline have been planted with pines and eucalyptus to consolidate the dunes.

Huelva★

In the 15C and 16C, the estuary formed by the Tinto and Odiel rivers saw the departure of numerous expeditions to the New World, notably those led by Columbus. A large monument, the **Monumento a la Fe Descubridora** (1929), has been erected near the harbour at Punta del Sebo in honour of the explorers who set out on these intrepid voyages.

Among Huelva's attractions note the unusual **Barrio Reina Victoria★**, an English-style district named after Queen Victoria; the **cathedral**, with its Renaissance façade and sculpture of the Virgen de la Cinta, the town's patron saint, by Martínez Montañés; and the paintings by Zurbarán in the **Iglesia de la Concepción** and **Museo Provincial.** (⏰ *Open 9am-8pm; Tue 2-8pm; Sun and public hols, 9am-2pm.* ⏰ *Closed Mon. No charge.* ☎ *959 25 93 00).*

Paraje Natural de las Marismas del Odiel★★

2km/1.2mi SE. ▶ *Exit Huelva along Avenida Tomás Domínguez.* This marshland (*marisma*) of outstanding beauty, situated at the mouth of the Tinto and Odiel rivers, close to one of the city's industrial chemical facilities, has been declared a World Biosphere Reserve. It provides a habitat for over 200 different species of bird and can be visited by **canoe** and small boat. (⏰ *Open Fri-Sun and public hols 10am-2pm and 3-6pm (reception office).* 🅿 *Advance booking required.* ☎ *959 50 05 12).*

La Rábida★

In 1484, the Prior of the **Monasterio de Santa Maria**, Juan Pérez, supported the theory put to him by Christopher Columbus that the world was round and helped him obtain the necessary commission from the Catholic Monarchs to set up his expedition.

The **church★** has managed to preserve old frescoes, wooden *artesonado* work and the delicate 14C alabaster statue of the **Virgen de los Milagros★** (Virgin of Miracles), in front of which Columbus is said to have prayed prior to setting off on his expedition. A small room to the right of the Flag Room (Sala de las Banderas), which exhibits the flag of every country on the American continent, displays a **mapamundi★**, a work by Juan de la Cosa, which outlined the coast of America for the first time. ⏰ *Open 1am-1pm and 4-6.15pm; summer, 10am-1pm and 4-7pm (10am-1pm and 4.45-8pm in Aug)* ⏰ *Closed Mon.* 🎟2.50€. ☎ *959 35 04 11.*

Life-size replicas of the three caravels which transported Columbus on his voyage of discovery to the New World are moored at the **Muelle de las Carabelas★**, a modern dock (muelle) on the banks of the Tinto Estuary. A small museum has also been established here. ⏰ *Open 10am-2pm and 5-9pm (21 Sep-19 Apr, 10am-7pm); Sat-Sun and public hols, 11am-8pm.* ⏰ *Closed Mon.* 🎟3€. ☎ *959 53 05 97/ 03 12.*

Palos de la Frontera★

This picturesque small town on the left bank of the Río Tinto was the birthplace of the Pinzón brothers, who sailed alongside Columbus on his epic adventure. The **Casa-Museo de Martín Alonso Pinzón** and the *azulejos* dotted around the town provide a reminder of this historic achievement. (⏰ *Open 10am-1.30pm and 5-7pm.* ⏰ *Closed Sat-Sun and public hols. No charge.* ☎ *959 35 01 99).*

The 15C **Iglesia de San Jorge** is fronted by an interesting Gothic-Mudéjar doorway.

Moguer★

The tranquil town with its elegant houses was another port from which expeditions ventured to the unknown. The memory of the poet **Juan Ramón Jiménez** (1881-1958), Moguer's most illustrious son and winner of the Nobel Prize for Literature in 1956, is kept alive through the verses adorning attractive *azulejo* panelling dotted around the town centre, as well as at his former home, now a museum, the **Casa-Museo Zenobia y Juan Ramón**★. (*Guided tours (45 min) 10am-2pm and 5-8pm; Sun public hols, 10am-2pm.* Closed Mon and public hols. 1.80€. 959 37 21 48).

The **town hall** *(ayuntamiento)*, with its fine Renaissance **façade**★, stands on plaza del Cabildo. From here, head along the pedestrianised **calle Andalucía**★, lined by several interesting buildings, including the Archivo Histórico Municipal and Biblioteca Iberoamericana; and the 15C Convento de San Francisco, with its Mannerist cloisters, Baroque main altarpiece and lofty belfry. The **tower**★ of the Iglesia de **Nuestra Señora de la Granada** calls to mind the Giralda in Sevilla.

Monasterio de Santa Clara★

Guided tours (50min), 11am-1pm and 5-7pm. Closed Mon. 1.80€. 959 37 01 07.

The church of this Gothic-Mudéjar monastery houses various objects of interest such as the Renaissance-style marble **tombs of the Portocarrero family**★, the lords of Moguer, a noteworthy set of **tombs**★ at the high altar, and some quite exceptional 14C **Nasrid-Mudéjar choir stalls**★★.

▶ *Return to the C 442, which follows the coast.*

Pine-covered sand dunes give way to endless beaches of fine sand dominated occasionally by cliffs as at **Mazagón** where there is a parador. Matalascañas is the main resort on this stretch of the coast.

Parque Nacional de Doñana★★★

Owing to its geographical position close to Africa, and the influence of both the Atlantic and the Mediterranean on its climate, this unique national park acts as a rest stop for many African and European migratory birds. Doñana is Spain's largest wildlife reserve with a total protected area (inner and outer park) of 73 000ha/ 180 390 acres.

The park's magnificent landscapes can be divided into three types of ecosystem: the salt marshes, coastal dunes and the former hunting grounds. The **salt marshes** cover the most extensive area within the park and are the ideal habitat for birds which migrate to Europe over the winter; the **sand dunes** are grouped together in formation parallel to the Atlantic and advance inland at a rate of 6m/20ft per year; while the stabilised sands or **cotos** are dry, undulating areas covered with heather, rockrose, rosemary and thyme, and various species of tree, including cork oak and pine.

Pink flamingoes in the Parco Nazionale de Doñana

H. Le Gac/MICHELIN

Address Book

The Doñana is home to several animal species including lynx, wild boar, deer and a wide variety of birds, including Spanish imperial eagles, flamingoes, herons, wild ducks and coots.

El Rocío

This small village is famous as the site of the **Santuario de Nuestra Señora del Rocío** (Sanctuary of the Virgin of the Dew), to which Spain's most popular religious pilgrimage *(romería)* is made during Whitsun weekend every year. This colourful event attracts a million visitors who come here to venerate the "Blanca Paloma" (White Dove), the name given to the Virgin Mary in El Rocío.

THE CÁDIZ COAST★

From Sanlúcar de Barrameda to Tarifa 160km/100mi – allow one day

The landscape is hillier south of the Guadalquivir and there are vineyards north of Cádiz.

Sanlúcar de Barrameda★

The fishing port of Sanlúcar, at the mouth of the Guadalquivir, is the home town of *manzanilla*, a sherry matured like Jerez *fino* but which has a special flavour thanks to the sea air. The *bodegas* (cellars) are in the old quarter on the hill around the massive **Castillo de Santiago**. The **Iglesia de Nuestra Señora de la O** close by has a fine Mudéjar **doorway**★★ and a 16C **Mudéjar artesonado ceiling**★.

Heading down into the modern town, pass the **Palacio de Orleans y Borbón**, a palace built in the 19C in neo-Moorish style, and now Sanlúcar's town hall, and the **covachas**★, a mysterious series of five ogee arches decorated with Gothic tracery. The lower town has two main churches: the **Iglesia de la Trinidad**, with its magnificent 15C Mudéjar **artesonado**★★; and the **Iglesia de Santo Domingo**, with the noble proportions of a Renaissance building. The **Centro de Visitantes Fábrica de Hielo**, a visitor centre in Bajo de Guía, near the mouth of the Guadalquivir, provides comprehensive information on the Parque Nacional de Doñana on the opposite bank. (🕐 Open 9am-2pm and 4-7pm (9pm in summer). ☎ 956 38 16 35).

Excursions into the park also depart from here.

Chipiona

This pleasant resort has a number of excellent beaches such as the **Playa da la Regla**★. The town's principal church, the **Iglesia de Nuestra Señora de la O**, is located in the old quarter.

Rota

The medieval-looking **old town**★ inside the ramparts is laid out around the **Castillo de la Luna** (nowadays the town hall) and the **Iglesia de Nuestra Señora de la O**★. Rota is known for its attractive beaches such as the **Playa de la Costilla**★. A large naval base is situated on the outskirts of the town.

El Puerto de Santa María★

The harbour, in Cádiz Bay, played an active role in trade with the New World. Today, fishing, the export of sherry (*bodegas* in the town include those owned by the Terry and Osborne companies) and tourism (beaches and golf courses) are the town's major sources of income.

A palm-shaded promenade overlooking the quays along the north bank leads to the 12C **Castillo de San Marcos**, a castle which was once the seat of the Dukes of Medinaceli. The late-15C **Iglesia Mayor Prioral** stands in the centre of the town. The **Portada del Sol**★, or Sun Gateway, in plaza de España, is a mix of Plateresque and Baroque styles. The **Fundación Rafael Alberti** nearby displays photos, letters, and manuscripts by the poet. (◔ *Open 10.30-2.30pm.* ◔ *Closed Mon (15 Sep-15 Jun), Sat-Sun and public hols.* ◉ *3€.* ☎ *956 85 07 11).*

Cádiz★★ (◔ *See CÁDIZ*)

To the south of Cádiz, there are good beaches at **La Barrosa**★★, Chiclana de la Frontera and **Conil de la Frontera (Playa de la Fontanilla** and **Playa de los Bateles)**.

Vejer de la Frontera★

Vejer, perched on a rocky crag, is one of the prettiest white villages of Andalucía. The best way to approach is along the road cut into the hillside from the south. There is a **view**★ from the car park at the north end of the town, down into the winding Barbate Valley. The **Iglesia Parroquial del Divino Salvador**, its three-aisle **interior**★ a mix of Romanesque and Gothic features, stands proudly inside the walls.

Between Vejer and Tarifa the road runs through the foothills of the Baetic range. The **Parque Natural La Breña y Marismas de Barbate**★, with its spectacular cliffs and picturesque coves, such as the **Cala de los Caños de Meca**★★, is situated 10km/6mi from Vejer.

Ruinas Romanas de Baelo Claudia★

◔ *Open 10am-2.30pm and 4-6pm; summer 10am-2pm and 5-7pm; Sun and public hols 10am-2pm. Last admission 30min before closing.* ◔ *Closed Mon, 1 and 6 Jan, 24- 25 and 31 Dec. 1.50€, no charge for citizens of the European Union.* ☎ *956 68 85 30.*

The remains of the important Roman city of Baelo Claudia date back to the 2C BC, when a salting factory specialising in the production of the famous Roman *garum* (a sauce made from the head, entrails, blood and other remains of fish) was established here. Vestiges of the basilica, forum and a small theatre are still visble on the site.

Tarifa

Tarifa stands on the most southerly point of the Iberian Peninsula. Atlantic and Mediterranean air masses converge over the area giving Tarifa the sea breezes ideal for windsurfing. It has become one of Europe's major centres for the sport.

The port of Tarifa

B. Kaufmann/MICHELIN

The **Castillo de Guzmán el Bueno**, a fortress which had been taken by the Christians in 1292, was under the command of Guzmán el Bueno whose son was captured by the Moors. When Guzmán had to choose between the death of his child and the surrender of his town, he replied by throwing his dagger to the enemy for the execution. The Muralla Sur (south wall) commands a fine **view**★★ of the Straits of Gibraltar and the coast of Morocco just 13.5km/8mi away. (🕐 *Open 10am-5pm (6pm in summer).* ☎ *956 68 46 89.*

The small plaza de Santa María is lined by the town hall *(ayuntamiento)* and the Museo Municipal. Tarifa's most important church is the **Iglesia de San Mateo Apóstol**, built at the beginning of the 16C in Gothic style with a central nave covered by a star vault.

🐾 The road heading north towards Cádiz runs parallel to the spectacular **Playa de los Lancesa**.

Costa del Sol ★

The Costa del Sol (Sun Coast) stretches along Andalucía's Mediterranean shore from Tarifa in the Straits of Gibraltar to the Cabo de Gata, a headland east of Almería. Every year, millions of visitors are attracted here by its wonderful climate, sandy beaches, whitewashed towns and villages and the diversity of leisure activities on offer. Although the coast is now a year-round holiday destination popular out of season with those escaping the harsh northern winter, the Costa del Sol comes to life during the summer, when the beaches are packed, hotels are fully booked and the nightlife continues until dawn.

Location

Because of its location, protected from the extremes of the inland weather systems affecting the Serranía de Ronda and the Sierra Nevada, the Costa del Sol enjoys a delightful climate with mild winters and hot summers. 🛈 *Estepona: Avenida San Lorenzo 1, 29680 Málaga, ☎ 95 280 20 02; Marbella: Glorieta de la Fontanilla, 29600 Málaga, ☎ 95 277 14 42; Nerja: Puerta del Mar, 29780 Málaga, ☎ 95 252 15 31; Salobreña: Plaza de Goya, 18680 Granada, ☎ 958 61 03 14.*

🐾 *Neighbouring sights are described in the following chapters: Straits of GIBRALTAR (to the SW), RONDA (50km/31mi N of San Pedro de Alcántara), ANTEQUERA (55km/34mi N of Málaga) and GRANADA (74km/46km N of Salobreña).*

Tours

THE WESTERN COASTLINE★★

From Estepona to Málaga *139km/86mi –* 🕐 *allow one day*
This highly developed strip of land between the mountains and the sea is a succession of beach resorts, hotels and apartments offering a huge range of amenities for the hundreds of thousands of annual visitors. In comparison, the mountain slopes inland harbour quieter, more traditional villages.

Estepona★
This popular large resort has a pleasant promenade as well as a fishing harbour and marina. The **old quarter**★ has retained the typical charm of a small Andalucían town. Its main attractions are the plaza de las Flores, the ruins of the castle and the 18C Iglesia de Nuestra Señora.
Casares★, 24km/15mi inland along the A 377 and MA 539, is a whitewashed town of Moorish origin with a maze of narrow streets clinging to a rock in the Sierra de Crestenilla.

San Pedro de Alcántara
Several archaeological remains have been discovered close to the beach. These include **Las Bóvedas** (thermal baths dating from the 3C AD) and the palaeo-Christian basilica

Address Book

For coin ranges, see the Legend at the back of the guide.

WHERE TO EAT

Pacomari – *La Gloria 4 - Nerja -* ☎ *952 52 01 38 - Closed Sun and 1-20 Dec.* With a sedate Andalucian patio and modest dining room, this is a good place to try regional specialties, such as *ajo blanco* (white gaspacho), though there are also economical prix fixe meals.

Vizcaya – *Paseo de las Flores (Playa de San Cristóbal.) – Almuñécar –* ☎ *95 863 57 12.* Although the coastline's sandy beaches are preferable, make sure you head for this stony beach to try the Vizcaya's paellas and grilled meat and fish dishes. Lively during the day and a more romantic setting at night.

Mesón Lorente – *Carretera 41 – Ojén –* ☎ *952 88 11 74 – Reservation recommended.* Many Andalucíans and tourists looking for a breather from the coast head for this restaurant, which is well known for its home cooking. The extended dining room looks onto the liveliest street in the town.

El Bodegón del Muro – *Santo Domingo 23 – Benalmádena –* ☎ *952 56 85 87 –* 📋 *– Reservation recommended.* A favourite with local families who come here to enjoy the good traditional cuisine on offer. The vaulted dining room is elegantly decorated in rustic style and has a terrace with views over the water.

Marisquería La Marea – *Plaza Cantarero – Nerja –* ☎ *95 252 57 78 –* 📋 *– Reservation recommended.* A good address for fish and seafood. The scallops and clams on display at the bar are grilled fresh when you order them and served either in the bar itself or in the nautically decorated restaurant.

Casa Eladio – *Virgen de los Dolores 6 (Old Town) - Marbella -* ☎ *95 277 00 83 - Closed Thu and 10 Jan-10Feb.* A longstanding family establishment where you can try traditional Spanish cooking at a fair price. Choices include delicious grilled fish and regional specialties such as *ajo blanco* (white gazpacho) and *pellejo de patata* (potato peel).

La Alcazaba – *Plaza de la Constitución - Mijas -* ☎ *952 59 02 53 - Closed Mon and 15-30 Jan.* Perched on the Arab walls of Mijas with fine vistas and careful decoration, La Alcazaba's best feature is its timeless *mozarabe* dining room, with flowing detailing and two venerable horseshoe arches framing an endless landscape.

El Padrastro – *Paseo del Compás 22 – Mijas –* ☎ *952 48 50 00 – Closed evening of 24 Dec – Reservation recommended.* If it's panoramic views of the town, the coast and the surrounding mountains you're after, there's no better place than El Padrastro. The menu here is original and the setting romantic, particularly when candlelit at night.

El Balcón de la Virgen – *Remedios 2 (Old quarter) – Marbella –* ☎ *95 277 60 92 – Dinner only. Closed Sun and 20 Dec-20 Jan..* In an attractive street lined by an endless succession of restaurant terraces. The restaurant, recognisable by the image of the Virgin Mary on its attractive façade, is mainly popular with tourists. Andalucían cuisine.

WHERE TO STAY

Hostal El Pilar – *Plaza de las Flores 10 – Estepona –* ☎ *952 80 00 18 – pilarhos@ anit.es – 20 rooms.* Time would appear to have stopped in this charming *hostal* on the main square. The interior, decorated with black and white family photos, has an impressive staircase leading up to the basic but pleasant rooms.

Hostal San Miguel – *San Miguel 36 – Nerja –* ☎ *952 52 72 17 –* 🛏 📋 *– 13 rooms. –* 🍽 *4.50€.* This hotel is in a recently restored town house near the centre, with modest but comfortable rooms. There's a bar-coffee shop, and a special feature is the top-floor terrace with small pool and sea and mountain views.

La Hostería de Don José – *Paseo del Nacimiento 1 (El Chifle) – Ojén –* ☎ *952 88 11 47 – hdonjose@Jjazzviajeros.com – 6 rooms.* A charming small hotel on the top of a hill overlooking the town. At the Don José everything you need for a comfortable stay is on hand: comfort, simple yet cosy furnishings, a friendly welcome and unforgettable views of Ojén's whitewashed houses set against the backdrop of the Mediterranean.

Casablanca Hotel – *Plaza San Cristóbal 4 – Almuñécar –* ☎ *958 63 55 75 –* 📋 ♿ *– 35 rooms –* 🍽 *2.50€ – Restaurant 7.49€.* With its cupola, raspberry-coloured façade and arches that imitate the architecture of Moroccan palaces, the Casablanca is a visual experience not to be missed! Once inside your room, the crystal chandeliers and marble decor add a decidedly Oriental touch. Make sure you book in advance.

La Carihuela

Hostal Marissal – *Paseo Balcón de Europa 3 - Nerja -* ☎ *952 52 01 99 - www. marissal.net -* ▭ *- 22 rooms -* ☟ *3€ - Restaurant. 15/30€.* In a privileged location, at the entry to the famed Balcony of Europe, with fine views to the passage from some rooms. Coffee Shop and restaurant.

Hotel La Fonda – *Santo Domingo 7 – Benalmádena -* ☎ *95 256 83 24 –* ⚓ *– 26 rooms -* ☟. A charming hotel in the Sierra de Castillejos, overlooking the Mediterranean. Spacious rooms, indoor pool, flower-filled patios and terraces with views of the hills and sea. Very reasonably priced given the standard.

Hotel La Morada Más Hermosa – *Montenebros 16 (Old Town) - Marbella -* ☎ *95 292 44 67 - www. lamoradamashermosa.com -* ▭ *- 6 hab -* ☟ *4€.* Find this hotel on a plant-bedecked alley right in the old part of town. The charming rooms have been decorated with care by the owner in a personal country Andalucian style with colonial details. Ask for room 2 with its pleasant terrace or wood-panelled room 5.

Hotel Marbella Club – *Boulevard Príncipe Alfonso von Hohenlohe -* ☎ *95 282 22 11 – hotelmarbellaclub.com –* P ▭ *– 84 rooms -* ☟ *28€ – Restaurant 58/69€.* One of the best hotels along the coast, built in the middle of a superb garden planted with palm trees. The bungalow accommodation here frequently hosts the rich and famous. The Marbella Club is the perfect place to unwind and enjoy the magnificent sports facilities available (swimming pool, beach, tennis etc).

SHOPPING

Marbella is one of the best places for shopping on the Costa del Sol with all the top names in international fashion represented here. Most of these stores are concentrated in Puerto Banús, where there is an impressive nucleus of modern, designer boutiques, and in the centre of Marbella, particularly along avenida Ricardo Soriano and calle Ramón y Cajal. The best indoor shopping centre on the Costa del Sol is also found in Puerto Banús.

Markets are an important feature of life on the Costa del Sol. The one in Marbella takes place on Saturday mornings next to the Nueva Andalucía bullring (plaza de toros) near Puerto Banús.

of Vega del Mar. 🚶 *Guided tours (1hr 45min), Tue, Wed and Fri at noon. Las Bóvedas is also open to the public.* 👁 *It is advisable to reserve a day ahead.* ☎ *95 278 13 60.* (👁 *For a description of the road from Ronda to San Pedro de Alcántara, see RONDA).*

Puerto Banús★★

The moorings at this magnificent marina attract some of the world's most luxurious sailing craft. It also has a huge choice of restaurants, bars and boutiques which are especially popular on summer evenings.

Marbella★★

The capital of the Costa del Sol is one of Spain's most famous tourist destinations and has developed into a resort popular with the international jet set.

Puerto Banús

Old quarter★

This picturesque district in the centre of the town is a maze of narrow, irregular whitewashed streets and alleyways in which old buildings stand side-by-side with a multitude of shops, bars and restaurants. The enchanting **plaza de los Naranjos**★, named after the orange trees *(naranjos)* in the square, is lined by the 16C town hall, the 17C Casa del Corregidor, and a small 15C chapel, the Ermita de Nuestro Señor Santiago. The other sights of interest in the old quarter are the 17C Iglesia de Santa María de la Encarnación and the **Museo del Grabado Español Contemporáneo**★. This museum, the only one in Spain devoted to contemporary prints, is housed in the town's 16C former hospital. (🕐 *Open 10am-2pm and 5.30-8.30pm; in summer, 10am-2pm and 6-9pm.* 🕐 *Closed Sun, Mon and public hols.* 🔙 *2.50€.* ☎ *95 282 50 35).*
Modern amenities for tourists include a marina, luxury accommodation complexes, excellent beaches, a long promenade, designer boutiques, health spas and several golf courses.

Fuengirola

The outline of the Castillo de Sohail, a castle of Moorish origin, dominates this large resort of high-rise apartment blocks. The remains of some Roman baths and villas have been discovered in the Santa Fe district.

▶ Head N from Fuengirola towards Mijas.

Mijas★

The **views**★ from this picturesque whitewashed town in the *sierra* of the same name encompass much of the coast. It is well worth strolling through its narrow, winding streets dotted with tiny squares and charming nooks and crannies. Its main architectural highlights are several sections of the old Moorish wall, and the 16C Iglesia de la Inmaculada Concepción, crowned by a Mudéjar tower. Its myriad shops display an extensive range of typical Andalucían arts and crafts (pottery, basketwork, woven goods) and other souvenirs. Mijas is also home to an unusual **miniatures museum**, known as the Carromato de Max. (🕐 *Open 10am-7pm (10pm in summer).* 🔙*3€).*

Benalmádena

The town of Benalmádena stands several kilometres inland from the resort of Benalmádena Costa. Its main sights of interest include several 16C watchtowers and a small **archaeological museum**. (🔙 *Closed for restoration).*

Torremolinos

This former fishing village developed into a huge tourist resort following the tourist boom in the 1960s and 1970s. The maritime promenade and the long beach are its main attractions.

Málaga★ (👆 *See MÁLAGA)*

THE EASTERN COASTLINE★

From Málaga to Almería 204km/127mi – allow one day

This, at times, beautiful coast is punctuated along its entire length by the ruins of Moorish towers – defences built after the Reconquest by local inhabitants against attacks by Barbary pirates.

Nerja★

Nerja, one of the main resorts along the coast to the east of Málaga, overlooks the Mediterranean from the top of a promontory. The **Balcón de Europa**★ is a magnificent mirador offering views of this dramatic coastline and occasional glimpses of North Africa in the distance.

Cueva de Nerja★★

4.5km/3mi E along the Motril road. 🕐 *Open 10am-2pm and 4-6.30pm (8pm Jul-Aug).* 🔙 *5€.* ☎ *95 252 95 20.*

RESTAURANTS – TAPAS

The pedestrianised district of **La Carihuela**, which runs alongside the beach, is the most attractive part of Torremolinos. It is also the town's main shopping area with dozens of bars, restaurants, hotels and shops of all descriptions. Two of the best restaurants here are Casa Juan, which has been specialising in fish and seafood for more than 30 years, and **El Roqueo**, with its terrace overlooking the promenade.

This enormous natural cave has been carved out of the marble landscape of the Sierra de Almijara. Paintings, weapons, jewels and bones discovered here indicate that the cave was inhabited in the Palaeolithic era. It is impressive both in terms of the size of its chambers and its spectacular stalactites and stalagmites. An annual festival of music and dance is held in the Sala de la Cascada (Cascade Chamber) the second and third weeks of July.

The road from Nerja to La Herradura★

The road follows a russet- and purple-coloured mountainside while the old scenic route commands delightful **views**★★ of the coastline.

Almuñécar

The amenities of this cosmopolitan resort include a palm-shaded promenade which skirts its pebble beach. Bananas, medlars, pomegranates and mangoes are grown on the small alluvial plain *(hoya)* behind the town. The **Cueva de los Siete Palacios** now houses an archaeological museum. (*Open 10.30am-1.30pm and 4-6pm; in summer, 10.30am-1.30pm and 6-9pm; Sun and public hols, 10.30am-1.30pm. Closed Mon, 1 Jan and 25 Dec. 2.02€. 958 63 11 25).*

The **Castillo de San Miguel** is also open to the public. (*Open 10.30am-1.30pm and 4pm-6pm; in summer, 10.30am-1.30pm and 6.30-9.30pm. Sun and public hols 10.30am-1.30pm. Closed Mon, 1 Jan and 25 Dec. 2€. 958 63 11 25).*

Salobreña★

Salobreña is probably the prettiest town along this stretch of coastline. Its houses, spread out across the hill, give the appearance of a white blanket occasionally punctuated by a purple splash of bougainvillea. An imposing Moorish **fortress** converted into a palatial residence by the Nasrid kings in the 14C stands proudly above the town.(*Open 10.30am-2pm and 4-7pm (5-9.30pm in summer). Closed Mon in winter 2€ (2.55€ with museum). 958 61 27 33 or 958 61 03 14).*

Motril

This is a large market centre for sugar cane. Motril's port is kept busy handling products from the local sugar refineries and produce from the Genil Valley.

The road from Calahonda to Castell de Ferro★

The road hugs the rocky coastline, offering views of the mountain and the sea.

After Balanegra the N 340 leaves the coast and turns inland through an immense sweep of greenhouses, a veritable sea of plastic around El Ejido, where flowers, vegetables and tropical fruit are grown.

The road from Aguadulce to Almería

Aguadulce was the pioneer beach for Almería's tourist industry. The sweeping view from the coast road takes in the town of Almería, with its bay, sheltered harbour and fortress.

Almería (*See ALMERÍA*)

Costa Vasca★★

MICHELIN MAP 574 B-C 21 TO 24

PAÍS VASCO (GUIPÚZCOA, VIZCAYA)

The Basque Coast (Costa Vasca) stretches from the Golfo de Vizcaya (Bay of Biscay) to the pointed headland of the Cabo de Machichaco. The steep shoreline, lined by cliffs and indented by estuaries, is an almost uninterrupted line of small fishing villages nestling in inlets below green hills.

Location

The Basque Coast runs from the French border to the city of Bilbao. ⓘ *Bermeo: Askatasun Bidea 2, 48370 Vizcaya, ☎ 94 617 91 54; Getaria: Parque Aldamar, 20808 Guipúzcoa, ☎ 943 14 09 57; Hondarribia: Javier Ugarte 6, 20280 Guipúzcoa, ☎ 943 64 54 58; Lekeitio: Independentzia Enparantaza, 48289 Vizcaya, ☎ 94 684 40 17; Zarautz: Nafarroa, 20800 Guipúzcoa; ☎ 943 83 56 28.*

Neighbouring sights are described in the following chapters: COSTA DE CANTABRIA (to the W), VITORIA-GASTEIZ (64km/40mi S of Bilbao) and PAMPLONA (79km/49mi SE of Donostia-San Sebastián).

Tours

FROM HONDARRIBIA TO BILBAO
247km/154mi – allow 2 days

Hondarribia/Fuenterrabía★

The main sights of interest In Fuenterrabía (Hondarribia in Basque), a popular seaside resort and large fishing port, are the interesting old town and **La Marina**, a bustling fishermen's quarter with characteristic wood balconies and numerous bars and cafés.

Address Book

For coin ranges, see the Legend at the back of the guide.

WHERE TO EAT

⊜ **Txiki Polit** – *Plaza de la Musika – Zarautz* – ☎ 943 83 53 57 – ▤. This simple tavern with paper tablecloths has an extensive, good-quality menu with specialities that include beef cutlets and a good choice of fish. It also has a number of reasonable guest rooms on the first floor.

⊜⊜ **Asador Almiketxu** – *Almike Auzoa 8 – Bermeo – 1.5km/1mi S of Bermeo* – ☎ 94 688 09 25 – *Closed Mon and 12 Nov-2 Dec.* This restaurant, offering a varied menu of traditional Basque cuisine, is located in a house on a hill on the outskirts of Bermeo, from where there are fine views of the town and the sea.

⊜⊜ **Iribar** – *Nagusia 34 – Getaria* – ☎ 943 14 04 06 – *Closed two weeks in Apr and two weeks in Oct* – ▤. The Iribar is a traditional restaurant serving reasonably priced grilled fish in the centre of this fishing village. The dining room, on two levels, is simply but pleasantly decorated.

WHERE TO STAY

⊜ **Pensión Itsasmin** – *Nagusia 32 – Elantxobe* – ☎ 94 627 61 74 – *15 rooms* – ☷ 4.21€. This small hotel in a pedestrian street in the upper part of town has 18 pleasant rooms with parquet flooring and exposed beams. Two of the rooms have dormer windows, while four have views of the port. Parking here is the only drawback.

⊜ **Hotel Emperatriz Zita** – *Avenida Santa Elena – Lekeitio* – ☎ 94 684 26 55 – Ⓟ – *42 rooms* – ☷ 7€ – *Restaurant 14€*. Between 1922 and 1931, this palatial building by the sea was occupied by the Empress Zita, the last empress of the Austro-Hungarian Empire. As you would expect, the rooms are spacious, comfortable and pleasantly decorated. The hotel also has its own thalassotherapy centre.

⊜⊜⊜ **Hotel Obispo** – *Plaza del Obispo 1 – Hondarribia* – ☎ 943 64 54 00 – *recepcion@hotelobispo.com* – ⅙ – *17 rooms* – ☷ 8.41€. The Obispo is a charming hotel housed in a 14C-15C palace located in the upper section of Hondarribia's old quarter. All the rooms are different, with the pleasant mix of exposed beams, stone walls, old furniture and fabrics creating a warm, cosy atmosphere.

As a reminder of its history, on 8 September every year Fuenterrabía holds a parade and festival in honour of the Virgen de Guadalupe, who is said to have delivered the town from a two-month siege by the French in 1638.

Old town

On the hill overlooking the River Bidasoa, the old fortified town, with its steep streets, has preserved its original 15C walls. These are punctuated by the **Puerta de Santa María**, a gateway surmounted by the town's coat of arms and twin angels venerating the Virgen de Guadalupe. The narrow and picturesque main street, **calle Mayor**, is lined with old houses with wrought-iron balconies and carved wooden cornices.

The **Iglesia de Santa María**, an impressive Gothic church remodelled in the 17C when it was given a Baroque tower, is supported round the apse by massive buttresses. It was in this church, on 3 June 1660, that the proxy wedding took place between the Spanish minister, Don Luis de Haro, on behalf of Louis XIV, and the Infanta María Teresa, six days before the solemnisation of the marriage in France.

The **Castillo de Carlos V**, a fortress built to help defend the Kingdom of Navarra, and now the town's parador, was constructed in the 10C by Sancho Abarca, King of Navarra, and subsequently restored by Charles V in the 16C.

Cabo Higuer★

4km/2.5mi N. ▶ *To reach this headland, leave Fuenterrabía on the road to the harbour and beach.* Turn left and as the road climbs, you will get a good **view**★ of the beach, the town and the quayside and from the end of the headland, the French coast and the town of Hendaye.

Ermita de San Marcial

9km/5.5mi SE. ▶ *Leave Fuenterrabía on the Behobia road and take the first right after the Palmera factory; bear left at the first crossroads.* A narrow road leads up to the wooded hilltop (225m/738ft). The **panorama**★★ from the hermitage terrace includes Fuenterrabía, **Irún** and the **Isla de los Faisanes** (Pheasant Island) in the mouth of the River Bidasoa which marks the frontier with France and has been the setting for several historic events including, in 1659, the signing of the Treaty of the Pyrenees which stipulated the marriage between Louis XIV and the Infanta María Teresa. In the distance you can see Donostia-San Sebastián and Hendaye beach.

Jaizkibel Road★★

The **drive**★★ along this road *(GI 3440)* is particularly impressive at sunset. After 5km/3mi you reach the Capilla de Nuestra Señora de Guadalupe (Chapel of our Lady of Guadalupe) where there is a lovely **view**★ of the mouth of the Bidasoa and the French Basque coast. The road overlooks the sea as it rises through pines and gorse to reach the Hostal de Jaizkibel at the foot of a 584m/1 916ft peak and a lookout with a superb **view**★★. The road down to Pasai Donibane affords **glimpses**★ of the indented coastline, the Cordillera Cantábrica range and the three mountains which dominate Donostia-San Sebastián – Ulía, Urgull and Igueldo.

Pasaia/Pasajes

17km/11mi W along the Jaizkibel road. Pasaia, in fact, comprises three villages around a sheltered bay connected with the open sea only by a narrow channel; **Pasai Antxo** is a trading port, **Pasai Donibane**★ and **Pasai San Pedro** are both deep-sea fishing

---

The Soldier of God

Ignatius de Loyola was born in 1491 in the Castillo de Loyola to an old family of the lesser nobility. He was bred to arms. It was while recovering from wounds received at the siege of Pamplona, that he heard the call of God and eight months later, in 1522, left the Loyola manor to go on a pilgrimage to Arantzazu and Montserrat. He next withdrew to a cave near Manresa in Catalunya where he began to write his **Spiritual Exercises**. In 1523 he set off in pilgrimage to Jerusalem from where, before returning to Spain, he journeyed to Paris (1528) and London (1530). After further wanderings and attendance at various universities, he and the compatriots he had met in Paris, Diego Laínez and Francis Xavier, were ordained (1537) and repaired to Rome. In 1540, the pope recognised the **Society of Jesus** which Loyola had conceived and for which he had drawn up the constitution.

Ignatius of Loyola died in 1556 and was canonised in 1622 at the same time as Francis Xavier and Teresa de Ávila.

Euskadi

Euskadi, or Euskal Herria, land of the Basques, corresponds more or less to the 11C Kingdom of Navarre. Historically, it consists of seven provinces: three of them make up the autonomous Spanish region of the Basque Country (Álava, Guipúzcoa and Vizcaya/Bizkaia), one of which has its own autonomous government (Navarra); and the three most northerly (Labourd, Basse-Navarre and Soule) form part of the French Pyrénées-Atlantiques *département*. These separate states nonetheless share a common race and language on both sides of the Pyrenees; their motto in Basque is *Zazpiak-bat* (the seven that make one).

The origins of the Basque people and their tongue remain something of a mystery, although recent genetic tests have shown links with both Welsh and Irish Celts. They are known to have been driven out of the Ebro Valley in Spain by the Visigoths and subsequently to have founded their own kingdom of Vasconia in the western Pyrenees. Those who settled in the plain intermarried with the people of Aquitaine and became known as the Gascons. But those who settled in the mountains fiercely defended their traditions, and in particular their language, from outside influences. It is above all the common language, **Euskara**, which binds the Basques together, although fewer than 20% of Spanish Basques – and fewer still of French – actually now speak it. Their distinctive culture sets them apart from the other peoples of Europe and nationalist feeling runs strong.

The Spanish Basque provinces traditionally enjoyed a large degree of autonomy, with their own Parliaments and special tax status. For centuries Spanish kings swore to respect the rights of Vizcaya beneath an ancient oak tree in Gernika (Guernica), the symbolic heart of the Basque country. The town was decimated on Franco's orders in 1937, crushing the fledgling Basque Republic declared in 1936 and bringing the Basque cause to worldwide attention. Basque nationalism in its modern form dates back to the founding of the now moderate Basque Nationalist Party by Sabino Arana in 1895, when Spanish unification threatened to undermine Basque autonomy. After Franco's victory, the Basque country was absorbed into Spain and efforts were made by the Spanish government to suppress Basque cultural identity. The separatist movement has been growing in strength since the 1960s, which is when the militant ETA (Euskadi Ta Askatasuna) began its terrorist activities. Since the death of Franco, some of the separatists' demands, such as a degree of regional autonomy, a Basque-language television station and language teaching in schools, have been granted, but full independence remains the aspiration of a solid core, with some 13% of the Basque population voting for Herri Batasuna, the Basque equivalent of Sinn Fein in Northern Ireland. The split between moderates and extremists was widened by the increased violence surrounding the issue of a Basque nation during the 1980s. The song Gernikako Arbola (The Tree of Guernica), in which the tree symbolises local freedom, has been adopted as the national anthem of the Spanish Basques.

ports, processing cod in the town. They hold the highest catch value along the Cantabrian coast. To get to **Pasai Donibane**★, either park the car at the entrance to the village or take a motorboat from San Pedro. The **view** from the water is picturesque – tall houses with brightly painted wooden balconies. The one and only village street winds between the houses and beneath arches offering glimpses of boats and landing stages. A path runs alongside the harbour to the lighthouse *(45min)*.

Donostia-San Sebastián★★ (See DONOSTIA-SAN SEBASTIÁN)

▷   *Take the N 1. 7km/4mi S of Donostia-San Sebastián bear right onto the Bilbao road (N 634).*

Zarautz

The resort has been fashionable since Queen Isabel II made it her summer residence in the 19C. The town is pleasantly situated in the centre of an amphitheatre of hills around a vast beach. Two **palaces** stand in the old quarter: the 16C property of the Marqués de Narros from which corner watchtowers look out over the beach, and the Luzea tower, on Plaza Mayor, with its mullioned windows and a machicolated corner balcony. The tower of the church of Santa María can be seen to one side.

Beyond Zarautz, the road rises to a picturesque **corniche section**★★ overlooking the sea as far as Zumaia. Getaria rock (Monte de San Antón), also known as *el ratón* (the mouse), soon comes into sight.

Getaria

Getaria is a small fishing village known locally for its *chipirones*, or squid, and its rock – *el ratón*, or Monte de San Antón – to which it is linked by an ancient, narrow road *(at present closed to traffic)*. From the rock you can see the harbour, the beach and Zarautz.

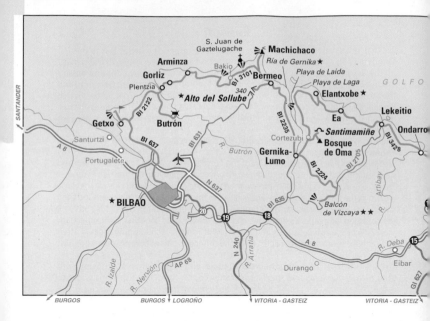

Long ago fishermen sailed from Getaria harbour to hunt whales, and navigators like **Juan Sebastián Elcano** set out on their voyages of discovery. A native of Getaria, Elcano sailed with Magellan and after the navigator died in the Philippines, brought his only surviving ship home, the first sailor to actually circumnavigate the world (1522). A narrow street, lined with picturesque houses, leads to the 13C-15C **Iglesia de San Salvador** (Church of our Saviour). The chancel rests on an arch beneath which an underground alley passes, from which one can see into the crypt. Inside is a Flamboyant Gothic gallery.

Zumaia

Zumaia is a large seaside resort situated at the mouth of the Urola with two fine beaches: Itzurun, a delightful beach nestled between cliffs, and Santiago, at the entrance to the town. Close to the latter is the house of the painter **Ignacio Zuloaga** (1870-1945), which has been converted into a **casa-museo** showing his own works – realistic and popular themes illustrated by brilliant colours and strong lines – and his personal collection of paintings by El Greco, Goya, Zurbarán and Morales. (○ Open 1 Apr-15 Sep, 4-8pm; at other times by prior arrangement. ○ Closed Mon and Tue. ๛ 5€. ☎ 943 86 23 41).

The 15C **Iglesia de San Pedro** (Church of St Peter) contains a 16C altarpiece by Juan de Anchieta.

▷ *Once past Zumaia, turn left onto the GI 631.*

Santuario de San Ignacio de Loyola

○ *Open 10am-1pm and 3-7pm.* ☎ *943 81 65 08.*

This **sanctuary** *(santuario)* was built by the Jesuits to plans by the Italian architect Carlo Fontana around the Loyola family manor house near Azpeitia at the end of the 17C. It has since become an important place of pilgrimage where large crowds attend the solemnities held annually on St Ignatius' day (31 July).

Santa Casa

The basement casemates of the 15C tower are vestiges of the original Loyola manor house. The rooms in which Ignatius was born, convalesced and converted have been transformed into profusely decorated chapels.

Basílica

The Baroque basilica is more Italian than Spanish in style. It is circular and surmounted by a vast cupola (65m/213ft high) attributed to Churriguera.

▷ *Return to the coast*

The journey by road to Deba is one of the most beautiful in the Basque country.

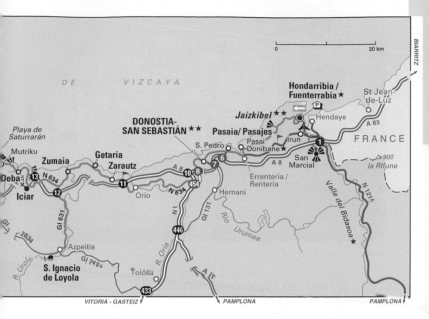

Icíar

The fortress-like church contains a Plateresque altarpiece in dark wood with, at the centre, a smiling 12C Romanesque Virgin, attired in a sumptuous mantle.

Deba

Deba is a small fishing port at the mouth of the Deba. The **Iglesia de Santa María la Real** conceals, beneath the porch in its fortified front, a superb Gothic portal decorated with extremely lifelike statues. The cloister galleries with their intricate tracery are particularly worthy of note.

There is a splendid **view**★ of the coast from the **cliff road**★ running between Deba and Lekeitio as it circles the promontory enclosing the Deva estuary.

The road then passes through **Mutriku**, which has one of the region's most delightful beaches, the **playa de Saturraran**.

Ondarroa

Ondarroa spreads over a spit of land between a hillside and a loop of the río Artibay. The church, upstanding like a ship's prow at one end, the tall Basque houses with washing at the windows, and the encircling river, make an attractive **picture**★. Canning and fish salting are the two main local industries.

The road between Ondarroa and Lekeitio is pleasant; on rounding a point you have a good **view**★ of Lekeitio, its beach and the island of San Nicolás, joined to the mainland at low tide.

Lekeitio

A deeply indented bay at the foot of Monte Calvario, divided by the island of San Nicolás, serves as the harbour for Lekeitio's long-standing fishing industry. The town is a resort with good sand beaches. The 15C **iglesia** guarding the harbour has three tiers of flying buttresses and a tall Baroque belfry.

Ea

This miniature harbour stands between two hills at the end of a quiet creek.

Elantxobe★

An attractive, peaceful village off the main road. Fishermen have long used the bay as a natural harbour and built their houses overlooking the water, against the steep side of Cabo Ogoño (300m/1 000ft).

Once beyond **Playa de Laga**, a vast expanse of rose-coloured sand circling the foot of Cabo Ogoño, you can see along the coastline, the peaceful waters of the **Gernika ría**★ (Estuary), the island of Izaro, the white outline of the town of Sukarrieta on the far bank, and the island of Chacharramendi.

Bermeo

The resort of **Playa de Laida**, on the *ría*, is popular with Gernika residents.

▶ *Bear left at Cortézubi.*

Cuevas de Santimamiñe

🔍 *Guided tours (1hr) at 10am, 11.15am, 12.30pm, 4.30pm and 6pm.* 🕐 *Closed Sat-Sun and public hols.* 🎫 *No charge.* ☎ *94 420 77 27.*

Wall paintings and engravings from the Magdalenian Period and interesting archaeological deposits were discovered in these **caves** in 1917. For conservation reasons, the caves containing the paintings are currently closed to visitors.
Nearby, a small road leads to the Bosque de Oma (3km/2mi).

Bosque de Oma

Fanciful geometric shapes, human silhouettes hiding behind tree trunks, and huge colourful canvases demonstrate the union between art and nature that Agustín Ibarrola wanted to create in this wood.

▶ *Return to the Gernika road.*

Gernika

Picasso's famous painting, *Guernica* (👁 *see MADRID and INTRODUCTION TO SPAIN*), has immortalised the tragic event that took place in this little town during the Civil War: on 26 April 1937, on Franco's orders, a Nazi German air squadron bombed the town and local inhabitants who had come to the market, killing more than 2 000.
In the Middle Ages, the Gernika oak was one of the four places where newly created lords of Biscay came to swear that they would respect the local fueros or privileges. Gernika was, on this account, visited by Queen Isabel in 1483. Today, the remains of the 1 000-year-old tree are in the small temple behind the **Casa de Juntas**.

Some 18km/11mi south *(via the BI 2224 and BI 3231)*, is the **Balcón de Vizcaya**★★ (Balcony of Biscay), a remarkable viewpoint overlooking the mountainous Biscay landscape, a chequerboard of meadows and forests.

▶ *Return to Gernika.*

Two viewpoints built beside the road at the mouth of the inlet before you reach Mundaka, enable you to take a last look back along its still waters. As the road drops downhill, you get a magnificent **view**★ of Bermeo.

Bermeo

Bermeo is an important inshore fishing port. The fishermen's quarter, still crowded onto the Atalaya promontory overlooking the old harbour, the Puerto Menor, was protected by the ramparts (traces remain), and the grim granite Torre de los Ercilla (now the Museo del Pescador, a fishermen's museum). In the Iglesia de Santa Eufemia, kings and overlords used to swear to uphold Biscay privileges.

▶ *Turn left towards Mungía.*

Alto del Sollube★ (Sollube Pass)

From the road up to the low pass (340m/1 115ft) there is a good view of Bermeo's semicircular site.

▶ *Return to Bermeo, follow the coast road left for 3km/1.8mi then turn right.*

Faro de Machichaco

From slightly left of this lighthouse there is a good view west along the indented coastline.

The road rises in a corniche to a **viewpoint**★ overlooking the **San Juan de Gazte-lugache** headland on which stands a hermitage *(access via a pathway)*, the goal of a local *romería* (pilgrimage) each Midsummer's Day.

There are extensive views from the **corniche road**★ between Bakio and Arminza. A belvedere commands an interesting **view**★ of the coast, Bakio, the valley farmlands and wooded hinterland.

Arminza

Arminza is the only harbour along a wild section of high, inhospitable coast.

Gorliz

Gorliz is an attractive beach resort at the mouth of the River Butrón. **Plentzia** nearby *(2km/1.2mi)*, once a fishing harbour and commercial port, is now an oyster farming centre and a resort. Upon exiting Plentzia, there is a good view of the river encircling the town.

Castillo de Butrón

🕐 *Open 10.30am-5.30pm; Sat-Sun and public hols, 11am-6pm; Mar-Sep, 10.30am-8pm daily.* 🕐*Closed Mon and Tue (in winter), 1 Jan and 24-25 and 31 Dec.* ⬤ *5€ (⬤⬤6€ including tour of main floor).* ☎ *94 615 11 10.*

This fantasy 19C castle is a good example of eclectic, picturesque architecture from the last century. It has been built on the remains of a 14C-15C construction, and provides visitors with an insight into life inside a medieval castle.

Getxo

A **paseo marítimo** or sea promenade overlooks the coast. From the road up to Getxo's well-known golf course there is an interesting view of the Bilbao inlet and on the far bank, Santurtzi and Portugalete.

Bilbao★ (🕐 *See BILBAO*)

Costa Verde★★★

MICHELIN MAPS 571 AND 572 (TOWN PLAN OF GIJÓN) B 8 TO 15 – ASTURIAS

The Green Coast of Asturias, one of Spain's most beautiful, is so called on account of the colour of the sea, the pine and eucalyptus trees along the shoreline, and the wooded pastures inland. Many of the towns and villages on the Costa Verde are nestled in picturesque coves, where fishing is the main source of income. On a clear day the Picos de Europa and Cordillera Cantábrica mountain ranges provide a stunning backdrop.

Location

The N 634 runs along the length of the Costa Verde, providing impressive views of both the sea and the mountains. *Gijón: Marqués de San Esteban 1, 33206, ☎ 98 534 60 46; Llanes: Alfonso IX (La Torre building), 33500; ☎ 98 540 01 64; Luarca: Olavarrieta (Capilla Palacio del Marqués de Ferrera), 33700, ☎ 98 564 00 83.*

> *Neighbouring sights are described in the following chapters: COSTA DE CANTABRIA (to the E), PICOS DE EUROPA (S of Ribadesella), OVIEDO (30km/19mi SW of Gijón) and RÍAS ALTAS (to the W).*

Tours

The coast from Unquera (to the E) to Castropol (to the W) is very rocky but follows an almost straight line due west except for where the Cabo de Peñas headland, west of Gijón, juts out to sea. The shore is lined by low cliffs interrupted by frequent sandy inlets; the estuaries are narrow and deep and although they are known locally as rías, they bear little resemblance to those in nearby Galicia. The coast from Cudillero westwards is steeper and more jagged; the coastal plain ends in a sheer line of cliffs overlooking small beaches tucked away in river mouths.

FROM LLANES TO GIJÓN 1
145km/90mi to the west

Llanes

A small peaceful fishing port (crayfish) and holiday resort. The clifftop promenade, paseo de San Pedro, affords a good view of the old, once fortified town, the rampart ruins and castle and the squat Iglesia de Santa María. If you can, be there for the St Roch festival in August to see the dances (the *Pericote* and in particular the children's *Prima* dance) in brilliant local costume.

The shoreline between Llanes and Ribadesella is a succession of sandy beaches sheltered by rock promontories: **Celorio, Barro** and **Cuevas del Mar**.

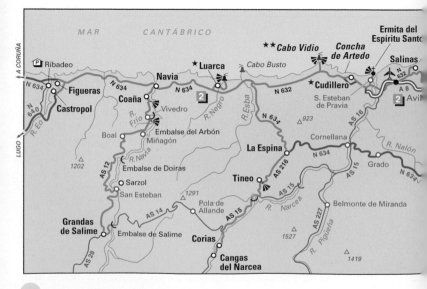

Ribadesella

The town and port of Ribadesella are on the right side of the estuary while opposite, a holiday resort has grown along the beach.

Cuevas de Tito Bustillo★

Guided tours (1hr) 10am-4.15pm. ○ *Closed Mon-Tue and 9 Sep-1Apr.* ◠ *3€, no charge Wed with prior reservation.* ☎ *98 586 11 20.*

These caves are famous for their **wall of paintings**★ decorated by the Palaeolithic inhabitants of 20 000 BC (between the Solutrean and the middle of the Magdalenian periods). A few animals – a horse, two stags, a doe, another stag and a horse – precede the smoothest area of rock, a sort of low ceiling where, in the hollows of the stone, there are animal shapes 2m/6.5ft long, painted red or ochre and outlined in black.

La Isla

Squat drying sheds or *hórreos*, typical of Asturias, stand beside the houses in the small, attractive village built on a rock headland close to the road. The vast bay is lined with beaches separated by rocks, one of which, lying offshore, gave the village its name.

Mirador del Fito★★★

12km/8mi SE of La Isla on AS 260. This magnificent viewpoint commands a spectacular panorama of the Picos de Europa and the coast.

Lastres

Lastres is a typical fishing village built against the side of a steep cliff between the beach and the harbour. It is known for its clams.

Priesca

The **Iglesia de San Salvador** has been restored. The chancel in this church contains capitals resembling those at Valdediós (◠ *see below*).

Villaviciosa

It was in Villaviciosa that the future **Emperor Charles V**, aged 17 and accompanied by a full escort of Flemish courtiers, landed in 1517 to take possession of his newly inherited kingdom. The ships' intended destination was Santander but by an error of navigation they sailed up the long *ría* to Villaviciosa harbour.

Modern visitors are greeted by a town with narrow streets, emblazoned houses and the **Iglesia de Santa María,** its west front decorated with a Gothic rose window and its Romanesque portal flanked by statue columns.

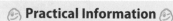

☺ **Practical Information** ☺

On the first Saturday in August every year, crowds of spectators flock to the area to watch the **Descenso Internacional del Sella**, a kayak race on the Sella river. The competition, which starts in Arriondas and ends in Ribadesella, can be followed from a train that runs parallel to the river.

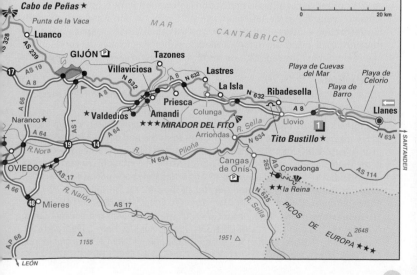

Address Book

For coin ranges, see the Legend at the back of the guide.

WHERE TO EAT

El Álamo – *Rapalcuarto – 10km/6mi E of Figueras along the N 634 – ☎ 98 562 86 49 – Closed 15-28 Feb –* 🖺. This roadside restaurant is renowned for its traditional cuisine and its copious, reasonably priced lunchtime menu. Eat in the modest dining room, the larger room is for groups.

Sport – *Rivero 9 - Luarca - ☎ 98 564 10 78 - Closed Wed (exc. summer and public hols) and Jan -* 🖺. This popular bar also has a dining area with a regional flavour, and a more formal area upstairs with views onto the estuary. The location near the fish market guarantees the freshness and quality of the fare.

El Jornu – *Cuetu Molin – Pancar – 1.5km/1mi SW of Llanes – ☎ 98 540 16 15 – Closed in Nov.* This popular and often noisy family-run restaurant serves simple but good-quality home cooking mainly based around fish and seafood.

Casa Tista – *Toriello 47 – Toriello – 5km/3mi E of Ribadesella along the AS 263 – ☎ 98 586 09 54 –* 🖺. This long-standing family-owned restaurant is famous for its excellent fish and seafood. Although prices have gone up here in the past few years, it still represents good value for money.

WHERE TO STAY

Hotel Rural Casa Manoli – *Carretera de Paredes – Almuña – 2km/1.2mi SE of Luarca along the Paredes road, then bear left – ☎ 98 547 00 40 – 13 rooms.*This small family hotel enjoys a peaceful rural setting on the outskirts of Luarca. Pleasant small garden and inexpensive, comfortable rooms.

Hotel Rural Camangu – *Camangu – 4.5km/3mi E of Camangu – ☎ 985 85 76 46 – 10 rooms –* 🖂 *5€.* This small family-run country hotel in a small village near Ribadesella is an excellent base for excursions into the local countryside. Pleasant decor, good value and a friendly welcome.

Hotel Carlos I – *Plaza Carlos I 1-4 – Villaviciosa – ☎ 98 589 01 21 - Closed Jan-Feb – 16 rooms –* 🖂 *€3€.* An 18C nobleman's house in the centre of the town is now home to this family-run hotel. The rooms here are spacious and attractively furnished and offer excellent value given the price. Highly recommended.

Hotel Palacete Peñalba – *El Cotarelo – Figueras – ☎ 98 563 61 25 –* 🅿 *– 12 rooms –* 🖂 *5€.* A unique, Modernist-style hotel with high ceilings and stylish furniture. This mansion is a listed artistic monument, although the garden could be better maintained.

La Posada de Babel – *La Pereda – 4km/2.5mi S of Llanes – ☎ 98 540 25 25 – Open Mar-Oct –* 🅿 *– 11 rooms –* 🖂 *7€ – Restaurant 24€.* This small hotel, with its rationalist-inspired architecture, is the perfect place for those seeking peace and quiet. The countryside around this former farm is delightful, and is enhanced by the extensive use of glass.

A short distance inland are Amandi and Valdediós with interesting churches.

Amandi – *3km/2mi S of Villaviciosa.* The bell gable of the **Iglesia de San Juan** can easily be picked out as it stands perched on high ground at the centre of the village. Though remodelled in the 18C the church still has its 13C portal and apse of which the **decoration**★ shows a high degree of sophistication. Inside the **apse**★, the frieze from the façade reappears to form a winding ribbon that follows the curves of the intercolumniation. The capitals have been beautifully and imaginatively carved.

Valdediós★

7km/4mi S of Villaviciosa. In the same valley are a small Asturian church, full of character and ancient charm, and a monastery.

The **Iglesia de San Salvador**, which was consecrated in 893 and is known locally as *El Conventín* or the little monastery, dates from the end of the Asturian period of architecture (8C-10C). The raised nave is abutted by narrow aisles; the capitals of the triumphal arch are decorated with the Asturian cord motif. The side portico was intended to serve as a covered walk or cloister; the strapwork capitals, arcaded windows and artistically sculpted *claustra* all show Mozarabic influence. ⏱ *Open 11am-1pm and 4.30-6pm; Nov-Apr, 11am-1pm.* ⏱ *Closed Mon.* ☎ *98 597 69 55.*

The **monasterio** (monastery) consists of a 13C Cistercian church and cloisters dating from the 15C, 17C and 18C. *Guided tours (40min), Apr-Sep, 11am-1.30pm and 4.30-7pm; Oct-Mar, 11.30am-1.30pm; Sat-Sun and public hols, 11.30am-1.30pm and 4-6pm.* ⏱ *Closed Mon, 1 Jan, Easter and 25 Dec.* 🎫 *1.20€.* ☎ *98 589 23 24.*

Tazones

This delightful little fishing village tucked away at the end of a protected inlet has a number of restaurants serving excellent local seafood.

Gijón

Gijón is a lively modern city with a population of over 250 000. It was originally built on the narrow Santa Catalina headland between two inlets which today serve as harbour (west) and beach, the vast Playa de San Lorenzo (east). **Plaza del Marqués**, near the port, is surrounded by well-proportioned buildings, among them the late-17C **Palacio de Revillagigedo**, with an elegant façade. The palace stands on the high Santa Catalina side of the square adjoining the fishermen's quarter known as Cimadevilla.

Gijón has preserved vestiges of its Roman past, including the **Termas Romanas del Campo Valdés**, Roman baths discovered in the old quarter of the city. An ingenious combination of walkways and information points enable visitors to explore and develop an understanding of this impressive archaeological find. (⏱ *Open 10am-1pm and 5-7pm (8pm Mar-Jun and Sep; 9pm Jul-Aug); Sun and public hols, 11am-2pm. and 5-7pm (8pm Jul-Aug).* 🎫 *2.20€ (3.60€ including visit of the Parque Arqueológico de la Campa de Torres).* ☎ *985 34 51 47).*

The **Torre del Reloj** is also well worth a visit, both for its displays relating to the prehistory and history of Gijón and for its splendid views of the city. (⏱ *Open 10am-1pm and 5-7pm (9pm Jul-Aug); Sun and public hols, 11am-2pm and 5-7pm (8pm Jul-Aug).* 🎫 *No charge.* ☎ *985 18 11 11 (ext.1329)).*

Gijón was the birthplace of **Gaspar Melchor de Jovellanos** (1744-1811), one of Spain's most eminent 18C men of letters. He was a poet, reformer, liberal economist, author and politician.

FROM GIJÓN TO CASTROPOL ②

179km/119mi to the west, excluding excursions inland

Luanco

Luanco harbour lies in a bay sheltered by the Punta de Vaca. It has a small beach and a sea promenade.

Cabo de Peñas★

The road runs through moorland to this cape, the northernmost point in Asturias. From the cliff and its large rock extension, all dominated by a lighthouse, there are fine **views** of the coast on either side of the cape.

Salinas

This is a rapidly expanding resort bordered to the east by a pine forest. The rock islet of La Peñona (footbridge) affords an overall **view**★ of the beach, one of the longest on the Costa Verde. Waves crash against the jagged rocks below.

Ermita del Espíritu Santo (Hermitage of the Holy Spirit)

As the road climbs there are glimpses through the eucalyptus trees of the Nalón estuary also known as Pravia ría and of waves lapping the immense San Juan de la Arena beach. The hermitage commands an extensive **view**★ west along the coastal cliffs. From this point, a scenic road follows the coastal heights toward Cudillero.

Cudillero★

The fishing village surrounded by steep hills makes an attractive **scene**★ from the end of the jetty: tall houses on the hillsides, white cottages with brown tiled roofs leading down to the small harbour nestling between two rock points, and a foreground of fishing boats, masts and nets drying in the sun.

Concha de Artedo

The beach is as beautiful as others in the area, but unfortunately pebbly.

Cabo Vidio★★

From near the lighthouse, the **views**★★ from this headland along the inhospitable coastline extend east to the Cabo de Peñas and west to Cabo Busto.

Excursion inland to the Narcea River

91km/57mi to Cangas de Narcea along the N 634 and AS 216, branching S at the Cabo Busto. The last section of this inland route runs parallel to the scenic River Narcea.

Tineo

The town perched 673m/2 208ft up the mountainside commands an immense **panorama**★★ of the surrounding sierras.

Corias

🕐 *Open 10am-12.30pm and 4-7.30pm.* ☎ *98 581 01 50.*

The large **monastery** *(monasterio)* re-erected in neo-Classical style after being burned down in the 19C, was founded in the 11C and occupied for 800 years by Benedictines. The main features of interest in the **church** are its ornate Churrigueresque altars.

Cangas de Narcea

The gateway to the upper Narcea Valley is popular with fishermen, hunters and tourists alike.

▶ *Return to the coast road (N 632).*

Luarca★

Luarca has a remarkable **site**★ at the mouth of the winding río Negro. The town, a distinctively attractive centre with its white houses and slate roofs, has seven bridges spanning the river, a sheltered fishing harbour and three beaches. At the end of the estuary, a lighthouse, church and cemetery stand on the headland once occupied by a fort. A narrow street leads to the top. For an interesting **view**★ of Luarca, take the lighthouse road left, then circle the church to the right and return to the harbour. On 15 August, the harbour fills with boats decked with flags.

Navia

This new town and fishing port stands on the right bank of the *ría*. A road follows the bank to a point overlooking the inlet where a **belvedere** dedicated to the Great Seafaring Discoverers gives a pleasant view.

Excursion inland along the Navia Valley

82km/51mi along the AS 12 (2hr 30min each way). The River Navia flows between Navia and Grandes de Salime, along a wild, enclosed valley at the foot of several high peaks. The route is via a winding, climbing road offering magnificent views of these impressive mountains.

▶ *After Coaña, turn right at a sign marked "castro."*

The circular foundations of a few houses and some paved streets remain from a **Celtic village** built on a mound.

For a striking **panorama**★★ of the **Arbón dam**, built just above a giant bend in the river, pause at the viewpoint.

Just past Vivedro, there is a **panoramic view**★★ extending from a loop in the river in the foreground to the mouth of the Navia in the far distance.

The **confluence**★★ of the Navia and the Frío is impressive as you look down on it from a giddy height. Beyond the bridge across the Frío, the road returns to the Navia which it follows to Miñagón. The squat drying sheds or *hórreos* you see from the road are the same rectangular shape as those in nearby Galicia.

The road descends beyond Boal to the level of the Navia, where 3km/2mi further on, the valley is blocked by the high **Doiras dam.**

The small village of **Sarzol**, perched on a hillside on the far bank from San Esteban, is surrounded by very steep slopes, all of which are cultivated.

Grandas de Salime

The main sight of interest in this large agricultural town is the **Museo Etnográfico.** Housed in a former presbytery, the museum traces aspects of traditional life in Asturias through reconstructed rooms, displays of objects found in a small agricultural holding or casería and tools used for various crafts.(🕐 *Open 11.30am-2pm and 4-6.30pm (7.30pm Jul-Sep).* 🕐 *Closed Mon.* ✍ *1.50€, no charge Tue.* ☎ *985 62 72 43).*

4km/2.5mi away is the **embalse de Salime**. There are viewpoints overlooking the dam wall and the power station.

▶ *Return to Navia, then continue W along the N 634.*

Figueras

From the port of Figueras on the ría Ribadeo you have a good view of Castropol which, from across the water, resembles an Austrian village casting its reflection in a lake.

Castropol

Castropol, the most westerly port in Asturias, lies along a promontory at the centre of a *ría* which marks the boundary with Galicia. This quiet village with a whitewashed main square *(plaza Mayor)* stands opposite Ribadeo, its Galician counterpart (& *see RÍAS ALTAS).*

Covarrubias ★

POPULATION: 629.

MICHELIN MAP 575 F 19 – CASTILLA Y LEÓN (BURGOS)

This historic Castilian village is partly surrounded by medieval ramparts guarded by the Doña Urraca tower, strangely shaped like a truncated pyramid. A Renaissance palace straddles the street to the picturesque old quarter, where half-timbered houses supported by stone columns have been restored. Covarrubias is the burial place of Fernán González, one of Castilla's great historic figures and the catalyst behind the kingdom's independence.

Location

Covarrubias stands on the banks of the River Arlanza, some 40km/25mi SE of Burgos. 🖪 *Monseñor Vargas, 09346 Covarrubias, ☎ 947 40 64 61.*

& *Neighbouring sights are described in the following chapters: BURGOS, PALENCIA (94km/59mi W) and SORIA (117km/73mi SE).*

WHERE TO STAY

⊜⊜ **Hotel Tres Coronas de Silos** – *Plaza Mayor 6 – Monastery of Santo Domingo de Silos – ☎ 947 39 00 47 – 16 rooms – ⊡ 7€.– Restaurant 15.63€.* A restored 18C seigniorial mansion on the main square now houses this pleasant hotel. It is decorated in typical Castilian style with exposed stone walls and plentiful wood, which combine to create a warm and inviting atmosphere.

Worth a Visit

Colegiata★

🔊 *Guided tours (30min), 10.30am-2pm and 4-7pm.* ☉ *Closed Tue.* ☞ *2€.* ☎ *947 40 63 11.*

This collegiate church, with a nave and two aisles and cloisters with ornamental vaulting, makes an impressive Gothic unit. It is also a pantheon containing some 20 medieval tombs, including those of Fernán González and the Norwegian Princess Cristina who married the Infante Philip of Castilla in 1258. The fine 17C church organ is worthy of particular note.

Museo-Tesoro (Museum and Treasury) – A painting by Pedro Berruguete and another by Van Eyck stand out from the collection of Primitives; note especially the 15C Flemish **triptych★** in which the central high relief of the Adoration of the Magi has been attributed to Gil de Siloé. There is also a splendid processional cross made by the goldsmiths of Calahorra in the 16C.

Excursions

Monasterio de Santo Domingo de Silos★★

18km/11mi SE. ☉ *Open 10am-1pm and 4.30-6pm; Sun-Mon and public hols, 4.30-6pm.* ☉ *Closed 1 Jan, 19 Mar, Maundy Thu afternoon-Easter Mon, 1 May, 15 Aug, 12 Oct, 1 Nov, and 8 and 20 Dec.* ☞ *2.40€, no charge Mon.* ☎ *947 39 00 49.*

The monastery owes its name to an 11C monk, Dominic, who reconstructed the conventual buildings of a former 6C-8C Visigothic abbey. The new buildings were abandoned in 1835 but were reoccupied by Benedictine monks from Poitou, in France, in 1880, who planted the magnificent cypress in the cloisters and a huge sequoia in front of the portal.

The monastery is also renowned for its concerts of Gregorian chant.

Claustro★★★ – The cloisters at Santo Domingo de los Silos are among the most beautiful in Spain. Large by Romanesque standards, they comprise two superimposed, architecturally similar galleries. The ground floor galleries have about 60 rounded arches supported by paired columns and, in the middle of each gallery, by a group of five columns. The eight low reliefs on the corner pillars are masterpieces of Romanesque sculpture.

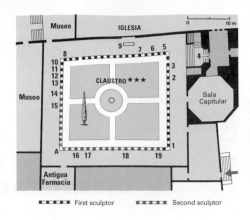

■■■■■ First sculptor   ■■■■■ Second sculptor

Careful study reveals that several major sculptors worked on the stone. The first and most original craftsman (mid- to late 11C) was primarily a linear artist who favoured hieratic postures and preferred Symbolism to Realism – his work extends along the east, north and part of the west galleries and includes the low reliefs on the southeast, northeast and northwest corner pillars. The second artist (early 12C) was more partial to volume than line and personified his figures. The third mason, again using a completely different style, carved the southwest pillar (12C).

The **capitals**, apart from those which are historiated, illustrate a fantastic bestiary which derives from the Mudéjar use of animal and plant motifs. *The most interesting have been numbered in the description of the galleries that follows.*

Southeast pillar

The Ascension is represented to the left, and Pentecost to the right. Its composition is similar to that of an ivory diptych.

East gallery

(1): strapwork, **(2)**: entwined plants, **(3)**: harpies defended by dogs.

Northeast pillar

This shows the Descent from the Cross and on the upper register, the earth and the moon on the point of being clouded over; on the other side is an original representation of the Entombment and the Resurrection as a single composition. Opposite the pillar is the fine doorway known as the **Puerta de las Vírgenes (4)** which led to the former Romanesque abbey church. Its horseshoe arch is flanked by columns with interesting capitals.

North gallery

(5): entwined plants, **(6)**: the Elders of the Apocalypse, **(7)**: harpies attacked by eagles, **(8)**: birds. The gallery also contains St Dominic's 13C tomb **(9)**: three Romanesque lions bear the recumbent figure of the saint.

Northwest pillar

This pillar, concerned with the doubts on the Resurrection in the minds of some disciples, shows Christ on the road to Emmaus and before St Thomas.

West gallery

(10): strapwork, **(11)**: birds with necks entwined, **(12)**: flamingoes, **(13)**: birds and lions ensnared by plant tendrils. The capitals that follow are by the second sculptor. **(14)**: the birth of Jesus, **(15)**: scenes of the Passion. Note the well-preserved 14C *artesonado* ceiling.

Southwest pillar (A)

By the third artist. On the left is an admirable Annunciation in which the Virgin Mary appears crowned by two angels; on the right is a Tree of Jesse.

South gallery

(16) and **(17)**: plant tendrils ensnaring birds in the first and stags in the second, **(18)**: eagles clutching hares, **(19)**: grimacing monster heads.

Museo

The museum displays some very old pieces, including an 11C chalice of St Dominic's with filigree decoration, an enamel reliquary, a 10C-11C manuscript of the Mozarabic rite and the tympanum from the portal of the original church.

Antigua Farmacia

The old pharmacy contains a fine collection of Talavera ceramic jars.

Iglesia

The present church (1756-1816), which is agreeably proportioned, combines the rounded volume of Baroque with the plain grandeur of the Herreran style.

Garganta de la Yecla

21km/13mi SE and 3km/2mi SW of Santo Domingo de Silos – ⛰ 20min. A footpath follows a deep narrow gorge cut into a thick layer of grey limestone.

Lerma

23km/14mi W along the C 110. Lerma owes its splendour to the **Duke of Lerma**, Philip III's ambitious favourite who ruled the country from 1598 until he was usurped by his son, the Duke of Uceda, in 1618. The period was one of untold extravagance and corruption, the court, dizzied by celebrations and balls, divided its time between Madrid and Valladolid; the duke, once having feathered his own nest, turned his attention to his home town which as a result became one of Spain's rare examples of Classical town planning.

The quarter built by the duke in the 17C, in the upper part of the town, retains its steep narrow cobbled streets and its houses, some of which are very old, with their wood or stone porticoes. The ducal palace, with its austere façade, stands on the spacious **plaza Mayor**★. The **Colegiata** church has a 17C gilded bronze statue by Juan de Arfe of the duke's nephew, the Archbishop Cristóbal de Rojas, shown at prayer. ○ *Open 10am-2pm and 4-7pm (8pm in summer); Sun and public hols 10am-2pm (and 4-7pm in summer).* ○ *Closed Mon, 1 Jan, 1 May and 25 and 31 Dec.* ⊕ *3€.* ☎ *947 17 70 02.*

Quintanilla de las Viñas

24km/15mi N. ▶ *Take the C 110, the N 234 towards Burgos, then bear right onto a small signposted road.* The road follows the Arlanza Valley out of Covarrubias into pleasant wooded gorges. You will see, below and to the right, the ruins of the **Monasterio de San Pedro de Arlanza** with beautiful Romanesque apses.

Iglesia de Quintanilla de las Viñas★

○ *Open 9.30am-2pm and 4-7pm (8pm Jul-Sep); Oct-Mar, 9.30am-5.30pm.* ○ *Closed Mon-Tue, last weekend in every month and holidays (check with church for precise dates).* ☎ *626 49 62 15.*

The church's great age – it is generally reputed to be 7C Visigothic – makes it of great archaeological interest. All that remains are the apse and transept, built of skilfully bonded blocks of stone. The outside walls are decorated with a frieze of bunches of grapes, leaves and birds as well as medallions and highly stylised motifs. The same foliated scrollwork is repeated inside on the keystones of the triumphal arch of which the imposts, on either side, are adorned with symbolic figures of the sun and moon.

Decorative frieze, Iglesia de Quintanilla de las Viñas

Cuenca★★

POPULATION: 46 047.

MICHELIN MAP 576 L 23 – CASTILLA-LA MANCHA (CUENCA)

Cuenca stands in a spectacular **setting**★★ hemmed in by the Júcar and Huécar ravines *(hoces)* on a rocky platform that appears to defy the laws of gravity. The magnificently preserved old city has been justifiably included on UNESCO's World Heritage List.

Location

▶ *Follow the signs to the historic quarter (casco antiguo). Cross the plaza Mayor and leave your car in the free car park in the upper section.* Cuenca is situated on the western part of the Montes Universales range which itself forms the eastern edge of the Meseta. Over time, this limestone massif has been eroded into a rugged terrain dotted with fantastic rock formations. Madrid and Albacete are located 164km/102mi and 145km/91mi from Cuenca respectively. ▯ *Plaza Mayor 1, 16001 Cuenca,* ☎ *969 23 21 19; Plaza de la Hispanidad 2, 16002 Cuenca,* ☎ *902 10 01 31.*

◔ *Neighbouring sights are described in the following chapter: TERUEL (151km/94mi NE).*

Special Features

Contemporary Art

Museo de Arte Abstracto Español★★

◷ *Open 11am-2pm and 4-6pm (8pm Sat); Sun, 11am-2.30pm.* ◷ *Closed Mon and public hols.* ▱*3€.* ☎ *969 21 29 83.*

The Museum of Abstract Spanish Art was inaugurated in 1966. Its setting and the views it commands are such that some of the windows are veritable works of art in themselves. The collection, put together by Fernando Zóbel and enriched since its foundation, is a fine selection of Spanish abstract art including works by Chillida, Tàpies, Saura, Zóbel, Cuixart, Sempere, Rivera and Millares.

Fundación Antonio Pérez

◷ *Open 10am-8pm (11am-8pm Sat-Sun and public hols).* ▱ *No charge.* ☎ *969 23 06 19.*

This foundation, housed in a former 17C Carmelite convent, exhibits part of the vast legacy of Antonio Pérez. In addition to work by Spanish artists such as Millares and

---

Address Book

For coin ranges, see the Legend at the back of the guide.

WHERE TO EAT

▱ **Mesón Mangana** – *Plaza Mayor 3* – ☎ *969 22 94 51 – Closed 15 Oct-15 Nov.* The perfect spot for a meal when visiting the old quarter. Good home cooking and local specialities, as well as excellent sausages, mature Manchego cheese and grilled meats. The comfortable dining room, with its decor of dark wood, is on the first floor .

▱▱ **Mesón Casas Colgadas** – *Canónigos 3* – ☎ *969 22 35 09 – Closed Mon evening* – ▤. A well-known local landmark which is worth eating in for its location alone. As its name suggests, the restaurant is housed in one of the city's famous hanging houses (casas colgadas), with a stupendous view of the Huécar ravine. The cuisine here is a pleasant fusion of modern and traditional.

WHERE TO STAY

▱ **Posada Huécar** – *Paseo del Huécar 3* – ☎ *969 21 42 01 – 22 rooms.* Behind the sober, salmon-coloured façade is a pleasant hotel with simply furnished but perfectly adequate rooms, all with TV, and a delightful garden. A good location in the old part of Cuenca.

▱ **Posada de San José** – *Julián Romero 4* – ☎ *969 21 13 00 – 29 rooms* – ▱ *7€.* This charming inn is housed in a former 17C seminary. All the rooms are different, although common features include an alcove, terrace and beds with canopies. Simple, elegant and totally peaceful.

FIESTAS

Holy Week processions are considerably enhanced by the site. At dawn on Good Friday the slow ascent to Calvary is enacted along the steep alleys to the accompaniment of drums. A festival of sacred music is also held throughout Holy Week.

Saura, the centre also displays the so-called *objetos encontrados* – objects and refuse which are part of daily life but which subsequently are classified works of art when recontextualised.

Walking About

CIUDAD ANTIGUA★★ (OLD TOWN) *2hr 30min*

▷ *From the car park in the castle district, pass through the 16C Renaissance-style Arco del Bezudo, then head down calle San Pedro to the church of the same name. From here, turn left onto ronda Julián Romero.*

Ronda Julián Romero

This delightful stepped alley with its small squares runs above the Huécar gorge and leads to the cathedral.

Convento de las Carmelitas

This former Carmelite convent is now home to the Fundación Antonio Pérez and the Museo Internacional de Electrografía (⚭ *see description under Special Features*).

Catedral★

🕐 *Open 10.30-1pm and 4-6pm (May-Sep 10am-2pm and 4-7pm); Sun and public hols 10am-6.30pm.* ⚭ *2.50€ (treasury).* ☎ *969 22 00 96.*

Construction of the cathedral, which fronts one side of the plaza Mayor, was started in the 13C in Norman-Gothic style. At the beginning of the 20C a fire destroyed the façade (which was subsequently rebuilt) and resulted in the collapse of one of the two towers flanking it, hence the lack of symmetry and gracefulness. The interior, a mix of Gothic architecture and Renaissance decoration, has several outstanding features, such as the superb wrought-iron chapel **grilles**★, a twin **ambulatory**, a **triforium** and an elegant Plateresque **door**★ into the chapter house with carved walnut panels by Alonso Berruguete.

The Hanging Houses of Cuenca

J. Balanya/MICHELIN

▷ *Walk along the right-hand side of the cathedral and take calle Canónigos.*

This street is lined by the Palacio Episcopal, housing the **Museo Diocesano**★, and the **Museo de Cuenca** (👁 *see descriptions under Worth a Visit*).

Casas Colgadas★ (Hanging Houses)

These famous 14C houses, now heavily restored, are home to the **Museo de Arte Abstracto** (👁 *see description under Special Features*) and a restaurant. The best **view**★ of these gravity-defying buildings can be enjoyed on the other side of the River Huécar, across the **Puente de San Pablo**, an iron bridge that leads to the Convento de San Pablo, nowadays the city's parador. This panorama is particularly enchanting at night when the scene is attractively illuminated.

▷ *Return to the cathedral and head along calle José T. Mena.*

Iglesia de San Miguel

This Gothic-style church, currently not used for worship, is one of the main venues for Cuenca's Religious Music Week.

▷ *Return to the plaza Mayor and follow calle Severo Catalina and calle Pilares.*

Plaza de las Angustias★

An 18C Franciscan monastery and a Baroque-style hermitage, known as the Virgin in Anguish, stands in this quiet, tree-lined square between the town and the Júcar ravine.

▷ *Return to calle San Pedro and continue to the church of the same name. Bear left into an alley which ends at the edge of the Júcar ravine, from where there is a good view of the valley.*

Worth a Visit

Museo Diocesano★

🕐 *Open 11am-2pm and 4-7pm (Apr-Sep 11am-2pm and 5-8pm); Sun and public hols, 11am-2pm.* 🕐 *Closed Mon.* 💶 *2€.* ☎ *969 22 42 10.*

The key exhibits in this small yet attractive museum are eight **panels**★ of an altarpiece by Juan de Borgoña (c 1510), two El Greco paintings, a Calvary by Gérard David and an exceptional collection of gold and silver plate. One of the most outstanding works is a 13C **Byzantine diptych**★ painted in a monastery on Mount Athos and covered in silver, pearls and precious stones. There is also the gilded bronze **Báculo de San Julián** (Crozier of St Julian) from Limoges (c 1200) decorated with enamel. Tapestries and carpets are displayed on the first floor.

Museo de Cuenca★

🕐 *Open 10am-2pm and 4-7pm; Sun and public hols, 10am-2pm.* 🕐 *Closed Mon.* 💶 *1.20€, no charge Sat pm and Sun.* ☎ *969 21 30 69.*

The first floor of this museum displays prehistoric objects. The second floor has the most interesting exhibits: sculpture, numismatic items and ceramics found in the Roman excavations at Segóbriga, Valeria and Ercávica. Note the top of a **Roman altar**★ found at Ercávica illustrating items used in sacred rites.

Museo de las Ciencias de Castilla-La Mancha

🕐 *Open 10am-2pm and 4-7pm (8pm May-Sep); Sun, 10am-2pm.* 🕐 *Closed Mon, 1 Jan, Maundy Thu, Good Fri and 25 Dec.* 💶 *1.20€ museum and 1.20€ planetarium.*

The regional science museum is located on plaza de la Merced, another of the many charming hidden secrets of Cuenca. Access is via the Iglesia de la Merced, built above the remains of several medieval cisterns. The museum is divided into various sections dedicated to subjects such as astronomy, the earth's treasures, the laboratory of life etc.

Excursions

Las Hoces (Ravines)

Roads which parallel the river on either side as it circles the bottom of the precipitous rock spur afford amazing views of the hanging houses.

Hoz del Júcar

The Júcar is the shorter and more enclosed ravine. Poplars stand reflected in the green river waters below the ochre-coloured cliff.

Hoz del Huécar

Round tour of 15km/9mi. The Huécar course swings from side to side between less steep slopes as it drains a small valley given over to market gardening. The Cuenca houses, seen from below, appear to defy gravity.

▶ *Turn left at the end of the ravine for Buenache de la Sierra and then left again for the Convento de San Jerónimo (monastery).*

Shortly afterwards, in a right bend, there's a remarkable **view**★ of the valley's tall grey rock columns and, in the distance, of Cuenca. Enter the town through a gateway set in the ramparts of the old quarter.

Las Torcas★

▶ *Take the N 420 then bear left after 11km/6.5mi.* The road passes through an attractive wood of conifers where the torcas, strange, circular depressions of earth which occasionally reach spectacular proportions, can be seen. The Torca del Lobo (Wolf's Hollow) is particularly interesting.

SERRANÍA DE CUENCA★

270km/168mi – 🕐*allow 1 day*

The unusual landscapes of this limestone area have been formed over the centuries by the infiltration of river water and wind erosion. The whimsical rock formations, the pine groves and the numerous streams all combine to form a sierra of unquestionable beauty.

Ventano del Diablo

25.5km/16mi from Cuenca along the CM 2105. The Devil's Window, an opening carved out of the rock, overlooks the depths of the **Garganta del Júcar** (Júcar Gorges).

Ciudad Encantada★

▶ *Follow the road signposted to the right of the CM 2105.* 🚶 The Enchanted City is a strange rock formation created by the shaping of limestone by the natural elements. An arrowed circuit directs visitors through this dreamlike forest of rocks, the most interesting of which are the Tobogán (Toboggan Slope) and the Mar de Piedras (Sea of Stones).

To reach the **Mirador de Uña** *(2km/1mi),* ▶ *continue along the road which leaves the car park.* Enjoy the extensive **view** of the Júcar Valley which is dominated along its entire course by towering cliffs, with, in the distance, Uña and its small lake.

Los Callejones

3km/2mi from Las Majadas. 🅿 *Leave your car on the esplanade.* Although less spectacular than the Ciudad Encantada, this isolated geological spot is a strange natural sight with unusual shapes in a maze of eroded blocks, arches and the narrow alleyways which lend their name to the area: The Alleyways.

Nacimiento del río Cuervo★ (Source of the Cuervo)

30km/19mi N of Las Majadas towards Alto de la Vega. 🅿 *Leave the car just after the bridge and walk up 500m.* A footpath leads to the **waterfalls**★ where water rushing through grottoes and out of moss-covered, hollowed-out rocks forms the beginnings of the Cuervo river.

Hoz de Beteta★ (Beteta Ravine)

30km/19mi NW along the CM 2106 and CM 2201 towards Beteta. This impressive ravine has been cut by the River Guadiela, which flows between towering vertical cliffs and lush vegetation. Upon reaching Vadillos, a road to the left leads to the famous spa of Solán de Cabras. The road (CM 210) then continues through the **valley of the River Escabas**. Before reaching Priego *(3km/2mi),* a road off to the right leads to the **Convento de San Miguel de las Victorias**, built in an impressive **setting**★.

Daroca ★

POPULATION: 2 630.

MICHELIN MAP 574 I 25 – ARAGÓN (ZARAGOZA)

Daroca is lodged between two ridges over which runs its 4km/2.5mi long perimeter of battlemented **walls**★. These were originally defended by more than 100 towers and fortified gateways like the impressive **Puerta Baja** (Lower Gate) flanked by square towers.

Location

Daroca stands at the crossroads of the N 234 and N 330, in close proximity to Calatayud (40km/25mi N), Zaragoza (85km/53mi NE) and Teruel (96km/60mi S). *Plaza de España 4, 50360 Daroca, ☎ 976 80 01 29.*

▸ *Neighbouring sights are described in the following chapters: TERUEL and ZARAGOZA.*

Worth a Visit

Colegiata de Santa María

Open 11am-1pm and 5.30-7pm; Apr-Oct, noon-1pm and 5.30-8pm; Sun and public hols, 11am-1pm and 6-8pm. Closed Mon. No charge. ☎ 976 80 07 61.

This collegiate church, built in the Romanesque period as a repository for the holy cloths, was modified in the 15C and 16C. In the north wall beside the belfry is a Flamboyant Gothic portal.

Interior

The late-Gothic nave includes several Renaissance features such as the cupola above the transept crossing.

The **south chapels**, partly faced with locally manufactured 16C *azulejos*, contain a series of interesting altarpieces. To the right of the entrance is a 15C **altarpiece**★ in multicoloured alabaster which is believed to have been carved in England – note the anecdotal detail. Gothic tombs stand on either side of the nave. The 15C **Capilla de los Corporales**★ (Chapel of the Holy Relics) is on the site of the original Romanesque apse. The altar, behind a kind of Flamboyant rood screen and framed by scenes of the miracle on the walls, includes a shrine enclosing the holy altar cloths. All around stand statues in delightful poses carved out of multicoloured alabaster. The painted Gothic **retable**★ is dedicated to St Michael.

Museo Parroquial★ (Parish Museum)

Open 11am-1pm and 5.30-7pm; Apr-Oct, noon-1pm and 5.30-8pm; Sun and public hols, 11am-1pm and 6-8pm. Closed Mon. 3€. ☎ 976 80 07 61.

Among the paintings on wood are two rare though badly damaged 13C panels and **altarpieces** to St Peter (14C) and St Martin (15C). All the gold and silver plate was made in Daroca except for the **reliquary** which once held the holy cloths, which was made by the 14C Catalan, Moragues. The figures are gold, the foundation silver. Most of the **chasubles**, many of them very old, were woven in the town, while others, dating from the 17C, are Mexican.

Iglesia de San Miguel

This fine church, outstanding both for the purity of its Romanesque east end and its 12C portal, has been restored to its original design. Unfortunately, the 13C wall paintings in the apse have faded. Outside, a short distance below, you can see the restored Mudéjar-style belfry of the **Iglesia de Santo Domingo**.

The Miracle of the Holy Alter Cloths

The miracle of the holy altar cloths took place in 1239, after the conquest of Valencia, when Christian troops in Daroca, Teruel and Calatayud were setting out to recover territory occupied by the Moors. Just as Mass was being celebrated, the Moors attacked and the priest had to hide the consecrated hosts between two altar cloths. Shortly afterwards, it was seen that the hosts had left bloodstained imprints on the linen. The three towns of Daroca, Teruel and Calatayud all claimed the precious relic. To settle the dispute the holy cloths were placed upon a mule which was then set free. It made straight for Daroca, dying, however, as it entered the Puerta Baja.

Donostia-San Sebastián★★

POPULATION: 176 019.

MICHELIN MAPS 573 (TOWN PLAN) OR 574 C 23 – 24

SEE PLAN OF COSTA VASCA IN COSTA VASCA – PAÍS VASCO (GUIPÚZCOA)

San Sebastián, or Donostia in Basque, stands in a glorious **setting**★★★ on a scallop-shaped bay framed by two hills (Monte Urgull and Monte Igueldo) and the small island of Santa Clara.

Two vast sand beaches follow the curve of the bay: La Concha and, beyond the promontory, the fashionable **Ondarreta**. Behind are gardens, promenades and luxury apartment blocks and, beyond the playa de Ondarreta, at the foot of Monte Igueldo, is the **Peine de los Vientos**, a work by the sculptor Eduardo Chillida.

Location

Donostia-San Sebastián is strategically located on the Gulf of Vizcaya, 25km/15mi W of the French border, 79km/49mi N of Pamplona, 102km/64mi E of Bilbao and 95km/59mi NE of Vitoria-Gasteiz. Because of the excellent road network, it is easy to travel to and from the main resorts and cities in the region. ▯ *Reina Regente 8, 20003 Donostia-San Sebastián,* ☎ *943 48 11 66.*

Address Book

For coin ranges, see the Legend at the back of the guide.

WHERE TO EAT

☞ **José Mari** – *Fermín Calbetón 5 –* ☎ *943 42 46 45 – Closed Tue and two weeks in Oct.* For the past 10 years and more this bar-restaurant has been serving a huge variety of tapas and sandwiches. The restaurant on the first floor has an excellent menu of local dishes.

☞☞ **Bodegón Alejandro** – *Fermín Calbetón 4 –* ☎ *943 42 71 58 – Closed Mon evening, Sunday, and Christmas week –* ▤. As befits a restaurant owned by the famous chef Martín Berasategui, the Alejandro serves excellent cuisine at surprisingly reasonable prices. Although there's just a single daily menu, the choice is quite varied. Its excellent location in the old town is an added bonus.

TAPAS

Txepetxa – *Pescadería 5 –* ☎ *943 42 22 27 – Closed Mon, two weeks in Jun and two weeks in Oct –* ▱▤. This traditional bar in the old town is worthy of its fine local reputation, particularly for its delicious anchovies, which are served in a variety of ways. The numerous prizes it has won go some way to explain its slightly expensive prices.

Ganbara – *San Jerónimo 21 –* ☎ *943 42 25 75 – Closed Sun evening, Mon, 15-30 Jun and 15-30 Nov –* ▤. This famous tapas bar behind the plaza de la Constitución is always full of customers here to enjoy the excellent selection on offer. The cosy restaurant in the basement is also recommended.

WHERE TO STAY

☞ **Pensión Anne** – *Esterlines 15, 2º –* ☎ *943 42 14 38 – 6 rooms.* A new, completely renovated pensión in the old town, in the midst of Donostia-San Sebastián's famous tapas bars. All the rooms look onto the street, although not all have their own bathroom.

☞☞ **Hotel Niza** – *Zubieta 56 –* ☎ *943 42 66 63 –* ▱ *– 41 rooms –* ☲ *7€.* This elegant hotel belonging to the Chillida family opened its doors in the 1920s and has remained a Donostia-San Sebastián institution. An unbeatable location overlooking the bay and beach. Homey decoration, renovated bathrooms.

☞☞ **Pensión Donostiarra** – *San Martín 6 1º –* ☎ *943 42 61 67 – www.pensiondonostiarra.com – 15 rooms.* The Donostiarra is one of the city's classic addresses and has recently benefited from a facelift. Close to the new cathedral, it occupies the first floor of an early-20C building, with comfortable rooms decorated with parquet flooring, simple furniture and modern bathrooms.

FIESTAS AND FESTIVALS

Donostia-San Sebastián's summer calendar includes the **Semana Grande** fiesta (August), an international jazz festival, Basque folklore festivals, golf and tennis tournaments, as well as horse racing and regattas.

The annual **International Film Festival** (September) is held in the new conference centre (Kursaal) designed by Rafael Moneo.

E. Baret/MICHELIN

La Concha Bay

▷ *Neighbouring sights are described in the following chapters: COSTA VASCA, BILBAO and PAMPLONA/IRUÑA.*

Background

The pioneer of tourism – Since the 19C, when Queen María Cristina of Habsburg chose Donostia-San Sebastián as her summer residence, the city has developed into one of Spain's leading resorts. The Palacio de Miramar, built on her orders, remains from this period.

A gastronomic capital – A feature of this city, where one eats well and copiously, are the 30 or so gourmet clubs. The all-male members prepare excellent meals which they then consume, accompanied by cider or the local *txacolí* wine. Basque specialities include fish dishes (hake, cod, bream and sardines) and the wonderful squid or *chipirones*.

Worth a Visit

Old Town

Although rebuilt following a fire in 1813, the narrow streets of the old town have considerable character and offer a sharp contrast to the wide avenues of modern Donostia-San Sebastián. The area comes alive at the evening aperitif hour when locals and tourists (especially the French, many of whom cross the border for a meal) crowd the bars and small restaurants in the *calles* Portu, Muñoa, 31 de Agosto and Fermín Calbetón to enjoy tapas (reputed to be among the best in Spain) and the excellent local seafood.

Plaza de la Constitución

The square is lined with houses with tall arcades and numbered balconies – a reminder of the days when they served as ringside seats for bullfights held in the square.

Iglesia de Santa María

⏰ *Open 8am-2pm and 5-8pm.* ☎ *943 42 31 24.*

> ## Panoramic Views
>
> **Monte Igueldo**★★★: ▷ *For access by car, follow the Concha and Ondarreta beaches and then bear left;* 🚡 *also accessible by funicular.* ⏰ *Open Nov-Mar, 11am-6pm (8pm Sat-Sun and public hols); Apr-Jun, 11am-8pm; Jul-Sep, 10am-10pm.* ⏰ *Closed Wed (in winter).* 🚠 *1.70€ (round trip).* ☎ *943 21 05 64.*
>
> At the top are an amusement park, hotel and restaurant. There is also a splendid **panorama** of the sea, the harbour with Santa Clara island and Donostia-San Sebastián itself, set within a mountain cirque. The view is beautiful in the evening when the town lights up.
>
> **Monte Urgull**★★: this hill, now a public park, is crowned by a fortress, the **Castillo de Santa Cruz de la Mota**. From the summit there is a good **panorama** of the monuments of the old town directly below and the Bahía de la Concha.

The church has a strikingly exuberant late-18C portal. Baroque altars adorn the vast sober interior.

Museo de San Telmo

🕐 *Open 10.30am-1.30pm and 4-7.30pm; April, 10.30-8pm; Sun and public hols, 10.30am-2pm.* 🕐 *Closed Mon, 1 and 6 Jan, 1 May and 25 Dec.* 🆓 *No charge.* ☎ *943 48 15 80.*

The museum is in an old 16C monastery. The Renaissance cloisters contain Basque stone funerary crosses carved in the traditional Iberian style and dating for the most part from between the 15C and the 17C. The cloisters' upper gallery is dedicated to the ethnographic section, with a reconstruction of a Basque interior. This gallery opens onto the rooms housing the museum's paintings, which include a Ribera, an El Greco, and a 19C art section. The chapel was decorated by **José María Sert** with historical scenes from the city's history, painted in sepia and gold.

Paseo Nuevo

The wide corniche promenade almost circles Monte Urgull and affords good **views** of the open sea and the bay. At the end is a bustling and colourful port with numerous fishing boats and pleasure craft.

Aquarium San Sebastián★

🕐 *Open 10am-7pm (8pm Holy Week-30 Oct, 9 pm Jul-Aug).* 🕐 *Closed 1 Jan and 25 Dec.* 🆓 *€.* ☎ *943 44 00 99.*

This complex houses an oceanographic museum and an aquarium. Although the museum contains an interesting collection of models, it is the newly designed aquarium, now one of the best in Europe, which is particularly impressive. A new tactile aquarium, in which visitors are actually able to touch harmless species of fish, two microworld aquariums, where cameras observe the underwater life of the very smallest fish, and, in particular, the **Oceanarium★**, an aquarium with a large 360° tunnel which is totally surrounded by water, are just some of the centre's new facilities which provide a valuable insight into the diversity of the world's oceans.

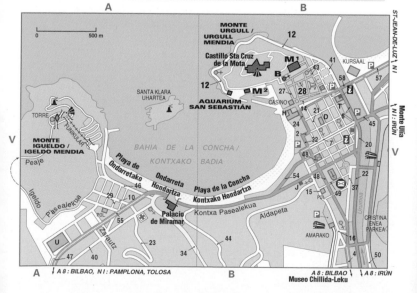

Museo Naval

🕐 *Open 10am-1.30pm and 4-7.30pm; Sun, 11am-2pm.* 🕐 *Closed Mon and public hols.* 🎟 *1.20€, no charge Thu.* ☎ *943 43 00 51.*

The ground floor of this plain 18C consular building, which now houses the city's naval museum, exhibits traditional construction tools and materials, while the first floor is dedicated to models and navigational instruments, all of which highlight the importance of the sea in Basque history.

Excursions

View from Monte Ulía★

7km/4mi E. ▶ *Follow the N 1 towards Irún and before reaching the summit and descending to Donostia-San Sebastián, take the first road on the right.*

While driving to the top via a series of hairpin bends there are good **views** of the town and its setting. A path at the top leads off to the right across a park to the Monte Ulía restaurant.

Museu Chillida-Leku

6km/4mi S. ▶ *Exit the N I, then take the GI 2132 from Rekalde towards Hernani and follow the signposts.* 🕐 *Open 10.30am-3pm; Holy Week-August to 7pm (to 3pm Sun and public hols).* 🕐 *Closed Tue, 1 Jan and 25 Dec. 7€.* ☎ *943 33 60 06.*

By creating this **museum**, Eduardo Chillida (b Donostia-San Sebastián, 1924-2002), one of the world's greatest contemporary sculptors, realised a dream: namely an open-air site in which he is able to exhibit his works and where visitors can slowly wander from one to the next. The 12ha/29-acre estate is the setting for 40 large sculptures and is a magnificent example of how art can be integrated into natural landscapes. The 16C Zabalaga country house has been carefully remodelled to exhibit Chillida's smaller sculptures and works on paper.

Monasterio de **El Escorial**★★★

MICHELIN MAPS 575 OR 576 K 17 – MADRID

The impressive monastery of San Lorenzo el Real, or El Escorial, stands at the foot of Monte Abantos on the southern slopes of the Sierra de Guadarrama at an altitude of 1 065m/3 494ft. This symbolic building, commissioned by King Philip II and designed by Juan de Herrera, heralded the creation of a style that combined the grandeur of a great palace with the austerity of a committed monastery.

Location

There is a good **view**★ of the monastery and the surrounding countryside from **Silla de Felipe II** (Philip II's Seat), from where the king oversaw its construction (▶ *turn left beyond the monastery into the road marked Entrada Herrería-Golf and follow signs to the Silla de Felipe II).* 🏛 *Grimaldi 2, 28200 San Lorenzo de El Escorial,* *91 090 53 13.*

😊 Fiestas 😊

The feast day of San Lorenzo (St Lawrence), the patron saint of the village and monastery, is celebrated on 10 August every year.

🚶 *Neighbouring sights are described in the following chapters: MADRID (49km/30mi SE), SEGOVIA (52km/32mi N), Sierra de GUADARRAMA (to the N) and Ávila (64km/40mi W).*

Background

In memory of San Lorenzo – On 10 August 1557, St Lawrence's Day, Philip II's forces defeated the French at the memorable battle of St-Quentin. In commemoration the king decided to build a monastery and dedicate it to the saint. It was consigned to the Hieronymites and served as the royal palace and pantheon.

The project was stupendous – there are nearly 1 200 doors and 2 600 windows; it required 1 500 workmen and was completed in a mere 21 years (1563-84) which is why the building has an exceptional unity of style.

The general designs of the first architect, Juan de Toledo, were followed, after his death in 1567 by his assistant **Juan de Herrera**, who, however, is responsible for the final overall elegance. Reaction to the sumptuous ornamentation fashionable in Charles V's reign spurred the architects to produce a sober monument with cleancut, majestic lines.

Monasterio de El Escorial

Special Features

Monastery 🕐 *allow half a day*
🕐 *Open 10am-5pm (6pm Apr-Sep); last admission 1hr before closing.* 🕐 *Closed Mon, 1 and 6 Jan, 1 May, 10 Aug,14 Sep, and 8, 24, 25 and 31 Dec.* ✆ *8€, no charge Wed for citizens of the European Union.* ☎ *91 890 78 18.*

It is said that the monastery recalls St Lawrence's martyrdom with its gridiron ground plan. It measures 206m x 161m (676ft x 528ft) and is built of grey granite – the austerity of the stone serving to emphasise, if anything, the severity of the architecture. When the king commanded an increase in height to accommodate a larger religious community, Herrera took the opportunity to position the rows of windows asymmetrically to lessen the monotony of horizontal lines which, otherwise, are only relieved by the pointed corner towers.

Palacios★★ (Royal Apartments)

While Philip II and the Spanish Habsburgs remained on the throne, El Escorial was a place of regal splendour: the king resided in apartments encircling the church apse, other royal apartments extended around the Patio de los Mascarones (Mask Courtyard). The Bourbons, who in fact preferred the palaces of La Granja, El Pardo and Aranjuez to El Escorial, when nevertheless in residence, occupied suites on the north side of the church. The palace took on renewed glory in the 18C in the reigns of Charles III and IV but lost its position as a centre of court life again later.

A staircase built in the time of Charles IV goes up *(3rd floor)* to the **Palacio de los Borbones** (Bourbon Apartments). These are sumptuous with Pompeian ceilings and fine **tapestries**★. The hangings include many made in the Real Fábrica (Royal Tapestry Works) in Madrid based on cartoons by Spanish artists, notably Goya, as in the series on popular subjects and pastimes. In later rooms are Flemish tapestries – a *Neptune* (from the Telemachus series) and several *(in the last room)* in realistic style by Teniers.

The style of decoration changes, introducing the austerity of the Habsburgs. The large **Sala de las Batallas** (Battle Gallery) contains frescoes (1587): on the south wall, of the Victory at Higueruela in the 15C against the Moors and on the north wall, the Victory at St-Quentin against the French.

The restraint of the **habitaciones de Felipe II** (Philip II's apartments) (2nd floor) is all the more striking after the luxury of the Bourbon rooms. Those of the Infanta Isabel Clara Eugenia, like those of her father, comprise a suite of relatively small rooms in which the principal decoration derives from dados of Talavera ceramic tiles. The king's bedroom, where he died in 1598, aged 71, is directly off the church. A communicating door allowed him to walk in at any time in the early years, and at the end, when he was dying of gangrene caused by advanced gout, to be present during services and contemplate the high altar from his bed. The paintings in the apartments include a *St Christopher* by Patinir and a portrait of the king in his old age by Pantoja de la Cruz. Facing the gardens and the plain, the Salón del Trono (Throne Room) is hung with 16C Brussels tapestries, the Sala de los Retratos (Portrait Gallery), which follows, with royal portraits. Finally, visitors are shown Philip's sedan chair in which he was carried when no longer able to walk.

Panteones★★ (Pantheons)

Access is through the Patio de los Evangelistas (Evangelists' Courtyard) in which the walls are painted with frescoes by Tibaldi (east wall) and his followers.

A marble and jasper staircase leads down to the **Panteón de los Reyes**★★★ (Royal Pantheon) which lies beneath the chancel. It contains the mortal remains of all the Spanish monarchs from the time of Emperor Charles V, with the exception of Philip V, Ferdinand VI and Amadeus of Savoy who are buried respectively in La Granja, Madrid and in Italy.

The chapel, which is octagonal in shape, was begun in 1617 in the reign of Philip III and completed in 1654. The main architect was Juan Bautista Crescenci. Facing the door is the jasper altar; on either side stand the 26 marble and bronze sarcophagi in wall niches. The kings are on the left and the queens whose sons succeeded to the throne, on the right. The sumptuous decoration is completed by an ornate chandelier, the work of an Italian artist.

The 19C **Panteón de los Infantes**★ (Infantes' Pantheon) includes not only royal children but also queens whose children did not succeed to the throne. The decoration includes delicately carved sculptures. Climatic conditions are such that the room has been well preserved.

Salas Capitulares★ (Chapter houses)

Two fine rooms, with ceilings painted by Italian artists with grotesques and frescoes, form a museum of Spanish (16C and 17C) and Italian (16C) religious painting.

The first room contains canvases by El Greco and Ribera, a *St Jerome* by Titian, and *Joseph's Tunic* painted by Velázquez in Rome.

The second room has works from the 16C Venetian School, including paintings by Tintoretto, Veronese and Titian *(Ecce Homo)*.

A room at the back contains works by Bosch and his followers: the *Haywain*, an example of his unbounded imagination, and the *Crown of Thorns (Los Improperios)*, of his satirical verve.

Basílica★★

Herrera based his final plan for the basilica on Italian drawings, introducing an architectural novelty, a **flat vault**, in the atrium. The church's interior owes much to St Peter's in Rome with a Greek cross plan, a 92m/302ft high cupola above the transept crossing supported by four colossal pillars, and barrel vaulting in the transept. The frescoes in the nave vaulting were painted by Luca Giordano in Charles II's reign. Wide, red marble steps lead to the sanctuary which has paintings on the vaulting of the lives of Christ and the Virgin by Cambiasso. The massive **retable**, designed by Herrera, is 30m/100ft tall and is composed of four registers of jasper, onyx and red marble columns between which stand 15 bronze sculptures by Leone and Pompeo Leoni. The tabernacle is also by Herrera. On either side of the chancel are the royal mausoleums with funerary figures at prayer by Pompeo Leoni. Charles V is shown with his Queen, Isabel of Portugal, their daughter María and her two sisters, while Philip II is portrayed in company with three of his wives, and his son, Don Carlos. The door at the end on the right is the one communicating with Philip II's room.

In the first chapel off the north aisle is the *Martyrdom of St Maurice* by Rómulo Cincinato, which Philip II preferred to that of El Greco (🕯 see below). In the adjoining chapel is a magnificent sculpture of Christ carved by Benvenuto Cellini in 1562.

Patio de los Reyes (Kings' Courtyard)

One of the three Classical gateways in the palace's principal façade opens onto this courtyard. The court is named after the statues of the kings of Judea which adorn the majestic west front of the church.

Biblioteca★★ (Library)

2nd floor. The gallery is 54m/177ft long and richly decorated; the shelving, designed by Herrera, is of exotic woods; the ceiling, sumptuously painted by Tibaldi, represents the liberal arts with Philosophy and Theology at each end. There are also magnificent portraits of Charles V, Philip II and Philip III by Pantoja de la Cruz, and one of Charles II by Carreño.

Philip II furnished the library with over 10 000 books of which many suffered in the 1671 fire and from the ravages of Napoleon's army. It is now a public library with over 40 000 books and some 2 700 manuscripts dating from the 5C to the 18C. The unusual presentation of the books on the shelves, with the spine facing inwards, is for preservation purposes.

In the cases, on the marble tables, are precious manuscripts including some in Arabic, autographs of St Teresa, the finely illuminated *Cantigas de Santa María*, a poem by King Alfonso the Wise, and an 11C Beatus.

Nuevos Museos★★ (New Museums)

The **Museo de Pintura** (Picture Museum) contains an interesting collection of works illustrating religious themes.

First room: canvases by Italian artists mainly from the 16C Venetian School (Titian, Veronese and Tintoretto). Second room: among others, two works by Van Dyck and a small painting by Rubens. Third room: works by Miguel de Coxcie, Philip II's Court Painter. Fourth room: Rogier Van der Weyden's outstanding *Calvary*, a sober and expressive painting, is flanked by an *Annunciation* by Veronese and a *Nativity* by Tintoretto. Fifth room: canvases by Ribera including *St Jerome Penitent*, the philosopher *Chrysippus* and *Aesop*, all with the artist's characteristic style of portraying especially vivid faces, together with two paintings by Zurbarán – *St Peter of Alcántara* and the *Presentation of the Virgin* – examples of his marvellous approach to light and subject matter. Last room: two paintings by Alonso Cano and various works by Luca Giordano.

The **Museo de Arquitectura** (Architectural Museum) in the vaulted basement outlines the construction of the monastery with biographies of the principal men involved, including craftsmen, as well as account books, Herrera's designs and so on.

On the ground floor, a continuation of the painting section, El Greco's *Martyrdom of St Maurice and the Theban Legionary*★ is given pride of place. The work, commissioned by Philip II but too original in composition, too acid in colouring to suit his taste, was rejected by the king. Nevertheless, this picture of the martyrdom of the legionary who refused to sacrifice to the gods, and of St Maurice trying to convince his companions that he should be executed in the other's place, is now considered one of El Greco's greater works.

Other Royal Buildings

Casita del Príncipe★ (Prince's or Lower Pavilion)

SE along the road to the station. ⏰*Visits by prior arrangement, 10am-1pm and 4-5.30pm (6.30pm Apr-Sep).* ⏰ *Closed Mon.* ⏳ *3.60€.* ☎ *91 890 59 02/3.*

Charles III commissioned Juan de Villanueva to build a leisure lodge for the future Charles IV in the Prince's Gardens, which stretch out below Philip II's apartments. Its exquisite decoration makes it a jewel of a palace, in miniature. There are painted **Pompeian**★ style ceilings by Maella and Vicente Gómez, silk hangings, canvases by Luca Giordano, chandeliers, porcelain and a beautiful mahogany and marble dining room.

Casita del Infante (Infante's or Upper Pavilion)

3km/2mi SW beyond the golf course. ⏰ *Only open during Holy Week (Tue-Sun) and Jull-Sep, 10am-6.45pm.* ⏰ *Closed Mon.* ⏳ *3.40€, no charge Wed for citizens of the European Union.* ☎ *91 890 59 03.*

Like the Prince's Pavilion, this lodge was designed by Villanueva. It was built for the Infante Gabriel, Charles IV's younger brother. The interior is furnished in the style of the period; the first floor was arranged as apartments for Prince Juan Carlos before his accession to the throne.

Excursions

Valle de los Caídos★★

16km/10mi NW on the M 600 and M 527. ⏰ *Open 10am-5pm; Apr-Sep, 10am-6.30pm; last admission 15min before closing.* ⏰ *Closed Mon, 1 and 6 Jan, 1 May, 17 Jul, 10 Aug and 24, 25 and 31 Dec.* ⏳ *5€ (9.50€ combined ticket with Palacio de El Escorial), no charge Wed for citizens of the European Union.* ☎ *91 890 56 11.*

The Valle de los Caídos, the Valley of the Fallen, built between 1940 and 1958, is a striking monument to the dead of the Spanish Civil War (1936-39). The road leads to the foot of the esplanade in front of the basilica, which is hollowed out of the rock face itself and is dominated by a monumental Cross.

Basílica★★

The basilica's west door in the austere granite façade is a bronze work crowned by a *Pietà* by Juan de Ávalos. At the entrance to the vast interior is a fine wrought-iron screen with 40 statues of Spanish saints and soldiers. The 262m/860ft nave (St Peter's, Rome: 186m/610ft; St Paul's, London: 152m/500ft) is lined with chapels between which have been hung eight copies of 16C Brussels tapestries of the Apocalypse. Above the entrances to the chapels are alabaster copies of the most famous statues of the Virgin Mary in Spain. A **cupola**★, 42m/138ft in diameter, above the crossing, shows in mosaic the heroes, martyrs and saints of Spain approaching both Christ in Majesty and the Virgin Mary. On the altar stands a painted wood figure of Christ Crucified, set against a tree trunk; it is the work of the sculptor Beovides. At the foot of the altar is the funerary stone of José Antonio Primo de Rivera, son of the dictator and founder of the Falangist Party, and that of Franco. Ossuaries contain coffins of 40 000 soldiers and civilians from both sides in the Civil War.

La Cruz★

The Cross by the architect Diego Méndez, is 125m/410ft high (150m/492ft including the base), the width from fingertip to fingertip, 46m/150ft. The immense statues of the Evangelists around the plinth and the four cardinal virtues above are by Juan de Ávalos. There is a good **view** from the base *(access by funicular)*. The large building showing Herreran influence on the far side of the valley from the basilica is a Benedictine monastery, seminary and social studies centre.

Estella/Lizarra★★

POPULATION: 13 569.

MICHELIN MAP 573 D 23 – NAVARRA

Estella (Lizarra in Basque) spreads over hilly ground on either side of the river Ega. The nobility of the brick and rough stone façades recalls the destiny intended for the city selected in the 12C by the kings of Navarra as their centre and in the 19C by the Carlists. The town is also an important staging post on the Way of St James.

Location

Estella is situated on the southern slopes of the Sierra de Andía and Sierra de Urbasa, along the N 111 linking Pamplona and Logroño (48km/30mi SW). ⓘ *San Nicolás 1, 31200 Estella,* ☎ *948 55 63 01.*

 Neighbouring sights are described in the following chapters: OLITE (44km/27mi SE), PAMPLONA (45km/28mil NE), The WAY OF ST JAMES and La RIOJA.

Walking About

Plaza de San Martín

The small square was originally at the heart of the freemen's parish, bustling with the comings and goings around its shops and inns; today nothing, apart from the splashing fountain, disturbs the peace. On one side stands the **former Ayuntamiento** (town hall) with an emblazoned front dating from the 16C.

Palacio de los Reyes de Navarra★ (Palace of the kings of Navarra)

The building is a rare example of 12C Romanesque civil architecture. Its long front is punctuated by arcades and twin bays with remarkable capitals.

Iglesia de San Pedro de la Rúa

 Guided tours (30min), 6.30-7pm; Sat 7.30-8pm (Jun-Oct 7.30-8pm); Sun and public hols, 11am-noon. ⓞ *Closed 1 and 6 Jan and 25 Dec.* ⓢ *2.20€.* ☎ *948 55 00 70.*

The church stands facing the royal palace on a cliff spur formerly crowned by the city castle. It retains outstanding 12C and 13C features.

There is an unusual **doorway**★ at the top of a steep flight of steps, in the north wall. The door's originality, with richly sculpted capitals and covings, lies in its equilateral scalloped arch, Caliphate influenced. Similar portals can be seen in Navarra at Puente la Reina and Cirauqui and in the Saintonge and Poitou regions of France. Inside are three Romanesque apses: note the transitional Romanesque Virgin and Child, a Gothic Christ and an unusual column of intertwined serpents in the central apse, and a Romanesque Crucified Christ in the apse on the left.

The Romanesque **cloisters** lost two galleries when the nearby castle was blown up in the 16C. The loss becomes all the more regrettable as one discovers the skill and invention of the masons who carved the remaining **capitals**★★; the north gallery series illustrates scenes from the lives of Christ and St Lawrence, St Andrew and St Peter, while plant and animal themes enliven the west gallery where the architect unexpectedly included a group of four slanting columns.

Calle de la Rúa

The pilgrim road. Note the **Palacio de Fray Diego de Estella**, at no7, a palace with an emblazoned Plateresque façade.

Estella La Bella

Such was the name pilgrims gave the town in the Middle Ages on their way to Santiago. As Estella was a major halt on the pilgrim road, it was endowed with several artistic buildings which date mainly from the Romanesque period. Moreover, in 1076, King Sancho Ramírez granted the town certain privileges which attracted tradesmen and innkeepers most of whom were freemen who settled on the right bank of the Ega. Pilgrims stopped to venerate Our Lady on the Hill whose shrine, now a modern church, stands on the site on which, according to tradition, on 25 May 1085, shepherds, guided by a shower of stars, found a statue of the Virgin. Of the town's many medieval hospices, the leper hospital of St Lazarus became the most famous.

Iglesia del Santo Sepulcro (Church of the Holy Sepulchre)

The church is remarkable for its portal which is purely Gothic. Superimposed above the door are the Last Supper, the three Marys at the Holy Sepulchre and Hell, and Calvary. The niches framing the doorway contain somewhat mannered figures of saints.

▶ *Take the Puente de la Cárcel (rebuilt in 1973) across the river.*

Iglesia de San Miguel

The church dominates a quarter that was inhabited by natives of Navarra at the end of the 12C and which still has a medieval atmosphere about its narrow streets. The north **portal**★ seems almost to have been designed as a challenge to the foreigners on the opposite bank of the river. On the tympanum is a figure of Christ surrounded by the Evangelists and other mysterious personages. Sculptures in the covings show censer-bearing angels, the Old Men of the Apocalypse, Prophets and Patriarchs, martyrs and saints, and scenes from the Gospels. The capitals illustrate the childhood of Christ and some hunting scenes. On the upper register of the walls are eight statue columns of the Apostles while on the lower register, two **high reliefs**★★, the most accomplished and expressive on the doorway show, on the left, St Michael slaying the dragon, and on the right, the three Marys coming from the Sepulchre. The noble bearing, the elegance of the draperies and the facial expressions, make the carving a masterpiece of Romanesque art.

Excursions

Monasterio de Irache★

3km/2mi SW. ◷ *Open 9.30am-1.30pm and 5-7pm; Sat-Sun and public hols, 8.30-1.30pm and 4-7pm.* ◷ *Closed Mon, Tue (afternoon) and in Dec.* ◐ *No charge.* ☎ *948 55 44 64.*

A Benedictine abbey was founded on the site as far back as the 10C. Later, Irache, a major halt on the Santiago pilgrim road, was a Cistercian community before becoming a university under the Benedictines, in the 16C, which was to close in 1833.

Iglesia★

This 12C-13C church's pure Romanesque style apse lies directly in line with the original intersecting ribs of the nave vaulting. During the Renaissance the dome on squinches was rebuilt and the *coro alto* added to the original structure. The main façade and most of the conventual buildings were rebuilt in the 17C.

Claustro

The Renaissance cloisters are decorated with brackets and capitals illustrating the lives of Christ and St Benedict.

TOUR THROUGH THE SIERRA DE ANDÍA AND SIERRA DE URBASA★

94km/58mi – about 3hr.

The pleasure of this tour lies in driving through beechwoods and, as you rise to the top of a pass, getting an extensive view over the countryside.

▶ *Leave Estella on NA 120 north towards the Puerto de Lizarraga (Lizarraga Pass).*

Monasterio de Iranzu

9km/6mi N of Estella. Signposted from NA 120. ◷ *Open May-Sep, 10am-2pm and 4-8pm; Oct-Apr, 10am-2pm and 4-6pm.* ◷ *Closed Mon, 20 Dec-10 Jan. 2.40€.* ☎ *948 52 00 47.*

The Cistercian monastery, built in lonely isolation in a wild **gorge**★ at the end of the 12C, is now a college. It is a good example of the Cistercian transitional style from Romanesque to Gothic in which robustness and elegance combine.

The cloister bays, where they have not been given a later florid Gothic fenestration, are typical, with Romanesque blind arcades, oculi and wide relieving arches. The church, with somewhat primitive vaulting, has a flat east end decorated with a triplet, or three windows, symbolising the Trinity, a feature found in many Cistercian churches.

Puerto de Lizarraga road★★

On emerging from the tunnel (alt 1 090m/3 576ft) pause briefly at the **viewpoint**★ overlooking the green Ergoyena Valley before beginning the descent through woods and pastures.

▶ *Continue to Etxarri-Aranatz where you take N 240 W to Olatzi and then turn left towards Estella.*

Puerto de Urbasa road★★

The fairly steep climb between great free-standing boulders and clumps of trees has a beautiful wildness in total contrast to the wide and lushly wooded valley which follows. Beyond the pass (alt 927m/3 041ft) tall limestone cliffs add character to the landscape before the road enters the series of gorges through which the sparkling river Urenderra flows.

Figueres★

POPULATION: 35 301.

MICHELIN MAP 574 F 38 – MAP 122 COSTA BRAVA –

SEE LOCAL MAP UNDER COSTA BRAVA – CATALUNYA (GIRONA)

Figueres, the capital of Alt Empordà, has developed into one of Catalunya's most important tourist destinations, due to its renown as the birthplace of **Salvador Dalí** (1904-89), the famous Surrealist artist. Dalí spent the last few years of his life in his home town, devoting his energies into building the extravagant museum dedicated to his work.

Location

Figueres is located 20km/12mi inland, in a fertile plain at the heart of the area known as the Ampurdán. It occupies a strategic position at the crossroads of routes leading to the Costa Brava and the French city of Perpignan, 58km/36mi N. 🄸 *Plaça del Sol, 17600 Figueres,* ☎ *972 50 31 55.*

⬧ *Neighbouring sights are described in the following chapters: GIRONA/GERONA (42km/26mi S), COSTA BRAVA and PIRINEOS CATALANES.*

Background

The end of the Spanish Civil War – On 1 February 1939 the last meeting of the Rebublican Cortes was held in the Castillo de Sant Ferrán. Three days later, Girona fell to the Nationalists, and two days after that the Republican leaders Azaña, Negrín and Companys crossed the French border on their journey into exile.

Address Book

For coin ranges, see the Legend at the back of the guide.

WHERE TO EAT

⊖⊖🍽 **Mas Pau** – *Avinyonet de Puigventós – 5km/3mi SW of Figueres on the N 260* – ☎ *972 54 61 54 – Closed evenings, Mon, Tue lunchtime (except in summer), and 7 Jan-15 Mar* – 🍽. A 16C farmstead sympathetically restored and decorated in exquisite taste with numerous antiques. A lovely locale in which to discover updated Catalan cuisine. Cosy terraces by the garden, and superb rooms are also available.

WHERE TO STAY

⊖⊖ **Hotel Duràn** – *Lasauca 5 –* ☎ *972 50 12 50 –* 🍽 *– 65 rooms –* ⌑ *6.60€ – Restaurant 28/37.35€.* This well-maintained hotel is located in the centre of the city, near the Dalí Museum. Cosy and comfortable, withe some spacious rooms, and adorned with numerous mirrors, rugs and paintings. The restaurant, decorated in similar style, specialises in Catalan dishes.

⊖⊖🍽 **Hotel Mas Falgarona** – *Avinyonet de Puigventós – 44.5km/3.5mi SW of Figueres on the N 260 –* ☎ *972 54 66 28 – Closed Jan –* 🄿 *– 8 rooms –* ⌑ *– Restaurant 43€.* This luxury hotel is housed in an old farmhouse. The minimalist decor, enhanced by various works of modern art, brings out the natural beauty of the stone, brick and wood. Delightful garden.

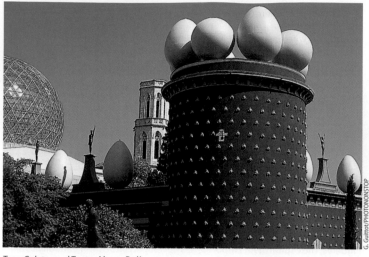

Torre Galatea and Teatre-Museu Dalí

A great inventor – **Narcís Monturiol**, the politician and inventor born in Figueres in 1819, has gone down in history as the man who, in 1859, developed the world's first submarine, the *Ictíneo* (see *Museo Naval; BARCELONA*), a steam-powered vessel capable of producing the oxygen necessary to enable occupants to breathe inside it.

Special Features

THE DALIAN WORLD

Salvador Dalí and Surrealism – Born into a well-to-do family in Figueres in 1904, Dalí was to become one of the world's most famous Surrealist aritists. His "paranoid-critical" method, based on an ironic vision of reality, resulted in his expulsion from the Surrealist ranks by its founder, André Breton. In his most famous paintings, *The Great Masturbator, The Persistence of Memory, Atomic Leda and Premonition of the Civil War*, Dalí expresses his personal world through bland forms loaded with sensuality in which sexual connotations, infantile traumas and the devotion for his wife Gala take on singular importance.

The two main Dalian attractions in Figueres are both located around the plaza de Dalí i Gala, a lively square with numerous souvenir shops and cafés.

Teatre-Museu Dalí★★

🕐 *Open 2 Jan- Jun and Oct-Dec, 10.30am-5.45pm; Jul-Sep, 9am-7.45pm; last admission 45min before closing.* 🕐 *Closed 1 Jan and 25 Dec.* 🖾 *9€.* ☎ *972 67 75 00.*

The Dalí theatre-museum, a world of folly and caprice which may charm or exasperate but never fails to impress, is a good reflection of the artist himself who said this of his creation: "The museum cannot be considered as such; it is a gigantic surrealist object, where everything is coherent, where nothing has eluded my design." It is housed in the former local theatre (1850) which was burnt down during the Civil War and restored in 1966. Dalí added an immense glass dome (beneath which he is now buried) and a vast patio, and decorated everything with fantasy objects: giant eggs, bread rolls – which cover the façade like the shells all over the Casa de las Conchas in Salamanca – basins and gilt dummies. He gave his eccentricity full rein in the squares around the museum where there are figures perched on columns of tyres, as well as inside – for instance in the Mae

> **Dalí in the Area Around Figures**
>
> Further examples of Dalí's creativity can be seen in two museums within a short distance of Figueres: the first, the **Casa-Museo Salvador Dalía**, is situated in the charming fishing village of **Cadaqués**★★ (see *COSTA BRAVA*), 31km/19mi E of Figueres on the C 260 and GI 614; the second, the **Casa-Museo Castell Gala Dalía** (see *GIRONA/GERONA*), in Púbol, 16km/10mi E of Girona on the C 66, is housed in the castle that Dalí gave to his wife, Gala, as a gift in 1970.

West sitting room where there is a lip-shaped sofa, a nose-chimney and eye-frames. Some of his canvases are exhibited in the museum (including a series showing him painting his wife Gala) as well as works by other artists such as Pitxot, Duchamp and Fortuny.

Torre Galatea★

The decoration of this tower was the work of Dalí, who introduced ornamental motifs of his choice (vivid colours and fantastic objects).

Worth a Visit

OLD TOWN

Figueres also has a pleasant historical centre with attractive small squares and narrow streets. The importance of the town at the beginning of the 20C is demonstrated by the town's own Rambla, a pleasant street full of outdoor bars and restaurants that runs through the old quarter.

Museu de Joguets★

🕐 Open 10am-1pm and 4-7pm; Sun and public hols 11am-1.30pm and 5-7.30pm; Sun and public hols, 11am-1.30pm and 5-7.30pm. 🕐 Closed Sun afternoon and Mon Oct-Jun (except public hols), 1 Jan and 25 Dec. 🖾 5€. ☎ 972 50 45 85.

The museum displays toys from many different countries and periods. Note the interesting collections of automata, puppets and teddy bears.

Museu de l'Empordà

🕐 Open 11am-7pm (8pm Sep-Dec); Sun and public hols, 11am-2pm. 🕐 Closed Mon, 1 Jan and 25-26 Dec. 🖾 3€. ☎ 972 50 23 05.

This building houses various collections devoted to the art, history and archaeology of the region. Of particular note is the exhibition of works by 19C and 20C painters (Nonell, Sorolla, Dalí and Tàpies).

Iglesia de Sant Pere

🕐 Open 9am-1pm and 4.30-8pm (9pm Sat); Sun 8.30am-1pm and 6-9pm. ☎ 972 50 03 25.

Built in the late 14C, this church has a single nave that reflects the influence of Gothic art in Catalan architecture. The apse, the transept and the belfry are all modern as the church was almost totally destroyed during the Spanish Civil War.

Excursions

Castillo de San Ferran★

🐾 Guided tours (2hr), 10.30am-2pm and 4-6pm; 1 Jul-16 Sep and Holy Week, 10.30am-8pm. 🕐 Closed 1 Jan, 30 May and 25 Dec. 🖾3€. ☎ 972 50 60 94.

This impressive fortress was built in the mid-18C to defend the border with France. The most advanced techniques of military architecture were used in its construction, including a large Vauban-style star-shaped perimeter ground plan. At the time, the castle was the second largest of its kind in Europe, with a parade ground alone that covered 12 000m2/14 340sq yd. The castle's **stables**★ are worthy of particular note. The delightful **views**★ from the walls encompass the expansive Empordà plain.

Gibraltar★

POPULATION: 28 339.

MICHELIN MAPS 578 X 13. BRITISH CROWN COLONY

One of the last remaining outposts of the British Empire and a self-governing Crown Colony, the towering bulk of Gibraltar is an impressive and distinctive sight, clearly visible from the foothills of neighbouring Andalucía some miles off. For many visitors, the first contact with Gibraltar is likely to be the incredible landing strip, which the main road into town actually crosses, physically linking the territory with mainland Spain.

Location

Gibraltar lies at the southwest tip of Spain and the northeast of the Straits of Gibraltar, only 24km/15mi away from the north African coast. *Algeciras: Juan de la Cierva, 11207 Cádiz, ☎ 956 57 26 36; Gibraltar: 158 Main Street, ☎ 9567 749 50/82; www.gibraltar.gi.*

🍂 *Neighbouring sights are described in the following chapters: COSTA DE LA LUZ, COSTA DEL SOL and MÁLAGA.*

Background

Historical notes – Archaeological discoveries on Gibraltar, for example in Gorham's Cave (⚷ *not open to the public*) on the east face of the Rock, testify to 100 000 years of human occupation, with periods of use by the Carthaginians, Phoenicians and even Neanderthal Man.

The Rock of Gibraltar, considered by the Ancient Greeks to be one of the **Pillars of Hercules** marking the western boundary of the Classical world, was transformed into an Islamic citadel after the Moors invaded it under **Tarik-ibn-Zeyad** in AD 711. The Moorish general named the rock Jebel Tarik (Tarik's Mountain), from which Gibraltar takes its name, and built a castle on it, now in ruins but still known as the Moorish Castle.

Geographical Features

The **Rock of Gibraltar**★ is a gigantic monolith of Jurassic limestone which forms a craggy promontory connected with mainland Spain to the north and stretching south into the Straits. It covers an area of about 6.5km2/2.5sq mi (4.5km/3mi long and 1.4km/0.9mi at its widest), rising to 423m/1 388ft at its highest point, Mount Misery. The east face of the Rock drops sheer into the sea, while the less steep west face has been partially reclaimed at the water's edge and forms the site of the town.

Gibraltar was recaptured by Spain on 20 August 1462, the feast of St Bernard, who was duly elected patron saint of the town. It was not until Columbus made his great voyage of discovery in 1492, heading west through the legendary Pillars, that Gibraltar ceased to be regarded as marker of the edge of the world. During the War of Spanish Succession, Anglo-Dutch naval forces, under **Admiral Rooke**, captured the Rock in 1704. Gibraltar was officially ceded to Britain in the Treaty of Utrecht in 1713. The citadel guarding the Straits of Gibraltar has remained in British hands ever since, despite a number of attempts by the Spanish and the French to seize it. The most notable of these was the **Great Siege of 1779-83**, during which the garrison under General Elliot heroically resisted all efforts by the Spanish and French to starve or bomb them into submission. Most of the old city of Gibraltar was destroyed during this epic struggle, but the Rock lived up to its reputation of being impregnable. Gibraltar became a British Crown Colony in 1830 and served as a naval base during both World Wars in the following century.

In 1967, Gibraltar's inhabitants voted resoundingly in favour of retaining their connection with Britain – by 12 138 votes to 44 – in a referendum proposing Spanish sovereignty. In 1969, Spain closed the border, cutting telephone lines and postal communications, a blockade it maintained until 1985. Gibraltar became a member of the European Economic Community in 1973 along with Britain.

Neanderthal Man or Gibraltar Woman?

Eight years before the discovery in 1856 of a 60 000-year-old skeleton in the Neander Valley, east of Düsseldorf, Germany, a skull of the same age, thought to be that of a woman, was discovered on Gibraltar. However, delays in publicising the Gibraltar findings meant that Gibraltar Woman is known as Neanderthal Man.

Practical Information

Customs and other formalities – Gibraltar is a British Crown Colony. The border is open 24hr a day and there are no restrictions on the number of crossings made. Visitors must be in possession of a valid passport. Holders of UK passports and citizens of other EU countries do not need a visa. Other nationalities should check visa requirements with the appropriate authorities (British consulate, high commission, or embassy). Gibraltar is a VAT-free shopping area.

Travel and accommodation – There are daily scheduled flights from London Heathrow, Gatwick and Luton and a daily ferry service between Gibraltar and Morocco. Regular flights also operate to and from North Africa. Hotel and bed and breakfast accommodation is available, but there are no campsites.

Money matters – The official currency is Gibraltar Government notes and coinage. The euro is accepted in most establishments. The territory offers a full range of UK and international banks, and credit cards and traveller's cheques are widely accepted.

Language – The official language spoken on the Rock is English, but most people speak Spanish as a second language.

Time – Gibraltar has the same time as in the rest of Europe (one hour ahead of GMT).

Motoring – Driving is on the right and the wearing of seatbelts is recommended but not compulsory. Drivers must have a current driver's licence, vehicle registration documents, evidence of insurance and nationality plates.

Telephoning – The international telephone code for Gibraltar is 350 (to call Gibraltar from Spain, however, dial 9567 before the five-digit local number).

Tourist information – Further tourist information is available from the Gibraltar Government Office, Arundel Great Court, 179 Strand, London WC2R 1EH; ☎ (020) 7836 0777; fax (020) 7240 6612; Gibraltar Information Bureau 1155 15th St NW, Washington, DC 20005 ☎202-452-1108;
Website – www.gibraltar.gi

Despite the reopening of the border, it is not unusual for Spanish customs officials to undertake thorough searches of vehicles which can cause lengthy delays. Most of the inhabitants of Gibraltar are united in their opposition to Spanish rule and they continue with their aspirations for self-determination with an overwhelming desire to become a British Crown dependency. With its people descended from a variety of races, religions and cultures, their identity shaped by years of resisting sieges, modern Gibraltar is an excellent example of a thriving, harmonious, multicultural society. Gibraltar's economy is based on a growing financial services sector and tourism, although the boom in these areas in the 1980s was slowed once recession hit Europe. The territory has retained its status as a free port and trade is based on transit and refuelling activities.

The naval and commercial ports, as well as the town with its mixture of English- and Spanish-style houses, pubs and shops, lie at the foot of the west face of the Rock. Numerous examples of Moorish architecture are still to be found, notably in the cathedral which has the ground plan of a mosque.

Worth a Visit

Tour of the Rock★

The top of the Rock can be reached on foot, by cable car and in official tour vehicles (🚫 *private cars are not allowed on the Upper Rock*). Go down Queensway and follow the signs to Upper Rock, designated a **nature reserve** and home to some remarkable flora and fauna and a number of Gibraltar's most interesting historical sites. The road leads first to **St Michael's Cave**, a natural cavern once inhabited by Neolithic man which features some spectacular stalactites and stalagmites. From here, it is possible to walk to the top of the Rock (🕐 *1hr there and back),* from where there are excellent viewsaa of both sides of the rock and of the Spanish and north African coasts.

Barbary Apes

The origin of the apes, one of Gibraltar's best-known attractions, is unknown. Legend has it that British rule will last as long as the apes remain in residence on the Rock. When it looked as if they might become extinct in 1944, Churchill sent a signal ordering reinforcements. The ape colony has since flourished – there are currently just under 200 of them. They are renowned for their charm and highly inquisitive natures. The apes, in reality tailless monkeys, are the protégés of the Gibraltar Regiment.

The road continues to the **Apes' Den**, home of the famous Barbary Apes.

Visitors interested in military history should not miss the **Great Siege Tunnels**, excavated in 1779 to make it possible to mount guns on the north face of the Rock, creating a defence system still impressive for its ingenuity. A military heritage centre is housed in Princess Caroline's Battery. Finally there are the ancient ruins of the **Moorish Castle** and the northern defences dominating the hillside.

Back down in town, the **Gibraltar Museum** contains extensive collections on local military and natural history. It also houses the well-preserved **Moorish Baths**. (🕐 *Open 10am-2pm and 4-7pm; Sat-Sun 10am-2.30pm.* 🞰 *No charge.* ☎ *956 36 07 15.)* The recently restored **Alameda Gardens** are home to many interesting and exotic plants, including Canary Islands dragon trees, cacti, succulents and a variety of Mediterranean vegetation. Gibraltar is home to some 600 species of flowering plant, which flourish in the subtropical climate, including a few unique to the Rock, such as its national flower, the Gibraltar Candytuft.

For those interested in seeing more examples of Gibraltar's plant- and bird-life, the **Mediterranean Steps**, leading from Jew's Gate (good view of the other Pillar of Hercules, Jebel Musa in Morocco) round the south of the Rock and up the east face of the Rock to the summit (🕐 *3hr walk from Jew's Gate to summit; wear good boots as some sections are quite steep)*, make a fascinating walk.

Straits of **Gibraltar** ★

MICHELIN MAP 578 X 13 –

ANDALUCÍA (CÁDIZ); GIBRALTAR: BRITISH CROWN COLONY

The Straits, the gateway to the Mediterranean and a mere 14km/9mi wide at the narrowest point, have always played an important strategic role in the history of this region. To the east, stands the natural port of the Bay of Algeciras, surrounded by the Spanish towns of Algeciras and La Línea de la Concepción, and the British outpost of Gibraltar.

Location

The Punta de Tarifa, at a latitude of 36º, occupies the southernmost tip of the Iberian Peninsula and is the closest point in Europe to the African continent. 🛈 *Algeciras: Juan de la Cierva, 11207 Cádiz,* ☎ *956 57 26 36; Gibraltar: 158 Main Street,* ☎ *9567 749 50/82.*

🔎 *Neighbouring sights are described in the following chapters: COSTA DE LA LUZ, COSTA DEL SOL and MÁLAGA.*

Tours

The 21km/13mi of road separating Tarifa from Algeciras provides some stunning **views**★★★ of the African coast. The best viewpoint is at the Mirador del Estrecho, 8km/5mi from Tarifa.

Tarifa (🔎 *see COSTA DE LA LUZ)*

Algeciras

Population 101 972. The Arabs arrived in Algeciras from Africa in 711 and remained until 1344, naming the town Al Djezirah (the island), after the Isla Verde, the Green Island, now joined to the mainland. The Bahía de Algeciras has always served the dual purpose of safe anchorage and vantage point overlooking the Straits of Gibraltar. Algeciras is Spain's busiest passenger port with crossings to Tangier and Ceuta several times a day (3.5 million passengers annually). The main sights of interest in the town are the the plaza Alta, the hub of the town, fronted by two churches: the 18C **Iglesia de Nuestra Señora de la Palma**, and the Baroque-style Iglesia de Nuestra Señora de la Aurora, and the **Museo Municipal**, displaying interesting exhibits on the **Siege of Algeciras** (1342-44). (🕐 *Open 10am-2pm and 5-8pm; 21 Jun-30 Sep, 10am-2pm.* 🕐*Closed Sat (21 Jun-30 Sep), Sun and public hols.* 🞰 *No charge.* ☎*956 57 06 72).*

Girona/Gerona★★

POPULATION: 70 409.

MICHELIN MAP 574 G 38 (TOWN PLAN) – MAP 122 COSTA BRAVA – CATALUNYA (GIRONA)

Girona stands on a promontory at the confluence of the Ter and Onyar rivers. Its strategic site has been so coveted and its history so eventful that it has become known as the city of a thousand sieges. Its ramparts were built and rebuilt by the Iberians, by the Romans and throughout the Middle Ages. Charlemagne's troops are described, in the *Song of Roland (Canción de Rolando)*, as assaulting the city; in 1809, under General Álvarez de Castro's command, Girona resisted attacks from Napoleon's troops for more than seven months.

Location

Because of its position on Roman and medieval roads connecting southern France with the Iberian Peninsula, Girona has always been an important crossroads. Nowadays, it stands on the N II and AP 7, which connect Barcelona (97km/60mi SW) with Figueres (42km/26mi N). In addition, the C 150 links Girona with Banyoles (19km/12mi NW), while the C 25 heads west to Vic (79km/49mi). Visitors heading to the coast can choose between the C 255 to Palafrugell (39km/24mi SW) or the C 250 to Sant Feliu de Guíxols (36km/22mi SW). 🏛 *Rambla de la Llibertat 1, 17004 Girona,* ☎ *972 22 65 75.*

ఉ *Neighbouring sights are described in the following chapters: FIGUERES, COSTA BRAVA and PIRINEOS CATALANES.*

Girona and Judaism

Girona's Jewish community, which settled on both sides of **calle de la Força** in the city's old quarter, was the second largest in Catalunya after Barcelona, and became famous in the Middle Ages for its prestigious Kabbalistic School, which existed for over 600 years from the 9C until the expulsions of 1492. This past can be felt in atmospheric narrow alleyways such as calle Cúndaro and calle Sant Llorenç, the latter home to the **Centro Bonastruc ça Porta**, dedicated to the town's Jewish history.

Address Book

For coin ranges, see the Legend at the back of the guide.

WHERE TO EAT

⊜⊜⊜ **El Celler de Can Roca** – *Carretera de Taialà 40 –* ☎ *972 22 21 57 – Closed Sun, Mon, 24 Dec-20 Jan and 1-15 Jul –* ▤. With its bold combinations, the creative cuisine here is a feast for the senses. Extensive wine list.

TAPAS

Boira – *Plaça de la Independencia 17 –* ☎ *972 20 30 96 –* ▤. This modern bar under the arcades of the square is the current in-place for Girona's young crowd. Good tapas and a great view of the colourful reflections in the river from the first floor.

WHERE TO STAY

⊜ **Hotel Condal** – *Joan Maragall 10 –* ☎ *972 20 44 62 – 38 rooms.* Recommended for its excellent location in a busy shopping street in the city centre more than anything else. Having said this, the Condal occupies a bourgeois mansion with rooms that are simple, yet clean and bright. Note that most bathrooms have shower only.

⊜⊜ **Hotel Ultonia** – *Gran Via de Jaume I 22 –* ☎ *972 20 38 50 –* ▤ *– 45 rooms –* ⌑. A hotel in classic style on one of the main streets. Public areas are rather reduced, but this is balanced by large, functionally comfortable rooms.

BARS AND CAFÉS

Cu-Cut – *Plaça de la Independència 10 –* ☎ *972 20 83 01.* An attractive, welcoming bar which often hosts concerts and poetry readings.

La Terra – *Ballesteries, 23 –* ☎ *972 21 92 54.* A pleasant bar overlooking the Onyar River.

GIRONA/ GERONA

Álvarez de Castro	AZ	2
Argenteria	BY	3
Ballesteríes	BY	4
Bellaire	BY	6
Berenguer Carnicer	AY	7
Bonastruc de Porta	AY	9
Carme	BZ	10
Ciutadans	BZ	12
Cúndaro	BY	13
Devesa Pas. de la	AY	14
Eduard Marquína Pl. de	AZ	15

General Fournàs	BY	16
General Peralta Pas. del	BZ	17
Joaquim Vayreda	AY	18
Juli Garreta	AZ	19
Llibertat Rambla de la	BZ	23
Nou	AZ	
Nou del Teatre	BZ	27
Oliva i Prat	BY	26
Palafrugell	BZ	28
Pedreres Pujada de les	BZ	29
Ramon Folch Av. d'en	AY	31
Rei Ferran el Católic	BY	33
Rei Martí Pujada del	BY	34

Reina Isabel la Católica	BZ	36
Reina Joana Pas. de la	BY	37
Sant Cristòfol	BY	39
Sant Daniel	BY	40
Sant Domènec Pl. de	BY	42
Sant Feliu Pujada de	BY	44
Sant Francesc Av. de	AZ	45
Sant Pere Pl. de	BY	48
Santa Clara	ABYZ	
Santa Eugénia	AZ	49
Ultònia	AZ	53

Banys Àrabs	BY	S
Centre Bonastruc ça Porta	BY	A
Colegiata de Sant Feliu	BY	R
Convento de Sant Domènec	BY	F
Edifici de Les Àligues	BY	U
Farinera Teixidor	AZ	K

Fontana d'Or	BY	E
Hospici	AZ	L
Museu d'Art	BY	M[1]
Museu del Cinema	AZ	M[2]
Pia Almoina	BY	N

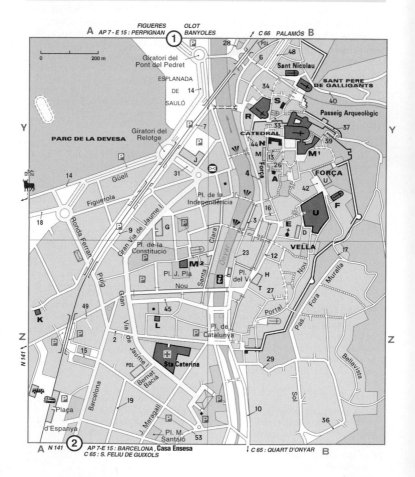

Special Features

FORÇA VELLA (OLD TOWN) ⏱ *Allow 3hr*

From footbridges over the Onyar, there are views of the picturesque orange and ochre-coloured buildings along the river banks, the cathedral tower and the spire of Sant Feliu.

Narrow alleys lead up to the cathedral which is preceded by a vast flight of 90 steps, known as the **Escaleras de la Pera**. The 14C **Pia Almoina** building on the right is an elegant example of Gothic architecture.

Catedral★

⏱ *Open 8am-2pm and 4-6pm (7pm Mar-Jun); Jul-Sep, 10am-8pm; Sun and public hols, 10am-2pm.* ⏱ *Closed Mon.* ⊛ *3€ (treasury).* ☎ *972 21 44 26.*

The Baroque façade has been designed like a stone altarpiece with a single huge oculus above. The rest of the building is Gothic: the chancel (1312) is surrounded by an ambulatory and radiating chapels; early in the 15C the decision was taken to add only a single **aisle**★★ but to make it outstandingly spacious (it is the largest Gothic nave in the world) and light. The two parts of the building have a similar, powerful, unadorned style, decoration having been restricted to the chapel arches, triforium niches and windows.

In the chancel, beneath a silver canopy symbolising the sky, is a silver-gilt embossed 14C **altarpiece**★, highlighted with enamelwork, which traces the Life of Christ. Among the chapels, many of which contain works of art, that of Sant Honorat (first north chapel), is outstanding for the tomb, in a Gothic niche, with three superimposed registers, of Bishop Bernard de Pau (d 1457).

Tesoro★★

⏱ *Same hours as Cathedral.* ⊛ *3€.* ☎ *972 21 44 26.*

The treasury houses an extraordinarily rich collection of religious art, including one of the most beautiful copies of the **Beatus**★★, *St John's Commentary on the Apocalypse*, written in the 8C. These miniatures, dated 975, by the monk Emeteri and the nun Eude, are notable for the bright colours and lively expressions used to illustrate the series of fantastic beasts. They are Caliphate influenced and show traces of Visigothic decoration. There is a 12C *Virgin of the Cathedral* (Virgen de la Seu) in the same room. Some splendid church plate is displayed in the rooms that follow, including a 14C enamel cross and, of particular interest, the 10C embossed silver **Hixem Casket**, a fine example of Caliphate art.

The end room contains the famous **Tapiz de la Creación**★★★ (Tapestry of the Creation), a unique work dating from about 1100. It is a marvellously delicate embroidery with well preserved colours which shows Christ in Majesty in a circular area at the centre, surrounded by the different stages of creation. The four winds fill the corners.

Claustro★

The 12C-13C Romanesque cloisters, irregular in shape, with a double line of columns, date – like the 11C Torre de Carlomagno (Charlemagne Tower) which dominates them – from the former Romanesque cathedral. The beautiful friezes on the pillars at the gallery corners and centres, illustrate, in most cases, scenes from Genesis. Note the finely drawn outlines, the delicate draperies and the serenity of the faces.

Houses overlooking the Onyar river

277

Museu d'Art de Girona★★

🕐 *Open 10am-6pm (7pm Mar-Sep); Wed, Sun and public hols, 10am-2pm.* 🕐 *Closed Mon, 1 and 6 Jan, Easter Sun and 25-26 Dec.* 📷 *2€.* ☎ *972 20 38 34.*

The museum is housed in the Palacio Episcopal and contains a comprehensive collection of art covering periods from the Romanesque to the 20C. The Romanesque section includes a 10C-11C altar from Sant Pere de Rodes of wood and stone faced with silver, and a 12C-13C **beam from Cruïlles**★. The Gothic section has a lovely alabaster Virgin of Besalù dating from the 15C. Among the richly decorated altarpieces displayed in the Throne Room is that of **Sant Miquel de Cruïlles**★★ by Luis Borrassá (15C), one of the most beautiful works of Catalan Gothic art. Note the splendid **Púbol altarpiece**★, executed in the Gothic style by Bernat Martorell in 1437. The **Sant Feliu altarpiece** by Juan de Borgoña marks the transition between the Gothic and Renaissance styles.

Colegiata de Sant Feliu★

This former collegiate church outside the town walls must originally have been a martyry built over the tombs of St Narcissus, Bishop of Girona, and St Felix, both patrons of the city.

A Gothic church with a tall east end was later built on the Romanesque foundations. In the apse are eight **early Christian sarcophagi**★ let into the walls. Two have outstanding carvings – on the right, the abduction of Proserpine, opposite, a spirited **lion hunt**★.

Baños Árabes★ (Arab Baths)

🕐 *Open 10am-2pm; Apr-Sep, 10am-7pm; Sun and public hols, 10am-2pm.* 🕐 *Closed Mon (Oct-Mar), 1 and 6 Jan, Easter Sun and 25-26 Dec.* 📷*1.50€.* ☎ *972 21 32 62.*

These late-12C baths were built in accordance with Muslim tradition. They consist of a central corridor giving onto four rooms: the **apoditerium**, a relaxation area with a central pool surrounded by columns supporting a lantern; the **frigidarium**, designed for cold baths; the **tepidarium**, a warm room where bathers could stay away from the intense heat or cold; finally, the **caldarium**, an area for hot baths.

Passeig Arqueològic (Archaeological Promenade)

Steps opposite the baths lead to gardens at the foot of the ramparts from which you can look along the Ter Valley.

Monasterio de Sant Pere de Galligants★

Not far from Sant Nicolau, with its clover leaf apse, stands the Romanesque church of Sant Pere. It has been repeatedly fortified; its east end appears embedded in the town walls and the belfry once served as a watchtower.

The church and cloisters house the **Museu Arqueològic de Girona** which has a collection of finds from excavations in the province. Hebrew memorial plaques from the 13C-14C are displayed in the cloisters while in the former sacristy there is Roman art from Empúries and the magnificent 4C **tomb of Las Estaciones**★ (the seasons; autumn in particular). (🕐 *Open 10am-2pm and 4-7pm; Jun-Sep, 10.30am-1.30pm and 4-7pm; Sun and public hols, 10am-2pm all year.* 🕐 *Closed Mon, 1 Jan, Easter Sun and 25-26 Dec.* 📷 *1.80€, no charge Sun.* ☎ *972 20 46 37).*

Museu del Cinema

🕐 *Open Oct-Apr, 10am-6pm; May-Sep, 10am-8pm; Sat 10am-8pm; Sun and public hols 11am-3pm.* 🕐 *Closed Mon, 1 Jan, 25-26 Dec.* 📷 *3€.* ☎ *972 41 27 77.*

Tomás Mallol's collection forms the nucleus of this original museum dedicated to the history of cinema. Visitors are taken on a journey to the world of illusion where they are able to admire the very first moving silhouettes, delicate light boxes, and the inventions which have led to the extraordinary developments in the film industry.

Parc de la Devesa★

This park contains the largest grove of plane trees in Catalunya.

Excursions

Casa-Museu Castell Gala Dalí★

In Púbol. ▶ *16km/10mi E along the C 66 towards La Bisbal d'Empordà. At a signposted intersection, turn right to Púbol.* 🕐 *Open 13 Mar-14 Jun and 16 Sep-Jan, 10.30am-6pm (closed Mon); 15 Jun-15 Sep 10.30am-8pm daily; 15 Mar-1 Nov by prior arrangement; last admission 45min before closing.* 🕐 *Closed 2 Nov-12 Mar.* 📷 *5.50€.* ☎ *972 48 86 55.*

Fortified bridge, Besalú

In 1970, Salvador Dalí bought the 14C castle that had once belonged to the barons of Púbol and gave it to his wife Gala as a present. The visit is full of surprises where you will discover a host of unusual objects in a Surrealist atmosphere. In the Heraldic Gallery on the first floor, note the huge fresco adorning the ceiling, painted by Dalí himself. Gala's bedroom *(Room 3)* features a strange chess game, in which the pawns are replicas of human fingers. On the second floor *(Room 7)* you can admire some of the clothes specially made for Dalí's favourite muse, along with designs by famous names from the fashion world: Chanel, Pierre Cardin, Christian Dior and even Dalí. Shrouded in a solemn atmosphere, the basement *(Room 11)* houses the mortal remains of Gala, together with various sculptures and a stuffed giraffe.

FROM GIRONA TO SANTA PAU

88km/55mi – ◷allow one day. ▶ *Head N from Girona along the C 66.*

Banyoles★

19km/12mi. This delightful town stands beside a **lake**★ carrying the same name, used as an important venue for nautical events. Among its many archaeological exhibits, the **Museu Arqueològic Comarcal**★, set up in a Gothic building, displays the famous Jaw of Banyoles, dating back to the Lower Palaeolithic era. *(◷ Open 10.30am-1.30pm and 4-6.30pm; Jul-Aug, 11am-1.30pm and 4-7.30pm; Sun and public hols all year, 10.30am-2pm. ◷ Closed Mon, 1 and 6 Jan and 24 and 31 Dec. ✆1.80€. ☎ 972 57 23 61).*

The neo-Classical Monasterio de Sant Esteve has preserved a Gothic portal and an altarpeice, also Gothic, from the Mare de Déu in L'Escala. A lively, popular market is held every Wednesday on the town's 13C arcaded main square.

A road 8km/5mi long circles the lake and, on the left bank, passes in front of the 13C **Iglesia de Santa Maria de Porqueres**★. The interior consists of a single nave separated from the apse by a huge central arch: the capitals and tops of the columns are carved with curious-looking characters. ◷ *Open 10am-8pm.* ☎ *972 57 32 17.*

▶ *Leave Banyoles heading towards the C 66 and continue for 13km/8mi to Besalú.*

Besalú★★

From the 11C to the 12C, Besalú was the capital of a county that stretched from Figueres to the Ter Valley. At the town entrance, spanning the Fluvià river, is an old Roman **fortified bridge**★, rebuilt during the medieval period. Of its past, Besalú has retained the **ancient city**★★ of Romanesque origin, with vestiges of ramparts and many medieval buildings with pretty paired windows. The Romanesque **Iglesia de Sant Pere**★ presents a fine window flanked by lions and an ambulatory – an unusual feature for the area. *(◷ Guided tour by prior arrangement ✆2.10€ (includes iglesia de Sant Vicenç). ☎ 972 59 12 40 (Tourism Office)).*

Traditional ritual baths, referred to as **Mikwa** (12C)can be found in the old Jewish quarter, cut across by narrow, winding streets. (👁️‍🗨️ *Guided tour by prior arrangement* 💶*1.05€.* ☎ *972 59 12 40 (Tourism Office).*
Other buildings of interest include the 12C-13C Iglesia de Sant Vicenç and the Casa Llaudes, with its attractive Romanesque patio.

▶ *Head 14km/9mi W along the N 260.*

Castellfollit de la Roca★

The village is perched on a basalt pile 60m/197ft high, in the midst of a spectacular volcanic setting that is part of the **Parc Natural de la Garrotxa**★, and includes a medieval town centre around the church of Sant Salvador. Following the orogenic movements triggered off by the subsidence of the Empordà (Ampurdán), the Olot plain became subject to volcanic eruption. The park features 30 volcanic cones of the Stromboli type and more than 20 basalt piles, which make for a somewhat surprising landscape.

▶ *Continue a further 8km/5mi W along the N 260.*

Olot★

Surrounded by mountains, many of which are volcanic craters, Olot is situated at the junction of three valleys formed by the Fluvià river. An important centre for both farming and crafts, it is well known for its cattle fairs, as well as for its production of religious imagery and miniature figurines for Christmas cribs.

The 18C neo-Classical **Iglesia de Sant Esteve**★, with its Baroque front and porch, houses a fine canopy, a Baroque retable and an unusual painting by El Greco – *Christ Bearing the Cross*★. 🕐 *Open 8am-1pm.* 🕐 *Closed Sun and public hols.* ☎ *972 26 04 74.*
The **Museu Comarcal de la Garrotxa**★, set up in a former hospice, displays a fine **collection of paintings and drawings**★★ by 19C and 20C Catalan artists. (🕐 *Open 11am-2pm and 4-7pm; Sun and public hols, 11am-2pm.* 🕐 *Closed Tue, 1 Jan and 25 Dec.* 💶 *3€., no charge first Sun of every month.* ☎ *972 27 91 30.*

Note also the splendid **Modernist façade**★ of the **Casa Solà-Morales**★, a work by Domènech i Montaner.

▶ *From Olot, head 9.5km/6mi E on the GI 524.*

Santa Pau★

This charming *pueblo*, spread out across a small hill, has an attractive arcaded square on which the Castillo de Santa Pau and the 15C-16C parish church (iglesia parroquial) both stand.

▶ *From here, return to Banyoles (24km/15mi) along the GI 524.*

Granada★★★

POPULATION: 241 471

MICHELIN MAP 578 U 19 (TOWN PLAN) MAP 124

COSTA DEL SOL – ANDALUCÍA (GRANADA)

Granada enjoys a glorious **setting**★★★ on a fertile plain overlooked by three hills – the Albaicín, Sacromonte and Alhambra – and crowned by the majestic peaks of the Sierra Nevada. Opposite the Albaicín, watching over the modern Christian city, stands the breathtaking Alhambra, one of the most magnificent monuments ever created by man and for many the highlight of any trip to Spain.

Location

Granada is situated along the A 44, at the confluence of the Genil and Darro rivers, and has excellent road links with all the main town and cities in the region. ☐ *Plaza Mariana Pineda, 18009 Granada, ☎ 958 24 71 28; Real de la Alhambra, ☎ 958 22 95 75.*

   Neighbouring sights are described in the following chapters: GUADIX (57km/35mi NE), JAÉN (94km/59mi N), ANTEQUERA (100km/62mi W) and COSTA DEL SOL (to the S).

Background

Historical notes – Granada began to gain importance in the 11C when the Caliphate of Córdoba declined. It became the capital of a kingdom founded by the Almoravids who were ousted a century later by the Almohads. It was in the 13C, however, that Granada reached the height of its glory when Muslims from Córdoba, which fell to the Christians in 1236, sought refuge here. In 1238, a new dynasty, that of the **Nasrids**, was founded by Mohammed in Nasr who acknowledged his position as vassal to Ferdinand III, thus ensuring a period of peace. For the next two and a half centuries (1238 to 1492) the kingdom of Granada flourished, becoming a symbol of economic, cultural and artistic prosperity, with magnificent buildings like the Alhambra.

The fall of Granada – In the 15C, as more of the Muslim-controlled territory in Spain was being lost to the Christians, the Catholic Monarchs were looking to conquer Granada, one of its last bastions. Internal divisions among the Nasrids would subsequently facilitate this task.

By 2 January 1492, after a six-month siege, the Catholic Monarchs had entered Granada; Boabdil, the last Nasrid king, gave them the keys of the city and went into exile. As he looked back on Granada from the Motril road his mother is said to have rounded on him, saying: "You weep like a woman for what you could not hold as a man"; the spot remains known as the Moor's Sigh – **Suspiro del Moro**. After 781 years the Moorish domination of Spain was ended.

Granada continued to flourish in the Renaissance which followed the Reconquest although the city's fortunes suffered an eclipse during the ruthless suppression of the Las Alpujarras revolt in 1570.

Modern Granada – There is a striking contrast between the old quarters of the town east of **plaza Nueva**, havens of peace and greenery on the Alhambra and Albaicín hills, and the noisy, bustling lower town with its network of shopping streets and the pedestrian quarter around the cathedral set between the city's two main avenues, **Gran Vía de Colón** and **calle de los Reyes Católicos**. Restaurants in the town centre serve Granada's speciality – a dish of ham and beans called *habas con jamón*.

Great Granadines – **Alonso Cano** (1601-67), architect, sculptor and painter, was the moving spirit behind the blossoming of art in 17C Granada. His art, eschewing Renaissance tradition, turned towards Classicism; he banished pathos from his sculpture and was in favour of restrained emotion. **Pedro de Mena** (1628-88), his follower, carved realistic sculptures on religious themes.

Eugenia de Montijo, future wife of Napoleon III (Empress Eugénie: 1853) was born in Granada in 1826, daughter of a grandee and, on her mother's side, granddaughter of William Kirkpatrick, Scots by birth, American by nationality and consul at Málaga.

Federico García Lorca, poet and dramatist, talented musician, friend of Dalí and Buñuel, was born 20km/12mi from Granada in Fuentevaqueros in 1899 (he died in 1936, shot by Franco's soldiers at the outbreak of the Spanish Civil War). His admirers will want to visit the summer home of the García Lorca family at **Huerta de San Vicente**. (☞ *Guided tours (30min), 10am-1pm and 4-7pm; Apr-Sep, 10am-1pm and 5-8pm. ☉ Closed Mon. ☞1.80€. ☎ 958 25 84 66.*

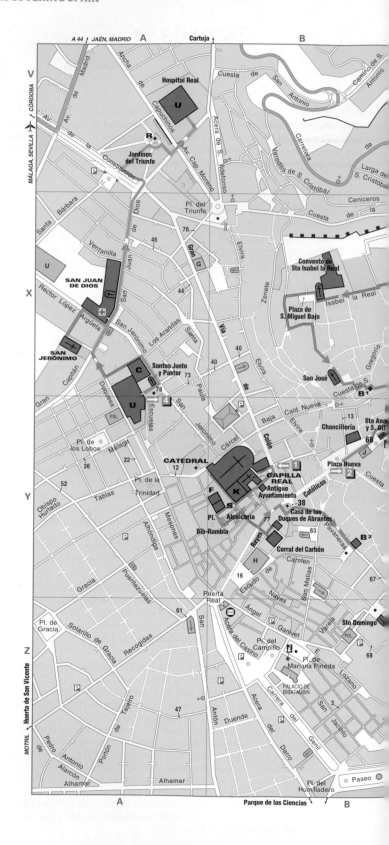

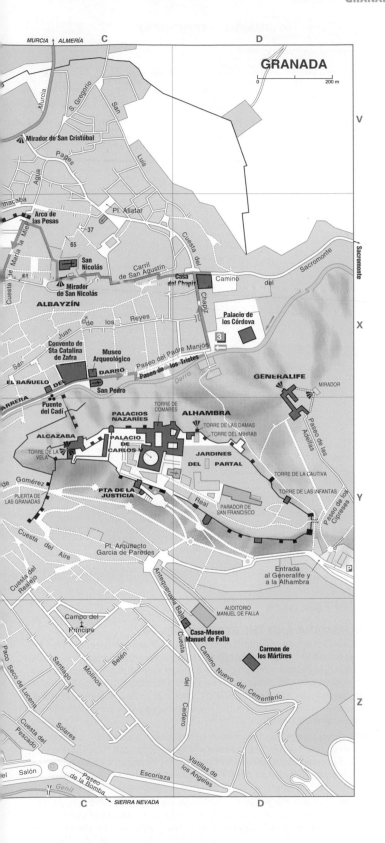

GRANADA

0   200 m

MURCIA   ALMERÍA   C   D

V

Mirador de San Cristóbal

Pages

S. Gregorio

San

Luis

Pl. Aliatar

Cuesta del

Sacromonte

Arco de
las Pesas

37

65

San
Nicolás

Carril
de San Agustín

Casa
del Chapiz

Camino   del

Mirador
de San Nicolás

Chapiz

Palacio de
los Córdova

X

ALBAYZÍN

de   los   Reyes

Juan

3

Convento de
Sta Catalina
de Zafra

Museo
Arqueológico

Paseo del Padre Manjón

EL BAÑUELO

DARRO

Paseo   de   los   Tristes

San Pedro

Darro

GENERALIFE

MIRADOR

CARRERA   DEL

Puente
del Cadí

PALACIOS
NAZARÍES

TORRE DE
COMARES

ALHAMBRA

Paseo de las Adelfas

ALCAZABA

PALACIO
DE
CARLOS V

TORRE DE LAS DAMAS

TORRE DEL MIHRAB

TORRE DE LA
VELA

JARDINES

DEL   PARTAL

TORRE DE LA CAUTIVA

de   Gomérez

PTA DE LA
JUSTICIA

TORRE DE LAS INFANTAS

PUERTA DE
LAS GRANADAS

Real

Paseo de los Cipreses

Y

Cuesta   del   Aire

PARADOR DE
SAN FRANCISCO

Pl. Arquitecto
García de Paredes

Cuesta del
Realejo

Entrada
al Generalife y
a la Alhambra

P

Antequeruela Baja

AUDITORIO
MANUEL DE FALLA

Campo del
Príncipe

Cuesta

Casa-Museo
Manuel de Falla

Paseo Seco de Lucena

Santiago

Molinos

Belén

Caldero

Camino Nuevo del Cementerio

Carmen de
los Mártires

Z

del

Cuesta del
Pescado

Solares

Vistillas de
los Ángeles

Salón

Paseo
de la Bomba

Escoriaza

Genil

C   D

SIERRA NEVADA

283

GRANADA — STREET INDEX

GRANADA — SITES INDEX

Special Features

THE ALHAMBRA AND THE GENERALIFE★★★

🕐 *Open Mar-Oct, 8.30am-8pm (and 10-11.30pm Tue-Sat: Nasrid Palace only); Nov-Feb, 8.30am-6pm (and 10-11.30pm Fri-Sat);* 🕐 *ticket office closes 1hr before last visit.* 🔎 *10€, advance purchases from any branches of the BBV bank in Spain or on the website: www. alhambratickets.com. One ticket covers the entire Alhambra and Generalife gardens and specifies entry time to the Nasrid Palace.* ☎ *958 22 75 25 or 902 44 12 21. Theme visits available for small groups if booked by the preceding Mon (for information and reservations,* ☎ *902 22 44 60).*

Nasrid architecture in Spain reached its climax in Granada, where it becomes the ultimate expression of aesthetic refinement by a sophisticated civilisation at its moment of decline. The Nasrid princes built for the moment, with no thought of posterity: beneath the fabulous decoration are ill-assorted bricks, plaster and rubble, so it is surprising how little time has diminished this masterpiece of Nasrid art.

Decoration was the main concern. Although wall hangings and carpets have disappeared and little furniture remains, the sculpture covering walls and ceilings everywhere reveals an art without equal since. This sculptural decoration is, in fact,

stuccowork, both outside and in. The finely modelled plaster, sometimes pierced, is worked in patterns in a low relief of flat planes to catch the light; another type of decoration was made by building up layers of plaster which were then cut away to form stalactites *(mocárabes)*. This type of ornament, painted in bright colours and even gilded in places, covered capitals, cornice mouldings, arches, pendentives and entire cupolas.

Ceramic tiles were used to provide a geometric decoration for most of the walls: *alicatados* formed a colourful marquetry, with lines of arabesque motifs making star designs; azulejos gave colour, different hues being separated by a thin raised fillet or a black line *(cuerda seca)*. **Calligraphy** employed the so-called Andalucían cursive which was particularly elegant; the more decoratively complicated Cufic was reserved for religious aphorisms which appear framed in scrollwork.

The Alhambra★★★

The beautiful Calat Alhambra (Red Castle) must be one of the most remarkable fortresses ever built. It stands at the top of a wooded hill commanding views of the town, the bleak Sacromonte heights, nearby hillsides and the gardens of the Albaicín.

The Alhambra's outer perimeter is entered through the Puerta de Las Granadas or the Pomegranate Gateway built by Emperor Charles V; a paved footpath then leads through to the **shrubbery**★.

Palacios Nazaríes★★★ (Nasrid Palace)

The Nasrid Palace was built around two courtyards, the Patio de los Arrayanes and the Patio de los Leones, in the 14C. Its richness and variety and the originality of its decoration defy description. The tour begins in the **Mexuar**, part of the first palace, which was used for government and judicial administration; an attractive frieze of *azulejos* and an epigraphic border cover its walls, and an oratory stands at one end. Cross the **Patio del Cuarto Dorado (1)**, in which the south wall, protected by a remarkable carved wood cornice, exemplifies the essentials of Granada art: windows are surrounded by panels covered with every variety of stucco and tile decoration. Opposite is the **Cuarto Dorado** (Golden Room), a wide room with tiled panelling, fine stuccowork and a beautiful wooden ceiling. The delightful **view**★ from its windows extends over the Albaicín.

Adjoining this is the beautiful oblong **Patio de los Arrayanes** (Myrtle Courtyard). A narrow central pool banked by myrtles runs the length of the court and reflects the massive bulk of the **Torre de Comares** (Comares Tower) which contrasts sharply with the light, slender porticoes that give onto the **Sala de la Barca** (a name arising from the Arabic word *barakha* meaning benediction) and the **Salón de Embajadores** (Hall of Ambassadors). This, the jewel of the Alhambra, was the audience chamber of the emirs and is crowned by a magnificent domed cedarwood ceiling. *Azulejos* and stucco bearing inscriptions, some from the Koran, others in honour of various princes, complete the decoration.

The Alhambra

Address Book

For coin ranges, see the Legend at the back of the guide.

WHERE TO EAT

🍴🍴 **La Ermita en la Plaza de Toros** – *Avenida Doctor Olóriz 25 (at the bullring)* – ☎ 958 29 02 57 – 📋. Its unusual location within the confines of the city's bullring and its tasteful decoration of exposed brickwork, wooden tables, rustic-style chairs and bullfighting memorabilia on the walls have made this a popular restaurant in which to enjoy typical Andalucían cuisine. The restaurant is on the first floor, and a tapas bar on the ground floor.

🍴🍴 **Chikito** – *Plaza del Campillo 9* – ☎ 958 22 33 64 – *Closed Wed* – *Reservation recommended*. A hugely popular restaurant and bar with locals and visitors alike, and renowned for serving local specialities and superb cured hams. It was here that artists and intellectuals such as García Lorca used to meet in the 1930s.

🍴🍴 **Mirador de Morayma** – *Pianista García Carrillo 2* – ☎ 958 22 82 90 – *Closed Sun July-Aug and Sun evening rest of year*. This restaurant in the Albaicín district has one of the best settings of any in the city. Rustic decor, a plant-filled terrace and magnificent views of the Alhambra.

TAPAS

Bodegas Castañeda – *Almireceros 1* – ☎ 958 21 54 64 – *Closed Sun* – 🚭 📋. The bar and tables in this typical bodega, its decor enhanced by the myriad bottles on display, are often full with customers enjoying the delicious tapas, hams and cheeses served here. A good central location just a few metres from plaza Nueva.

Casa Enrique – *Acera del Darro 8* – ☎ 958 25 50 08 - *Closed Sun* - 🚭 📋. This tavern dates from 1870 and has become a symbol of the city. Its small size and careful decoration make it a good meeting-point. Outstanding wine cellar.

Pilar del Toro – *Hospital de Santa Ana 12* – ☎ 958 22 38 47. Housed in an old 17C house, the Pilar del Toro is worth a visit for its distinctive architecture alone. The iron gate leads to the bar with a small counter to the left and a large Andalucían patio to the right, with an attractive restaurant on the first floor.

La Trastienda – *Plaza de Cuchilleros 11* – ☎ 958 22 69 95 - 🚭. Founded in 1836. Once through the small entrance door, head down some steps to the former grocery store, which has retained its original counter, where you can enjoy excellent chorizo and tapas, either at the bar or in the small room to the rear.

WHERE TO STAY

🛏 **Hotel Los Tilos** – *Plaza Bib-Rambla 4* – ☎ 958 26 67 12 – 📋 - *30 rooms* – 🍽 *5€*.

This no-frills hotel fronts a charming square filled with flower stalls, just a few metres from the cathedral. Although on the basic side, the rooms are comfortable, some with the bonus of a view over the plaza.

🛏 **Hotel Maciá Plaza** – *Plaza Nueva 4* – ☎ 958 22 75 36 – 📋 – *44 rooms* – 🍽 *5.30€*. A recently renovated hotel occupying a four-storey building with an attractive façade in a central square at the foot of the Alhambra. Standard-quality rooms with carpets and wicker furniture.

🛏🛏 **Hotel América** – *Real de la Alhambra 53* – ☎ 958 22 74 71 – *Closed Mar-Nov* – *14 rooms* – 🍽 *7€*. *Restaurant 16€*. A small, family-run hotel superbly located within the confines of the Alhambra. A warm welcome and friendly service are the trademarks of the América, which also has a pleasant patio.

🛏🛏 **Carmen de Santa Inés** – *Placeta de Porras 7* – ☎ 958 22 63 80 – 📋 – *9 rooms* – 🍽 *8€*. Elegant rooms, attentive staff and impressive views of the Alhambra are the highlights of this charming hotel in a typical villa in the Albaicín.

🛏🛏🛏 **Hotel Palacio de Santa Inés** – *Cuesta de Santa Inés 9* – ☎ 958 22 23 62 – 📋 – *13 rooms* – 🍽 *8€*. This 16C Mudéjar-inspired building is situated in the Albaicín district, with several rooms enjoying views of Granada's number one attraction. In the charming colonnaded patio, you can still make out what's left of the building's original Renaissance frescoes.

BARS AND CAFÉS

El Tren – *Carril del Picón, 22* – *Open 8am-10pm*. This unusual bar has a warm and friendly atmosphere and an extensive choice of teas, coffees and cakes. The bar has an electric train running on tracks suspended from the ceiling, hence the name. A varied clientele which changes according to the time of day.

Teterías – *Calderería Nueva*. Calle Calderería Nueva, between the city centre and the Albaicín, is a typical example of a street found in the Moorish quarter of any city. The small and cosy teterías are typical cafés which give a welcoming feel to this particular street. Two are worth mentioning: the quiet and pleasant Pervane, with its huge selection of teas, coffees, milk shakes and cakes; and Kasbah, decorated with cushions and rugs on the floor in true Moorish coffee shop style.

NIGHTLIFE

La Fontana – *Darro 19* – *Open 4pm-3am*. Housed in an old residence at the foot of the Alhambra and Albaicín hills, this inviting antique-adorned café is an ideal place for a quiet drink in an atmosphere dominated by lively conversation. An excellent choice of coffees, herbal teas and cocktails.

El 3er Aviso – *Plaza de Toros 1-18 – Open 4pm-5am*. A surprising location inside the city's bullring, where its spacious design combines with modern, tasteful decor. The café is located on several floors, and from each floor it is possible to look down onto the floors below. Good chart music popular with the 25-45 crowd, and also quiet areas for those wanting to enjoy a chat.

El Camborio – *Sacromonte 47 (in the Sacromonte district) – Open Tue-Sat, midnight-6am*. One of Granada's oldest and most established nocturnal haunts El Camborio has been open for the past 30 years. Best approached by car or taxi as it is located in one of the city's least salubrious districts. The venue itself is quite unique with four interconnected

caves and with good dance music. Popular with an eclectic crowd, though predominantly frequented by students. A good place to end the night.

El Príncipe – *Campo del Príncipe 7 – ☎ 958 22 12 17 – Open Tue-Sun in summer, 11pm-6am; Wed-Sun in winter*. This large venue is the place to be seen for the city's in-crowd, hosting regular concerts by leading Spanish groups. Always crowded with a mix of ages.

FIESTAS

The city's religious festivals are lively, colourful events, especially those held in Holy Week and at Corpus Christi. The city also holds an annual **music and dance festival** in June and July in the delightful surroundings of the Generalife gardens.

Another opening off the Patio de los Arrayanes leads to the second palace, the residence of the royal family, at the heart of which stands the justly famous **Patio de los Leones** (Lion Courtyard) built by Mohammed V. Twelve rough stone lions support an ancient low-lying fountain while delicate arcades of slender columns around the court lead to the main state apartments.

The **Sala de los Abencerrajes**, so called after Boabdil had ordered the massacre of the Abencerraje family and piled their heads into the room's central basin, has a splendid star-shaped *mocárabe* cupola.

Adorning the end of the **Sala de los Reyes** (Kings' Chamber) are alcoves containing vaulting painted to illustrate the pastimes of Moorish and Christian princes – the style is so atypical that it is not known whether the artist was a Christian working for the sultan before the Reconquest or later.

The **Sala de las Dos Hermanas** (Hall of the Two Sisters), named after the two large white identical marble slabs in the pavement, is renowned for its honeycomb cupola vaulting. Beyond are the **Sala de los Ajimeces** and the **Mirador de Lindaraja**, both equally resplendent. After passing through the room once occupied by the American writer Washington Irving, exit onto a gallery with views of the Albaicín, then head down to the Patio de la Reja **(2)** and Patio de Lindaraja.

▶ *Cross the Patio de Lindaraja to the Partal gardens.*

Gardens and perimeter towers★★

Spreading to the east of the royal palaces are the terraced Jardines de Partal which descend to the gracefully *artesonado* porticoed **Torre de las Damas** (Lady Tower), built in the early 14C.

The Torre de Mihrab on the right, is a former Nasrid oratory – a rarity since the princes were not notably pious. The Torre de la Cautiva and Torre de las Infantas (Captive's and Infantas' towers) are sumptuously decorated inside.

▶ *Enter the Palacio de Carlos V from the Partal gardens.*

Palacio de Carlos V★★ (Emperor Charles V's Palace)

In 1526, Pedro Machuca, who studied under Michelangelo, was commissioned with the design of a suitable palace to be financed from a tax levied on the Moors. Their uprising in 1568 interrupted the building and the palace was completed at a much later date. This purely Classical style building, always thought one of the most successful creations of the Renaissance period in Spain, is the only construction of Machuca's to remain. Although in comparison with the Nasrid Palaces the building may at first appear somewhat lacking, its grandeur soon becomes apparent, so perfect are its lines, so dignified its appearance, so simple its plan of a circle within a square. The palace contains two museums:

Museo de la Alhambra★

This museum is entirely devoted to Hispano-Moorish art. Its exhibits range from ceramics, wood carvings and panels to *azulejos* and *alicatados*, stuccowork, bronzes, fabric etc. Outstanding objects include the famous 14C **blue** (or **gazelle**) **amphora**★ and the Pila de Almanzor, decorated with lions and deer.

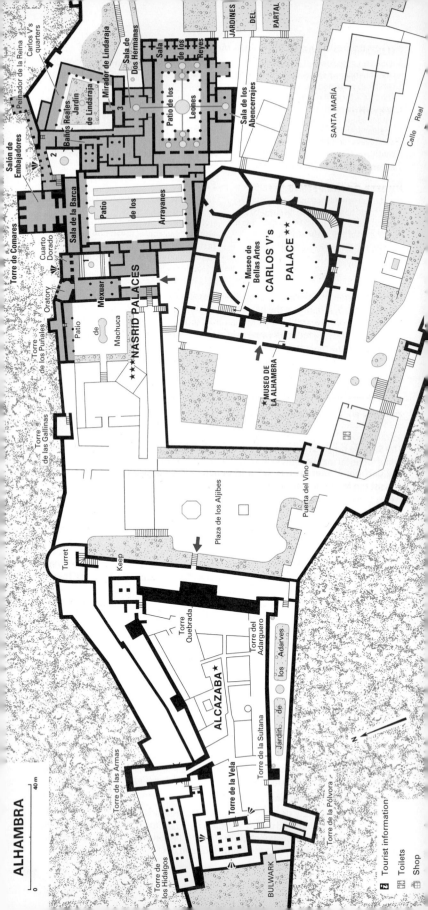

ALHAMBRA

0   40 m

Peinador de la Reina

Carlos V's quarters

Sala de Dos Hermanas

Mirador de Lindaraja

Sala de los Reyes

Sala de los Abencerrajes

Baños Reales

Jardín de Lindaraja

3

Patio de los Leones

JARDINES DEL PARTAL

SANTA MARÍA

Calle Real

Salón de Embajadores

2

Torre de Comares

Cuarto Dorado

Sala de la Barca

Patio de los Arrayanes

Oratory

Mexuar

CARLOS V's PALACE ★★

Museo de Bellas Artes

Torre de los Puñales

Patio de Machuca

★★★NASRID PALACES

★ MUSEO DE LA ALHAMBRA

Torre de las Gallinas

Puerta del Vino

Plaza de los Aljibes

Turret

Keep

Torre Quebrada

Torre del Adarguero

los Adarves

ALCAZABA ★

Jardín de

Torre de las Armas

Torre de la Sultana

Torre de la Vela

BULWARK

Torre de la Pólvora

Torre de los Hidalgos

N

ℹ Tourist information

🚻 Toilets

🏛 Shop

Museo de Bellas Artes (Fine Arts Museum)

Religious sculpture and paintings of the 16C to the 18C predominate, with works by Diego de Siloé, Pedro de Mena, Vicente Carducho and Alonso Cano, as well as a magnificent still life, *Thistle and Carrots*★★, by Brother Juan Sánchez Cotán.

Alcazaba★

This austere fortress is the oldest part of the Alhambra. The two towers overlooking the Plaza de los Aljibes (Cistern Court) date back to the 13C. The lofty Torre de la Vela (Watchtower) commands a magnificent **panorama**★★ of the palace, the Generalife, Sacromonte, Granada and the Sierra Nevada.

Puerta de la Justicia★

The massive Justice Gateway is built into a tower in the outer walls. Of note on the external façade is a wide strip of delightful 16C *azulejos* bearing the image of the Virgin and Child.

The Generalife★★

One of the most enjoyable aspects of the 14C Generalife, the summer palace of the kings of Granada, is its cool, green, terraced water **gardens**. Both the Patio de los Cipreses (Cypress Alley) and the Patio de las Adelfas (Oleander) lead to the palace. The main nucleus of the complex is the **Patio de la Acequia** (Canal Court), a large pool with fountains, a pavilion at either end, and a *mirador* in the middle commanding fine views of the Alhambra. The pavilion through the portico to the rear contains the Sala Regia, a room decorated with some fine stuccowork.

The upper gardens above the palace contain the famous **escalera del agua**, or water staircase.

CATHEDRAL QUARTER ⏱45min

Capilla Real★★ (Chapel Royal)

🕐 *Open 10.30am-1pm and 3.30-6.30pm; Apr-Oct, 10.30am-1pm and 4-7pm; Sun and public hols, 11am-1pm and 3.30-6.30pm.* 🕐 *Closed 2 Jan (morning), Good Fri and 12 Oct (morning).* 🎟 *3€.* ☎ *958 22 78 48.*

The **Catholic Monarchs** wanted to be buried on the site of their definitive victory against the Moors and ordered the construction of this Isabelline Gothic chapel by Enrique Egas. It was begun in 1506 and completed under Emperor Charles V in 1521. Its unity of style, richness of decoration and the art objects it contains, lend the chapel a unique interest. To enter *(by the south door)*, cross the courtyard of the old **Lonja** (Exchange), also designed by Egas. The chapel's south front has an elegant Renaissance façade of two superimposed arcades with turned columns. Every conceivable decoration of the Isabelline style is to be seen inside the chapel: ribbed vaulting, walls emblazoned with the arms of the Catholic Monarchs, the yoke and fasces (revived in 1934 by the Falange), a monogram of the initials of their first names, and the eagle of St John. Beautiful wrought-iron grilles close two chapels. The chancel, closed by a spectacular gilded **screen**★★★ by Master Bartolomé, contains the **mausoleums**★★★ of the Catholic Monarchs on the right, and of Philip the Handsome and Juana the Mad, the parents of Charles V, on the left. The first was carved by Fancelli in Genoa in 1517, the second, which is magnificent in proportion and workmanship, by Bartolomé Ordóñez between 1519 and 1520 (the sarcophagi are in the crypt). In the high altar **retable**★ (1520) Felipe Vigarny created a work with great movement and expression. The lower register of the predella depicts the siege of Granada and the baptism of the moriscos. Note also the praying statues of the Catholic Monarchs, attributed to Diego de Siloé.

Museo

Numerous objects of incalculable historical value can be seen in this museum which is situated in the sacristy. Among exhibits on display are **Queen Isabel's sceptre and crown, King Ferdinand's sword,** plus an outstanding **collection of paintings**★★ by Flemish (Rogier Van der Weyden, Memling), Italian (Perugino, Botticelli) and Spanish (Bartolomé Bermejo, Pedro Berruguete) artists. In the rear of the museum can be found the famous *Triptych of the Passion*, the central section of which was painted by the Fleming Dirk Bouts, and two sculptures of the Catholic Monarchs at prayer by Felipe Vigarny.

Opposite is the 18C Baroque-style former **town hall** *(ayuntamiento)*, built on the site of the former 14C Muslim *madraza* or university of Yusuf I.

Catedral★

Enter from Gran Vía de Colón. ◔ *Open 10.45am-1.30pm and 3.30-6.30pm; Sun, 3.30-6.30pm; Apr-Sep, 10.30am-1.30pm and 4-7pm; Sun, 4-7pm.* ◕ *3€.* ☎ *958 22 29 59.*

Construction of the cathedral was started in 1518. However, the architect Diego Siloé, who replaced Enrique Egas and was entrusted with the project from 1528 until his death in 1563, made changes to the design and introduced the Renaissance style to the building. The façade (1667), overlaid by three tall arcades, is by Alonso Cano. The **Capilla Mayor**★ is the first thing you notice inside, for its plan and decoration are surprising. Siloé designed a rotunda circled by an ambulatory, the whole cleverly linked to the nave and four aisles of the basilica. The rotunda combines two superimposed orders, the uppermost with paintings by Alonso Cano of the Life of the Virgin and beautiful 16C stained glass in paired windows. Marking the rotunda entrance on twin facing panels, are the figures at prayer of the Catholic Monarchs by Pedro de Mena and, in a medallion by Alonso Cano, those of Adam and Eve. The impressive **organ** in the nave dates from about 1750 and was made by Leonardo of Ávila. The finely carved Isabelline doorway in the south transept is the original **north portal**★ of the older Capilla Real.

Alcaicería

The area, which has been reconstructed and is now a kind of *souk* or oriental bazaar with craft and souvenir shops, was a silk market in Moorish times.

Corral del Carbón

This 14C former Moorish storehouse has preserved a harmonious doorway with a horseshoe arch adorned with an *alfiz* surround and panels bearing *sebka* decoration. The sober internal patio is home to the city's tourist office.

Worth a Visit

⊛ *The routes marked on the plan offer suggestions for various walks through the city.*

Albaicín★★

The quarter, on the right bank of the Darro, covers a slope facing the Alhambra. It was here that the Moors built their first fortress, the refuge to which they retreated when the Christians reconquered the city. The alleys are lined by white-walled houses or the long walls that enclose luxuriant gardens of prosperous town houses called *cármenes*. Go to the **Iglesia de San Nicolás** (Church of St Nicholas) *(access by the Cuesta del Chapiz)*, if possible at sunset, for a really beautiful **view**★★★ of the Alhambra and the Generalife. The Sierra Nevada beyond is particularly spectacular in winter when covered in snow.

Baños Árabes★ (El Bañuelo)

◔ *Open 10am-2pm.* ◔ *Closed Sun, Mon and public hols.* ◕ *No charge.* ☎ *958 02 78 00 or 958 24 23 39.*

Despite their age, these 11C Moorish baths are the best preserved in Spain. Star-pierced vaulting decorates a room surrounded by columns.

Monasterio de San Jerónimo★

◔ *Open 10am-1.30pm and 3-6.30pm; Apr-Sep, 10am-1.30pm and 4-7.30pm.* ◕ *3€.* ☎ *958 27 93 37.*

This 16C monastery was principally designed by Diego de Siloé. Fine Plateresque and Renaissance doorways lead onto its harmonious cloisters, characterised by their sturdy pillars. The **church**★★ contains the tomb of Gonzalo Fernández de Córdoba, the Gran Capitán. The richness of its Renaissance style apse, magnificently illuminated by the transept windows, and the roof with its superb coffers and vaulting adorned with saints, angels and animals, stands out. The **retable**★★, the work of a number of artists, is a jewel of the Granadine School. The paintings on the walls are from the 18C.

Iglesia de San Juan de Dios★

⟜ *Guided tours (50min), 10am-1pm; open afternoons by prior arrangement.* ◔ *Closed Sun, public hols and in Aug.* ◕ *2.40€.* ☎ *958 22 21 44.*

The Church of St John of God is one of Granada's most important churches. The interior, access to which is through a beautiful carved mahogany doorway, is magnificent in both its richness and its stylistic uniformity. Behind the massive Churrigueresque altarpiece of gilded wood, is a lavishly decorated *camarín* which contains the funerary urn of **San Juan de Dios**. He founded the Order of Knights Hospitallers and died in Granada in 1550.

Cartuja★

🕐 *Open 10am-1pm (noon Sun and public hols) and 3.30-6pm; Apr-Oct, 10am-1pm and 4-8pm.* 🎟 *2.10€.* ☎ *958 16 19 32 (10am-noon only).*

The Carthusian monastery is northwest of town, near the university. Leave the centre of town on the Gran Vía de Colón or the calle San Juan de Dios. Go through the cloisters into the church, exuberantly decorated with Baroque stucco in 1662. At

the back of the apse is the early-18C Holy of Holies (Sancta Sanctorum), a *camarín* decorated with multicoloured marble; beneath the cupola, painted in false relief, is a marble Sagrario which contains the Tabernacle.

The **sacristy**★★ (1727-64) is an outstanding example of Late Baroque. Some call it the Christian Alhambra on account of the intricate white stuccowork on the walls and vaulting, where straight lines and curves form never-ending patterns on mouldings and cornices. This stucco ornamentation contrasts sharply with the cupola paintings and the strong colours of the marble ogee moulding. The magnificent door and cedarwood furnishings inlaid with tortoiseshell, mother-of-pearl and silver, are by a Carthusian monk, Brother José Manuel Vásquez.

Sacristy, Cartuja

B. Kaufmann/MICHELIN

Parque de las Ciencias★

Kids 🕐 *Open 10am-7pm; Sun and public hols, 10am-3pm.* 🕐 *Closed Mon, 1 Jan, 1 May, 15-30 Sep and 24-25 Dec.* 🎟 *4€, 2€ planetarium.* ☎ *958 37 78 10.*

This large science park comprises an interactive museum, a planetarium, an astronomical observatory and a tropical butterfly collection.

Museo Arqueológico

🕐 *Open 9am-8.30pm (Tue, 2.30-8pm; Sun, 9am-2.30pm).* 🕐 *Closed Mon and public hols.* 🎟 *1.50€, no charge for citizens of the European Union.* ☎ *958 22 56 40.*

The archaeological museum is housed in Casa Castril, a Renaissance palace with a fine **Plateresque doorway**★. It contains an outstanding collection of Egyptian alabaster vases found in a necropolis in Almuñecar, a bull figure from Arjona and a selection of decorative Roman and Moorish art.

Sacromonte

The hillside opposite the Generalife is covered by a network of paths which lead past clumps of prickly pears to the gypsies' caves. Flamenco dancing and singing is performed in these troglodyte dwellings in the evenings.

Hospital Real

The royal hospital, now the university rectorate, was founded by the Catholic Monarchs. The ground plan, similar to those in Toledo and Santiago de Compostela, is of a cross within a square and provides four spacious courtyards. Four Plateresque windows adorn the façade, while a Virgin and Child flanked by statues of the Catholic Monarchs at prayer, by Alonso de Mena, dominates the main doorway. Of interest in the interior are the two harmonious *patios* in the left wing, decorated with heraldic motifs.

Carmen de los Mártires

🕐 *Open 10am-2pm and 4-6pm; in summer, 10am-2pm and 5-7pm; Sat-Sun and public hols, 10am-7pm.* 🕐 *Closed in Aug.* 👁 *No charge.* ☎ *958 22 79 53.*

This Carmelite monastery is situated on the Alhambra hill. The romantic terraced **gardens**★, embellished with fountains and sculptures, provide a beautiful setting for a stroll.

Excursions

SIERRA NEVADA★★

The Sierra Nevada range lies just 80km/50mi from the Costa del Sol and lines Granada's horizon to the south; it is massive, beautiful, often snow-capped and in season preceded by a wave of pink almond blossom. There is 🎿 skiing in winter at **Solynieve**★★, one of Spain's best ski resorts with over 60km/37mi of slopes, 45 runs, 20 ski lifts, and there are excellent hotel facilities at **Pradollano**.

The recent designation of the Sierra Nevada as a **National Park** in 1999 has resulted in severe restrictions on the use of the old road. Two control posts, one on the northern section (Borreguiles crossroads), the other to the south (Hoya del Portillo), limit access within the park for private vehicles. As a result, the best way to tour the area is on foot. For further information contact the **El Dornajo Visitor Centre**. (🕐 *Open 10am (9.30am in summer) to 2.30pm and 4.30-7pm (8pm in summer).* ☎ *958 34 06 25).*

The most interesting routes are the ascents to the Laguna de la Yeguas, **Mulhacén** (3 482m/11 424ft) and **Veleta** (3 394m/11 132ft).

The panorama from the top is wonderful, extending north to the Cordilleras Béticas, north-east to the Sierra de la Sagra, east to the wall of lofty summits dominated by the Mulhacén and Alcazaba, and south to the Mediterranean. Finally, in the west lie the jagged outlines of the Sierra de Tejeda and the Sierra de Almijara.

Alhama de Granada★

60km/37mi SW on the A 92 and A 335. Alhama de Granada is an attractive small town of whitewashed houses and narrow streets built above an impressive gorge. It is dominated by the imposing tower of the **Iglesia de la Encarnación**★, a well-proportioned church built of golden stone. The stunning **view**★ from the belvedere behind the Iglesia del Carmen encompasses the canyon of the Alhama River. On the outskirts of the town, baths dating from the Roman period can still be seen in an attractive verdant setting. The town's magnificent Moorish **cistern**★, into which flowed the thermal waters of the area, bears witness to the great importance of Alhama during the period of Arab domination in Andalucía.

TOUR THROUGH THE ALPUJARRAS★★

90km/56mi – 🕐*allow one day.*

This mountainous region offering a variety of landscapes stretches across the southern slopes of the Sierra Nevada between the Gádor and Controviesa massifs. Because of its isolation from the rest of Spain it has managed to retain its traditional character.

From Lanjarón to Valor

The High Alpujarras encompass the valley of the Guadalfeo river, where the houses blend in perfectly with the landscape. Their most typical feature is the flat roof terrace, known as a *terrao*, made using large beams of chestnut and battens (*alfarjías*), on top of which a layer of bluish-grey clay (*launa*) is added. In the past, these flat roof terraces were used as meeting areas, although nowadays they are predominantly used for drying.

Lanjarón

This popular resort is famous for its medicinal mineral water and spa. The town's other main attraction is its 16C castle, affording fine views of the entrance to the valley from its superb elevated position.

The Alpujarran Uprising

In 1499 the Arabs who did not wish to leave Spain were forced to renounce their religion and to convert to Christianity. They were known as moriscos. In 1566 Philip II forbade them their language and traditional dress, which sparked off a serious uprising, especially in Las Alpujarras where the moriscos proclaimed as king Fernando de Córdoba under the name Abén Humeya. In 1571 Philip II sent in the army under Don Juan of Austria who crushed the rebellion. However, a tense feeling of unrest remained, and in 1609 Philip III ordered the expulsion of all the Moriscos (who numbered about 275 000) from Spain.

▶ *9km/5.5mi from Lanjarón, before reaching the town of Órgiva, take the GR 421. Caution is required when driving along this narrow mountain road.*

Pampaneira★★

Of the three villages in the **Poqueira Valley**★★, namely Bubión, Capileira and Pampaneira, the latter has succeeded in preserving its traditional architecture to best effect. The 17C Iglesia de Santa Cruz stands along one side of the plaza de la Libertad.

The village of **Bubión**, an important centre of *morisco* resistance during the revolt of 1569, is situated 5km/3mi further along the valley. **Capileira** is home to the **Museo Alpujarreño de Artes y Costumbres Populares**, a museum re-creating 19C Alpujarran life through its popular arts and customs.(⊙ *Open 11.30am-2.30pm; Sat, 4-7pm (8pm in summer).* ⊙ *Closed Mon.* ☎ *958 76 30 51).*

A narrow alleyway in Pampaneira

B. Kaufmann/MICHELIN

▶ *Return to the GR 421.* The road passes through the settlements of **Pitres, Pórtugos** and **Busquístar**, traversing an area of outstanding beauty as it gradually enters the **Trevélez Valley**★.

Trevélez★

Trevélez has been famous for its excellent cured hams and dried sausages since Queen Isabel II extolled their virtues in the 19C. The town is divided into three districts of narrow streets and is the highest municipality in Spain (1 600m/5,248ft). Behind the village the impressive silhouette of **Mulhacén**, the highest peak on the Iberian Peninsula (3,482m/11 424ft), stands guard.

Beyond Trevélez, the valley opens out and the verdant landscape gives way to a wilder, drier terrain planted with the occasional vineyard, and populated by the villages of **Juviles, Mecina Bombarón** and **Yegen**. The latter owes it fame to the Englishman Gerald Brenan, the author of *South from Granada* who lived in the village for several years in the 1920s and 1930s.

Don Fernando de Córdoba, known as **Abén Humeya**, was born and lived in Válor, the next village after Yegen. Its church, the 16C Iglesia de San José, is, like many in the region, built in Mudéjar style.

WHERE TO STAY

⊖ **Hotel Alcazaba de Busquístar** – *Busquístar – 4km/2.5mi S of Trevélez along the Juviles road –* ☎ *958 85 86 87 –* 🅿 *– 43 rooms –* 🍽 *4€ – Restaurant 12€.* A hotel which has used typical local materials in its construction, including stone slabs, baked clay floors and whitewashed walls. The rooms are spacious and have terraces with superb views over the *sierra*.

Sierra de **Gredos**★★

MICHELIN MAPS 575 OR 576 K 14, L 14 – CASTILLA Y LEÓN (ÁVILA)

The granite massif of the Sierra de Gredos, which includes the Pico de Almanzor (2 592m/8 504ft), the highest peak in the Cordillera Central, is bordered by four rivers: Tormes and Alberche to the north, Tiétar to the south and Alagón to the west. The contours of the sierra are dissimilar, the north face being marked by the remains of glacial features such as mountain cirques and lakes, the south, a steep granite wall, by eroded gullies. The valleys are fertile; those in the north produce fruit (mainly apples) and French beans (the speciality of Barco de Ávila); those in the south, sheltered by the sierra, grapes, olives and tobacco. In order to preserve the trout in the Alberche and Tormes rivers, the deer and the *capra hispánica*, a type of mountain goat, which haunt the upper heights, the Reserva Nacional de Gredos was created.

Location

There are various ways of travelling to this impressive mountain range: from Madrid, the best route is along the M 501 towards San Martín de Valdeiglesias; from Ávila, take the N 502 towards the Puerto del Pico; and from Plasencia, follow the EX 203 towards Jarandilla de la Vera. *Arenas de San Pedro: Generalísimo 1, 5400 Ávila,* ☎ *920 37 23 68.*

Neighbouring sights are described in the following chapters: ÁVILA, La ALBERCA and MADRID.

Special Features

San Martín de Valdeiglesias

This old market town, dominated by the walls of the 14C castle built by the Lord High Constable Álvaro de Luna, serves as an excellent departure point for local excursions.

Toros de Guisando

6km/4mi NW. The *Bulls of Guisando*, as they are called, four rudimentarily carved figures in granite, stand in an open field. Similar figures may be seen throughout the province of Ávila. They are obviously ancient and remain an enigma though one theory is that they form a commemorative monument, a Celt-Iberian idol. They have certain similarities to the stone sows or *porcas* that may be seen in villages in the Trás-os-Montes region of Portugal.

Embalse de Burguillo★ (Burguillo Reservoir)

20km/12mi NW. The man-made lake on the Alberche river, amid hills covered in sparse vegetation, provides a fine setting for water sports enthusiasts.

Pantano de San Juan

8km/5mi E. As the road descends to this artificial lake there are attractive **views**★ of the narrow part of the Alberche reservoir where the banks are deeply indented and covered in pine trees. The area is popular with Madrileños in summer on account of its water sports facilities.

Safari Madrid

27km/17mi SE at **Aldea del Fresno**.

Kids This is one of Spain's largest game parks, where wild animals from the world over may be observed. The main attraction is a demonstration by trained birds of prey. (⏲ *Open 10.30am-6.30pm (9.30pm in summer).* ≈*10€, 6€ children aged 3-10.* ☎ *91 862 23 14).*

▸ *From San Martín de Valdeiglesias, take the M 50 (which then becomes the C 501), towards Arenas de San Pedro.*

Arenas de San Pedro

This attractive small town at the foot of the Sierra de Gredos is another good base for local excursions. Its main monument of note is the Gothic **Iglesia de Nuestra Señora de la Asunción.**

Cuevas del Águila★ (Águila Caves)

9km/5.5mi S of Arenas de San Pedro. ▶ *Bear right immediately beyond the village of Ramacastañas and continue for 4km/2.5mi along the unsurfaced road.*

A single vast chamber is open to the public. Among the many concretions are lovely frozen streams of calcite, ochre crystals coloured by iron oxide and massive pillars still in process of formation. ○ *Open 10.30am-1pm and 3-6pm (7pm in summer).* ∞*4€.* ☎ *920 37 71 07.*

Puerto del Pico road★

29km/18mi NE of Arenas de San Pedro. The road cuts through the centre of the sierra. After crossing **Mombeltrán** (15C castle with well-preserved exterior), the road rises to a corniche, paralleling the old Roman road, used for years as a stock route, which one can see below. From the pass (1 352m/4 436ft) there is a good **view**★ of the mountains and, in the foreground (south), of the Tiétar Valley and, beyond, the Tajo. Beyond the pass the landscape becomes austere with granite boulders crowning the hilltops.

The **Parador de Gredos**, the first in Spain (1928), stands in a magnificent **setting**★★ commanding far-reaching views.

Laguna Grande★

12km/7.5mi S of Hoyos del Espino. ⊛ *Park the car at the end of the road.* 🚶 A well-defined path leads up to Laguna Grande (2hr), a glacial basin fed by mountain torrents. Halfway along the walk, there is an unforgettable **panorama**★ of the Gredos cirque.

Guadalajara

POPULATION: 67 847

MICHELIN MAP 576 K 20 – MAP 121 ALREDEDORES DE MADRID –

CASTILLA-LA MANCHA (GUADALAJARA)

Guadalajara, which takes its name from the Arabic meaning river of stones, has developed into a satellite town on account of its proximity to Madrid.

The town became the fief of the **Mendozas** in the 14C, a name famous in Spanish history. It includes among its members Íñigo López de Mendoza, first **Marquis of Santillana** (1398-1458), poet and author of the pastoral *Serranillas*; his son, **Cardinal Pedro González de Mendoza** (1428-95), adviser to the Catholic Monarchs; and the second Duke of Infantado, who built the palace at the north entrance to the town in the 15C.

Location

The town is situated close to Madrid and Alcalá de Henares, on the A 2 linking the Spanish capital with Barcelona. 🛈 *Plaza de los Caídos 6, 19001 Guadalajara,* ☎ *949 21 16 26.*

Neighbouring sights are described in the following chapters: MADRID (55km/34mi SW), ALCALÁ DE HENARES (25km/15mi SW) and SIGÜENZA (75km/47mi NE).

Worth a Visit

Palacio del Infantado★ (Palace of the Duke of Infantado)

○ *Open 10.30am-2pm and 4.15-7pm; Sun and public hols, 10.30am-2pm.* ○ *Closed Mon, 1 Jan, Good Fri, 8 and 15 Sep, and 24 and 31 Dec.* ∞ *1.20€.* ☎ *949 21 33 01.*

The palace, built at the end of the 15C by Juan Guas, is a masterpiece of civil Isabelline architecture in which the Gothic and Mudéjar styles combine. The magnificent **façade**★ is adorned with diamond stonework and a large crest, the Mendoza family coat of arms, above the doorway. The upper gallery consists of a series of paired ogee windows interposed between corbelled loggias. The effect of the whole is splendid in spite of the later windows, which were added in the 17C. The two-storey **patio**★ is just as remarkable with its multifoil arches resting on turned columns and its extremely delicate Mudéjar ornamentation. The decoration of the palace interior, equally sumptuous at the outset, was damaged during the Spanish Civil War.

When Francis I of France, captured at Pavia in 1525, was on his way to imprisonment in Madrid, he was received at the palace with the pomp due to his station.

Nowadays it houses the **Museo Provincial de Guadalajara**. ○ *Open 10am-2pm and 4-7pm; Sun and public hols, 10am-2pm.* ○ *Closed 1 and 6 Jan, Good Fri, 1 May, 8 and 9 Sep and 25 Dec.* ⊗ *1.20€.* ☎ *949 21 33 01.*

Excursion

Pastrana

42km/26mi SE on the N 320. This delightful town, once a ducal city, retains memories of the **Princess of Eboli**, favourite of Philip II. The **Palacio Ducal,** with its plain rough-hewn stone façade, stands on Hour Square or Plaza de la Hora, so named because the duke, the princess's husband, confined her to the palace for the last five years of her life, allowing her to appear at the window for only an hour a day.

The **Colegiata**, a collegiate church built by the dukes in the 16C, contains, in the sacristy, four Gothic **tapestries**★ woven in Tournai after cartoons by Nuno Gonçalves which illustrate the capture of Arzila and Tangier by Alfonso V of Portugal in 1471. They reveal the Portuguese painter's mastery of composition, love of detail (armour and costume) and talent for portraiture. *(○ Open 11.30am-2pm and 4.30-6.30pm; Sun and public hols, 1-2.30pm and 4.30-6.30pm.* ⊗ *2.50€.* ☎ *949 37 00 27).*

Guadalupe★★

POPULATION: 2 447

MICHELIN MAP 576 N 14 – EXTREMADURA (CÁCERES)

Guadalupe appears suddenly before you as the road climbs. The monastery, bristling with battlements and turrets, stands above the village which clusters around the foot of its austere ramparts. The road above the village commands a good view★ of the monastery.

The old village★ with its steeply pitched brown tile roofs is attractively picturesque, particularly in spring when flowers bring colour to the balconies.

Location

Guadalupe stands on the southeastern slopes of the mountain range of the same name. ⓘ *Plaza Santa María de Guadalupe 1, 10140 Guadalupe,* ☎ *927 15 41 28.*

Neighbouring sights are described in the following chapters: TRUJILLO (82km/51mi W) and TALAVERA DE LA REINA (106km/66mi NE).

Patron of Todas Las Españas (All the Spains)

The first shrine is believed to have been built following the discovery of a miraculous Virgin by a cowherd in 1300. Alfonso XI, having invoked the Virgin of Guadalupe, as she was known, shortly before his victory over the Moors at the **Battle of Salado** (24 October 1340) had a grandiose monastery built in gratitude and entrusted it to the Hieronymites. The pilgrimage centre, richly endowed by rulers and deeply venerated by the people, exercised a great influence in the 16C and 17C when it became famous for craftsmanship – embroidery, gold and silversmithing, illumination – and more importantly, situated as it was at the heart of the kingdom of the Conquistadors, the symbol of the **Hispanidad** – that community of language and civilisation which links the Spanish of the Old and New Worlds. Christopher Columbus named a West Indian island after the shrine; the first American Indians converted to Christianity were brought to the church for baptism and Christians freed from slavery came in pilgrimage to leave their chains as votive offerings.

Solemn processions on 12 October celebrate the day of the Hispanidad.

Special Features

MONASTERIO★★ ⏱1hr 15min

🚶 *Guided tours (1hr), 9.30am-6.30pm.*
👥 *3€.* ☎ *927 36 70 00.*

The monastery, abandoned in 1835, was taken over by Franciscans in 1908 and restored. The heart of the building dates from the Gothic period, late 14C-early 15C, but with rich donations, numerous additions were made in the 16C, 17C and 18C. The resulting plan appears confused because the monks had to crowd ever more buildings within the fortified perimeter. The monastery contains some very valuable artistic treasures.

ARTS AND CRAFTS

The traditional craft of copper smelting (jugs and pots) is still very much alive in Guadalupe.

Façade

15C. The façade, golden in colour, exuberant in its Flamboyant Gothic decoration, overlooks a picturesque square. It is set between tall crenellated towers of rough stone like the sombre defensive walls on either side. Moorish influence, characteristic of Mudéjar Gothic, can be seen in the exaggeratedly sinuous decoration in imitation of Moorish stuccowork. Bronze reliefs on the 15C doors illustrate the Lives of the Virgin and Christ.

Iglesia (Church)

14C. The church was one of the first monastery buildings to be erected, but in the 18C additions were made such as the gilt Baroque decoration on the vaulting and the pierced balustrade above the nave to take votive lamps in honour of the Virgin. An intricate iron grille, wrought at the beginning of the 16C by two famous Valladolid ironsmiths, closes the sanctuary, which is ornamented with a large classically ordered retable carved by two 17C sculptors, Giraldo de Merlo and Jorge Manuel Theotocopuli, son of El Greco. The Virgin of Guadalupe stands in the middle of the altarpiece **(1)** but can be seen more clearly from the *Camarín*.

Sala Capitular (Chapter house)

The chapter house contains a remarkable collection of 87 **antiphonaries and books of hours with miniatures**★ by the monks of Guadalupe. The richly illuminated works cover a period from the 14C to the 18C, most of them dating from the 16C.

Monasterio de Guadalupe

B. Brillion/MICHELIN

Claustro Mudéjar

The 14C-15C cloisters are remarkable for their great size and the two storeys of horseshoe-shaped arches. There is a small Mudéjar Gothic temple in the middle and in a corner, a lavabo faced with multicoloured tiles.

Museo de Bordados (Embroidery Museum)

The museum, in the former refectory, displays a fine collection of richly decorated **copes and altarfronts**★★, skilfully embroidered by the monks between the 15C and the 19C.

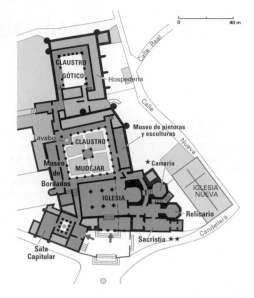

Museo de Pinturas y Esculturas (Painting and Sculpture Museum)

The works include a 16C triptych of the *Adoration of the Magi* by Isembrandt, an ivory Christ attributed to Michelangelo, an *Ecce Homo* by Pedro de Mena, eight small canvases of the monks by Zurbarán, and another small painting by Goya, *Prison Confession*.

Sacristía★★ (Sacristy)

17C. Canvases by Carreño de Miranda hang in the antechamber. The sacristy is a magnificently successful combination of Classical style architecture and highly ornate Baroque decoration. The unexpected harmony and rich colouring set off the well-known series of **paintings by Zurbarán**★★ to perfection. The 11 canvases, painted in a serene yet forceful style between 1638 and 1647, are of the Hieronymite monks and scenes from the Life of St Jerome including *The Temptation* in which he is shown resisting beautiful lady musicians.

Relicario (Reliquary Cabinet)

This contains a collection of the Virgin of Guadalupe's mantles and the crown, which is worn only in solemn processions.

Camarín★

18C. A chapel-like room where the Virgin of Guadalupe rests. Riches of every description abound: jasper, gilded stucco and marble and precious wood marquetry frames for nine canvases by Luca Giordano. The Virgin herself sits on an enamelwork throne (1953), a small 12C figure carved in now darkened oak, almost obscured beneath a richly embroidered veil and mantle.

Claustro Gótico (Gothic Cloisters)

In the *hospedería* (hostelry). The cloisters were built in the 16C in an elegant Flamboyant Gothic style to serve as a dispensary for the four hospitals then in the monastery's care.

Excursions

Puerto de San Vicente (San Vicente Pass)

40km/25mi E on the C 401. The **road**★ to the pass crosses the Las Villuercas mountain ranges. During the climb *(8km/5mi)* beyond the Guadarranque Valley, there are wonderful **views**★ of green mountain ranges, their jagged crests aligned like the waves of the sea in the wild, moorland landscape.

Sierra de **Guadarrama**★

MICHELIN MAP 575 OR 576 J 17-18 – CASTILLA Y LEÓN (SEGOVIA), MADRID

The Sierra de Guadarrama is a green oasis in the desert of Castilla, so close to Ávila, Segovia and Madrid that you can see the range's snow-capped peaks from these towns in winter. The countryside here comprises granite and gneiss outcrops, steep slopes covered up to halfway in evergreen oaks and pinewoods but above, near the crests, are traces of glaciation. Abundant rainfall in the upper heights gives rise to streams which feed the province's four reservoirs (Pinilla, Navacerrada, Santillana and El Atazar).

Mountain towns and resorts, such as Navacerrada, Cercedilla, Guadarrama and El Escorial, have developed in recent years, providing refuge for Castilians fleeing the torrid summer heat of the Meseta. The sierra is also home to two ski resorts: Puerto de Navacerrada and Puerto de los Cotos.

Location

The mountain range stretches for around 100km/62mi from Puerto de Malagón (Ávila) to Puerto de Somosierra (Madrid), and acts as a natural border for the province of Madrid to the northwest. The sierra is easily accessible from both Madrid and the province of Segovia. *Puerto de Navacerrada: Caseta Punto de Información (information post), 28180 Puerto de Navacerrada, ☎ 91 852 33 02.*

☝ *Neighbouring sights are described in the following chapters: MADRID, SEGOVIA and Monasterio de EL ESCORIAL.*

Tours

FROM MANZANARES EL REAL TO SEGOVIA

106km/66mi – ⏱ *allow one day excluding visits to Segovia and Riofrío.*

Manzanares el Real

The **castillo**★ standing at the foot of the Sierra de la Pedriza was built by the Duke of Infantado in the 15C. This gem of civil architecture is a well-proportioned fortress, the austerity of its lines relieved by bead mouldings on the turrets and the Plateresque decoration applied to the south front, which could be the work of Juan Guas. ⏱ *Open 10am-5.15pm (10am-1.15pm and 4-7.15pm Jul-Aug).* ⏱ *Closed Mon and public hols.* ☞ *1.80€,* ☎*91 853 00 08.*

Sierra de la Pedriza★

This granite massif, foothill to the Sierra de Guadarrama, which presents by turns a chaos of rose-coloured rock and eroded screes with mountain streams, is popular with rock climbers, particularly in the Peña del Diezmo area (1 714m/5 623ft).

▷ *Continue along the M 608, which runs alongside the Santillana reservoir, as far as Soto del Real; from here, follow the M 611.*

Address Book

For coin ranges, see the Legend at the back of the guide.

WHERE TO EAT

☺☺ **Asador Felipe** – *Del Mayo 3 – Navacerrada* – ☎ *91 853 10 41 - Open Jul-Sep and public hols rest of year.* The popular Asador Felipe is just a few metres from the Restaurante Felipe, owned by the same proprietor and in business for over 20 years. Delicious grilled meats cooked over an open fire, typically Castilian decor, and a pleasant terrace for the summer months.

WHERE TO STAY

☺☺ **Hotel La Posada de Alameda** – *Grande 34 – Alameda del Valle – 6km/4mi NE of El Paular along the M 604 –* ☎ *91 869 13 37 – www.laposadadealameda.com –* 🅿 *– 22 rooms –* ☲ *4.81€ – Restaurant 25/30€.* This attractive rural inn started life as a dairy farm before its conversion to a modern-style hotel adorned with designer furniture. The lounge areas and bedrooms, some with dormer windows, are simple yet cosy, with stone floors and functional bathrooms. The *posada* also has a bright, attractive restaurant.

Miraflores de la Sierra

Summer resort. Attractive view from a lookout on the village outskirts.

▷ *Continue along the M 611 towards La Morcuera and then Rascafría.*

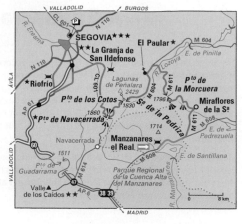

Puerto de la Morcuera

As you reach the pass (1 796m/5 892ft), an extensive view which includes the El Vellón reservoir, opens to the south.
A descent through bare moorland brings you to the wooded Lozoya depression. In the distance by Lozoya town, is the La Pinilla dam, supplied by the río Lozoya, a well-known trout stream.

Real Monasterio de Santa María de El Paular★

2km/1.2mi from Rascafría. Castilla's earliest Carthusian monastery stands in the cool Lozoya Valley. It was founded in 1390 and was subsequently enriched by the kings of Castilla and those of unified Spain in the 15C and 16C.

In 1954, the Benedictines began reconstruction of the complex, which comprises a monastery, a church and a hotel (a former palace). The **church** has a Flamboyant doorway by Juan Guas. Inside is a finely wrought Gothic screen and a magnificent 15C alabaster **altarpiece**★★ illustrating the Lives of the Virgin and Christ and which, from its emphasis on the picturesque and detail in costume and bourgeois interiors, is certainly Flemish. In contrast, the Tabernáculo (Tabernacle), behind the high altar, is decorated in exuberant Baroque. (☞ *Guided tours (45min), at noon, 1pm and 5pm; Sun and public hols at 1pm, 4pm, 5pm and 6pm.* ◑ *Closed Thu afternoon.* ☜ *No charge.* ☎ *91 869 14 25).*

▷ *The road continues through dense pine woods.*

Puerto de los Cotos

1 830m/6 004ft. The pass is the departure point for ski-lifts to the slopes. 🎿 From the upper chair-lift terminus at Zabala, excursions may be made in summer to the Laguna de Peñalara *(15min)*, occupying a former glacial cirque, the Picos de Dos Hermanas (Summit of the Two Sisters) *(30min)* and Peñalara (2 429m/7 967ft), the highest point in the sierra *(45min)*.

Puerto de Navacerrada★

1,860m/6,102ft. The pass, on the borders of the two Castillas, commands a beautiful **view**★ of the Segovian plateau and the line of the valley, hidden beneath dense pines, through which the road to Madrid runs. The pass is a popular ski resort and is linked by train to Cercedilla.

▷ *Take the CL 601 towards Valsaín and La Granja.*

Palacio de La Granja de San Ildefonso★★

◑ *Open 10am-1.30pm and 3-5pm; Sun and public hols, 10am-2pm; Easter-15 Oct, 10am-6pm.* ◑*Closed Mon, 1, 6 and 23 Jan, 1 May, 25 Aug, and 8, 24, 25 and 31 Dec.* ☜*5€, no charge Wed for citizens of the European Union.* ☎ *921 47 00 19.*

The palace of La Granja is a little Versailles at an altitude of 1 192m/3 911ft at the foot of the Sierra de Guadarrama in the centre of Spain. It was built in 1731 by Philip V, grandson of Louis XIV, in pure nostalgia for the palace of his childhood.

The palace

Galleries and chambers, faced with marble or hung with crimson velvet, are lit, beneath painted ceilings and gilded stucco mouldings, by ornate chandeliers, made by the local royal workshops which became renowned in the 18C. A **Museo de Tapices**★★ (Tapestry Museum) on the first floor contains principally 16C Flemish hangings, notably *(3rd gallery)* nine of the *Honours and Virtues* series and a 15C Gothic tapestry of *St Jerome* after a cartoon by Raphael.

Gardens, Palacio de La Granja

Philip V and his second wife, Isabel Farnese, are buried in a chapel in the collegiate church.

Gardens★★

 Open Nov-Feb, 10am-6pm (6.30pm Oct and Mar; 7pm Apr; 8pm May, first two weeks of Jun, and Sep; 9pm second two weeks of Jun, and Jul-Aug). The fountains operate from 5.30pm Sat-Sun and public hols from Holy Week to middle of Aug, subject to sufficient water; all the fountains operate on 30 May, 25 Jul and 25 Aug. 3.40€ (if fountains are operating). 921 47 00 19.

Rocks were blown up and the ground levelled before the French landscape gardeners (Carlier, Boutelou) and sculptors (Dumandré, Thierry) could start work in the 145ha/358-acre park which is to a great extent inspired by the gardens and parkland of Versailles. The woodland vistas are more natural, however, the rides more rural, the intersections marked by less formal cascades. The chestnut trees, brought from France at great expense, are magnificent. The **fountains**★★ begin at the Neptune Basin, go on to the New Cascade (Nueva Cascada), a multicoloured marble staircase in front of the palace, and end at the Fuente de la Fama, or Fame Fountain, which jets up a full 40m/131ft (*see also INTRODUCTION TO SPAIN: GARDENS OF SPAIN).*

Real Fábrica de Cristales de La Granja (Royal Glass Factory)

 Open 10am-6pm; Sat, 10am-6pm (7pm 15 Jun-15 Sep); Sun and public hols, 10am-3pm.
 Closed Mon, 1 and 6 Jan and 25 December. 3.50€. 921 01 07 00.

Although the glass-works dates back to the reign of Philip V, the present building was built in 1770, under Charles III. It is one of the few examples of industrial architecture in Spain and is now the headquarters of the National Glass Centre. A glass museum (Museo del Vidrio) with exhibits and machinery from the royal factory is now housed inside the building.

Riofrío★ *See SEGOVIA*

Segovia★★★ *See SEGOVIA*

Guadix★

POPULATION: 20 322

MICHELIN MAP 578 U 20 – ANDALUCÍA (GRANADA)

Guadix, a farming centre, stands where the irrigated plain meets the dry plateau. The plateau's soft stone has been deeply ravined into fantastic shapes by erosion. The town, whose origins date back to prehistoric times, became important under the Romans and the Visigoths due to its strategic position at the junction of several important roads. Its importance grew under the period of Moorish domination and lasted until the 18C, when the town experienced its period of greatest artistic splendour. Guadix is also renowned for having one of the largest complexes of cave dwellings in Spain.

Location

Guadix is situated at the centre of the depression *(hoya)* of the same name, 57km/35mi from Granada along the A 92. The town is also a good base from which to explore the Alpujarras (Puerto de la Ragua is just 30km/18mi to the south) and the eastern fringe of the province (Baza, Orce etc). ◪ *Avenida Mariana Pineda, 18500 Guadix,* ☎ *958 66 26 65.*

> **The River of LIfe**
>
> It was the Moors who gave this old Roman camp the poetic name of Guadh-Haix, which translates as "the river of life".

☙ *Neighbouring sights are described in the following chapter: GRANADA.*

Worth a Visit

Catedral★

🕓 *Open 8.30am-1pm and 4-6pm* ☙ *2€ (cathedral and museum); no charge Fri.* ☎ *958 66 51 08.*

The east end of the cathedral is by Diego de Siloé, but the 17C Renaissance tower and Baroque **façade**★ (Fachada de la Incarnación), dating from 1713, are later additions. In the interior, the Gothic naves lead to the apse and the large lantern above the transept, both Renaissance in style.

Plaza de la Constitución

This pretty arcaded square dates from the 16C and 17C; along one of its sides stands the town hall, built at the beginning of the 17C during the reign of Philip III.

Barrio de Santiago★

This is one of the most typical districts in Guadix. Monuments of note here include the **Iglesia de Santiago**, its lovely Plateresque **doorway**★ leading to a pleasant square; and numerous seigniorial mansions such as the **Palacio de Peñaflor**. The views of the town and troglodyte quarter from the adjacent Moorish **alcazaba** *(entrance via the seminary)*, are particularly impressive. (🕓 *Open 9am-2pm and 4-7pm; Sat, 9am-2pm.* 🕓 *Closed Sun and public hols.* ☙ *0.60€.* ☎ *958 66 01 60).*

Barrio de las Cuevas★ (Troglodyte Quarter)

▸ *Walk up the street leading to the Iglesia de Santiago.* Beyond the church is an area of dwellings which have been hollowed out of the soft tufa hillside. The rocks round the entrances are whitewashed and the homes have conical chimneys built to emerge on a level with the paths. The exceptional conditions within these unique dwellings enables the temperature to be kept constantly warm in winter and cool in summer. One of the caves has been converted into a **museum**. (🕓 *Open 9am-2pm and 4-6pm; Sat, 10am-2pm.* 🕓 *Closed Sun and public hols.* ☙*1.35€).*

Excursions

Purullena

6km/4mi NW. The **road**★★ winds through tufa rocks to reach the **troglodyte village** of Purullena. Pottery-making is a well-developed cottage industry as the many stalls along the roadside testify.

B. Morandi/MICHELIN

Castillo de La Calahorra

Beyond Purullena, the Granada road rises in a corniche, affording extensive **views**★ over the plateau, cut deep by canyons. It then enters a wild landscape to reach the **Puerto de Mora** (Mora Pass) at 1 390m/4 560ft.

La Calahorra★

18km/11mi SE along the A 92. La Calahorra stands in a vast plain which lies between the Sierra Nevada and the Sierra de Los Filabres.

It is dominated by a **castillo**★★ imprisoned by four round towers with such an austere appearance that the graceful interior is completely unexpected. Park the car in the village and walk up to the castle. A heavy door opens onto a delightful Renaissance **patio**★★, a masterpiece of refinement. The design of the arcades and balustrade, the Italian-style carving surrounding the windows and the skilful proportions of the **staircase**★ convey a highly sophisticated artistic style. (*Wed, 10am-1pm and 4-6pm. No charge.* ☎ *958 67 70 98*).

Huesca★

POPULATION: 50 085

MICHELIN MAP 574 F 28 – SEE LOCAL MAP UNDER JACA – ARAGÓN (HUESCA)

Huesca, the capital of Alto Aragón (Upper Aragón), has a tranquil, provincial appearance which belies its turbulent historical past. The old town is huddled around the top of a promontory crowned by the imposing silhouette of its cathedral.

Location

Huesca stands on a plain, 72km/45mi N of Zaragoza, 91km/57mi S of Jaca and 123km/77mi NW of Lleida/Lérida, and is a good base for excursions into the Pyrenees. From Huesca, the N 330 heads north to Sabiñánigo (54km/34mi), while the A 132 runs northwest to Puente la Reina de Jaca (72km/45mi). *Plaza de la Catedral 1, 22002 Huesca,* ☎ *974 29 21 70.*

Neighbouring sights are described in the following chapters: BARBASTRO (52km/32mi SE), JACA and PIRINEOS ARAGONESES.

Background

Historical notes – In Roman times, the town was made capital of an independent state by praetor Sertorius, then became an important Moorish stronghold and was finally reconquered by **Pedro I of Aragón** in 1096. It was capital of Aragón until 1118 when Zaragoza was awarded the privilege.

The origins of a well-known Spanish saying – "Resounding like the bell of Huesca" is a Spanish expression for describing a dire event with far-reaching effects. The saying goes back to the 12C, when the King, **Ramiro II**, weary at the insolence of his nobles, summoned them to his palace ostensibly to watch the casting of a bell *(compana)* which he promised would be heard throughout Aragón. When the lords assembled, the king had the most rebellious beheaded – thereby making the fame of the bell indeed resound throughout his kingdom.

Worth a Visit

OLD QUARTER

The old hilltop city is ringed by a belt of streets, among them the **calle del Coso**, which run over the site of the former ramparts.

Catedral★

🕐 *Open 8am (10am museum) to 1.30pm and 4-7.30pm.* 🕐 *No visits during religious services.* ⊚ *3€ (museum).* ☎ *974 22 06 76.*

The cathedral's 13C façade is elegant, ornate Gothic and is divided unusually by a gallery and a typically Aragonese carved wood overhang. A narrow gable encloses a small rose window and the portal covings where the statues, carved out of friable limestone, are weatherworn. On the tympanum are the Magi and Christ appearing before Mary Magdalene.

The late-Gothic (15C-16C) church, on a square plan, is divided into a nave and two aisles covered by star vaulting. The high altar, alabaster **altarpiece**★★ dates from 1533. In this masterpiece by Damián Forment (one of Donatello's followers), three scenes of the Crucifixion appear in high relief in the middle of Flamboyant canopy and frieze decoration. Facing the cathedral is the Palacio Municipal or *Ayuntamiento* (town hall), a tastefully decorated Renaissance town house.

Museo Arqueológico Provincial★

🕐 *Open 10am-2pm and 5-8pm; Sun and public hols, 10am-2pm.* 🕐 *Closed Mon, 1 and 6 Jan, 6 and 24-25 Dec.* ⊚ *No charge.* ☎ *974 22 05 86.*

The museum is in the old university on an attractive old square. The university itself was built in 1690 as a series of eight halls round a fine octagonal patio. Parts of the former royal palace were incorporated in the building, including the gallery in which the Campana de Huesca massacre took place.

The museum contains archaeological items (mainly from the prehistoric period) and paintings, in particular a **collection**★ of Aragonese Primitives. Among the most interesting works are several by the Maestro de Sigena (16C).

Iglesia de San Pedro el Viejo★

🕐 *Open 10am-2pm.* ☎ *974 22 23 87.*

Although restored, the 11C monastery's **cloisters**★, with their historiated capitals, remain a major example of Romanesque sculpture in Aragón. On the side facing the church, the tympanum of the cloister doorway has an unusual Adoration of the Magi with all the emphasis on the giving of gifts. The capitals in the east gallery are the least restored. A Romanesque chapel contains the tombs of Kings Ramiro II (Roman sarcophagus) and Alfonso I, the Battler, the only Aragonese kings not to be buried in the royal pantheon in San Juan de la Peña.

Excursions

Monasterio de Monte Aragón

5km/3mi E along the N 240. The monastery ruins are visible from the road. It was originally built as a fortress by Sancho I Ramírez when investing the Moorish stronghold of Huesca.

TOUR THROUGH LOS MALLOS DE RIGLOS AND THE SIERRA DE LOARRE

▶ *Leave Huesca on the A 132 to Ayerbe. Continue a further 9km/5.5mi, then turn left to Agüero.*

Agüero

The setting of the village with its tiled roofs is made spectacular by a background of upstanding *Mallos* (👁 *see below*). Half a mile before Agüero, a road leads off, right, to the Romanesque **Iglesia de Santiago** where the three aisles of the church are covered by three separate stone roofs. Note the carvings on the tympanum (Epiphany, Joseph Asleep) and the covings (Salome's Dance, left).

▶ *Return to the A 132 heading back towards Huesca, then turn left onto the HU 310 in the direction of Riglos.*

Los Mallos de Riglos★★

The road becomes more enclosed and the Río Gállego soon comes into view, banked by tall crumbling cliffs, red ochre in colour. **Los Mallos**, as they are called, are a formation of rose pudding-stone, highly vulnerable to erosion, which has here created sugar loaf forms – the most dramatic group stands to the right of the road, its flamboyant mass completely dominating the small village of **Riglos**. Further up the valley is the Peña reservoir.

▶ *Head back to Ayerbe on the A 132, then turn left to Loarre along the A 1206.*

Castillo de Loarre★★

🕐 *Open 11am-2pm and 4-5.30pm; Apr-Oct, 11am-2pm and 4-7pm.* 🕐 *Closed Mon, 1 and 6 Jan, 25 and 29 Jun and 25 Dec.* ◉4€. ☎974 38 26 27.

As you approach the castle, the sheer beauty and tranquillity of the site, a veritable eyrie, becomes ever more compelling. In the 11C, Sancho Ramírez, King of Aragón and Navarra, had this impenetrable fortress built at an altitude of 1 100m/3 609ft and then installed a religious community within it. The walls, flanked by round towers, command a vast **panorama**★★ of the Ebro depression. After the massive keep and fine covered stairway, turn to the church which was completed only in the 12C. Standing over a crypt are a tall nave, a cupola and an apse adorned with blind arcades, all in the purest Romanesque style. The capitals with stylised motifs are very beautiful.

▶ *Continue SE on the A 1206 toward Esquedas.*

Bolea

The main **altarpiece** in the village church is a superb example of 15C Hispano-Flemish art.

▶ *Return to Huesca on the A 132.*

Iruña★  👁 *see Pamplona*

Jaca★

POPULATION: 14 426

MICHELIN MAP 574 E 28 –ARAGÓN (HUESCA)

Jaca stands at the foot of the Pyrenees, overlooked by the Peña de Oroel. Because of its strategic position, it developed into a prominent enclave in the fledgling Kingdom of Aragón, and became its capital in the 9C. Nowadays, Jaca is a busy crossroads and an excellent base all year round for excursions into the Pyrenees.

Location

Jaca's road links include the A 23, running from Huesca to El Puerto de Somport, and the N 240, heading to Pamplona (111km/69mi NW). The town is situated at one end of the wide Aragón river valley. 🔲 *Avenida Regimiento de Galicia 2, 22700 Jaca,* ☎ *974 36 00 98.*

👁 *Neighbouring sights are described in the following chapters: PIRINEOS ARAGONESES, Monasterio de LEYRE (70km/44mi W) and HUESCA (91km/57mi S).*

Worth a Visit

Catedral★

🕐 Open 8am-1pm and 4-8pm. ☎ 974 35 63 78.

This, Spain's oldest Romanesque cathedral, dates back to the 11C. Its carved decoration was to influence the Romanesque craftsmen who worked on the churches along the pilgrim route to Santiago de Compostela. Outside, note the **historiated capitals**★ of the south porch and behind it the south doorway where great attention has been given to the draperies on the figures in the Sacrifice of Isaac and in King David and his musicians. Gothic vaulting, regrettably embellished with ornate keystones in the 16C, covers the aisles which are unusually wide for the period. The apse and side chapels are profusely decorated with Renaissance sculpture but the cupola on squinches over the transept crossing has retained its original simplicity.

Museo Diocesano (Diocesan Museum)

⚲ Closed for restoration. ☎ 974 36 18 41.

The cloisters and adjoining halls contain Romanesque and Gothic **wall paintings**★ from village churches in the area: Urríes, Sorripas, de Ruesta, Navasa, Bagüés and a reconstitution of the Osia church apse. There is also a collection of Romanesque paintings of the Virgin and Christ.

Castillo de San Pedro

🕐 Open 11am-noon and 5-6pm. ☎ 974 36 30 18.

Built in 1595 during the reign of Philip II, the castle formed part of the defensive system consisting of citadels (Jaca and Pamplona) and military towers (Fiscal) erected to protect the border with France. This fortress, of limited height and surrounded by a moat, has a perfect pentagonal plan, with defensive bulwarks at each vertex.

Tours

Tour through Serrablo ▢1

54km/34mi – allow half a day.

▶ Leave Jaca on the A 23 towards Sabiñánigo.

This excursion runs almost entirely along the left bank of the River Gallego, where an extraordinary series of Mozarabic churches dating from the 10C and 11C have been preserved.

Museo de Dibujo

In Larrés, 18km/11mi E of Jaca along the A 23. 🕐 Open 11am-1pm and 4-7pm. ⚲ 2€. ☎ 974 48 29 81.

This museum, dedicated exclusively to sketches, is housed in the 14C Castillo de Larrés and displays work by artists such as Martín Chirino, Vázquez Díaz and Salvador Dalí. It also contains a section devoted to graphic humour, comics and short stories.

▶ Return to the A 23. Once you reach Cartirana, take the N 260 as far as Puente Oliván. Follow signs to Oliván, then turn off towards Orós Bajo, the starting point for this tour. Follow directions.

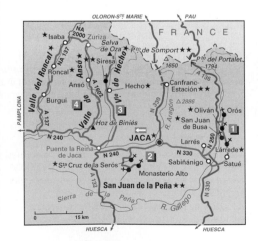

Mozarabic churches

The churches of the Serrablo share many common characteristics: they are all small with a common rectangular ground plan, with the addition of a semicircular apse; some are also crowned by a bell-tower. The walls are generally devoid of bays, while the arches used are either horseshoe or semicircular in design; occasionally, doors are framed by an alfiz surround. The most impressive of these churches are those in Orós Bajo, San Martín de Oliván, **San Juan de Busa**★ (with its unfinished apse), **San Pedro de Lárrede**★ and Satué.

▶ *From Satué, head towards Sabiñánigo.*

Museo Ángel Oresanz y Artes de Serrablo★

This museum is located in Sabiñánigo, to the S of the town centre, in the district known as Puente de Sabiñánigo. 🕐 *Open 10.30am-1.30pm and 3.30-6.30pm; Sun and public hols, 10.30am-1.30pm and 4-7pm. Apr-Sep, 10.30am-1.30pm and 4-7pm. Jul-Aug,10.30am-1.30pm and 5-9pm.* 2€. ☎ 974 48 42 61.

This, the best ethnographic museum in the Huescan Pyrenees, has been established in a delightful house built in traditional Serralbo style. The most impressive room is undoubtedly the kitchen.

Monasterio de San Juan de la Peña★★ ②

25km/15mi – 🕐*allow half a day.*

▶ *Leave Jaca on the N 240. After 11km/7mi, turn off towards Santa Cruz de la Serós*

🕐 *Open 10am-2pm and 4-7pm; Jun-Aug, 10am-2.30pm and 3.30 (4pm in June)-8pm; 16 Oct-15 Mar, 11am-2pm and 4-5.30pm.* 3.50€. ☎ 974 35 51 19 .

Santa Cruz de la Serós★

This famous convent, founded late in the 10C, was richly endowed by nobles and princesses. The nuns abandoned the convent in the 16C. Only the **Romanesque church**★, surrounded by small, typically Aragonese houses, remains. The stout belfry, crowned by an octagonal turret abuts on the lantern. The portal with its Chi-rho (sacred monogram) decorated tympanum recalls that of Jaca Cathedral. Inside, a column and capitals have been assembled to form an unusual stoup.

San Caprasio, the small church at the entrance to the village, has a nave adorned with Lombard bands and a low apse, typical of the 11C. The belfry is late 12C.

▶ *Beyond Santa Cruz de la Serós the road winds its way through the Sierra de la Peña.* 🅿 *Leave your car in the car park next to the Monasterio Alto.*

Monasterio de San Juan de la Peña★★

The most spectacular feature of this monastery is undoubtedly its **setting**★★ in a hollow beneath overhanging rocks. The site was initially settled by a group of hermits who gradually developed a monastic complex. In the middle of the 9C, they adopted the rule of St Benedict and the monastery was chosen as a pantheon for the kings

Church, Monasterio de San Juan de la Peña

B. Juge/MICHELIN

and nobles of Aragón and Navarra. In the 11C, the order incorporated itself into the Cluniac Reform. Following this, another church, the Romanesque Upper Church (Iglesia Alta), and the cloisters (12C), were built above the existing church.

The oldest preserved architectural features can be seen on the lower storey, where the Lower Church dates from the early Mozarabic monastery. It consists of two adjoining aisles divided by wide arches and ending in twin niche-apses hollowed out of the living rock. Traces of mural painting can be seen on the walls and on the undersides of the arches. The **Sala de Concilios** (Council Chamber) was built by King Sancho Garcés around the year 922.

The upper storey contains the Pantheon of the Aragón nobility, the museum, the upper church and the cloisters. The 11C-14C **Panteón de Nobles Aragoneses** houses funerary niches emblazoned with coat of arms, sacred monograms and in many cases a cross with four roses, the emblem of Iñigo Arista, founder of the Kingdom of Navarra. A door opposite leads into the **museum**.

The late-11C **Iglesia Alta** (Upper Church) comprises a single aisle, while the three apsidal chapels, decorated with blind arcades, are hollowed out of the cliff face. The **Panteón de Reyes** or Royal Pantheon, where the kings of Aragón and Navarra were buried for 500 years, opens off the north wall. The present decor is 18C.

The 12C **cloisters**★★, accessed via a Mozarabic door are cornered between the precipice and the cliff face. Here, just two galleries with historiated capitals and fragments of another remain. The mason who carved the **capitals**★★ developed a personal style and use of symbolism, apparent in his chronological survey of man from the Creation to the coming of the Evangelists, which was to influence sculpture throughout the region for years to come.

Valle de Hecho★ 3

60km/37mi – allow one day.

▷ *Leave Jaca on the N 240. In Puente la Reina de Jaca, turn right on the A 176.*

The road follows the course of the Aragón Subordán. The settlement of major interest in this area is **Hecho**★, whose houses are fine examples of traditional architecture with their stone doorways, often adorned with coats of arms, flat tiled roofs, chimneys etc. Hecho has two museums, the **Museo de Escultura al Aire Libre**, devoted to open-air sculpture, next to the Tourist Office, and the **Museo Etnológico**. (*Open 1 Jul-15 Sep, 10.30am-1.30pm and 5-9pm. 1.20€*).

2km/1.2mi further north is the village of Siresa and the **Iglesia de San Pedro**★★, which was originally part of a monastery of the same name. It is known that it existed before the 9C since we are told that it was visited by **St Eulogus of Córdoba** who was martyred in 859. It was reformed at the end of the 11C and admitted Augustinian monks. The **church**, dating from the same period, has a fine elevation and walls decorated by the ornamental use of blind arcades and buttresses. The interesting **altarpieces**★ are principally 15C. (*Open 11am-1pm and 3-5pm; in summer, 11am-1pm and 5-8pm. 1.50€*).

▷ *The road continues through a narrow valley towards* **Selva de Oza.**

Tour Through the Roncal and Ansó Valleys★ 4

161km/100mi – allow one day.

These two high valleys played an important part in the Reconquest. They have for a long time lived self-sufficiently, preserving an ancient economy based on sheep rearing with common pastureland for grazing. Religious festivals are still celebrated in traditional costume.

▷ *Leave Jaca on the N 240, heading W.*

For 47km/29mi the road runs along the valley of the River Aragón through a landscape of clay hills.

▷ *Turn right onto the NA 137.*

The road goes up the green **Roncal Valley**★ watered by the River Esca. It crosses a narrow humpbacked bridge just before its arrival in **Burgui. Roncal**★, which lends its name to the valley and the famous local cheese, has a number of fine examples of seigniorial architecture, in addition to a museum dedicated to the tenor **Julián Gayarre.** The road passes *(to the left)* the unusual fortified tower of the Iglesia de Nuestra Señora de San Salvador de Urzainqui, before reaching **Isaba/Izaba**★, without doubt the biggest tourist centre in the whole valley.

▷ *A little further N, take the NA 2000 towards the Zuriza tourist complex.*

Once in the **Ansó Valley**★, this spectacular **road**★ runs along the course of the River Veral as far as the town of **Ansó**, its houses clustered around the church, inside of which there is an interesting Museo Etnológico, dedicated to local ethnology. (◷ *Open May–Oct, 10.30am–1.30pm and 3.30–8pm; otherwise by prior arrangement. ↝ 2€. ☎ 974 37 00 22).*

▶ *To return south, follow the narrow, winding A 1602 through the Veral Valley.*

Before reaching the plain, the river flows for 3km/2mi through the gorge known as the **Hoz de Biniés**.

Jaén★

POPULATION: 107 117

MICHELIN MAP 578 S 18 – ANDALUCÍA (JAÉN)

Jaén is dominated by the Cerro de Santa Catalina (St Catherine Hill), crowned by an imposing fortress, and surrounded by a vast swathe of olive groves, from which the famous local olive oil is produced. The name of the town derives from the Arabic *geen* (on the caravan route). Its architectural heritage includes Moorish remains and a number of Renaissance buildings, many of which were designed by Vandelvira.

Location

The town extends across the foot of the Sierra de Jabalcuz. Its main road link is the A 44, which heads south to Granada (94km/59mi S) past the Parque Natural de la Sierra Mágina. ⊟ *Maestra 13 bajo, 23002 Jaén, ☎ 953 24 26 24.*

⟲ *Neighbouring sights are described in the following chapters: BAEZA (48km/30mi NE), ÚBEDA (57km/35mi NE), PRIEGO DE CÓRDOBA (67km/42mi SW) and GRANADA.*

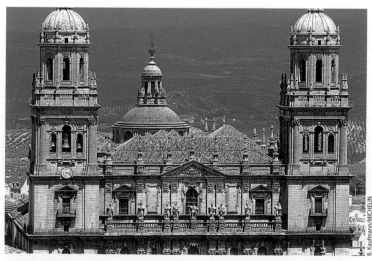

Cathedral, Jaén

B. Kaufmann/MICHELIN

Worth a Visit

Catedral★★

🕐 *Open 8.30am-1pm and 4.30-7pm; in summer, 8.30am (10am museum) to 1pm and 5-8pm.* 🕐 *Closed Sun afternoon in Jul-Aug.* 🎟 *3€.* ☎ *953 22 46 75.*

The cathedral's impressive outline dominates the town's historical quarter. It was built in the 16C and 17C by **Andrés de Vandelvira**, the most representative architect of Andalucían Baroque. The immense façade with its Baroque decoration of statues, balconies and pilasters resembles that of a palace.

The triple-nave **interior**★★ is crowned by some fine ribbed vaulting and an imposing cupola above the transept. Behind the high altar is a chapel containing the **Reliquía de Santo Rostro**★, said to hold one of the veils used by St Veronica to wipe Christ's face.

Note also the **choir stalls**★★, richly carved in the Berruguete style, the chapter house, and the sacristy, also a work by Vandelvira, which now houses the cathedral museum *(museo)*.

Museum

Access via the right arm of the transept. The cathedral treasure includes two canvases by Ribera, a delightful Flemish *Virgin and Child*, some large bronze candelabra by Master Bartolomé, and miniature choir books.

Baños Árabes★★

The Moorish baths, the largest in Spain (470m2/5 059sq ft), are beneath the 16C **Palacio de Villardompardo** and have been restored to their 11C appearance. 🕐 *Open 9am-8pm; Sat-Sun, 9.30am-2.30pm; last admission 30min before closing time.* 🕐 *Closed Mon and public hols.* 🎟 *No charge.* ☎ *953 24 80 00 (ext 4166).*

The **Museo de Artes y Tradiciones Populares** (Museum of Popular Art and Traditions) and **Museo de Arte Naïf** (Museum of Naive Art) are situated around a charming **patio**★ inside the palace.

Capilla de San Andrés★ (St Andrew's Chapel)

The **Capilla de la Immacula**★★ (Chapel of the Immaculate Conception), with a minutely decorated drum supporting its star vaulting, is a masterpiece of Plateresque art. The gilded wrought-iron **screen**★ which stands before the chapel, worked as delicately as a curtain of gold lace, is by **Master Bartolomé** (16C), a native son of Jaén.

Iglesia de San Ildefonso★

This large church, built in the 14C and 15C, has three portals, each in a different style: Gothic, Renaissance (Vandelvira) and neo-Classical (Ventura Rodríguez). The interior has several outstanding features including a magnificent **main altarpiece**, a fine tabernacle, and the **Capilla de la Virgen**, a chapel decorated with stained glass and fresco paintings, housing a statue of Jaén's patron saint.

Real Monasterio de Santo Domingo

The headquarters of the Archivo Histórico Provincial, the province's historical archives, is adorned with a well-proportioned Renaissance façade (Vandelvira) and a delightful 17C **patio**★.

Iglesia de la Magdalena

This 16C church, built above the remains of a former Arab mosque, has preserved an exquisite **ablutions patio**★.

Museo Provincial★

🕐 *Open 9am-8pm; Tue, 3-8pm; Sun and public hols, 9am-3pm.* 🕐 *Closed Mon.* 🎟 *1.50€, no charge for citizens of the European Union.* ☎ *953 25 06 00.*

This museum, housed in a building constructed in 1920 which has incorporated two 16C portals (from the old granary (pósito) and the Iglesia de San Miguel), consists of two sections: fine arts, on the first floor; and archaeology, on the ground floor, including 4C BC **Iberian sculptures from Porcuna**★, a Roman mosaic from Bruñel, and the 4C AD **Martos sarcophagus**★, a palaeo-Christian work illustrating the Seven Miracles of Jesus.

Castillo de Santa Catalina★ (St Catherine's Castle)

5km/3.1mi W. This imposing Moorish fortress, which sits impressively on the top of the hill of the same name, was restored by Ferdinand III following the reconquest of Jaén. From the castle (now Jaén's parador) the magnificent **views**★★ encompass the blue-tinged Sierra de Jabalcuz and the extensive swathes of olive groves encircling the town.

Jerez de la Frontera★★

POPULATION: 181 602

MICHELIN MAP 578 V 11 – ANDALUCÍA (CÁDIZ)

Jerez is situated with its back to the sea, looking out at the fertile countryside which surrounds it. It is a refined, elegant city and is the perfect counterpoint to the bustling provincial capital, Cádiz. At fiesta time, however, Jerez springs into life, proudly sharing with visitors those traditions for which it is justifiably famous: wine, equestrian art and flamenco.

Location

Jerez is situated in the middle of the Andalucían countryside at the heart of the Jerez-Xerz-Sherry appellation. It is just 35km/22mi from the provincial capital, Cádiz, 30km/19mi from Arcos de la Frontera, and 90km/56mi from Sevilla.

▮ *Larga 39, 11403 Jerez de la Frontera,* ☎ *956 33 11 50/62.*

Ġ *Neighbouring sights are described in the following chapters: CÁDIZ, Costa de la LUZ and PUEBLOS BLANCOS.*

Special Features

Bodega Domecq

🕭 *Visits by prior arrangement.* 🞑 *3€ weekday mornings, 4.51€ afternoons, Sat-Sun and public holidays.* ☎ *956 15 15 00.*

Historical Notes

Jerez was one of the first towns to be founded by the Moors on the Iberian Peninsula. A number of vestiges remain from the Moorish "Sahrish", including sections of the old walls, the fortress *(alcazaba)* and a mosque. In 1264, Jerez was conquered by the troops of Alfonso X, and developed into a settlement of strategic importance as well as a leading commercial centre. The economic resurgence experienced by the province of Cádiz in the 18C left its mark on Jerez, with the construction of fine Baroque buildings and its famous wine cellars, some of which can still be seen today.

Sherry

History would appear to show that the vine was first brought to this part of Spain by the Phoenicians, and that the Romans later exported large quantities of wine from the region during their long period of occupation. It is also known that despite the law of prohibition laid down in the Koran, the production and consumption of wine continued during the period of Moorish occupation. Following the Reconquest of 1264 by the troops of Alfonso X, and then once again at the end of the 16C, two varieties of grape were introduced here; namely Palomino and Pedro Jiménez, both of which provide sherry with a particular character.

Sherry is a blended white wine which is divided into five main types: **Fino** (15-17º), or extra dry, the lightest in body and strawlike in colour; **Amontillado** (18-24º), an older fino; **Oloroso** (18-24º), a medium, fragrant, full bodied and golden wine; **Dulce**, an oloroso with a higher concentration of sugar; and **Manzanilla**, a dry, light sherry from the coastal town of Sanlúcar de Barrameda. Their quality is the result of two principal factors: the region's special climate, and a careful maturing process which involves gradual blending and the use of solera or mother wines, with three or four American oak barrels placed one on top of the other. Each year a specific quantity of new wine is transferred to the top barrel; the same amount is then transferred from this barrel to the one immediately below it. This process continues until the very last barrel, which contains the desired wine. A visit to a **bodega**★ (a wine storehouse) is an interesting experience: **Domecq, González Byass, Sandeman** and **Williams&Humbert**.

JEREZ DE LA FRONTERA

Alcázar	AZ	Iglesia de San Juan de los Caballeros	AY
Bodega Domecq	AZ B²	Iglesia de San Lucas	AY
Bodega González Byass	AZ B⁴	Iglesia de San Marcos	ABY
Bodega Harvey	BZ B⁶	Iglesia de San Mateo	AZ
Bodega Sandeman	ABY B⁸	Iglesia de San Miguel	BZ
Bodega Williams & Humbert	BY B¹⁰	La Cartuja	BZ
Cabildo	BZ C²	Museo Arqueológico de Jerez	AY M
Casa Domecq	BY C⁴	Museo de Relojes	AY
Casa de los Ponce de León	AY C⁶	Palacio de Riquelme	AY V
Catedral	AZ	Palacio del Marqués de Bertemati	AZ R
Centro Andaluz de Flamenco	AY E	Real Escuela Andaluza de Arte Ecuestre	BY
Convento de Santa María de Gracia	AY F	Teatro Villamarta	BZ T
Convento de Santo Domingo	BY	Yeguada de la Cartuja	BZ
Iglesia de San Dionisio	BZ K	Zoo-Jardín Botánico	AY

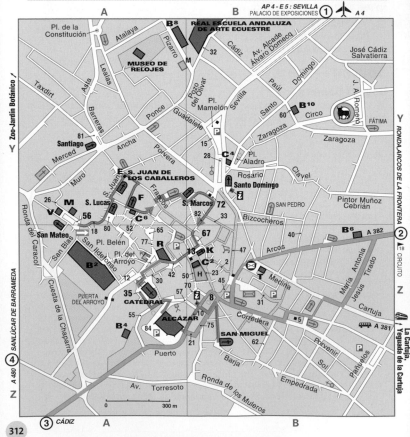

Address Book

For coin ranges, see the Legend at the back of the guide.

WHERE TO EAT

Gaitán – *Gaitán 3 – ☎ 956 16 80 21 - Closed Sun evenings in winter and Sun noon in summer–* . This well-respected restaurant serves good-quality, innovative regional cuisine. The small whitewashed dining room is long and narrow and abundantly embellished with decorative objects.

TAPAS

Juanito – *Pescadería Vieja 8-10 – ☎ 956 33 48 38 – Closed Sun and midday Monday in summer and Sun evening and Mon the rest of the year –* . The Casa Juanito, located in a pedestrianised street lined with outdoor terraces, has been serving its huge choice of tapas in Jerez for the past 50 years or more. The decor could not be more Andalucían, with its ceramic tiles and bullfighting-inspired pictures.

WHERE TO STAY

Serit – *Higueras 7 – ☎ 956 34 07 00 –* – 35 rooms. 6€. A centrally located, family-run hotel, functional and up-to-date. Best rooms, in the annex, have wood floors and wrought-iron furniture.

Hotel Doña Blanca – *Bodegas 11 – ☎ 956 34 87 61 –* – 30 rooms – 5.70€. This unpretentious hotel in an attractive Andalucían-style building has the great advantage of a superb location between the market and post office in the centre of Jerez. The bedrooms here are on the spacious side with all the usual creature comforts.

BARS AND CAFÉS

Cafetería Bristol – *Plaza Romero Martínez – Open 9am-midnight*. The presence of the Teatro Villamarta in the square explains the busy nature of this café, whose relaxing atmosphere is popular with theatregoers. One of the city's favourite haunts for afternoon coffee.

Cafetería La Vega – *Plaza Estévez – ☎ 956 32 36 18 – Open 9am-11pm*. Tourists and locals mingle on the pleasant terrace of this cafetería, situated on one of the busiest squares in central Jerez. Highly recommended at any time of day.

La Rotonda – *Larga 40 – Open 9am-11pm*. This is a classic venue is every sense of the word, in terms of its decor, atmosphere and character. It has a pleasant outdoor terrace and excellent service. A fine selection of wines, cheeses and dried sausages, as well as a small shop selling delicious sweets.

ENTERTAINMENT

The **Teatro Villamarta** (*plaza Romero Martínez*, ☎ 956 32 93 13) offers a full programme of opera, music, dance and theatre, including flamenco. The city's best-known **flamenco clubs** (*peñas flamencas*) are the Peña Tío José de Paula, at calle Merced 11 (☎ 956 30 32 67), and the popular Peña el Garbanzo, at calle Santa Clara 9 (☎ 956 33 76 67).

FERIAS AND FESTIVALS

Horses are no less important than sherry in Jerez and, in the region, locally bred mounts are equally famous. In the 16C, the Carthusian monastery (Cartuja) crossed Andalucían, Neapolitan and German breeds, giving rise to the famous **Cartujana** horse. Annually in April or May there is the **Feria del Caballo**, or Horse Fair, with racing as well as dressage and carriage competitions.

In September the **Fiesta de la Vendimia** (Wine Harvest Festival) showcases a cavalcade and a flamenco festival; the cante jondo is particularly alive and popular in Jerez, a town which is home to such famous singers as **Antonio Chacón** (1870-1929) and **Manuel Torres.**

Founded in 1730, this *bodega* is the oldest in Jerez. The visit includes some of the company's most renowned storehouses, such as the Bodega El Molino, where a whole host of celebrities have signed their names.

Bodega González Byass

Tours at 11am, noon, 1pm, 5pm, 6pm and 7pm; Sun at 10am, 11am, noon and 1pm. 6€. ☎ 956 35 70 16/ 70 00.

Established in 1835. Its most famous storehouse is the spectacular La Concha bodega, designed by Gustave Eiffel in 1862.

Walking About

The Medieval Town

The tour below passes through a labyrinth of narrow streets and highlights Jerez's importance between the 13C and 16C.

Bodega González Byass

J. Malburet/MICHELIN

Plaza del Mercado

The former medieval market is now a tranquil square surrounded by fine buildings such as the **Palacio de Riquelme**, with its imposing Renaissance façade, the 15C **Iglesia de San Mateo**, and the **Museo Arqueológico de Jerez**, a sober 18C edifice.

▶ *Follow calle Cabezas to the **Iglesia de San Lucas**, and from here continue to the Iglesia de San Juan via calle Ánimas de Lucas, plaza de Orbaneja and calle San Juan.*

Iglesia de San Juan de los Caballeros★

The interior of this medieval church has a magnificent nine-sided 14C **polygonal apse**★, topped by a ribbed cupola with jagged decoration.

▶ *Head initially along calle Francos and then calle Canto to plaza de Ponce de León.*

Note the fine **Plateresque window**★★ on one of the corners.

▶ *Continue along calle Juana de Dios Lacoste, cross calle Francos once more, then follow calle Compañía to the Iglesia de San Marcos.*

Iglesia de San Marcos

This late-15C church has a single nave crowned by a beautiful 16C **star vault**. The apse is hidden by a 16C polygonal **altarpiece**★ showing strong Flemish influence. Behind the church is the attractive plaza de Rafael Rivero.

▶ *From the square, calle Tonería leads to plaza de Plateros.*

Plaza de Plateros

This atmospheric square was an important commercial centre in the Middle Ages. The **Torre de Atalaya**, a 15C watchtower, is adorned with Gothic windows with multifoil arches.

Plaza de la Asunción★

On one side of this pleasant square stands the **Casa del Cabildo**★★ (1575), its Renaissance façade adorned with grotesque figures, cupids and Corinthian columns. The Gothic **Iglesia de San Dionisio** shows clear Mudéjar influence. Note the main door and roof, so typical of the architectural techniques employed during the reign of Alfonso X.

▶ *Head down calle José Luis Díez.*

Plaza del Arroyo

One end of the square is fronted by the **Palacio del Marqués de Bertemati**★, with its attractive façade and fine Baroque balconies.

Catedral★★

🕐 *Open 11am-1pm and 6-8pm; Sat 10am-2pm and 6-8pm; Sun 11am-2pm.* ☎ *956 34 84 82.*

This monumental cathedral, reached via a large staircase, combines both Renaissance and Baroque features. The interior of the church is extravagantly decorated and comprises five aisles. The transept is crowned by a cupola embellished with bas-reliefs of the Evangelists. The annual wine harvest festival is held in **plaza de la Asunción**, in front of the cathedral.

Alcázar★

Open 16 Sep-30 Apr, 10am-6pm; 1 May-15 Sep, 10am-8pm; last admission 30min before closing. Closed 1 and 6 Jan and 25 Dec. 1.30€. ☎ 956 31 97 98.

This impressive fortress, built by the Almohads in the 12C, is situated along alameda Vieja, from where there is an excellent **view**★★ of the cathedral. It is accessed via the **Puerta de la Ciudad** (City Gateway), a typical Almohad gate built at a 90° angle. The prayer room in the **mosque**★★, located within the walls of the Alcázar, is covered by a delightful **octagonal cupola**. A **camera obscura** has been installed in the **Palacio de Villavicencio**, providing visitors with a unique view of Jerez via its ingenious arrangement of mirrors and lenses.

Plaza del Arenal

This square, a popular meeting-place since Moorish times, is adorned with a statue of **Miguel Primo de Rivera**, a native son of the city, by Mariano Benlliure.

Iglesia de San Miguel★★

Visits at 7pm daily. ☎ 626 78 54 48.

Construction of this attractive church began in Gothic style in the late 16C although it was not completed until two centuries later. The Baroque tower above the main façade dates from this later period. In contrast, the San José façade, the oldest part of the church, is a fine example of the Hispano-Flemish style predominant in the 15C. In the interior, the highlight is a Renaissance **altarpiece**★ by Martínez Montañés.

Worth a Visit

Museo de Relojes★★

Open 10am-2pmAbre and 5-6pm; Sun and public hols 10am-2pm. Closed Mon. 5.10€. ☎ 956 18 21 00.

This clock museum is housed in the 19C Palacete de la Atalaya, surrounded by pleasant gardens. The collection numbers some 300 varied timepieces in perfect working order, mainly French and English in provenance, from the 18C and 19C. The oldest exhibit is a 17C clock in **Italian casing**.

Real Escuela Andaluza del Arte Ecuestre★

Guided tour (30 min) including facilities and training sessions, Mon, Wed and Fri, 10am-1pm (also Tue, Nov-Feb); horse show other days. Closed Sat-Sun and public hols. 6€; show: 13€ or 21€ (18€ or 24€ during fairs). ☎ 956 31 80 08.

The **Royal Andalucían School of Equestrian Art** is housed in the Recreo de las Cadenas, a 19C French-style palace. The school was founded in 1973 by Álvaro Domecq Romero to train riders in classical horsemanship on the famous Cartujana horse. The stables and tack rooms are open to the public. A weekly **show**★★ entitled "A Horse Symphony" takes place in the main arena, where these impressive beasts hold centre stage. The combination of Spanish music, riders dressed in 18C costume, and magnificent horses is a spectacle not to be missed.

Museo Arqueológico de Jerez

Open 10am-2pm and 4-7pm; 15 Jun-30 Sep, 10am-2.30pm; Sat-Sun and public hols, 10am-2.30pm. Closed Mon, 1 and 6 Jan, Good Fri, 25 Dec. 1.75€, no charge first Sun of every month. ☎ 956 34 13 50.

The archaeological museum provides an interesting overview of the history of the Jerez region. The outstanding exhibit is an elegant **Greek helmet**★ dating from the 7C BC.

La Cartuja★

6km/3.5mi SE.

This Carthusian monastery, founded in 1477, has a Greco-Roman style portal attributed to Andrés de Ribera. The Flamboyant Gothic church has a richly decorated Baroque **façade**★★★. Inside, the high altar was originally adorned with the famous canvases by Zurbarán which are now exhibited in museums in Cádiz and Grenoble (France).

La Cartuja Stud Farm★ (Yeguada de la Cartuja)

At the Finca Fuente del Suero, 6.5km/4mi from Jerez on the Medina Sidonia road. Visits (1hr 30min-2hr), Sat, 11am. Closed 16 Dec-14 Jan. 10€; 6€ (child). ☎ 956 16 28 09.

Members of the public are able to visit the stud farm's facilities and get a closer look at the famous Cartujana horses.

▸ Convento de Santo Domingo; Casa Domecq (18C, doorway★).

León★★

POPULATION: 147 625

MICHELIN MAP 575 E 13 (TOWN PLAN) – CASTILLA Y LEÓN (LEÓN)

León, one-time capital of the kingdom of León, stretches along the banks of the Bernesga and is surrounded on all sides by the Meseta. The city was an important halt along the Way of St James and has preserved many fine monuments from its prestigious past, including masterpieces of Romanesque (San Isidoro), Gothic (cathedral) and Renaissance architecture (San Marcos).

Location

The city is situated on the southern fringes of the Cordillera Cantábrica, the northern boundary of the Meseta. The nearby AP 66 motorway runs north to Oviedo (121km/75mi). Palencia and Valladolid are located 128km/80mi and 139km/87mi respectively to the southeast. *Plaza Regla 3, 24003 León, ☎ 987 23 70 82.*

Neighbouring sights are described in the following chapter: The WAY OF ST JAMES.

Background

The medieval town – In the 10C, as their territory expanded, the kings of Asturias moved their capital from Oviedo to León. They built a walled city on the site of earlier Roman fortifications and peopled it with Mozarabs, Christian refugees from Córdoba and Toledo; by the 11C and 12C León had become virtually the centre of Christian Spain.

The east part of the city recalls the early medieval period clearly in the still-evident remains of the ramparts and the houses fronting alleys where peeling roughcast reveals brickwork façades. The most evocative quarter, known as the Barrio Húmedo (wet quarter or watering-hole) on account of its many small bars and restaurants, lies between the arcaded **Plaza Mayor** and **Plaza de Santa María del Camino**, a particularly attractive square with wooden porticoes, a fountain and church belfry.

The modern city – As León flourishes thanks to its industry, the city limits are extending westwards along the river banks. Its development has depended on hydroelectric power from the basin of the Esla river, local mineral resources (iron and coal) and livestock farming.

León's artistic tradition has also been maintained, as can be seen in Gaudí's neo-Gothic palace, **Casa de Botines** on plaza de San Marcelo.

Address Book

For coin ranges, see the Legend at the back of the guide.

WHERE TO EAT

☞ **Rancho Chico** – *Plaza San Martín 7 –* ☎ 987 26 04 83 – *Closed Wed, 15-30 Sep and 15-end Feb –* ▨ . For more than 20 years this restaurant has been earning plaudits from locals for its reasonably priced, simple, traditional fare. Its location on the pleasant and lively plaza de San Martín is an added bonus. Possible to eat on the terrace in fine weather.

☞☞ **Casa Pozo** – *Plaza San Marcelo 15 –* ☎ 987 22 30 39 – *Closed evenings –* ▨ . This is one of the oldest restaurants in León, in business without a break since 1936. The two entries lead to separate tapas bars and assorted dining areas. A good place to sample the best of regional dishes.

WHERE TO STAY

☞☞ **La Posada Regia** – *Regidores 11 –* ☎ 987 21 31 73 – 20 rooms – ▭ . A small, welcoming hotel in the old quarter of León, just a stone's throw from the cathedral. The building itself dates from the 14C and is an attractive mix of open brickwork and stone. Spacious, attractively furnished bedrooms.

☞☞☞ **Parador Hotel San Marcos** – *Plaza San Marcos 7 –* ☎ 987 23 73 00 – P ▨ – ▭ 10.30€ – *Restaurant 26.50€.* Few hotels can claim to have a façade that is a masterpiece of Plateresque art! The interior continues the visual feast with its magnificent church and impressive Renaissance cloisters. Every corner of this former convent and pilgrims' hostel is a piece of art and history, in what is the most exclusive establishment in the parador chain.

Special Features

Catedral★★★

🕐 *Open 10am-2pm and 4-7pm; Jun-Sep, 10am-2pm and 5-8pm.* 🕐 *Closed Mon and 24 and 31 Dec.* ✍ *1.20€.* ☎ *987 23 64 05.*

The cathedral, built mainly between the mid-13C and late 14C, is true Gothic in style even to the very high French-inspired nave with vast windows.

Main façade

The façade is pierced by three deeply recessed and richly carved portals separated by unusual, sharply pointed arches. The gently smiling Santa María Blanca *(a copy: original in the apsidal chapel)* stands at the pier of the central doorway in which the lintel carries a carving of the Last Judgement with graphic portraits of the blessed and the damned. The left portal tympanum illustrates scenes from the Life of Christ, while the right portal, the Puerta de San Francisco, includes the Dormition and the Coronation of the Virgin.

South façade

The statues decorating the jambs of the central doorway are extremely fine.

Interior

The outstanding **stained-glass windows**★★★ – 125 windows and 57 oculi with an area of 1 200m2/12 917sq ft – are unique in Spain but by their sheer mass endangers the resistance of the walls (the last restoration was at the end of the last century). The west front rose and the three central apsidal chapels contain the oldest, 13C-15C glass; the Capilla de Santiago (St James's Chapel) has glass in which the Renaissance influence is already apparent while the nave windows, which were made much later (some are even considered modern), illustrate three major themes: the vegetable and mineral kingdoms (below), historic personages and heraldic crests (behind the triforium) and, high up, the blessed.

The Renaissance **trascoro**★ by Juan de Badajoz, includes four magnificent alabaster high reliefs framing Esteban Jordán's triumphal arch through which there is an attractive view down the length of the nave.

The high altar **retable**, painted by Nicolás Francés, is a good example of the 15C international style. To the left is a remarkable **Entombment**★, which shows a Flemish School influence and is attributed to the Master of Palanquinos. At the foot of the altar, a silver reliquary contains the relics of San Froilán, the city patron.

Several Gothic tombs can be seen in the ambulatory and transept, in particular that of Bishop Don Rodrigo – in the Virgen del Carmen Chapel to the right of the high altar – which is surmounted by a multifoil arch.

Claustro★

Before entering the cloisters, note the well-preserved, sheltered north transept doorway dedicated to the figure of the Virgin with the Offering, at the pier.

The galleries are contemporary with the 13C-14C nave but the vaulting, with its ornately carved keystones, was added at the beginning of the 16C. The galleries are interesting for the frescoes by Nicolás Francés and the tombs dating from the Romanesque and Gothic periods.

Museo

📷 *Guided tours (30min), 9.30am-1.30pm and 4-6.30pm; Jun-Sep, 9.30am-2pm and 4-7.30pm;* 🕐 *Closed Sat afternoon Oct-May, Sun and public hols. Last admission 1 hr before closing.* ✍ *3.50€.* ☎ *987 87 57 70.*

This museum collection includes a French-inspired 15C statue of St Catherine, a Christ carved by Juan de Juni in 1576 (proportioned in such a way as to be viewed from below), a Mozarabic Bible, with miniatures, from 920, an antiphonary dating from the same period, a 13C codex illustrated with engravings, and the Plateresque staircase which used to lead up to the chapter house.

Worth a Visit

San Isidoro★

The **basilica**, built into the Roman ramparts, its belfry like a watchtower overlooking the walls, was dedicated in 1063 to Isidore, Archbishop of Sevilla and Doctor of the Visigothic Church, whose ashes had been brought north for burial in Christian territory since Sevilla was then under Moorish rule. Of the 11C church there remains only the

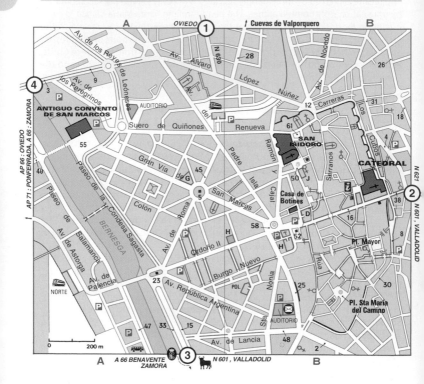

LEÓN

Alcalde Miguel Castaño	B	2	González de Lama	B	18	Quevedo Av. de	A	40
Almirante Martín-			Guzmán el Bueno			Ramiro Valbuena	A	45
Granizo Av. del	A	3	Glorieta de	A	23	Rúa	B	
Ancha	B	16	Independencia Av. de	B	25	Sáez de Miera Pas. de	A	47
Arquitecto Ramón			Inmaculada Pl. de	A	5	San Francisco Pas. de	B	48
Cañas del Rio	B	4	Jorge de Montemayor	B	26	San Isidoro Pl. de	B	50
Caño Badillo	B	8	Mariano Andrés Av. de	B	28	San Marcelo Pl. de	B	52
Cruz Roja de León	A	9	Murias de Paredes	B	30	San Marcos Pl. de	A	55
Espolón Pl. de	B	12	Ordoño II	A		San Pedro	B	38
Facultad Av. de la	A	15	Padre Isla Av. del	AB		Santo Domingo Pl. de	B	58
			Palomera	B	31	Santo Martino Pl. de	B	61
			Papalaguinda Pas. de	A	33			

pantheon. Construction of the present basilica began at the very end of the 11C and it underwent modifications at a later date: the apse and transept are Gothic while the balustrade and the pediment on the south front were added during the Renaissance. The sculptures on the Romanesque portals, depicting Abraham's Sacrifice and the Descent from the Cross, are contemporary with those of the church at Frómista.

Panteón Real★★

Guided tours (40min), 10am-1.30pm and 4-6.30pm; Sun and public hols, 10am-1.30pm; Jul-Aug, 9am-8pm; Sun and public hols, 9am-2pm. Closed 1 Jan and 25 Dec. 2.40€, no charge Thu afternoon. 987 87 61 61.

The Royal Pantheon is one of the earliest examples of Romanesque architecture in Castilla. The **capitals**★ crowning the short, thick columns bear traces of the Visigothic tradition yet at the same time introduce great novelty into Romanesque carving in Spain. Some, with plant motifs, show influences from Asturian art, while others are fully historiated.

The beautifully preserved 12C **frescoes**★★ are outstanding. They illustrate not only classic themes from the New Testament but also scenes from country life; note, on the inside of an arch, a calendar of seasonal tasks.

The pantheon is the resting place of 23 kings and queens and many children.

Tesoro★★

The treasury contains works of great artistic value. The 11C reliquary containing the relics of San Isidoro is made of wood, faced with embossed silver and covered in a Mozarabic embroidery. Other items include the famous **Cáliz de Doña Urraca**★, or Doña Urraca's chalice, comprising two Roman agate cups mounted in the 11C in a

Panteón Real de San Isidoro, León

gold setting inlaid with precious stones, the 11C **Arqueta de los Marfiles**★ (Ivory Reliquary) in which each finely carved plaque represents an Apostle, and another reliquary decorated with Limoges enamelwork (13C). The library contains over 300 incunabula and a large number of manuscripts adorned with miniatures, including a Mozarabic Bible dating from 960.

Antiguo Convento de San Marcos★ (Former Monastery of St Mark)

Part of the monastery has been converted into a parador. The site has been connected with the Knights of the Order of Santiago or St James since the 12C First it was the site of the mother house of the soldier friars, protectors of pilgrims on the way to Santiago de Compostela; three centuries later, when the Catholic Monarchs did away with the privileges of the Military Orders and became the Grand Masters themselves it was the site of the monastery planned by Ferdinand as being worthy of the dignity and riches acquired by the knights during the Reconquest. This resulted in the present sumptuous edifice, built finally at the height of the Renaissance. The church was completed in 1541 but work continued right up to the 18C.

The 100m/328ft long **façade**★★ has a remarkable unity of style in spite of the addition of a Baroque pediment in the 18C. It consists of two storeys of windows and niches set within a regular layout of friezes and cornices, engaged columns and pilasters. Medallions in high relief, of people from the Bible, ancient Rome, or Spain, provide additional decoration: Lucretia and Judith flank Isabel the Catholic, Trajan and Augustus, and Charles V. Carving above the main entrance traces St James' life from the legend of his slaying of the Moors to his apotheosis (at the apex of the pediment). The **church** front (on the extreme right), emblazoned with scallop shells, symbols of the pilgrimage to Santiago de Compostela, remains incomplete. The shell theme is repeated inside, on the wall behind the high altar.

Museo de León★

🕐 *Open 10am-2pm and 4-7pm; Jul-Sep, 10am-2pm and 5-8pm; Sun and public hols, 10am-2pm.* 🕐 *Closed Mon, 6 Jan and 24 and 31 Dec.* 🔸 *1.20€, no charge Sat-Sun, 23 Apr, 18 May, 12 Oct and 6 Dec.* ☎ *987 23 64 05.*

The first gallery of the museum, with its star vaulting, displays among its works of art from the Mozarabic to the Late Gothic period, the 10C Votive Cross of Santiago de Peñalba and an outstanding 11C ivory crucifix, the **Cristo de Carrizo**★★★. A Byzantine influence is apparent in the small figure's great presence and penetrating gaze, the formally dressed hair and beard and the arrangement of the loincloth. Through a window can be seen the *artesonado* Renaissance ceiling of the old chapter house (now part of the parador). The **cloister** galleries, built between the 16C and 18C, now serve as a lapidary museum (note the fine medallions on the keystones). The northeast corner contains a low relief of the Nativity with an interesting architectonic perspective by Juan de Juni.

The **sacristy**★, a sumptuous creation by Juan de Badajoz (1549), has ribbed vaulting decorated with scallop shells, ribands, cherubim and bosses carved as masks. Several works by Juan de Juni are displayed.

Excursions

San Miguel de Escalada★

28km/17mi W. Leave León via ③ on the town plan.

In the 11C, Alfonso III made a gift of an abandoned monastery to a group of monks who were expelled from Córdoba, enjoining them to rebuild. Of their work only the church remains (at the centre of a terrace) but even so, it is one of the few Mozarabic edifices in Spain and the best preserved. The **exterior gallery**★, built in 1050, has horseshoe-shaped arches resting on carved capitals at the top of smoothly polished columns. The monastery church (**iglesia**★) building is considerably earlier, dating from 913. The nave and two aisles, covered with wooden vaulting, are divided from the apses by a triple-arched portico and a balustrade of panels carved with Visigothic (birds pecking seeds, bunches of grapes) and Moorish (stylised foliage) motifs. (🕐 Open 10am-2pm and 4-6pm; May-Sep, 10am-2pm and 5-8pm; *Sun and public hols, 10am-2pm.* 🕐 *Closed Mon.* 👁 *No charge.* ☎ *987 23 70 82).*

Cuevas de Valporquero★★ (Valporquero Caves)

47km/29mi N on the LE 311. 👁 *Guided tours (1hr 15min), Jun-Sep, 10am-2pm and 3.30-7pm; Oct-May, Fri-Sun and public hols only, 10am-5pm.* 👁 *€5.90.* ☎ *987 57 64 08.*

The caves hollowed out by underground streams are still in the process of formation (be careful not to slip). The temperature is constant at 7°C/45°F. Neutral lighting sets off the extraordinary shapes of the concretions – there is a stalactite "star" hanging from the roof of the large chamber – and the variety of tones (35 have been counted) of red, grey and black of the mineral oxide stained stone. The tour ends with a walk along a narrow passage 1 500m/1 640yd long cut obliquely by subterranean waters through a 40m/131ft thick layer of soft rock.

Lérida★ 👁 see Lleida

Monasterio de Leyre★

MICHELIN MAPS 573 OR 574 E 26 – NAVARRA

A splendid **panorama**★★ opens out at the end of a steeply winding approach road to the monastery, over the man-made embalse de Yesa (lake); on all sides are marl hills, their limestone crests forming majestic ramparts while in the Sierra de Leyre itself, great walls of mixed ochre-coloured stone and local rock hang suspended, halfway up the ridge face.

Location

The monastery is situated on the southern slopes of the Sierra de Leyre, close to the Yesa Reservoir. 🅘 ☎ *948 88 41 50.*

👁 *Neighbouring sights are described in the following chapters: SANGÜESA/ZANGOZA (15km/9mi SW), PAMPLONA (51km/32mi NW) and JACA (68km/42mi E).*

Background

Historical notes – By the early 11C, the Abbey of San Salvador de Leyre had established itself as the uncontested spiritual centre of Navarra; Sancho III, the Great, and his successors made it their pantheon and gave their blessing to the building of a church which, with its crypt, was to be one of the earliest examples of Romanesque art in Spain (consecrated 1057). Bishops of Pamplona were, by tradition, former abbots of Leyre which held dominion over some 60 villages and 70 churches and monasteries.

Crypt

In the 12C, however, when Navarra was joined to Aragón, the royal house neglected Leyre in favour of San Juan de la Peña; in the same period the Pamplona bishops sought greater authority and instituted a lawsuit which considerably reduced both the finances and the prestige of the old monastery. In the 13C, the monastery was home to the Cistercian Order but by the 19C it had been abandoned. In 1954, however, a Benedictine community from Silos took it over. They restored the 17C and 18C conventual buildings which have now been converted into a hostelry.

Special Features

Iglesia★★ (Church) ○ 30min
○ *Open 10.15am-2pm and 3.30-7pm (6pm Nov-Feb).* ○ *Closed 1 and 6 Jan and 25 Dec.* ⊙ *1.80€.* ☎ *948 88 41 50.*

East end

11C. Three apses of equal height, together with the nave wall surmounted by a turret and a further square tower with treble windows, make a delightful group. The beautiful smoothness of the walls and the absence of decoration, apart from several modillions, indicate the building's great age.

Crypt★★

The crypt, built in the 11C to support the Romanesque church above (with which it shares the same ground plan), looks even older, so roughly robust and archaic is its appearance. The vaulting is relatively high but divided by arches with enormous voussoirs and, in some cases, double ribs, curving down onto massive capitals, incised only with the most rudimentary lines. Unusually these capitals stand on short shafts of unequal height, practically at ground level.

Interior★

In the 13C when the Cistercians rebuilt the church's central aisle to include a bold Gothic vault, they nevertheless retained the first bays of the earlier Romanesque church as well as the chancel and semicircular apses. The three aisles which have come down to us intact have barrel vaulting with double ribs springing throughout from the same height. The decorative elegance arises from engaged pillars, finely designed capitals and beautifully assembled blocks of rough-hewn stone. In the north bay a wooden chest contains the remains of the first kings of Navarra.

West portal★

12C. The portal's rich decoration has won it the name of Porta Speciosa. Carvings cover every available space. On the tympanum are archaic statues – Christ (centre), the Virgin Mary and St Peter *(on His right)* and St John *(on His left)*; the covings are alive with monsters and fantastic beasts. Above, the spandrels show (on the right) the Annunciation and the Visitation.

Excursions

Hoz de Lumbier★

14km/9mi W. The gorge cut by the Irati through the Sierra de Leyre foothills between Lumbier and Liédana is barely 5km/3mi long and so narrow that it appears at either end as a mere crack in the cliff face. There is a good **view** of the gorge from a lookout point on the road (N 240).

Hoz de Arbayún★

31km/19mi N along the N 240 and NA 211. The river Salazar is so steeply enclosed within the limestone walls of the Sierra de Navascués that the road has to diverge from the river course and the only way to see it is by going to the viewpoint north of Iso. From there a splendid **view**★★ opens onto the end of the canyon where the cliff walls are clad, at their base, in lush vegetation through which flows the sparkling stream.

Lizarra★★   *see Estella*

Lleida/Lérida★

POPULATION: 119 380

MICHELIN MAP 574 H 31 – CATALUNYA (LLEIDA)

Lleida was once a citadel, built on high ground to command a point where communications crossed. Caesar's and Pompey's legions stormed it savagely; the Moors occupied it from the 8C to the 12C.

The ancient fortress, the Zuda or Azuda, sited like an acropolis, and occupied in the 13C by the counts of Catalunya, was destroyed by artillery fire in 1812 and 1936, but the fortifications which surround it remain. The glacis has been converted into gardens. From the terraces there is an extensive view of the town, the green Segre plain and, to the southeast, the Sierra la Llena. Lleida stands at the heart of a fertile plain and is an important fruit-growing centre.

Location

Lleida is the capital of the only province in Catalunya that is not bordered by the sea. The city is an important communications hub, linked to Barcelona by the AP 2 motorway and A 2 highway, the Pyrenees by the C 1313 and N 240, and Huesca via the N 240. *Avenida de Madrid 36, 25002 Lleida, ☎ 902 25 00 50 or 973 27 09 97.*

Neighbouring sights are described in the following chapters: MONTBLANC (61km/38mi SE), TARRAGONA (97km/60mi SE), ZARAGOZA (150km/94mi W) and the PIRINEOS ARAGONESES.

Address Book

WHERE TO EAT

Santbernat – *Saracíbar* – ☎ 973 27 10 31 – 🍽 – *Reservation recommended*. Although the Santbernat is located above the bus station, don't be put off by first appearances as the restaurant is one of the best in the city. Attractive decor, albeit a bit kitsch, plus an excellent choice of local specialities.

WHERE TO STAY

Hotel Goya – *Alcalde Costa 9* – ☎ 973 26 67 88 – 🛏 – *18 rooms*. This pleasant small hotel is located in a lively district near the main shopping area and city centre. Although lacking in luxuries, the rooms are bright, clean and functional. Excellent value for money.

Worth a Visit

🕐 *To reach the cathedral, take the lift from plaza de Sant Joan.*

Seu Vella★★★ (Old Cathedral)

🕐 *Open 10am-1.30pm and 3-5.30pm; Jun-Sep, 10am-1.30pm and 4-7.30pm; last admission 20min before closing.* 🕐 *Closed Mon, 1 Jan and 25 Dec.* ☞ *2.40€, no charge Tue.* ☎ *973 23 06 53.*

The cathedral stands on a remarkable **site**★, dominating the city from inside the walls. It was built between 1203 and 1278 on the site of a mosque; the tall, octagonal belfry was added in the 14C. Philip V converted it into a garrison fortress in 1707.

Iglesia★★

The outstanding decoration in this transitional style church occurs in its great variety of **capitals**★, many of which are historiated. Those in the apses and transept illustrate themes from the Old Testament, those in the nave and aisles, scenes from the New Testament. Moorish influences can be seen in the exterior decoration, particularly in the carvings of the Puerta de Els Fillols (Godchildren's Doorway) off the south aisle and in the Puerta de la Anunciata (Annunciation Doorway), in the corresponding transept. Above is a lovely rose window. The extremely delicate style of carving, reminiscent of Moorish stuccowork, on the capitals of the church doorways, has come to be known as the Romanesque School of Lleida and may be seen throughout the region, in particular on the superb **portal**★★ from the Iglesia de **Agramunt** *(52km/32mi NE).*

Claustro★★

The cloisters have an unusual position in front of the church. Their galleries, completed during the 14C, are remarkable for the size of the bays and the beautiful stone tracery, different in each case. Although the cloisters are Gothic in style, the delicately carved decoration of plant motifs on the **capitals**★ and friezes is Moorish- influenced. There is a fine view from the south gallery extending over the town and surrounding countryside.

In the southwest corner stands the **bell tower**★★, an interesting Gothic construction 60m/197ft high.

The calle Major is lined by several buildings of interest: the 13C **Palau de la Paeria**, now the town hall *(ayuntamiento)*, with its fine façadea; the **Hospital de Santa María**, adorned with a **patio**★ showing Renaissance influence; and the 18C **Seu Nova** (new cathedral).

▶ *Exit through the Puerta del Lleó towards calle Sant Martí*

Iglesia de Sant Martí★

🕐 *Open 10am-1.30pm and 4-8pm; Sun and public hols, 10am-1.30pm.* 🕐 *Closed Mon, 1 and 6 Jan, Good Fri, 1 May and 25-26 Dec.* ☞ *1.80€, no charge Tue.* ☎ *973 28 30 75.*

Although built in the 12C, this church was substantially remodelled three centuries later. It was subsequently used as both a barracks and a prison. An interesting **collection**★ of sacred art from the Museo Diocesano is on display in the nave.

Iglesia de Sant Llorenç

🕐 *Open 8.30am-1pm and 5-8.30pm (7pm Sun and public hols).* ☎ *973 26 79 94.*

The late Romanesque church (13C) shows heavy Gothic influence, illustrated by its belfry and the pointed arches separating the central nave from the side aisles. Note the fine collection of Gothic retables.

Hospital de Santa María

🕐 *Open 9.30am-2pm and 5.30-8.30pm; Sat and public hols, noon-2pm and 5.30-8.30pm; Sun, noon-2pm; Jun-Sep, noon-2pm and 6-9pm; Sat and public hols, 11am-2pm and 7-9pm; Sun, 11am-2pm.* 🕐 *Closed Mon, 1 and 6 Jan, 1 May and 24-25 Dec.* ☞ *No charge.* ☎ *973 27 15 00.*

The most impressive feature in this former hospital, dating from the 15C, is the fine **patio**★, showing clear Renaissance influence. Nowadays the building is the headquarters of the Institut d'Estudis Illerdencs.

Palau de la Paeria

🕐 *Open 11am-2pm and 5-8pm; Sun and public hols, 11am-2pm.* ☎ *973 70 03 94.*

This 13C building in calle Major is renowned for its splendid **façade**★. The palace is now Lleida's City Hall, with a museum devoted to local archaeology in the basement.

🝙 Palacio Episcopal (Museo Diocesano).

Lugo★

POPULATION: 87 605

MICHELIN MAP 571 C 7 (TOWN PLAN) – GALICIA (LUGO)

Under the Romans Lugo was capital of the province of Gallaecia, from which period the town's walls, old bridge and thermal baths still survive. Today, the administrative centre of the modern province of Lugo is a pleasant town with wide shopping streets such as the rúa da Raíña and plaza de Santo Domingo and a distinguished old quarter huddled around the cathedral.

Location

Lugo enjoys a lofty setting (485m/1 591ft) on the left bank of the River Miño, at the heart of Galicia, 97km/61mi from A Coruña/La Coruña along the A 6, 96km/60mi from Orense/Ourense on the N 540, and 107km/67mi from Santiago de Compostela on the A 6 and A 54. ⛳ *Praza Maior 27, 27001 Lugo, ☎ 982 23 13 61.*

  ◔ *Neighbouring sights are described in the following chapters: RÍAS ALTAS, The WAY OF ST JAMES and A CORUÑA/La CORUÑA.*

Special Features

Old Town

Murallas★★

The walls were built by the Romans in the 3C, although they have undergone significant modifications since that time, particularly during the Middle Ages. They are made of schist slabs levelled off at a uniform 10m/33ft to form a continuous perimeter over 2km/1.2mi long with 10 gateways into the old quarter. In 2000, the walls were declared a World Heritage Site by UNESCO.

Catedral★

The Romanesque church (1129) was modified in later years by Gothic and Baroque additions. The Chapel of the Wide-Eyed Virgin at the east end, by Fernando Casas y Novoa who built the Obradoiro façade of the cathedral in Santiago de Compostela, has a Baroque rotunda enhanced by a stone balustrade. The north doorway, sheltered

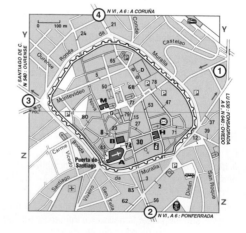

by a 15C porch, has a fine Romanesque **Christ in Majesty**✶. The figure is above a capital curiously suspended in mid-air and carved with the Last Supper.

Inside, the Romanesque nave is roofed with barrel vaulting and lined with galleries, a feature common in pilgrimage churches. There are two immense wooden Renaissance altarpieces at the ends of the transept – the south one is signed by the sculptor Cornelis de Holanda (1531). A door in the west wall of the south transept leads to the small but elegant **cloisters**.

City squares

The 18C **Palacio Episcopal**, facing the north door of the cathedral on **praza de Santa María**, is a typical *pazo*, one storey high with smooth stone walls, advanced square wings framing the central façade and decoration confined to the Gil Taboada coat of arms on the main doorway.

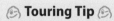

😊 Touring Tip 😊

A stroll along the sentry path on the walls. Any of the flights of steps leading from the town's gateways, as well as the ramp at the Puerta de Santiago, opposite the cathedral, will take you up to the path, from where there are some fine views of Lugo and its surrounding countryside.

Plays and concerts are given in the square in summer. **Praza del Campo**, behind the palace, is lined by old houses and has a fountain at its centre. Calle de la Cruz with its bars and restaurants, and **praza Maior**, dominated by the 18C **town hall,** with its gardens and esplanade, are popular with the townspeople as places to meet and stroll. The rúa da Raiña is home to the Alejo Madarro sweet shop, which first opened its doors in the middle of the 19C.

Museo Provincial

🕐 *Open 10.30am-2pm and 4.30-8.30pm (8pm Sat); Sun, 11am-2pm; Jul-Aug, 11am-2pm and 5-8pm; Sat, 10am-2pm.* 🕐 *Closed Sun and public hols (Jun-Aug) and 1 Jan, 22 May and 24-25 and 31 Dec.* 🖾 *No charge.* ☎ *982 24 21 12.*

This museum, which is dedicated to various aspects of Lugo art, is housed in the 18C kitchens of the former Monasterio de San Francisco. It has managed to re-create the atmosphere of a traditional country kitchen similar to those found in some of the more remote villages in the area (🖝 *see Santa Eulalia de Bóveda, below*). The museum is on two floors and includes one room devoted to ceramics from Sargadelos, in addition to coins and numerous exhibits from the Roman period. The former cloister of San Francisco contains an interesting collection of sundials, as well as several altars and sarcophagi. Several entrances connect with the **Museo Nelson Zúmel**, dedicated to Spanish paintings from the 19C and 20C.

Excursion

Santa Eulalia de Bóveda

14km/9mi SW. ▶*Take the Orense road and turn right after 4km/2.5mi. After 2km/1.2mi turn left towards Burgo, and then right, in Poutomillos, after a further 7km/4.5mi.*
🕐 *Open 11am-2pm and 3.30-7.30pm; Jun-Sep, 11am-2pm and 4.30-8.30pm; Sun and public hols all year, 11am-2pm.* 🕐 *Closed Mon.* ☎ *609 23 77 79.*

This attractive Galician village still has granite farm buildings with tile-stone roofs and drying sheds or *hórreos*. The **palaeo-Christian monument** discovered at the beginning of the 20C and excavated in 1924, consists of a vestibule (now open to the sky), a rectangular chamber with a basin and round-arched niche and frescoes of birds and leaves, doubtless of Christian origin, on the walls. The dating and purpose of the monument continue to intrigue archaeologists.

Madrid★★★

POPULATION: 3 084 673

MICHELIN MAPS 575 OR 576 K 18-19 (TOWN PLAN) –

MAP 121 ALREDEDORES DE MADRID –

MICHELIN CITY PLAN MADRID 42 AND 2042 – MADRID

Madrid is one of Europe's most hospitable, cosmopolitan and lively cities, with wide avenues, attractive parks and a great sense of joie de vivre. It became the country's capital in the 16C at a time when Spain ruled over a vast empire. The city's main monuments, Classical and Baroque in style, were built during the 17C, 18C and 19C. As a result of the artistic legacies of the Habsburgs and Bourbons, Madrid is home to an exceptional wealth of paintings, enhanced considerably in recent years by the superb collections on display in the Museo Thyssen-Bornemisza and Centro de Arte Reina Sofia.

Location

Europe's highest capital stands at an altitude of 646m/2 119ft at the centre of the Iberian Peninsula, to the southeast of the Sierra de Guadarrama mountain range. The city has a dry, continental climate characterised by hot summers and cold, sunny winters. ⃞ *Plaza Mayor 3, 28013 Madrid, ☏ 91 588 16 36; Duque de Medinaceli 2, 28014 Madrid, ☏ 91 429 49 51/31 77; Madrid-Barajas Airport, 28042 Madrid, ☏ 91 305 86 56. www.munimadrid.es*

⃠ *Neighbouring sights are described in the following chapters: ALCALÁ DE HENARES (32km/20mi E), Monasterio de EL ESCORIAL (49km/30mi NW), ARANJUEZ (47km/29mi S), TOLEDO (71km/44mi SW), SEGOVIA (98km/61mi NW) and Sierra de GUADARRAMA.*

Background

Madrid in the past – Madrid, an unimportant village until the Moorish invasion, owes its name to the fortress *(alcázar)* of Majerit built under Mohammed I on the banks of the Manzanares in the 9C. In 1083 it was captured by Alfonso VI, who, it is said, discovered a statue of the Virgin by a granary *(almudín)* as he entered the town. He then converted the town mosque into a church, dedicating it to the Virgin of the Almudena who was declared the city patron. From the 14C the kings of Castilla came regularly to Madrid; Emperor Charles V rebuilt the Muslim *alcázar* and in 1561 Philip II moved the court from Toledo to Madrid. The medieval town expanded rapidly and the population tripled. Its layout of winding streets can still be seen today around Plaza Mayor.

The town really began to develop under the last of the Habsburgs, in the middle of Spain's Golden Age (16C). During the reign of Philip III, Juan Gómez de Mora undertook a series of reforms and from then on Plaza Mayor was to be the heart of the city. The town plan drawn up in 1656 by Pedro Texeira, gives a good impression of Madrid under Philip IV, when it had a large number of convents and churches. The king was an art lover who gave his patronage to many artists including Velázquez and Murillo, as well as men of letters such as Lope de Vega, Quevedo, Calderón and Tirso de Molina.

From a town to a city – It was in the 18C under the Bourbons that the town underwent its greatest transformations. Philip V decided to build a royal palace, and Charles III, inspired by ideas from European courts, provided Madrid with a splendour hitherto unknown. This was the Prado and the Puerta de Alcalá, magnificent examples of neo-Classical town planning. In turn, the nobility began building **palaces**, such as **Liria** and **Buenavista**, which they surrounded with gardens.

The 19C began with occupation by the French and the Madrid rebellion of May 1808 and the brutal reprisals it provoked. In the second half of the 19C, Madrid underwent great alteration: in 1857 the remaining ramparts were demolished and a vast expansion plan *(ensanche)* gave rise to the districts of Chamberí, Salamanca and Argüelles, and, at the end of the century, **Arturo Soria's** *Ciudad Linea*, a revolutionary town planning project, provided for a residential quarter for 30 000 inhabitants around today's avenida de Arturo Soria.

At the beginning of the 20C, architecture was French-inspired, as can be seen in the Ritz and Palace hotels; the neo-Mudéjar style was also popular and brick façades so characteristic of Madrid went up all over the city **(plaza de Toros de las Ventas)**. The **Gran Vía**, a fast thoroughfare which crosses the centre of town to link Madrid's new districts, was inaugurated in 1910 and has since been popularised in an operetta *(zarzuela)*.

Madrid today – As capital, Madrid is Spain's leading city as far as banks, insurance companies, universities, administrative bodies and political institutions are concerned. It is also an important industrial and technological centre with most of these activities developing on the outskirts of the city.

The business district, centred around the Puerta de Alcalá and paseo de la Castellana, was modified extensively between 1950 and 1960 when traditional mansions were demolished to make room for new buildings. The city's most modern edifices may be seen in the **AZCA** area, the result of one of Madrid's most revolutionary projects, designed to fulfil various administrative, residential and commercial functions. Among its most noteworthy buildings are the avant-garde **Banco de Bilbao-Vizcaya** and the **Torre Picasso**.

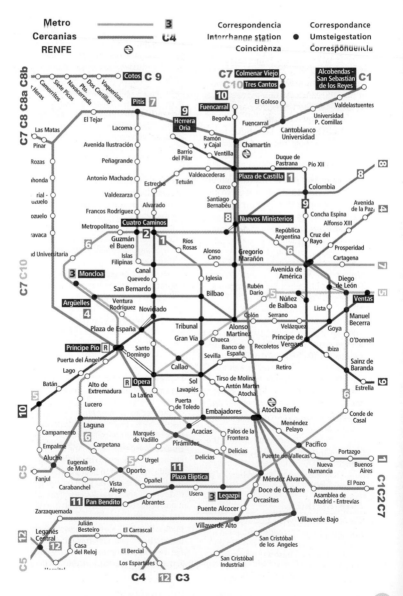

Address Book

GETTING ABOUT

✈ **Airport** – Madrid-Barajas airport is located 13km/8mi east of the city, alongside the N II highway. A shuttle bus operates to the airport from plaza de Colón, with six pick-up points along its route. It runs from 4.45am until 1.30am with a departure every 10min between 7am and 10pm. For further information, call ☏ 91 431 61 92.

🚇 Metro line no8, which links up with line no4, connects the airport with the city. Airport information ☏ 902 35 35 70. Info-Iberia ☏ 902 400 500.

🚂 **RENFE (Spanish State Railways)** – The city's main railway stations are Atocha and Chamartín. For information and reservations, call ☏ 902 24 02 02 (24-hr information; reservations from 5.30am-11.50pm); or log on to www.renfe.es. The AVE high-speed train departs from Atocha, taking just 2hr 30min to reach Sevilla via Córdoba. Madrid also has a comprehensive suburban train network (*Cercanías*) which can be used to get to El Escorial, the Sierra de Guadarrama, Alcalá de Henares and Aranjuez.

🚌 **Inter-city buses** – Most buses to other cities depart from the Estación Sur, calle Méndez Álvaro. ☏ 91 468 42 00.

Taxis – Madrid has a huge number of registered taxis with distinctive white paintwork with a red diagonal stripe on the rear doors. At night, the green light indicates that the taxi is for hire.

🚌 **Local buses** – For information, call ☏ 91 406 88 00. A good way of getting to know the city, although traffic jams are a major problem. Passengers should also beware of pickpockets. Times vary from line to line, but generally buses operate between 6am and 11.30pm. Night buses operate from 11.30pm onwards, with most departing from plaza de Cibeles. In addition to single tickets, passengers can also purchase a 10-trip **Metro-bus** ticket (*un bono de 10 viajes*) valid on both the bus and metro network, as well as a zone-based monthly ticket (*abono mensual*) which is valid for an unlimited number of bus and metro journeys for one month.

🚇 **Metro** – *Metro stations are shown on the maps in this guide.* For information, call ☏ 902 444 403. The metro system is the fastest way to get around the city and consists of 11 lines. It operates from 6am to 1.30am. Passengers should beware of pickpockets.

SIGHTSEEING

The Guía del Ocio (www.guiadelocio.com/madrid) is a weekly guide containing a list of every cultural event and show in the city. It can be purchased at newspaper stands.

Bus turístico Madrid Visión – This tourist bus offers three different routes around the city (historic Madrid, modern Madrid and monumental Madrid). Tickets, which can be purchased on board, in hotels or via a travel agent, are valid for 1 or 2 days. During the period of validity, passengers can hop on and off as much as they like as well as change their route. Services operate from 10am-7pm in winter, 10am-9pm in spring and autumn, and 9.30am-midnight in summer. Stops include the Puerta del Sol, plaza de Cibeles, paseo del Prado and Puerta de Alcalá. For information and prices, call ☏ 91 779 18 88.

DISTRICTS

Madrid is a city that is full of charm, with its own magnificent parks and impressive buildings. It is a city best explored by strolling through its streets and squares, discovering the delights of its many districts and getting to know its inhabitants.

Centro – This district is made up of several areas, each with their own individual character. It has a reputation for being noisy, chaotic and full of people, although visitors are often surprised by its narrow alleyways and small squares. **Sol-Callao** is the shopping area par excellence, packed with locals and visitors out for a stroll, heading for the main pedestrianised precinct (Preciados district) or for a drink or dinner in one of the many local cafés and restaurants. A number of cinemas are also located in this area. Visitors should take particular care in the evening, especially in streets such as Valverde and Barco.

Barrio de los Austrias – Madrid's oldest district is wedged between calles Mayor, Bailén, Las Cavas and the plaza de la Cebada. Its origins are medieval and it still retains its evocatively named streets and Mudéjar towers. An excellent area for tapas, dinner or a drink. On Sundays, the famous **Rastro** flea market (🕯 *see Rastro*) is held nearby.

Lavapiés – This district is located around the square of the same name with many houses dating from the 17C. It is considered to be Madrid's most colourful district with a mix of locals, students and a large immigrant population.

Huertas – Huertas was home to the literary community in the 17C and the Movida movement in the 1980s. Nowadays, it is packed with bars and restaurants and is particularly lively at night, attracting an interesting mixture of late-night revellers.

Malasaña – This part of Madrid, which used to be known as Maravillas, is situated between Las glorietas de Bilbao y Ruiz Jiménez and around plaza del Dos de

Mayo. In the mornings, this 19C *barrio* is quiet and provincial, but it is transformed at night by the legions of young people heading towards Malasaña's many bars. For those in search of a quieter night out, the district also has a number of more tranquil cafés.

Alonso Martínez – The average age and financial standing of this district's inhabitants is somewhat higher than in neighbouring Bilbao and Malasaña, as shown by the myriad upmarket bars and restaurants frequented by the city's rich and famous.

Chueca – This district covers an area around the plaza de Chueca; its approximate outer limits are the paseo de Recoletos, calle Hortaleza, Gran Vía and calle Fernando VI. At the end of the last century it was one of Madrid's most elegant districts. Today it is the city's gay area with a multitude of small and sophisticated boutiques.

Salamanca – In the 19C, Salamanca was Madrid's principal bourgeois district designed by the Marquis of Salamanca in the shape of a draughts board with wide streets at right angles. Nowadays, the district is one of the capital's most expensive areas and is home to some of Spain's leading designer boutiques (Serrano and Ortega y Gasset) and an impressive collection of stores selling luxury goods.

For coin ranges, see the Legend at the back of the guide.

WHERE TO EAT

La Finca de Susana – *Arlaban 4 (Huertas)* – Sevilla – ☎ 91 369 35 57 – 🍽. Centrally located with food that's good for the price, so it's always full with a with-it young crowd that doesn't mind waiting. Food is traditional, with some *nouvelle* touches. Go early, you can't reserve.

La Bola – *Bola 5 (Centro)* – Ópera – ☎ 91 547 69 30 – *Closed Sat evening, Sunday in Jul-Aug, Sun evenings the rest of year* – 🚫 🍽. If you're hoping to try a traditional cocido madrileño, look no further than this famous tavern which has been serving up this traditional dish in earthenware pots for over a century.

La Vaca Verónica – *Moratín, 38* – ☎ 91 429 78 27 –*Closed midday Sat* – 🍽. The outstanding decor re-creates a cosy, intimate space, with spider lamps, ceiling mirrors, candles and soft lighting. Posters recall Pop Art and Art Nouveau. Specialties include grilled meats and the delicious *pasta con carabineros*.

Teatriz – *Hermosilla 15 (Salamanca)* – Serrano – ☎ 91 577 53 79 – 🍽. Designed by Philippe Starck, this former theatre has been converted into an impressive-looking restaurant where you can choose between eating in the orchestra or enjoying a drink at the stage

Cocido Madrileño at La Bola

J.-D. Sudres/PHOTONONSTOP

bar. The good, reasonably priced menu is based on Mediterranean dishes and Italian specialities.

Zerain – *Quevedo 3 (Huertas)* – Antón Martín – ☎ 91 429 79 09 – *Closed Sun, August and Holy Week* – 🍽. One of the typical menus at this Basque cider bar near plaza de Santa Ana includes *tortilla de bacalao* (cod omelette) and *chuletón* (meat cutlets). Rustic, but pleasant decor. The cider here is served directly from the barrel.

Casa Lucio – *Cava Baja 35 (La Latina)* – La Latina – ☎ 91 365 32 52 – *Closed Sat lunchtime and Aug* – 🍽. One of Madrid's best-known addresses frequented by politicians, actors and visitors alike. Typical Castilian decor. Famous for its *huevos estrellados* (fried eggs).

El Amparo – *Puigcerdá 8 (Salamanca)* – Retiro – ☎ 91 431 64 56 – *Closed Sat lunchtime, Sun and Holy Week* – 🍽. Top-class restaurant with an original design including split-level dining rooms and roof skylights. Very pleasant atmosphere. Fine cuisine and polished service with prices to match.

TAPAS

Casa Labra – *Tetuán 12 (Centro)* – Sol – ☎ 91 531 00 81. This old tavern dating back to the middle of the 19C is a Madrid institution. It was here that Pablo Iglesias founded the Spanish Socialist Party (PSOE) in 1879. Its house speciality is fried cod *(bacalao frito)*, which you can enjoy standing up on the street or at the marble tables inside. Also a restaurant with menu.

Taberna Almendro 13 – *Almendro 13 (La Latina)* – La Latina – ☎ 91 365 42 52 – 🚫 🍽. Although it has only been in business for 8 years, this new tavern with an old atmosphere is always packed. Its tapas include cheese and sausage pastries *(roscas de queso y embutido)*, fried eggs *(huevos estrellados)* and its potato-based *patatas emporradas*.

La Venencia – *Echegaray 7 (Huertas)* – Sevilla – ☎ 91 429 73 13 – 🚫. If your taste is for sherry, then this is the place for you.

La Venencia is a small, narrow bar in the Huertas district which more than makes up in atmosphere and cuisine what it lacks in size. The yellowish walls and wooden bar provide added character. Cold tapas only.

Prada a Tope – *Príncipe 11 (Huertas)* – 🚇 *Sevilla* – *Closed Mon and in Aug* – ☎ *91 429 59 21* – 🍽️. A warm locale in the spirit of El Bierzo, a traditional part of León. Outstanding rustic decor of wood and slate, with long bar, large tables, and walls covered with photos. Great variety of local products on sale.

Taberna de la Daniela – *General Pardiñas 21 (Salamanca)* – 🚇 *Goya* – ☎ *91 575 23 29* – 🍽️. A new bar with traditional decoration. *Azulejos* on the outside with vermouth on tap and a wide selection of canapés and *raciones* inside. Specialities here include *cocido madrileño*.

José Luis – *Serrano, 89 (Salamanca)* – 🚇 *Núñez de Balboa* – ☎ *91 563 09 58* – 🍽️. A Salamanca institution. In two parts, each with its distinct style, but sharing the same bar. A wide choice of superb tapas; its Spanish omelette is the most famous in the city. Tables outside in summer.

WHERE TO STAY

🛏️ **Hostal Miguel Ángel** – *San Mateo 21 2ºD (Bilbao)* – 🚇 *Tribunal* – ☎ *91 447 54 00* – *16 rooms*. Next to the Museo Romántico. The somewhat darkened brick conceals a well-maintained hotel with a fabulous wooden staircase leading to the reception on the second floor. Friendly staff and spotless, more than adequate rooms with TV and en-suite bathroom.

🛏️ **Hotel Centro Sol** – *Carrera de San Jerónimo 5 2º-4º (Centro)* – 🚇 *Sol* – ☎ *91 522 15 82* – 🍽️ – *35 rooms*. A hotel very close to the Puerta del Sol occupying the second and fourth floors of a building somewhat lacking in charm. However, its rooms, all with TVs and good bathrooms, are very reasonably priced and have been recently refurbished.

🛏️ **Hotel Plaza Mayor** – *Atocha 2 (Centro)* – 🚇 *Sol* – ☎ *91 360 06 06* – 🍽️ – *20 rooms*. – 🛏️ *3.50€*. An unpretentious hotel, but with a great location right by the city's main square. Behind the modern brick façade, the rooms are small, functional but attractively decorated.

🛏️🛏️ **Hotel Mora** – *Paseo del Prado 32 (Retiro)* – 🚇 *Atocha* – ☎ *91 420 15 69* – *60 rooms* – 🛏️. The Mora enjoys a superb location in an impressive building opposite the botanical gardens on paseo del Prado. Comfortable, recently renovated rooms and reasonable rates.

🛏️🛏️ **Hotel Inglés** – *Echegaray 8 (Chueca)* – 🚇 *Sevilla* – ☎ *91 429 65 51* – 📇 – *58 rooms* – 🛏️ *5€*. There's no doubting the character of this hotel built in 1853. A good central and moderately priced option in the Chueca distrct, an area renowned for its lively nightlife. Clean, comfortable rooms.

🛏️🛏️ **Hotel París** – *Alcalá 2 (Centro)* – 🚇 *Sol* – ☎ *91 521 64 96* – *120 rooms* – 🛏️. At the time it was built (1863) the París was one of the most elegant and prestigious hotels in the city. Today, it is one of the oldest in Madrid and despite losing some of its former splendour still retains its old-world charm. Large, adequate rooms, albeit on the antiquated side.

🛏️🛏️ **Hotel La Residencia de El Viso** – *Nervión 8 (República Argentina)* – 🚇 *República Argentina* – ☎ *91 564 03 70* – 🍽️ – *12 rooms* – 🛏️ *9€* – *Restaurant €30.80/56.40*. This small hotel occupies an early-20C mansion in a residential area near plaza de la República Argentina. Elegant decor and a charming patio.

🛏️🛏️🛏️ **Hotel Casón del Tormes** – *Río 7 (Centro)* – 🚇 *Plaza de España* – ☎ *91 541 97 46* – 🍽️ – *63 rooms* – 🛏️ *6.50€*. Located in a small, quiet street in the centre of the city, just behind the Senate building. Built in the middle of the 1960s, the hotel has large, comfortable rooms which have been recently renovated.

🛏️🛏️🛏️ **Hotel Carlos V** – *Maestro Vitoria 5 (Centro)* – 🚇 *Sol* – ☎ *91 531 41 00* – 🍽️ – *67 rooms* – 🛏️. A good central option in a pedestrianised street away from the noise of the city. Although small, the English-style rooms are pleasant and well appointed. An eclectic cafeteria on the first floor.

🛏️🛏️🛏️ **Hotel Ritz** – *Plaza de la Lealtad 5 (Retiro)* – 🚇 *Banco de España* – ☎ *91 701 67 67* – 🍽️ ♿ – *137 rooms* – 🛏️ *30€* – *Restaurant €62/79*. A magnificent early-20C building superbly located near paseo del Prado. The hotel has all the elegance, tradition and comfort you would expect from such a famous name, plus prices to match. The terrace-garden here is an additional delight.

CAFÉS

Café de Oriente – *Plaza Oriente 2* – 🚇 *Ópera* – ☎ *91 5 41 39 74* – *Open 8.30am-2am*. This classic institution, located in the plaza de Oriente opposite the Royal Palace, is a delightful place for a drink at any time of day. Pleasant terrace.

Café del Círculo de Bellas Artes – *Marqués de Casa Riera 2* – 🚇 *Banco de España, Sevilla* – ☎ *91 3 60 54 00* – *Open Mon-Thu and Sun 9am-midnight, Fri-Sat 9am-3am*. The marked 19C atmosphere of this great café with its enormous columns and large windows is in sharp contrast to its young, intellectual clientele. Outdoor terrace in summer. Highly recommended.

El Espejo – *Paseo de Recoletos 21* – 🚇 *Colón* – ☎ *913 19 11 22* – *Open 9am-2am*. An attractive, Modernist-style café close to the Café Gijón (below) with a charming wrought-iron and glass canopy.

Café Gijón – *Paseo de Recoletos 31* – ⚇ *Banco de España* – ☎ *91 5 21 54 25* – *Open 7am-2am*. This café, which has long been famous as a meeting point for writers and artists, continues the tradition to this day. Outdoor terrace in summer.

NIGHTLIFE

Café Central – *Plaza del Ángel 10* – ⚇ *Antón Martín* – ☎ *91 3 69 41 43* – *Open 2pm-3.30am*. One of the city's main haunts for jazz-lovers since the early 1980s.

Los Gabrieles – *Echegaray 17* – ⚇ *Sevilla* – ☎ *91 429 62 61* – *Open Mon-Thu 12.30pm-2am, Fri-Sat 12.30pm-3.30am*. Tapas by day and a bar by night. A favourite haunt for foreign students in Madrid, attracted, no doubt, by the historical chronicles on its *azulejo*-decorated panelling.

Irish Rover – *Avenida de Brasil 7* – ⚇ *Santiago Bernabeu* – ☎ *91 5 55 76 71* – *Open Mon-Thu and Sun 11am-2.30pm and Fri-Sat 11am-3.30am*. A pub within a pub. A section which looks as though it has come straight out of one of Joyce's novels and a tiny lounge are just two of the features of this Irish home-from-home. Daily performances and a small market on Sundays. Young clientele.

Joy Eslava – *Arenal 11* – ⚇ *Ópera, Sol* – ☎ *913 66 37 33* – *Open Mon-Thu 11.30pm-5am, Fri-Sat 11.30pm-6am*. This well-known club, occupying a former 19C theatre, has been attracting a colourful crowd of club-goers and famous faces for several decades. On your way home, why not pay a visit to the famous Chocolatería de San Ginés, in the street of the same name.

Libertad, 8 – *Libertad 8* – ⚇ *Chueca* – ☎ *9 15 32 73 48* – *Open 1am-4am*. A building over a century old is the setting for this atmospheric café, renowned for its poetry readings and storytellers, attracting young, bohemian audiences.

Palacio de Gaviria – *Arenal 9* – ⚇ *Sol* – ☎ *91 5 26 60 69* – *Open Sun-Wed 8pm-3am, Fri-Sat 11pm-6am*. A fascinating club which has been converted from one of Madrid's old palaces. Also famous for its ballroom dancing. Its Thursday-night fiesta internacional is very popular with foreigners.

Del Diego – *La Reina 12* – ⚇ *Gran Vía* – ☎ *91 5 23 31 06* – *Open Mon-Thu 7pm-3am, Fri-Sat 7pm-4am*. A pleasant bar serving some of the city's best cocktails.

SHOPPING

Casa Mira – *Carrera San Jerónimo 30* – ⚇ *Sevilla* – ☎ *91 429 88 95* - *Open 10am-2pm and 5-9pm*. The best *turrones*, *mazapanes* (marzipan) and homemade sweets in Madrid. Founded in 1842, it has passed from father to son. The wares are of the highest quality, without preservatives or additives, cut and weighed at time of sale.

La Violeta – *Pl. de Canalejas 6* - ⚇ *Sevilla* - ☎ *91 522 55 22* - *Open 9.30am-2pm and 4.30-8.30pm* - *Closed Sun, public hols and in Aug*. This establishment has served such luminaries as King Alfonso XIII and writers Jacinto Benavente y Valle Inclán since 1915. The bonbons and caramels are popular but the *marron glacé* and glazed violets take the cake.

Capas Seseña – *Cruz 23 (Huertas)* - ⚇ *Sevilla or Sol* - ☎ *91 531 68 40* - *www. sesena.com* - *Open 10am-1.30pm and 4.30-8pm* - A family firm that dates from 1901, where traditional and contemporary **capes** are crafted by hand from fine fabric. Photos show such clients as Hemingway, Picasso, Catherine Deneuve, Rodolfo Valentino and Marcelo Mastroianni.

Art Galleries – A number of galleries can be found in and around Atocha, close to the Centro de Arte Reina Sofía, in the Salamanca district (near the Puerta de Alcalá) and on the left side of the paseo de la Castellana, close to the calle Génova.

ENTERTAINMENT

Madrid has over 100 cinemas, including one **Imax** cinema, 20 or so theatres, numerous concert halls and one casino. The **Auditorio Nacional** (opened in 1988) has a varied programme of classical music, the **Teatro de la Zarzuela** hosts a wide range of shows including Spanish operettas *(zarzuelas)* and ballets, while the **Teatro Real** offers a season of opera. The **Veranos de la Villa** and the **Festival de Otoño** are two events held in the summer and autumn respectively with an interesting mix of cultural performances. The **Festival Internacional de Jazz** is another event also held during November.

Berlín Cabaret – *Costanilla de San Pedro 11* – ⚇ *La Latina* – *Open Mon-Thu and Sun, 11pm-5am and Fri-Sat, 11pm-6am*. One of Madrid's famous venues. Live acts (magicians, drag queens etc) and a fun atmosphere.

Café de Chinitas – *Torija 7* – ⚇ *Callao* – ☎ *91 5 47 15 02* – *Open Mon-Sat, 10.30pm-5am*. Very popular with tourists. Dinner shows also available.

Casa Patas – *Cañizares 10* – ⚇ *Antón Martín* – ☎ *91 3 69 04 96* – *Open Mon-Sun, noon-5pm; Fri-Sat, 8pm-2.30am and Sun-Thu, 8pm-1.30am*. One of the best venues in which to enjoy a night of flamenco.

FIESTAS

On 15 May, the city commemorates the feast day of **San Isidro**, its patron saint. The day is celebrated in a variety of ways: an outdoor picnic, impromptu dancing, rock concerts and above all through its famous bullfighting festival, which lasts for some six weeks. It is also traditional for *madrileños* to eat traditional pastries *(rosquillas)* on this special day.

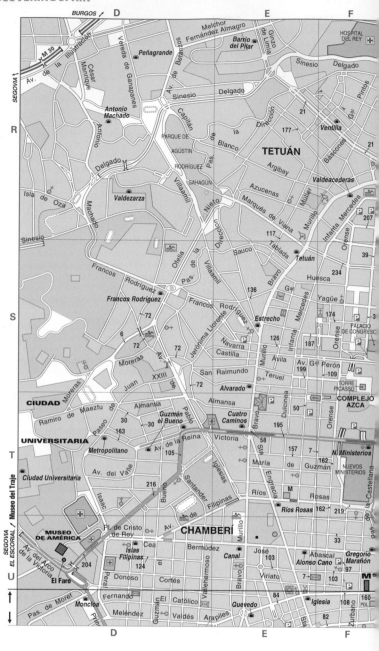

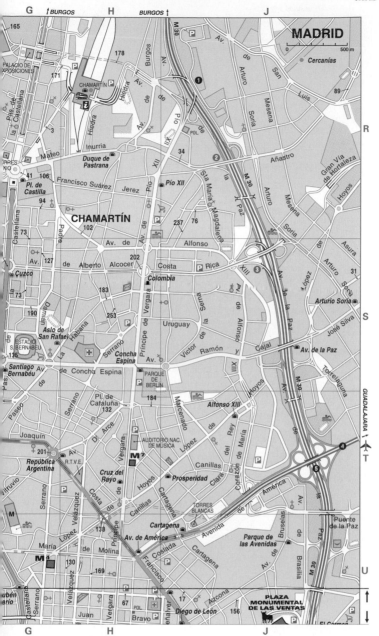

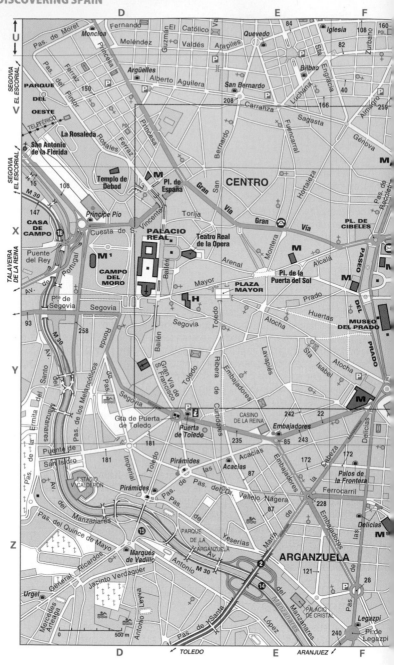

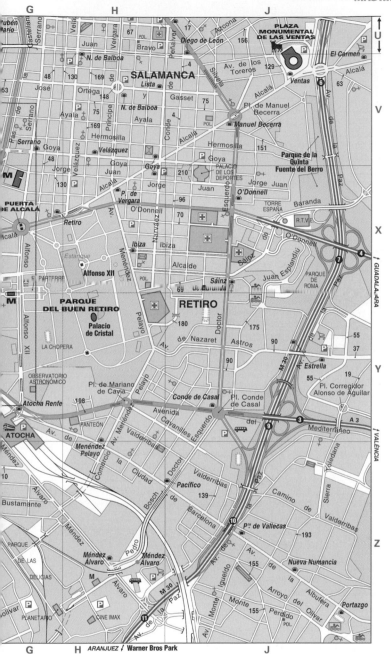

MADRID — STREET INDEX

MADRID — SITES INDEX

Special Features

MUSEO DEL PRADO★★★ ⏱3hr

⏰ *Open Tue-Sun 9am-7pm. Last admission 1hr before closing.* ⏰ *Closed Mon, 1 Jan, Good Fri, 1 May and 25 Dec.* ⊛3€, *no charge Sun, 18 May, 12 Oct, 6 Dec.* ☎ *91 330 28 00.*

The Prado is probably the greatest gallery of Classical paintings in the world. The neo-Classical building was designed by Juan de Villanueva under Charles III to house the Natural Science Museum. After the War of Independence (the Peninsular War), Ferdinand VII altered the project and instead installed the collections of Spanish painting made by the Habsburg and Bourbon kings, which reflect the development of royal artistic taste over the centuries. The Prado also contains precious collections of work by Flemish painters, acquired by the Catholic Monarchs, as well as a great many paintings from the Italian School favoured by Emperor Charles V and Philip II.

😊 The Paseo del Arte 😊

This poetic name refers to the imaginary axis linking Madrid's three greatest museums (the Prado, Thyssen-Bornemisza and the Reina Sofía), which form a close triangle in the same part of the city. The **Bono Arte**, a combined ticket on sale in each of the museums, entitles the holder to admission to all three of these magnificent art galleries. Cost: 7.66€.

😊 Museum Collections 😊

El Museo del Prado está is currently completing a significant expansion. Given the large number of works in stock, some paintings are only displayed in temporary exhibitions.

Spanish School★★★ (15C-18C)

Bartolomé Bermejo (*Santo Domingo de Silos* – with his costume rich in gold) and **Yáñez de la Almedina**, who developed the style and technique of Leonardo *(Santa Catalina),* stand out as two painters who cultivated an international style. Masip and his son **Juan de Juanes** *(The Last Supper)* are more associated with the style of Raphael, while Morales' favourite subject, a *Virgin and Child*, is also outstanding.

In those rooms devoted to the **Golden Age**, two painters stand out: **Sánchez Coello**, a disciple of the portrait painter Antonio Moro, and his pupil **Pantoja de la Cruz**, who was another portraitist at the court of Philip II. The personality of **El Greco**, who followed strong Byzantine traditions during his studies in Venice, stands apart within the Spanish School. Here, works dating from his early Spanish period *(Trinity)* through to his maturity *(Adoration of the Shepherds)* can be seen and the evolution of his style studied. Other works are proof that he was a great portraitist; pay particular note to the **Gentleman with his Hand on his Breast**. **Ribalta** is the Spanish Baroque artist who first introduced tenebrism to Spain with its chiaroscuro technique already seen in Caravaggio's work. **José (Jusepe) de Ribera**, also known as **Lo Spagnoletto**, is represented by his major work, the *Martyrdom of St Felipe* – which was originally thought to be of St Bartholomew – in which the artist's vigorous use of chiaroscuro emphasises the dramatic, horrifying nature of the scene. Both the portraits and still-life paintings of **Zurbarán** are peaceful compositions in which the use of chiaroscuro and realism are triumphant. In the Prado we discover the lesser known aspect of the style of this "Painter of Monks", both in the series of *The Labours of Hercules* which he painted for the Casón del Buen Retiro and in the portrait of *St Isabel of Portugal*. **Murillo**, who mainly painted Marian religious scenes, also cultivates popular subjects with delightful realism; note his enchanting child portraits *(The Good Shepherd and The Boys of the Shell)*.

Velázquez (1599-1660)

The Prado possesses the greatest paintings of Velázquez. This artist of genius, born in Sevilla, was apprenticed first to Herrera the Elder and then to Francisco Pancheco whose daughter he married in 1618. He later moved to Madrid where he was called to the court by Philip IV in 1623 and subsequently painted a great many portraits. On the suggestion of Rubens he spent some time in Italy (1629-31) where he painted **The Forges of Vulcan.** Influenced by Titian and Tintoretto he began to use richer, more subtle colours and developed his figure compositions as can be seen in his magnificent **Christ on the Cross.** On his return he painted **The Surrender of Breda** in which his originality emerges and where, as is borne out by the composition, the

Derechos Reservados – ©Museo del Prado, Madrid

Las Meninas, by Velázquez

emphasis rests on the psychological relationship between the protagonists. The use of light in his pictures is crucial, setting off figures and objects yet also giving life to the space between them; on the strength of this Velázquez developed his famous aerial perspectives in which parts of the picture are left hazy in order to further highlight the central figures. He strove towards naturalism, as is shown in his royal hunting portraits of **Philip IV** and **Prince Baltasar Carlos, the Hunter** (1635, a wonderful rendering of a child) and his equestrian portraits of the royal family, in particular that of **Prince Baltasar Carlos on Horseback** with the *sierra* in the background. His predilection for realism is evident in his pictures of Aesop, as well as of buffoons and dwarfs, his favourite themes. In 1650 he returned to Italy where he painted two light, modern landscapes, the **Gardens of the Villa Medici.** During the last years of his life, when he was laden with honours and all manner of official functions, he portrayed the young princes and princesses very freely, as in the picture of the **Infanta Margarita of Austria** (1659) in tones of pink and grey. In his masterpiece, **The Maids of Honour (Las Meninas)** (1656), a magnificent display of light and colour, the Infanta Margarita is shown in the artist's studio accompanied by her maids and dwarves while the king and queen are portrayed in a mirror in the background. In **The Spinners** (1657), Velázquez has combined myth and reality in a wonderful interplay of oblique lines and curves.

Among the disciples of Velázquez was the court painter **Carreño de Miranda** (*Monstrua Naked and Clothed*). Mention should also be made of **Alonso Cano** who painted scenes of the *Immaculate Conception*.

Goya (1746-1828)

Spanish painting maintained its supremacy in the 18C and 19C with Goya (born in Fuendetodos, Aragón, in 1746) who is magnificently represented in several rooms. His many portraits of the royal and famous, his war scenes, his depiction of everyday life which served as a model for tapestries, and finally his **Majas**, all widely illustrate his extraordinary Realism and his enthusiasm for colour. The museum contains some 40 cartoons painted in oil between 1775 and 1791 for weaving at the Real Fábrica (Royal Tapestry Works). The colourful naturalness of the scenes gives a delightful picture of life in 18C Madrid. A little further on are the canvases of the **2 May** and the **Execution of the Rioters on 3 May 1808** painted by Goya in 1818. Here he was inspired by the rebellion in Madrid in 1808 against the French occupying forces when the people wished to prevent the departure of the queen and princes for Bayonne (see ARANJUEZ). The reprisal by Murat that ensued was terrible. Goya condemned the horror of that night and the executions that took place on Príncipe Pío hill. The two paintings bring out the violence and cruelty of war as do Goya's brutal etchings of the *Disasters Of War* (1808) and *La Tauromaquia*. The so-called *Black Paintings* (1820-22) on the ground floor, which Goya made for his house, the Quinta del Sordo, are the anguished reactions of a visionary to the reality of life in Spain at the time (*The Witches' Coven, Cronus Swallowing his Son*).

The Prado's Major Works

SCHOOL	ARTIST	PAINTING
Spanish	Juan de Juanes	Ecce Homo
16C-18C	El Greco	Gentleman with his Hand on his Breast
		Adoration of the Shepherds
	Zurbarán	Still Life
		St Isabel of Portugal
	Velázquez	The Surrender of Breda
		The Spinners
		The Maids of Honour (Las Meninas)
		Prince Baltasar Carlos on Horseback
		Infanta Doña Margarita of Austria
		The Forges of Vulcan
		Christ on the Cross
	Murillo	Holy Family with a Little Bird
		Immaculate Conception of Soult
		The Good Shepherd
	Goya	Family of Charles IV
		Maja Naked, Maja Clothed
		Executions at Moncloa
		The Second of May
		The Witches' Coven
Flemish	Robert Campin	St Barbara
15C-17C	Van der Weyden	Deposition
	Hans Memling	Adoration of the Magi
	Bruegel the Elder	Triumph of Death
	Hieronymus Bosch	Garden of Earthly Delights
	Rubens	The Three Graces
Italian	Fra Angelico	Annunciation
15C-17C	Andrea Mantegna	Dormition of the Virgin
	Botticelli	Story of Nastagio degli Onesti
	Titian	Venus with the Organist
	Tintoretto	Washing of the Feet
	Veronese	Venus and Adonis
German and Dutch	Albrecht Dürer	Self-portrait
16C-17C	Rembrandt	Artemisa

Flemish School★★★ (15C-17C)

The Prado has an exceptional collection of Flemish painting due to the close relations Spain developed with the Low Countries in the past.

Among the Flemish Primitives is the noticeable interest in interiors (*St Barbara* by Robert Campin known as the Master of Flemalle) to which **Van der Weyden** added great richness of colour, a sense of composition and the pathetic *(Descent from the Cross, Pietà)*. The dramatic aspect is interpreted differently, through melancholy, by his successor, **Memling** *(Adoration of the Magi)*. There follow the weird imaginings of **Hieronymus Bosch**, known as El Bosco *(The Garden of Earthly Delights)* which influenced his disciple Patinir *(Crossing the Stygian Lake)*, and a painting by **Bruegel the Elder,** the *Triumph of Death*.

Notable in the collection of Flemish paintings from the 16C and 17C are **Ambrosius Benson's** religious pictures, the portraits of personalities at the court of Philip II by the Dutchman, **Antonio Moro** (16C), the series of the *Five Senses* by Brueghel the Younger (17C) and his and **David Teniers the Younger's** colourful scenes of everyday life.

The most Baroque of painters, **Rubens** (who was born in Germany), breathed new life into Flemish painting *(The Three Graces)*. There is a rich collection of his work in the museum completed by that of his disciples: **Van Dyck**, excellent portraits, **Jordaens**, everyday-life scenes, and animal paintings by their contemporaries, Snyders and Paul de Vos.

Dutch School (17C)

There are two interesting works by **Rembrandt**: a *Self-portrait* and *Artemesia*.

Italian School★★ (15C-17C)

The Italian School is particularly well represented from the 15C and is especially rich in works by Venetian painters.

The Italian Renaissance brought with it elegance and ideal beauty as in paintings by **Raphael** *(The Holy Family, Portrait of a Cardinal)*, Roman nobility and monumental bearing in the work of **Mantegna** *(Dormition of the Virgin)* and melancholic dreaminess in **Botticelli** *(Story of Nastagio degli Onesti)*. On the other hand, the spirituality of the magnificent *Annunciation* by **Fra Angelico** belongs to the Gothic tradition. The collection also includes soft-coloured works by Andrea del Sarto, and others by Correggio, an artist from the Parma School who used *chiaroscuro*.

The triumph of colour and sumptuousness comes with the Venetian school: **Titian** with his exceptional mythological scenes *(Danae and the Golden Shower, Venus with the Organist)* and his admirable portrait of *Emperor Charles V*; **Veronese** with his fine compositions set off by silver tones; Tintoretto's golden-fleshed figures springing from shadow *(Washing of the Feet)* and finally **Tiepolo's** paintings intended for Charles III's royal palace.

French School (17C-18C)

The French are represented by **Poussin** landscapes and canvases by **Lorrain** (17C).

German School

This is represented by a selection of **Dürer's** figure and portrait paintings *(Self-portrait, Adam and Eve)* and two hunting scenes and a religious canvas by Cranach.

Casón del Buen Retiro★

▶ *Entrance in calle Alfonso XII, no28.* ⊶ *Closed for restoration.* This annexe to the Prado has an exceptional collection of the most innovative artistic trends in 19C Spain on exhibition (neo-Classicism, Romanticism, Realism, Impressionism etc).

The central **Gran Salón** (former Salón de Baile or Ballroom of the old Palacio del Buen Retiro) has preserved the beautiful roof decoration painted by Lucas Jordán. Exemplary works from Spanish historical painting hang from its walls, including *The Last Will and Testament of Isabel the Catholic* by Rosales, *Juana the Mad* by F Pradilla and *The Execution of Torrijos and his companions on the beaches of Málaga* by A Gisbert. Other artists represented elsewhere in the museum include José de Madrazo *(The Death of Viriato)*, V López *(Portrait of Goya)*, E Lucas, Alenza, Esquivel *(Contemporary Poets)*, Federico de Madrazo, M Fortuny *(The artist's children in the Japanese Hall)*, Rosales, I Pinazo *(Self-portrait)*, Sorolla *(Children at the beach)*, Regoyos, Rusiñol, Chicharro *(Pain)*, Zuloaga etc.

MUSEO THYSSEN-BORNEMISZA★★★

🕐 *Open 10am-7pm; last admission 30min before closing.* 🕐 *Closed Mon, 1 Jan, 1 May, 25 Dec.* ⬗≈6€. ☎ *91 369 01 51.*

The neo-Classical Palacio de Villahermosa has been magnificently restored by the architect Rafael Moneo to house an outstanding collection acquired by the Spanish State from **Baron Hans Heinrich Thyssen-Bornemisza.** The collection was assembled in the 1920s by his father, Baron Heinrich, and bears witness to what is considered to be one of the largest and most inspired collections ever brought together in the private art world.

The museum contains approximately 800 works (mainly paintings) from the late 13C to the present day. They are exhibited in chronological order on three floors (the visit should start on the second (top) floor where the collection's oldest exhibits are displayed), and provide an overview of the main schools of European art (Italian, Flemish, German, Dutch, Spanish, French) including examples of Primitive, Renaissance, Baroque, Rococo and neo-Classical works. The gallery also devotes space to 19C American painting, the 20C European Romanticism and Realism movements and presents a representative selection from the Impressionist, Post-Impressionist and Expressionist periods. The visit concludes with paintings from both the European and American avant-garde movements.

Second floor

The visit begins with the Italian Primitives *(Gallery 1)*: **Duccio di Buoninsegna's** *Christ and the Samaritan Woman*, in which concern for scenic realism – one of the predominant themes of the Renaissance – can be seen, stands out. **Gallery 3** displays some splendid examples of 15C Dutch religious painting such as **Jan van Eyck's** *The Annunciation Diptych*, in which the artist parades his prodigious technique by giving the finely-proportioned Angel and the Virgin the appearance of high reliefs carved in stone; next to it is the small *Our Lady of the Dry Tree* by **Petrus Christus** in which the Virgin and Child symbolise the flowering of the dry tree.

The museum possesses a magnificent **portrait collection**. It is worth spending some time in **Gallery 5** which contains some superb examples of the Early Renaissance which encompass its values of identity and autonomy. These come to the fore in the beautiful and well-known *Portrait of Giovanna Tornuaboni* by the Italian painter **D Ghirlandaio.** The room also houses a further dozen portraits of exceptional quality which emanate from various schools from the period, notably *A Young Man at Prayer* by **Hans Memling**, *A Stout Man* by **Robert Campin**, *Henry VIII* by **Hans Holbein the Younger** and **Juan of Flanders'** extremely delicate *Portrait of an Infanta (Catherine of Aragón?).*

Raphael's *Portrait of an Adolescent* can be seen in the Villahermosa Gallery *(Gallery 6)* while **Gallery 7** (16C) reveals **Vittore Carpaccio's** *Young Knight in a Landscape* in which the protagonist's elegance stands out from a background heavy with symbolism. The *Portrait of Doge Francesco Vernier* by **Titian** should not be missed, with its sober, yet diverse tones. After admiring **Dürer's** *Jesus Among the Doctors (Gallery 8)*, where the characters are portrayed in a surprising way given the period (1506), move on to **Gallery 9**, which contains an excellent selection of portraits from the 16C German School including **The Nymph from the Fountain**, one of several paintings by **Lucas Cranach the Elder**, and the *Portrait of a Woman* by **Hans Baldung Grien**, in which the original expression and the delicacy of contrasts give the portrait an attractive air. The display of 16C Dutch paintings in **Gallery 10** includes **Patinir's** *Landscape with the Rest on the Flight into Egypt* while **Gallery 11** exhibits several works by **El Greco** as well as **Titian's** *St Jerome in the Wilderness* (1575), with its characteristic use of flowing brush-strokes, painted the year before his death. One of the splendid early works of **Caravaggio** – the creator of tenebrism – *St Catherine of Alexandria*, can be admired in **Gallery 12**. In the same gallery is a splendid sculpture (St Sebastian) by Baroque artist **Bernini**, executed at the tender age of 17. Also displayed here is the *Lamentation over the Body of Christ* (1633) by **Ribera** – one of Caravaggio's followers – which captures the Virgin's suffering with great subtlety. After passing through several rooms dedicated to 17C Baroque art (including **Claude Lorrain's** *Pastoral Landscape with a Flight into Egypt* and **Zurbarán's** superb *Santa Casilda*), you reach the 18C Italian Painting section *(Galleries 16-18)* with its typical Venetian scenes by **Canaletto** and **Guardi**. The remaining galleries on this floor (19-21) are consecrated to Dutch and Flemish works from the 17C. **Van Dyck's** magnificent *Portrait of Jacques le Roy*, **De Vos'** *Antonia Canis*, and two memorable **Rubens**, *The Toilet of Venus* and

Portrait of a Young Woman with a Rosary, all hang from the walls of **Gallery 19**, while **Gallery 21** possesses the fine *Portrait of a young Man Reading a Coranto* by **Gerard ter Borch,** skilfully representing the model pictured in his daily environment.

First floor

The first few galleries *(22-26)* represent Dutch paintings from the 17C with scenes of daily life and landscapes. Pay particular note to **Frans Hals'** *Family Group in a Landscape*, a fine example of a collective portrait. The century is completed by the still-life paintings in **Gallery 27.**

Several interesting portraits stand out from the 18C French and British schools, such as **Gainsborough's** *Portrait of Miss Sarah Buxton* in **Gallery 28**. 19C North-American painting, virtually unknown in Europe, takes pride of place in the next two rooms *(29 and 30)* with works by the Romantic landscape artists Cole, Church, Bierstadt and the Realist Homer. The European Romanticism and Realism of the 19C is best expressed by **Constable's** *The Lock*, **Courbet's** *The Water Stream* and **Friedrich's** *Easter Morning*, together with the three works in the collection by **Goya** *(Gallery 31)*.

Galleries 32 and **33** are dedicated to Impressionism and Post-Impressionism. Here, admire the magnificent works by the principal masters of these movements: Monet, Manet, Renoir, Sisley, Degas, Pissarro, Gauguin, Van Gogh, Toulouse-Lautrec and Cézanne. *At the Milliner* by **Degas** is considered to be one of his major canvases. Other works which equally stand out include **Van Gogh's** *"Les Vessenots" in Auvers*, a landscape painted in the last year of his life and which displays the explosion of brush-strokes synonymous with some of his later works, *Mata Mua* by **Gauguin**, from his Polynesian period, and **Cézanne's** *Portrait of a Farmer*, in which his particular use of colour is used to build volumes, a style which opened the way to Cubism. Expressionism is represented in **Galleries 35-40**, following a small display of paintings from the Fauve movement in **Gallery 34**. The Expressionist movement, the best represented in the entire museum, supposes the supremacy of the artist's interior vision and the predominance of colour over draughtsmanship. The works exhibited illustrate the different focal points of German Expressionism. Two highly emblematic paintings by **Grosz**, *Metropolis* and *Street Scene*, hang in **Gallery 40**.

Ground floor

The first few galleries *(41-44)* contain exceptional Experimental avant-garde works (1907-24) from the diverse European movements: Futurism, Orphism, Suprematism, Constructivism, Cubism and Dadaism. **Room 41** displays Cubist works by **Picasso** *(Man with A Clarinet)*, **Braque** *(Woman with a Mandolin)* and **Juan Gris** *(Woman Sitting)*, while *Proun 1C* by **Lissitzky** and *New York City, New York* by **Mondrian** merit special mention in Room 43.

Gallery 45 shows post-First World War European works by **Picasso** *(Harlequin with a Mirror)* and **Joan Miró** *(Catalan Peasant with a Guitar)*, as well as a 1914 abstract composition by **Kandinsky** *(Picture with Three Spots)*. In the next gallery, mainly dedicated to North American painting, can be seen *Brown and Silver I* by **Jackson Pollock** and *Green on Maroon* by **Mark Rothko**, two different examples of abstract American Expressionism. The last two galleries *(47 and 48)* are given over to Surrealism, Figurative Tradition and Pop Art. The following are worthy of particular note: *The Key to the Fields* by the Surrealist artist **Réne Magritte**, *Hotel Room* by the Realist **Edward Hopper**, *Portrait of George Dyer in a Mirror* by **Francis Bacon**, *Express* by **Robert Rauschenberg** and *A Woman in a Bath* by **Roy Lichtenstein**.

Carmen Thyssen-Bornemisza Collection

The collection of the Baroness opened to the public in this new wing in the summer of 2004. The more than 250 works on exhibit build on those in the original wing of the museum. Notable are 17C Dutch painting, Impressionism and Post-Impressionism, North American painting, and early Avant-Garde works, especially German.

MUSEO NACIONAL CENTRO DE ARTE REINA SOFÍA (Queen Sofia Art Center)

🕐 *Open 10am-9pm; Sun, 10am-2.30pm.* 🕐 *Closed Tue.* ⌦ *3€ (7.66€ for Paseo del Arte ticket (Bono Arte) in combination with Museo del Prado and Museo Thyssen), no charge Sat from 2.30pm and all day Sun.* ☎ *91 467 50 62.*

The former Hospital de San Carlos was refurbished to house this outstanding museum of contemporary art, which, in addition to its permanent collection, organises a continuing programme of outstanding cultural exhibitions.

Permanent collection★
Avant-garde movements

Second floor. The 16 rooms exhibit canvases illustrating leading avant-garde movements in Spanish painting and the international events that prompted them, running from the late 19C to the years following the Second World War. Some of the rooms cover the work of a single artist. In Room 4, which displays Cubist works by the great artist **Juan Gris,** note the remarkable *Portrait of Josette.* In the gallery devoted to **Picasso** *(Room 6),* one is strongly impressed by **Guernica**★★★, commissioned for the Spanish Pavilion at the 1937 World Fair. Inspired by the appaling bombing of Gernika and much commented on because of its expressiveness and powerful symbolism, this monumental black and white picture is a stark denunciation of the atrocities of war. Among other works is the magnificent *Still Life (dead birds),* a 1912 cubist painting. Room 7 shows a retrospective of the work of **Joan Miró,** with *Snail, Woman, Flower, Star* (1934) and *Woman, Bird and Star (Tribute to Picasso)* (1970); his sculptures can be seen in Room 16. There are lovely sculptures by **Julio González** (1920-40s) in Room 8. **Dalí** is represented in Room 10, where you can admire some of his early works *(Little Girl at the Window* – 1925), together with later examples taken from his Surrealist period *(The Great Masturbator).* Surrealist works from other countries are shown in Room 11. After the room dedicated to cineaste Luis Buñuel and his contemporaries is Room 13, which traces the evolution of Spanish art between 1920 and 1930 through the works of P. Gargallo, D. Vázquez Díaz, María Blanchard, Benjamín Palencia and F. Bores, among others.

  Additions

An expansion programme continues at the Centro de Arte Reina Sofía. The new wing, designed by Jean Nouvel, will house temporary exhibitions. As a result, more works from the permanent collection will be shown on the third floor of the former hospital

Post-Civil War movements

Fourth floor (Rooms 18 to 45). Here you can see works reflecting major artistic movements from the late 1940s to the present. Room 19 displays works by artists belonging to **Dau al Set** and **Pórtico**, the two main trends to have emerged in Spain in the wake of the Civil War. Rooms 20 to 23 cover the Abstract movement spanning the 1950s and the early 1960s, illustrated by Guerrero, Ràfols Casamada, Hernández Mompó, Oteiza, Sempere and members of the **Equipo Crónica**. Informalism is extremely well represented in Rooms 27 to 29 with a fine collection of paintings, divided into those associated with **El Paso** (Millares, Saura, Rivera, Canogar, Feito and Viola) or with the **Cuenca Group** (Zóbel and Torner). An interesting selection of works by **Tàpies** can be seen in Rooms 34 and 35; take note of the Motherwell. Figurative art is shown in Room 31 with canvases by Antonio López García, Julio López Hernández, Carmen Laffón, Francisco López and Xavier Valls. The next room is dedicated to P. Palazuelo. The works of Genovés, Villalba, Alfaro, Arroyo, Pérez Villalta, Luis Gordillo and the Equipo Crónica *(Rooms 36 to 39)* demonstrate the similarities and differences between Pop Art and figurative, narrative works.

The collage series *Gravitaciones* by **Eduardo Chillida** in Rooms 42 and 43 is shown with examples of his sculptures *(Mesa de Omar Khayyan II* and *Homenaje a San Juan de la Cruz).*

Works of the sixties by important U.S. artists (D. Judd, B. Nauman, B. Newman, E. Kelly) are shown in Room 41. Room 44 is dedicated to video, a characteristic form of the end of the 20C. Also in the permanent collection is a selection of recent Spanish and foreign works *(Rooms 40 and 45),* showing the diversity of language and artistic expression in contemporary art: figurative (Barceló, García Sevilla, Katz, Kuitca, etc.), abstrac (Broto, Sicilia, Uslé, Ritcher, Lasker, etc.), installations and sculpture (Navarro, Iglesias, Kapoor, Schlosser) and photographs.

Walking About

OLD MADRID★ ⏱ *2hr 30min – see town plan*

Steep, narrow streets, small squares, 17C palaces and mansions, houses with wrought-iron balconies dating from the 19C and early 20C provide the backdrop to this walk through Old Madrid, the very heart of the city, which first developed around plaza Mayor and plaza de la Villa.

The old town is best visited early in the morning or late in the afternoon when the churches are open.

Plaza Mayor★★

This was built by Juan Gómez de Mora during the reign of Philip III (1619) and forms the architectural centre of **Habsburg Madrid**.

On the north side, flanked by pinnacled towers, stands the **Casa de la Panadería** (a former bakery) which was reconstructed by Donoso in 1672. Its mural decoration, the third since it was built, is the work of the artist Carlos Franco. The 17C equestrian statue of Philip III in the middle of the square is by Giambologna and Pietro Tacca. The vast square was the setting for *autos-da-fé*, mounted bullfights, and the proclamations of Kings Philip V, Ferdinand VI and Charles IV. Its present appearance is a result of the work carried out by Juan de Villanueva at the end of the 18C.

A stamp and coin market is held under the arches on Sunday mornings while at Christmas, stalls are set up selling religious and festive decorations. The shops around the square, hatters in particular, have retained their look of yesteryear.

Pass through the **Arco de Cuchilleros** into the street of the same name, fronted by tall, aged houses with convex façades. The **Cava de San Miguel** provides a rear view of the houses which look onto the square and gives an indication of the steep slopes around Plaza Mayor. The name *cava* derives from the ditches or moats that once stood here. This area is crowded with small restaurants (mesones) and bars (tavernas). The **Mercado de San Miguel**, an indoor market built early this century, has preserved its elegant iron structure.

▶ *Head down the calle Conde de Miranda, cross the pleasant plaza del Conde de Barajas and the calle de Gómez de Mora to get to plaza de San Justo or Puerta Cerrada, an old city gate. Continue right along the calle de San Justo.*

Iglesia Pontificia de San Miguel★

🕐 *Open 11.15am-12.30pm and 7.30-9pm.* 🕐 *Closed Sun and public hols.* ☎ *91 548 40 11.*

The basilica by Bonavia is one of the rare Spanish churches to have been inspired by 18C Italian Baroque. Its convex façade, designed as an interplay of inward and outward curves, is adorned with fine statues. Above the doorway is a low relief of St Justus and St Pastor to whom the basilica was previously dedicated. The interior is graceful and elegant with an oval cupola, intersecting ribbed vaulting, flowing cornices and abundant stuccowork.

▶ *Follow calle Puñonrostro – to the left of the church – and calle del Codo, in former times one of Madrid's most dangerous streets because of its reputation for drunkards, to plaza de la Villa.*

Plaza de la Villa★

The quiet pedestrian square is presided over by a statue of Álvaro de Bazán, hero of Lepanto, by Benlliure (1888). Several famous buildings are arranged around the square including the **Ayuntamiento** (town hall), built by Gómez de Mora in 1617, the **Torre de los Lujanes** (Luján Tower), one of the rare examples of 15C civil architecture preserved in Madrid and in which Francis I was imprisoned after the battle of Pavia, and the **Casa de Cisneros**, built several years after the death of the cardinal of the same name, which is connected to the Ayuntamiento by an arch. Of the original 16C edifice only an attractive window giving onto plazuela del Cordón remains.

Calle Mayor

The name of this street, literally Main Street, gives us an indication of its historical importance. It has preserved several interesting buildings such as n° 61, the narrow house in which the 17C playright, **Pedro Calderón de la Barca**, lived. The Antigua Farmacia de la Reina Madre (Queen Mother's Pharmacy), close by, has preserved a collection of old chemist's jars and pots. The **Instituto Italiano de Cultura** (n°86) occupies a palace dating from the 17C which has undergone more recent restoration. The Palacio Uceda opposite, a building dating from the same period, is now the military headquarters of the **Capitanía General** (Captaincy General). This brick-and-granite palace is a fine example of civil architecture of the time. In front of the **Iglesia Arzobispal Castrense** (17C-18C) is a monument commemorating the attack on Alfonso XIII and Victoria Eugenia on their wedding day in 1906. In the nearby calle de San Nicolás, the Mudéjar tower of San Nicolás de los Servitas can still be seen.

▶ *Follow calle del Sacramento, which passes behind plaza de la Villa, to plazuela del Cordón.*

Plazuela del Cordón

Just before you reach the square, stop to admire the back of the Casa de Cisneros. From the centre of the *plazuela* there is an unusual view of the façade of the Iglesia de San Miguel.

▷ *Return to calle del Cordón and continue to calle de Segovia.*

Across the street rises the 14C **Mudéjar tower** of the **Iglesia de San Pedro** (Church of St Peter), which, apart from the Torre de San Nicolás, is the only example of the Mudéjar style in Madrid.

▷ *Go along calle del Príncipe Anglona to plaza de la Paja.*

Plaza de la Paja

This calm, irregularly built square was, along with the plaza de los Carros, the commercial centre of Madrid in the Middle Ages. The Palacio Vargas, on one side of the square, obscures from view the Gothic **Capilla del Obispo**, a chapel built in the 16C by Gutiérrez Carvajal, Bishop of Palencia. Close to it, in plaza de los Carros, is a chapel, the Capilla de San Isidro, part of the Iglesia de San Andrés, built in the middle of the 17C in honour of Madrid's patron saint. The **Museo de San Isidro**, a museum containing a miracle well and a fine Renaissance patio, is situated next to this complex group of religious buildings. There is also an exhibit on Madrid from its prehistory to the installation of the royal court in the 16C. (🕐 *Open 9.30am-8pm (2.30pm Aug); Sat-Sun, 10am-2pm.* 🕐 *Closed Mon and public hols.* 🚻 *No charge.* ☎ *91 366 74 15).*

▷ *Cross calle de Bailén and take the first street on the right leading to the Jardines de los Vistillas.*

Jardines de las Vistillas (Vistillas Gardens)

From the part of the gardens closest to the calle Bailén there is a splendid **panorama**★, especially at sundown, of the Sierra de Guadarrama, Casa de Campo, the Catedral de la Almudena and the viaduct.

Iglesia de San Francisco El Grande

🕐 *Guided tours (30min), 11am-12.30 and 4-7pm (5-6.30pm in summer); last tour 30min before closing; no tours Sun-Mon.* 🚻 *3€.* ☎ *91 365 38 00.*

The church's vast neo-Classical façade is by Sabatini but the building itself, a circular edifice with six radial chapels and a large dome 33m/108ft wide, is by Francisco Cabezas. The walls and ceilings of the church are decorated with 19C frescoes and paintings except those in the chapels of St Anthony and St Bernardino which date from the 18C. The Capilla de San Bernardino, the first chapel on the north side, contains in the centre of the wall, a St Bernardino of Siena preaching before the king

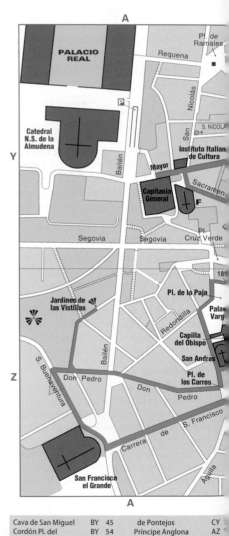

Paseo del Prado

With the 18C drawing to a close, Charles III wanted to develop a public area which would be worthy of Madrid's position as capital of Spain and called upon the court's best architects for his project. In an area outside of the city at the time, Hermosilla, Ventura Rodríguez, Sabatini and Villanueva designed, drained, embellished and built a curved avenue with two large fountains, Cybele and Neptune, at each end, and a third, Apollo, in the centre. To complete the project, the **Botanical Gardens, Natural History Museum** (now the Museo del Prado) and the **Observatory**, were also built. The result was a perfect combination of the functional and the ornate dedicated to science and the arts. Since the 16C, the paseo del Prado has been a favourite place for Madrileños to meet and to relax. Today, the avenue retains its dignified air, and provides locals and visitors alike with an opportunity to pass judgement on the vision and imagination of Charles III.

of Aragón (1781), painted by Goya as a young man. Some of the Plateresque **stalls**★ from the Monasterio de El Parral outside Segovia may be seen in the chancel. The 16C **stalls**★ in the sacristy and chapter house come from the Cartuja de El Paular (🕭 *see Sierra de GUADARRAMA*), the Carthusian monastery near Segovia.

▶ *Walk along carrera de San Francisco and Cava Alta to calle de Toledo.*

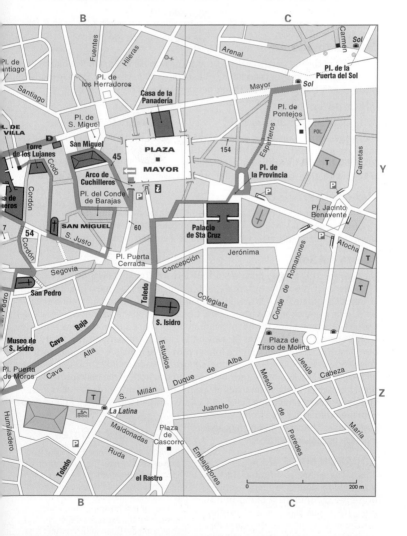

| Ayuntamiento | BY H | Iglesia Arzobispal Castrense | AY F |
| Casa de Pedro Calderón de la Barca | BY D | | |

Plaza de Cibeles and Palacio de Comunicaciones at night

Calle de Toledo

This is one of the old town's liveliest streets. The popular **El Rastro** flea market sets up in neighbouring streets and along Ribera de Curtidores every Sunday morning and on public holidays. *Visitors should beware of pickpockets here.*

Iglesia de San Isidro

🕐 *Open 10am-noon and 6-8pm.* 🕐 *Closed Fri.* ☎ *91 369 20 37.*

The church with its austere façade and twin towers is by the Jesuits Pedro Sánchez and Francisco Bautista. Formerly the church of the Imperial College of the Company of Jesus (1622), it was the cathedral of Madrid from 1885 until 1993. It contains the relics of Madrid's patron saint, Isidro, and those of his wife, Santa María de la Cabeza.

Plaza de la Provincia

Note the well-proportioned façade of the 17C **Palacio de Santa Cruz,** former court prison (Lope de Vega was incarcerated here) and present Ministry for Foreign Affairs. It was from here that prisoners were taken to be executed in the nearby Plaza Mayor.

Puerta del Sol

The itinerary ends at the Puerta del Sol, the liveliest and best-known square in Madrid. It has been a crossroads for historical events in the city over the ages although its present layout only dates back to the 19C. A small monument illustrating Madrid's coat of arms – a bear and an arbutus (strawberry) tree – stands on the point at which calle del Carmen joins the square. In front of this monument is an equestrian statue of Charles III. At its base, the major works for which the king was responsible in the city have been highlighted. The clock on the former post office (now the headquarters of the Presidencia de la Comunidad de Madrid) chimes the traditional 12 strokes at midnight on New Year's Eve. Kilometre Zero, on the ground in front of the building, marks the point from which all the main roads of Spain radiate and distances are measured. The many streets leading into Puerta del Sol are crowded with small traditional shops with their colourful wood fronts where customers can just as easily find fans and mantillas as cooked delicacies.

BOURBON MADRID★★

This is the smart, residential part of Madrid with wide tree-lined avenues bordered by opulent-looking buildings, luxurious palaces and former mansions which now house museums. It is a pleasant area to stroll around in between a visit to the Prado and a walk in the Retiro.

Historical Notes

Philip IV commissioned the construction of a palace near the **monasterio de los Jerónimos** (of which only the church remains). It was subsequently destroyed during the Peninsular War and as a result only the building that formerly contained the Museo del Ejército and the Casón del Buen Retiro remain. The Duke of Olivares had the palace grounds developed into a park.

Plaza de Cibeles★

Standing in the centre of the square is one of the emblems of the city and Madrid's most famous fountain, the 18C Cybele, goddess of fertility who rides a lion-drawn chariot.

The square, the nerve centre of the city, stands at the junction of calle de Alcalá, Gran Vía, paseo del Prado and paseo de Recoletos with its continuation, paseo de la Castellana. Many an artist has been inspired to paint the perspectives opening from the square and the impressive buildings surrounding it such as the **Banco de España** (1891), the 18C **Palacio de Buenavista**, now the Ministry for Defence, the late-19C **Palacio de Linare**s, now the home of the Casa de América, and the **Palacio de Comunicaciones** or Post and Telegraph Office (1919).

Paseo del Prado★

This fine, tree-lined avenue runs between plaza de Cibeles and plaza del Emperador Carlos V. Heading south from plaza de Cibeles, the road passes the Ministerio de la Marina and Museo Naval (*see description under Worth a Visit),* before reaching, in the centre of the avenue, the Fuente de Apolo (Apollo's Fountain), designed by Ventura Rodríguez. The **plaza de la Lealtad**, to the left, with its obelisk dedicated to the heroes of the 2 May, is surrounded by seigniorial buildings such as the neo-Classical **La Bolsa** (Stock Exchange) and the emblematic **Hotel Ritz**.

Plaza de Canóvas del Castillo

This square, embellished by the splendid Fuente de Neptuno (Neptune's Fountain), is overlooked by the **Palacio de Villahermosa**, a late-18C to early-19C neo-Classical palace that is now home to the **Museo Thyssen-Bornemisza★★★** (*see description under Special Features),* and the Hotel Palace.

Continuing south, the left-hand side of the paseo del Prado between plaza de Neptuno and plaza del Emperador Carlos V is occupied by the Prado Museum and the **Real Jardín Botánico** (Royal Botanical Gardens), both projects the work of Juan de Villanueva. ◷ *Garden open 10am-6pm Nov-Feb (7pm Mar and Oct, 8pm Apr and Sep, and 9pm May-Aug); last entry 30min before closing; to greenhouse 1hr before closing.* ◷ *Closed 1 Jan and 25 Dec.* ▧ *2€.* ☎ *91 420 04 38.*

Museo del Prado★★★

This neo-Classical building now home to one of the world's finest art museums was built during the reign of Charles III as the headquarters for the Institute of Natural Sciences. However, following the War of Independence (Peninsular War), Ferdinand VII changed the plans and decided to use it to house the art collections belonging to the Spanish Crown (*see museum description under Special Features).*

Plaza del Emperador Carlos V

The impressive glass and wrought-iron façade of **Atocha railway station** dominates this square at the southern end of the paseo. It is well worth looking inside this remodelled station to view the unusual tropical garden created within it, and to catch a glimpse of the AVE – the high-speed train connecting Madrid with Córdoba and Sevilla.

The former **Hospital de San Carlos**, opposite the station, was created by Charles III, although today it houses the **Museo Nacional Centro de Arte Reina Sofía★** (*see description under Special Features).* This imposing granite building with its austere façade is lightened only by the external glass lifts built to provide access to the museum.

▷ *Return in the direction of the Jardín Botánico and walk up cuesta de Claudio Moyano, renowned for its second-hand booksellers.*

Parque del Buen Retiro ★★(Retiro Park)

◷ *Open 7am-10pm (midnight in summer).* ☎ *010 (municipal information).*

The Retiro, bordered to the west by the impressive calle de Alfonso XII as far as the Puerta de Alcalá, is close to the heart of every *madrileño*. The park, which covers 130ha/321 acres), is a beautiful island of greenery in the middle of the city with dense clumps of trees (La Chopera at the south end), elegant, formal flower-beds (El Parterre at the north end) and a sprinkling of fountains, temples, colonnades and statues. Beside the lake (Estanque) where boats may be hired, is the imposing **Monumento a Alfonso XII.** Near the graceful **Palacio de Cristal**★, in which exhibitions are held, are a pool and a grotto.

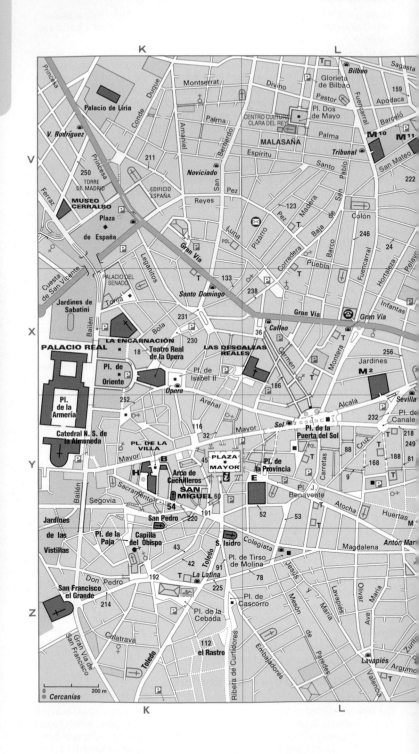

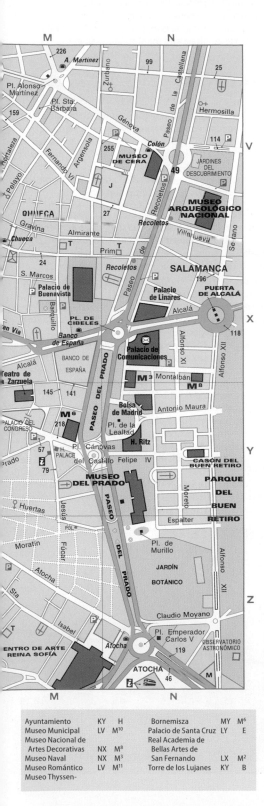

Puerta de Alcalá★ (Alcalá Arch)

The arch, which stands at the centre of plaza de la Independencia, was built by Sabatini between 1769 and 1778 to celebrate the triumphant entrance of Charles III into Madrid. The perspective from here, particularly at night, is one of the most beautiful in the city, taking in plaza de Cibeles, calle de Alcalá and the start of the Gran Vía.

Worth a Visit

AROUND THE ROYAL PALACE★★ ◷1 day

Plaza de la Armería

The vast arcaded square is bounded to the south by the incomplete façade of the **Catedral de la Almudena**. This cathedral, which has taken over a century to complete (the first construction project began in 1879), has a neo-Baroque façade which is in complete harmony with the palace and the excessively cold neo-Gothic interior. It was consecrated by Pope John Paul II in 1993.

The view from the west side of the square extends over the Casa de Campo and the Campo del Moro gardens which slope down to the Manzanares river.

Palacio Real★★ (Royal Palace)

Unaccompanied or guided tours (40min), 9.30am-5pm (9am-6pm Apr-Sep); Sun and public hols, 9am-3pm (3pm Apr-Sep). ◷ Closed 1 and 6 Jan, 1, 5 and 15 May, 12 Oct, 24-25 and 31 Dec and during State receptions. ⊛ 8€ (9€ guided tours), no charge Wed for citizens of the European Union. ☎ 91 454 88 00 or 91 542 00 03 (reservations).

The best view of the palace, which overlooks the Manzanares river, is from paseo de Extremadura and from the gardens of the **Campo del Moro**★.

The palace, an imposing edifice built by the Bourbons, was the royal family's official residence until 1931. Today, it is run by the Patrimonio Nacional (Spain's National Trust) and used by the king for state receptions.

On Christmas Day in 1734, while the royal family was staying at the Parque del Buen Retiro, a fire burnt the old Habsburg Alcázar to the ground. Philip V replaced it with a new palace, the present edifice, designed originally by the Italian architect Felipe Juvarra. When Juvarra died, work continued under Sacchetti, who modified his plans, and then under Ventura Rodríguez until completion in the reign of Charles III.

It forms a quadrilateral made of Guadarrama granite and white stone, measuring some 140m/459ft on the sides, on a high bossaged base. The upper register, in which Ionic columns and Doric pilasters alternate, is crowned by a white limestone balustrade. Colossal statues of the kings of Spain from Ataulf to Ferdinand VI were originally intended to be placed above this, but under Charles III they were put in Plaza de Oriente and the Retiro gardens.

The north front gives onto the **Jardines de Sabatini**, the west the **Campo del Moro**. **Plaza de la Armería** stands to the south between the west and east wings of the palace. The east façade gives onto **plaza de Oriente**.

Palacio Real

Palacio★ (Palace)

A monumental staircase with a ceiling painted by Giaquinto leads to the Salón de Alabarderos (Halberdier Room), the ceiling of which was painted by Tiepolo. This leads to the **Salón de Columnas** (Column Room) in which the treaty for Spain's membership of the European Community was signed on 12 June 1985, and where royal celebrations and banquets are held. The next room is the **Salón del Trono**★ (Throne Room), which was known as the Salón de Reinos (Kingdom Room) in the 18C. It has totally preserved its decoration from the period of Charles III and is resplendent with crimson velvet hangings and a magnificent ceiling painted by Tiepolo in 1764 symbolising *The Greatness of the Spanish Monarchy*. The consoles, mirrors and gilded bronze lions are of Italian design. The following three rooms were the king's quarters, occupied by Charles III in 1764. The Saleta Gasparini was the king's dining room; only the ceiling painted by Mengs remains from its original, primitive decoration. The Gasparini antechamber, with a ceiling also painted by Mengs, and Goya portraits of Charles IV and Queen María Luisa of Parma, is followed by the **Cámara Gasparini**, covered from floor to ceiling in pure Rococo decoration.

The Salón de Carlos III was the king's bedroom. It was here that he died in 1788. The décor is from the period of Ferdinand VII. The **Sala de Porcelana** is, along with its namesake in Aranjuez Palace, the masterpiece of the Buen Retiro Porcelain Factory. Official banquets are held in the Alfonso XII **Comedor de Gala** or Banqueting Hall (for 145 guests), which is adorned with 16C Brussels tapestries. Subsequent rooms display various silver objects, table and crystalware used by the monarchs. The two music rooms contain a collection of instruments including several made by **Stradivarius**★. In the chapel are frescoes by Corrado Giaquinto and paintings by Mengs *(Annunciation)* and Bayeu *(St Michael the Archangel)*.

The Queen María Cristina rooms display an unusual mix of styles ranging from the Pompeian decor in the Salón de Estucos (Stucco Room) to the neo-Gothic appearance of the Salón de Billar (Billiard Room).

Real Farmacia (Royal Pharmacy)

Several rooms have been redesigned to display a number of 18C-20C jars, including a fine 18C Talavera glass jar. The inside of a distillation room has also been re-created with retorts, glass flasks, scales and distillation equipment.

Real Armería★★ (Royal Armoury)

The collection of arms and armour put together by the Catholic Monarchs, Emperor Charles V and Philip II, is outstanding. The key pieces of the display are Charles V's suit of armour and the weapons and armour belonging to Philip II and Philip III. A vaulted hall in the basement contains an excellent collection of Bourbon shotguns, ranging from those made by Philip V's armourer to the Winchester given to King Alfonso XII by the President of the United States.

Museo de Carruajes Reales★ (Royal Carriage Museum)

⊶*Closed for restoration.* ☏ 91 542 00 59.

A pavilion built in 1967 in the middle of the **Campo del Moro** winter garden, which commands a good view of the palace, houses the old royal horse-drawn carriages, most of which date from the reign of Charles IV, in the late 18C. Among the exhibits are the late-17C Carroza Negra or Black Coach made of stained beech and ash, and some 18C berlins, including that used by the Marquis of the House of Alcántara. The coronation coach (drawn by eight horses with accompanying footmen), was built in the 19C for Ferdinand VII and still bears marks of the assassination attempt made on Alfonso XIII and his bride, Victoria Eugenia, in May 1906.

Plaza de Oriente

This attractively landscaped square lies between the east façade of the Palacio Real and the main façade of the Teatro Real. Following redesign as a pedestrian way, it has become a pleasant place for a stroll. At the heart of the gardens, decorated with statues of Gothic kings, stands the magnificent equestrian statue of Philip IV, the work of Pietro Tacca (17C).

Teatro Real

This hexagonal neo-Classical building by architect López de Aguacio was inaugurated as an opera house in 1850 for Isabel II. It has two façades each overlooking a square, one the plaza de Oriente and the other the plaza de Isabel II. The building was fully refurbished during the 1990s.

Monasterio de las Descalzas Reales★★

Guided tours (45min), Tue, Wed, Thu and Sat, 10.30am-12.45pm and 4-5.45pm; Fri, 10.30am-12.45pm; Sun, 11am-1.45pm. Closed Mon, 1 and 6 Jan, Wed-Sat during Holy Week, 1 and 15 May, 15 Jul, 15 Aug, 9 Nov, and 24-25 and 31 Dec. *5€ (combined ticket with Monasterio de la Encarnación: 6€), no charge Wed for citizens of the European Union.* 91 542 00 59.

Although the convent stands in one of the liveliest parts of Madrid, the moment one steps inside, one is taken right back to the 16C. It was Joanna of Austria, daughter of Emperor Charles V, who founded the convent of Poor Clares here in the palace in which she was born. For centuries it served as a retreat for nobles who wished to retire from the world. Their gifts allowed the order to amass the works of art that have made this an outstanding museum.

The magnificent grand **staircase**★ is totally decorated with frescoes. In a former nuns' dormitory is an extraordinary collection of **tapestries**★★ depicting the Triumph of the Church, woven in Brussels in the 17C to cartoons by Rubens. Beyond are the **33 small chapels**, sumptuously decorated; among the most outstanding are those of the Virgin of Guadalupe (Baroque) and that of *Christ Recumbent* by the 16C sculptor Gaspar Becerra.

Other convent treasures include, in rooms on the entresol, various portraits of the royal family (by Rubens, Sánchez Coello, Morales and Pantoja de la Cruz), and a *St Francis* by Zurbarán; *The Adoration of the Kings and Shepherds* by Brueghel the Older, the magnificent *Evangel of the Coins* by Titian, and a *Virgin and Child* by Morales as well as sculptures by Pedro de Mena (a *Dolorosa* and an *Ecce Homo)* and Gregorio Hernández (*Magdalene*).

Real Monasterio de la Encarnación★
(Royal Convent of the Incarnation)

Guided tours (45min), Tue, Wed, Thu and Sat, 10.30am-12.45pm and 4-5.45pm; Fri, 10.30am-12.45pm; Sun, 11am-1.45pm. Closed Mon, 1 and 6 Jan, Wed-Sat during Holy Week, 1 and 15 May, 27 Jul, 9 Nov, and 24-25 and 31 Dec. *3.60€ (combined ticket with Monasterio de las Descalzas: 6€), no charge Wed for citizens of the European Union.* 91 542 00 59.

The convent stands on a delightful square of the same name near the former Alcázar with which it was once connected by a passageway. It was founded in 1611 by Margaret of Austria, wife of Philip III, and occupied by Augustinian nuns. The generosity of each successive Spanish monarch may be seen today in its impressive display of art works.

The collection of paintings from the 17C Madrid School is particularly rich and includes the historically interesting *Exchange of Princesses on Pheasant Island* in 1615 by Van der Meulen and a *St John the Baptist* by Ribera. There is a noteworthy polychrome sculpture of *Christ at the Column* by Gregorio Hernández on the first floor.

The **Relicario**★, with a ceiling painted by Vicencio Carducci, contains some 1 500 relics. Among the most notable are the Lignum Crucis and the phial containing the blood of St Pantaleon which is said to liquify each year on 27 July.

The church with its sober quasi-Herreran style portal was originally by Gómez de Mora (1611) but was reconstructed by Ventura Rodríguez in the 18C after the fire in the Alcázar.

Plaza de España

Every visitor to Madrid is bound to spend some time on the large esplanade during a tour of the city centre. The monument to Cervantes in the middle of the square, and the figures of Don Quixote and Sancho Panza, appear overwhelmed by the size of the skyscrapers built in the 1950s, in particular the **Torre de Madrid** and the **Edificio España.**

Starting from the square is the **Gran Vía,** a wide avenue lined by shops, cinemas and hotels, and calle Princesa, popular with the young and with students, which leads towards the **Ciudad Universitaria**★ (University City).

MONCLOA – CASA DE CAMPO DISTRICT

Museo Cerralbo★

Open 9.30am-3pm; Sun and public hols, 10am-3pm. Closed Mon. *2.40€, no charge Wed and Sun.* 91 547 36 46.

The museum, installed in a late 19C mansion, displays the collection left to the Spanish State by the Marquis of Cerralbo, a man of letters and patron of the Arts, on his death in 1922. A wide range of exhibits can be seen in the mansion's rooms and galleries, including an extensive collection of mainly Spanish paintings, furniture, fans, clocks, armour and weaponry, porcelain, archaeological finds, photographs and personal mementoes belonging to the marquis.

Parque del Oeste★ (Park of the West)

This delightful landscaped garden, extending across slopes overlooking the Manzanares, was designed at the beginning of the 20C. In the southern part, on Príncipe Pío hill, stands the small 4C BC Egyptian **Temple of Debod**. It once stood beside the Nile in Nubia and was rescued from the waters when the Aswan Dam was being built. Note the hieroglyphs on the interior walls.

The **paseo del Pintor Rosales** nearby, stretching northwestwards, acts as a balcony overlooking the park. Its pavilions and pavement cafés command wonderful views of Velázquez-like sunsets. **La Rosaleda**, a rose garden, holds flower shows in June.

Casa de Campo★

This extensive park was reafforested under Philip II in 1559 and today is very popular with *madrileños*,

A **teleférico** (cableway) offering superb views connects the Parque del Oeste with the **Casa de Campo★**. ◷*Open noon (11am in spring and summer) to nightfall.* ◉*4.20€ round trip.* ☎ *91 541 11 18 or 91 541 74 50.*

Attractions within the confines of the Casa de Campo include a lake, a swimming pool and an **amusement park**. 🄺 *Consult timetables. Admission to the park:* ◉*5.10€; ticket for all rides: 21.40€, 12.20€ for children under 7.* ☎ *91 463 29 00.*

The **zoo-aquarium**★★ here is said to house one of the largest assortments of animals anywhere in Europe. (🄺 ◷ *Open 10.30am-nightfall.* ◉*13.10€, 10.55€ for children under 7.* ☎ *91 512 37 70).*

Museo de América★ (Museum of the Americas)

◷ *Open 9.30am-3pm; Sun and public hols, 10am-3pm.* ◷ *Closed Mon, 1 and 6 Jan, 1 and 15 May, 24-25 and 31 Dec.* ◉*3€, no charge Sun.* ☎ *91 543 94 37.*

This archaeological and ethnological museum, which provides a general overview of European ties with the American continent, has brought together historical, geographical, cultural, artistic and religious aspects of the Americas, at the same time retaining the vision of the New World held by Europe since its discovery. Over 2 500 objects are on display on two floors and are accompanied by explanations, maps, models, reconstructions of dwellings etc. Among the exhibits of great historical value on display, the following stand out: the 17C *Conquest of Mexico*, the *Stele of Madrid* (Mayan), the powerful **Treasure of Los Quimbayas★** (Colombian) and two manuscripts, the *Tudela Manuscript* (1553) and the 13C-16C **Tro cortesiano Manuscript★★★,** one of four remaining Mayan manuscripts in existence and the museum's prized historical work.

Faro de la Moncloa (Moncloa Beacon)

🄺 ◷ *Open 10am-2pm and 5-7pm (8pm Spring and autumn, 9pm summer). Sat-Sun and public hols, 10.30am-5.15pm. Closed Mon, 1 Jan and 25 Dec.* 1€. ☎ *91 544 81 04.*

Completed in 1992. From its 76m/250ft high **observatory**★★, there is a wonderful view of Madrid and its surrounding area. To the northeast, the outline of the Sierra Madrileña can be seen.

Museo del Traje (Costume Museum)

♿ *Avenida Juan Herrera 2.* ◷ *Open 9.30am-7pm; Sun and public hols 10am-3pm.* ◷ *Closed Mon.* ◉*3€.* ☎ *91 549 71 50.*

This interesting museum covers everyday clothing through the years, as well as the designs of couturiers Mariano Fortuny and Balenciaga. A **timeline** traces clothing from before the 18C through the 20C, and ends with a re-creation of the the world of the fashion runway.

SALAMANCA – RETIRO

Museo Arqueológico Nacional★★ (National Archaeological Museum)

▶ *Entrance in calle Serrano.* ◷ *Open 9.30am-8.30pm; Sun and public hols, 9.30am-2.30pm. Closed Mon, 1 and 6 Jan, and 24.* ◉ *3€, no charge Sat (after 2.30pm) and Sun.* ☎ *91 577 79 12.*

Founded in 1867 by Queen Isabel II. Since 1895 the archaeological museum has occupied the same building as the **Biblioteca Nacional** (National Library). It is one of the city's most impressive museums and is without doubt the best of its type in Spain.

Prehistoric, Egyptian and Greek Art★

Galleries 1-18. The art of the Upper Palaeolithic period is represented by the reproduction, in the garden, of the **Cuevas de Altamira** (🌜*see Altamira Caves*) and their paintings of bison. This section introduces the history of mankind. The arrival of metal in the Iberian Peninsula (around the middle of the 3rd millennium BC) coincided with the development of the Los Millares culture. The galleries that follow are devoted to the Bronze Age (2nd millennium BC); the so-called Bell Beaker and El Argar. The Age of Iron is represented by the warlike cultures of the northeast and their outstanding gold- and silver-smithing, Note the splendid bronze Costix **bulls**★ of the Megalithic culture (Talayots) of the Balearic Islands Several galleries exhibit numerous finds from beyond the Iberian peninsula. The gallery dedicated to **Ancient Egypt**, displays objects of a mainly funerary nature, including sarcophagi such as that of Amenemhat from the 21st Tebas dynasty. Classical Athens is also represented by the magnificent collection of **Greek vases**★.

Iberian and Roman Antiquities★★

Galleries 19-26. Exhibits in the Iberian galleries illustrate the origin of local techniques and the artistic influence of the Phoenicians, the Greeks and the Carthaginians. The works displayed at the beginning of the section show an Eastern tendency: note the terracottas from Ibiza, including the *Dama de Ibiza*, which perhaps represents the goddess Tanit. The second gallery, where the influence of Carthage is obvious, shows sculpture at a high peak of artistic expression: standing out from the greatest Iberian sculptures is the the **Dama de Elche**★★★ (Lady of Elche), a stone bust, with a sumptuous head-dress and corsage, mysterious and imposing in expression. In the same gallery are the **Dama de Baza**★★, a realistic goddess figure of the 4C BC which has preserved much of its colour, and the woman bearing an offering discovered at Cerro de los Santos. Other galleries illustrate Spain's adoption, when under Roman domination, of the invader's techniques – bronze law tablets, sculptures, mosaics (including the 3C Labours of Hercules), sarcophagi, ceramics and, in particular, a hydraulic pump made of bronze – and later how she developed a Hispanic palaeo-Christian art which incorporated ideas from Byzantium.

Medieval Decorative Art★

Archivo Fotográfica/Museo Arqueológico Nacional

Galleries 27-35. In this section are the magnificent **votive crowns of Guarrazar**★★ dating from the Visigothic period. Most of them were offered by the 7C Visigothic King Recceswinth and are made of embossed gold plaques decorated with pearls, revealing a mixture of Germanic and Byzantine techniques.

This section is also devoted to the incomparable art of Muslim Spain. Among other objects, ivory caskets are displayed. Gallery 31 shows the Romanesque portal from the Monasterio de San Pedro de Arlanza (12C) and contains some of the treasures from San Isidoro de León, in particular the magnificent 11C ivory **processional cross**★★ of Don Fernando and Doña Sancha. Rooms 32 and 33 display various exhibits of Romanesque and Gothic art, including engravings, grilles and capitals. The 14C polychrome wooden chairs from the Monasterio de las

Votive Crown

Clarisas de Astudillo (Palencia) are particularly worthy of note. Romanesque tombs and capitals, together with Gothic sculpture in subsequent galleries, continue to show deep Moorish influence. Gallery 35 is a reconstruction of a Mudéjar interior, complete with carved desks and a magnificent **artesonado**★★ ceiling.

16-19C Art

Galleries 37-38. Porcelain, furniture, jewels and arms are on display from the Kingdom of the Austrias (1516-1700). The building and furnishing of royal palaces under the Bourbons in the 17C, 18C and 19C encouraged the decorative arts, particularly porcelain (Buen Retiro) and crystal (Reales Fábricas) which are represented here.

North of the Museo Arqueológico are the **Jardines del Descubrimiento** (Discovery Gardens), an extension to **plaza de Colón** with massive carved stone blocks, monuments to the discovery of the New World. Directly underneath the gardens is Madrid's **Centro Cultural** (cultural centre).

Museo Lázaro Galdiano★★

🕐Open 10am-4.30pm. 🕐 Closed Tue, 1 Jan, 1 Nov, 6 and 25 Dec. ☎ 91 561 60 84

The mansion of José Lázaro Galdiano (1863-1947), outstanding editor and art lover, houses this magnificent museum of the valuable **collections**★★ he assembled during his life and which he left to the state. On the **lower level**, both collector and collection are introduced through a sample of outstanding works from different fields and eras: Spanish art (*San Lázaro and his Sisters*, by the Master of Perea; *Portrait of Charles III*, by Mengs; *St James of Alcalá*, by Zurbarán; *Anne of Austria*, by Sánchez Coello), the treasury (gold, silver, gems) and European art (*Christ Tied to the Column*, by Naccherino; *Lady Sondes*, by Reynolds). The **main floor** –which retains ceilings painted by Villamil and some lovely items of furniture – is entirely devoted to Spanish Art from the 15C to 19C, with magnificent Gothic and Renaissance panels; paintings by Zurbarán, El Greco, Carreño de Miranda, Claudio Coello; a *Girl's Head* attributed to Velázquez and a small gallery with works by Goya (*Aquelarre, The Witches Conjure*, among others). On the **second floor**, dedicated to European art, are works of the **Flemish School**, outstanding in both quality and number (Bosch, Benson, Metsys, Brueghel the Younger, Moro, etc.); there are also Italian works (*The Adolescent Saviour*, work by Leonardo da Vinci; bronze items), German (Lucas Cranach), Dutch, French (paintings and decorative art) and English (18C portraits and a small Constable painting). The **third floor** houses most of the collections of decorative arts (some 4 000 items): **ivories and enamel**★★★, ceramics, numismatics, arms, fabric and archaeological artifacts.

Museo Nacional de Artes Decorativas

🕐 Open 9.30am-3pm (2.30pm Jul-Sep); Sat-Sun, 10am-2pm. ⊜2.40€. ☎ 91 532 64 99.

This museum is housed in a 19C mansion. It contains a splendid collection of furniture and decorative objects (porcelain, lamps, clocks, tapestries). The collection ranges from Mudéjar rugs (15C) and Castilian carved desks to Avant Garde European pieces (1880-1940) to an exquisite 18C Neapolitan-style Nativity. Several rooms have also been re-created such as a chapel with a Mudéjar ceiling and walls and panels covered with **embossed leather**★ and an 18C Valencian kitchen.

Museo Naval

🕐 Open 10am-2pm. 🕐 Closed Mon, 1 and 6 Jan, 1 May, Aug, and 25 Dec. ⊜ No charge. ☎ 91 379 52 99.

On display are ship **models**★, books, nautical instruments, weapons, portraits, navigation charts and paintings of naval battles. Of particular interest is the **map of Juan de la Cosa**★★, an invaluable document drawn in 1500, on which the American continent appears for the very first time.

Museo de Cera (Waxworks Museum)

🔳 🕐 Open 10.30am-2.30pm and 4.30-8.30pm; Sat-Sun and public hols, 10am-8.30pm; last admission 30min before closing. ⊜ 10€. ☎ 91 319 46 81.

This museum contains wax figures from Spanish history and contemporary celebrities in a realistic setting.

CENTRO

Real Academia de Bellas Artes de San Fernando★
(San Fernando Royal Fine Arts Academy)

🕐 Open 9am-7pm; Sat-Sun and Mon, 9am-2.30pm (2pm public hols). 🕐 Closed 1 and 6 Jan, 1 and 30 May, 24-25 and 31 Dec and local public hols. ⊜ 2.40€, no charge Wed. ☎ 91 524 08 64.

Founded in 1752, during the reign of Ferdinand VI, the picture gallery has a valuable collection of 16C-20C paintings. Of particular interest are the Spanish paintings from the Golden Age, with works by Ribera, Zurbarán, Murillo, Alonso Cano (*Christ Crucified*) and Velázquez. The 18C is also present with works by artists with Bourbon connections (Van Loo, Mengs, Giaquinto, Tiepolo and Bayeu) and above all Goya, including his *Self-portrait* and a series of studio paintings (*The Asylum, Inquisition Scene*). Worthy of note in the collection of European paintings are the enigmatic *Spring* by Arcimboldo and the *Descent* by Martín de Vos. Artists of the 20C are also represented (Picasso, Juan Gris, Chillida, Tàpies).

Museo Municipal

🕐 *Open 9.30am-8pm; August, 9.30am-2.30pm. Sat-Sun, 10am-2pm.* 🕐 *Closed Mon and public hols.* ⬚ *No charge.* ☎ *91 588 86 74.*

This interesting museum is housed in the former city hospice, an 18C building with a superb **portal**★★ built by Pedro de Ribera in Churrigueresque style. The different sections of the museum retrace the history of the city from its origins to the present day, with particular emphasis on the periods under the Habsburgs and Bourbons. Its wide-ranging collections (paintings, ceramics, furniture, coins etc) include porcelain from the Buen Retiro factory and an **1830 model of Madrid**★, by Gil de Palacio.

Museo Romántico

⚰ *Closed for renovation.* ☎ *91 448 10 71.*

This museum paints an accurate picture of life in the 19th century. Its exhibits include a collection of paintings, miscellaneous objects and furniture.

OTHER DISTRICTS

San Antonio de la Florida★

🕐 *Open 10am-2pm and 4-8pm; Sat-Sun and Aug, 10am-2pm.* 🕐 *Closed Mon and public hols.* ⬚ *No charge.* ☎ *91 542 07 22.*

The chapel, built in 1798 under Charles IV, and painted by Goya, contains the remains of the famous artist. The **frescoes**★★ on the cupola illustrate a religious theme, the miracle of St Anthony of Padua – but the crowd witnessing the miracle is of a far more worldly nature, as Goya used the beautiful women of 18C Madrid as models. The result is a marvellous portrait of Madrid society at the time.

Museo Sorolla★

🕐 *Open 9.30am-3pm; Sun and public hols, 10am-3pm.* 🕐 *Closed Mon. 1 and 6 Jan and 24-25 and 31 Dec.* ⬚ *2.40€.* ☎ *91 310 15 84.*

The museum is the lovely onetime Madrid home of Joaquín Sorolla (1863-1923), the great Valencian Luminista painter known for his magnificent treatment of light and the brilliant palette in his maritime scenes. The ground floor includes the painter's studio, while the exhibits are upstairs. Some of the works on exhibit are *The Mother* (1895), *Clotilde with Nightgown* (1910), *The Smock* (1909), *The Pink Dressing Gown* (1916), *Noria, Jávea* (1900), *Instantánea, Biarritz* (1906), and *La Siesta* (1911).

Plaza Monumental de las Ventas★ (Bullring)

The bullring (1931), known as the cathedral of bullfighting, is Spain's largest, with a seating capacity of 22 300. Adjoining it is a **Museo Taurino** (Bullfighting Museum) in honour of the great bullfighters. (🕐 *Open 9.30am-2.30pm; Sun and public hols, 10am-1pm.* 🕐 *Closed Mon in summer, Sat all year and Sun in summer.* ⬚ *No charge.* ☎ *91 725 18 57).*

Museo de la Ciudad (City Museum)

🕐 *Open 10am-2pm and 4-7pm; Jul-Aug, 10am-2pm and 5-8pm; Sat-Sun all year, 10am-2pm.* 🕐 *Closed Mon and public hols.* ⬚ *No charge.* ☎ *91 588 65 99.*

A stroll through the museum's rooms (third and fourth floors) provides the visitor with a journey through the history of Madrid, from prehistory to the present day. Special mention should be made of the superb **models**★ of various parts of the city and of some of the city's most emblematic buildings.

Museo del Ferrocarril (Railway Museum)

🄺🄸🄳🄸 🕐 *Open 10am-3pm.* 🕐 *Closed Mon and in Aug.* ⬚ *3.50€, no charge Sat.* ☎ *902 22 88 22.*

Installed in the Delicias station, the oldest in Madrid. This wrought-iron and glass station, built in 1880, has a collection of steam engines, a restaurant car in which visitors can still enjoy a cup of coffee, electric locomotives etc. It is an ideal museum for children, who will have an opportunity to climb inside some of the exhibits.

Museo Nacional de Ciencia y Tecnología (National Science and Technology Museum)

🕐 *Open 10am-2pm and 4-6pm; Jul-Aug, 9am-3pm; Sun and public hols, 10am-2pm.* 🕐 *Closed Mon, 1 and 6 Jan, 1 and 15 May, 9 Nov and 24-25 and 31 Dec.* ⬚ *No charge.* ☎ *91 530 31 21.*

The museum has put on show just a small percentage of its extraordinary collection of scientific objects. In one room, where a view of the sky has been reproduced, the museum has set out instruments used for navigation and astronomy. These include a **cross-staff**★★ and a 16C astrolabe by the Flemish astronomer Arsenius.

Faunia

▶ *7km/4.5mi from Madrid along the A 3. Once past the M 40, turn off to Valdebernardo.*

Kids ◐ *Open 10.30am-7pm (8pm Jun, 9pm Jul-Aug); 10am-9pm Sat-Sun and public hols.* *17.50€, 12€ children under 10 and senior citizens over 60.* ☎ *91 301 62 10.*

This nature-themed park re-creates the planet's ecosystems on 140 000m²/167 300sq yd, with some 4 500 small- and medium-sized animals and over 70 000 trees and plants. The pavilions, half-buried in the earth, are dedicated variously to tropical jungles, Mediterranean forests, the north and south poles, pollination and insects, the world at night, the underground world, animal food resources, and biodiversity. The park also has a good selection of shops and restaurants.

Excursions

Warner Bros Park★

Kids ◐ *Check seasonal schedule.* *32€ (1 day), 48€ (2 days); children: 24€ (1 day), 36€ (2 days).* ☎ *91 821 12 34.*

This theme park is a great getaway and fun trip to the world of Warner Bros. Aside from its five different areas and numerous attractions, it has assorted bars, restaurants and shops.

Hollywood Boulevard – Your first encounter is with the glitter and glamour of the most famous streets of Hollywood.

Movie WB World Studios – Inspired by Warner studio productions, you'll participate in car chases, explosions, and all kinds of risky deeds. Don't miss the *Hotel Embrujado* (Bewitched Hotel) for chilling special effects, or the performances of *Loca Academia de Policía* (Police Academy) and *Arma Letal* (Lethal Weapon).

Super Heroes World – Live the passionate adventures of comic-strip heroes, in Superman's Metrópolis and Batman's shadowy Gotham City. Roller-coaster rides include Superman: *La Atracción del Acero* (The Attraction of Steel), *La Fuga de Batman* (Batman's Escape) and *Venganza del Enigma* (Vengeance of Enigma, including a 100m/330ft free fall).

The Old West Territory – You'll feel like a real cowboy out here in the West. Test your bravery on the wooden Wild Wild West ride or rafting the dizzying *Cataratas salvajes* (Wild Waterfalls). Live the *Aventura de Río Bravo* in a gold mine.

Cartoon Village – An enchanting voyage through the world of fantasy for the smallest visitors. Sylvester the Cat, Bugs Bunny, Road Runner, and Tom and Jerry come to life in this little town. Attractions include Tom and Jerry's roller coaster and the ACME factory tour on river rapids.

El Pardo

17km/10.5mi NW. The town, now on the outskirts of Madrid, has grown around one of the royal residences. Its surrounding forests of holm oak were once the traditional hunting preserve of Spanish monarchs.

Palacio Real★

Guided tours (35min), 10.30am-5.45pm; Sun and public hols, 9.55am-2.25pm; Apr-Sep, 10.30am-6.45pm; Sun and public hols, 9.25am-1.40pm. ◐ *Closed 1 and 6 Jan, 1 and 15 May, 9 Nov and 24-25 and 31 Dec and for State receptions.* *5€, no charge Wed for citizens of the European Union.* ☎ *91 376 15 00.*

The royal palace was built by Philip III (1598-1621) on the site of Philip II's (1556-98) palace which had been destroyed in a fire in 1604, save for the Torreón de la Reina (Tower of the Queen). It was remodelled by Sabatini in 1772. Franco lived here for 35 years; today, it is used by Heads of State on official visits. As you walk through the reception rooms and private apartments you will see elegant ensembles from Charles IV's collections including furniture, chandeliers and clocks. More than 200 **tapestries**★ hang on the walls; the majority are 18C from the Real Fábrica de Tápices (Royal Tapestry Factory) in Madrid based on cartoons by Goya, Bayeu, González Ruiz and Van Loo. Frescoes from the 16C by Gaspar Becerra (a disciple of Michelangelo) have recently been restored in the Torreón de la Reina.

Casita del Príncipe (The Prince's Pavilion)

☛ Closed for restoration. ☎ *91 376 03 29.*

The pavilion, built in 1772 for the children of the future Charles IV and his wife María Luisa, was completely remodelled by Juan de Villanueva in 1784. It is a single-storey building of brick and stone decorated in the extremely ornate, refined taste fashionable in the late 18C with silk hangings and Pompeian style ceilings.

La Quinta

☛ Closed for restoration. ☎ *91 376 03 29 / 15 00.*

The former residence of the Duke of Arcos became Crown property in 1745. Inside, elegant early-19C wallpaper embellishes the walls.

Convento de Capuchinos (Capuchin Monastery)

🕐 *Open 8am-1pm and 5-8pm.* ☎ *91 376 08 00.*

A chapel contains one of the major works of Spanish sculpture, a polychrome wood figure of **Christ Recumbent**★ by Gregorio Fernández, commissioned by Philip III in 1605.

Málaga★

POPULATION: 534 683

MICHELIN MAP 578 V 16 (TOWN PLAN) MAP 124 COSTA DEL SOL –

SEE COSTA DEL SOL – 59KM/37MI E OF MARBELLA

AND 124KM/77MI SW OF GRANADA – ANDALUCÍA (MÁLAGA)

After its founding by the Phoenicians, the town became an important Roman colony and, under the Moors, the main port for the kingdom of Granada.

Today, Málaga is the lively capital of the Costa del Sol and enjoys a particularly pleasant climate. Some of the districts have retained a distinctive character, such as **La Caleta** in the east, with its old houses and gardens, bearing witness to Málaga's economic importance during the 19C. The city's beaches stretch eastwards from La Malagueta, at one end of the Paseo Marítimo, to **El Palo** *(5km/3mi E)*, a former fishermen's quarter known for its seafood restaurants.

Location

Málaga is nestled between the Parque Natural de los Montes de Málaga and the Mediterranean. The descent into Málaga from the north offers a good view of this whitewashed city at the mouth of the Guadalmedina. The city is dominated by the Gibralfaro (Lighthouse Mountain), a hill crowned by 14C ramparts which command a fine viewaa of the town, the port and the surrounding area. *Echegaray 2, 29005,* ☎ *952 06 13 80; Av. Cervantes 1, 29106 Málaga,* ☎ *95 213 47 50.*

Málaga Wine

This aperitif or dessert wine is predominantly produced from Pedro Ximénez and Moscatel grapes. The main types are Málaga Negro, Lágrima and Color. Large quantities of currants are also produced in the Málaga area, mainly for export.

Address Book

For coin ranges, please see the Legend at the back of the guide.

WHERE TO EAT

⊜⊜ **El Chinitas** – *Moreno Monroy 4 –* ☎ *95 221 09 72 –* ▤ . Ceramic murals, photos and pictures of popular personalities and artists make this one of the most characteristic restaurants of Málaga. The terrace on a pedestrian street is pleasant, and there are dining areas on three floors.

⊜⊜⊜ **Restaurante-Museo La Casa del Ángel** – *Madre de Dios 29 (facing Teatro Cervantes) –* ☎ *95 260 87 50 - Closed Mon and 2 weeks in Jun -* ▤ . Ángel Garó captures the senses by conjuring up the best of Andalucian gastronomy in a unique artistic setting. Enjoy delicious cuisine while surrounded by original works by the likes of Picasso, Dalí, Miró, Sebastiano del Piombo and Julio Romero de Torres, master on canvas of the beauty of the Spanish woman.

TAPAS

Bar La Mesonera – *Gómez Pallete 11.* This small bar fills up with stars and the rich and famous before and after flamenco performances at the Teatro Cervantes opposite. Delicious tapas and a colourful, typically Andalucían atmosphere.

La Posada de Antonio – *Granada 33 –* ☎ *95 221 70 69 –* ▤ . This typical bar decorated with wooden barrels is at the heart of Málaga's main area for nightlife. Specialities include local dishes as well as grilled meats prepared in front of customers. A favourite meeting point for young *malagueños.*

WHERE TO STAY

⊜ **Hotel Castilla y Guerrero** – *Córdoba 7 –* ☎ *95 221 86 35 –* ▤ – *36 rooms.* Plain but comfortable and well-located, with everything needed for a good rest, and adequate bathrooms. Go up the stairs to check in. Good for the price.

⊜ **Hotel Elcano** – *Avenida Juan Sebastián Elcano 103 –* ☎ *952 20 43 03 –* ▤ – *12 rooms.* This charming family-run hotel along the coast road is housed in an attractive mansion built in the style of the 1900s. The bedrooms here are large, bright and airy. Breakfast is served in an air-conditioned conservatory.

⊜⊜ **Hotel Monte Victoria** – *Conde de Ureña 58 –* ☎ *952 65 65 25 – hotelmontevictoria.com –* ▤ – *Reservations advised – 8 rooms –* ⊡ *5.35€.* Quiet family hotel in a villa.Best assets are the garden terrace with impressive city views and the carefully kept rooms. Located on a narrow, climbing street where it's hard to park, though only 15 min on foot from the Casco Viejo (Old Quarter).

TAKING A BREAK

Café Central – *Plaza de la Constitución 1 – Open 8am-10pm*. One of Málaga's most typical and long-standing coffee houses, frequented by a faithful batch of regulars. Although the terrace on the square is particularly pleasant, the large tea-room stands out as the café's most impressive feature.

Casa Aranda – *Herrería del Rey* – ☎ *952 22 12 84 – Open 9am-9pm*. This lively, atmospheric café has taken over every building on this narrow street. A great place for a chat with friends over chocolate con churros.

NIGHTLIFE

El Pimpi – *Granada 6 – Open 4pm-4am*. El Pimpi, on two floors with a number of rooms, is located in a pedestrianised street in the heart of Málaga. This unmissable bar is a favourite haunt for a quiet beer, coffee or tapas in the late afternoon and early evening. Later on, the atmosphere livens up considerably with the occasional burst into song in a wine cellar-type atmosphere. The chilled sweet Málaga wine here is well worth trying.

Liceo – *Beatas 26 – Open 10pm-5am*. This lively bar, installed in one of Málaga's old town houses is popular with an international crowd, particularly those in their thirties. This old mansion with its 19C feel really comes to life at the weekend.

Puerta Oscura – *Molina Lario 5* – ☎ *95 222 19 00 - Closed 20 Aug-1 Sep - Open 6pm-3am*. Excellent for a cup of coffee or something stronger, while you listen to chamber music. The setting is classically elegant, intimate and distinguished. During Málaga's fiesta, the decorations of religious imagery transform the space.

ENTERTAINMENT

Teatro Cervantes – *Ramos María* – ☎ *952 22 41 00*. Teatro Cervantes, which first opened its doors in 1870, offers an extensive programme of theatre and concerts.

FIESTAS

Málaga's major celebrations are **Holy Week** and the **Feria** (the week of August 15).

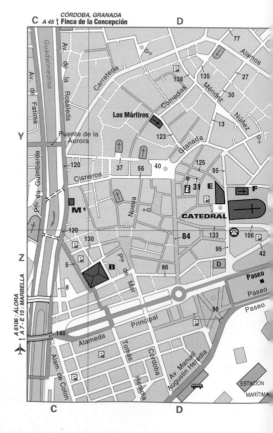

✆ *Neighbouring sights are described in the following chapters: COSTA DEL SOL and ANTEQUERA (48km/30mi N).*

Worth a Visit

Museo Picasso (Picasso Museum)★★

🕐 *Open 10am-8pm (9pm Fri-Sat).* 🕐 *Closed 1 Jan and 25 Dec.* ⊜ *6€.* ☎ *902 44 33 77.*

The 16C Palacio de Buenavista houses the permanent collection of this magnificent museum. The wide selection of Picasso works (over 200) comes from the private collections of Christine and Bernard Ruiz-Picasso, daughter-in-law and grandson of the artist. Oils, sketches, engravings, sculptures and ceramics make up the collection, arranged chronologically and covering the stages of a long artistic trajectory. Among the paintings are *Olga Kokholva with Mantilla* (1917), *Mother and Child* (1921-1922), *Portrait With White Cap* (1923), *Bust of Woman, Arms Crossed Behind Head* (1939), *Woman in Armchair* (1946), *Still Life With Skull and Three Hedgehogs* (1947), *Jacqueline Seated* (1954), *The Bather* (1971) and *Man, Woman and Child* (1972).

Alcazaba★

🕐 *Open 8.30am-7pm (9.30am-8pm in summer).* 🕐 *Closed Mon, 1 Jan and 24-25 and 31 Dec.* ⊜ *1.80€ (3€, joint ticket with Gibralfaro).* ☎ *952 22 51 06.*

This 11C fortress was one of the most important military constructions of the Moors. The winding approach is lined with the ruins (fortified gateways, columns and capitals) of the **Roman theatre** unearthed at the foot of the fortress. Inside the final gateway, Puerta del Cristo (Christ's Door), where the first Mass was celebrated on the town's reconquest (1487), are Moorish gardens. There is a **view**★ of the harbour and city from the ramparts.

The former palace, located inside the inner perimeter, currently houses the **Museo Arqueológico**★, displaying artefacts running from the prehistoric era to the Middle Ages. The galleries devoted to Roman art and Arabic art (exhibits dating back from the 10C to the 15C) deserve special mention. Models of the Alcazaba and cathedral are also on display.

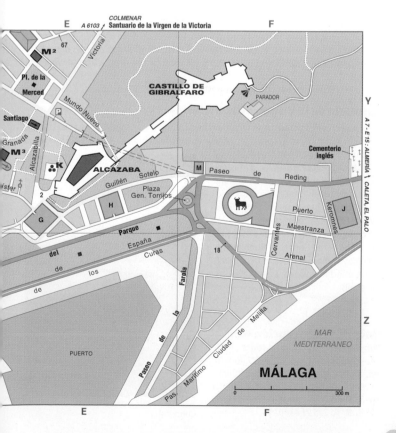

Catedral★

🕐 *Open 9.30am-6.45pm; Sat, 9.30am-6pm; Sun and public hols, open for worship only.* 📷 *1.80€.* ☎ *95 222 03 45.*

Construction of the cathedral spanned three centuries (16C-18C) but is still incomplete to this day as the south tower lacks its full elevation. Because of this, it is locally nicknamed *La Manquita* (the Missing One). The three aisles of the vast hall-church are covered inside with highly decorative **oven vaulting**★. The classically ordered Corinthian columns, entablatures and cornices add to the interior's monumental appearance. The decoration includes **choir stalls**★ with figures by Pedro de Mena, 17C marble pulpits 17C and two 18C Baroque organs. The **side chapels** also feature several works of interest (Dolorosa, Virgin and Child) in addition to an impressive early-15C carved and painted **Gothic retable**★ in the ambulatory.

The 18C **Palacio Episcopal** (Episcopal Palace) on the cathedral square is built in Baroque style and has a lovely marble façade.

El Sagrario

This unusual 16C rectangular church in the cathedral gardens features a fine **north portal**★ built in Isabelline Gothic style. The 18C interior is Baroque; at its end it presents a beautiful **Mannerist altarpiece**★★, crowned by a well-preserved Calvary.

Museo-Casa Natal Picasso (Picasso's Birthplace)

🕐 *Open 10am-8pm; Sun, 10am-2pm.* 🕐 *Closed 1 Jan and 25 Dec.* 📷 *No charge.* ☎ *95 226 02 15.*

The house is located in a mid-15C building on the **plaza de la Merced**. The first floor contains a number of Picasso's drawings as well as a collection of ceramics. The rest of the building houses the offices of the Pablo Ruiz Picasso Foundation, as well as a room used for temporary exhibitions.

Museo de Artes y Costumbres Populares (Museum of Popular Art and Costume)

🕐 *Open 10am-1.30pm and 4-7pm; 15 Jun-30 Sep, 10am-1.30pm and 5-8pm; Sat, 10am-1.30pm.* 🕐 *Closed Sun and public hols.* 📷 *2€.* ☎ *95 221 71 37.*

The museum is housed in a restored 17C inn, the Mesón de la Victoria. The ground floor displays objects used in the past for work on the land or sea, such as ploughing implements, a sardine fishing boat, and tools used for the production of wine and olive oil.

On the first floor is a collection of statuettes in 18C and 19C costumes.

Santuario de la Virgen de la Victoria★

At the end of calle Compás de la Victoria. The sanctuary was founded by the Catholic Monarchs in the 15C and rebuilt two centuries later. The church is dominated by a large 17C carved altarpiece at the centre of which stands the **camarín**★★, a masterpiece of exuberant Baroque architecture completely covered by stuccowork and presided over by a fine 15C *Virgin and Child* of German provenance.

The **crypt**★, a pantheon created to house the tombs of the Counts of Buenavista, could not be more sombre, with its black background festooned with skeletons and skulls.

Excursion

Finca de la Concepción★

7km/4mi N. 🚌 *Guided tours (1hr), 1 Apr-20 Jun, 10am-6.30pm; 21 Jun-10 Sep, 10am-7.30pm; 11 Sep-20 Oct, 10am-5.30pm; 21 Oct-10 Dec, 10am-4.30pm; 11 Dec-31 Mar, 10am-4pm.* 🕐 *Closed Mon. 2.95€.* ☎ *95 225 21 48/ 07 45.*

A romantic corner of the Finca de la Concepción

B. Kaufmann/MICHELIN

These lovely gardens were designed on the occasion of a wedding for an upper-class Málaga family. Visitors will enjoy strolling through this delightful jungle, planted with more than 300 tropical and subtropical species and charmingly dotted with streams, ponds, waterfalls and Roman ruins.

Melilla

POPULATION: 63 670.

MICHELIN MAP 742 FOLDS 6 AND 11 – NORTH AFRICA

The Spanish enclave of Melilla is a calm yet lively town which exudes an opulent air with its wide avenues and large buildings. The market-gardening area which surrounds the town to the south and west, the two parks in the centre of the city and the sailing and fishing vessels all hold greater interest for the visitor than the port area.

Location

Melilla is situated at the entrance to a peninsula, its rugged landscape jutting into the Mediterranean for a length of 20km/12mi culminating in the Cabo de Tres Forcas (Three Forks headland). *Fortuny 21, 52001 Melilla, ☎ 95 267 54 44.*

Worth a Visit

OLD TOWN★

▶ *At the end of avenida del General Macía, climb the steps which go through the ramparts.*

The old town, built on a rocky peninsula and encircled by 16C and 17C fortifications, dominates the port area. Monuments worthy of interest include the tiny **Capilla de Santiago** *(at the end of a covered passageway)*, recognisable by its Gothic vault, and the Puerta de Santiago, a gateway bearing the escutcheon of Emperor Charles V on its façade.

 Getting to Melilla

By ferry – Trasmediterránea operates services to and from Almería (7hr) and Málaga (8hr). For information and bookings, call ☎ 902 45 46 45.
By plane – Iberia has daily flights to Melilla from Málaga. For information and bookings, call ☎ 902 400 500.

Museo Municipal

◷ Open 10am-2pm and 4-8.30pm; 1 May-1 Oct, 10am-2pm and 5-9.30pm; Sun, 10am-2pm. ◷ Closed Mon, 1 Jan and 25 Dec. ⊜ No charge. ☎ 95 268 13 39.

In the Baluarte de la Concepción (bastion). Exhibits on display in this museum include pottery, vases, coins and jewels from the Carthaginian, Phoenician and Roman periods which have been discovered in the area; 17C-19C Spanish weaponry hangs from the walls.

From the museum's terrace there are panoramic **views**★ of the old and new towns, the port and, to the north, the Cabo de Tres Forcas.

A Spanish Possession Since the 15C

In 1497, under the reign of the Catholic Monarchs, the Duke of Medinaceli's troops seized this town which then became Spanish territory. In the past, like many towns along the North African coast, Melilla fell prey to the waves of navigators and conquerors in the Mediterranean (Carthaginians, Phoenicians, Romans).

Mérida★

POPULATION: 51 135

MICHELIN MAP 576 P 10 – EXTREMADURA (BADAJOZ)

This tranquil, historic town at the heart of Extremadura, on the right bank of the River Guadiana, was the former capital of the Roman province of Lusitania. The remains surviving from this period bear witness to the town's importance during this illustrious era.

Location

Mérida is situated close to the A 5 highway linking Madrid with Portugal via Trujillo and Badajoz. ▪ *Paseo José Álvarez Saénz de Buruaga, 06800 Mérida,* ☎ *924 31 53 53.*

⚲ *Neighbouring sights are described in the following chapters: BADAJOZ (62km/39mi W), ZAFRA (66km/41mi S), CÁCERES (71km/44mil N) and TRUJILLO (88km/55mi NE).*

Special Features

ROMAN MÉRIDA★★ *3hr*

In 25 BC, the Roman governor of Augustus founded the township of *Emerita Augusta* in this hitherto uncolonised region. It was well situated on the River Guadiana and at the junction of major Roman roads and as a result soon became the capital of Lusitania. The Romans lavished upon it temples, a theatre, an amphitheatre and even a 400m/437yd circus.

Museo Nacional de Arte Romano★★ (National Museum of Roman Art)

🕐 *Open 10am-2pm and 4-6pm; Mar-Nov, 10am-2pm and 4-9pm; Sun and public hols all year, 10am-2pm.* 🕐 *Closed Mon, 1 and 6 Jan, 1 May, 10, 24-25 and 31 Dec.* ⮑ *2.40€, no charge Sat afternoon and Sun.* ☎ *924 31 19 12.*

This museum is housed in an imposing **building**★ designed by the architect Rafael Moneo Vallés to display Mérida's rich Roman archaeological collections. The vast construction, its sober, majestic lines reminiscent of edifices built under the Roman Empire, is made entirely of brick, an ideal material as its warm colour sets off the marble statues inside. A ramp leads up to the main hall which is separated into bays by nine semicircular arches. Its structure is similar to the main entrance of the amphitheatre. The skilfully designed complex also includes two upper floors of galleries and light passageways, suspended, as it were, above the hall. The museum is organised according to theme in a clear, didactic manner.

Among the sculptures in the hall are statues from the Roman theatre including the strong-featured head of Augustus *(at the end of the second bay)* and in the last bay, parts from the portico of Mérida's *forum*: statues of important people, caryatids and giant medallions (Medusa and Jupiter) which made up the frieze. The upper floors display jewellery, coins and pottery. Wonderful **mosaics**★ may be admired at close range from the passageways.

The basement, the excavation site around which the museum was built, contains the remains of Roman villas and tombs.

Teatro Romano★★ (Roman Theatre)

🕐 *Open 9.30am-2pm and 4-6.30pm; Jun-Dec, 9.30am-2pm and 5-7.30pm.* 🕐 *Closed 1 Jan and 24-25 and 31 Dec.* ⮑ *5.50€ (7.50€ combined ticket with church of Santa Eulalia and Alcazaba).* ☎ *924 31 20 24.*

The theatre was built by Agrippa, Augustus' son-in-law, in the Classical style of the great theatres in Rome, in 24 BC. A semicircle of stone tiers afforded seating for 6 000, the front row being reserved for high dignitaries; a pit held the orchestra; a high stage wall was decorated during Hadrian's reign (2C AD) with a covered colonnade and statues. Behind the stage, overlooking the gardens, is a portico where the audience could walk during intervals. The great blocks of granite in the vaulting of the passageways to the tiers are secured by drystone construction alone.

Anfiteatro★ (Amphitheatre)

The arena dates from the 1C BC and held, it is estimated, 14 000 spectators. It staged chariot races and the *naumachiae* or mimic sea battles, for which the amphitheatre was specially flooded. The steps to the audience seats and the *vomitoria*, the great covered passageways through which the crowd left, can still be seen. The tiers have disappeared apart from those reconstituted on either side of the east *vomitorium* (right coming from the theatre). Round the chariot course is a wall crowned by a cornice which protected the front row of spectators – usually notables – from wild beasts when there were gladiatorial combats. The open ditch in the centre presumably contained arena machinery and workshops.

COMBINED ENTRANCE TICKET

This ticket, on sale at all the city's major monuments, allows entry to the theatre, amphitheatre, Roman houses, Alcazaba and the Iglesia de Santa Eulalia.

CLASSICAL THEATRE FESTIVAL

During the months of July and August the Roman theatre reverts to its original function to host this prestigious festival which has been running for almost 50 years. For information, log onto www. festivaldemerida.es.

Casa Romana del Anfiteatro (Roman Villa)

🕓 *Open 9.30am-2pm and 4-6.30pm; Jun-Dec, 9.30am-1.45pm and 5-7.30pm.* 🕓 *Closed 1 Jan and 24-25 and 31 Dec.* 📷 *7.50€ (combined ticket).* ☏ *924 31 20 24.*

The remains of various constructions, including water channels, pavements and bases of walls, which formed part of a patrician villa built around a peristyle and dependent rooms, can be seen here. The pavements and mosaics are in remarkably good condition. Some show intricate geometrical motifs while others illustrate scenes from everyday life. One in particular, called *Autumn*, depicts grape-treading.

Casa del Mitreo

▷ *Next to the bullring.* This patrician villa was built outside the town at the end of the 1C. It is laid out around three open patios with a dual purpose: the distribution of light to the internal rooms and the collection of rainwater. Some of the rooms have preserved the remains of paintings and mosaics, which include the **Cosmological Mosaic**★.

Templo de Diana

▷ *Calle Romero Leal.* The remains of a Roman temple dedicated to imperial worship built under Augustus. A large part of the peristyle of Corinthian columns and fluted shafts is still visible. In the 16C its materials were used to build the palace of the Count of Corbos.

Two Roman **bridges** still span the River Albarregas and River Guadiana (where an adjoining quay was also built). Water for the colony was brought by means of two **aqueducts**, San Lázaro and Los Milagros, of which a few elegant polychrome brick and stone arches remain. The water was fed from two reservoirs, the Cornalvo and Proserpina, north of the town.

Worth a Visit

Alcazaba

🕓 *Open 9.30am-2pm and 4-6.30pm; Jun-Dec, 9.30am-2pm and 5-7.30pm.* 🕓 *Closed 1 Jan and 24-25 and 31 Dec.* 📷 *7.50€ (combined ticket).* ☏ *924 31 20 24.*

The Moors built the fortress in the 9C to defend the 792m/866yd **Puente Romano**★ (Roman Bridge) across the islet-strewn Guadiana river. Inside the walls is an interesting **cistern** dug to the same depth as the bed of the river. To decorate the fortress, the Moors took Corinthian capitals and Visigothic marble friezes from former buildings or ruins.

Iglesia de Santa Eulalia★

🕓 *Open 10am-2pm and 4-6.30pm; in summer, 9.10am-2pm and 5-7.30pm.* 📷 *2.80€ (7.50€ , combined ticket with Alcazaba and Teatro).* ☏ *924 31 20 24.*

The excavations carried out in the basement of this church have brought to light the interesting history of this particular site which has been occupied by a succession of Roman houses, a palaeo-Christian necropolis, a 5C basilica and, from the 13C, this Romanesque church.

Montblanc★★

POPULATION: 5 612

MICHELIN MAP 574 H 33 – CATALUNYA (TARRAGONA)

Hidden behind the stones of Montblanc's ancient walls are the vestiges of a town with an important medieval past. From the road, the imposing profile of its battlements provides a contrast with the tranquillity of the fertile surrounding area planted with vines and almond trees. Within the walls, its narrow, cobbled streets, fronted by stone buildings, perpetuate arcane legends and deep secrets, while its peaceful streets, the silence punctuated by the occasional pealing of a church bell, recall the town's golden age back in the 14C.

Location

Montblanc, the capital of the Conca de Barberà, is located in an impressive settingaa on top of a small hill, at the crossroads of the N 240, linking Tarragona and Lleida, and the C 240 from Reus (29km/18mi S). ⓘ *Miquel Alfonso (Iglesia de Sant Francesc.), 43400 Tarragona,* ☎ *977 86 17 33.*

ⓘ *Neighbouring sights are described in the following chapters: TARRAGONA (36km/22.5mi SE) and LLEIDA/LÉRIDA (61km/38mi NW).*

> **WHERE TO STAY**
>
> ⊖ **Fonda dels Àngels** – *Plaça Els Àngels 1* – ☎ *977 86 01 73 – Closed 1-20 Sep, Christmas and 1 Jan –* ⊞ *– 12 rooms -* ⊡ *4€ - Restaurant 12/16€.* This small, family-run inn at the heart of the former Jewish quarter has been converted from a Gothic-style house, of which an original ogival window has been preserved. Simple but pleasant rooms, plus a popular restaurant serving interesting local cuisine.

Special Features

THE RAMPARTS★★

The ramparts were originally commissioned by Peter IV, king of Aragón (also known as Peter the Ceremonious) in the middle of the 14C. Nowadays two thirds of the original walls (1 500m/5 000ft) are still extant, along with 32 square towers and two of the four doors: that of Sant Jordi (S) and that of Bover (NE).

Iglesia de Santa Maria★★

🕐 *Open 11am-1pm and 4.30-6pm; Sun and public hols, 11am-1pm.* ☎ *977 86 17 33 .*

Poised on a promontory overlooking the old city, this beautiful Gothic church has a single nave and radiating chapels that come right up to the foothills. The unfinished façade is Baroque. The interior features a sumptuous 17C **organ**★★, a Gothic altarpiece in polychrome stone (14C) and an elegant silver monstrance.

Museu d'Art Frederic Marès

☛ *Temporarily closed.* ☎ *977 86 03 49.*

This museum housed in a late-19C former prison contains interesting religious paintings and sculptures from the 14C to the 19C, in particular fine 14C wooden statues. From the plaza de Santa Bárbara, a little higher up, there are pleasant views of the town.

View of the town

Museu Comarcal de la Conca de Barberà★

🕐 *Open 10am-2pm and 4-7pm; Jun-Sep, 10am-2pm and 5-8pm; Sun and public hols all year, 10am-2pm.* 🕐 *Closed Mon, 1 Jan and 25-26 Dec.* 👓 *2.40€.* ☎ *977 86 03 49.*

Set up in a 17C house, the museum displays archaeological and ethnographical artefacts discovered in the area as well as a fine collection of 18C ceramic flasks belonging to an apothecary.

Montblanc in the Middle Ages

Until 1489, Montblanc was a thriving town with a prosperous Jewish community *(calle dels Jueus).* Its golden age was the 14C, when its economic supremacy was reflected in the political arena with several Estates General being held in the town at the instigation of Catalan-Aragonese monarchs.

Plaza Mayor

The town's main square is fronted by arcades sheltering small shops, cafés and outdoor terraces. The major monuments of note here are the town hall *(ayuntamiento)* and the Gothic-style Casa dels Desclergue.

Iglesia de Sant Miquel★

🔎 *Guided tours by prior arrangement.* ☎ *977 86 17 33 (tourism office).*

Fronted by a Romanesque façade, this small 13C church is built in the Gothic style with pure, sober lines. It was chosen by the Court of Catalunya to host the Estates General in 1307, 1333, 1370 and 1414.

Next to the church on the same square stands the **Palau del Castlà**, formerly the residence of the king's representative, which houses the 15C prison on its ground floor.

Call Judío (Jewish Quarter)

The only remains from the former Jewish district are the Calle dels Jueus (Street of the Jews) and the remains of a Gothic house in plaza dels Àngels.

Another interesting building is the 14C **Casa Alenyà**, a Gothic house of slender proportions.

OUTSIDE THE WALLS

Convento de la Serra★

🕐 *Open 10am-7pm.* ☎ *977 86 17 33 (tourism office).*

This old convent, formerly occupied by nuns belonging to the Order of St Clare, stands on a small hill offering lovely views of the surrounding countryside. The convent once enjoyed the protection of several kings and popes. It houses the much-venerated **Mare de Déu de la Serra**, an alabaster statue made in the 14C.

Hospital de Santa Magdalena★

Despite their smallness, the 15C **cloisters**, illustrating the transitional period between Gothic and Renaissance, are truly remarkable. The vertical perspective on the ground floor, featuring fluted columns and pointed arches, is broken in the upper section.

Museu Molins de la Vila

1km/0.6mi toward Prenafeta. 🔎 *Guided tours (1hr) by prior arrangement. 1.80€.* ☎ *977 86 03 49.*

The museum's two medieval mills provide visitors with an insight into the traditional activity of flour milling.

Tour

THE CISTERCIANS ROUTE

90km/56mi – 🕐 *allow one day*

This suggested tour visits the most important Cistercian monasteries in Catalunya. These were founded in the middle of the 12C, once the reconquest of Catalunya had been completed by Ramón Berenguer IV. The most spectacular is undoubtedly the Monasterio de Poblet, although a visit to Santes Creus may be more memorable. The Monasterio de Santa María de Vallbona, the only one of the three to be inhabited by nuns, is renowned for its tranquillity and elegant simplicity.

▸ *Exit Montblanc on the N 240 to l'Espluga de Francolí. From here, follow the T 700 for 4km/2.5mi.*

Monasterio de Poblet★★★

🎧 *Guided tours (45min), 10.30am-1.30pm and 4.30-6.30pm (5.30pm Nov-Feb).*
🕐 *Closed 1 Jan and 25 Dec.* 🎫*3€ (6.50€ combination ticket with Vallbona de les Monges and Santes Creus Monasteries.* ☏ *973 33 02 66.*

Located in a splendid **site**★ sheltered by the Prades mountains, Poblet is one of the largest and best preserved Cistercian monasteries. Founded by Ramón Berenguer IV in the 12C, it enjoyed the protection of the crown of Aragón.
An outer perimeter 2km/1mi long was built to protect the land and vegetable gardens belonging to the monastery.

Capilla de Sant Jordi★★

To the right of some sheds set aside for agricultural and industrial purposes, stands the precious 15C chapel. The Late Gothic interior of this tiny building features splendid broken barrel vaulting.
A second, inner wall fortified by polygonal towers enclosed the conventual annexes where visitors from the outside world were received. It is pierced by the 15C **Porta Daurada** (Golden Door), named after the gilded bronze sheets that form its covering, commissioned by Philip II when he visited the monastery in 1564.

Plaça Major★

On this main square, of irregular design, stands the 12C **Capilla de Santa Caterina**, flanked by various shops, a hospital for pilgrims and a carpentry workshop. On the right are the ruins of the 16C Abbatial Palace and the large **stone cross** erected by Abbey Guimerà, dating from the same century.
A third wall, built by Peter the Ceremonious, surrounds the monastery proper. These crenellated walls, fortified by 13 towers, are an imposing sight (608m/1 995ft long, 11m/36ft high and 2m/6.5ft thick). On the right stands the **Baroque façade of the church**, built around 1670 and flanked, 50 years later, by heavily ornate windows. Although this façade presents pleasing proportions, it breaks with the overall austerity of the monastery.

Porta Reial★

This doorway opens onto the conventual buildings. Because of its somewhat forbidding appearance, squeezed in between two massive towers, it looks more like the entrance to a fortress than to a monastery.

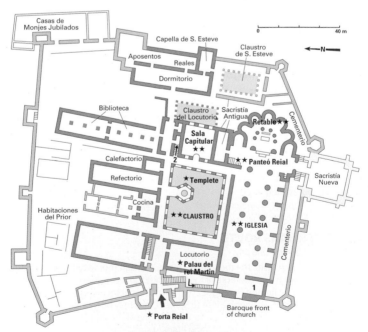

SANTA MARIA DE POBLET: THIRD PERIMETER WALL

Periods of contruction ▮ 12C-13C ▮ 14C ▮ 16C ☐ 17C-18C

Palacio del Rei Martin★

Beyond the door, to the right, a narrow staircase leads up to this 14C Gothic palace built above the west wing of the cloisters. Its splendid rooms are wonderfully light thanks to the pointed bay windows.

Locutorio

Originally used as a dormitory for Catholic converts, this room later became a wine press. The 14C vaulting rests directly onto the walls, without any other form of support.

Cellar

This magnificent Gothic cellar *(celler)* below the monks' sleeping quarters has been transformed into a concert hall.

Claustro★★

The size of these cloisters (40 x 35m/131 x 115ft) and their sober lines give some indication of the monastery's importance. The south gallery (c 1200) and huge lavabo or **templete**★ with its marble fountain and 30 taps are in pure Romanesque style; the other galleries, built a century later, have a floral motif tracery; beautiful scrollwork adorns the **capitals**★ throughout.

The **kitchen** *(cocina)* and the huge **monk's refectory** *(refectorio de los monjes)*, both built around 1200 and still in use, open onto the cloisters. The **library** *(biblioteca)* – the former scriptorium – is crowned by ogival vaulting supported by a row of 13C columns at its centre. The 13C **chapter house**★★ *(sala capitular)*, accessed via a Romanesque doorway, is adorned with four slender octagonal columns beneath palm-shaped vaulting.

Iglesia★★

The light, spacious church, imbued with serenity, is typically Cistercian. It has pure architectural lines, broken barrel vaulting over the nave, two storeys in elevation, and unadorned capitals. The only decorative note lies in the windows and wide arches joined beneath an arch which dissolves into the piers of the engaged columns. In contrast to the lack of ornament, the church had to incorporate numerous altars because of the growing community; the apse was therefore ringed by an ambulatory and radiating chapels, a feature more commonly found in Benedictine churches.

The **royal pantheon**★★ *(panteó reial)*, the church's major ornament and its most original feature, has immense shallow arches spanning the transepts on either side of the crossing, surmounted by the alabaster, royal tombs. These were constructed in about 1350 to provide a repository for the kings of Aragón, buried at Poblet between 1196 and 1479. The sepulchres were desecrated in 1835 but were restored by the sculptor Frederic Marès.

The **retable**★★ *(retablo)* at the **high altar** *(altar mayor)* is a monumental marble Renaissance altarpiece carved by Damián Forment in 1527. Figures in four superimposed registers can be seen glorifying Christ and the Virgin.

In the narthex, an opening to the outside world added in 1275, is the Renaissance **altar of the Holy Sepulchre (1)**.

A wide flight of stairs leads from the north transept to the monks' dormitory.

Dormitorio

Massive central arches support the ridge roof above the vast, 87m/285ft long gallery. Part of the dormitory has been converted into monks' cells.

▶ *Leave Poblet on the T 232 towards Maldà. From here, take the road to Vallbona.*

Monasterio de Vallbona de les Monges★★

🚶 *Guided tours (45min), 10.30am-1.30pm and 4.30-6.30pm (5.30pm Nov-Feb).* 🕐 *Closed Mon, 1 Jan and 25 Dec.* 🎫 *3€ (6.50€ combination ticket with Poblet and Santes Creus Monasteries).* ☎ *973 33 02 66.*

The Cistercian **Monasterio de Santa Maria**, in the heart of the village, completes the Cistercian Trinity along with the abbeys of Poblet and Santes Creus. The convent was founded in 1157 by the hermit Ramón de Vallbona and became a Cistercian community for women. In 1563, when, as a result of the Council of Trent, a decree was passed stipulating that convents could not remain isolated, the nuns of Vallbona encouraged inhabitants from the neighbouring village to settle around the abbey.

Iglesia★★

Built chiefly in the 13C and the 14C, this church is a fine example of transitional Gothic architecture. The interior is simple and surprisingly light thanks to two octagonal lantern towers: one (13C) lies above the transept crossing while the other, dating from the 14C, overlooks the centre of the nave. The church contains the beautiful tombs of Queen Violante of Hungary, wife of James I the Conqueror of Aragón, and her daughter, as well as a huge polychrome Virgin from the 15C. The abbesses' tombstones are inlaid in the floor.

Cloisters★

The east and west galleries are Romanesque (12C-13C). The 14C Gothic north wing features pretty capitals with plant motifs. In the south gallery (15C but built in Romanesque style) note the 12C statue of Nuestra Señora del Claustro (Our Lady of the Cloisters), which was restored in the 14C.

▶ *Leave Vallbona in the direction of Rocallaura and from here return towards Montblanc along the C 240 to link up with the AP 2. Turn off onto the TP 2002 at exit 11.*

Monasterio de Santes Creus★★★

46km/29mi SE of Vallbona. Tour: 2hr. ⊙ Open 15 Mar-15 Sep, 10am-1.30pm and 3-7pm (6pm 16 Jan-15 Mar; 5.30pm 16 Sep-15 Jan); last admission 20min before closing. ⊙ Closed Mon exc public hols, 1 Jan and 25 Dec. ⊚ 3€ (6.50€, joint ticket with Vallbona de les Monges and Poblet Monasteries. ☏ 977 63 83 29.

From the road, the Monasterio de Santes Creus appears as a vast complex of buildings set in undulating countryside. The monastery was founded in the 12C by monks from Toulouse and, like Poblet, came under the protection of the great families of Catalunya and into the favour of the kings of Aragón.

Santes Creus hosts an interesting festival of classical and sacred music as well as an international competition for Gregorian chant.

The monastery plan is similar to that of Poblet in that it has three perimeter walls. A Baroque gateway leads to the principal courtyard where the monastic buildings, enhanced with fine *sgraffiti*, now serve as shops and private residences. To the right is the abbatial palace, with its attractive patio, which is now the town hall; at the end stands the 12C-13C church. The façade is plain apart from a rounded doorway, a large Gothic window and battlements added a century later.

🎧 *The visit starts with an audio-visual presentation on the history and daily life of the monastery.*

Gran Claustro★★★ (Great Cloisters)

Construction began in the year 1313 on top of earlier cloisters, of which there remain a fountain as well as the chapter house. The ornamentation, consisting of capitals and bands, is a perfect illustration of Gothic motifs: plants and flowers, animals, biblical, mythological and satirical themes. The scenes are executed with remarkable refinement and creativeness. The Puerta Real or Royal Gate on the south side of the church opens onto cloisters with Gothic bays which, although much restored, still have lively carvings – note the illustration of Adam and Eve on the south-west corner where Eve is shown emerging out of Adam's rib, and the fine tracery of the arches (1350-1430). In contrast, the transitional style of the **lavabo**, which incorporates a marble basin, appears almost clumsy. Carved tombs of the Catalan nobility fill the gallery niches.

The Great Cloisters

The chapter house★★ (*sala capitular*) is an elegant hall with arches supported on four pillars. Abbots' tombstones have been inlaid in the pavement.

Stairs next to the chapter house lead to the 12C **dormitory** *(dormitorio)*, a long gallery divided by diaphragm arches supporting a timber roof presently used as a concert hall.

Iglesia★★

The church, begun in 1174, closely follows the Cistercian pattern of a flat east end and overall austerity; the square ribbed ogive vaulting, replacing the more usual broken barrel vaulting, does nothing to soften its severity. The lantern (14C), the stained glass in the great west window, and the superb apsidal **rose window**★, partially hidden by the high altar retable, do, however, relieve the bareness. The ribbed vaults rest on pillars which extend back along the walls and end in unusual consoles with rich corbelling. Gothic canopies at the transept openings shelter the **royal tombs**★★: on the north side (c 1295) that of **Pedro the Great** (III of Aragón, II of Barcelona) and on the south (14C), that of his son, **Jaime II**, the Just, and his queen, **Blanche d'Anjou**. The Plateresque decoration below the crowned recumbent figures in Cistercian habits, was added in the 16C.

Claustro Viejo (Old Cloisters)

Although they were built during the 17C, these "old cloisters" occupy the site of former cloisters dating back to the 12C. The design of the old cloisters is simple with a small central fountain and eight cypresses in the close, imparting a cool, contemplative atmosphere. Leading off the cloisters are the kitchens, refectory and the **royal palace** (note the splendid 14C **patio**★).

Morella

POPULATION: 2 717

MICHELIN MAP 577 K 29 – COMUNIDAD VALENCIANA (CASTELLÓN)

Morella has an amazing **site**★: 14C ramparts, punctuated by towers, form a mile-long girdle round a 1 004m/3 294ft hill on which the town has been built in tiers. Crowning the rock summit are the ruins of a medieval castle.

Location

Morella nestles at the heart of the Maestrazgo, a rugged and mountainous region. The town's road link to the coast is via the N 232, connecting Morella with Peñíscola (78km/49mi) and Castellón de la Plana (98km/61mi). The town of Alcañiz is situated 67km/42mi to the N. 🗐 *Plaza de San Miguel, 12300 Morella,* ☎ *964 17 30 32.*

🜟 *Neighbouring sights are described in the following chapters: COSTA DEL AZAHAR and ALCAÑIZ.*

Worth a Visit

A stroll around Morella's concentric streets reveals a number of noteworthy noble houses and religious buildings. One of the gateways in the walls, the Puerta de San Miguel, houses a small **museum** dedicated to the time of the dinosaurs. (🕐 *Open 11am-2pm and 4-6pm (7pm in summer).* 🕐 *Closed Mon.* 🜷 *1.80€.* ☎ *964 17 31 17, ext 3.*

Basílica de Santa María la Mayor★

🕐 *Open noon-2pm and 4-6pm (11am-2pm and 4-7pm Jul-Sep). No visits during religious services.* 🕐 *Closed 1 and 6 Jan and 25 and 31 Dec.* `🜷 1.50€.* ☎ *964 16 07 93.*

The basilica is one of the most interesting Gothic churches in the Levante. It has two fine portals surmounted by gables: the 14C Apostle Doorway, and the later Virgins' Doorway with an openwork tympanum. The unusual raised Renaissance

El Maestrazgo

Morella lies at the heart of the mountain region which was the fief *(maestrazgo)* of the Knights of Montesa, a military order founded by James II of Aragón. The order, which had its seat at San Mateo *(40km/25mi SE of Morella)* as of 1317, fortified all villages in the region so as to be better defended against the Moors. Each community at the foot of its castle had a main porticoed square and narrow streets lined by balconied houses. Most occupy attractive sites in isolated, strongpoint positions and have retained considerable character.

coro at the nave centre has a spiral stair-case magnificently carved by a local artist (biblical scenes) and a delicate balustrade with a frieze illustrating the Last Judgement. The sanctuary was sumptuously decorated in Baroque style in the 17C and an elegant organ loft introduced in the 18C. There is a small **museum** with a beautiful Valencian *Descent from the Cross* and a 14C *Madonna* by Sassoferrato.

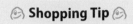

☺ Shopping Tip ☺

Truffles, honey, cheese and rugs are just some of the typical local products on sale in the shops lining the town's streets, in particular Virgen del Pilar, Segura Barreda, Marquesa Fuente del Sol and Blasco de Alagón.

Castillo

On the way up there are good **views**★ of the town, the 13C-14C ruins of the Convento de San Francisco with its Gothic cloisters, the 14C-15C aqueduct and the reddish heights of the surrounding sierras.

Excursions

Santuario de la Balma

25km/15.5mi NW along the CV 14. This unusual Marian sanctuary has been built into a rock wall in an impressive setting overlooking a meander in the River Bergantes. The cave in which the Virgin appeared has been enclosed by a side wall dating from the 13C (subsequently restored), and a 17C façade. Access to the sanctuary is via a narrow gallery excavated into the rock.

Mirambel

30km/19mi W on the CS 840. ▶*Bear left after 11km/7mi.*

This small, well-preserved maestrazgo village has retained its medieval character, with a number of houses bearing their original coats of arms.

Murcia★

POPULATION: 338 250

MICHELIN MAP 577 S 26 (TOWN PLAN) – MAP 123 COSTA BLANCA – MURCIA.

Murcia lies on either side of the Segura, at the centre of a fertile market-gardening area (huerta). Today it is a lively university city which in recent times has experienced spectacular growth around its old quarter with the construction of new districts and wide avenues such as the paseo del Malecón.

Location

Murcia is located less than 50km/31mi from the coast. The A 7 motorway runs north-east to Elx/Elche (59km/37mi) and Alicante.  *San Cristóbal 6, 30001 Murcia,* ☎ *968 36 61 00.*

🕭 *Neighbouring sights are described in the following chapter: ALACANT/ALICANTE (81km/51mi NE).*

Background

Historical notes – The city, founded in the reign of Abd ar-Rahman II in 831 as Mursiya, was finally captured during the Reconquest in 1266 and was soon sufficiently secure for the pope to transfer the episcopal seat to it from Cartagena, a city always vulnerable to pirate attack. Up to the 18C, Murcia prospered from agriculture and silk weaving.

Two famous 18C sons of Murcia – **Francisco Salzillo** (1707-83), the son of an Italian sculptor and a Spanish mother, is the last famous name in Spanish polychrome wood sculpture. *Pasos*, or processional groups, were his speciality (although he did do other types of carving); 1 800 works are attributed to the artist.

The other notable 18C Murcian was the statesman, Don José Moñino, **Count of Florida-blanca** (1728-1808), minister to Charles III and IV. If Murcia owes him much, Spain owes him more, for it was by his counsel that the country's economy was put on its feet.

Worth a Visit

Catedral★

Currently closed for renovation. ⊙ *Open 7am-1pm and 5-8.30pm (10pm in summer); museum, 10am-1pm and 5-8.30pm.* ⊙ *Closed during the Virgen de la Fuensanta pilgrimage (dates vary).* ☎ 968 21 63 44.

The original cathedral, built in the 14C, is camouflaged outside by Renaissance and Baroque additions. The **façade★**, with an arrangement of columns and curves as successful architecturally as decoratively, is a brilliant example of Baroque.
The impressive 18C belfry, 95m/311ft in height, was completed by Ventura Rodríguez in the 18C.
The interior, however, beyond the entrance covered by a cupola matching the façade, is preponderantly Gothic, apart from the 16C **Capilla de los Junterones** *(fourth south chapel)* which has rich Renaissance decoration. The **Capilla de los Vélez★** *(off the ambulatory)* is sumptuous Late Gothic with splendid star vaulting and wall decoration which clearly includes Renaissance and Mudéjar motifs.
The sacristy, approached through two successive Plateresque doors (note the beautiful panels of the first), is covered by an unusual radiating dome. The walls are richly panelled with Plateresque carving below and Baroque above.
The interesting carved **stalls** (1567) in the *coro* are from an old Castilian monastery.

Museo

At the entrance to the museum there is part of a Roman sarcophagus showing Apollo and the Muses, while the silver monstrance (1678) is the third largest in Spain, measuring over 2m/6.5ft in height and weighing 600kg/1,320lb. The side rooms contain Salzillo's **St Jerome★** and a 14C altarpiece by Barnaba da Modena of St Lucy and the Virgin. The treasure, in the chapter house, includes monstrances and chalices as well as the crowns of Murcia's venerated Virgen de la Fuensanta.

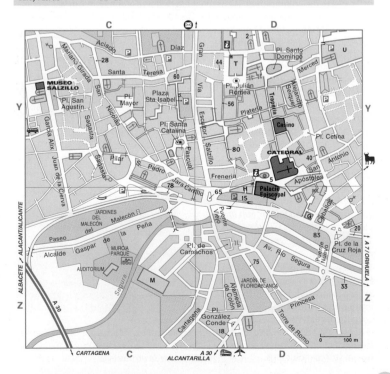

Ascent of the tower

A ramp leads up to the top of this belfry which commands an interesting **panorama**★ of Murcia and its market gardens.

In the cathedral square is the Italianate **Palacio Episcopal**, with elegant cloisters.

Calle de la Trapería★

The pedestrianised main street in the old quarter is fronted by one of the most sumptuous **casinos** in Spain, a late-19C building with an inner Moorish patio and elaborate decoration and a great glassed-over gallery.

Museo Salzillo★

🕐 Open 9.30am-1.30pm and 4-7pm; Sun and public hols, 11am-1pm. 🚫 Closed Mon, and Sat-Sun in Jul-Aug. 🎫 3€. ☎ 968 29 18 93.

The museum possesses many of Salzillo's masterpieces including the eight polychrome wood sculptures of **pasos** carried in the Good Friday procession during Holy Week. They stand in the side chapels off the rounded nave of the Church of Jesus. The deep emotion on the faces in the groups of the Last Supper and Christ's Arrest and the majesty of St John and the Angel in the Agony in the Garden are truly impressive. The museum also contains 565 of Salzillo's vivid terracotta pieces, used to create scenes from the life of Jesus.

Excursions

Orihuela★

24km/15mi NE on the A 7. The peaceful town of Orihuela, with its many churches, lies along the banks of the Segura at the foot of a deeply scored hill. The river provides water for the town's fertile market gardens *(huertas)* and for the local **palm grove**. In the 16C Orihuela was made an episcopal see and for two centuries was a university town. The poet and dramatist Miguel Hernández was born in the town in 1910; his house is now a museum.

Catedral★

📷 Guided tours (30min), 10.30am-1.30pm and 4pm (5pm in summer) to 7.30pm; Sat, 10.30am-1.30pm. 🎫 1.20€ (museum, tower and reliquary). ☎ 96 530 06 38.

Constructed from the 14C-16C, the cathedral has a Renaissance -style north doorway dedicated to the Annunciation. The interior has three cruciform Gothic naves, ambulatory, and unusual vaulting with spiral ribs. The stalls of the choir in the central nave are carved in Baroque style. There are notable Renaissance **grilles** around the choir and presbitery. The small cloister leads to a convento. The **Museo de la Catedral** houses a *Temptation of St Thomas Aquinas* by Velázquez, a *Christ* by Morales and a *Mary Magdalene* by Ribera.

The **Palacio del Obispo** on calle Ramón y Cajal behind the cathedral has a magnificent 18C patio.

Colegio de Santo Domingo

North of the City

🕐 Open 10am-2pm and 4-7pm; Jun-Sep 10am-2pm and 5-8pm; Sun and public hols 10am-2pm. 🚫 Closed Mon, 1 and 6 Jan and 25 Dec. ☎ 96 530 27 47.

This monumental building (16C-18C), formerly the university, started out in Renaissance style and transformed into Baroque. The long façade of the college conceals two sober cloisters (17C and 18C). The 18C **church**★ is totally covered with murals and exuberant stucco mouldings.

Colegio de Santo Domingo

J. Malburet/MICHELIN

Address Book

WHERE TO EAT

🍴🍴 **Acuario** – *Plaza Puxmarina 3 –* ☎ *968 21 99 55 – Closed Sun, 15-30 Aug and Holy Week –* 🍴. This established family restaurant offers regional cuisine with contemporary touches, based on local recipes and produce. Good for the price.

WHERE TO STAY

🛏🛏 **Hispano 2** – *Radio Murcia 3 –* ☎ *968 21 61 52 - hotel@hotelhispano.net –* 🍴 *– 35 rooms -* 🗐 *5€ -* A local classic, known for its excellent location by the cathedral among the winding lanes and pedestrian streets. Rooms are of a basic comfort level, and public areas are limited but cosy.

SHOPPING

Pastelería Bonache – *Plaza de las Flores 8 –* ☎ *968 21 20 83 - Closed Sat Jul-Aug - Open 9.30am-2.30pm and 5-10pm.* A tradition since 1828. Don't leave Murcia without trying a *pastel de carne* (meat pie), known throughout the province and beyond for its exquisite and unique flake pastry.

FIESTAS

Murcia's **Holy Week** processions are particularly solemn: on the morning of Good Friday, penitents in mauve robes bear eight Salzillo floats *(see below)* in procession through the town. The week after the **Spring Festival** is the occasion for general rejoicing with processions of floats and finally the Entierro de la Sardina, or Burial of the Sardine, which symbolises the end of Lent.

Museo de la Muralla

🕐 *Open 10am-2pm and 4-7pm; Sep-Jun 10am-2pm and 5-8pm; Sun and public hols 10am-2pm.* ☎ *96 530 46 96.*

This little museum takes you down below street level to the remains of the city wall and dwellings and baths from the Moorish era, as well as a Gothic palace and a Baroque building.

The **Iglesia de Santiago,** near the town hall, is built in Gothic style, with Renaissance transept and apse. It was founded by the Catholic Monarchs whose yoke and arrow emblems, together with a statue of St James, may be seen on the Gothic portal; the doorway on the right is Baroque. In the interior, note the statues attributed to Salzillo in the side chapels. 🕐 *Open 10am-1.30pm and 4pm (5pm in summer) to 7.30pm.* 🎫 *0.60€.* ☎ *96 530 27 47.*

Santuario de la Fuensanta (La Fuensanta Shrine)

7km/4mi S. ▶ *Follow the signs from Puente Viejo.*

From the shrine of the Virgen de la Fuensanta, patron saint of Murcia, are fine **views** of the town and the *huerta*.

Cartagena

62km/39mi SE along the N 301. Cartagena occupies a unique position in the curve of a deep bay sheltered by fortified promontories. In 223 BC the settlement was captured by the Carthaginians; it was subsequently colonised by the Romans, who named it *Cartago Nova*, under whom it developed into a prosperous colony (traces of the forum have been discovered beneath plaza de los Tres Reyes). Following a long period of decline, it returned to favour during the reign of Philip II, who fortified the surrounding hilltops, and that of Charles III, who built the Arsenal.

The city is known for its solemn and dramatic Holy Week processions.

City life centres around calle Mayor, the main street. Near plaza del Ayuntamiento is the early **submarine** invented by a native of the city, Lieutenant Isaac Peral, in 1888.

From the top of the **Castillo de la Concepción**, a former fort which is now a public garden (Parque Torres), there is a good general **view** of the harbour and the ruins of the former Romanesque cathedral of Santa María la Vieja.

Museo Nacional de Arqueología Marítima

▶ *Navidad jetty, in the harbour. Take the Algameca road and when you reach the Empresa Nacional Bazán, turn onto the road on the right and follow it to the end.* 🕐 *Open 9.30am-3pm.* 🚫 *Closed Mon, 1 and 6 Jan, 1 May, 24-25 and 31 Dec and local festivals.* 🎫 *2.40€, no charge Sun.* ☎ *968 12 11 66.*

This museum of maritime archaeology displays finds from various underwater excavations, notably a rich collection of Phoenician, Punic and Roman amphorae. Seafaring activity during Antiquity is illustrated by maps and small-scale models of vessels (galleys, biremes and triremes) as well as a model of the Mediterranean sea bed.

Mar Menor
At La Manga: 81km/51mi SE via the N 301 and MU 312 and 33km/21mi from Cartagena.

Mar Menor, or Little Sea, is a lagoon separated from the open Mediterranean by **La Manga**, a sand bar 500m/1 640ft wide which extends northwards for 20km/12mi from the eastern end of the rocky Cabo de Palos headland. Gilt-head, mullet and king prawns are fished from its shallow salt-water. The low-lying hinterland is cloaked in almond trees with here and there a palm or a windmill.

La Manga del Mar Menor is a large, elongated seaside resort with surrealistic tower blocks stretching for miles along the sand bar. Its sandy beaches and calm water are ideal for sailing, windsurfing and water-skiing.

In **Santiago de la Ribera**, where there is no natural beach, pontoons with changing cabins line the seafront. **San Javier**, nearby, is the seat of the Academia General del Aire (General Air Academy).

Alcantarilla
9km/6mi W on the N 340. The **Museo de la Huerta**, on the Murcia road, is a museum dedicated to local **agriculture and irrigation**. Displays include an ethnographic pavilion providing background information, while outside, dispersed among the orange trees, visitors can admire white rustic dwellings *(barracas)* and a **noria**, the giant waterwheel devised for irrigation by the Moors. ○ *Open 10.30am-6.30pm; Sat-Sun and public hols, 10.30am-1pm and 3-6pm; 4 Apr-Oct, 10am-8pm (1.30pm Aug); Sat-Sun and public hols, 10am-1.30pm and 4-6pm.* ○ *Closed Mon, 1 and 6 Jan, Good Fri, 1 May, 1 Nov and 25 Dec.* ☎ *968 89 38 66.*

Lorca
67km/42mi SW along the N 340-E 12. Lorca lies in a fertile valley, irrigated by the Guadalentín, a marked contrast with the remainder of this extremely arid region. The city is sited at the foot of a hill crowned by as **castle**, the **Fortaleza del Sol**, where visitors may spend the day back in the Middle Ages. *Open 10.30am (10 am Jun-Sep) to 5pm. Last admission 1h before closing.* ○ *Closed Jan-Feb and 24 and 31 Dec.* ⊛9€. ☎ *902 40 00 47.*

The main sights of interest in town are the **plaza de España,** surrounded by the fine Baroque façades of the **Ayuntamiento** (town hall), the **Juzgado** (Law Courts), embellished with a corner sculpture, and the **Colegiata de San Patricio**, a collegiate church built in the 16C and 18C, and the **Casa de los Guevara**, the doorway of which, although in poor condition, is, nevertheless, an outstanding example of Baroque sculpture (1694).

"Blancos" and "Azules"
Lorca is one of the cities of Spain where Holy Week is celebrated with full traditional panoply. Sumptuous embroideries, the pride of a local craftsmanship that is old and famous, adorn the *pasos*. Biblical and imperial Roman characters in full costume join penitents in long processions, the brilliant colours of the former contrasting with the sombre robes of the latter. Finally, there is friendly rivalry between the White and Blue Brotherhoods who compete for solemnity and magnificence.

Caravaca de la Cruz
70km/44mi W along the C 415. Caravaca stretches around the foot of a hill crowned by castle ramparts. In May each year, the town celebrates the miracle which took place within its walls in 1231. Then, it is said, a priest named Chirinos was celebrating Mass before the Moorish king who had taken him prisoner, when the Cross, which had been missing from the altar, suddenly reappeared; the Moor was moved to immediate conversion and the Cross, believed to be part of the True Cross, became an object of great popular veneration. It was stolen in 1935.

Castillo-Iglesia de la Santa Cruz
Guided tours (45min), 11am-1pm and 4-7pm (Aug, 10am-1pm and 5-8pm). ○ *Closed Mon (except Aug), 1 Jan and 1-5 May.* ⊛ *2.40€.* ☎ *968 70 77 43.*

The restored ramparts of the 15C castle enclose the church which for so long sheltered the Holy Cross (Santa Cruz). The 1722 doorway in local red marble has a surprisingly bold Baroque character. Estípites, or inverted balusters, and delicately twisted pillars add to the vertical effect of the entrance without detracting from the robustness and, in fact, give it something of a Latin-American appearance. Inside there is a strictly Herreran elegance. From the battlements at the top of the building there is an interesting view of the surrounding town.

Olite★

POPULATION: 3 049.

MICHELIN MAP 573 E 25 – NAVARRA.

Olite, the favourite residence of the kings of Navarra in the 15C, lives in the shadow of its castle which has all the appearance and size of a medieval city. Superb views of the town can be enjoyed on the approach by road from both San Martín de Unx and Beire. The fairy-tale castle visible today is the result of restoration work carried out at the beginning of the 20C. During the summer months, Olite attracts large numbers of visitors who come to the town to enjoy the impressive setting, lively atmosphere and myriad activities on offer.

Location

Olite stands at the heart of the Navarran plain, 4km/2.5mi from the A 15 motorway linking Zaragoza and Pamplona/Iruña. ⚑ *Mayor 1, 31390 Olite,* ☎ *948 74 17 03.*

🕭 *Neighbouring sights are described in the following chapters: PAMPLONA(43km/27mi N), ESTELLA and SANGÜESA/ZANGOZA (44km/27.5mi NE).*

Worth a Visit

Castillo de los Reyes de Navarra★★ (Fortress of the Kings of Navarra)
Entrance on plaza de Carlos III el Noble. 🕐 *Open 10am-2pm and 4-6pm (to 7pm Apr-Jun and Sep; to 8 pm Jul-Aug).* 🕐 *Closed 1 and 6 Jan, and 25 Dec.* ⊛ *2.70€.* ☎ *948 74 00 35.*

The fortress is divided into two parts: the Palacio Viejo (Old Palace), nowadays Olite's parador, and the Palacio Nuevo (New Palace), the construction of which was ordered by Charles III, the Noble, in 1406. The French origins of the prince – he was a Count of Evreux and native of Mantes – explain the foreign-style fortifications, a transition between the massive stone constructions of the 13C and the royal Gothic residences of the late 15C with galleries and small courtyards. During the Peninsular War, a fire almost completely destroyed the building. Behind the 15 or so towers marking the perimeter were hanging gardens, along with inner halls and chambers decorated with *azulejos*, painted stuccowork and coloured marquetry ceilings. The most impressive rooms are the Guardarropa (Wardrobe), now housing an exhibition, the Sala de la Reina (Queen's Room) and the Galería del Rey (King's Gallery).

Iglesia de Santa María la Real
Visits by prior arrangement. ☎ *948 71 24 34 or 948 43 04 97.*

The church is the former chapel royal. An atrium of slender multifoil arches precedes the 14C **façade**★, a beautiful example of Navarra Gothic sculpture. The only figurative carving on the portal is on the tympanum which illustrates the lives of the Virgin and Christ. A painted 16C retable above the high altar frames a Gothic statue of Our Lady.

Iglesia de San Pedro
The church façade below the tapering octagonal spire has a somewhat disparate appearance. The portal covings are set off by tori (large convex mouldings). Eagles on either side symbolise, right and left respectively, Gentleness and Violence. Inside the church, at the beginning of the north aisle, is a stone, carved to represent the Trinity (15C).

Excursions
▶ *Head 19km/12mi NE along the NA 5300 to San Martín de Unx, then follow the NA 5310.*

Detail, church façade

Ujué★

Ujué, perched on a summit overlooking the Ribera region, remains, with its tortuous streets and picturesque façades, much as it was in the Middle Ages.

Iglesia de Santa María

A Romanesque church was built on the site at the end of the 11C. In the 14C, Charles II, the Bad, undertook the building of a Gothic church but work must have been interrupted for the Romanesque chancel remains to this day. The central chapel contains the venerated **Santa María la Blanca**, a wooden Romanesque statue, plated in silver. On the Sunday after St Mark's Day (25 April), a traditional **romería** (pilgrimage) is held in her honour.

Fortaleza (Fortress)

The church towers, invariably used for military purposes, command a view which extends to Olite, the Montejurra and the Pyrenees. Of the medieval palace there remain lofty walls and a covered watch path circling the church.

Monasterio de La Oliva★

34km/21mi SE. Leave Olite on the N 121. ▶ *After 14km/9mi, turn left onto the NA 124 to Carcastillo and from here follow the NA 5500.* ◷ *Open 9am-12pm and 3.30-5.45pm; Sun and public hols, 9-11.15am and 4-5.45pm.* ⊜ *1.80€.* ☎ *948 72 50 06.*

La Oliva was one of the first Cistercian monasteries to be built by French monks outside France during the lifetime of St Bernard (1090-1153). The monastery's influence was considerable in the Middle Ages. The buildings, now stripped of treasure and trappings, retain the beauty of the pure Cistercian style.

Iglesia★★

Apart from a triangular coping and the turret (17C), the façade of this late-12C church is unadorned – a perfect setting for the interplay of lines of the portal and two rose windows. The interior is surprisingly deep with pillars and pointed arches lined with thick polygonal ribs in austere Cistercian style.

Claustro★

The bays in these late-15C cloisters appear exceptionally light. Gothic additions were simply grafted onto an older construction, as can be seen by the arch springs which, in part, obscure the entrance to the 13C **Sala Capitular** (chapter house).

Oñati/Oñate

POPULATION: 10 264

MICHELIN MAP 573 C 22 – PAÍS VASCO (GUIPÚZCOA).

Oñati, with its seigniorial residences, monastery and old university, is nestled amid the wild beauty of the Udana Valley. Twice during the First Carlist War the town served as Don Carlos' headquarters. Finally it fell to **General Espartero**, obliging the Carlists to sign the Convention of Vergara which put an end to the war.

Location

Oñati stands at the foot of Monte Alona (1 321m/4 333ft), 45km/28mi NE of Vitoria-Gasteiz and 74km/46mi SW of Donostia-San Sebastián. *Foruen Enparantza 4, 20560 Oñati,* ☎ 943 78 34 53.

Neighbouring sights are described in the following chapters: VITORIA-GASTEIZ, DONOSTIA-SAN SEBASTIÁN and COSTA VASCA.

Worth a Visit

Antigua Universidad (Old University)

Open 9am-5pm (2pm Fri) Closed Sat-Sun and public hols. ☎ 943 78 34 53.

The university, now administrative headquarters of the Guipúzcoa province, was founded in 1542 by a native prelate of Oñati and closed early this century; it was the only university in the Basque country and enjoyed considerable cultural prestige. The gateway by the Frenchman, Pierre Picart, is surmounted by pinnacles and crowded with statues. Among the figures is the founding bishop (at the centre) and St Gregory and St Jerome (right and left respectively). The exuberant decoration reappears at the corner of each tower and again in the exceedingly elegant patio.

Ayuntamiento (Town Hall)

This fine 18C Baroque building was designed by the architect Martín de Carrera. At Corpus Christi, unusual traditional dances and processions which date back to the 15C are held in the square.

Iglesia de San Miguel

Visits by prior arrangement. ☎ 943 78 34 53.

The Gothic church facing the university was modified in the Baroque period. A Renaissance chapel off the north aisle, closed by beautiful iron grilles, contains an interesting gilded wood altarpiece and the marble tomb of the founder of the university. The golden stone cloister exterior with gallery tracery, ogee arches, and statue niches is Isabelline Plateresque in style.

Excursions

Santuario de Arantzazu★

9km/5.5mi S along the GI 3591. Open 8am-8pm. No charge. ☎ 943 78 09 51.

The **scenic cliff road**★ follows the course of the River Arantzazu which flows through a narrow gorge. The **shrine** is perched at an altitude of 800m/2 625ft in a mountain **setting**★ facing the highest peak in the province, Mount Aitzgorri (1 549m/5 082ft). Dominating the church is an immense bell tower 40m/131ft high, built, like the towers framing the façade, with diamond-faceted stone symbolising the hawthorn bush (*arantzazu* in Basque) in which the Virgin appeared to a local shepherd in 1469. A hermitage was then built on the spot and occupied by Franciscans in the 16C but the present building only dates from 1955. Inside, a statue of the Virgin, patron of the province, stands at the centre of a huge wooden altarpiece painted by Lucio Muñoz.

Elorrio

18km/11mi NW on the Durango road.

This small, ancient town in which many houses are emblazoned with coats of arms, possesses a collection of 15C and 16C crucifixes unique in the Basque country. The one at the town's west entrance is decorated with a frieze of people, the one at the east with a cabled column. The **Iglesia de la Concepción** (Church of Our Lady of Holy Conception), which is a typically Basque church with its thick round pillars and star vaulting, contains an exuberant Churrigueresque altarpiece.

Parque Nacional de
Ordesa y Monte Perdido★★★

MICHELIN MAP 574 E 29-30 –

100KM/62MI FROM HUESCA – ARAGÓN (HUESCA).

The Ordesa Valley is a grandiose canyon cutting through vast, layered limestone folds. The escarpments, which rise nearly 1 000m/3 280ft from the valley floor, are divided into steel, grey or red, ochre strata. In spring, cascades of melted snow streak the vertical rock face. Along the valley bottom, the River Arazas, a turbulent trout stream, rushes beneath flourishing beech and maple trees. Growing up the lower slopes are pines, larches, firs – some 25m/82ft tall – and a carpet of box, hawthorn and service trees.

The park is also home to other valleys of equal beauty such as the Valle de Pineta and the Cañón de Añisclo, towered over by impressive peaks such as Monte Perdido (3 355m/11 004ft).

Location

Nestled in the NE of Spain at the centre of the Pyrenees, this national park can be approached from Torla to the W or Aínsa from the SE. The Parc National des Pyrénées, with which it is twinned, stands on the French side of the border. The best time to visit the park is from May to September as some roads may be closed due to snow at other times of year. ⓘ Torla: ☏ 974 48 64 72, Aínsa: ☏ 974 50 07 67.

The National Park

The Valle de Ordesa was declared a national park in 1918 and was expanded in 1982 to cover an area of 15 608ha/ 38 569 acres, including the Monte Perdido massif and the Ordesa, Añisclo, Escuain and Pineta valleys. The purpose of the park is to safeguard the region's outstanding natural beauty – the massif's limestone relief of canyons, cliffs and chasms – as well as the variety and richness of its flora and fauna (Pyrenean ibex, golden eagle and izard, a goatlike antelope of the Pyrenees).

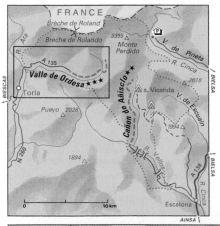

PARQUE NACIONAL
DE ORDESA Y
MONTE PERDIDO

- – – – Path described
- – – – Other path
- ⌂ Refuge
- ✗ Restaurant
- ⓘ Tourist Information Centre
- P Car park
- ℗ Parador

👆 *Neighbouring sights are described in the following chapters: PIRINEOS ARAGONESES and JACA (62km/39mi S).*

Walking Tours

VALLE DE ORDESA★★★

A viewpoint on the road into the park offers a general panorama of the reserve, and a little further on, a second point looks over the 60m/197ft high **cascada de Tamborrotera** ① (waterfall). As the road soon comes to an end, the rest of the park may only be visited on foot.

The best route for inexperienced walkers or families with young children is along the path that runs through the bottom of the canyon beside the Arazas river itself, which makes for a pleasant, shady walk.

👁 *Allow a day for a round tour from the car park to the end of the canyon and back.*

The three walks below are feasible for experienced, well-equipped hikers.

Circuito del Circo de Soaso (Tour of the Soaso Cirque)

🚶 *Start from the Cadiera refuge beyond the car park; 7hr.*

The first part of the walk as far as the valley floor is easy and can be attempted by anyone. The second part, via the Cola de Caballo (Horse's tail) is more difficult, however, and is only recommended to those who are well equipped and in good physical condition (steep climbs).

This walk provides the best and most complete tour of the Ordesa Valley. From the Circo de Soaso path several waterfalls can be seen including the **Gradas de Soaso** ②, or Soaso Steps, followed by the impressive, 70m/230ft high **Cola de Caballo** ③. The path continues along the **Faja de Pelay** overlooking the canyon to a depth of 2 000m/6 550ft at the foot of the Sierra de Cutas. Continue along the **Senda de los Cazadores** (Huntsman's Path) ⑤, from where there is a wonderful view of the canyon. The best panorama can be had from the **Mirador de Calcilarruego** 🚲. The path back to the refuge drops sharply (almost 1,000m/3,300ft).

Circo de Cotatuero (Cotatuero Cirque)

🚶 *Start from the restaurant; 4hr.*

On the park's northern border are the **Cotatuero** ⑥ and the **Copos de Lana** (Tufts of Wool) *cascadas* (waterfalls) ⑦ with a drop of 250m/820ft.

Circo de Carriata

🚶 *Start from the Centro de Información; 4hr.*

The walk is worth doing although the *clavijas*, or mountaineering peg track, is difficult and not recommended for those who suffer from vertigo.

A long hike is possible to Monte Perdido via the Goriz refuge, and beyond, along paths leading to the Cirque de Gavarnie in France via the Brecha de Rolando (Roland Gap) *(ask at the Centro de Información).*

CAÑÓN DE AÑISCLO★★

Access from Escalona village on the Bielsa-Ainsa road – a 13km/8mi drive.

The Añisclo Canyon, narrower than that of Ordesa, is a cool, attractive valley with pine trees clinging to the limestone walls.

Walk to Ripareta

🚶 *Start from the San Urbez bridge. 5hr there and back.*

The wide, well-defined path follows the course of the enclosed Río Vellos which cascades down the valley to its confluence with the Pardina.

Orense/Ourense

POPULATION: 108 382

MICHELIN MAP 571 E 6, F 6 (TOWN PLAN) – GALICIA (ORENSE)

Since Antiquity, Orense (Ourense in Galician) – the name is said to come from the legendary gold believed to exist in the Miño Valley – has been famous for its waters which pour out from three springs, Las Burgas, at a temperature of 65°C/150°F. The town has preserved an old bridge, Puente Romano, which dates from the 13C when it was rebuilt on Roman foundations to provide a crossing for pilgrims on their way to Santiago de Compostela.

Location

Orense is the capital of the only land-locked province in Galicia. It straddles the banks of the River Miño, 101km/63mi from Vigo (to the E) along the A 52 motorway, 100km/62mi from Pontevedra (to the SE) via the N 541, and 111km/69mi from Santiago de Compostela (to the SE) on the N 525 and the A 53. ⓘ *Curros Enríquez 1 (Torre de Orense), 32003 Orense,* ☎ *988 37 20 20.*

ⓖ *Neighbouring sights are described in the following chapters: SANTIAGO DE COM-POSTELA, PONTEVEDRA and RÍAS BAJAS.*

Worth a Visit

Catedral★

🕐 *Open 11am-1.30pm and 4-7.30pm; Sun and public hols, 5-7pm.* 👓 *1.20€ (Capilla del Santísimo Cristo); 1.20€ museum.* ☎ *988 26 64 38.*

The cathedral, which took from the 12C to the 13C to build, has been constantly modified over the ages. The **Portada Sur** (South Door), in the Compostelan style, lacks a tympanum, but is profusely decorated with carvings on covings and capitals. The **Portada Norte** (North Door) has two statue columns and, beneath a great ornamental arch, a 15C Deposition framed by a Flight into Egypt and statues of the Holy Women.

The interior is noteworthy for its pure lines. At the end of the 15C, a Gothic-Renaissance transitional style **lantern**★ was built above the transept. The high altar has an ornate Gothic retable by Cornelius de Holanda. The 16C and 17C **Capilla del Santísimo Cristo** (Chapel of the Holy Sacrament), decorated with exuberant sculpture in the Galician Baroque style, opens off the north transept. The triple-arched **Pórtico del Paraíso**★★ (Paradise Door) at the west end, with its beautiful carvings and bright medieval colouring, illustrates the same theme as the Pórtico de la Gloria in Santiago Cathedral. The central arch shows the 24 Old Men of the Apocalypse; to the right is the Last Judgement. The pierced tympanum above, like the narthex vaulting, is 16C.

A door in the south aisle opens onto the 13C chapter house, now a **museum (Museo Catedralicio)**. Among the items displayed are church plate, statues, chasubles and a 12C travelling altar.

Museo Arqueológico y de Bellas Artes (Archaeological and Fine Arts Museum)

⚁ *Closed for renovation.* ☎ *988 22 38 84.*

The finely emblazoned façade overlooking plaza Mayor belongs to the former episcopal palace, now a museum. The collections inside include prehistoric specimens, cultural objects (mainly statues of warriors) and a section of fine arts with, in particular, an early-18C wood carving of the **Camino del Calvario**★ (Stations of the Cross).

Claustro de San Francisco★

⚁ *Closed for renovation.* ☎ *988 38 81 10.*

The elegant 14C cloisters consist of horseshoe-shaped Gothic arches resting on slender, paired columns to which a diamond and leaf decoration adds simple sophistication. Some of the **capitals** illustrate scenes of the hunt or historic personages.

Excursions

Monasterio de Santa María la Real de Oseira★

34km/21mi NW. Leave Orense on the N 525. After 23km/14mi turn right towards Cotelas.

Address Book

🍃 *Guided tours (45min), 9.30am-12.30pm and 3-5.30pm (6.30pm in spring and summer); Sun and public hols, only at 12.30pm.* ☜ *1.20€.* ☎ *988 28 20 04.*

The grandiose Cistercian monastery, commonly known as the Escorial of Galicia, was
founded by Alfonso VII in the middle of the 12C. It stands in an isolated position in
the Arenteiro Valley, a region that once abounded in bears (osos) as the monastery's
name suggests.

The **façade** (1708) consists of three sections. In a niche below the statue of Hope
which crowns the doorway is the figure of a Nursing Madonna with St Bernard at
her feet. Of note inside the monastery are an **escalera de honor** (grand staircase)
and the **Claustro de los Medallones** (Medallion Cloisters) decorated with 40 busts
of famous historic personages.

The **church** (12C-13C), hidden behind the Baroque façade of 1637, has retained the
customary Cistercian simplicity modified only by the frescoes in the transept which
were painted in 1694.

The **chapter house**★ dates from the late 15C and early 16C and is outstanding for
its beautiful vaulting of crossed ribs descending like the fronds of a palm tree onto
four spiral columns.

Verín

69km/43mi SE along the A 52. Verín is a lively, picturesque town with narrow paved
streets, houses with glassed-in balconies, arcades and carved coats of arms.
Its thermal springs, already famous during the Middle Ages, are reputed for their
treatment of rheumatic and kidney disorders.

Castillo de Monterrei

6km/4mi W. There is a parador next to the castle. It played an important role throughout the Portuguese-Spanish wars, having been strategically built on the frontier for
the purpose. It was more than a castle, since included within the perimeter were a
monastery, a hospital and a town which was abandoned in the 19C. The approach is
up an avenue of lime-trees which commands a full **panorama**★ of the valley below.
To enter the castle you pass through three defence walls, the outermost dating from
the 17C. Inside, at the centre, stand the square 15C Torre del Homenaje (Keep) and the
14C Torre de las Damas (Lady's Tower); the palace courtyard is lined by a three-storey
arcade and is less austere. The 13C church has a **portal**★ delicately carved with a
notched design and a tympanum showing Christ in Majesty between the symbols
of the Evangelists.

Celanova

26km/16mi S on the N 540. The large, imposing **monastery** on plaza Mayor was
founded in 936 by San Rosendo, Bishop of San Martín de Mondoñedo.
The **church** is a monumental late-17C edifice built in Baroque style. The coffered vaulting
is decorated with geometrical designs, the cupola with volutes. An immense altarpiece
(1697) occupies the back of the apse. Note also the choir stalls, Baroque in the lower part
and Gothic in the upper, as well as the fine organ. 🍃 *Guided tours (45min) at 11am,
noon, 1pm, 4pm and 5pm (and 6pm Apr-Oct).* ☜ *1.20€.* ☎ *988 43 22 01.*

The **cloisters**★★, among the most beautiful in the region, took until the 18C to
complete even though construction began in 1550. The majestic staircases here are
particularly worthy of note.
The **Capilla de San Miguel**, a chapel behind the church, is one of the monastery's earliest buildings (937) and one of the rare Mozarabic monuments still in good condition.

Santa Comba de Bande

52km/32.5mi S along the N 540 (26km/16mi S of Celanova). 10km/6mi beyond Bande, head along a road to the right for 400m/440yd.

The small 7C Visigothic **iglesia**★ overlooks the lake. Inside the church, the plan is that of a Greek cross, lit by a lantern turret. The apse is square and is preceded by a horseshoe-shaped triumphal arch resting on four pillars with Corinthian capitals. Pure lines and perfect wall masonry add a rich quality to this unique building.

TOUR ALONG THE RÍO SIL★

65km/40mi E. ▶ *Head along the C 536; after 6km/4mi, turn left towards Luintra and continue for a further 18km/11mi. The monastery is signposted.*

Monasterio de San Estevo de Ribas de Sil

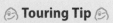 *Work to convert the building into a hotel is currently under way; as a result the monastery is closed. Before starting your journey, check with the tourist office in Orense.* The monastery appears suddenly in a majestic **setting**★, spread over a great spur, against a background of granite mountains deeply cut by the Sil. The church's Romanesque east end remains, as do the three cloisters, built to grandiose proportions largely in the 16C, although one still has Romanesque galleries surmounted by elegant low arches.

>  **Touring Tip**
>
> Another way of discovering the wild beauty of this area is to take a **boat trip** along the River Sil. To get to the embarkation point, leave Orense on the C 536, turning left after 6km/4mi towards Luintra and Loureiro and following signs to San Estevo, from where the boat departs *(duration: 1hr 30min)*. For times and prices, call ☎ 988 21 51 00.

Gargantas del Sil★ (Gorges of the Sil River)

▶ *Return on the downhill road on the left towards the Sil (do not take the signposted turning to the embalse de San Estevo).*

Two dams, one vaulted, the other a buttressed type, control the waters of the Sil which flow through deep gorges. The sides of the valley are dotted with vineyards and small villages.

▶ *Continue along the left bank of the river until you reach the N 120. Turn left towards Orense.*

Osuna★★

POPULATION: 17 306

MICHELIN MAP 578 U 14 – ANDALUCÍA (SEVILLA).

This elegant Andalucían town, built on a hill at the heart of the Sevillan countryside, has preserved a beautiful **monumental centre**★ inherited from its former status as a ducal seat. The dukedom was created in 1562 and the house of Osuna was to become one of the most powerful on the Iberian Peninsula. The prosperity that Osuna was to enjoy in subsequent centuries is reflected in the fine examples of civil and religious architecture embellishing the town.

Location

Osuna rises above a gently undulating landscape to the south of the Guadalquivir depression, near the A 92 highway linking Granada (160km/100mi E) with Sevilla. 🅘 *Sevilla 22, 41013 Osuna,* ☎ *95 481 18 53.*

🔎 *Neighbouring sights are described in the following chapters: ANTEQUERA (67km/42mi SE), CÓRDOBA (85km/53mi NE) and SEVILLA (92km/57mi W).*

Worth a Visit

ZONA MONUMENTAL★

▶ *Follow directions to Centro Ciudad (Town Centre) and Zona Monumental.*

Colegiata★

🎧 *Guided tours (45min), Oct-Apr, 10am-1.30pm and 3.30-6.30pm; May-Sep, 10am-1.30pm and 4-7pm.* 🕐 *Closed Mon, 1 and 6 (afternoon) Jan, Maundy Thu, Good Fri, and 24 (afternoon), 25 and 31 (afternoon) Dec.* 🎫 *2€.* ☎ *95 481 04 44.*

This 16C Renaissance style collegiate church houses five **paintings**★★ by **José (Jusepe) de Ribera "El Españoleto"** (1591-1652), including The Expiration of Christ, in the side chapel off the Nave del Evangelio. The remainder are exhibited in the sacristy.

Panteón Ducal★★ (Ducal Pantheon)

The ducal pantheon was built in Plateresque style in 1545 as the burial place for the Dukes of Osuna. It is approached by a delightful patio, designed in the same style. The chapel (1545), also Plateresque, stands just below the Colegiata's main altar and is crowned by a blue and gold polychrome coffered ceiling which has been blackened by candle smoke. Another crypt below, built in 1901, contains the tombs of the most important dukes.

Nearby stand the 16C **former university** (Antigua Universidad) and the 17C **Monasterio de la Encarnacióna**, in which the highlight is the magnificent **dado**★ of 17C Sevillian *azulejos* in the patio. The nuns here produce and sell several types of delicious biscuits and pastries. (🕐 *Open 10am-1.30pm and 3.30-6.30pm; in summer, 10am-1.30pm and 4-7pm.* 🕐 *Closed Sun-Mon.* ☎ *95 481 11 21).*

On the descent into the town centre, note the 12C-13C Torre del Agua, a former defensive tower now home to a small **archaeological museum.** (🕐 *Open 11am-1.30pm and 4.30-6.30pm; May and Sep, 11.30am-1.30pm and 5-7pm (Jul-Aug 10am -2pm.* 🎫 *1.60€.* ☎ *95 481 12 07.*

TOWN CENTRE

Mainly around plaza del Duque and plaza España. Osuna's streets are lined by numerous Baroque **mansion houses and palaces**★★, whose massive wooden doors, darkly shining and copper nailed, reveal fine wrought-iron grilles and cool green patios. Of particular note are the **calle San Pedro**★ (Cilla del Cabildo, Palacio de los Marqueses de la Gomera), the Antigua Audencia (former Law Courts), the Palacio de los Cepeda, the former Palacio de Puente Hermoso, several fine churches (Santo Domingo, la Compañía) and the **belfry of the Iglesia de la Merced**★, built by the same architect as the **Cilla del Cabildo**.

Cilla del Cabildo

B. Kaufman/MICHELIN

Excursion

Écija★

34km/21mi N along the A 351. The town lies in the Guadalquivir depression and is renowned for its lofty Baroque belfries decorated with ceramic tiles, such as the 18C **Torre de San Juan★.**

🅿 *Park in plaza de España.*

Écija has some interesting popular architecture, including several delightful small squares, and houses adorned with decorative columns, coats of arms and charming patios. The streets adjoining the avenida Miguel de Cervantes have preserved several old palaces with fine **façades**★: the 18C Baroque **Palacio de Benamejí**; the concave and fresco-adorned **Palacio de Peñaflor**, its portal built on columns; and the Plateresque-style **Palacio de Valdehermoso**. Several churches are also worthy of mention: **Los Descalzos**, renowned for the exuberant decoration of its **interior**★; **Santa María**, crowned by an impressive tower; the **Iglesia de Santa Cruz**, with its unusual series of patio-like areas and **palaeo-Christian sarcophagus**★; the Convento de los Marroquíes, with its lofty **bell tower**★, where the delicious *marroquíes* biscuits are still produced and sold by the nuns; and the **Iglesia de Santiago**★, which has preserved the Mudéjar windows of an earlier building and a Gothic **retable**★ at the high altar illustrating the Passion and the Resurrection.

Ourense  *see Orense*

Oviedo★★

POPULATION: 204 276

MICHELIN MAPS 572 B 12 (TOWN PLAN) – ASTURIAS.

Built on a rise at the foot of Monte Naranco, the capital of the Principality of Asturias has a long and eventful history. The modern city conceals a magnificent and well-preserved old quarter huddled around the cathedral. Oviedo is sprinkled with enchanting plazas and lanes set with frozen pedestrians, who turn out to be an assortment of sculptures. Strolling about is a delight. The impressive examples of typical Asturian architecture make this a World Heritage Site.

Location

Oviedo is located in an important mining and industrial area. The A 66 motorway provides a fast link with the coast (Gijón is situated 29km/18mi to the N) and with León (121km/75mi to the S). *Plaza Alfonso II El Casto 6, 33003 Oviedo, ☎ 98 521 33 85; Calle Marqués de Santa Cruz 1 (El Escorialín), 33003 Oviedo, ☎ 98 522 75 86.*

Neighbouring sights are described in the following chapter: COSTA VERDE.

Background

The capital of the Kingdom of Asturias (9C-10C) – All that the Muslims left of the small city built by Fruela I (722-68) around a Benedictine monastery on a hill named Ovetum, was a pile of ruins. Fruela's son, Alfonso II, the Chaste (791-842), transferred the court from Cangas de Onís and Pravia, where it had been previously, to Oviedo. He rebuilt the town, encircling it with ramparts and embellishing it with religious buildings of which only traces remain – the Cámara Santa, the east end of San Tirso Church and Santullano Church. His successor Ramiro I (842-50) continued the royal patronage and built a splendid summer palace which remains, in part, on the slopes of nearby Monte Naranco (*see Worth a Visit below*).

But in 914, with the extension of the kingdom's boundaries southwards, the king, Don García, transferred the court to León. The Asturias-León kingdom existed briefly from 1037 to 1157 and then in 1230 was finally incorporated into Castilla. Recognition of a sort returned to the old kingdom in 1388 when the heir apparent to the Castilian throne took the title, Prince of Asturias. The heir to the Spanish throne still carries the same title today.

Two Battles of Oviedo: 1934 and 1936-37 – In 1934, following the insurrection in the Asturian mining area, the town was heavily damaged during fighting between insurgent miners and right-wing government forces: the Cámara Santa was destroyed, the university set on fire and the cathedral damaged. In 1937, Oviedo was once more the scene of heavy fighting, this time during the Civil War.

Special Features

OLD TOWN ⏱ *1hr 30min*

Follow the route marked on the town plan..

▸ *Enter by Calle San Francisco, and proceed along the right side of the street.*

Address Book

For coin ranges, see the Legend at the back of the guide.

WHERE TO EAT

Las Campanas de San Bernabé – *San Bernabé 7 – ☎ 98 522 49 31 – Closed Sun and in Aug –* 🖻. This restaurant is located in the middle of the main shopping area, five minutes from the cathedral. A pleasant decor of brick walls and oak beams, and good, reasonably priced regional cuisine.

El Raitán y El Chigre – *Plaza Trascorrales 6 – ☎ 98 521 42 18 – Closed Sun evening –* 🖻. This rustic-style restaurant at the heart of the historic quarter serves delicious Asturian dishes. The set menus are recommended.

WHERE TO STAY

Hotel Isla de Cuba – *Isla de Cuba 7 – ☎ 985 29 39 11 – 8 rooms –* 🖾. Despite lacking a great deal of charm, this small but adequate family-run hotel is moderately priced and enjoys a good location just five minutes' walk from the old quarter.

Hotel Casa Camila – Fitoria de Arriba 28 – ☎ *98 511 48 22 – 7 rooms –* 🖾 *– Restaurant 20€*. This charming, well-maintained hotel on Monte Naranco is the perfect hideaway if you're looking for peace and quiet away from the city. Impressive views of Oviedo and rooms that are more than comfortable.

LOCAL SPECIALITIES

Typical gastronomic treats in Oviedo include *carbayones*, large delicious pastries made with almonds and egg yolks, and the savoury *bollos preñaos*, filled with chorizo. The best *carbayones* in the city can be bought at the *Camilo de Blas* pastry shop (calle Jovellanos 7) and the *Los de Peñalba* sweet shop (Calle Milicias Nacionales 4).

Antigua Universidad (Former University)

The austere, stone-fronted building was completed in the 17C. The neoclassical court was restored after the civil war, and displays a statue of Don Fernando de Valdés Salas, founder of the university.

Opposite the façade of the universidad is *Mujer Sentada (Seated Woman)* by Manolo Hugué, one of the many sculptures set in the old town.

Plaza de Porlier

From this vantage point, one can see the façade and tower of the cathedral in the next plaza. Two fine palaces border the square: the palace of the **Count of Toreno**, dating from 1673, on the right; and the **Camposagrado** opposite, a magnificent 18C edifice now the Law Courts (note the spread eaves).

Plaza de de Alfonso II el Casto (Plaza de la Catedral)

As you enter this great square, you'll see the 17C **Palacio de Valdecarzana.** Note the monumental coat of arms at the top of the façade. The majestic cathedral rises at the far end of the square. Opposite, at Calle de La Rúa, is the **Palacio de la Rúa**, built at the end of the 15C.

Catedral★

The cathedral occupies the site of earlier pre-Romaneque and Romanesque churches. Although constructed over an extended period, the main work was carried out between 1412 and 1565 in Flamboyant Gothic style. Note the asymmetric façade. The south tower rises to 60m/197ft and tapers into a delicate openwork spire. Three 17C Gothic portals pierce the asymmetrical façade; figures of the Transfiguration are above the central portal. The walnut-panelled doors (also 17C) bear figures of the Saviour and St Eulalia.

Interior – The cathedral has three aisles, the triforium surmounted by tall stained-glass windows, and an ambulatory. The open vista down the nave enhances the splendid 16C polychrome **high altarpiece**★★, carved with scenes from the Life of Christ.

On either end of the transepts are 18C Baroque panels, and in the south transept, next to the main chapel, the 17C polychromed stone image of The Saviour.

The **Capilla de Alfonso II el Casto** (Alfonso II was known as The Chaste) stands on the site of the original church and is the pantheon of the Asturian kings. The decoration inside the gate (*end of north transept*) is Late Gothic. In the embrasures are the figures of the Pilgrim St James, St Peter, St Paul and St Andrew, as well as saints and musicians, and on a mullion, a Virgin of Milk. Renaissance and Baroque elements intermingle in the decoration of this chapel, where the illustrious kings of Asturias are interred.

Cámara Santa

Access by the south transept. ◷ *Open 10am-1pm; afternoons: Nov-Feb, 4-6pm (7pm in summer).* ◷ *No visits Sun and public hols.* ⬷ *1.90€ (2.40€ complete visit).* ☏ *98 520 31 17.*

The Cámara Santa was built by Alfonso II early in the 9C and reconstructed in the Romanesque period, when the barrel vault and six pairs of columns were added.

These 12 **statue columns**★★ representing the Apostles are among the most masterly sculptures of 12C Spain. The artist was obviously influenced by the Pórtico de la Gloria (Doorway of Glory) in Santiago Cathedral. Column capitals illustrate the marriage of Joseph and Mary, the Holy Women at the Tomb and lion and wild boar hunts. Note the heads of Christ, the Virgin and St. John above the entry; it is believed that they once formed part of a Calvary scene along with painted figures, now lost.

The **tesoro**★★ (treasury) in the apse includes an outstanding collection of ancient gold and silver plate: the **Cruz de los Ángeles** (Cross of the Angels), a gift from Alfonso II in 808, made of cedar wood and studded with precious gems, Roman cabochons and cameos; the **Cruz de Victoria** (908), faced with chased gold, precious stones, and enamel, which was supposedly carried by Pelayo at the victory of Covadonga; the **Arqueta de las Ágatas** or Agate Reliquary, a gift by Fruela II in 910; and the 11C **Arca Santa**, a silver-plated reliquary casket with Latin and Cufic decoration and inscriptions.

OVIEDO

			Constitucíon Pl. de la	B 22	Riego Pl.	AB53
			Daoiz y Velarde Pl. de	AB23	San Antonio	B 56
Alcalde G. Conde	B 2		Jesús	AB28	San Vicente	B 59
Alfonso II El Casto Pl. de	B 5		Juan Escalante	B 29	Santa Clara	A 60
Calvo Sotelo	A 12		Martínez Marina	A 33	Schultz	B 62
Canóniga	B 17		Palacio Valdés	A 40	Trascorrales Pl. de	B 64
Carbayón Pl. de	A 18		Pelayo	A	Uría	A
Cimadevilla	B 20		Pérez de la Sala	A 43	Victor Chávarri	B 66
Conde de Toreno	A 21		Postigo Alto	B 48		

Ayuntamiento	B	H	Palacio de Camposagrado	B	J
Museo Arqueológico	B	M²	Palacio de Toreno	B	B
Museo de Bellas Artes de Asturias	B	M¹	Palacio de Valdecarzana	B	A

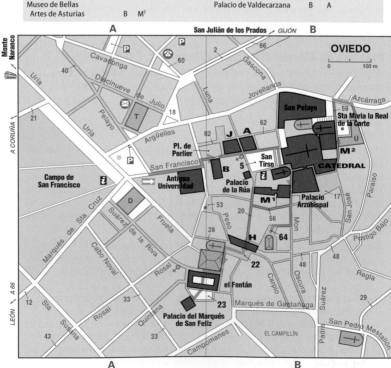

Claustro

The cloisters, in Gothic style (14-15C) have intersecting pointed arches and delicate tracery in the bays. The **Capilla de Santa Leocadia** *(to the left on entering)* is in fact the Cámara Santa crypt. It is decorated outside *(garden)* with blind arcades and covered inside with barrel vaulting and contains an altar, tombs from the time of Alfonso II and an unusually small stone cubicle. The Gothic **sala capitular** (chapter house) contains fine stalls dating from the late 15C.

▶ *Return to the Plaza de Alfonso II el Casto.*

To the right of the cathedral *(as you leave)* the low reliefs and busts compose an homage to the kings of Asturias. To the left, at the opening of Calle Santa Ana, opposite the cathedral walls, note the Moorish *alfiz* window enclosure in the east wall of the **Iglesia de San Tirso**, all that remains from the orignal 9C church. Its presence in a building of that date remains a mystery.

▶ *Turn left onto Calle Tránsito de la Virgen alongside the cathedral.*

Beyond the arch that connects the cathedral to the Palacio Arzobispal (archbishop's palace), on the left, is the Romanesque Torre Vieja (old tower) of the former cathedral. Just ahead is the Plaza de la Corrada del Obispo. To the right is the rather loud façade of the **Palacio Arzobispal** (late 16C), and to the left, the imposing 18C **Puerta de la Limosna** (alms gate) connecting to the cathedral cloister.

▶ *Continue along Calle San Vicente and just after the arch, the Museo Arqueológico will come into view.*

Museo Arqueológico (Archaeological Museum)

⚷ *Closed for renovation.* ☎ 985 26 91 04 or 985 26 13 58

The museum is housed in the former Convento de San Vicente (16C-18C).

Two galleries opening off the 15C Plateresque cloisters at ground level contain pre-Romanesque art. Small fragments and reproductions provide striking evidence of the delicate sophistication of monumental decoration in the Asturian period. Among the exhibits are altars such as that of Naranco surmounted by its original stone, reconstructions of chancel screens, low reliefs often showing Byzantine influence, column bases from San Miguel de Lillo and pierced bays inlaid in walls.

Local prehistoric finds, coins and carved wood objects, including old musical instruments, are on view in the upper cloister.

*After the museum, go under the arch and cross the Plaza de Feijoo, where the **Iglesia de Santa María la Real de la Corte** and the Faculty de Psychology are located. Just beyond, at the corner of Calle Jovellanos is the attractive façade of the 18C **Monasterio de San Pelayo**, looking more like a place than a religious edifice.*

▶ *Turn right onto Jovellanos, and from the next corner (calle Paraíso), take a look at the old city wall.*

▶ *Return to Calle Santa Ana (by the way you came, or by Jovellanos and Calle del Águila) to reach the Museo de Bellas Artes.*

Museo de Bellas Artes de Asturias
(Fine Arts Museum of Asturias)

🕐 *Open 10.30am-2pm and 4.30-8.30pm; Sat, 11.30am-2pm and 5-8pm; Sun and public hols, 11.30am-2.30pm; Jul-Aug, 11am-2.30pm and 5-9pm; Sat-Sun and public hols, 11am-2.30pm.* 🕐 *Closed Mon, 1 and 6 Jan, Good Fri, 8 and 22 Sep, 12 Oct, 1 Nov and 6 and 25 Dec.* 🎫 *No charge.* ☎ 98 521 30 61.

The museum takes up three buildings in the old town, including the elegant 18C Palacio de Velarde and the 17C Casa de Oviedo-Portal. The basis of the museum, which ranges from the Middle Ages to the present day, is a collection of Spanish painting, enriched by notable foreign works (mostly Italian and Flemish) and a magnificent representation of Asturian painting. There is also a good sculpture collection.

Among the works in **Palacio de Velarde** worthy of mention are a complete **Apostolado** by El Greco (ground floor); the Gothic panels of the *Santa Marina Retable* (on the stairway); the *Triptych of Don Alvaro de Carreño* by the master of the *Legend of Mary Magdalene;* a *Burial of Christ* and a magnificent *Apostle* by **Ribera**; a dramatic *Crucifixion* by **Zurbarán**; a *San Pedro* by Murillo; the portrait of *Charles II at Ten Years* by Carreño de Miranda, two portraits by **Goya** *(Jovellanos* and *Charles IV)* and assorted works of Luis Meléndez in the galleries on the first floor. The second floor is devoted to Asturian and Spanish art of the 19C and early 20C (Realism, Romanticism, Modernism). Notable are a portrait by F. Madrazo, *Study of Light* by Ramón Casas, *Green Wall* by S. Rusiñol, and works by *Anglada-Camarasa*.

A passageway leads to the second floor of the **Casa Oviedo-Portal**. Worth seeing are the gallery dedicated to the paintings of **J. Sorolla;** a *Musketeer with Sword and Cupid* by **Picasso**; and paintings by Gutiérrez-Solana, Regoyos and Nonell. On the first floor of this building are Asturian works of the latter part of the 20C, and on the ground floor, some interesting examples of **contemporary Spanish art** of the same period (Palazuelo, Tàpies, Barceló, Sicilia, Broto) and a collection of glassware and vases of the 19 and 20C.

As you leave, take a look at the enchanting Plaza de Trascorrales, with its brightly coloured houses and its sculpture of *The Milkmaid.*

▶ *Take Calle Cimadevilla to reach Plaza de la Constitución.*

Along **Plaza de la Constitución** are the **Ayuntamiento** (City Hall), a long building with 17 and 18C porticoes, and the Iglesia de San Isidoro, from the same era.

▶ *Take Calle Fierro, where there is a covered market, to Calle Fontán.*

Fontán is one of the more picturesque parts of the ciy. This block of houses, with porticoes supported by columns, has an enchanting courtyard, which can be reached by an archway in each façade.

▶ *Leave by the archway that faces Plaza Daoíz y Velarde.*

The first sight in **Plaza Daoíz y Velarde** is the sculpture ensemble, **Las vendedoras del Fontán**, erected to honor the women who have sold goods in the outdoor market of these streets over the years. The beautiful tree-set plaza is the site of the noble **Palacio de Camposagrado**. Beside it is the Biblioteca de Asturias (library), with its unusual façade.

Worth a Visit

Campo de San Francisco

This downtown park was the garden of the former Convento de San Francisco. A place for strolling and gathering, it still retains parts of a Romanesque portal near the pond.

OUTSIDE THE OLD QUARTER

Antiguo Hospital del Principado (Former Hospital of the Principality)

▶ *Leave Oviedo on calle Conde de Toreno (marked on the plan).*

The façade of the 18C hospital, which is now the Hotel Reconquista, is emblazoned with a fine Baroque **coat of arms**★.

Iglesia de Santullano or San Julián de los Prados★

🕐 *Open May-Sep, 10am-1pm and 4-6pm; Sat, 9.30-11.30am; Oct-Apr, 9.30am-noon;; Mon, 10am-3pm.* 🕐 *Closed 25 Dec and 1 Jan.* 🎟 *1.20€.* ☎ *607 35 39 99.*

The outstanding work of Asturian art, constructed under Alfonso the Chaste in the first half of the 9C, has a characteristic porch, nave and twin aisles, wide transept and, at the east end, three chapels with barrel vaults. The walls are covered in **frescoes**★ with geometrical and arquitectonic motifs of clear Roman influence. There is a fine transitional Romanesque **Christ in Glory**★ in the central apse. Outside, the east end is typical with a window with a triple arcade and lattice.

Santuarios del Monte Naranco★
(Mount Naranco Church and Chapel)
4km/2.5mi along Avenida de los Monumentos to the NW.

Of the summer palace built by Ramiro I on the south side of the mountain in the 9C, there remain the former audience chamber, now the Iglesia de Santa María, and part of the royal chapel, San Miguel.

Centro de Recepción e Interpretación del Prerrománico Asturiano
Just above the parking area, to the left.

🕐 *Open 10am-1pm and 3-5pm; Apr-Oct 9.30am-1.30pm y 3.30-7.30pm. Last admission 30 min before closing.* 🕐 *Closed Sun afternoon-Mon.* ☎ *98 511 49 01.*

Interesting panels explain Asturian art (in Spanish only). A video is narrated in English, Spanish, French and German.

Iglesia de Santa María del Naranco★★

🕐 *Open 9.30am-1pm and 3-5pm (7pm 1 May-15 Oct); Sun and public hols, 10am-1pm.* 🎟 *1.50€, no charge Mon.* ☎ *98 529 56 85.*

This harmonious and attractive church is square, two-storeyed, supported by grooved buttresses and lit by vast bays. The lower floor is a vaulted crypt. On the upper floor, a former reception hall, two loggias open off the great chamber covered by barrel vaulting. The decoration is delicate and unified. Clusters of slender cabled colonnettes adorn the pillars. The loggia capitals are Corinthian, those abutting the walls polygonal. Arch ribs descend on fluted pilasters to to the medallions minutely decorated in Byzantine style.

From outside, there is a fine **view** of Mount Aramo, with Oviedo in the foreground.

Iglesia de San Miguel de Lillo★

15 min on foot. 🕐 *Open 10am-1pm and 3-5pm (7pm 1 May-15 Oct); Sun and public hols, 10am-1pm.* 🎟 *1.50€, no charge Mon.* ☎ *98 529 56 85.*

What remains today is probably only a third of the original church, whose outline is traced by wooden markers. It is believed that a large part of the church collapsed in the 13C.

The narrowness of the aisles accentuates the height of the walls in which several claustra type windows remain. The delicacy of the interior carving is a delight: on the door **jambs**★★ are identical scenes in relief of a consul, surrounded by dignitaries, presiding over contests in an arena. An Asturian cord motif is repeated on the capitals and on the vaulting in the nave and gallery.

Excursions

Iglesia de Santa Cristina de Lena★

34km/21mi S on the A 66 (junction 92). ▶*At Pola de Lena, head for Vega del Rey and there take the signposted road.* 🅿 *Park the car before the rail viaduct and walk up the steep path (15min).* 🕐 *Open 11am-1pm and 4.30-6.30pm.* 🕐 *Closed Mon.* 🎟 *1.20€, no charge Tue.* ☎ *985 49 05 25.*

Santa Cristina de Lena (9C) is a well-proportioned church built of golden stone. It stands on a rocky crag from which there is a **panoramic view**★ of the green Caudal Valley.

The little building, which is later than those on Monte Naranco, has a Greek cross plan unusual in Asturias, but the traditional stone vaulting remains, with blind arcades, in which the columns have pyramid-shaped capitals emphasised by a cord motif, sculpted medallions extending the arch ribs and cabled columns in the choir. The nave is separated from the raised choir by an iconostasis in which the superimposed arches increase the impression of balance. The low reliefs in the chancel are Visigothic sculptures, recognisable by their geometric figures and plant motifs, which have been placed in a new setting.

Teverga

43km/27mi SW on the N 634 and AS 228. The road follows the River Trubia which, after Proaza, enters a narrow gorge. As you emerge, glance back for a **view**★ of the Peñas Juntas cliff face which marks the end of the gorge. Beyond the Teverga fork the road penetrates the enclosed **desfiladero de Teverga**★ (Teverga Defile).

The **Colegiata de San Pedro de Teverga** is just outside La Plaza village. This collegiate church, which is late 12C, has had a porch and tower added. The architecture is an obvious continuation of the pre-Romanesque Asturian style. The building includes a narthex, a tall narrow nave and a flat east end, originally three chapels. The narthex capitals are carved with stylised animal and plant motifs. 🕐 *Open noon-2pm and 4-6pm (7pm Sat-Sun).* 🎟 *1.20€.* ☎ *98 576 42 75.*

Palencia

POPULATION: 81 988.

MICHELIN MAP 575 F 16 – CASTILLA Y LEÓN (PALENCIA).

Palencia is a tranquil provincial capital situated in the fertile Tierra de Campos region. The centre of the town is built along a north-south axis, hemmed in to the west by the río Carríon and to the east by the railway. It was here that Alfonso VIII created the first Spanish university in 1208.

In the area around Palencia, irrigation by the Canal de Castilla and other waterways has led to the development of an important horticultural industry.

Location

Palencia is situated close to the A 62 heading northwest to Burgos (88km/55mi) and southeast to Valladolid (50km/31mi) and Salamanca (166km/104mi). *Mayor 105, 34001 Palencia,* ☎ *979 74 00 68.*

Neighbouring sights are described in the following chapters: The WAY OF ST JAMES, VALLADOLID and BURGOS.

Worth a Visit

Catedral★★

🕐 *Open 10.30am-1.30pm and 4-6.30pm; 1 Jul-20 Sep, 10.30am-1.30pm and 4.30-730pm; Sun, 11.15am-3pm.* ☞ *3€ (museum)* ☎ *979 70 13 47.*

Palencia's beautiful, unknown cathedral – the townspeople believe the monument is not given sufficient recognition – is a 14C-16C Gothic edifice with a good many Renaissance features. In the 7C a chapel was built on the site to enshrine the relics of a Visigothic saint, Antolín. The chapel lay forgotten during the Moorish occupation and for long after, until, according to tradition, Sancho III de Navarra came upon it while hunting wild boar. The king erected a Romanesque chapel (1034) over the ruins which survives today as the crypt to the cathedral.

Interior★★

The centre of the cathedral contains an incredible concentration of works of art in all the different styles of the early 16C: Flamboyant Gothic, Isabelline, Plateresque and Renaissance. This wealth is due to Bishop Fonseca who gathered round him in the early 16C a group of highly skilled artists. The monumental high altar **retable** (early 16C), with its many compartments, was carved by Felipe Vigarny, painted by Juan of Flanders and is surmounted by a Crucifix by Juan de Valmaseda. The 16C tapestries on the sides were commissioned by Bishop Fonseca. The *coro* grille, with a delicately wrought upper section, is by Gaspar Rodríguez (1563); the choir stalls are Gothic, the organ gallery, above, is dated 1716. The **Capilla del Sagrario** (Chapel of the Holy Sacrament) behind the high altar and closed by a fine Romanesque grille, is exuberantly Gothic with a rich altarpiece by Valmaseda (1529). To the left, and slightly higher up, is the sarcophagus of Queen Urraca of Navarra (d 1189). The sculptures in the *trascoro* are the work of Gil de Siloé and Simon of Cologne; the central **triptych**★ is a masterpiece, painted in Flanders by Jan Joest de Calcar in 1505 – the donor, Bishop Fonseca, is depicted at its centre.

A Plateresque staircase beside the *trascoro* leads to the Romanesque **crypt** which retains several vestiges (arches and capitals) of the 7C Visigothic chapel.

Museo★

To the right of the west door. 🔍 *Guided tours (1hr) 10.30am-1.20pm and 4-6.30pm; 16 May-30 Sep, 10.30am-1.20pm and 4.30-7.20pm; Sun and public hols, 11.15am-1pm.* ☎ *979 70 13 47.*

The collection includes a *St Sebastian* by El Greco and four 15C Flemish **tapestries**★ of the Adoration, the Ascension, Original Sin and the Resurrection of Lazarus. They were commissioned by Bishop Fonseca who had his crest woven into the corners.

Excursions

Iglesia de Frómista★★

29km/18mi NE along the N 611. 🕐 *Open 10am-2pm and 3-6.30pm; in summer, 10am-2pm and 4.30-8pm.* ☎ *979 81 01 44.*

Many pilgrims on the way to Santiago de Compostela used to at Frómista. The only vestige of the famous Benedictine **Monasterio de San Martín** is the church at the centre of a large square.

Built in 1066, with beautifully matched rough-hewn stone blocks of considerable size, the church marks a climax in the development of Romanesque architecture in Castilla and was used as a model for many of the region's churches.

Outside, note the classic east end, rising from the apses up over the transept walls, almost imperceptibly to the **cupola** squinches and finally to the lantern. The decorative features are all there – billets outlining the windows, engaged columns and cornices with ornately carved modillions.

The **interior** has a perfect basilica design with a nave, two aisles and a transept which does not project outside. The pure Romanesque lines of the exterior are apparent inside, in the barrel vaulting, apsidal oven vaults, the dome on squinches and double ribbed arches. The richly carved **capitals** with human figures or plant motifs provide indispensable decorative relief.

Baños de Cerrato
14km/9mi SE

▷ *Cross the railway at Venta de Baños before turning right towards Cevico de la Torre. Bear left at the first crossroads.*

Basílica de San Juan Bautista★

🔍 *Guided tours (20min), 10.30am-1.30pm and 4-7pm; in summer, 10.30am-1.30pm and 5-8.30pm.* 🕐 *Closed Mon.* ☎ *988 77 08 12 (town hall).*

This Visigothic basilica is the oldest church in Spain in a good state of preservation. It was built by the Visigothic King, Recceswinth, while he was taking the waters in Baños de Cerrato, in 661. The date is shown beneath the apsidal arch. The church consists of three aisles covered in timber vaulting, a transept and three apses. The horseshoe arches separating the aisles are supported on marble columns. The capitals are carved with a stylised foliage motif which includes the long, ribbed leaf which later appeared widely in Asturian art. Note the decorative frieze in the central apse.

Pamplona/Iruña★

POPULATION: 191 197.

MICHELIN MAP 573 D 25 (TOWN PLAN) – NAVARRA.

The old quarter of Pamplona (Iruña in Basque) has retained its medieval appearance of narrow streets and small arcaded squares such as the plaza Consistorial and plaza de Los Burgos. The busy streets around the attractive plaza del Castillo are named after the old trades practised in them, such as Zapatería (*zapato* is the Spanish for shoe) and Tejería (*teja* meaning tile). This area is also full of bars and restaurants.

Location

The old town is demarcated to the north and east by the River Arga. As a result, modern Pamplona, with its wide streets, high buildings, gardens and fountains, extends southwards. Two important cross-border routes depart from the town: one through Roncesvalles to the French Pyrenees, the other via the Puerto de Velate to Hendaye. 🗊 *Eslava 1, 31001 Pamplona,* ☎ *948 20 65 40.*

The "Sanfermines"

The *feria* of San Fermín is celebrated with joyous ardour from 6 to 14 July each year. Visitors pour in, doubling the town's population, to see the great evening bullfights and enjoy the carefree atmosphere (described by Hemingway in *The Sun Also Rises*). The most spectacular event, and the one most prized by "Pamploneses", however, is the **encierro** or early morning *(around 8am)* running of the bulls. The beasts selected to fight in the evening are let loose with a number of steers to rush through the streets along a set route leading to the bullring (🔍 *see route on town plan*).

PAMPLONA IRUÑA		García Castañón	ABY 30	Sancho el Mayor	ABZ 60
		Juan de Labrit	BY 33	Sangüesa	BZ 69
		Leyre	BYZ 36	Santo Domingo	AY 70
Amaya	BYZ 4	Mayor	AY 40	Sarasate Paseo de	AY 72
Ansoleaga	AY 5	Mercaderes	BY 43	Taconera Recta de	AY 73
Bayona Av. de	AY 13	Navarrería	BY 48	Vínculo Pl. del	AYZ 78
Carlos III Av. de	BYZ	Navas de Tolosa	AY 50	Zapatería	AY 89
Castillo de Maya	BZ 16	Paulino Caballero	BZ 51		
Chapitela	BY 17	Príncipe de Viana Pl. del	BZ 54		
Conde Oliveto Av. del	AZ 19	Reina Cuesta de la	AY 56		
Cortes de Navarra	BY 20	Roncesvalles Av. de	BY 59		
Cruz Pl. de la	BZ 22	San Fermín	BZ 63		
Esquiroz	AZ 25	San Francisco Pl. de	AY 65		
Estafeta	BY 26	San Ignacio Av. de	BYZ 66		

Ayuntamiento	AY H		Museo de Navarra	AY M

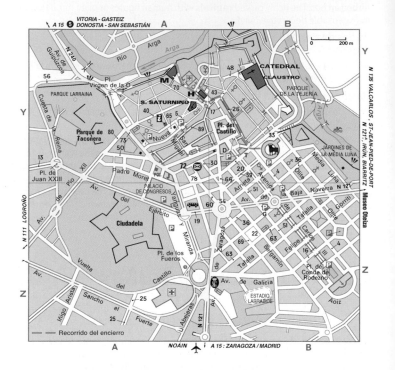

🐾 *Neighbouring sights are described in the following chapters: DONOSTIA-SAN SEBAS-TIÁN (94km/59mi N), ESTELLA/LIZARRA (43km/29mi SW), SANGÜESA/ZANGOZA (46km/29mi SE) and Monasterio de LEYRE (61km/38mi SE).*

Background

Historical notes – Pamplona dates back to Roman times and is said to have been founded by Pompey who, tradition has it, gave the town his name. In the 8C, the Moors occupied the town briefly before being expelled with the help of Charlemagne, who, however, took advantage of the weakness of the native forces to dismantle the city walls. In revenge the people of Navarra took part in the historic massacre of Charlemagne's rearguard in the Roncesvalles pass.

In the 10C Pamplona became the capital of Navarra. Throughout the Middle Ages, the city was troubled by disputes between the citizens of the old quarter – the Navarrería – who supported an alliance with Castilla, and the freemen who lived on the city outskirts in the districts of San Cernín and San Nicolás and favoured the retention of the Navarra crown by a French line. The disputes were settled in 1423 when Charles III, the Noble, promulgated the union between the three municipalities. They joined to become a single city and Pamplona reached the peak of its power. Building of the citadel began during the reign of Philip II in 1571.

Address Book

For coin ranges, see the Legend at the back of the guide.

WHERE TO EAT

Rodero – *Arrieta 3* – ☎ *948 22 80 35* – *info@restauranterodero.com* - *Closed Sun and Mon evening* – 🍽. This luxury restaurant behind the bullring is one of the best in the whole province. Family-run with high-quality service and creative, innovative cuisine with prices to match.

TAPAS

Baserri – *San Nicolás 32* – ☎ *948 22 20 21* - *info@restaurantebaserri.com* - 🍽 - *4€.* The Baserri is widely recognised as being one of the best place for tapas in Pamplona, as witnessed by its numerous prizes and the huge number of locals who come here. Make sure you try the sirloin with roquefort (*solomillos al roquefort*).

WHERE TO STAY

Hotel Yoldi – *Avenida de San Ignacio 11* – ☎ *948 22 48 00* - *yoldi@ hotelyoldi.com* - 🍽 - *50 rooms.* – 🛏 *8€.* A modern, featureless hotel, but a good option nevertheless in the centre of Pamplona. Comfortable and functional rooms and a good location near the bullring. As with everywhere in the city at fiesta time, not easy to get a room here.

Worth a Visit

Catedral★★

🕐 *Open 10.30am-1.30pm and 4-7pm; Sat 10am-1.30pm; 15 Jul-15 Sep, 10am-7pm; Sat, 10am-2pm.* 🕐 *Closed Sun and public hols.* 🎟*3.61€.* ☎ *948 21 08 27.*

The present Gothic cathedral was built in the 14C and 15C over an earlier Romanesque edifice whose only remains (doorway and cloister capitals) are now in the Museo de Navarra. At the end of the 18C, Ventura Rodríguez rebuilt the west front in the Baroque and neo-Classical style then fashionable.

Interior★

The nave, only two tiers high, has wide arches and windows and, with plain ribbing and great bare walls, the unadorned appearance typical of Navarra Gothic.

In front of the finely wrought grille closing the sanctuary stands the alabaster **tomb**★★, commissioned in 1416 by Charles III, the Noble, founder of the cathedral, for himself and his queen. The expressive reclining figures and **mourners** were carved by the Frenchman, Janin Lomme. Note the late-15C Hispano-Flemish altarpiece (south ambulatory chapel).

Claustro★

The 14C-15C cloisters have a delicate appearance, with elegant Gothic arches surmounted, in some cases, by gables. Sculptured tombs and doors add interest; note the Dormition of the Virgin on the tympanum of the cloister door which is almost Baroque in expression.

Off the east gallery is the Capilla Barbazán – a chapel named after the bishop who had it built to house his tomb – which has beautiful 14C star vaulting. On the south side, the doorway of the Sala Preciosa is a key piece in the sculpture of the period, with tympanum and lintel beautifully carved with scenes from the Life of the Virgin and, on either side of the door, two statues together forming a fine Annunciation.

In the southeast corner note the former lavabo, transformed into a shrine commemorating the Battle of Las Navas de Tolosa.

Museo Diocesano★

🕐 *Open 10am-1.30pm and 4-7pm; Sat, 10am-1.30pm; 15 Jul-15 Sep, 10.30am-7pm; Sat, 10am-2.30pm.* 🕐 *Closed Sun and public hols.* 🎟 *4€.* ☎ *948 21 08 27.*

The Diocesan Museum is in the old refectory and adjoining kitchen, which date from 1330. The refectory, a lofty hall with six pointed arches, contains a reader's rostrum decorated with an enchanting scene of a unicorn hunt. The square kitchen, with a fireplace in each corner, has a central lantern rising to a height of 24m/79ft. The museum displays religious objects including a 13C *Reliquary of the Holy Sepulchre* donated by St Louis (Louis IX of France) and polychrome wood statues of the Virgin and Christ from all parts of the province.

▶ *On leaving the cathedral follow the narrow, picturesque calle del Redín to the ramparts.*

Murallas (Ramparts)

A small bastion, now a garden, commands a view of the fortified Puerta de Zumalacárregui (a gate which is visible below and to the left) and a stretch of the old walls and, further away, a bend in the Río Arga and Monte Cristóbal.

Museo de Navarra★

🕐 *Open 9.30am-2pm and 5-7pm (Thu to 9pm); Sun and public hols, 11am-2pm.*
🕐 *Closed Mon, 1 Jan, Good Fri, 7 Jul and 25 Dec.* 2€, *no charge Sun and public hols.* ☎ *948 42 64 92.*

This brick structure occupies the site of the 16C Hospital de Nuestra Señora de la Misericordia, of which only the Renaissance gateway and the chapel, the latter now housing an exhibition of sacred art, have been preserved.

The Roman period *(basement and first floor)* is represented by lapidary exhibits such as funerary steles, inscriptions and **mosaic**★ pavements from 2C and 4C villas. The mosaics are principally geometric and often in black and white.

The main exhibit in the Hispano-Moorish section *(Room 1.8)* is an ivory **casket**★ from San Salvador de Leyre which was sculpted in Córdoba in the early 11C. Pride of place is given to the Romanesque period with **capitals**★ from the former 12C cathedral of Pamplona on which an unknown artist carved three biblical scenes – the Passion, the Resurrection and the Story of Job – with a care for detail only equalled by his mastery of composition and brilliance of imagination.

The museum also contains a large collection of **Gothic wall paintings**★ from various corners of the province: Artaíz (13C), Artajona (14C), Pamplona (14C), Gallipienzo (14C-15C) and Olleta (15C). Although by different masters, the works share common characteristics (the unobtrusive emphasis on faces and features; the crowds; pronounced curves) so reminiscent of French miniaturists. Note also the fine mural in the cathedral refectory. This work, painted by Juan Olivier in 1330, shows similar traits.

Renaissance art is evident in the reconstruction of the interior of the **Palacio de Oriz**, decorated with 16C monochrome painted panels depicting the story of Adam and Eve and the wars of Emperor Charles V.

A section of the third floor is devoted to 17C-18C paintings. Here, prominence is given to Luis Paret and Francisco de Goya; the work of the latter includes the portrait of the *Marqués de San Adrián.*

The museum's comprehensive collection of 19C-20C Navarran art is also worthy of note.

Iglesia de San Saturnino★

This composite church at the centre of a tangle of narrow streets in the old quarter has a mingled architecture of Romanesque brick towers, 13C Gothic **portals**★ and vaulting and numerous later additions.

Ayuntamiento (Town Hall)

This has a reconstructed **Baroque façade**★ originally dating from the late 17C with statues, balustrades and pediments.

Excursions

Museo Oteiza

En Alzuza, 7 km/4.5mi E. ▶ *Take the NA 150, then immediately turn left.*
🕐 *Open 10am-8pm.* 🕐 *Closed Mon, 1 Jan and 25 Dec.* 3€. ☎ *948 33 20 47.*

The museum brings us into the creative universe of Jorge Oteiza (1908-2003), one of the key figures of modern Spanish sculpture. The building, next to the artist's house, was conceived by his friend the architect Saénz de Oiza. Oteiza, after abandoning representation at the beginning of the fifties, began an abstract period of geometric and metaphysical experimentation which converted him into the great sculptor of the "void."

Santuario de San Miguel de Aralar★

45km/28mi NW.
▶ *Follow the A 15, then shortly before Lecumberri, turn onto the NA 751.*
The NA 751 crosses the Sierra de Aralar through a magnificent landscape of beech woods to reach this sanctuary. From here the extensive views encompass the Araquil Valley and the foothills of the Sierra de Andía. 🕐 *Open 10am-2pm and 4pm-dusk.* ☎ *948 39 60 28.*

The sanctuary consists of a two-sided Romanesque **church** that encloses a totally independent chapel. Some specialists date the church to the 8C and others to the late 12C. The building has a magnificent gilt and enamel **altar front**★★, now considered one of the major works of European Romanesque gold- and silverwork, and which some archaeologists attribute to a late-12C Limoges workshop. It consists of various gilded bronze plaques adorned with enamel and mounted precious stones arranged in the form of an altarpiece, although it is not known whether this was its original purpose. The outstanding multicoloured honeycomb enamelwork is adorned with a variety of delicate decoration including arabesques and plant motifs.

Roncesvalles/Orreaga★

47km/29mi NE along the N 135. This vast, grey-walled mass of buildings with bluish zinc roofs, dating back to the 12C, appears hidden by dense vegetation.
The buildings served formerly as an important hostelry for pilgrims heading to Santiago de Compostela, with a funerary chapel, square in plan, now the Capilla del Sancti Spiritus (Chapel of the Holy Spirit), and a collegiate church rich in relics.

Iglesia de la Real Colegiata

This Gothic collegiate church, inspired by those of the Paris region, was consecrated in 1219, since when it has been repeatedly, and unfortunately, restored. Beneath the high altar canopy is the statue of **Nuestra Señora de Roncesvalles,** carved in cedar wood and plated in silver, and created in France in the late 13C or early 14C.

Sala Capitular (Chapter house)

The beautiful Gothic chamber, off the cloisters, contains the tombs of the founder, Sancho VII, the Strong (1154-1234), King of Navarra and his queen.

Museo★

🕐 *Open 10am-2pm and 3.30-5.30pm (7pm 5 Apr-25 Oct); Jan, 10.30am-2.30pm.* 🕐 *Closed Wed in Jan, 1 and 6 Jan, 8 Sep and 25 Dec.* 🎫 *2€.* ☎ *948 79 04 80.*

Housed in the old stables, the museum contains fine pieces of ancient plate: a Mudéjar casket, a Romanesque book of the Gospel, a 14C enamelled reliquary which, doubtless on account of its chequered design, is known as "Charlemagne's chessboard", a 16C Flemish triptych, an emerald, said to have been worn by Sultan Miramamolín el Verde in his turban on the day of the Battle of Las Navas de Tolosa in 1212, and a lovely *Holy Family* by Morales.

Epic Poems

According to legend, Roncesvalles was the site where the Basques of Navarra massacred the rearguard of Charlemagne's army in 778 as Roland was leading it back through the Pyrenees to France. The late 12C to early 13C Poem of **Bernardo del Carpio** describes Bernardo as a national hero who fought alongside his Basque, Navarra and Asturian companions in arms to avenge the Frankish invasion of Spain; the 12C **Song of Roland**, the first French epic poem, on the other hand, glorifies the heroic but ultimately despairing resistance of a handful of valiant Christian knights against hordes of Saracen fanatics.

TOUR THROUGH THE VALLE DEL BIDASOA★

100km/62mi N – 🕐 *allow one day.*

The Bidasoa has cut a course through the lower foothills of the western Pyrenees, where villages of typical Basque houses lie surrounded by lush meadows and fields of maize. The Bidasoa river is renowned for its salmon and trout.

▶ *Exit Pamplona along avenida de la Baja Navarra and continue on the N 121A.*

The road winds its way through hilly country over the Velate Pass.

▶ *Follow the NA 2540.*

Elizondo, the capital of the **Valle del Baztán**, is a wealthy seigniorial town with numerous houses decorated with armorial bearings.

▶ *Return to Irutia and follow the N 121B to rejoin the N 121A, heading N towards Berrizaun.*

This road then heads into the ancient confederation of the **Cinco Villas**, comprising the towns of **Etxalar, Arantza, Igantzi, Lesaka** and **Bera**, where many of the houses bear noble coats of arms. The house façades, typical of Basque architecture, have deep eaves which shelter wooden balconies with delicate balustrades.
At this point, close to the French border, the River Bidasoa carves its way through a narrow gorge, the Garganta de Endarlaza.

Pedraza de la Sierra★★

POPULATION: 448

MICHELIN MAPS 575 OR 576 I 18 – CASTILLA Y LEÓN (SEGOVIA).

Pedraza, perched on a hill and encircled by medieval walls, is a delightful village that has retained much of its original seigniorial atmosphere. At the weekend, numerous visitors head for the village to wander through its enchanting streets and to eat roast lamb or suckling pig in one of its traditional restaurants.

Location

The village stands on the northern slopes of the Sierra de Guadarrama. ⓘ *Real 5, 40172 Pedraza,* ☎ *921 50 86 66.*

⚲ *Neighbouring sights are described in the following chapters: SEGOVIA (35km/22mi SW) and Sierra de GUADARRAMA.*

Walking About

The **Puerta de la Villa**, a fortified gateway, opens into a maze of steep, narrow alleys bordered with country-style houses, many with family crests. The first medieval building of interest is the **Cárcel de la Villa**, the town's former jail. ⓞ *Open Sat-Sun and public hols, 11.30am-2pm and 3.30-6pm (7pm autumn-winter).* ⚲ *€2.50€.* ☎ *921 50 98 77 or 921 50 99 55.*

Calle Real leads to the splendid **plaza Mayor**, surrounded by ancient porticoes topped by wide balconies and the slender Romanesque bell tower of San Juan. From here, it is possible to approach the restored 16C **castle** which now houses a small collection of works by one of Pedraza's illustrious native sons, the artist **Ignacio Zuloaga**. ⚲ *Guided tours (30min) in winter, Sat-Sun and public hols, 11am-2pm and 4-6pm (at other times by prior arrangement); in summer, Wed-Sun, 11am-2pm and 5-8pm.* ⚲ *4€.* ☎ *921 50 98 25.*

Plaza Mayor

F. Gouverneur/MICHELIN

Excursion

Sepúlveda

25km/16mi N. By approaching Sepúlveda from Pedraza you will get a good view of its magnificent terraced **site**★ on the slopes of a deep gorge in the Duratón river valley.

Leave the car in the town hall square, overlooked by the old castle ruins, and walk up to the **Iglesia de San Salvador** from which there is a fine view of the town and surrounding countryside. The church itself is typical Segovia Romanesque with a multiple-storey belfry with paired bays and an east end decorated with a carved cornice. It has one of the oldest side doors in Spain, dating from 1093.

Centro de Recepción e Interpretación del Parque Natural de las Hoces del Duratón (Duratón Gorges) – ◐ *Open 10am-5pm; Jul-Sep 10am-2pm and 4-7pm; Sat and public hols Jul-Sep, 10am-2pm and 4-7pm.* ☎ *921 54 05 86.*

This centre, housed in the former Iglesia de Santiago, is able to provide all the information visitors need to know about the park, including hiking routes and details of canoe companies.

The **park** itself runs along the middle stretch of the river, hemmed in on either side by spectacular 70m/230ft walls. The last section of the river is a series of enclosed meanders. This stunning landscape is watched over by the simple Romanesque hermitage *(ermita)* of San Frutos.

Picos de Europa★★★

MICHELIN MAP 572 C 14-15-16 –

CASTILLA Y LEÓN, ASTURIAS AND CANTABRIA.

The Picos de Europa, the highest range in the Cordillera Cantábrica, stand at an average distance of 30km/18mi from the sea. The impressive landscape is one of deep gorges cut by gushing mountain rivers, as well as high snow-capped peaks, jagged with erosion.

In 1995, the **Parque Nacional de los Picos de Europa** was created to protect and preserve the precious flora and fauna of the region. Covering a total area of 64 660ha/159 775 acres, it also incorporates the former Parque de la Montaña de Covadonga.

Location

The range extends from the Valle de Sella to the Liébana depression and is divided into three blocks: the western or Covadonga massif, the central or Naranjo de Bulnes massif and the eastern or Andara massif. The south face is less steep than the north, where the higher peaks are congregated, and looks out over a less abrupt, harsher terrain of outstanding beauty. *Cangas de Onís: Avenida de Covadonga (Plaza del Ayuntamiento), 33550 Asturias,* ☎ *98 584 80 05; Covadonga: Explanada de la Basílica, 33589 Cantabria,* ☎ *98 584 60 35; Potes: Independencia 30, 39570 Cantabria,* ☎ *942 73 07 87.*

Neighbouring sights are described in the following chapters: COSTA VERDE and COSTA DE CANTABRIA.

Tours

DESFILADERO DE LA HERMIDA★★ (LA HERMIDA DEFILE) 1

From Panes to Potes – *27km/17mi –* ◐ *about 1hr*

The outstanding feature of the drive is the **ravine**★★, some 20km/12mi long in all, which extends either side of a basin containing the hamlet of La Hermida. The gorge is narrow and so lacking in sunlight as to be bare of vegetation; the Deva has sought out weaknesses in the rock wall to carve out a sawtooth course.

Iglesia de Nuestra Señora de Lebeña

◐ *Open 10am-8.30pm in summer; by prior arrangement in winter.* ☎ *942 74 43 32.*

Address Book

For coin ranges, see the Legend at the back of the guide.

WHERE TO EAT

El Bodegón – *San Roque – Potes –* ☎ *942 73 02 47.* El Bodegón is a converted old stone-fronted house in the centre of town. The rustic, wood-adorned interior is pleasant, although the tables are somewhat close together. A good, traditional menu.

El Corral del Indianu – *Avenida de Europa 14 – Arriondas –* ☎ *98 584 10 72 – Closed 24 Dec-24 Jan, Sun and Wed evenings and Thu (except in Aug) -* 🖼. A pleasant surprise in the centre of Arriondas. The building's stone walls enclose a restaurant that successfully combines the modern and traditional, in terms of both decor and cuisine. A gastronomic treat.

WHERE TO STAY

Hotel Del Oso – *Cosgaya – 9km/5.5mi SE of Fuente Dé along the Potes road –* ☎ *942 73 30 18 – Closed 7 Jan-15 Feb –* 🅿 🏊 *– 51 rooms –* 🛏 *5.80€ – Restaurant 37.90€.* This hotel is located at the very heart of the Picos de Europa on the banks of the River Deva, amid a spectacular landscape of high peaks. Behind the sober brick façade, the rooms are both spacious and comfortable, particularly those in the annexe. The hotel restaurant specialises in regional cuisine.

La Tahona de Besnes – *Besnes – Alles – 10km/6mi W of Panes on the AS 114 –* ☎ *98 541 57 49 – Closed 10-30 Jan – 13 rooms –* 🛏 *5.70€ – Restaurant 12.50€.* This former mill in Besnes, near Alles, has been transformed into an inviting country hotel. Stone and exposed wood beams are the order of the day here, with agricultural implements providing the decoration. Wood is also the predominant material on the floors and ceilings of the guest rooms.

Parador de Cangas de Onís – *Villanueva – Cangas de Onís – 3km/2mi NW of Cangas de Onís along the Arriondas road –* ☎ *98 584 94 02 –* 🅿 🖼 ♿ *– 64 rooms –* 🛏 *10€ – Restaurant 25.90€.* Benedictine monks chose to settle on this very spot next to the River Sella in their search for tranquillity and beauty. Nowadays, the monastery has been converted into a delightful parador offering a combination of history, nature and art. Luxurious surroundings, including elegant, comfortable rooms.

The small 10C Mozarabic church stands surrounded by poplars at the foot of tall cliffs. The belfry and porch are later additions. The semicircular vaulting over the three aisles rests on horseshoe-shaped arches decorated with beautifully carved Corinthian style capitals.

The church houses a venerated 15C sculpture of the Virgin Mary.

Potes

Potes is a delightful village in a pleasing **site**★ set in the hollow of a fertile basin against a background of jagged crests, the peaks of the central massif. From the bridge there is a view, reflected in the Deva, of old stone houses and the austere 15C **Torre del Infantado**, a restored tower which now serves as the town hall *(ayuntamiento)*.

THE CLIMB TO FUENTE DÉ★★ ②

30km/19mi along the N 621– 🕐 *about 3hr*

Monasterio de Santo Toribio de Liébana

▶ *Approach along a signposted road on the left.* 🕐 *Open 10am-1pm and 4-7pm.* ☎ *942 73 05 50.*

The monastery now occupied by Franciscans, was founded in the 7C and grew to considerable importance in the following century when a fragment said to be of the True Cross, brought from Jerusalem by Turibius, Bishop of Astorga, was placed in its safekeeping. A *camarín (access through the north aisle of the church)* now contains the fragment (the largest known piece of the True Cross) in the *lignum crucis* reliquary, a silver gilt Crucifix. The church, transitional Romanesque in style, has been restored to its original harmonious proportions. The monastery was also the house of **Beatus**, the 8C monk famous for his **Commentary on the Apocalypse**, which was copied in the form of illuminated manuscripts (🖼 *see illustration under INTRODUCTION TO SPAIN: LITERATURE).*

There is a **view**★ of Potes and the central range from the lookout point at the end of the road.

Fuente Dé★★

The parador is at 1 000m/3 300ft. Nearby is the starting point of the 🚠 cableway **(teleférico)** which rises an additional 800m/2 625ft to the terminal at the top of the sheer rock face. (🕐 *Only operates in fine weather, 10am-6pm; Holy Week and Jul-Sep, 9am-8pm.* 🎫 *10€.* ☎ *942 73 66 10).*

During the **ascent** you may see wild chamois. The **Mirador del Cable★★** at the terminal commands a splendid panorama of the upper valley of the Deva and Potes, and the peaks of the central range. A path leads to the Aliva refuge. The effect of erosion on the upper heights of karst limestone are spectacular, producing long stony plateaux and huge sink-holes known as **hoyos**.

PUERTO DE SAN GLORIO★ (SAN GLORIO PASS) 3

From Potes to Oseja de Sajambre *83km/52mi –* 🕐*about 3hr*

The road crosses the green Quiviesa Valley with its poplar woods, then begins to climb through mountain pastures. 10km/6mi beyond Bores, a series of bends affords a changing panorama on the left. The drive up to the San Glorio pass is through silent, lonely countryside.

Puerto de San Glorio★

Alt 1 609m/5 279ft. A track leads north *(*🕐*1hr there and back)* to near the Peña de Llesba, where the **Mirador de Llesba** forms a magnificent natural **viewpoint★★** for the highest crests: to the right is the east range and to the left the central massif with its steep south face dominating the Fuente Dé. The peak in the left foreground is the Coriscao (2 234m/7 330ft).

The scenery remains austere until you come to the village of **Llánaves de la Reina**, tucked into the opening of the **Gargantas de Yuso** (Yuso Gorge) which is spectacular for its rock colouring.

▶ *At Portilla de la Reina, bear right onto LE 243.*

Puerto de Pandetrave★★

An ascent through the high mountains brings you to the pass (1 562m/5 125ft) and a **panorama** of the three ranges with, in the right foreground, the Cabén de Remoña and Torre de Salinas, both part of the central massif, and in the distance, lying in a hollow, the village of Santa Marina de Valdeón.

🚗 *The road between Santa Marina de Valdeón and Posada de Valdeón is narrow but passable.*

Puerto de Panderruedas★

The road climbs to mountain pastures at an altitude of 1 450m/4 757ft. 🚶 Walk up the path to the left *(15min there and back)* to the **Mirador de Piedrafitas★★** *(viewing table)* from where there is an impressive view of the immense cirque which closes

The impressive landscapes around Fuente Dé

J. Balanya/MICHELIN

off the Valdeón Valley. To the northeast can be seen the Torre Cerredo (2 648m/8 688ft), the highest peak in the range.

Puerto del Pontón★

Alt 1 280m/4 200ft. From the pass you will get a picturesque **view**★★ of the Sajambre Valley. The descent to Oseja de Sajambre (& see below) begins with tight hairpin bends in full view of the western range; it continues as a spectacular road cut into the mountain side (tunnels) during which you can see the formidable rock wall through which the Sella has hollowed its course.

DESFILADERO DE LOS BEYOS★★★ (LOS BEYOS DEFILE) 4

From Oseja de Sajambre to Cangas de Onís – 38km/24mi – ① about 1hr

Mirador de Oseja de Sajambre★★

There is an awe-inspiring **view**★★ of the Oseja de Sajambre basin with the sharp Niaja peak at its centre rising to 1 732m/5 682ft, and of the Los Beyos defile opening between walls of broken rock strata.

Desfiladero de Los Beyos★★★

The defile, one of the most beautiful in Europe, is 10km/6mi long, cut by the Sella through an exceptionally thick layer of limestone. Though wide enough to allow sunlight to penetrate, it is too precipitous for anything other than an occasional tree to have gained a hold on its sides.

Cangas de Onís

An elegant humpbacked **Roman bridge** (puente romano) across the Sella lies west of the town.
The Capilla de Santa Cruz, also west of the town, was built in Contranquil, to celebrate the victory of Covadonga and was rebuilt after the Civil War. The chapel houses the region's only dolmen of which one stone is engraved.

Villanueva

The 17C Benedictine **Monasterio de San Pedro** stands at the end of the village. The monastery was built around an already existing Romanesque church of which there remain the apse and an elegantly decorated side portal – note on the left the capitals illustrating the farewell of King Favila and his sad end, apparently being devoured by a bear. Inside there are further capitals to be seen in the apse and at the triumphal arch. Imaginatively ornamented stone modillions decorate the apse exterior.

THE ROAD TO COVADONGA AND THE LAKES★★ 5

From Cangas de Onís to Covadonga 35km/22mi – ① about 3hr

Cueva del Buxu

🔈 Guided tours (30min), 9am-1pm and 3-5.30pm; entry restricted to 25 visitors per day; tickets cannot be booked in advance. ① Closed Mon, Tue, in Nov, 1 Jan and 24-25 and 31 Dec. ☞ 1.35€, no charge Wed. ☎ 608 17 54 67.

The cave in the cliff face contains charcoal drawings and rock engravings dating back to the Magdalenian period. There are a stag, horse and bison scarcely larger than the size of a hand.

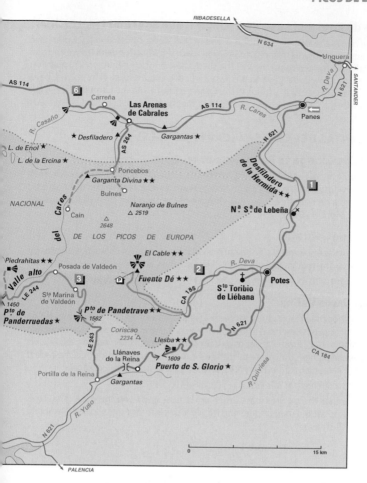

The approach to Covadonga *(from a road to the right)* gradually reveals the town's impressive mountain setting.

Covadonga

This famous shrine and landmark in Spanish history is nestled in a magnificent **setting**★★ at the bottom of a narrow valley surrounded by impressive peaks. The legendary Battle of Covadonga (722), in which **Don Pelayo** defeated the Moors, heralded the beginning of the Spanish Reconquest.

La Santa Cueva

🕑 *Open 9am-6.30pm (8pm in summer).* ☎ *98 584 61 15.*

The cave is dedicated to the Virgin of the Battlefield and contains the deeply venerated 18C wooden statue of the Virgin, patron of Asturias. It is known as **La Santina** and is the centrepiece of a major procession on 8 September.

Basílica

🕑 *Open 9am-6.30pm (8pm in summer); no visits during religious services.* ☎ *98 584 60 35/ 96.*

In front of the neo-Romanesque basilica built between 1886 and 1901 stands a statue of Pelayo beneath the Cruz de la Victoria (Cross of Victory) which Pelayo brandished during the battle (the original is on display in the Cámara Santa in Oviedo).

The **museo** contains the gifts to the Virgin of Covadonga including the magnificent **crown**★ with more than 1 000 diamonds. 🕑 *Open 10.30am-2pm and 4-6.30pm (7.30pm in summer).* 🕑 *Closed Tue, and in Nov.* 👝 *2€.* ☎ *98 584 60 96.*

Lago de Enol and Lago de Ercina★ (Lake Enol and Lake Ercina)

▶ *Continue to the lakes along the CO 4.* The road is steep; on looking back you have an extensive panorama. After 8km/5mi, you reach the **Mirador de la Reina**★★ from where there is a picturesque view of the succession of rock pyramids which make up the Sierra de Covalierda. Beyond the pass, two rock cirques formed by *hoyos* (👁 *see above)*, provide beautiful settings to the **Lago de Enol**★ and the **Lago de Ercina** (alt 1 232m/4 042ft). On 25 July, the Lago de Enol Shepherd's Festival draws large crowds for the dances and kayak races.

GARGANTAS DEL CARES★★ (CARES GORGES) ⑥

From Covadonga to Panes *90km/56mi – 🕐 allow one day*

As you come out of Las Estazadas village there is a splendid **panorama**★★ of the rock wall which closes off the Río Casaño Valley. From a viewpoint on the right, shortly after Carreña de Cabrales, there is a glimpse of the fang-like crest of **Naranjo de Bulnes** (2 519m/8 264ft).

Arenas de Cabrales

Arenas, as its name suggests, is the main production centre for *cabrales*, a blue ewes' milk cheese. The road now, for a while, skirts the Río Cares.

▶ *Bear right onto AS 264 which runs through the Upper Cares Valley.*

Upper Cares Valley

The Poncebos road leads south, through a pleasant **ravine**★. After the embalse de Poncebos (Poncebos Reservoir) a track *(3hr there and back on foot)* leads to the mountain village of Bulnes. 🚶 From Poncebos to Caín *(3hr 30min walk one way)* a path follows the Cares and plunges down into the **defile**★★ before reaching the foot of the central massif (😊 *here you can hire a car with a driver to take you back to Poncebos).*

▶ *Return to Arenas de Cabrales.*

Beyond Arenas the **gorges**★ are green with moss and even the occasional tree. Narrow humpbacked road bridges and fragile looking footbridges span the emerald waters of the river.

Monasterio de Piedra★★

MICHELIN MAPS 574 OR 575 I 24 – ARAGÓN (ZARAGOZA).

Hidden in a fold of this arid plateau is a green oasis fed by the River Piedra. The best approach to the monastery is via Ateca, along a road that crosses a parched landscape of red earth above the Tranquera Reservoir. Just before the monastery, the village of Nuévalos comes into view high up against a clay hillside.

Location

This magnificent area is situated some 25km/15mi S of the N II-E 90 highway linking Madrid and Zaragoza (104km/65mi).

👁 *Neighbouring sights are described in the following chapter: Monasterio de SANTA MARÍA DE HUERTA (63km/39mi NW).*

Walking About

The site was discovered and settled by Cistercian monks, who generally chose pleasant surroundings for their retreats. The monks in this case came from the Abbey of Poblet in Tarragona and established a monastery on the spot in 1194. This was rebuilt several times and suffered damage in the 19C. The conventual buildings have been reconstructed as a hotel.

Park and Waterfalls★★

🚶 *Open 9am-5pm (8pm in summer).* 🎫 10€. ☎ 902 19 60 52.

Waterfalls and cascades are to be seen along the marked footpath through the heart of the forest *(follow the red signposts to go and the blue ones to return).* The paths, steps and tunnels laid out last century by **Juan Federico Muntadas** have transformed an

impenetrable forest into a popular park. The first fall is the **Cola de Caballo** (Horse's Tail), a cascade of 53m/174ft. You first look down on this fall from a viewpoint and come on it again at the end of your walk if you descend the steep and slippery steps into the beautiful **Cueva Iris** (Iris Grotto), where you will see it from the back.
Baño de Diana (Diana's Bath) and the romantic **Lago del Espejo** (Mirror Lake), cupped between tall cliffs, are both worth a halt.
The signposted route ends outside the park at the monastery ruins. Of the Gothic buildings there remain the kitchen, refectory and cloisters.

Pirineos Aragoneses★★

MICHELIN MAP 574 D 28-32, E 29-32 AND F 30-31 – ARAGÓN (HUESCA).

The central Spanish Pyrenees, in the northern part of the province of Huesca, include the highest peaks in the Pyrenean chain: Aneto (3 404m/11 165ft), Posets (3 371m/11 060ft) and Monte Perdido (3 355m/11 004ft). The foothills are often ravined and covered only with sparse vegetation; the landscape at the heart of the massif, accessible up the river courses, is on a different scale altogether. The valleys, whether wide and lush or narrow and gullied, lead to mountain cirques well worth exploring.

Address Book

For coin ranges, see the Legend at the back of the guide.

WHERE TO EAT

⊜ **Casa Ruba** – *Esperanza 18 – Biescas –* ☎ *974 48 50 01 – Closed Sun evings (exc in summer) –* ▤. This Pyrenean-style house is home to one of the most renowned restaurants in the area. With over a century of history and tradition behind it, the Casa Ruba serves well-prepared, good-quality dishes, in addition to a range of tapas at the bar. If you're looking for somewhere to stay, 29 inexpensive rooms are also available here. Highly recommended.

⊜⊜ **Deth Gormán** – *Met Día 8 - Vielha –* ☎ *973 64 04 45 – Closed Tue and in Jun –* ▤. A small restaurant in the center of the village. The wooden front suggests the rustic, simple inteior, where regional specialties are served.

⊜⊜ **Bodegas del Sobrarbe** – *Plaza Mayor 2 – Aínsa –* ☎ *974 50 02 37 – Closed Jan-Feb*. This restaurant in the basement of a building lining the main square of this medieval town is decorated in traditional country style and serves excellent game and grilled steaks.

WHERE TO STAY

⊜ **Hotel-Restaurante Casa Frauca** – *Carret. de Ordesa – Sarvisé –* ☎ *974 48 63 53 – Closed 9 Jan-1 Mar – 12 rooms –* ⊑ *3.50€ – Restaurant 14/50€*. This hotel is well maintained with cosy rooms in which the wood floors and beams add to the overall mountain atmosphere. The small, rustic-style restaurant has an extensive menu of unpretentious offerings.

⊜ **Hotel Pradas** – *Avenida Ordesa 7 – Broto –* ☎ *974 48 60 04 · info@hotelpradas. com -* ▣ *– 24 rooms –* ⊑ *5€ - Restaurant €15/40*. The attractive stone façade is the first thing you notice as you approach this partially renovated hotel on the main road into Broto. Several rooms have their own lounge area, albeit with a more expensive price tag.

⊜ **Hotel Villa de Torla** – *Plaza Aragón 1 – Torla –* ☎ *974 48 61 56 56 - Closed 8 Jan-6 Mar – 38 rooms –* ⊑ *4.50€*. The rooms in this recently renovated, attractive stone house in the centre of Torla are rustic, pleasant and comfortable. The swimming pool and terrace are welcome in summer.

⊜ **Hostal Dos Ríos** – *Avenida Central 2 – Aínsa –* ☎ *974 50 01 06 – Open Apri-Oct and 26 Dec-6 Jan – 17 rooms –* ⊑ *4.50€*. This *hostal* and the neighbouring hotel of the same name are easily the best medium-priced options in Aínsa. From its location in the lower part of the town, the main square is easily accessible on foot or by car. The guest rooms here are clean and perfectly adequate.

⊜⊜ **Llanos del Hospital** – *Camino del Hospital – Benasque – 15km/9mi N of Benasque along the A 139. Follow a road to the right, signposted Los Llanos del Hospital. -* ☎ *974 55 20 12 -* ▣ *– 57 rooms –* ⊑ *– Restaurant 14€*. Wood and stone are the order of the day in this charming hotel established in a former pilgrims' hospital. The setting, at the foot of the Pico de Maladeta and close to the Pico de Aneto, is quite spectacular. Cosy, pleasantly decorated rooms.

Location

The route described below covers the entire Pirineos Aragoneses from east to west – to make travelling easier, it has been divided into six independent sections. This area of the Pyrenees is accessible from numerous points: from Pamplona/Iruña it is advisable to follow the N 240 to Jaca (111km/69mi SE); from Huesca the quickest route is the N 330, also to Jaca (91km/57mi N); while the best approach from Barbastro is along the N 123 and the A 138 to Aínsa (52km/32.5mi N). *Aínsa: Avenida Pirenaica 1, 22330 Huesca, ☏ 974 50 07 67.*

Neighbouring sights are described in the following chapters: JACA, HUESCA and PIRINEOS CATALANES.

Background

Structure and relief – The geological division of the Pyrenees into vast longitudinal bands can be clearly seen in this region. The **axis of Palaeozoic terrain** comprises the Maladeta, Posets, Vignemale and Balaïtous massifs, where there are still remains of the Quaternary glaciers. There follows the **Pre-Pyrenees** or Monte Perdido region where the deep **Mesozoic limestone** layer has been deeply eroded to form an area of sharp relief: the canyons, gorges and cirques of the upper valleys. The limestone area, which extends in broken mountain chains as far as the Ebro Basin (Sierras de Guara and de la Peña) is divided at Jaca by a long depression through which the River Aragón flows. Tertiary sediment has accumulated into hills, some of which remain bare of vegetation, affording an unusual blue marl landscape like that around the **Yesa Reservoir.**

Life in the valleys – The upper valleys of the Kingdom of Aragón developed an independent political and pastoral way of life based on self-contained communities very early in their history. In spite of improved roads, local individuality remains, folklore is still followed and native costume is still worn in certain valleys. Sadly, emigration has led to the abandonment of a number of villages.

Tourism is becoming one of the major economic activities in the region with the development of winter sports resorts such as Candanchú, Astún, Canfranc, Panticosa, El Formigal and Benasque.

Tours

FROM VIELHA TO BENASQUE 1
122km/76mi – ⏱ about 3hr

Vielha (*See PIRINEOS CATALANES*)

The road cuts through the Maladeta massif by way of the Vielha tunnel which ends in the lonely upper valley of the Noguera Ribagorçana where the attractive hamlet of **Vilaller** stands huddled around a hillock.

▶ *Take the N 260 to Castejón de Sos, an important paragliding centre. From here, follow the A 139 through the valley.*

Valle de Benasque★

Benasque (1 138m/3 734ft) lies in an open valley, lush and green in spite of its altitude, overshadowed by the Maladeta massif. The town serves as a base for walkers, climbers (ascending the Aneto) and skiers (Cerler 5km/3mi away). Benasque's streets are lined with old seigniorial mansions. It is also well worth visiting **Anciles**, 1.6km/1mi away, a village known for its attractive

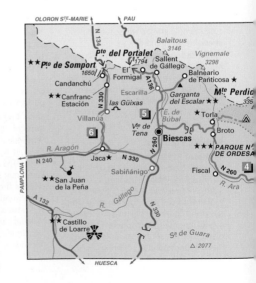

houses. The road continues 15km/9.5mi farther north; just before it ends, a turn-off leads to the Hospital de Benasque, the departure point for excursions into the Parque Natural Posets-Maladeta.

FROM BENASQUE TO AINSA ②

180km/112mi – ⏱ *allow half a day*

As the road heads south through the Esero Valley, it first passes through the village of Villanova, with its two 11C-12C Lombard-Romanesque-style churches, before continuing past Castejón de Sos on the left-hand side. It then follows the **Congosto de Ventamillo**★★, a defile of 3km/2mi with sheer limestone rock walls.

Ainsa★

Ainsa, one of the prettiest towns in the Pyrenees, stands on a promontory still girded by a wall, commanding the juncture of the River Cinca and River Ara. In the 11C the town was the capital of the small kingdom of Sobrarbe. Today, its arcaded **Plaza Mayor**★★ in the upper part of town, dominated by the tower of a Romanesque church, is a gem of Aragonese architecture. It is also home to the interesting and modern **Museo de Oficios y Artes Tradicionales**★, a museum devoted to traditional arts and crafts. ⏱ *Open May-Jun, 10.30am-2pm and 4.30-8pm; Jul-15 Sep 10am-2pm and 4-9pm;* ⏱ *Closed Mon (and Tue July-Aug) and 16 Sep-Apr.* ✇ *2.40€.* ☎ *974 51 00 75.*

FROM AINSA TO MONTE PERDIDO ③

73km/45mi – ⏱ *about 4hr*

The A 138 follows the course of the Cinca River northwards, passing through an attractive landscape that becomes more dramatic at a defile known as the **Desfiladero de las Devotas**★.

Cañón de Añisclo★★ (👣 *see Parque Nacional de ORDESA Y MONTE PERDIDO*)

Valle de Gistaín★

▶ *Exit the A 138 at Salinas de Sin.* This valley, also known as the Valle de Chistau, has been formed by the erosion of the Cinqueta River, and is the setting for some of the most picturesque villages in the Pyrenees, including **Plan**, San Juan de Plan and **Gistaín**.

Bielsa and Valle de Pineta

From the pleasant mountain village of Bielsa, a narrow road climbs the valley of the Cinca River, traversing the impressive landscapes of the **Valle de Pineta**★★ to the Parador de Bielsa, nestled in a spectacular glacial cirque.

FROM AÍNSA TO BIESCAS ④

81km/51mi – ⏱ *about 3hr*

Between **Boltaña** (16C church) and **Fiscal** (medieval tower), the river course has uncovered uneven earth strata which now rise out of the water curiously like dorsal fins. The road then reaches the village of **Broto**, whose church is fronted by an interesting Renaissance doorway. Beyond Broto, the great mass of the Mondarruego (alt 2 848m/9 341ft), closing the Ordesa Valley to the north, provides a backdrop for the spectacular **landscape**★★ in which the small village of **Torla**★ can be seen massed against the western slope of the Ara Valley. The village church, the Iglesia de San Salvador, houses several noteworthy 18C altarpieces, while the castle-abbey in Torla is now home to an **ethnographic museum.** (*For information, call* ☎ *974 48 61 52 (town hall).* ✇*1€*).

Parque Nacional de Ordesa y Monte Perdido★★★ *(See Parque Nacional de ORDESA Y MONTE PERDIDO)*

THE PORTALET ROAD 5
52km/32mi – about 2hr

The **Tena** Valley beyond Biescas is at first narrow and boulder strewn but widens out majestically to be filled by the vast Búbal reservoir.

▶ *A short distance before Escarilla, bear right onto HU 610 for Panticosa.*

Garganta del Escalar★★ (Escalar Gorge)

The gorge is so narrow that the sun seldom penetrates its depths; the stream below hollowed out a bed first through limestone and later through lamellar schists and granite. The road cuts down the west slope by long ramps and tight hairpin bends to an austere mountain cirque, the setting for the **Balneario de Panticosa★**, a spa with six sulphurous and radioactive springs renowned for their curative powers. The hotels and treatment centres here, overlooked by the Vignemale peak, exude a charming 19C air.

▶ *Return to Escarilla and continue to the Portalet Pass.*

The mountain town of **Sallent de Gállego**, a little east of the A 6 at a height of 1 305m/4 281ft, hosts a large summer music festival and is renowned as a centre for trout fishing and mountaineering. **El Formigal** (alt 1 480m/4 856ft), further on, is a well-equipped ski resort.

Carretera del Portalet

Alt 1 794m/5 886ft. The pass lies between the Portalet peak and the sharply pointed Aneu summit to the west. The view northwest extends towards the Aneu cirque and the Pic du Midi d'Ossau in France (alt 2 884m/9 462ft).

FROM BIESCAS TO THE PUERTO DE SOMPORT 6
58km/36mi – about 2hr

▶ *Continue S along the N 260 as far as Sabiñánigo – from here it is possible to follow the tour through the Serrablo (see JACA: EXCURSIONS) – and then take the N330 to Jaca (see JACA). From Jaca, the N 330 continues northwards.*

The **Cueva de las Güixas**, a cave in Villanúa opened to the public in 1927, has some 300m/330yd of underground galleries. (*For information, call ☎ 974 37 81 39.* 3.60€).

Beyond the village of Canfranc, the road reaches the impressive abandoned shell of the **Canfranc international resort★★**, an extraordinary example of early-20C architecture that is awaiting restoration. The road then continues to **Candanchú**, the best-known ski resort in Aragón, less than 1km/0.6mi from the Puerto de Somport. The **Puerto de Somport★★** (alt 1 632m/5 354ft), beside the Somport tunnel (opened in 2003), is the only pass in the Central Pyrenees which generally remains snow-free all year. Its history as a thoroughfare goes back to the Romans who built a road over it which was trodden by Pompey's legions, Saracen hordes and, later, cohorts of pilgrims on their way to Santiago de Compostela.

Climb the mound to the right of the monument commemorating the building of the road for an extensive **panorama★★** of the Spanish Pyrenees.

Pirineos Catalanes★★★

MICHELIN MAP 574 D 32, E 32-37 AND F 32-37 – CATALUNYA (GIRONA, LLEIDA).

The mountains are deeply cut across by side valleys – Arán, Ribagorça, Pallars, Alt Urgell, Cerdanya, Ripollès, Garrotxa and Empordà (Ampurdán) – which makes communication extremely difficult. As a result, these regions have developed separately from each other, acquiring their own individuality, personality and traditions. This applies more particularly to local art, especially during the Romanesque period. All, however, offer delicious regional cuisine and provide countless opportunities for leisure and sporting activities: skiing, hunting, fishing, mountain climbing and adventure sports.

Location

This mountain chain forms a wide, almost unbroken barrier 230km/143mi long extending from the Mediterranean Sea to the Arán Valley, which, due to its proximity to the Maladeta massif, is situated at quite a high altitude exceeding 2 500m/8 202ft (Pica d'Estats: 3 145m/10 318ft; Puigmal: 2 910m/9 547ft). The last range, the Montes Alberes, reaches the Cabo de Creus, plunging into the water from a height of about 700m/2 297ft. South of this granite axial ridge are the Cadí, Boumort and Montsec, forming a calcareous pre-Pyrenean chain. *Camprodon: Plaça d'Espanya 1, 17867 Girona, ☎ 972 74 00 10; Puigcerdà: Querol 1, 17520 Girona, ☎ 972 88 05 42; La Seu d'Urgell: Avinguda Valls d'Andorra 33, 25700 Lleida, ☎ 973 35 15 11; Tremp: Plaça de la Creu 1, 25620 Lleida, ☎ 973 65 00 09; Vielha: Sarriulera 10, 25530 Lleida, ☎ 973 64 01 10.*

Neighbouring sights are described in the following chapters: PIRINEOS ARAGONESES, Principat d'ANDORRA and GIRONA/GERONA.

Tours

UPPER VALLEY OF THE TER★ 1

From the Collado de Ares to Vall de Núria *106km/66mi – allow one day*
The Ripollès area features a large mountainous ensemble towering at around 3 000m/10 000ft and dominated by Puigmal. Sheltered by this rocky amphitheatre, the upper valley of the Ter is split into two large valleys: Camprodon and Ribes. The countryside surrounding the Collado de Ares (1,610m/5,283ft) features pleasant, rolling hills with green pastures.

Vall De Camprodon

Molló
The 12C Romanesque church has a lovely Catalan belfry.
Take the narrow, winding road which goes through Rocabruna and leads to Beget.

Beget★★
This attractive mountain village, with its stone houses and wooden balconies, enjoys an extremely pleasant **setting**★, in the deep recesses of a peaceful valley, where the silence is broken only by the burbling of a stream.
The **Romanesque church**★★ (10C-12C), presenting an apse adorned with Lombard arcatures and a slender lantern-tower, houses the **Majestad de Beget**★, a magnificent figure of Christ carved in the 12C. *Ask for the keys from Señora María Vila, opposite the church.* ☎ 972 74 12 72.
▸ *Return to the C 38 and proceed in the direction of Camprodon.*

Camprodon★
Camprodon stands at the confluence of the Ritort and Ter rivers and is crossed by a fine 12C humpbacked bridge, **Pont Nou**★, renovated in the 14C. The community developed around the **Monestir Sant Pere**, of which there remains only the 12C **Romanesque church**★, with its five apses and graceful belfry above the transept crossing.

Monasterio de Sant Joan de les Abadesses★★
Open Nov-Feb, 10am-2pm; Mar-Apr and Oct, 10am-2pm and 4-6pm (7pm May-Sep); Jul-Aug, 10am-7pm; Sat-Sun and public hols, 10am-2pm and 4-6pm (7pm, May-Aug). 1.80€. ☎ 972 72 23 53.

Address Book

For coin ranges, see the Legend at the back of the guide.

WHERE TO EAT

Can Jan – *Sant Roc 10 – Camprodon – ☎ 972 13 04 07 - Closed 1-15 Nov*. The overriding features of this centrally located restaurant are the friendly welcome and service, colourful wood decor and works by local artists on display. The menu includes typical dishes from the valley based on local products.

Grau de l'Ós – *Jaume II de Mallorca 5 – Bellver de Cerdanya – ☎ 973 51 00 46 – Closed Mon and Tue*. This village home has been carefully restored without losing its rustic feel. Despite its traditional bent, the menu occasionally comes up with original combinations such as chicken with wild mushrooms and cheese salad with apple vinegar.

Cal Teo – *Avinguda Pau Claris 36 – La Seu d'Urgell – ☎ 973 35 10 29 – Closed Sun evenings and Mon –* 🍴. A well-known traditional restaurant on the town's main avenue. Once you've been served the excellent grilled meats or the house speciality, bacalao a la catalana (Catalan-style cod), the slightly outdated decor is quickly forgotten. A good option after visiting the cathedral.

Casa Perú – *Sant Antoni 6 – Bagergue – 2km/1.2mi N of Salardú – ☎ 973 64 54 37 – Closed 1-15 Jul and Wed in winter*. For many, the Casa Perú is the perfect mountain restaurant; with its excellent location in a small village of stone houses, low ceilings, rustic tableware and deliciously flavoured cuisine. Make sure you try the *olla aranesa*, a local stew, as well as the wide selection of game dishes.

Els Puis – *Avinguda Dr. Morelló 13 – Esterri d'Àneu – ☎ 973 62 61 60 – Closed Mon and in May*. A family-run restaurant on the outskirts of the village, popular with locals and tourists alike. The menu focuses on high-quality local specialities, the wine cellar is varied and the service attentive. Seven reasonably priced rooms also available.

La Cabana – *Carretera de Tahüll – Boí – ☎ 973 69 62 13 – Closed May-23 Jun, Oct, Nov and Mon (exc summer) –* 🍴. A pleasant setting with fine views of the village and valley. The tastefully decorated restaurant serves typically Catalan dishes including a wide choice of meats.

WHERE TO STAY

Hotel Roya – *Mayor – Espot – ☎ 973 62 40 40 - Closed 3 Nov-3 Dec - 34 rooms –* 🛏 *5€ - Restaurant 13.50/30€*. Well located between the ski slopes and hiking paths and in the middle of the resort's shops. Comfortable, bright and attractive rooms, some with views of the charming local church. Reasonably priced given the quality and location.

Hotel Casa Peyró – *Coll – 13km/8mi S of Caldes de Boí on the L 500 – ☎ 973 29 70 02- Closed May and Oct - 8 rooms –* 🛏 *7.50€ – Restaurant 15/35€*. A pretty stone-built house with rooms decorated in pastel shades. A particularly pleasing feature is the quality of the bed linen and towels. Sauna on the first floor, although it is only open in winter. At night, nothing disturbs the peace of this village buried in the depths of the valley.

Hotel Fonda Biayna – *Sant Roc 11 – Bellver de Cerdanya – ☎ 973 51 04 75 - Closed 25 Dec – 17 rooms –* 🛏 *- Rest. 14/30€*. An attractive mansion in a large village of stone houses, with simple yet comfortable rooms which have kept their original furniture. The only drawback is the size of the bathrooms.

Hotel Cal Teixido – *Sol de Vila 33 – Estamariu – 4km/2.5mi E of La Seu d'Urgell on the N 260, then turn left – ☎ 973 36 01 21 - Closed Jan and Nov (last weeks) –* 🍴 *– 14 rooms –* 🛏 *– Restaurant 18/24€*. This large chalet decorated with brick and wood has 11 bright, comfortable rooms. With its isolated location on the side of a hill, peace and quiet is guaranteed.

Maristany – *Avinguda Maristany 20 - Camprodon – ☎ 972 13 00 78 - Closed in Dec –* 🅿 *– 10 rooms –* 🛏 *9.02€ - Restaurant 18.03€*. On the outskirts of town, in a quiet and well-kept area. Rooms are modern and comfortable. The cosy restaurant is in an annex.

Parador de Arties – *Carretera de Baqueira - Arties – ☎ 973 64 08 01 –* 🅿 ♿ *– 54 rooms –* 🛏 *9.70€ Restaurant 24€*. This handsome building includes parts of the architectural legacy of the Portalà family, including a 16C tower and chapel. Its exterior combines wood, stone and slate, in perfect harmony with the Pyrenees all around.

SPORT

Skiing is without doubt the most popular sport in the Pirineos Catalanes. Nowadays, the region has numerous resorts, some of which are home to large hotels with huge capacities. The best known include La Molina, in the province of Girona, and Baqueira-Beret, popular with the Spanish royal family, in the Val d'Aran (Lleida). For general information on skiing in Catalunya, contact the **Associaciò Catalana d'Estacions d'Esquí i Activitats de Muntanya** (ACEM), ☎ 93 416 01 94 or www.acem-cat.com

La Molina ski resort: ☎ 972 89 20 31 or www.lamolina.com

Baqueira-Beret ski resort: ☎ 973 64 44 55 or www.baqueira.es.

Descent from the Cross

The monastery, which has lent its name to the town, was founded in the 9C by Count Wilfred the Hairy, whose daughter Emma was the very first Abbess of this Benedictine monastery. However, it soon closed its doors to women and was subsequently occupied by male religious orders.

Iglesia★

Before entering, note the east end with its three storeys. The arches and columns with carved capitals recall those of southwest France.

Following an earthquake in 1428, local masons repaired the church by extending the nave, placing columns where previously the ambulatory had been. The decoration of the apses echoes that of the east end, the motifs on the richly carved capitals those of Oriental fabrics.

A magnificent **Descent from the Cross**★★, a group in polychrome wood carved in 1251, in which the figures are shown with great realism, presides over the central apse. In 1426 an unbroken host was discovered on the Christ figure's head, which has made the statue an object of particular veneration to this day.

Among the church's other treasures are the lovely 14C Gothic altarpiece in alabaster of Santa María la Blanca, the tomb of Miró de Tagamanent and the Gothic altarpiece of San Agustín.

Claustro★

These cloisters are simple and elegant; the sweeping arches and slender columns with capitals decorated with plant motifs replaced those of an earlier Romanesque cloister in the 14C. The **museum** houses an interesting collection of embroidered fabric.

Antiguo Palacio de la Abadía

Opposite the church on the square stands the 14C former Abbatial Palace. Note the small patio and its carved capitals.

Upon leaving the town towards Ripoll, admire the pretty **medieval bridge**★ spanning the Ter river.

Ripoll, A Centre of Learning in the Middle Ages

Ripoll owes its celebrity to the Benedictine monastery founded in the 9C by **Wilfred the Hairy**, Count of Barcelona. The monastery was the pantheon of the counts of Barcelona, Besalú and Cerdaña until the 12C.

The library at Ripoll was one of the richest in Christendom: not only did it possess texts of the scriptures and theological commentaries but also works by non-Christian authors such as Plutarch and Virgil as well as scientific treatises. The learning of Antiquity was restored by the Arabs, who treasured and disseminated the works of the Greeks which they discovered when they captured Alexandria and, with it, its incredible library. Ripoll, previously overrun by the Moors, became, under Abbot Oliba, a link between Arab and Christian civilisations, a centre of culture, ideas and exchange to which came such men as Brother Gerbert, the future Pope **Sylvester II** (999).

VALL DE RIBES

Ripoll★

Antiguo Monasterio de Santa María★

All that remains of the original monastery are the church portal and the cloisters.

Iglesia★

🕐 *Open 9am-1pm and 3-8pm; cloisters: 10am-1pm and 3-7pm.* 🕐 *Closed Mon, except in summer.* ⊙ *1.20€.* ☎ *972 70 02 43.*

The 9C monastery church soon had to be enlarged. In 1032, the famous Abbot Oliba consecrated another church, a more majestic edifice, and a jewel of early Roman-esque art. An earthquake in 1428, various remodellings over the ages and a fire in 1835, all destroyed the 11C building. It was rebuilt at the end of the 19C according to the original plan, with a nave and four aisles cut by a great transept on which seven apses abutted.

The south transept contains the 12C tomb of Ramón Berenguer III, the Great, while in the north is the funerary monument to Wilfred the Hairy.

Portada★★★

The 12C portal, built a century after the church, is weather worn in spite of the late-13C overhang, and the figures are difficult to decipher.

The portal design, comprising a series of horizontal registers, has been compared to that of a triumphal arch crowned by a large frieze. The carving may be seen to illustrate the glory of God and his people, victorious over his enemies (Passage of the Red Sea), a symbol of special significance at the time of the Reconquest.

The low reliefs cover not only the doorway but also the surround. The result is an exceptionally intricate series of carvings illustrating biblical personages and events.

Claustro★ (Cloisters)

Only the gallery abutting the church dates back to the 12C. It was the only gallery until the 14C when the others were added, their later date being betrayed only by the carving on some of the capitals.

▶ *Head N along the N 152.*

Ribes de Freser

This famous spa stands at the confluence of three rivers – the Freser, the Rigard and the Segadell – and is well known for its abundant waters and their healing properties. A rack railway takes you from Ribes to the Vall de Núria.

Vall de Núria★

The valley is surrounded by a rocky amphitheatre stretching from Puigmal to the Sierra de Torreneules.

The Virgin of Núria the patron saint of Pyrenean shepherds, is venerated in a sanctuary located in the upper part of the valley.

Getting to the Valley

🚎 The only **access** to the valley is by **rack railway** from Ribes de Freser, with a stop in Queralbs. Opened in 1931, this train service covers a 12.5km/8mi route and spans a height of 1 000m/3 300ft, offering wonderful **views**★★ of the mountain range, the streams and the ravines. The 45 min trip is accompanied by a recorded commentary in several languages. 🕐 *Call for hours.* 🕐 *Closed 2 Nov-2Jan.* ⊙ *6€ round trip (12.94€ rack railway and cable cars).* ☎ *972 73 20 20.*

LA CERDANYA★★ ②

From Vall de Núria to La Seu d'Urgell *72km/45mi –* 🕐 *about 2hr 30min*

The Cerdanya Basin, located between the Andorran massifs and the Sierra de Cadí, was formed by subsidence. It owes its fertility to the fact that it is watered by the River Segre, a tributary of the Ebro. Since 1659 Cerdanya has been divided: the northern part, known in French as La Cerdagne, was ceded to France under the Treaty of the Pyrenees.

In 1984 the opening of the **Túnel del Cadí**, which cuts across the mountainous barrier formed by the Sierra del Cadí and the Sierra de Moixeró, has facilitated access to Cerdanya from Manresa.

From Ribes de Freser to Puigcerdà, the road is cut into the cliff face for almost its entire length up to the Collado de Toses, commanding impressive **views**★ of the Segre and its luxuriant slopes.

La Molina

This is one of Catalunya's most important ski resorts. The nearby village of Alp is a popular place for tourists, both in winter and in summer.

▷ *Leaving La Molina, the N 152 joins up with the E 09, which follows an upward course, offering a sweeping view of the vast Cerdanya plain.*

Puigcerdà

The capital of Cerdanya, which developed on a terrace overlooking the River Segre, is one of the most popular holiday resorts of the Pyrenees. Its old-fashioned shops, ancient streets and balconied buildings have retained all of their picturesque charm. The lofty, early-20C mansions are hidden beside the artificial lake. The **bell tower**★, serving as the town's symbol and landmark, is all that remains of the Gothic Iglesia de Santa María.

Llívia

The existence of this small 12km2/5sq mi Spanish enclave in France, 6km/4mi from Puigcerdà, can be ascribed to an administrative subtlety. Under the Treaty of the Pyrenees, France was to be granted the Roussillon area as well as 33 villages from Cerdanya. Since Llívia was considered to be a town, it did not qualify and was to remain part of Spanish territory.

Llívia features charming narrow streets, the ruins of a medieval castle, perched on a mound overlooking the town, and several old towers. Among its many interesting exhibits, the **Museu Municipal** contains a famous chemist's shop known as the **Farmacia de Llívia**★, said to be one of the oldest in Europe. ◷ *Open 10am-4.30pm Oct-Mar (6pm Apr-Jun, 7pm Jul-Sep); Sun and public hols, 10am-2pm. ◷ Closed Mon.* ☞ *1€. ☎ 972 89 63 13.*

▷ *Return to Puigcerdà and take the N 260 towards La Seu d'Urgell.*

Bellver de Cerdanya★

Poised on a rocky crag dominating the Vall del Segre, Bellver de Cerdanya has a fine main square with beautiful balconied stone houses and wooden porches.

La Seu d'Urgell/Seo de Urgel★

This city of prince-archbishops stands in peaceful countryside where the Valira, which rises in the mountains of Andorra, joins the Segre River.

Catedral de Santa Maria★★

◷ *Open 10am-1pm and 4-6pm (7pm Jun-Sep); Sun and public hols, 10am-1pm. ☞ 1€. ☎ 973 35 32 42.*

The cathedral, whose construction was started in the 12C, shows strong Lombard influence. The central section of the west face, with its pediment crowned by a small campanile, is typically Italian

Inside, the elevation is spectacular, the nave rising on cruciform pillars, surrounded, in the French style, by engaged columns. A most effective twin arched gallery decorates the east transept wall and then reappears outside to circle the apse.

Claustro★

The cloisters are 13C, although the east gallery had to be rebuilt in 1603. The granite capitals illustrating human figures and animals were carved with consummate artistry and humour by masons from the Roussillon. The Santa Maria door (southeast corner) opens into the 11C **Iglesia de Sant Miquel**★, the only remaining building of those constructed by St Ermangol.

Museo Diocesano★

The Diocesan Museum has a wonderful collection of works of art dating from the 10C to the 18C. The most precious work is a beautifully illuminated 11C **Beatus**★★, one of the best preserved copies of St John's Commentary on the Apocalypse written in the 8C by the priest, Beatus of Liébana.

Of note also are an interesting **papyrus**★ belonging to Pope Sylvester II, the 13C enamelled Romanesque crucifix from the Monasterio de Silos which shows a Byzantine influence, the 14C **Abella de la Conca**★ altarpiece by Pere Serra also with a Byzantine influence as well as characteristics from the Siena School, and the 14C *St Bartholomew Altarpiece* in coloured stone which illustrates scenes with great realism. The crypt contains church plate and the 18C funerary urn of St Ermangol. ◷ *Open*

Oct-May, noon-1pm; Sun and public hols, 11am-1pm; Jul-Sep, 10am-1pm and 4-6pm; Sat-Sun and public hols, 11am-1pm. 🎫 *2.10€.* ☎ *973 35 32 42.*

VALL DEL SEGRE★ ③

From La Seu d'Urgell to Tremp *73km/45mi –* 🕐 *allow 3hr*

At the point where it flows into the Valira, the River Segre forms a huge basin sheltered by mountains. The massif is cut across by many side valleys, all quite different from each other.

▶ *Take the N 260 towards Organyà.*

Garganta de Tresponts★★

As it flows past, the Segre winds its way through dark-coloured rocks (puzolana) and green pastures. Further downstream the topography changes: the limestone rocks of Ares and Montsec de Tost offer a typically Pyrenean landscape extending down to a small cultivated basin, where the river disappears.

Coll de Nargó

This typical Pyrenean hamlet has one of the most splendid Romanesque churches in Catalunya, dating back to the 11C: **Sant Climent**★ has a single nave and a pretty apse adorned with Lombard bands. Its sober **bell tower**★ is pre-Romanesque.

Embalse de Oliana★

The dam, which looks more like a wide river, is surrounded by grey rocks with lively waterfalls in spring. From the road the sight is quite spectacular.

Collado de Bòixols Road★★

Between the Coll de Nargó and Tremp, the L 511 follows a series of canyons which it overlooks for the whole stretch, either from slopes clad in pine and holm oak, or barren hillsides. Further on, the road proceeds up the slope, halfway between the river and the yellow and pink crests, offering lovely views and **landscapes**, especially from the Collado de Bòixols.

Then the road leads into a wide U-shaped valley, where terraced cultivation extends to the foot of the glacial ridge of Bòixols, onto which cling the church and a few nearby houses. The road continues to descend the valley until it eventually merges into the Conca de Tremp.

VALL DEL NOGUERA PALLARESA ④

From Tremp to Llavorsí *143km/89mi –* 🕐 *allow one day*

Pallars is situated in the uppermost region of the Catalan Pyrenees, where the highest summit is Pica d'Estats (3 145m/10 318ft). It is divided into two different areas: to the north, **Pallars Sobirà**, lying at the heart of the Pyrenees; to the south, **Pallars Jussà**, incorporating the vast pre-Pyrenean zone formed by Conca de Tremp. The road follows the bed of the Noguera Pallaresa. After La Pobla de Segur, it cuts across a limestone landscape of remarkable uniformity.

Tremp

Located in the centre of the Conca de Tremp – a huge basin with lush Mediterranean vegetation and crops – the village has retained its old quarter and three towers from the former walls. The **Iglesia de Santa María**★ houses an astonishing 2m/6.5ft high Gothic statue in polychrome wood: **Santa María de Valldeflors**★ (14C). The municipality of Tremp has its own reservoir, the **pantano de Sant Antoni**★.

▶ *The C 13 follows the river course and spans the pantano de Sant Antoni.*

La Pobla de Segur

This popular tourist resort has been dubbed the gateway to the Pyrenees as it is the only means of access to the Valle de Arán, Alta Ribagorça and Pallars Sobirà.

Vall Fosca★

Hemmed in by high peaks, this valley is dotted with delightful hamlets, each with its Romanesque church: **Torre de Cabdella, Espui** and **Cabdella**. In the upper part of the valley, you can tour a large lake area, whose main attraction is the **lago Gento**.

▶ *Return to La Pobla de Segur and proceed upwards along the N 260.*

Desfiladero de Collegats★★

Eroded by the torrent waters, the red, grey and ochre limestone rocks have taken on the appearance of spectacularly steep cliffs. Note the **Roca de l'Argenteria**★, a stalactite-shaped rock formation near the Gerri de la Sal.

Sort

The resort has become famous throughout Europe because of its wild waters and the canoeing events that are held on this stretch of the Noguera Pallaresa.

▶ *When you reach Rialp, turn left towards Llessui.*

Vall de Llessui★★

The road winds its way up to the northwest, taking you through a steep granite landscape featuring a great many ravines.

UPPER VALLEY OF THE NOGUERA PALLARESA★ 5

From Llavorsí to Puerto de la Bonaigua

▶ *105km/65mi –* 🕓 *allow half a day*

The mountain summits dominate a wild, secluded landscape.

Llavorsí

It lies at the confluence of the three main basins of the upper valley of the Noguera Pallaresa: Aneu, Cardós and Ferrera.

▶ *Take the L 504 and proceed N.*

Vall de Cardós★

The Noguera de Cardós constitutes the central axis of this valley. The capital Ribera de Cardós presents a 12C Romanesque church with a belfry similar to those found in the Valle de Boí.

▶ *Return to Llavorsí and take the C 13 towards Baqueira.*

Vall d'Aneu★★

The Noguera Pallaresa crosses the valley with, on its left, the underlying valley of **Espot**, a picturesque village which has developed near the banks of a mountain stream. It is also the gateway to the Pallars section of the **Parc Nacional d'Aigüestortes i Estany de Sant Maurici**★★ (🕓 *see Parc Nacional d'AIGÜESTORTES I ESTANY DE SANT MAURICI).*

Beyond Esterri d'Aneu the road cuts across a breathtaking landscape, dotted with Romanesque churches such as the **Iglesia de Sant Joan d'Isil**★, glimpsed between high summits, and follows a corniche up to **puerto de la Bonaigua** (2 072m/6 799ft), circled by many peaks. On the left lies a magnificent glacial cirque.

LA VALL D'ARÁN★★ 6

From Puerto de la Bonaigua de Bòssost *45km/28mi –* 🕓 *allow half a day*

The **Arán Valley**, situated in the north-west tip of the Catalan Pyrenees, occupies the upper valley of the Garonne river. Because of its Atlantic climate, it is more humid and less sunny than the southfacing valleys of the Pyrenean range.

Although the area has been subject to Spanish rule since the Middle Ages (13C), its isolated location has helped it to preserve its local traditions and language (*aranes* is a variation of the *langue d'oc*, or old southern French). Surrounded by mountains reaching an altitude of 3 000m/9 850ft, communications between the Arán Valley and neighbouring localities were difficult and for a long time passes like the puerto de la Bonaigua or the Bòssost Portilhon were their only link with the outside world. The opening of the Vielha Tunnel in 1948 put an end to this state of seclusion.

Today, pastures have been replaced by cultivated fields and much time and money have been devoted to the exploitation of local forests, rivers and mines. However, such developments have in no way jeopardised the beauty of this natural site: the green meadows of the valley are dotted with the grey slate roofs of its 39 villages, often clustered around a Romanesque church. In recent years the region has seen the creation of several ski resorts.

Baqueira Beret

This Pyrenean ski resort, sloping from 1 500m/4 900ft up to 2 510m/8 230ft, offers excellent sporting facilities, lodging and services.

Salardú★

Salardú is a charming village with granite and slate houses gathered around the **Iglesia de Sant Andreu★** (12C-13C), whose interior contains some interesting 16C **Gothic paintings★★** and a fine 12C **Christ in Majesty★★**, a stylised wooden statue 65cm/25in high displaying remarkable anatomical precision. Note the slender belfry, of octagonal design (15C).

Arties★

It lies at the confluence of the Garonne and Valarties rivers. The Romanesque church has an apse decorated with painted scenes illustrating the Last Judgement, Heaven and Hell.

Escunhau

The **Iglesia de San Pedro★** has preserved a fine 12C **portal★★** bearing an expressive Christ and some unusual capitals decorated with human faces.

Betrén

The main building of interest in this popular village is the **Iglesia de San Esteve★**, built during the period of transition from Romanesque to Gothic. Note the archivolts on the **portal★★**, decorated with human faces showing great realism and alluding to the Last Judgement and the Resurrection.

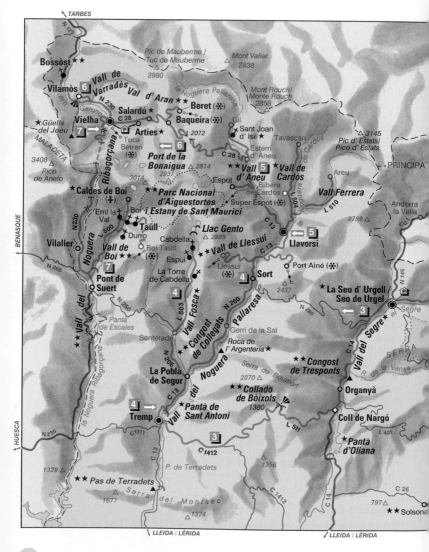

Vielha

At an altitude of 971m/3 186ft, the capital of the Arán Valley is a large holiday resort laid out along the banks of the Garonne. The old part of town still features many pretty houses dating from the 16C and 17C. Note the **Iglesia Parroquial de Sant Miquèu**★, a parish church with a fine 14C octagonal bell tower and a 13C Gothic doorway representing the Last Judgement. The interior contains the splendid **Cristo de Mijaran**★, a famous fragment belonging to a 12C Descent from the Cross, the features of which are carved with painstaking precision. The **Musèu dera Val D'Aran** provides an introduction to the culture of the valley. (🕐 *Open 5-8pm; Jul-Sep, 10am-1pm and 5-8pm; Sat, 10am-1pm and 5-8pm; Sun, 10am-1pm.* 🕐 *Closed Mon.* ⌖ *2€.* ☎ *973 64 18 15).*
The Parador del Valle de Arán is a belvedere above Vielha commanding a superb **view**: in the distance lies the cirque closing off the Arán Valley to the south and, on the right, looms the formidable barrier of the Maladeta massif.

Bossòst

16km/10mi N of Vielha. The **Iglesia de la Purificació de Maria**★★ is probably the area's most typical example of Romanesque architecture (12C). Its three naves are separated by sturdy columns which support the barrel vaulting for the massive roof. Its three apses are adorned with Lombard bands and the pretty, colourful north **doorway** features archaic relief work in its tympanum, depicting the Creator surrounded by the Sun, the Moon and symbols of the Evangelists.

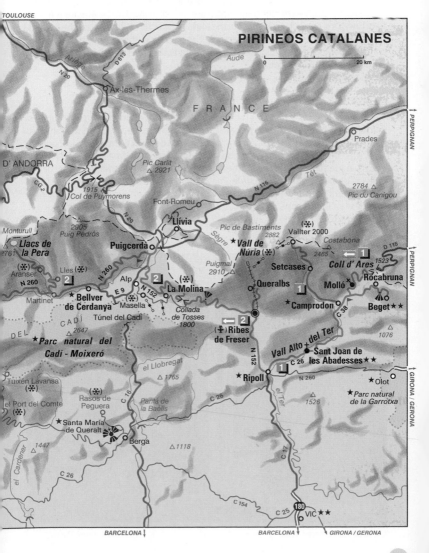

VALL DEL NOGUERA RIBAGORÇANA★★ [7]

From Vielha to Caldes de Boí *54km/34mi –* ⏱ *about 3hr*

The Upper Ribagorça region has a very abrupt landscape, with summits exceeding 3 000m/10 000ft, vast glacial cirques, pretty lake areas and steep valleys with small villages nestling below.

The vielha tunnel was constructed through the Maladeta massif in 1948.

Vilaller

Poised on a rocky outcrop, the village is dominated by the octagonal belfry of its 18C Baroque church, the Iglesia de Sant Climent.

El Pont de Suert

The locality is dotted all over with attractive hamlets – **Castelló de Tor, Casòs, Malpàs** – located in a secluded setting that has kept its rustic appearance and charm.

▶ *Take the road that climbs up towards Caldes de Boí.*

Vall de Boí★★

Watered by the Noguera de Tor and the Sant Nicolau, this valley is renowned for its cluster of Lombard **Romanesque churches** (11C-12C), the finest in the Pyrenees. Characterised by slate roofing and irregular masonry, they stand out for their pure, sober lines and for the wall frescoes which once decorated them *(several reproductions can be admired in the churches)* and which are now displayed in the **Museu d'Art de Catalunya** (👁 *see BARCELONA*). Note the highly distinctive silhouette of the belfries, separate but nonetheless resting against the nave, and their ornamentation with Lombard bands. Of particular interest are Santa Eulàlia at Erill la Vall, La Nativitat at Durro and Sant Joan at Boí.

▶ *Beyond Erill la Vall turn right onto a narrow road leading to Boí.*

Taüll★

This typical mountain village is famous for the frescoes adorning its two churches. Considered to be unique masterpieces of Romanesque art, they are currently exhibited in Barcelona's Museu d'Art de Catalunya. The **Iglesia de Sant Climent**★★, just outside Taüll, was consecrated on 10 December 1123, only one day before Santa María (👁 *see below*). In the southeast corner of the sanctuary stands the slender six-storey belfry, built in Lombard Romanesque style. The interior used to be entirely decorated with frescoes dating from the same period. A replica of the famous Pantocrator of Taüll can be seen in the apse. (🕐 *Open 10.30am-2pm and 4-7pm (8pm Jun-Sep).* ⊘ *1€.* ☏ *973 69 40 00).*

Iglesia de Sant Climent, Taüll

With its labyrinthine streets, stone houses and wooden balconies, the village is clustered around the **Iglesia de Santa Maria**★, a Romanesque church with three naves separated by cylindrical pillars.

▶ *Return to the road leading to Caldes de Boí.*

Parc Nacional d'Aigüestortes i Estany de Sant Maurici★★

Access by the road linking Boí to Caldes de Boí (*(& see Parc Nacional d'AIGÜESTORTES I ESTANY DE SANT MAURICI).*

Caldes de Boí★

Situated at an altitude of 1 550m/5 084ft, Caldes de Boí is an important thermal spa with 37 springs spurting out water at temperatures between 24ºC and 56ºC (75ºF to 133ºF). In the close vicinity lies **Boí-Taüll**, a satellite resort designed for downhill skiing.

Plasencia★

POPULATION: 36 826

MICHELIN MAP 576 L 11 – EXTREMADURA (CÁCERES).

The old quarter of this tranquil provincial town is home to a number of interesting Renaissance buildings such as the new cathedral. Between February and July the nests of the numerous storks that migrate here are an attractive addition to Plasencia's rooftops and towers.

Location

The town stands on the banks of the River Jerte, at the point where the last granite foothills of the Sierra de Gredos meet the Extremadura plain. ▯ *Plaza de la Catedral, 10600 Plasencia, ☎ 927 42 38 43.*

& *Neighbouring sights are described in the following chapters: CÁCERES (85km/53mi SW), TRUJILLO (83km/52mi SE) and La ALBERCA (117km/73mi N).*

Walking About

BARRIO VIEJO (OLD QUARTER)

The streets around the cathedral and plaza Mayor, well worth a walk, are lined by noble façades and houses with wrought-iron balconies.

Catedral★

The cathedral is in fact two buildings from different periods. A Romanesque-Gothic edifice was built in the 13C and 14C. At the end of the 15C, its east end was demolished and a new cathedral with a bolder architectural design was begun. Only the chancel and transept were completed. Enter the cathedral by the north door which has a rich Plateresque decoration. A door left of the *coro* opens into the **old cathedral** (now the parish church of Santa María). The cloisters have pointed arches and Romanesque capitals while the chapter house is covered by a fine dome on squinches which is disguised outside by a pyramid-shaped belfry covered in tiles. The shortened nave houses a museum of religious art.

Inside the **Catedral Nueva** (New Cathedral), the tall pillars and slender ribs extending into network vaulting illustrate the mastery of the famous architects responsible for the design: Juan de Java, Diego de Siloé and Alonso de Covarrubias.

The **altarpiece**★ is decorated with statues by the 17C sculptor Gregorio Fernández; the **choir stalls**★ were carved in 1520 by Rodrigo Alemán – look on the backs and misericords of the lower row for scenes, on the right, from the Old Testament, and on the left, of everyday life.

Start from plaza de la Catedral and leaving on your right the **Casa del Deán** (Deanery) with its unusual corner window, and the **Casa del Dr Trujillo**, now the Law Courts (Palacio de Justicia), make for the Gothic **Iglesia de San Nicolás**, a church which faces the beautiful façade of the **Casa de las Dos Torres** (House with Two Towers).

Continue straight ahead to the **Palacio Mirabel**. This palace, flanked by a massive tower, contains a fine two-tiered patio and the Museo de Caza (Hunting Museum). A passage beneath the palace *(door on right-hand side)* leads to the **calle Sancho Polo** and the more popular quarter near the ramparts where there are stepped alleys, white-walled houses and washing hanging from the windows – a scene typical of villages further south. Turn right for **plaza Mayor,** an asymmetrical square surrounded by porticoes, which is the bustling town centre.

Excursions

La Vera

To the E of Plasencia along the EX 203. This fertile valley is given over to tobacco grow-ing and market-gardening. Villages like **Cuacos de Yuste** where Don Juan of Austria grew up, have managed to preserve their picturesque character. The 15C castle in **Jarandilla de la Vera** has been converted into a parador.

Monasterio de Yuste★

1.8km/1mi from Cuacos de Yuste. ◥ *Guided tours (30min), 9.30am-12.30pm and 3-6pm (3.30-6.30pm Apr-Oct).* ◉ *2.50€, no charge Wed morning.* ☎ *927 17 21 30.*

In 1556, when Emperor **Charles V** had grown weary of power, he abdicated and retired to this modest Hieronymite monastery. He died on 21 September 1558. Even today, the serene atmosphere, particularly of the beautiful surrounding countryside, makes one understand why the great emperor chose this retreat in which to pass his last years.

The monastery which was devastated during the War of Independence and during the period following the passing of Mendizábal's decrees, has been partially restored. Of Charles V's small palace one sees the dining hall, the royal bedroom built to adjoin the chapel so that the emperor could hear Mass without having to rise, the Gothic church and, lastly, the two fine cloisters, one Gothic, the other Plateresque.

Parque Natural de Monfragüe

25km/16mi S along the EX 208. ▣ *Centro de Información del Parque (Park Information Centre) in Villareal de San Carlos. Various itineraries on foot or by car.* ◷ *Open 9am-2.30pm and 3.30-6.30pm; in summer, 9am-2.30pm and 4.30-7.30pm.* ◷ *Closed 1 Jan and 25 Dec.* ☎ *927 19 91 34.*

Some parts of the hills flanking the Tajo river at its confluence with the Tiétar are situated within the park (17 842ha/44 089 acres). The ecological importance of these areas is determined by their typically Mediterranean flora (rockrose, cork oak, gall oak, lavender, arbutus etc); and their rich and varied fauna, with, in this park, a large number of protected species (black and tawny vultures, imperial eagles, Iberian lynx, mongooses etc).

Coria

42km/26mi W. ▶ *Take the N 630 S and after 7km/4.5mi turn right onto the EX 108.*

This town overlooking the Alagón Valley has preserved its Roman walls and gateways; these were subsequently rebuilt in the Middle Ages.

Catedral★

The cathedral, a Gothic edifice embellished with elegant Plateresque decoration in the 16C, is crowned with a Baroque tower and has a sculptured frieze along the top of its walls.

Inside, the tall, single aisle has vaulting adorned with lierne and tierceron ribs which are typical of the region. Note the 18C altarpiece and, in the coro, the wrought-iron grilles and the Gothic choir stalls.

Pontevedra★

POPULATION: 75 148

MICHELIN MAP 571 E 4 – LOCAL MAP SEE RÍAS BAJAS

Pontevedra is a quiet provincial town where life continues in an ordered and unhurried fashion. The architecture here is a pleasant mix of fine buildings, plain arcades, cobbled streets, squares embellished with the occasional stone cross, and attractive parks and gardens. The town's bars and cafés, their outdoor terraces teeming in summer, offer a cosy retreat in the cool of winter.

Location

Pontevedra is situated at the head of the estuary (ría) of the same name, and is linked by motorway with Vigo (27km/17mi S) and Santiago de Compostela (57km/35mi N). The N 541 heads inland through attractive countryside to Orense/Ourense (100km/62mi SE). ▌ *Gutiérrez Mellado 1 bajo, 36001 Pontevedra, ☎ 986 85 08 14.*

◔ *Neighbouring sights are described in the following chapters: RÍAS BAJAS and SAN-TIAGO DE COMPOSTELA.*

Special Features

CASCO ANTIGUO★ (OLD QUARTER)
🕐 *Allow 1hr 30min*

In spite of extensive development, the new town has respected the old, a kernel tucked into the area between calles Michelena, del Arzobispo Malvar and Cobián, and the river, where life continues peacefully in the shadow of glazed house fronts, squares occasionally adorned with a Calvary **(plaza de la Leña; del Teucro; de Mugártegui)** and streets near the Lérez **(Pedreira, Real, San Nicolás)**. The town comes to life in **calle Sarmiento** on market days.

> **An Important Port**
>
> Pontevedra was once a busy port lying sheltered at the end of its *ría*; fishermen, merchants, overseas traders lived there as did sailors and explorers such as **Pedro Sarmiento**, skilled navigator of the 16C, wise cosmographer and author of *Voyage to the Magellan Straits.* The Lérez delta, however, silted up so that by the 18C Pontevedra had begun to decline and the new port at Marín was taking its place.

Plaza de la Leña★

This is a delightful square with its asymmetrical shape, its Calvary and the beautiful façades that surround it. Two 18C mansions on the square have been converted into a museum.

Plaza de la Leña

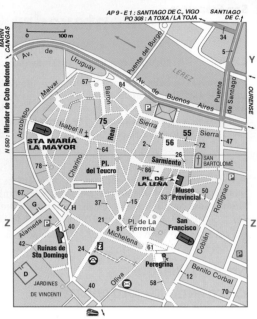

Museo Provincial

🕐 *Open 10am-1.30pm and 4.30-8pm; Jun-Sep, 10am-2.15pm and 5-8.45pm; Sun and public hols, 11am-2pm.* 🕐 *Closed Mon, 1 and 6 Jan and 25 Dec.* ∞ *1.20€, no charge for citizens of the European Union.* ☎ *986 85 14 55.*

The ground floor of the museum contains prehistoric collections, in particular the **Celtic treasures**★ from A Golada and Caldas de Reis which date from the Bronze Age, and that of Foxados from the 2C and 1C BC, as well as the pre-1900 silverware collection of Fernández de la Mora y Mon, containing over 600 hand-worked pieces from a number of countries. The first floor, which is dedicated to paintings, has several 15C Aragonese Primitives on display.

The second mansion includes a reconstruction of a stateroom from the Numancia, the frigate captained by Admiral Méndez Núñez during the disastrous Battle of Callao (Peru's chief sea port) in 1866. When told that it was folly to attack a port so well defended, the admiral replied, "Spain prefers honour without ships to ships without honour." On the museum's upper floor are an interesting antique kitchen and 19C Sargadelos ceramics. A large collection of interesting trinkets is also on display in this building.

Iglesia de Santa María la Mayor★

🕐 *Open 10am-1pm and 5-9pm; no visits during religious services.* ☎ *986 86 61 85.*

Old alleyways and gardens surround this delightful Plateresque church which was built by the mariner's guild in the fishermen's quarter between approximately the late 1400s and 1570. The **west front**★ is carved like an altarpiece, divided into separate superimposed registers on which are reliefs of the Dormition and Assumption of the Virgin and the Trinity. At the summit is the Crucifixion at the centre of an openwork coping finely carved with oarsmen and fishermen hauling in their nets. A sculpture of St Jerome can be seen to one side.

The **interior** is a generally successful mingling of Gothic (notched arches), Isabelline (slender cabled columns) and Renaissance (ribbed vaulting) styles. The back of the west façade is covered in naive low reliefs of scenes from Genesis (Adam and Eve, Noah's Ark) and the New Testament.

San Francisco

The church's simply styled Gothic façade looks onto the gardens of plaza de la Herrería. The interior features timber vaulting.

Capilla de la Peregrina (Pilgrim's Chapel)

🕐 *Open 8am-1pm and 4.30-9pm.* ☎ *986 85 68 85.*

This small church, with its scallop-shaped floor plan and convex façade, dates from the end of the 18C. Its interior contains a statue of the patron saint of Pontevedra.

Ruinas de Santo Domingo (Santo Domingo Ruins)

🕐 *Open 10.15am-1.30pm and 5-8.30pm; Oct-May, by prior arrangement.* 🕐 *Closed Sat-Sun and public hols.* 🎟 *No charge.* ☎ *986 85 14 55.*

These ruins are a perfect example of medieval romanticism. The church's Gothic east end still remains, its tall bays overgrown with ivy. Arranged inside is a lapidary museum of Roman steles, Galician coats of arms and tombs, in particular, tombs of craftsmen showing the tools they used, and tombs of noblemen.

> **Touring Tip**
>
> **CAFETERÍA CARABELA**
>
> This coffee house on the lively Plaça de la Ferrería, with its attractive view of both the Iglesia de San Francisco and the Capilla de la Peregrina, is a pleasant place for a drink or a bite to eat.

Excursions

Mirador Coto Redondo★★

14km/9mi S on the N 550. Take the Vigo road; after 6km/4mi, turn right towards the Lago Castiñeiras and then follow the signposts. The hill climb through pine and eucalyptus woods, with occasional good views, is pleasant. The **panorama**★★ from this viewpoint extends over both the Pontevedra and Vigo *rías*.

Priego de Córdoba★★

POPULATION: 22 196

MICHELIN MAP 578 T 17 – ANDALUCÍA (CÓRDOBA).

This lovely town, the capital of Cordoban Baroque, reached its economic and artistic zenith in the 18C as a result of the silk industry. With its impressive fountains, magnificent churches and delightful old Moorish quarter, the town comes as a pleasant surprise in this isolated part of Andalucía.

Location

Priego sits on a plain at the heart of the Subbética Cordobesa mountain range, away from the major road and rail links. ▯ *Río 33, 14800 Priego de Córdoba, ☎ 957 70 06 25.*

  Neighbouring sights are described in the following chapters: JAÉN (67km/42mi NE), GRANADA (79km/49mi SE) and ANTEQUERA (85km/53m SW).

Worth a Visit

Fuentes del Rey y de la Salud★★ (Fountains of the King and of Health)

At the end of calle del Río. The sight created by these two fountains, the most well-known in the town, is a surprising one. The older, the **Fuente de la Salud**, is a Mannerist frontispiece built in the 16C. Next to it is the lavish **Fuente del Rey** which was completed at the beginning of the 19C. Both the dimensions and the richness of its design evoke the gardens of a Baroque palace. It has a total of 139 jets spouting water from the mouth of the same number of masks. The central display represents Neptune's chariot and Amphitrite.

Barrio de la Villa★★

This charming quarter, dating back to medieval and Moorish times, has narrow, winding streets and flower-decked whitewashed houses.

El Adarve★

This delightful viewpoint which looks out onto the Subbética mountain range encircles the Barrio de la Villa to the north.

Parroquia de la Asunción★ (Parish Church of the Assumption)

At the end of paseo del Abad Palomino. 🕔 *Visits by prior arrangement, 10.30am-1.30pm and 4-7pm; in summer, 11am-2pm and 5.30-8pm; no visits during religious services.* 🕔 *Closed Sun afternoon and Mon.* ☎ 606 17 16 53.

This 16C church was remodelled in Baroque style in the 18C. The presbytery is dominated by an impressive carved and painted 16C Mannerist-style **altarpiece**.

El Sagrario★★

The chapel, which opens on to the Nave del Evangelio, is a masterpiece of Andalucían Baroque. It comprises an antechamber leading into an octagonal space surrounded by an ambulatory. Light plays an important part in the effect of the scene; intensified by the whiteness of the walls and ceiling, it shimmers over the extensive and lavish **yeserías**★★★ (plasterwork decoration), creating a magical atmosphere. In spite of this excessive adornment, the overall effect is one of delicacy.

From the paseo del Abad Palomino the remains of the imposing Moorish **fortress**, subsequently modified in the 13C and 14C, are visible.

Priego is embellished with numerous churches: the charming Rococo-style **Iglesia de las Angustias**; the **Aurora**, with its fine portal; and **San Pedro**, adorned with a number of interesting statues. Also noteworthy amid this Baroque splendour is the 16C **royal abattoir** (Carnicerías Reales), built along classical lines and now used as an exhibition centre.

Puebla de Sanabria

POPULATION: 1 969

MICHELIN MAP 575 F 10 – CASTILLA Y LEÓN (ZAMORA).

Puebla de Sanabria is an attractive mountain village near the Portuguese border, a short distance from Galicia and the province of León. Its white-walled houses with tile-stone roofs and the occasional emblazoned façade are dominated by the 15C castle of the Count of Benavente. The church is a late-12C, reddish granite construction with a west door simply outlined with a large bead motif. The view from the castle esplanade takes in the Río Tera and part of the lake.

Location

Puebla de Sanabria stands alongside the A 52 motorway, close to the Embalse de Cernadilla (reservoir) and the Lago de Sanabria (lake). ⓘ *Plaza Mayor, 49300 Puebla de Sanabria, ☎ 980 62 00 02.*

ⓘ *Neighbouring sights are described in the following chapters: ZAMORA (110km/69mi SE) and The WAY OF ST JAMES (to the N).*

Worth a Visit

Valle de Sanabria

19km/12mi NW. Follow the lake road, then turn right after 14km/9mi; after a further 6km/4mi turn left. This valley of glacial origin, now a nature reserve, was hollowed out at the foot of the Sierras de Cabrera Baja and Segundera. It is a delightful area, well-known for its hunting and fishing, that owes much of its appeal to the many streams running through the light bush vegetation.

Lago de Sanabria

Sanabria, the largest glacial lake in Spain, lies at an altitude of 1 028m/3 373ft. It is used for all types of water sports, and for salmon-trout fishing.

San Martín de Castañeda

There are attractive **views**★ of the rushing stream of the Tera and the mountain-encircled lake all the way to this Galician-looking village. The first distinguishable sight of it is the east end of its noble 11C Romanesque **church**.

Rías Altas★

MICHELIN MAP 571 A 5-7, B 4-8, C 2-5, D 2 –

GALICIA (LUGO, A CORUÑA/LA CORUÑA).

Although indented by *rías* – inlets made by the Atlantic into the coastline, like the sea lochs of Scotland or the *fjords* of Norway – the northern coast of Galicia from Ribadeo to Cabo Finisterre is generally low-lying. The rocks, bare and smooth, the granite houses with slate roofs, give the impression that the climate must be grim – yet holidaymakers arrive with the fine season, attracted by the scenery and small sandy creeks. Galicia's *rías* are described below from east to west.

Location

This series of inlets, best approached from either A Coruña/La Coruña or Lugo, is situated in the far northwest corner of the Iberian Peninsula. ⓘ *Ferrol: Plaza Camilo José Cela, 15403 Coruña, ☎ 981 31 11 79; Foz: Avenida de Lugo 1, 27280 Lugo, ☎ 982 14 06 75; Mondoñedo: Plaza de la Catedral 34, 27740 Lugo, ☎ 982 50 71 77; Ribadeo: Plaza de España, 27700, ☎ 982 12 86 89; Viveiro: Avenida de Ramón Canosa, 27850 Lugo, ☎ 982 56 08 79.*

ⓘ *Neighbouring sights are described in the following chapters: RÍAS BAJAS, A CORUÑA/La CORUÑA, COSTA VERDE and LUGO.*

Special Features

RÍAS ALTAS

The Rías Altas comprise a succession of deep inlets backed by thick forests of pine and eucalyptus.

Ría de Ribadeo

(⚅ *See also under COSTA VERDE*(). The ría de Ribadeo is formed by the estuary of the Eo. After a headlong course, the River Eo, forming the border between Galicia and Asturias, slackens its pace to wind gently between the wide green banks of its lower valley. There is a beautiful **view**★ up the estuary from the bridge across the mouth of the river.

The old port of **Ribadeo** is now an important regional centre and summer resort.

Ría de Foz

Foz, at the mouth of its ría, is a small port with a coastal fishing fleet. Its two good Atlantic beaches are popular in summer.

Iglesia de San Martín de Mondoñedo

5km/3mi W. ▶ *Take the Mondoñedo road, then immediately turn right.* 🕐 *Open 11am-1pm and 4-8pm.* ☎ *982 14 06 75.*

Standing almost alone on a height is the church, once part of a monastery of ancient foundation and an episcopal seat until 1112 when this was transferred to Mondoñedo. The style of the church is archaic and, most unusually in this region, shows no sign of Compostelan influence. The east end, decorated with Lombard bands, is supported by massive buttresses; inside, the transept **capitals**★ are naively carved and rich in anecdotal detail: the one illustrating the parable of the rich man who allows Lazarus to die of hunger, shows the table overflowing with food while a dog beneath it is licking Lazarus's feet as he lies stretched out on the ground. The capitals, believed to date from the 10C, bear Visigothic influence in the plant motifs.

Mondoñedo

23km/14mi SW along the N 634. Mondoñedo rises out of the hollow of a lush, well cultivated valley. The streets of the old town are lined with stylish white-walled houses ornamented with armorial bearings and wrought-iron balconies. The cathedral square is particularly delightful with its arcades and solanas (glassed-in galleries).

The immense façade of the **cathedral**★ combines the Gothic grace of the three large portal arches and the rose window, all dating from the 13C, with the grandiose Baroque style of the towers added in the 18C.

On the sober **interior**, transitional Romanesque in style, the most noteworthy features include a series of late-14C frescoes one above the other (below the extraordinary 1710 organ) illustrating the Massacre of the Innocents and the Life of St Peter; the Rococo retable at the high altar; and a polychrome wood statue of the Virgin in the south ambulatory, known as the English Virgin, as the statue was brought from St Paul's, London, to Mondoñedo in the 16C. Off the south aisle is the burial niche of Bishop Juan Muñoz who gave the church its present façade.

The classical **cloisters** were added in the 17C.

Ría de Viveiro

Sea, countryside and mountain combine in a varied landscape, a coastline of white sand beaches and lofty headlands sung by **Nicomedes Pastor Díaz**, 19C politician and poet.

All **Viveiro** retains of its town walls is the Puerta de Carlos V (Charles V Gateway), emblazoned with the emperor's arms. In the summer months the port is transformed into a holiday resort. On the 4th Sunday in August, visitors from all over Galicia come for the local Naseiro Romería festival.

Ría de Santa María de Ortigueira

The *ría* is deep and surrounded by green hills while **Ortigueira** port has quays bordered by well-kept gardens.

Ría de Cedeira

A small, deeply enclosed ría with beautiful beaches. The road gives good **views** of **Cedeira** (summer resort) and the surrounding countryside.

Ría de Ferrol

The *ría* forms a magnificent natural harbour entered by way of a narrow 6km/4mi channel guarded by two forts. In the 18C, on account of its exceptional site and favourable position for trade with America, King Ferdinand VI and King Charles III decided to make the port of Ferrol a naval base. The symmetry of the town plan evident in the old quarter dates from the same period.

Ferrol today is one of Spain's major naval bases and is also a dockyard.

Betanzos★

Betanzos, a one-time port which has now silted up as a result of alluvium from the Mandeo river, stands at the end of the *ría* of the same name. Built on a hill, its old quarter has retained substantial reminders of its former prosperity in the form of three richly ornamented Gothic churches and its steep streets and old houses with glassed-in balconies.

Iglesia de Santa María del Azogue★

🕐 *Open 10.30am-2pm and 4-7.30pm; no visits during religious services.* ☎ *981 77 07 02.*

The name of the 14C-15C church comes from *suk* or market-place in Arabic. The gracefully asymmetrical façade is given character by a projecting central bay pierced by a rose window and a portal with sculptured covings. Niches on either side contain archaic statues of the Virgin and the Archangel Gabriel, symbolising the Annunciation. Inside, three aisles of equal height, beneath a single timber roof, create an effect of spaciousness.

Iglesia de San Francisco★

🕐 *Open 10.30am-2pm and 4-7.30pm.*

This Franciscan monastery church, in the shape of a Latin Cross embellished with a graceful Gothic east end, was built in 1387 by the powerful Count Fernán Pérez de Andrade, Lord of Betanzos and Puentedeume. It is chiefly remarkable for the many tombs aligned along its walls, the carved decoration on its ogives and chancel arches and the wild boar sculpted in the most unexpected places. Beneath the gallery to the left of the west door is the **monumental sepulchre★** of the founder, supported by a wild boar and a bear, his heraldic beasts. Scenes of the hunt adorn the sides of the tomb; his hounds lie couched at his feet, while at his head an angel greets his soul.

Iglesia de Santiago

The church, built in the 15C by the tailors' guild, stands on higher ground than the two mentioned above. Its interior resembles that of Santa María. Above the main door is a carving of St James Matamoros or Slayer of the Moors, on horseback. The 16C **ayuntamiento** (town hall) abutting the east end is embellished with an arcade and a fine sculpted coat of arms.

Ría de La Coruña (🕐 *See A CORUÑA/La CORUÑA*)

Costa de la Muerte

Costa de la Muerte (Coast of Death)

The landscape between La Coruña and Cabo Finisterre is of a wild, harsh and majestic coast. It has long been whipped by stormy weather and owes its inhospitable name to the many ships that have run aground or been smashed to pieces against its rocks. Tucked away in its more sheltered coves, however, are small fishing villages like **Malpica de Bergantiños** which is protected by the Cabo de San Adrián (opposite the Islas Sisargas, islands on which there is a bird sanctuary) or **Camariñas** which is famous for its bobbin-lace.

Cabo Finisterre or Fisterra★ (Cape Finisterre)

Corcubión★, near Cabo Finisterre, is an attractive old harbour town of emblazoned houses with glassed-in balconies. The coast **road★** to the cape looks down over the Bahía de Cabo Finisterre, a bay which is enclosed by three successive mountain chains. The lighthouse on the headland commands a fine **panorama★** of the Atlantic and the bay.

Rías Bajas★★

MICHELIN MAP 571 D 2-3, E 2-3, F 3-4 (TOWN PLAN OF VIGO) –

GALICIA (A CORUÑA/LA CORUÑA, PONTEVEDRA).

The Rías Bajas, a coastline well supplied by the sea (renowned for its seafood) and with deep inlets affording safe anchorages, is Galicia's most privileged and attractive region. In the season, holidaymakers, Spanish for the most part, come to enjoy the beaches and resorts like those of A Toxa.

Location

The Rías Bajas are a series of four inlets: the ría de Muros y Noia, the smallest, forming the estuary of the River Tambre; the ría de Arousa, the delta of the River Ulla and separated from the former by the Barbanza Peninsula, from where the Mirador de la Curota provides stunning views; the ría de Pontevedra, surrounded by delightful beaches; and the ría de Vigo, with the Islas Cíes at its mouth. *Baiona: Paseo de Ribeira, 36300 Pontevedra, ☎ 986 68 70 67; Sanxenxo: Madrid, 36960 Pontevedra, ☎ 986 72 02 85; Vigo: Dársena de la Estación Marítima de Trasantlánticos, 36201 Pontevedra, ☎ 986 43 05 77; Tui: Puente de Tripes, 36700 Pontevedra, ☎ 986 60 17 89.*

⊙ *Neighbouring sights are described in the following chapters: RÍAS ALTAS, PONTEVEDRA and SANTIAGO DE COMPOSTELA.*

Address Book

For coin ranges, see the Legend at the back of the guide.

WHERE TO EAT

⊜ **Tasca Típica** – *Cantón 15 – Noia –* ☎ *981 82 12 70.* This old stone building in the centre of Noia has been converted into a typical bar serving tapas and a good-value daily menu. In fine weather, customers can also eat on the terrace.

⊜⊜ **Anduriña** – *Calvo Sotelo 58 – A Guarda –* ☎ *986 61 11 08 – Closed 3-27 Nov* – ▤. Despite its simple appearance, this well-known local restaurant has an excellent menu, including reasonably priced fish.

⊜⊜ **La Oca** – *Purificación Saavedra 8 (opposite Teis market) – Vigo –* ☎ *986 37 12 55 Closed Sat-Sun, Mon and Tue evenings, Holy Week and 3 weeks in Aug.* Don't be put off by the slightly out-of-the-way location or the neglected façade of this small family-run restaurant, as the food here is innovative and creative with notable French influences. A true pleasure for the palate!

⊜⊜ **Posta do Sol** – *Ribeira de Fefiñans 22 - Cambados –* ☎ *986 54 22 85 – Closed 15-31 Jan, 15-31 Oct and Wed (exc. Jun-Dec).* An attractive little restaurant in a one-time bar. The dining room, with fireplace, is decorated in regional style – the Camariñas lace curtains are lovely. The specialty is seafood.

⊜ **Casa Ramallo** – *Castro 5 – Rois – 4km/2.5mi N of Padrón on the AC 301 –* ☎ *981 80 41 80 – Closed Mon and 24 Dec-7 Jan –* ▤ *– Reservation recommended.* This small, family-run hotel has an excellent reputation locally for its delicious home cooking, in particular its stews, meat dishes and seafood. Highly recommended.

WHERE TO STAY

⊜ **Casa do Torno** – *Lugar do Torno 1 – Noia – 1.1km/0.7mi S of Noia on the Boiro road. –* ☎ *981 84 20 74 – 8 rooms –* ⊠ *4.21€.* A rural hotel in an unpretentious whitewashed village house with a garden at the rear. Cosy rooms with wood floors and antique furniture. Although on the small side, the bathrooms are pleasant with good attention to detail. The perfect base for a few days of relaxation.

⊜⊜ **Hotel Convento de San Benito** – *Plaza de San Benito – A Guarda –* ☎ *986 61 11 66 - Closed Jan– 23 rooms –* ⊠ *5€.* This former convent near the fishing port of A Guarda was founded in the 16C and originally housed an order of Benedictine nuns. A haven of peace and quiet with sober yet elegant rooms, and fine classical-style cloisters.

⊜⊜ **Hotel Pazo de Mendoza** – *Elduayen 1 – Baiona –* ☎ *986 38 50 14 – 11 rooms –* ⊠ *4.50€ – Restaurant €10.50.* A modern hotel built within the walls of an 18C house facing the sea in the centre of Baiona. The rooms are comfortable and well-furnished with attractive wood floors. The creative restaurant menu is based on high-quality local products.

⊜⊜ **Pazo de Hermida** – *Trasmuro 21 – Lestrove – 1km/0.6mi SW of Padrón along the C 550. –* ☎ *981 81 71 10 – Closed 21 Dec-7 Jan –* 🅿 *– 6 rooms –* ⊠ *6€.* This Galician manor house (*pazo*), built in the 17C above two former defensive towers, was for a short time home to the 19C poet Rosalía de Castro, who was undoubtedly attracted here by the tranquillity of the setting. Comfortable rooms and a highly recommended address.

Tours

RÍA DE MUROS Y NOIA★★ ①

From Muros to Ribeira *71km/44mi –* 🕐 *about 1hr 15min*

The *ría* is especially delightful for its wild scenery. The coastline, lower than in other *rías*, is strewn with rocks. The wooded northern bank is particularly attractive. **Muros** is a seaside town with a harbour and typical local style houses, while **Noia** is notable for its main square looking out to sea, upon which stands the Gothic **Iglesia de San Martín**★ with a magnificently carved portal and rose window.

RÍA DE AROUSA ②

From Ribeira to A Toxa *115km/71mi* – 🕐 *about 3hr*

Ría de Arousa, at the mouth of the River Ulla, is the largest and most indented of the inlets.

Ribeira

A large fishing port with vast warehouses.

Origins

The *rías* are river valleys that have been invaded by the sea. In the case of the Galician coast, its formation is the result of tectonic movements which caused the collapse of the coastline and the advance of the sea.

The port of Muros

Mirador de la Curota★★

10km/6mi from Puebla del Caramiñal. ▶ *Take the LC 302 W towards Oleiros and after about 4km/2.5mi turn right onto a narrow road up to the viewpoint.*

From a height of 498m/1 634ft there is a magnificent **panorama**★★ of the four inlets of the Rías Bajas. On a clear day the view extends from Cabo Finisterre to the River Miño.

Padrón

It was to this village that the legendary boat came which brought St James to Spain. The boat's mooring stone *(pedrón)* can be seen beneath the altar in the **iglesia parroquial** (parish church) near the bridge. The town, renowned for its green peppers, is also home to the residence in which the poet **Rosalía de Castro** (1837-85) lived. Her house has now been converted into a **museum**. ⊙ *Open 10am-1.30pm (2pm in summer) and 4-7pm (8pm in summer); Sun and public hols, 10am-1.30pm (2pm in summer).* ⊙ *Closed Mon, 1 and 6 Jan and 25 Dec.* ⊛ *1.40€.* ☏ *981 81 12 04.*

Vilagarcía de Arousa

A garden-bordered promenade overlooking the sea gives the town the air of a resort. The Convento de Vista Alegre, founded in 1648, stands on the outskirts on the Cambados road. It is an old pazo with square towers, coats of arms and pointed merlons.

Mirador de Lobeira★

4km/2.5mi S. ▶ *Take a signposted forest track at Cornazo.*

The view from the lookout takes in the whole *ría* and the hills inland.

Cambados★

Cambados has retained an old quarter of alleyways bordered by beautiful houses. At the town's northern entrance is the magnificent, square **plaza de Fefiñanes★,** lined on two sides by the emblazoned Fefiñanes *pazo*, on the third by a 17C church with lines harmonising with the *pazo*, and on the fourth by a row of arcaded houses. Also worthy of note on the other side of the village are the romantic ruins of **Santa Mariña de Dozo**, a 12C parish church which is now a cemetery. Cambados is the place to try the local white Albariño wine which has a light fruity flavour.

A Toxa★

A sick donkey abandoned on the island by its owner was the first living creature to discover the health-giving properties of the spring in A Toxa. The stream has run dry but the pine-covered island in its wonderful **setting**★★ remains an ideally restful place. It is the most elegant resort on the Galician coast, with luxury villas and an early 20C palace. There is a small church covered in scallop shells.

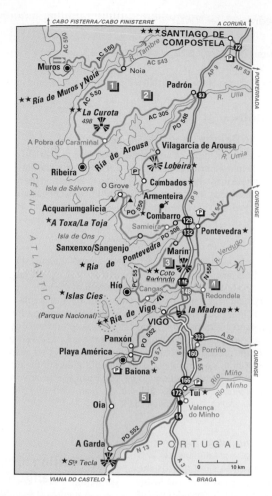

The seaside resort and fishing harbour of **O Grove** on the other side of the causeway is renowned for its seafood.

Aquariumgalicia

Kids *From O Grove head towards San Vicente and turn off at Reboredo.* 🕐 *Open 10am-8pm (9pm Sat-Sun and public hols).* � *€9, children €6.* ☎ *986 73 15 15.*

This, the only aquarium in Galicia, has over 15 000 exhibits representing more than 150 species on display in 18 tanks which re-create different marine habitats. The complex also includes a marine farm where species of commercial interest, such as the unusual turbot and the gilthead, are bred.

The **road**★ from A Toxa to Canelas affords a succession of views of sand dunes and extensive, rock enclosed beaches like that of **La Lanzada.**

RÍA DE PONTEVEDRA★ ③

From A Toxa to Hío *62km/39mi –* 🕐 *about 3hr*

Sanxenxo

A very lively resort in summer with one of the best climates in Galicia.

Monasterio de Armenteira

🕐 *Visits by prior arrangement.* ☎ *986 71 83 00.*

In Samieira a small road leads to this Cistercian monastery, where a 12C church and 17C classical-style cloister can still be visited.

Combarro★

This small, typical fishing village with winding alleyways has a good many Calvaries and is famed for its **hórreos**★ (drying sheds) on the seafront.

433

Pontevedra★ (👣 *See PONTEVEDRA*)

Marín

Headquarters of the Escuela Naval Militar or Naval Academy.

Hío

The village at the tip of the Morrazo headland has a famous and intricately carved **Calvary★**.

RÍA DE VIGO★★ ④

From Hío to Baiona *70km/43mi –* 🕐 *about 3hr*

Although smaller than the ría de Arousa, the Vigo inlet is deeper and better protected, remarkably sheltered inland by hills and out to sea by islands, the Islas Cíes. In addition, by Domaio, where the steep, wooded banks draw together and the narrow channel is covered in mussel beds, it becomes really beautiful. From Cangas and Moaña you can see the white town of Vigo covering the entire hillside on the far side of the inlet.

Vigo

Michelin Town Plan Vigo

Vigo, Spain's principal transatlantic port, is the country's leading fishing port and one of its most important industrial and commercial centres. Legend has it that treasure dating from the time of Philip V lies at the bottom of the inlet. Vigo's **setting**★ is outstanding: built in an amphitheatre on the south bank of the ría and surrounded by parks and pinewoods. There are magnificent **views**★★ of Vigo and its bay from El Castro hill behind the town. Berbés, Vigo's oldest quarter and home to fishermen and sailors, is a picturesque part of town. Beside it is the unusual A Pedra market where fishwives sell the oysters which may be tasted in the many bars nearby.

At Punta do Muíño, a beautiful place for splendid **views** of the *ría*, is the **Museo del Mar** (Maritime Museum), designed by Aldo Rossi and César Portela, where the relationship of Vigo and the sea is explored. 🕐 *Open 11am-8pm (Fri-Sat to 11.30pm, Sun to 9pm).* 🎫 *No charge.* ☎ *986 24 76 95.*

Islas Cíes★

🚢 *By boat from Vigo.* The beautiful archipelago of crystalline water and immaculate white sand guards the entrance to the ría de Vigo. The archipelago, a bird sanctuary, was decreed a nature reserve in 1980, and as of 2002 is part of **Parque Nacional de las Islas Atlánticas de Galicia**. There are three islands: Monteagudo, El Faro and San Martiño. The first two are linked via a sandy beach, the playa de Rodas.

> ### 🐚 Getting to the Cíes Islands 🐚
>
> From June to September, daily boat services operate from Cangas and Vigo (journey time: 30min). For information, call ☎ *986 22 52 72.*

Mirador la Madroa★★

6km/4mi. ▶ *Exit Vigo along the airport road. After 3.5km turn left, following signposts to the "parque zoológico" (zoo).* The esplanade commands a fine **view**★★ of Vigo and the *ría*.

The Alcabre, Samil and Canido beaches stretch down the coast south of Vigo.

Panxón

14km/9mi SW along the C 550. A seaside resort at the foot of Monte Ferro.

Playa América

A very popular, elegant resort in the curve of a bay.

Baiona/Bayona★

It was here, on 10 March 1493, that the caravel *Pinta* – one of the three vessels in Christopher Columbus's fleet – captained by **Martín Alonso Pinzón,** sailed into Baiona bringing news of the discovery of the New World.

Today, Baiona has grown into a lively summer resort with a harbour for fishing boats and pleasure craft fronted by a promenade of terrace cafés. In the old quarter houses may still be seen with coats of arms and glassed-in balconies. The **ex-colegiata** (former collegiate church) at the top of the town was built in a transitional Romanesque-Gothic style between the 12C and 14C. Symbols on the arches of chisels, axes and knives represent the various guilds that contributed to the building of the church. Note also the stone pulpit dating from the 14C. ◐ *Open 11am-12.30pm and 4.30-6.30pm.* ☎ *986 68 70 67.*

Monterreal

◐ *Open 10am-dusk.*👝 *0.60€, 3€ vehicles.* ☎ *986 35 63 85.*

The Catholic Monarchs had a defence wall built around Monterreal promontory at the beginning of the 16C. The fort within, which became the governor's residence, has been converted into a parador, surrounded by a pleasant pinewood. A **walk round the battlements**★ *(about 30min)*, rising sheer above the rocks, is well worthwhile for the splendid **views**★★ of the bay, Monte Ferro, the Estela islands and the coast with its sandy coves stretching south to the cabo Silleiro headland.

THE ROAD FROM BAIONA TO TUI★ ⑤ *58km/36mi*

The coast between Baiona and A Guarda is a flat, semi-deserted area indented by the sea.

Oia

The houses in the fishing village are clustered around the former Cistercian abbey of **Santa María la Real** with its Baroque façade. On the other side of the road are the outlying slopes of green hills where wild horses roam. Festivals known as *curros*, during which the wild foals are rounded up for branding, are held in the hills on certain Sundays in May and June.

A Guarda/La Guardia

This small fishing village stands at the extreme southern end of the Galician coastline. To the south, **Monte Santa Tecla**★ (341m/1 119ft) rises above the mouth of the Miño, affording fine **views**★★ from the top. (▶ *Follow signs for Citania de Santa Trega.*) On the slopes are the extensive remains of a **Celtic city,** testimony to human habitation from the Bronze Age to the 3C AD. Two round huts with stone walls and thatched roofs have been reconstructed on the side of the road.

▶ *From A Guarda, the C 550 heads inland parallel to the Miño River.*

Tui/Tuy★

Tui stands just across the border from Portugal in a striking **setting**★. Its old quarter, facing the Portuguese fortress of Valença, stretches down the rocky hillside to the right bank of the River Miño. The **Parque de Santo Domingo** (Santo Domingo Park), in which stands a Gothic church of the same name, commands a good view of Tui and the Portuguese coast.

Since 1884, when a bridge was built by Gustave Eiffel across the Miño, Tui has served as a gateway to Portugal.

The historic town is one of the oldest in Galicia; its emblazoned houses and narrow stepped alleys climbing towards the cathedral testify to its rich past.

Catedral★

◐ *Open 9.30am-1.30pm and 4-7pm (8pm 22 Apr-Oct).* ◐ *The Museo Diocesano is closed in winter.* 👝 *2€ (winter), 2.50€ (summer) including visit to Museo Diocesano.* ☎ *986 60 05 11.*

The low-lying cathedral, fringed with crenellations and flanked by towers, still resembles the fortress it was for so long. It was consecrated in 1232 having been built, for the most part, in Romanesque-Gothic style. The Romanesque north door, marked only by arches cut into the wall stone, is almost austere. In contrast the west front is adorned with a 14C porch which, while remaining defensive in character, is highly decorative with equilateral arches preceding a richly sculptured **portal**★. The tympanum, beneath the carved covings, glorifies the Mother of God; above the Adoration of the Magi and Shepherds are the towers of heavenly Jerusalem rendered ethereal by the interplay of mass and void.

Inside are the impressive reinforcing beams the cathedral was given in the 15C and 18C to compensate for the slant of the pillars. The transept plan of three aisles is Compostelan and, in Spain, is found only in this church and that of Santiago de Compostela. Modifications were made to the chapels from the 16C to the 18C. The choir stall carvings recount the life and miracles of San Telmo, patron of Tuy.

The sentry path over the wide galleries in the **cloisters**, soberly decorated in Cistercian style, commands good views of the river valley and Portugal on the opposite bank.

Capilla de San Telmo (San Telmo Chapel)

A Portuguese-style reliquary shrine has been built below the cathedral on the site of the house of **San Pedro González Telmo**, a Dominican who lived in Tuy and died in 1240. Pilgrims visit the alcove in the crypt where the saint died *(entrance: rúa do Corpo Santo)*.

La Rioja★

MICHELIN MAP 573 E 20-23, F 20-24 –

LA RIOJA, NAVARRA, PAÍS VASCO (ÁLAVA).

As it passes through La Rioja, the Ebro Valley is carpeted in endless vineyards and fields of vegetables. The high peaks of the Sierra de Cantabria and Sierra de la Demanda look down upon the valley, providing a permanent presence on the horizon. This picturesque natural landscape is dotted with towns and villages with a rich artistic heritage, largely as a result of the Way of St James that runs through the region.

Location

The wine region covers an area of approximately 5 000km2/1 930sq mi across the provinces of La Rioja, Álava and Navarra. 🅱 *Haro: Plaza Monseñor Florentino Rodríguez, 26200 La Rioja, ☏ 941 30 33 66; Logroño: Paseo Príncipe de Vergara (Espolón), 26071 La Rioja, ☏ 941 29 12 70; Nájera: Constantino Garrán 8, 26300 La Rioja, ☏ 941 36 00 41; San Millán de la Cogolla: Monasterio de Yuso (edificio Aula de la Lengua), 26326 La Rioja, ☏ 941 37 32 59; Santo Domingo de la Calzada: Mayor 70, 26250 La Rioja, ☏ 941 34 12 30.*

🔾 *Neighbouring sights are described in the following chapter: The WAY OF ST JAMES.*

Background

La Rioja owes its name to the Río Oja, a tributary of the Ebro. **Rioja Alta** (Upper Rioja), to the west around Haro, is devoted principally to wine-growing while **Rioja Baja** (Lower Rioja), with **Logroño** and Calahorra as its main towns, has unusual tableland relief and is given over to the extensive growing of early vegetables (mainly asparagus, artichokes, peppers and tomatoes), which has spawned a large local canning industry. La Rioja flourished culturally and economically early in its history thanks to its position on the pilgrim route to Santiago de Compostela. Since then it has become famous for its wine.

Worth a Visit

Logroño

The capital of the Rioja region is situated on the banks of the Ebro. Pilgrims on their way to Santiago de Compostela would have entered this pleasant town through the stone gateway, which still retains an attractive view over the old town with the Baroque tower of the cathedral, the spired tower of Santa María del Palacio and the Mudéjar tower of **San Bartolomé**.

> **TAPAS**
>
> The small **calle del Laurel** is without doubt one of the main attractions in Logroño with its huge choice of bars serving delicious local specialities (sweet peppers, mushrooms etc).

Santa María la Redonda

The church of Santa María dates from 1435, but has only been the town's cathedral since 1959. It has three naves, three polygonal apses and chapels in its side aisles. These include the Plateresque-style Chapel of Our Lady of Peace (Nuestra Señora de la Paz), founded in 1541 by Diego Ponce de León. The extraordinary grille enclosing the choir is particularly worthy of note.

THE WINES OF LA RIOJA

Rioja is the only Spanish appellation with the Denominación de Origen Calificada (DOC) quality label. The wine is the result of over seven centuries of tradition and a superb position in the Ebro Valley between the Sierra de la Demanda and the Sierra de Cantabria. The wine region is traditionally divided into three sub-zones: Rioja Alavesa, Rioja Baja and Rioja Alta. Although seven grape varieties are permitted, the two most commonly used are Tempranillo and Grenache. Red wine accounts for 75% of production and is produced according to two different processes: **carbonic maceration** and **ageing**. The first produces young, fresh wines which are best consumed in the year of production, whereas the ageing process, in Bordeaux oak barrels, results in three different wines, classified according to the time spent in the barrel and the time which has elapsed between the harvest and the moment the wine leaves the cellars: **Crianza** (12 months in the barrel, one year in the bottle), **Reserva** (12 months in the barrel, two years in the bottle) and **Gran Reserva** (24 months in the barrel, three years in the bottle).

Museo de la Rioja

🕐 Open 10am-2pm and 4-9pm; Sun and public hols, 11.30am-2pm. 🕐 Closed Mon, 1 Jan, Good Fri and 25 Dec. 👁 No charge. ☎ 941 29 12 59.

This regional museum is housed in a fine 18C Baroque palace in which General Espartero lived during the last century. The collection mainly originates from disentailments during the 19C. The Romanesque carvings and Gothic retable from Torremuña are particularly interesting, as is a superb Hispano-Filipino marble sculpture from the Baroque period representing an expiring Christ.

Laguardia★

With its situation on a hill at the foot of the Sierra de Cantabria, Laguardia is perhaps the most attractive town in Rioja Alavesa. Its fortified appearance from the main road is enhanced as you approach, as its walls and two imposing towers, San Juan to the south, and the 12C tower of the abbey to the north, come into view; the latter was connected to the Gothic Iglesia de Santa María de los Reyes. Laguardia retains its medieval urban plan and noble houses. The house where the fabulist Samaniego was born is now the Tourist Office.

Iglesia de Santa María de los Reyes

👁 Guided tours, 10am-2pm and 4-7pm; Sat, 10am-2pm and 5-7pm; Sun, 10.45am-2pm. 🕐 Closed public hols. For information on visits, contact the Tourist Office in Laguardia. 👁 2€. ☎ 941 60 08 45.

This splendid church is adorned with a superb late-14C **portal**★★ which has completely preserved its 17C polychrome decoration. The tympanum is divided into three scenes relating events from the life of the Virgin. Note the figure of Christ holding a small child in his hands representing the soul of the Virgin. Saints and singing angels adorn the arches.

The interior is a strange mix of Gothic and Renaissance styles; the Renaissance vault in the central nave is of particular interest.

The walkway around the village commands views over vast sweeps of vineyard.

Centro Temático del vino Villa Lucía (Villa Lucía Wine Centre)

Outside of Laguardia on the way to Logroño.

🕐 Open 9am-2pm and 4.30-8pm. 👁 5.50€. ☎ 945 60 00 32.

The museum on this lovely estate traces the history of the cultivation of vines and elaboration of wines. Wine tastings and banquets are held as well.

The **panorama** from the **Balcón de Rioja**★★ or Rioja Balcony 12km/8mi northwest of Laguardia near the Puerto de Herrera (Herrera Pass, 1 100m/3 609ft), is incredibly extensive, particularly along the length of the Ebro Valley, flat and arid in appearance apart from the winding silver thread of the river's own course.

Haro

This small but prosperous farming and commercial centre is famous for its wines. There are countless cellars and taverns in the old quarter where seigniorial mansions with elegant 16C and 18C façades recall the town's prestigious past. In **plaza de la Paz** the simple lines of the neo-Classical town hall (Ayuntamiento), built by Juan de Villanueva in 1769, are particularly impressive, as is the Baroque tower of the **Iglesia de Santo Tomás** behind it. This church, which was constructed by Felipe Birgany in 1516, has preserved its fine Renaissance doorway.

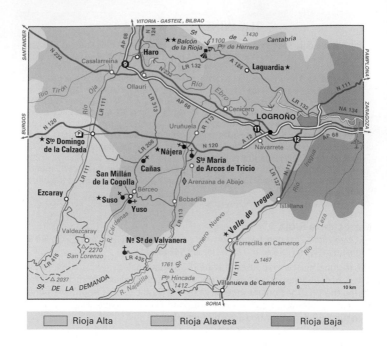

| Rioja Alta | Rioja Alavesa | Rioja Baja |

Museo del Vino de la Rioja

🕐 *Open 10am-2pm and 4-8pm; Sun, 10am-2pm. Last admission 1hr before closing.*
🕐 *Close 1 and 6 Jan, 15 May, 25 and 29 Jun, 8 Sep and 24-25 and 31 Dec.* ✆ *2€, no charge Wed.* ☎ *941 31 05 47.*

Without doubt, wine is one of the biggest attractions of the Rioja region. This museum is entirely devoted to this art with descriptions and explanations on wine production from cultivation all the way through to the bottling process. An interesting and worthwhile visit for wine-lovers.

Santo Domingo de la Calzada★

This historical town, an important staging post on the Way of St James, was founded on the banks of the Oja river in the 11C and owes its name to a hermit, Dominic, who built a bridge to help pilgrims on their way to Santiago de Compostela, a causeway (*calzada*: road, causeway) to Burgos, a hospice and a hospital. Parts of the 14C ramparts can still be seen.

The **old town**★ is huddled around the **plaza del Santo,** dominated by the cathedral and the former hospital, which has now been converted into a parador. The streets around the square, particularly the calle Mayor, have preserved a number of 16C and 17C stone houses with fine doorways. The 18C Ayuntamiento (town hall), the major monument in the nearby plaza de España, is crowned by an impressive escutcheon.

> ### 😊 Medieval Market 😊
>
> A colourful medieval market is held every year in the old town to coincide with festivities commemorating the Constitution and the Immaculate Conception (6 and 8 December).

Catedral★

🕐 *Open 9am1.30pm and 4-6.30pm.* 🕐 *Closed Sun and public hols.* ✆ *2€.* ☎ *941 34 00 33.*
▶ *Entrance via the 14C cloisters, housing the cathedral museum.*

The church is Gothic, apart from the ambulatory and one of the apsidal chapels which are Romanesque (second half of the 12C). The saint's tomb (13C), beneath a 1513 canopy, is in the south transept, and opposite is a sumptuous **Gothic cage**. This contains a live white cock and hen in memory of a miracle attributed to the saint. According to legend, a pilgrim was unjustly accused of theft and hanged. After a month on the gallows, he was still alive and, on seeing his parents, said "Tell the judge to let me down; St Dominic has protected me". The judge, on hearing the news just as he was about to begin a meal of roast chicken, declared "He must be as alive as this bird", whereupon the cockerel stood up and, fully feathered, crowed aloud to proclaim the pilgrim's innocence.

The **retable**★★ at the high altar (1538) is an unfinished work by Damián Forment. The artist has used the human body as a decorative element, making this an original work and one of the 16C's major sculptures. The second chapel off the north aisle contains a fine 15C Hispano-Flemish altarpiece.

The cathedral contains other works of great interest, including the **Capilla de la Magdalena**★ (Evangelist's nave) with its fine Plateresque decoration and magnificent screen. Note the delicate 15C Flemish statue of La Verónica. In the Epistle nave, opposite the Capilla de la Magdalena, the **Capilla de San Juan Bautista or Santa Teresa** contains an impressive screen, interesting noble tombs and a magnificent retable with Hispano-Flemish paintings. A large imperial escutcheon crowns the Plateresque decoration in the Capilla de la Inmaculada.

On the exterior, a Baroque-style 18C **tower** can be seen. In the same square, opposite the cathedral, the small **Ermita del Santo** (Saint's Hermitage) has an attractive Gothic interior.

Abadía de Cañas

🕐 *Open 1030am (11.30am Sun)-1.30pm and 4-6pm; in summer, 10am-1.30pm and 4-7pm.* 🕐 *Closed Sun during Eucharist (10am).* 👁 *3€.* ☎ *941 37 90 83.*

This monastery has been inhabited by Cistercian monks since its foundation in 1170. The 16C church and chapter house are extraordinary examples of the purity and simplicity of Cistercian art, with elegant pointed arches, floral decoration and simple fan vaulting. A magnificent 16C sculpted and painted Renaissance altarpiece stands at the foot of the church. The abbey's works of art (altarpieces, canvases, sculptures etc) are displayed in the former granary. A collection of reliquaries is exhibited in a separate room.

Ezcaray

This delightful village, situated at the foot of the Sierra de la Demanda range close to Logroño and surrounded by superb natural countryside on the banks of the Oja river, has become a summer resort and a popular ski area. It has preserved its quaint mountain style, its stone and wood porticoes, seigniorial mansions and the church of **Santa María la Mayor** as well as the buildings of a former tapestry factory founded by Charles III in 1752. Today the tradition lives on in the manufacture of blankets.

Nájera

Reconquered by Sancho Garcés I in 920, Nájera became the capital of the kingdom of Navarra until 1076. The town is an important staging-post on the Way of St James.

Monasterio de Santa María la Real★

🕐 *Open 10am-1pm and 4-6pm; Apr-Oct, 9.30am-1.30pm and 4-7.30pm; Sun and public hols, 10am-1pm and 4-7.30pm; last admission 30min before closing.* 🕐 *Closed Mon (except in summer), 1 and 6 Jan, 17 Sep and 24-25 and 31Dec.* 🎟 *2€.* ☎ *941 36 36 50.*

The monastery was founded by Don García III, King of Navarra, in 1032. According to legend, the site is that of a cave which the king stumbled upon (while following a vulture and a partridge) and where he found a statue of the Virgin. It fell into total ruin in the 15C, but was rebuilt in the same century.

The salient features of the **cloisters**★ are the bays in the lower gallery, filled with Plateresque stone tracery (1520), each to a different arabesque pattern.

Beneath the gallery of the **church**★, two soldiers bearing the colours of King García and his queen, Estefanía of Barcelona, guard the entrance to the **Panteón Real**★ (Royal Pantheon) of princes of Navarra, León and Castilla of the 11C and 12C. The recumbent statues were carved in the 16C. At the centre, between the kneeling figures of the founders, is the entrance to the cave where the Virgin was found. The present polychrome figure of the Virgin is 13C. Among the royal sarcophagi in the Epistle aisle is the **tomb of Doña Blanca de Navarra**★, a jewel of Romanesque sculpture.

In the choir, note the beautiful carving and infinite variety of the misericords and armrests in the **stalls**★ (1495), particularly the central seat on which the founder king is depicted majestically in full armour beneath a delicate canopy.

Basílica de Santa María de Arcos de Tricio

3km/2mi SW of Nájera. 🚶 *Guided tours (15-20min), in summer, 10.30am-1.30pm and 4.30-7.30pm; Sat-Sun and public hols, 10.30am-2.30pm; in winter, Sat-Sun and public hols only, 10.30am-1.30pm and 4.30-7.30pm.* ☎ *636 82 05 89.*

This unusual church, with its basilical ground plan, was built in the 5C above a Roman mausoleum. Its most noteworthy features are the thick tambours of the impressive Roman columns supporting the Baroque vaults; the remains of the 12C Romanesque frescoes at the east end; and the Roman, palaeo-Christian and medieval tombs beneath the metal floor grille in the nave.

San Millán de la Cogolla

The most attractive approach is via the turn-off from the LR 113 at Bobadilla. Declared a World Heritage Site in December 1997, San Millán de la Cogolla was already famous in the 5C when Millán or Emilian de Berceo and his followers settled here as hermits. In the 10C, a monastery and Mozarabic church were built in the mountains (Suso) and then, in 1053, another monastery was built in the valley (Yuso). The first known manuscripts in Castilian Spanish, the *Glosas Emilianenses*, were written at San Millán. **Gonzalo de Berceo**, the first cult Castillian poet, who wrote *La Vida de San Millán* (The Life of St Millan) and *Los Milagros de Nuestra Señora* (The Miracles of Our Lady), was educated here.

Monasterio de Suso★

🕐 *Open 10am-1.30pm and 4-6.30pm (7.30pm spring-summer).* 🕐 *Closed Mon.* 🎟 *No charge.*

The monastery stands on a hillside overlooking the Monasterio de Yuso and the Cárdenas Valley. It is a magnificent Mozarabic building partly hollowed out of the rock with a cubic apse and large carved corbels. The church has two aisles separated by three horseshoe-shaped arches. The aisles were extended westwards in the Romanesque era. A cave necropolis for the burial of the monks was discovered near the church.

Monasterio de Yuso

🚶 *Guided tours (1hr)10am-1pm (1.30 Tue) and 4-6.30pm; May-23 Sep 10.30am-1.30pm and 4-6.30pm.* 🕐 *Closed Mon except in Aug.* 🎟 *3.50€* ☎ *941 37 30 49.*

The monastery was built between the 16C and 18C, in Renaissance style in the case of the church, neo-Classical and Baroque respectively for the portals and sacristy. In the treasury are splendid **ivories**★★ from two 11C reliquaries. These were robbed of their gold mounts and precious stones by French soldiers and are now shown as sets of ivory plaques – San Millán's (1067-80), consisting of 24 Romanesque pieces, is carved with great human expression, while San Felices' (1090), consists of five pieces with a distinctly Byzantine hieratic style.

Monasterio de Nuestra Señora de Valvanera

Access via the LR 113. This monastery is nestled in a delightful, isolated mountain **setting**★★, surrounded by extensive woods and dominated by the peaks of the Sierra de San Lorenzo. The church houses a statue of the patron saint of La Rioja, the Virgen of Valvanera, a fine sculpture dating from the 12C. A hostel for pilgrims is also located here (☎ 941 37 70 44).

Valle del Iregua★

50km/31mi S of Logroño on the N 111. For 15km/9mi the road skirts orchards and market-gardens in the Ebro plain, until, near Islallana, appear the first **rock faces**★ of the Sierra de Cameros, overlooking the Iregua Valley from a height of more than 500m/1 640ft. Two tunnels later, the valley narrows, squeezed between massive reddish-coloured boulders. It opens out into an island of greenery and narrows again upstream with the torrent running at the bottom of a deep ravine while the mountain road dominates the site of Torrecilla en Cameros. In the village of **Villanueva de Cameros** the half-timbered houses are roofed with circular tiles.

Ronda★★

POPULATION: 35 788

MICHELIN MAP 578 V 14 – ANDALUCÍA (MÁLAGA).

Ronda stands at the heart of the Serranía de Ronda in a delightful setting surrounded by lush river valleys. Its dramatic position above a deep ravine, its geographical isolation, and the legends of local highwaymen made the town a place of pilgrimage for Romantic writers during the 19C. Despite its huge popularity, it has retained its delightful character, typified by cobbled streets, whitewashed houses and impressive mansions.

Location

The town occupies an extraordinary site on a rocky platform overlooking a deep ravine. The River Guadalevín divides Ronda into two parts, connected by the 18C Puente Nuevo, offering an impressive **view**★ of the ravine El Tajo: to the south, the **Ciudad**, the old quarter, with its concentration of sights of interest; and, to the north, the **Mercadillo**, the old market area, nowadays extended by the modern town. The Camino de los Molinos road provides impressive views of the town's steep cliffs and the stunning profile of the **Tajo**★. ⏸ *Ronda: Plaza de España 9, 29400, ☎ 95 287 12 72; Arcos de la Frontera: Cuesta de Belén, 11630, ☎ 956 70 22 64.*

   🔖 *Neighbouring sights are described in the following chapters: Costa del SOL, MÁLAGA (96km/60mi SE) and ANTEQUERA (94km/59mi NE).*

Walking About

LA CIUDAD★★

🔖 *Tour:* ⏱ *2hr. Depart from Puente Nuevo.*

The old walled town, a vestige from the Moorish occupation which lasted until 1485, is a picturesque quarter of narrow alleys and whitewashed houses with wrought-iron balconies.

  ▶ *Cross the bridge and follow calle Santo Domingo.*

Ronda – The Cradle of Bullfighting

Ronda is indelibly linked with the world of bullfighting. **Francisco Romero**, who was born here in 1695, laid down the rules of bullfighting, which until then had been only a display of audacity and agility. He became the father of modern bullfighting by his introduction of the cape and the **muleta**. His son Juan introduced the *cuadrillo* or supporting team and his grandson, **Pedro Romero** (1754-1839), became one of Spain's greatest bullfighters. He founded the **Ronda School**, known still for its classicism, strict observance of the rules and *estocada a recibir*.

Address Book

For coin ranges, see the Legend at the back of the guide.

WHERE TO EAT

◎◎ **Doña Pepa** – *Plaza del Socorro 10 - Ronda* – ☎ *952 87 47 77 – Closed evenings 24 and 31 Dec –* ▤ *– Reservation recommended.* Try the best of Ronda cooking, such as *rabo de toro* (bull's tail), In a house with all the charm and style of Andalucia. Meals from the set menu are reasonably priced.

◎◎◎ **Tragabuches** – *José Aparicio 1 –* ☎ *95 219 02 91 – Closed Sun evening and Mon –* ▤. This restaurant, considered by many locals to be the best in Ronda, is just a stone's throw from the parador and the bullring. Its kitchen, run by Sergio López, a prize-winning young chef, offers guests modern cuisine in an avant-garde setting.

WHERE TO STAY

◎◎ **Hotel San Gabriel** – *Marqués de Moctezuma 19* – ☎ *95 219 03 92 – Closed 21 Dec-7 Jan and 21-31 Jul –* ▤ *– 16 rooms –* ⊇ *6.50€.* A delightful, magnificently decorated mansion dating from 1736. Some of the rooms look onto a charming patio. The hotel prides itself on its friendliness and attention to detail.

Casa del Rey Moro

The current building was erected in the 18C in neo-Mudéjar style (👣 *see description under Worth a Visit).*

Palacio del Marqués de Salvatierra

This small mansion is graced with an exceptional Renaissance **portal**★★ and an attractive wrought-iron balcony decorated with two pairs of pre-Columbian-inspired statues.

▶ *From the Arco de Felipe V, by the Puente Viejo, a stone path leads to the Baños Árabes.*

Baños Árabes★

🕙 *Open 10am-7pm; Sat-Sun and public hols 10am-3pm.* 🕙 *Closed Mon 1 Jan and 24 Dec.* ◎ *2€.* ☎ *95 287 38 89.*

Built at the end of the 13C in the artisans' and tanners' district, the Moorish baths comprise three rooms topped with barrel vaults and illuminated by star-shaped lunettes.

▶ *Follow a stone staircase running parallel to the walls, then pass through a 13C gateway, the Puerta de la Acijara.*

Minarete de San Sebastián★

This graceful minaret is the only one remaining from the 14C Nasrid mosque which stood on this spot. The horseshoe arch framing the door is particularly worthy of note.

Santa María la Mayor★

🕙 *Open 10am-7pm). 2€.* ☎ *95 287 22 46.*

The Collegiate Church of St Mary was built over the town's former main mosque. Today, only a 13C horseshoe arch, decorated with *atauriques* and calligraphic motifs, and a minaret remain from the original building. The interior is divided into three distinct architectural styles: Gothic (aisles); Plateresque (high altar); and Baroque (choir stalls). On the exterior, note the double balcony used as a tribune by local dignitaries.

▶ *Continue along calle Manuel Montero.*

Palacio de Mondragón

The palace's noble Renaissance façade is crowned by two small Mudéjar towers. Nowadays, the palace houses the **Museo de la Ciudad** (👣 *see below).*

Worth a Visit

Museo de la Ciudad★★

🕙 *Open 10am-7pm (6pm Nov-Mar); Sat-Sun and public hols, 10am-3pm.* 🕙 *Closed 1 Jan, Good Friday and 25 Dec.* ◎ *2€.* ☎ *952 87 84 50.*

Puente Nuevo and the ravine (El Tajo), Ronda

The outstanding feature on the inside is the charming **Mudéjar patio**★★ with the remains of *azulejos* and stuccowork between its arches. The collection includes an exhibition on the natural habitats of the Serranía de Ronda.

Plaza de Toros: Museo Taurino★

🕐 *Open in winter, 10am-6pm (7pm spring and autumn; 8pm summer).* ⌗ *5€.* ☏ *95 287 41 32.*

The bullring, dating from 1785 and with a capacity for 6 000 spectators, is one of Spain's oldest and most beautiful arenas. It is entered through an elegant gateway and is surrounded by fine arcades. Traditional *Corridas Goyescas*, fights in period costumes from the time of Goya, are held annually. The museum contains sumptuous costumes and various mementoes and photographs of generations of Ronda matadors including those from the Romero and Ordóñez families.

Casa del Rey Moro

Open 10am-6pm (8pm spring and summer). 4€. 95 218 73 00.

The interior contains an impressive set of Moorish steps, known as **La Mina,** which descend to the river. The **gardens**★ were laid out in 1912 by the French landscapist **Jean-Claude Forestier,** who also designed the María Luisa Park in Sevilla.

Museo del Bandolero

Open 10am-6pm (8pm summer). 2.70€. 95 287 77 85.

The Serranía de Ronda mountain range was one of the main areas of activity for bandits, brigands and outlaws in the region. This museum provides visitors with an insight into these legendary figures in Andalucían history.

▶ **Templete de la Virgen de los Dolores**★ **(1734)**

Excursions

Iglesia Rupestre de la Virgen de la Cabeza★

2.7km/1.7mi along the A 369 towards Algeciras. *Open 10am-2pm.* *Closed Sun, 1 Jan and 24 Dec.* 1.20€. 649 36 57 72.

This 9C Mozarabic monastery was excavated out of rock. The frescoes in the church were painted in the 18C. The **views**★★ of Ronda from here are particularly impressive.

Ruinas de Acinipo

19km/11.5mi along the A 376 towards Sevilla. *Open 9am-4.30pm.* *Closed Mon, 1 Jan and 24 Dec.* No charge. 952 22 75 60 or 630 42 99 49.

Known popularly as Ronda la Vieja, the old ruined settlement of Acinipo has preserved a 1C AD theatre, including part of the stage and the terraces.

Cueva de la Pileta★

20km/12mi SW. ▶ *Leave Ronda on the A 376 towards Sevilla, then take the MA 555 towards Benaoján. From here, bear onto the MA 561.* *Guided tours (1hr), 10am-1pm and 4-5pm.* 6.50€. 95 216 73 43.

The cave, a limestone formation with over 2km/1.2mi of galleries and natural concretions, was discovered in 1905 and is of immense geological and artistic interest. The red and black wall paintings span an extensive period of prehistory, predating those discovered at Altamira, with figurative motifs from the Palaeolithic era (20 000 BC) and symbolic art and animal drawings (goats, panthers etc) from the Neolithic period (4 000 BC).

RONDA TO SAN PEDRO DE ALCÁNTARA BY ROAD★★

49km/30mi SE on the C 339 – *about 1hr.*

For 20km/12mi the road travels through a bare mountain landscape; it then climbs steeply into a **corniche**★★ above the Guadalmedina valley and its smaller tributary valleys. The route is deserted, there's not a single village.

RONDA TO ALGECIRAS BY ROAD★

118km/73mi SW on the C 341, C 3331 and A 7 – *about 3hr.*

The Ronda-Gaucín section is particularly interesting when the road climbs steeply to overlook the Genal valley. It then continues, winding around the foot of **Jimena de la Frontera** perched on a hill and crossing the **Parque Natural de los Alcornocales**★, one of the largest forests of cork oaks in Spain. After another 22km/14mi, a narrow road on the right leads to **Castellar de la Frontera**★, a village of flower-filled alleyways huddled within the castle grounds.

PUEBLOS BLANCOS★★
(WHITEWASHED VILLAGES OF ANDALUCÍA)

The mountainous region to the west between Ronda and Arcos de la Frontera is formed by the Sierras de Grazalema, Ubrique and Margarita. In these often weirdly shaped mountains, ranging from desolate heights to lush green valleys, are the remains of the *pinsapos* forest of native pines dating from the beginning of the Quaternary Era.

The beauty of the countryside is set off by the delightful white villages *(pueblos blancos)*, often perched on rocky crags or stretched out along escarpments, their narrow streets of whitewashed houses dominated by a ruined castle or a church. The inhabitants make a living from farming, stock raising and local crafts.

From Ronda to Arcos de la Frontera

By the northern route; 130km/81mi – ⏱ about 4hr. Leave Ronda along the MA 428 towards Arriate, then continue on the CA 4211.

Setenil★

This unique village, nestled in the gorge carved out by the Guadalporcún river, has a number of troglodyte dwellings built into the rock. Fine examples of these are the Cuevas del Sol (Caves of the Sun) and the Cuevas de la Sombra (Caves of the Shade). Other sights of interest here include the **tourist office**, housed in an impressive building with a handsome 16C **artesonado ceiling**, the keep (torre del homenaje), and the Iglesia de la Encarnación.

Olvera

Olvera enjoys an impressive **site**★★ amid a landscape of olive groves. The village's network of steep streets and alleyways is laid out across the hillside, which is crowned by the keep of its triangular-shaped **castle** and the Iglesia de la Encarnación. Olvera is renowned for its superb olive oil. ⏱ *Open 10.30am-2pm and 4-6.30pm (7pm 1 Jun-14 Oct).* ⏱ *Closed Mon.* ⊕ *1.20€ (museum).* ☎ *956 12 08 16 (Tourist Office).*

▶ *Take the A 382 towards Algodonales, then turn off to the right onto the CA 531.*

Zahara de la Sierra★

The village enjoys an extraordinary **setting**★★ on top of a hill. Zahara was an important defensive enclave for the Nasrids, and subsequently the Christians. The outline of the 12C **castle** and the 18C Baroque **Iglesia de Santa María de Mesa** stand out above Zahara's whitewashed rooftops.

▶ *Return to the A 382 and continue towards Villamartín.*

Villamartín

The **Alberite dolmen**, dating from around 4 000 BC, can be visited on the outskirts of Villamartín, 4km/2.5mi to the south. It consists of a gallery 20m/65ft long formed by large stone slabs, and a funerary chamber.

Bornos

Bornos is unlike many of its fellow villages along this route in that it is not surrounded by mountains, nor is it completely white. It does, however, have some of the best architecture in the whole area. The plaza del Ayuntamiento is fronted by the **Castillo-Palacio de los Ribera★**, a castle-cum-palace which is now home to the tourist office. The inside of the building has an attractive Renaissance-style **patio** and a 16C garden. Also lining the square is the **Iglesia de Santo Domingo**, a Gothic church built in the late 15C.

Espera
10km/6mi NW of Bornos along the CA 402.

The village stands on a small outcrop and is dominated by the ruins of a Moorish castle, the **Castillo de Fatetar**.

Arcos de la Frontera★★

Arcos has a remarkable **site**★★ atop a crag enclosed by a loop in the Guadalete river. The old town, right at the top of the rock, is huddled against the formidable crenellated castle walls and those of the two churches.

👀 *It is advisable to park your car below the village in plaza de Andalucía. Ascend the cuesta de Belén, a hill which connects modern Arcos with the medieval town.*

Once past the callejón de Juan del Valle, note the 15C Gothic-Mudéjar **façade**★ of the **Palacio del Conde del Águila.**

▶ *Continue to the right along calle Nueva to plaza del Cabildo.*

Plaza del Cabildo

One side of the large square overhangs the deep river precipice. The **view**★ extends to a wide meander of the Guadalete which encloses fields of cereals and fruit trees. The plaza is lined by the town hall *(ayuntamiento)*, the parador, occupying a former palace, and the castle (closed to visitors).

Iglesia de Santa María★

🕐 *Open 10am-1pm and 4-7pm; Sat, 10am-2pm.* 🕐 *Closed Sun and public hols.* 👓 *1.50€.* ☎ *956 70 00 06.*

This church was built around 1530 on the site of the former main mosque. The **west façade**★, a work by Don Alonso de Baena, is a good example of the Plateresque style. The interior, with its mixture of Gothic, Mudéjar, Plateresque and Baroque, has some fine star-vaulting and a 17C **altarpiece** representing the Ascension of the Virgin.

An alleyway, the **callejón de las Monjas**, runs along the north side beneath the church's flying buttresses.

A charming maze of narrow alleys leads to the other side of the cliff, where the Capilla de la Misericordia, the Palacio del Mayorazgo (nowadays a music conservatory) and the **Iglesia de San Pedro** can be seen.

Iglesia de San Pedro

The church dates from the early 15C and for many years rivalled Santa María in importance. The façade is crowned by an impressive neo-Classical bell tower.

From Arcos de la Frontera to Ronda
By the southern route; 102km/63mi – 🕐 about 3hr

Leave Arcos along the A 372 towards **El Bosque**. This small town is home to the Parque Natural Sierra de Grazalema visitor centre.

▶ *Leave El Bosque on the A 373.*

Ubrique

The **road**★ now enters the heart of the Sierra de Grazalema in what is undoubtedly the most beautiful part of the tour, passing through this sleepy town which extends in a white swathe across the Cruz del Tajo Hill. Today, Ubrique has developed into the main industrial and commercial centre in the area, specialising in leather goods. The upper section of the town, beyond the **plaza del Ayuntamiento**, is the more interesting, dominated by the 18C parish church of **Nuestra Señora de la O**.

▶ *From Ubrique, continue 10km/6mi E along the A 374.*

Villaluenga del Rosario

This small, tranquil village is the highest in Cádiz province. Its most unusual feature is its irregularly shaped **bullring** *(plaza de toros)* built on top of a rock.

▶ *Head 15km/9.5mi NE along the A 374.*

Grazalema★★

Grazalema is without doubt one of Andalucía's most charming villages. It also has the dubious distinction of being the wettest place in the whole of Spain.

The name Grazalema comes from the Arabic *Ben-Zalema*. The village has retained the layout of its streets from the Moorish period, as well as the tower of the **Iglesia de San Juan**. The pretty **plaza de España**, around which the village has developed, is fronted by the 18C **Iglesia de la Aurora**, and adorned with an unusual fountain. Grazalema is famous for its white and brown woollen blankets; today, it is still possible to visit a traditional **hand loom** in operation at the entrance to the town.

▶ *Return to Ronda on the A 372.*

Salamanca★★★

POPULATION: 186 322

MICHELIN MAPS 575 AND 576 J 12-13 –

CASTILLA Y LEÓN (SALAMANCA).

To spend time in Salamanca today is to be continually reminded of its illustrious past. This delightful university city of golden stone, narrow streets, splendid buildings and exuberantly rich façades has a long tradition of learning. Blessed with perhaps the most magnificent main square in Spain, Salamanca has long been a favoured destination for foreign students and visitors alike, who come here to enjoy the delights of one of Europe's most attractive cities.

Location

Situated on the western fringes of the Castilla y León region, Salamanca is easily accessible from Ávila (98km/61mi SE on the N 501), Valladolid (115km/72mi NE on the A 62) and Zamora (62km/39mi N on the N 630). The city is an excellent base from which to explore one of the most beautiful mountain ranges in Spain, the Sierra de la Peña de Francia. The old city, for the most part pedestrianised, stands on a slight rise on the right bank of the River Tormes. *Rúa Mayor 70 (Casa de las Conchas), 37008 Salamanca, ☎ 923 26 85 71; Plaza Mayor 14, 37002, ☎ 923 21 83 42.*

Neighbouring sights are described in the following chapters: CIUDAD RODRIGO (89km/55mi SW), ZAMORA (62km/39mi N) and La ALBERCA (94km/59mi S).

Background

A tumultuous past – Iberian in origin, Salamanca was conquered by Hannibal in the 3C BC, flourished under the Romans who built the **Puente Romano** (Roman bridge) across the Tormes, and invaded repeatedly by the Moors. Alfonso VI took the city from the Moors in 1085; Raymond of Burgundy subsequently repopulated it with Franks, in addition to incomers from Asturias, León and Portugal. From this period on, the walls, old cathedral and numerous other monuments were built. In 1218, Alfonso IX established a centre for study, later to become an important university. In the 14C and 15C, the city was to see a rise in disturbances and confrontations between noble factions. In 1520, Salamanca rose against the royal authority of Emperor Charles V (*see SEGOVIA*). The 16C saw Salamanca enjoy one of its greatest artistic and intellectual periods, only to fall into a sustained crisis that would last until the 20C.

Los Bandos – During the 15C, rivalry between noble factions *(bandos)* saw the city's streets bathed in blood. The most famous incident took place when two Monroy brothers of the Santo Tomé Bando were killed by Manzano brothers of the San Benito Bando after an argument at a game of *pelota*. Their mother, Doña María, and the Santo Tomé faction immediately took their revenge, planting the decapitated Manzano heads triumphantly on the Monroy tomb – after which the mother was known as **María La Brava**. Her 15C house, which remains to this day, can be found in the lively Plaza de los Bandos with its numerous 19C buildings. The *bandos* remained active until 1476.

Salamanca was occupied by the French during the War of Independence; when the French evacuated the town, Wellington entered it in June 1812 but within days had moved south to the **Arapiles Valley** where, on 22 July, he won the resounding Victory of Salamanca which proved to be a major turning point in the war.

The university – The university was founded in 1218 (about 50 years after Oxford University) and grew under the patronage of kings of Castilla, high dignitaries and learned men such as the antipope Benedict XIII. Its teaching was soon widely renowned (it took part in the reform of the Catholic Church) and by the 16C it numbered 70 professors of studies and 12 000 students. Its great and famous members include the Infante Don Juan, son of the Catholic Monarchs; St John of the Cross and his teacher, the great humanist **Fray Luis de León** (1527-91); and **Miguel de Unamuno** (1864-1936), Professor of Greek, University Rector for a number of years, and a philosopher of international standing.

Art in Salamanca – In the late 15C and early 16C, two major painters were working in Salamanca: **Fernando Gallego**, one of the best Hispano-Flemish artists (much influenced in precision of line and realism by Dirk Bouts) and **Juan of Flanders** (b 1465),

Plaza Mayor

who settled in the city in 1504 and whose elegant and gentle work is outstanding for the subtle delicacy of its colours.

The 15C also saw the evolution of the original Salamanca patio arch, a mixtilinear arc in which the line of the curve, inspired by Mudéjar design, is broken by counter curves and straight lines. The 16C brought decoration to an ebullient climax in **Plateresque** art, the purest examples of which may be seen in Salamanca.

Special Features

MONUMENTAL CENTRE★★★ 🕐 *allow one day*
Follow the itinerary on the town plan.

Plaza Mayor★★★

The Plaza Mayor is unquestionably the life and soul of Salamanca. All the city's major streets converge on the square, where locals and visitors alike meet for a drink at its lively café terraces or for an evening stroll. It was built for the city by Philip V between 1729 and 1755 in gratitude for its support in the War of Succession, and is among the finest in Spain. It was designed as a homogeneous unit principally by the Churriguera brothers: four ground-level arcades with rounded arches, decorated by a series of portrait medallions of the Spanish kings from Alfonso XI to Ferdinand VI and famous men such as Cervantes, El Cid, Christopher Columbus and Hernán Cortés, support the three storeys which rise in perfect formation to an elegant balustrade. On the north and east sides are the pedimented fronts of the **Ayuntamiento** (town hall) and the Pabellón Real (Royal Pavilion), the latter distinguished by a bust of Philip V.

▶ *Exit the plaza Mayor along calle Prior and head for plaza de Monterrey.*

Casa de las Muertes (House of Death)

The early-16C façade, one of the first examples of Plateresque, is attributed, complete with its design of medallions, foliated scrollwork and decorative putti, to Diego de Siloé.

Convento de las Úrsulas (Ursuline Convent)
🕐 *Open 11am-1pm and 4.30-6.30pm.* 🕐 *Closed last Sun of every month.* 👛 *2€.*
☎ *923 21 98 77.*

Address Book

For coin ranges, see the Legend at the back of the guide.

WHERE TO EAT

El Bardo – *Compañía 88* – ☎ *923 25 92 65*. A typical student haunt with vaulted ceilings and a lively atmosphere. A good bet for a bite to eat after visiting the nearby Casa de las Conchas. Vegetarian items available.

La Fonda del Arcediano de Medina – *Reja 2* – ☎ *923 21 57 12* – *Reservation recommended*. This restaurant has a solid local reputation as a result of its cuisine and good wine list. Meats and *bacalao* (cod) are the specialties. Pleasant decor, including subtle lighting and an interesting collage of images on the ceiling.

El Patio Chico – *Meléndez 13* – ☎ *923 26 86 16* - 🖵. Decorated in traditional style with brick walls, exposed beams and a terracotta floor. A pleasant atmosphere with a background of the latest chart hits. The house speciality is chanfaina, the city's signature dish.

TAPAS

Momo – *San Pablo 13* – ☎ *923 28 07 98*. The contemporary version of a tapas bar, with minimalist decoration and allusions to the clocks in the novel *Momo*. Tapas and skewers come cold and hot, and there's a dining room in the basement.

Mesón Cervantes – *Plaza Mayor 15* – ☎ *923 21 72 13* – 🖵. A bar with typical Castilian decor and fine views of plaza Mayor serving modern, innovative cuisine. Popular with Salamanca's young crowd at night.

WHERE TO STAY

Hostal Catedral – *Mayor 46 1ºB* – ☎ *923 27 06 14* – 🖵 – *Reservation recommended* – *6 rooms* – 🖾 *2.50€*. Because of its location (some of its windows open directly onto the cathedral), it would have been impossible to give this hostal any other name! Occupying the first floor of an attractive stone building, it is tastefully decorated with spotless bathrooms and unexpected touches such as embroidered bed linen.

Hotel Emperatriz – *Compañia 44* – ☎ *923 21 92 00* – 🍴 – *61 rooms* – 🖾 *2.50€* – *Restaurant 7.50/9.50€*. The name of the street refers to the Society of Jesus, as the Clerecía is located just a few metres from the hotel. The façade has a noble appearance, yet the interior is somewhat simple in style.

Hostal Plaza Mayor – *Plaza del Corrillo 20* – ☎ *923 26 20 20* – *19 rooms*. Ideal if you want to stay in the centre of Salamanca as it is situated just behind Plaza Mayor, opposite the Romanesque church of San Martín. The hotel's interior design highlights the main features of the house, such as its attractive wooden beams.

Hotel Rector – *Rector Esperabé 10* – ☎ *923 21 84 82* – 🖵 – *14 rooms* – 🖾 *10€*. A charming small hotel with spectacular views of the cathedral and elegant, well-appointed rooms.

TAKING A BREAK

Café Novelty – *Plaza Mayor 2* – ☎ *923 21 49 56*. A famous Salamanca café where Miguel de Unamuno used to meet his friends and colleagues. The wooden chairs and marble tables conjure up images of the philosopher engaged in animated discussion, while its terrace on plaza Mayor offers a wonderful view of one of Spain's finest squares.

Café Tío Vivo – *Clavel 5* – *Open from 8am*. The name originates from the tío vivo (merry-go-round) on the bar. The cine-camera, spotlights and the objects decorating the bar give it an American feel.

Capitán Haddock – *Concejo 13-15* – *Open 8am-1am*. The entrance is through a narrow passageway which gives no hint of the stylish decor and subdued lighting inside.

La Regenta – *Espoz y Mina 19* – ☎ *923 12 32 30* – *Open 10am-noon and 2-8pm*. This typical café with a 19C atmosphere has an older feel than those above.

The 16C church contains the **tomb**★ of Alonso de Fonseca on which the incredibly delicate carved low reliefs are attributed to Diego de Siloé. The **museum**, with its artesonado and coffered ceilings, houses panels and fragments of an altarpiece by Juan de Borgoña, one of which illustrates *St Ursula and the Virgins*. There are also two noteworthy works by Morales the Divine, an *Ecce Homo* and a *Pietà*.

Palacio de Monterrey

Built in 1539, this typical Renaissance palace has an openwork balustrade crowning a long top floor gallery, between corner towers.

SALAMANCA

Álvaro Gil	BY	3
Anaya Pl.	BZ	4
Ángel Pl.	BY	6
Azafranal	CY	
Bandos Pl. de los	BY	7
Bordadores	BY	9
Caldereros	BZ	10
Calderón de la Barca	BZ	12
Carmen Cuesta del	BY	13
Comuneros Av. de los	CY	16
Concilio de Trento Pl.	BZ	18
Condes de Crespo Rascón	BY	19
Constitución Pl. de la	CY	21
Corillo Pl.	BY	22
Dr. Torres Villarroel Pas. del	BY	25

Espoz y Mina	BY	28
Estación Pas. de la	CY	30
Federico Anaya Av. de	CY	31
Filiberto Villalobos Av. de	AY	33
Fray Luis de Granada	BY	34
Fuente Pl. de la	BY	36
Juan de la Fuente	BZ	37
Libertad Pl. de la	BY	39
Libreros	BZ	40
María Auxiliadora	CY	42
Marquesa de Almarza	CZ	43
Mayor Pl.	BY	
Meléndez	BY	45
Monterrey Pl. de	BY	46
Palominos	BZ	51
Patio Chico	BZ	52
Poeta Iglesias Pl.	BY	57

Pozo Amarillo	BY	58
Ramón y Cajal	AY	60
Rector Lucena	BY	15
Reina Pl. de la	CY	61
Reyes de España Av.	BZ	63
San Blas	AY	64
San Isidro Pl. de	BYZ	66
San Julián Pl.	CY	67
Sancti Spiritus Cuesta	CY	75
Santa Eulalia Pl.	CY	69
Santa Teresa Pl. de	BY	70
Santo Domingo Pl.	BZ	72
Serranos	BZ	76
Toro	BCY	
Tostado	BZ	78
Wences Moreno	BY	79
Zamora	BY	

Casa de Doña Maria la Brava	BY	Q
Casa de las Muertes	BY	S
Convento de las Dueñas	BZ	F
Convento de las Úrsulas	BY	X

Escuelas menores	ABZ	U¹
Museo Art Nouveau y Art Déco	BZ	M¹
Palacio de Fonseca (Diputación)	BY	D

Palacio de Monterrey	BY	R
Purísima Concepción	BY	P
Universidad	BZ	U

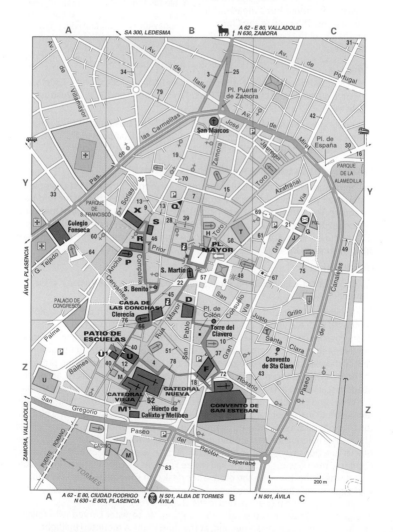

Iglesia de la Purísima Concepción (Church of the Immaculate Conception)

🕐 *Open Fri-Sat noon-1pm and 5-7pm (8pm summer).* 🕐 *Closed Sun-Thu except for worship.* ☎ *923 21 27 38.*

The church contains works by Ribera, including one of his most famous paintings, the **Immaculate Conception**★, which hangs above the high altar.

Plaza de San Benito

Surrounding this delightful square, at the centre of which stands the **Iglesia de San Benito**, are the mansions of Salamanca's old noble rival families. The church itself, dating from 1490, was the Maldonado family pantheon.

Casa de las Conchas★ (House of Shells)

This late-15C house with its 400 scallop shells, carved in the same golden stone as the wall, its line of highly decorative Isabelline windows and, lower down, beautiful wrought-iron window grilles, composes a timelessly decorative and unique façade. Its interior now houses a public library. The **patio** has delicate mixtilinear arches, openwork balustrades, carved lions' heads and coats of arms. The view of the Clerecía from the top of the stairs is particularly attractive.

A Secular Tradition

The red inscriptions which appear on most of the town's monuments, in particular those of the university, are part of an old tradition that dates back to the 15C: on graduating, students would take part in a bullfight and, with the blood of the bull they had killed, write the word Victor and the date on a wall. Today the same is done with paint.

Clerecía

🕐 *Open 10.30am-1.30pm and 4-6.30pm; Apr-Oct 10.30am-1.30pm and 5-7.30pm. Last admission 40 min before closing.* 🕐 *Closed Sun afternoon and Mon; 1 and 6 Jan and 25 Dec.* 🎫 *1.50€.* ☎ *923 27 71 22.*

This impressive Jesuit College was begun in 1617 and was only finished with the completion of the Baroque towers by Andrés García de Quiñones in 1755. There are Baroque cloisters beside the church.

Patio de las Escuelas★★★ (Schools' Square)

This small square, off the old Calle Libreros, is surrounded by the best examples of Salamanca Plateresque. A bronze statue of Fray Luis de León stands in the middle of the square. The former university principals' residence is now the **Museo Unamuno**, a museum dedicated to this famous philospher. *Guided tours (30min), 9.30am-1.30pm and 4-7.30pm; Sat, 10am-1.30pm and 4-7pm; Sun, 10am-1.30pm; last admission 30min before closing.* 🎫 *1.80€.* ☎ *923 29 44 00 (ext. 1196).*

Universidad

🕐 *Open 9.30am-1.30pm and 4-6.30pm; Sun and public hols, 10am-1pm.* 🎫 *4€.* ☎ *923 29 44 03.*

The university's sumptuous **entrance**★★★ of 1534 is a brilliant piece of sculpture, composed with the utmost care for detail, as in the goldsmith's art. Above the twin doors, covered by basket arches, the carving is in ever greater relief as it rises through the three registers, to compensate for the increasing distance from the ground. A central medallion in the first register shows the Catholic monarchs who presented the doorway; in the second, above crowned escutcheons and medallions, are portrait heads in scallop shell niches; in the third, flanking the pope supported by cardinals, are Venus and Hercules (in square frames) and the Virtues (in roundels). The most famous motif in this outstanding ensemble is the death's head surmounted by a frog (on the right pilaster, halfway up) symbolising the posthumous punishment of lust. The lecture halls are located around the **patio**: the **Paraninfo** or Large Hall, where official functions were held, is hung with 17C Brussels tapestries and a portrait of Charles IV from Goya's studio; the hall where Fray Luis de León lectured in theology is as it was in the 16C, with the professor's desk and sounding-board overlooking the rough-hewn students' benches – a luxury in days when students usually sat on the floor. Fray Luis' ashes are buried in the chapel (1767).

The grand staircase rises beneath star vaulting, its banister carved with foliated scrollwork and imaginary scenes and, at the third flight, a mounted bullfight.

A gallery on the first floor has its original, rich **artesonado ceiling** with stalactite ornaments and a delicate low relief frieze along the walls. A Gothic style door with a fine 16C grille opens into the 18C library which contains 40 000 16C-18C volumes as well as incunabula and manuscripts, some of which date back to the 11C.

Hospital del Estudio (Students' Hospice)

Now the University Rectorate. The hospice, completed in 1533, has an interesting Gothic entrance with two basket-handle arches. Visible on its upper part are two escutcheons of Spain, made before 1492 given that the pomegranate, the symbol of the Catholic Monarchs, does not feature on them, and a trefoil arch framed by an *alfiz*.

Escuelas Menores (Minor Schools)

🕐 *Open 9.30am-1pm and 4-6.30pm (7.30pm in summer); Sun and public hols, 10am-1.30pm.* ⬡ *4€.* ☎ *923 29 44 03.*

Standing to the right of the hospital and crowned by the same openwork Renaissance frieze, is the entrance to the Minor (preparatory) Schools – a Plateresque portal decorated with coats of arms, roundels and scrollwork. The typical Salamanca **patio**★★ (1428) inside, has lovely lines. To the right of the entrance is a new exhibition room with a fine Mudéjar ceiling; the University Museum opposite exhibits what remains of the ceiling painted by Fernando Gallego for the former university library. This section of the **Cielo de Salamanca**★ (Salamanca Sky) illustrates constellations and signs of the zodiac. The interest of this remaining part gives an idea of what the whole must have been like in the 15C. Several works by Juan of Flanders and Juan of Burgundy stand out in the museum.

Catedral Nueva★★ (New Cathedral)

🕐 *Open 9am-2pm and 4-6pm (8pm in summer); Sun, 9am-2pm.* ⬡3€. ☎ *923 21 74 76.*

Construction, begun in 1513, was largely completed by 1560, although additions continued to be made until the 18C – hence the variety of architectural styles: Gothic, Renaissance and Baroque.

The **west front**★★★ is divided below the windows into four wide bays which correspond to the ground plan. The bays are outlined by pierced stonework, carved as minutely as the keystones in the arches, the friezes and the pinnacled balustrades. The Gothic decoration of the central portal, which in retable style includes scenes such as a Crucifixion shown between St Peter and St Paul, overflows the covings and tympanum.

The **north doorway,** facing the **Colegio de Anaya**, is adorned with a delicate low relief of Christ's entry into Jerusalem (Palm Sunday). The doorway was recently restored and the lower section of the last archivolt now contains the somewhat surprising figure of a small astronaut as well as a mythological animal eating an ice-cream.

The **interior**, in particular the pattern of the vaulting, the delicacy of the cornices and the sweep of the pillars, strikes one immediately on entering. The eight windows in the lantern are given added effect by a drum on which scenes from the Life of the Virgin were painted in the 18C by the Churriguera brothers who also designed the ornate Baroque stalls in the *coro*, the *trascoro* and the organ loft above the stalls on the north side; the south loft is Plateresque (1558).

Catedral Vieja★★★ (Old Cathedral)

🕐 *Open 10am-12.30pm and 4-5.30pm (10am-7.30pm in summer).* ⬡3€; no charge Sun 10am-noon. ☎ *923 21 74 76.* ▶ *Enter through the first bay off the south aisle in the new cathedral.*

Fortunately the builders of the new cathedral respected the fabric of the old which, nevertheless, is almost totally masked outside by its larger descendant. It was built in the 12C and is a good example of the Romanesque, the pointed arching being a legitimate, if unusual, innovation; the **cimborrio** (lantern), or Torre del Gallo, with two tiers of windows and ribbing, is outstanding. High up beneath the vaulting, the capitals are carved with scenes of tournaments and imaginary animals. The Capilla de San Martín (St Martin's Chapel) at the base of the tower is covered in 13C frescoes by Antón Sanchez de Segovia.

The **altarpiece**★★ in the central apsidal chapel was painted by Nicholas of Florence in 1445 and comprises 53 compartments decorated in surprisingly fresh colours in vivid detail – an interesting testimony to the architecture and dress of the times – beneath a Last Judgement in which the dark background enhances the brilliance of the Risen Christ. The Virgin of the Vega at the retable centre is a 12C wooden statue, plated in gilded and enamelled bronze.

Recesses in the south transept contain French-influenced 13C recumbent figures and frescoes.

Claustro – Some of the capitals from earlier Romanesque galleries destroyed during the Lisbon earthquake in 1755 remain in these cloisters, forming a surprising contrast to the Plateresque decoration. The adjoining **Capilla de Talavera**, with a Mudéjar dome on carved ribs, was where the ancient Mozarabic rite was celebrated – the altarpiece is in the style of Pedro Berruguete. The Capilla de Santa Barbara was formerly used for university examinations. A museum occupying three rooms and the Capilla de Santa Catalina contains works by Fernando Gallego and his brother Francisco as well as others by Juan of Flanders (St Michael altarpiece).

The **Capilla Anaya** contains the outstanding 15C alabaster **tomb**★★ of Diego de Anaya, archbishop first of Salamanca and then of Sevilla. The sides are decorated with saints and their emblems. Surrounding the tomb is a magnificently wrought Plateresque grille. There is also a 15C **organ**★ and the superb 16C recumbent statues of Gutierre de Monroy and Constancia de Anaya.

From the **Patio Chico** you can see the old cathedral apse and the scallop tiling on the **Torre del Gallo** (Cockerel Tower). From here, calle Arcediano leads to the delightful **Huerto de Calixto y Melibea.**

Museo de Art Nouveau y Art Déco

🕐 *Open 11am-2pm and 4-7pm; Sat-Sun and public hols, 11am-8pm; 1 Apr-15 Oct, 11am-2pm and 5-9pm; Sat-Sun and public hols, 11am-9pm.* 🕐 *Closed Mon, 1 and 6 Jan and 24-25 and 31 Dec.* 💷 *2.50€, no charge Thu morning.* ☎ *923 12 14 25.*

This modern art museum is housed in the Casa Lis, a Modernist building dating from the beginning of the 20C. It is one of the few museums in Spain devoted to Art Nouveau and Art Deco. Its collection includes works by R Lalique, vases by E Galle and small sculptures by Hagenauer. The view of the building from the Tormes river is particularly impressive.

Convento de San Esteban★ (St Stephen's Monastery)

🕐 *Open 9am-1.30pm and 4-6pm (8pm in summer).* 💷 *1.50€.* ☎ *923 21 50 00.*

Gothic and Renaissance styles are mingled in this 16C and 17C building, so that while typically Gothic pinnacles decorate the side buttresses, nothing could be more Plateresque in style than the sculpture of the impressive **façade**★★. The low relief of the *Martyrdom of St Stephen* is by Juan Antonio Ceroni (1610).

In the 17C **cloisters**★, note the prophets' heads in **medallions** and the grand staircase (1553).

The large **church** has star vaulting in the gallery and a central altarpiece by José Churriguera with an abundance of carving and gilt decoration. Crowning it is a painting The Martyrdom of St Stephen, by Claudio Coello.

Convento de las Dueñas

🕐 *Open 10.30am (11.30am Sun)-12.45pm and 4.30-5.30pm (6.45pm in summer).* 💷 *1.50€.* ☎ *923 21 54 42.*

The Renaissance **cloisters**★★ of this convent have profusely carved capitals which are extraordinarily forceful in spite of their small size. Among the sculptures are the figures of symbolic animals, distorted human shapes as well as medallions decorated with the heads of majestic old men or delicately featured women.

Cloisters, Convento de las Dueñas

J. Malburet/MICHELIN

Torre del Clavero

The tower, all that remains of a castle built in 1450, is an octagonal keep, crowned with sentry turrets decorated underneath with Mudéjar trellis-work.

Palacio de Fonseca or Diputación (Fonseca Palace or Council)

The **patio**★ of this Renaissance palace combines Salamanca mixtilinear arches at one end with a corbelled gallery – supported by distorted atlantes – on the right and an arcade on the left in which the capitals resemble those in the Convento de las Dueñas. The view of the palace is particularly pleasant at night.

Iglesia de San Martín

The Romanesque church has a north door with dog-tooth covings in the Zamora style.

▶ Colegio Fonseca (Gothic chapel, Renaissance **patio**★); Iglesia de San Marcos (12C); Convento de Santa Clara (Museum: 13C-16C murals, artesonado work).

Excursion

Alba de Tormes

23km/14mi SE on the N 501 and C 510. The small town stands on the banks of the Tormes river. Only the massive keep remains of the castle of the dukes of Alba. The town boasts of possessing the mortal remains of St Teresa of Ávila in the church of the Carmelite Convent.

The **Iglesia de San Juan,** a church with a Romanesque-Mudéjar east end, contains an outstanding 11C **sculpture ensemble**★ in the apse. It illustrates Christ and the Disciples seated in a semicircle, all equally noble in expression and stance.

San Sebastián★★ (♨ *See DONOSTIA)*

Sangüesa/Zangoza★

POPULATION: 4 447.

MICHELIN MAP 573 E 26 – NAVARRA.

Sangüesa (Zangoza in Basque) stands in arable country (mostly cereals) on the left bank of the River Aragón. It still seems to guard the bridge which in the Middle Ages brought the town prosperity. Its artistic heritage, including its picturesque streets fronted by impressive mansions, is the result of the role played by the Way of St James during the course of Sangüesa's history.

Location

Sangüesa is situated 5km/3mi from the N 240, linking Jaca with Pamplona. 🚩 *Mayor 2, 31400 Sangüesa,* ☎ *948 87 14 11.*

♨ *Neighbouring sights are described in the following chapters: The WAY OF ST JAMES, Monasterio de LEYRE (15km/9mi NE), OLITE (44km/27mi SW), PAMPLONA (46km/29mi NW) and JACA (81km/51mi E).*

Sangüesa and the Way of St James

Fear of the Moors compelled Sangüesans to live until the 10C on the Rocaforte hillside; by the 11C, however, the citizens had moved down to defend the bridge and clear a safe passage for pilgrims. Sangüesa reached its zenith at the end of the Middle Ages when prosperous citizens began to build elegant residential mansions. These contrasted with the austere Palacio del Príncipe de Viana (Palace of the Prince of Viana), residence of the kings of Navarra, now the Ayuntamiento (town hall), with its façade (seen through the gateway) flanked by two imposing battlemented towers.

The main street, the former rúa Mayor which was once part of the pilgrim road, is lined with comfortable brick houses with the Classical carved wood eaves and windows with rich Gothic or Plateresque surrounds. In the second street on the right coming from the bridge can be seen the Baroque front of the Palacio de Vallesantoro, a palace protected by monumental overhangs carved with imaginary animals.

Worth a Visit

Iglesia de Santa María la Real★

The church, begun in the 12C, was completed in the 13C with the construction of the splendid south portal, the octagonal tower and its spire.

Portada Sur★★ (South Portal) – Late 12C to 13C. The portal is so crowded with sculpture that one stands amazed at the number of subjects depicted and the variety of ways in which they have been illustrated. At least two artists worked on the masterpiece: the Master of San Juan de la Peña and a certain Leodegarius.

The **statue columns**, already Gothic, derive from those at Chartres and Autun. On the **tympanum**, God the Father at the centre of a group of angel musicians receives the chosen at his right, , but with his down-pointing left arm reproves the sinners. In a corner, weighing souls, is St Michael.

The **covings** swarm with motifs; the second innermost shows the humbler trades: clog-maker, lute-maker and butcher.

The older **upper arches**, marked by an Aragonese severity of style, show God surrounded by the symbols of the four Evangelists, two angels and the 12 disciples.

Excursions

Castillo de Javier★

7km/4mi NE on the NA 541. **St Francis Xavier**, the patron saint of Navarra, who was born here in 1506, founded the Society of Jesus, along with his Basque compatriot, Ignatius Loyola. He was later sent as a missionary by the Portuguese, first to Goa and then to Japan. He died in 1552 on his way to China. He was canonised in 1622.

⚷ *Closed for reconstruction.* ☎ *948 88 40 24.*

The fortress, birthplace of the saint, was in part destroyed by Cardinal Cisneros in 1516. The visit includes the Patio de Armas (Parade Ground), the **oratorio**★ (oratory), which contains a 13C Christ in walnut and an unusual 15C fresco of the Dance of Death, the Sala Grande (Great Hall) and, among the oldest parts of the castle dating from the 10C-11C, the Cuarto del Santo (Saint's bedroom).

B. Juge/MICHELIN

Ayuntamiento

Sos del Rey Católico★

13km/8mi SE along the A 127. It was here, in the **Palacio de los Sada** (Sada Palace), that Ferdinand the Catholic, who was to unite Spain, was born in 1452. The houses, palaces, walls and doorways which line the narrow cobbled streets and alleys leading to the keep and the church give the town a medieval air.

On the **plaza Mayor,** an irregularly shaped square, stand the imposing 16C Ayuntamiento (town hall), which like the Palacio de los Gil de Jaz has large carved wood overhangs, and the Lonja (Exchange) with wide arches.

Iglesia de San Esteban★ – *Open 10am-1pm and 3.30-5.30pm; Jun-Sep, 10am-1pm and 4-6pm; Sun and public hols, 10am-noon and 4-6pm. 0.60€.* ☎ *948 88 82 03.*
The Church of St Stephen is reached through a vaulted passageway. The 11C **crypt**★ beneath the church is dedicated to Our Lady of Forgiveness (Virgen del Perdón). Two of the three apses are decorated with fine 14C **frescoes**. The central apse contains outstanding carved capitals carved with the figures of women and birds. The statue columns at the **main door** have the stiff and noble bearing of those at Sangüesa. The church itself, built in the transitional style, has a beautiful Renaissance **gallery**★. A chapel contains a 12C Romanesque figure of Christ with eyes open wide.

Uncastillo

34km/21mi SE. 21km/13mi from Sos del Rey Cátolico. The Romanesque **Iglesia de Santa María** has an unusual 14C tower adorned with machicolations and pinnacle turrets. The rich and delicate carving on the **south portal**★, depicting imaginary beasts for the most part, makes it one of the most beautiful doorways of the late Romanesque period. The church gallery with Renaissance **stalls**★ and the **cloisters**★ are 16C Plateresque.

Monasterio de
Santa María de Huerta★★

MICHELIN MAP 575 I 23 –

CASTILLA Y LEÓN (SORIA).

In 1144, on the request of Emperor Alfonso VII, a Cistercian community came to settle in what was to become the Soria region on the border between Castilla and Aragón. Monks settled in Huerta in 1162 and shortly afterwards laid the foundations of the present buildings.

The sober Cistercian style was slightly modified by Renaissance innovations. From 1835 to 1930 the monastery buildings stood empty before being reinhabited and restored.

Location

The monastery stands close to the A 2 highway linking Madrid and Zaragoza (131km/82mi NE).

⚭ *Neighbouring sights are described in the following chapters: Monasterio de PIEDRA (53km/33mi E), SIGÜENZA (67km/42mi SW) and SORIA (85km/53mi NW).*

Tour

🕐 *Approximately 1hr. Open 10am-1pm and 4-6.30pm; Sun and public hols, 10-11.15am; last admission 15min before closing.* ☜ *2€.* ☎ *975 32 70 02.*

The monastery is entered through a 16C **triumphal arch**.

CLOISTERS AND MONASTIC BUILDINGS

Claustro Herreriano (Herreran Cloisters)

16C-17C. The buildings surrounding the cloisters are the monks' living quarters.

Claustro de los Caballeros★ (Knights' Cloisters)

13C-16C. The cloisters owe their name to the many knights who lie buried there. The two storeys of the cloisters have very different styles: the arches at ground level are elegant, pointed and purely Gothic while above, the gallery added in the 16C has all the exuberance and imagination of the Plateresque *(it is a copy of the gallery in the Palacio de Avellaneda in Peñaranda de Duero).* The decorative medallions are of Prophets, Apostles and Spanish kings.

Sala de los Conversos (Lay brothers' Hall)

12C. This is divided down its length by stout pillars, crowned with stylised capitals.

Cocina

The kitchen has a monumental central chimney.

Refectorio★★

The refectory, a masterpiece of 13C Gothic, impresses by its sheer size – it has sexpartite vaulting rising 15m/50ft above the 35m/115ft long hall – and the amount of light shining through the windows, in particular, the wonderful rose window in the south wall. Leading up to the **reader's lectern** is a beautiful staircase carved out of the wall with small arches supported by slender columns.

IGLESIA

The church has been restored to its original state although the royal chapel has kept its sumptuous Churrigueresque decoration. Between the narthex and the aisles there is an intricate 18C wrought-iron screen.

The **coro alto** (choir) is beautifully decorated with Renaissance panelling and woodwork. The Talavera *azulejos* on the floor are very old.

Santander★

POPULATION: 196 218.

MICHELIN MAP 572 B 18 (ALSO TOWN PLAN) – CANTABRIA.

Santander enjoys a magnificent location★★ on a delightful bay bathed by the azure waters of the Cantabrian Sea and overlooked by verdant hills. It is a city best enjoyed on foot, with its long maritime front – one of the finest in Spain – lined by attractive gardens offering incomparable views.

During the summer, Santander is transformed into a lively, cosmopolitan resort with its superb beaches, prestigious International Festival and the renowned courses at the Universidad Internacional Menéndez Pelayo, attracting students from around the world.

Location

Santander stands to the west of the bay, enclosed by the rocky Magdalena headland and the sandy Somo point. The city covers an extensive area, with the central area fanning out to the west of the Magdalena peninsula, and the El Sardinero residential district to the north. The A 8 motorway runs SE to Bilbao (116km/72mi). *Jardines de Pereda, 39003 Santander, ☎ 942 21 61 20; Plaza de Velarde 5, 39001 Santander, ☎ 942 31 07 08.*

Neighbouring sights are described in the following chapters: SANTILLANA DEL MAR (26km/16mi W) and COSTA DE CANTABRIA.

Worth a Visit

CITY CENTRE

The seigniorial **paseo de Pereda**★, along the seafront, is lined by the imposing Banco de Santander building and the small Palacete del Embarcadero, used as an exhibition centre. Along with the avenida de Calvo Sotelo, a major shopping street, this area forms the heart of the city centre.

Museo Regional de Prehistoria y Arqueología★

Open 9am (10am 16 Jun-15 Sep) to 1pm and 4-7pm; Sun and public hols all year, 11am-2pm. Closed Mon, 1 Jan, Good Fri, 1 May and 25 Dec. No charge. ☎ 942 20 71 09.

The archaeological museum in the basement of the Diputación consists mainly of finds excavated in prehistoric caves in Cantabria (particularly El Castillo, El Pendo and El Valle), although remains of extinct animals from the Quaternary Era are also on display here. The richest period is the Upper Palaeolithic from which there are bones engraved with animal silhouettes and **batons**★ (from El Pendo) made of horn and finely decorated for a purpose still unknown. The swords, spear tips and large Cabárceno cauldron all date from the Bronze Age. Also worthy of note are the three large circular steles, used for funerary purposes, which are representative of the apogee of the Cantabrian culture (Bronze Age). Finally, one gallery is devoted to remains of the Roman occupation. The finds are mostly from Julióbriga (*see AGUILAR DE CAMPOO: Tours)* and Castro Urdiales, and include coins, bronzes and pottery figurines. The most outstanding exhibit from the Middle Ages is a Mozarabic belt clasp made from bone and dating from the 10C.

Catedral

Entry is through the restored Gothic cloisters. The fortress-like cathedral stands on a slight rise at the end of paseo de Pareda. The cathedral was badly damaged as a result of a fire in 1941, but has been rebuilt in its original Gothic style. A Baroque altarpiece dominates the presbytery; the **font** to the right of the ambulatory was brought here from the

A Time of Crisis

At the end of the 19C, the Cabo Machichaco cargo boat disaster, killing more than 500 people, caused widespread shock in Spain.

Half a century later, on 15 February 1941, at a time when the city was attempting to recover from the Civil War, a tornado struck Santander: the sea swept over the quays and a fire broke out, almost completely destroying the centre. Reconstruction was undertaken to a street plan of blocks of no more than four or five storeys, and space was allocated to gardens beside the sea, promenades such as the paseo de Pereda which skirts the pleasure boat harbour known as Puerto Chico, and squares such as plaza Porticada.

Address Book

BOAT TRIPS

Throughout the year, vessels known as *reginas* provide a shuttle service between Santander and Somo and Pedreña (two districts on the other side of the bay). In summer, excursions around the bay and along the Cubas River are also available for visitors, with departures from the Embarcadero del Palacete dock on paseo de Pereda. ☎ *942 216 753*.

For coin ranges, see the Legend at the back of the guide.

WHERE TO EAT

☺ **Mesón Rampalay** – *Daoíz y Velarde 9 – ☎ 942 31 33 67 – Closed Tue*. This bar-restaurant is located in a street running parallel to paseo Pereda, next to the Iglesia de Santa Lucía. A long bar and a number of tables, where you can enjoy traditional specialities such as red peppers with tuna, seafood salad, and mushrooms with cod.

☺☺ **Bodega del Riojano** – *Río de la Pila 5 – ☎ 942 21 67 50 – Closed Sun evening and Mon*. This charming, tavern-style bar-restaurant is decorated with numerous painted barrels both at the entrance to the bar and in the spacious dining room, giving the place a rustic feel. The cuisine here revolves around traditional local dishes.

WHERE TO STAY

☺☺ **Hotel Carlos III** – *Avenida Reina Victoria 135 (El Sardinero) – ☎ 942 27 16 16 – Open 15 Mar-Oct – 20 rooms – ⊑ 4€*. The Carlos III is a small hotel housed in an impressive early-20C mansion opposite the playa del Sardinero. A pleasant mid-range option.

☺☺☺ **Las Brisas** - *La Braña 14 (El Sardinero) – ☎ 942 27 50 11 – 13 room*. An attractive building with a tower, in the El Sardinero district next to the beach. Sitting rooms have lovely decorative details, and the service and attention in this small establishment are personalised.

FIESTAS

In addition to the International Music and Dance Festival held during August in the Palacio de Festivales (designed by Saénz de Oiza, 1991), Santander also hosts the fiesta of St James (Santiago) in July, with its bullfights and range of popular concerts and performances.

---

garden of a house in Sevilla by soldiers from Santander who helped Ferdinand III, the Saint, conquer Sevilla in 1248.

Iglesia del Cristo★ – Access to the cathedral's fine 13C crypt, comprising three low aisles separated by solid cruciform pillars, is through the south portal. Excavations in the Evangelist nave have brought to light the remains of a Roman house where, it would seem, the relics of St Emeterio and St Celedonio, patron saints of the city, were buried; these are currently displayed in the apse to the left. The Baroque Christ at the high altar is from the Castilian School.

Museo de Bellas Artes (Fine Arts Museum)

🕐 *Open 10.15am-1pm and 5.30-9pm (Sat, mornings only); 15 Jun-15 Sep, 11.15am-1pm and 5.30-9pm (Sat, mornings only).* 🕐 *Closed Sun and public hols.* ⬤ *No charge.* ☎ *942 23 94 85/ 7.*

Major works on display include a portrait of Ferdinand VII by **Goya**; a series of the latter's etchings entitled *Disasters of War, La Tauromaquia* and *Caprichos*; and several 16C-18C paintings by Flemish and Italian artists. The majority of the museum's collection is dedicated to canvases and sculptures by 19C-20C Spanish (and local) artists such as Madrazo, Solana, Cossío, Riancho, Blanchard, Oteiza and Miró. The room on the ground floor is devoted to temporary exhibitions.

Biblioteca Menéndez y Pelayo

🔍 *Guided tours (20min), 9.30-11.30am (every half hour).* 🕐 *Closed Sat-Sun and public hols.* ☎ *942 23 45 34.*

Marcelino Menéndez y Pelayo (1856-1912), one of Spain's greatest historians and indefatigable writers, bequeathed to his native city this fabulous library of nearly 43 000 books and manuscripts by great Castilian authors, in addition to the building that now houses it, on the condition that it retained its original appearance. The Casa-Museo to the rear *(open to the public)*, will soon house the library of another great Spanish literary figure, Gerardo Diego.

J. Malburet/MICHELIN

The beach at El Sardinero

PENÍNSULA DE LA MAGDALENA★★

[Kids] With its magnificent position and sublime views, this peninsula is one of Santander's major sights. An oasis of greenery overlooking the sea, it is an ideal place for a stroll, and is popular with children, in particular for the small zoo (seals, penguins, polar bears etc) on the El Sardinero side, and the replicas of the galleons in which Francisco de Orellana explored the Amazon.

A palace, the **Palacio de la Magdalena,** stands to the rear of the park. At the end of the 19C, the royal family – along with the elite of Spanish society – made bathing in the sea fashionable here, with the result that the municipality built this palace as a summer residence for Alfonso XIII. Today, the building is occupied by the Menéndez Pelayo International University.

EL SARDINERO★★

With its three magnificent **beaches** – separated by two promontories but linked at low tide – along with those of El Promontorio and Magdalena, and leafy promenades, the residential and resort area of El Sardinero is deserving of its reputation as one of Santander's main attractions. Plaza de Italia, the heart of the district, is fronted by the Casino (1916) and the Parque de Mataleñas, with access to the city's municipal golf course.

Walk to Cabo Mayor★

allow 2hr; 4.5km/3mi round trip from the junction of calle García Lago and calle Gregorio Marañón, at the far end of El Sardinero. By car, 7km/4.5mi N.

This attractive walk, adjoining the Mataleñas golf course, runs along the coast, passing through Cabo Menor before reaching Cabo Mayor, offering magnificent views of the coast and bay along its entire length.

Museo Marítimo del Cantábrico (**maritime museum**), Calle San Martín de Bajamar, ☎ 942 27 49 62.

Excursions

Muriedas

7km/4mi S on the Burgos road. The house of Pedro Velarde, hero of the War of Independence, has been restored and is now the home of the **Museo Etnográfico de Cantabria** (Cantabrian Ethnographic Museum). A typical, Cantabrian gateway opens onto grounds in which may be seen a *hórreo* (squat drying shed) from the Liébana region and a Cantabrian stele. The 17C residence contains furniture, utensils and tools from all parts of the province. Mementoes of Velarde are displayed in his former bedroom and another large room on the first floor. *Guided tours (40min), 10am-1pm and 4-6pm (7pm 21 Jun-20 Sep); Sun and public hols all year, 11am-2pm; last admission 30min before closing.* ○ *Closed Mon, 1 Jan, Good Fri, 1 May and 25 Dec.* *No charge.* ☎ 942 25 13 47.

Parque de la Naturaleza de Cabárceno (Cabárceno Nature Reserve)

15km/9.5mi S. [Kids] *Open 9.30am-6pm (7pm May-Sep).* *12€.* ☎ 942 56 37 36.

An old iron mine in the Sierra de Cabarga that had been worked from Roman times until 1989, is now part of an environmental rehabilitation project (750ha/1 853 acres) which includes a superb **game park** where animals from the world over may be seen.

Castañeda

24km/15mi SW via the N 623 and N 634. The **antigua Colegiata**, a former collegiate church dating from the end of the 12C, stands in the small, pleasant valley through which the Pisueña runs. The unusually deep doorway is given considerable elegance by a simple decoration of alternate convex and concave covings.

Inside, the central area has retained its original plan with semicircular arches in the nave and the cupola on squinches. ○ *Visits by prior arrangement.* ☎ *942 59 21 57 (Señor Luis Carlos Fernández Ruiz).*

Puente Viesgo★

26km/16mi SW along the N 623. The caves (El Castillo, Las Chimeneas, Las Monedas and La Pasiega) hollowed out of the limestone mountain sides all round Puente Viesgo provide ample proof of their habitation in prehistoric times.

Cueva del Castillo★ – 👣 *Guided tours (45min), Oct-Apr, 9.30am-4pm; May-Sep, 10am-1pm and 4-7.30pm.* ○ *Closed Mon, Tue (Apr-Oct), 1 Jan, 23 May, 29 Sep and 25 and 31 Dec.* 👛 *3€.* ☎ *942 59 84 25.*

Cave dwellers began engraving and painting the walls towards the end of the Palaeolithic Age (from the Aurignacian to the Magdalenian period). The many designs – 750 have been counted – outlines only and sometimes incomplete, are widely scattered and some are difficult to get to. Many remain enigmatic, particularly the hands dipped in ochre and pressed against the wall, or outlined in red, to form negatives. It is thought they may symbolise man's superiority or possess magical powers. Of the almost 50 discovered only three are right hands.

The meaning of the parallel lines and point alignments also remains obscure. They may refer to weapons or traps for catching animals.

Santiago de Compostela★★★

POPULATION: 105 851.

MICHELIN MAP 571 D 4 (TOWN PLAN) – GALICIA (A CORUÑA/LA CORUÑA).

In the Middle Ages, Santiago de Compostela, the third most important city of pilgrimage after Jerusalem and Rome, attracted pilgrims from all parts of Europe. It remains one of Spain's most enchanting cities with its old quarters and maze of narrow streets. It is also a lively city, a reputation enhanced by its numerous bars and taverns, thousands of university students, and the throng of annual visitors. And with its artistic and musical heritage, its traditions and and its history, Santiago has something for everyone.

Contrary to all expectations, however, the styles of architecture that predominate here are Baroque and neo-Classical, rather than Romanesque, lending an air of solemnity to the city, a sensation that can be best appreciated from the paseo de la Herradura.

Location

This important pilgrimage city and junction of major historical routes remains well connected by road with the AP 9 leading to Vigo (84km/52mi S) and A Coruña/La Coruña (72km/45mi N), the N 547 heading to Lugo (107km/67mi E) and the AP 53 running SE to Orense/Ourense (111km/69mi). The city's airport is located at Km 11 along the Santiago-Lugo road. 🛈 *Vilar 43, 15705 Santiago de Compostela,* ☎ *981 58 40 81; Plaza de Galicia, 15706 Santiago de Compostela,* ☎ *981 57 39 90.*

🔎 *Neighbouring sights are described in the following chapters: A CORUÑA/La CORUÑA, PONTEVEDRA (57km/35mi S), RÍAS BAJAS, RÍAS ALTAS and The WAY OF ST JAMES.*

Background

History, tradition and legends – The Apostle **James the Greater**, known as the Thunderer on account of his temper, crossed the seas, so the legend goes, to convert Spain to Christianity. His boat was cast ashore at the mouth of the Ulla and he preached for seven years throughout the land before returning to Judaea where he fell an early victim to Herod Agrippa. His disciples, forced to flee, returned to Spain with his body which they buried near the earlier landing place. Invasions by the barbarians and later the Arabs caused the grave to be lost to memory. A star is believed to have pointed out the grave to some shepherds early in the 9C. This legend was to reinforce the theory that Compostela derived from *campus stellae* or field of stars although a more recent thesis, following the discovery of a necropolis beneath the cathedral, holds that the derivation is from compostela, the Latin for cemetery. In 844 Don Ramiro I was leading a handful of Spaniards in a bold attack against the Moors grouped at **Clavijo** near Logroño, when a knight in armour mounted on a charger and bearing a white standard with a red cross upon it, is said to have appeared on the battlefield. As he beat back the infidels the Christians recognised St James, naming him from that time *Matamoros* or Slayer of the Moors. The Reconquest and Spain had found a patron saint. During the crusade, it is said that one of the Christian leaders, the Lord of Pimentel, had to swim across a *ría*. He emerged from the sea covered in shells which were then adopted as the pilgrim symbol.

In the 11C devotion spread abroad until a journey to St James' shrine ranked equally with one to Rome or Jerusalem, particularly perilous since the invasion of the Holy Land by the Turks. St James had a particular appeal for the French who felt united with the Spanish in face of the Moorish threat, but English, Germans, Italians and even Scandinavians made the long pilgrimage, travelling for the most part through France along the routes organised to a considerable degree by the Benedictines and Cistercians of Cluny and Cîteaux.

Special Features

PRAÇA DO OBRADOIRO.

The dimensions of the square and the architectural quality of its surrounding buildings make it a fitting setting for the cathedral.

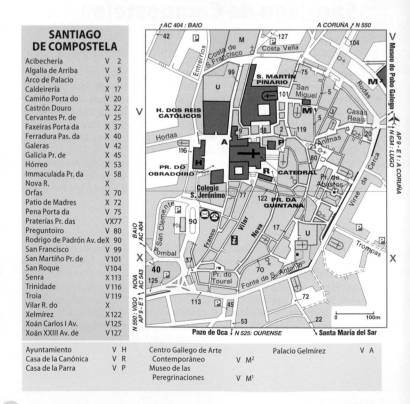

SANTIAGO DE COMPOSTELA

Catedral★★★

🕐 *Open 10.30am-1.30pm and 4-6.30pm (8pm Jun-Sep).* ☎ *981 56 05 27.*

The present cathedral, built upon the same site as the first basilica erected over the Apostle's tomb shortly after its discovery, and that of Alfonso III destroyed by Al-Mansur in 997, dates almost entirely from the 11C, 12C and 13C, although from the outside it looks more like a Baroque building.

Fachada del Obradoiro★★★ (Obradoiro façade) – This Baroque masterpiece (its name means work of gold) by **Fernando Casas y Novoa** has lent magnificence to the cathedral entrance since 1750. The central area, richly sculptured and given true Baroque movement by the interplay of straight and curved lines, rises to what appears almost to be a long tongue of flame. The upward triangular lines are emphasised by high flanking towers, slender and slightly in recess but sumptuously ornate.

Pórtico de la Gloria★★★ (Doorway of Glory) – Behind the Baroque façade stands the narthex and the Pórtico de la Gloria, a late-12C wonder by **Maestro Mateo**, leading to the nave. The statues of the triple doorway are exceptionally beautiful both as a composition and in detail, for the master used all his artistry to give variety of expression, style and colour.

The doorway is slightly more recent than the rest of the Romanesque cathedral and shows features of the Gothic style. Mateo, who also built bridges, had the crypt below reinforced to bear the weight of the portico. The central portal is dedicated to the Christian Church, the one on the left to the Jews, that on the right to the Gentiles. The central portal tympanum shows the Saviour surrounded by the four Evangelists while on the archivolt are the 24 Elders of the Apocalypse. The engaged

Cathedral

J. Malburet/MICHELIN

Address Book

For coin ranges, see the Legend at the back of the guide.

WHERE TO EAT

O Dezaseis – *Rúa de San Pedro 16 –* ☎ *981 577 633 – Reservation recommended.* Near the Porta do Camiño and the Museo do Pobo Galego, this restaurant has carved an impressive niche in Santiago gastronomy with its delicious tapas and excellent wines, which can also be enjoyed beneath the vines on the terrace. Attractive decor of wood and local stone.

San Clemente – *San Clemente 6 –* ☎ *981 58 08 82 – Closed Mon –* 🍽. Very close to the cathedral but in a quiet part of the city off the tourist track, serving what have become legendary fish dishes.

Casa Marcelo – *Rúa Hortas 1 –* ☎ *981 55 85 80 – Closed Sun, Mon, Tue, 1-15 Feb and 1-15 Oct –* 🍽. This charming restaurant just off praça do Obradoiro has a deserved reputation for its innovative cuisine. Just the one fixed tasting menu, but well-balanced and varied. A pleasant dining environment, splendid wine list and excellent value for money.

TAPAS

Adega Abrigadorio – *Carrera del Conde 5 –* ☎ *981 56 31 63 –* 🍴. This bar of long-standing tradition near the parque de la Alameda serves a good range of chorizos, to a backdrop of exposed stone, wood barrels and even a small mill.

La Bodeguilla de San Roque – *San Roque 13 –* ☎ *981 564 379.* Despite its simple appearance, this bodega has earned a good reputation for its scrambled egg dishes, chorizos and wines. If you prefer something more substantial, there's also a pleasant restaurant on the first floor.

WHERE TO STAY

Hostal Mapoula – *Entremurallas 10, 3º –* ☎ *981 58 01 24 – 12 rooms.* A small, family-run hostal in a narrow street in the old quarter, near praça do Toural. Nothing luxurious, but good service and clean rooms with en-suite bathrooms. A recommended choice, both for its location and value for money.

Hotel San Clemente – *San Clemente 28 –* ☎ *902 40 58 58 – 10 rooms -* 💤 *5.35€.* The San Clemente enjoys an enviable location a couple of minutes' walk from the praça do Obradoiro. With its ideal size, sympathetically decorated rooms based on brick and wood, and moderate prices, the hotel comes highly recommended.

Casa Grande de Cornide – *Cornide – Teo-Casalonga – 11.5km/7mi SW of Santiago on the N 550 towards Padrón –* ☎ *981 80 55 99 – Closed Jan –* 🅿 *– 10 rooms –* 💤 *6€.* For those who prefer peace and quiet away from the city, this large, traditional-style Galician house offers the perfect solution. The decor and furnishings are a pleasant fusion of the classic and the modern, creating a comfortable, cosy atmosphere. In summer, guests can take advantage of the pool in the lovely garden surrounding the house.

Parador Hotel Reyes Católicos – *Praça do Obradoiro 1 –* ☎ *981 58 22 00 –* 🍽 ♿ *– 131 rooms from –* 💤 *12.80€.* The former Royal Hospital founded by the Catholic Monarchs in 1499 has now been converted into a luxury parador. Particularly worthy of note are its inner patios which trace the typology of hospitals in the 16C. Elegant rooms, some with four-poster beds.

TAKING A BREAK

Cafetería Paradiso – *Rúa do Vilar 29 –* ☎ *981 58 33 94 – Open 8am-2am.* A café with a 19C atmosphere.

Café Derby Bar – *Rúa das Orfas 29 –* ☎ *981 58 59 04.* A timeless bar said to have been popular with the writer Valle Inclán.

Café Literario – *Praça da Quintana.* A stylishly decorated café with a young clientele, located at the top of a flight of steps with a fine view of both the square and the cathedral.

Vinatería Don Pinario – *Plazuela de San Martín.* A combination of interesting decor and a good selection of wines in this delightful square.

---

pillars are covered in statues of Apostles and Prophets. Note the figure of Daniel with the hint of a smile, a precursor to the famous Smiling Angel in Reims Cathedral in France. The pillar beneath the seated figure of St James, bears finger marks upon the stone; traditionally, on entering the cathedral, exhausted pilgrims placed their hands here in token of safe arrival. On the other side of the pillar, the statue known as the saint of bumps is believed to impart memory and wisdom to whoever bumps his forehead against it.

Interior – The immense Romanesque cathedral into which pilgrims crowded in the Middle Ages has remained intact with all the characteristics of pilgrim churches at the time: a Latin cross floor plan, vast proportions, an ambulatory and a triforium. The nave and transept, complete with aisles, are plain yet majestic, aesthetic yet functional. Galleries open onto the aisles through twin bays beneath a supporting arch. The side

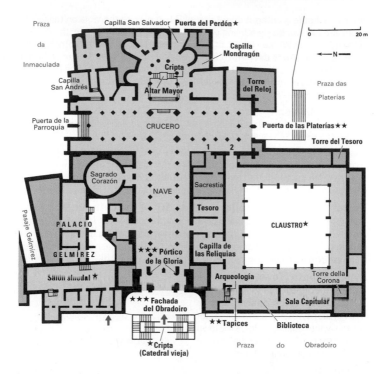

aisles are covered with 13C groin vaults. At major festivals a huge incense burner, the **botafumeiro** *(displayed in the library)*, is hung from the transept dome keystone and swung to the eaves by eight men pulling on a rope.

The decoration in the sanctuary is surprisingly exuberant for a Romanesque setting. The **altar mayor** or high altar, surmounted by a sumptuously apparelled 13C statue of St James, is covered by a gigantic baldaquin. (Pilgrims mounting the stairs behind the altar may kiss the saint's mantle.) Beneath the altar is the **cripta**, a crypt built into the foundations of the 9C church which contained St James' tomb and now enshrines the relics of the saint and his two disciples, St Theodore and St Athanasius.

Particularly beautiful among the cathedral's many outstanding features is the Gothic vaulting of the Capilla Mondragón (1521), and the 9C Capilla de la Corticela, which at the time of its construction was separate from the cathedral. The Renaissance doors to the **sacristía** (sacristy) **(1)** and *claustro* (cloisters) **(2)** on the right arm of the transept are also worthy of note.

Museo – ⏰ *Open Oct-May, 10am-1.30pm and 4-6.30pm; Jun-Sep, 10am-2pm and 4-8pm; Sun and public hols, mornings only.* ⬠5€. ☎ 981 56 05 27.

The museum consists of three distinct parts. Access to the **tesoro** (treasury), occupying a Gothic chapel to the right of the nave, is via the inside of the cathedral. Exhibits on display include a gold and silver monstrance by Antonio de Arfe (1539-66). To visit the **cripta**★ (crypt), built in the 11C to compensate for differences in floor level and to support the Pórtico de la Gloria, exit to the Plaza del Obradoiro. The entrance to the crypt is partially obscured by the large staircase beneath the Obradoiro façade. This is in fact a small Romanesque church with a Latin cross plan and attractive columns and sculpted capitals. Access to the rooms devoted to the cathedral's archaeological excavations, the **biblioteca** (library), where the *botafumeiros* are displayed, the **sala capitular** (chapter house) with its impressive granite vault and walls hung with 16C Flemish tapestries, and the balcony rooms, displaying **tapestries**★★ by Goya, Bayeu, Rubens and Teniers, is via a side entrance.

Claustro★ – *Access via the museum.* This Renaissance cloister was designed by Juan de Álava who, in line with architectural trends at the beginning of the 16C, combined a Gothic structure with Plateresque decoration. The cloister was completed by Rodrigo Gil de Hontañón and Gaspar de Arce.

Puerta de las Platerías★★ (Silversmiths' Doorway) – This is the only 12C Romanesque doorway to have been preserved. Not all of the entrance we see today is original, as many of the sculptures were taken from the Puerta de la Azabachería. The most impressive figure is without doubt that of David playing the viola on the left door. Adam and Eve can be seen being driven out of the Garden of Eden; the Pardoning of the Adulterous Woman is also distinguishable on the right-hand corner of the left tympanum. The **Torre del Reloj** (Clock Tower), on the right, was added at the end of the 17C. To the left, stands the **Torre del Tesoro** (Treasury Tower). The façade of the **Casa del Cabildo**, opposite the *fuente de los caballos,* or horse trough, is a Baroque feature built in the 18C.

Palacio Gelmírez

🕐 *Open Holy Week-Sep, 10am-1.30pm and 4.30-7.30pm; otherwise by prior arrangement.* 🕐 *Closed Mon.* 🜸 *5€.* ☎ *981 57 23 00.*

This is the bishops' palace, to the left of the cathedral. Some 12C and Gothic style apartments are open to the public, including the vast **Salón Sinodal**★ (Synod Hall) which is more than 30m/98ft long and has sculptured ogive vaulting. Carved in high relief on the bosses are scenes from the wedding banquet of Alfonso IX de León.

Hostal de los Reyes Católicos★ (Hostelry of the Catholic Monarchs)

The hostelry, founded by Ferdinand of Aragón and Isabel of Castilla as a pilgrim inn and hospital and now a parador, has an impressive **façade**★ with a splendid Plateresque doorway. The hospital's plan of a cross within a square, which affords four elegant Plateresque *patios*, was common to hospitals of the period.

Ayuntamiento (Town hall)

Opposite the cathedral is the severely Classical 18C façade of the former Palacio de Roxoi by the French architect Charles Lemaur. Today, the building serves as the town hall and the headquarters of the regional government, the Xunta de Galicia.

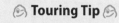

😊 Touring Tip 😊

For one of the best views of the cathedral, descend the steps in avenida de Rajoi, to the left of the town hall.

Colegio de San Jerónimo

The college, a 17C building on the square's south side, has an elegant 15C gateway with a strong Romanesque influence.

CASCO ANTIGUO★★ (OLD TOWN)

Present-day Santiago is the result of superimposing Renaissance rationale and Baroque theatricality on a medieval structure. Despite this, the old part of the city continues to be a maze of delightful narrow streets which open out onto lively squares such as Fonseca, Platerías, Feijóo, San Martín and San Roque.

Rúa do Franco

This busy street is lined by old colleges, such as the Colegio de Fonseca, numerous shops and typical bars. The Porta da Faxeiras leads to the paseo de la Herradura, the landscaped hill that is the setting for the city's fairs. The excellent **view**★ from here encompasses the cathedral and the rooftops of Santiago.

Rúa do Vilar

The street leading to the cathedral is bordered by arcaded and ancient houses, as is the **rúa Nova** which runs parallel, although this has more shops.

Plaza de la Quintana★★

The square surrounding the east end of the cathedral bustles with lingering students. The lower part is bordered by the former **Casa de la Canónica** (Canon's Residence) with a plain but harmonious arcade and, at right angles, by the 17C Monasterio de San Pavo de Antealtares, whose windows barred by beautiful old wrought ironwork embellish an otherwise austere construction.

Opposite, the doorway in the cathedral's east end, known as the **Puerta del Perdón**★ (Door of Pardon) or Puerta Santa (Holy Door), designed by Fernández Lechuga in 1611 and opened only in Holy Years (when the feast day of St James, 25 July, falls on a Sunday), incorporates all the statues of the Prophets and Patriarchs carved by Maestro Mateo for the original Romanesque *coro*. At the top of a large flight of stairs is the **Casa de la Parra,** House of the Bunch of Grapes, a fine late-17C Baroque mansion.

Museo de las Peregrinaciones (Pilgrimage Museum)

🕐 *Open 10am-8pm; Sat, 10am-1.30pm and 5-8pm; Sun, 10.30-1.30pm.* 🕐 *Closed Mon, 1 and 6 Jan, 1 May, 25 Jul, 16 Aug, and 24-25 and 31 Dec..* 🜸 *2.40€.* ☎ *981 58 15 58.*

This small museum, devoted to the origins and history of pilgrimages to Santiago, occupies what is said to have been the house of King Don Pedro I (14C). Due to its heavy restoration, hardly any of its original medieval features remain.

Monasterio de San Martín Pinario★

🕐 *Open 10am-2pm and 4-6pm.* 🕐 *Closed Mon.* ➝ *No charge.* ☎ *981 58 40 81.*

The monastery church overlooking plaza San Martín, preceded by a double flight of stairs, has an ornate front composed like a Plateresque altarpiece.

The interior consists of a surprisingly wide single aisle covered by coffered barrel vaulting. It is lit by a Byzantine-style lantern without a drum. The high altar **retable★**, in the most ornate Churrigueresque manner, is by the great architect Casa y Novoa (1730). On either side are Baroque pulpits canopied by cottage-loaf-shaped sounding boards. A grand staircase beneath an elegant cupola leads to three 16C-18C cloisters, one of which is the Claustro de las Procesiones (Processions Cloister).

The monastery façade overlooking plaza de la Inmaculada is colossal in style with massive Doric columns in pairs rising from the ground to the roof. Plaza de la Azabachería opposite is so named because of the guild of jet ornament craftsmen (azabacheros) who had their workshops in this square.

<table>
<tr><td>

Holy Years

This denomination is given to the feast of St James (25 July) on days when it falls on a Sunday. In recent years, the religious ceremonies in Santiago took on even greater solemnity with the approach of the Jubilee.

</td></tr>
</table>

Worth a Visit

Museo do Pobo Galego (Museum of the Galician People)

🕐 *Open 10am-2pm and 4-8pm; Sun and public hols, 11am-2pm. Last admission 30 min before closing.* ➝ *No charge.* ☎ *981 58 36 20.*

This regional museum is in the former Convento de Santo Domingo de Bonaval (17C-18C). It provides visitors with a general introduction to Galician culture, with the emphasis on its diversity. Rooms are devoted to the sea, crafts, musical instruments and dwellings. The building has a particularly impressive triple **spiral staircase★**, which provides access to the exhibition rooms. The **Centro Gallego de Arte Contemporáneo** (Galician Contemporary Art Centre), designed by the Portuguese architect Álvaro Siza, is situated opposite this museum.

Colegiata de Santa María del Sar★

Calle Castrón de Ouro. Entrance via the apse. 🕐 *Visits by prior arrangement, 10am-1pm and 4-7pm.* 🕐 *Closed Sat-Sun and public hols.* ➝ *0.60€.* ☎ *981 56 28 91.*

The 12C Romanesque collegiate church appears anachronistic by the addition in the 18C of its buttresses. The strength of the latter, however, is not superfluous when one looks inside at the astonishing slant of the pillars caused by the pressure of the vaulting. The only cloister gallery to remain abuts the church and is exceedingly elegant, with paired **arches★** richly decorated with carved floral and leaf motifs.

Excursions

Pazo de Oca★

25km/16mi S on the N 525. 🕐 *Open 9am-8pm (9pm in summer); only gardens open to the public.* ➝ *4€, no charge Mon (except public hols) until 12.30pm.* ☎ *986 58 74 35.*

This austere Galician **manor**, or *pazo*, with a crenellated tower, lines two sides of a vast square in which stands a Calvary. The romantic **park★★** behind comes as a complete surprise (⌖ *see INTRODUCTION TO SPAIN: Spanish Gardens*). There are shady arbours, terraces covered with rust-coloured lichen, pools, and a silent lake on which a stone boat floats idly.

Monasterio de Sobrado dos Monxes

56km/35mi W. 🕐 *Open 10.30am-1pm and 4.15-7pm; Sun and public hols, 12.15-1pm and 4.15-7pm.* ➝ *0.60€.* ☎ *981 78 75 09.*

Sobrado is a vast Galician **monastery**, built between the Renaissance and Baroque periods. It is badly weatherworn but is in the process of restoration by the Cistercian community now living within its walls. Preoccupation with size brought a certain severity in the decoration of the church façade. On the other hand, the interior displays fertile imagination in the design of the **cupolas** in the transept, the sacristy and the Capilla del Rosario (Rosary Chapel) as well as in the Claustro de los Medallones (Medallion Cloisters).

Of the monastery's medieval buildings, there remain a kitchen with a monumental fireplace, a chapter house and the Capilla de la Magdalena (Mary Magdalene Chapel).

Santillana del Mar★★

POPULATION: 3 839.

MICHELIN MAP 572 B 17 –

COSTA DE CANTABRIA – CANTABRIA.

The name Santillana del Mar is something of a contradiction in terms as this small, delightful town is in fact located a few kilometres inland. Santillana has managed to preserve its former medieval appearance, as witnessed by the noble mansions, their façades embellished with family coats of arms, that line its cobbled streets.

Location

Santillana sits in a hollow, surrounded by verdant hills, between Santander and Comillas (16km/10mi to the W). *Plaza Mayor, 39330 Santillana del Mar, ☎ 942 81 82 51.*

Neighbouring sights are described in the following chapters: SANTANDER (26km/16mi E) and COSTA DE CANTABRIA.

Walking About

The **town**★★ has two main streets, both leading to the collegiate church. Between the two lies a network of communicating alleys. Most of the noblemen's residences, with plain façades of massive rough stone, date from the 15C, 16C and 17C. Almost all have wrought-iron balconies or wooden galleries *(solanas)* and the majority sport traditional crests or coats of arms.

Start the walk in **calle de Santo Domingo**, with the 17C Casa del Marqués de Benemejís to the left and the Casa de los Villa, distinguishable by its semicircular balconies, to the right.

▶ *Turn left at the fork into calle de Juan Infante.*

Plaza de Ramón Pelayo

This vast, aesthetically pleasing triangular square is bordered by several fine buildings: to the right, the **Parador Gil Blas** and the 14C **Torre de Merino** (Merino Tower); to the rear, the **Torre de Don Borja** (now an exhibition room), with its elegant pointed doorway; and to the left, the 18C Ayuntamiento (town hall), the Casa del Águila and the Casa de la Parra (exhibition room).

Calle de las Lindas *(at the end of the square on the right)* runs between massive-looking houses with austere façades to join **calle del Cantón** and **calle del Río**, which lead to the collegiate church. On the corner, note the escutcheon of the Casa de Valdivieso (nowadays the Hotel Altamira). Many of the houses along these streets have now been taken over by restaurants and shops selling signature local products, such as cheese, chocolates, and arts and crafts; several pleasant garden terraces have also been laid out here.

As you approach the church, you will see several noblemen's residences on the right-hand side: the Casa del **Marqués de Santillana,** with its impressive windows; the **Casa de los Hombrones**, named after the two knights supporting the Villa coat of arms (an eagle with its wings spread out and the motto: a good death honours an entire life); and, opposite the drinking fountain, the **Casa de Quevedo** and the **Casa de Cossío**, both

---

Historical Notes

Santillana grew up around a monastery which sheltered the relics of St Juliana, who was martyred in Asia Minor – the name Santillana is a contraction of Santa Juliana. Throughout the Middle Ages, the monastery was famous as a place of pilgrimage and was particularly favoured by the Grandees of Castilla. In the 11C it became powerful as a collegiate church; in the 15C, the town, created the seat of a marquisate, was enriched by the fine mansions which still give it so much character.

WHERE TO STAY

🍽 **Hotel Colegiata** – *Carretera Los Hornos 20 – 1km/.6mi N of Santillana on the S 474, towards Suances – ☎ 942 84 02 16 – 🅿 – 27 rooms – ▱ 3.61€ – Restaurant 24.58/28.39€*. This rural country house in a hilly setting overlooking Santillana has been converted into a delightful hotel with comfortable rooms and a popular restaurant. An excellent alternative for those hoping to escape the hustle and bustle of Santillana.

with magnificent coats of arms. The next house after the Casa de los Hombrones is now home to the **Museo de la Tortura**, a museum devoted to torture. 🕐 *Open 10am-8pm (9pm in summer).* ⌾ *3.61€.* ☎ *942 84 02 73.*

On the left, just before the Colegiata, stands the **house of the Archduchess of Austria,** adorned with three coats of arms. The building opposite is the *casa-museo* (home-museum) of the sculptor Jesús Otero.

Colegiata★

🕐 *Open 10am-1.30pm and 4-7.30pm (6.30pm 15 Jun-15 Sep).* 🕐 *Closed Mon (winter), 28 Jun, 16 Aug and 25 Dec.* ⌾ *3€ (includes visit to Museo Diocesano).* ☎ *942 84 03 17.*

The collegiate church dates from the 12C and 13C. While the design of the east end is pure Romanesque, that of the west to some extent lacks unity, although the harmonious placing of the windows and towers and the golden colour of the stone make it blend in well with the overall architecture of the square. On the portal, above the Romanesque Christ Pantocrator, is a Baroque niche with a statue of St Juliana.

Claustro★

These cloisters are a fine example of the 12C Romanesque style. Each pair of twin columns is covered by a capital carved by a master craftsman. Though plant and strapwork motifs predominate, the **capitals★★** in the south gallery, which do illustrate a scene, often in allegory, are very expressive: look out for Christ and six of the disciples, Christ's baptism and the ordination of a priest; the beheading of John the Baptist and Daniel in the Lion's Den; a Descent from the Cross; fidelity, represented by a dog between a nobleman and his wife; the struggle between Good (a knight) and Evil (a beast); that between Good and Temptation (a snake); and the Good Shepherd.

Interior

The vaulting in the aisles was rebuilt at the end of the 13C when it was given intersecting ribs, but that above the transept and apses is original. The aisles and apses are out of line and the cupola, unusually, is almost elliptical. The pillars are crowned by highly stylised capitals. St Juliana's memorial sarcophagus, carved in the 15C, stands at the centre of the nave. The chancel contains a 17C Mexican beaten **silver altarfront** and Romanesque stone figures of **four Apostles★**, carved in the hieratic style. The 16C carved and sculpted Hispano-Flemish **altarpiece★** has the original polychrome wood predella which is carved to show the Evangelists in profile. In the chapel at the foot of the church, admire a Christ Pantocrator and a large 11C baptismal font decorated with Daniel in the Lions' Den.

Skirt around the exterior of the Colegiata's east end to appreciate the Romanesque style of the apses and the restored **Palacio de los Velarde**, which has retained its Renaissance air.

Convento de Regina Coeli

▶ *Retrace your steps to return to the starting-point of the walk.*

The restored 16C Convento de Clarisas (Convent of the Poor Clares) is nowadays occupied by the **Museo Diocesano** (museum of the diocese), with its interesting collection of paintings, sculptures and pieces of religious gold and silver work from around the province. The collection of Baroque carvings and ivory is worthy of particular note. 🕐 *Open 10am-2pm and 4-7pm (7.30pm 15 Jun-15 Sep). Last admission 30 min before closing.* 🕐 *Closed Mon (winter), 28 Jun, 16 Aug and 25 Dec.* ⌾ *2.50€ (includes entry to the Colegiata).* ☎ *942 84 03 17.*

A large coat of arms adorns the fine 18C **Casa de Los Tagle** at the end of the street.

Children will be interested by the **zoo** at the exit to Santillana along the Puente San Miguel road. 📷 🕐 *Open 9.30am-dusk.* ⌾ *9€, 5€ (child).* ☎ *942 81 81 25.*

Special Features

MUSEO DE ALTAMIRA★★

2km/1.2mi SW. 📷 🕐 *Guided tours 9.30am-5pm; Jun-Sep, 9.30am-7.30pm (5pm Sun and public hols). Visiting times for the Neocueva are posted at the entrance.* ⌾ *€2.40, no charge Sat afternoon and Sun.* ☎ *942 81 80 05.* 🕐 *Tickets should be purchased in advance at the Banco de Santander.*

This extensive complex dedicated to the prehistoric world encompasses the original cave, the new cave (neocueva) and a museum.

Cueva de Altamira

As a protective measure, the original cave is not open to visitors.

The Altamira caves consist of several galleries which have preserved wall paintings and engravings dating back to the Solutrean Age, 20 500 years ago. The most impressive paintings are those in the Sala de los Polícromos (Polychrome Chamber). Known as the **Sistine Chapel of Quarternary Art**, this 18m/59ft long and 9m/30ft wide cave has an outstanding **ceiling**★★★ painted mainly during the Magdalenian Period (15000-12000 BC) like the Lascaux cave paintings in the Dordogne (France). Numerous polychrome bison are shown asleep, crouched, stretching and galloping with extraordinary realism. The natural bulges on the rock face were used with great skill to bring out body shape and to give the impression of movement.

1879: The Year of Great Discovery

It was in this year that the archaeologist **Marcelino Sanz de Sautuola** noticed rock paintings on a cave roof which he eventually dated as prehistoric. These were the first such paintings ever to be discovered and as they were in such good condition there was widespread disbelief and scepticism about their authenticity. Only after 20 years and the discovery of similar paintings in the Dordogne Valley in France was the highly developed pictorial art of the Upper Palaeolithic period fully recognised.

The artists – who must have been in a crouched position to paint (the floor level has been lowered to enable the ceiling to be seen more easily) – used natural pigments, chiefly ochre, red and brown which they reduced to a powder and mixed with animal fat. They outlined their subjects in black (with the use of charcoal) to give a firm edge to their colourwork.

Neocueva

An informative guided tour (30min) using the very latest in technology introduces visitors to replicas of the cave entrance and the Sala de los Polícromos, with their extraordinary wall paintings.

Museo

The museum provides visitors with an educational and informative insight into the life of man in the Upper Palaeolithic period through audio-visual aids, animated drawings, explanatory panels etc.

The exhibition begins with a short introduction to the world of archaeology and a presentation of the evolution of man through to *Homo sapiens*. The daily life of man in the Upper Palaeolithic period is also covered, outlining methods for producing tools, showing the types of art created at the time, as well as providing an explanation of the process by which art was produced (engraving, colouring techniques etc). Various examples of other caves with wall paintings in Cantabria are also displayed.

Segovia★★★

POPULATION: 57 617

MICHELIN MAPS 575 OR 576 J 17 – MAP 121 ALREDEDORES DE MADRID –
LOCAL MAP SEE SIERRA DE GUADARRAMA – CASTILLA Y LEÓN (SEGOVIA).

This austere, imposing city, situated at an altitude of 1 000m/3 280ft, has a unique site perched on a triangular rock rising like an island out of the surrounding Castilian plain at the confluence of the River Eresma and River Clamores. Enclosed within its sturdy walls is a complicated maze of narrow streets dotted with impressive Roman monuments and noble mansions.

Location

For the best overall view of the city, drive along cuesta de los Hoyos and paseo de Santo Domingo de Guzmán. *Plaza Mayor 10, 40001 Segovia, ☏ 921 46 03 34; Plaza de Azoguejo, 1, 40001 Segovia, ☏ 921 46 29 06.*

Neighbouring sights are described in the following chapters: PEDRAZA (35km/22mi NE), Sierra de GUADARRAMA, ÁVILA (67km/42mi SW) and MADRID (98km/61mi S).

Background

The noble Castilian city of Segovia, former residence of King Alfonso X, the Wise, and King Henry IV, was an important economic and political centre in the Middle Ages and was to play a decisive role in the history of Castilla. The 15C marked the Golden Age of Segovia, when its population numbered 60 000 citizens.

Isabel the Catholic, Queen of Castilla – On the death of Henry IV in 1474 many grandees refused to recognise the legitimacy of his daughter, Doña Juana, known as **La Beltraneja** after her mother's favourite, Beltrán de la Cueva. In Segovia in her stead, the grandees proclaimed Henry's half-sister, Isabel, Queen of Castilla – thus preparing the way for Spain's unification since Isabel was already married to Ferdinand, heir apparent of Aragón. La Beltraneja, aided by her husband, Alfonso V of Portugal, pressed her claim, but renounced it in 1479 after the defeats at Toro and Albuera.

The "Comuneros" – In 1520, just three years after he had landed in the Asturian port of Tazones to take possession of the crowns of Castilla and Aragón, the Habsburg Charles I was forced to depart his new kingdom in order to be proclaimed Holy Roman Emperor (as Charles V). The same year, an uprising started in the towns and cities of Castilla that was to become known as the revolt of the Comunidades (town forces). The catalysts of the uprising included the aforementioned absence of Charles V, his eagerness to surround himself with a Flemish court to the detriment of Castilian nobles, and his attempt to impose new taxes to pay for the pomp and splendour of his

---

Address Book

For coin ranges, see the Legend at the back of the guide.

WHERE TO EAT

☏☏ **Narizotas** – *Plaza de Medina del Campo 1* – ☏ *921 46 26 79.* In this traditional restaurant, customers can choose between the classic roast suckling pig (cochinillo asado) or a more original menu comprising specialities such as local sausages (embutidos) and fricassée of lamb (cochifrito). During the summer, there's also the option of eating on the pleasant street terrace.

☏☏ **Mesón de Cándido** – *Plaza Azoguejo 5* – ☏ *921 42 59 11 –*. Surely the most famous and traditional restaurant in the entire province, in a 15C house right under the aqueduct. Its rustic

Castillian interior is the perfect setting for enjoying roast suckling pig, the indisputable star of the menu.

WHERE TO STAY

☏ **Hotel Don Jaime** – *Ochoa Ondátegui 8* – ☏ *921 44 47 90 – 16 rooms* – 3€. The bedrooms in this welcoming Castilian mansion, magnificently located at the foot of the Roman aqueduct, are simple, bright and quiet.

☏ **Hotel Las Sirenas** – *Juan Bravo 30* – ☏ *921 46 26 63* – 39 *rooms*. This hotel from another age, at the heart of Segovia's old quarter, has an elegant stone façade and rooms that are comfortable, albeit lacking in luxuries. The attractive staircase and old hairdressing salon are reminders of its better days.

new empire. At the root of the Comuneros movement was the opposition of Castilian towns, the middle classes and merchants to the alliance established between Charles V and the landowning aristocracy. Numerous town forces, under the leadership of Juan de Padilla in Toledo, Francisco Maldonado in Salamanca and Juan Bravo in Segovia, rose up against royal authority, but were finally crushed at Villalar in 1521.

Special Features

CIUDAD VIEJA★★ (OLD TOWN)
🕐 4hr – Follow the itinerary on the plan

Acueducto romano★★★

This aqueduct is one of the finest examples of Roman engineering still standing today. The simple, elegant structure was built during the reign of Trajan in the 1C to bring water from the River Acebeda in the Sierra de Fuenfría to the upper part of the town. It is 728m/2 388ft long, rises to a maximum height of 28m/92ft in plaza del Azoguejo where the ground is lowest, and consists throughout of two tiers of arches.

Casa de los Picos

The house, faced closely with diamond pointed stones, is the most original of Segovia's 15C mansions.

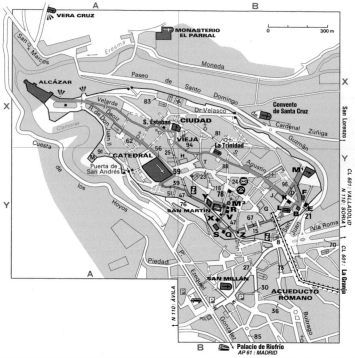

Casa del Conde de Alpuente

The elegant façade of this 15C Gothic house is adorned with *esgrafiado* designs.

Alhóndiga

This 15C granary has been transformed into an exhibition room.

Plaza de San Martín★

The square in the heart of the old aristocratic quarter is the most evocative of historic Segovia. It is formed of two small squares joined by a flight of steps. The statue is of Juan Bravo. Around the square stand the **Casa del Siglo XV** (15C House), also known as Juan Bravo's

> ## Esgrafiados
>
> Geometric designs, or *esgrafiados*, are one of the most characteristic features of Segovian architecture. The word derives from the Italian *graffiare*, meaning "to scratch". The technique consists of scratching – following a pre-existing design – an outer layer, to expose an underlying layer of a different colour tone. The range of motifs could cover simple geometric decoration to biblical and mythological scenes. In Segovia's case, the black stains on some of the city's walls are in fact iron scoria, the purpose of which is purely decorative.

house, with a gallery beneath the eaves, the 16C tower of the **Casa de los Lozoya** as a reminder of the family's power in former times, the Plateresque façade of the **Casa de Solier** (Solier Mansion, also known as Casa de Correas) and the ornate entrances to big houses. In the middle of the square is the 12C **Iglesia de San Martín★,** a church framed on three sides by a covered gallery on pillars with carved strapwork and animal figures on the capitals.

Museo Esteban Vicente

🕐 *Open 11am-2pm and 4-7pm; Sun and public hols, 11am-2pm.* 🕐 *Closed Mon.* 🎟 *2.40€, no charge Thu.* ☏ *921 46 37 38.*

The museum is housed in the palace of Henry IV in the so-called Hospital de Viejos (Old People's Hospital). The only trace of the original building is the fine chapel with a Mudéjar ceiling which has been converted into an auditorium. The museum was created following a donation by the artist Esteban Vicente and exhibits his work from 1925 to 1997.

The 17C **antigua cárcel** (Old Prison) has a decorative Baroque pediment.

Plaza Mayor

Dominated by the impressive cathedral, the arcaded square with its terrace cafés is a popular meeting-place with Segovians. Among the buildings surrounding the square are the Ayuntamiento (town hall) and the Teatro Juan Bravo.

Catedral★★

🕐 *Open 9.30am-6pm (7pm Apr-Oct); no visits during religious services.* 🎟 *2€ (museum).* ☏ *921 46 22 05.*

This was built during the reign of Emperor Charles V to replace the cathedral that had been destroyed during the Comuneros' Revolt in 1511. It is an example of the survival of the Gothic style in the 16C when Renaissance architecture was at its height. The beautiful golden stone, the stepped east end with pinnacles and delicate balustrades and the tall tower, bring considerable grace to the massive building. The width of the aisles combines with the decorative lines of the pillars and ribs in the vaulting, to make the interior both light and elegant. Among the chapels, which are closed by fine wrought-iron screens, the first off the south aisle contains as altarpiece an *Entombment* by Juan de Juni. The *coro* stalls, in the late-15C Flamboyant Gothic style, are from the earlier cathedral.

Claustro★ – The 15C cloisters from the former cathedral, which stood near the Alcázar, were transported stone by stone and rebuilt on the new site. The Sala Capitular (chapter house) has beautiful 17C Brussels **tapestries★** which illustrate the story of Queen Zenobia.

Alcázar★★

🕐 *Open 10am-6pm (7pm Apr-Sep and Fri-Sat in Oct).* 🕐 *Closed 1 and 6 Jan and 25 and 31 Dec.* 🎟 *3.50€, no charge Wed for citizens of the European Union.* ☏ *921 46 07 59.*

The Alcázar, standing on a cliff overlooking the valley, was built above a former fortress in the early 13C and modified in the 15C and 16C by Henry IV and Philip II respectively. In 1764, Charles III converted the building into a **Real Colegio de Artillería** (Royal Artillery School), but in 1862 it suffered a devastating fire which spared the academy's library and very little else. Reconstruction was completed at

Alcázar

the end of the 19C, during the reign of Alfonso XII, hence its neo-Gothic appearance today. The furniture and richly decorated Mudéjar artesonado work, mostly dating from the 15C, are original and were brought from various Castilian towns. Its keep is flanked by corbelled turrets. The main rooms of note are the Chamber Royal (Cámara Real) and the Sala de los Reyes (Monarchs' Room). The Sala del Cordón and terrace command a fine **panorama** of the fertile Eresma Valley, the Monasterio de El Parral, the Capilla de la Vera Cruz and the meseta beyond. The rooms of the artillery school now house a museum reminding visitors of the importance of the chemical laboratory established here in the 18C and the French chemist **Louis Proust**, who formulated his law of constant proportions in Segovia. The **views** from the keep (152 steps) stretch across the city to the Sierra de Guadarrama.

Iglesia de San Esteban (St Stephen's Church)

⊶ *Not open to visitors.* ☎ *921 46 00 27.*

One of the latest (13C) and most beautiful of Segovia's Romanesque churches. The porticoes running along two of its sides have finely carved capitals.
The five-storey **tower**★ has elegant bays and slender columns on the corners. The interior is in Renaissance style. Inside, the altar in the south transept has a 13C Gothic figure of Christ in polychrome wood.

Iglesia de la Trinidad (Holy Trinity Church)

This somewhat austere Romanesque church has a decorated apse where there is blind arcading and capitals carved with imaginary beasts and plant motifs.

Romanesque Churches

These beautiful churches of golden stone have common architectural features: well-rounded apses, frequently a tall square belfry beside the east end and a covered gallery where weavers' or merchants' guilds used to meet.

Iglesia de San Juan de los Caballerosa

🕐 *Open 10am-2pm and 4-7pm; Sun, 10am-2pm.* 🕐 *Closed Mon and public hols.*
💰 *1.20€, no charge Sat-Sun and public hols.* ☎ *921 46 33 48.*

This is Segovia's oldest Romanesque church (11C). Its outstanding feature is the portico (taken from the church of San Nicolás) with its carvings of portrait heads, plant motifs and animals. The church, which was almost in ruins at the turn of the 20C, was bought by Daniel Zuloaga, who converted it into his home and workshop. Today it houses the **Museo Zuloaga**, exhibiting drawings by the artist and paintings by his nephew, Ignacio Zuloaga.

Plaza del Conde de Cheste

On the square stand the palaces of the **Marqués de Moya**, the **Marqués de Lozoya**, the **Condes de Cheste** and the **Marqués de Quintanar**.

Iglesia de San Sebastián

This small Romanesque church stands on one side of a quiet square.

Worth a Visit

OUTSIDE THE WALLS

Iglesia de San Millán★

🕐 *Open 10am-2pm and 4.30-7.30pm.* 🕐 *Closed Sun, Mon and public hols.* ☎ *921 46 38 01.*

The early-12C church stands in the middle of a large square which allows a full view of its pure, still primitive Romanesque lines and two porticoes with finely carved modillions and capitals. Inside, the three aisles have alternating pillars and columns as in Jaca Cathedral. The apse has blind arcading and a decorative frieze which continues throughout the church. The transept has Moorish ribbed vaulting.

Monasterio de El Parral★

🕐 *Open 10am-12.30pm and 4-6.30pm; Sun and public hols, 10-11.30am and 4.30-6.30pm; no visits during religious services.* ☎ *921 43 12 98.*

The monastery was founded by Henry IV in 1445 and later entrusted to the Hieronymites. The **church**, behind its unfinished façade, has a Gothic nave with beautifully carved doors, a 16C altarpiece by Juan Rodríguez and, on either side of the chancel, the Plateresque tombs of the Marquis and Marchioness of Villena.

Capilla de la Vera-Cruz★

🕐 *Open 10.30am-1.30pm and 3.30-6pm (7pm in spring and summer).* 🕐 *Closed Mon and in Nov.* 👝 *1.50€, no charge Tue to citizens of the European Union.* ☎ *921 43 14 75.*

The unusual polygonal chapel was erected in the 13C, probably by the Templars; it now belongs to the Order of Malta. A circular corridor surrounds two small chambers, one above the other, in which the order's secret ceremonies were conducted. The Capilla del Lignum Crucis contains an ornate Flamboyant Gothic altar. There is a good view of Segovia.

Convento de Santa Cruz

The convent pinnacles, the decorated Isabelline **entrance** with a Calvary, a *Pietà*, and the emblems of the Catholic Monarchs, can be seen from the road.

Iglesia de San Lorenzo

The Romanesque church with its unusual brick belfry stands in a picturesque square surrounded by corbelled half-timbered houses.

Excursions

LA GRANJA DE SAN ILDEFONSO★★ (👝 *see Sierra de GUADARRAMA*)

Riofrío★

11km/7mi S on the N 603. 🕐 *Open 10am-1.30pm and 3-5pm; Sun and public hols, 10am-2pm; Holy Week-Oct, 10am-6pm.* 🕐 *Closed Mon, 1, 6 and 23 Jan, and 25 and 31 Dec.* 👝 *5€, no charge Wed for citizens of the European Union.* ☎ *921 47 00 19.*

The Palacio Real (Royal Palace) can be seen through the holm oaks where deer roam, below the Mujer Muerta (the Dead Woman), a foothill of the Sierra de Guadarrama.

Palacio

Riofrío was planned by Isabel Farnese as the equal of La Granja which she had to vacate on the death of her husband, Philip V. Construction began in 1752 but though it was very big – it measures 84m x 84m (276ft x 276ft) – it was nothing more than a somewhat pretentious hunting lodge. This palatine construction was never completed and Isabel Farnese never lived in it. The furniture belongs to the period of Francisco de Asís de Borbón, the husband of Isabel II, and Alfonso XII, both of whom spent considerable periods of time in the palace.

It is built around a Classical-style grand central courtyard. The green and pink façade reveals the Italian origins of the wife of Philip V. A monumental staircase leads to sumptuously decorated apartments. A **Museo de Caza** (Hunting Museum) illustrates the development of hunting methods since prehistoric times with the aid of paintings and display cases of animals in their natural habitat.

J. Malburet/ MICHELIN

Castillo de Coca

Castillo de Coca★★

52km/32mi NW along the C 605 and SG 341. ✎ *Guided tours (45min-1hr), 10.30am-1.30pm and 4.30-6pm (7pm Apr-Jun, 7.30pm Jul-Sep); last admission 30min before closing.* ○ *Closed two weeks in Jan and first Tue of every month.* 2.50€. ☎ *921 57 35 54.*

This **castillo** (fortress), on the outskirts of Coca village, is the most outstanding example of Mudéjar military architecture in Spain. It was built in the late 15C by Moorish craftsmen for the archbishop of Sevilla, Fonseca, and consists of three concentric perimeters, flanked by polygonal corner towers and turrets with, at the centre, a massive keep. It is the epitome of all fortresses, but with the sun mellowing the pink brick and the interplay of shadows on battlements and watchtowers, it can be attractive as well as awesome.

The torre del *homenaje* (keep) and *capilla* (chapel), which contains Romanesque wood carvings, are open to the public.

Arévalo

60km/37mi NW along the C 605. Isabel the Catholic spent her childhood in the 14C **castle** with its massive crenellated keep that dominates the town. Of note also in the town are the Romanesque-Mudéjar churches built of brick, and several old mansions.

Plaza de la Villa★, the former Plaza Mayor, is one of the best-preserved town squares in Castilla with its half-timbered brick houses resting on pillared porticoes. They blend in perfectly with the Mudéjar east end of the Iglesia de Santa María and its blind arcading.

Sevilla★★★

POPULATION: 701 927

MICHELIN MAP 578 T 11-12 (TOWN PLAN) – ANDALUCÍA (SEVILLA).

Sevilla, standing in the plain of the Guadalquivir, is capital of Andalucía and Spain's fourth largest city. It has all the characteristics of a bustling metropolis but has many moods and facets which may escape the visitor in too much of a hurry. It is well worth taking the time to stroll along the narrow streets of old quarters like Santa Cruz, or ride slowly through the city's peaceful parks and gardens in a horse-drawn carriage.

Sevilla is also the great centre of flamenco, famous too for its bullfights held in the 18C plaza de la Maestranza, and for its myriad cafés and tapas bars.

Location

Sevilla is the hub of a comprehensive network of motorways and dual carriageways linking it with other major provincial towns and cities in Andalucía, including Huelva (92km/57mi W), Jerez de la Frontera (90km/56mi SW), Cádiz (123km/77mi SW) and Córdoba (143km/89mi NE). ▯ *Paseo de las Delicias 9, 41012 Sevilla,* ☎ *95 423 44 65 ; Plaza Triunfo 1-3, 41004,* ☎ *954 21 00 05.*

◔ *Neighbouring sights are described in the following chapters; JEREZ DE LA FRONTERA, OSUNA, HUELVA, ARACENA (93km/58mi NW) and COSTA DE LA LUZ.*

Background

Historical notes – Sevilla's history is neatly summed up by the lines carved long ago on the Puerta de Jerez (Jerez Gate): "Hercules built me; Caesar surrounded me with walls and towers; the King Saint took me." Sevilla, known as Hispalis under the Iberians, was chief city of Roman Baetica and, before Toledo, became the capital of the Visigothic kingdom. In 712 the Moors arrived; in the 11C, on the fall of the Córdoban caliphs, the city was created capital of a kingdom which gained in prosperity a century later under the Almohads. In 1195 **Sultan Yacoub al-Mansur** (1184-99), builder of the famous Giralda, won victory over the Christians at the Battle of Alarcos. On 19 November 1248, **King Ferdinand III of Castilla**, the Saint, as he was known (and is referred to in the lines above) and who was cousin to St Louis of France, delivered the city from the Moors who were all expelled.

The discovery of America in 1492 brought new prosperity to Sevilla. Expeditions to the New World set out from the port: **Amerigo Vespucci** (1451-1512), the Florentine who determined to prove that Columbus's discoveries were not the Indies but a new continent to which his own name was ultimately given; **Magellan**, who set out in 1519 to circumnavigate the world. By 1503 the city's trade with ports far and near had become such that Isabel the Catholic created the *Casa de contratación* or Exchange to encourage and also to control all trade with America. This monopoly lasted until 1717 when the silting up of the Guadalquivir brought about the transfer of the Casa concession to Cádiz.

Art and architecture in Sevilla – The ramparts on the north side of the town, the lofty Alcázar, the **Torre del Oro** *(Golden Tower)* – built in 1220 on the banks of the Guadalquivir to guard the port which could be closed by a chain stretched across the

A Tradition of Fiestas

The great festivals, when vast crowds flock to the city from all over Spain and overseas, reveal the provincial capital in many guises. During **Semana Santa**, or **Holy Week**, *pasos* processions are organised nightly in each city quarter by rival brotherhoods. *Pasos* are great litters sumptuously bejewelled and garlanded with flowers on which are mounted religious, polychrome wood statues; these constructions are borne through the crowd on the shoulders of between 25 and 60 men. Accompanying the statues are penitents, hidden beneath tall pointed hoods; from time to time a voice is raised in a *saeta*, an improvised religious lament.

During the **April Fair or Feria,** which began life in the middle of the 19C as an animal fair, the city becomes a fairground with horse and carriage parades. The women in flounced dresses and the men in full Andalucían costume ride up to specially erected canvas pavilions to dance *sevillanas*.

river to another tower, since vanished, on the far bank – and finally, the Giralda, are all reminders of Sevilla's Moorish occupation. Interestingly, Sevilla was, in fact, Christian at the time the Nasrids were building the Alhambra in Granada and so the use of the **Mudéjar style,** that mixture of Moorish and Christian, long after the reconquest of the town in 1248, reflected this fascination for Arab design – as exemplified in the Alcázar built under Peter the Cruel, the Casa de Pilatos, the **Palacio de las Dueñas** and the **Torre de San Marcos** (San Marcos Belfry).

In Spain's Golden Age, the **Seville School** of painters brought renown to the city. Three generations of artists corresponded to the three reigns: under Philip III (1598-1621) **Roelas** and **Pacheco**, portraitist and Velázquez' master; under Philip IV (1621-65) **Herrera the Elder,** whose paintings have an epic touch, and **Zurbarán** (1598-1664) who, after having studied in the city, remained here and portrayed motionless figures with rare spiritual intensity. Finally under Charles II (1665-1700) there was **Murillo** (1618-82), a Baroque artist, author of numerous gently radiant Immaculate Conceptions and, also, of brilliantly depicted everyday scenes, particularly those including young women, children and characters common to every town and village, such as the water carrier. Also of this period was **Valdés Leal** (1622-90), who had a violent Baroque technique, and whose best work can be seen in the Hospital de la Caridad (Hospital of Charity). **Velázquez** (1599-1660) was born in Sevilla; he entered Pacheco's Academy and later became his son-in-law; on moving to Madrid he became court portraitist and, laden with honours, spent the rest of his life painting the royal family.

Sevilla's statues, many the work of the 17C sculptor **Martínez Montañés**, are dispersed throughout the city's churches. The best known are the **Cristo del Gran Poder** (Christ of Great Power) by **Juan de Mesa,** the **Cachorro** by Francisco Antonio Gijón in the **Capilla del Patrocinio,** calle Castilla, named after the gypsy who served as the sculptor's model, and finally, the **Macarena Virgin**, the most popular figure in Sevilla, which stands, when not in procession, in a special chapel.

Sevilla today – Modern Sevilla, the only river port in Spain, is an exuberant, passionate and festive city which has benefited from huge investment in recent years.

The **1992 World Fair** was held on the **Isla de la Cartuja** (Island of the Carthusian Monastery) between two branches of the Guadalquivir. This great event, which has left an indelible mark on Sevilla, not only resulted in a large-scale urban modernisation programme for the city (bridges, communications etc), but also involved the incorporation of the land on the Isla de la Cartuja into the urban structure of Sevilla. This is also the location of the **Isla Mágica** theme park, which retraces the discovery of the New World by the Spanish, taking as its point of departure 16C Sevilla, and the **Centro Andaluz de Arte Contemporáneo**, housed in the former Cartuja monastery.

Special Features

Sevilla's two most important monuments, the cathedral and the Alcázar, as well as its most typical district, the famous Santa Cruz quarter, are all located within a short distance of each other in the centre of the city.

THE GIRALDA AND CATHEDRAL★★★ ⏱1hr 30min

🕐 Open 11am-5pm; Sun, 2.30-6pm. 🕐 Closed 1 and 6 Jan, 30 May, Corpus Christi, 15 Aug and 8 and 25 Dec. Restricted opening times on Tue, Maundy Thu and Good Fri during Holy Week. ⊛ 6€, no charge Sun. ☎ 95 421 49 71.

La Giralda

B. Kaufmann/MICHELIN

Address Book

TRANSPORT

Airport – Aeropuerto de San Pablo, 8km/5mi toward Madrid on the N IV motorway, ☎ 95 444 90 00. A bus service operates from the airport to the railway station and city centre.

Trains – Estación de Santa Justa, ☎ 95 441 41 11. The high-speed AVE (Tren de Alta Velocidad) departs from this station, taking just 45min to Córdoba and 2hr 30min to Madrid. For bookings, call ☎ 95 454 03 03 or visit www.renfe.com. For **RENFE** (Spanish State Railways) information, call ☎ 95 454 02 02.

Inter-city buses – Sevilla has two bus stations: **Estación Plaza de Armas**,☎ 95 490 77 37; and **Estación del Prado de San Sebastián**, ☎ 95 441 71 11.

Taxis – Radio Taxi ☎ 95 458 00 00/95 457 11 11.

SIGHTSEEING

Publications – Two free bilingual publications (Spanish-English) are published for tourists every month. These brochures, **Welcome Olé** and **The Tourist**, can be obtained from major hotels and tourist sites around the city. Sevilla City Hall's Department of Culture **(NODO)** also publishes a monthly brochure listing all the city's cultural events. A monthly publication covering the whole of Andalucía, **El Giraldillo,** contains information on the region's fairs, exhibitions and theatres, as well as details on cinemas, restaurants and shops. www. elgiraldillo.es

Horse-drawn carriages – It is well worth taking a trip in one of the numerous horse-drawn carriages operating in the city. They can normally be hired by the cathedral, in front of the Torre del Oro and in the María Luisa park.

Boat trips on the Guadalquivir– Boat trips lasting 1hr during the day and 1hr 30min at night depart every half-hour from the Torre del Oro. ☎ 95 456 16 92

For coin ranges, see the Legend at the back of the guide.

WHERE TO EAT

○○ **Bodegón La Universal** – *Betis 2 (Triana)* – ☎ *95 433 47 46 – Closed Wed –* 🗒. The terrace, cooled by the fresh air rising from the Guadalquivir, provides a great view of the city and bullring. Traditional cuisine and a pleasant place to eat either before or after exploring the Triana quarter.

○○ **Corral del Agua** – *Callejón del Agua 6* – ☎ *95 422 48 41 - Closed 15 Jan-1 Mar.* A pleasant, refreshing surprise awaits you in this quiet, atmospheric alley. The terrace, with its abundant vegetation, is delightful in the heat of summer. Classic Andalucían cuisine.

○○🍽 **Taberna del Alabardero** – *Zaragoza 20 – ☎ 95 450 27 21 – Closed Aug –* 🗒. This 19C mansion houses one of the best restaurants in Sevilla, a high-class hotel with a dozen or so rooms, a very pleasant tea-room and the city's school of hotel management.One of the best tables in Sevilla.

TAPAS

Bar Europa – *Siete Revueltas 35 – ☎ 95 422 13 54 –* 🗒. The Europa, situated in a street behind plaza del Salvador, is a traditional bar that has retained its Belle Epoque feel. Popular with a young crowd who head here in the early evening for tapas and people watching.

Bodega San José – *Adriano 10 – ☎ 95 422 41 05 –* 🍴. Given its location close to the Maestranza bullring, it's not surprising that this typical bodega is popular with aficionados of bullfighting and good fino sherry. The air of authenticity is enhanced by the dirt floor and the odours emanating from the huge barrels.

Casa Morales – *García Vinuesa 11 – ☎ 95 422 12 42 –* 🍴. In this bodega founded in 1850 make sure you consult the experienced waiters when choosing your wine or sherry. Excellent home-made tapas.

Las Teresas – *Santa Teresa 2 (Santa Cruz) – ☎ 95 421 30 69.* This small, typically Sevillian tavern, whose doors open onto a picturesque narrow street, is one of the oldest in the Barrio Santa Cruz. Attractive early-19C decor and delicious tapas. The Casa Plácido opposite is a good place for cold tapas.

Sol y Sombra – *Castilla 149-151 – ☎ 95 433 39 35 – Closed Mon-Tue lunchtime and Aug –* 🗒. One of the most popular bars in the city. This bustling bar with its characteristic aromas of fine cheeses, cured hams and cigarette smoke, and walls covered with old and modern brightly coloured bullfighting posters is a must for visitors.

El Rinconcillo – *Gerona 40 – ☎ 95 422 31 83 – Closed 17 Jul-2 Aug –* 🗒. One of

A typical tapas bar

R. Mattes/ MICHELIN

the oldest and most attractive bars in Sevilla. Although its origins date back to 1670, the current decor is from the 19C, including the attractive *azulejo* panelling and the wooden ceiling and counter.

Bodeguita Romero – *Harinas 10* – ☎ *95 421 41 78 - Closed Mon and 15-31 Aug* – 🖃. Held in high esteem by residents. Its bar bursts with tapas and larger portions, all made with quality ingredients. The decor has a local flair.

WHERE TO STAY

Sevilla has a huge range of accommodation for visitors, but beware Holy Week and the Feria, when prices are likely to double or even triple. If you're planning to stay in the city for these events, make sure you check the room rate carefully beforehand.

☞ **Hotel Londres** – *San Pedro Mártir 1* – ☎ *954 50 27 45 - www.londreshotel.com* – 🖃 – *25 rooms*. Near the Museo de Bellas Artes. This centrally located hotel has basic but clean rooms, some with balcony. The best rooms have balconies and overlook the street. The hotel is slowly upgrading, while maintaining its traditional charm.

☞ **Hotel Doña Blanca** – *Plaza Jerónimo de Córdoba 14* – ☎ *95 450 13 73* – 🖃 – *19 rooms*. The rooms in this attractive mansion, with its distinctive red façade, are very reasonably priced given its size, decor and comfort. The other major plus is its central location in a bustling part of the city near the Iglesia de Santa Catalina.

☞ **Hotel Sevilla** – *Daóiz 5* – ☎ *95 438 41 61 - www.hotel-sevilla.com - 30 rooms*. 🖃. An excellent location in a pleasant small square near the Palacio de la Condesa de Lebrija. A good option for those looking for basic comfort at budget prices. The faded decor here adds to the hotel's overall charm.

☞🍽 **Hotel Simón** – *García Vinuesa 19* – ☎ *95 422 66 60* – 🖃 – *29 rooms* – 🖳 *4.20€*. This whitewashed mansion, arranged around a cool internal patio, seems to be from a different era, with corridors decorated with antique furniture and large mirrors. All the bedrooms are comfortable, with the best adorned with colourful azulejos. An excellent location close to the cathedral.

☞🍽 **Hostal Van Gogh** – *Miguel de Mañara 4* – ☎ *95 456 37 27* – 🖃 – *14 rooms*. Despite its name, this *hostal* is typically Sevillian, with a bull's head over the entrance, brightly coloured walls and pots of geraniums on the balconies. Simple, clean rooms and a good location in the Santa Cruz district.

☞🍽 **Hotel Amadeus** – *Farnesio 6* – ☎ *954 501 443 – www. hotelamadeussevilla.com* – 🖃 – *14 rooms* – 🖳 *7€*. A family of musicians converted this typically Sevillian house with courtyard in the heart of the Santa Cruz

district into a delightful small hotel, in which the decor enhances the building's original architectural features.

🍽🍽 **Hotel Las Casas de la Judería** – *Callejón Dos Hermanas 7* – ☎ *95 441 51 50 – www.casasypalacios.com -* 🖳 🖃 – *119 rooms* – 🖳 *15€*. A pleasant surprise in the city's old Jewish quarter. Elegant, traditional and full of colour, this charming, old hotel is housed in the former mansion of the Duke of Béjar.

🍽🍽 **Hotel Alfonso XIII** – *San Fernando 2* – ☎ *95 491 70 00* – 🖃 – *127 rooms* – 🖳 *20€*. Built in 1928 in neo-Mudéjar style, the Alfonso XIII is Sevilla's most luxurious and famous hotel. An excellent location opposite the gardens of the Alcázar.

TAKING A BREAK

Café de la Prensa – *Betis 8* – ☎ *954 33 34 30* – Open 10am-1am. This modern café with a young and intellectual ambience is located alongside the riverbank. Its outdoor tables offer a magnificent view of both the Guadalquivir and the monumental heart of the city. Perfect for whiling away the late afternoon or for a few drinks to start the evening.

Horno San Buenaventura – *Avenida de la Constitución 16* – ☎ *954 45 87 11* – Open 8am-10pm. Part of a network of old furnaces over six centuries old. Particularly popular because of its proximity to the cathedral and its spacious lounge on the top floor. Its cakes are justifiably famous.

La Campana – *Plaza de la Campana 1* – ☎ *954 56 34 33* – Open 8am-10pm. One of Sevilla's classic cafeterias. The Rococo decor creates a pleasant atmosphere in which to enjoy La Campana's pastries, which are famous throughout the city. Varied clientele ranging from the district's senior citizens to tourists passing through the centre.

NIGHTLIFE

Paseo de las Delicias – This avenue is home to four venues (Chile, Líbano, Alfonso and Bilindo). Although not open all year round, these venues become lively in summer, when they are perfect for those who prefer to move from bar to bar. On winter afternoons they are ideal for a quiet drink in the middle of the María Luisa park, surrounded by buildings used during the 1929 Ibero-American Exhibition, while in the summer, drinking and dancing outdoors into the early hours is more the scene. The age range is between 25 and 40, but varies from one venue to the next.

El Tamboril – *Plaza de Santa Cruz* – Open 10pm-5am. Tucked away in a corner of the Santa Cruz district, this taberna is always heaving with its faithful clientele who occasionally burst into song with an impromptu sevillana or rumba. Always busy until the early hours of the morning. The Salve Rociera, a prayer to Our Lady of El Rocío, is sung at midnight every day.

Abades – *Abades 13 – ☎ 954 22 56 22 – Open 5pm-early hours of the morning.* This 18C palatial residence in the heart of the Barrio Santa Cruz has a number of Baroque lounges filled with antiques. A select crowd, who can enjoy a relaxing drink in elegant surroundings to the background strains of classical music.

La Carbonería – *Levíes 18 – ☎ 954 56 37 55 – Open 8pm-4am.* One of Sevilla's institutions and the key to the culture of the city's alternative crowd. Housed in a former coal warehouse in the Jewish Quarter (Judería), La Carbonería is split up into a number of different areas, where you can listen to a musical recital in intimate surroundings around a chimney or to authentic lively flamenco (live music every night). The venue also hosts art and photography exhibitions. A must!

Calle Sierpes

H. Le Gac/ MICHELIN

ENTERTAINMENT

Teatro de la Maestranza – *Paseo de Cristóbal Colón 22 – ☎ 954 22 65 73* – This theatre offers a full season of theatre and dance, including performances by leading international stars, particularly in the field of opera.

SHOPPING

Most of the city's smartest shops and large department stores are located in and around the following streets: **Sierpes**, O'Donnell and San Pablo. A less upmarket shopping area can also be found behind the Iglesia de San Salvador.

Antique-lovers are best advised to wander through the historic centre of the city, particularly through the Santa Cruz district.

The **Jueves** (Thursday) is an interesting small market which takes place once a week along the calle Feria. On Sundays there are other local markets on the alameda de Hércules.

Arts and crafts – Sevilla has a rich tradition of arts and crafts. Potters can still be found in the Santa Cruz and **Triana** districts; the latter contains the aptly named calle Alfarería, literally Pottery Street. The "La Cartuja" factory is the heir to this tradition which dates back to Roman times and the period of Moorish occupation of the city. Other typical products from Sevilla include inlaid woodwork, shawls, fans, flamenco costumes, wrought iron, harnesses, guitars and castanets.

La Giralda★★★

The Giralda – 98m/322ft high – was once a minaret; its name, literally weather vane, comes from the revolving bronze statue of Faith at its summit. When the Giralda was built in the 12C, it resembled its Moroccan sisters, the Koutoubia in Marrakesh and the Hassan Tower in Rabat, and was surmounted by four decorative gilded spheres. The top storey and Renaissance style lantern were added in the 16C. The delicate ornament is typical of the style of the Almohads, a dynasty of strict religious belief, opposed to ostentation, whose members created monumental grandeur in exact accordance with their ideals of utter simplicity. A gently sloping ramp *(accessible from inside the cathedral)*, interrupted at intervals by platforms, leads to the top at 70m/230ft from which there are excellent **views**★★★ of the town.

Cathedral★★★

"Let us build a cathedral so immense that everyone, on beholding it, will take us for madmen", the chapter is said to have declared when they were knocking down the mosque. They succeeded, for Sevilla's cathedral is, in terms of floor space, the third largest in Europe after St Peter's in Rome and St Paul's in London. The exterior is massive.

As one of the last to be built in the Gothic style, the cathedral shows obvious Renaissance influence. The main portals are modern though harmonising with the whole. However, the Puerta de la Natividad (Nativity Doorway) on the right and the Puerta del Bautismo (Baptism) on the left, on either side of the west door, include beautiful sculptures by Mercadente de Bretaña, or Brittany (c 1460), while the Gothic Puerta

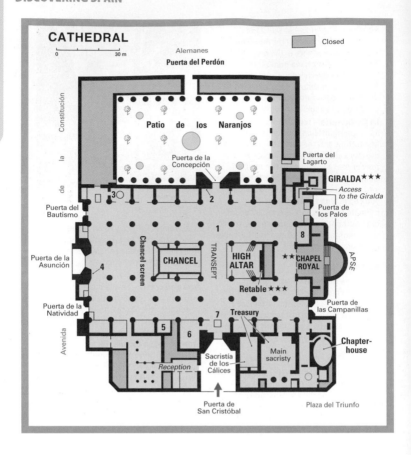

CATHEDRAL

0 — 30 m

Alemanes
Puerta del Perdón

Closed

Constitución

Patio de los Naranjos

Puerta de la Concepción

Puerta del Lagarto

GIRALDA★★★

Access to the Giralda

3

2

Puerta del Bautismo

Puerta de los Palos

1

8

Chancel screen

CHANCEL

TRANSEPT

Puerta de la Asunción

4

HIGH ALTAR

★★CHAPEL ROYAL

APSE

Retable ★★★

Puerta de la Natividad

Puerta de las Campanillas

7 Treasury

5

6

Chapter-house

Avenida

Sacristía de los Cálices

Main sacristy

Reception

Puerta de San Cristóbal

Plaza del Triunfo

de Los Palos and Puerta de las Campanillas, on either side of the rounded Capilla Real (Royal Chapel) (1575) at the east end, have Renaissance style tympana in which Maestro Miguel Perrin (1520) has made full play of perspective in true Renaissance style.

▶ _Enter through the Puerta de San Cristóbal._

The **interior** is striking in size and richness. The massive column shafts, supporting huge arches, appear slender because they are so tall; the magnificent Flamboyant vaulting rises 56m/184ft above the transept crossing. A **mirror (1)** on the floor provides visitors with a striking view of these magnificent stone vaults.

Capilla Mayor (Chancel)

The chancel is unbelievably rich. Splendid Plateresque **grilles**★★ (1518-33) precede the immense Flemish **altarpiece**★★★, profusely but delicately carved with scenes from the life of Christ and the Virgin Mary and gleaming with gold leaf (1482-1525).

Coro

Partly hidden by a grille (1519-23) by Brother Francisco of Salamanca, are some fine 15C and 16C choir stalls. The **trascoro**, a screen of multicoloured marble, jasper and bronze, is 16C.

Tesoro

The **Sacristía de los Cálices** (Chalice Sacristy) contains various paintings and sculptures including canvases by Goya _(Santa Justa and Santa Rufina)_, Valdés Leal, Murillo and Zurburán, and a triptych by Alejo Fernández. The anteroom displays the 15-branch Tenebrario or Plateresque candelabrum, measuring 7.80m/25ft in height, used during Holy Week celebrations.

In the 16C **Sacristía Mayor**, the main exhibits are a Renaissance **monstrance** by Juan de Arfe, measuring 3.90m/13ft in height and weighing 475kg/1 045lb, a _Santa Teresa_ by Zurbarán, and _The Martyrdom of San Lorenzo_ by Lucas Jordán.

😊 Chapels And Altars 😊

- 😊 **Altar de Nuestra Señora de Belén (2)** (Our Lady of Bethlehem): on the north side, to the left of the Puerta de la Concepción. A fine portrayal of the Virgin Mary by Alonso Cano.
- 😊 **Capilla de San Antonio (3)**: this chapel contains several interesting canvases dominated by Murillo's *Vision of St Anthony of Padua,* on the right-hand wall. Also worthy of note are *The Baptism of Christ,* also by Murillo, and two paintings of St Peter by Valdés Leal.
- 😊 **Altar del Santo Ángel (4)** (at the foot of the cathedral, to the left of the Puerta Mayor): this altar is dominated by a fine *Guardian Angel* by Murillo.
- 😊 **Capilla de San Hermenegildo (5)** (next to the Capilla de San José): the 15C alabaster tomb of Cardinal Cervantes sculpted by Lorenzo Mercadante.
- 😊 **Capilla de la Vitrgen de la Antigua (6)** (the next chapel): larger than the others and covered with an elevated vault. A fine 14C fresco of the Virgin adorns the altar.
- 😊 **19C funerary monument to Christopher Columbus (7)**: the explorer's coffin is borne by four pallbearers, each with the symbol of one of the kingdoms of Castilla, León, Navarra and Aragón on his chest.
- 😊 **Capilla de San Pedro (8):** canvases by Zurbarán.

Sala Capitular

The vast 16C Renaissance chapter house has an elliptical dome and an *Immaculate Conception* by Murillo.

Capilla Real★★ (Chapel Royal)

🔒 *Closed to visitors.* The Chapel Royal opens through an enormous entrance arch. It is covered by an elegant, richly ornamented Renaissance dome and is decorated with carved busts. On either side are the tombs of Alfonso X of Castilla (d 1284) and his mother, Beatrice of Swabia.

At the centre of the high altar is the robed figure of the **Virgen de los Reyes**, patron of Sevilla, given, according to legend, by St Louis of France to his cousin St Ferdinand of Spain, who lies buried in a silver gilt shrine below the altar. The chapel screen dates from 1771.

Patio de los Naranjos (Orange Tree Court) – This impressive rectangular patio served as the ablutions area in the former mosque. It is flanked on the north side by the cathedral.

The exit from the cathedral is through the **Puerta del Perdón**, an Almohad arch decorated with stuccowork and two statues by Miguel Perrin.

REAL ALCÁZAR★★★

🕐 *Open Oct-Mar, 9.30am-5pm (1.30pm Sun and public hols); Apr-Sep, 9.30am-7pm (5pm Sun and public hols); last admission 1hr before closing time.* 🕐 *Closed Mon, 1 and 6 Jan, Good Fri, 25 Dec and for official ceremonies.* 😊 *5€; Cuarto Alto: 3€.* ☎ *95 450 23 24.*

The royal palace visible today is the result of several phases of construction. All that remains of the 12C Alcázar of the Almohads are the **Patio de Yeso** and the section of wall dividing the Patio de la Montería from the Patio del León. The rest of the building dates from the Christian period. In the 13C, Alfonso X, the Wise, built a palace on top of the Almohad remains, known today as **Charles V's rooms**. Then, in the 14C, **Peter the Cruel** (1350-69) erected the main nucleus of the building on view today. This part, which is known as **Peter the Cruel's Palace,** was built in 1362. It is a masterpiece of Mudéjar art, built by masons from Granada; as a result, the decoration is highly influenced by the Alhambra which dates from the same period, making the building, in spite of later modifications under Juan II, the Catholic Monarchs, Charles V and Philip II, one of the purest examples of the Mudéjar style.

Cuarto del Almirante (Admiral's Apartments)

Right side of the Patio de la Montería. It was here that Isabel

😊 The Cuarto Real Alto 😊

An optional 30min guided tour enables visitors to view the King and Queen of Spain's official residence in Sevilla, The various rooms, with their fine artesonado ceilings, contain an impressive display of 19C furniture and clocks, 18C tapestries and French lamps. Of particular note are the **Capilla de los Reyes Católicos** (Chapel of the Catholic Monarchs) – an exquisite oratory with a ceramic font, by Nicola Pisano – and the Mudéjar **Sala de Audiencias**.

SEVILLA

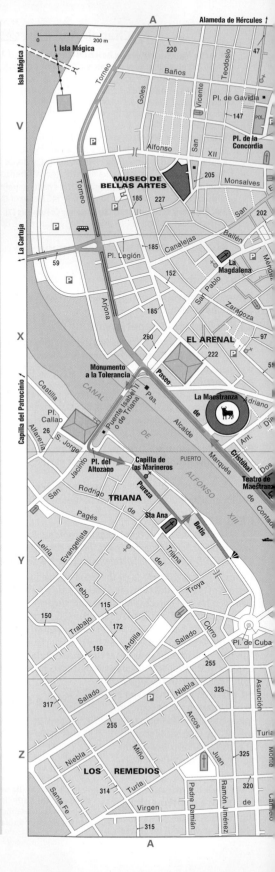

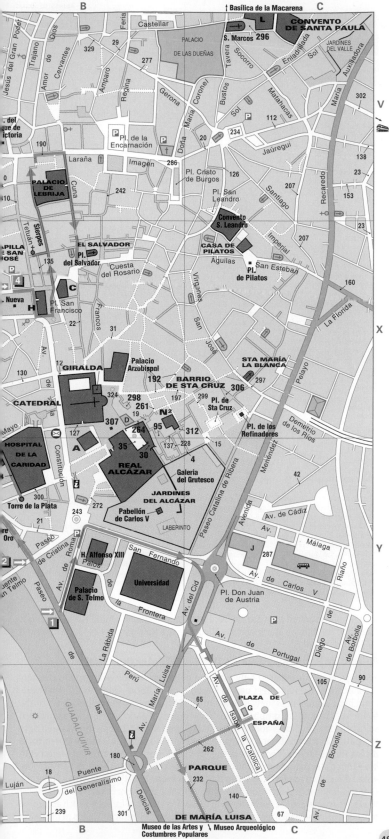

† Basílica de la Macarena

B   C

CONVENTO
DE SANTA PAULA

L

Castellar

PALACIO
DE LAS DUEÑAS

S. Marcos 296

JARDINES
DEL VALLE

Feria

329

29

277

Amparo

Regina

Gerona

Doña María Coronel

Bustos

Sol

Socorro

Enladrillada

Sol

Matahacas

302

María Auxiliadora

V

Jesús del Gran Poder

Trajano

Amor de Dios

Cervantes

. del
que de
ictoria

190

Pl. de la
Encarnación

20

234

112

Jaúregui

138

23

153

23

Recaredo

Laraña

Imagen

286

Cuna

242

Pl. Cristo
de Burgos

126

Pl. San
Leandro

Santiago

207

207

Imperial

PALACIO
DE
LEBRIJA

10

Sierpes

Tetuán

APILLA
E SAN
OSÉ

135

EL SALVADOR

Pl.
del Salvador

Cuesta
del Rosario

Convento
S. Leandro

CASA DE
PILATOS

Águilas

Pl.
de Pilatos

San Esteban

160

La Florida

X

4

Nueva

H

C

Pl. San
Francisco

22

Francos

31

Virgenes

San José

STA MARÍA
LA BLANCA

297

Pelayo

Demetrio
de los Ríos

Av. de

130

12

GIRALDA

Palacio
Arzobispal

192

324

298

261

BARRIO
DE STA CRUZ

197

306

299

Pl. de
Sta Cruz

CATEDRAL

Constitución

307

D

N²

95

312

Pl. de los
Refinadores

42

127

A

264

137

228

15

Menéndez

Mayo

HOSPITAL
DE LA
CARIDAD

35

30

4

Galería
del Grutesco

REAL
ALCÁZAR

JARDINES
DEL ALCÁZAR

Paseo Catalina de Ribera

Avenida

Av. de Cádiz

300

Torre de la Plata

243

272

Pabellón
de Carlos V

LABERINTO

Av.

Av. de Carlos V

J

287

Málaga

Riaño

Y

21

re
Oro

Paseo

2

uente
an Telmo

de Cristina

Paseo

H. Alfonso XIII

Palos

San Fernando

ap la Frontera

Universidad

Av. del Cid

Pl. Don Juan
de Austria

de

Diego

Av.
de Borbolla

1

Palacio
de S. Telmo

La Rábida

Perú

Av. de Portugal

P

GUADALQUIVIR

18

Luján

Puente

del Generalísimo

239

301

Delicias

Av. María Luisa

65

180

262

PARQUE

232

DE MARÍA LUISA

PLAZA DE

G

ESPAÑA

105

90

Av. de Isabel la Católica

Borbolla

Av. de

140

67

Z

Museo de las Artes y \ Museo Arqueológico
Costumbres Populares

B   C

Gerona	BCV	Niebla	AZ	San Leandro Pl.	CV
Gloria	BXY137	Nueva Pl.	BX	San Pablo	AX
Goles	AV	O'Donnell	BV210	San Pedro Pl.	BV286
Gonzalo Bílbao	CV138	Padre Damián	AZ	San Sebastián Pl.	CY287
Hernán Cortés Av.	CZ140	Pagés del Corro	AY	San Telmo Puente	BY
Imagen	BV	Palos de la Frontera	BY	San Vicente	AV
Imperial	CX	Pascual de Gayangos	AV220	Santa Cruz Pl. de	CX
Isabel II o de Triana		Pastor Landero	AX222	Santa Fe	AZ
Puente	AX	Pedro del Toro	AV227	Santa Isabel Pl. de	CV296
Isabel la Católica		Perú	BZ	Santa María La Blanca	CX297
Av. de	CZ	Pilatos Pl. de	CX	Santa Marta Pl. de	BX298
Jaúregui	CV	Pimienta o Susona	BCY228	Santa Teresa	CX299
Jesús de la Vera Cruz	AV147	Pizarro Av.	CZ232	Santander	BY300
Jesús del Gran Poder	BV	Ponce de León Pl.	CV234	Santiago	CV
José Laguillo Av.	CV302	Portugal Av. de	CYZ	Santiago Montoto Av.	BZ301
José María Martínez		Presidente Carrero		Sierpes	BVX
Sánchez Arjona	AY150	Blanco	BZ239	Socorro	CV
Juan Ramón Jiménez	AZ	Puente y Pellón	BV242	Sol	CV
Juan Sebastián Elcano	BZ	Puerta de Jerez	BY243	Temprado	BY304
Julio César	AX152	Pureza	AY	Teodosio	AV
Júpiter	CV153	La Rábida	BY	Tetuán	BX
Laraña	BV	Recaredo	CV	Torneo	AV
Leiria	AY	Refinadores Pl. de los	CX	Trabajo	AY
Luis Montoto	CX160	Regina	BV	Trajano	BV
Málaga Av.	CY	República Argentina Av.	AYZ255	Tres Cruces Pl. de las	CX306
Marcelino Champagnat	AY172	Reyes Católicos	AX260	Triunfo Pl. del	BX307
María Auxiliadora	CV	Rodrigo Caro Callejón de	BX261	Troya	AY
María Luisa Av.	BZ	Rodrigo de Triana	AY	Turia	AZ
Marineros Voluntarios		Rodríguez Caso Av.	CZ262	Velázquez	BV310
Glorieta	BZ180	Roma Av. de	BY	Venerables Pl. de los	BCX312
Marqués de Paradas Av.	AVX185	Romero Morube	BX264	Virgen de África	AZ314
Martín Villa	BV190	Rosario Cuesta del	BX	Virgen de Fátima	AZ317
Matahacas	CV	Salado	AYZ	Virgen de Loreto	AZ320
Mateos Gago	BX192	Salvador Pl. del	BX	Virgen de los Reyes	
Méndez Núñez	AX	San Eloy	AV	Pl. de la	BX324
Menéndez Pelayo	CXY	San Esteban	CX	Virgen de Luján	ABZ
Mesón del Moro	BX197	San Fernando	BY	Virgen del Águila	AZ315
Miño	AZ	San Francisco Pl.	BX	Virgen del Valle	AZ325
Monsalves	AV	San Gregorio	BY272	Vírgenes	CX
Monte Carmelo	AZ	San Jacinto	AY	Viriato	BV329
Murillo	AV202	San Jorge	AX	Zaragoza	AX
Museo Pl. del	AV205	San José	CX		
Navarros	CVX207	San Juan de la Palma	BV277		

Alameda de Hércules	BU		Iglesia de San Marcos	CV	Costumbres Populares	BCZ M²
Archivo General			Iglesia de Santa		Museo de Bellas Artes	AV
de Indias	BXY A		Maria la Blanca	CX	Palacio Arzobispal	BX
Ayuntamiento	BX H		Iglesia de la Magdalena	AX	Palacio de San Telmo	BY
Barrio de Santa Cruz	BCX		Iglesia del Salvador	BX	Palacio de la Condesa	
Basílica de la Macarena	CV		Isla Mágica	AV	de Lebrija	BV
Caja de Ahorros			Itálica	AVX	Parque de María Luisa	CZ
San Fernando	BX C		Jardines del Alcázar	BCY	Parroquia de Santa Ana	AY
Capilla de San José	BX		La Cartuja-Centro		Plaza de España	CZ
Capilla de los Marineros	AY		Andaluz de Arte		Real Alcázar	BXY
Capilla del Patrocinio	AY		Contemporáneo	AVX	Teatro de la Maestranza	AY
Casa de Pilatos	CX		La Giralda	BX	Torre de la Plata	BY
Catedral	BX		La Maestranza	AX	Torre del Oro	
Convento de San Leandro	CVX		Monumento a la		(Museo de la Marina)	BY
Convento de Santa Isabel	CV		Tolerancia	AX	Triana	AY
Convento de Santa Paula	CV		Museo Arqueológico		Universidad	BY
Hospital de la Caridad	BY		de Sevilla	CZ		
Hospital de los Venerables	BX		Museo de Artes y			

the Catholic founded the Casa de Contratación. The Sala de Audiencias (Audience Chamber) contains an altarpiece, the **Virgin of the Navigators**★ (1531-36), painted by Alejo Fernández.

Palacio de Pedro el Cruel★★★ (Palace of Peter the Cruel)

The narrow façade, sheltered by a carved polychrome pine overhang, is strongly reminiscent of the Patio del Cuarto Dorado (Golden Room Court) in the Alhambra. From here, a small passageway leads to the **Patio de las Doncellas** (Court of the Maidens), a beautifully proportioned, Moorish arched patio which is still exquisite in spite of the upper storey added in the 16C. A number of Mudéjar rooms open onto this patio. On the right-hand side, an elevated round arch leads to the **Dormitorio de los Reyes Moros** (Bedroom of the Moorish Kings), two rooms decorated with blue-toned stucco and a magnificent *artesonado* ceiling. Pass through a small room with a flat ceiling to reach the **Patio de las Muñecas** (Dolls' Court) with its delicate, Granada-influenced decoration. The gallery on the upper floor dates from the 19C. On the arch to the left of the north side two medallion faces can be seen which according to legend give the patio its name. The Catholic Monarch's bedroom leads to the **Salón**

Mercurio pool and Galería del Grutesco

de Felipe II (Philip II's Salon), with its magnificent Renaissance coffered cedar ceiling; this in turn connects, via the **Arco de los Pavones** (Peacocks' Arch), with the **Salón de Embajadores** (Ambassadors' Hall), the most sumptuous room in the Alcázar, with its remarkable 15C half-orange cedarwood **cupola**★★★. The tour is completed around the Patio de las Doncellas with the **Sala del Techo de Carlos V** (Charles V's Room), the former palace chapel, crowned by a magnificent Renaissance ceiling.

▷ *Come out of the palace into the Patio de la Montería and through a vaulted passage on the right.*

Palacio Gótico or Salones de Carlos V (Gothic Palace or Charles V's Rooms)

These rooms correspond to the Gothic palace built under the reign of Alfonso X. The structure and groin vaults date from this period. It was here that Charles V married Isabel of Portugal. The rooms house a magnificent collection of **tapestries**★★ from the Real Fábrica de Tapices de Madrid illustrating Emperor Charles V's conquest of Tunis in 1535.

Jardines★

These gardens are one of the best examples of this magnificent Moorish art. Leave Charles V's rooms to reach the Mercurio pool and the 17C **Galería del Grutesco**★, from where there is an impressive view of the gardens, laid out in terraces with numerous ornamental basins. The most enchanting parts of the garden are **Charles V's pavilion**, the maze and the English garden.

A twin-columned *apeadero*, a covered room in Baroque style, leads to the Patio de Banderas.

Patio de Banderas (Flag Court)

The small enclosed square is bordered by elegant façades which stand out against the background of the Giralda tower.

BARRIO DE SANTA CRUZ★★★ (SANTA CRUZ QUARTER)

This former Jewish quarter or Judería was the quarter favoured by Sevilla nobility in the 17C; it remains well worth visiting for its character, its alleys, wrought-iron grilles, flower-filled patios and squares shaded by orange trees and palms. It is even more delightful in the evenings when cafés and restaurants overflow into the squares like those of Doña Elvira, los Venerables Sacerdotes, Alfaro, Santa Cruz and Las Cruces.

Hospital de los Venerables★

🞸 *Guided tours (25min), 10am-2pm and 4-8pm.* 🕐 *Closed 1 Jan, Good Fri and 25 Dec.* 🞖 *4.75€.* ☎ *95 456 26 96.*

This building, located in the lively plaza de los Venerables, is one of the best examples of 17C Sevillian Baroque art. It now serves as the headquarters for the Cultural Focus Foundation. Its fine **church**★ is covered with frescoes painted by Valdés Leal and his son Lucas Valdés.

Patio, Casa de Pilatos

Worth a Visit

NORTH OF THE CATHEDRAL

Museo de Bellas Artes★★★ (Fine Arts Museum)

🕐 *Open 9am-8.30pm; Tue, 3-8pm; Sun and public hols, 9am-2pm.* 🕐 *Closed Mon.*
💶 *1.50€, no charge for citizens of the European Union.* ☎ *95 422 18 29/ 07 90.*

This excellent museum in the former Convento de la Merced (Merced Friary) was built in the 17C by Juan de Oviedo around three beautiful patios. It houses an important collection of paintings covering Spain's Golden Age. The Baroque doorway was added in the 18C.

The first of the museum's 14 rooms (**Sala I**) contains examples of medieval art. **Room II** is dedicated to Renaissance art, in particular a fine sculpture of *St Jerome* by Pietro Torrigiani, a contemporary of Michelangelo. Other works of note include Alejo Fernández's *Annunciation*, with its Flemish and Italian influence clearly evident, and a diptych of *The Annunciation and Visitation* by Coffermans. Two magnificent portraits of *A Lady and a Gentleman* by Pedro Pacheco are the highlight in **Room III**.

Room V★★★ is undoubtedly the museum's star attraction. The church, its walls decorated with paintings by the 18C artist Domingo Martínez, provides a stunning backdrop to an outstanding collection of work by Murillo and one of Zurbarán's masterpieces, *The Apotheosis of St Thomas Aquinas* (in the nave), with its skilfully executed play between light and shade. **Murillo** is the great painter of religious subjects and idealised figures, such as beggar children, with a strong popular appeal; his style is characterised by soft forms, delicate colouring and sweetness of mood, earning it the label *estilo vaporoso*. His works can be found in the transept and in the apse where his monumental *Immaculate Conception*, with its energetic movement, holds pride of place, surrounded by several saints. On the right-hand side of the transept a kindly *Virgen de la Servilleta* is particularly interesting (admire the effect of the Child moving towards you). Note also *St Francis Embracing Christ on the Cross* and a further *Immaculate Conception*, also known as *The Child*. Among several paintings on its left-hand side, *St Anthony and Child*, *Dolorosa* and *St Felix of Cantalicio and Child* are all worth a closer look.

Upper Floor: Room VI (a gallery) displays a fine, richly decorated collection of saints (anonymous, though some painted by followers of Zurbarán). **Room VII** contains further works by Murillo and his disciples while **Room VIII** is entirely devoted to the other great Baroque artist, Valdés Leal. European Baroque is represented in **Room IX** with, among others, canvases by Brueghel, the supreme *Portrait of a Lady* by Cornelis de Vos, and a powerful *St James the Apostle* by Ribera. **Room X★★** merits special attention, with its walls mostly set aside for **Zurbarán** (1598-1664), including a *Christ on the Cross*, in which the body of Christ, painted against a dark background, almost appears as if sculpted in relief. However, in some of his compositions, his lack of concern for perspective results in the occasional inaccuracy, as can be seen in *St Hugh and Carthusian Monks at Table* which is otherwise quite outstanding. His preoccupation with the treatment of the canvas can be admired in the splendid velvet brocade in *San Ambrosio*. In addition to his paintings of saints, his *Virgin of the Caves* and *San Bruno's visit to Urbano II* are also of interest. On display in the same room is the sculpture of *The Penitent St Dominic* by Martínez Montañés. The ceiling of the inner room should not be missed. **Room XI** (a gallery), with its collection of 18C works, is enlivened by Goya's *Portrait of Canon José Duato*. The following two rooms **(XII and XIII)** display 19C art with, in particular, some superb portraits by Esquivel, while the final room **(XIV)** shows several 20C canvases (Vázquez Díaz, Zuloaga).

Casa de Pilatos★★ (Pilate's House)

🕐 *Open 9am-7pm (6pm 22 Sep-20 Mar).* 📷 *8€ (5€ ground floor only).* 📞 *95 422 52 98.*

The palace, built between the late 15C and early 16C by Don Fadrique, the first Marquis of Tarifa, is thought to be based on Pontius Pilate's house in Jerusalem. It is a mixture of Mudéjar, Renaissance and Flamboyant Gothic styles.

The large patio, in which the Mudéjar style predominates, resembles an elegant Moorish palace with finely moulded stuccowork and magnificent lustre *azulejos*★★. The statues, some Antique and the rest 16C, portray, among others, Roman emperors and Athena. The ground floor rooms with *artesonado* ceilings, the chapel with Gothic vaulting and *azulejo* and stucco decoration on the altar, and the remarkable wood **dome**★ over the grand **staircase**★★ illustrate the vitality of the Mudéjar style in civil architecture during the Renaissance. Among the painted ceilings on the first floor is that by Francisco Pacheco (1603) illustrating the Apotheosis of Hercules. The gardens are also open to the public.

At the nearby **Convento de San Leandro** it is possible to buy the convent's famous **yemas** – delicious sweets made with egg yolk and sugar.

Iglesia de San Luis de los Franceses★

This church, the work of Leonardo de Figueroa, is one of the best examples of Sevillian Baroque architecture. The exuberant **interior**★★ is a mix of outstanding murals, sumptuous retables and fine azulejos.

Convento de Santa Paula★

🕐 *Open 10.30am-12.30pm and 3.30-6.30pm.* 🕐 *Closed Mon and for certain religious ceremonies.* 📞 *95 453 63 30.*

This 15C convent is one of the most beautiful and lavish in the city. The church's breathtaking **portal**★ (1504) is adorned with ceramics. Despite the obvious mix of styles (Mudéjar, Gothic and Renaissance), the overall effect is a harmonious one. **Inside**★, the nave is covered by a 17C roof and the chancel by a Gothic vault covered with attractive frescoes. The church also contains sculptures and paintings of interest.

Museum★

Entrance through n°11 on the plaza. It has some fine works on display by important artists such as Ribera, Pedro de Mena, Alonso de Cana etc.

Capilla de San José★ (St Joseph's Chapel)

The intimate, profusely gilded, Baroque chapel, gleams at night by the lights of evening service. The overpowering altarpiece, organ and ornate galleries are typical of the period (1766).

Palacio de la Condesa de Lebrija★

🕐 *Open (including public hols) 11am-1pm and 4.30-7pm (8pm Apr-Sep); Sat, 10am-1pm.* 🕐 *Closed Sun.* 📷 *3.60€ (6.60€ both floors).* 📞 *95 422 78 02.*

The structure of the building is a typical example of an Andalucían palace-residence, with a patio and interior garden. The decoration is perhaps more of a surprise with **Roman mosaics**★ from nearby Itálica, Mudéjar artesonado ceilings, 16C and 17C *azulejos*, and a sumptuous **stairway**★.

Iglesia del Salvador★

This 17C-18C church rises majestically on one side of the square which gives it its name. The sensation of vastness pervades the whole of the interior. It contains some of the city's most impressive 18C **Baroque retables**★★.

Ayuntamiento (Town Hall)

The hall's attractive **east façade**★ (1527-34) is Renaissance in style and adorned with delicate scrollwork decoration. Star vaulting covers the vestibule.

AROUND THE CATHEDRAL

Iglesia de Santa María la Blanca★

This former synagogue was transformed into a church in the 14C and was almost totally rebuilt three centuries later. In the **interior**★, the Baroque exuberance of the ceilings is balanced by the lightness of the pink marble columns supporting them.

Hospital de la Caridad★ (Hospital of Charity)

🕐 *Open 9am-1.30pm and 3.30-7.30pm; Sun, 9am-1pm.* 🕐 *Closed on some public hols.* ◉ *4€.* ☎ *95 422 32 32.*

Plaza de España

R. Mattès/MICHELIN

The hospital was founded in 1625 by Miguel de Mañara who called upon the great Sevillian artists of the time to decorate the **church**★★ with the themes of Death and Charity. Valdés Leal illustrated the first with a striking sense of the macabre, Murillo the second in two large paintings: *The Miracle of the Loaves and Fishes* which faces Moses *Smiting Water from the Rock*, as well as in *St John of God* and *St Isabel of Hungary Caring for the Sick*. Pedro Roldan's **Entombment**★★ adorns the high altar.

Archivo General de Indias (Archives of the Indies)

🔒 *Temporarily closed for restoration.*

The building, dating from 1572, was designed by Juan de Herrera, architect of the Escorial, as an Exchange *(lonja)*. It now houses a unique collection of priceless documents on America at the time of its discovery and conquest, including maps and charts, plans of South American towns and their fortifications as well as the autographs of Columbus, Magellan, Cortés and others.

SOUTH OF THE CATHEDRAL

Parque de María Luisa★★

The 19C park with its beautiful trees, pools and fountains, once formed the grounds of the Palacio de San Telmo. Several buildings remain from the 1929 Ibero-American Exhibition including the semicircular edifice surrounding the vast **plaza de España**★. Each of the benches around the square with their *azulejo* decoration represents a province of Spain and illustrates an episode from its particular history. There is rowing in the canals on the square.

Museo Arqueológico★

🕐 *Open Tue, 2.30-8pm; Wed-Sat, 9am-8pm; Sun, 9am-2pm.* 🕐 *Closed Mon and public hols.* ◉ *1.50€, no charge for citizens of the European Union.* ☎ *954 23 24 01.*

The archaeological museum in the neo-Renaissance palace on plaza de América houses interesting collections of objects from prehistoric through to Phoenician, Punic and Roman times. The 7C-6C BC **Carambolo Treasure**★ includes gold jewellery from the ancient Tartessos civilisation, and a statue of Astarte with a Phoenician inscription. The exhibits in the **Roman section**★, most of which come from Itálica (👣 *see below*), consist mainly of statues (Venus, Diana the Huntress, Trajan, a head of Alexander the Great, a beautiful Hispania), as well as mosaics and bronzes.

Palacio de San Telmo

The palace (1682-1796), once a naval academy and residence of the Dukes of Montpensier and now a seminary, has a grand Baroque **portal**★ (1722), three storeys high, by Leonardo de Figueroa. It now serves as the headquarters of the regional government, the Junta de Andalucía.

Universidad

The university with its harmonious Baroque façades and elegantly laid-out patios, is in the old tobacco factory (18C).

ISLA DE LA CARTUJA (LA CARTUJA ISLAND)

Isla Mágica★ (Magic Island)

Kids ⓒ *Open 2 Apr-1 Nov: all day May-mid Sep (11am-10 pm or midnight); check opening times for rest of season and public hols.* ⚬ *21€, 14.50€ (child and over 65); children under 5 no charge; less outside of high season. Includes all rides and shows.* ☎ *902 16 17 16; reservations, 902 16 00 00; www.islamagica.es.*

Cross the symbolic Puente de La Barqueta to reach this theme park which takes visitors on an adventure back to the Century of Discovery. The 40ha/99 acre site is divided into six theme areas: **Sevilla, the Gateway to the Indies; The Gateway to America; Amazonia; The Pirates' Den; The Fountain of Youth;** and **El Dorado.** Theatrical performances are held throughout the park, which also offers such impressive attractions as the **Anaconda**, a breathtaking water ride, **The Rapids of the Orinoco** for rafting enthusiasts, and **The Jaguar**, the most exciting attraction of them all. The park also has a whole host of restaurants and shops to help you catch your breath as you continue along your magical journey.

La Cartuja–Centro Andaluz de Arte Contemporáneo

ⓒ *Open 10am-8pm (9pm Apr-Sep); Sat, 11am-8pm (9pm Apr-Sep); Sun, 10am-3pm; last admission 30min before closing time.* ⓒ *Closed Mon and public hols.* ⚬ *3€, no charge Tue for citizens of the European Union.* ☎ *95 503 70 70.* 🚌 *Buses C-1 and C-2*

This contemporary art museum is in the former Monasterio de la Cartuja, of which some **convent buildings**★ remain. In the 19C, the monastery was used as a ceramics factory, the ovens and chimneys of which can still be seen today. The museum now houses a permanent collection of notable 20C artists (including Miró and Chillida) and younger Andalucians. As well, it mounts temporary exhibitions.

👣Triana district★; Iglesia de la Magdalena (interior★); Iglesia de San Marcos (Mudéjar tower★).

Excursions

Itálica★

9km/6mi NW on the N 630. ⓒ *Open Oct-Mar, 9am-5.30pm; Sun, 10am-4pm; Apr-Sep, 8.30am-8.30pm; Sun, 9am-3pm.* ⓒ *Closed Mon.* ⚬ *1.50€, no charge for citizens of the European Union.* ☎ *955 99 73 76/ 65 83.*

Standing on a cypress-covered hillside overlooking the Guadalquivir plain are the remains of a **Roman town**, the birthplace of the emperors Hadrian and Trajan and the poet Silius Italicus. The great size of the amphitheatre illustrates the importance of the town at the time. By following the network of streets covering the hillside you see mosaics, among others of birds and Neptune, in their original sites.

Anfiteatro

This amphitheatre was one of the largest in the Roman Empire with seating for 25 000 spectators. Parts of both the seating area and the pit beneath the stage remain from its original elliptical design.

The remains of the theatre can be seen in the centre of the town of Santiponce.

Carmona★★

40km/25mi W along the A 4. Carmona rises up on the edge of the plateau overlooking the fertile valley of the River Corbones. The town's old quarter is notable for its delightful palaces, mansion houses and religious buildings.

🅿 *Park near the Puerta de Sevilla in the lower part of town.*

Old town★

Before entering the old town through the fortified **Puerta de Sevilla**★, with its double Moorish arch, note the **Baroque tower**★ of the **Iglesia de San Pedro**★, a church containing a sumptuous sacrarium chapel (Capilla del Sagrario) and, a little further along, the **Convento de la Concepción** with its fine cloisters and Mudéjar church.

▷ *Walk through the Puerta de Sevilla.*

The **Iglesia de San Bartolomé**, built in the 17C and 18C, houses a chapel adorned with Renaissance *azulejos*. The *capilla mayor* in the Mudéjar church of **San Felipe**★ at the end of the street of the same name is also covered with colourful 16C ceramics.

Plaza de San Fernando is fronted by a number of Mudéjar and Renaissance buildings. The Baroque **town hall** *(ayuntamiento)*, the entrance to which is along calle de El Salvador, has preserved a mosaic dating from the period of Roman occupation. Next door stands the 17C-19C **Iglesia del Salvador**, adorned with a magnificent Churrigueresque altarpiece and an interesting collection of paintings, retables and silverwork. ◔ *Open Thu-Mon, 11am-2pm; Mon, Thu and Fri, also open 4-6pm.* ◔ *Closed Tue and Wed.* ⊛ *1.20€.* ☎ *954 14 12 70.*

The 15C Gothic **Iglesia de Santa María la Mayor**★, later restored in Renaissance and Baroque styles, can be seen nearby. The church has preserved the ablutions patio from the former mosque standing on the site, as well as a monumental **Plateresque altarpiece**★ illustrating the Passion of Christ, fine Plateresque wrought-iron grilles, and a valuable collection of gold and silverwork. A little further along note the **Convento de las Descalzas**★, a stunning example of 18C Sevillian Baroque, and the **Convento de Santa Clara**, whose Mudéjar church contains paintings by Valdés Leal in addition to a collection of female portraits influenced by the style of Zurbarán.

The **Puerta de Córdoba** stands at the end of the street, with its two towers of Roman origin and a gateway added in the 17C.

Alcázar de Arriba (Upper Fortress)

This old Roman fortress (alcázar) offers superb **views**★ of the countryside around Carmona. It was extended by the Almoravids, later converted into the palace of Peter I, and now houses the town's parador.

Necrópolis Romana★

😊 *Access to the Roman necropolis is indicated along the road to Sevilla.*

◔ *Open 9am-5pm; 16 Jun-16 Sep, 8.30am-2pm; Sat-Sun in winter, 10am-2pm.* ◔ *Closed Mon and public hols, and Sun in winter.* ⊛ *1.50€, no charge for citizens of the European Union.* ☎ *95 414 08 11.*

More than 300 1C tombs, mausoleums and crematoria have been discovered. Most comprise a vaulted funerary chamber with niches for the urns. The most interesting are the **Tumba del Elefante** (so called on account of the statue of an elephant) with three dining rooms and a kitchen, and the **Tumba de Servilia**, which is the size of a patrician villa. The complex also includes an amphitheatre and a small museum.

Sigüenza★

POPULATION: 5 426.

MICHELIN MAP 576 I 22 – CASTILLA-LA MANCHA (GUADALAJARA).

The pink and ochre coloured town of Sigüenza, dropping in tiers from the hilltop on which it is built, is dominated by its imposing cathedral fortress and castle (parador). A stroll through the old quarter reveals a maze of narrow streets fronted by seigniorial mansions and Romanesque doorways framed by elegant archivolts.

Location

Sigüenza is situated 22km/14mi from the A 2 road linking Madrid and Zaragoza.
🏠 *Paseo de la Alameda (Ermita del Humilladero), 19250 Guadalajara,* ☎ *949 34 70 07.*

🚶 *Neighbouring sights are described in the following chapters: Monasterio de SANTA MARÍA DE HUERTA (67km/42mi NE), GUADALAJARA (73km/45mi SW) and SORIA (95km/59mi N).*

Worth a Visit

The **plaza Mayor**, extending from the south wall of the cathedral in the centre of Sigüenza, is a delightful square with its 16C arcaded gallery and Renaissance town hall *(ayuntamiento)*.

Catedral★★

🕐 *Open 11am-1pm and 4.30-6.30m; Sun, 11am-1pm and 5.30-7pm; public hols, noon-1pm and 5.30-7pm.* 🎫 *3€, no charge Mon.* ☎ *619 36 27 15.*

The nave, begun to a Cistercian plan in the 12C, was only completed in 1495, the end of the Gothic period; the ambulatory and cloisters are slightly later. The roof and transept dome were rebuilt after the boming of Sigüenza during the Civil War in 1936.

The façade appears more like that of a fortress than a church as it stands flanked by crenellated towers and powerful buttresses until you notice its great rose and Romanesque windows with their old stained glass.

Interior

The nave with sober lines and high vaulting supported on massive pillars graced by slender engaged columns, conveys an impression of solid strength.

In the **north aisle**, the **doorway**★ into the Capilla de la Anunciación (Chapel of the Annunciation) is decorated with Renaissance pilasters, Mudéjar arabesques and Gothic cusping. The 15C triptych beside it by the Castilian School is dedicated to St Mark and St Catherine.

In the **north transept** is a fine **sculptured unit**★★: a 16C **porphyry doorway** opens onto the cloisters of multicoloured marble. The 16C **Santa Librada altar**, designed by Covarrubias as a retable, features a central niche containing an altar surmounted by painted panels of the martyrdom of the saint and her eight sisters, all born, according to legend, on the same day. Beside it, note the 16C **sepulchre of Dom Fadrique of Portugal**, a more ornate monument adorned with Plateresque decoration.

The **sacristy** by Covarrubias has an amazing **ceiling**★ – a profusion of heads and roses between which peer thousands of cherubim; the panelling and woodwork of doors and furniture are delicately carved in ornate Plateresque. The 16C **Capilla de las Reliquias** (Reliquary Chapel) is covered with a **dome**★.

A chapel off the **ambulatory** contains a 16C wooden **Crucifix**★.

The **chancel** (*presbiterio*) has a beautiful 17C wrought-iron grille framed by two alabaster **pulpits**★, one Gothic (on the right), the other Renaissance (on the left). The altarpiece is 17C.

The Capilla del Doncel in the south transept was designed for the **Doncel tomb**★★ commissioned by Isabel the Catholic for her young page, Don Martín Vázquez de Arce, who died at the gates of Granada in 1486. The figure, considered a major work of sepulchral art in Spain, shows the youth reclining on one elbow and reading serenely; it is extraordinarily realistic. In the centre of the room is the mausoleum of the Doncel's parents.

Claustro

The 16C Gothic cloisters are surrounded by chapels with Plateresque doors, among them the 16C-17C Puerta de Jaspe (Jasper Doorway) which communicates with the transept.

The **Sala Capitular** (chapter house) displays books, manuscripts and a collection of 17C Flemish tapestries.

Museo de Arte Antiguo (Museum of Ancient Art)

▶ *Opposite the cathedral.*

🕐 *Open noon-2pm and 5-6pm.* 🕐 *Closed Mon.* 🎫 *No charge.* ☎ *949 39 10 23.*

Among the many works displayed are sculptures by Pompeo Leoni (Room C), a *Pietà* attributed to Morales, an *Immaculate Conception* by Zurbarán (Room E) and a fiery statue of the *Prophet Elijah* by Salzillo (Room N).

Excursion

Atienza

31km/19mi NW on the C 114. Atienza is a typical Castilian village built at the foot of a castle of which only the keep remains proudly upright on its rock. **Plaza del Trigo,** surrounded by porticoes, is attractively medieval. The town, an important commercial enclave during the Middle Ages, was granted protection by Alfonso VIII of Castila in recognition for the support its citizens gave him in 1162 when, as a child, he sought refuge from his uncle, Ferdinand II of León who hoped to secure the Castilian throne. The event is commemorated annually in the Whitsun **Caballada** festival.

Atienza once had seven churches but since the Civil War all that remains of interest are the Churrigueresque altarpiece in the **parish church** on plaza del Trigo and the Rococo chapel in the **Iglesia de la Trinidad** (Holy Trinity Church) near the cemetery.

Sitges★★

POPULATION: 13 096

MICHELIN MAP 574 I 35 – CATALUNYA (BARCELONA).

Sitges has become a popular holiday resort famous for its two lovely, carefully kept beaches. Its 2km/1mi long Passeig Marítim, an avenue that joins up with the beach at Ribera, is dotted with hotels, luxury residences and various other establishments. During the Modernist movement Sitges was an important cultural centre and many examples of architecture dating from those days can be seen in the city.

Location

Sitges is a coastal resort halfway between Barcelona and Tarragona, with which it has excellent road links. *Morera 1, 08870,* ☎ *93 894 05 84/42 51.*

Neighbouring sights are described in the following chapters: BARCELONA (45km/28mi NE), TARRAGONA (53km/33mi SW) and MONTBLANC (81km/51mi W).

Worth a Visit

OLD TOWN★★ ◷ *1hr 30min*

Dominating the breakwater of La Punta, sheltering the fishing harbour, stands the parish church. All around are the streets of the old town lined with white-walled houses, their balconies brilliant with flowers. Local museums housed in neo-Gothic mansions contain canvases from the late 19C, when Rusiñol and Miguel Utrillo (father of the French painter) painted in this quarter.

Museo del Cau Ferrat★★

◷ *Open 10am-1.30pm and 4-6.30pm; Sat, 9.30am-7pm; 15 Jun-30 Sep, 10am-2pm and 5-9pm; Sun and public hols, 10am-3pm.* ◷ *Closed Mon, 1 Jan, 25 Aug and 25-26 Dec.* ⊙ *3€ (combined ticket: 5.40€); no charge first Wed of month.* ☎ *93 894 03 64.*

The painter **Santiago Rusiñol** (1861-1931) converted two 16C fishermen's houses, to which he added a number of Gothic features. He bequeathed large collections of ceramics, paintings, sculptures and wrought-iron works to the town for exhibition in this museum, which opened in 1933.

Painting

Note two remarkable works by El Greco: *Penitent Mary Magdalene* and *The Repentance of St Peter.* The gallery also contains canvases by Picasso, Casas, Nonell, Llimona, Zuloaga and Rusiñol himself *(Poetry, Music and Painting).*

Sitges

Wrought iron

This collection, which has given its name to the museum *(cau ferrat)*, consists of various exhibits of different styles and periods. Among the objects on display are a set of 16C braziers.

Ceramics

The exhibition rooms are decorated with numerous ceramic objects.

Museo Maricel del Mar★

🕐 *Open 10am-1.30pm and 3-6.30pm; Sat, 10am-5pm; 15 Jun-30 Sep, 10am-2pm and 5-9pm; Sun and public hols all year, 10am-3pm.* 🕐 *Closed Mon, 1 and 6 Jan, 25 Aug and 25-26 Dec.* ⚬ *3€ (combined ticket: 5.40€), no charge first Wed of month.* ☎ *93 894 03 64.*

The museum is in a former 14C hospital, converted by the American Charles Deering in 1913 under the supervision of Miguel Utrillo. It is linked by a footbridge to another mansion, the Maricel de Terra. The collections displayed are of medieval and Baroque works of art.

Casa Llopis-Museu Romàntic★

🕐 *Open 10am-1.30pm and 3-6.30pm; Sat, 10am-7pm (15 Jun-30 Sep, 10am-2pm and 5-9pm); .* ⚬ *3€ (combined ticket, 5.40€), no charge first Wed of month.* ☎ *93 894 29 69.*

This bourgeois house built at the end of the 18C illustrates the considerable wealth accumulated by the city in the 19C and gives a good idea of the life of the middle and upper classes during the Romantic period with frescoes on the walls, English furniture, various mechanical devices and musical boxes. Dioramas on the ground floor supplement the picture with scenes of private, social and popular activities. The museum also houses the **Lola Anglada collection,** an outstanding display of 17C, 18C and 19C dolls from all over Europe.

Excursions

Vilanova i la Geltrú★

7km/4mi SW. Situated in a small bay, this locality is both an important fishing harbour and a popular holiday resort for tourists. Its fine sandy beaches and shallow waters are its main attraction.

Museu Romàntic Casa Papiol★

🕐 *Open 10am-1.30pm and 3-6.30pm; Sat, 10am-7pm; 15 Jun-15 Oct 10am-2pm and 5-7pm; Sun and public hols 10am-3pm.* 🕐 *Closed Mon, 1 Jan, 25 Aug and 25-26 Dec.* ⚬ *3€ (combined ticket, 5.40€), no charge first Wed of month.* ☎ *93 894 03 64.*

The large mansion built by the Papiol family between 1780 and 1801 gives a good idea of the values cherished by the devout yet well-to-do industrial middle classes in the 19C. A certain austerity reigns in the library with its 5 000 or so 16C to 19C volumes, in the Deputy's office, in the chapel with its strange relic of St Constance and in the reception rooms where the walls are covered in biblical scenes executed in grey monochrome. On the other hand, the opulence of the house is evident in the rich furnishings, the ballroom and the Louis XVI apartment where the French General, Suchet, once stayed. The kitchen is spick and span, gleaming with ceramic tiles. Workrooms and annexes on the entresol and ground floors contain equipment and stores: the stove, olive oil reserve, servants' kitchen and the stables.

Biblioteca-Museu Balaguer★

🕓 Open 10am-1.30pm and 4-6.30pm; Jun-Sep, 10am-1.30pm and 4.30-7pm; Thu, 6-8.30pm; Sun and public hols, 10am-1.30pm all year. 🕓 Closed Mon, 1 Jan, Holy Week, 1 May, 5 Aug and 25-26 Dec. ⊜ 1.80€, no charge Thu afternoon and first Sun of month. ☎ 93 815 42 02.

Set up in a curious building of Egyptian and Greek inspiration, this library-museum was founded at the instigation of the poet, historian and politician **Víctor Bala-guer** (1824-1901). The library boasts around 40 000 titles. The museum houses an impressive **contemporary art collection,** with works from the 1950s and 1960s by Catalan artists (Legado 56); small works outlining the evolution of painting from the end of the 14C to the beginning of the 20C; an interesting collection of **16C and 17C paintings** (El Greco, Murillo, Carducho, Maino, Carreño etc) and examples of Egyptian and Asian art.

Museu del Ferrocarril★

Kids 🕓 Open 15 July-15 Sep, 11am-2pm and 5-8pm; rest of the year, 10.30am-2.30pm; Sat, 4-6pm; Sun and public hols, 10.30am-2.30pm. 🕓 Closed Mon, 1 and 6 Jan and 25-26 Dec. ⊜ 4€. ☎ 93 815 84 91.

The museum houses one of the most impressive collections of railway engines in Spain.

Solsona★★

POPULATION: 6 601

MICHELIN MAP 574 G 34 – CATALUNYA (LLEIDA).

Solsona is a calm, tranquil town endowed with a noble air and a fine array of elegant medieval residences along its gently sloping streets. The town is also dotted with several attractive squares, such as the plaza de Sant Joan and plaza de la Ribera, which have managed to retain the atmosphere of bygone days.

Location

Solsona is the capital of the Solsonès region and stands on the C 1410 road linking Manresa with the C 1313 heading into the Pyrenees. 🗋 Solsona: Carretera Basella 1, 25280, ☎ 973 48 23 10; Cardona: Avenida del Rastrillo, 08261, ☎ 93 869 27 98.

👣 Neighboring sights are described in the following chapters: PIRINEOS CATALANES, LLEIDA/LÉRIDA (108km/67mi SW) and VIC (97km/60mi E).

Worth a Visit

Museo Diocesano y Comarcal★★ (Diocesan and Regional Museum)

🕓 Open 10am-1pm and 4-6pm; May-Sep, 10am-1pm and 4.30-7pm; Sun and public hols, 10am-2pm. 🕓 Closed Mon (except public hols), 1 Jan and 25 Dec. ⊜ 2€. ☎ 973 48 21 01.

Corpus Christi

Corpus Christi is the occasion for young men, dressed in ancient costumes, to parade through the streets firing salvoes from blunderbusses, for giant pasteboard figures to appear and children to dance the local dance, the "Bal de Bastons", in the streets.

The Romanesque and Gothic style **paintings**★★ in the museum housed in the Palacio Episcopal (Episcopal Palace, an 18C Baroque building), are excellent examples of Catalan art.

The fresco collection of works from throughout the province includes a painting from the **Sant Quirze de Pedret church**★★, discovered beneath an overpainting done 100 years later. This fresco, executed in an archaic style, shows God, with arms outstretched, in a circle which represents heaven, surmounted by a phoenix symbolising immortality. Another circle features a peacock proudly pecking at a bunch of grapes. The narrative talent of the 12C Maestro de Pedret can be seen in the theme of the Apocalypse, painted in a style obviously of Byzantine influence in a reconstituted Mozarabic apse. Totally different are the thinly outlined, elegant 13C paintings from **Sant Pau de Caserres**★ – in particular, some wonderful **angels**★★ of the Last Judgement – and the already Gothic-style 14C works from Cardona.

The museum is also known for its collection of **altar fronts** which includes a frontal from Sagars, in which all decoration is omitted to heighten the symbolism of the scenes illustrated, and a realistic painting of the Last Supper, **La Cena de Santa Constanza**★ by Jaime Ferrer (15C).

The **Museo de la Sal** (Salt Museum), another department, is possibly unique. Everything displayed on the table has been carved out of rock salt from Cardona: the setting, the repast and the weird, pinnacled centrepiece.

Catedral★

🕐 *Open 8am-1pm and 4-8pm, Jul-Aug, 9am-1pm and 5-9pm;* 🕐 *no visits during religious services on Sun and public hols.* ☏ *973 48 06 19.*

Only the belfry and the apse remain of the Romanesque church; the rest is Gothic with Baroque additions such as the portals and the sumptuous 18C Capilla de la Virgen (Lady Chapel) off the south transept. This chapel houses the **Mare de Déu del Claustro**★, a beautifully carved Romanesque figure of the Virgin Mary in black stone.

▶ Museo del Ganivet; Ayuntamiento (town hall – 16C).

Excursions

Cardona★

20km/12mi SE along the C 55. The town of Cardona, with its attractive old quarter, sits at the foot of an imposing castle.

Castillo de Cardona★

The origins of this spectacular fortress, perched on top of a hill at an altitude of 589m/1 933ft, date back to the 8C. Of the original 11C buildings there remain only a truncated tower, the **Torre de la Minyona**, and the collegiate church. It is surrounded by distinct Vauban-style walls and bulwarks built during the 17C and 18C. Nowadays the castle is home to the parador, commanding a marvellous **view**★ of the **montaña de sal**★★, a salt mine worked since Roman times, with some galleries more than 1km/0.6mi deep. 🔳 *Guided tours (1hr), 10am-3pm; Sat-Sun and public hols, 10am-6pm (8pm in Aug).* 🕐 *Closed Mon exc public hols and 15 Dec-15Jan.* 🎟 *9€.* ☏ *902 40 04 75.*

Colegiata de Sant Vicenç★★

🕐 *Open 10am-1.30pm and 3-5.30pm (6.30pm Jun-Sep); last admission 30min before closing.* 🕐 *Closed Mon exc public hols, 1 Jan and 25 Dec.* 🎟 *2.40€, no charge Wed.* ☏ *93 868 41 69.*

The collegiate church was built in 1040 and has several features from the Lombard style of architecture which flourished at the time in Catalunya. The smooth, unadorned walls, the lantern over the transept crossing, the different types of vaulting – barrel in the nave with its impressive elevation, and groined in the aisles – all testify to a skilful mastery of the art. Below, the groined vaulting in the **crypt**★ rests on six graceful columns. The interior was used as a backdrop by Orson Welles when he shot *Chimes at Midnight*. Outside, the charming Gothic cloisters date from the 15C.

Soria ★

POPULATION: 35 540

MICHELIN MAP 575 G 22 – CASTILLA Y LEÓN (SORIA).

This tranquil provincial capital stands on the banks of the Duero, the river that provides the town with its greenery and a modicum of cool during the harsh Castilian summer. Over the centuries, the desolate scenery and medieval atmosphere of the old town have been immortalised by numerous poets such as Antonio Machado.

Location

Soria is situated at an altitude of 1 050m/3 445ft on a plateau buffeted by the winds of the Meseta. ⌷ *Plaza Ramón y Cajal, 42003 Soria,* ☎ *975 21 20 52.*

ꙮ *Neighbouring sights are described in the following chapters: El BURGO DE OSMA (56km/35mi SW) and Monasterio de SANTA MARÍA DE HUERTA (85km/53mi SE).*

Worth a Visit

Iglesia de Santo Domingo★

The attraction of this church's west front lies in its two tiers of blind arcades, its window and richly carved **portal**★★. The overall French air is explained by the fact that the church's founders were Alfonso VIII and his queen, Eleanor Plantagenet, who appear on either side of the portal. The carving on the tympanum is less cluttered than that of the archivolt where the figures have been carved with great attention to detail. The scenes so realistically illustrated include the early chapters of Genesis (on the capitals of the jamb shafts), the 24 Elders of the Apocalypse playing stringed instruments, the Massacre of the Innocents, and Christ's childhood, Passion and Death (in ascending registers on the archivolt).

Palacio de los Condes de Gómara
(Palace of the Counts of Gómara)

The long façade, part Renaissance, part Classical, the bold upstanding tower and double patio are a proud example of late-16C opulence.

Iglesia de San Juan de Rabanera

The Romanesque portal taken from a ruined church dedicated to St Nicholas, recalls the events of the saint's life in the capitals on the slender columns on the right and on the tympanum. The unusual decoration at the church's east end shows both Byzantine and Gothic influences. Inside are two interesting Crucifixes – Romanesque over the altar and Baroque in the north transept.

Museo Numantino (Numancia Museum)

🕐 *Open 9am-2pm and 4-9pm; Jul-Sep 10am-2pm and 5-8pm; Sun and public hols, 10am-2pm.* 🕐 *Closed Mon (except Jul-Aug), 1 Jan, local festivals in Jun (Jueves La Saca and Domingo de Calderas), 2 Oct and 25 Dec.* ⊜ *1.20€, no charge Sat-Sun.* ☎ *975 22 13 97.*

The collections in the recently restored museum illustrate the historical development of Soria from the Palaeolithic Age to modern times. Most of the items displayed come from local excavations – note the artefacts from Celt-Iberian necropolises and the coloured pottery from Numancia (ꙮ *see below*).

"Soria Pura, Cabeza de Extremadura"

The motto in the city arms recalls events in the 10C when Soria and its dependent countryside marked the limits of Castile in the face of the Muslim-conquered south. Gradually the Christians built a **fortified line** along the Duero reinforced by bastions such as **Soria, Berlanga, Gormaz, Peñaranda** and **Peñafiel**.

In the Middle Ages, the town grew prosperous partly through its role in the **Mesta**, a powerful association of sheep farmers that organised the seasonal migration of flocks between Extremadura, Castilla and pastures in the north of the country.

Address Book

For coin ranges, see the Legend at the back of the guide.

WHERE TO EAT

⊜⊜ **Casa Augusto** – *Plaza Mayor 5 –* ☎ *975 21 30 41 –* 🍽️. This centrally located restaurant on the town's main square serves traditional, high-quality regional cuisine in an attractive stone-walled dining room. A daily fixed menu is also available.

WHERE TO STAY

⊜ **Hostería Solar de Tejada** – *Claustrilla 1 –* ☎ *975 23 00 54 – 18 rooms*. This charming small hotel in the centre of Soria is attractively decorated with a mix of materials, modern design features, bright colours and well-crafted furniture. Excellent value for money.

Catedral de San Pedro

🕐 *Open 11am-1pm; Apr-Oct, 10.30am-1.30pm and 4.30-7.30pm (5.30pm in Oct).* 🕐 *Closed Mon in winter.* ⊜ *1€.* ☎ *975 24 01 79.*

The 16C Gothic cathedral is light and spacious; the **cloisters**★ are older, possessing three Romanesque galleries. The capitals have been delicately re-sculpted in a pure Romanesque style that recalls the work in Santo Domingo de Silos. In the gallery walls are the funerary niches in which the monks are buried.

Monasterio de San Juan de Duero

🕐 *Open 10am-2pm and 4-7pm; Jul-Sep, 10am-2pm and 5-8pm; Sun and public hols, 10am-2pm.* 🕐 *Closed Mon, 1 Jan, 22 Jun, 2 Oct and 24-25 and 31 Dec.* ⊜ *0.60€, no charge Sat-Sun.* ☎ *975 22 13 97.*

The monastery founded by the Hospitallers of St John of Jerusalem stands in a rustic setting on the far bank of the Duero. Only the graceful gallery arcading, with four different orders, remains of the 12C-13C **cloisters**★. The intersecting, overlapping arches owe much to Moorish art. The church contains a small lapidary museum. Two small chambers with beautiful historiated capitals stand at the entrance to the apse; the ciborium effect is unusual, like one might find in an Orthodox church.

Aguirre	B	5	García Solier	A	33	Ramón Benito Aceña Pl.	A	66
Alfonso VIII	A	8	Hospicio	B	36	Ramón y Cajal Pl.	A	63
Caballeros	A	12	Logroño Carret	B	39	San Benito	A	67
Campo	A	15	Mariano Granados Pl.	A	42	San Blás y el Rosel Pl.	A	69
Cardenal Frías	A	18	Mariano Vicén Av.	A	45	San Clemente	A	70
Casas	A	21	Mayor Pl.	B	48	San Juan de Rabanera	B	71
Collado	A	24	Nuestra Señora de			Sorovega	B	75
Condes de Gómara	B	27	Calatañazor	B	54	Tirso de Molina	B	78
Espolón Pas. del	A	29	Obispo Augustín	B	57			
Fortún López	B	31	Pedrizas	A	60			

Iglesia de San Juan de Rabanera	A R		Museo Numantino	A M	Palácio de los Condes de Gómara	B J

Parque del Castillo (Castle Park)

The lines composed about the Soria countryside by the Sevillian poet, Antonio Machado (1875-1939), who wrote *Campos de Castilla,* come alive in this park: "violet mountains, poplars beside green waters."

Ermita de San Saturio (San Saturio Hermitage)

1.3km/0.8mi S of the N 122. A shaded path beside the Duero leads to the cave where the holy man sat in meditation. The octagonal chapel built into the rock and covered with frescoes is 18C.

Excursions

Ruinas de Numancia

7km/4mi NE via ① *on the town plan.* ◷ *Open Nov-Mar, 10am-2pm and 3.30-6pm; Apr-May, 10am-2pm and 4-7pm; Jun-Aug, 10am-2pm and 5-9pm; Sun and public hols, 10am-2pm.* ◷ *Closed Mon.* ⬭ *0.60€, no charge Sat-Sun.* ☎ *975 22 13 97.*

There are few signs of the events which took place in Numancia in 133 BC. The Romans were in Spain at the time and thought that having pacified the peninsula their legions would suffer little opposition; Numancia, however, resisted them. **Scipio Aemilianus,** who had destroyed Carthage, directed the siege against Numancia. After eight months the Numantines could resist no more but, unwilling to submit, they burned their city and perished one and all.

The present ruins are of the Numancia rebuilt by the Romans.

SIERRA DE URBIÓN★★

⊛ *Roads are liable to be blocked by snow between November and May.*

It seems surprising that this part of the Sistema Ibérico mountain range, which at one point rises to 2 228m/7 310ft and is so close to the Soria plateau and the flat, ochre-coloured Ebro Valley, should be hilly and green, filled with streams rushing through pinewoods and meadows. One of these streams is the source of the Duero, one of Spain's longest rivers *(910km/565mi).*

Laguna Negra de Urbión★★

53km/33mi NW by ⊚ *on the plan and the N 234.* ◷ *About 1hr.*

▷ *At Cidones bear right towards Vinuesa; continue for 18km/11mi before turning onto the Montenegro de Cameros road. After 8km/5mi bear left onto the Laguna road (9km/6mi).*

The **road**★★, after skirting the Cuerdo del Pozo reservoir (embalse), which is ringed by tall stone cliffs, rocks and holm oaks, continues through pines to the **Laguna Negra** (alt 1 700m/5 600ft). The lagoon is a small glacial lake at the foot of a semicircular cliff over which cascade two waterfalls.

Laguna Negra de Neila★★

About 86km/53mi NW by ⊚ *on the plan and the N 234.*

▷ *At Abejar turn right towards Molinos de Duero; continue to Quintana de la Sierra where you bear right for Neila (12km/7mi) and then left for Huerta de Arriba; 2km/1mi on the left is the road to Laguna Negra.*

The **road**★★ through green, picturesque countryside commands changing views of the valley and Sierra de la Demanda. The lake lies at an altitude of 2 000m/6 500ft.

Talavera de la Reina

POPULATION: 69 136

MICHELIN MAP 576 M 15 – CASTILLA-LA MANCHA (TOLEDO).

The name of this Castilian town is forever synonymous with the azulejos (ceramic tiles) which brought it fame and prosperity in the past. Talavera stands on the right bank of the River Tagus, spanned by a 15C bridge, and has preserved part of its medieval walls and several churches of interest, such as the Colegiata de Santa María la Mayor and the Iglesia de Santiago el Nuevo, both built in Mudéjar style.

Location

Talavera is situated on the A 5 highway linking Madrid (120km/80mi NE) and Badajoz.
🖪 *Ronda del Cañillo (Torreón), 45600 Talavera de la Reina,* ☎ *925 82 63 22.*

🖄 *Neighbouring sights are described in the following chapters: TOLEDO (80km/50mi E), Monasterio de GUADALUPE (106km/66mi SW) and Sierra de GREDOS (to the N).*

Special Features

TALAVERA CERAMICS

Since the 15C, the name Talavera has been associated with the **ceramic tiles** used to decorate the lower walls of palaces, mansions and chapels. Talavera *azulejos* were always recognisable by their blue and yellow designs.

Today, tiles have been largely replaced by the manufacture of domestic and purely decorative ware such as plates, vases and bowls. Green indicates that an object was made in **El Puente del Arzobispo,** a small village *(34km/21mi SW)* which now specialises in the mass production of pottery drinking jars *(cacharros).*

The **Museo Ruiz de Luna** displays an interesting collection of ceramics dating from the 15C through to modern times. ◷ *Open 10am-2pm and 4-6.30pm (including public hols); Sun, 10am-2pm.* ◷ *Closed Mon, 1 Jan, 1 May and 25 Dec.* ⊜ *0.60€.* ☎ *925 80 01 49.*

Basílica de la Virgen del Prado (Basilica of the Prado Virgin)

In a park at the entrance to the town coming from Madrid. The church, which is virtually an *azulejos* museum, gives a good idea of the evolution of the local style. The oldest tiles, dating from the 14C to 16C, yellow coloured and with geometric designs, are in the sacristy *(access through the north door)*; 16C to 18C tiles, blue coloured and with narrative designs, are in the church proper and the portal.

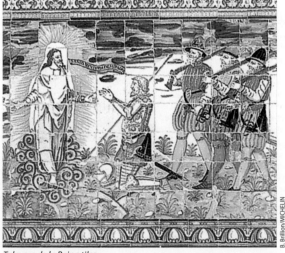

B. Brillion/MICHELIN

Talavera de la Reina tiles

Excursion

Oropesa

32km/20mi W. Two churches and a castle rise above the town. The **castle**★ retains its proud bearing of 1366; the annexes were built in 1402 and are now a parador. A plaque in the stairwell recalls that a Count of Oropesa, **Francisco de Toledo**, was Viceroy of Peru from 1569 to 1581.

The village of **Lagartera**, 2km/1.2mi west of Oropesa, has been known for several centuries for the embroidery done by its women who, during the summer months, may be seen sitting at their front doors working. They embroider long skirts and vividly coloured bonnets in peasant style, tablecloths and subtly toned silk hangings with scatterings of flowers – every cottage has its own display.

Tarragona★★

POPULATION: 112 801

MICHELIN MAP 574 I 33 – CATALUNYA (TARRAGONA).

Tarragona, a city rich in reminders of Antiquity and the Middle Ages, is also a modern town with wide, verdant avenues, attractive small squares and a lively commercial centre. Its seafront, rising in tiers up the cliffside, is embellished by delightful gardens overlooking the Mediterranean. This promenade skirts the old city, encircling the tower of the Palace of Augustus, before following the city's walls, behind which stands the imposing silhouette of the cathedral.

Location

Since Roman times, Tarragona has taken full advantage of its maritime position and is still one of Spain's major ports. With over 15km/9.5mi of sandy beaches, the city has also developed into a popular destination for summer visitors. 🛈 *Fortuny 4, 43001 Tarragona, ☎ 977 23 34 15; Major 39, 43003, ☎ 977 24 52 03.*

Address Book

SIGHTSEEING

Port Aventura – This theme park is located 10km/6mi S of Tarragona and is easily accessible via the A 7 motorway (exit 35) and the N 340.

For coin ranges, see the Legend at the back of the guide.

WHERE TO EAT

⬡ **Taverna Catalana de Julia** – *Nazaret 6* – ☎ *977 22 29 06 – Closed Tue and Mon midday in summer.* A cosy restaurant in a pleasant plaza by the city walls, popular with young people. Choose the rustic dining room or the pleasant terrace, where you can enjoy the *llesques* (slices of bread rubbed with tomato and drizzled with olive oil).

⬡⬡⬡ **Merlot** – *Cavallers 6* – ☎ *977 22 06 52 – Closed 1-15 Feb, Sun, and Mon lunchtime* – ▦. The vaulted ceiling, subtle lighting and high-quality rustic furniture combine to create a refined, intimate ambience. The menu covers a range of Catalan dishes (rice dishes, in particular) as well as an excellent selection of home-made desserts.

WHERE TO STAY

⬡ **Urbis** – *Reding 20 bis* – ☎ 977 24 01 16 - ▦ – *44 rooms* – ☟. Situated near the convention centre, this modest family hotel offers functional rooms with updated (though small) bathrooms.

⬡⬡⬡ **Hotel Imperial Tarraco** – *Passeig de les Palmeres* – ☎ *977 23 30 40 – imperialtinet.fut.es* – 🅿 ▦ – *155 rooms* – ☟ *10 €– Restaurant 15€.* Despite its luxury tag, the rates here are not extortionate. The hotel is housed in a half-moon-shaped modern building near the city's Roman ruins, overlooking the amphitheatre. Many of the international-style rooms enjoy views of the Mediterranean.

TAKING A BREAK

Pla de la Seu – *Plaça de la Seu.* The best feature of this establishment is its terrace facing the cathedral. Perfect for a refreshment before or after your visit.

Sumpta – *Avinguda Prat de la Riba 34* – ☎ *977 22 61 58.* The impressive choice at this prestigious wine bar includes a huge selection of sparkling wines from Catalunya. The Sumpta also has its own restaurant.

ⓘ *Neighbouring sights are described in the following chapters: BARCELONA (109km/68mi to the NE), LLEIDA/LÉRIDA (97km/60mi to the NW) and SITGES (53km/33mi to the NE).*

Special Features

ROMAN TARRAGONA★★

Passeig Arqueològic★ (Archaeological Promenade)

🕐 *Open Oct-Mar, 9am-5pm; Apr-Sep, 9am-9pm; Sun and public hols, 10am-2pm (3pm Apr-Sep, 9pm public hols).* 🕐 *Closed Mon, 1 and 6 Jan, 1 May and 25-26 and 31 Dec.* 👝 *1.90€.* ☎ *977 24 22 20.*

It was the Scipios, according to Livy and Pliny, who built Tarragona's city walls in the 3C BC. They were erected on existing Cyclopean bases, the great boulders being held in position by their sheer size. They were so massive that they were for a long time thought to have been barbarian or pre-Roman. The medieval inhabitants extensively raised and rebuilt the ramparts; the 18C citizens remodelled them but still left us with walls bearing the marks of 2 000 years of history. A pleasant walk has been laid out through the gardens at the foot of the walls.

Museu Nacional Arqueològic de Tarragona★★ (Archaeological Museum)

🕐 *Open Jun-Sep, 10am-8pm; Oct-May, 10am-1.30pm and 4-7pm; Sun and public hols, 10am-2pm.* 👝 *2.40€ (includes visit to Museu y Necrópolis Paleocristianas).* ☎ *977 23 62 09.*

The exhibits are all from Tarragona or its immediate environs; most date from the Roman period.

Roman architecture

(Room II, ground floor). Gathered here are vestiges of the most imposing buildings in Tarraconensis.

TARRAGONA						
		Enginyer Cabestany	CZ 14	Ramón i Cajal Av.	CZ	40
		López Peláez	CZ 19	Roser Portal del	DZ	43
Àngels Pl.	DZ 2	Mare de Déu del Claustre	DZ 22	Sant Agustí	DZ	
Baixada de Misericòrdia	DZ 3	Nova Rambla	CDZ	Sant Antoni Portal de	DZ	46
Baixada de Toro	DZ 5	Pau Casals Av.	CZ 27	Sant Joan Pl.	DZ	52
Baixada Roser	DZ 8	Pla de la Seu	DZ 29	Unió	CZ	
Cavallers	DZ 9	Pla de Palau	DZ 32	William J. Bryant	DZ	55
Civadería	DZ 10	Ponç d'Icart	CZ 33			
Coques Les	DZ 12	Portalet	DZ 34			

Antic Hospital	DZ E	Museo d'Art Modern	DZ M²	Museu-Casa Castellarnau	DZ M³
Fòrum Romà	CZ B	Museu Nacional		Recinte Monumental del Pretori i	
Fòrum provincial	DZ D	Arqueològic	DZ M⁴	Circ Romà	DZ M¹

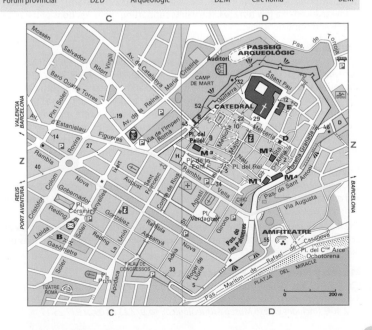

Capital of Tarraconensis

The history of Tarragona dates back many centuries. The imposing ramparts built of enormous Cyclopean blocks of stone, indicate that it was founded by peoples from the eastern Mediterranean early in the first millennium BC. In due course it suffered occupation by the Iberians. The Romans, who by 218 BC had control of the larger part of the peninsula, developed Tarraconensis into a major city and overseas capital. Although it could never equal Rome, it enjoyed many of the same privileges as the imperial capital and Augustus, Galba and Hadrian did not disdain to live in it.

Conversion to Christianity, often attributed to the work of St Paul, brought it appointment as a metropolitan seat, and its dignitaries, the primacy of Spain. This honour was retained throughout the barbarian invasions of the 5C and the destruction of the Moors in the 8C but lost finally to the ambition of Toledo in the 11C. The city was then abandoned until the 12C, when it reverted to the Christians.

Roman mosaics★★

The museum presents the finest collections in Catalunya. The exhibits displayed in Rooms III *(first floor)* and VIII *(second floor)* testify to the high degree of craftsmanship achieved by the Romans in this field. The most extraordinary piece is unquestionably the **Mosaic of the Medusa**★★ (late 2C), with its penetrating gaze.

Roman sculpture★

(Rooms VI to X, second floor). The **funerary sculptures** *(Room IX)* are superb and extremely well preserved. Note *(Room VI)* the bust of Lucius Verusa, executed in the 2C, a perfect example of the art of that period, and the small **votive sculpture of Venus**★, whose tiny proportions in no way detract from its overall beauty and grace.

Recinto Monumental del Pretorio y Circo Romano★ (Praetorium and Roman Circus)

🕐 *Open Oct-Mar, 9am-7pm; Apr-Sep, 9am-9pm; Sun and public hols, 10am (9am Apr-Sep)-2pm.* 🕐 *Closed Mon, 1 and 6 Jan, 1 May and 25-26 Dec.* 🎟 *2€.* ☎ *977 24 22 20.*

This site includes a tall square tower from the 1C BC which has since undergone heavy restoration. You can visit the **vaulted underground galleries**★ or else go to the top and enjoy the sweeping **view**★★ of the ruins and the town.

The most important exhibit is **Hippolyte's sarcophagus**★★, which was discovered virtually intact on the bed of the Mediterranean sea in 1948; its sculptured ornamentation is at once lively, varied and finely executed.

Roman Circus

Designed originally for chariot races, this vast building (325m × 115m/1 066ft × 378ft) is now reduced to a few terraces, the vaults supporting them, sections of the outer façade and some doorways.

Amfiteatre★★

🕐 *Open Oct-Mar, 10am-1pm and 3-5pm; Apr-Sep, 9am-8pm; Sun and public hols 10am-2pm (3pm Apr-Sep).* 🕐 *Closed Mon, 1 and 6 Jan, 1 May, and 25-26 Dec.* 🎟 *2€.* ☎ *977 24 22 00.*

Shaped as an ellipse, the amphitheatre is situated at the water's edge, in a naturally sloped **site**★ which was put to good use when the tiers were built. It was here that Bishop Fructuosus and his deacons, Augurius and Eulogius, were martyred in 259. Traces of the commemorative Visigothic basilica have been discovered within the Romanesque walls of the Iglesia de Santa María del Miracle, a church which replaced the original Visigothic basilica in the 12C and is itself now in ruins.

Forum Romà

🕐 *Open Oct-Mar, 9am-5pm; Sun and public hols, 10am-3pm; Jun-Sep, 9am-9pm (3pm, Sun and public hols).* 🕐 *Closed Mon, 1 and 6 Jan, 1 May, 11 Sep and 25-26 and 31 Dec.* 🎟 *1.87€.* ☎ *977 23 34 15.*

The Roman Forum was the core of the city's political, religious, commercial and legal activities. Today all that remain are a few reliefs, pieces of frieze and sections of a public thoroughfare.

Museo y Necrópolis Paleocristiana

🕐 *Open 16 Jun-15 Sep, 10am-1pm and 4-8pm; 16 Sep-15 Jun, 10am-1.30pm and 3-5.30pm; Sun and public hols, 10am-2pm.* 🕐 *Closed Mon, 1 and 6 Jan and 25-26 31 Dec.* 🎟 *2.40€ (includes visit to Museo Arqueológico).* ☎ *977 23 62 09 or 977 25 15 15.*

Altarpiece, Capilla de la Virgen de Montserrat

The museum is currently undergoing major restoration. As a result, only a few rooms are open to the public.

Worth a Visit

CIUDAD MEDIEVAL (MEDIEVAL QUARTER)

Catedral★★

🕐 *Open 16 Mar-30 May, 10am-1pm and 4-7pm; 1 Jun-15 Oct, 10am-7pm; 16 Oct-15 Nov, 10am-5pm; 16 Nov-15 Mar, 10am-2pm.* 🕐 *Closed Sun and public hols.* ⊛ *2.40€.* ☎ *977 23 86 85.*

Construction began in 1174 on top of the former site of Jupiter's Temple, in what is now the heart of the medieval quarter. The cathedral was built in transitional Gothic style, although the side chapels are both Plateresque and Baroque.

Façade★

Approached by a flight of steps, the façade can be divided into three parts: a typical Gothic central section flanked by two Romanesque side sections. The **main doorway** represents the Last Judgement, with highly expressive relief work. The archivolts are carved with Apostles and Prophets and, on the pier, the Virgin (13C) receives the Faithful. Note the large Gothic rose window.

Interior★★

It is based on the plan of a Latin cross, with three naves and a transept crossing. The Romanesque apse has semicircular arches. Each end of the transept crossing opens onto rose windows with stained glass dating from the 14C. The three naves were built mostly in the Gothic style.

The cathedral interior houses many works of art but the finest piece is undoubtedly the **altarpiece of Santa Tecla**★★★ *(Capilla Mayor, 1430)*, closing off the central apse, which is reached by two Gothic doorways open on either side. Santa Tecla (St Thecla) is the city's patron saint. According to legend, she was converted to Christianity by St Paul, persecuted on many occasions, but was spared torture and death through divine intervention. This work by Pere Joan shows a marked talent for detail, ornamentation and the picturesque. To the right of the altar lies the 14C **Tomb of the Infante Don Juan de Aragón**★★, attributed to an Italian master.

The **Capilla de la Virgen de Montserrat** *(second chapel on the left)* houses a **retable**★ by Luis Borrassà (15C), and **reliefs**★ recounting the life story of the city's saint can be admired in the Capilla de Santa Tecla (third chapel in the right-hand aisle). The **Capilla de los Sastres**★★ *(to the left of the Capilla Major)* is one of the most impressive in all the cathedral, featuring intricate ribbed vaulting, a pretty altarpiece and paintings. This superb ensemble is further enhanced by the sumptuous tapestries hanging from the ceiling, most of which are decorated with allegorical motifs.

Claustro★★

The cloisters are very unusual and large – each gallery is 45m/148ft long. They were built in the 12C and 13C and the arches and geometric decoration are clearly Romanesque, but the vaulting is Gothic, as are the large supporting arches which divide the bays into groups of three.

Moorish influence is evident in the *claustra* of geometrically patterned and pierced panels filling the oculi below the arches, the line of multifoil arches at the base of the cathedral roof and the belfry in one corner, rising 70m/230ft above the ground. Inlaid in the west gallery is a *mihrab*-like stone niche, dated 960.

Note the remarkable **Romanesque doorway**★, dominated by a Christ in Majesty, which links the cathedral to the cloisters.

Museo Diocesano★★

🕐 *Open 16 Mar-30 May, 10am-1pm and 4-7pm; 1 Jul-15 Oct, 10am-7pm; 16 Oct-15 Nov, 10am-5pm; 16 Nov-15 Mar, 10am-2pm.* 🕐 *Closed Sun and public hols.* ⊜ *2.40€.* ☎ *977 23 86 85.*

The museum occupies four rooms in the capitular outbuildings. These contain religious vestments, paintings, altarpieces and reliefs of a very high standard. The fine collection of tapestries in Room III includes **La Buena Vida**★, a Flemish work dating back to the 15C. In the Capilla del Corpus Christi, one of the most beautiful exhibits is n°105, a richly ornate **monstrance**★, and a polychrome alabaster relief work depicting St Jerome (16C).

Antiguo Hospital★

This former 12C-14C hospital is a surprising mix of architectural styles, in which its modern features contrast with the original Romanesque façade and doorway. The building is now used as the headquarters of the local council.

Museu-Casa Castellarnau★

🕐 *Open Oct-Mar 9am-5pm; Apr-Sep 9am-9pm; Sun and public hols, 10am-2pm (3pm Apr-Sep, 9pm Public hols).* 🕐 *Closed Mon, 1 and 6 Jan, 1 May and 25-26 Dec.* ⊜ *1.87€.* ☎ *977 24 22 20.*

During a visit to Tarragona, the Emperor Charles V is said to have stayed in this wealthy 14C-15C residence, which became the property of the Castellarnau family in the 18C. It features a pretty Gothic patio and many fine examples of 18C furniture.

♿ El Serrallo★ (19C fishermen's district; fish market)

Excursions

Acueducto de Las Ferreres★★

Leave the city along rambla Nova. 4km/2.5mi from Tarragona you will see the Roman aqueduct up on your right. It is a well-preserved two-tier structure, 217m/712ft long, known as the Puente del Diablo (Devil's Bridge). 🚶 *You can walk (30min)* through the pines to the base.

Mausoleo de Centcelles★★

5km/3mi NW. Exit the city along avenida Ramón i Cajal.

▸ *Take the Reus road, then bear right after crossing the Francolí. Turn right in Constanti into the calle de Centcelles, and continue an additional 450m along an unsurfaced road, turning left just before the village of Centcelles.*

🕐 *Open 10am-1.30pm and 3-5.30pm; Jun-Sep, 10am-1.30pm and 4-7.30pm; Sun, 10am-2pm all year.* 🕐 *Closed Mon and public hols.* ⊜ *2.40€.* ☎ *977 52 33 74.*

The mausoleum, which now stands in a vineyard, takes the form of two monumental buildings faced in pink tiles. They were built in the 4C by a wealthy Roman near his summer residence which was also vast and included private thermal baths. The first chamber in the mausoleum is covered by an immense cupola (diameter: 11m/36ft), decorated with **mosaics**★★ on themes favoured by the early Christians such as hunting scenes, Daniel in the lion's den etc. The adjoining chamber, which is the same size only square, has an apse on either side. The group of buildings is obviously outstanding although its symbolism remains obscure.

Torre de los Escipiones★

▸ *Leave Tarragona along vía Augusta. After 5km/3mi turn left.*

This square, sober-looking funerary tower (1C) is made up of three sections. The upper and central parts both present reliefs portraying two characters. It was first thought, mistakenly, that these were the Escipion brothers, after whom the tower was named. However, it later transpired that they in fact portrayed Atis, a Phrygian divinity associated with death rituals.

Villa Romana de Els Munts★

12km/7.5mi E along the N 340. Leave Tarragona along vía Augusta. ◷ *Open 10am-1.30pm and 3-5.30pm; Jun-Sep, 10am-1.30pm and 4-7.30pm; Sun and public hols, 10am-2pm all year; last admission 20min before closing.* ◷ *Closed Mon, 1 Jan and 25 Dec.* ⊛ *1.80€, no charge Tue.* ☎ *977 23 62 09.*

Nestling in the locality of Altafulla, in a privileged **site**★★ perched on top of a hillock gently sloping towards the sea, stands this old Roman villa. You can visit the L-shaped arcaded passage that was flanked by gardens and the Roman **baths**★, whose complex plan are proof of the city's former prosperity.

Arco de Berà★

▸ *Leave Tarragona along the vía Augusta. The arch is situated in the locality of Roda de Berà, 20km/12mi along the N 340.* The Vía Augusta used to pass under this imposing, well-proportioned arch (1C). It features a single opening and eight grooved pilasters crowned by Corinthian capitals.

Port Aventura★★

Kids *10km/6mi SW towards Salou.* Universal Studios Port Aventura is a huge amusement park that takes visitors on a fascinating and entertaining world tour. It is divided into five different geographical zones, each focusing on a particular theme: Mediterranean, Polynesian, Chinese, Mexican and the Wild West.

Besides the performances and demonstrations, each country has its own souvenir shops and a great many places where you can sample local cuisine.

Visitors are provided with a guide to the park at the main ticket office.

The park features numerous attractions; the following is a list of the most interesting.

Mediterrània

At the main entrance to the park, where all the services are concentrated (exchange, facilities for hiring wheelchairs and video cameras etc).

Mediterranean culture and atmosphere are encapsulated in this small coastal town. Here you will discover some of the fascinating secrets of the sea, such as how to tie sailors' knots or how to understand the movements of the tide. On the pier of this small bay, the shops sell more than 40 articles with Port Aventura motifs (ties, T-shirts, pencils, swimming costumes etc).

Polynesia★

Beyond the Estación Norte (North Station), a path winds its way among tropical vegetation, brilliantly coloured exotic birds and mini-paradise islands. Grass-skirted musicians and dancers perform along the way. An outdoor stage is the setting for the **Makamanu Bird Show**, where parrots, cockatoos and magpies perform amazing acrobatic acts while they squawk amusing sentences.

In **Tutuki Splash**★★, the Polynesian barge travels into the entrails of a volcano before hurtling into a cataract at a speed of over 55kph/35mph.

China★★

The heart of the theme park, this area symbolises all the magic and mystery of a millenary civilisation. The town of **Ximpang** houses the **Jing Chou Temple**, where you can admire the **Magic Fantasy of China** show. It's a never-ending succession

Practical Information

The park is open from 15 Mar to 6 Jan as follows: 15 Mar-22 Jun and 17 Sep-6 Jan, 10am-8pm (10pm Sat-Sun); 23 Jun-16 Sep, 10am-midnight. ☎ *902 20 22 20.*

Tickets can be purchased 24hr in advance through the services of Servi-Caixa or at the park ticket offices: adults (12-60 years of age): 28.85€/day (43.27€ for two consecutive days); children (5-12 years old) and over-60s: 21.64€ (33.06€ for two consecutive days); children under 5: no charge. Parking: cars: 4.21€; motorbikes: 2.40€/day; caravans: 4.81€.

of attractions: butterflies, multicoloured fish, shadows that turn into the most unexpected shapes etc. The Great Wall of China encloses this whole area but beyond it lies the most exciting attraction of all.

The star attraction of Port Aventura is undoubtedly **Dragon Khan**★★★, shaped like a large hook. Only the bravest visitors risk a ride on the world's most spectacular roller coaster and its eight gigantic loops. This unforgettable experience is reserved for those with nerves of steel and a head for heights!

Mexico★★

Treat yourself to a picturesque tour of Mexico, spanning centuries of culture. Admire the ruins of the legendary Mayan civilisation or the sights of colonial Mexico, enjoy the lively strains of Mariachi music and sample the spicy dishes of traditional Mexican cuisine. The imposing replica of the **Chichen-Itzá Pyramid** houses the **Gran Teatro Maya**, where ritual pre-Colombian dances are performed.

On the **Tren del Diablo**★, visitors' shouts and laughter mingle with the creaking of the carriages of this outdoor mining train that rushes through tunnels and along bridges and ravines.

Far West★★

Penitence, an old village of the American West, is the setting for all your dreams come true: playing the lead role in a western or dancing in the local saloon amid a bunch of pretty girls and reckless adventurers. Do not miss a ride on the **Union Pacific Steam Engine** which will take you on a tour round the park until you reach Mediterrània.

On the **Stampede**★, two wagons compete with each other on a high-speed wooden roller-coaster ride. An exhilarating white-knuckle experience.

The **Grand Canyon Rapids**★★, meanwhile, offers a frenzied white-water rafting experience.

Costa Caribe

🕐 *Open 10am-7pm (in winter, only Gran Caribe section).* 🎟 *Adults 13-59: 18€, children 5-12 and adults over 60: 14.50€.* ☎ *902 20 22 20*

Located next to Port Aventura, this is a magnificent water park with a Caribbean island theme. One covered and heated section remains open right through the winter.

Teruel ★

POPULATION: 31 068

MICHELIN MAP 574 K 26 – 96KM/60MI FROM DAROCA, ARAGÓN (TERUEL).

As a result of its somewhat isolated position and poor communication links, Teruel has retained its unquestionable charm, characterised by splendid buildings and narrow streets that have withstood the test of time and transport visitors back over the centuries. It is a tranquil town with the honour of being the smallest provincial capital in the country. In 1986, Teruel was declared a World Heritage Site by UNESCO for its magnificent Mudéjar architecture.

Location

The capital of Bajo (Lower) Aragón stands at an altitude of 916m/3 005ft. The town occupies a tableland on the left bank of the Turia river amid an impressive **landscape**★ of rugged hills and deeply etched ravines. 🛈 *Tomás Nougués 1, 44001 Teruel,* ☎ *978 60 22 79.*

🚶 *Neighbouring sights are described in the following chapters: CUENCA (152km/95mi SW) and Costa del AZAHAR.*

Worth a Visit

Plaza del Torico, in the heart of the town, is the traditional meeting-place for locals. The square, lined with Rococo-style houses, gets its name from the small statue of a bull calf on a pillar at its centre.

Where to Eat

🍽🍽 **Ambeles** – *Ronda Ambeles 6 –* ☎ *978 61 08 06 - Closed 15 July-7Aug –* 🍴. The bar gives way to a large dining area in updated classical style. The wide-ranging menu combines traditional cuisine with Basque specialties and regional dishes, all at moderate prices.

The Legend of the Lovers of Teruel

In the 13C, **Diego de Marcilla** and **Isabel de Segura** were in love and wished to marry but Isabel's father had set his sights on a richer suitor. Diego thereupon went to the wars to win honour and riches. The day of his return, five years later, was Isabel's wedding day to his rival. He died in front of her in despair and the following day Isabel was overcome with grief and died in her turn. This drama inspired many 16C poets and dramatists including Tirso de Molina.

Museo Provincial★

🕐 *Open 10am-2pm and 4-7pm (including public hols); Sat-Sun, 10am-2pm.* 🕐 *Closed Mon, 1 Jan, 1 May, 10-13 Jul and 24- 25 and 31 Dec .* 🔖 *No charge.* ☎ *978 60 01 50.*

The museum, housed in a mansion with an elegant Renaissance façade crowned by a gallery, displays ethnological and archaeological collections. The former stables in the basement display tools and other everyday objects from the region; note the reconstitution of a forge and the 15C Gothic door knocker.

The first floor is given over to ceramics, an industry for which Teruel has been renowned since the 13C. Green and purple designs adorn the oldest pieces, blue those produced in the 18C (as is the case for pots and jars from a pharmacy in Alcalá).

The upper floors contain archaeological collections from different periods: prehistoric (an Iron Age sword from Alcorisa), Iberian, Roman (a catapult) and Arab (an 11C censer).

Catedral

🕐 *Open 11am-2pm and 4-8pm.* 🔖 *1.80€.* ☎ *978 61 99 50.*

The cathedral, originating in the 13C with the tower, was enlarged in the 16C and further increased by a lantern and ambulatory in the 17C. The late-13C **artesonado ceiling★**, hidden in the 17C beneath star vaulting and so preserved, has now once more been revealed and is a precious example of Mudéjar painting. Its beams and consoles are painted with decorative motifs, people at court and hunting scenes.

The cathedral possesses a 15C **altarpiece** of the Coronation of the Virgin (north transept) in which the scenes depicted along the second band are shown in perspective suggesting Flemish influence. The **retable at the high altar,** carved in the 16C, is by **Gabriel Joli.** Joli was known for his powerful portraits and his skilful way of illustrating movement by a marked turn of the body.

Iglesia de San Pedro

🕐 *Open 10am-2pm and 5-7.30pm.* 🔖 *1€.* ☎ *978 61 99 30.*

In spite of 18C reconstruction, the church has kept its original Mudéjar style in its tower and east end.

Torre de San Martín

Mudéjar Towers

The great richness of **Mudéjar architecture★** in Teruel arises because Christians, Jews and Muslims all lived peacefully together in the town until the 15C – the last mosque was closed only in 1502. There are five towers in all, built between the 12C and 16C, in each case to a three-storey plan: at the base, an arch provided access to the street; the centre, pierced only by narrow Romanesque openings, was decorated with Moorish-influenced ornamental brickwork and ceramics, while at the top was a belfry, pierced by bays in pairs below and quadruples above. The two best examples, the **Torre de San Martín** and the **Torre del Salvador**, are both 13C.

The **Mausoleo de los Amantes de Teruel** (The Mausoleum of the Teruel Lovers) adjoins the church. They are shown in an alabaster relief by Juan de Ávalos (20C). Through the glass walls of the tomb, also in the chapel, the lovers' actual skeletons can be seen.

Excursions

Albarracín★

38km/24mi W along the N 234 and A 1512. Hidden away in the Sierra de Albarracín, this medieval city tinged with pinkish hues stands in an exceptional **site**★, perched on a cliff above the Guadalaviar river. The ramparts extending up the hill behind the town were built by the Moors in the 10C then restored to a large extent by the Christians in the 14C. Several of the caves in the surrounding sierra contain **rock engravings** from the Upper Palaeolithic era, such as the sites at Callejón del Plou and Cueva del Navaza *(5km/3mi SE towards Bezas and Valdecuenca).*

A random wander through the narrow, steep and winding, cobbled streets will reveal a different aspect of the town at every corner. Starting out from the **plaza Mayor,** you come to a quarter where the houses have ground floors built of limestone and overhanging upper storeys faced with rose-coloured roughcast. Fine woodwork balconies, wrought-iron grilles at the windows and the occasional coat of arms add character to the façades. The covered roof galleries are quite different from those to be found on houses elsewhere in Aragón.

Catedral

🕐 *Open 10.30am-2pm and 4.30-6.30pm.* 👝 *1.80€ (museum).* ☎ *978 71 00 84.*

The belfry, crowned by a smaller lantern, marks the position of the cathedral slightly south of the town centre. One of the chapels off the vast 16C nave contains a small wooden altarpiece (1566) carved with scenes from the life of St Peter. The chapter house is well worth a visit for its **treasure** which includes gold- and silverwork as well as some 16C **tapestries**★, of which seven were woven in Brussels and recount the life of Gideon.

Toledo★★★

POPULATION: 63 561

MICHELIN MAP 576 M 17 (TOWN PLAN) – MAP 121 ALREDEDORES DE MADRID –

CASTILLA-LA MANCHA (TOLEDO).

Toledo stands out dramatically against the often luminously blue Castilian sky: a golden city rising from a granite eminence, encircled by a steep ravine filled by the green waters of the Tajo (Tagus). It is as spectacular as it is rich in history, buildings and art; every corner has a tale to be told, every aspect reflects a brilliant period of Spanish history when the cultures of east and west flourished and fused: one is constantly aware of this imprint of Christian, Jewish and Moorish cultures which, as in Granada, productively co-existed during the Middle Ages.

Location

The city's incomparable **site**★★★ can be seen particularly well from the *carretera de circunvalación*, a ring-road which for a couple of miles parallels, on the far bank, the almost circular loop of the Tajo which flows all the way round from the Puente de Alcántara (Alcántara Bridge) to the Puente de San Martín. For truly memorable views of the city, couched between the Alcázar and the Monasterio de San Juan de los Reyes (Monastery of St John of the Kings), it is worth going to the **viewpoints** on the surrounding hills. These are covered by extensive olive groves in which country houses *(cigarrales)* stand half concealed. The terrace of the parador, set above the *carretera de circunvalación*, commands a superb view. 🖪 *Puerta Bisagra, 45003 Toledo, ☎ 925 22 08 43; Plaza del Ayuntamiento 1, 45001 Toledo, ☎ 925 25 40 30.*

⚑ *Neighbouring sights are described in the following chapters: ARANJUEZ (47km/29mi NE), MADRID (71km/44mi NE) and TALAVERA DE LA REINA (80km/50mi NW).*

Background

From a Roman town to a Holy Roman city – The Romans, appreciating the site's strategic and geographic advantage at the centre of the peninsula, fortified and built up the settlement into a town they named Toletum. It passed, in due course, into the hands of the barbarians, and in the 6C to the Visigoths who ultimately made it a monarchal seat. The Visigoths, defeated at Guadelete in 711, abandoned the town to the Moors who incorporated it in the Córdoba Emirate, until the successful revolt of the *taifas* in 1012 raised it to the position of capital of an independent kingdom. In 1085 Toledo was conquered by Alfonso VI de León. Two years later, the king moved his capital to it from León. It is to Alfonso VII, crowned emperor there, that Toledo owes its title of imperial city. Toledo, with its mixed Moorish, Jewish and Christian communities, began to prosper richly. The Catholic Monarchs gave it the Monastery of St John but lost interest in the

Toledo

Address Book

For coin ranges, see the Legend at the back of the guide.

WHERE TO EAT

La Abadía – *Plaza de San Nicolás 3 – ☎ 925 25 11 40.* The owners of this restaurant have successfully transformed the basement of this former 16C palace. The complex lighting and modern furniture combine to create a highly original overall effect and a pleasant backdrop to some creative cuisine. Not for those suffering from claustrophobia.

Casón de los López de Toledo – *Sillería 3 – ☎ 925 25 47 74 – Closed Sun evenings – .* Time seems to have stood still in this stone mansion built around a fountain-adorned patio. A delightful setting in which to try local specialities such as partridge stew (*perdiz estofada*) and wild boar (*jabalí*). The bar on the ground floor serves a range of tapas.

WHERE TO STAY

Hotel La Almazara – *3.5km/2mi SW along the Cuerva road – ☎ 925 22 38 66 – Closed 11 Dec-Feb – 📇 – Reservation recommended – 28 rooms – 3.50€.* This former cardinal's residence is reached via a lane planted with olive trees. The building's sturdy walls are clad with ivy, while the bedrooms are spacious and bright, some with terrace in the shade of magnificent gardens.

Hostal del Cardenal – *Paseo Recaredo 24 – ☎ 925 22 49 00 – 🍽 – 28 rooms – 6.90€ – Restaurant 23.24/36.25€.* This charming hotel, half-hidden in a delightful garden full of fountains, low walls and flowers, stands at the foot of the city walls. Behind the splendid stone façade, the bedrooms are elegantly decorated with wood furnishings and antiques. The restaurant here is superb.

SHOPPING

Toledo is renowned for its **damascene ware** (black steel inlaid with gold, silver and copper thread) as well as its culinary specialities including braised partridge and marzipan.

FIESTAS

Toledo's streets provide a splendid setting for the **Corpus Christi** procession, one of the largest in Spain, held on the first Sunday following Corpus Christi.

---

city when they began to compare it with Granada, reconquered under their own aegis in 1492. Emperor Charles V had the Alcázar rebuilt. Also during his reign the city took part in the Comuneros' Revolt led by **Juan de Padilla,** a Toledan.

Progress was halted in 1561 when Philip II named Madrid as Spain's capital, leaving Toledo as the spiritual centre, the seat of the primacy. The siege of the Alcázar in 1936 during the Civil War brought it briefly into the limelight of history.

Toledo and the Visigoths – Toledo played a key role during the Visigothic supremacy in the peninsula which began in 507. By 554 they had made it their capital and Councils of State, which had met in Toledo as early as 400, were resumed; that of 589, following upon the conversion of King Reccared two years previously, established Visigothic hegemony and the religious unification of Spain. The Visigoths, torn by internal strife, however, were unable to resist the Moors and abandoned Toledo in 711; it took Pelayo and a small band of Christians to reinstate the dynasty.

Toledo and the Jews – Toledo would appear to have been by far the most important Jewish town in Spain: in the 12C the community numbered 12 000.

Under **Ferdinand III** (1217-52), a tolerant monarch who encouraged the intermingling of the races which brought about a cultural flowering, the city developed into a great intellectual forum. This well-being reached its climax under his son, **Alfonso X, the Wise** (1252-84), who gathered round him a court of learned Jews and established the *School of Translation*. Jewish prosperity and immunity suddenly and brutally ceased in 1355 with a pogrom instigated by the supporters of Henry IV of Trastamara; at the same time many conversions followed the preaching of the Dominican, **San Vicente Ferrer.** The final blow came in 1492 with the Catholic Monarchs' decree of expulsion.

Mudéjar art in Toledo – It was following the Reconquest that the Mudéjar style established itself in Toledo, with the construction of palaces (Taller del Moro), synagogues (El Tránsito, Santa María la Blanca) and churches. Brick was widely used in place of stone, and typical Moorish features such as stuccowork, *artesonado* and *azulejos* became commonplace. In the 13C and 14C, most Toledan churches were given Romanesque semicircular **east ends**, blind arcades took on variations unknown elsewhere, and **belfries** were built square and decorated until they appeared strongly reminiscent of minarets. The edifices often have a nave and two aisles – a Visigothic influence – tripartite apses – a Romanesque souvenir – and wood vaulting carved in the Moorish style.

Special Features

CATEDRAL★★★

🕐 *Open 10.30am-6.30pm; Sun and public hols, 2-6.30pm.* 🕐 *Closed mornings of 6 Jan, Palm Sun, Holy Tues, Easter Sun, Corpus Christi, 15 Aug, 1 Nov and 8 Dec; afternoons of Maundy Thu, Good Fri and 24, 25 and 31 Dec.* ⊛ *4.21€ museum.* ☎ *925 22 22 41.*

The cathedral dominates the **plaza del Ayuntamiento,** in the heart of Toledo's old quarter. Construction began in the reign of Ferdinand III (St Ferdinand) in 1227, under Archbishop Rodrigo Jiménez de Rada. Unlike other churches in the vicinity, the design was French Gothic but as building continued until the end of the 15C, plans were modified and the completed edifice presents a conspectus of Spanish Gothic, although considerably masked by additions. The church, nevertheless, remains of outstanding interest for its sculptured decoration and numerous works of religious art.

Exterior

The **Puerta del Reloj** (Clock Doorway), in the north wall, is the old entrance, dating from the 13C although modified in the 19C.

The **main façade** is pierced by three tall 15C portals of which the upper registers were completed in the 16C and 17C. At the centre is the **Puerta del Perdón** (Pardon Doorway), crowded with statues and crowned with a tympanum illustrating the legend according to which the Virgin Mary, wishing to reward San Ildefonso, Bishop of Toledo in the 7C, for his devotion, appeared, at Assumption, in the episcopal chair, to present him with a magnificent embroidered chasuble.

The harmonious tower is 15C; the dome, which replaces the second tower, was designed by El Greco's son in the 17C. In the south wall, the 15C **Puerta de los Leones** (Lion Doorway) designed by Master Hanequin of Brussels and decorated by Juan Alemán was flanked in 1800 by a neo-Classical portal.

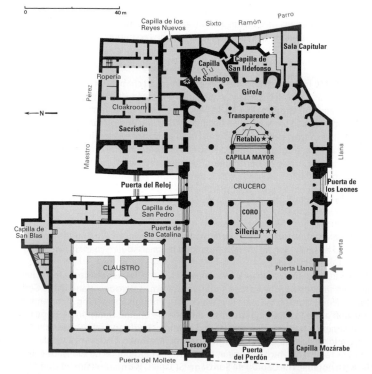

Plaza del Ayuntamiento

El Greco

Domenikos Theotokopoulos, the Greek – El Greco – one of the great figures in Spanish painting, was born in Crete in 1541. After an apprenticeship painting icons, he went to Italy where he worked under Titian and studied Michelangelo before journeying to Spain in 1577 and settling in Toledo where he remained until he died in 1614. Although he did not always succeed in pleasing Philip II he found favour and fortune with Toledans. His work, with its acquired Italian techniques, retained considerable Byzantine influence which appeared as a lengthening of forms – a mannerism which increased as the painter aged. A recurring feature in illustrated scenes was the division of the canvas into two – earth and heaven – demonstrating El Greco's belief that this life was but preparation for an exalted hereafter. The supernatural is a constant preoccupation, figures convey an intense spiritual inner power – all is seen with the eye of the visionary and portrayed sometimes by means of apparent distortion, by brilliant, occasionally crude colours, often by violent, swirling movement so that some pictures have the aspect of hallucinations. But the portraits by contrast are still, the colours deep, expressions meditative in the religious, watchful in the worldly.

▶ *Enter through the Puerta del Mollete, left of the west front, which opens onto the cloisters.*

Interior

The size and sturdy character of the cathedral rather than its elevation are what strike one as one gazes up over the five unequal aisles and the great supporting pillars. A wonderful collection of stained glass (1418-1561) colours the windows; magnificent wrought-iron grilles enclose the chancel, *coro* and chapels. The attention is also drawn to the cardinals' hats hanging from the vaults above the tombs of those cardinals who were primates of Spain.

Capilla Mayor

The chancel, the most sumptuous part of the cathedral, was enlarged in the 16C by Cardinal Cisneros.

The immense polychrome **retable**★★, carved in Flamboyant style with the Life of Christ depicted in detail on five registers, is awe inspiring. The silver statue of the Virgin at the predella dates from 1418. The marble tomb of Cardinal Mendoza in Plateresque style on the left is by Covarrubias. The recumbent figure is the work of an Italian artist.

Coro

A series of 14C high reliefs and wrought-iron enclosed chapels form the perimeter of the choir which is itself closed by an elegant iron screen (1547). Within are magnificent 15C and 16C **choir stalls**★★★ of which the lower parts, in wood, were carved by Rodrigo Alemán to recall, in 54 beautifully detailed and picturesque scenes, the conquest of Granada; the 16C upper parts, in alabaster, portraying Old Testament figures, are by Berruguete *(left)* and Felipe Vigarny *(right)*. The central low relief, the Transfiguration, is also by Berruguete. The style of his work creates the impression of movement while that of Vigarny is more static. The pipes of a sonorous organ dominate the central area, occupied by two bronze lecterns and a Gothic eagle lectern. The 14C marble *White Virgin* is French.

Girola

The double ambulatory, surmounted by an elegant triforium with multifoil arches, is bordered by seven apsidal chapels separated by small square chapels. The vaulting is a geometrical wonder.

There is little room to step back for a good look at the **Transparente**★, the contentious but famous work by Narciso Tomé which forms a Baroque island in the Gothic church. Illuminated by the sun's rays which pour through an opening in the ambulatory roof (made to allow light to fall on the tabernacle), the *Transparente* appears as an ornamental framework of angels and swirling clouds and rays surrounding the Virgin and the Last Supper. The **Capilla de San Ildefonso** (Chapel of San Ildefonso) contains tombs, of which the one in the centre, of Cardinal Gil de Albornoz (14C), is the most notable. The **Capilla de Santiago** (St James) is a mausoleum for Don Álvaro de Luna, Constable of Castilla, and his family.

Sala Capitular (Chapter house)

The antechamber is adorned with an impressive Mudéjar ceiling and two Plater-esque carved walnut wardrobes. Remarkable Mudéjar stucco doorways and carved Plateresque panels precede the chapter house where there is a particularly beautiful multicoloured **Mudéjar ceiling**★. Below the frescoes by Juan de Borgoña, are portraits of former archbishops including two by Goya painted in 1804 and 1823.

Sacristía (Sacristy)

The first gallery, with its vaulted ceiling painted by Lucas Jordán, includes a powerful group of **paintings by El Greco**★ of which **El Expolio** (*The Saviour Stripped of His Raiment*), painted soon after the artist's arrival in Spain, is outstanding. It conveys a dominating, exalted personality, set against the swirling folds of robes in vivid, often acidic tones, which establish a rhythmical movement akin to Baroque, on the canvas. Also among the collection is one of El Greco's series of portraits of the Apostles. Works by other artists in the sacristy include a remarkable portrait of *Pope Paul III* by Titian, a *Holy Family* by Van Dyck, a *Mater Dolorosa* by Morales and the *Taking of Christ* by Goya which displays to advantage his skill in composition, in the use of light and in portraying individuals in a crowd. There is also one of Pedro de Mena's (17C) most characteristic and famous sculptures, *St Francis of Assisi* (in a glass case). In the vestry are portraits by Velázquez *(Cardinal Borja),* Van Dyck *(Pope Innocent XI)* and Ribera. The old laundry *(ropería)* contains liturgical objects dating back to the 15C. Continuing on from the sacristy you reach the **Nuevas Salas del Museo Catedralicio** (Cathedral Museum's New Galleries), installed in the Casa del Tesorero (Treasurer's House). The rooms display works by Caravaggio, El Greco, Bellini and Morales.

Tesoro (Treasury)

A Plateresque doorway by Covarrubias opens into the chapel under the tower. Beneath a Granada style Mudéjar ceiling note the splendid 16C silver-gilt **monstrance**★★ by Enrique de Arfe, which, although it weighs 180kg and is 3m high (just under 400lb and 10ft high), is paraded through the streets at Corpus Christi. The pyx at its centre is fashioned from gold brought from America by Christopher Columbus.
There is also a 13C Bible given by St Louis of France to St Ferdinand (Ferdinand III of Castilla).

Capilla Mozárabe (Mozarabic Chapel)

The chapel beneath the dome was built by Cardinal Cisneros (16C) to celebrate Mass according to the Visigothic or Mozarabic ritual which had been threatened with abolition in the 11C.

Claustro (Cloisters)

The architectural simplicity of the 14C lower gallery contrasts with the bold mural deco-ration by Bayeu of the Lives of Toledan saints (Santa Eugenia and San Ildefonso).

CENTRE OF OLD TOLEDO★★★

🕓 *Allow 1 day – see itinerary on town plan*

There is something to see and enjoy at every step in Toledo. Walking along the maze of narrow, winding lanes you pass churches, old houses and palaces.
Ringing the square before the cathedral are the 18C **Palacio Arzobispal** (Archbishop's Palace), the 17C **Ayuntamiento** (Town Hall) with its classical façade and the 14C **Audiencia** (Law Courts).

Iglesia de Santo Tomé

🕓 *Open 10am-6pm (7pm 1 Mar-15 Oct); last admission 30 min before closing.* 🕓 *Closed 1 Jan and 25 Dec.* 🎟 *1.50€.* ☎ *925 25 60 98.*

The church, like that of San Román (see below), has a distinctive 14C Mudéjar tower. Inside is El Greco's famous painting **The Burial of the Count of Orgaz**★★★ executed for the church in about 1586. The interment is transformed by the miraculous appear-ance of St Augustine and St Stephen waiting to welcome the figure from earth, sym-bolised by a frieze of figures in which, as he highlighted faces and hands and painted vestments with detailed biblical references, El Greco made every man an individual portrait – he is said to have painted a self-portrait in the sixth figure from the left.

Casa y Museo de El Greco★ (El Greco House and Museum)

🕓 *Open 10am-2pm and 4-7pm (6pm Dec-Jan); Sun and public hols, 10am-2pm; last admission 30min before closing.* 🕓 *Closed Mon, 1 Jan, 1 May and 24-25 and 31 Dec.* 🎟 *2.40€.* ☎ *925 22 40 46.*

TOLEDO

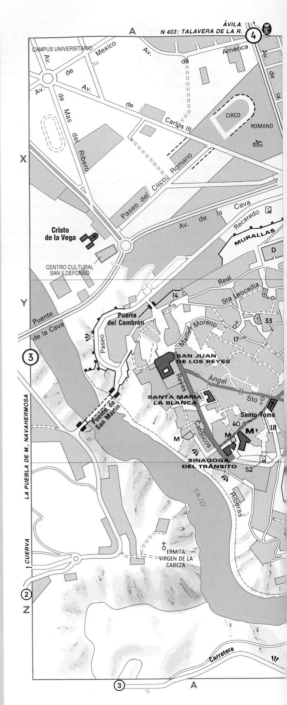

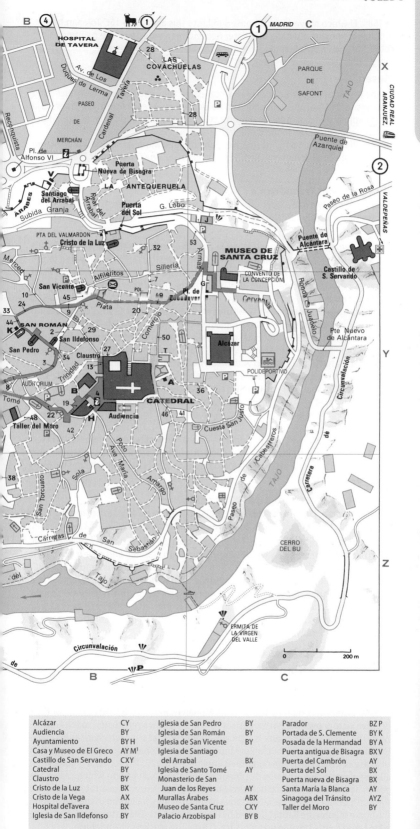

Alcázar	CY	Iglesia de San Pedro	BY	Parador	BZ P
Audiencia	BY	Iglesia de San Román	BY	Portada de S. Clemente	BY K
Ayuntamiento	BY H	Iglesia de San Vicente	BY	Posada de la Hermandad	BY A
Casa y Museo de El Greco	AY M¹	Iglesia de Santiago		Puerta antigua de Bisagra	BX V
Castillo de San Servando	CXY	del Arrabal	BX	Puerta del Cambrón	AY
Catedral	BY	Iglesia de Santo Tomé	AY	Puerta del Sol	BX
Claustro	BY	Monasterio de San		Puerta nueva de Bisagra	BX
Cristo de la Luz	BX	Juan de los Reyes	AY	Santa María la Blanca	AY
Cristo de la Vega	AX	Murallas Árabes	ABX	Sinagoga del Tránsito	AYZ
Hospital de Tavera	BX	Museo de Santa Cruz	CXY	Taller del Moro	BY
Iglesia de San Ildefonso	BY	Palacio Arzobispal	BY B		

In 1585, El Greco moved into a house similar to this attractive 16C Toledan **house**. In the first floor studio hang a St Peter Repentant, a version of the painting in the cathedral and, in what would have been the artist's workroom, a signed *St Francis and Brother León*.

Museo

On the first floor of the museum are an interesting *View and Plan of Toledo* (including a likeness of his son, one with various differences from the version in the Prado) and the complete series of individual portraits of the Apostles and Christ (a later, more mature series than that in the cathedral).

The **capilla** on the ground floor, with a multicoloured Mudéjar ceiling, has a picture in the altarpiece of *St Bernardino of Siena* by El Greco. *The Crowning of Thorns* is Hispano-Flemish.

Sinagoga del Tránsito★★

🕐 *Open 10am-2pm and 4-6pm; Sun and public hols, 10am-2pm; last admission 30min before closing.* 🕐 *Closed Mon, 1 Jan, 1 May and 24- 25 and 31 Dec.* 🎟 *2.40€.* ☎ *925 22 36 65.*

Of the 10 synagogues that once stood in the old Jewish quarter (Judería), only this and Santa María la Blanca remain. Money for its construction was provided in the 14C by Samuel Ha-Levi, treasurer to King Peter the Cruel. In 1492 it was converted into a church and dedicated soon afterwards to the Dormition (Tránsito) from which it gets its name.

It appears from the outside as a small unpretentious building but inside, an amazing **Mudéjar decoration**★★ covers the upper part of the walls and all the east end. Above the rectangular hall is an *artesonado* ceiling of cedarwood; just below, are 54 multifoil arches, some blind, others pierced with delicate stone tracery. Below again runs a frieze, decorated at the east end with *mocárabes* and on the walls, bearing the arms of Castilla, with inscriptions in Hebrew to the glory of Peter the Cruel, Samuel Ha-Levi and the God of Israel. The three arches at the centre of the east wall are surmounted by a panel in relief of roses surrounded by magnificent strapwork and, at either side, by inscriptions describing the synagogue's foundation. The women's balcony opens from the south wall.

The adjoining rooms, at one period a Calatrava monastery, have been converted into a **Museo Sefardí** (Sephardic Museum) displaying tombs, robes, costumes and books. Several are presents from Sephardim, descendants of the Jews expelled from Spain in 1492.

Sinagoga de Santa María la Blanca★

🕐 *Open 10am-5.45pm (6.45pm Mar-Sep).* 🕐 *Closed 1 Jan, 24 Dec (afternoon), 25 Dec and 31 Dec (afternoon).* 🎟 *1.50€, no charge Wed afternoon.* ☎ *925 22 72 57.*

This was the principal synagogue in Toledo in the late 12C; in 1405, however, it was given to the Knights of Calatrava who converted it into a church and gave it its present name. Subsequent vicissitudes, including modification of the east end in the 16C, incredibly left the Almohad-style mosque unharmed so that the hall appears as before with five tiered aisles, separated by 24 octagonal pillars supporting horseshoe-shaped arches. The plain white of the pillars and arches is relieved by the intricately carved **capitals**★ adorned with pine cones and strapwork. Above, the decoration is equally outstanding. The polychrome wood altarpiece is 16C.

Monasterio de San Juan de los Reyes★
(St John of the Kings Monastery)

🕐 *Open 10am-6pm (7pm in summer).* 🕐 *Closed 1 Jan and 25 Dec.* 🎟 *1.50€.* ☎ *925 22 38 02.*

The monastery was built by the Catholic Monarchs in thanksgiving to God for their decisive victory over the Portuguese at Toro in 1476. It was entrusted to the Franciscans. The overall architecture is typically Isabelline, that style which includes in the Flamboyant Gothic style touches of Mudéjar and even Renaissance art, particularly in this case since construction continued until the early 17C. The exterior is somewhat austere despite the ornamental pinnacles and stone balustrade which crown the edifice and, in the latter instance, circle the octagonal lantern. Covarrubias designed the north portal during the later stages of construction, including in the decoration the figure of John the Baptist flanked by Franciscan saints. The fetters from the façade were taken from Christian prisoners freed from the Muslims in Andalucía.

Claustro

Although restored, the cloisters remain extremely attractive with Flamboyant bays and the original Plateresque upper galleries (1504) crowned with a pinnacled balustrade. The upper gallery has Mudéjar artesonado vaulting.

Iglesia

The church, rebuilt after being fired by the French in 1808, has the single wide aisle typical of Isabelline churches; at the crossing are a dome and a lantern. The **sculptured decoration**★ by the church's Flemish architect, Juan Guas, provides a delicate stone tracery *(crestería)* which at the transept forms twin tribunes for Ferdinand and Isabel. The transept walls are faced with a wonderful frieze of royal escutcheons, supported by an eagle, the symbol of St John. Other decoration includes Mudéjar *mocárabes* on the bosses in the transept vaulting and heads in picturesque high relief on the triumphal arches. The original altarpiece has been replaced by a 16C Plateresque retable.

Not far away are a Visigothic palace and gateway, which were once part of the town perimeter. The gateway was rebuilt in the 16C. The **Puerta del Cambrón** is named after the *cambroneras* or hawthorns which once grew around it.

▷ *Turn left out of calle Santo Tomé onto the picturesque Travesía de Campana alley.*

Before you, in the small shaded plaza del Padre Mariana, stands the monumental Baroque façade of the **Iglesia de San Ildefonso** and higher up, that of the **Iglesia do San Pedro.**

Iglesia de San Román: Museo de los Concilios de Toledo y de la Cultura Visigoda★
(Museum of the Councils of Toledo and Visigothic Culture)

🕐 *Open 10am-2pm and 4-6.30pm; Sun and public hols, 10am-2pm.* 🕐 *Closed Mon, 1 Jan and 25 Dec.* 👓 *0.60€, no charge Sat afternoon and Sun.* ☎ *925 22 78 72.*

The 13C Mudéjar church, at the highest point in the town, has a fine upstanding tower closely resembling that of Santo Tomé. Inside, the three aisles divided by horseshoe-shaped arches are reminiscent of Santa María la Blanca. The walls are covered in 13C frescoes of the raising of the dead, the Evangelists and, on the far wall, one of the Councils of Toledo. The apse was modified in the 16C when a cupola was built over it by Covarrubias. Note the 18C **altarpiece**.

The Visigothic collections include, in glass cases, fine bronze jewellery and copies of votive crowns decorated with cabochon stones from Guarrazar (originals in the Museo Arqueológico, Madrid). On the walls are steles, fragments from capitals, balustrades from the choir and pilasters decorated with geometric motifs or scrollwork.

The Plateresque **doorway** *(portada)* opposite the church belongs to the Convento de San Clemente.

In plaza de San Vicente, note the Mudéjar east end of the **Iglesia de San Vicente** before continuing up calle de la Plata with its houses with carved entrances.

Plaza de Zocodover

This bustling triangular square is the heart of Toledo. It was rebuilt after the Civil War as was the Arco de la Sangre (Arch of Blood) which opens onto calle de Cervantes.

Museo de Santa Cruz★★ (Santa Cruz Museum)

🕐 *Open 10am-6.30pm; Mon, 10am-2pm and 4-6.30pm; Sun and public hols, 10am-2pm.* 🕐 *Closed 1 Jan and 25 Dec.* 👓 *1.20€, no charge Sat afternoon and Sun.* ☎ *925 22 10 36.*

Cardinal Pedro González de Mendoza, Archbishop of Toledo, died before fully realising his ambition to build a hospital for the sick and orphaned, but his project was completed by Queen Isabel. The result is a fine group of Plateresque buildings begun by Enrique Egas and completed by Covarrubias who was responsible for the **façade**★★. On the gateway tympanum Cardinal Mendoza kneels before the Cross supported by St Helena, St Peter, St Paul and two pages; on the arches are the cardinal virtues while above, two windows frame a high relief of St Joachim and St Anne.

The museum which is large but well arranged, is known for its **collection of 16C and 17C pictures**★ which includes 18 paintings by **El Greco**★.

Inside, the architecture is outstanding for the size of the nave and transept – forming a two-tiered Greek cross – and for the beautiful coffered ceilings.

Ground floor

The first part of the nave contains 16C Flemish tapestries, **primitive paintings**★, and the *Astrolabios* or *Zodiac* tapestry, woven in Flanders in the mid-15C for Toledo cathedral, which fascinates still by its originality and modern colouring. Note, in the south transept, the *Ascension* and the *Presentation of Mary in the Temple* by the Maestro de Sijena. In the second part of the nave hangs the immense pennant flown by Don Juan of Austria at the Battle of Lepanto. Before it is a 17C Crucifix, recalling the one believed to have been present at the battle and which is now in Barcelona Cathedral. The north transept contains a *Christ at the Column* by Morales.

First floor

A staircase leads to the upper gallery of the north transept which displays the **paintings by El Greco**★. There are gentle portraits of the Virgin and St Veronica as well as a version of the *Expolio*, later than the original in the cathedral. The most famous painting in the collection is the **Altarpiece of the Assumption**★, which dates from 1613, the artist's final period. The figures are particularly elongated, the colours rasping.

The south transept contains a *Holy Family at Nazareth* by Ribera, the specialist in tenebrism (term applied to paintings in dark tones) who here showed himself to be a master of light and delicacy.

In the first part of the nave are 16C Brussels tapestries illustrating the life of Alexander the Great. There are also 17C statues from the studio of Pascual de Mena of a *Mater Dolorosa* and an *Ecce Homo*.

The **Plateresque patio**★ has bays with elegant lines complemented by the openwork of the balustrade and enhanced by beautiful Mudéjar vaulting and, even more, by the magnificent **staircase**★ by Covarrubias. Adjoining rooms house a museum of archaeology and decorative arts.

Worth a Visit

WITHIN THE CITY WALLS

Alcázar

⚬━ *Closed for restoration.* ☎ *925 22 16 73.*

The Alcázar, destroyed and rebuilt so many times, stands massive and proud as ever, dominating all other buildings. It was Emperor Charles V who decided to convert the 13C fortress, of which El Cid had been the first governor, into an imperial residence. The conversion was entrusted first to Covarrubias (1538-51) and subsequently to Herrera, who designed the austere south front. The siege and shelling of 1936 left the fortress in ruins. From 21 July for eight weeks, infantry cadets under Colonel Moscardó, resisted the Republicans. Their families, about 600 women and children, took refuge in the underground galleries.

Puerta Nueva de Bisagra

Reconstruction has restored the Alcázar to its appearance at the time of Charles V – an innovation is the *Victory Monument* by Ávalos in the forecourt. Inside, you see the underground galleries which sheltered the cadets' families, and the office above in which Colonel Moscardó was ordered by phone to surrender or see his son shot. His son died on 23 August; the Alcázar was relieved on 27 September.
Weapons and uniforms are displayed in museum rooms off the patio.

Posada de la Hermandad (House of the Brotherhood)

A 15C building which used to be a prison.

Puerta del Sol

The Sun Gate in the town's second perimeter, rebuilt in the 14C, is a fine Mudéjar construction with two circumscribing horseshoe arches. At the centre a later low relief shows the Virgin presenting San Ildefonso with a chasuble. At the top, the brick decoration of blind arcading incorporates an unusual sculpture of two girls bearing the head of the chief *alguacil* (officer of justice) of the town on a salver; the story goes that he had been condemned for raping them.

Cristo de la Luz (Christ of the Light)

In AD 1000 the Moors built a mosque on the site of a ruined Visigothic church; in the 12C this mosque was converted into a Mudéjar church. Legend has it that the church was named Christ of the Light because when Alfonso VI was making his entry into Toledo, El Cid's horse in the royal train suddenly knelt before the mosque in which, within a wall, a Visigothic lamp was discovered lighting up a Crucifix. Three series of arches of different periods, intersecting blind arcades, and a line of horizontal brickwork surmounted by Cufic characters make up the façade. Inside, pillars, for the most part Visigothic, support superimposed arches, similar in design to those in the mosque in Córdoba. Nine domes, each different, rise from square bays.
The adjoining gardens lead to the top of the Puerta del Sol from which there is a unique view of the city.

Iglesia de Santiago del Arrabal (St James on the Outskirts)

This beautifully restored Mudéjar church contains the ornate Gothic Mudéjar pulpit from which San Vicente Ferrer is said to have preached. The altarpiece is 16C.

Puerta Nueva de Bisagra (New Bisagra Gate)

The gate was rebuilt by Covarrubias in 1550 and enlarged during the reign of Philip II. Massive round crenellated towers, facing the Madrid road, flank a giant imperial crest.

Puerta Antigua de Bisagra (Old Bisagra Gate)

According to tradition, Alfonso VI entered through this gate in the former Moorish ramparts when he reconquered Toledo in 1085.

Taller del Moro

o— *Closed for reconstruction.* ☎ *925 22 45 00.*

This workshop *(taller)*, used by a Moor as a collecting yard for building material for the cathedral, is in fact an old palace. The Mudéjar decoration can still be seen in rooms lit by small openwork windows, interconnected through horseshoe-shaped openings ornamented with *atauriques* or Almohad style stucco.

BEYOND THE CITY WALLS

Hospital de Tavera★

Guided tours (30min), 10.30am-1.30pm and 4-5.45pm (6.30pm in summer). � *Closed Mon, 1 Jan and 25 Dec.* ☜ *3.60€.* ☎ *925 22 04 51.*

The hospital, founded in the 16C by Cardinal Tavera, was begun by Bustamante in 1541 and completed by González de Lara and the Vergaras in the 17C.
After the Civil War, the Duchess of Lerma rearranged certain **apartments**★ in 17C style, where paintings of great artistic value may be seen.

Ground floor

In the vast library, the hospital archives contain volumes bound in leather by Moorish craftsmen. Among the paintings displayed, El Greco's *Holy Family* is arresting, the portrait of the Virgin perhaps the most beautiful the artist ever painted. Note also the *Birth of the Messiah* by Tintoretto, the *Philosopher* by Ribera and, in an adjoining room, his strange portrait of the *Bearded Woman*.

First floor

The reception hall contains another El Greco, the sombre portrait of *Cardinal Tavera*, painted from a death mask. Beside it are *Samson and Delilah* by Caravaggio and two portraits of the *Duke and Duchess of Navas* by Antonio Moro.

A gallery to the **church** leads off from the elegant twin patio. The Carrara marble portal is by Alonso Berruguete who also carved the tomb of Cardinal Tavera. The retable at the high altar was designed by El Greco whose last work, a **Baptism of Christ**★ is displayed in the church. It is an outstanding painting in which the artist's use of brilliant colours and elongated figures is at its most magnificent.

Giving onto the patio is the hospital's former pharmacy, which has been restored.

Puente de Alcántara

The 13C bridge ends respectively to west and east in a Mudéjar tower and a Baroque arch. On the far side of the Tajo, behind battlemented ramparts, the restored 14C **Castillo de San Servando** (San Servando Castle), an advanced strongpoint in medieval times, can be seen.

A plaque on the town wall by the bridge recalls how **St John of the Cross** (1542-91) escaped through a window from his monastery prison nearby.

Puente de San Martín

The medieval bridge, rebuilt in the 14C following damage by floodwaters, is marked at its south end by an octagonal crenellated tower; the north end is 16C.

Cristo de la Vega

The Church of Christ of the Vega, formerly St Leocadia, stands on the site of a 7C Visigothic temple, the venue of early church councils and, according to legend, the site of St Leocadia's apparition before San Ildefonso and the king. Although considerably modified in the 18C, it still has a fine Mudéjar apse. Inside, a modern Crucifix now stands in place of the one around which many legends had gathered, including one in which the figure offered an arm to a jilted girl who had come to seek comfort.

Excursions

Guadamur

15km/9mi SW. Leave Toledo by T on the map, bearing left onto the CM 401. The **castillo** (castle) overlooking the village was built in the 15C and restored in the late 19C. The apartments, occupied for a period by Queen Juana the Mad and her son, the future Emperor Charles V, have been furnished with Spanish period furniture. ⚷ *Currently undergoing restoration. ☎ 925 29 13 01.*

Tortosa★

POPULATION: 29 717

MICHELIN MAP 574 J 31 – 65KM/40MI FROM PEÑÍSCOLA – CATALUNYA (TARRAGONA).

Tortosa, for centuries the last town before the sea, was charged in those times with guarding, from the heights overlooking the Ebro, the region's only river bridge. From the Castillo de la Suda, a castle which has been converted into a parador, there is a fine view of the town, the Ebro and the valley. Today, Tortosa is endowed with an impressive artistic heritage, whch ranges from stunning Gothic monuments to fine examples of Modernism.

Location

Tortosa stands on the banks of the Ebro, close to the river delta and 14km/9mi from the Mediterráneo motorway running along the coast. 🛈 *Plaza del Bimil.lenari, 43500,* ☎ *977 51 08 22.*

🔍 *Neighbouring sights are described in the following chapters: TARRAGONA (83km/52mi NE), ALCAÑIZ (94km/59mi NW and COSTA DEL AZAHAR, to the S.*

Worth a Visit

CIUDAD ANTIGUA★ (OLD TOWN) *3hr*

Catedral★★

🕐 *Open 10am-1pm and 4-8pm. No visits during religious services.* ☎ *977 44 17 52.*

The cathedral was built in pure Gothic style even though construction, begun in 1347, continued for 200 years. The 18C **façade**★ built in the Baroque style is lavishly decorated: capitals with plant motifs, curved columns and outstanding reliefs.

In Catalan tradition the lines of the **interior**★★ are plain, the arches high and divided into two tiers only in the nave. Note the double ambulatory. The chancel is framed by radiating chapels which, as was originally planned, should be divided by fenestration like that at the north entrance to the ambulatory.

The retable at the high altar has a large wood **polyptych**★ painted in the 14C, illustrating the Life of Christ and the Virgin Mary. Another interesting work is the 15C **altarpiece of the Transfiguration**★, attributed to Jaime Huguet, presenting lavish ornamentation and delicately carved figures. The two stone 15C **pulpits**★ in the nave are beautifully carved with low reliefs: those on the left illustrate the Evangelists and their symbols, those on the right the Doctors of the Roman Church, Saints Gregory, Jerome, Ambrose and Augustine.

Capilla de Nuestra Señora de la Cinta★ (Chapel of Our Lady of the Belt)

Second chapel off the south aisle. This was built in the Baroque style between 1642 and 1725 and is decorated with paintings and local jasper and marble; at its centre is the relic, the belt of Our Lady *(services of special veneration: first week in September).*

Font

First chapel off the south aisle. The stone basin is said to have stood in the garden of the antipope Benedict XIII, Pedro de Luna, and bears his arms. A great many funerary steles and reliefs can be found in the austere cloisters (14C) adjoining the right side of the temple.

View of Tortosa from the Castillo de la Suda

T. Vidal/GC (DICT)

Palacio Episcopal★ (Bishop's Palace)

🕐 *Open 10am-1pm.* 🕐 *Closed Sat, Sun and public hols.* ☎ *977 44 07 00.*

The 14C Catalan patio of this palace, built in the 13C-14C, is memorable for the straight flight of steps which completely occupies one side and the arcaded gallery, lined with slender columns. On the upper floor, the **Gothic chapel**★, entered through a carved doorway from a well-proportioned anteroom, has ogive vaulting in which the ribs descend on to figured bosses. The final decorative touch is given by the false relief windows built into the walls on either side.

Reales Colegios de Tortosa★

🕐 *Open 10am-1pm and 4-7pm; 1 Jun-15 Sep, 8am-3pm.* 🕐 *Closed Sat-Sun and public hols.* ⏴ *No charge.* ☎ *977 44 15 25.*

In 1564 the Emperor Charles V founded this lovely Renaissance ensemble, consisting of the Colegio de Sant Lluís and the Colegio de Sant Jordi y Sant Domingo.

The **Colegio de Sant Lluís**★ was at one time used for educating newly converted Muslims: the door of the main façade features two sphinxes symbolising knowledge, flanked by the imperial coat of arms. In the section above are sculptures of St James and St Matthew, who were the patrons of the College. The fine oblong **patio**★★ is curiously decorated with characters in relief, representing an incredibly wide range of expressions and attitudes.

The Renaissance façade of the **Colegio de Sant Jordi y de Sant Domingo** bears a Latin inscription *(Domus Sapientiae,* meaning House of Knowledge), indicating the vocation of this institution.

Iglesia de Sant Domingo

Built in the 16C, this church was once part of the Reales Colegios.

Llotja de Mar

A fine Gothic building (16C) with two rectangular naves separated by semicircular arches. The old maritime exchange was moved to its current premises in 1933.

Excursions

Parque Natural del Delta del Ebro★★
(Ebro Delta Nature Reserve)

25km/16mi E. Visitors are advised to contact the tourist information office in Deltebre. ▣ *Centro de Información: Calle Doctor Martín Buera 22, Deltebre.* ☎ *977 48 96 79.* The boat trip from Deltebre to the mouth of the Ebro is highly recommended (45min round trip). 🕐 *Open 10am-2pm and 3-6pm (19 May-Sep); Sun and public hols, 10am-2pm.* 🕐 *Closed 1 Jan and 25 Dec.* ⏴ *1.20€.*

There are boat trips between Deltebre and the river mouth (45min there and back). The reserve, covering an area of 7 736ha/19 116 acres, was created in 1983 to protect the birds that shelter there and to encourage local economic development. The vast delta, closed by the Isla de Buda (Buda Island), is a swampy stretch of alluvium deposits collected by the Ebro from the Montes Cantábricos range, the Pyrenees and the Aragón plateaux. Three-quarters of the land is given over to the growing of rice and early fruit and vegetables.

Trujillo★★

POPULATION: 8 919

MICHELIN MAP 576 N 12 – EXTREMADURA (CÁCERES).

The modern town gives little idea of the originality and charm of the old town, built on a granite ledge higher up the hillside. This was hastily fortified by the Moors in the 13C against attack by the Christians and, as the centuries passed, had superimposed on its Arabic appearance, noble mansions built in the 16C and 17C by the Indianos – those who had journeyed across the Atlantic and returned with a fortune.

Location

Trujillo is situated on the A 5 linking Madrid and Badajoz.  *Plaza Mayor, 10200 Trujillo,* ☎ *927 32 26 77.*

Neighbouring sights are described in the following chapters: CÁCERES (47km/29mi W), PLASENCIA (80km/50mi NE), Monasterio de GUADALUPE (82km/51mi E) and MÉRIDA (89km/55mi SW).

Background

The land of the Conquistadores – "Twenty American nations", it is said, "were conceived in Trujillo". Accurate or not, it is certainly true that the city can claim to have fathered numbers of conquerors and colonisers of the New World: **Francisco de Orellana** who left in 1542 to explore the legendary country of the Amazons; **Diego García de Paredes,** nicknamed the Samson of Extremadura on account of his Herculean strength; and **Francisco Pizarro** (1475-1541), the conqueror of Peru and the most famous of them all. Pizarro amassed a huge fortune, plundering the riches of the Emperor Atahualpa and occupying his capital, Cuzco (1533). The early discovery of the Potosí silver mines made Peru the most important colony in the Spanish Empire, but an implacable rivalry between Pizarro and his companion in arms, Almagro, brought about the death first of Almagro in 1538 and then of Pizarro, murdered amid untold riches in his own palace.

Special Features

OLD QUARTER

The old quarter of Trujillo is less austere than Cáceres, the mansions generally having been built later in the 16C and 17C, and decorated with arcades, loggias and corner windows. The widespread use of whitewash on house fronts and the steeply inclined alleys bring additional interest to the town. Those visiting Trujillo in late spring or at any time throughout the summer will hear the flapping wings and see the outline of many a high-perched stork.

Plaza Mayor★★

The square, one of the most beautiful in Spain, is unusual for its irregular shape and different levels linked by wide flights of steps and the great variety of seigniorial mansions overlooking it. Worth examining in detail, it evokes a way of life long gone and at night its appearance is positively theatrical.

Address Book

WHERE TO EAT

Mesón La Cadena – *Plaza Mayor 8 –* ☎ *927 32 14 63 –* . The dining room of this popular family-run restaurant is on the first floor, with good views of the main square. The menu features a good choice of traditional Extremadura dishes. Bar on the ground floor. Eight reasonably priced bedrooms are also available.

WHERE TO STAY

Hotel Victoria – *Plaza del Campillo 22 –* ☎ *927 32 18 19 –* &. *– 27 rooms. –* *4.50€– Restaurant €10.* The Hotel Victoria is housed in a renovated building with comfortable rooms arranged around an interior patio.

Equestrian statue of Pizarro

This bronze by the American sculptors, Charles Runse and Mary Harriman, dates from 1927.

Iglesia de San Martín

16C. The rubble and freestone walls of the church enclose a vast nave chequered with funerary paving stones. The south parvis served in the past as a public meeting ground.

Palacio de los Duques de San Carlos★ (Palace of the Dukes of San Carlos)

17C. Now an enclosed convent. The tall granite façade, decorated in the transitional Classical Baroque style has a corner window surmounted by a crest with a double-headed eagle. Visitors have access to the **patio** with two tiers of rounded arches and a fine staircase of four flights.

Palacio del Marqués de Piedras Albas (Palace of the Marquis of Piedras Albas)

The Renaissance loggia has been accommodated into the original Gothic wall.

Palacio del Marqués de la Conquista (Palace of the Marquis de la Conquista)

The palace was built by Hernando Pizarro, the conquistador's brother. It has an exceptional number of windows with iron grilles and a Plateresque corner **window★**, added in the 17C with, on the left, the busts of Francisco Pizarro and his wife, and on the right Hernando and his niece, whom he married. Above is the family crest. Crowning the façade is a series of statues representing the months of the year.

Ayuntamiento Viejo (Former town hall)

16C. Three tiers of Renaissance arcades from a nearby patio have been reconstructed to form the façade of what is now the Palacio de Justicia (Law Courts).

Casa de las Cadenas (House of Chains)

The chains are said to have been brought by Christians freed from Moorish serfdom.

Torre del Alfiler (Alfiler Tower)

The so-called needle tower, visible from the square, is a Mudéjar belfry and a favourite spot with storks.

Palacio de Orellana-Pizarro

This 16C palace has a beautiful Plateresque upper gallery.

Iglesia de Santiago

This church's 13C Romanesque belfry and the tall seigniorial tower belonging to the Palacio de los Chaves stand on either side of the Arco de Santiago (St James' Arch), one of the town's seven original gateways. The nave of the church was modified in the 17C.

Iglesia de Santa María★

🕐 *Open 10am-2pm and 4.30-7pm (7.30pm in summer).* 🎫 *1.30€.* ☎ *927 32 26 77.*

This 13C Gothic church, in which the network vaulting was reconstructed in the 15C, is the pantheon of Trujillo's great men. In the coro alto, lit by a wide rose window, are the two stone seats in which the Catholic Monarchs sat during Mass when in residence in the city. The 24 panels of the Gothic **retable**★ at the high altar are attributed to Fernando Gallego.

From the top of the belfry there is a delightful **view** of brown tile roofs, the Plaza Mayor arcades and the castle.

Castillo

The castle stands out prominently on the granite ledge from which the blocks were hewn for its construction. The massive crenellated curtain wall is reinforced by numerous heavy square towers. Above the keep the patron of Trujillo, Our Lady of Victory, can still be seen keeping vigil. The view from the walls takes in the town and its Plaza Mayor.

Tudela ★

POPULATION: 26 163

MICHELIN MAP 573 F 25 – NAVARRA.

In the 9C the town was a dependency of the Córdoba Caliphate. From this time, it has preserved a large Moorish quarter, the Morería, in addition to several Mudéjar-style houses. A number of interesting Christian churches were also built in Tudela following the Reconquest of the town in the 12C.

Location

Tudela stands on the right bank of the River Ebro at the heart of the Ribera, an area which, as a result of widespread irrigation, has developed into a prosperous market-gardening centre growing mainly asparagus, haricot beans, artichokes and peppers.

🏛 *Plaza Vieja, 31500 Tudela,* ☎ *948 84 80 58.*

👁 *Neighbouring sights are described in the following chapters: ZARAGOZA (81km/51mi SE), PAMPLONA (84km/52mi N), SORIA (90km/56mi SW) and La RIOJA (NW).*

Worth a Visit

Catedral ★

⊶ *Currently closed for restoration.*

The 12C-13C cathedral is an excellent example of the transitional Romanesque-Gothic style. The **Last Judgement Doorway** ★ (Portada del Juicio Final) difficult to see through lack of space, is an incredibly carved unit with nearly 120 groups of figures illustrating the Last Judgement.

The **interior**, Romanesque in the elevation of the nave, is Gothic in its vaulting and clerestory. Excepting the coro enclosure and several side chapels, which are Baroque, the church is rich in Gothic works of art including early-16C choir stalls, the retable at the high altar and the stone reliquary statue of Byzantine appearance dating from about 1200 of the White Virgin. Just beside it, the **Capilla de Nuestra Señora de la Esperanza** ★ (Chapel of our Lady of Hope) has several 15C masterpieces including the sepulchre of a chancellor of Navarra and the central altarpiece.

The 12C-13C **cloisters** ★★ *(claustro)* are exceedingly harmonious with Romanesque arches resting alternately on groups of two or three columns with historiated capitals. Most of them relate scenes from the New Testament and the lives of the saints in a style inspired by the carvings of Aragón. A door of the mosque which once stood on the site has been preserved in one of the gallery walls.

Iglesia de San Nicolás

When the church in calle Rúa in the old quarter was rebuilt in the 18C a tympanum of Romanesque origin was placed in the façade built of brick in the Mudéjar style. God the Father is shown seated, holding his Son and surrounded by the symbols of the Evangelists.

Excursions

Tarazona

21km/13mi SW on the N 121. In the Middle Ages, Tarazona was for a time the residence of the kings of Aragón. Round the former royal mansion, now the **Palacio Episcopal** (Episcopal Palace), an old quarter still remains with narrow streets overlooking the quays of the River Queiles.

Catedral

⊶ *Currently closed for restoration.* ☎ *948 40 21 61.*

The cathedral was largely rebuilt in the 15C and 16C. Several architectural styles may be seen: Aragón Mudéjar in the belfry tower and lantern, Renaissance in the portal and, in the **second chapel** ★ as you walk left round the ambulatory, delicately carved Gothic **tombs** of the two Calvillos cardinals from Avignon.

😊 Fiestas 😊

St Anne's feast day (26 July) is celebrated annually, as at Pamplona/Iruña, with several days of great rejoicing including *encierros* and bullfights. During Holy Week, an event known as the Descent of the Angel takes place on the picturesque **plaza de los Fueros**, which served as a bullring in the 18C.

The **Mudéjar cloisters** have bays filled with 16C Moorish plasterwork tracery. Not far away, a small enclosed square surrounded by houses, the 18C **Plaza de Toros Vieja**, was once a bullring.

Monasterio de Veruela★★

▶ *39km/24mi S from Tudela and 17km/11mi from Tarazona. From Tarazona, take the N 122 towards Zaragoza then bear right onto the Z 373.*

🕐 *Open Oct-Mar, 10am-1pm and 3-6pm; Apr-Sep, 10am-2pm and 3-6pm. Apr-Sep 10am-2pm and 4-7pm.* 🕐*Closed Mon, 1 Jan and 25 Dec.* 📷 *1.80€.* ☎ *976 64 90 25.*

Cistercian monks from southern France came in the middle of the 12C to this spot where they founded a monastery and surrounded it with a fortified perimeter wall. Seven centuries later the Sevillian poet **Bécquer** was to stay while writing his *Letters from My Cell*, in which he described the Aragón countryside much in the manner of later guide books!

Iglesia★★

The church, built in the transitional period between Romanesque and Gothic, has a sober but attractive façade with a single oculus, a narrow band of blind arcades strangely lacking a base line, and a doorway decorated with friezes, billets and capitals.

The interior, with pointed vaulting, is an amazing size. The vault groins are pointed over the nave and horseshoe-shaped over the aisles and ambulatory. A Plateresque chapel with a multicoloured carved door was built onto the north transept in the 16C. Opposite, the sacristy door is in a surprising Rococo style.

Claustro★

The cloisters are ornate Gothic. At ground level the brackets are carved with the heads of men and beasts; above are three galleries with Plateresque decoration. The **Sala Capitular★** (chapter house), in pure Cistercian style, contains the tombs of the monastery's first 15 abbots.

Úbeda★★

POPULATION: 32 524

MICHELIN MAP 578 R 19 – ANDALUCÍA (JAÉN).

Úbeda is one of Andalucía's architectural treasures, with numerous monuments of interest. It enjoyed its period of greatest splendour during the 16C, when the majority of its magnificent Renaissance buildings were built. It is well worth spending time exploring this delightful provincial town to discover its palaces, churches and fine squares.

Location

Like the neighbouring town of Baeza, Úbeda stands amid extensive olive groves, between the River Guadalquivir and River Guadalimar. 🛈 *Plaza Baja del Marqués 4 (Palacio de Contadero), 23400 Úbeda, ☎ 953 75 08 97.*

🕐 *Neighbouring sights are described in the following chapters: BAEZA (9km/5.5mi W), JAÉN (57km/35mi SW) and Parque Natural de las SIERRAS DE CAZORLA, SEGURA Y LAS VILLAS (to the E).*

Walking About

BARRIO ANTIGUO★★ (OLD QUARTER) 🕐 *allow one day*

Plaza Vázquez de Molina★★

The square, the monumental centre of Úbeda, is lined with old, historic buildings like the **Palacio del Deán Ortega**, which has been converted into a parador.

Palacio de las Cadenas★ (House of Chains)

The mansion, now the Ayuntamiento (town hall), named after the chains round the forecourt, was designed in 1562 by Vandelvira, who was also responsible for the construction of the Jaén Cathedral.

The majestic but not overly ornate **façade**★★ is relieved by alternating bays and pilasters and decorated above with caryatids and atlantes.

The outstanding feature of the interior is the delightful Renaissance patio. The upper floor is home to the Archivo Histórico Municipal, commanding pleasant views of the square and surrounding area.

Iglesia de Santa María de los Alcázares★

The church was built in the 13C above the remains of a former mosque. Its main interest lies in the harmonious façade; the main door; the late-16C Puerta de la Consolada on the left side; and the fine 16C Renaissance cloisters. Although the interior was badly damaged during the Spanish Civil War, it has preserved several delightful **chapels**★, adorned with sculptures and profuse decoration and enclosed by impressive **grilles**★, most of which are the work of Master Bartolomé.

Capilla de El Salvador★★

🕐 *Open 10.30am-2pm and 4.30-7pm.* 🕐 *Closed Mon.* ⊛ *2.25€.* ☎ *953 75 08 97.*

Diego de Siloé designed this homogeneous and sumptuous church in 1536. Its façade is ornamented with Renaissance motifs.

The **interior**★★ is frankly theatrical: the single nave has vaulting outlined in blue and gold and is closed by a monumental wrought-iron grille. Beyond, the Capilla Mayor (chancel) forms a kind of rotunda in which an immense 16C altarpiece includes a baldaquin with a sculpture by Berruguete of the Transfiguration (only the figure of Christ remains).

The **sacristy**★★, by Vandelvira, is ornamented with coffered decoration, medallions, caryatids and atlantes with all the splendour of the Italian Renaissance style.

Casa de los Salvajes (House of the Savages)

Two very odd savages, dressed in animal skins held together with belts of blackberry branches, may be seen on the façade, supporting a bishop's crest.

Iglesia de San Pablo★

The church is a harmonious mixture of Gothic architecture, as seen in the west door, and the Isabelline style, to be seen in the **south door** (1511). The **chapels**, adorned in several instances with fine wrought-iron grilles, are the church's chief interior feature: the Capilla de las Calaveras (Chapel of the Skulls) was designed by Vandelvira; the Capilla de las Mercedes, a typical example of the Isabelline style, is enclosed by an extraordinary **grille**★★ – note the highly imaginative scene depicting Adam and Eve.

The plaza Primero de Mayo is bordered by the 17C former town hall, showing clear Palladian influence.

Convento de San Miguel

This former convent houses the **Museo de San Juan de la Cruz** (Museum of St John of the Cross), retracing the final days of this great mystical poet who died in Úbeda.

🕐 *Open 11am-1pm and 5-7pm.* 🕐 *Closed Mon.* ⊛ *1.20€.* ☎ *953 75 06 15.*

Address Book

For coin ranges, see the Legend at the back of the guide.

WHERE TO STAY

🍽 **Hotel Victoria** – *Alaminos 5* – ☎ *953 75 29 52* – ▦ – *15 rooms.* Clean and reasonably priced are the key words to describe this small family-run hotel. Despite being on the basic side, the bedrooms are comfortable and well maintained. The best option in town for those on a tight budget.

🍽🍽 **Palacio de la Rambla** – *Plaza del Marqués 1* – *Closed 15 Jul-15 Aug* – ☎ *953 75 01 96* – ▦ – *8 rooms* 🍽. This fine 16C palace, once the home of an aristocratic family, has opened its doors to guests, who are treated like family friends in an atmosphere that is refined yet relaxed. Its most impressive architectural features are the magnificent Renaissance patio and the life-size warriors bearing weapons on the façade.

FIESTAS

The nocturnal procession on Good Friday is known for its great solemnity.

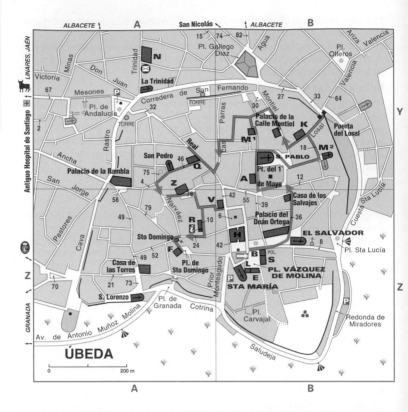

ÚBEDA

Casa del Obispo Canastero (Bishop Canastero's Mansion)

Among the figures decorating the mansion's diamond pointed stone façade are two soldiers bearing the owner's coats of arms.

Palacio de la Calle Montiel

This palace was one of the town's first Renaissance buildings and has a monumental gate flanked by twisted columns.

Casa Mudéjar

This recently restored 14C Mudéjar house is home to the town's **Museo Arqueológico**, displaying archaeological exhibits discovered in Úbeda and the surrounding area. ⏰ *Open 9am-8.30pm; Sun, 9am-2.30pm.* 🚫 *Closed all day Mon and Tue morning. 1.50€, no charge for citizens of the European Union.* ☎ *953 75 37 02.*

Palacio del Conde de Guadiana

Built in the early 17C, the Palace of the Count of Guadiana is crowned by a fine **tower**★ with angular balconies.

Palacio de la Vela de los Cobos

Although the palace's façade dates from the late 18C, its Renaissance appearance bears witness to the long survival of this style in Úbeda.

Palacio del Marqués del Contadero (Palace of the Marquis of Contadero)

The late-18C façade, crowned by a gallery, is also Renaissance in style.

Iglesia de Santo Domingo

The church's delicate south door, overlooking a small picturesque square of the same name, is decorated with Plateresque reliefs. The plaza is also fronted by the Casa de los Morales.

▷ Antiguo Hospital de Santiago (Museo de la Semana Santa); Palacio de los Bussianos; Iglesia de la Trinidad; Palacio de la Rambla; Casa de las Torres; Iglesia de San Lorenzo.

Uclés

POPULATION: 297

MICHELIN MAP 576 M 21 – CASTILLA-LA MANCHA (CUENCA).

The massive castle-monastery *(castillo-monasterio)* of Uclés stands impressively on a hill overlooking the village. From 1174 to 1499 it was the headquarters of the Order of Santiago. Because of its strategic value, the little village was the scene of numerous conflicts such as the Battle of Uclés in 1108, when the Almoravids defeated the army of Alfonso VI of Castilla.

Location

Uclés is well situated in the SE corner of the province of Cuenca near the A 3 linking Madrid and Valencia. *www.ucles.org and www.monasteriodeucles.com*

Neighbouring sights are described in the following chapters: CUENCA (70km/44mi E) and ARANJUEZ (77km/48mi W).

Worth a Visit

Castillo-Monasterio

Open 10am-6pm (8pm in summer). 3€. 969 13 50 58.

The present building was begun in 1529 in the Plateresque style, but the greater part of the work was undertaken by Herrera's disciple, **Francisco de Mora** (1560-1610), who tried to build his own Escorial – the building is, in fact, known as the Little Escorial. Entry is by a beautiful Baroque **portal**★★. Worth noting are the well (also Baroque), and the magnificent **artesonado**★ ceiling in the refectory. The sacristy has two lovely windows. The church is in the Herreran style.
The ramparts command an extensive panorama.

Excursion

Roman town of Segóbriga

In Saelices, 14km/9mi S of Uclés. Leave the A 3 at exit 103/104 and follow signs towards Casas de Luján. Open 9am-2pm and 4-6pm. No charge. 696 67 05 14.

To best appreciate this former Roman town, it is recommended that you first head for **Saelices** to visit the **museum** dedicated to the site. This former Celtiberian settlement, whose history dates back to the 5C BC, was transformed into an important town in Roman times due to its role as an important crossroads. It reached its zenith in the 1C AD, a period in which the theatre and, above all, its imposing, well-preserved **amphitheatre**★, with a capacity for 5 000 spectators, were built. Remains of the Roman baths and the old walls surrounding the city are also still visible.

Valencia★★

POPULATION: 777 427

MICHELIN MAP 577 N28 (TOWN PLAN) OR 574 N 28 –

COMUNIDAD VALENCIANA.

Valencia, Spain's third largest city, has all the character of a large Mediterranean town and is notable for its pleasant, mild climate and the quality of its light. Its wide avenues, lined with palms and fig trees, encircle the old quarter with its fortified gateways, churches and narrow streets with quaint, old-fashioned shop fronts and Gothic houses, of which some have attractive *patios*. However, Valencia is also a city in the process of change, as witnessed in two works designed by Santiago Calatrava – the Ciutat de les Arts i les Ciències (Arts and Science City) and the bridge over the former bed of the River Turia – and the **Palacio de Congresos** (Conference Centre) by Sir **Norman Foster**, all of which have propelled this historic medieval city to the forefront of Spanish architectural design.

Location

Valencia, which for many years turned its back on the sea and tourism, has made up for lost time with the development of an excellent infrastructure and superb beaches, such as the **Playa de las Arenas** (also known as the **Playa de Levante**) and the **Playa de la Malvarrosa**, both linked to the city centre by bus and a modern tram service. The latter, which inspired artists such as Joaquín Sorolla, is home to the casa-museo of **Vicente Blasco Ibáñez** (1867-1928), who described the life and customs of the Valencian huerta in works such as *La Barraca* (The Cabin) and *Entre Naranjos* (Among the Orange Trees). *Plaza del Ayuntamiento 1, 46002 Valencia, ☎ 96 351 04 17; Poeta Querol, 46002 Valencia, ☎ 96 351 49 07; Paz 48, 46003 Valencia, ☎ 96 398 64 22.*

Neighbouring sights are described in the following chapters: COSTA DEL AZAHAR, COSTA BLANCA and ALACANT/ALICANTE (174km/109mi S).

Background

2 000 years of history – The city, founded by the Greeks in 138 BC, passed successively into the hands of the Carthaginians, Romans, Visigoths and Arabs. In 1094 it was reconquered by **El Cid**, who was titled Duke of Valencia but lived only five years in the city before dying there in 1099. The Moors recaptured it three years later and held it until 1238 when it was repossessed, this time by James the Conqueror, who declared it the capital of a kingdom which he allied to Aragón. Valencia then enjoyed a long period of prosperity until the end of the 15C when, following the discovery of America and the development of ports in Andalucía, it began to decline. A silk renaissance in the 17C renewed its fortunes.

Over the past two centuries, Valencia has been involved in every war and insurrection in Spain. During the War of the Spanish Succession (1701-14), the city sided with the Archduke, Charles of Austria, but found itself stripped of its privileges; in 1808, it rebelled against the French and was then taken by Suchet in 1812; in 1843 it rose under **General Narváez** to restore the regency of María Cristina of Naples; finally

Las Fallas

The origins of this festival date back to the Middle Ages when on St Joseph's Day, the carpenters' brotherhood, one of the town's traditional crafts, burned their accumulated wood shavings in bonfires known as *Fallas* (from the Latin *fax*: torch). The name became synonymous with a festival for which, in time, objects were made solely for burning – particularly effigies of less popular members of the community! In the 17C single effigies were replaced by pasteboard groups or floats produced by quarters of the town – rivalry is such that the figures today are fantastic in size, artistry and satirical implication. Prizes are awarded during the general festivities, which include fireworks, processions, bullfights etc, before everything goes up in the fires or *cremá* on the evening of 19 March. Figures *(ninots)* dating from 1934 to the present day which have been spared from the bonfires are on display in an interesting museum, the **Museo Fallero.** ⏲ *Open 9.15am-2pm and 4.30-8pm (5.30-9pm, Apr-9 Sep); Sun and public hols, 9.15am-2pm.* ⏲ *Closed Mon, 1 and 6 Jan, 1 May and 25 Dec.* ⊛ *2€. ☎ 96 352 54 78 (ext. 4625).*

during the Civil War in March 1939, after the fall of Catalunya, the city became the last refuge of the Republican forces.

Art in Valencia – Valencia enjoyed a period of brilliance, both economically and artistically, in the 15C. Examples of Gothic architectural flowering are to be seen in the old city's palaces, mansions, gates, the cathedral and the Lonja (Exchange). In painting, several artists won renown: **Luis Dalmau**, influenced by Flemish painting, who developed a Hispano-Flemish style; **Jaime Baço**, known as **Jacomart**, and his fellow artist **Juan Reixach** who were both influenced by Flanders and Italy; and the **Osonas**, father and son, who also showed Flemish austerity in their work.

Valencia craftsmen of the 15C were also outstanding in the decorative arts: wrought ironwork, gold- and silversmithing, embroidery and particularly ceramics, for which special centres were established at Paterna and Manises (see the Museo de Cerámica in Worth a Visit).

The Valencia huerta and Albufera – The city lies along the banks of the Turia at the heart of fertile countryside known locally as **La Huerta.** On this expanse, watered by an irrigation system laid down by the Romans and improved by the Moors, are the countless citrus trees and market gardens which produce the fruit and early vegetables exported throughout Europe.

South of Valencia lies a vast lagoon, the **Parque Natural de La Albufera** (see COSTA DEL AZAHAR).

Special Features

CIUDAD VIEJA★ (OLD TOWN) Allow 3 hr (see route on town plan)

Valencia's old quarter is one of the most extensive in Europe and bears witness to the city's importance during the 15C. The best starting point for a tour of this district is El Miguelete, the bell tower of the cathedral, in plaza de la Reina.

El Miguelete★

Open 10am-1pm and 5pm-dusk. 1.20€. 96 391 81 27.

The main bell of this octagonal Gothic bell tower was consecrated on the feast day of St Michael in 1418, and owes its name to the diminutive form of Miguel (Micalet in Valencian). From the top there is a bird's-eye view of the cathedral roofs and the town with its countless glazed ceramic domes.

Catedral★

Open 7.30am-1pm and 5-8.30pm (7pm Jun-Sep). 1.20€. 96 391 81 27.

The cathedral stands on the site of a former mosque. Although work began in 1262, the major part of the building dates from the 14C and 15C. The Gothic style was completely masked in the late 18C by a neo-Classical renovation. Subsequent restoration work and the removal of this neo-Classical decoration has returned the cathedral to its original Gothic appearance.

Plaza de la Virgien

Address Book

For coin ranges, see the Legend at the back of the guide.

WHERE TO EAT

⊖ **Asador del Carme** – *Plaza del Carme 6 – ☎ 96 392 24 48 – ▤ – Closed lunchtime except Sun.* Customers are attracted here by the pleasant covered terrace, extensive menu of grilled meats and copious salads, the peace and quiet of the square from which it takes its name, and the attractive views of the Iglesia del Carmen.

⊖ **Casa Chimo** – *Avenida Neptuno 40 – ☎ 96 371 20 48 – Closed Wed – Reservation recommended.* This well-established restaurant is popular with Valencian families who come here to enjoy a traditional paella by the sea. The dining room inside, with its high ceilings and tiled walls, provides a cool retreat from the summer sun.

⊖⊖ **La Riuá** – *Del Mar 27 – ☎ 96 391 71 72 – Reservation recommended.* A heavy wooden door provides access to one of the city's best-known restaurants. The split-level dining room is adorned with attractive *azulejos*, although it can be slightly on the noisy side. A good address in which to discover local Valencian cuisine.

TAPAS

Las Cuevas – *Samaniego 9 – ☎ 96 391 71 96 – Closed in Aug.* It's just like a cave: tiny windows, narrow doors and beams. Nothing but tapas are served here, prepared according to typical Valencian traditions: mussels, stuffed red peppers, sardines etc. At weekends, the atmosphere at Las Cuevas becomes somewhat more lively as it fills up with the city's youngsters.

WHERE TO STAY

⊖ **Hostal Antigua Morellana** – *En Bou 2 – ☎ 96 391 57 73 – ▤ – 18 rooms (doubles only).* A stone's throw from the Lonja and main market, this family-run hotel offers excellent value for money. The comfortable and bright rooms provide the best views of the picturesque narrow streets in the Carmen district.

⊖ **Hostal Londres** – *Barcelonina 1 – ☎ 96 351 22 44 – 61 rooms – ⊊ 5€.* This famous hostal has maintained a certain faded charm and as such is often full. Rooms are modest with such touches as wrought-iron headboards and full baths. Those facing the street can be particularly noisy at the weekend.

⊖⊖ **Hostal Venecia** – *Plaza Ayuntamiento (enter through Llop 5) – ☎ 96 352 42 67 – ▤ 🛆 – 62 rooms – ⊊ 3.90€.* The building is outstanding, with classic façade and balconies facing the plaza del Ayuntamiento, Valencia's social

and cultural centre. Rooms are well furnished and there are some apartments. The breakfast room enjoys fine views.

⊖⊖⊖ **Hotel Reina Victoria** – *Barcas 4 – ☎ 96 352 04 87 – 94 rooms – ⊊ 10€ – Restaurant 15€.* It's worth making a journey here if only to admire the immaculate white stone Baroque façade. The interior lives up to expectations, with its charming entryhall set with marble and mirrors. Rooms are Rococo inspired but not over the top.

TAKING A BREAK

El Siglo – *Plaza Santa Catalina 11 – ☎ 96 391 84 66 – Open 10am-1pm and 4pm-midnight.* Founded in 1836, El Siglo (The Century) is a chocolate-maker, ice-cream producer and horchata specialist rolled into one. The extensive building is adorned with *azulejos* from Manises. Another typical confectioner, the less-frequented *Santa Catalina*, is just ten metres away.

Café de las Horas – *Conde de Almodóvar 1 – ☎ 963 91 73 36 – Open 4.30am-1.30am (3am on public hols).* This café with a 19C atmosphere is just steps from the Plaza de la Virgen. The high point is the decor, including trompe-l'œil scenes on the walls, a little fountain, and finely tuned lighting that goes with the music to create an intimate atmosphere.

Café del Negrito – *Plaza Negrito – Open 4pm-3am.* This artists' café, situated in a small square in the old town, is a popular meeting-place for friends who come here to enjoy the best "Valencian water" and to enjoy the Negrito's famous orange juice and champagne cocktails. Note the bar opposite, the *Ghecko*, which is completely covered in shells.

NIGHTLIFE

Calle Caballeros – This street is the hub of Valencia's nightlife. Between plaza de la Virgen, with its numerous outdoor cafés, and plaza Tossal, a popular square for tapas, you'll pass by the *Johnny Maracas* salsa bar, the *Babal Hanax* disco, and the fashion *Café Bolsería* with its jet-set clientele.

Clot – *Plaza Redonda 1 – ☎ 96 391 81 23 – Open 10am-1pm and 4-midnight.* This typical tavern beneath the arcades of plaza Redonda serves a fine selection of tapas, including some delicious sausages (*salchichas*).

La Marxa – *Cocinas 5 – Open Tue-Sat from 11pm.* At the heart of the famous Carmen district, La Marxa is the emblem of Valencian nightlife, and has been instrumental in developing Valencia's reputation as a city with a vibrant club scene.

Pilar – *Moro Zeit 13 – ☎ 96 391 04 97 – Open daily (except Wed) noon-midnight.*

VALENCIA

Founded in 1918, Pilar is one of the best tapas bars in the city. The house speciality is *clochinas*, a mussels-based dish. Another local tapas institution, *El Molino*, is located directly opposite, making this a good area in which to discover Valencian nightlife.

ENTERTAINMENT

Palau de la Música – *Paseo de la Alameda* – ☎ *96 337 50 20*. This venue dedicated to classical music is the focus of the city's cultural life.

SHOPPING

Lladró – *Poeta Querol 9* – ☎ *963 51 16 25* – *Open Mon-Sat, 10am-1pm and 4-8pm*. This internationally famous porcelain manufacturer has boutiques around the world selling stunning works of art across a broad price range.

Mercadillo de la Plaza Redonda – *Open 9am-1pm and 4-9pm*. This typical small market in plaza Redonda is the place to buy a whole range of clothes and bric-a-brac, or else simply to watch the world go by over a coffee. On Sundays, animals and pets can also be bought here.

Turrones Ramos – *Sombrerería 11 (next to Plaza Redonda) - Closed Sat-Sun and in Aug - Open 10am-2pm and 5-8pm*. This shop has sold hand-made *turrón* since 1890. The marzipan is worth trying too, especially *casca de batata* and *casca de yema* made with sweet potato or egg yolk."

FIESTAS

During the week of 12-19 March, the city celebrates the festival of St Joseph, with its famous **Las Fallas** (☝ *see below*).

Exterior

The elegant and slender early-18C west face is in imitation of the Italian Baroque style, after plans by a German architect. The Assumption on the pediment is by Ignacio Vergara and Esteve.

The south door opening to calle Palau is Romanesque, while the north, the **Portada de los Apóstoles** (Apostles' Door), opening to Plaza de la Virgen, is Gothic, decorated with numerous, but time-worn sculptures. The statue of the Virgin and Child, which once stood against the pier, is now on the tympanum surrounded by angel musicians.

Interior

Although the elevation of the Gothic vaulting is not very great, plenty of light filters in through the alabaster windows in the beautiful Flamboyant Gothic **lantern**.

The **retable** in the capilla mayor (chancel), the major work of Fernando de Llanos and Yáñez de la Almedina (early 16C), illustrates the Lives of Christ and the Virgin in a style markedly influenced by Leonardo da Vinci.

The high altar, a Renaissance portico hides a translucent alabaster relief of the Resurrection (1510). Opposite is the 15C late Gothic Virgen del Coro (Chancel Virgin) in polychrome alabaster and, in a chapel, a Crucifixion known as the Cristo de la Buena Muerte (Christ of Good Death).

Capilla del Santo Cáliz or Sala Capitular★ (Chapel of the Holy Grail or Chapter house)

Last chapel along the north aisle, at the end of the cathedral. The chamber, which in the 14C served as a reading room, has elegant star vaulting. Behind the altar, 12 alabaster low reliefs by the Florentine sculptor, Poggibonsi, are part of a fine Gothic structure in the centre of which can be seen a magnificent 1C carnelian agate cup, said to be the Holy Grail (the vessel traditionally used by Jesus Christ at the Last Supper and in which a few drops of his blood are said to have fallen). The cup, according to legend, was brought to Spain in the 3C and belonged first to the Monasterio de San Juan de la Peña then to the crown of Aragón which, in the 15C, presented it to Valencia Cathedral. This chapel provides access to the **museum**, which contains a monumental monstrance made after the Civil War and two large paintings by Goya of San Francisco de Borja. ◷ *Open 9am-1pm and 5-7pm; Sun and public hols 10am-1pm.* ◷ *Closed afternoons Oct-Mar.* ☎ *96 391 81 27.*

TRIBUNAL DE LAS AGUAS

Since the Middle Ages disputes in the huerta have been settled by the Water Tribunal: every Thursday at noon, representatives of the areas irrigated by the eight canals, accompanied by an *alguazil* (officer of justice), meet in front of the Portada de los Apóstoles (Apostles' Door) of the cathedral; the offence is read out, judged (the judges all in black) and the sentence pronounced immediately (a fine, deprivation of water) by the most senior judge. The proceedings are oral and there is no appeal.

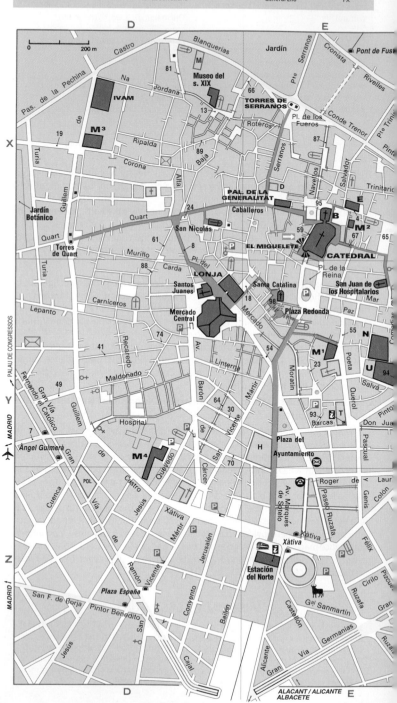

Street map of Valencia

↑ PUIG

F

Jardines del Real

U

Av. Blasco Ibáñez

MUSEO DE BELLAS ARTES SAN PÍO V

San Pío V

del

López

Jardín de Monforte

X

General Elío

Llano del Real

Micer Mascó

Pl. del Temple

Puente del Real

Pas. de la

Turia

Pas. de la

Convento de Santo Domingo

Alameda

Puente Calatrava

Alameda

Pl. de Tetuán

Paz

LA GLORIETA

Pl. Alfonso el Magnánimo

Av. Navarro Reverter

Ciudadela

el Pontó

Y

Plaza Porta de la Mar

Sorolla

Colón

Conde Salvatierra de Álava

Grabador Esteve

Plaza

Austria

Colón

Sorni

Plaza América

Jorge Juan

Puente de Aragón

Av. Jacinto Benavente

Isabel la Católica

Amorós

Hernán Cortés

Cirilo Amorós

Pizarro

Turia

Altea

Cortés

Maestro Gozalbo

Conde

Ciscar

Salamanca

Burjana

Almirante Cadarso

Regne

Reina Doña Germana

Reina

València

F

Platja de Malva-Rosa ↑

Z

TARRAGONA

ALACANT / ALICANTE

Ciutat de les Arts i les Ciències

537

▶ *Exit the cathedral via the Puerta del Palau (right-hand side of the transept) and continue as far as plaza del Arzobispo.*

At the left, in a large plot, are ruins dating from the Roman era up to Medieval times.

▶ *Retrace your steps along calle Palau to la plaza de Nápols i Sicilia and turn right ontoTrinquete de los Caballeros*

Iglesia de San Juan de los Hospitalarios (Church of St John of the Hospital Brother★

Access through courtyard. This attractive church in early Gothic style was founded in 1238. It consists of a single nave with pointed barrel vault, and interesting side chapels.In the first chapel are beautiful 13C murals; in another is a 16C Renaissance altarpiece. There are also a Baroque chapel (at the front of the church), and, in the last chapel, a magnificent Calvary of three 12C and 14C wood sculptures.

▶ *Return to the plaza del Arzobispo*

Museo de la Ciudad (City Museum)

🕐 *Open 9.15am-2pm and 4.30-8pm (5.30-9pm in summer); Sun and public hols, 9.30am-2pm.* 🕐 *Closed Mon, 1 Jan, 1 May and 25 Dec.* 🆓 *No charge.* ☎ *96 352 54 78, ext 4126.*

This museum is housed in the 19C Palacio del Marqués de Campo. It contains the city's art gallery and a small section devoted to the history of Valencia from its foundation through to the Christian period.

Cripta Arqueológica de la Cárcel de San Vicente (San Vicente Jail Archaeological Crypt)

🕐 *Open 9.15am-2pm and 4.30-8pm (Oct-Mar, 5.30-9pm); Sun and public hols, 9.15am-2pm.* 🕐 *Closed Mon.* 🆓 *No charge.* ☎ *96 352 54 78, ext. 1184.*

A small Visigothic chapel with a sepulchre surrounded by four finely decorated screens and two Visigothic stone sarcophagi. The visit also includes an audio-visual presentation.

Almudín

This is a 14C-16C granary with popular-style frescoes covering the walls and two 19C *azulejos* altars. It is now used as a venue for temporary exhibitions.

▶ *Return to plaza de la Virgen.*

Iglesia de Nuestra Señora de los Desamparados

🕐 *Open 7am-2pm and 4-9pm.* ☎ *96 391 92 14.*

This church, overlooking plaza de la Virgen, dates from the second half of the 17C and is linked to the apse of the cathedral via a Renaissance arch. The floor plan is oval. Beneath the painted cupola stands the venerated statue of the patron of Valencia, known as the Virgin of the Abandoned *(desamparados)*, which receives a steady flow of devotees.

Palau de la Generalitat★

🕐 *Open 9am-2pm.* 🕐 *Cosed Sat-Sun and public hols, and 10-20 Mar.* 🆓 *No charge.* ☎ *96 386 34 61.*

This fine 15C Gothic palace to which one tower was added in the 17C and a second identical one added in the 20C, was until 1707 the meeting place of the Valencia Cortes charged with the collection of tax.

Visitors enter an attractive Gothic patio decorated with a sculpture by Benlliure of Dante's *Inferno* (1900). Then they see a golden saloon with a wonderful gilt and multicoloured **artesonado ceiling**★ and a large painting of the Tribunal de las Aguas, or Water Tribunal (🕯 *see above).* On the first floor are the Sala de los Reyes (Royal Hall) displaying portraits of the Valencian kings, the Oratorio (Oratory) with its altarpiece by the local 16C painter, Juan Sariñena, and the Gran Salón de las Cortes Valencianas (Valencian Grand Council Chamber). The *azulejos* frieze and the coffered ceiling are 16C. Members of the Cortes are portrayed in several 16C canvases.

The rear façade gives onto the pleasant **plaza de Manises**.

Torres de Serranos★

At the end of calle Serranos, which runs from the plaza de Manises. The towers, now considerably restored, are, nevertheless, a good example of late-14C military architecture; they guarded one of the entrances to the medieval city. The defensive features all face outwards. Note the flowing lines of the battlements and the delicate tracery above the gateway.

▶ *Return to plaza de Manises.*

Calle de Caballeros

This street, starting from plaza de Manises, heads into the traditional Carmen district. In former times, calle de Caballeros was the most important street in the old town. Some of the houses along it have preserved their Gothic patios (numbers 22, 26 and 33).

▶ *Head along the street that runs from opposite n°26.*

Iglesia de San Nicolás

🕐 *Open 9.30-11am and 6.30-8pm. Sun and public hols 10am-1pm.* 🕐 *Closed Mon and Mon-Fri in Aug.* ☎ *96 391 33 17.*

This, one of the town's oldest churches, has been completely renovated in the Churrigueresque style. Among the 16C paintings are an altarpiece by Juan de Juanes *(chapel to the left on entering)* and a *Calvary* by Osona the Elder *(by the font).*

▶ *Continue as far as plaza del Esparto, then, follow calle Quart.*

Torres de Quart

These 15C towers, again a fine example of military architecture, guard another entrance to the city. In the 19C they were badly damaged by Napoleon's cannons. *Return to plaza del Esparto and head along calle Bolsería.*

Lonja★ (Silk Exchange)

🕐 *Open 9.15am-2pm and 4.30-8pm (5.30-9pm Apr-Sep); Sun and public hols, 9.15am-2pm.* 🕐 *Closed Mon, 1 Jan, 1 May and 25 Dec.* ☎ *96 352 54 78, ext. 4153.*

The present building was erected on the request of the Valencia silk merchants in the 15C to replace an earlier commodities exchange similar to those of Barcelona and Palma. The prosperity which required a larger building was well reflected in the style of the new edifice: Flamboyant Gothic.

The Lonja, topped by a crenellated roof ridge, has an impressive Gothic entrance. The left wing, separated from the entrance by a tower, is crowned by a gallery decorated with a medallion frieze. The old commercial silk **hall**★★ is lofty, with ogival arches supported on slender, elegantly cabled columns; the bays in the walls are filled with delicate tracery.

Iglesia de los Santos Juanes

🕐 *Open 8am (7.30am in summer) to 1pm and 6-8pm.* ☎ *96 391 63 54.*

This is a vast church with a Baroque façade. The single aisle, originally Gothic, was modified in the 17C and 18C by the addition of exuberant Baroque stuccowork. The small tower crowning the Baroque façade can be seen to best effect from the Lonja.

Mercado Central (Central Market)

The enormous metal and glass construction, built in 1928, is a good example of Modernist architecture. Try going there in the mornings when it is at its busiest with stalls of glistening fish and great piles of fruit and vegetables fresh from the *huerta*.

Iglesia de Santa Catalina

The church, built over a mosque after the Reconquest, is notable for its 17C **Baroque belfry**★.

Plaza Redonda

A passageway leads to this unusual little round square, more like a patio, surrounded by stalls selling lace and haberdashery.

▶ *Go out to calle San Vicente Mártir and turn left by the Abadía de San Martín.*

Palacio del Marqués de Dos Aguas★★

This magnificent Baroque building houses the Museo Nacional de Cerámica y de las Artes Suntuarias González Martí (*see Worth a Visit*). The marble portal, constructed in the 18C by Ignacio Vergara after a plan by the painter Hipólito Rovira, was covered by paintings until the 19C.

▶ *Return to calle San Vicente Mártir and continue to the plaza del Ayuntamiento*

Plaza del Ayuntamiento

This great square is the busiest part of the modern city, and the meeting point of *Valencianos,* with a showy flower market always in bloom.

Worth a Visit

Ciutat de les Arts i les Ciències★★

This great cultural and recreational complex (350 000 m²/420 000 sq yd)), is made up of a series of spectacular avant-garde white buildings that reflect onto great turquoise sheets of water. Its components focus on the themes of art, science and nature.

L'Oceanogràfic★★

Kids *At the eastern end.* ◷ *Open 9.30am-1.30pm.* ⊜ *20.50€ (28€ with L'Hemisfèric and Museu de les Ciències Príncipe Felipe).* ☎ *902 100 031.*

The largest maritime centre of Europe is the work of architect Félix Candela. The ensemble of buildings and facilities is set around a lake and joined by gardens, passages and tunnels. The magnificent and entertaining exhibit focuses on marine life in the climactic zones of the planet: Mediterranean, marshland (🐾 *10 min tour*), temperate and tropical zones (turtles and grey seals outside and a great 70m/230ft tunnel-aquarium below), the Arctic (with belugas and walruses), the Antarctic (penguins) and Oceans (including a 30m/100ft aquarium-tunnel with sharks and rays). The large dolphin centre hosts 15-20min performances throughout the day which are a treat for kids and others. Restaurants and bars provide locales for a break.

L'Umbracle★

An unusual arrangement of white parabolic arches shelters this pleasant palm garden (note the teak floor), located on a terrace facing the Museu de les Ciències. From the Umbracle, there is a fine **view** of the entire complex.

Museu de les Ciències Príncipe Felipe★★

◷ *Open 10am-8pm (9pm Sun and public hols).* ⊜ *7€ (10.50€ combined with L'Hemèsferic, 22.50€ with l'Oceanogràfic).* ☎ *902 10 00 31.*

This colossal and surprising building, the work of Santiago Calatrava, houses the largest interactive museum in Europe. The aim is to create a friendly encounter with science and the latest in technology, through experiments and demonstrations. Themes are wide-ranging, including the human genome, space travel, astronomy, sports, lasers, water, magnetism, and much more.

L'Hemisfèric★

⊙ *Check programmes and prices by calling* ☎ *902 10 00 31.*

Also the work of Calatrava, this building symbolizes a human eye open to the world. It is situated in the centre of a 24 000 m²/28 800 sq yd pool, and houses a planetarium and Omnimax cinema.

L'Hemisfèric (Ciutat de les Arts i les Ciències)

Palau de les Arts

Along the same architectural lines as the other buildings, and also by Calatrava, this great and as yet-unfinished centre of the performing arts mounts exhibits on opera, music, theatre and dance.

Museo Nacional de Cerámica y de las Artes Suntuarias González Martí★★ (National Museum of Ceramics and Decorative Art)

○ Open 10am-2pm and 4-8pm; Sun and public hols, 10am-2pm. ○ Closed Mon, 1 Jan, 1 May and 24-25 and 31 Dec. ⊗ 2.40€. No charge Sat afternoon and Sun. ☎ 96 351 63 92.

This museum occupies the lovely Baroque **Palacio del Marqués de Dos Aguas★★**.

On the **ground floor**, in addition to temporary exhibitions, is the **carriage★** of the Marquis of Dos Aguas (1753), with surprisingly rich decoration, along with a more modest vehicle from 1800

On the **first floor**, palatial décor remains intact (lovely painted ceilings, marble floors, and splendid furniture). Rooms include the Chinese salon, the dining room, the *fumoir*, the chapel, and a room restored with Gothic elements where the paintings of the Pinazos are on display.

The **ceramic collection** on the **second floor** is displayed in chronological sequence: Moorish ceramics (the basis of the craft in Spain), green and black porcelain, and later pieces from Málaga, Murcia and Manises. Christian ceramics of the 13C and 14C evidence continuity from the Moorish. Outstanding examples include green and manganese ceramics from **Paterna** (*6km/3.8mi N of Valencia*), the latter showing brown streaks. The golden age of ceramics in **Manises** (*8km/5mi N of Valencia*) in the 15C is represented by lovely pieces, along with a Virgin and

Detail, façade of the Palacio del Marqués de Dos Aguas

Child of the same period and a 16C Majolica vase from a Florentine workshop.

In the room housing 16 and 17C pieces, one can see how Valencian lustreware technique spread to Cataluña and Aragon. The influence of silversmithing in Italian reliefs and polychromes is evident. Also on display are Chinese porcelain and European imitations. There is an impressive urn from Toledo (15C-16C).

By the 18C, Italian, French and Chinese porcelana came into fashion. Also shown are items from Manises and Talavera. The **Real Fábrica de Alcora**, established in 1727, became the centre of innovation in Spain, spreading the Louis XIV, Classic and Baroque styles. Pieces from 19C **Manises** evidence later styles that spread through southern and eastern Spain. There is also a Valencian kitchen with 18C and 19C tilework. New forms arose in the 20C as ceramics went beyond their traditional function, in the work of Blat, Picasso, Cumella and Colmeiro.

Back on the ground floor are additional palatial rooms, including a bedroom with polychrome stucco work, the porcelain room with pieces from Dresden, and the ballroom, largest in the palace.

Colegio del Patriarca o del Corpus Christi★ (Patriarch or Corpus Christi College)

○ Open 11am-1.30pm. ○ Closed Good Fri. ⊗1.20€. ☎ 96 351 41 76.

This former seminary, founded by the Blessed Juan de Ribera, Archbishop of Valencia and Patriarch of Antioch, dates back to the 16C. The **church** is one of the few examples of Renaissance churches in Spain with frescoes painted on the walls; the lower sections are covered with tiles from Manises. In the Capilla de la Purísima hang four 15C Flemish tapestries.

The patio, which is architecturally harmonious and decorated with Talavera *azulejo* friezes, has, at the centre, a statue of the founder by the modern sculptor Benlliure. The small **museum** has an interesting collection of 15C-17C works and includes paintings by Juan de Juanes, a precious **triptych of the Passion**★ by Dirk Bouts, an admirable 14C Byzantine crucifix from the Monasteriy of Athos, a 13C Romanesque *Christ*, a portrait (on pasteboard) of the founder, Ribera, by Ribalta, and other paintings by Ribalta, Morales and El Greco (one of the many versions of the *Adoration of the Shepherds).*

In the same plaza is the **Universidad** (University), its buildings grouped round a vast Ionic quadrangle.

Museo de Bellas Artes San Pío V★

◷ *Open 10am-8pm.* ◷ *Closed Mon, 1 Jan, Good Fri and 25 Dec.* ☞ *No charge.* ☎ *96 360 57 93.*

This Fine Arts museum near the Jardines del Real (Royal Gardens) is especially interesting for its **collection of Valencian Primitives**★★ and other works by major Spanish artists. Countless altarpieces prove the vitality of the Valencia School of the 15C. Among the many artists are Jacomart, Reixac and the Osonas, Elder and Younger. Some of the retables are by less well-known artists such as Gonzalo Pérez, the author of the Flemish-influenced altarpiece of San Martín, or by anonymous artists like that of Fray Bonifacio Ferrer. The triptych of the *Passion* by Hieronymus Bosch is an extraordinarily expressive work; the central panel is a copy of *Los Improperios* – the Mocking of Christ – in El Escorial.

Representing the Renaissance are Macip, Juan de Juanes, Yáñez de la Almedina and Fernando de Llanos whose use of colour recalls that of Leonardo da Vinci. Tenebrism (term applied to paintings in dark tones) made its first appearance in Spain at the beginning of the 17C in the works of Ribalta and came to full fruition in those of Ribera *(St Sebastian).* Spain's Golden Age is also represented with works by El Greco, Morales and Velázquez. Goya's mastery of portrait is also evident in his pictorial portrayal of *Francisco Bayeu.*

Valencian art from the 19C and 20C is comprehensively covered with works by Joaquín Sorolla, Pinazo and Muñoz Degrain. Various sculptures by Mariano Benlliure are also exhibited throughout the museum.

Jardines del Real (Royal Gardens)

The city's biggest park is close to the pleasant **Jardín de Monforte**. The **Puente del Real** (Royal Bridge), which crosses the **Jardín del río Turia**, is 16C.

Instituto Valenciano de Arte Moderno (IVAM)

Centro Julio González: ◷ *Open 10-8pm (10pmJun-Sep).* ◷ *Closed Mon, 1 Jan, Good Fri and 25 Dec.* ☞ *2€. No charge Sun.* ☎ *96 386 30 00.*

This modern building houses a permanent collection of more than 7 000 works of contemporary art, which are on rotating display *(Galleries 3 and 4, upper level)*. It also owns the largest collection of the works of **Julio González** (1876-1942), one of the major sculptors of the 20C *(Gallery 2, lower level)*. There is also a permanent collection of the paintings of **Ignacio Pinazo** (1849-1916) *(Gallery 5, upper level)* , a notable artist of the 19-20C transition from the academic tradition to more modern styles.

Centro de la Beneficencia

This former Augustinian convent was converted into a welfare centre in 1840. Today, it is a cultural complex comprising the Museo de Prehistoria, Museu d'Etnologia and Sala Parpalló, a room used to host temporary exhibitions.

Museo de Prehistoria

◷ *Open 10am-8pm (9pm Apr-Sep).* ◷ *Closed Mon, 1 Jan, 1 May and 25 Dec.* ☎ *96 388 35 65.*

An attractive presentation of the most important archaeological discoveries found in the region from the Palaeolithic to Roman periods. Exhibits include reproductions of Parpalló cave paintings, a collection of Neolithic ceramics and rooms devoted to Iberian art.

Museu d'Etnologia

◷ *Open 10am-8pm (9pm Apr-Sep).* ◷ *Closed Mon, 1 Jan, 1 May and 25 Dec.* ☎ *96 388 35 65.*

This ethnographic museum is dedicated to increasing the awareness of Valencian culture.

Jardín Botánico

○ *Open 10am-6pm (9pm Apr-Sep).* ○ *Closed Mon.* ⊜ *0.50€.* ☎ *96 315 68 18.*

Valencia was one of the first cities to adopt the 16C Italian trend of creating gardens for botanical study. The present garden dates from 1802 and is still used for research purposes.

Museo del Siglo XIX (Museum of the 19 C)

○ *Open 10am-8pm.* ⊜*No charge.* ☎*96 360 57 93.*

Temporary expositions are held in this old Carmelite convent, a mix of Gothic, Renaissance and Classical styles.

Convento de Santo Domingo

The monastery's Classical style entrance, with statue niches for saints, was designed by Philip II (1527-98).

⟩ Museo Valenciano de la Ilustración y la Modernidad (Museum of Illustration and Modernism)

Located in the Modernist Estación del Norte, with attractive display. (⬝⬝ *Guided tours by appointment.* ☎*96 388 37 30.*)

○ *Open 10am-2pm and 4-8pm; Sun and public hols, 10am-2pm.* ☎ *96 388 37 30.*

Excursion

Puig

18km/11mi N on the V 21. ⬝⬝ *Guided tours (1hr) 10 and 11 am, noon, and 4 and 6 pm.* ○ *Closed Mon, afternoons Sun and public hols and in Jan,* ⊜ *1.80€.* ☎ *96 147 02 00.*

The **Monasterio de la Virgen del Puig,** occupied by the Order of Mercy, overlooks the village. The monastery's foundation in the 13C was prompted by the discovery, in 1237, of a 6C Byzantine style marble low relief of the Virgin which had lain hidden in the earth beneath a bell since the barbarian invasion. James the Conqueror chose the Virgin as patron of the Kingdom of Valencia and ordered the building of a convent in her honour.

In the church, the Gothic vaulting is no longer hidden by its 18C stucco overlay. The Byzantine Virgin can be seen at the high altar. The present monastery was built between the 16C and 18C; paintings from the Valencia School are displayed in the upper 18C cloisters.

Valladolid★

POPULATION: 345 891

MICHELIN MAP 575 H 15 (TOWN PLAN) – CASTILLA Y LEÓN (VALLADOLID).

The former capital of the court of Castilla and of a large empire stands amid an expansive landscape of vineyards and cereal crops. Today, this important provincial capital still preserves interesting architectural vestiges that bear witness to its rich and illustrious past.

Location

The city is situated at the confluence of the River Pisuerga and River Esgueva, at the centre of the northern section of the Spanish Meseta. ⓘ *Santiago 19 bis, 47001 Valladolid, ☎ 983 34 40 13.*

 Neighbouring sights are described in the following chapters: PALENCIA (47km/29mi NE) and ZAMORA (98km/61mi W).

Background

Historical notes – From the 12C, Castilla's kings frequently resided at Valladolid and the Cortes (Parliament) often assembled there. Peter the Cruel married there in the 14C, as did Ferdinand and Isabel in 1469; it was the birthplace of Philip IV and his sister Anne of Austria, mother of Louis XIV.

The city was also deeply involved in the 16C Comuneros Revolt during the reign of Emperor Charles V (*see SEGOVIA).*

Castillo de Simancas *(11km/7mi SW)* – This castle was converted by Emperor Charles V into a repository for state archives. The collection represents a complete history of Spanish administration from the 15C to the 19C.

Address Book

For coin ranges, see the Legend at the back of the guide.

WHERE TO EAT

 Covadonga – *Zapico 1 –* ☎ *983 33 07 98.* The uninspiring modern appearance of this restaurant is quickly forgotten once inside, where the welcome is friendly, the service excellent and the cuisine wholesome and plentiful. Make sure you try the house speciality of roast suckling lamb *(lechazo).*

 El Figón de Recoletos – *Acera de Recoletos 3 –* ☎ *983 39 60 43 – Closed Sun evening and 20 Jul-10 Aug –* . This typically Castilian restaurant with its dark wood decor and sturdy chairs is frequented by businessmen and women, families and tourists alike. The roast peppers *(pimientos asados)*, brisket of lamb *(falda de cordero)* and grilled chops *(chuletitas)* tend to be the most popular choices on the menu here.

WHERE TO STAY

 Hotel El Nogal – *Conde Ansúrez 10 –* ☎ *983 34 03 33 – – 26 rooms – 2.50€ – Restaurant 12.50€.* This small, recently renovated hotel is located within the triangle of the plaza Mayor, cathedral and Museo de Escultura. The international-style rooms here are bright and airy and are reasonably priced given the quality. The hotel restaurant is pleasant with an often lively ambience.

 Hotel Imperial – *Peso 4 –* ☎ *983 33 03 00 – – 79 rooms – 4€ – Restaurant 16/26€.* An authentic Valladolid institution of the Renaissance, set in the 16C Gallo mansion, impeccably maintained while meeting mcontemporary requirements. The green marble lobby is popular for afternoon tea.

SHOPPING

Confiterías Cubero – *Pasión 7 -* ☎ *983 35 60 77.* This shop has not only delicious patries and authentic local sweets, but also a unique *Museo del Dulce* (museum of sweets) where the sights of Valladolid are re-created in sugar.

Manuel Iborra – *Lencería 2 -* ☎ *983 35 11 21.* The best-known shop for *turrón* and homemade ice cream in Valladolid. Outstanding for *tortas imperiales* (imperial cakes) and *sopa de almendras* (almond soup).

FIESTAS

The city's Holy Week processions are renowned for their solemnity and impressive statues and floats.

VALLADOLID			Colegio de Santa Cruz Pl.	CY	40	Pasión	BY	30
			Doctrinos	BY	16	Portillo de Balboa	CX	32
Arco de Ladrillo Pas. del	BZ	2	Duque de la Victoria	BY	17	San Ildefonso	BY	36
Arzobispo Gandásegui	CY	3	España Pl. de	BY	18	San Pablo Pl. de	BX	37
Bailarín Vicente Escudero	CY	5	Fuente Dorada Pl. de	BY	20	Santiago	BY	41
Bajada de la Libertad	BCY	6	Gondomar	CX	21	Santuario	CY	42
Cadenas de San Gregorio	CX	8	Industrias	CY	23	Sanz y Forés	CXY	45
Cánovas del Castillo	BCY	9	Jorge Guillén	BXY	24	Teresa Gil	BY	
Cardenal Mendoza	CY	10	Maldonado	CY	25	Zorrilla Pas. de	BZ	47
Chancillería	CX	13	Marqués del Duero	CXY	26			
Claudio Moyano	BY	14	Miguel Iscar	BY	29			

Casa de Cervantes	BY	R	Patio Herreriano-		Universidad	CY	U
Iglesia de Las Angustias	CY	L	Museo de Arte				
Museo Oriental	BZ	M¹	Contemporáneo				
			Español	BY M²			

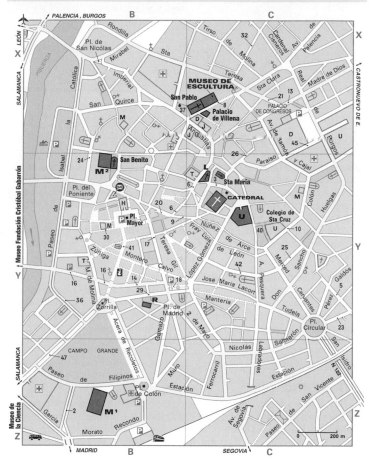

Special Features

THE ISABELLINE STYLE

This style, which emerged in the late 15C, is a mixture of Flamboyant Gothic and Mudéjar tradition, the ultimate stage before Plateresque. The decorative focus on entrances produced rectangular panels which eventually extended from ground level to cornice and were compartmented like an altarpiece.

The most characteristic examples of the style in Valladolid are the Colegio de San Gregorio and the façade of the Iglesia de San Pablo.

Whereas the Salamanca Plateresque fronts, abundantly and delicately decorated with a hint of the Renaissance, are outstanding, those of Valladolid, being earlier, demonstrate a less sophisticated but more vigorous art.

Iglesia de San Pablo – detail of the façade

Colegio de San Gregorio

This building is the most impressive example of the Isabelline style in the city. The **entrance**★★★, attributed to Gil de Siloé and Simon of Cologne, is one of the marvels of Spanish art. The decoration is unbelievably rich; every fantasy from savages to interwoven branches of thorn, is somehow felicitous in its inclusion in the strongly hierarchical composition which focuses first on the doorway and then rises to the magnificent heraldic motif above.

The college is the official home of the **Museo Nacional de Escultura**★★★ (⚷ *closed for refurbishment: the exhibition can be seen at the Palacio de Villena;* ♿ *see description under Worth a Visit*).

Iglesia de San Pablo (St Paul's Church)

The **façade**★★★ is outstanding. The lower section, by Simon of Cologne, consists of a portal with an ogee arch all framed within a segmental arch, and above, a large rose window and two coats of arms supported by angels. The upper façade, from a later date, is a less exuberant composition in the Plateresque style, divided into panels adorned with inset statues and armorial bearings.

Worth a Visit

IN THE CENTRE

The historical centre of Valladolid, where most places of interest are located, is a blend of carefully tended plazas, lively pedestrian ways, bustling commerce, and a pleasant park, the Campo Grande. The Plaza Mayor, where the Ayuntamiento stands (an eclectic building from 1908), is the city's nervous centre. The lovely and spacious columned plaza dates from the 16C.

Museo Nacional de Escultura★★★
(National Museum of Sculpture)

⚷ *The museum is scheduled to be closed for refurbishment until the end of 2005. The collection's temporary home is the nearby Palacio de Villena.* ⏰ *Open 10am-2pm and 4-6pm; (9pm Apr-Sep) Sun and public hols, 10am-2pm.* ⏰ *Closed Mon, 1 and 6 Jan, 1 May, 8 Sep, and 24-25 and 31 Dec.* ⊙ *2.40€, no charge Sat afternoon and Sun.* ☎ *983 25 03 75.*

From the 16C to the 17C Valladolid was one of Spain's major centres for sculpture. This museum is a reflection of this with its wonderful collection of religious statues in polychrome wood, a material which, because both carved and painted, was particularly well suited to the expression of the dramatic.

The Palacio de Villena houses an excellent selection from the museum. On the ground floor, aside from paintings (including an attractive *Pieta* by Pedro Berruguete) are the magnificent sculptures of two 16C Mannerist masters: **Alonso Berruguete** and

Juan de Juni. The former is represented by a remarkable altarpiece designed for the church of San Benito, shown here dismantled, and the latter by *The Crucifixion* and the portentous and impressive ensemble, **Burial of Christ**. Outstanding works by **Gregorio Fernández**, leading 16C exponent of Castillian Baroque, include *Passage to the Sixth Agony* (note the imploring face of the Virgin) and **Christ Recumbent**, a formidable anatomical study of a body exhausted by suffering. There are also works of the Andalucian School (Martínez Montañés, Pedro de Mena, Alonso Cano and others).

Outstanding works on the second floor include those of the two major exponents of the Spanish Renaissance: **Diego Siloé** (*The Holy Family*) and **Felipe Vigarny** (*Virgin and Child*, a model of grace and elegance). There is also an excellent painting by **Rubens** (*Democritus and Heraclitus*).

On the third floor are Late Baroque (18C) works, such as *St Francis of Assisi* by *Salzillo* and *Head of St Paul* by Juan Alonso de Villabrille y Ron. There is also an odd set of bulls from the 18C and early 19C. On the way down, admire the magnificent **Neapolitan nativity** with more than 180 figures.

Capilla del Colegio de San Gregorio★

Designed by Juan Guas, this lovely Gothic chapel with elevated choir contains an altarpiece by Berruguete, a tomb by Felipe Vigarny and carved choir stalls.

Catedral★

▶ *Enter by the Puerta de Santa María in Plaza Universidad.* ⏱ *Open 10am-1.30pm and 4.30-7pm; Sat-Sun and public hols, 10am-1.30pm.* 🕐 *Closed Mon.* ☎ *983 30 43 62.*

The cathedral project, commissioned in about 1580 by Philip II from Herrera, was only realised very slowly and was distorted to some degree by the architect's 17C and 19C successors – as in the octagonal tower, and the upper part of the façade, filled with Baroque ornament by Alberto Churriguera.

Although never completed, the **interior** remains one of Herrera's major successes. The altarpiece (1551) in the central apsidal chapel, where the interplay of perspective and relief makes the figures come to life, is by Juan de Juni.

Museo Diocesano y Catedralicio★

Located in the funerary chapels of the former Gothic cathedral; note the Mudéjar cupolas in the Capilla de San Llorente. There is an interesting **collection★** of sculptures, tombs, paintings, silverware, and ornaments. Note two busts by Pedro de Mena (*Ecce Homo* and *Dolorosa*), two 13C tombs, two Christs of the same century (one Protogothic with four nails), a superbly dramatic *Ecce Homo* by Gregorio Fernández, the sculpture group *Lament for Christ* (c 1500) and a silver monstrance by Juan de Arfe (16C).

Upon leaving the cathedral, note the lovely Baroque façade of the university, with sculptured and heraldic decoration, the work of Narciso and Antonio Tomé.

Colegio de Santa Cruz

This lovely college, dating from the end of the 15C, is one of the first Renaissance buildings in Spain; the finely carved decoration at the entrance, in fact, is still Platateresque but the rusticated stonework is of entirely Classical inspiration. The Neoclassic balconies and windows were part of an 18C reconstruction.

Iglesia de Santa María la Antigua

The only Romanesque features in this otherwise Gothic church, are its tall slender Lombard tower and its portico with triple columns along the north wall.

Iglesia de las Angustias

Facing the Teatro Calderón de la Barca. The church, built by one of Herrera's disciples, contains in its south transept Juan de Juni's masterpiece, the **Virgen de los Siete Cuchillos★** (Virgin of the Seven Knives).

Patio Herreriano - Museo de Arte Contemporáneo Español (Museum of Contemporary Spanish Art)

Entry by calle Jorge Guillén. 🕐 *Open 11am-8pm* 🕐 *Closed Mon (except public hols) 1 Jan and 25 Dec.* 🎟 *6€.* ☎ *983 36 29 08.*

The lovely **Herreran patio★** of the former monastery of San Benito and a newer annex house this museum, which has an interesting permanent collection of contemporary Spanish art (since 1917). There are also temporary exhibitions.

Iglesia de San Benito (St Benedict's Church)

Enter from calle San Benito. The 15C church of the former monastery has a massive porch that lends a fortress-like air. The interior is Gothic with three aisles and a large grille.

Museo Oriental

🕐 *Open 4-7pm; Sun and public hols, 10am-2pm.* 🆓 *3€.* ☎ *983 30 68 00.*

The museum, located in a neo-Classical college (18C) designed by Ventura Rodríguez, houses a collection of **Chinese art**★ (bronze, porcelain, lacquerware, coins and silk embroidery) and Philippine art with important **ivory pieces**★.

Casa de Cervantes

Enter from calle Rastro 🕐 *Open 9.30am-3.30pm; Sun and public hols, 10am-3pm.* 🕐 *Closed Mon, 1 and 6 Jan, 1 and 13 May, 8 Sep and 24-25 and 31 Dec.* 🆓 *2.40€, no charge Sun.* ☎ *983 30 88 10.*

The author of *Don Quixote* lived in this house from 1603 to 1606. It looks much as it did at that time with whitewashed walls and some of the writer's own simple furnishings.

BEYOND THE CENTRE

Museo Fundación Cristóbal Gabarrón

Calle Rastrojo at the corner of Barbecho, 20 min on foot from Plaza Mayor or by bus 3 from Plaza Mayor. 🕐 *Open 11am-2pm and 5-8pm; Sat-Sun 11am-2pm.* 🕐 *Closed Mon and public hols.* 🆓 *6€.* ☎ *983 36 24 90.*

This singular museum, the creation of artist Cristóbal Gabarrón, groups several small collections from the Pillars of History (Egypt, Etruria and Roma), Prehispanic cultures, black Africa, religious art, 16-19C painting, Picasso as a ceramist, world graphics and Gabarrón himself.

Museo de la Ciencia (Science Museum)

🧒 🕐 *Open 10am-7pm; summer 11am-9pm.* 🆓 *9€.* 🕐 *Closed Mon, 1 Jan and 25 Dec.* ☎ *983 14 43 00.*

An interactive science museum, with a room just for kids from 3 to 9. It also includes a modern planetarium.

Excursions

Peñafiel★

55km/34mi E along the N 122. Peñafiel was one of the strong points in the fortified line built along the Duero during the Reconquest.

Castillo★

The village of Peñafiel is dominated by its redoubtable 14C castle, built to massive proportions at the meeting point of three valleys. The fortress consists of two concentric oblong perimeters built along the ridge. Crowning it, within the second, fairly well preserved perimeter, is an imposing keep, reinforced at its summit by machicolated turrets.

Nowadays, the castle is home to the **Museo Provincial del Vino de Valladolid**, providing a fascinating insight into the local wine industry. 🕐 *Open 11.30am-2.30pm and 4.30-7.30pm (8.30pm in summer).* 🆓 *5€ (castle and museum).* ☎ *983 88 11 99.*

Iglesia de San Pablo

The church (1324) has a Mudéjar east end and inside, Renaissance vaulting over the 16C Capilla del Infante (Infante Chapel).

Plaza del Coso

The vast, typically Castilian square is almost completely ringed by houses with wide balconies which serve as galleries for viewing bullfights held below.

Tordesillas

30km/19mi SW along the A 62. It was here, in this historic town, massed upon the steep bank of the Duero in 1494, that the kings of Spain and Portugal signed the famous **Treaty of Tordesillas** dividing the New World between them. All lands west of a line of longitude 370 leagues west of Cape Verde were to be Spanish, all to the east, Portuguese – a decision which gave Spain all Latin America except Brazil.

Juana the Mad locked herself away here on the death of her husband Philip the Fair in 1506. On her own death 46 years later, she was buried in the Convento de Santa Clara. Her body was later removed to Granada.

Convento de Santa Clara★

Guided tours (1hr), 10.30am-1.15pm and 4-5.45pm; Apr-Sep, 10.30am-1.30pm and 4-6.30pm; Sun and public hols, 10.30am-1.30pm and 3.30-5.30pm. ◐ Closed Mon, 1 and 6 Jan, Maundy Thu (afternoon), Good Fri, 1 May, Corpus Christi, 2 local holidays in Sep (dates vary), and 24, 25 and 31 Dec. ⌾ 3.60€, no charge Wed for citizens of the European Union. ☎ 983 77 00 71.

The old palace, built by Alfonso XI in 1350 in commemoration of his victory at the Battle of Salado, was converted into a convent by his son, Peter the Cruel, who installed María de Padilla here, to whom he may have secretly been married even though Blanche de Bourbon was his queen. For María, who in this distant heart of Castilla was homesick for the beauty of Sevilla, he commissioned Mudéjar decoration.

The **patio**★, with multifoil and horseshoe-shaped arches, has strapwork decoration and multicoloured ceramic tiles. The **Capilla Dorada** (Gilded Chapel) with a fine Mudéjar cupola, exhibits mementoes and works of art including Juana's organ, Charles V's virginal, Philip II's clavichord and a 13C altarfront.

The **church** is on the site of the former throne room; the choir has a particularly intricate **artesonado ceiling**★★. In the Flamboyant Gothic **Capilla de los Saldaña** (Saldaña Chapel) are the founders' tombs and a 15C retable, originally a travelling altar.

Medina del Campo

54km/34mi SW along the A 62 and the A 6; 24km/15mi from Tordesillas. In the Middle Ages the town was an important commercial centre famous for its fairs. Today, a large market is held here on Sundays. Isabel the Catholic died in the town in 1504.

Castillo de la Mota★

This impressive 13C-15C castle on a hill overlooking the town has retained its imposing appearance. Juana the Mad often stayed here and Cesare Borgia was imprisoned in the keep for two years.

Villa de Almenara-Puras: Museo de las Villas Romanas (Museum of Roman Villas)

51 km/31.8mi S by the N 601. Turn at Almenara and continue 3km/1.9mi S. ◐ Open 10.30am-2pm and 4-6pm (4.30-8pm in summer). ◐ Closed Mon and 24-25 and 31 Dec. ⌾ 3€. ☎ 983 62 60 36.

This attractive museum uses audiovisual methods, dioramas and models to bring the world of the Romans, and especially life in their rural villas, into the present. Continue to the remains of a sumptuous villa of the 4C and the underlying 3C structure which retains numerous mosaics.

Medina de Rioseco

40km/25mi NW along the N 601. Medina de Rioseco is the agricultural centre of the Tierra de Campos, the granary of Castilla. The picturesque narrow main street, or **Rúa,** is lined by porticoes supported by wooden pillars.

In the 16C, the town benefited from the work of Castilian sculptors, mainly from the Valladolid School, such as Juan de Juni, Del Corral and Jordán, who have left their mark in its churches.

Iglesia de Santa María

◐ *Open 11am-2pm and 4-7pm; in summer, 11am-2pm and 5-8pm. ◐ Closed Mon, 1 and 6 Jan and 25 Dec. ⌾ 1.80€ (includes Iglesia de Santiago). ☎ 983 72 50 26.*

The 15C-16C church's central altarpiece was carved by Esteban Jordán. The **Capilla de los Benavente**★ (Benavente Chapel, 16C), to the left of the high altar, contains a 16C retable by Juan de Juni. The decoration on its walls and cupola by Jerónimo del Corral illustrates scenes from the Last Judgement and the Garden of Eden. The treasury contains ivories and gold- and silverwork including a 16C monstrance by Antonio Arfe.

Iglesia de Santiago

◐ *Open 11am-2pm and 4-7pm; in winter, 11am-2pm and 5-8pm. ◐ Closed Mon, 1 and 6 Jan and 25 Dec. ⌾ 1.80€ (includes Iglesia de Santa María). ☎ 983 70 03 27.*

The altarpieces in the three apsidal chapels of this 16C-17C church form a spectacular Churrigueresque group.

Vic★★

POPULATION: 29 113

MICHELIN MAP 574 G 36 – CATALUNYA (BARCELONA).

This important commercial centre and thriving industrial town (leather goods, food processing and textiles) was formerly occupied by the Romans, who named it Ausa. Vic is embellished with several monumental buildings which are testament to its historical significance.

Location

Vic is situated at the centre of the Vic Plain, at the crossroads of the River Gurri and River Mèder, and at the intersection of the C 17, C 25 and C 25D roads. The town is an excellent base from which to explore cities such as Barcelona and Girona, as well as the stunning scenery of the Pyrenees. ▯ *Ciutat 4, 08500 Vic, ☎ 93 886 20 91.*

 Neighbouring sights are described in the following chapters: BARCELONA (66km/41mi S), GIRONA/GERONA (79km/49mi NE) and PIRINEOS CATALANES.

Worth a Visit

OLD QUARTER★

Vic's historical district is demarcated by a series of wide avenues (ramblas) that follow the route of the old walls, of which a few remnants remain (rambla del Bisbat).

Museu Episcopal★★★

 Open 10am-7pm; Oct-Mar, 10am-1pm and 4-7pm; Sun and public hols, 10am-2pm. Last admission 30 min before closing. Closed Mon, 1 and 6 Jan, Easter Sun and 25-26 Dec. 4€, no charge first Thu of every month. ☎ 93 886 93 60.

This magnificent museum, founded in 1891, displays a rich collection of Romanesque and Gothic works, along with valuable fabrics and costumes. Sections are also devoted to archaeology, leather, jewelry, ironwork, and ceramics, among others. The current museum building opened in 2002.

Romanesque statue of the Virgin, Museo Episcopal

Sala del románico★★★ (Romanesque Gallery)

Among the works on exhibit are the *Descent of Erill la Vall*, a sculptural ensemble of five figures, the painting *Canopy of Ribes de Freser*, and an outstanding group of **altar fronts**. The *Lluça Altar* marks the transition to the Gothic style. There are also murals from the apse of Santa María de El Brull and de Sant Sadurní d'Osomort and wood sculptures of the Virgin and Christ.

Salas del gótico★★★ (Gothic Galleries)

The Gothic reached Cataluña around 1275 and lasted until the 15C. From the early period, there is a magnificent marble altarpiece by **Bernat Saulet** ; a set of Virgins with Child, notably the *Virgin of Boixadors* ; the fine altar front of Bellver de Cerdanya and parts of an altarpiece by **Pere Serra**.

The 15C saw the introduction of the international Gothic style. The collection of altarpieces from this period is impressive. Notable pieces include the **Santa Clara** and *Sant Antoni i Santa Margarida* altars, both by Borrasà, the *de Guimerà* altar, the work of Ramón de Mur, and the *Verdú* altarpiece of Jaume Ferrer II.

The paintings of *Jaume Huguet* mark the start of the transition to the Renaissance.

Tejido e indumentaria★★ – (Textiles and Costumes)

A magnificent display of 13C-18C textiles and, above all, of liturgical wear (14-19C).

Catedral★

🕐 *Open 10am-1pm and 4-7pm. No visits during religious services.* 🕐 *Closed Mon.* 🎫 *2€.* ☎ *93 886 44 49.*

> **Local Specialities**
>
> Vic is the centre of the Llonganissa quality label, producing delicious sausages and meat products such as *salchichones* (salami-type sausages), *butifarras* (Catalan sausages) and *fuets*.

The elegant Romanesque belfry and the crypt, both built in the 11C, are all that remain of the present church's forerunners.

The cathedral was built in the neo-Classical style between 1781 and 1803. In 1930 the famous Catalan artist **José María Sert** decorated the **interior**★ with wall paintings which were lost when the church was burned during the Civil War. Sert took up his brushes again in 1939, and by 1945, when he died, the walls were once more covered with vast murals.

The **paintings**★★ have an intensity, a power reminiscent of Michelangelo, and also a profound symbolism. They evoke the mystery of the Redemption *(chancel)* from the time of Adam's original sin *(transept)* to the Passion *(apse)*, the Evangelists and the Martyrs *(nave)*. Three scenes on the back of the west door illustrate the triumph of human injustice in the Life of Christ and in the history of Catalunya: Jesus chasing the moneylenders from the temple *(right)*; Jesus condemned *(in the centre)* and the road to Calvary *(left)*. The monochrome golds and browns in the murals lend the effect of a relief, and deepen the emotion of the work.

The former high altar **retable**★★, at the end of the ambulatory, is a 15C alabaster work. Its 12 panels, divided by statues of the saints and by mouldings, are devoted to the glorification of Christ, the Virgin and St Peter. Opposite, lies the canon who commissioned the retable in a Gothic tomb by the same sculptor.

Claustro★ (Cloister)

Wide, tracery-filled 14C arches surround the small close in which stands the monumental tomb of the philosopher, **Jaime Balmes** (1810-48), native of Vic. In a cloister gallery one can see the tomb of the painter JM Sert, surmounted by his last and unfinished work, a *Crucifixion*, intended by the artist to replace the one in the cathedral.

Palau Episcopal

The episcopal palace was initially built in the 12C but has been subject to significant modification over the centuries. The **Sala dels Sínodes**, decorated in 1845, and the patio are the main features of note.

Plaça Major★

The pretty façades with Modernist, Gothic and Baroque details, add a touch of class to this great arcaded square where the many shops and café terraces attract a lively crowd. A popular market is held in the square every Saturday.

▷ Ayuntamiento (Gothic and Baroque town hall); Templo Romano (Roman Temple, 2C); Museo del Arte de la Piel (Museum of Leatherwork).

Excursions

Monasterio de Sant Pere de Casserres★

🕐 *Open 10am-1.30pm and 3.30-5pm (6pm Mar-Jun and Sep-Oct; 7 pm Jul-Aug). Last admission 30 min before closing.* 🕐 *Closed Mon, 15 Jan-14 Feb, 1 Jan and 25-26 and 31 Dec.* 🎫 *4€.* ☎ *93 744 71 18.*

▶ *17/11.6mi NE. Travel NE from Vic and take the C 153, then turn right immediately toward Tavernoles and Parador. At Parador take a paved lane to the left (3.5km/2.2mi).*

Just before Parador, stop along the right of the road to enjoy a fine **view**★★ of the marsh of Sau, framed by high banks.

The small Romaneque montastery of Sant Pere de Casseres enjoys a privileged **location**★★ at the end of a long and narrow peninsula in the Sau marsh.

Monasterio de Santa Maria de L'Estany★

🕐 *Open 10am-1pm and 4-7pm (6.30pm in winter).* 🎫 *1.20€.* ☎ *93 830 31 39.*

▶ *24km/15mi SW. Leave Vic along the C 25 towards Manresa. Turn right at exit 164 and follow the BP 4313.*

The small village of **L'Estany**★ grew up around this medieval Augustinian monastery. Still in existence are the 12C Romanesque church, whose bell tower was rebuilt in the 15C, and the beautiful **cloisters**★ whose arcades are supported by matching columns and decorated with 72 remarkable **capitals**★★. The north gallery is Romanesque and narrative in style; the west, decorative with palm fronds and gaunt griffons; the south, geometrical and interlaced although the sophisticated execution and heraldic positions of the animals indicate a later date; the east features wedding scenes and musicians.

EXCURSIONS THROUGH THE SIERRA DE MONTSENY★

The Sierra de Montseny, a mighty range of Pyrenean foothills in the heart of Catalunya, is a vast granite dome covered in beeches and cork oaks and crossed by numerous creeks. To the southeast lies the **Parque Natural de Montseny,** covering a total area of 17 372ha/42 600 acres; its highest peaks are Matagalls (1 695m/5 560ft) and **Turó de l'Home** (1 707m/5 601ft).

From Vic to Sant Celoni via the northern road

▶ *60km/37.5mi. Leave Vic to the S and turn left after 6km/3.6mi along the B 520.*

The road goes through pine and beechwoods and the delightful village of **Viladrau** before beginning a gradual descent with mountain views off to the right. The view opens out onto the steep Montseny slopes as the road (*GI 552*) continues its hillside descent. After the attractively sited **Arbúcies**, it runs beside the river for a distance before turning off for **Breda**, dominated by the **monasterio de Sant Salvador**★ and its Romanesque tower, and Sant Celoni.

From Sant Celoni to la ermita de Sant Marçal★★

Beyond Campins, the road rises in hairpin bends, affording **views** of the coastal plain; it continues in a magnificent **corniche** (2km/1mi) to the lake *(embalse)* of Santa Fè (alt 1 130m/3 707ft). The road then climbs up (7km/4mi) to the Ermita de Sant Marçal (alt 1 260m/4 134ft), a hermitage perched on the side of the lofty Matagalls ridge.

From Sant Celoni to Tona via Montseny★

43km/27mi. There are good views of the sierra from the **route** across the plain irrigated by the Tordera. Beyond Montseny, the road rises, reaching a wild area, before descending to Tona past the Romanesque church in **El Brull** and the tower of **Santa Maria de Seva.**

Vitoria-Gasteiz★

POPULATION: 209 704

MICHELIN MAP 573 D 21-22 (TOWN PLAN) – PAÍS VASCO (ÁLAVA).

Vitoria-Gasteiz is the capital of the largest Basque province and the seat of the Basque government. The city was founded in the 12C, when it was surrounded by defensive walls. Nowadays, it is a pleasant, elegant city which has preserved an attractive old quarter in its upper section.

Location

The city sits at an altitude of 524m/1 718ft at the centre of the Llanada Alavesa, a vast cereal-covered plateau far closer in appearance to the plains of Castilla than the green hills of the Basque country. ▯ *Plaza del General Loma, 01005 Álava, ☎ 945 16 15 98.*

⌖ *Neighbouring sights are described in the following chapters: BILBAO (64km/40mi N), PAMPLONA (93km/58mi E) and La RIOJA.*

Walking About

CIUDAD VIEJA★★ (OLD TOWN) ⏱ *1hr 30min*

Seigniorial houses with balconies and fronts bearing family coats of arms stand in concentric streets – each named after a trade – around the cathedral. The liveliest streets, full of charming shops and bars, are those to the left of the plaza de la Virgen Blanca. The **Iglesia de San Pedro**, with its interesting Gothic façade, can also be found in this part of the old town.

Plaza de la Virgen Blanca

The square is the most characteristic feature of Vitoria-Gasteiz and its historic centre. It is dominated by the Iglesia de San Miguel (St Michael's Church) and is surrounded by house fronts with glassed-in balconies, or *miradores*, framing the massive monument at the square's centre which commemorates Wellington's decisive victory at the Battle of Vitoria on 21 June 1813, after which King Joseph and 55 000 of his men fled north of the Pyrenees. It acts as a link between the old and new towns and communicates with the nobly ordered 18C **plaza de España** also known as plaza Nueva.

The square's attractive 18C and 19C buildings are fronted by several attractive cafés (Café Marañón, Café Vitoria).

Iglesia de San Miguel

A jasper niche in the church porch exterior contains the polychrome statue in Late Gothic style of the Virgen Blanca, patron of the city. The church is entered through a late-14C portal. Its tympanum illustrates the Life of St Michael. Also worthy of note inside are the chancel altarpiece by Gregorio Fernández and, to its right, a Plateresque sepulchral arch.

Plaza del Machete

This small, elongated square lies at the back of the **Arquillos**, a tall arcade which links the upper and lower towns. A niche in the east end of San Miguel church contains the *machete* or cutlass, on which the procurator general had to swear to uphold the town's privileges *(fueros)*. The 16C **Palacio de Villa Suso,** on its right-hand side, has been converted into a meeting centre.

▶ *Climb the steps adjoining the palace.*

A stroll along the **calle Fray Zacarías Martínez,** with its old wood-framed houses and former palaces, is particularly pleasant. The Renaissance north doorway of the Palacio de los Escoriaza-Esquivel, built on a section of the former town walls, is worthy of special note; if you find it open, enter to view the lovely covered courtyard.

VITORIA-GASTEIZ		España Pl. de	BZ 18	Pascual de Andagoya	
		Gasteiz Av. de	AYZ	Pl. de	AY 39
		Herrería	AY 24	Portal del Rey	BZ 42
Angulema	BZ 2	Independencia	BZ 27	Postas	BZ
Becerro de Bengoa	AZ 5	Machete Pl. del	BZ 30	Prado	AZ 45
Cadena y Eleta	AZ 8	Madre Vedruna	AZ 33	San Francisco	BZ 48
Dato	BZ	Nueva Fuera	BY 34	Santa María Cantón de	BY 51
Diputación	AZ 12	Ortiz de Zárate	BZ 36	Virgen Blanca Pl. de la	BZ 55
Escuelas	BY 15				

Casa del Portalón	BY L	Museo "Fournier" de		Museo de Arqueología	BY M¹
Catedral Nueva	AZN	Naipes de Álava	BY M⁴	Museo de Bellas Artes	AZM²

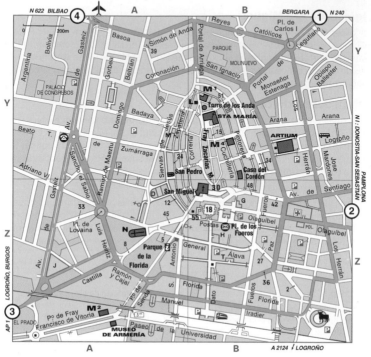

Catedral de Santa María

☞ *Closed for restoration.* ☞ *Open for guided tours.*

The construction of the Gothic church-fortress, part of the city's first defensive ring, began at the end of the 13C, though most of the work was achieved in the 14C. It remains open to guided tours (& see Worth a Visit) while extensive restoration work is under way.

Beyond the cathedral, the wood and brick **Casa Godeo-Guevara-San Juan**, a house rebuilt in the 16C, is home to a small archaeological museum (& *see description under Worth a Visit*). The **Casa del Portalón,** opposite, is a typical late 15C-early 16C shop which is now occupied by a well-known local restaurant. The **Torre de los Anda,** the lower part of which was built as part of the town's medieval defences, forms a triangle with the two houses.

In calle Cuchillería, the **Palacio de Bendaña,** a building noted for its corner turret and plain doorway with *alfiz* surround, is home to a museum devoted to playing cards (& *see description under Worth a Visit*). Inside, a part of the delightful **Renaissance patio** has been preserved.

The **Casa del Cordón**, a 16C house at nº24 in the same street, is used for temporary exhibitions.

CIUDAD NUEVA (MODERN TOWN)

As Vitoria-Gasteiz grew in the 18C, neo-Classical constructions began to appear such as the **Arquillos** arcade (& *see above*) and **plaza de España.** In the 19C, the town expanded southwards with the **Parque de la Florida** (Florida Park) – near to which the **Catedral Nueva** (New Cathedral) was built in 1907 in neo-Gothic style – and two wide avenues: the paseo de la Senda and the paseo de Fray Francisco. The latter was built up in the late 19C to early 20C and is lined with mansions and large town houses, such as the Palacio de Ajuria Enea, now the seat of the Lehendakari, or Basque government, and two museums, the Museo de la Armería and the Museo de Bellas Artes.

Close by the Plaza de España is the modern Plaza de los Fueros, the work of architect José Luis Peña Ganchegui and sculptor Eduardo Chillida.

Worth a Visit

Restoration Work at Catedral de Santa María★★
🕐 *Open 11am-2pm and 5-8pm.* ☎ *945 25 51 35.*

Due to its location, this Gothic cathedral has experienced serious subsidence problems, and there has been a centuries-long struggle to keep it from falling down. An ambitious program to realign its walls was started in 2000 and will run at least to 2010. A visit affords the opportunity to witness the enormous task of the restoration of a monument of incalculable historic and artistic value, and to track its progress. An innovative hard-hat tour takes visitors along metal walkways and through construction passages to discover the secrets of this temple fortress and along with it, to understand the evolution of the historic centre of the city.

Museo "Fournier" de Naipes de Álava★
🕐 *Open 10am-2pm and 4-6.30pm; Sat, 10am (11am Sun and public hols) to 2pm.* 🕐 *Closed Mon, 1 Jun, Good Fri and 25 Dec* ⊚ *No charge.* ☎ *945 18 19 18.*

The famous playing card factory of Heraclio Fournier was established in Vitoria-Gasteiz in 1868. The grandson of the founder, Félix Alfaro Fournier, has assembled a valuable collection of playing cards which was acquired by the Town Council of Álava in 1986. The present collection, from all over the world, numbers over 15 000 packs, dating from the late 14C to the present day illustrating history (wars, battles, revolutions), geography, politics (caricatures of personalities) and local customs (traditional dress and pastimes). There is also a display of a variety of materials (paper, parchment, cloth, metal etc) demonstrating printing and engraving techniques.

Artium★
🕐 *Open 11am-8pm; Sat-Sun and public hols 10.30am-8pm.* 🕐 *Closed Mon exc public hols, 1 Jan and 25 Dec.* ⊚ *3.50€.* ☎ *945 18 19 25.*

This important museum and cultural centre, opened in 2002, aims to make modern art accessible by focusing on its foundations and by mounting temporary exhibitions.

A significant selction from its **magnificent collection**★ is shown on a rotating basis (changing twice a year). The museum owns more than 1 800 works of Spanish artists, ranging from the Avant Garde of the twenties and thirties (the greater part of the collection) to the most recent. Names are of the stature of Miró, Gargallo, Tàpies, Canogar, Palazuelo, Oteiza and Chillida as well as others who have earned recognition more recently (Barceló, Iglesias, Urzay, Badiola, Sicilia and Broto).

Museo de Armería★ (Museum of Arms and Armour)
🕐 *Open 10am-2pm and 4-6.30pm; Sat, 10am (11am Sun and public hols) to 2pm.* 🕐 *Closed Mon, Good Fri and 25 Dec.* ⊚ *No charge.* ☎ *945 18 19 20.*

The well-presented collection housed in a modern building traces the tradition and evolution of weaponry in the Basque country from prehistoric axes to early-20C pistols. Note the 15C-17C **armour**, including suits of 17C **Japanese armour,** and various exhibits from the Battle of Vitoria and the Peninsular War.

Museo Fournier de Naipes de Álava

A Spanish playing card dating from 1570

Address Book

For coin ranges, see the Legend at the back of the book.

WHERE TO EAT

⊖⊜ **La Peseta** – *Plaza San Bartolomé 3 – Astorga – ☎ 987 61 72 75 – Closed Sun evening and 15-31 Oct –* ▤. This popular, family-run restaurant has a simple, somewhat antiquated dining room, where the cuisine is traditional and reasonably priced. The *cocido maragato* (a stew of assorted animal parts) is popular. There are also 19 modest guest rooms.

⊖⊜⊜ **Mesón del Peregrino** – *Irunbidea 10 – Puente la Reina – 1km/0/6mi NE of Puente la Reina on the Pamplona/Iruña road – ☎ 948 34 00 75 – Closed 23 Dec-15 Jan –* ▤. A charming restaurant housed in a magnificent large stone house with dining rooms overlooking the garden and swimming pool. The tasteful decor is rustic in style, creating the perfect atmosphere in which to enjoy the creative cuisine on offer here. The restaurant also has 13 rooms, with prices in the mid- to high price range.

WHERE TO STAY

⊖ **Hostal Infanta Doña Leonor** – *Condes de Toreno 1 – Villalcázar de Sirga – ☎ 979 88 80 15 –* ▣ *– 9 rooms – ⛭ 3.50€.* If you're hoping for a good night's sleep in a peaceful setting, this modern hostal in the small town of Villalcázar de Sirga is ideal, with its cosy rooms, parquet floors and wooden furniture.

⊖ **Hotel San Martín** – *Plaza San Martín 7 – Frómista – ☎ 979 81 00 00 – Closed Jan –* ▣ *– 12 rooms – ⛭ 3.60€ – Restaurant €7.80.* Despite its simplicity, this hotel on two floors close to the Romanesque church of San Martín has 12 comfortable, well-equipped rooms, all with private bathroom and TV. Much of the cooking in the restaurant is done in the traditional wood-fired oven.

⊖ **Hotel Madrid** – *Avenida de La Puebla 44 – Ponferrada – ☎ 987 41 15 50 – 45 rooms – ⛭ 4.21€ – Restaurant 10€.* A good central location, friendly staff and clean, comfortable rooms are the main features of this well-established hotel, which has been welcoming guests for more than half a century, and whose longevity is reflected in the overall decor.

⊖⊜ **Hotel Real Monasterio San Zoilo** – *Obispo Souto – Carrión de los Condes – ☎ 979 88 00 50 –* ▣ *– 35 rooms – ⛭ 5.50€.* This former Benedictine monastery has dispensed with the austerity of former times and is now a delightful hotel where the welcome is both warm and friendly. The architecture – a mix of brick, stone and wood – is soberly elegant, the rooms extremely comfortable and the prices unbeatable.

⊖⊜ **Pousada de Portomarín** – *Avenida de Sarria – Portomarín – ☎ 982 54 52 00 – hpousadalander.es –* ▣ *– 32 rooms – ⛭ 7.60 €– Restaurant 12.50€.* A peaceful hotel in a modern stone building with fine views of the River Miño. Spacious, comfortable rooms with wood floors and attractive furniture. Some rooms have the added bonus of a terrace. A good restaurant serving traditional cuisine.

Museo Diocesano de Arte Sacro (Diocesan Sacred Art Museum)

🕐 *Open 10am-2pm and 4-6.30pm; Sat, 10am (11am Sun and public hols) to 2pm and 5-8pm.* ⊜ *No charge.* ☎ *945 15 06 31*

Located in the ambulatory of the **Catedral Nueva**, this museum exhibits works belonging to the Diocese of Vitoria and the historical territory of Álava. A visit proceeds from Romanesque works to lovely Gothic images, interesting Flemish works on panels (*Descent from the Cross* by Van der Goes, *The Crucifixion* by Ambrosius Benson), 16C-18C canvases (*St Francis* by El Greco, several Riberas, *The Immaculate Conception* by Alonso Cano) and a good collection of silverware, with pieces from the Romanesque and Gothic eras to the present.

Museo de Bellas Artes (Fine Arts Museum)

🕐 *Open 10am-2pm and 4-6.30pm; Sat, 10am (11am Sun and public hols) to 2pm and 5-8pm.* 🕐 *Closed Mon, 1 Jan, Good Fri and 25 Dec.* ⊜ *No charge.* ☎ *945 18 19 18.*

The museum, housed in the early 20C Historicist Palacio de Agustí, displays Spanish art of the 18 and 19C and a comprehensive selection of Basque *costumbrista* painting by such artists as Iturrino, Regoyos and Zuloaga. The collection witnesses the evolution of the Academic style into Romanticism and, finally, Realism.

Museo de Arqueología (Archaeological Museum)

🕐 *Open 10am-2pm and 4-6.30pm; Sat, 10am (11am Sun and public hols) to 2pm .* 🕐 *Closed Mon, 1 Jan, Good Fri and 25 Dec.* ⊜ *No charge.* ☎ *945 18 19 22.*

This small museum, housed in the Casa Godeo-Guevara-San Juan in a half-timbered and brick house rebuilt in the 16C, displays finds from excavations in Álava province, covering the period from the Palaeolithic to the Middle Ages. Note the dolmen collections and Roman steles and sculptures, including the *Estela del Jinete* (Knight's stele).

Excursions

Santuario de Estíbaliz

10km/6mi E. ▶ *Leave Vitoria-Gasteiz by* ② *on the town plan and then take the A 132. Bear left after about 4km/2.5mi.* ◷ *Open 9.30am-1pm and 4-6.30pm.* ◷ *No visits during religious services.* ☎ *945 29 30 88.*

The shrine, a popular pilgrimage with the Basques, comprises a Late Romanesque sanctuary **(santuario)**. The south front has an attractive wall belfry. Inside, the 12C Romanesque statue of the Virgin has been restored.

TOUR EAST OF VITORIA-GASTEIZ: MEDIEVAL PAINTINGS

25km/16mi. ▶*Leave Vitoria-Gasteiz by* ② *on the town plan and follow the N 1 as far as junction 375.*

Gaceo

⌕ *Ask for the key at house n°10 in Gaceo.* ☎ *945 30 02 37.*

Superb 14C **Gothic frescoes**★★ decorate the chancel of the church **(iglesia)**. The south wall shows Hell in the form of a whale's gullet, the north, the Life of the Virgin with the Crucifixion and Last Judgement at the centre and a Trinity above. On the roof are scenes from the Life of Christ.

Alaiza

▶ *Follow the A 411 for 3km/2mi, turn right, then left after a few metres.* ◷ *Visits by prior arrangement or ask for the key at house n°26 in Alaiza.* ☎ *945 30 10 42 or 945 31 25 35 (Señor López de Aguilar).*

In 1982 obscure **paintings**★ were discovered on the walls and roof of the church **(iglesia)** apse. The paintings, which probably date from the late 14C, consist of a series of strange rough red outlines representing castles, churches, soldiers and many other personages. They remain an enigma.

TOUR WEST OF VITORIA-GASTEIZ

105km/65mi. ▶ *Leave Vitoria-Gasteiz along calle Beato Tomás de Zumárraga, then bear left onto the A 3302.*

Mendoza

In the heart of the village stands the Castillo de Mendoza, a fortress with embrasures, a stout outer wall lacking battlements but flanked by four towers. The castle commands an impressive view of the surrounding plain. This former residence of the Duke of Infantado is now the **Museo de Heráldica Alavesa** (Álava Heraldry Museum) with a collection of the coats of arms of all the nobility of the region. ◷ *Open 10am-2pm and 4-6.30pm; Sat, 11am-3pm; Sun and public hols, 10am-2pm.* ◷ *Closed Mon, 1 Jan and Good Fri.* ⌕ *No charge.* ☎ *945 24 00 30.*

▶ *Head S back towards the N 1 and after 1.5km/1mi bear right onto the A 2622 towards Pobes.*

Salinas de Añana

The salt pans rising in tiers up the hillside in the form of an amphitheatre next to the village produce a most unusual effect – water from several local springs is channelled between the ridges. The **church** contains a Flemish picture of the *Annunciation* with sensitively painted faces. At Easter all the salt makers walk in a procession known traditionally as the *Quema de Judas*.

Tuesta

The **Romanesque church,** dating from the 13C and later modified, has an interesting portal with a pointed arch and a decoration of archivolts and historiated capitals, one of which shows a man hunting a boar *(left)*. Above is the Epiphany. Inside, note the naive wood sculpture of St Sebastian *(north wall of the nave)* and a 14C figure of the Virgin.

▶ *Follow the A 2625 N towards Orduña.*

Once over the **Puerto de Orduña** (Orduña Pass) (900m/2 953ft), a beautiful **panorama**★ opens up of the lush hollow in which Orduña town nestles; in the distance are Amurrio and the Basque mountains (viewpoint). The descent to the plain is down a series of hairpin bends.

▶ *In Orduña, take the A 2621 and return to Vitoria-Gasteiz via Murguía.*

The Way of St James★★

MICHELIN MAPS 571, 573 AND 575 D-E-F 4-26 –

NAVARRA, LA RIOJA, CASTILLA Y LEÓN, GALICIA.

The discovery of the body of the Apostle James in Santiago de Compostela transformed this city into the most important pilgrimage centre in Europe during the Middle Ages. From the 11C onwards, the veneration of relics – a fundamental feature of religious devotion during this period – gave rise to the development of a path that led to this Galician city, where pilgrims could worship the body of the Apostle.

Today, thousands of pilgrims continue to walk the Way of St James, and although for some at least the journey has lost its religious significance, it offers the opportunity to explore the history and culture of this fascinating part of the Iberian Peninsula.

Location

The Way of St James, which runs east to west from the Pyrenees to Santiago de Compostela through the interior of Northern Spain, passes through several autonomous communities. ▪ *www.xacobeo.es; Astorga: Plaza Eduardo de Castro 5, 24700, ☎ 987 61 82 22; Ponferrada: Gil y Carrasco 4, 24400, ☎ 987 42 42 36; Puente de la Reina: Plaza Mena, 31100, ☎ 948 34 08 45.*

Background

The relics of St James (Santiago) discovered early in the 9C soon became the object of a local cult and then of pilgrimage. In the 11C devotion spread abroad until a journey to St James' shrine ranked equally with one to Rome or Jerusalem – the last particularly perilous since the invasion of the Holy Land by the Turks. St James had a particular appeal for the French who felt united with the Spanish in the face of the Moorish threat, but English, Germans, Italians and even Scandinavians made the long pilgrimage. They travelled for the most part through France along the routes organised to a considerable degree, by the Benedictines and Cistercians of Cluny and Cîteaux and the Knights Templars of the Spanish Order of the Red Sword who assured the pilgrims' safety in northern Spain, provided them with funds and flagged the route with cairns. Hospitals and hospices in the care of the Hospitallers received the sick, the weary and the stalwart alike who travelled almost all in the pilgrims' uniform of heavy cape, 8ft/2.4m stave with a gourd attached to carry water, stout sandals and broad-brimmed felt hat, turned up in front and marked with three or four scallop shells. A Pilgrim Guide of 1130, the first tourist guide ever written, probably by Aimeri Picaud, a Poitou monk from Parthenay-le-Vieux, describes the inhabitants, climate and customs of different regions, the most interesting routes, and the sights on the way – the pilgrim in those days was in no hurry and frequently made detours which took weeks or months to complete, to visit a sanctuary or shrine. Churches, therefore, both on and off the way, benefited, as did the associated towns, from the pilgrims who numbered between 500 000 and two million a year.

In 1175, Pope Alexander III recognised the statutes of the Military Order of Santiago, drawn up to ensure the protection of pilgrims.

Of those who "took the cockleshell", the English, Normans and Bretons often came part of the way by boat, embarking from Parson's Quay in the Plymouth estuary, in the case of the English, then disembarking at Soulac and following the French Atlantic coast south through Bordeaux to the Pyrenees, or they landed directly in Spain at La Coruña, on the north coast or in Portugal. Mediterranean pilgrims landed in Catalunya and Valencia and crossed the peninsula. The land routes through France began at Chartres, St-Denis and Paris; joining at Tours, they continued south to Bordeaux, at Vézelay and Autun to go through Limoges and Périgueux, and at Le Puy and Arles. The stopping places along the way formed a main street or calle Mayor around which a village would develop. Farming communities grew into towns and some were settled by foreigners or minority groups (often French or Jewish), who consolidated the recovered territory and brought with them a wealth of culture.

With the passage of time, however, the faith that made people set out on pilgrimages began to diminish; those seeking gain by trickery and robbery, and known as false pilgrims, among whom was the poet Villon, increased; the Wars of Religion, when

Christians fought among themselves, reduced the faithful even more. Finally in 1589, Drake attacked La Coruña and the bishop of Compostela removed the relics from the cathedral to a place of safety. They were lost and for 300 years the pilgrimage was virtually abandoned. In 1879 they were recovered, recognised by the pope and the pilgrimage recommenced. In Holy Years, when the feast day of St James (25 July) falls on a Sunday, there are jubilee indulgences and thousands of pilgrims once more visit the shrine.

Special Features

THE WAY IN SPAIN – MAIN HALTS

The diverse ways through France met at Roncesvalles, Behobia and Somport to cross the Pyrenees and continued through northeastern Spain as two routes only – the Asturian, from Roncesvalles, which until the 15C was considered extremely dangerous because of possible attack by brigands, and a more southerly route from Somport, known as the **Camino Francés**, or French Way, on account of the number of French pilgrims who followed it. It became marked over the centuries by churches and monasteries in which French architectural influence is obvious. The two routes converged at Puente la Reina.

The route from **Roncesvalles** to Puente la Reina was the shorter of the two with only one main stop: **Pamplona**; the longer Somport-Puente la Reina way stopped at **Jaca, Santa Cruz de la Serós, San Juan de la Peña,** the **Monasterio de Leyre** and **Sangüesa** (◑ see index).

Puente la Reina★

The venerable humpbacked bridge which spans the River Arga and gives the town its name, was built in the 11C for the pilgrims on their way to Santiago. Standing at the entrance to the town, on the Pamplona road, is a bronze pilgrim, marking the point at which the two routes converged.

The wide N 111 circles the old town outside whose walls stands the **Iglesia del Crucifijo** (Church of the Crucifix). The porch communicated with the pilgrims' hospice. A second nave was added to the existing 12C main aisle in the 14C and now contains the famous Y-shaped Cross with the profoundly Expressionist **Christ**★ carved in wood and said to have been brought from Germany by a pilgrim in the 14C. (◑ Open 8.30am-8.30pm. ◑ No visits during religious services. ☎ 948 34 00 50).

▶ Leave the church to walk along the narrow but extremely elegant main street, the calle Mayor, fronted by houses of golden brick and carved wood eaves, to the bridge. On the way you will see the **Iglesia de Santiago** (Church of St James) with its **doorway**★ crowded with carvings, now almost effaced. Inside, the nave, remodelled in the 16C, was adorned with altarpieces. Note also the two statues placed facing the entrance: St James the Pilgrim in gilded wood, and St Bartholomew. ◑ Open 9am-1pm and 5-8.30pm. ☎ 948 34 01 32.

Iglesia de Santa María de Eunate★★

5km/3mi E of Puente la Reina. The origin of this delightful, isolated 12C **Romanesque** chapel, so harmonious in proportion and design, remains unknown. The finding of human bones supports the theory of the building having been a funerary chapel on the pilgrim road like that of Torres del Río (◑ see below). The ground plan is octagonal, with a pentagonal apse on the outside of the building and a semicircular one inside. It is likely that the outside gallery encircling the church formerly led to adjoining buildings used to provide shelter for pilgrims.

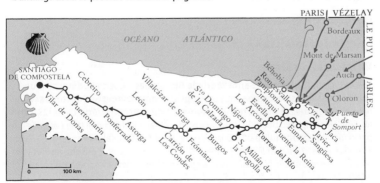

O. Torres/MARCO POLO

Iglesia de Santa María de Eunate

Cirauqui★

The village's steep, winding alleyways are lined by steps and closely crowded by houses, their lower walls whitewashed, with rounded doorways, and their upper fronts adorned with iron balconies and further embellished with coats of arms and carved cornices. At the top of the village *(difficult climb)* stands the **Iglesia de San Román** with a multifoil 13C **portal**★ similar to that of San Pedro de la Rúa in Estella/Lizarra.

Estella★ and Monasterio de Irache★ (ⓒ *See ESTELLA*)

Los Arcos

The **Iglesia de Santa María de los Arcos** (Church of St Mary of the Arches), visible from a distance by its high tower, is Spanish Baroque inside. The effect is overwhelming with stucco, sculpture and painting covering every available space; the transept, with its imitation Córdoba leather decoration, is particularly noteworthy. Above the high altar, pure Baroque in style, rises the 13C polychrome wood statue of the Black Virgin of Santa María de los Arcos. The cloisters with Flamboyant bays illustrate the elegance and lightness of 15C Gothic.

Torres del Río

The **Iglesia del Santo Sepulcro**★ (Church of the Holy Sepulchre) is an unusual Romanesque building, tall in height, octagonal in plan and dating from about 1200. Its resemblance to the chapel in Eunate has given rise to speculation that it is also a funerary chapel. Inside, vertical lines predominate; the magnificent Mudéjar-inspired, star-shaped **cupola** is geometrical perfection. The decoration is sparse, consisting only of minute windows at the points of the star, modillions and historiated capitals. Note also the fine 13C crucifix.

Nájera and Santo Domingo de la Calzada★ (ⓒ *See La RIOJA*)

Burgos★★★ (ⓒ *See BURGOS*)

Iglesia de Frómista★★ (ⓒ *see PALENCIA*)

Villalcázar de Sirga

The vast Gothic **Iglesia de Santa María la Blanca** has a fine carved **portal**★ on its south front and inside, in the south transept, two outstanding Gothic **tombs**★. The recumbent statues of the brother of Alfonso X, who had him murdered in 1271, and his wife Eleanor, have been delicately carved with an eye for detail (the costumes in particular) as has the tomb of the prince showing the funeral procession. ⓒ *Open Mon-Sat 10am-2pm and 5-8pm (May-Oct); Sun and public hols 6-8pm. Rest of year only Sat-Sun and public hols noon-2pm and 5-7pm, other days by appointment.* ☎ *979 88 80 76.*

Carrión de los Condes

The Poema de Mío Cid narrates the events of the weddings in Valencia of the daughters of El Cid, Doña Elvira and Doña Sol, to the counts of Carrión, the latter attracted by the rich dowries promised. Upon returning to Carrión, the daughters were mistreated and then abandoned. Having requested justice from the king, El Cid issued a challenge to the counts and then executed them for their sins.

The 11C **Monasterio de San Zoilo**, rebuilt during the Renaissance, has **cloisters**★ designed by Juan de Badajoz with distinctive vaulting. The keystones and bosses are adorned with figurines and medallions. (🕐 *Open 10.30am-2pm; Sat-Sun and public hols, 10.30am-2pm and 4-6.30pm; Apr-Oct, 10.30am-2pm and 4.30-8pm.* 🕐 *Closed 15 Dec-15 Jan.* ⊘*1.35€.* ☎ *979 88 09 02).*

The **Iglesia de Santiago** has beautiful 12C carvings on the façade including, on the portal's central coving, an architect with his compass, a barber with his scissors, a potter at his wheel, a cobbler, and so on. The high reliefs on the upper part show a Gothic influence.

León★★ (🕐 *See* LEÓN)

Astorga

Astorga is renowned for its delicious *mantecadas*, a type of light bread roll.

Catedral★

🕐 *Open 9.30am (9am in summer) to noon and 4.30-6pm (5-6.30pm in summer); Sat-Sun and public hols, 10am-8pm.* ☎ *987 61 58 20.*

Building began with the east end of the church in a Flamboyant Gothic style in the late 15C and was not completed until the 18C, which explains the rich Renaissance and Baroque work on the façade and towers. The front **porch**★ low reliefs illustrate specific events in the Life of Christ such as the Expulsion of the Moneylenders from the Temple and the Pardoning of the Adulterous Woman. Above the door is a beautiful Deposition.

The **interior** is surprisingly large, with an impressive upsweeping effect created by the innumerable slender columns soaring from the pillars. Behind the high altar is a 16C **retable**★ by three artists named Gaspar – Gaspar de Hoyos and Gaspar de Palencia were responsible for the painted, gilt decoration, and **Gaspar Becerra** (1520-70), an Andalucían, for the low reliefs. After studying in Renaissance Italy, Gaspar Becerra developed a personal style of humanist sensitivity far removed from the Baroque Expressionism of the Spanish sculptors.

The **Museo de la Catedral** contains a rich collection of gold and silver plate, including a 13C gold filigree Holy Cross reliquary and a 10C reliquary of Alfonso III, the Great. There is also a beautiful 13C Romanesque painted wood chest. 🕐 *Open 11am-2pm and 3.30-6.30pm; Mar-Sep, 10am-2pm and 4-8pm.* 🕐 *Closed 1-15 Jan.* ⊘ *2.50€ (Combined entrance with the Museo de los Caminos:* ⊘*2.40€).* ☎ *987 61 58 20.*

Palacio Episcopal

This fantastic pastiche of a medieval palace was dreamed up by **Gaudí** in 1889. The original, brilliant interior decoration, especially that in the neo-Gothic chapel on the first floor, is a profusion of mosaics, stained glass and intersecting ribbed vaults. The palace houses the **Museo de los Caminos** (Museum of the Way of St James), a collection of medieval art reflecting the theme of pilgrimage. (🕐 *Open 11am-2pm and 4-6pm; 21 Mar-18 Sep, 10am-2pm and 4-8pm; Sun and public hols, 11am (10am in summer) to 2pm; last admission 45min before closing.* 🕐 *Combined entrance with the Museo de la Catedral: 4€.* ☎ *987 61 68 82.*

Ponferrada

The centre of a mining area and capital of the fertile Bierzo, a subsided basin, Ponferrada owes its name to an iron bridge built at the end of the 11C across the Sil to help pilgrims on their way to Santiago de Compostela. The town is dominated by the ruins of the **Castillo de los Templarios** (Templars' Castle).

La Maragatería

Long ago an ethnic group of unknown origin, but possibly of mixed Gothic-Moorish blood, settled in this part of the Astorga region. These Maragatos led an isolated existence in the heart of an inhospitable region where they became muleteers. They may still be seen at religious festivals or weddings in their national costume of voluminous knee breeches, shirt front and wide embroidered belt. Jacks in full Maragato dress can be seen striking the hours on the clock of the **town hall** on the **plaza Mayor** in Astorga.

Peñalba de Santiago★

21km/13mi SE. Peñalba stands isolated in the heart of the so-called Valle del Silencio (Valley of Silence). Its characteristic architecture of schist-walled houses with wooden balconies and slate tile-stone roofs, remains intact. The village has grown up around the Mozarabic **Iglesia de Santiago**, a church which is all that remains of a 10C monastery. Note the portal with its paired horseshoe arch set off by an *alfiz*. There are fine views from the belfry of the village and the valley beyond.

Las Médulas★

22km/14mi SW. Declared a World Heritage Site in 1997. The northwest slopes of the Aquilianos mountains on the left bank of the Sil have been transformed into a magic landscape of rocky crags and strangely shaped hillocks of pink and ochre by debris from a gold-mine worked in Roman times. Over the ages this has been covered by a vegetation of gnarled old chestnut trees.

Cebreiro

Cebreiro, not far from the Puerto de Piedrafita (Piedrafita pass, 1 109m/3 638ft), is one of the places where one can best imagine the hardships pilgrims underwent on their long tiring journey. The unusual drystone and thatched houses *(pallozas)*, inhabited until recently, go back in construction to ancient Celtic huts; one houses an **Ethnographic Museum** (Museo Etnográfico). Still offering shelter to the traveller is an inn beside the small 9C mountain church where pilgrims venerated the relics of the miracle of the Holy Eucharist which took place c1300, when the bread was supposedly turned to flesh and the wine to blood. The holy relics are preserved in silver caskets presented by Isabel the Catholic and may be seen together with the miraculous chalice and paten.

Portomarín

The village of Portomarín had stood for centuries beside a bridge spanning the Miño when modern civilisation required the construction of a dam at Belesar. Before the old village was drowned, however, the **church**★ of the Knights of St John of Jerusalem was taken down and re-erected stone by stone on the new site. It is square in shape, fortified and ornamented with massive supporting arches and Romanesque doors with delicately carved covings. The west door depicts Christ in Majesty with the 24 Old Musicians of the Apocalypse.

Vilar de Donas

6.5km/4mi E of Palas de Rei. The **church**, slightly off the main road, is entered through a Romanesque doorway. Lining the walls **inside**, are the tombs of the Knights of the Order of St James, slain in battle against the infidels. **Frescoes**★ painted in the 15C still decorate the apse, illustrating Christ in Majesty with St Paul and St Luke on his left and St Peter and St Mark on his right and, on the chancel walls, the faces of the elegant young women who gave the church its name – *(donas* in Galician).

Santiago de Compostela★★★ *(◎ see SANTIAGO DE COMPOSTELA)*

Zafra

POPULATION: 14 065

MICHELIN MAP 576 Q 10 – EXTREMADURA (BADAJOZ).

A 15C *alcázar* (now a parador) stands guard at the entrance to this white-walled town, one of the oldest in Extremadura. It was built by the Dukes of Feria with nine round towers crowned by pyramid-shaped merlons. The white marble patio is Renaissance and the delightful gilded saloon, Mudéjar.

Location

Zafra is situated in the southern section of the Extremadura region, close to the border with Andalucía, 7km/4.5mi W of the N 630, which runs north-south through the Iberian Peninsula along the former Silver Road (Ruta de la Plata). ▯ *Plaza de España 8, 06300 Zafra,* ☎ *924 55 10 36.*

 ✆ *Neighbouring sights are described in the following chapters: MÉRIDA (58km/36mi N), BADAJOZ (76km/47mi NW) and ARACENA (98km/61mi S).*

Worth a Visit

Squares★

The town's two squares, the large 18C **plaza Grande** and the adjoining and much smaller 16C **plaza Chica**, with their fine arcaded houses, form an attractive precinct.

Iglesia de la Candelaria

The 16C church in transitional Gothic-Renaissance style can be identified by its massive red-brick belfry. In the shallow south transept stands an **altarpiece** by Zurbarán painted in 1644.

😋 Fiestas 😋

Zafra's cattle fairs are famous locally, especially the Feria de San Miguel (St Michael's Fair) during the week of 5 October.

Excursions

Llerena

42km/26mi SE along the N 432. The **plaza Mayor** of this modest country town is one of the most monumental in all Extremadura. On one side stands the **Iglesia de Nuestra Señora de Granada** (Church of Our Lady of Granada) in which the composite façade is harmonised by the colourful interplay of white limestone and brick; the delicacy of two superimposed arcades contrasts with the mass of a great Baroque belfry. A pomegranate (*granada* in Spanish) and the emblem of the Catholic Monarchs – decorates the escutcheon on the tympanum over the main door.

Jerez de los Caballeros

42km/26mi SW along the EX 101 and EX 112. Jerez de los Caballeros is the birthplace of the conquistador, **Vasco Núñez de Balboa** (1475-1517), who crossed the Darien Isthmus (now Panama) and in 1513 discovered the Southern Sea (the Pacific Ocean). The town's name, tradition and atmosphere stem from the Knights Templar – Caballeros del Temple – to whom the town was given by Alfonso IX of León on its recapture from the Moors in 1230.

Jerez stands in a fortified position on a hillside, its exuberantly Baroque decorated belfries and towers pointing to the sky. On the summit is the even more ornate San Bartolomé with its façade and belfry faced with painted stucco, molten glass mosaics and *azulejos*. With its steep narrow streets lined by white-walled houses, Jerez gives a foretaste of Andalucían architecture.

Zamora★

POPULATION: 68 202

MICHELIN MAP 575 H 12 – CASTILLA Y LEÓN.

The genteel town of Zamora stands on the banks of the River Duero at the heart of an extensive plain. It played an important role in the Middle Ages, particularly during the 12C and 13C, a period which saw the construction of the cathedral and numerous Romanesque churches which are still visible in the old quarter.

Location

The old quarter of Zamora, in the upper section of the town, commands an impressive view of the River Duero at is feet. 🅸 *Plaza de España 8, 49015 Zamora, ☎ 980 53 18 45.*

🖎 *Neighbouring sights are described in the following chapters: SALAMANCA (62km/39mi S) and VALLADOLID (95km/59mi E).*

Background

Historical notes – Only traces remain of the walls which made Zamora the westerly bastion of the fortified Duero line during the Reconquest. The town played its part in the repeated struggles for the throne of Castilla: in the 11C when Sancho III's sons fought for his kingdom, and in the 15C, when La Beltraneja unsuccessfully disputed the rights of Isabel the Catholic.

Worth a Visit

Catedral★

🕐 *Open Oct-2 Mar, 10am-2pm and 4.30-6.30pm; 3 Mar-30 Sep, 10am-1pm and 5-8pm.* 🕐 *Museum closed Mon.* 🖎 *2€ (museum). ☎ 980 53 06 44.*

The cathedral was built between 1151 and 1174 and subsequently underwent additions and alterations. The north front is neo-Classical in keeping with the square it overlooks; it contrasts, however, with the Romanesque bell tower and the graceful cupola covered in scallop tiling which recalls the Torre del Gallo in Salamanca. The south front, the only original part of the building, has blind arcades and a Romanesque portal with unusual covings featuring openwork festoons.

The aisles are transitional Romanesque-Gothic, the vaulting ranging from broken barrel to pointed ogive. Slender painted ribs support the luminous **dome**★ on squinches above the transept. At the end of the Gothic period, master woodcarvers and wrought-iron smiths worked in the church – there are fine **grilles** enclosing the coro, two 15C Mudéjar pulpits, and **choir stalls**★★, decorated with biblical figures on their backs and with allegorical and burlesque scenes on armrests and misericords.

Museo Catedralicio (Cathedral Museum)

The museum, off the Herreran-style cathedral cloisters, displays a collection of 15C Flemish **tapestries**★★ illustrating the life of Tarquin and the Trojan War; others, dating from the 17C, are of Hannibal's campaigns.

The **Jardín del Castillo** (Castle Garden) behind the cathedral, commands fine views of the Duero river below.

Romanesque churches★

The 12C saw a series of originally designed Romanesque churches built in Zamora province. Particular features included portals without tympana, surrounded by mul-tifoil arches and often possessing heavily carved archivolts; the larger churches also

---

Semana Santa

Zamora's Holy Week solemn celebrations are renowned for the numbers who attend and for the spectacular *pasos* street processions. On Palm Sunday a children's procession escorts a paso of Christ's entry into Jerusalem; on Maundy Thursday evening a totally silent, torchlight procession follows the poignant *Recumbent Christ,* a sculpture by Gregorio Fernández, borne by white-robed penitents through the streets in imitation of the walk to Golgotha. Most of these *pasos* may be seen in the **Museo de la Semana Santa.** 🕐 *Open 10am-2pm and 4-7pm; in summer, 10am-2pm and 5-8pm; Sun and public hols, 10am-2pm.* 🖎 *2.70€. ☎ 980 53 22 95 or 980 53 60 72.*

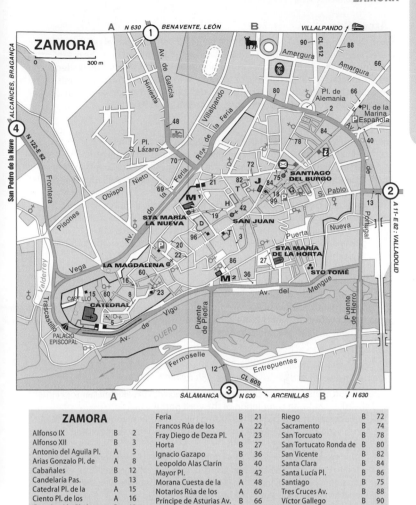

ZAMORA			Feria	B	21	Riego	B	72
			Francos Rúa de los	A	22	Sacramento	B	74
Alfonso IX	B	2	Fray Diego de Deza Pl.	A	23	San Torcuato	B	78
Alfonso XII	B	3	Horta	B	27	San Tortucato Ronda de	B	80
Antonio del Aguila Pl.	A	5	Ignacio Gazapo	B	36	San Vicente	B	82
Arias Gonzalo Pl. de	A	8	Leopoldo Alas Clarín	A	40	Santa Clara	B	84
Cabañales	B	12	Mayor Pl.	B	42	Santa Lucía Pl.	B	86
Candelaría Pas.	B	13	Morana Cuesta de la	A	48	Santiago	B	75
Catedral Pl. de la	A	15	Notarios Rúa de los	A	60	Tres Cruces Av.	B	88
Ciento Pl. de los	A	16	Príncipe de Asturias Av.	B	66	Víctor Gallego	B	90
Constitución Pl. de	B	18	Puebla de Sanabria	A	70	Viriato Pl.	B	96
Corral Pintado	B	19	Puentica Pl. de la	A	69	Zorilla Pl. de	B	99
Damas	A	20						

Casa de los Momos	B	J	Casa del Cordón	B	M²	Museo de la Semana Santa	B	M¹

had domes on squinches over the transept crossing. The best examples of the style in Zamora are the **Magdalena, Santa María la Nueva, San Juan, Santa María de la Orta, Santo Tomé** and **Santiago del Burgo.**

Seigniorial mansions

Casa del Cordón and **Casa de los Momos** have elegant Isabelline windows.

Excursions

San Pedro de la Nave★

▶ *19km/12mi NW. Leave Zamora by ④ on the town plan. Follow the N 122 for 12km/7mi then turn right.*

The Visigothic **church** *(iglesia)*, in danger of being submerged on account of the damming of the Esla, has been rebuilt at El Campillo. It is late 7C and is artistically remarkable for the carving on the transept **capitals** with its strong sense of composition: *Daniel in the lion's den, the Sacrifice of Isaac* etc. The frieze, halfway up the wall, presents Christian symbols including grapes and doves. ⏰ *Open Mon-Fri, 4.30-6.30pm.* 🔑 *Ask for the keys at the nearby bar.* ☎ *980 55 57 09.*

Arcenillas

7km/4mi SE on the C 605. In the village church *(iglesia)*, 15 **panels**★ depicting the Life, Death and Resurrection of Christ have been reassembled from the great Gothic altarpiece designed for Zamora Cathedral by late-15C artist **Fernando Gallego**, one of the greatest Castilian painters of this age, who adopted a Hispano-Flemish style in which there are echoes of Van der Weyden but with stronger colours and softer facial expressions. ◷ *Open 9am-2pm and 4-6pm.* ☏ *980 53 40 05.*

Benavente

66km/41mi N along the N 630. During the Middle Ages the town was a prosperous commercial centre. Several fine monuments remain from that period. The Renaissance style **Castillo de los Condes de Pimentel** (Castle of the Counts of Pimentel), now a parador, has preserved its 16C Torre del Caracol (snail-shell tower). From the terrace are **views** of the valley.

The transitional **Iglesia de Santa María del Azogue** is a church with a wide east end with five apses and two Romanesque portals typical of the local Zamora style. Inside, a beautiful 13C *Annunciation* stands at the transept crossing.

The **Iglesia de San Juan del Mercado** has a 12C carving on the south portal illustrating the journey of the Magi.

Toro

33km/21mi E along the N 122-E 82. The town, which stands on the banks of the Duero, is endowed with a number of Romanesque churches (albeit in a poor state of repair) built in brick with interesting Mudéjar decoration. The collegiate church, on the other hand, is built of limestone and is in better condition.

Colegiata★

◷ *Open 10am-1pm and 5-8pm; Oct-Feb, 10am-2pm and 4-6.30pm.* ◷ *Closed Mon, Fri, 10am-1pm (winter) and Jan.* ⊗ *0.60€.* ☏ *980 10 81 07.*

Construction of the collegiate church began in 1160 with the elegant transept lantern and ended in 1240 with completion of the west portal.

The Romanesque **north portal** illustrates typical themes: above, the Old Men of the Apocalypse and below, angels linked together by a rope symbolising the unity of Faith.

The Gothic **west portal**★★, repainted in the 18C, is the church's great treasure. It is dedicated to the Virgin; the Celestial Court is shown on the archivolt, an expressive Last Judgement on the coving. The statues on the jambs of the pier and tympanum, although a little stiff, have very youthful faces.

Start beneath the **cupola**★, one of the first of its kind in Spain, with two tiers of windows in the drum. Polychrome wood statues stand against the pillars at the end of the nave on consoles, one of which is carved with an amusing version of the birth of Eve (below the angel). In the sacristy is the **Virgin and the Fly**★, a magnificent Flemish painting by either Gérard David or Hans Memling.

Iglesia de San Lorenzo – ⊶ *Closed for restoration.* ☏ *980 10 81 07.* This is the best preserved of Toro's Romanesque churches made of local brick. With its stone base, blind arcading and dog-tooth decoration on the upper cornice, it has much of the Mudéjar style of Castilla and León. Inside, the Gothic **altarpiece** flanked by Plateresque tombs, was painted by Fernando Gallego.

San Cebrián de Mazote

57km/35mi NE along the N 122-E 82 or on the C 519 from Toro. The 10C **Iglesia de San Cebrián de Mazote,** built to a cruciform plan with three aisles divided by horseshoe-shaped arches, is a rare Mozarabic church. The modillions are typical but some of the capitals and low reliefs bear traces of an earlier, Visigothic style. ☙ *Guided tours by prior arrangement.* ☏ *983 78 00 77.*

Zangoza ⊙*see Sangüesa*

Zaragoza★★

POPULATION: 622 371

MICHELIN MAP 574 H 27 (TOWN PLAN) – ARAGÓN.

The towers and domes of the Basílica del Pilar, dominating the urban skyline, are the most characteristic features of Zaragoza, which enjoys a splendid location on the right bank of the River Ebro. The city was largely rebuilt in the 19C after the War of Independence and although not especially striking, pleases on account of its historic monuments and the bustling life along its modern boulevards.

Zaragoza is both a major university and religious centre, veneration of the Virgen del Pilar (Virgin of the Pillar) making it the leading Marian shrine in Spain.

Location

Although the region surrounding Zaragoza is particularly arid, the city stands in the middle of a fertile area irrigated by the Aragón canal and the Ebro, Gállego, Jalón and Huerva rivers. 🛈 *Glorieta Pio XII Torreón de la Zuda, 50003 Zaragosa, ☎ 976 20 12 00; Plaza Nuestra Señora del Pilar, 50001; ☎ 976 39 35 37.*

👌 *Neighbouring sights are described in the following chapters: HUESCA (72km/45mi NE) and TUDELA (82km/51mi NW).*

Background

Caesaraugusta-Sarakusta – Salduba, well situated at the confluence of the Ebro and its tributaries, the Gállego and the Huerva, became, in the year 25 BC, a Roman colony named Caesaraugusta after the Emperor Caesar Augustus. On 2 January in AD 40, according to tradition, the Virgin appeared miraculously to St James, leaving as proof of her apparition the pillar around which the **Basílica de Nuestra Señora del Pilar** was later built. In the 3C the city is said to have suffered persecution at the hands of Diocletian – it still honours from that time the memory of the Uncounted Martyrs, interred in the crypt of **Santa Engracia.**

Four centuries of Muslim occupation would appear to have left the city, renamed Sarakusta, with but a single major heirloom. From the brilliant but shortlived *taifa* kingdom established under the Benihud dynasty in the 11C, there remains the **Aljafería**, a palace, built by the first monarch of the line and a unique and very precious example of Hispano-Muslim art.

Zaragoza, the capital of Aragón – The Aragón kings, after freeing the city from the Moors, proclaimed Zaragoza, the great agricultural town on the Ebro, as capital. The city, however, jealous of its autonomy, voted itself the most democratic Fueros in the whole of Spain and increased its prosperity through wise administration and the establishment of the **Lonja** (Commodities Exchange). Tolerant by tradition, it protected its Muslim masons, so that the Mudéjar style could be used to embellish its churches: the apse of **La Seo** (Cathedral), **San Pablo** and **Magdalena** towers. Houses in the old town with elegant patios and *artesonado* ceilings give a good idea of the city's prosperity in the 16C.

Two heroic sieges – Zaragoza's resistance before Napoleon's army in the terrible years 1808-09 shows the Spanish people's desire for independence and the determination of those of Aragón in particular.

In June 1808 the city was invested for the first time by the French, the siege only being lifted on 14 August. The exultant Zaragozans sang "The Virgin of Pilar will never be French." Alas! On 21 December General Lannes appeared with his men who remained until the town capitulated on 20 February. By the end, half the inhabitants, some 54 000, had died. From that appalling siege there remains the shrapnel-pitted **Puerta del Carmen** (Carmen Gate).

Worth a Visit

Plaza de la Seo and plaza del Pilar are fronted by some of the city's most important buildings.

La Seo★★

🕐 *Open 10am-2pm (noon Sun) and 4-5.30pm (7pm in summer).* 🕐 *Closed Mon.* 💿 *1.50€.* ☎ *976 29 12 31.*

Address Book

For coin ranges, see the Legend at the back of the guide.

WHERE TO EAT

Casa Portolés – *Santa Cruz 21* – ☎ *976 39 06 65* – *Closed Sun evening and Mon.* This tavern-style restaurant has a bar at the entrance where you can enjoy a range of tapas and *raciones*. The restaurant itself, a pleasant mix of arches and exposed brick, serves mainly traditional cuisine. A good location close to the plaza del Pilar in a small square by calle Espoz y Mina.

Antonio – *Plaza. San Pedro Nolasco 5* – ☎ *976 39 74 74* – *Closed Sun evenings and Sun all day in Jul-Aug* - 🍽. A good restaurant that compensates for its modest size with attentive service. Have a drink at the bar while wating for a table. Often filled up with regulars.

TAPAS

Bodeguilla de la Santa Cruz – *Santa Cruz 3* – ☎ *976 20 00 18* – *Closed Sun evening and Mon* – 🍽. The decor in this pleasant, centrally located bar is a throwback to wine cellars of years gone by. Small, but full of atmosphere, with tapas served at the bar.

Los Victorinos – *José de la Hera 6* – ☎ *976 39 42 13* – *Closed 15-30 Nov* – 🍽. This small, lively bar adorned with bullfighting memorabilia is located in a narrow street near the plaza del Pilar and plaza de la Seo. The great selection of delicious, beautifully presented tapas on the bar is not to be missed.

WHERE TO STAY

Hotel Las Torres – *Plaza del Pilar 11* – ☎ *976 39 42 50* – 🍽 – *54 rooms* – 🛏 *6€.* An agreeable hotel, albeit lacking great charm, but with a magnficent location in front of the basilica in plaza del Pilar. Although on the basic side, the rooms are carefully maintained.

Hotel Sauce – *Espoz y Mina 33* – ☎ *976 39 01 00* – 🅿 🍽 – *43 rooms* – 🛏 *8€.* This friendly, family-run hotel enjoys a good position in the centre of the city, a few metres from Zaragoza's two main squares. The rooms are all different and are perfectly adequate despite being on the small side.

PILAR FESTIVALS

In the week of 12 October, Zaragozans extol their Virgin with incredible pomp and fervour: on the 13th at about 7pm the **Rosario de Cristal** procession moves off by the light of 350 carriage-borne lanterns. Other festivals during the week include the **Gigantes y Cabezudos** procession (cardboard giants and dwarfs with massive heads), *jota* dancing and the famous bullfights.

The Cathedral of Zaragoza, La Seo, is remarkable for its size and includes all the decorative styles from the Mudéjar to the Churrigueresque, although it is basically Gothic in design. In the 17C, the tall belfry which harmonises with those on the Pilar Cathedral nearby, was added; in the 18C the Seo was given a Baroque façade. Walk into calle del Sepulcro to see the Mudéjar decoration on the **east end.**

The interior is impressive with its five aisles of equal height. Above the high altar is a Gothic **retable**★ with a predella carved by the Catalan, Pere Johan, and the three central panels of the Ascension, Epiphany and the Transfiguration sculpted by Hans of Swabia (the stance of the figures and the modelling of the faces and robes strike a German note).

The **surrounding wall of the chancel** *(trascoro)* and some of the side chapels were adorned in the 16C with groups of carved figures, clear evidence of the vitality of Spanish sculpture during the Renaissance. Other chapels, ornamented in the 18C, show the all too excessive exuberance of the Churrigueresque style. One exception is the **Parroquieta**, a Gothic chapel containing a 14C tomb influenced by the Burgundian style and, in particular, a **cupola**★ in the Moorish style, in polychrome wood with stalactites and strapwork (15C).

Museo Capitular★

In the sacristy. Exhibited are paintings, an enamel triptych, religious objects and a large amount of church plate including silver reliquaries, chalices and an enormous processional monstrance made up of 24 000 pieces.

Museo de Tapices★★

An outstanding collection of Gothic hangings. All were woven in Arras or Brussels; titles include the *Sailing Ships*, the *Crucifixion* and the *Passion*.

La Lonja★

Currently being used as a temporary exhibition centre. 🕐 *Open 10am-2pm and 5-9pm; Sun and public hols, 10am-2pm.* 🕐 *Closed Mon, 1 Jan, 24 (afternoon), 25 and 31 (afternoon) Dec.* ☎ *976 39 72 39.*

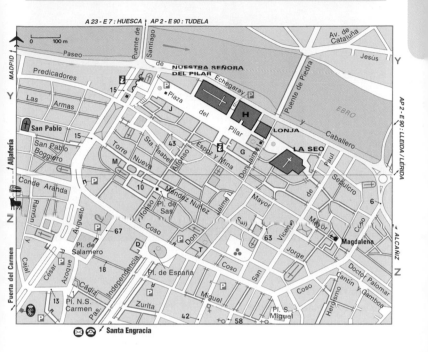

Zaragoza, like the other major trading towns of Valencia, Barcelona and Palma de Mallorca in the Kingdom of Aragón, founded a commercial exchange as early as the 16C. These buildings, in a transitional style between Gothic and Plateresque, include some of the finest examples of civil architecture in Spain. In this instance the vast hall is divided into three by tall columns, their shafts ornamented with a carved band of grotesques. Coats of arms supported by cherubim mark the start of the ribs which open out into star **vaulting**.

The **Ayuntamiento** (town hall) has been rebuilt in traditional Aragón style with ornate eaves. Two modern bronzes stand at the entrance.

Basílica de Nuestra Señora del Pilar★
🕐 *Open 6.45am-8.30pm (9.30pm in summer).* ☏ *976 29 95 64.*

Several sanctuaries have been built successively on this site to enshrine the miraculous pillar *(pilar)* above which the Virgin Mary was said to have appeared. The present building, Zaragoza's second cathedral, was designed by Francisco Herrera the Younger in about 1677. It takes the form of a buttressed quadrilateral lit by a central dome. The cupolas, with small lantern towers, whose ornamental tiles may be seen reflected in the waters of the Ebro, were added by Ventura Rodríguez in the 18C.

The interior is divided into three aisles by giant pillars with fluted pilasters. Some of the frescoes decorating the cupolas were painted by Goya as a young man.

The **Capilla de la Virgen** (Lady Chapel) by Ventura Rodríguez is, in fact, virtually a miniature church on its own. It contains, in a niche on the right, the pillar and a Gothic wood statue of the Virgin. The Virgin's mantle is changed every day except on the 2nd of the month, which is the anniversary of the Apparition (2 January), and the 12th of the month, which is the celebration of the Hispanidad (12 October). Pilgrims go to kiss the pillar through an opening at the rear.

The **high altar** in the centre of the church is surmounted by a **retable**★ carved by Damián Forment of which the predella is outstanding. The **coro** is closed by a high grille and adorned with Plateresque stalls.

Basílica de Nuestra Señora del Pilar

Museo Pilarista★

🕐 *Open 9am-2pm and 4-6pm.* 🎫 *1.50€.* ☎ *976 29 95 64.*

Displayed are the sketches made by Goya, González, Velázquez and Bayeu for the cupolas of Our Lady of the Pillar, a model by Ventura Rodríguez, and some of the jewels which adorn the Virgin during the Pilar festivals. Among the very old ivory pieces are an 11C hunting horn and a Moorish jewellery box.

Aljafería★

Access by calle Conde de Aranda. 🕐 *Open 10am-2pm and 4.30-6.30pm (8pm Apr-Oct); Sun and public hols, 10am-2pm. Last admission 30 min before closing.* 🕐 *Closed Sun and afternoons of public hols in winter, and 1 Jan and 25 Dec.* 🎫 *3€, no charge Sun.* ☎ *976 28 96 84/5.*

This palace is something of a surprise, as it is highly unusual to find such a magnificent example of Moorish architecture in this part of Spain. Built in the 11C by the Benihud family, it was subsequently modified by the Aragonese kings (14C) and Catholic Monarchs (15C) before being taken over by the Inquisition and later converted into a barracks.

The Moorish palace is centred around a rectangular patio bordered by porticoes with delicate tracery and carved capitals. The **musallah**, a form of private mosque for the emirs, has been restored complete with *mihrab* and all the accustomed Moorish fantasy of multifoil arches and floral decoration. The stuccowork is brightly painted.

The first floor and the staircase transport the visitor 400 years ahead to the sumptuous style of the Catholic Monarchs when Flamboyant Gothic reigned supreme. Only the ornate **ceiling**★, its cells divided by geometric interlacing and decorated with fir cones, remains of the throne room. Another *artesonado* ceiling can be seen in the room in which **Santa Isabel**, daughter of Pedro III of Aragón and future Queen of Portugal, was born in 1271.

Excursion

Fuendetodos

▶ *45km/28mi SW along the N 330; after 21km/13mi bear left onto the Z 100.* It was in a modest house (**Casa-Museo de Goya**) in this village that the great painter Francisco Goya y Lucientes was born in 1746. 🕐 *Open 11am-2pm and 4-7pm.* 🕐 *Closed Mon (except public hols).* 🎫 *1.80€.* ☎ *976 14 38 30.*

The **Museo de Grabados** next door displays a collection of his work in the field of engravings. 🕐 *Open 11am-2pm and 4-7pm.* 🕐 *Closed Mon (except public hols).* 🎫 *1.80€.* ☎ *976 14 38 30.*

Mallorca, Playa de Portals Nous

BALEARIC ISLANDS★★★

POPULATION: 825 000

MICHELIN MAP 579.

To many visitors, the Balearics evoke thoughts of summer sunshine and frenetic nightlife, yet this deceptive façade masks a historical past and natural beauty that are as impressive as those of any island in the Mediterranean.

Although the archipelago is one of the most popular tourist destinations in the world, note that over 40% of its verdant landscapes are protected by law.

Location

The Balearic Archipelago is situated in the Western Mediterranean, off the coast of the Levante region on the Spanish mainland. It covers a land area of 5 000km²/1 900sq mi and is made up of three large islands – Mallorca, Menorca and Ibiza – each with a character distinct from the others, two small ones – Formentera and Cabrera – as well as many islets. The Comunidad Autónoma Balear (Balearic Autonomous Community) is one of Spain's 50 provinces, with Palma as administrative capital. The language, Balearic, is derived from Catalan but has kept ancient roots (such as the articles *Se*, *Sa* and *Ses* from the Latin *Ipse*). The average annual temperature in the Balearics is 17.6°C/63.6°F.

MALLORCA★★★

POPULATION: 659 000

MICHELIN MAP 579 – BALEARES.

Mallorca is an island paradise where the stunning beauty of its steep and indented north shore, characterised by delightful coves, contrasts with the flatter, more gentle south coast, with its extensive beaches and crystal-clear turquoise waters. Over the decades, these attractions have seen the island develop into one of Europe's most popular tourist destinations. However, away from the beaches, in Mallorca's picturesque towns and villages, visitors will discover the less-heralded aspects of the island, in which history and architecture proudly come to the fore.

Location

Mallorca is the largest of the Balearic Islands, covering an area of 3 640km²/1 405sq mi. The island's airport is located 11km/7mi SW of Palma de Mallorca. *Palma de Mallorca: Plaza de la Reina 2, 07012, ☎ 971 71 22 16.*

Background

Landscape – A relief map of Mallorca shows three different zones:
The **Sierra de Tramuntana** in the northwest rises in limestone crests – the highest is **Puig Major** (1 445m/4 740ft) – running parallel to the coast. In spite of its low altitude, the chain, its cliffs plunging spectacularly into the sea, forms a solid rock barrier against offshore winds from the mainland.
Pines, junipers and holm oaks cover the slopes, interspersed here and there by the gnarled and twisted trunks of Mallorca's famous olive trees. Villages, perched halfway up hillsides, are surrounded by terraces planted with vegetables and fruit trees.
The central plain, **El Pla**, is divided by low walls into arable fields and fig and almond orchards; the market towns, with outlying windmills to pump water, retain the regular plan of medieval fortress towns.
The **Sierras de Levante** to the east have been scoured by erosion, hollowed out into wonderful caves. The coast is rocky and indented with sheltered, sand-carpeted coves.

The Short-lived Kingdom of Mallorca (1262-1349) – On 5 September 1229, James (Jaime) I of Aragón set sail from Salou to recapture Mallorca, an important commercial bastion in the Mediterranean, from the Muslims, hoping to quell unrest among his nobles by offering them land. The decisive battle took place in the Bay of Palma on 31 December 1229.

Thirty years later James united Mallorca-Baleares, Roussillon and Montpellier in a single independent kingdom which he presented to his son, James II. He and his successor, Sancho, brought prosperity to the island, founding new towns, building strongholds and peopling the territory with Catalan immigrants. Nor did it apparently suffer when Pedro IV seized the archipelago in 1343, killing the young prince at Llucmajor, to reunite it to the crown of Aragón.

Churches were built, a merchant navy was established which brought local prosperity, and a school of cartography was founded which rapidly became famous.

The Mallorcan Primitives (14C-15C) – Gothic Mallorcan painting, characterised by a marked gentleness of expression, was wide open to external influences: the so-called **Master of Privileges** (Maestro de los Privilegios) showed, even in the 14C, a Sienese preference for miniaturisation and warm colours; later, both **Joan Daurer** and the talented **Maestro de Obispo Galiana** became inspired by Catalan painting; the end of the century saw the assertion of personal characteristics in **Francesch Comes,** whose mannerism was to portray figures with full lips.

In the 15C, artists on the island included some who had studied in Valencia such as **Gabriel Moger**, the suave **Miguel de Alcanyís** and **Martí Torner.** The **Maestro de Predelas** is distinguishable by his attention to detail, **Rafael Moger** by his realism. There were also two master painters, both from abroad, **Pedro (Pere) Nisart** and **Alonso de Sedano**, who introduced the Flemish style which was to dominate Mallorcan painting in the 16C (*see Palma; Museo de Mallorca).*

Famous Mallorcans and Illustrious Visitors – **Ramón Llull** (1232-1316) is a good example of the cosmopolitan outlook of Mallorca in the 13C. A reformed libertine, he became a great humanist, learning foreign languages and studying philosophy, theology and alchemy. A defender of the Christian faith, he travelled widely and was later beatified.

Fray Junípero Serra (1713-83) left to do missionary work in California, where he founded a number of missions including those of San Francisco and San Diego. He was beatified in 1988.

Among the foreign writers, poets and savants to visit the island in the 19C, were **Frédéric Chopin** and **George Sand** who spent the winter of 1838 in the Cartuja de Valldemossa (Valldemosa Carthusian Monastery).

Robert Graves (1895-1985), the strongly individualistic English poet, novelist and critic whose works include *I, Claudius, Good-bye to All That* and *The White Goddess,* lived (from 1929 onwards) and died here.

The Austrian archduke, **Ludwig Salvator** (1847-1915), spent most of his 53 years' stay on the west coast where he compiled the most detailed study ever made of the archipelago. He was patron to the French speleologist, E.A. Martel, who explored many of the island's caves in 1896.

Economy – Tourism is the major force in the economy, with shoe manufacturing second and an artificial pearl industry at Manacor now finding foreign outlets. Horticulture supplies the fresh fruit canning and dried fruit industries (figs and apricots), while the almond crop is largely exported.

Worth a Visit

PALMA★★
 See maps on p 580.

The visitor who has the good fortune to arrive in Palma by boat discovers a city spread across the curve of a wide bay, its proud cathedral standing guard as in foregone days of maritime glory. The town's many ancient buildings testify to its former heyday. The city's residential quarters with their hotels stretch out on either side of the historic centre and along the seafront, in avinguda Gabriel Roca, shaded by palms, which leads to the harbours. The old harbour, bordered by passeig Sagrera, serves both passenger and merchant ships. The new harbour, at the southern tip of El Terreno quarter, accommodates the largest liners.

The Bahía de Palma

The bay, protected from north and west winds by the Puig Major range, has a mild climate all the year round. Hotels and tourist apartment blocks stretch along the seafront for 20km/12mi. To the west, the hotels stand along the indented Bendinat coastline where there is little sand, except at the two beach areas of **Palmanova** and **Magaluf.** The coast to the east is less sheltered, being straight, but has mile upon mile of fine sand with a series of resorts – **Can Pastilla, ses Meravelles** and **s'Arenal** whose beaches are known collectively as the Platjas de Palma.

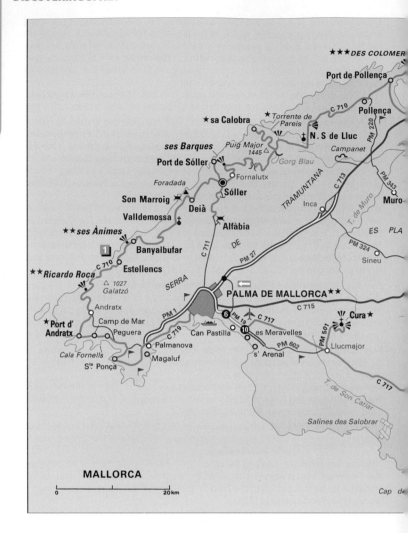

MALLORCA

0   20 km

The "Ciutat de Mallorca"

This was the name by which the city was known after its liberation on 31 December 1229 and during its most prosperous period when trade links were forged with Barcelona, Valencia, the countries of Africa and the kingdoms of northern Europe; Jews and Genoese established colonies in the town, the latter even founding an exchange, and James II (Jaime II) and his successors endowed the city with beautiful Gothic buildings. Finally, the Aragón policy of expansion in Naples and Sicily enabled Palma to extend her commercial interests also.

Palma's old mansions

In the 15C and 16C, the great families of Palma, descended from rich merchants and members of the aristocracy, favoured the Italian style. They built elegant residences with stone façades, relieved by windows with Renaissance style decoration. It was only in the 18C that a characteristic Mallorcan *casa* (house) appeared, with an inner court of massive marble columns, wide shallow arches and incorporating stone steps to a high and graceful loggia. Balustrades of stone or wrought iron completed the decoration. The same families built themselves luxurious summer villas in the mountains to the north of Palma.

Modern Palma

The city of Palma is home to a large proportion of the total population of the island and is one of the most popular cities in Spain in terms of visitor numbers.

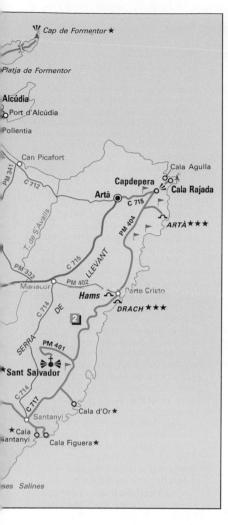

Tourists congregate in and around **El Terreno** – especially in plaza Gomila – and **Cala Major** quarters in the west of town, but the native heart of the city remains the **passeig des Born.** This wide *rambla*, known as **El Born**, followed the course of the Riera river before this was diverted in the 16C to run outside the walls on account of its devastating floodwaters. The shops selling pearls, glassware, leather goods, clothes and local craftwork are in the old town east of El Born in pedestrian streets around Plaça Major and in avinguda Jaume III.

Barrio de la Catedral★ (Cathedral Quarter) ⏱ 3hr

Catedral★★

⏱ *Open 10am-3.15pm; Apr-Oct, 10am-5.15 pm (6.15pm Jun-Sep); Sat, 10am-2pm.* ⏱ *Closed Sun and public hols.* ⏳ *3.50€.* ☎ *971 72 31 33.*

The bold yet elegant cathedral, its tall buttresses surmounted by pinnacles, rises above the seafront. The Santanyi limestone of its walls changes colour according to the time of day: ochre, golden or pink. The cathedral, which was begun in the early 14C on the site of a former mosque, is one of the greatest constructions of the late Gothic period.

The west face was rebuilt in neo-Gothic style in the 19C after an earthquake but its 16C Renaissance portal has remained intact. The south door, known as the **Portada del Mirador** (Viewpoint Doorway), overlooks the sea, the delicate Gothic decoration dating from the 15C preserved beneath a porch. On the tympanum is a scene of the Last Supper while the statues of St Peter and St Paul on either side prove that Sagrera, architect of the Llotja (Exchange), was also a talented sculptor.

The **interior** is both large and light, measuring 121m x 55m (397ft x 180ft) with a height of 44m/144ft to the top of the vaulting above the nave. Fourteen tall, incredibly slender octagonal pillars divide the nave from the aisles. The lack of adornment increases the impression of spaciousness. The Capilla Mayor or Real (Royal Chapel), itself the size of a church, contains at its centre an enormous wrought-iron baldaquin by Gaudí (1912) with Renaissance choir stalls on either side. The tombs of the kings of Mallorca, James II and Jaime III, lie in the Capilla de la Trinidad (Trinity Chapel).

Museo-Tesoro (Treasury Museum)

The Gothic chapter house contains the Santa Eulàlia altarpiece by the Maestro de los Privilegios (1335). In the oval, Baroque chapter house are a number of reliquaries including that of the True Cross, decorated with precious stones. There are also two Baroque candelabra in embossed silver by Joan Matons.

La Almudaina

⏱ *Open 10am-2pm and 4-5.15pm; Apr-Sep, 10am-5.45pm; Sat and public hols, 10am-1.15pm.* ⏱ *Closed Sun, 1, 6 and 20 Jan, 12 Apr, 1 May and 24-25 and 31 Dec.* ⏳ *3.20€; Wed, no charge for citizens of the European Union.* ☎ *971 21 41 34.*

This ancient Moorish fortress, dating from the Córdoba caliphate, was converted in the 14C and 15C by the kings of Mallorca into a royal palace. Today, as one of the

Address Book

For coin ranges, see the Legend at the back of the guide.

WHERE TO EAT

⊖ **Ca's Cuiner** – *Plaça Cort 5 – Palma –* ☎ *971 72 12 62 – Closed Sun –* 🖼 – 🍴. This shop selling ready-made meals also has its own restaurant (or vice-versa) and is considered the temple of Mallorcan cuisine. The menus on offer are simple but delicious, ranging from *empanadas de cordero,* (lamb pastries), *tumbet* (a local vegetable stew) to *sobrasada* (a sausage). Mainly popular with locals.

⊖⊖ **S'Assecados** – *Mar 11 – Porto Cristo –* ☎ *971 82 08 26.* This charming restaurant on a square overlooking the Porto Cristo marina is housed in an early-20C colonial-style building. The decorative focus here is the ceramic chimney and the old *azulejos.*

⊖⊖ **Cás Cosi** – *Baronia 1-3 – Banyalbufar* – ☎ *971 61 82 45 – Closed Tue Nov-Mar –* 🍴. A high-quality restaurant in Banyalbufar, an attractive village surrounded by mountains. The pleasant atmosphere is created by the successful combination of the modern and traditional, a mix that is also evident in the copious cuisine.

⊖⊖ **Sa Plaça Petra** – *Plaça Ramón Llull 4 - Petra - About 10 km E or Manacor by the PM 332 –* ☎ *971 56 16 46 – Closed Tue and in Nov –* 🍴. This attractive restaurant, a combination of old and new, exemplifies what Mallorcans mean by "isle of calm." It has a pleasant terrace, as well as three guest rooms.

⊖⊖ **Es Baluard** – *Plaça Porta de Santa Catalina, 9 – Palma –* ☎ *971 71 96 09 – Closed Sun –* 🍴 *– Reservation recommended.* With its attentive service, elegant decor, wooden terrace and refined Mallorcan cuisine, the Es Baluard has become a local favourite. An extensive wine list and a good location close to the port.

⊖⊖ **Stay** – *Estación Marítima - Port de Pollença –* ☎ *971 86 40 13 – stay@ stayrestaurant.com.* Well-known to locals, this restaurant has a fine location, with two dining areas and a serene seaside terrace.

WHERE TO STAY

⊖ **Santuari de Lluc** – *Depatx de cel.les – Lluc –* ☎ *971 87 15 25 –* 🅿 *– 110 room.* A number of cells in the oldest monastery on the island (dating to 1286) have been converted into modest but comfortable guest rooms. Monastic silence guaranteed for those searching for complete peace and quiet, along with a daily children's concert.

⊖ **Hotel Rosamar** – *Avinguda Joan Miró 74 – Palma –* ☎ *971 73 27 23 – www. rosamarpalma.com – Closed Tue and 1 Dec* – 🍴 *– 40 rooms.* This attractive yellow building facing the sea is located in the upper section of the El Terreno district, alongside the road leading to the Castillo de Bellver. With its pleasant garden, lively bar, and bedrooms with spacious terraces, the Rosamar is an ideal bolt-hole for a few days' rest and relaxation.

⊖⊖ **Hotel Born** – *Sant Jaume 3 – Palma* – ☎ *971 71 29 42 – 25 rooms.* A good central option if you're planning on staying in Palma itself. The hotel occupies a former 16C palace which was subsequently restored in the 18C and is accessed via a delightful Ibizan-style patio. On the whole the rooms are quiet with tasteful decor.

⊖⊖ **Hotel Mar i Vent** – *Major 49 – Banyalbufar –* ☎ *971 61 80 00 – Closed Dec-Jan –* 🅿 *– 29 rooms –* 🍽 *– Restaurant 21€.* A quite charming hotel converted from an old stone house with views of the wooded mountains to the west and the Mediterranean to the north. Beautifully maintained both inside and out.

⊖⊖⊖ **Hotel Son Trobat** – *Carretera Manacor-Sant Llorenç – Sant Llorenç des Cardassar – 4.8km/3mi NE of Manacor on the C 715.* – ☎ *971 56 96 74 - Closed 1 Dec-31 Jan –* 🏊 🍴 *– 25 rooms –* 🍽 *– Restaurant 24€.* This large property in the heart of the Mallorcan countryside successfully combines the rustic charm of an old building with the facilities of the modern age (two swimming pools, jacuzzi, Turkish bath, sauna etc). Reasonably priced given the standard.

SHOPPING

Mallorca's two gastronomic specialities are **ensaimada**, a light spiral roll dusted with sugar, and **sobrasada**, a hot pork sausage.

official residences of the King of Spain, several rooms have recently been restored and elegantly furnished with Flemish tapestries, clocks and paintings. In the courtyard, note the carved overhanging eaves and the doorway of the Iglesia de Santa Ana (St Anne's Church), one of the rare examples of Romanesque architecture in the Balearics. There is a 15C altarpiece inside.

Ayuntamiento

Carved wooden eaves overhang the 17C façade of the town hall.

A view of Palma's marina and cathedral

R. Mattes/ MICHELIN

Iglesia de Santa Eulàlia

13C-15C. The tall nave is unusually bare for a Gothic church. The first chapel off the south aisle contains a 15C altarpiece.

Between the churches of Santa Eulàlia and Sant Francesc, at no2 Carrer Savellà, is the 18C **Can Vivot,** its beautiful patio decorated with marble columns.

Iglesia de Sant Francesc

🕐 *Open 9.30am-12.30pm and 3-6pm; Sun and public hols, 9am-1pm.* 🕐 *Closed 1 Jan, Good Fri and 24-25 Dec.* ⌨ *0.60€.* ☎ *971 71 26 95.*

13C-14C. The church's façade, rebuilt in the late 17C, has an immense Plateresque rose window and a Baroque portal with a beautifully carved tympanum by Francisco Herrera. The interior consists of a vast single aisle. The first apsidal chapel on the left contains the tomb of Ramon Llull: a recumbent statue of the philosopher lies upon a frieze of imaginary beasts supported by seven Gothic niches.

The **cloisters**★ (claustro), begun in 1286 and completed in the 14C, are extremely elegant. Apart from one side of trefoil openings, the architect divided the remaining galleries into multifoil bays supported on groups of slender columns which he varied in diameter, together with the decoration on the capitals, to achieve diversity and grace. The ceiling is painted throughout.

Casa Marqués del Palmer

In the middle of the aristocratic Carrer del Sol stands the impressive Casa Marqués del Palmer, a mansion built in 1556 in stone and now blackened by age. Renaissance decoration around the upper-floor windows mellows the austerity of its Gothic walls. The upper gallery, protected by the traditional deep eaves, is a replica of the one adorning the Llotja.

The former old Jewish quarter, **La Portella**, lies close against the town wall.

Baños Árabes

🕐 *Open 9.30am-7.30pm (7pm Dec-Mar).* ⌨ *1.20€.* ☎ *971 72 15 49.*

The Moorish baths are the only relic to have remained intact from the time of the caliphate in Palma. The baths, beneath their small circular windows and classical dome, supported on 12 columns with rudimentary capitals, were used after the Reconquest by Jews and Christians alike.

Museo de Mallorca

🕐 *Open 10am-7pm; Sun and public hols, 10am-2pm.* 🕐 *Closed Mon.* ⌨ *2.40€; Sat-Sun, no charge.* ☎ *971 71 75 40.*

The museum consists of three sections: Archaeological, Fine Arts (Bellas Artes) and Ethnographical *(for this last section, 👣 see Tours: Muro).*

PALMA DE MALLORCA

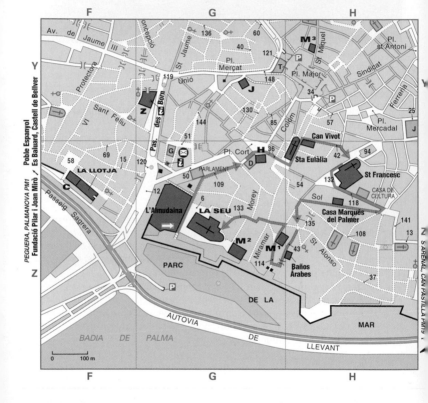

Muslim archaeology

Palma was occupied by the Muslims from the 8C to 1229 when it was known as Medina Mayurqa. The only architectural vestiges from the 12C, when it was one of the most important towns in all *Al-Andalus*, are the Almudaina, Arco de la Almudaina (Almudaina Arch) and the Baños Árabes. The ground floor displays capitals, *artesonado* ceilings and ceramics from this period.

Fine Arts★

See also Background: Mallorcan Primitives. This section of the museum has an excellent collection of Mallorcan Gothic paintings from the 14C and 15C. Works from the early 14C show a clear Italian influence; among them is the Santa Quiteria altarpiece by the Maestro de los Privilegios. Catalan works begin to appear after 1349 when Mallorca was annexed by Aragón: the *Crucifixion* by Ramón Destorrents, interesting for its composition and expression, was to influence other paintings. In Room 2 are the *Annunciation, St Lucy* and *Mary Magdalene* by Maestro del Obispo Galiana (late 14C). Room 3: Francesch Comes, one of the most prestigious of the early-15C painters, is represented here by his **St George**★, remarkable for the depth and detail of the landscape. There is also the 15C *San Onofre Altarpiece* by the Maestro de Predellas. In the rooms devoted to 16C, 17C and 18C art, note the paintings of St Michael and St John by Juan de Juanes.

Museo Diocesano (Diocesan Museum)

On the square behind the cathedral. ○ *Open 10am-1pm and 3-6pm (8pm in summer); Sat-Sun and public hols, 10am-1pm.* ⊙ *2€.* ☎ *971 71 28 27.*

Among the many Gothic works displayed is Pere Nisart's outstanding **St George**★ (1568) which shows the saint slaying the dragon against a backdrop of the town of Palma, as it was in the 16C.

To the west of El Born ○ *1hr*

La Llotja (La Lonja)★

○ *Only open during exhibitions: 11am-2pm and 5-9pm; Sun and public hols, 11am-2pm.* ○ *Closed Mon.* ⊙ *No charge.* ☎ *971 71 17 05.*

The designer of this 15C commodities exchange was **Guillermo Sagrera**, a famous architect who was a native of Mallorca. The Llotja's military features are only for the sake of appearances: the openwork gallery made to look like a sentry path never served as one; the merlons and turrets are not for defence but decoration. But such devices distract the eye from the inevitable buttresses and the austerity of the outer walls which were further modified by Gothic windows with delicate tracery. The interior, in which cross vaults outline the pointed arches which descend onto six beautiful, spirally fluted columns, is exceptionally elegant.

Antiguo Consulado del Mar (Former Maritime Consulate)

The early-17C building adorned with a Renaissance balcony was the meeting-place of the Tribunal de Comercio Marítimo (Merchant Shipping Tribunal). Today it houses the administration (*presidencia*) of the Comunidad Autónoma de las Islas Baleares (Autonomous Community of the Balearic Islands).

▶ *Walk up the passeig des Born.*

Palau Solleric

○ *Open 10.30am-1.30pm and 5.30-8.30pm; Sun and public hols, 10.30am-1.30pm.* ○ *Closed Mon.* ☎ *971 72 20 92.*

The decoration of the front of this 18C palace overlooking the Born is completed by an elegant loggia; behind this front *(follow the narrow covered way round the building)* is the most perfect **patio**★ in Palma, complete with a beautifully proportioned double flighted staircase set off by delicate wrought ironwork. Exhibitions are held in the palace rooms.

Outside the Centre

Museu d'Art Espanyol Contemporani (Col·lecció March)★ (Museum of Contemporary Spanish Art (March Collection)

○ *Open 10am-6.30pm; Sat 10.30am-2pm* ○ *Closed Sun and public hols.* ⊙ *No charge.* ☎ *971 71 35 15.*

The former main branch of the Banca March, an 18C mansion in regional style, now houses a **permanent collection**★ of 52 works of contemporary Spanish artists. A visit offers a tour of 20C Spanish art, from the Avant Garde (Picasso, Miró, Dalí and J. González) to the most recent figures.

Casa Berga

The mansion dating from 1712 now houses the Palacio de Justicia (Law Courts). The façade is encumbered uncharacteristically with stone balconies but the inner courtyard, although vast, is a typical Mallorcan patio.

Pueblo Español★ (Spanish Village)

Off the town plan, along passeig de Sagrera. ○ *Open 9am-5.30 pm (7.30 pm in smmer).* ⊙ *4.81€.* ☎ *971 73 70 75.*

This village, where the most typical houses of every region of Spain have been reconstructed, differs from its counterpart in Barcelona; here the buildings are exact reproductions of actual famous houses or monuments: the Patio de los Arrayanes (Myrtle Court) from the Alhambra in Granada, the Casa de El Greco in Toledo, the Plaza Mayor in Salamanca etc. Craftsmen at work in the alleys, and folk dancing and singing in the streets bring the village to life.

Features of all the major Roman constructions in Spain have been incorporated in the monumental **Palacio de Congresos** (Convention Centre) facing the village.

Castillo de Bellver★

▶*Leave Palma along passeig de Sagrera.* ◷ *Open 8am-7.15pm (8.30pm Apr-Sep); Sun and public hols, 10am-5pm (7pm Apr-Sep); last admission 45min before closing.* ◷ *Closed 1 Jan and 25 Dec.* ⊜*1.80€.* ☎ *971 73 06 57.*

The castle, built by the Mallorcan kings of the 14C as a summer residence, was converted not long afterwards into a prison, which it remained until 1915.

Among those incarcerated was the poet, dramatist and politician **Jovellanos**, known also at the time for his progressive system of education. He was released in 1808, just as French officers, captured by the Spanish at the Battle of Bailén, arrived.

The castle's circular perimeter, round buildings and circular inner court are highly original; a free-standing keep dominates all. The arcade on the ground floor is set off by a series of tall Roman statues. These were donated by Cardinal Despuig together with his Italian collections, and belong to the **Museo Municipal de Historia** (Municipal History Museum). Also displayed in the museum are finds from excavations in Pollença.

A full **panorama**★★ of the Bahía de Palma can be seen from the terrace.

Fundació Pilar i Joan Miró (Pilar and Joan Miró Foundation)

▶*Leave the town centre via the passeig de Sagrera.* ◷ *Open 10am-6pm; 16 May-15 Sep, 10am-7pm; Sun and public hols throughout the year, 10am-3pm.* ◷ *Closed Mon, 1 Jan and 25 Dec.* ⊜ *4.80€.* ☎ *971 70 14 20.*

The museum was born from the desire of Joan Miró (1893-1983) and his wife to provide the city of Palma with a lively cultural and artistic centre. In the shadow of Son Abrines, Miró's private residence from 1956, the works donated by the artist are displayed in a part of the building called the Espacio Estrella, a satellite section of Moneo, an amalgam of the Museo de Arte Romano, Mérida, and the Museo Thyssen-Bornemisza in Madrid. Visitors to the foundation are also provided with an introduction to one of the most wide-ranging and original artists in contemporary art. The large studio provided for him by his friend JL Sert and the San Boter studio are also shown.

Es Baluard - Museu d'Art Modern i Contemporani de Palma (Museum of Contemporary Art, in the baluarte de Sant Pere (bastion), facing the port)

Tours

LA COSTA ROCOSA★★★ (THE ROCKY COAST) ①

From Palma to Alcúdia

264km/165mi. Allow 2 days. See map of island on pp 576–577.

Mallorca's west coast, known as the Rocky Coast, is dominated by the limestone barrier of the Sierra de Tramuntana which reaches an altitude of 1 436m/4 711ft at

Port de Sóller

J. Malburet/ MICHELIN

Puig Major. The mountain range, its wild terrain softened only by the occasional pinewood, drops dramatically to the deep, translucent sea. In the south, around the villages of Estellencs and Banyalbufar, the slopes have been terraced into *marjades* where olives, almonds and vines are grown. In the more fertile valleys further inland, fincas, or large estates with seigniorial mansions such as Granja and Alfàbia, were established from the 17C to the 19C.

▶ *Leave Palma along passeig Sagrera.*

The indented coast between Palma and Port d'Andratx with its wide sandy creeks and coves has been built up into a series of resorts: **Palmanova, Santa Ponça** where a Cross commemorates the landing of James I of Aragón in 1229, **Peguera, Cala Fornells** and **es Camp de Mar.**

Port d'Andratx★

The small fishing port now also used by pleasure craft lies well sheltered in the curve of a narrow harbour. The town of Andratx, surrounded by almond plantations some distance behind the harbour, is scarcely distinguishable against the grey mountain background, dominated by the 1 026m/3 366ft high Galatzó peak.

The C 710 between Andratx and Sóller is an extremely winding **scenic road**★★★, cutting mostly along the edge of the cliff that extends all the way to the indented northwest coast. It commands outstanding views and is shaded along its length by pine trees.

Mirador Ricardo Roca★★

The **view** from this lookout point drops sheer to tiny coves below, lapped by the wonderfully limpid sea.

Estellencs

The village is surrounded by terraces of almond and apricot trees.

Banyalbufar

The tall stone village houses stand in terraces surrounded by fields of tomatoes and vines. There is swimming in the harbour.

Mirador de Ses Ánimes★★

The **panorama** from the watchtower stretches along the coast from the Isla de Dragonera to the south and as far north as Port de Sóller.

Cartuja de Valldemossa (Valldemossa Carthusian Monastery)

🕐 *Open Mar-Oct, 9.30am-6pm (4pm Nov-Feb); Sun, 10am-1pm.* 🕐 *Closed 1 Jan and 25 Dec.* 🎫 *7.50€.* ☎ *971 61 21 06.*

The monastery, set in the heart of Valldemossa village, was made famous by the visit George Sand and Chopin paid in the winter of 1838-39. The bad weather and local hostility to their unorthodox way of life left George Sand disenchanted, although the beauty of the countryside did evoke enthusiastic passages in her book, *A Winter in Majorca,* and Chopin regained his inspiration during the stay. From the monks' cells there are pleasant **views** of the surrounding olive groves, carob trees and almond orchards.

An 18C **pharmacy**, built into one of the cloister galleries, has a fine collection of jars and boxes. A small **museum** displays xylographs (wood engravings).

The road beyond Valldemossa runs along cliffs more than 400m/1 300ft high.

Son Marroig

🕐 *Open 9.30am-6pm (8pm Apr-Sep).* 🕐 *Closed Sun, 1 Jan and 25 Dec.* 🎫 *3€.* ☎ *971 63 91 58.*

The former residence of Archduke Ludwig Salvator includes an exhibition of archaeological finds and Mallorcan furniture collected by the author, and his volumes on the Balearic Islands. A small marble belvedere in the garden affords a view of the locally famous pierced rock rising out of the sea, the **Foradada**.

Deià

The village of reddish-brown houses perched on a hillside amid olive and almond trees has attracted a number of writers and painters. All around are higher hills, covered in holm oaks and conifers giving it almost a mountain setting. There is a pleasant walk from the village down to a creek with a small beach.

Sóller

The delightful 19C houses of Sóller are spread out in a quiet valley of market gardens, orange trees and olives groves.

Port de Sóller

Port de Sóller lies in the curve of an almost circular bay, its sheltered harbour ideal for pleasure boats. With the advantages of a sand beach and low mountain hinterland, it is now the major seaside resort of the west coast. A small train runs between Port de Sóller and Sóller. Boat trips along the coast set off from the harbour.

▷ *Take the C 711 from Sóller to Alfàbia.*

The road twists steeply up the hillside commanding views westwards of Sóller, the harbour and the sea before descending the range's southern slopes towards the plain.

Jardines de Alfàbia (Alfàbia Gardens)

🕐 *Open 9.30am-5.30pm (6.30pm May-Sep); Sat, 9.30am-1pm.* 🕐 *Closed Sun and public hols in winter.* 🎫 *4.50€.* ☎ *971 61 31 23.*

The estate was originally a Moorish residence although all that now remains of the 14C period is the *artesonado* ceiling over the porch.
Follow the signposted path through the gardens with their bowers, fountains and luxuriant palms, bougainvillaea and clumps of bamboo.
A visit to the **library** and grand saloon conveys the atmosphere of a traditional seigniorial residence.

▷ *Return to Sóller.*

Take the narrow mountain road from Sóller via the picturesque villages of Biniaraix and Fornalutx, their ochre-coloured stone houses set off by green shutters.

▷ *Follow the C 710.*

Mirador de Ses Barques

From this viewpoint there is an interesting **panorama** of Port de Sóller.

The road leaves the coast to head inland through mountainous countryside. It runs through a long tunnel before following the upper valley of the Pareís. All the while the landscape is dominated to the west by the impressive **Puig Major** *(military base on the summit).*

▷ *After skirting the Gorg Blau reservoir, take the Sa Calobra road.*

Sa Calobra road★★★

The magnificently planned road plunges towards the Mediterranean, dropping 900m/3 000ft in 14km/9mi. It drops vertiginously through a weird and desolate landscape of steep, jagged rocks, above which towers the Puig Major.

Sa Calobra★

Pleasure boats from Port de Sóller are often to be seen moored in the rocky creek beside which stand the few houses of Sa Calobra village. Nearby is the mouth of the **Pareís river★**, its clear water pouring over the beach of round white shingle which lies in its path to the sea. The river bed is accessible for a couple of hundred metres along a track which passes through two underground galleries; a 2-3km/1.5-2mi walk along the course gives an idea of how enclosed the stream is.

▷ *Return to the C 710.*

About 1km/0.6mi north of the Sa Calobra fork, a small **mirador★** *(lookout, alt 664m/2 178ft)* gives a good view over a length of the cleft hollowed out by the Pareís. The road then passes through a lovely forest of holm oaks.

Monasterio de Nuestra Señora de Lluc

🕐 *Open 8am-10pm.* ☎ *971 87 15 25.*

The origin of the monastery dates back to the 13C when a young shepherd found a statue of the Virgin on the site and a shrine was subsequently built. The present buildings date from the 17C (church) and early 20C (hostelry). *La Moreneta*, as the dark stone Gothic statue of the Virgin is known, is patron of Mallorca and venerated by a great many pilgrims.
From a pass 5km/3mi north of Lluc, you can see right across to the Bahía de Pollença.

Pollença

The town stands between two hills, the Puig (333m/1 092ft) to the east, and a hill to the west crowned by a Calvary *(access up a long flight of steps bordered by cypresses)*. The streets are picturesque, lined with low ochre-coloured houses with rounded arches over the entrances.

Port de Pollença

This large resort has a perfect **setting**★ in a sheltered bay between the Cabo Formentor headland to the north and the Cabo del Pinar to the south, and provides a vast expanse of calm water for water-skiing and sailing. There are moorings in the harbour for pleasure craft and a pleasant promenade skirts the beach.

Cabo de Formentor road★

The road commands spectacular views as it twists and turns, rising several times to the edge of the clifftops and, at one point, following a narrow jagged crest. The **Mirador des Colomer viewpoint**★★★ *(access along a stepped path)* overlooks, in an impressive, vertical drop, what is known as Mallorca's Costa Brava where great rock promontories plunge to the sea.

The **Platja de Formentor** is a well sheltered beach facing Pollença bay. It is further enhanced by the flowered terraces of the grand Hotel Formentor, built in 1928, and once famous for its casino and millionaire guests.

The road continues towards the cape and, once through the tunnel which temporarily hides the Cala Figuera to the north, it passes through a steep and arid landscape. The **Cabo de Formentor**★, dominated by a lighthouse, is the most northerly point of the island. It drops sheer to the sea, 200m/650ft, in a formidable rock wall.

▶*Return to Port de Pollença, then skirt the bay until you reach Alcúdia.*

Alcúdia

Alcúdia, still encircled by 14C ramparts, guards access to the promontory which divides the bays of Pollença and Alcúdia. The **Puerta del Muelle** or **Xara** (Quai Gate), which led to the harbour, and the **Puerta de San Sebastián** or **Puerta de Mallorca** on the other side of town, remain of the early fortified walls; they were reconstructed and incorporated into the ramparts when they were strengthened in the 14C. The streets in the shadow of the walls have a distinctive medieval air as have the town's houses, brightened by Renaissance surrounds to their windows.

About 2km south is the site of the ancient Roman town of **Pollentia** founded in the 2C BC. All that remains of the city are the theatre ruins.

Museo Monográfico de Pollentia (Pollentia Monographic Museum)

🕐 *Open 10am-1.30pm and 3.30-5.30pm; Sat-Sun, 10.30am-1pm.* 🕐 *Closed Mon and public hols.* 🎟 *2€. No charge first Sun of month.* ☎ *971 89 71 02.*

A chapel in Alcúdia's old quarter houses the museum with its collections of statues, oil lamps, bronzes and jewellery from the site of the ancient city of Pollentia.

A number of sights around Alcúdia are also worth a visit.

Port d'Alcúdia

2km/1.2mi E. The port of Alcúdia overlooks a vast bay built up with hotels and tower blocks. A long beach stretches away to the south as far as Can Picafort. The marshy hinterland of La Albufera is a nature reserve.

Cuevas de Campanet

17km/11mi SW along the C 713 and a secondary, signposted road. These caves were discovered in 1947. About half of them along the 1 300m/1 500yd-long path have ceased formation, their massive concretions now totally dry. In the area which is still waterlogged, the most common features are straight and delicate stalactites. 🚶 *Guided tours (45min), 10am-6pm (7pm 26 Apr-Oct).* 🕐 *Closed 1 Jan and 25 Dec.* 🎟 *9€.* ☎ *971 51 61 30.*

Muro

▶ *Follow the C 713 SW for 11km/7mi and then bear left for another 7km/4mi via Sa Pobla.*

The road crosses countryside bristling with windmills. The **ethnological section** of the **Museo de Mallorca**, housed in a large 17C nobleman's residence, displays collections of traditional furniture, dress and farm implements as well as an old pharmacy and island ceramics including whistles (*xiurels*). An annexe houses exhibitions on various craftsmen: a blacksmith, cabinetmaker, gilder, engraver, welder, goldsmith and cobbler. (🕐 *Open 10am-1pm and 4-6pm; in summer, 10am-2pm and 4-7pm; Sun throughout the year, 10am-2pm.* 🕐 *Closed Mon and public hols.* 👁 *1.80€.* ☎ *971 71 75 40.*

EAST COAST AND CAVES★★②

From Artà to Palma
165km/103mi. Allow one day. 👣 *See map on pp 576–577.*

Artà

The town of Artà with its narrow streets may be distinguished from a distance by its high rock site crowned by the Iglesia de Sant Salvador (Church of our Saviour) and the ruins of an ancient fortress. The Artà region is rich in **megalithic remains** (👣 *see MENORCA*), particularly *talayots* which sometimes can be seen over the low walls dividing the fields.

▶ *Continue along the C 715.*

Capdepera

Access to the fortress: by car, along narrow streets; on foot, up steps. The remains of a 14C fortress still girding the hilltop give Capdepera an angular silhouette of crenellated walls and square towers. The buttressed ramparts now enclose only a restored **chapel**, but it is still possible to walk the old sentry path, **viewing**★ the sea and the nearby calas (coves).

Cala Rajada

Cala Rajada with its delightful fishing village and pleasure boat harbour, has grown into a seaside resort on account of the creeks which lie on either side of it.

Casa March – 🚶 *Guided tours (2hr) by prior arrangement.* 👁 *3€.* ☎ *971 56 30 33.* The gardens of this vast residence on the hillside facing the port have become an outdoor museum of modern sculpture. Over 40 sculptures, blending in perfectly with the vegetation, are the works of famous artists such as Henry Moore, Sempere, Otero Besteiro, Berrocal, Barbara Hepworth, Eduardo Chillida and Arman.

By crossing the pinewood towards the lighthouse, you come to two rocky inlets, so far relatively wild, but 2km/1mi further north, is **Cala Agulla**, well known for its sandy beach.

▶ *Return to Capdepera and follow the signs to the Coves d'Artà.*

Coves d'Artà★★★
🚶 *Guided tours (45min), 10am-5pm (7pm Jul-Oct); last admission 30min before closing.* 🕐 *Closed 1 Jan and 25 Dec.* 👁 *8€.* ☎ *971 84 12 93.*

The caves, magnificently sited in the cape closing Canyamel bay to the north and accessible by a cliff road, were largely hollowed out by the sea – the giant mouth overlooks the sea from a height of 35m/115ft. The chambers themselves are impressively lofty and contain massive concretions. The vestibule is blackened by smoke from 19C visitors' torches but the caves that follow are varied and equally impressive, containing the **Reina de las Columnas** (Queen of Columns) 22m/72ft tall, Dantesque surroundings cleverly highlighted in the **Sala del Infierno** (Chamber of Hell) and a fabulous decoration of concretions in the **Sala de las Banderas** (Hall of Flags), 45m/148ft high.

▶ *Return to the PM 404 and bear left. At Portocristo, take the Manacor road off which you soon turn for the Coves dels Hams.*

Coves dels Hams
🚶 *Guided tours (45min), Nov, 11am-5pm; Dec-Feb, 11am-4.30pm; Mar, 10.30am-5pm; Apr, May and Oct, 10.30am-5.30pm; Jun-Sep, 10am-6pm.* 🕐 *Closed 25 Dec.* 👁 *9.80€.* ☎ *971 82 09 88.*

The caves, following the course of a former underground river, communicate directly with the sea, so that the water level in several of the small clear pools rises and falls with the slight Mediterranean tide. The concretions are delicate and some, such as the stalactites in the **Sala de los Anzuelos**★ (Fish-hook Chamber), are as white as snow.

▶ *Return to Portocristo and bear right.*

Coves del Drach★★★
🚶 *Guided tours (1hr) at 10.45am, noon, 2pm and 3.30pm; 15 Mar-Oct at 10am, 11am, noon, 1pm, 2pm, 3pm, 4pm and 5pm.* 🕐 *Closed 1 Jan and 25 Dec.* 👁 *8.50€.* ☎ *971 82 07 53.*

Four chambers succeed one another over a distance of 2km/1.2mi, their transparent pools reflecting richly decorative concretions. The marine origins of the caves seem unquestionable in spite of their size: the French speleologist, **Édouard-Alfred Martel,** who first explored them in 1896, believed that infiltration through the limestone subsidence and faults had caused the cavities in which several pools are slightly salty. Rainfall dissolved the soft Miocene limestone, forming as it did so countless concretions. In the words of Martel: "On all sides, everywhere, in front and behind, as far as the eye can see, marble cascades, organ pipes, lace draperies, pendants of brilliants hang suspended from the walls and roof." It is the **roofs**, above all, which are amazing, glittering with countless, sharply pointed icicles. The tour ends with a look at the limpidly translucent **Lago Martel**. The vast chamber in which the lake lies has been converted into a kind of concert hall; musicians in boats rise up seemingly from the depths and, in a dreamlike atmosphere, glide across the water as they play.

▶ *Continue along the road towards Santanyí and turn right onto the PM 401.*

Monasterio de Sant Salvador★

🕐 *Open 8am-9pm.* ☞ *No charge.* ☎ *971 58 00 56.*

The monastery perched on a rise 500m/1 640ft above the plain (🚗 tight hairpin bends), commands a wide **panorama**★★ of the eastern part of the island.

It was founded in the 14C although the **church** and buildings, now used for pilgrims, were rebuilt in the 18C. In the church behind the Baroque high altar is a deeply venerated **Virgin and Child**, while in the south chapels are three **Nativities** set in dioramas and a multicoloured stone **altarpiece** carved in the 14C in low relief with scenes of the Passion.

▶ *Return to the Santanyí road.*

Secondary roads lead off this road to a series of resorts built up in the creeks along the coast, namely **Cala d'Or**★, with fully developed tourist facilities, **Cala Figuera**★, which is still a delightful little fishing village, and **Cala Santanyí**★.

▶ *From Santanyí follow the C 717 towards Palma. In Llucmajor, bear right onto the PM 501.*

Santuario de Cura★

🕐 *Open 10am-1.30pm and 3.30-6pm.* ☎ *971 12 02 60.*

The road climbs from Randa up tight hairpin bends to the monastery high on the hillside. The buildings have been restored and modernised by the Franciscans who have occupied them since 1913. You may visit the 17C **church**, the Sala de Gramática (Grammar Room) and a small **museum**.

From the terrace on the west side of the monastery there is a **panorama**★★ of Palma, the bay, the Puig Major chain and, in the northeast, Cabo de Formentor headland, the northernmost point on the island.

▶ *Return to Llucmajor and continue W along the C 717 to Palma.*

MENORCA★★

POPULATION: 70 000

669KM2/258SQ MI – MICHELIN MAP 579.

Menorca has managed to remain on the margins of major tourist development, thus avoiding the rampant construction that has blighted other Mediterranean islands and preserving its picturesque villages and delightful coastline dotted with creeks of crystal-clear water. Other attractions of the island include its unspoilt wildlife, plentiful sunshine, superb cuisine and high standard of hotel accommodation.

Location

Menorca is the second largest and most populated of the Balearic islands and the farthest from the mainland. ▯ *Ciutadella: Plaça de la Catedral 5, 07760, ☎ 971 38 26 93; Maó: Plaça Explanada 40, 07703, ☎ 971 36 37 90.*

Background

Landscape – Menorca divides into two distinct zones, determined by relief and geological origin. The island's highest point, Monte Toro, 358m/1 174ft, is in the northern part of the island, known as the Tramuntana, where there are outcrops of dark slate rock from the Palaeozoic and Mesozoic geological eras. Along the coast, these ancient, eroded cliffs have been cut into a saw's edge of *rías* (inlets) and deep coves. The second zone, south of the Maó-Ciutadella dividing line, is the Migjorn limestone platform of light-coloured rock which forms tall cliffs along the coast cut by creeks.

The vegetation is typically Mediterranean with pinewoods, wild olives battered into gnarled and twisted shapes by the north wind, together with mastic trees, heather and aromatic herbs such as rosemary, camomile and thyme.

Throughout the island, fields are divided by drystone walls punctuated by gates made from twisted olive branches.

Historical notes – After settlement by prehistoric peoples, whose monuments may be seen throughout the island, Menorca was colonised by the Romans, conquered by Vandals in 427, and then came under Muslim control. In the 13C, Alfonso III of Aragón invaded the island, made Ciutadella capital and encouraged settlers from Catalunya and Aragón. In the 16C, Barbary pirates attacked first Maó and then Ciutadella, leaving both cities in virtual ruin.

In 1713, Menorca, which had begun to prosper through sea trade in the late 17C, was ceded to the English crown by the Treaty of Utrecht. Maó became England's economic

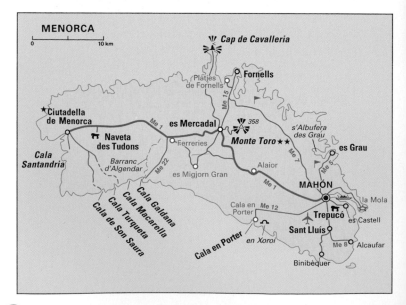

stronghold in the Mediterranean. Apart from a short period of French rule from 1756 to 1763, the island remained throughout the 18C under the British, who built houses and, under an enlightened governor, Kane, roads. The island's first road, between Maó and Ciutadella, still exists (north of the C 721) and is known as camino Kane. At the beginning of the 19C, Menorca was restored definitively to Spain.

The island's economy has gradually been oriented towards the leather industry and jewellery-making while cattle raising provides the island with dairy products, particularly its well-known cheeses.

The Megalithic monuments – In the second millennium BC, at the end of the Bronze Age, the Balearics were populated by settlers similar to those who inhabited Sardinia during the same period. The cavernous nature of the Minorcan countryside offered natural shelter both for the living and the dead; some of the caves, such as **Calascoves**, are even decorated. At the same time, **talayots** began to appear (over 200 have been identified). They take the form of great cones of stones, possibly covering a funeral chamber and forming, it is believed, the base for a superimposed wooden house. Other characteristic monuments of the civilisation include **taulas**, consisting of two huge stone blocks placed one on top of the other in the shape of a T, possibly serving as altars, and **navetas**, single monuments which take the form of upturned boats and contain funeral chambers.

For more detailed information on local archaeology, a map may be bought on the island showing the sites of the monuments: Mapa Arqueológico de Menorca, by J Mascaró Pasarius.

Minorcan architecture – The walls and even the roofs of Minorcan houses are brightly whitewashed; the low dividing walls so typical of the island also have a white band along the top. Tiles are used for roofing, chimneys and guttering. Houses are built facing south, their fronts characterised by wide, open bays while the northern walls, exposed to fierce *tramontana* winds, have very small windows.

English influence on architecture is evident in the towns, where many of the houses have sash windows and some of the seigniorial mansions are in the Palladian style fashionable in Britain in the 18C.

Address Book

For coin ranges, see the Legend at the back of the guide.

WHERE TO EAT

Itake – *Moll de Llevant 317 (Puerto) – Mahón – ☎ 971 35 45 70 – Closed Sun evening, Mon and 23 Dec-2 Jan – ▤ – Reservation recommended.* Understandably, given its location near the port, the colourful decor in this small and inviting restaurant takes its inspiration from the sea and the theme of long ocean voyages. The cuisine here is simple yet original, with signature dishes such as potatoes stuffed with *sobrasada* (sausage), ostrich and kangaroo.

El Horno – *Des Forn, 12 - Ciudadela – ☎ 971 38 07 67 – Open Holy Week-Oct – ▤.* A modest family operation in cosy surroundings. The ground floor is rustic, with a French-inspired menu at moderate prices.

Binisues – *2km/1.2mi from Ferreries on the Ciutadella road. Camino de Ets Alocs – ☎ 971 37 37 28 – ▱.* The interior of this magnificent castle, with its impressive yellow façade, is shared between an exhibition of antiques (entry fee) and a select restaurant specialising in quality seafood (lobster, prawns etc). The views of the surrounding area from the terrace are quite spectacular.

WHERE TO STAY

Hotel Del Almirante – *El Fonduco (Puerto) – es Castell – ☎ 971 36 27 00 – ▣ ▥ – 39 rooms – ▱.* The antique furniture, paintings adorning the walls and "very British" clientele confer a special feel to this old mansion. It is also said that the ghost of Admiral Collingwood continues to haunt its walls. Excellent value for money.

Son Triay Nou – *Carretera de Cala Galdana – Ferreries – 3km/2mi from Ferreries towards Cala Galdana – ☎ 971 15 50 78 – ▣ ▥ – 6 rooms (doubles only).* This Italianate mansion with its raspberry-coloured façade stands in a romantic setting surrounded by greenery. The bedrooms are both comfortable and attractive although the bathrooms are on the small side.

Hotel Biniali – *Carretera S'Ullastrar-Binibèquer 50 – Sant Lluís – 1.5km/1mi SW – ☎ 971 15 17 24 – Closed Holy Week-Nov – ▣ ▥ – 9 rooms – ▱ 8.50€.* This fine example of typically Menorcan architecture occupies a former farm encircled by a small park. The comfortable rooms are all individually decorated and furnished, some with terraces offering expansive views of the local countryside.

J. Hidalgo, C. Lopesino/ MARCO POLO

Harbour, Ciutadella

The fields around Ciutadella are scattered with curious stone constructions shaped like ziggurats (the pyramidal stepped towers of ancient Mesopotamia); these *barracas*, vaulted inside with false ceilings, served as shelters for shepherds.

Worth a Visit

CIUTADELLA/CIUDADELA★

In the Middle Ages, Ciutadella, the citadel, and capital of Menorca, was ringed with walls. The ramparts were demolished in 1873 but their layout can still be distinguished in the circle of avenues around the old quarter. The fortified aspect of the city becomes evident when viewed from the harbour.

After being sacked by Turkish pirates in the 16C, Ciutadella was partly rebuilt in the late 17C and 18C. Today, the atmosphere in the alleys of the old quarter and in the harbour, give the town a calm and indefinable charm.

Each year the **Midsummer's Day Festivities** or **Fiestas de San Juan,** are celebrated with traditional rejoicing. On the preceding Sunday, a man representing John the Baptist, dressed in animal skins and carrying a lamb, runs through the town to the sound of *fabiols* (small flutes) and *tambourins*. On 24 and 25 June, over 100 horsemen take part in jousting tournaments and processions.

Barrio Antiguo (Old Quarter)

Plaza del Born, the former parade ground, is flanked by the eclectic 19C façade of the **Ayuntamiento** (town hall) and the early-19C **Palacio de Torre-Saura,** a palace with side loggias. In the centre of the square is an obelisk commemorating the townspeople's heroic stand against the Turks in the 16C.

Catedral

⚷ *Closed for renovation.* ☏ *971 38 07 39.*

The late-14C fortified church has kept part of the minaret of the mosque which once stood on the site. Inside, the single aisle is ogival and the apse pentagonal. You will be able to see the church's Baroque doorway from calle del Rosario facing the cathedral. At the end of the street, turn left into calle del Santísimo where two fine late-17C mansions may be seen on opposite sides of the street: **Palacio Saura** has a Baroque façade adorned with a cornice, while **Palacio Martorell** is of a more sober design. By way of calle del Obispo Vila, in which stand the Claustro de Socorro (Socorro Cloisters) and the Iglesia de Santo Cristo (Church of the Holy Christ), you come to the main street which leads to **plaza de España** and the arcaded **carrer de Ses Voltes**.

Puerto (Harbour)

The ramp approach to the harbour, which is well sheltered and serves mainly pleasure craft, is along a former counterscarp. The buildings along the quays are bustling with cafés and restaurants. The esplanade beyond, pla de Sant Joan, the centre for Midsummer's Day festivities, is bordered by boat shelters hollowed out of the living rock. The whole area comes alive at night.

Excursions

Nau or Naveta des Tudons

5km/3mi E of Ciutadella. This funerary monument, shaped like an upturned ship, is notable for the vast size of the stones in the walls and, more particularly, those lining the floor inside.

Cala Santandria

3km/2mi S. This is a small sheltered beach in a creek.

Cala Torre-Saura, Cala Turqueta, Cala Macarella

Ask locally for directions. The three beaches are set in small, beautifully unspoilt creeks fringed by sweet-smelling pines.

MAÓ/MAHÓN

Maó's **site**★ is most striking when approached from the sea: it appears high atop a cliff in the curve of a deep, 5km/3mi long roadstead or natural harbour.

Maó reached its height during the English occupation from 1713 to 1782 when it was endowed with Palladian-style mansions.

On the north side of the harbour is the Finca de San Antonio – the Golden Farm – where Admiral Nelson lived during a brief stay on the island, and where he put the finishing touches to his book, *Sketches of My Life* (October 1799).

The town gave its name to a sauce which we now know as mayonnaise.

Most of the town's shops are in the network of streets between **plaza del Ejército**, a large, lively square lined with cafés and restaurants, and the quieter **plaza de España** with its two churches: **Santa Maria**, with a beautiful Baroque organ, and **Carmen**, the Carmelite church, whose cloisters have been converted to hold the municipal market.

Museo de Menorca

🕐 *Open 9.30am-2pm; Sa-Sun 10am-2pm (Apr-Sep, 10am-2pm and 6-8.30pm; Sun 10am-2pm)*. 🕐 *Closed Mon and public hols.* 👓 *2.40€, no charge Sat (afternoon) and Sun.* ☎ *971 35 09 55.*

The museum occupies a former Franciscan monastery. The rooms are laid out around a sober 18C cloister and display prehistoric and other objects relating to Menorcan history, including a room dedicated to the local *talayot* culture.

Puerto (Harbour)

Walk down the steep ramp from carrer de Ses Voltes, cut by a majestic flight of steps, and follow the quay to the north side of the roadstead. Look across the water for a view of the town at its most characteristic, with its larger buildings lining the top of the cliff and below, the open-air dance halls, the restaurants, shops and coloured fishermen's cottages, snug against the foot.

Excursions

La Rada★ (Roadstead)

The south side consists of a series of coves and villages, among them Cala Figuera with its fishing harbour and restaurants. **Es Castell**, further along, was built as a garrison town by the English when it was called Georgetown. It has a grid plan, with the parade ground at its centre. The islands in the natural harbour include Lazareto and, beside it, Cuarentena, which, as its name suggests, was a quarantine hospital for sailors. A road follows the northern shore to the Faro de la Mola (Mola Lighthouse) affording views of Maó.

Talayot de Trepucó

1km/0.6mi S of Maó. This megalithic site is famous for its *taula* which is 4.80m/16ft high.

Sant Lluís

4km/2.5mi S. The town with its narrow streets was founded by the French during their occupation of the island.

Small resorts have grown up nearby: at **Alcalfar** where the houses stand a short distance inland beside a creek between two rocky promontories, and **Binibèquer**, a small, completely new village which, with its alleyways, small squares, and dazzling white houses, has been made to look like a fishing hamlet.

Es Grau

8km/5mi N. Beside the attractive white village with its long beach is a vast lagoon, **Albufera de es Grau,** 2km/1mi long and 400m/437yd wide. It is an ideal spot to watch the rich migrant bird life (rails, ducks and herons).

Cala en Porter

12km/8mi W. High promontories protect a narrow estuary inlet, lined by a sandy beach. Houses stand perched upon the left cliff. From their lofty position, ancient troglodyte dwellings, the **Coves d'en Xoroi**, overlook the sea. A bar has been installed in one of them.

MERCADAL

Mercadal, a small town of brilliantly whitewashed houses halfway between Maó and Ciutadella, is the point where roads to the coast meet on the north-south axis.

Excursions

Monte Toro

3.5km/2mi along a narrow road. On a clear day, the **view**★★ from the church-crowned summit (358m/1 175ft) is of the entire island. You can see the indented Bahía de Fornells (Fornells Bay) to the north, the straight line of the coastal cliffs to the south and Maó to the southeast.

Fornells

8.5km/5mi N on the C 723. Fornells, a small fishing village of whitewashed houses with green shutters, lies at the mouth of a deep inlet, surrounded on all sides by bare moorland. The village lives off crayfish fishing, as can be seen from the single-sail craft moored in the harbour. The local speciality, crayfish soup or caldereta, is a food-lover's delight.

Cap de Cavalleria

12km/8mi N along the PM 722. The drive to the cape, the northernmost point on the island, is through windswept moorland, battered by the *tramontana* from the north, with large, white, elegant country houses, like that at Finca Santa Teresa. The **view** from the lighthouse is of a rocky, indented coast, more Atlantic than Mediter-ranean.

Cala Santa Galdana

16km/10mi SW via Ferreries. The beauty of this magnificent cove set in a limpid bay flanked by tall cliffs, has been somewhat marred by the construction of large hotels.

🚶 It is also possible to walk to the cove from **the Algendar ravine** *(on leaving Ferreries, take the track left towards Ciutadella).* The path (🕐 *3hr there and back)* winds through a ravine beside a stream which is enclosed in places by cliffs up to 50m/160ft tall.

IBIZA★

POPULATION: 88 000

572 KM2/221SQ MI – MICHELIN MAP 579 – BALEARES.

The modern face of Ibiza is that of an island frequented by young hedonists who come here to enjoy the renowned nightlife. Yet, despite this image and the subsequent over-development, many parts of the island remain a natural paradise. There are stunning beaches, hidden coves and delightful villages with narrow streets lined by whitewashed houses and simple churches, all of which combine to forge a personality that is unique in the Balearics.

Location

Ibiza is the closest of the Balearic islands to the Spanish mainland (83km/52mi). In total, the "island of pines", as the Greeks named it, has 210km/131mi of coastline.
🚌 *Eivissa: Plaça d'Antoni Riquer 2, 07800, ☎ 971 30 19 00.*

Background

Historical notes – Ibiza's history dates from the beginnings of trade development throughout the Mediterranean: in the 10C BC, Phoenicians made the island a staging-post for ships loaded with Spanish metal ores returning to Africa; in the 7C BC, Carthage grew all-powerful and founded a colony on the island; under the Romans the capital grew in size and prosperity to judge from the necropolis discovered at Puig des Molins.

Landscape – Ibiza, the **Isla Blanca** or White Island, as it has been called, is the largest of the Pityuses Islands (the name given to Ibiza and Formentera by the ancient Greeks). It lies 52 miles from the peninsula, 45 miles southwest of Mallorca, and measures 41km/25mi in length.

Dazzling whitewashed walls, flat roof terraces, tortuous alleys and an atmosphere similar to that of a Greek island give Ibiza its unique character within the Balearics. It is a mountainous island where the muddled lines of relief leave little space for cultivation between the limestone hills. Among pines and junipers on the hillsides stand the cube-shaped houses of many small villages. The shore appears wild and indented, guarded by high cliffs; promontories are marked by rocks out to sea, some standing as high as the amazing limestone needle known as **Vedrá**★ (almost 400m/1 300ft).

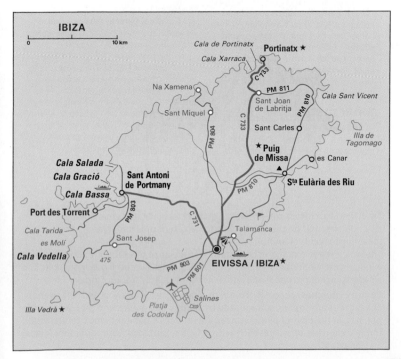

Address Book

For coin ranges, see the Legend at the back of the guide.

WHERE TO EAT

◉ **Sa Caleta** – *Playa Es Bol Nou (Sa Caleta) – Sant Josep – ☎ 971 18 70 95 – Only noon-7pm (Jul-Sep noon-midnight)*. The Sa Caleta enjoys a splendid position by the sea in an unspoilt bay surrounded by red earth. Its faithful customers come here in the knowledge that only the freshest fish is served, including seafood produced in the restaurant's own seawater nurseries.

◉◉ **El Chiringuito es Cavallet Playa** – *Playa Es Cavallet – Ibiza – ☎ 971 39 53 55 – Only open at lunchtime in summer*. A *chiringuito* is generally an informal beach-side shack, although in this instance the description is somewhat wide of the mark. For many years the place to meet, this restaurant is popular with the rich and famous who come here to eat on the huge terrace overlooking the beach. The quality of the cuisine doesn't disappoint, living up to the restaurant's well-earned reputation.

◉◉ **C'an Pujol** – *Carretera Vieja a Port des Torrent (Bahía de San Antonio) – Sant Antoni de Portmany – ☎ 971 34 14 07 – Closed Wed and in Dec – Reservation recommended*. This family-run restaurant is hidden amid the concrete of Sant Antoni. If you're planning on trying the house speciality (*bullit de peix*), a delicious fish stew served with rice made from a broth using the same fish, make sure you call ahead of time.

◉◉ **Villa Mercedes** – *Passeig del Mar – Sant Antoni de Portmany – ☎ 971 34 85 43 – ▦*. The Villa Mercedes is an exclusive restaurant in an attractive Modernist-style house. The views from the dining room windows encompass the ever-changing harbour, which is particularly busy at night. The menu here is on the original side and should satisfy even the most demanding of gourmets.

WHERE TO STAY

◉ **Sa Pensió** – *Carrrer de Sa Cala 11 – Sant Joan – ☎ 971 33 30 12 – 12 rooms*. This modest town house to the north of the island has a dozen farily basic but perfectly acceptable rooms, a few with their own terrace. The pleasant dining room offers an attractive setting for a relaxed evening meal.

◉◉ **Hostal Parque** – *Plaça del Parque 4 – Ibiza – ☎ 971 30 13 58 – ▦ – 34 rooms*. Small but pleasing rooms with excellent sound-proofing to block out the noise from the plaza del Parque, a popular meeting-point for local youngsters.

◉◉ **Hotel Montesol** – *Passeig Vara de Rei 2 – Ibiza – ☎ 971 31 01 61 – ▦ – 55 rooms – ⌁ 5*. Nothing in the town can compare with this large, mustard-coloured building dating from the beginning of the last century, with its comfortable rooms overlooking the streets of the old quarter. Make sure you enjoy a drink on the hotel's terrace café, which continues to be one of Ibiza's famous locations.

◉◉ **La Colina** – *5.5km/3.5mi SW of Santa Eulalia del Río – ☎ 971 33 27 67 – Closed in Dec – 🅿 – 16 rooms – ⌁*. This traditional, Ibizan-style country house stands on the side of a small hill. Now a quiet, family-run hotel, it is increasingly popular with foreign visitors. Pleasant outdoor areas, including a swimming pool.

◉◉ **Can Jondal** – *Sant Josep – Carretera de San José a Ibiza. – ☎ 971 18 72 70 – beashabteleline.es – ⇥ ⌁ – 6 rooms – ⌁*. A pleasant Ibizan house with whitewashed walls, numerous terraces and tastefully decorated rooms. A haven of peace and quiet on the slopes of a hill in the midst of nature. A friendly welcome guaranteed.

◉◉◉ **Hotel Rural Es Cucons** – *Santa Agnès de Corona –1km along Corona - Camí des Plà de Corona - ☎ 971 80 55 01 – escuconsretemail.es – ⌁ ▦ – 14 rooms – ⌁ – Restaurant 10/32€*. The young couple who own this hotel have succeeded in converting this former Ibizan farm into an architectural jewel that has been magnificently decorated in keeping with its origins. A superb combination of luxury and simplicity at the heart of an expansive valley carpeted in almond trees.

Traditional architecture – While the architecture inland has managed to preserve its traditions, that on the coast tends to have suffered from overdevelopment to meet the demands of tourism.

The typical Ibizan cottage, or **casament**, is made up of several white cubes with few windows; each represents a single room and opens off a central common room. The arcaded porches provide shade and a sheltered area for storing crops.

Country churches are equally plain with gleaming white exteriors and dark interiors. The façades are square, surmounted by narrow bell gables and pierced by wide porches. In the days of pirate attacks, the island's inhabitants took refuge in the fortified churches of villages such as Sant Carles, Sant Joan, Sant Jordi, Sant Miquel and Puig de Missa.

Folklore and traditional costume – Ibiza's uncomplicated folklore lives on in the everyday practices of its modern inhabitants. Women are still to be seen wearing the traditional long gathered skirt and dark shawl. At festivals the costume is brightened with fine gold filigree necklaces or **emprendades**. The island dances are performed to the accompaniment of flute, tambourine and castanets, by groups whose skill becomes evident as they perform the steps faster and faster.

Economy – Ibiza's main resource is its tourism, an industry that has unfortunately marred some of the island's sites. The **salt pans** *(salinas)* in the south, exploited since Carthaginian times, produce about 50 000t of salt a year.

Worth a Visit

EIVISSA/IBIZA★

Eivissa's colourful beauty and impressive **site**★★ are best appreciated for the first time if seen from the sea; alternatively take the **Talamanca** road out of town and look back *(3km/2mi NE)*. The town, built on a hill overlooking the sea, consists of an old quarter ringed by walls, the lively Marina district near the harbour, and, further out, residential and shopping areas. All along the shoreline are large hotels.

Upper town★ (Dalt Vila) 🕐 *1hr 30min*

The Dalt Vila, enclosed by the 16C walls built under Emperor Charles V, is the heart of the old city and retains even today a certain rustic, medieval character. There remain many noble houses worth looking at particularly for their vast patios and Gothic windows.

Enter the quarter through the **Porta de Taules**, a gateway which is surmounted by Philip II's crest, and either continue by car up a steep slope to the cathedral square or take a leisurely stroll through the quiet meandering streets with their shops and art galleries.

Catedral

🔒 *Closed for restoration.* ☎ *971 31 27 73*

The cathedral's massive 13C belfry, which closely resembles a keep but for its two storeys of Gothic bays, totally dominates the town. The nave was rebuilt in the 17C. An ancient bastion behind the east end has been converted into a lookout point from which you can get a good **panoramic view**★ of the town and harbour.

Museo Arqueológico de Ibiza y Formentera★

🕐 *Open 9am-3pm; in summer, 10am-2pm and 6-8pm; Sun 10am-2pm.* 🕐 *Closed Mon and public hols.* 💶 *2.40€, no charge Sat afternoon and Sun.* ☎ *971 30 12 31.*

The museum's most impressive exhibits are those from Punic art, which developed around the Mediterranean from the 7C BC to the 3C AD. Particularly impressive are the ex-votos discovered on Ibiza and Formentera, predominantly from excavations at Illa Plana and the Es Cuiram cave. The cave is believed to have been a temple to the goddess **Tanit**, who was venerated there from the 5C BC to the 2C BC. Also worthy of note are the examples of polychrome moulded glass and Punic, Roman and Moorish ceramics.

The goddess Tanit

J. Malburet/ MICHELIN

Lower town

Museu Monogràfic de Puig des Molins★ (Puig des Molins Monographic Museum)

🔒 *Closed for restoration.* ☎ *971 30 17 71.*

The Puig des Molins hillside necropolis was a burial-ground for the Phoenicians from the 7C BC and then for the Romans until the 1C AD. There is a model of the site in Room IV and some of the hypogea, or underground funerary chambers, of which over 3 000 have been discovered, may be visited.

The objects displayed were found in the tombs and include articles from everyday life as well as items used in funerary rituals which represented symbols of resurrection. The outstanding, partly coloured, 5C BC **bust of the goddess Tanit**★, a Punic version of the Phoenician Astarte, is a perfect example of Greek beauty. A second bust is more Carthaginian.

La Marina

The Marina district near the municipal market and the harbour, with its restaurants, bars and shops, stands in lively contrast to the quieter Dalt Vila.

Sa Penya★

The former fishermen's quarter, now the centre of Ibiza's nightlife, is built on a narrow rock promontory at the harbour mouth and is quite different from the rest of the town. Within the limited space available, white cubic houses overlap and superimpose on one another in picturesque chaos, completely blocking streets in places and compelling them to continue by means of steps cut out of the rock.

SANT ANTONI DE PORTMANY/SAN ANTONIO ABAD

Sant Antoni with its vast, curved bay has been extensively developed by the tourist industry. The old quarter, hidden behind modern apartment blocks, centres around a fortified 14C church rebuilt in the 16C. There is a large pleasure boat harbour. Several coves and creeks are within easy distance of the town.

Excursions

Cala Gració

2km/1.2mi N. A lovely, easily accessible, sheltered creek.

Cala Salada

5km/3mi N. The road descends through pines to a well sheltered beach in a cove.

Port des Torrent and Cala Bassa

5km/3mi SW. Port des Torrent is all rocks; Cala Bassa a long, pine-fringed beach. In this part of the coast the rocks are smooth and separate and just above or just below the water line, providing perfect underwater swimming conditions.

Cala Vedella

15km/9mi S. A road skirts the shoreline through pine trees between the beaches of Cala Tarida (rather built-up), Es Molí (unspoiled) and Cala Vedella in its enclosed creek. You can return to Sant Antoni along a mountain road cut into the cliffs as far as Sant Josep.

SANTA EULÀRIA DES RIU/SANTA EULALIA DEL RÍO

Santa Eulària des Riu, standing in a fertile plain watered by Ibiza's only river, has grown into a large seaside resort with modern buildings. Beaches in the vicinity, like that at **Es Canar**, have also been developed.

Puig de Missa★

▶ *Bear right off the Eivissa/Ibiza road 50m/55yd after the petrol station (on the left).*

This minute, fortified town crowning the hilltop provides a remarkable overview of the island's traditional peasant architecture; the town is a surviving example, in fact, of those easily defended hills, where, in case of danger, the church (16C) served as a refuge.

Excursions

Portinatx★

27km/17mi N on the PM 810, PM 811 and C 733. The road passes through **Sant Carles** which has a fine church and is a departure point for quiet local beaches. It then descends to the vast **Sant Vicent** creek *(cala)* with a beautiful sandy beach and opposite, the Isla de Togomago, before crossing an almost mountainous landscape covered in pines. The last section of the approach road is picturesque as it threads its way between holm oaks and almond trees looking down on **Cala Xarraca.** Creeks sheltered by narrow cliffs with pine trees fringing the sandy beaches, make **Cala de Portinatx** one of the island's most attractive areas.

J. Malburet/ MICHELIN

Portinatx

FORMENTERA

POPULATION: 6 000

84KM2/32SQ MI – MICHELIN MAP 579.

Formentera, christened the "Wheat Island" by the Romans (*frumentum*: wheat in Latin), is the smallest island in the archipelago, and is the ideal retreat for those in search of peace and quiet, impressive scenery and beautiful beaches lapped by crystal-clear water.

Location

Formentera lies just 7km/4.5mi south of Ibiza. It has an overall length from west to east of 14km/9mi although it is in fact two islets joined by a sandy isthmus. The "capital", Sant Francesc de Formentera, the passenger port, Cala Savina, the salt pans, Cabo de Barbaria and the dry open expanse on which cereals, figs, almonds and a few vines are grown, are on the western islet; the island's 192m/630ft high "mountain", its slopes covered in dwarf pines, rises from the **Mola** promontory on the eastern islet. Rock cliffs and sand dunes alternately line the shore.
Access to the island is exclusively by sea, and the best way of exploring Formentera is by bicycle. ◻ *Port de Sabina, 07870 Formentera, ☎ 971 32 20 57.*

Special Features

The Beaches (Playas or Platjas)

The white sandy beaches with their clear water are the island's main attraction. Long beaches stretch along either side of the isthmus, the rocky Tramuntana to the north and the sheltered, sandy Migjorn to the south. Other, smaller beaches around the island include Es Pujòls (the most developed), Illetas and Cala Saona.

Cala Savina

Your landing point on the island is in the main harbour: a few white houses stand between two big lagoons, salt-marshes glisten in the distance on the left.

Sant Francesc (San Francisco Javier)

Chief and only town on the island. Its houses are clustered around the 18C church-fortress.

> ### Historical Notes
>
> Formentera's inhabitants arrived comparatively recently, the island having been abandoned in the Middle Ages in the face of marauding Barbary pirates and only repopulated at the end of the 17C. Most of the present population consists of fishermen and peasant farmers, shipping figs and fish to Ibiza and salt to Barcelona.

El Pilar de la Mola

The hamlet at the centre of the Mola promontory has this geometrically designed church which is similar to those on Ibiza, only smaller.

Faro de la Mola

The lighthouse overlooks an impressive cliff. There is a monument to Jules Verne who mentioned this spot in one of his books.

CANARY ISLANDS ★★★

POPULATION: 1 600 000

7 273KM²/2 808SQ MI.

These volcanic islands, where nature has been at its most generous, provide visitors with myriad contrasts: exuberant vegetation and desert landscapes; steep cliffs and seemingly endless beaches; and picturesque villages and bustling resorts.

These attractions, coupled with a fantastic climate, have turned the "Fortunate Islands" into one of the world's leading tourist destinations, particularly during the winter months, when hundreds of thousands of visitors descend on the Canaries from northern Europe.

Location

The Canary Islands lie slightly north of the Tropic of Cancer – average latitude 28° – in the Atlantic, 10 times nearer to the coast of Africa (115km/70mi) than to Spain to which they belong (1 150km/700mi). The total surface area of the seven islands together with six smaller islets is 7 273 km2/2 808sq mi (compare with Madrid province: 7 995 km2/3 086sq mi). The archipelago is divided into two provinces: the eastern, called **Las Palmas**, consists of Gran Canaria, Fuerteventura and Lanzarote; the western, called **Santa Cruz de Tenerife,** consists of Tenerife, La Palma, La Gomera and El Hierro. The Canary Islands are one of Spain's autonomous communities, in which Santa Cruz de Tenerife and Las Palmas de Gran Canaria share the status of capital. Each island has its own local council (Cabildo Insular), which, in reality, acts as its own governing body.

Background

Volcanic creation – The islands were thrust up from the Atlantic seabed by volcanic eruptions well before the Tertiary Era. La Gomera and Gran Canaria have the typical conic silhouette and most of the islands, except for Fuerteventura and Lanzarote, are very hilly and end in steep cliffs on the coast. The height of the Pico del Teide, or El Teide, at 3 718m/12 195ft the highest point in the archipelago and indeed in all Spain, slightly exceeds the average depth of the sea round the islands, 3 000m/16 640 fathoms. Despite its small area, La Palma reaches a height of 2 426m/7 959ft. Erosion and successive eruptions (the most recent was on La Palma in October 1971) have altered the islands' configuration; lava streams (of the Hawaiian type), slag deserts (of the Stromboli type) and fields and cones of cinder (of the Vulcanian type) form what is known locally as the **malpaís** which is most extensive on Lanzarote.

Mount Teide (Tenerife)

Getting To The Canary Islands

BY PLANE

All the islands have an airport (Tenerife has two), offering easy, rapid access to the Spanish mainland and the rest of Europe, which is where most of the islands tourists come from. A number of inter-island routes also operate throughout the year. The two airports handling the greatest number of flights are Tenerife and Gran Canaria, whereas the airports at El Hierro and La Gomera offer scheduled flights on smaller planes between the different islands.

Iberia ☏ 902 400 500; www.iberia.com

Binter Canarias: Inter-island flights only. Contact Iberia for information and reservations.

Spanair ☏ 902 13 14 15; www.spanair.com (flights to Gran Canaria, Tenerife and Lanzarote).

Air Europa ☏ 902 40 14 01; www.air-europa.com (flights to Gran Canaria, Tenerife and Lanzarote).

By ferry – For those intending to visit the Canary Islands from mainland Spain, there is a two-day boat trip leaving from Cádiz and travelling to Santa Cruz de Tenerife and Las Palmas de Gran Canaria. There are also ferry, jet-foil and hydrofoil services to travel from one island to the other.

Trasmediterránea ☏ 902 45 46 45; www.trasmediterranea.es

TIME

Clock times on the Canary Islands are the same as Greenwich Mean Time (so one hour behind mainland Spain).

ACCOMMODATION

Refer to the Address Book section under each island.

Visitors must bear in mind that on these islands the **high season** runs from 1 November to 30 April. During this period tourists come here to enjoy the wonderful climate and forget their cold, continental winters and springs. The more touristy areas feature big hotels belonging to well-known hotel chains. It has become difficult for people to book rooms independently, as most of the hotels cater to clients on package tours sent by travel agents. On the two larger islands, the south coast boasts particularly pretty beaches and a very sunny climate. La Palma, El Hierro and La Gomera are perfect resorts for those seeking a quiet, secluded spot.

The Fortunate Islands – Every year over 10 million tourists visit the islands to enjoy their wonderful climate and magnificent scenery. Although the Canary Islands are located in a subtropical zone, they enjoy a mild climate because of two characteristics: the persistence of trade winds and the presence of a cold current watering their shores. Without their influence, the Islands would be far hotter and far drier. While El Teide is snow-capped for several months in the year, the coasts bask in a very pleasant climate; the average temperature rarely drops below 18°C/65°F.

The islands closer to Africa can be hotter but temperatures rarely exceed 30°C/86°F thanks to the cold Canary current. Rain is practically unknown in the archipelago; the eastern islands sometimes experience whole years of drought.

The vegetation on the main islands and on the south side of the smaller islands, which is protected from the wind (sotavento), consists mainly of xerophils, plants adapted to dry conditions: cactus (cardón) and **nopal** (tunera), a type of Barbary fig which is attractive to the cochineal fly from which a popular red dye is extracted. On the hilly north coasts, however, which are exposed to the northeast trade winds (barlovento), the humidity in the atmosphere sustains a luxuriant vegetation (laurel and giant ericas). The volcanic soil is rich in natural minerals and very fertile. Irrigation enables a great variety of plants to be grown. Water draining from the mountain peaks is stored in huge cisterns. Banana plantations now cover the lowland in the north of Gran Canaria and Tenerife while tomatoes are cultivated in the south. In the eastern islands peasant ingenuity makes up for the absence of surface water.

The only species of the original flora to survive is the age-old **dragon tree** (dracaena), of which there are many fine specimens on the islands. The tree sap was used for medicinal purposes by the Guanches (🕯 see below).

Barely 30 or 40 years ago, the economy of the Canary Islands was predominantly agricultural, specialising in export crops (bananas, oranges, tomatoes and tobacco), but today under 8% of the population live off farming. In fact, the islands' main source of income is tourism. The expansion of this area of activity has brought about an increase in the services sector, which employs 60% of the working population.

The Conquest – The islands are alluded to in Greek literature, referred to more exactly by Plutarch and described in some detail by Pliny the Elder who called them the Isles of the Blest or the Fortunate Islands. Many explorers landed in the archipelago but none stayed, not even **Lancelloti Malocello** from Genoa, although Lanzarote took

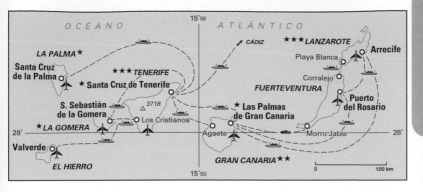

its name from him. The first expedition worthy of the name was made in 1402. The native population put up a fierce resistance and after several years of effort, **Jean de Bethencourt** and **Gadifer de la Salle** had subdued only four islands: Lanzarote, Fuerteventura and, to a lesser degree, La Gomera and El Hierro. The archipelago finally came under the control of Spain at the end of the century with the conquest of Gran Canaria by **Pedro de Vera** in 1483, of La Palma in 1492 and Tenerife in 1496 by **Alonso Fernández de Lugo**.

The origin of the name "Canaries" remains obscure, although some think it is derived from the Latin *canis* (dog), alluding to the very large dogs to be found on the islands.

The Guanches – When they arrived in the islands in the 15C the explorers found that the native population was still living in the Stone Age. The **Guanches** (the name of the inhabitants of Tenerife was extended to the rest of the archipelago) grew crops and kept cattle. They lived in caves in the volcanic rock, wore goats' skins and ate meal **(gofio)**, made from grilled cereals, and cheese made from goats' or sheep's milk. Their utensils were rudimentary. Only the way in which they buried their dead, almost always mummified and sewn up in goat skins, showed any sign of sophistication. Little is known about the origins of these people. From a study of their dead they appear to have belonged to the Cro-Magnon human type (who go back to the Ice Age); certain traits are typical of the Berbers of North Africa. No explanation has been found for the presence among them of fair-skinned, blond people. Conquest, and more particularly, natural disasters (plague, famine and volcanic eruptions) have left few survivors.

Local cuisine – Canary Island gastronomy is renowned for its *papas arrugadas* (literally wrinkled potatoes: tiny potatoes cooked in their skins in a small amount of heavily salted water so that a salt crust is formed around the potatoes as the water evaporates) and for its sauces made with olive oil: *mojos verdes* (flavoured with coriander) or *mojos rojos* (flavoured with paprika). Fish is also a popular dish and is caught locally – sama, sea bass, grouper, *vieja* – and cooked in a variety of manners (on one side, in a stew, baked in a crust of cooking salt etc). Two traditional dishes are *potaje* (a vegetable stew) and *sancocho* (stewed grouper with bananas, potatoes and a spicy sauce). The islands are also renowned for the variety and quality of their fruit: besides the tasty banana, try their delicious papayas, guavas and mangoes.

TENERIFE★★★

POPULATION: 685 583.

2 036KM²/786SQ MI.

The impressive snow-capped silhouette of El Teide, the highest peak in the whole of Spain (3 718m/12 195ft), is undoubtedly the most famous symbol of this beautiful island, whose name in the local Guanche language translates as "snow-covered mountain". Around this peak, the spectacular Las Cañadas crater bears witness to Tenerife's volcanic past. The island's magnificent climate and stunning beauty are its major assets, attracting those in search of sea, sand and sunshine as well as visitors who prefer to explore Tenerife's outstanding natural landscapes.

Location

Tenerife is the largest of the Canary Islands. As in Gran Canaria, the south is arid, while the steeper north coast is lush with banana plantations. Strangely, it is the north that is home to the largest resort on the island, Puerto de la Cruz. 🖪 *Santa Cruz de Tenerife: Plaza de España, 38003, ☎ 922 23 98 97; Playa de las Américas: Avenida Rafael Puig Llubina 1, 38660, ☎ 922 75 06 33; Puerto de la Cruz: Plaza de Europa, 38400, ☎ 922 38 60 00.*

Address Book

For coin ranges, see the Legend at the back of the guide.

WHERE TO EAT

⊜⊜ **Régulo** – *San Felipe 16 - Puerto de la Cruz – ☎ 922 38 45 06 – Closed Sun, lunchtime Sun and in Jul.* This traditional island house retains all its charm, with a lovely patio and dining areas on two floor. Antiques and plants are prominent in the decor.

⊜⊜ **Casa del Vino** – *Finca La Baranda. El Sauzal – 21km/13mi from Santa Cruz de Tenerife along the Autopista del Norte – ☎ 922 56 38 86 – Closed holiday evenings, Sun evenings and Mon.* This attractive restaurant in an old country house is decorated in rustic style with exposed wooden beams. Owned by the local town council, it serves a range of high-quality Canarian cuisine. A wine museum can also be visited within the same complex.

⊜⊜ **El Bacalao de la Cazuela** – *General Goded 11 – Santa Cruz de Tenerife – ☎ 922 29 32 49 – Closed Sat at lunch and Sun –* 🖾. Although its location near the bullring is a little away from the main centre and the menu slightly limited, this cheery restaurant is worth a visit for its high-quality cuisine, excellent daily specials and good wine list. A good balance between traditional meat and fish dishes, enlivened by the occasional modern flourish.

WHERE TO STAY

⊜⊜ **Monopol Hotel** – *Quintana 15 - Puerto de la Cruz – ☎ 922 38 46 11 – 92 rooms –* 🖾 *– Restaurant 12€.* This attractive four-storey whitewashed building adorned with wooden balconies stands in a pedestrianised street in a lively shopping district near the seafront. Comfortable rooms, arranged around a Canarian-style patio.

⊜⊜ **Hotel Aguere** – *Obispo Rey Redondo (Calle Carrera) 55 - La Laguna – ☎ 922 25 94 90 – 21 rooms –* 🖾. One of the few hotels on the island to have retained its old seigniorial charm. The wooden entrance door provides access to a large, patio-style open hall area around which all the rooms are laid out. The wooden floors, antique furniture and somewhat antiquated bathrooms provide further old-world charm. Highly recommended.

EXPENSIVE

⊜⊜⊜ **San Roque Hotel** – *Esteban de Ponte 32 – Garachico – ☎ 922 13 34 35 –* 🖾 *– 20 rooms –* 🖾. This luxury hotel is tucked away in a street in the centre of Garachico. The entrance patio, painted in a warm Pompeii red and adorned with a wooden balcony, sets the tone of the hotel, a fusion between the old and the contemporary, and traditional and Avant Garde design. The bedrooms, some of which are split-level, are both spacious and comfortable.

Special Features

PICO DEL TEIDE★★★

This impressive volcano rises imperiously in the centre of the island, with various access options available. Clouds often enshroud Mount Teide, preventing visitors from enjoying the superb panoramas from designated viewpoints.

When visiting the mountain, ensure that you have comfortable footwear and a warm jacket, as at this altitude the temperature and weather can change dramatically in a short time.

La Esperanza Approach★

The road climbs to the crest which divides the island into two, looking down on the north and south coasts alternately.

Pinar de la Esperanza★

The road runs for several miles through this extensive pinewood.
In the centre of a clearing, at a place known as **Las Raíces**, an obelisk commemorates the alliance of the local military chiefs in July 1936 under General Francisco Franco, then Captain-General of the Canary Islands, against the Spanish Republican Government. (Franco was posted to the Canaries in February 1936 after the triumph of the Popular Front.)

Belvederes★★

The road is punctuated by a series of belvederes (Montaña Grande, Pico de las Flores, Ortuño, Chipeque). When the mass of cloud which frequently surrounds El Teide disperses, admire the stark contrast between the lushness of the north coast and the aridity of the Güimar Valley to the south.
After La Crucita, the road enters into a high-mountain landscape. The Astronomical Observatory at Izaña is visible to the left.

El Portillo

Alt 2 030m/6 660ft. The pass, which joins up here with the TF 21 road from La Orotava, is the gateway to the mineralogically extraordinary world of Las Cañadas.

Mount Teide

J. Malburet/ MICHELIN

Parque Nacional del Teide★★★

At the entrance to the park is the El Portillo visitor centre which contains an informative exhibition on volcanism, as well as information on the network of local paths; the Cañada Blanca centre is located next to the parador. ⊙ *Open 9am-2pm.* ☁ *Guided walking tours (2hr) by prior arrangement.* ☎ *922 29 01 29/83.*

About 350m/1 150ft below the summit of El Teide lies Las Cañadas plateau, a spectacular volcanic crater at an altitude of over 2 000m/6 560ft which had fallen in on itself before El Teide was created. The Pico del Teide rises up from its northern side. In the centre of the park, opposite the hotel (parador), are a few boulders of lava **(Los Roques)**, laid bare by erosion. Other rocks **(Los Azulejos)** are covered with copper oxide which glints blue-green in the sun.

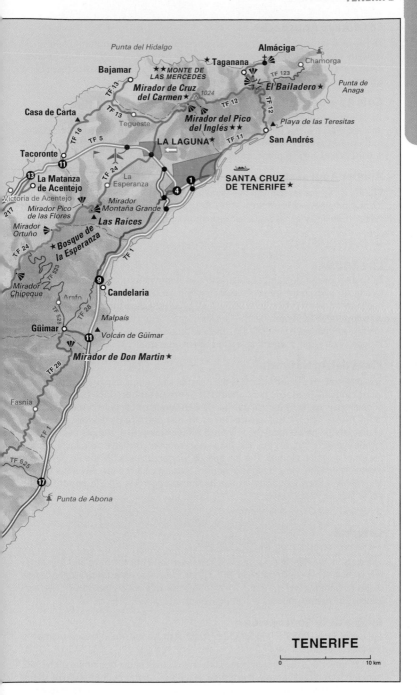

Punta del Hidalgo
Almáciga
★Taganana
Chamorga
Bajamar
★★MONTE DE
LAS MERCEDES
TF 123
Punta de
Anaga
Mirador de Cruz
del Carmen ★
El Bailadero ★
TF 13
TF 12
Casa de Carta
1024
TF 13
Mirador del Pico
del Inglés ★★
TF 12
Playa de las Teresitas
TF 16
Tegueste
TF 12
LA LAGUNA ★
TF 5
TF 11
San Andrés
Tacoronte
TF 24
①
SANTA CRUZ
DE TENERIFE ★
⑬ La Matanza
de Acentejo
La
Esperanza
④
Victoria de Acentejo
Mirador Pico
de las Flores
Mirador
Montaña Grande
217
Mirador
Ortuño
★ Las Raíces
★ Bosque de
la Esperanza
TF 24
TF 523
TF 1
Mirador
Chipeque
Arafo
⑨
TF 525
TF 28
Candelaria
Güimar
Malpaís
⑪
Volcán de Güimar
Mirador de Don Martín ★
TF 28
Fasnia
TF 1
TF 625
⑰
Punta de Abona

TENERIFE

0   10 km

Pico del Teide★★★

🚠 *Ascent by* **cable car** *from La Rambleta (2 356m/7 728ft): not suitable for those with respiratory or heart problems (the cable car climbs 1 199m/3 932ft in 8min).* 🕐 *Operates 9am-4pm (5pm in summer), weather permitting.* 🕐 *Closed 1 Jan and 25 Dec.* ⊗ *20€ round trip.* ☎ *922 53 37 20.*

🚶 From the top (3 555m/11 660ft), a steep 30min walk across loose volcanic scree leads to the summit *(the path to the summit is currently closed)*. The top of the cone is occupied by a crater, almost 25m/82ft deep and 50m/164ft in diameter, swathed in wisps of sulphurous smoke. On a clear day, the view covers the whole of the Canaries archipelago.

La Orotava Approach★

The vegetation on the north coast (bananas, fruit trees, corn, potatoes and vines) is clearly visible during the climb. The extensive pinewoods begin in **Aguamansa**. Beyond the village at the side of the road there is a huge basalt formation resembling a daisy.

Guía Approach

The climb via Guía is more mountainous. The narrow road crosses two Pico Viejo defiles, Las Narices del Teide (last eruption in 1798) and the Chinyero volcano (1909). As these are the last volcanoes to have erupted, the contrast between the pinewood and the defiles is more pronounced.

Vilaflor Approach

Vilaflor is the highest town on the island (1 466m/4 806ft). The road passes through a beautiful pinewood and then, at the **Boca de Tauce pass**★★ (2 055m/6 742ft), reveals a striking view of Las Cañadas dominated by El Teide.

Worth a Visit

LA LAGUNA★

La Laguna, once the island's capital and now home to its university, was founded by Lugo in 1496 on the edge of a lagoon which has since disappeared, The original quadrilateral plan is still evident. On the feast of Corpus Christi the streets are carpeted with flowers; on 14 September the Crucifix from San Francisco monastery, dedicated to the town's patron, is venerated in a massive procession and general festivities which include Canary Island wrestling, a sport which goes back to Guanche times.

Plaza del Adelantado

This pleasant, tree-lined square is the heart of La Laguna. It is fronted by several interesting buildings: the old **Convent of Santa Catalina**, which has retained its original upper gallery, a local feature rarely seen nowadays but once common enough in the islands; the 17C **Palacio de Nava** with its stone façade, reminiscent in style of the bishop's palace, and the town hall, or **ayuntamiento**, with its neo-Classical façade *(entrance for visits on calle Obispo Rey Redondo)*. The latter is in fact a combination of several buildings. The 16C and 18C portals on calle Obispo Rey Redondo, a street lined with some delightful houses, are particularly impressive. *Guided tours (45min), 8am-3pm (2pm Jul-Sep) by prior arrangement.* ○ *Closed Sat-Sun and public hols.* ☏ *922 63 11 94.*

▶ *Follow calle Obispo Rey Redondo.*

Catedral

⊶ *Closed for restoration.* ☏ *922 25 89 39.*

The elegant neo-Classical façade was erected in 1819 but the nave and four aisles were rebuilt in neo-Gothic style in 1905. Of particular note is the retable in the Capilla de los Remedios *(right transept)*, which also contains a 16C Virgin and 17C Flemish panels. The treasury houses rich liturgical objects.

Iglesia de la Concepción★

○ *Open 8.30am-7.30pm (7pm Sat); Sun 7.30am-8pm. No visits during religious services.* ◌ *0.60€.* ☏ *922 25 91 30.*

The 17C grey stone tower stands over this church, built at the beginning of the 16C, but with later modifications. It is typical of the sanctuaries built at the time of the conquest. In contrast to the sober style of the architecture, the interior has retained several Mudéjar ceilings, a ceiling with Portuguese influence, a Baroque pulpit and choir stalls, and a beaten silver altar *(Capilla del Santísimo)*.

▶ *Take calle Belén, then head down calle San Agustín.*

Palacio Episcopal or Antigua Casa de Salazar

The bishop's palace, also known as the House of Salazar, has a beautiful stone façade dating from the 17C and an attractive flower-decked patio.

Museo de Historia de Tenerife

○ *Open 9am-7pm.* ○ *Closed Mon, 1 and 6 Jan, Carnival Tue, and 24-25 and 31 Dec.* ◌ *3€, no charge Sun.* ☏ *922 82 59 49.*

The late-16C **Casa Lercano**, with its fine patio, is home to this museum. Its exhibits provide an overview of the island's social, economic, religious and institutional history from the 15C to the present day.

Santuario del Cristo

At the end of calle Nava Grimón. The church contains a much venerated 15C Crucifix at the centre of a typical beaten silver altarpiece.

SANTA CRUZ DE TENERIFE★

The capital of the island began life as a small port serving La Laguna, developed further in the 19C, and has since become the island's maritime and industrial centre. It is a port of call for ocean liners and cargo vessels, a role it shares with Puerto de la Luz in Las Palmas. An oil refinery, tobacco factory and other industrial plants contribute to the local economy.

From the harbour breakwater there is a **view**★ of the town: a stepped semicircle of high-rise buildings against the backdrop of the Pico del Teide and the Anage massif.

SANTA CRUZ DE TENERIFE			Doctor Guigou	CX	12	Imeldo Seris	CY	31
			Doctor José Naveiras	CX	13	José Murphy	CY	34
			Domínguez Alfonso	CY	15	Numancia	BX	39
Alférez Provisional Pl.	CY	3	General Galcerán Puente	BY	19	Pérez Galdós	CY	43
Bethencourt Alfonso	CY	5	General Gutiérrez	DY	20	Saludo	DX	46
Bravo Murillo Av. de	DY	6	General O'Donnell	DY	23	San Francisco Pl.	DY	49
Candelaria Pl. de la	DY	8	General Serrador Puente	CY	24	San Isidro	DX	50
Castillo	CY		General Weyler Pl. del	BY	26	Santo Domingo Pl.	CY	51
Costa y Grijalba	BY	10	Iglesia Pl. de la	DY	30	Valentín Sanz	CY	53

The Guimera theatre, new auditorium (designed by Santiago Calatrava) and exhibition buildings bear witness to the city's cultural interests and tradition.

This quiet, peaceful town takes on quite a lively, even frenzied appearance during **Carnival**. That of Santa Cruz de Tenerife is probably the most famous and colourful in all of Spain. The whole city takes part in this hugely popular celebration. Children and grown-ups alike dress up and join the mounted procession that involves many groups of performers and onlookers.

Iglesia de la Concepción

The few houses with balconies built around the 16C-18C church are all that remains of the old city. The most impressive features of the church's exterior are the high tower and balconies; its interior contains some fine Baroque retables.

Museo de la Naturaleza y el Hombre★
(Museum of Nature and Man)

🕐 Open 9am-7pm. 🕐 Closed Mon, 1 an 6Jan, Carnival Tuesday and 24-25 and 31 Dec. 🖂 3€, no charge Sun. ☎ 922 53 58 16.

This interesting museum is in the former Hospital Civil, a large neo-Classical building. Its exhibits include well-presented collections from the fields of archaeology and natural science.

Palacio de Carta

This 18C palace is situated on plaza de la Candelaria, close to the monumental plaza de España. Although it has now been converted into the headquarters of a bank, it retains its delightful patio with wooden arches and galleries.

Iglesia de San Francisco

The church was built in the 17C and 18C and displays the characteristics of Canary Island churches from this period: naves with wooden roofs and cylindrical pillars. The chancel contains a Baroque retable.

Parque Municipal García Sanabria★

This alluring tropical and Mediterranean garden is close to La Rambia, a large land-scaped boulevard and one of the city's main arteries.

Museo Militar

It was when attacking the town and castle on 24 July 1797 that Nelson lost both the battle ... and his right arm. Among the cannon on view is one known as the Tiger, which fired the fatal ball.

Parque Marítimo César Manrique★

▶ Leave by ② on the town plan. 🄺🄸🄳🄸 🕐 Open 10am-6pm (7pm spring and summer); last admission 1 hr before closing. 🖂 2.50€. ☎ 922 20 29 95.

This large leisure complex by the sea is a series of swimming pools and restaurants. Based on a design by the artist César Manrique, it successfully combines water, volcanic rock and vegetation.

PUERTO DE LA CRUZ★

The mushroom growth of Puerto de la Cruz, at the heart of the banana region on the north coast, is due not to the fishing on which it once relied but to tourism. The sun and the Pico del Teide look down on an exuberant proliferation of high-rise buildings going up side by side along the rock-strewn and reef-outlined coast. A pleasant, lively **seafront promenade★**, lined with outdoor terraces, shops and flower-hung viewpoints, and which includes the small 18C San Telmo hermitage, provides the main attraction of Tenerife's premier resort. The old part of the town (the pedestrian area between the Plaza de la Iglesia and Plaza del Charco) has preserved the typical architecture of the 17C and 18C with its balconied houses and attractive churches.

Lago Martiánez★ (Martiánez Lake)

🄺🄸🄳🄸 🕐 Open 10am-5pm (6pm Jun-Sep). 🕐 Partially Closed in May. 🖂 3.30€. ☎ 922 38 59 55 or 922 37 13 21.

This large complex of swimming pools by the sea is surrounded by vegetation and volcanic rock. It is a fine example of the successful combination of aesthetics and leisure which characterises many of the works of its creator, the artist César Manrique.

Jardín de Aclimatación de la Orotava★★

▶ *Follow signs to Jardín Botánico.* ◯ *Open 9am-6pm (7pm Apr-Sep).* ◯ *Closed 1 Jan, Good Fri and 25 Dec.* ⊗ *0.60€.* ☎ *922 38 35 72.*

The botanical gardens, which cover only 2ha/5 acres, contain an extraordinary profusion of all sorts of trees and flowers from the Canary Islands and elsewhere in the world. The garden was created in the 18C by the Marquis of Villanueva del Prado on the orders of Charles III. It contains a wide variety of palm trees, although its most impressive exhibit is the rubber plant, which is over 200 years old and perches on adjacent roots as if on stilts.

Playa Jardín★ (Garden Beach)

▶ *To the W of the town; follow signposts.* This attractive, black sandy beach is surrounded by well-tended gardens. The **Castillo de San Felipe**, an old watchtower which is now used for cultural functions, can be seen to its eastern end.

Loro Parque (Parrot Park)

▶ *W of Playa Jardín; well signposted.* ◼Kids ◯ *Open 8.30am-6.45pm; last admission at 5pm.* ⊗ *17.21€.* ☎ *922 37 38 41.*

This subtropical 50 000m2/59 800sq yd garden has a comprehensive collection of parrots and animals (gorillas, monkeys, crocodiles etc), as well as a dolphinarium. Parrot and dolphin shows are regularly held for visitors.

LA OROTAVA▲▲

This ancient town, arranged in terraces at the foot of the mountain, dominates the fertile valley of the same name. It has preserved an impressive historic centre with fine mansions from different periods. Its balconies are some of the most beautiful in the Canary Islands.

On the Thursday after Corpus Christi, the streets are strewn with flowers and the main square is decorated with a gigantic variegated sand and pebble picture. On the second Sunday after the feast the people of the neighbouring villages meet for a pilgrimage *(romería de San Isidro)* dressed in traditional costume and riding in bullock carts (St Isidore was a farm labourer). Their attractive costumes and colourful carts add a picturesque note to this festival, which has been declared an event of national tourist interest.

▶ *Leave your car in plaza de la Constitución and continue your visit on foot.*

Plaza de la Constitución

The square, which is fronted by the 17C Baroque church of San Agustín and the Liceo Taoro cultural centre, acts as a viewpoint.

▶ *Follow calle Carrera, then descend the street to the right.*

Iglesia de la Concepción

◯ *Open 9am-1pm and 4-8pm; Sun and public hols, 10am-1pm.* ◯ *Closed Wed afternoon.* ☎ *922 33 01 87.*

La Orotava, with a dragon tree in the foreground

J. Malburet/ MICHELIN

The 18C church, built on the site of an earlier construction, has a graceful Baroque façade between flanking towers. The treasury is open to the public.

▶ *Return to calle Carrera.*

Calle Carrera

The street passes in front of the **plaza del Ayuntamiento**, with its neo-Classical style Palacio Municipal. The **Hijuela del Jardín Botánico** behind it, a lush park created in the 19C, used to act as a nursery for the Botanical Gardens in Puerto de la Cruz. ◷ *Open 9am-2pm. Closed Sat-Sun and public hols. No charge.* ☎ *922 38 35 72.*

Calle de San Francisco★

This street is adorned with some of the town's most beautiful balconies.

La Casa de los Balcones

Despite the name, this is in fact two 17C houses (nos 3 and 5), both with magnificent balconies and delightful patios. A craftwork shop *(ground floor)* and a small **Museo** *(first floor)* which shows the inside of a traditional bourgeois house have been created inside n°3. ◷ *Open 8.30am-7.30pm (1.30pm Sun).* ☜ *1.50€ (museum).* ☎ *922 33 06 29.*

La Casa Molina

Another craftwork shop has been established in this 16C-17C Renaissance-style house, which offers a fine view from its terrace.

▶ *Return to calle Carrera, then follow calle Tomás Zerolo to the left.*

Museo de Artesanía Iberoamericana

◷ *Open 9am-6pm; Sat, 9am-2pm.* ◷ *Closed Sun and public hols.* ☜ *2.10€.* ☎ *922 32 33 76.*

The museum is housed in the former Convento de Santo Domingo (17C). It displays a varied collection of Spanish and Latin-American handicrafts, including musical instruments, ceramics, textiles etc.

Excursions

MONTE DE LAS MERCEDES★★
Round trip of 49km/30mi from La Laguna. ◷ *Allow 3hr*

The mountainous Anaga headland is high enough to trap the clouds from the north so that the area is sufficiently humid for woodlands of tree laurel, giant heather and *fayas*, a local species, to flourish. The winding roads which carve their way through this part of the island offer some superb views.

Mirador de Cruz del Carmen★

A good view of La Laguna Valley can be enjoyed from this viewpoint which is situated inside the Parque Rural de Anaga. The visitor centre has an interesting exhibition on the park. ◷ *Open 9.30am-3pm (4pm in winter).* ☎ *922 63 35 76.*

Mirador del Pico del Inglés★★

An impressive panorama spreads out from the 1 024m/3 360ft peak of the Anaga headland to the distant Pico del Teide.

El Bailadero★

The road crossing this pass commands good views in both directions.

Taganana★

On the way downhill there are magnificent **views**★★ of the village's picturesque setting between two ravines. It is worth visiting the **Iglesia parroquial de Nuestra Señora de Las Nieves** for its Hispano-Flemish altarpiece. ◷ *Open 10 am-7pm; no visits during religious services.* ☎ *922 59 00 75.*

Almáciga
View of the coast and the Anaga headland from the hermitage.

San Andrés
Small fishing village; nearby is the golden sand beach of Las Teresitas.

Anaga mountains

TOUR OF THE ISLAND
310km/194mi – ⏱ *about 3 days*

👓 *This tour can be divided into three parts: the first section runs along the north coast from La Laguna to Garachico (100km/62mi); the second along the west coast from Garachico to Los Cristianos (77km/48mi); and the third to the south and west, ending up in Santa Cruz de Tenerife (133km/83mi).*

Bajamar
Large resort on a picturesque stretch of rocky coast with natural pools.

Casa de Carta
⏱ *Open 9am-7pm.* 🚫*Closed Mon, 1 and 6 Jan, Carnival Tue, and 24- 25 and 31 Dec.* 💰 *3€.* ☎ *922 54 63 00/8.*

The property is a typical Canary Island farm. An 18C building houses the **Museo de Antropología de Tenerife.**

Tacoronte
Here the lordly summit of El Teide comes into view. In the **Iglesia de Santa Catalina** there is a fine Mudéjar roof in the chancel. ⏱ *Visits by prior arrangement.* ☎ *922 56 06 91.*

Tacoronte is home to a handsome specimen of the dragon tree.

La Matanza de Acentejo
Here in La Matanza de Acentejo (Acentejo Massacre) in 1495, Lugo and his troops were soundly beaten by the Guanches; soon afterwards, however, Lugo got his revenge at the place now known as La Victoria (Victory) de Acentejo.

Mirador de Humboldt★★★
The lookout point is named after the German naturalist, Alexander Humboldt, who visited Tenerife in 1799 and was especially struck by the **Orotava Valley**. This immense depression at the foot of El Teide extends all the way to the sea, covered by a dense green carpet of banana trees broken only by gleaming water and the buildings of La Orotava town and Puerto de la Cruz.

La Orotava★★ 👣 *See La Orotava.*

Puerto de la Cruz★ 👣 *See Puerto de la Cruz.*

Los Realejos
From the town hall terrace of the upper village, there is a view of the villages along the coast; the nearby **Iglesia de Santiago Apóstol** has interesting vaulting. There is a dragon tree growing in the cemetery, which is perched on a tall rock spike. ⏱ *Open 6-9pm; Sun and public hols, 9am-1pm; otherwise by prior arrangement.* ☎ *922 34 02 61.*

Icod de los Vinos★
The town of Icod, which dates from the conquest (15C), is at the centre of a wine-producing area (*vinos* means wines). It boasts a **dragon tree**★ which is several thousand years old, the oldest and the most imposing in the Canary Islands *(signposted once*

you enter the town). The **Iglesia de San Marcos** is worth visiting, as is the nearby landscaped square which is surrounded by elegant houses with wooden balconies.

San Marcos

The road runs through banana plantations to reach this seaside resort which is sited in a rocky creek and backed by jagged black cliffs.

Garachico

Before the volcanic eruption in 1716 Garachico was an important town on the north coast. Little remains: a cluster of old houses and a fortress, the **Castillo de San Miguel.** A promenade has been built on the rough pointed rocks.

Valle de El Palmar★★

Take the TF 42 to the W of Garachico. Just beyond the El Palmar Valley, there is a tiny village built on a volcanic chimney in the centre of a crater which is neatly terraced for cultivation.

▶ *Return to Garachico.*

Drive south to **San Juan del Reparo** for a good **view**★ of Garachico.

Santiago del Teide

Picturesque domed church.

Masca

⊙ *Very dangerous road in poor state of repair.* Remote but charming hamlet set in delightful **countryside**★.

El Retamar

South of the village the road begins a long descent through lava fields produced by the eruption of the Chinyero volcano in 1909.

Acantilado de Los Gigantes★

The Teno mountain range ends here in enormous black cliffs which are rightly called Los Gigantes, the giants, because of their 400m/1 300ft vertical drop.

Adeje

Within walking distance of the village *(2km/1.2mi E)* lies the grandiose beauty of Hell Valley, **Barranco del Infierno**★, an enormous open crevice with a small watercourse running through it.

Playa de las Américas

A large resort with beaches of black sand and a multitude of hotels, apartments, restaurants, bars, nightclubs etc.

Los Cristianos

Once a fishing village, it is now one of the island's largest and busiest resorts. The Playa de las Vistas, in the centre of Los Cristianos, is one of its best beaches, with an attractive promenade running along it.

Parque Ecológico de Las Águilas del Teide

3km/2mi on the Los Cristianos-Arona road.
Kids ⊙ *Open 10am-6pm.* ⊛ *19€.* ☎ *922 72 90 10.*

This wildlife park has a large number of exotic birds and other animals on display across 75 000m²/89 700sq yd of lush gardens. The park also organises parrot shows and birds of prey demonstrations.

Cactus and Animal Park

▶ *Motorway exit 26 (Guaza), then take the signposted road to the left.*
Kids ⊙ *Open 10am-6.30pm.* ⊛ *10€.* ☎ *922 79 54 24.*

These cactus gardens are laid out in a desert-like setting. The park also contains a small animal area and an interesting reptilarium.

Jardines del Atlántico

4km/2.5mi on the Guaza-Valle de San Lorenzo road; the turn-off is indicated to the right.

🕐 *Open 9am-5.30pm.* 🚶 *Guided tours (recommended) at 10am, 11.30am, 1pm and 3.30pm.* 🕐 *Closed 1 Jan and 25 Dec.* 🎟 *10€.* ☎ *922 72 04 03.*

A stroll through this estate provides visitors with an introduction to the indigenous flora and traditional crops on the island (bananas, tomatoes, papayas, avocados etc). The gardens also displays a collection of agricultural and domestic tools.

▷ *Follow the TF 82 in the Valle de San Lorenzo.* Although longer and more winding than the motorway, the inland road (TF 82) is more beautiful and punctuated by many fine views.

Mirador de la Centinela★

Like a sentinel, the viewpoint is positioned on a rocky projection commanding a vast area of the plain pitted with craters.

El Médano

The beach, one of the best on the island for windsurfing, lies in the shelter of an eroded volcanic cone and is bordered by an attractive promenade.

▷ *Return to the inland road.*

Mirador de Don Martín★

The belvedere provides a view of the Güimar rift valley, the slopes of which are mainly covered in tropical fruit plantations. Between the town and the sea stands the imposing Güimar volcano.

Güimar

A major town on the south coast.

Candelaria

This coastal town is a well-known place of pilgrimage. In 1390 two Guanche shepherds found a statue of the Virgin Mary washed up on the beach. It was set up in a cave but in 1826 a storm swept it away. A **basílica** (1958) houses the new statue of the patron and the archipelago to which islanders make a pilgrimage on 14 and 15 August. In the square outside are nine statues of the Menceyes, the ancient Guanche chiefs of Tenerife.

GRAN CANARIA★★

POPULATION: 715 994.

560KM2/602SQ MI.

Because of the diversity of its landscapes, it is often said that Gran Canaria is a continent in miniature. This huge massif is dominated by the Pozo de las Nieves (1 949m/6 393ft) at its centre, around which a multitude of ravines fan out in all directions to the sea. The mountain relief, which acts as a cloud barrier and divides the island into two distinct climate zones, is the catalyst for the huge contrasts between the wetter landscapes of the north and west, and the extensive desert-like areas in the south of the island. The north and west coast is steep and rocky, in contrast to the more accessible south, with its long sandy beaches and major tourist resorts.

Location

Gran Canaria is an almost circular island wedged between Tenerife and Fuerteventura. It is the third largest Canary island in terms of area and has the largest city on the archipelago, Las Palmas de Gran Canaria. The airport, 20km/12mi from the capital, and Puerto de la Luz provide communication links with other islands, mainland Spain and abroad. 🄸 *Las Palmas de Gran Canaria: Parque Santa Catalina, 35007,* ☎ *928 22 09 47.*

Worth a Visit

LAS PALMAS DE GRAN CANARIA★

Las Palmas de Gran Canaria was founded in a palm grove in 1478 by Juan Rejón; it is now capital of the province of Las Palmas de Gran Canaria and is one of Spain's major ports.

Address Book

WHERE TO EAT

⊖⊖ **Mesón de la Montaña** – *Arucas* – ☎ *928 60 14 75* – 🍽. Despite the informal service, this restaurant represents good value for money. A recommended address for traditional Canarian cuisine served at large round tables in a pleasant location offering good views of Arucas.

⊖⊖ **Casa de Galicia** – *Salvador Cuyás 8 – Las Palmas de Gran Canaria* – ☎ *928 27 98 55* – 🍽. High-quality Galician cuisine where the emphasis is on freshness. A good position between the Playa de las Canteras and the Parque de Santa Catalina. The El Anexo restaurant next door is run by the same owners.

WHERE TO STAY

⊖ **Hotel Rural Casa de Los Camellos** – *Progreso 12 (on the corner of Retama)* – *Agüimes* – ☎ *928 78 50 03* – *11 rooms* – 🛏 *3.79€.* This small hotel, located in the old part of Agüimes, has been recently restored in a welcoming, rustic style, with wooden floors and furniture, and pleasant, attractively decorated bedrooms. The hotel also has two patios and its own restaurant.

⊖⊖ **Hotel Rural El Refugio** – *Cruz de Tejeda - Cruz de Tejeda* – ☎ *928 66 65 13* – 🅿 🍽 - *10 rooms* – 🛏 *4.50€.* The somewhat difficult access to this small country hotel is rewarded by its extraordinary setting in an area of lush vegetation near the Roque de Nublo and Roque de Bentayga. An excellent base for excursions through the centre of the island. Cosy bedrooms with wooden floors and attractive furniture.

⊖⊖ **Tenesoya** – *Sagasta, 98 - Las Palmas de Gran Canaria* – ☎ *928 46 96 08 - 42 rooms* – 🛏 *5.€* The best part of this hotel is its value. It's just a step from the beach and offers comfortable rooms with updated, well-equipped bathrooms.

It extends for nearly 10km/6mi between the Guiniguada Ravine *(S)* and the Isleta Peninsula *(N)* which forms a natural breakwater to the harbour.

Las Palmas de Gran Canaria comprises three districts: the old city, **Vegueta**, dates from the time of the conquest; **Puerto de la Luz**, the tourist district, is flanked by the harbour and Alcaravaneras beach on the east side and Canteras beach on the west; between them lies the residential garden city, **Ciudad Jardín.** Beyond the cliff which once formed the western limit to the city, new housing developments are proliferating. The airport *(25km/16mi)* and Las Palmas harbour are on the air and sea routes between Europe and South America and bring the island many visitors.

Vegueta – Triana★ 🕑 *2hr – see plan of old city*

These two districts form the historic centre of Las Palmas. It was only from the 19C onwards that the city began to extend beyond these areas with the development of Puerto de La Luz.

Plaza de Santa Ana

The pleasant palm-bordered square is overlooked by the fine façade of the town hall (1842) on one side, and by the cathedral on the other. The bronze dogs recall the possible derivation of the name of the archipelago. To the side are the Bishop's Palace (Palacio Episcopal), with an *alfiz*-decorated portal showing clear Mudéjar influence, and the Renaissance-style Casa del Regente. During the Corpus Christi procession, the square and adjacent streets are carpeted with flowers, sawdust and salt.

Catedral – 🕑 *Open 7-10.30am; Sat, 7-9pm; Sun and public hols, 7am-1.30pm and 6.30-8pm.* 🕑 *Closed Mon.* ⊗ *2€.* ☎ *928 31 49 89.*

Christopher Columbus

It is often maintained that, but for the Canary Islands, Columbus (1451-1506) would never have reached America. His persistence in trying to convince the sovereigns of Portugal, England, France and Castile of the existence of a westerly passage to Asia is well known. Eventually their Catholic Majesties of Castile provided him with three ships – the *Niña*, the *Pinta* and the *Santa María* – for an expedition to the Indies. He set sail westwards from Palos in August 1492 but was forced to put into Las Palmas and La Gomera for repairs to the *Pinta*. On 12 October 1492 he spied land and set foot for the first time on the American continent – on the Caribbean Island of San Salvador. On each of his three subsequent voyages he landed at Las Palmas or on La Gomera before going on to discover the other islands of the Antilles (1493), the Orinoco delta (1498) and the shores of Honduras (1502).

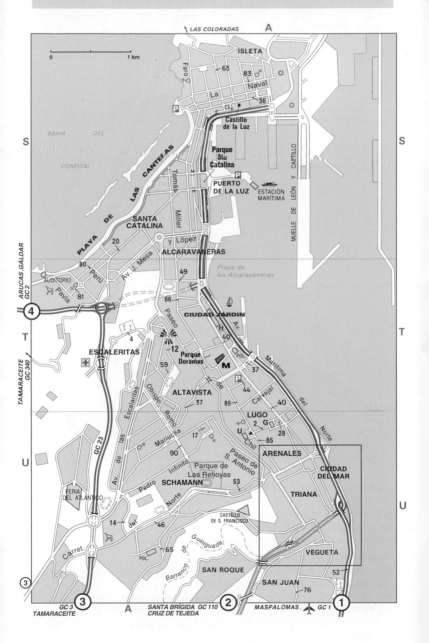

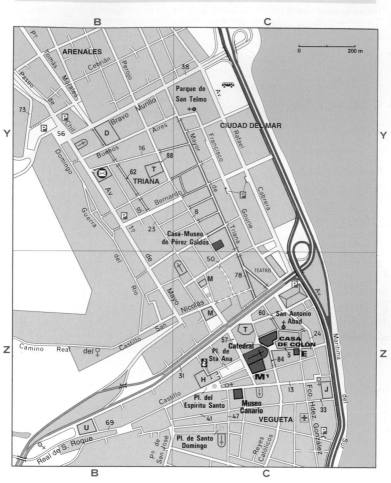

The cathedral was begun at the beginning of the 16C but not completed until the 19C. The façade is strictly neo-Classical; the interior, however, is more Gothic. It has three elegant aisles with tierceron vaulting and several side chapels. In the transept are statues by the Canary Island sculptor, **José Luján Pérez** (1756-1815): St Joseph and the Mater Dolorosa *(right)* and the Virgin and Child *(left)*.

Museo Diocesano de Arte Sacro
Entrance in calle Espíritu Santo. ◔ *Open 10am-2.30pm; Sat, 10am-1.30pm.* ◔ *Closed Sun and public hols.* ⊛ *2.40€.* ☎ *928 31 49 89.*

The museum, which is dedicated to sacred art, is housed in cathedral buildings around the 16C Patio de los Naranjos. It contains a collection of 16C-19C engravings and pieces of gold and silverwork. The chapter house contains a mosaic from Manises (Valencia).

Casa de Colón★
Entrance in calle Colón. ◔ *Open 9am-7pm; Sat, 9am-3pm.* ◔ *Closed Sun and public hols.* ☎ *928 31 23 84.*

The palace of the island's first governors, where Columbus himself stayed in 1502, now houses a museum in a typical Canary Island setting: maps and navigational instruments evoke Columbus' expeditions. Note the fine *artesonado* ceilings. The upper floor contains a collection of 16C-19C paintings.

Nearby is the **Iglesia de San Antonio Abad** on the site of the chapel in which Columbus attended Mass. The present church has an elegant Baroque interior.

Centro Atlántico de Arte Moderno

🕐 *Open 10am-9pm; Sun, 10am-2pm.* 🕑 *Closed Mon and public hols.* ☎ *902 31 18 24.*

The **calle de los Balcones** has preserved several 18C buildings with fine doorways. The centre is in one of these and has been completely converted by the architect Sáenz de Oíza. It was originally founded with the aim of fostering cooperation between Europe, Africa and America and providing strong links between these three continents. It hosts interesting temporary exhibitions. Its permanent collections present works by 20C artists from the Canary Islands, the Spanish mainland and abroad. The centre will soon be extended with an annexe.

Museo Canario★

🕐 *Open 10am-8pm; Sat-Sun and public hols, 10am-2pm.* 🕑 *Closed 1 Jan and 25 Dec.* 🎟 *3€.* ☎ *928 33 68 00.*

The isolation of the Canary Islands prolonged their prehistory until the end of the Middle Ages. This museum displays a collection of anthropological and archaeological artefacts from the islands' pre-Hispanic culture, including mummies, idols, skins, ceramics etc. Particularly interesting is the collection of terracotta seals *(pintaderas)* found only on Gran Canaria, whose purpose remains a mystery (were they for body paint, branding or sealing harvests?), and a re-creation of the cave, Cueva Pintada, in Gáldar.

Two squares, **plaza del Espíritu Santo** and **plaza de Santo Domingo,** are worth visiting for their picturesque charm.

Casa-Museo Pérez Galdós

🕐 *Guided tours (30-45min), 9am-9pm; Sat, 9am-6pm; Sun, 10am-3pm.* 🕑 *Closed public hols.* 🎟 *No charge.* ☎ *928 37 37 45.*

Manuscripts, photographs, drawings and personal objects belonging to the writer, Pérez Galdós (1843-1920) are displayed in the house where he was born.

Parque de San Telmo

The street starting in the southwest corner of this pleasant park, calle Mayor de Triana, is the bustling main shopping street in the old town. The interior of the small **Iglesia de San Bernardo** is full of character with its Baroque altars and paintings on the walls of the east end. An unusual Modernist kiosk stands in another corner of the park.

Modern Town 🕐 *2hr – see plan of city*

▶ *Drive along avenida Marítima del Norte. The road skirts the town on land reclaimed from the sea.*

Parque Doramas

This large central park encloses the Santa Catalina Hotel with its casino, and the **Pueblo Canario**, a Canary Island village created by the painter Néstor de la Torre (1888-1938). 🕐 *Open 10am-8pm; Sun, 10.30am-2.30pm. Closed Mon, 1 Jan, Holy Thu, Good Fri and 25 Dec.* 🎟 *2€.* ☎ *928 24 39 11.*

Folklore festivals are also held in the complex, which includes several craftwork shops and the **Museo Néstor**. 🕐 *Open 10am-8pm; Sun and public hols, 11am-2pm.* 🕑 *Closed Mon.* 🎟 *0.90€.* ☎ *928 24 51 35.*

Parque Santa Catalina

The park is at the centre of the tourist district in **Puerto de la Luz**, and the neighbouring streets are lined with restaurants, bars and nightclubs thronged

Puerto de la Luz

The port of Las Palmas de Gran Canaria is the engine behind the city's development and is one of the largest in Spain. Its privileged position on the transatlantic routes between Europe, Africa and America has resulted in the development of an international port with a high volume of passenger and goods traffic. It is also one of the largest fishing ports in the region due to its proximity to the rich fishing grounds off the African coast, and the leading distribution centre for goods in the Canary Islands. The port area also includes a large naval repair centre which is able to offer a full range of services to vessels calling into the port.

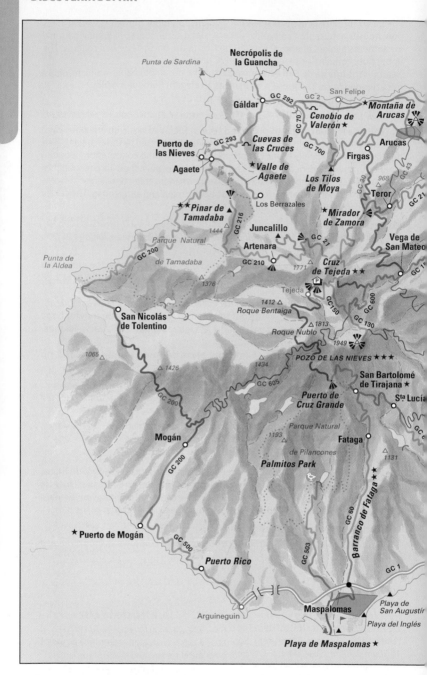

with tourists. Equally numerous are the Indian bazaars selling all sorts of Asian goods, and particularly cameras, radios, tapes and videos at low prices because the port of Las Palmas enjoys privileged customs regulations.

Playa de las Canteras★

This superb broad curving beach slopes gently into the water; it is sheltered from rough seas by a line of rocks offshore and backed by a pleasant 3.5km/2mi promenade with a multitude of popular restaurants and outdoor cafés.

At its southeastern end stands the **Auditorio Alfredo Kraus**, a building designed by Oscar Tusquets. The auditorium, which was opened in 1998, hosts an opera season and major concerts.

Castillo de la Luz

⚔ *Closed for restoration.* ☎ *928 44 66 23.*

The fort, which was built at the end of the 15C to protect the town against pirates, organises temporary exhibitions.

Paseo Cornisa

This avenue in the modern Escaleritas district above the garden city provides a fine **panorama**★ of Puerto de la Luz and La Isleta.

Excursions

THE NORTH COAST

From Las Palmas to San Nicolás de Tolentino – *128km/79mi – allow 1 day.*

▶ *Leave Las Palmas on the GC 2, 𝗈̄ on the plan. Take exit 8 and head towards Arucas.*

Arucas

After Las Palmas and Telde, Arucas is the third largest town on the island. A narrow road leads from the north wall of the main church to the top of **Montaña de Arucas,** which is shaped like a sugar loaf, offering a vast **panorama**★ as far east as Las Palmas de Gran Canaria. At the foot of the mountain the town's black cathedral stands out against white houses.

▶ *Take the C 813. At Buenlugar, 6km/4mi beyond Arucas, turn left.*

Firgas

This is the source of a sparkling mineral water which is very popular throughout the archipelago. The paseo de Gran Canaria, next to the landscaped plaza de San Roque, which is fronted by a church and Ayuntamiento (town hall), pays a picturesque homage to the island's local communities.

▶ *Return to the main road.*

Los Tilos de Moya

The winding road runs to the side of the mountain, passing Moya 2km/1mi to the left. Los Tilos is a protected area with a wood of wild laurel trees.

▶ *At Guía, turn right to join C 810. Head toward Las Palmas for a few metres, then turn off to Cenobio de Valerón.*

GRAN CANARIA

0 _____ 10 km

Cenobio de Valerón★

🕐 *Open 10am-5pm.* 🕐 *Closed Mon, Tue and 24 and 31 Dec.* ☎ *928 21 94 21.*

In a remarkable location on the edge of a ravine caves have been hollowed out of the volcanic tufa; they are protected by a layer of basalt. Although tradition has it that in the time of the Guanches the caves were a type of convent (cenobio) where girls prepared for their role as Sacred Virgins, they were in fact used as a large collective granary. On the top of the mountain the chiefs met in council (Tagoror).

▶ *Return to the C 810 and head towards Gáldar.*

Gáldar

At the foot of Mount Gáldar the Guanche king held his court *(guanarteme)*; there are a few precious traces of this mysterious civilisation. A cave **(Cueva Pintada)** was discovered in 1881 containing some **mural paintings**★ which have not yet been interpreted. Various Guanche objects are on display. ⚬━ *Closed for restoration.* ☎ *928 55 10 90.*

Necrópolis de la Guancha

On the coast 2km/1.2mi N of Gáldar. 🛈 *For information, telepone* ☎ *928 21 94 21.*

Excavations in the archaeological area have brought to light the remains of a Guanche settlement and necropolis. The burial ground consists of circular constructions of great blocks of lava and a large burial mound.

▶ *Return to Gáldar and take the C 810 S.*

Cuevas de las Cruces

Halfway between Gáldar and Agaete. These are attractive natural cave formations in the volcanic tufa.

Agaete

This charming white-walled village is situated in the heart of a fertile region. On 4 August the village celebrates the **Fiesta de la Rama**, one of the island's most popular festivals.

Los Berrazales road★

SE of Agaete. The road runs parallel to the **Agaete Valley**★, which is sheltered by high mountains and covered in lush vegetation.

Puerto de las Nieves

W of Agaete. This little fishing harbour was also used for shipping bananas in the days when land transport to Las Palmas de Gran Canaria was difficult. From the quay there is a good view in front of the cliff of the famous **Finger of God** *(Dedo de Dios)*, a pointed rock which resembles a finger.

The hermitage **(ermita)** contains some 15C Flemish paintings. 🕐 *Visits by prior arrangement.* ☎ *928 55 43 82.*

San Nicolás de Tolentino

A highly spectacular road, which follows the steep cliffs along the coast and crosses several ravines, leads to San Nicolás, a village in a fertile basin growing sugar cane and tomatoes.

THE CENTRE OF THE ISLAND

From Las Palmas de Gran Canaria to Cruz de Tejeda – *156km/97mi* – 🕐 *allow 1 day.*

▶ *Leave Las Palmas de Gran Canaria on the C 811,* ② *on the plan*

Tejeda and the Roque Nublo

Tafira

A holiday resort favoured by the inhabitants of Las Palmas, the town is also home to the island's university.

Jardín Canario★

🕐 *Open 9am-6pm.* 🕐 *Closed 1 Jan and 25 Dec.* ☎ *928 21 95 80.*

The tropical garden, which is arranged in terraces, makes a pleasant walk.

▶ *In Monte Lentiscal turn left.*

Mirador de Bandama★★

A road leads to the top of Bandama (569m/1 867ft). The summit provides a superb view of the enormous Caldera de la Bandama, a volcanic crater with its eruption formations intact, inside of which can be seen a small cultivated area. The **panorama** is impressive, taking in Tafira, the Montaña de Arucas and Las Palmas to the north, the crater, Las Palmas golf club (the oldest in Spain) and Telde to the south, and the island's mountainous centre to the west.

▶ *Return to the C 811.*

Santa Brígida

This village sits close to a ravine planted with palm trees. A colourful plant and flower market is held at weekends.

Vega de San Mateo

The village is situated in an important agricultural area. A large fruit and vegetable market is held here on Saturdays and Sundays. The **Casa-Museo Cho Zacarías**, in a series of traditional houses, two of which date from the 17C, displays a comprehensive ethnographic collection which includes pottery, furniture, textiles, traditional implements etc. 🕐 *Open 10.30am-12.30pm;* 🕐*Closed Sun.* 🎫 *3.60€.* ☎ *928 66 17 95.*

▶ *Continue along the C 811 for 6km/4mi, then bear left.*

Pozo de las Nieves★★★

From the summit (1 949m/6 394ft), which is sometimes snow-capped, there is a spectacular **panorama**★★★ of the whole island. To the south the view stretches as far as the Playa de Maspalomas, with San Bartolomé de Tirajana in the foreground; to the west, the unusual shapes of the **Roque Nublo** to the left and the **Roque Bentayga** to the right are also visible. On a clear day, Mount Teide (Tenerife) stands out on the horizon.

Cruz de Tejeda★★

NW of Pozo de las Nieves. Near the hotel (parador) which has been built at the top of the pass (1 450m/4 757ft) lies the village of **Tejeda** in a huge volcanic basin. From the chaotic landscape, which the Spanish writer Unamuno described as a "petrified tempest", rise two volcanic necks: Roque Bentaiga and Roque Nublo which have been objects of veneration among the indigenous people of the Canary Islands.

▶ *Bear W to Artenara along the GC 110.*

The drive includes attractive **views**★ of the troglodyte village of **Juncalillo** where most of the people live in caves formed by a lava flow.

Artenara

This small, well-kept village is the highest on the island (1 230m/4 035ft). The enchanting **Ermita de la Cuevita**, a hermitage dug into the rock, contains a statue of the Virgin with Child. From here, the **panorama**★ of the Bentaiga and Nublo peaks, Tejeda and Pozo de las Nieves is particularly impressive. From the restaurant (Mesón de la Silla), which is in a cave on the edge of the village, there is a **view**★ of Roque Bentaiga.

Pinar de Tamadaba★★

The road passes through this magnificent wood of Canary pines extending to the edge of a cliff which drops sheer to the sea.

▶ *After a left hand bend, continue to the end of a tarred road, following signs to the Zona de Acampada, then park the car and walk 200m/220yd through the pine trees to the edge.*

On a clear day, the **view**★★ of Agaete, Gáldar and the coast, with the Pico del Teide on the horizon, is superb.

▶ *Return by the same road and turn left onto the GC 110 to Valleseco.*

Mirador de Zamora★

Just north of Valleseco there is an attractive **view**★ of Teror, nestled in a wide valley surrounded by impressive mountains.

Teror

The majesty of the façade of the 18C **Iglesia de Nuestra Señora del Pino** perfectly befits a town which has such a distinguished air and retains many fine mansions with wooden balconies. The church houses a statue of Our Lady of the Pine Tree, the island's venerated patron, who is said to have appeared in the branches of a pine tree in 1481. The treasury contains various embroidered cloaks belonging to the statue and other rich gifts. (🕐 *Open 9am-noon and 2.30-8.30pm; Sun and public hols, 7.30am-8.30pm.* 🎟 *0.60€ (treasury). ☎ 928 63 01 18).*

There is an extraordinary atmosphere at the annual pilgrimage (8 September) when thousands of islanders gather in Teror to present their gifts and join in worship. On Sundays a lively market attracts a large crowd.

THE SOUTH COAST

From Las Palmas de Gran Canaria to Maspalomas – *59km/37mi* – 🕐 *about 2hr.*

▶ *Leave Las Palmas de Gran Canaria along the GC 1,* ① *on the plan, and then take exit 8 (Telde).*

Telde

Like Gáldar, this city was a capital of the island's indigenous people. In the lower town stands the **Iglesia de San Juan Bautista**, a 15C church, subsequently rebuilt in the 17C and 18C, which contains a 16C Flemish retable depicting the Life of the Virgin. The figure of Christ was made in Mexico out of reeds and a light, paper-based paste.

▶ *From the square in front of the church take calle Inés Chimida.*

The road leads to the quiet **San Francisco district** which has retained its old-fashioned character with narrow paved streets and whitewashed houses. For centuries this district has been known for its traditional craftwork.

▶ *Follow the C 813 towards Ingenio. Beyond the junction with the C 816 turn left, immediately after some cottages, into a rough track; the last 250m/270yd is on foot.*

Cuatro Puertas★

The cave, which has four openings or doors *(cuatro puertas),* is a place where the council for the indigenous population of the island *(Tagoror)* used to meet. The east face of the mountain is riddled with caves where the Guanche embalmed their dead. The view over the east coast is impressive. The summit (to the east) is a sacred site.

Ingenio

Ingenio is a traditional centre for embroidery.

Dunes of Maspalomas

Maspalomas

The largest resorts are situated along the flat, sandy coastline to the south: **Maspalomas, Playa del Inglés** and **Playa de San Agustín**. These tourist centres are home to countless hotels, apartments, chalets, shopping centres, restaurants, nightclubs, outdoor cafés, water parks and a whole host of other leisure facilities for the huge numbers of visitors who come here to enjoy the superb beaches and wonderful climate in this part of the island.

Maspalomas has developed around its spectacular dunes and **beach**★, which are part of a 400ha/990-acre protected zone. Other attractions in this area include natural pools and a palm grove.

Excursions from Maspalomas

Palmitos Park

13km/8mi N. 🧒 🕐 *Open 10am-6pm.* 🎫 *17€ (12€ children aged 3-12).* ☎ *928 14 02 76.*

The arid ravine contains an oasis where exotic birds from Australia and South America can be seen at liberty. The park also contains an aquarium, a cactus garden and a greenhouse with myriad butterflies.

Mogán

38km/24mi NW. The road (C 812) runs northwest along the steep, built-up coast, passing through **Puerto Rico**, a resort with apartment buildings clinging to the slopes of a ravine, and **Puerto de Mogán**★, a picturesque resort and fishing centre built around an attractive marina and port. The road then turns inland up a ravine (**barranco**) to Mogán.

San Bartolomé de Tirajana★

48km/30mi N on the GC 520. The way up to San Bartolomé passes through the **Barranco de Fataga**★★, an impressively beautiful ravine. The road passes close to Arteara, in an oasis at the bottom of a ravine, and then through Fataga, a picturesque village surrounded by orchards, before reaching San Bartolomé, which is set in a magnificent green mountain cirque at the foot of tall cliffs, probably the inner walls of an old volcanic crater.

Puerto de Cruz Grande – Fine view of the mountains south of Roque Nublo.

▶ *Return to San Bartolomé and take the C 815 going SE.*

Santa Lucía – The small **Museo Guanche** displays objects excavated to the east of the village from a hill which has been shaped by erosion to look like a fortress (fortaleza). 🕐 *Open 9am-6pm.* 🎫 *1.80€.* ☎ *928 77 30 80.*

LANZAROTE★★★

POPULATION: 88 849

846KM2/326SQ MI.

Lanzarote, which has been designated a Biosphere Reserve, is the most unusual of the Canary Islands. Its black earth landscape, dotted with oases of vegetation and crops, and lapped by the deep blue waters of the Atlantic, is full of contrasting textures and colours. Although tourism has seen the development of some resorts along the island's fine white sandy beaches, Lanzarote has managed to preserve much of its natural landscape, despite having to adapt to the difficult natural conditions which have shaped the character and activities of its inhabitants over the centuries.

Location

This flat island, whose maximum altitude is just 66m/216ft, is located a little over 100km/62mi from the African coast. The airport, close to the capital, and the port of Arrecife provide links with the other islands in the archipelago. Frequent ferry services also operate to nearby Fuerteventura from Playa Blanca. 🛈 *Arrecife: Parque José Ramírez Cerdá, 35500,* ☎ *928 80 15 17.*

Address Book

For coin ranges, see the Legend at the back of the guide.

WHERE TO EAT

Casa'l Cura – *Nueva 1 – Haría* – ☎ *928 83 55 56 – Lunchtime only*. This restaurant in the Haría Valley, the wettest part of the island, occupies an old country house with an attractive patio. The cuisine here is typically Canarian and reasonably priced. If you prefer not to eat à la carte, you may want to try the buffet on the first floor.

La Era – *Barranco 3 – Yaiza* – ☎ *928 83 00 16*. A family-run restaurant in a lovely 17C country house. There are several attractive dining rooms and a tapas bar. Traditional Canarian fare is offered along with a fixed menu.

WHERE TO STAY

Hotel Miramar – *Coll 2 – Arrecife* – ☎ *928 80 15 22* – ♿ – *85 rooms* – ⌕ *4.80€– Restaurant 9€*. Although this 1980s-style building is lacking in architectural charm, its location, by the sea and opposite the Castillo de San Gabriel in the centre of Arrecife, couldn't be better. As you would expect given its name, the bedroom balconies offer good sea views, although the bedrooms themselves are on the basic side with somewhat antiquated furniture.

El Hotelito del Golfo – *Golfo 10 – Yaiza* – ☎ *928 17 32 72* – 🅿 ⌣ – *9 rooms* – ⌕. Although offering limited creature comforts, this hotel has a pool, garden and a spectacular location on a volcanic cliff. The rooms are fairly rudimentary but adequate nonetheless. A good option for those seeking peace and quiet.

Finca de las Salinas – *La Cuesta 17 – Yaiza* – ☎ *928 83 03 25* – 🅿 ▤ – *17 rooms* – ⌕ – *Restaurant (guests only) 16.25/26€*. This charming country hotel appears like an oasis in this most arid, yet most impressive part of the island, near the Parque de Timanfaya. Delightful attention to detail throughout, in addition to cool and comfortable bedrooms with rustic-style floors and light-coloured walls.

Background

From the 14C to the present – The island owes its name to Lancelloti Malocello from Genoa, who landed here in the 14C. Actual conquest came in 1401 with the arrival of the Normans, **Gadifer de la Salle** and **Jean de Bethencourt**, who met little resistance with the result that before long Bethencourt was able to present the island to the King of Castile. Lanzarote then became the base for expeditions against the other islands which met with no success until finally Fuerteventura was also subdued. When Bethencourt left Lanzarote in 1416, much mourned by the local inhabitants, to return to his native France, he entrusted the government of the island to his cousin, Maciot.

Once the main islands had been conquered, Lanzarote was largely left to its own devices and, as its coast was open and its mountains low, it became a prey to marauding pirates in search of slaves. Calamity of a different nature occurred in 1730 in the form of a massive volcanic eruption. Near the village of Timanfaya a flaming mountain range, the **Montañas del Fuego,** suddenly appeared. The eruption lasted six years and covered one third of the island in a sea of lava. In 1824 there was another eruption in the north where a new volcano, Tinguatón, spewed molten lava over the southwest part of the island engulfing the fields and houses.

Gradually the people re-established themselves in the lunar landscape: the lava fields *(malpaís)* and the thick black layers of ash and pebbles are pitted with over 100 craters. In **La Geria**, where volcanic pebbles (lapilli) are plentiful, vines have been planted and low semicircular walls have been built to protect them from the northeast wind. The grapes produce an excellent light white wine – Malvasía – with a distinctive bouquet. Throughout the island the fields are covered with a deep layer of the lapilli (*picón* in the local dialect) as they retain moisture, a precious attribute on an island where it scarcely ever rains. Another feature of this arid land is the dromedary; its humpbacked silhouette is an integral element in the landscape.

Worth a Visit

ARRECIFE

The administrative centre is on the coast facing offshore reefs; it was defended by the **Castillo de San Gabriel** which was built in the 16C on an islet and linked to the town by two bridges, one of which, the Puente de Bolas, is a drawbridge.

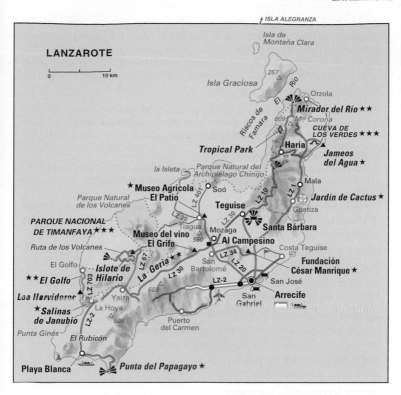

Arrecife has a pleasant beach and a picturesque maritime lagoon, the Charca de San Ginés, where fisherman tie up their small boats. To the north, at the end of the avenue bordering the sea, the 18C **Castillo de San José** stands on a small promontory. The castle has been restored by the artist César Manrique and now houses the **Museo Internacional de Arte Contemporáneo.** (🕐 Open 11am-9pm. ⊗ No charge. ☎ 928 81 23 21).

The gallery's cafeteria-restaurant offers fine views of the Puerto de Naos and Arrecife to the right, and the Los Mármoles quay to the left.

Excursions

The three tours suggested below all depart from Arrecife.

THE CENTRE OF THE ISLAND
62km/39mi through the centre of the island.

Fundación César Manrique★
In Taro de Tahíche. 🕐 *Open 10am-6pm; Sun, 10am-3pm; Jul-Oct, 10am-7pm. Last admission 30 min before closing.* 🕐 *Closed 1 Jan.* ⊗ *7€.* ☎ *928 84 31 38.*

César Manrique (1920-92)

César Manrique is intimately linked to Lanzarote and its tourist development; it was towards the latter that he channelled the very best of his artistic talent, promoting a new standard to regulate property speculation and urban growth in order to avoid the disastrous consequences of uncontrolled development.

Manrique was born on Lanzarote, and everywhere on the island visitors can see the importance of the work he carried out. He was responsible for the Island Council's **Art, Culture and Tourism Centres**, in which he introduced his ideas on the integration of art and nature. These centres and the **Fundación César Manrique** bear witness to the passion he felt for Lanzarote and his concerns for the preservation of its natural heritage.

In total, seven centres have been created: the Museo de Arte Contemporáneo Castillo de San José; the El Diablo restaurant in the Parque Nacional de Timanfaya; the Casa-Museo and the Monumento al Campesino (Peasants' Monument); the Cueva de Los Verdes; the Jameos del Agua; the Mirador del Río and the Jardín de Cactus (🍃 see descriptions in the text).

The foundation was set up in 1968 in a house that was built on top of five volcanic bubbles formed during the eruptions of 1730 to 1736. César Manrique was an original artist who deliberately chose this location for his Foundation to demonstrate the bond between architecture and nature. Besides his own work, visitors can admire an exhibition of contemporary art (Miró, Tàpies, Mompó, Guerrero, Chirino etc).

Monumento al Campesino

This monument near **Mozaga**, in the centre of the island, has been erected as a homage to the peasant farmers of Lanzarote. Next to it, the **Casa-Museo del Campesino** is an example of the island's typical architecture.

Museo Agrícola El Patio★

In Tiagua. ◷ *Open 10am-5.30pm (including public hols); Sat, 10am-2.30pm. Last admission 30 min before closing.* ◷ *Closed Sun.* ◉ *5€ (including wine tasting and one tapa).* ☏ *928 52 91 34.*

This agricultural museum is in an old farm. Its outbuildings display ethnographic and ethnological exhibits which provide an overview of the traditional way of life and culture of the island's farmers. A tasting of Malvasía wine is also offered to visitors.

Museo del Vino El Grifo

◷ *Open 10.30am-6pm (7pm Jul-Sep).* ◉ *No charge.* ☏ *928 52 49 51.*

The 18C El Grifo wine storehouses have been converted into a museum explaining traditional wine production methods.

La Geria★★

La Geria lies between Yaiza and Mozaga in a weird landscape of blackish desert pockmarked with craters. The village is an important centre for wine production.

THE SOUTH OF THE ISLAND

Round trip of 124km/77mi from Arrecife – about 1 day

Parque Nacional de Timanfaya★★★

🚐 *Tours of the park by coach are available from 9am until 5.45pm; last tour at 5pm.* ◉ *6.60€ (including Ruta de los Volcanes).* ☏ *928 84 00 57 or 928 80 15 00.*

The range, which emerged during the eruptions of 1730-36, and stands out sometimes red, sometimes black, in a lunar landscape of volcanic cinder and slag, is undoubtedly the major natural attraction on the island. The **Montañas de Fuego** form the central part of this massif.

Dromedaries wait by the roadside 5km/3mi north of Yaiza; they provide an exotic if somewhat swaying and jolting ride up the mountainside, from where there is a good view of the next crater. Although the volcanoes have not erupted since 1736, their inner fires burn and bubble still. At **Islote de Hilario** some strange phenomena still occur: twigs dropped into a hole in the ground 50cm/20in deep catch fire; water poured into a pipe set into the lava evaporates immediately into steam because of the high temperature of the subsoil (140°C/254°F at 10cm/4in, over 400°C/752°F at 6m/20ft). From the El Diablo restaurant, where the kitchen uses the heat of the earth for its cooking, there are some fine views of the surrounding area. Buses leave Islote to follow the **Ruta de los Volcanes**, a special 14km/9mi road through the lava fields and craters, providing extraordinary views of the landscape.

From a natural lookout point there is a view over an immense lava field pitted with volcanoes stretching to the sea. The road passes through the Valley of Tranquillity, a region of ashes. In the inhospitable solitude of these mountains, lichens are the only sign of life.

Los Hervideros

In the caverns at the end of the tongue of lava, the sea boils (*hervir*: to boil) in an endlessly fascinating spectacle.

El Golfo★★

A lagoon, retained by a sandbank in the crater, is filled with vivid emerald green water; a steep cliff of pitted black rock forms an impressive backdrop.

Salinas de Janubio★

To form these salt pans, the sea has entered a disused crater producing myriad contrasts in colour and form – the gleaming white pyramids of salt, the deep blue still water and the geometrically square pans in the semicircular lagoon.

El Golfo

Playa Blanca

This pleasant resort has a pedestrianised promenade which separates the old fishermen's houses from the attractive white sandy beach. Ferries operate regularly to Fuerteventura, which is visible in the distance.

Punta del Papagayo★

The Rubicón region was where Bethencourt originally settled. The only trace of the conquest is the Castillo de las Colaradas, an old tower standing on the edge of the cliff. From "parrot" point *(access along a road at the entrance to Playa Blanca, through which you reach the* **Espacio protegido de los Ajaches**, *a protected area),* with its magnificent rocky creeks, there are good **views**★ of the Playa Blanca and Fuerteventura. (⏱ *Open 9am-7pm.* ⌨ *3€ (vehicle entry fee).* ☎ *928 17 34 52).*

▶ *Return to Arrecife via the LZ 2.*

THE NORTH OF THE ISLAND
Round trip of 77km/47mi from Arrecife – about half a day

Jardín de Cactus★
In Guatiza. ⏱ *Open 10am-6pm.* ⌨ *3€.* ☎ *928 52 93 97.*

This cactus garden has been aesthetically designed to display a large selection of species from the Canary Islands, America and Madagascar. It is laid out in terraces in an old quarry; an old windmill has also been added to the site. It is situated in an area with an abundance of prickly pears, a cactus which attracts cochineal beetles; in the past these insects were crushed to obtain a crimson dye.

Cueva de los Verdes★★★
Guided tours (1hr), 10am-6. ⌨ *7€.* ☎ *928 17 32 20 or 928 84 84 84.*

At the foot of the Corona volcano are underground galleries where the Guanches used to take refuge from marauding pirates. The galleries were formed during successive eruptions when lava streams cooled and hardened into dense basalt layers, diverting or allowing subsequent streams to flow around or over earlier flows. There are 2km/1mi of galleries at different levels, illuminated to show the kaleidoscope of colours and shapes in the underground phantasmagoria.

Jameos del Agua★
⏱ *Open 10am-6.30pm; Tue, Fri and Sat, 6.30pm-2am, including a folklore show at 11pm.* ⌨ *6.60€ (day), 7.20€ (evening).* ☎ *928 84 80 20.*

This attractive leisure complex has a restaurant, bar, dance floor and auditorium. A *jameo* is a cavity which is formed when the top of a volcanic tube collapses. The natural lagoon in the cave is the habitat of a minute, albino millenary crab which is born blind. The **Casa de los Volcanes** on the upper level presents interesting information on volcanism.

Mirador del Río★★

🕐 *Open 10am-5.45pm.* 🎟 *2.70€.* ☎ *928 52 65 51.*

At the north end of the island, a steep headland, **Riscos de Famara**, stands isolated above the waves. The belvedere blends superbly into the cliff and commands a superb **panorama**★★ across the azure waters of the **El Río** strait to La Graciosa and its neighbouring islands (Montaña Clara, Alegranza, Roque del Oeste and Roque del Este); immediately below are the local salt pans. A **passenger ferry** operates from Orzola to La Graciosa. ⛴ *Crossing from Orzola to La Graciosa (15min): departures at 10am, noon and 5pm (and 6.30pm in summer); crossing from La Graciosa to Orzola: departures at 8am, 11am and 4pm (and 6pm in summer).* 🎟 *12.02€ round trip.* ☎ *928 84 20 70/55.*

Tropical Park

🧒Kids 🕐*Open 10am-5pm. 9€.* ☎ *928 83 55 00.*

The park contains 45 000m²/53 820sq yd of tended gardens devoted to exotic birds. Regular events are held for visitors, including the ever-popular parrot shows.

Haría

As on all the islands, the northern end is the least arid. Some 5km/3mi south of the village there is a fine **view**★, from a lookout point, of the lush Haría Valley with its hundreds of palm trees. In the distance rises the Corona volcano.

Teguise

Teguise, once the island's capital, is the home of the *timple*, a miniature guitar which is a vital element in Canary Island folklore. Nearby is the **Castillo de Santa Bárbara**, built in the 16C on the Guanapay volcano, which houses the **Museo del Emigrante**, containing an interesting collection of documents and mementoes relating to the emigration of Canary Islanders to America. (🕐 *Open 10am-5pm.* 🎟 *1.80€.* ☎ *928 84 50 01*).

From the summit there is a vast **panorama**★ including Teguise in the foreground and the island of La Graciosa on the horizon.

FUERTEVENTURA

POPULATION: 49 542

1 731KM2/668SQ MI.

The island's attraction lies in the beauty of its bare landscape and in the immense beaches of white sand with turquoise water which make up almost the entire shoreline. A mild climate, moderate winds and a calm sea especially on the east coast, make this tranquil island the ideal resort for sailing, diving, fishing and, in particular, windsurfing. To prove the point, the world windsurfing championships are held here in July and August.

Address Book

For coin ranges, see the Legend at the back of the guide.

WHERE TO EAT

🍽🍽 **Casa Santa María** – *Plaza Santa María – Betancuria –* ☎ *928 87 82 82.* This 16C house with its tiled roof, whitewashed walls and at times over-the-top local decoration is set amid lush vegetation with stupendous views. Canarian cuisine at its best.

WHERE TO STAY

🛏🛏 **Hotel Fuerteventura** – *(Playa Blanca) – Puerto del Rosario – 3.5km/2mi S of Puerto Rosario –* ☎ *928 85 11 50 –* 🅿 ⛵ – *50 rooms –* 🍴 *7.21€. Restaurant 21€.* This hotel occupies the building originally housing the parador. Although slightly old-fashioned, the moderately priced rooms are still pleasant (some have been recently refurbished), with wooden floors and good-quality furniture. Its best feature is undoubtedly its location facing the sea.

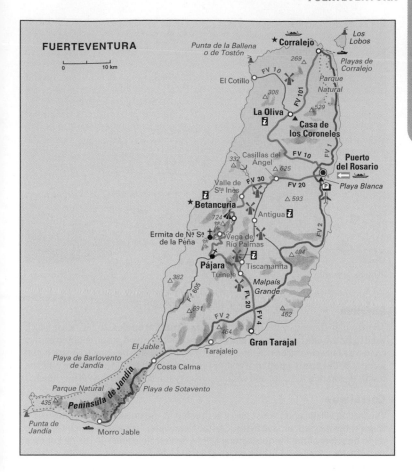

FUERTEVENTURA

0   10 km

Punta de la Ballena
o de Tostón
★ Corralejo
Los Lobos
269
Playas de Corralejo
El Cotillo
FV 10
308
FV 101
Parque Natural
La Oliva
529
Casa de los Coroneles
332
Casillas del Ángel
FV 10
625
Puerto del Rosario
FV 30
Valle de Stª Inés
FV 20
Playa Blanca
★ Betancuria
593
724
Antigua
FV 2
Ermita de Nª Sª de la Peña
Vega de Río Palmas
Pájara
494
Tiscamanita
382
Tuineje
Malpaís Grande
F 605
691
FL 20
462
FV 2
FV 4
464
El Jable
Tarajalejo
Gran Tarajal
Playa de Barlovento de Jandía
Costa Calma
Parque Natural
Playa de Sotavento
Península de Jandía
435
Punta de Jandía
Morro Jable

Location

Fuerteventura is the largest island after Tenerife in the Canary Archipelago and, with the exception of El Hierro, is the least densely populated (28 inhabitants per km²/73 inhabitants per sq mi). Unlike the other islands in the group, its coastline is flat with long beaches. *Puerto del Rosario: Avenida de la Constitución 5, 35600, ☎ 928 53 08 44.*

Background

Landscape – Fuerteventura is an arid land dotted with countless bare crests and mostly extinct volcanoes, and was described as a "skeletal island" by the Spanish writer and humanist, **Miguel de Unamuno**, who was exiled here in 1924. In this desert-like landscape, the terrain is only suitable for the grazing of goats. The sites of villages scattered in the vast plains and in the ravines are marked by palm trees and numerous windmills, drawing water from the subsoil for the cultivation of cereals and tomatoes.

Fuerteventura shares the climate of its near neighbour, Africa; the continent's sand, blown across the sea, gave the island its present form by building up an isthmus, El Jable, between the originally separate islets of Maxorata and Jandía.

The stretch of sea separating the island from Africa is a popular area for deep-sea fishing.

Tours

Both in **Puerto del Rosario** and at the airport, taxis and hire cars are available to tour the island. A long beach, Playa Blanca, is located south of the capital.

CORRALEJO★
39km/24mi N of Puerto del Rosario along the FV 10 and FV 101.

Playa de Sotavento

La Oliva

Take the path starting by the church. The **Casa de los Coroneles**, an 18C house which used to be the official residence of the governor of the island, is surmounted by two crenellated towers and ornamented with attractive wooden balconies. Nearby *(right)* stands the **Casa del Capellán**, a minute house enclosed within a drystone wall; the motifs decorating the door and window are very similar to those in Pájara church.

Corralejo★

The fishing village and tourist resort is situated at the northern end of the island beyond the *malpaís*, or lava fields. Crystal-clear water laps at the immense white dune **beaches** of the Parque Natural Dunas de Corralejo and the Isla de Lobos, a paradise for underwater fishing which can be reached by boat. Lanzarote is visible to the north.

GRAN TARAJAL

67km/42mi S.

▷ *Leave Puerto del Rosario along the FV 20. Beyond Casillas del Angel, turn right onto the FV 30.*

South of Valle de Santa Inés there is a fine view of Betancuria.

Betancuria★

This quiet town in the valley was founded in 1404 by the explorer Jean de Bethencourt, who chose this remote spot in the heart of the mountains as the capital of the island.

🙂 Centros de Turismo y Ocio 🙂

🕐 Open 10am-6pm. ☎ 928 87 80 49.

These **leisure and tourist centres** are housed in buildings with typical island architecture and introduce visitors to the traditional ways of life, culture and gastronomy of the island.

La Cilla "Museo del Grano", in La Oliva – The museum has been installed in an old granary and provides explanations on traditional agriculture.

Mirador de Morro Velosa, in Betancuria – A belvedere with a superb view of the centre of the island. The restaurant serves typical dishes from the Canary Islands.

Centro de Artesanía Molino de Antigua, in Antigua – This arts and crafts centre is in an old mill encircled by a garden of palm and cactus trees. It also contains a craftwork shop and a general information centre providing details on the island.

Centro de Interpretación de los Molinos, in Tiscamanita – A traditional cottage alongside a mill is the setting for this information centre which explains the history of mills *(molinos)* on Fuerteventura.

Betancuria retains not only a certain urban style from the early years of the conquest but also a ruined Franciscan monastery and an ancient **cathedral**, with white walls and a picturesque wooden balcony, now called the **Iglesia de Santa María la Antigua.** The interior consists of a nave and two aisles; the baptistery contains an interesting crucifix; the sacristy has retained its attractive ceiling with panel ornament.

On the south side of the town there is a small **Museo Arqueológico** which displays several Guanche exhibits. (🕐 *Open 10am-5pm (4.30pm in summer); Sun, 11am-2pm.* ⌾ 🕐*Closed Mon and public hols.* ⌾ *1.20€.* ☎ *928 87 82 41).*

The road south provides an attractive contrast between the wide horizon of bare rose-tinted peaks and the village of Vega de Río Palmas nestling in its green valley-oasis. Not far away stands the hermitage of the Virgen de la Peña, a place of pilgrimage, where the islanders gather every year on the third Saturday in September to venerate Fuerteventura's patron saint.

Pájara

The carvings on the church doorway betray signs of Aztec inspiration (plumed heads, pumas, snakes and suns).

▶ *In Pájara take the FV 20 to the left.*

Gran Tarajal

Tamarisk trees surround the port which exports its tomato production and which is the second largest town on the island.

PENÍNSULA DE JANDÍA
Morro del Jable: 54km/34mi SW of Gran Tarajal.

This natural park is famous for its magnificent beaches; half of the island's total can be found within it. On the windward side of the island the beaches are wilder, while those on the leeward side tend to be wider and flatter.

LA PALMA★

POPULATION: 78 198

706KM2/272SQ MI.

With a total surface area of just 706km²/272sq mi and its highest peak rising to 2 426m/7 949ft at the centre, in proportional terms La Palma has the highest average altitude of any island in the world. Rain is also more abundant here than in the rest of the Canaries, resulting in numerous streams and springs. It is known alternatively as the "Beautiful Island" or the "Green Island" because of its lush vegetation, characterised by woods of laurel and pine and numerous banana plantations. La Palma has distanced itself from the major tourist development on neighbouring islands and as such will appeal to nature-lovers and those seeking peace and quiet far from the madding crowds.

Location

La Palma is located in the far northwest of the archipelago. The huge central crater, the Caldera de Taburiente, with a diameter of over 10km/6mi and a depth of 1 500m/4 920ft, was probably produced by the volcano which created the island. A chain of peaks, Las Cumbres, extends south; deep ravines cut into the steep slopes produce an indented coastline. In the mountains, where the rainfall is plentiful, the water is collected to irrigate the lower terraces. 🛈 *Santa Cruz de la Palma: O'Daly 22 (Casa Salazar),* ☎ *922 41 21 06.*

Worth a Visit

SANTA CRUZ DE LA PALMA

The administrative centre of the island was founded by Lugo in 1493 at the foot of a tall cliff which is, in fact, a half-eroded crater, the Caldereta. In the 16C, with rising cane sugar exports and the expansion of the dockyards using local hardwood timber, Santa Cruz was one of Spain's major ports; nowadays, it is a peaceful city where mansions with elegant façades and great wooden balconies line the seafront promenade. At Playa de Los Cancajos, 5km/3mi to the south, the beach and rocks are black.

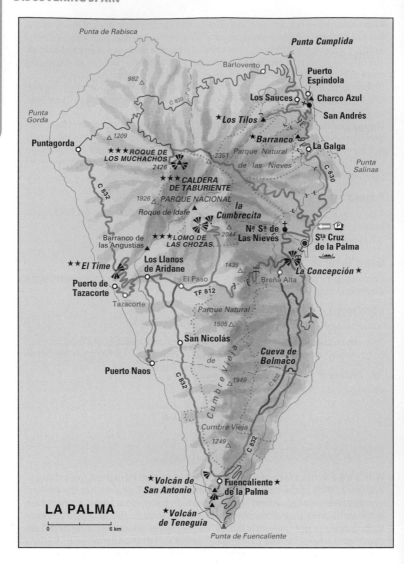

Punta de Rabisca
Punta Cumplida
Barlovento
Puerto Espíndola
982 △
C 830
Los Sauces ○ ▲ Charco Azul
Punta Gorda
★Los Tilos ▲
San Andrés
Puntagorda
△ 1209
★Barranco ▲
La Galga
★★★ROQUE DE LOS MUCHACHOS ✹
2426 ▲
Parque Natural
2351
de las Nieves
Punta Salinas
C 830
★★★ CALDERA DE TABURIENTE
1926 △ PARQUE NACIONAL
Roque de Idafe ▲
la Cumbrecita
C 832
Barranco de las Angustias
★★★LOMO DE LAS CHOZAS
2044 ▲
Nª Sª de Las Nieves ●
Stª Cruz de la Palma ○ ⇐ P
★★El Time ✹
Los Llanos de Aridane
1435
La Concepción ★
Puerto de Tazacorte ○
El Paso
Breña Alta
TF 812
Tazacorte
Parque Natural
1505 △
San Nicolás ○
Cueva de Belmaco
Puerto Naos ○
C 832
de
Cumbre Vieja
1949 △
C 832
Cumbre Vieja
1249 △
C 832
LA PALMA
0   6 km
★Volcán de San Antonio ○
Fuencaliente ★ de la Palma
★Volcán de Teneguía
Punta de Fuencaliente

Plaza de España

Several of the buildings date from the Renaissance. The 16C **Iglesia de El Salvador** has beautiful ceilings with **artesonado ornament**★; the sacristy has Gothic vaulting. Opposite stand the 16C town hall and a line of houses in the colonial style.

Walk uphill to the delightful **plaza de Santo Domingo**. Next to a further education college stands the **chapel** of a former monastery; it is furnished with some beautiful Baroque altars. ⌖ *To visit the chapel, ask for the keys at the Iglesia de El Salvador.* ☎ *922 41 32 50.*

Tours

The two tours suggested below both depart from Santa Cruz de la Palma.

THE NORTH OF THE ISLAND

Observatorio Roque de los Muchachos★★★

36km/22mi NW. ◷ *About 1hr 45min for the ascent.*

Laurel bushes and pine trees line the winding road which offers extensive views as it climbs to the **astrophysical observatory**, one of the world's most important, at an altitude of 2 432m/7 949ft. (◷ *Visits by prior arrangement,* ☎ *922 40 55 00*).

From the Roque de los Muchachos the impressive **panorama**★★★ encompasses the Caldera, Los Llanos de Aridane, the island's mountain chain, the islands of El Hierro and La Gomera, as well as Mount Teide on Tenerife.

Punta Cumplida

36km/22mi N. There are very fine views of the coast from the cliff road which crosses some deep ravines *(barrancos)* which are part of the Los Tiles Biosphere Reserve. Note also the impressive number of craters.

La Galga – North of the village, on emerging from the tunnel, the road crosses a steep and well-wooded **ravine**★.

San Andrés – In the church there is a beautiful Mudéjar ceiling in the chancel.

Charco Azul – Natural seawater pools.

Puerto Espíndola – A tiny fishing village where the boats are drawn up onto a shingle beach in a breach in the cliff face.

Punta Cumplida – Walk round the lighthouse on the promontory to see the waves breaking on the basalt rock piles. The attractive Fajana swimming pools are located north of here.

Los Sauces – The main agricultural centre in the north of the island.

Los Tilos★ – Make a detour up the Agua ravine to reach the forest of lime trees which covers the picturesque ravine. The **Centro de Investigación e Interpretación de la Reserva de la Biosfera de Los Tilos**, provides interesting details on the flora to be found in the Biosphere Reserve. 🕐 *Open 9am-4pm (6pm in summer).* 🕐 *Closed 1 Jan and 24, 25 and 31 Dec.* ⊗ *No charge.* ☎ *922 45 12 46.*

THE CENTRE AND SOUTH OF THE ISLAND

Via Los Llanos and Fuencaliente – *190km/118mi.*

▶ *Head N out of Santa Cruz. After the ravine, take the first turning on the left.*

Ahead is the **Barco de la Virgen**, a cement reproduction of Columbus' Santa María, which contains a small **naval museum**. (🕐 *Open 9.30am-2pm and 4-7pm; Jul-Sep, 9.30am-2.30pm.* 🕐 *Closed Sat-Sun and public hols.* ⊗ *1€.* ☎ *922 41 65 50).* The road passes the Fuerte de la Virgen, a fortress which defended the town in the 16C.

Las Nieves

At the foot of Pico de las Nieves, shaded by the great laurel trees in the square, stands the **Santuario de Nuestra Señora de las Nieves** which houses the statue of the island's patron saint. Every five years the figure is carried in procession to the boat built in her honour and then to the Iglesia de El Salvador in Santa Cruz.

La Cumbrecita

Mirador de la Concepción★

The summit of the Caldereta commands a wonderful **bird's-eye view**★ of Santa Cruz de la Palma, the harbour and the mountains.

▶ *Take the TF 812 toward the W.*

Parque Nacional de la Caldera de Taburiente★★★

4km/2.5mi W of the tunnel on the right is the **Centro de Visitantes**, *containing information on the waymarked footpaths within the park (length, timings, difficulty etc).*
🕐 *Open 9am-2pm and 4-6.30pm.* ☎ *922 49 72 77.*

▶ *A little further on, turn right towards La Cumbrecita.*

The **Cumbrecita Pass** (1 833m/6 014ft) and the **Lomo de las Chozas Pass** *(1km/0.6mi further on)* provide a splendid **panorama**★★★: the depths of La Caldera de Taburiente, dotted with Canary Island pines and crowned by rose-tinted peaks (Roque de los Muchachos – opposite). Standing up from the sharp stone spine dividing the crater floor is a rock spike, Roque de Idafe, which was sacred to the Guanches.

Los Llanos de Aridane

The island's second largest town lies at the centre of an attractive plain which is planted with banana palms and avocado trees.

El Time★★

From the top of El Time cliff there is a remarkable **panorama**★★ of the Aridane plain, a sea of banana palms, and of the Barranco de las Angustias, an impressive rock fissure which is the only outlet for the water which collects in the Caldera de Taburiente.

Puntagorda

The beauty of the landscape makes this drive particularly worthwhile.

▶ *Return to El Time.*

Puerto de Tazacorte

Small harbour where Lugo landed in 1492. The beach is popular on Sundays with the citizens of La Palma.

Puerto Naos

A picturesque descent first through the lava fields which date from the eruption in 1949 and then through the banana plantations. A seaside resort has developed beside the vast black sandy beach.

San Nicolás

The lava stream from the Nambroque volcano which cut the village in two in 1949 still scars the landscape.

Fuencaliente★

Before reaching Fuencaliente, look back from the Mirador de las Indias for a **glimpse**★ of the coast through the pines. The sunny village was a spa until its hot water spring disappeared during the eruption of the **San Antonio volcano**★ in 1677. Circle the volcano to see the impressive craters of the **Teneguía volcano**★, which appeared in October 1971, and the lava stream which flowed towards the sea and separated the lighthouse from the village. The surrounding land, which is now covered in ash, is cultivated as before and glasshouses have been erected at the very foot of the new volcano.

Cueva de Belmaco

5km/3mi from the airport fork. At the back of the cave are several rocks engraved with enigmatic labyrinthine Guanche inscriptions.

LA GOMERA★

POPULATION: 16 790

378KM²/1 46SQ MI.

La Gomera is the ideal island for visitors seeking peace and quiet, contact with nature and outdoor activities. This round island rises steeply from coastal cliffs, cut by deep ravines, to a *meseta* with a single peak, Mount Garajonay (alt 1 487m/4 879ft). Few traces remain of early volcanic activity apart from the blocks of solidified volcanic material known locally as roques and the basalt cliffs, Los Órganos, visible only from the sea. The fertile red soil is carefully husbanded: even the steepest hillsides are industriously terraced.

Location

La Gomera is the second smallest island in the Canaries; only El Hierro has a smaller surface area. The recently opened airport has improved communications to the island, which, until recently, was only accessible by sea.
🛈 *San Sebastián de la Gomera: Real 4, 38800, ☎ 922 14 15 12.*

F. Brocal/ MICHELIN

Worth a Visit

San Sebastián de la Gomera

Christopher Columbus stopped off here, in what is now the administrative centre of the island, before going on to discover America in 1492. His route can be traced down the main street from the corner house where he took on water *(ask to see the well (el pozo) in the country courtyard/patio)*, past the **Iglesia de la Asunción** where he heard Mass, to the two-storey white house, a little before the post office, where he is said to have slept. In 1488

The Whistling Language

In former times, the steep terrain in the interior of the island posed huge communication problems for the inhabitants of La Gomera. As a result, an unusual whistling language was created by the Guanches to provide contact from valley to valley. Despite its ancient roots, this language continues to be used today.

Doña Beatriz de Bobadilla took refuge in the **Torre del Conde de Gomera** to escape from the Guanches who had just killed her husband because of his cruelty and for seducing one of their women. The countess was only delivered from attack by the arrival of Pedro de Vera who massacred the besiegers.

To Parque Nacional de Garajonay★★

▶ *15km/9mi. Leave San Sebastián de la Gomera on the TF 711.* The road emerges from the first tunnel into the **Hermigua valley**★★: the white houses, palm trees and banana plantations at the foot of the high cliffs make a picturesque scene.

Agulo★

Very picturesque site beside the sea in the north of the island. Tenerife is visible on the horizon.

Parque Nacional de Garajonay★★

A visit to the Juego de Bolas visitor centre is recommended. ⏱ *Open 9.30am-4.30pm; guided walking tours on Wed and Sat by prior arrangement.* ⏱ *Closed Mon, 1 Jan and 25 Dec.* ☎ *922 80 09 93.*

The national park, created in 1981, is covered by a thick forest of laurels, traces of the Tertiary Era, and giant heathers, punctuated by rocks (roques). The almost permanent mist, caused by the trade winds, lends the region an air of mystery.

Valle Gran Rey★★

55km/34mi from San Sebastián de la Gomera on the TF 713. The road ascends the slopes to the south of the island; the climb up to the central *meseta* inside the national park is less steep.

Chipude – A potters' village in an attractive setting.

Arure – From the far side of the bridge there is a good **panorama**★ of Taguluche.

Barranco del Valle Gran Rey★★ – The ravine, at the end of which are the village houses, is the most spectacular on the island.

EL HIERRO

POPULATION: 6 995

278KM2/107SQ MI.

This small island, which has preserved intact its magnificent natural landscapes, is a combination of fertile farmland, spectacular cliffs plunging into the sea from heights of 700m/2 300ft, volcanic cones, fields of lava carpeted in forests of laurel, and an impressive underwater world popular with divers.

Location

El Hierro is situated in the far southwest of the archipelago and is shaped like a half crater open to the north. The airport is very close to the capital, whose port, La Estaca, provides ferry links with neighbouring islands. *Valverde: Dr. Quintero Magdaleno 4, 38900 Valverde, ☎ 922 55 03 02.*

Tours

The excursions suggested below all depart from **Valverde**, the capital of the island, at an altitude of 571m/1 873ft.

Tamaduste

8km/5mi NE. A large sandbank has dammed the sea inlet by the small seaside resort and formed a quiet lagoon.

El Golfo★★

8km/5mi W. There is an excellent **view**★★ of El Golfo from the **Mirador de La Peña.** The depression is probably an ancient crater. The rim is covered with laurels and giant heather while the level floor is cultivated. La Fuga de Gorreta, near the Salmor rocks *(NE)*, is the habitat of a primeval lizard.

Where to Eat

WHERE TO EAT

☻ **La Higuera de Abuela** – *In Echedo - 5km/3mi NW – Valverde – ☎ 922 55 10 26 – ▨▨.* This small, family-run restaurant revolves around its cosy terrace, but there's also a lovely rustic dining area with colonial details in the decor.

Tour through La Dehesa

▶ *105km/65mi. Head S from Valverde along the TF 912.*

Tiñor – Until 1610, when it was blown down in a storm, a Garoé tree stood on the northeast side of the village. It was venerated by the native tribesmen since its leaves collected water by condensation and they made use of the supply.

Sabinosa – The village has a spa-hotel where diseases of the skin and the digestion are treated.

La Dehesa – A track begins 3km/2mi further on which crosses the arid pastoral region called La Dehesa and provides extensive **views**★ of the south coast of the island where the fiery red earth, pitted with craters, slopes steeply to the sea, which has been named Mar de las Calmas in view of its still waters.

Punta de Orchilla – Orchilla Point was designated as the original meridian in 2C AD long before Greenwich. Beyond the lighthouse lies a wood of sabine trees, conifers with twisted trunks which are found only on El Hierro.

Ermita de Nuestra Señora de los Reyes – The Hermitage of Our Lady of the Kings, the patron saint of El Hierro, contains statues of the three Wise Men (los Reyes) and one of the Virgin Mary which is carried in procession every four years to Valverde. Dancers from the villages it passes through take turns to carry the Virgin along the route.

El Pinar – A pleasant **pine forest**★ extends all over this region.

INDEX

ACSJ / Michelin

a. 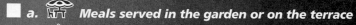 _Meals served in the garden or on the terrace_

b. _A particularly interesting wine list_

c. _Cask beers and ales usually served_

Find out all the answers in the Michelin Guide "Eating Out in Pubs"!

A selection of 500 dining pubs and inns throughout Britain and Ireland researched by the same inspectors who make the Michelin Guide.

- for good food and the right atmosphere
- in-depth descriptions bring out the feel of the place and the flavour of the cuisine.

The pleasure of travel with Michelin Maps and Guides.

MAPS AND PLANS

Legend

Selected monuments and sights

 Tour - Departure point

🏛 ✝ Catholic church

🏛 ✝ Protestant church, other temple

🕍 ☪ Synagogue - Mosque

Building

■ Statue, small building

✝ Calvary, wayside cross

◎ Fountain

●—●—■ Rampart - Tower - Gate

⋈ Château, castle, historic house

∴ Ruins

⌣ Dam

☼ Factory, power plant

☆ Fort

∩ Cave

▣ Troglodyte dwelling

⊓ Prehistoric site

▾ Viewing table

Ⅻ Viewpoint

▲ Other place of interest

Special symbols

⊛ Civil Guard (Guardia Civil)

Ⓟ Parador (hotel run by the State)

🐂 Bullring

🌳 Olive grove

🍊 Orange grove

Sports and recreation

🏇 Racecourse

⛸ Skating rink

♨ ▦ Outdoor, indoor swimming pool

🎥 Multiplex Cinema

⛵ Marina, sailing centre

⌂ Trail refuge hut

□—■—■—□ Cable cars, gondolas

□—⊥—⊥—□ Funicular, rack railway

🚂 Tourist train

◆ Recreation area, park

🎢 Theme, amusement park

🐂 Wildlife park, zoo

❋ Gardens, park, arboretum

🐦 Bird sanctuary, aviary

🚶 Walking tour, footpath

👶 Of special interest to children

Abbreviations

D Provincial Council (Diputación)

G Central government representation (Delegación del Gobierno)

H Town hall (Ayuntamiento)

J Law courts / Courthouse (Palacio de Justicia)

M Museum (Museo)

POL. Police station (Policía)

T Theatre (Teatro)

U University (Universidad)

Highly recommended	★★★	
Recommended	★★	
Interesting	★	

Additional symbols

🛈		Tourist information
═══	═══	Motorway or other primary route
❶	❶	Junction: complete, limited
⊞═══	═══	Pedestrian street
⊺ ═ ═ ═ ⊺		Unsuitable for traffic, street subject to restrictions
▥▥▥	----	Steps – Footpath
🚉	🚋	Train station – Auto-train station
🚌	S.N.C.F.	Coach (bus) station
•——•——•		Tram
Ⓜ		Metro, underground
🅟🆁		Park-and-Ride
♿		Access for the disabled
✉		Post office
☎		Telephone
✉		Covered market
•⤬•		Barracks
△		Drawbridge
⛏		Quarry
✗		Mine
Ⓑ	Ⓕ	Car ferry (river or lake)
⛴		Ferry service: cars and passengers
⛴		Foot passengers only
③		Access route number common to Michelin maps and town plans
Bert (R.)...		Main shopping street
AZ B		Map co-ordinates

Hotels and restaurants

	Hotels- price categories:	
	Provinces	Large cities
⊖	<40 €	<60 €
⊖⊖	40 to 65 €	60 to 90 €
⊖⊖⊖	65 to 100 €	90 to 130 €
⊖⊖⊖⊖	>100 €	>130 €

	Restaurants- price categories:	
	Provinces	Large cities
⊖	<14 €	<16 €
⊖⊖	14 to 25 €	16 to 30 €
⊖⊖⊖	25 to 40 €	30 to 50 €
⊖⊖⊖⊖	>40 €	>50 €

20 rooms *118.79 €/* *180.70 €*	Numbers of rooms: price for one person/two people including breakfast
"double rooms"	Double occupancy only
🍽 *5.16 €*	Price of breakfast when it is not included in the price of the room
100 apart/ room week. *200/300 €*	Number of apartments or rooms, minimum/maximum price per week (units rented on a weekly basis only, in summer)
100 beds *15.49 €*	Number of beds (youth hostels, refuges, etc) and price per person
150 sites *19.63 €*	Number of camp sites and cost for two people with a car
10/26 €	Restaurant: minimum/maximum price for a full meal (not including drinks)
⊘	No credit cards accepted
🅟	Reserved parking for hotel patrons
⊱	Swimming Pool
▤	Air conditioning
♿	Rooms accessible to persons of reduced mobility

The prices correspond to the higher rates of the tourist season

NOTES

NOTES

NOTES

NOTES

NOTES

NOTES

NOTES

NOTES

NOTES

NOTES

NOTES

NOTES

NOTES

Manufacture française des pneumatiques Michelin

Société en commandite par actions au capital de 304 000 000 EUR
Place des Carmes-Déchaux – 63000 Clermont-Ferrand (France)
R.C.S. Clermont-Fd B 855 200 507

No part of this publication may be reproduced in any form
without the prior permission of the publisher.

© Michelin et Cie, Propriétaires-éditeurs
Dépot légal mars 2006 – ISSN 0763-1383

Pre-Press : Nord Compo à Villeneuve-d'Ascq
Printing and Binding: IME à Baume-les-Dames
Printed in France, janvier 2006

Made in France